The Juvenile Justice System

Delinquency, Processing, and the Law

Fifth Edition

Dean John Champion
Texas A & M International University

PEARSON

Prentice Hall

Upper Saddle River, New Jersey 07458

Library of Congress Cataloging-in-Publication Data
Champion, Dean J.
    The juvenile justice system: delinquency, processing, and the law /
        by Dean John Champion.—5th ed.
            p. cm.
        ISBN 0-13-219374-4
1. Juvenile justice, Administration of—United States. 2. Juvenile
courts—United States. I. Title.
    KF9779.C425 2007
    345.73'08—dc22

                                                                        2006004210

Executive Editor: Frank Mortimer, Jr.
Associate Editor: Sarah Holle
Marketing Manager: Adam Kloza
Production Editor: Patty Donovan, Pine Tree Composition, Inc.
Production Liaison: Barbara Marttine Cappuccio
Director of Manufacturing and Production: Bruce Johnson
Managing Editor: Mary Carnis
Manufacturing Manager: Ilene Sanford
Manufacturing Buyer: Cathleen Petersen
Senior Design Coordinator: Mary Siener
Cover Designer: Eva Ruutopold
Cover Image: Paul Conklin; PhotoEdit
Formatting and Interior Design: Pine Tree Composition, Inc.
Printing and Binding: R.R. Donnelley & Sons

Pearson Prentice Hall™ is a trademark of Pearson Education, Inc.
Pearson® is a registered trademark of Pearson plc
Prentice Hall® is a registered trademark of Pearson Education, Inc.

Pearson Education LTD.
Pearson Education Singapore, Pte. Ltd
Pearson Education, Canada, Ltd
Pearson Education-Japan
Pearson Education Australia PTY, Limited
Pearson Education North Asia Ltd
Pearson Educaçion de Mexico, S.A. de C.V.
Pearson Education Malaysia, Pte. Ltd

10 9 8 7 6 5 4 3 2

ISBN 0-13-219374-4

Contents

Chapter 5

The Legal Rights of Juveniles

Chapter 6

Juveniles and the Police

Chapter 7

Intake and Preadjudicatory Processing   276

Chapter 8

Prosecutorial Decision Making in Juvenile Justice   308

Chapter 9

Classification and Preliminary Treatment: Waivers and Other Alternatives

338

Chapter 10

The Adjudicatory Process: Dispositional Alternatives

392

Chapter 11

Nominal Sanctions: Warnings, Diversion, and Alternative Dispute Resolution   444

Chapter 12

Juvenile Probation and Community-Based Corrections   495

Chapter 13

Juvenile Corrections: Custodial Sanctions and Parole   555

Preface

The Juvenile Justice System: Delinquency, Processing, and the Law, Fifth Edition, is a complete examination of the juvenile justice system. It examines how juvenile offenders are defined and classified and draws on current literature to depict significant stages of juvenile processing.

Current juvenile cases are used to illustrate the legal bases for decisions about juveniles. Landmark Supreme Court cases are included, although persuasive decisions from various state courts are presented to show juvenile justice trends. A legalistic perspective is used, therefore, to highlight the different rights juveniles have acquired and how different components of the juvenile justice system relate to them. An integral feature of this book is the distinction between status offenses and delinquent offenses. This difference has significant consequences for all juveniles affected.

The history of juvenile courts is described, including crucial events that have influenced the course of juvenile justice. Increasingly, juveniles are extended rights commensurate with the rights of adults. An indication of this trend is the growing use of waivers (certifications or transfers) to criminal court. This option is intended to expose more serious juvenile offenders to more severe punishment forms compared with the possible punishments that juvenile judges may impose. However, the spreading use of waivers has not always achieved the intended result of more severe penalties for juveniles, since many juveniles who are waived to criminal courts receive minimal punishments, if punished at all.

One explanation is that most juveniles who are transferred to criminal courts are not necessarily the most serious, dangerous, or violent juvenile offenders. A majority of those transferred continue to be property offenders, drug users, or public order and status offenders. Once juveniles are waived to the jurisdiction of criminal courts, their age becomes a mitigating factor. Quite often, this factor trivializes the seriousness of their offending and lessens the punishments imposed. Many cases against juveniles are dropped or reduced to less serious charges. Thus, many juveniles who are tried as adults receive sentences that are comparatively less severe than those that would otherwise be contemplated and imposed by juvenile judges. However, one potential penalty that receives increasing attention is the death penalty applied to juveniles. Current case law about imposing the death penalty as a punishment for juveniles is examined, and several juvenile death penalty cases are described.

Juveniles are not only classified according to type of offense, but they are also tracked according to the nature of offenses committed across years. Delinquency is defined and measured according to several popular indices, such as the *Uniform Crime Reports* and the *National Crime Victimization Survey.* The fact is that no single resource discloses the true amount of delinquency in the United States.

The major components of the juvenile justice system are featured, including law enforcement, prosecution and the courts, and corrections. Corrections is presented in a broad context, with each correctional component described. Correctional strategies ranging from diversion to full-fledged incarceration are featured, together with a discussion of the favorable and unfavorable dimensions of such programs. One interesting feature is a section devoted to recidivism among juveniles, depending on the nature of the treatment program described. Thus, community-based correctional programs are assessed, together with probation and parole alternatives for managing a growing juvenile offender aggregate. Electronic monitoring and home confinement are described as strategic and technological means of coping with growing numbers of juvenile offenders.

Each chapter contains information about the juvenile justice system of a foreign country. Thus, 13 countries are featured as separate chapter box materials. Their juvenile justice systems are explained, and their defining criteria for juvenile offenders and their offenses are described. These international portrayals are designed to provide interesting contrasts with the U.S. juvenile justice system. Each country throughout the world has its definition of who juveniles are and the nature of their offending, including proscriptions for how such offending should be punished. Some countries are more lenient with their youths than other countries. One continuing theme is that every country continues to evolve new and improved standards for dealing with youthful offenders, for delinquency prevention, rehabilitation, and punishment.

Each chapter also contains career snapshots of persons who work with juvenile offenders in different capacities. Some of these persons are juvenile court judges, while others are juvenile probation and parole officers and counselors. These profiles are intended to show why juvenile justice professionals have chosen their careers and what they find rewarding about them. At the same time, they set forth what they believe are requirements and characteristics persons should possess who plan to enter the field of juvenile justice as a career. Not just anyone can work with juvenile offenders effectively. Special training, preparation, and education are required. On-the-job experiences with juveniles are described by most of these professionals, and such experiences help students understand some of the situational difficulties these persons experience. Their work is often frustrating, but at the same time, it is rewarding in various ways. More than a few success experiences are reported, as these professionals relate how some of their juvenile clients have gone on to lead law-abiding, productive lives.

Every effort has been made to include the most up-to-date sources, references, and other materials. Thus, at the time this book went into production, the most currently available material was used as the bases for tables, figures, and juvenile justice statistics. The most current material is not always that current, however. For instance, government documents about juvenile justice statistics are published 12–18 months from the time the information is actually collected and analyzed. Therefore, it is not unusual for a government document published in 2007 to report "recent" juvenile delinquency statistics for 2005 or earlier. This situation is common, since governmental compilation and reporting of such information is a slow and tedious process. It is not possible, therefore, for the government to report 2007 information in 2007. The historical factual information about juveniles and the juvenile justice system does not change, however. Also, there are few changes in juvenile laws from year to year. Of course, new information is constantly being generated by researchers and government agencies. As a textbook ages, therefore, those seeking more current information about juvenile delinquency trends and other statistical information can obtain this data from several sites on the Internet. But the reader should be assured that for the most part, most textbooks are replete with rather constant or consistent information about the juvenile justice system. I have sought to provide the reader with the best and most recent information available at the time this manuscript was prepared.

PEDAGOGY

There are several important ancillaries that have been prepared for this book. First, there are chapter objectives that outline what each chapter is designed to accomplish. Key terms that are fundamental to understanding the juvenile justice system, the criminal justice system, and various programs and processes are highlighted in **boldface.** A complete glossary of these terms is provided in an appendix. Each chapter contains a summary, highlighting the chapter's main points.

Also included at chapter ends are questions for review. Students are encouraged to study these questions and learn to answer them based on chapter information provided. These questions may also be used in preparation for semester or quarter examinations. At chapter ends, Internet sites are listed that will prove to be useful in looking up significant historical events or factual information relevant to juvenile justice and its many organizations and agencies. As is the case with just about every information source, the Internet is constantly changing. New sites are being added, almost daily, while older, even established sites are discontinued or changed. Again, every effort has been made to include relevant Internet sites that were functional and up and running at the time of this book's publication. In the event some of these Internet sites are no longer in existence, various Internet search engines can be used to locate most topics of student interest.

Supplements for instructors include an Instructor's Manual, TestGen, and PowerPoint CD. The Instructor's Manual includes chapter outlines, summary information, and short answer essay questions. Any instructor who adopts this book can order the supplements from their Prentice Hall sales rep. The TestGen includes selections of true/false and multiple choice questions that can be used for examination purposes. Any questions about the text or factual information, as well as any inadvertent inaccuracies, may be made directly to the author through the contact information below:

ACKNOWLEDGMENTS

Any textbook is the result of the hard work of many persons. First, I wish to acknowledge the reviewers who took the time to examine the previous edition of this book and make helpful and insightful suggestions for its improvement and revision. These reviewers include Jim Jengeleski, Shippensburg University Shippensburg, PA and Michael Leiber, University of Northern Iowa Cedar Falls, IA.

I am also indebted to Frank Mortimer, my editor, who has always been supportive of my projects. A special thanks is extended to Sarah Holle, Associate editor, who was always there to chase down important book details and make sure all aspects of the production process ran smoothly. Finally, the entire editorial and production staff at Prentice Hall should be acknowledged. Their various efforts, both large and small, helped to shape and improve the present edition.

Dean John Champion
Department of Behavioral, Applied Sciences,
and Criminal Justice
Texas A & M International University
5201 University Blvd.
Laredo, TX 78041
(956) 326-2611 (O)
E-mail: dchampion@tamiu.edu

About the Author

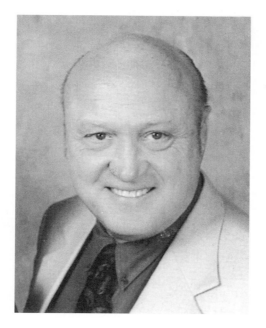

Dean John Champion is Professor of Criminal Justice at Texas A & M International University in Laredo, Texas. Dr. Champion has taught at the University of Tennessee–Knoxville, California State University–Long Beach, and Minot State University. He earned his Ph.D. from Purdue University and B.S. and M.A. degrees from Brigham Young University. He also completed several years of law school at the Nashville School of Law.

Dr. Champion has written over 30 texts and/or edited works and maintains memberships in eleven professional organizations. He is a lifetime member of the American Society of Criminology, Academy of Criminal Justice Sciences, and the American Sociological Association. He is a former editor of the Academy of Criminal Justice Sciences/Anderson Publishing Company Series on *Issues in Crime and Justice* and the *Journal of Crime and Justice.* He is a contributing author for the *Encarta Encyclopedia 2000* for Microsoft. He has been a Visiting Scholar for the National Center for Juvenile Justice and is a former president of the Midwestern Criminal Justice Association. He has also designed and/or offered numerous online courses for the University of Phoenix, Excelsior College, and the University of Alaska–Fairbanks.

Among his published books for Prentice Hall include *Administration of Criminal Justice: Structure, Function, and Process* (2003); *Basic Statistics for Social Research* (1970, 1981); *Research Methods for Criminal Justice and Criminology* (1993, 2000, 2006); *The Juvenile Justice System: Delinquency, Processing, and the Law* (1992, 1998, 2001, 2004, 2007); *Corrections in the United States: A Contemporary Perspective* (1990, 1998, 2001, 2005); *Probation, Parole, and Community Corrections* (1990, 1996, 1999, 2005); and *Policing in the Community* (w/George Rush) (1997). Dr. Champion's specialty interests include juvenile justice, criminal justice administration, corrections, and statistics/methods.

| CHAPTER I | *An Introduction to Juvenile Justice in the United States* |

Chapter Outline

Key Terms

1

juvenile courts
juvenile justice system
law enforcement agencies
New York House of Refuge
Philadelphia Society for
    Alleviating the Miseries of
    the Public Prisons

Poor Laws
prosecution, and the courts
reeve
reform schools
shires
Society for the Prevention of
    Pauperism

solitary confinement
sweat shops
transportation
truants
Walnut Street Jail
workhouses

Chapter Objectives

When you finish reading this chapter, you will have accomplished the following objectives:

1. Understand the basic components of the juvenile justice system.
2. Know about the early origins of juvenile courts in the United States.
3. Understand significant historical events in the evolution of the juvenile justice system.
4. Become familiar with the doctrine of *parens patriae* and how juveniles continue to be affected by this doctrine.
5. Understand the legal basis for governmental intervention in matters of child discipline and parental control.
6. Understand the increasing bureaucratization of juvenile justice and growing criminalization of juvenile processing.
7. Become familiar with the get-tough movement and implications for juveniles..

• *Two 12-year-olds, Mark G. and Reed M., were playing ball one afternoon in their Salt Lake City, Utah, neighborhood. When Mark G. chased the ball into a neighbor's yard, he passed the neighbor's new SUV parked in the driveway. The keys were in the ignition. Mark G. told Reed M. about this, and the boys decided to take a ride in the neighbor's car. The neighbor also had left her purse on the front seat of the car, which contained credit cards and some cash. The boys drove around Salt Lake for an hour or so and then decided to go to Denver, about 500 miles away. In the meantime, the car was reported stolen. Both children were reported missing. Early the next morning, the stolen car was spotted by a Colorado State Trooper, primarily because he couldn't see the head of the driver of the vehicle. When he stopped the car on the outskirts of Denver, he discovered two 12-year-olds. He took them both into custody. Subsequently, the FBI investigated, since the vehicle had been driven across state lines in violation of federal law. The parents of both boys were required to pick up their children in person, which meant driving to Denver. The stolen car was impounded, and it was subsequently returned to Salt Lake to the lawful owner. The towing expense was in excess of $800, and the impound fees were approximately $300. Some car damage had been sustained, where the youths had carelessly side-swiped some Interstate guard railing on their way to Denver. The juvenile court judge heard the case, declared the boys delinquent on the stolen car charges, and placed both boys on probation, primarily because they were first-offenders. As one condition of their probation, the boys and their families were ordered to pay restitution to the neighbor for her car damage, impound costs, and towing fees. Furthermore, the boys were ordered to perform 100 hours of community service by cutting city park lawns and doing clean-up tasks.* [Source: Adapted from the Associated Press, "12-Year-Old Car Thieves Placed on Probation Following Federal Investigation," June 14, 2005.]

• *Gabriel M. was an 11-year-old at a middle school in a Phoenix, Arizona, suburb. During one weekend, he assisted his father in replacing a windshield glass on the family car. Gabriel M. helped to glue the glass in place and removed excess glue with a small cutting device. Placing the glue tube and cutting device in his pants pocket while he worked with his father, Gabriel M. forgot to remove them when he went to school the following Monday. While he was in the lunch line, he reached in his pocket for some change and the glue tube fell out on the floor. Gabriel M. retrieved it and put it back in his pocket. Shortly thereafter, a teacher on lunch duty approached Gabriel M. and ordered him to the principal's office. Gabriel M. was advised that a female student had seen him in possession of a glue tube and he was ordered to empty his pockets onto the principal's desk. In the process, the cutting device and glue tube were discovered. Gabriel M. explained that he had helped his dad over the weekend with the car windshield and had simply failed to remove these objects from his pocket. Nevertheless, the principal called the parents and asked them to come to the school to pick up their son. The police were also notified, and an officer was dispatched to the school to investigate. The principal summarily suspended Gabriel M. for "substance abuse" and "possession of a dangerous weapon," and the police officer wrote up a brief report of the incident and left with the confiscated glue and cutting device. Gabriel M.'s father explained to the principal that Gabriel M. had assisted him with the car windshield that previous weekend and that it was a "simple mistake." The principal didn't see it that way and advised that Gabriel would be suspended from school until a children's protective services officer investigated. The following day, a woman from the children's protective services agency, Janice R., appeared at Gabriel M.'s home and asked Gabriel M.'s mother if she wanted an attorney present. The mother called the father, who rushed home. The father didn't believe that the case was serious enough to merit an attorney and asked when his son could return to school. Janice R. advised that Gabriel M. would be required to submit to a urinanalysis because of the "substance abuse" notation in the police report. If Gabriel M. tested "clean," then he would have to be interviewed at a later hearing by a youth officer at the juvenile probation office concerning the "dangerous weapon" also noted in the report. If everything went well, according to Miss R., Gabriel would be permitted to reenter the school. Mr. M. hired an attorney, had his son drug-tested, and appeared with his son before a youth officer with the juvenile court later. The youth worker asked Mr. M. if he owned any firearms. Mr. M., a hunter, said that he owned two rifles. The youth officer said that he would sign a release for Gabriel M. to return to his school once proof was shown that Mr. M. had disposed of these dangerous weapons and paid a processing fee of $250 to the juvenile court. Mr. M. sold his hunting rifles, showed the youth worker the bill of sale, and paid the fee, thus enabling Gabriel to reenter the school about a week after he had been suspended. Both the school and the juvenile court retained records of Gabriel M.'s alleged "substance abuse" and "possession of a dangerous weapon," and officials refused to remove any documentation from Gabriel M.'s file. Mr. M. estimated that his legal fees and costs amounted to over $3,000.* [Source: Adapted from Joan Henry and the Associated Press, "School Suspension of 11-Year-Old for Possessing Glue Proves Costly," July 22, 2005.]

• *Maria G., a 15-year-old Hispanic girl, is a member of a female gang in Paramount, California. One day at her school, Maria G. was the subject of an ethnic slur by Angie E., a 14-year-old female member of a rival female gang. That evening Angie E. was walking down the street with two girlfriends in her neighborhood when a car approached and gunfire erupted. Angie E. was wounded in the arm by a 9 mm bullet, while her two companions were unharmed. The car sped off, but Angie E. told police that Maria G. had been the shooter. Maria G. was arrested later that evening at her home and charged with attempted murder. Three of Maria G.'s friends, also gang members, were taken into custody. Subsequently the juvenile court adjudicated Maria G. delinquent and ordered her confined for up to 18 months at a juvenile facility operated by the California Youth Authority. Maria G. was ordered to make restitution payments to the juvenile court to offset some of Angie E.'s medical expenses. As a part of her disposition to the Youth Authority, Maria G. was required to participate in group and individual counseling as well as work toward her GED. Maria G. was released from the Youth Authority in June 2005 into the custody of juvenile paroling authorities. Further counseling and close supervision were recommended.* [Source: Adapted from Leo G. Hall and the Associated Press, "Female Gang Shooter Returns to the Community: How Safe Are We from Youth Violence?" July 4, 2005.]

INTRODUCTION

Each of these cases is different. Each of these cases is the same. These are the differences. Youths steal a car and drive it hundreds of miles away across state lines and damage it. A court finds the boys guilty of vehicular theft and places them on probation with conditions. A boy is suspended from school for possessing a dangerous substance and a weapon, and he is subsequently processed by the juvenile court probation office. A female gang member is involved in a drive-by shooting where a victim is injured. She is subsequently incarcerated. This is the similarity. All of these persons are juveniles. Each of them has committed one or more offenses that has placed them within the juvenile justice system.

This book is about the juvenile justice system and describes each and every one of its primary components. The organization of this chapter is as follows. First, the juvenile justice system as a concept is described. Some of those who work with juveniles believe that the use of the word *system* is inappropriate. Rather, the term *process* is preferred. This is because of the extensive amount of fragmentation and differentiation in the juvenile justice process. Also, juvenile courts and procedures for processing juvenile offenders vary greatly among jurisdictions. There are as many different juvenile justice apparatuses in the United States as there are cities and counties and states. At the same time, there are many similarities relating to how juveniles are processed. Some of the types of differences and similarities among such systems are noted and described in greater detail in later chapters.

The next section of this chapter describes the history of juvenile justice in the United States. Compared with other countries, the United States is a young nation with a past spanning less than 400 years. In 1999 the first centennial of juvenile courts in the United States was celebrated. The contemporary formality that characterizes many juvenile courts did not emerge until the 1960s and 1970s. The historical antecedents of our present system of juvenile justice are rooted in England during the 1500s. Youthful offenders were figuratively under the jurisdiction of the King of England, who, as father of the country, dispensed justice to youths through his political appointees who were called chancellors. These persons made decisions about juveniles using their best judgment and in accordance with what they believed to be in a child's best interests. When the American Colonies were established, the influence of England on how youths were treated continued to be reflected in both formal and informal policies toward them developed by the citizenry and political figures. Between the early 1600s and late 1800s, an evolution of sorts transpired relating to youthful offenders and their treatment. From grim beginnings and conditions of despair,

American youths increasingly attracted the attention of various concerned persons and groups, particularly religious organizations. Many of the significant events that molded our contemporary system of processing youthful offenders are noted and described.

Two legal cases, *Ex parte Crouse* (1839) and *People ex rel. O'Connell v. Turner* (1870), are described. These cases were particularly influential in shaping subsequent policies about child welfare, questions of guardianship, and the nature of punishments for certain types of juvenile behaviors. During the 40-year period following the Civil War, several philanthropists, religious groups, and political entities contributed in different ways in promoting a number of important youth reforms. The child-saving movement was created, and houses of refuge were constructed and operated. Crucial legislation in different states was enacted, establishing both truancy laws and juvenile courts. Gradually, children gained greater recognition and were given special treatment, moving them well beyond their early conceptualization as chattel and their unfair and unilateral treatment in primitive children's tribunals. These and other critical events are described.

Early juvenile courts were noted particularly for their paternalistic views toward youths. These paternalistic views are manifested in the doctrine of *parens patriae,* which is essentially a perpetuation of early sixteenth-century English philosophy and clearly establishes the traditional nature of many contemporary juvenile courts. Traditionalism continues to be pervasive among juvenile court judges who most frequently make decisions about youthful offenders according to what is believed to be in their best interests rather than justice or fairness. The inherent inequality of individualized justice for juveniles is clearly at odds with due process and equal protection under the law. These contrasting and incompatible philosophies of juvenile justice continue to affect a juvenile's life chances. The chapter concludes with an examination of the *parens patriae* doctrine, upon which traditional juvenile court philosophy is based. This philosophy is explained, as well as how it has come into conflict with a growing get-tough movement dedicated to the idea that juveniles, especially more serious and violent ones, will get their just desserts.

THE JUVENILE JUSTICE SYSTEM

The **juvenile justice system,** similar to **criminal justice,** consists of a more or less integrated network of agencies, institutions, organizations, and personnel that process juvenile offenders. This network is made up of **law enforcement agencies, prosecution, and the courts;** corrections, probation, and parole services; and public and private community-based treatment programs that provide youths with diverse services. This definition is qualified by the phrase "more or less integrated" because the concept of juvenile justice has different meanings for individual states and the federal government. Also, in some jurisdictions, the diverse components of the juvenile justice system are closely coordinated, while in other jurisdictions, these components are at best loosely coordinated, if they are coordinated at all. There is no single nationwide juvenile court system. Instead, there are 51 state systems, including the District of Columbia, and most of them are divided into local systems delivered through

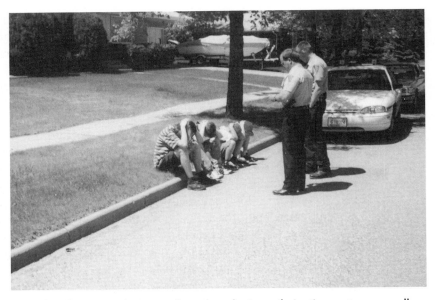

Over 2 million juveniles are referred to the juvenile justice system annually in the United States.

either juvenile or family courts at the county level, local probation offices, state correctional agencies, and private service providers. These systems, do, however, have a common set of core principles that distinguish them from criminal courts for adult offenders, including:

1. Limited jurisdiction (up to age 17 in most states)
2. Informal proceedings
3. Focus on offenders, not their crimes
4. Indeterminate sentences; and
5. Confidentiality (Wood, 2001:117).

A Process or System?

Many **criminologists** and **criminal justice professionals** express a preference for the word *process* rather than the word *system* when they refer to juvenile justice. This is because *system* connotes a condition of homeostasis, equilibrium, or internal balance among system components. In contrast, *process* focuses on the different actions and contributions of each of these components in dealing with juvenile offenders at various stages of the processing through the juvenile justice system. Furthermore, *system* implies coordination among elements in an efficient production process; but in reality, communication and coordination among juvenile agencies, organizations, and personnel in the juvenile justice system are often inadequate or nonexistent (Guarino-Ghezzi and Loughran, 2004).

Further clouding the concept of juvenile justice is the fact that different criteria are used to define the broad classes of juveniles among local, state, and federal jurisdictions. Within each of these jurisdictions, certain mechanisms exist for redefining particular juveniles as adults so that they may be legally processed by the adult counterpart to juvenile justice, the criminal justice system. Despite these definitional ambiguities and systemic interfaces among jurisdictions, most scholars who investigate juveniles understand what is meant by juvenile justice (Roberts and Gabor, 2004). As with pornography, these scholars and investigators recognize the juvenile justice process whenever they see its components, even if they may not always be able to define it precisely.

THE HISTORY OF JUVENILE COURTS

Juvenile courts are a relatively recent American creation. However, modern American juvenile courts have various less formal European antecedents. In biblical times, Roman law vested parents with the almost exclusive responsibility for disciplining their offspring. One's age was the crucial determinant of whether youths were subject to parental discipline or to the more severe penalties invoked for adult law violators. While the origin of this cutting point is unknown, the age of 7 was used in Roman times to separate infants from those older children who were accountable to the law for their actions (Musick, 1995). During the Middle Ages, English **common law** established under the monarchy adhered to the same standard. In the United States, several state jurisdictions currently apply this distinction and consider all children below the age of 7 to be not accountable for any criminal acts they may commit.

Under the laws of England during the 1500s, **shires** (counties) and other political subdivisions were organized to carry out the will of the king. Each shire had a **reeve,** or chief law enforcement officer. In later years, the term "shire" was combined with the term "reeve" (shire-reeve) to create the word *sheriff* a term that is now applied to the chief law enforcement officer of most U.S. counties. While reeves enforced both criminal and civil laws and arrested law violators, other functionaries, called **chancellors,** acted on the king's behalf and dispensed justice according to his wishes. These chancellors held court and settled disputes that included simple property trespass, property boundary disagreements, and assorted personal and property offenses, including public drunkenness, thievery, and vagrancy. The courts conducted by chancellors were known as **chancery courts** or **courts of equity.** Today, some jurisdictions in the United States such as Tennessee have chancery courts where property boundary disputes and contested wills may be adjudicated by chancellors. These courts have other jurisdiction as well, although they deal primarily with equity cases (e.g., breaches of contract, specific performance actions, and child custody cases).

In eighteenth-century England, no distinctions were made regarding age or gender when punishments were administered. Youthful offenders age 7 or older experienced the same harsh punishments imposed on adults. Stocks and pillories, whipping posts, branding, ducking stools, and other forms of corporal punishment were administered to juveniles as well as to adult offenders for many different types of crimes. In some instances, **banishment** was used as a way of punishing more serious offenders. Some offenders were transported to Pacific islands that were owned by the British and converted into penal colonies. This was known as **transportation.** Many prisoners died in these colonies. The death penalty was invoked frequently, often for petty crimes. Incarceration of offenders was particularly sordid, as women, men, and youths were confined together in jails for lengthy periods. No attempts were made to classify these offenders by gender or age, and all prisoners slept on hay loosely thrown on wooden floors.

Workhouses and Poor Laws

Eighteenth-century jails were patterned largely after **workhouses** that were still common nearly two centuries earlier. In 1557, for example, **Bridewell Workhouse** was established in London. Although the manifest aim of such places was to punish offenders, Bridewell and other similar facilities were created primarily for the purpose of providing cheap labor to satisfy mercantile interests and demands. Interestingly, jailers and sheriffs profited greatly from leasing their inmates to various merchants in order to perform semiskilled and skilled labor (Spruit et al., 1998). These same jailers claimed that the work performed by inmates for mercantile interests was largely therapeutic and rehabilitative, although in reality the primary incentive for operating such houses was profit and personal gain. Exploitation of inmates for profit in these and other workhouses was perpetuated by jailers and sheriffs for many decades, and the general practice was accepted by an influential constituency of merchants and entrepreneurs.

At the time of the Bridewell Workhouse, English legislators had already established several statutes known as the **Poor Laws.** These laws targeted debtors who owed creditors, and sanctions for those unable to pay their debts were imposed. Debtors' prisons were places where debtors were incarcerated until they could pay their debts. Since debtors needed to work to earn the money required to pay off their debts, and since opportunities for earning money for prison labor were almost nonexistent, imprisonment for debts was tantamount to a life sentence. Many offenders were incarcerated indefinitely, or until someone, perhaps a relative or influential friend, could pay off their debts for them.

The Poor Laws were directed at the poor or socioeconomically disadvantaged. In 1601, additional statutes were established that provided constructive work for youths deemed by the courts to be vagrant, incorrigible, truant, or neglected. In general, education was not an option for these youths—it was an expensive commodity available almost exclusively to children from the upper social strata, and it provided a major means of achieving still higher status over time. For the masses of poor, education was usually beyond their reach; they spent most of their time earning money to pay for life's basic necessities. They had little or no time to consider education as a realistic option (Moak and Wallace, 2003).

Indentured Servants

Many youths during this time became apprentices, usually to master craftsmen, in a system of involuntary servitude. This servitude was patterned in part after the **indentured servant system. Indentured servants** entered voluntarily into contractual agreements with various merchants and businessmen to work for them for extended periods of up to seven years. This seven-year work agreement was considered by all parties to be a mutually beneficial way of paying for the indentured servant's passage from England to the colonies. In the case of youthful apprentices, however, their servitude, for the most part, was compulsory. Furthermore, it usually lasted until they reached adulthood or age 21.

During the Colonial period, English influence on penal practices was apparent in most New England jurisdictions. Colonists relied on familiar traditions for administering laws and sanctioning offenders. It is no coincidence, therefore, that much criminal procedure in American courts today traces its origins to legal customs and precedents inherent in British jurisprudence during the 1600s and 1700s (Moak and Wallace, 2003). However, relatively little attention was devoted to the legal status of juveniles during this period and to how to manage them. In fact, more than a few juveniles were summarily executed for relatively petty offenses (Musick, 1995).

Hospital of Saint Michael

In other parts of the world during the same era, certain religious interests were gradually devising institutions that catered primarily to youthful offenders. For example, in Italy, a corrective facility was established in 1704 to provide for unruly youths and other young people who violated criminal laws. This facility was the **Hospital of Saint Michael,** constructed in Rome at the request of the Pope. The institution was misleadingly named, however, since the youths it housed were not ill. Rather, they were assigned various tasks and trained to perform semiskilled and skilled labor—useful tools that would enable them to find employment more easily after their release from Saint Michael. During rest periods and evening hours, youths were housed in individual cells (Griffin and Griffin, 1978).

The Quakers and Walnut Street Jail

Reforms relating to the treatment and/or punishment of juvenile offenders occurred slowly. Shortly after the Revolutionary War, religious interests in the United States moved forward with various proposals designed to improve the plight of the oppressed, particularly those who were incarcerated in prisons and jails. In 1787, the Quakers in Pennsylvania established the **Philadelphia Society for Alleviating the Miseries of the Public Prisons.** This largely philanthropic society was comprised of prominent citizens, religious leaders, and philanthropists who were appalled by existing prison and jail conditions. Adult male, female, and juvenile offenders continued to be housed in common quarters and treated like animals. The High Street Jail in Philadelphia was one eyesore that particularly attracted the Society's attention. Because members of the Quaker faith visited this and other jail facilities regularly to bring food, clothing, and religious instruction to inmates, they were in strategic positions to observe the totality of circumstances in which those confined found themselves.

In 1790, an older Philadelphia jail facility originally constructed in 1776 was overhauled and refurbished. It was renamed the **Walnut Street Jail.** This facility has considerable historical significance for corrections, since it was the first real attempt by jail authorities to classify and segregate offenders according to their age, gender, and crime seriousness. The Walnut Street Jail was innovative in at least three respects. First, it pioneered what is now known as **solitary confinement.** Sixteen large solitary cells were constructed to house prisoners on an individual basis during evening hours. Second, prisoners were segregated from other prisoners according to offense seriousness. More violent criminals were placed with others like them. First-offenders or petty offenders were similarly grouped together and segregated from more violent convicts. Third, women and children were maintained in separate rooms during evening hours, away from male prisoners (Rogers, 1993).

The Walnut Street Jail promoted rehabilitation. It attempted to train its inmates for different types of labor, such as sewing, shoemaking, or carpentry. Unskilled laborers were assigned tasks such as beating hemp for ship caulking. Most prisoners received modest wages for their skilled or unskilled labor, although much of this pay was used to pay for their room and board. Finally, religious instruction was provided to inmates by Quaker teachers. This provision is indicative of the dramatic influence of religion in shaping prison policies and practices relating to inmate treatment and benefits (Guarino-Ghezzi and Loughran, 2004).

The Child Savers and Houses of Refuge

As more families gravitated toward large cities such as New York, Philadelphia, Boston, and Chicago during the early 1800s to find work, increasing numbers of children roamed the streets, most often unsupervised by working parents who could not afford child care services. Lacking familial controls, many of these youths committed acts of vandalism and theft. Others were simply idle, without visible means of support, and were designated as vagrants. Again, religious organizations intervened in order to protect unsupervised youths from the perils of life in the streets. Believing that these youths would subsequently turn to lives of crime as adults, many reformers and philanthropists sought to save them from their plight.

Thus, in different cities throughout the United States, various groups were formed to find and control these youths by offering them constructive work programs, healthful living conditions, and, above all, adult supervision. Collectively, these efforts became widely known as the **child-saving movement. Child savers** came largely from the middle and upper classes, and their assistance to youths took many forms. Food and shelter were provided to children who were in trouble with the law or who were simply idle. Private homes were converted into settlements where social, educational, and other important activities could be provided for needy youths. The child savers were not limited to the United States. In Scotland and England during the 1850s, child-saving institutions were abundant, with similar philosophies and interests compared with U.S. child-saving organizations. In England particularly, middle-class values were imposed on the children of the working class through institutional education, training, and discipline. Eventually several juvenile reformatories were established for the purpose of institutional control (Moak and Wallace, 2003).

In the United States, more than a few child-saver organizations sought to impose their class, ethnic, and racial biases on the poor, immigrants, and minority women. A middle-class gender ideology of maternal care was imposed upon working-class and lower-class mothers. Many of these mothers were declared unfit and in need of state control, since they did not conform to the cultural ideal espoused by middle- and upper-class child savers. Thus, there was the general charge that child savers sought to control and resocialize the children of the dangerous classes for the benefit of the capitalist entrepreneurs. But not everyone agrees that child savers exploited children. In certain cities, such as Wilmington, Delaware, the child-saving movement emphasized education rather than work (Offutt, 1995). Furthermore, the ultimate aims of this movement in Delaware and several other states were largely altruistic and humanitarian. Even in contemporary youth corrections, the child-saver orientation influences the care and treatment strategies of contemporary personnel (Blevins, 2005).

The **New York House of Refuge** was established in New York City in 1825 by the **Society for the Prevention of Pauperism** (Guarino-Ghezzi and Loughran, 2004). Subsequently imitated in other communities, **houses of refuge** were institutions largely devoted to managing status offenders, such as runaways or incorrigible children. Compulsory education and other forms of training and assistance were provided to these children. However, the strict, prison-like regimen of this organization was not entirely therapeutic for its clientele. Many of the youthful offenders who were sent to such institutions, including the House of Reformation in Boston, were offspring of immigrants. Often, they rebelled when exposed to the discipline of these organizations, and many of these youths eventually pursued criminal careers as a consequence. It would appear that at least some of these humanitarian and philanthropic efforts by child savers and others had adverse consequences for many affected juveniles.

Another facility with a notorious reputation for how it treated juveniles was the Western House of Refuge (WHR) in Rochester, New York, which operated during the 1880s. Juvenile inmates of this facility were considered deviant and criminal. In reality, the youths institutionalized at the WHR were primarily orphaned, abused, or neglected. Their treatment consisted of hard labor and rigid discipline (Smith, 1989). Not all houses of refuge were like the Western House of Refuge, however. In California, for instance, several houses of refuge were operated in ways that stressed vocational training, educational instruction, and some amount of aftercare when youths were ultimately released (Schlossman and Pisciotta, 1986).

Up until the late 1830s, there was little or no pattern to the division of labor between parental, religious, and state authority. As private interests continued to include larger numbers of juveniles within the scope of their supervision, various jurisdictions sought to regulate and institutionalize these assorted juvenile assistance, treatment, and/or intervention programs. In many communities, city councils sanctioned the establishment of facilities to accommodate youths who were either delinquent, dependent, or neglected.

Ex Parte Crouse

In 1839, a decision in a state case gave juvenile authorities considerable power over parents in the management and control of their own children. *Ex parte Crouse* (1839) was a case involving a father who attempted to secure the release of his daughter, Mary Ann Crouse, from the Philadelphia House of Refuge (Shelden, 1998). The girl had been committed to the Philadelphia facility by the court because she was considered unmanageable. She was not given a trial by jury. Rather, her commitment was made arbitrarily by a presiding judge. A higher court rejected the father's claim that parental control of children is exclusive, natural, and proper, and it upheld the power of the state to exercise necessary reforms and restraints to protect children from themselves and their environments. While this decision was only applicable to Pennsylvania citizens and their children, other states took note of it and sought to invoke similar controls over errant children in their jurisdictions. Essentially, children in Pennsylvania were temporarily deprived of any legal standing to challenge decisions made by the state in their behalf.

Reform Schools and *People ex rel. O'Connell v. Turner*

Throughout the remainder of the nineteenth century, different types of institutions were established to supervise unruly juveniles. At roughly mid-century, **reform schools** in several jurisdictions were created. One of the first state-operated reform schools was opened in Westboro, Massachusetts, in 1848. By the end of the century, all states had reform schools of one sort or another. All of these institutions were characterized by strict discipline, absolute control over juvenile behavior, and compulsory work at various trades. Another common feature was that they were controversial (Guarino-Ghezzi and Loughran, 2004).

The primary question raised by reform school critics was, "Do reform schools reform?" Since many juveniles continued to commit delinquent acts after being released from these schools and eventually became adult criminals, the rehabilitative value of reform schools was seriously challenged. The Civil War exacerbated the problem of unruly youths, since many families were broken up. Orphans of dead soldiers were commonplace in the post–Civil War period. Such children were often committed to reform schools, regardless of whether they had committed criminal offenses. Many status offenders were sent to reform schools, simply because they were vagrants. Many of these children did not need to be reformed. Rather, they needed homes and noninstitutional care.

One state, Illinois, was particularly aggressive when it came to confining juveniles in reform schools. Many of these incarcerated juveniles were children of immigrant workers in and around Chicago, and often they were rounded up and imprisoned for simple loitering or playing in the city streets. The Chicago Reform School was especially notorious as a site where such youths were sent and confined. In 1870, however, the Illinois Supreme Court heard and decided a case that ultimately prohibited such juvenile arrests by police and incarcerations. This was the case of *People ex rel. O'Connell v. Turner* (1870). Few legal challenges of state authority were made by complaining parents, because of the awesome power of the state and its control over juvenile matters. However, an Illinois case paved the way for special courts for juveniles and an early recognition of their rights. A youth, Daniel O'Connell, was declared vagrant and in need of supervision and committed to the Chicago Reform School for an unspecified period. O'Connell's parents challenged this court action, claiming that his confinement for vagrancy was unjust and untenable. Existing Illinois law vested state authorities with the power to commit any juvenile to a state reform school as long as a "reasonable justification" could be provided. In this instance, vagrancy was a reasonable justification. The Illinois Supreme Court distinguished between misfortune (vagrancy) and criminal acts in arriving at its decision to reverse Daniel O'Connell's commitment. In effect, the court nullified the law by declaring that reform school commitments of youths could not be made by the state if the "offense" was simple misfortune. They reasoned that state's interests would be better served if commitments of juveniles to reform schools were limited to those committing more serious criminal offenses rather than those who were victims of misfortune. The Illinois Supreme Court further held that it was unconstitutional to confine youths who had not been convicted of criminal conduct or afforded legal due process to be confined in the Chicago Reform School (Shepherd, 2002:2). One result of this decision was the eventual closure of the Chicago Reform School two years later. As one alternative to incarceration, Chicago and other Illinois youths without adult supervision were placed under the care of social service agencies and benevolent societies. Both individuals and groups established settlements for displaced or wayward youths.

Community-Based Private Agencies

In 1889, **Jane Addams** established and operated Hull House in Chicago. Hull House was a settlement home used largely by children from immigrant families in the Chicago area. In those days, adults worked long hours, and many youths were otherwise unsupervised and wandered about their neighborhoods looking for something to do. Using money from various charities and philanthropists, Addams supplied many children with creative activities to alleviate their boredom and monotony. Addams integrated these activities with moral, ethical, and religious teachings. In her own way, she was hoping to deter these youths from lives of crime with her constructive activities and teaching (Ayers, 1997). Thus, her approach was consistent with the philosophy of **Cesare Beccaria,** the father of classical **criminology.** Beccaria wrote in 1764 that the purpose of punishment was deterrence, and that punishment should be measured according to the seriousness of the criminal acts committed.

Truancy Statutes

Truants were created as a class of juvenile offenders in Massachusetts in 1852, where the first compulsory school attendance statute was passed. Many other states adopted similar statutes, until all jurisdictions had compulsory school attendance provisions by 1918 (Bazemore, Stinchcomb, and Leip, 2004). Some historians have erroneously credited Colorado as having drafted the first juvenile court provisions. In fact, the Colorado legislature passed the Compulsory School Act of 1899, the same year that the first juvenile court was established in Illinois. The Colorado action was aimed at preventing truancy, specifically mentioning those youths who were habitually absent from school, wandered about the streets during school hours, and had no obvious business or occupation. Colorado legislators labeled such youths juvenile disorderly persons, but this action did not lead to the creation of a Colorado juvenile court (von Eye and Schuster, 2001).

The Illinois Juvenile Court Act. The Illinois legislature established the first juvenile court on July 1, 1899 by passing the **Act to Regulate the Treatment and Control of Dependent, Neglected and Delinquent Children,** or the **Illinois Juvenile Court Act.** This act provided for limited courts of record, where notes might be taken by judges or their assistants, to reflect judicial actions against

Status offenses include runaway behavior, truancy, curfew violation, and underage drinking.

juveniles. The jurisdiction of these courts, subsequently designated as **juvenile courts,** would include all juveniles under the age of 16 who were found in violation of any state or local law or ordinance. Also, provision was made for the care of dependent and/or neglected children who had been abandoned or who otherwise lacked proper parental care, support, or guardianship. No minimum age was specified that would limit the jurisdiction of juvenile court judges. However, the act provided that judges could impose secure confinement on juveniles 10 years of age or over by placing them in state-regulated juvenile facilities such as the state reformatory or the State Home for Juvenile Female Offenders. Judges were expressly prohibited from confining any juvenile under 12 years of age in a jail or police station. Extremely young juveniles would be assigned probation officers who would look after their needs and placement on a temporary basis.

Illinois's Juvenile Court Act says much about the times and how the legal status of juveniles was interpreted and applied. The full title of the Act is revealing. According to the Act, it was applicable only to

"... children under the age of sixteen (16) years not now or hereafter inmates of a State institution, or any training school for boys or industrial school for girls or some institution incorporated under the laws of this State, except as provided [in other sections]. ... For purposes of this act the words dependent child and neglected child shall mean any child who for any reason is destitute or homeless or abandoned; or dependent upon the public for support; or has not proper parental care or guardianship; or who habitually begs or receives alms, or who is found living in any house of ill fame or with any vicious or disreputable person; or whose home, by reason of neglect, cruelty or depravity on the part of its parents, guardian or other person in whose care it may be, is an unfit place for such a child; and any child under the age of eight

(8) years who is found peddling or selling any article or singing or playing any musical instrument upon the streets or giving any public entertainment. The words delinquent child shall include any child under the age of 16 years who violates any law of this State or any city or village ordinance. The word child or children may mean one or more children, and the word parent or parents may be held to mean one or both parents, when consistent with the intent of this act. The word association shall include any corporation which includes in its purposes the care or disposition of children coming within the meaning of this act."

Even more insightful is what happens when such children are found. What are the limits of court sanctions? Illinois law authorized juvenile court judges to take the following actions in their dealings with dependent and neglected children:

"When any child under the age of sixteen (16) years shall be found to be dependent or neglected within the meaning of this act, the court may make an order committing the child to the care of some suitable State institution, or to the care of some reputable citizen of good moral character, or to the care of some training school or an industrial school, as provided by law, or to the care of some association willing to receive it embracing in its objects the purpose of caring or obtaining homes for dependent or neglected children, which association shall have been accredited as hereinafter provided . . ."

For juvenile delinquents, similar provisions were made. Judges were authorized to continue the hearing for any specific delinquent child "from time to time" and "may commit the child to the care and guardianship of a probation officer." The child might be permitted to remain in *its* own home, subject to the visitation of the probation officer. Judges were also authorized to commit children to state training or industrial schools until such time as they reach the age of their majority or adulthood.

Juveniles as Chattel

The choice of the word *it,* used here in reference to children, shows how youths were viewed in those days. In early English times, children were considered chattel, lumped together with the cows, pigs, horses, and other farm property one might lawfully possess. The Act itself was sufficiently ambiguous so as to allow judges and others considerable latitude or discretion about how to interpret juvenile behaviors. For example, what is meant by proper parental care or guardianship? What is habitual begging? Is occasional begging acceptable? Would children be subject to arrest and juvenile court sanctions for walking city streets playing a flute or other musical device? Who decides what homes and establishments are unfit? Where are the criteria that describe a home's fitness? It has almost always been presumed that juvenile court judges know the answers to these questions, and their judgments, regardless of their foundation, rationality, or consistency with due process, are seldom questioned.

These statements reflect the traditionalism that juvenile court judges have manifested over the years (Guarino-Ghezzi and Loughran, 2004). Taking dependent and neglected or abandoned children and placing them in training or industrial schools is the functional equivalent of adult incarceration in a prison or jail. By a stroke of the pen, the Illinois legislature gave juvenile court judges

BOX 1.1

James Bueche
Director of the Division of Youth Services
Office of Youth Development, Baton Rouge, LA

Statistics:

B.A. (criminal justice) Southeastern Louisiana University; M.S.W., Louisiana State University; Certified Corrections Executive, American Correctional Association

Background and Interests

I grew up in Baton Rouge, Louisiana, where I currently live and work. I graduated from Southeastern Louisiana University (SLU) in 1990 with a degree in criminal justice. SLU is located in Hammond, Louisiana. At the time I attended SLU, the Criminal Justice Program was fairly small and intimate, as everyone in the program knew each other well. Upon graduation I obtained a job in the Parish jail in Baton Rouge where my primary duties included watching inmates who were either there for pretrial or awaiting movement to a long-term facility. Being directly out of college, this experience really opened my eyes to what the real world looked like, since I had spent the last four years learning through books and lectures. This job was a harsh introduction as to what type of individuals found their way into the jail. I worked many mornings on the intake unit, and there were many days when I would get the inmates up for breakfast and they did not know where they were or how they got there. Many of them could not bond out on minor charges, since they were homeless or had no family with resources to assist them. It was at that time that I felt a need to do more. Even though the position at the jail was an important one, I wanted to become more involved in the system with youth in the community prior to them coming into the juvenile justice system.

I was hired as a juvenile probation officer with the Office of Youth Development in 1991. Again this was an eye-opening experience because at the time, training for this position was almost nonexistent. I was handed

a caseload of 80 youth who primarily lived in a rural area approximately 60 miles outside of Baton Rouge. My first challenge was to find all of these kids' homes and meet with them and their parents. This sounds easy enough, but when I began going through the files, I found that all the addresses were in the form of Post Office boxes. After several telephone calls and many hours of becoming lost and asking for directions, I became familiar with the area and found the kids now under my supervision. When I finally got my bearings and realized what I was doing, I was astonished at the manner in which many of these kids lived in rural Louisiana. Many of them lived in houses with dirt floors with little heat, usually provided by a stove, and air conditioning was nonexistent. Again I made a commitment to see what I could do to better my skills to improve the conditions of these and any other youth I may come into contact with. I enrolled part time in a Masters of Social Work (M.S.W.) program through Louisiana State University (LSU). The program involved two nights a week, and everyone in class was in a similar situation as me. We were all practitioners in an area of the people-helping system, and everyone brought their real-life situations and experiences into the classroom. I learned more in this program from the others in the class than from any of the instructors. I finally received my M.S.W. in 1995 and was extremely glad that I had finished the program.

I have worked in many positions with the Office of Youth Development, ranging from community-based program development to intensive aftercare of youth coming out of our secure facilities. Presently, I am the Director of the Division of Youth Services. We oversee 11 Regional Offices around the state that provide community supervision to approximately 6,000 youths. Additionally, we have approximately 72 contracted community-based programs that range from intensive in-home services to restricted residential programming. The oversight of these offices and programs delivers daily challenges that require a lot of delegation to a wonderful staff. One thing that is always consistent when working with this high-risk population is that the staff becomes extremely frustrated, since many days are filled with negative telephone calls, complaints from parents, and judicial inquiries better known as orders. However, whenever we can assist a youth to make a small step in the right direction or turn their life around, this is what keeps the staff coming back to work and try to make a difference.

Interesting Experiences

Throughout my career I have had many experiences working in community-based settings. I have been to homes where a mother answered the door practically nude and proceeded to invite me inside. I have been involved in family fights, literally physical, in a living room with very little room to move. I have also been involved in the apprehension of numerous youths in the community with nothing more than a pair of handcuffs, later to learn the youths had access to weapons or had large amounts of drugs on them. When I look back at a lot of the serious cases I have had to deal with, I am especially reminded of interviewing the violent offenders for reports or progress on supervision. Their presence was so disarming that it was difficult to match the youths with the crimes they had previously committed. I am surprised that my education and experience have brought me to this position in my life. I am also surprised that I made it through most of these crazy days without being seriously hurt.

While I have had a number of occurrences in the community, one of my most memorable experiences was when I did my internship at the Louisiana State Penitentiary. At the time, the prison housed over 5,000 inmates. I worked in a mental health unit of the facility and it became very difficult for me to determine who had a mental condition or who was malingering to get out of work or should be moved to another area of the facility. The operation at the adult prison was immense and it was amazing to see how well the day operated with inmates being fed, going to work and back in their housing areas at the end of the day.

Advice to Students

The best advice I can give to students is to go into a field they really enjoy and have a great deal of interest in exploring. There is nothing worse than going to a job that you do not look forward to going to or are not interested in learning more about every day. Additionally, during school I would suggest that students should involve themselves in internships or even get a part-time job in the field they are pursuing. This will give them a knowledge base of what they might expect when they finally get into the workforce. I wish I had done this, since I was kind of shell-shocked for a period of time after graduation. Also, even though you are in a career and are happy with your position, this is not the time to sit back and become comfortable. People need to use every opportunity they have to learn new skills; volunteer for new projects or even take classes that could eventually help you to advance in your career. Believe me, the more skills you have, the more you will be able to do in the field of juvenile justice, or any field for that matter.

absolute control over the lives of all children under age 16 in the State of Illinois. During the next 10 years, 20 states passed similar acts to establish juvenile courts. By the end of World War II, all states had created juvenile court systems. However, considerable variation existed among these court systems, depending on the jurisdiction. Not all of these courts were vested with a consistent set of responsibilities and powers.

Children's Tribunals

Earlier versions of juvenile courts were created in Massachusetts in 1874. For instance, there were **children's tribunals,** sometimes referred to as **civil tribunals.** These informal mechanisms were used to adjudicate and punish children charged with crimes. They were entirely independent from the system of criminal courts for adults. Usually judges would confer with the equivalent of a social worker and then decide how best to deal with a wayward youth. Under the tribunal system, youths were not entitled to representation by counsel, and the proceedings occurred in secret, away from public view. Furthermore, there were no formal presentations of evidence against the accused youth, no transcripts, no cross-examination of witnesses, and no right to appeal a judicial decision (Pratt and Grimshaw, 1985).

Some years later, Colorado implemented an education law in 1899 known as the **Compulsory School Act.** Although this act was primarily targeted at youths who were habitually absent from school, it also encompassed juveniles who wandered the streets during school hours, without any obvious business or occupation. These youths were termed "juvenile disorderly persons," and they were legislatively placed within the purview of truant officers and law enforcement officers who could detain them and hold them for further action by other community agencies. While both Massachusetts and Colorado created these different mechanisms specifically for dealing with juvenile offenders, they were not juvenile courts in the same sense as those established by Illinois in 1899. Furthermore, these truancy-oriented courts were not an exclusively American creation. In England, for example, pre-court tribunals have been established to decide whether families should be taken to court because of a child's nonattendance at school. The intent of such tribunals is to normalize families and destroy deviant identities juveniles might acquire because of their school absences. Both parents and children must reassure the judge that regular school attendance will be forthcoming (Pratt and Grimshaw, 1985).

Informal Welfare Agencies and Emerging Juvenile Courts

The juvenile court has evolved from an informal welfare agency into a scaled-down, second-class criminal court as the result of a series of reforms that have diverted less serious offenders from juvenile court and moved more serious offenders to criminal courts for processing (Feld, 1993b). Several policy responses have been recommended as options. These include (1) restructuring the juvenile courts to fit their original therapeutic purposes; (2) accepting punishment as the purpose of delinquency proceedings, but couple it with criminal procedural safeguards; and/or (3) abolishing juvenile courts altogether and trying young offenders in criminal courts, with certain substantive and procedural modifications (Cohn et al., 2002).

The Lack of Juvenile Court Uniformity

Little uniformity exists among jurisdictions regarding juvenile court organization and operation. Even within state jurisdictions, great variations exist among counties and cities relating to how juvenile offenders are processed. Historically, family or domestic courts have retained jurisdiction over most, if not all, juvenile matters. Not all jurisdictions have juvenile courts, per se. Rather, some jurisdictions have courts that adjudicate juvenile offenders as well as decide child custody. Thus, while it is true that all jurisdictions presently have juvenile courts, these courts are not always called juvenile courts (Guarino-Ghezzi and Loughran, 2004).

From *Gemeinschaft* to *Gesellschaft* and Reconceptualizing Juveniles

Before the establishment of juvenile courts, how were juvenile offenders processed and punished? How were dependent and neglected children treated? Social scientists would probably describe village and community life in the 1700s and 1800s by citing the dominant social and cultural values that existed then. The term **gemeinschaft** might be used here to describe the lifestyle one might find in such settings. It is a term used to characterize social relations as being highly dependent upon verbal agreements and understandings and informality. Ferdinand Tonnies, a social theorist, used *gemeinschaft* to convey the richness of tradition that would typify small communities where everyone was known to all others. In these settings, formal punishments, such as incarceration in prisons or jails, was seldom used. More effective than incarceration were punishments that heightened public humiliation through stocks and pillars and other corporal measures. There was sufficient social pressure exerted so that most complied with the law. Thus, in *gemeinschaft* communities, people would probably fear social stigma, ostracism, and scorn more than their loss of freedom through incarceration (Hogg and Carrington, 2003).

In these communities, children would remain children through adolescence, eventually becoming adults as they commenced to perform trades or crafts and earned independent livings apart from their families. Children performed apprenticeships over lengthy periods under the tutorship of master craftsmen and others. Many of the terms we currently use to describe delinquent acts and status offenses were nonexistent then. As the nation grew, urbanization and the increasing population density of large cities changed social relationships gradually but extensively. Tonnies described the nature of this gradual shift in social relationships from a *gemeinschaft* type of social network to a **gesellschaft** type of society. In *gesellschaft* societies, social relationships are more formal, contractual, and impersonal. There is greater reliance on codified compilations of appropriate and lawful conduct as a means of regulating social relations.

As urbanization gradually occurred, children were reconceptualized. During the period of Reconstruction following the Civil War, there were no child labor laws, and children were exploited increasingly by industry and business.

Children were put to work in factories in their early years, where they were paid low wages in **sweat shops,** usually manufacturing companies where long hours were required and persons worked at repetitive jobs on assembly lines. By the end of the nineteenth century, in part because of these widespread nonunionized and unregulated sweat-shop operations and compulsory school attendance for youths in their early years, loitering youths became increasingly visible and attracted the attention of the general public and law enforcement.

Specialized Juvenile Courts

Special courts were subsequently established to adjudicate juvenile matters. The technical language describing inappropriate youthful conduct or misbehaviors was greatly expanded and refined. These new courts were also vested with the authority to appoint probation officers and other persons considered suitable to manage juvenile offenders and enforce new juvenile codes that most cities created. Today, most larger police departments have specialized juvenile sections or divisions, where only juvenile law violations or suspicious activities are investigated. In retrospect, Platt (1969) suggests that the original aggregate of child savers had much to do with inventing delinquency and its numerous, specialized subcategories as we now know them. At least they contributed to the formality of the present juvenile justice system by defining a range of impermissible juvenile behaviors that would require an operational legal apparatus to address. Once a juvenile justice system was established and properly armed with the right conceptual tools, it was a relatively easy step to enforce a fairly rigid set of juvenile behavioral standards and regulate most aspects of their conduct. This seems to be a part of a continuing pattern designed to criminalize the juvenile courts and hold juveniles accountable to the same standards as adult offenders (Blevins, 2005).

As juvenile court systems became more widespread, it was apparent that these proceedings were quite different from criminal courts in several respects. Largely one-sided affairs, these proceedings typically involved the juvenile charged with some offense; a petitioner claiming the juvenile should be declared delinquent, a status offender, dependent, or neglected; and a judge who would weigh the evidence and decide the matter (Costello, 2003; Patrick et al., 2004). Juveniles themselves were not provided with opportunities to solicit witnesses or even give testimony in their own behalf. Defense attorneys were largely unknown in juvenile courtrooms, since there were no significant issues to defend (Arthur, 2004).

Juvenile court proceedings were closed to the general public, primarily to protect the identities of the youthful accused. While these proceedings were conducted behind closed doors for this manifest purpose, a latent function of such secrecy was to obscure from public view the high-handed and discriminatory decision making that characterized many juvenile court judges. In short, they didn't want the general public to know about the subjectivity and arbitrary nature of their decisions. On the basis of allegations alone, together with uncorroborated statements and pronouncements from probation officers and others, juvenile court judges were free to declare any particular juvenile either delinquent or nondelinquent. The penalties that could be imposed were wide-ranging, from verbal reprimands and warnings to full-fledged incarceration in a secure juvenile facility. Virtually everything depended on the opinions and views of presiding juvenile court judges. And their decisions were not appealable to higher courts.

Throughout much of the twentieth century, juveniles had no legal standing in American courts. Their constitutional rights were not at issue, because they did not have any constitutional protections in the courtroom. No rules of evidence existed to govern the quality of evidence admitted or to challenge the reliability or integrity of testifying witnesses. In most jurisdictions, juveniles were not entitled to jury trials, unless the juvenile court judge approved. And most juvenile court judges opted for bench trials rather than granting jury trials to juvenile defendants. Because these proceedings were exclusively civil in nature, the rules of criminal procedure governing criminal courts did not apply. Juveniles did not acquire criminal records. Rather, they acquired civil adjudications of delinquency. Yet, the incarceration dimension of the juvenile justice system has almost always paralleled that of the criminal justice system. Industrial or training schools, reform schools, and other types of secure confinement for juveniles have generally been nothing more than juvenile prisons. Thus, for many adjudicated juvenile offenders sentenced to one of these industrial schools, these sentences were the equivalent of imprisonment.

Kangaroo Courts in Action

Such unchecked discretion among juvenile court judges continued well into the 1960s. One explanation is mass complacency or apathy among the general public about juvenile affairs. Juvenile matters were relatively unimportant and trivial. Another explanation is the prevalent belief that juvenile court judges knew what is best for adjudicated offenders and usually prescribed appropriate punishments. Juvenile court judges and others often viewed juveniles as victims of their environment and peer associations. It might be easier to justify why new environments are required, including incarceration for the purpose of training, education, and rehabilitation, if the adverse effects of former environments can be illustrated. However, in 1967, the U.S. Supreme Court decided the case of *In re Gault*. This was perhaps the first major Supreme Court case that applied more stringent standards to juvenile court judge decision making, thus making them more accountable to the general public.

Briefly, Gerald Gault was a 15-year-old Arizona youth who allegedly made an obscene telephone call to an adult female neighbor. The woman called the police, suggested that the youth, Gault, was the guilty party, and Gault was summarily taken into custody and detained for nearly two days. The woman was never brought to court as a witness, and the only evidence she provided was her initial verbal accusation made to police on the day of Gault's arrest. Gault himself allegedly admitted that he dialed the woman's number, but he claimed that a friend of his actually spoke to the woman and made the remarks she found offensive. Partly because Gault had been involved in an earlier petty offense and had a "record," the judge, together with the probation officer, decided that Gault was dangerous enough to commit to the Arizona State Industrial School, Arizona's main juvenile penitentiary, until he reached 21 years of age or until juvenile corrections authorities decided he was rehabilitated and could be safely released. According to Arizona law, the sentence was unappealable. Any adult convicted of the same offense may have been fined $50 and/or

Conventional classroom settings are found in both public and private institutions for delinquents.

sentenced to a 30-day jail term. But in Gault's case, he received six years in a juvenile prison, complete with correctional officers with firearms, high walls, locked gates, and barbed wire.

Appropriately, the U.S. Supreme Court referred to the court of the judge who originally sentenced Gault as a kangaroo court. Gault's sentence was reversed and several important constitutional rights were conferred upon all juveniles as a result. Specifically, all of Gault's due process rights had been denied. He had been denied counsel, had not been protected against self-incrimination, had not been permitted to cross-examine his accuser, and had not been provided with specific notice of the charges against him. Now all juveniles enjoy these rights in every U.S. juvenile court. It is important to note that Arizona was not alone in its harsh and one-sided treatment of juvenile offenders. What occurred in the Gault case was occurring in juvenile courts in most other jurisdictions at the time. The Gault case served to underscore the lack of legal standing of juveniles everywhere, and substantial juvenile justice reforms were occurring (D'Angelo and Brown, 2005).

The Increasing Bureaucratization and Criminalization of Juvenile Justice

After the *Gault* case and several other important Supreme Court decisions affecting juveniles, the nature of juvenile courts began to change. But this transformation was anything but smooth. Even the U.S. Supreme Court continued to view juvenile courts as basically rehabilitative and treatment-centered apparatuses, thus reinforcing the traditional doctrine within the context of various constitutional restraints. Nevertheless, episodic changes in juvenile court procedures and the juvenile justice system generally suggested that it was becoming increasingly criminalized. Furthermore, many juvenile courts have moved away from traditional methods of conducting adjudicatory hearings for juveniles. Instead of individualized decision making and a rehabilitative orientation, many judges are increasingly interested in mechanisms that streamline the processing of juvenile cases and offenders. In fact, some juvenile courts have used mathematical models to establish profiles of juvenile offenders to expedite the adjudicatory process. This has been termed **actuarial justice** by some authorities, and it means that the traditional orientation of juvenile justice and punishment has been supplanted by the goal of efficient offender processing (Kempf-Leonard and Peterson, 2000). In Minnesota and other jurisdictions, the development of new Rules of Procedure for Juvenile Court and the current administrative assumptions and operations of these courts, with limited exceptions, often render them indistinguishable from criminal courts and the procedures these courts follow.

PARENS PATRIAE

Parens patriae is a concept that originated with the king of England during the twelfth century. It means literally the father of the country. Applied to juvenile matters, *parens patriae* means that the king is in charge of, makes decisions about, and has the responsibility for all matters involving juveniles. Within the scope of early English common law, parental authority was primary in the early upbringing of children. However, as children advanced beyond the age of 7, they acquired some measure of responsibility for their own actions. Accountability to parents was shifted gradually to accountability to the state, whenever youths 7 years of age or older violated the law. In the name of the king, chancellors in various districts adjudicated matters involving juveniles and the offenses they committed. Juveniles had no legal rights or standing in any court. They were the sole responsibility of the king or his agents. Their future often depended largely on chancellor decisions. In effect, children were wards of the court, and the court was vested with the responsibility to safeguard their welfare (Lamb, Weinberger, and DeCuir, 2002).

Chancery courts of twelfth- and thirteenth-century England and later years performed many tasks, including the management of children and their affairs, as well as the management of the affairs of the mentally ill and incompetent. Therefore, an early division of labor was created, involving a three-way relationship between the child, the parent, and the state. The underlying thesis of *parens patriae* was that the parents are merely the agents of society in the area of childrearing, and that the state has the primary and legitimate interest in the upbringing of its children. Thus, *parens patriae* established a type of fiduciary or trust-like parent–child relation, with the state able to exercise the right of intervention to delimit parental rights (Fader et al., 2001).

Since children could become wards of the court and subject to their control, a key concern for many chancellors was for the future welfare of these children. The welfare interests of chancellors and their actions led to numerous rehabilitative and/or treatment measures. Some of these measures included placement of children in foster homes or their assignment to various work tasks for local merchants. Parental influence in these child placement decisions was minimal. In the context of *parens patriae,* it is fairly easy to trace this early philosophy of child management and its influence to subsequent events in the United States, such as the child-saver movement, houses of refuge, and reform schools. These latter developments were both private and public attempts to rescue children from their hostile environments and meet some or all of their needs through various forms of institutionalization.

 **BOX 1.2**

James D. Rankin, Jr.
CSU Director, Virginia Department of Juvenile Justice 31st District Court Service Unit, Manassas, VA

Statistics:

B.S. (social work), Madison College; M.S. (administration of justice and public safety), Virginia Commonwealth University

Background

I grew up in New Market, a small, rural community in the Shenandoah Valley of Virginia. Upon completion of high school I attended Blue Ridge Community College, graduating with an Associate of Arts degree in 1969 and graduated in 1971 from Madison College (now James Madison University) in Harrisonburg, Virginia, with a Bachelor's degree in social work. One week later I began my juvenile justice career as a probation officer with Prince William County, Virginia, where I have been fortunate to serve in various capacities. As a probation officer for five years, I encountered many interesting, challenging, and amusing cases. Some of the people I supervised went on to tragic ends, that is, being executed on death row for criminal offenses. Others have gone on to better and more pleasant accomplishments having become commissioned officers in the military and serving in police departments and other public safety venues.

Following my tenure as a probation officer, I became a probation supervisor and fortunate to be a part of one of the fastest growing communities in the nation at the time. From the beginning, our small office was able to cope due to the existence of a family-friendly work environment where flexibility and teamwork continues to be emphasized. I recall my reluctance at leaving the front line for a mid-management position as I felt my true skill and love was to work directly with people. It became evident to me after a few years that I possessed the leadership and managerial skills that allowed me to continue to work with people and develop programs, resources, and poli-

cies. One of my greatest pleasures has been watching the growth and development of young and enthusiastic officers as they become proficient and competent in their abilities and truly enjoy their jobs. In 1982, I was promoted to Assistant Director and held that position for 10 years until being promoted to my current position as Director of the Court Service Unit, from where I direct the work of about 60 employees and related programs and services. En route to the position of Director, I was able to attend graduate school while working full time and in 1980 received a master's degree in the Administration of Justice and Public Safety from Virginia Commonwealth University in Richmond, Virginia.

My juvenile justice involvement has provided me with varied and numerous experiences. I have worked every aspect of juvenile probation to include intake, parole, probation, and domestic relations where I served for 10 years as a mediator dealing with custody, support, and visitation matters. Some of those experiences include having been a witness at a Navy Court Martial hearing, presenting before the Virginia General Assembly, walking the halls at a high school to ease racially tense conditions, and serving on numerous local and state boards and committees.

Reflections

I was initially attracted to juvenile justice from an undergraduate experience where one of my advisors asked me to serve as a mentor for a young man at the local high

school. I felt the experience would help prepare me for social work, but it also gave me
exposure to the juvenile justice system and
piqued my interest. I had been awarded a
scholarship in social work that required me
to work two years in social work upon graduation. Based on limited availability of social work positions and my request, that
requirement was waived to allow me to work
in juvenile justice. During my employment
in Prince William County for the past 30
years, I've been uniquely placed to observe
significant changes in terms of population,
demographics, social needs, and resource
and program development. In the early
1970s, Prince William County was one of the
fastest growing communities in the nation
and experienced challenges meeting infra-
structure demands associated with such
rapid growth. It has been a pleasure and a
joy to watch the community grow, adjust,
and respond to its juvenile justice needs,
which include a day reporting center, secure
detention, group homes, emergency shelter
facilities, diversion programs, intensive supervision, specialized sex offender programming, and a Juvenile Drug Court. Resources
have been allocated to provide and purchase
intervention services for juveniles that might
otherwise have had their service needs go
unmet or face incarceration in a correctional
facility. Over the years the faces of the young
people have changed, however, not their
basic needs or how we respond to them. We
are seeing more violent offenses and gang-
involved behavior coming before the courts.
Additionally, more juveniles with mental
health issues are making their way into the
justice system.

For all the positives and gains that
have been made, clearly there are some negatives. Salaries have always been a concern
in the failing to keep pace with salaries of
positions requiring similar job skills and educational backgrounds. The attempt to
maintain adequate work conditions and
identify sufficient resources to address the
unique needs of some of our clientele have
not been as successful as desired. In terms
of program development, not every initiative that we embarked upon was successful
nor supported. Nonetheless, I thoroughly
enjoy the challenges we faced and continue

to face. The Court Service Unit has been creative and resourceful in planning, developing, directing, and coordinating the delivery
of services in the 31st Judicial District,
which include the Cities of Manassas and
Manassas Park, Virginia, and a total population of about 386,000. The level of my success in my position is for others to
determine, but my degree of job satisfaction
is my responsibility and without hesitation I
can think of no other position I would have
rather held.

The role of the Director is critical in
the overall effectiveness of a Court Service
Unit. The Director certainly must model a
respect for the position, departmental policy, and initiatives, and have a vision for
what the unit can and should accomplish.
Being attentive and responsive to trends and
to input from knowledgeable individuals
and being surrounded by a quality management team all lead to the work of effective
management. Policies that are developed
and implemented and program strategies all
bear the influence of the Director. The position carries undeniable stressors; recognition of staff needs, recruitment, budget
development, performance compliance, and
sometimes having to make the final decision
as when the "buck stops here."

Changes and Trends

In the early 1970s, Prince William County
was a rural, bedroom community to the metropolitan Washington, DC, area. Even though
small by comparison to the metropolitan
area, the rapid growth soon saw the county
being faced with a shortage of schools, teachers, public safety personnel, highways, and
other government support to meet the demands of the community. The need to
rapidly fill those positions and create resources kept, and to some extent, continues
to keep Prince William County in a reactive
mode. Technology, media, and the influences of the modern age, where families are
more of an amalgamation than a single unit,
have made a significant impact on our client
profile. Juveniles enter the system at a
younger age, many with mental health issues,
having committed more violent and gang-
(continued)

related offenses. The influence of the Latino community has been profound, resulting in additional pressures on the system to respond to the resource needs of that unique population.

Advice to Students

Students interested in juvenile justice careers are encouraged, as a part of their academic education, to participate in field placements or internships related to the field. It is often said that "book smarts" do not make one proficient at working with people and to some extent it is true; however, a solid educational foundation is important. Probation officers have always worn many different "hats," serving as mentor, advocate, prosecutor, attorney, "the man," and judge, to name a few. The role of probation officer has not changed but delivery of probation services has become much more sophisticated over the years. There is a need to have a specialized skill set to include knowledge of adolescent growth and development, an awareness of mental health illness (signs and symptoms), as well as a practical knowledge of juvenile and criminal law. In seeking internships, students should seek those that afford them ample opportunity to participate in an experiential initiative as opposed to one based on observation. While academic preparation is encouraged, some of the innate abilities that are critical in this field must be assessed on an individual basis. A probation officer should have the ability to listen, empathize, model good character, hold juveniles accountable, and communicate effectively, as these abilities will influence their effectiveness and overall job performance and satisfaction.

Future Challenges

My career has encompassed three-plus decades, and looking to the future, one of the challenges I see for the system is more emphasis on prevention. As previously mentioned, rapidly growing Prince William County was in a position of constantly react-

ing to identified needs within the community. Prevention, quite often, is difficult to measure and thus many prevention programs do not receive financial support. This is an element that must receive more attention. In addition, with the influx of diversity in our populations, such as the Latino community in some areas, human service agencies will be in need of additional skill sets, to include the ability to apply cultural awareness and sensitivity in order to communicate effectively with those individuals. Another growing concern for the future is that of gangs. For a long time there was an effort to repress or even deny the concern about gang activity. Now that it is being more openly and readily recognized, efforts need to be extended to provide successful interventions as well as gang suppression and abatement activities.

Finally, a major trend or future challenge is the need for collaboration. The success of the Court Service Unit is based on our ability to establish partnerships within the human services community. Such partnerships will be critical for the future. No longer can the courts, police, and juvenile justice community solely be expected to address juvenile delinquency nor can the police deal independently with public safety. Schools cannot stand alone in the education of our youth. These aspects of life are intertwined and all human service agencies, public and private, have an investment in addressing them. This concept/trend is being more readily embraced in communities where initiatives are multijurisdictional, multidisciplinary in makeup, where partners and key stakeholders come to the table sharing resources, information, integrity, and efforts to address anticipated needs of a community. Issues around territory and "turf" must become secondary and the need to collaborate become primary. True and meaningful collaborations will be the way that communities deliver effective juvenile justice, public safety, education, and other human service needs in the future.

MODERN INTERPRETATIONS OF *PARENS PATRIAE*

Parens patriae in the 1990s is very much alive throughout all juvenile court jurisdictions in the United States, although some erosion of this doctrine has occurred during the past three or four decades. The persistence of this doctrine is evidenced by the wide range of dispositional options available to juvenile court judges and others involved in earlier stages of offender processing in the juvenile justice system. Most of these dispositional options are either nominal or conditional, meaning that the confinement of any juvenile for most offenses is regarded as a last resort. Nominal or conditional options involve relatively mild sanctions (e.g., verbal warnings or reprimands, diversion, probation, making financial restitution to victims, performance of community service, participation in individual or group therapy, or involvement in educational programs), and these sanctions are intended to reflect the rehabilitative ideal that has been a major philosophical underpinning of *parens patriae* (Sanborn, 2001).

The Get-Tough Movement

However, the strong treatment or rehabilitative orientation reflected by the *parens patriae* concept is in conflict with the contemporary juvenile justice themes of accountability, justice, and due process (Inciardi, 2003). Contemporary juvenile court jurisprudence stresses individual accountability for one's actions. Increasingly there is a trend toward just-deserts and justice in the juvenile justice system. This **get-tough movement** is geared toward providing law violators with swifter, harsher, and more certain justice and punishment than the previously dominant rehabilitative philosophy of American courts (Flory and Hutchinson-Wallace, 2005).

Stereotypical views of juvenile corrections inaccurately portray these institutions as largely warehouses for youths where rehabilitation is largely ignored.

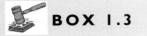 **BOX 1.3**

Crime in Sweden has increased substantially since World War II. Since the 1970s law-breaking behavior has continued to increase. A small portion of this increase has been committed by juvenile offenders. Sweden has traditionally adopted a rehabilitative position toward juvenile offending. One of the first industrialized countries besides the United States to recognize the special status of juveniles, Sweden passed several laws in 1902 declaring that juveniles should be separated from adult offenders. This separation pertained not only to confinement with adult offenders, but to all varieties of measures applied to juveniles and treatments for their behaviors, illegal or otherwise. Throughout the twentieth century, Sweden's policy toward juveniles has been to insulate them from any aspect of the criminal justice process, largely through diversion. This diversion includes separation from both correctional treatment and prison. Since World War II, there has been a subtle shift from treatment to punishment in programs involving delinquent offenders.

In the pre–World War II period, criminal youths were subjected to forced care under the Act on Child Care of 1935. Forced care applied to juveniles between the ages of 15 and 17, although this act was expanded to include those between 18 and 21 as well. Youth prisons were established for young people, and these prisons were more like treatment centers providing medical, social, educational, and other forms of assistance, depending on individual youth needs. Placement in such forced-care facilities was indeterminate, and the needs of each youth determined the length of stay in these facilities. Following World War II, forced care was abolished and replaced by protective foster care in community homes. Prison sentences were drastically shortened for those under age 18. Youth welfare was increasingly oriented toward preventive and supportive measures. Institutional placement was a last resort in any juvenile decision making. The thinking reflected a shift toward treatment and away from punishment.

In 1965 the laws were changed to provide a greater variety of treatments for juvenile offenders. Youth prisons were only for those youths who committed a crime for which the penalty was prison. Perpetrators had to be between the ages of 18 and 20, although in a few exceptional cases, a few persons under age 18 were imprisoned. Subsequently the age was extended to include youths between ages 21 and 23. The time spent in prison was unspecified. For younger youths ages 15–17, these youths were diverted from the criminal justice system to be treated through community child care. During the 1970s placing youths in prisons or forced care was avoided as much as possible. Youth prisons were eventually abolished in 1980, and according to the 1982 Social Services Act, decisions about youths would be made according to their best interests, consistent with the *parens patriae* doctrine in the United States. Forced-care provisions were continued for only the most violent youthful offenders under the Act with Special Provisions on the Care of Young People (LVU) in 1982, although the theme continued to be whatever was in the youth's best interests.

Community homes were created and operated by county councils. These became specially approved youth homes. They were located in communities near where youths lived in order for youths to maintain normal friendships with their peers. In 1989, partially in response to growing juvenile violence and perceived lenient treatment, the LVU was changed to provide more serious consequences proportional to the seriousness of the acts committed. Citizen protection was stressed by the 1993 Commission on Juvenile Crime (SOU), resulting in the establishment of the National Board for Institutional Care (SIS). In 1994 the state assumed responsibility for youth welfare in specially approved youth homes. Today SIS has the responsibility for all youths under age 18 sentenced to institutional care. The length of time for institutional care is no less than 14 days and no more than 4 years.

Punishment is indeterminate but intentionally abbreviated. Institutional youth care replaced prison sentences for juveniles under age 18. Those between ages 18 and 21 can still receive prison sentences depending on the circumstances of their offense.

The major type of crime committed by juveniles is theft. Violent crimes are rare. Juvenile violence has been exaggerated by the media. Significant changes in the method of reporting crimes have shown marked declines in the amount of juvenile violence. Today it accounts for a very small amount of youthful offending. Crime among youths escalated during the 1980s and until the mid-1990s, when it became stable and began to decline. Subsequently there was a marked drop in charges among juveniles relating to theft. Sweden has been progressive to the extent that it has implemented several self-report studies of juvenile crime. It has tracked juvenile and general criminal offending since 1971 through self-reports. Overall the level of theft offending has declined between 1995–2005.

The juvenile justice system in Sweden is particularly unique because there is no juvenile court. The responsibility for responding to crimes committed by young people is shared by the social services and the adult judicial system. For those under age 15, the responsibility for treatment lies with social services. Between 15–17 years of age, the responsibility is divided equally between social services and the judiciary. From ages 18–20, the judicial authorities have the primary responsibility over juvenile offenders.

Whenever a criminal act occurs, police investigate. Swedish police have considerable discretionary power. In fact, police officers have the right in certain cases to direct youths to repair the damage caused by their behavior toward victims, much like victim–offender reconciliation or through mediation. Police prevent, discover, and investigate crimes. The police are empowered to investigate all crimes for those over the age of 12. However, for youths under age 18 and over age 12, it is expected that a close collaboration will occur between police and social services to ensure the proper treatments and measures will be applied where needed. When police interrogate youths, their par-

ents are usually present. If the suspect is under age 15, social services assumes jurisdiction over the case. The prosecutor gets any case where the offender is age 15 or older. However, if the suspect is age 15 or over but under age 18, social services are still informed.

Where youths are age 15 or older, prosecutors have extraordinary discretionary powers. They decide whether a preliminary investigation should be discontinued; whether a prosecution waiver should be issued; whether a summary sanction order should be issued; or whether a suspect should be prosecuted in court. Waivers of cases in Sweden have nothing to do with U.S. waivers. In these Swedish cases, a prosecutorial waiver means that the guilty party will not be subjected to further measures within the court apparatus, contingent upon the youth's agreement not to reoffend. Such waiver rights are given to prosecutors under the Swedish Young Offenders Act (LUL) for any suspect under age 18, and in certain cases up to age 20. Such waivers may be revoked if youths reoffend. Social services usually advise prosecutors before they issue waivers. Prosecutors also determine the sanctions to be imposed for various crimes. Summary sanction orders are usually day fines, where the number of days is determined by crime seriousness and the amount of the fine is determined by the family's economic circumstances. About a third of all youths receive day fines.

In those instances where the prosecutor decides to prosecute, over 60 percent of prosecuted youths receive convictions from prosecutors. All youth convictions are determined by the general court. Only 11 percent of all registered offenders in Sweden are sentenced to prison. For persons under age 18, imprisonment is only rarely used. Only about 50 persons a year are imprisoned who were under age 18 at the time they committed their offense. In these cases, imprisonment is usually for a very short period of a few months. Probation follows imprisonment, often for an indeterminate period until authorities are satisfied that the youth will not reoffend. Thus, the most frequently used sanctions are fines (37 percent

(continued)

of all juveniles sentenced), waived prosecution (24 percent), and community care (18 percent).

Social services do not punish youths. They determine social and educational needs on an individual basis and see that they are implemented. Thus, all offending by those under age 15 is a social welfare problem. The aim of social services, therefore, is to help young offenders out of the social situations that led them to commit crimes. A broad range of therapies is available to social services in their treatment of youths. Social services may make out-of-home placements of youths, if the parents are deemed unfit to raise their children properly or if the youths' guardians are unsuitable. In about 80 percent of all social services cases, these measures are voluntary. The most common form of placement used with compulsory care orders by social services is placement in a youth care facility. Educational, vocational, and social programs are offered to those in need of such services.

Swedish schools have a great deal of power as well to deal with unruly students. Most Swedish schools have their own mechanisms for dealing with juvenile problems. Ordinarily some collaboration should occur between school authorities and social services when treating specific youths, particu-

larly where mental illness treatments are recommended. Parents are almost always involved in such decision making as well.

In sum, police or prosecutors conduct preliminary investigations of all youths under age 21, with a wide variety of coercive measures possible. Court proceedings are swift. A six-week time limit exists for prosecutors to complete their investigations; guardians and social services are advised as to the results of such investigations. General courts are responsible for implementing any type of coercive measures, depending on individual needs. Proceedings against juveniles are closed to the public. Guardians and social services may attend. If imprisonment is the sentence, extraordinary reasons must exist for such action. In less serious cases involving persons under age 15, evidentiary proceedings are possible but never used; investigation is done if needed; local social welfare boards implement special measures if recommended; searches for goods may be conducted, and for special reasons; and limited coercive measures, such as the search and seizure of goods, may be taken by local social welfare boards. The net effect is to insulate most juveniles from contact with the criminal justice system and thus avoid adverse labeling. Diversion is the guiding philosophy.

[*Sources:* Adapted from Jerzy Sarnecki and Felipe Estrada, "Juvenile Crime in Sweden." Department of Criminology, University of Stockholm, Unpublished paper, 2004; *Crime Statistics 2004*. Stockholm, SE, 2005; Utredningen Om Oversyn Av Det Allmannas Ingripanden Vid Ungdomscbrott, "Institutional Care of Youths," Unpublished paper, 2005.]

For juveniles, this means greater use of nonsecure and secure custody and incarcerative sanctions in state group homes, industrial schools, or reform schools. For those juveniles charged with violent offenses, this means transferring larger numbers of them to the jurisdiction of criminal courts for adults, where more severe sanctions such as life imprisonment or the death penalty may be imposed. Not everyone agrees that this is a sound trend, however. It has been suggested that while many people favor a separate juvenile justice system different from the criminal justice system, they exhibit a strong preference for a system that disposes most juveniles to specialized treatment or counseling programs in lieu of incarceration, even for repeat offenders (Merlo and Benekos, 2003).

Influencing the *parens patriae* doctrine are the changing rights of juveniles. Since the mid-1960s, juveniles have acquired greater constitutional rights commensurate with those enjoyed by adults in criminal courts. Some researchers believe that as juveniles are vested with greater numbers of constitutional rights, a gradual transformation of the juvenile court is occurring toward one of greater criminalization (D'Angelo and Brown, 2005). Interestingly, as juveniles obtain a greater range of constitutional rights, they become less susceptible to the influence of *parens patriae.*

Another factor is the gradual transformation of the role of prosecutors in juvenile courts. As prosecutors become more involved in pursuing cases against juvenile defendants, the entire juvenile justice process is perceived by some researchers as weakening the delinquency prevention role of juvenile courts (Herring, 2005). Thus, more aggressive prosecution of juvenile cases is perceived as moving away from delinquency prevention for the purpose of deterring youths from future adult criminality. The intentions of prosecutors in most cases are to ensure that youths are entitled to due process, but the social costs may be to label these youths in ways that will propel them toward adult criminality rather than away from it (Schaffner, 2005).

SUMMARY

The juvenile justice system is a more or less integrated network of agencies, institutions, and organizations that process juvenile offenders. Its essential components include law enforcement, prosecution and the courts, community and institutional corrections, aftercare, and parole. Social service agencies, both public and private, supplement governmental organizations in processing and supervising youths. Because juvenile justice is most often administered at the city and county levels throughout the United States, there is considerable diversity among jurisdictions about its structure and operations. Some authorities regard this network of agencies as a process rather than a system, since there is much fragmentation and less precise coordination between agencies and juvenile justice personnel.

The first juvenile court was established in 1899 in Illinois. Prior to juvenile courts, juveniles were subject largely to parental supervision and/or informal social welfare agencies whose goals were to make decisions for juveniles according to whatever was in their best interests. Early English common law established the age of 7 as one's age of accountability, and those under the age of 7 were considered not responsible for their actions. In fifteenth-century English counties or shires, reeves or local law enforcement officers would maintain order, and chancellors appointed by the King would make decisions about juveniles who violated the law. During the mid- to late 1500s, workhouses and other facilities were used to house criminals, including women and juveniles. In the colonies, many jails and lockups were fashioned after similar English facilities, and accommodations for inmates were poor.

Pennsylvania was one of the first states to make substantial improvements in facilities where prisoners of all types were maintained, and the Walnut Street Jail in Philadelphia was a pioneering effort in penal reform in 1790. This facility provided for separate quarters for women and children from male prisoners, together with other innovations. Significant improvements in the treatment of prisoners were promoted by the Quakers, who sought conditions that would contribute to one's rehabilitation and eventual reintegration into society.

During the early 1800s, various philanthropists and religious groups joined forces to establish the child savers, a general movement dedicated to providing food, shelter, and other services to children who wandered about the streets unsupervised. Often both parents had to work to provide for their families, and few if any alternatives were available to families for child care. Child-saving organizations were found in other countries besides the United States. Often these child-saving organizations sought to impose their middle-class ideologies and beliefs on the children they protected, and not everyone supported their efforts. Houses of refuge were established in different cities as well. Although some houses of refuge were privately operated, many were state-operated and functioned like training schools, offering compulsory education and vocational training. Some houses of refuge, such as the Western House of Refuge in Rochester, New York, were custodial institutions for youths considered deviant, orphaned, abused, or neglected. The power of the state in regulating juvenile affairs was established by court decisions such as *Ex parte Crouse* in 1839, which usurped parental control over unmanageable children.

In Illinois and other states, institutions known as reform schools were created, and were little more than prisons for juveniles. These institutions proliferated following the Civil War, when many children were orphaned. Simple vagrancy, begging, or wandering the streets aimlessly were sufficient grounds to commit youths to such facilities, which were notorious for their harsh conditions, strict discipline, and compulsory labor. In 1870, the case of *People v. ex rel. O'Connell v. Turner* was decided. This case resulted in the successful removal of a juvenile from an Illinois reform school whose only offense was that he was vagrant and in need of supervision. More than a few states were quick to recognize the unfavorable consequences of locking up vagrant juveniles with hardcore youths in prison-like settings like reform schools. More community-based public and private agencies were spawned in the aftermath of the removal of such children from these institutions, such as Hull House, a settlement home operated by Jane Addams in Chicago in the 1880s. For juveniles who committed crimes, children's tribunals were established in states such as Massachusetts during the 1870s. These tribunals were informally conducted and were forerunners of today's juvenile courts.

During the 1890s compulsory education became the rule rather than the exception for youths, and Colorado passed the first truancy statute in 1899 that provided for the compulsory education of juveniles. Other states quickly followed suit and passed similar laws. These statutes performed both manifest and latent functions. One manifest function was to ensure that all children received educational instruction and could learn how to read and write. A latent function was to keep children occupied during daytime hours and under the close supervision of school authorities.

The emergence of the first juvenile court in 1899 was an official recognition of a special class of persons for which a unique set of laws would be applicable. This new type of court was vested with a great deal of power over juvenile affairs, and for many decades, this and similar courts in other jurisdictions functioned like social welfare agencies. Decisions were almost always made on behalf of juveniles and in their best interests, a traditional philosophy rooted in early English jurisprudence called *parens patriae*. Thus, juvenile courts perpetuated a long-standing pattern of treating juveniles as entities in need of care, protection, and supervision. These courts also established an assortment of punishments and imposed such punishments most often in closed proceedings. Children had no legal standing, and therefore juvenile rights were never regarded as an issue for juvenile court judges to consider. Juvenile proceedings were civil in nature and one-sided.

As more juvenile courts were created in different jurisdictions and greater numbers of juvenile offenders were processed by them, considerable organizational restructuring was necessary as a means of streamlining case processing and disposing of juvenile cases. Gradually juvenile courts and the juvenile justice system acquired many of the characteristics of large bureaucracies replete with rules and regulations. As greater bureaucratization occurred, juvenile courts assumed many of the characteristics that typify contemporary criminal courts, with judge's benches, tables for the defense and prosecution, seats for audiences, and in some instances, jury boxes. These physical characteristics of such courts made them appear criminal-like, and growing numbers of concerned citizens regarded them as criminogenic environments.

Despite these physical similarities to criminal courts, juvenile courts processed juveniles quite differently and continue to do so. On a state-by-state basis, each juvenile court gradually defined the age limits of its jurisdiction and delineated the types of cases it heard and decided. Different types of juveniles fell within the jurisdiction of these courts, including status offenders, delinquent offenders, and children in need of supervision. Status offenders included juveniles who committed offenses not defined as criminal but rather as violations of laws applicable only to juveniles. Such laws pertained to truancy, runaway behavior, curfew violation, and a litany of other types of minor offending. Delinquents were juveniles who committed acts that would be crimes if adults committed them. Children in need of supervision included a large class of juveniles who lacked adequate parental control or guardianship, were orphans in need of state protection, or who suffered from different psychological or physical conditions requiring special care and supervision. Presently juvenile courts exercise jurisdiction over most persons charged with delinquency, although many of these courts have divested themselves of jurisdiction over other types of juveniles, such as status offenders or children in need of supervision.

Juvenile courts have perpetuated the *parens patriae* doctrine through their traditional orientation toward and treatment of juvenile offenders. However, during the 1960s and 1970s juveniles acquired several important constitutional rights similar to those enjoyed by adults. Greater attorney representation of juvenile interests followed, and juvenile proceedings became more adversarial. Today juvenile courts have a strong due process focus, attributable in part to a get-tough movement or ideology that espouses more punishment-centered orientations toward juveniles. Juvenile court judges reflect a mixed set of philosophical principles that guide their decision making about juvenile offenders. Many of these judges attempt to balance the aims of due process and justice with individualized treatments and therapies intended to rehabilitate and reintegrate youthful offenders.

QUESTIONS FOR REVIEW

1. What are the principal components of the juvenile justice system? Why do some persons view juvenile justice as a process rather than as a system?
2. What were workhouses and their functions? How did the poor laws influence those confined to workhouses?

3. Who were child savers, and how did the child-saving philosophy influence the subsequent development of juvenile courts?

4. What were the cases of *Ex parte Crouse* and *People ex rel. O'Connell v. Turner?* What was their significance for juvenile justice?

5. What was the Illinois Juvenile Court Act and what was its significance for juvenile courts?

6. What is the age jurisdiction of most juvenile courts in the United States? Who are juvenile offenders?

7. What is the doctrine of *parens patriae?* What are its origins? Does *parens patriae* continue to influence juvenile courts today? Why or why not?

8. Why is there a general lack of uniformity among juvenile courts in the United States?

9. What were houses of refuge and reform schools? Were they successful in accomplishing their objectives? Why or why not?

10. Are juvenile courts primarily treatment centered or punishment centered? What is the get-tough movement and what are some reasons for its existence?

Internet Connections

American Bar Association's Juvenile Justice Center
http://www.abanet.org/crimjust/juvjus/home.html

American Civil Liberties Union
http://www.aclu.org

Building Blocks for Youth
http://www.buildingblocksforyouth.org/issues/jjdpa/factsheet.html

National Center for Missing and Exploited Children
http://www.missingkids.com

National Clearinghouse on Child Abuse and Neglect Information
http://nccanch.acf.hhs.gov/

Open Society Institute
http://www.soros.org/crime/

Youth Change (problem-youth problem solving)
http://www.youthchg.com

CHAPTER 2

Measuring Delinquency: Types of Offenders and Trends

Chapter Outline

Key Terms

at-risk youths
career escalation
chronic offenders
cleared by arrest
decarceration
deinstitutionalization of status
    offenses
delinquent child
dependent and neglected children
divestiture
DSO
felonies
gangs
hidden delinquency
incident
index crimes
Index Offenses

infants
jurisdiction
juvenile delinquency
juvenile delinquent
juvenile delinquents
Juvenile Justice and Delinquency
    Prevention Act of 1974
    (JJDPA)
juvenile offenders
misdemeanor
Monitoring the Future Survey
National Crime Victimization Survey
    (NCVS)
National Juvenile Court Data
    Archive
National Youth Survey
net-widening

Office of Juvenile Justice and
    Delinquency Prevention
    (OJJDP)
pathways
relabeling
runaways
self-report information
self-reports
Sourcebook of Criminal Justice
    Statistics
status offenses.
stigmas
stigmatization
stigmatize
truancy courts
Uniform Crime Reports (UCR)
victimization

Chapter Objectives

As the result of reading this chapter, you will have accomplished the following objectives:

1. Determine what is meant by juvenile delinquency.
2. Distinguish between juvenile delinquents and the broad class of status offenders, including runaways, truants, and curfew violators.
3. Understand the deinstitutionalization of status offenders.
4. Learn important differences between the *Uniform Crime Reports* and *National Crime Victimization Survey* as key indicators of delinquent behavior.
5. Learn about other important sources of information about juvenile offending, including the *National Juvenile Court Data Archive,* self-report information, and the *Sourcebook of Criminal Justice Statistics.*
6. Learn about violent and nonviolent delinquent conduct, and whether there is any career escalation among juvenile offenders.
7. Determine some of the major differences between male and female juveniles and their offending patterns.

• *An upstate New York county deputy was patrolling a suburban neighborhood of a large city one wintry evening and spotted some suspicious lights in a large vacant home. He called for backup and was soon joined by another deputy. They investigated and discovered a broken window at the rear of the home. They entered and encountered four youths huddled near a fireplace in the living room. According to the youths, they were from North Carolina and had hitchhiked to New York. They walked off the main highway nearby and discovered the vacant home. They found some wood stacked in the backyard and gained entry to the home by breaking the window. They were cold and wanted to get warm. They were planning on going to Canada. The deputies obtained identifying information for all four youths, two boys and two girls. They ranged in age from 12 to 14. They told the deputies that their parents had forbid them from seeing each other, and that they wanted to be together. Running away from home was their only solution. They planned on getting jobs at fast-food restaurants once they got to Canada, but other than that, they had no specific plans and just wanted to be together. The parents of the youths were contacted and retrieved their children from the local social services office in the New York community the following day. The youths were cited by the deputies for breaking and entering, but a juvenile court judge in New York ordered restitution for the broken window to the vacant home and other minor carpet damage.* [*Source:* Adapted from Gene Forsythe and the Associated Press, "North Carolina Runaways Caught Near Canadian Border," June 11, 2005.]

• *Three black men were drinking beer and eating pizza in an Ocala, Florida, Pizza Hut one evening near Interstate 75. The waitress asked for IDs before serving these persons the beer, and each person produced out-of-state driver's licenses showing that they were over age 21. The men sat at their table and continued to drink, talking more loudly and disturbing other patrons. Finally the Pizza Hut manager approached the men and asked them to pay for their meal and leave. One of the men produced a wad of $100 bills and put two bills on the table. "Keep the change," he said. This was an excessive amount for a $85 tab. The manager observed the men get into a dark, late-model Mercedes sedan and drive off. He copied down the Georgia license plate number and called Florida police. Within minutes they located these men and their car heading south on Interstate 75 and stopped them. The "men" looked more like boys, and a closer inspection of their Georgia driver's licenses disclosed that they were fake. The police asked the men to open their trunk. Inside the trunk was a large plastic bag containing several wallets, watches, rings, and other jewelry. Two loaded firearms were also recovered. Unable to give a believable account of why these items were in their position, the persons were placed in a local jail cell to await further investigation. The driver was also charged with driving under the influence. It turned out that the men were actually three boys, ages 14, 15, and 16. They were from a suburb of Atlanta and the recovered evidence linked them with several robberies that had recently occurred outside of a gay Atlanta nightclub. The Mercedes was a stolen vehicle and belonged to one of the robbed nightclub patrons. The 16-year-old had an extensive juvenile record, while the 14-year-old and 15-year-old were apparently first-offenders. The younger boys were brothers and the older boy was their close friend. They were returned to Atlanta and turned over to juvenile authorities where robbery, vehicular theft, and interstate transportation of stolen property charges were pending against them.* [*Source:* Adapted from the Associated Press, "Georgia Teen Robbers Found in Florida," April 29, 2005.]

• *A convenience store manager in Baltimore, Maryland, called police to investigate a group of teenagers who had congregated in his store parking lot at about 11:30 P.M. one evening. A police car entered the parking lot and two officers approached the small crowd of 10–12 loitering youths. Most of the youths were boys, although there were three girls in the group. Several of the boys wore the same types of jackets with a popular professional basketball team logo. Although these youths weren't causing any trouble, it was apparent to the store manager that some potential customers who pulled into the parking lot to do late-night shopping at his store left the lot once they saw the milling youths. Police asked for identification, and the youths became belligerent, insisting they hadn't done anything wrong and that they were entitled to be anywhere they wanted. Another police cruiser joined the first, and several other officers became involved in the informal investigation. Eventually the youths gave their names, ages, and other identifying information to police. The youths ranged in age from 11 to 17, and the 17-year-old seemed to be the center of attention. The police asked if these youths were a gang, largely because of the basketball jackets they were wearing. The youths denied being a gang or belonging to one. It turned out that several of the older youths attended a local school and were "hanging out" after attending a school basketball game. Other kids in the group had joined them. The older youths were told to leave the parking lot or face arrest on public order charges and curfew violations. The youngest youths under age 16 were taken to the police station where their parents eventually picked them up. A record was made and nothing more was made of the incident.* [*Source:* Adapted from the Associated Press, "'Hanging Out': A Growing Community Problem?" February 6, 2005.]

INTRODUCTION

These cases vary greatly in their seriousness. In the first instance, police officers encountered several youths who were running away from home. They had an argument with their parents about who they could date, and they decided to run away so that they could be together. They had broken into a vacant home on a cold night to get warm. The three boys drinking beer and eating pizza in a Florida restaurant presented a far darker picture for police officers, who eventually connected them with several Atlanta, Georgia, assaults and robberies. The third case may or may not have involved members of a gang. A group of teens was hanging out in front of a convenience store, being disorderly and making potential store customers feel unsafe and leave. Each of the cases was investigated by police, with three different outcomes. The circumstances of each situation seemed to determine how authorities interpreted what they saw and the action taken.

This chapter is about different kinds of juveniles and the types of offenses they commit. The first section examines juveniles and how they are defined. Every jurisdiction throughout the United States has its own criteria for determining who juveniles are and whether they should fall within the jurisdiction of the juvenile court. A majority of the states classify juveniles as ranging in age from 7 to 17, and juvenile courts in these states have jurisdiction over these juveniles. Some states have no minimum-age provisions and consider each case on its own merits, regardless of the youthfulness of the juvenile.

All juveniles are subject to the laws and ordinances of their respective jurisdictions. If they violate one or more of these laws, they may come to the attention of law enforcement officers, who investigate a broad range of offenses. Because juveniles are not yet considered adults and are not fully responsible for some of their actions, special laws have been established that pertain only to them. Adults are exempt from these special laws. Therefore, when juveniles offend, their "offenses" may or may not be criminal ones. Every state and the federal government has differentiated between all juveniles according to the seriousness of the offenses they commit. One objective of this section is to distinguish between juveniles who commit crimes and those who commit other types of offenses simply because they are juveniles. Juveniles who commit crimes are classified as delinquents, and these actions are categorically classified as juvenile delinquency.

The next section of this chapter examines several types of status offenses. These are offenses committed by juveniles that would not be crimes if adults committed them. Several types of status offenses, such as runaway behavior, truancy, and curfew violation, are defined and explained. The characteristics of youths involved in such behaviors are described.

During the first half of the twentieth century, virtually every juvenile court had jurisdiction over both delinquent and status offenders. Often, both types of offenders would be punished by juvenile court judges in similar ways by being confined in reform schools or training schools for short periods. More than a few persons were concerned that status offenders were being treated the same as juvenile delinquents and made to live and interact with them in prison-like juvenile institutions. In 1974, the U.S. Congress passed the Juvenile Justice and Delinquency Prevention Act. This act, which was not binding on the states, encouraged all jurisdictions to remove their status offenders from institutions where they were being held for more or less lengthy periods. Subsequently a growing number of states removed their status offenders from these institutions and placed these juveniles in different communities under the care of social service or welfare agencies. This process has been called the deinstitutionalization of status offenders (DSO) and is described in some detail. DSO has several meanings, including decarceration, divestiture of jurisdiction, and diverting dependent and neglected children to social services. Each of these meanings of DSO will be defined and described. As the result of DSO, several important outcomes and implications for youths have been observed. Several of these outcomes are listed and are described. These include net-widening, relabeling, removal of status offenders from institutional placement, an expansion of community services, and a modest influence on recidivism rates among status offenders.

How much delinquency and status offending are there in the United States? While no one knows for sure the answer to these questions, various measures exist that purportedly depict their frequency. The next chapter section describes several official measures used in tracking juvenile offending. These include *The Uniform Crime Reports, The National Crime Victimization Survey, The National Juvenile Court Data Archive,* and *The Sourcebook of Criminal Justice Statistics.* These are considered official documents with a high degree of authenticity. However, each compendium has weaknesses and strengths. These are listed and described. Other, less official surveys of juvenile offending exist, including *The National Youth Survey* and the *Monitoring the Future Survey.* These national surveys are also defined and described. An important source of unreported delinquency and status offense information is through the use of self-reports, or disclosures by juveniles to private researchers about the nature and extent of their offending. Often, there are vast discrepancies between official reports and the information disclosed about delinquency through self-reports. However, self-report information is flawed in several respects and not perfectly reliable. Some of the weaknesses as well as some of the strengths of self-reports are listed.

Classifying juvenile offending has led to a distinction between violent offenses and property offenses. Certain violent offenses, such as murder, rape, aggravated assault, and robbery, are described, and juvenile involvement in these delinquent acts is elaborated. In recent years, several incidents of school violence have been reported by the media and given extensive coverage. Thus, school violence and school violence patterns and trends are depicted. This section also describes certain youths who are considered at risk of becoming delinquent. Several risk factors, such as family instability, poor school adjustment, lower socioeconomic status, low self-control and self-esteem, and antisocial behaviors, are described. Some violent offending is gang-related and is described as well. Juvenile gangs often form along racial or ethnic lines. Such parallels are examined. While their numbers are few, some juveniles are murderers. These juveniles are described.

One concern of criminologists and others is whether less serious offenders, such as status offenders, progress to commit more serious offenses over time. This is known as career escalation. For many decades, it was believed that less serious juvenile offending, if not detected and corrected, would necessarily lead to more serious offending. Today, it is uncertain whether career escalation occurs for most juveniles who commit less serious offenses. Career escalation and juvenile violence trends are examined.

The chapter concludes with an examination of female juveniles and how they have emerged in recent years as a proportionately greater minority among serious juvenile offenders. Female juvenile offenders are profiled and several trends among these females are described. Female juveniles have increasingly become involved in gang activities, and juvenile female gang formation is examined. Because more female juvenile offenders have come to the attention of police, several myths and misconceptions about female juveniles have been started and perpetuated. These myths and misconceptions are described.

WHO ARE JUVENILE OFFENDERS?

Juvenile Offenders Defined

Juvenile offenders are classified and defined according to several different criteria. According to the 1899 Illinois Act that created juvenile courts, the **jurisdiction** of such courts would extend to all juveniles under the age of 16 who were found in violation of any state or local law or ordinance (Gittens, 1994). About a fifth of all states place the upper age limit for juveniles at either 15 or 16. In most other states, the upper age limit for juveniles is 17, except for Wyoming, where the upper age limit is 18. Ordinarily, the jurisdiction of juvenile courts includes all juveniles between the ages of 7 and 18 (Black, 1990:867). Federal law defines juveniles as any persons who have not attained their 18th birthday (18 U.S.C., Sec. 5031, 2005).

The Age Jurisdiction of Juvenile Courts

The particular age jurisdiction of juvenile courts over juveniles depends on the established legislative definitions of them among the states. The federal government has no juvenile court. Although upper and lower age limits are prescribed, these age limits are far from uniform among jurisdictions. Common law has been applied in many jurisdictions where the minimum age of accountability for juveniles is 7. It is presumed that youths under the age of 7 are incapable of formulating criminal intent and are thus not responsible under the law. While this presumption may be rebutted, in most cases, it isn't. Thus, if a 6-year-old child kills someone, deliberately or accidentally, he or she will likely be treated rather than punished. In some states, no lower age limits exist to restrict juvenile court jurisdiction. Table 2.1 shows upper age limits for most U.S. jurisdictions.

Those states with the lowest maximum age for juvenile court jurisdiction include Connecticut, New York, and North Carolina. In these states, the lowest maximum age for juvenile court jurisdiction is 15. Those states having the lowest maximum age of 16 for juvenile court jurisdiction are Georgia, Illinois,

TABLE 2.1

Age at Which Criminal Courts Gain Jurisdiction over Young Offenders

Age of Offender When Under Criminal Court Jurisdiction (years)	States
16	Connecticut, New York, North Carolina
17	Georgia, Illinois, Louisiana, Massachusetts, Missouri, South Carolina, Texas
18	Alabama, Alaska, Arizona, Arkansas, California, Colorado, Delaware, District of Columbia, Florida, Hawaii, Idaho, Indiana, Iowa, Kansas, Kentucky, Maine, Maryland, Michigan, Minnesota, Mississippi, Montana, Nebraska, Nevada, New Hampshire, New Jersey, New Mexico, North Dakota, Ohio, Oklahoma, Oregon, Pennsylvania, Rhode Island, South Dakota, Tennessee, Utah, Vermont, Virginia, Washington, West Virginia, Wisconsin, Federal districts
19	Wyoming

Source: Jeffrey A. Butts et al. (1996). *Juvenile Court Statistics 1993:* Statistics Report. Washington, DC: Office of Juvenile Justice and Delinquency Prevention. Updated 2005 by author.

Louisiana, Massachusetts, Michigan, Missouri, South Carolina, and Texas. All other states and the federal government use age 18 as the minimum age for criminal court jurisdiction. Under the Juvenile Justice and Delinquency Prevention Act of 1974, juveniles are persons who have not attained their 18th birthday (18 U.S.C., Sec. 5031, 2005).

Juvenile offenders who are especially young (under age 7 in most jurisdictions) are often placed within the control of community agencies such as departments of human services or social welfare. These children frequently have little or no responsible parental supervision or control. In many cases, the parents themselves may have psychological problems or suffer from alcohol or drug dependencies. Youths from such families may be abused and/or neglected, and in need of supervision and other forms of care or treatment. Instead of punishing those under the age of 7, various kinds of treatment, including social therapy and psychological counseling, are most frequently required. Some states have further age-accountability provisions. Tennessee presumes, for instance, that juveniles between the ages of 7 and 12 are presumed accountable for their delinquent acts, although this presumption may be overcome by their attorneys through effective oral arguments and clear and convincing evidence.

Some states have no minimum age limit for juveniles. Technically, these states have the power to decide matters involving children of any age. This control often involves placement of children or infants in foster homes or under the supervision of community service or human welfare agencies. Neglected, unmanageable, abused, or other children in need of supervision are placed in the custody of these various agencies, at the discretion of juvenile judges. Thus, juvenile courts generally have broad discretionary powers over most persons under the age of 18. Under certain circumstances that are discussed in a later chapter, some juveniles, particularly young ones such as 11-year-olds and 12-year-olds, may be treated as adults for the purpose of prosecuting them in criminal court for alleged serious crimes.

JUVENILE DELINQUENTS AND DELINQUENCY

Juvenile Delinquents

In law, juveniles are referred to as **infants.** Legally, therefore, a **juvenile delinquent** is any infant of not more than a specified age who has violated criminal laws or engages in disobedient, indecent, or immoral conduct, and is in need of treatment, rehabilitation, or supervision (Black, 1990:777). These youths are **juvenile delinquents.** Black (1990:428) also says that a juvenile delinquent is a **delinquent child.** These definitions are somewhat ambiguous. What is "indecent" or "immoral conduct"? Who needs treatment, rehabilitation, or supervision? And what sort of treatment, rehabilitation, or supervision is needed? What is a "specified age"? These ambiguities have never been fully resolved.

Juvenile Delinquency

Federal law says that **juvenile delinquency** is the violation of any law of the United States by a person prior to his 18th birthday, which would have been a crime if committed by an adult (18 U.S.C., Sec. 5031, 2005). A broader, legally applicable, definition of juvenile delinquency is a violation of any state or local law or ordinance by anyone who has not yet achieved the age of majority (adapted from Black, 1990:428). Although not especially perfect, these definitions are qualitatively more precise than the former ones.

Juvenile courts most often define juveniles and juvenile delinquency according to their own standards. For many jurisdictions, a delinquent act is whatever a court says it is. To illustrate the implications of such a definition for any juvenile, consider the following scenarios.

Scenario #1:   It is 10:15 P.M. on a Thursday night in Detroit. There is a curfew in effect for youths under age 18, prohibiting them from being on city streets after 10:00 P.M. A police officer in a cruiser notices four youths standing at a street corner, holding gym bags and conversing. One youth walks toward a nearby jewelry store, looks in the window, and returns to the group. Shortly thereafter, another boy walks up to the same jewelry store window and looks in it. The officer pulls up beside the boys, exits the vehicle, and asks them for identification. Each of the boys has a high school identity card. The boys are 16 and 17 years of age. When asked about the jewelry store interest, one boy says that he plans to get his girlfriend a necklace like one in the store window, and he wanted his friends to see it. The boys explain that they are waiting for a ride, since they are members of a team and just finished a basketball game at a local gymnasium. One boy says, "I don't see why you're hassling us. We're not doing anything wrong." "You just did," says the officer. He makes a call on his radio for assistance from other officers, and makes all the youths sit on the curb with their hands behind their heads. Two other cruisers arrive shortly and the youths are transported to the police station where they are searched. The search turns up two small pocket knives and a bottle opener. The youths are charged with "carrying concealed weapons" and "conspiracy to commit burglary." Juvenile authorities are notified.

Scenario #2:   A highway patrol officer spots two young girls with backpacks attempting to hitch a ride on a major highway in Florida. He stops his vehicle and asks the girls for IDs. They don't have any ID but claim they are over 18 and that they are trying to get to Georgia to visit some friends. The officer takes both girls into custody and to a local jail where a subsequent identification discloses that they are 13- and 14-year-old runaways from a Miami suburb. Their parents are looking for them. They are detained at the jail until their parents can retrieve them. In the meantime, a nearby convenience store reports that two young girls from off the street came in an hour earlier and shoplifted several items. Jail deputies search the backpacks of the girls and find the shoplifted items. They are charged with "theft." Juvenile authorities are notified.

Scenario #3:   A 15-year-old boy who has been suspended from a local Atlanta school for pushing another student is being held in a juvenile psychiatric wing of a mental hospital while undergoing some juvenile court-ordered tests to determine his mental condition. During the night, he sneaks away from the facility but is caught by police the next day. He is charged with "escape." Juvenile authorities are notified.

These and a thousand other scenarios could be presented. Are these scenarios the same? No. As the facts are presented, some of these scenarios are not especially serious. Can each of these scenarios result in a finding of delinquency by a juvenile court judge? Yes. Whether juveniles are "hanging out" on a street corner late at night, whether they have shoplifted, or whether they have run away from a psychiatric institution, it is possible in *some* juvenile court *somewhere* that all of them could be defined collectively as delinquent or delinquency cases. Some juvenile offending is more serious than other types of juvenile offending. Breaking windows or violating the town curfew would certainly be less serious than armed robbery, rape, or murder. The wide range of offense seriousness has caused many jurisdictions to channel less serious cases away from juvenile courts and toward various community agencies where the juveniles involved can receive assistance rather than punishment. Should one's age, socioeconomic status, ethnicity or race, attitude, and other situational circumstances influence police response one way or another? The fact is that regardless of the offenses alleged, all juveniles are confronted by subjective appraisals and judgments from the police, prosecutors, and juvenile court judges on the basis of both legal and extralegal factors. Because of their status as juveniles, youths may also be charged with various noncriminal acts. Such acts are broadly described as **status offenses.**

STATUS OFFENDERS

Status offenders are of interest to both the juvenile justice system and the criminal justice system. Status offenses are any acts committed by juveniles that would (1) bring the juveniles to the attention of juvenile courts and (2) not be crimes if committed by adults. Typical status offenses are running away from home, truancy, and curfew violations. Adults would not be arrested for running away from home, being truant from school, or walking the streets after some curfew time for juveniles. However, if juveniles do these sorts of things in particular cities, they may be grouped within the broad delinquency category, together with more serious juvenile offenders who are charged with armed robbery, forcible rape, murder, aggravated assault, burglary, larceny, vehicular theft, or illicit drug sales.

Runaways

In 2005, it was estimated there were over 200,000 **runaways** in the United States reported to police (Office of Juvenile Justice and Delinquency Prevention, 2005). This represents less than 1 percent of all offenses charged that year. Over half of these runaways are 15–17 years of age. Runaways consist of those youths who leave their homes, without permission or their parents' knowledge, and who remain away from home for prolonged periods ranging from several days to several years. Many runaways are eventually picked up by police in different jurisdictions and returned to their homes. Others return of their own free will and choice. Some runaways remain permanently missing, although they are likely a part of a growing number of homeless youths roaming faraway city streets throughout the United States. Information about runaways and other types of status offenders is compiled annually through various statewide clearinghouses and the federally funded National Incidence Studies of Missing, Abducted, Runaway, and Thrownaway Children (NISMART).

   Runaway behavior is complex and difficult to explain, although researchers tend to agree that many runaways generally have serious mental health needs (Cocozza and Skowyra, 2000). Many of these youths seek out others like them for dependency and emotional support. Some runaways regard

Increasing numbers of youths become runaways and eventually disappear into large cities where they live lives of uncertainty.

others like them as role models and peers, and often, delinquency among them occurs and increases through such peer modeling (Lindstrom, 1996). Studies of runaways indicate that many boys and girls have psychological and/or familial adjustment problems and have been physically and sexually abused by their parents or close relatives. Evidence suggests that many runaways engage in theft or prostitution to finance their independence away from home and are exploited (Hwang and Bedford, 2004).

Although all runaways are not alike, there have been attempts to profile them. Depending on how authorities and parents react to children who have been apprehended after running away, there may be either positive or negative consequences. Empathy for runaways and their problems is important for instilling positive feelings within them. Various runaway shelters have been established to offer runaways a nonthreatening residence and social support system in various jurisdictions. These shelters often locate particular services for runaways that will help meet their needs. Many children accommodated by these shelters report that they have been physically and sexually abused by family members. Thus, there is some coordination of these homes with various law enforcement agencies to investigate these allegations and assist parents in making their homes safer for their children (Harris, 2000; Reynolds et al., 1999).

Truants and Curfew Violators

Truants.   Other types of status offenders are truants and curfew and liquor law violators. Truants are those who absent themselves from school without either school or parental permission. Very little is known about the numbers or characteristics of truants in the United States (Baker, Sigmon, and Nugent, 2001). Several reasons are that each school district defines truancy differently from other districts; sociodemographic characteristics of truants are not normally maintained, even by individual schools; and no consistent, central reporting mechanisms exist for data compilations about truants. For instance, in Wisconsin, a truant may be a youth who absents himself/herself from school without excuse for five or more consecutive school days. In other states, a truant may be defined as someone who misses one day of school without a valid excuse.

There are probably 200,000 or more truants in the United States on any given day. This figure is most likely an underestimate of the actual number of truants. On a city-by-city basis, where records of truants are maintained, we can glean much about the true magnitude of truancy. For instance, in Pittsburgh, Pennsylvania, on any given day, there are 3,500 students absent from school, with about 70 percent of these absences unexcused. In Philadelphia, there are 2,500 students truant each day. And in Milwaukee, Wisconsin, there are 4,000 students absent from school each day without an excuse. One disturbing dimension of truancy is that about two-thirds of all juvenile males arrested while truant have tested positive for drug use (Witmer, 2002:1–2).

Truancy is not a crime. It is a status offense. Youths can be charged with truancy and brought into juvenile court for a status offense adjudication. Truancy is taken quite seriously in many jurisdictions, since evidence suggests that daytime crime and truancy are highly correlated. In Minneapolis, for example, when police officers began to cite truant students and take them into custody, daytime crime dropped by 68 percent. And in San Diego, California, about half of all violent juvenile offending occurs between 8:30 A.M. and 1:30 P.M. (Witmer, 2002:2). Several states have acted to establish more formal truancy policies in order to compel students to attend school regularly, with possible institutionalization as a serious sanction imposed for violating court orders for compulsory school attendance. An example is the Rhode Island Truancy Court.

Rhode Island Truancy Court.   Several states, such as Rhode Island, have established formal mechanisms to deal with the problem of truancy. The Family Court system of Rhode Island has established **truancy courts** for the purpose of heightening status offender accountability relating to truancy issues. Chronic truants are referred to the Truancy Court where their cases are formalized. This formal process dealing with truancy involves truants, their parents/guardians, a truant officer, and a Truancy Court magistrate. Participants must sign a "Waiver of Rights Form," illustrated in Figure 2.2. This form outlines the rights of truants, including the right to challenge any truancy accusation against them. Several important due process rights are included on the form. The purpose of the Truancy Court is to avoid formal juvenile court action by obeying the behavioral requirements outlined. These include (1) attending school every day; (2) being on time; (3) behaving; and (4) doing classroom work and homework. Failure to comply with one or more of these requirements may result in a referral to Family Court or placement in the Department of Children, Youth, and Families and removal from the home. This means possible institutionalization if one's truancy persists following the Truancy Court hearing.

The Truancy Court also requires parents to sign a form that permits the release of confidential information about the truant. This information is necessary in devising any type of treatment program and providing any counseling or services the truant may require. Thus, the Family Court is vested with the power to evaluate, assess, and plan activities for the truant that are designed to prevent further truancy. Various interventions are attempted in an effort to heighten the youth's awareness of the seriousness of truancy and the importance of staying in school. This form is illustrated in Figure 2.3.

Two other documents are required by the Truancy Court. Figures 2.4 and 2.5 illustrate a Treatment Reference Sheet and an Official Family Court Order.

The Treatment Reference Sheet shown in Figure 2.4 is an informational document designed to provide the Truancy Court magistrate with valuable information about the student's progress prior to the Truancy Court hearing. Some of this information pertains to the parents and whether they have any criminal history, the status of their mental health, and their own educational attainment. It is believed that the background of parents is a significant consideration in any treatment recommendation made for the truant. For instance, information is acquired relating to whether the youth has any disabilities or mental health problems, which could account for his or her truant conduct. The youth's grades in different subjects are also recorded for the magistrate's inspection. Figure 2.5 is a formal court order outlining any sanctions the magistrate believes will heighten the truant's accountability. These include possible home confinement and any special conditions the court chooses to impose. Rhode Island Family Court officers are pleased with the results of the Truancy Court process thus far.

Rhode Island Truancy Court
Waiver of Rights Form

Juvenile Name: _____
School: _____
Juvenile ID: _____
Petition Number: _____

I understand that I have the right to a trial on the truancy offense filed against me and recognize that I have the following rights should I decide to go to trial:

1. My right to a trial by a Judge and my right to appeal to the Supreme Court from any decision or finding of delinquency or waywardness.
2. The right to have the City/Town prove each and every element of the offense(s) against me by evidence and by proof beyond a reasonable doubt.
3. My right to the presumption of innocence.
4. My privilege against self-incrimination.
5. My right to confront and cross-examine the City/Town witnesses against me.
6. My right to present evidence and witnesses on my behalf and to testify in my own defense if I choose to do so.
7. My right to appeal to the Rhode Island Supreme Court from any sentence imposed by the Court after the entry of my ADMISSION OF SUFFECIENT FACTS or ADMISSION.

I understand that the Court has jurisdiction over me until my 21st birthday. I also understand that if I go to trial and am found wayward on the Truancy charge, I could be sent to the Rhode Island Training School if I refuse to obey a valid court order to attend school after I have been sentenced by a Family Court Judge.

I understand that I will have the right to an attorney if it appears that I could receive a sentence to the Rhode Island Training School.

I understand that by staying in the Truancy Court I will not go to trial and will have to abide by the Truancy Court requirements of:

1. Attending School Every Day.
2. Being on Time.
3. Behaving.
4. Doing My Classroom Work and Homework.

I agree that I will present a doctor's note or nurse's note if I am absent from school due to illness.

I understand that if I do not obey the Truancy Court requirements my case may be referred to the Family Court for trial or that I can be placed in the custody of the Department of Children, Youth, and Families and be removed from my home.

I understand that I may request a trial or hearing before a Justice of the Family Court at any time during my Truancy Court participation.

I/we have discussed the content of this document with the Truancy Court Magistrate who has explained this to me.

_____   _____
Participant's Signature   Date   Responsible Adult   Date

                                             _____
                                             Responsible Adult   Date

_____   _____
Truancy Court Magistrate   Date   Truant Officer   Date

TCW-1 (4/03)

FIGURE 2.2   Rhode Island Truancy Court Waiver of Rights Form.

RHODE ISLAND FAMILY COURT
TRUANCY COURT
CHIEF JUDGE JEREMIAH S. JEREMIAH, JR.

<u>RELEASE OF CONFIDENTIAL INFORMATION</u>

CLIENT'S NAME_____ DATE OF BIRTH_____

PARENT' S NAME _____

CLIENT'S ADDRESS _____

I hereby authorize all school, educational and treatment providers to release to The Rhode Island

Family Court or its representative any records concerning me and/or my children relating to

educational and school records, mental health, psychological and medical/physician records,

counseling, any treatment records, or other related documents and/or evaluations that relate to

said individuals.

This authorization is needed for the purpose of evaluation, assessment and planning by the

Rhode Island Family Court.

I understand that these records are protected by law and cannot be released without written

consent. This information may not be relayed to any other agency/facility/individual not

specified above. I understand that I may revoke this consent at any time.

_____   _____
SIGNATURE of CLIENT/ PARENT   WITNESS

_____
DATE

FIGURE 2.3   Rhode Island Release of Confidential Information Form.

RI Family Court / Truancy Court
TREATMENT REFERENCE SHEET

JUVENILE NAME_____ D.O.B._____

DATA: 1. Advised Child / Parent of right to trial and consequences of Truancy Court
       ❑ YES   ❑ NO

     2. Number of days absent before Arraignment: _____ out of _____ days

     3. Grades at Time of Arraignment:
         a. English_____   d. Math_____
         b. Reading_____   e. History_____
         c. Science_____   f. Others_____

     4. Single Parent Family   ❑   Two Parent Family   ❑

     5. Sibling Information (age, educational status)_____
_____

     6.   Parent(s) graduated from high school: ❑ YES   ❑ NO

     7.   Parent(s) has/have criminal history: ❑ YES   ❑ NO

     8.   Parent(s) has/have mental health history: ❑ YES   ❑ NO

     9.   Child disabilities (mental health)_____

     10.   Medication_____

     11.   Child's Educational Status: ❑ Regular Education   ❑ 504   ❑ IE
                                          ❑ Alternative placement
     12.   Does child want to graduate from high school: ❑ YES   ❑ NO

FIGURE 2.4   Rhode Island Truancy Court Treatment Reference Sheet (public domain).

Curfew Violators. Curfew violators are those youths who remain on city streets after specified evening hours when they are prohibited from loitering or not being in the company of a parent or guardian. In 2005, there were over 220,000 youths charged with violating curfew and loitering laws in the United States (Office of Juvenile Justice and Delinquency Prevention, 2005). This is less than 1 percent of all offenses reported to police that year.

RHODE ISLAND FAMILY COURT
FAMILY AND JUVENILE DRUG COURT
<u>OFFICIAL FAMILY COURT ORDER</u>

Please be advised that:

PARENT'S NAME: _____

CHILD'S NAME: _____   **DATE OF BIRTH:** _____

ADDRESS: _____

_____

Has been ordered on this _____ **day of** _____ **, in the year 2005, the following:**

☐ **HOME CONFINEMENT**

    From _____ **Until** _____

☐ **SPECIAL CONDITIONS:** _____

_____

_____

_____

BY ORDER OF THE COURT:

_____   _____

DATE   **Associate Justice Kathleen A. Voccola**

FIGURE 2.5 Rhode Island Official Family Court Order (public domain).

Curfew violators tend to differ from runaways in that they are more serious offenders. However, truants and liquor law violators are more inclined to become **chronic offenders** and to engage in more serious, possibly criminal, behaviors. This is because truancy and curfew violations are viewed as undisciplined offenses. Some state jurisdictions, such as Maryland, have established programs to deal with chronic truancy. In Maryland, for example, Project Attend creates partnerships between local school systems and law enforcement agencies in school clusters where chronic truancy is a problem. Through arbitration, the attendance and academic achievement of identified chronic truants is improved significantly by including families and matching them with appropriate service providers.

In an effort to decrease the incidence of juvenile crime, many cities throughout the United States have enacted curfew laws specifically applicable to youths. The theory is that if juveniles are obliged to observe curfews in their communities, then they will have fewer opportunities to commit delinquent acts or status offenses (Urban, 2005). For example, in New Orleans, Louisiana, in June 1994, the most restrictive curfew law went into effect. Under this law, juveniles under age 17 were prohibited from being in public places, including the premises of business establishments, unless accompanied by a legal guardian or authorized adult. The curfew on weeknights is 8:00 P.M. and 11:00 P.M. on weekends. Several exceptions were made for youths who might be traveling to and from work or who were attending school, religious, or civil events. A study of the impact of this strict curfew law was conducted, and it revealed that juvenile offending shifted to non-curfew hours. Furthermore, the enforcement of this curfew law by New Orleans police was difficult, since curfew violations often occurred outside of a police presence. If anything, the curfew law tended to induce rebelliousness among those youths affected by the law. Curfew laws have not been an especially effective deterrent to status offending or delinquency generally (Urban, 2005).

Juvenile and Criminal Court Interest in Status Offenders

Among status offenders, juvenile courts are most interested in chronic or persistent offenders, such as those who habitually appear before juvenile court judges. Repeated juvenile court exposure by status offenders may eventually be followed by adult criminality, although there is little support for this view in the research literature. The chronicity of juvenile offending seems to be influenced by the amount of contact youths have with juvenile courts. Greater contact with juvenile courts is believed by some persons to **stigmatize** youths and cause them to acquire labels or **stigmas** as delinquents or deviants (Faulkner and Faulkner, 2004; Hartwell, 2004). Therefore, diversion of certain types of juvenile offenders from the juvenile justice system has been advocated and recommended to minimize **stigmatization.**

One increasingly popular strategy is to remove certain types of offenses from the jurisdiction of juvenile court judges (Trulson, Marquart, and Mullings, 2005). Because status offenders are comparatively less serious than juvenile delinquents who commit crimes, status offenders have been targeted by many state legislatures for removal from juvenile court jurisdiction. The removal of status offenders from the discretionary power of juvenile courts is a part of what is generally known as the **deinstitutionalization of status offenses,** or **DSO.**

BOX 2.1

Susan Steidler-Ehlis
Juvenile Corrections Specialist, Northwest Regional Office Division of Juvenile Services, North Dakota Department of Corrections and Rehabilitation, Williston, ND

Statistics:

B.S. (social work, psychology), University of Mary (Bismarck, ND); A.A., Bismarck State College

Background

I grew up in North Dakota in the Bismarck-Mandan area and am the 4th of 11 children. I suppose that mine was a very strong, conservative, and supportive family and that our spiritual faith was an important part of my upbringing. I attended a private grade school, and from as early as I started to think about my future, I wanted to be a nun and a social worker, and I wanted to work with and assist children and their families. As life often goes, things didn't work out quite like I had imagined as a little girl. Instead, I grew up, was definitely not a nun, graduated from high school, worked for a time, and was accepted to start college at Creighton University, where I met my husband. College was put off, I married the love of my life, had three children, and then several years later, I returned to school and began the work of becoming educated as outlined above. I put a lot of effort into college and found it a rewarding experience. I am convinced that a positive educational performance assisted me in achieving my employment goals. At the age of 38 I began my professional career in the juvenile justice system and I have loved almost every minute of it. At times my associates have heard me ask loudly, "Do I get paid enough to do this?" And the answer is generally, "No," and then I usually do it anyway!

Experiences

I remember a young man and his family who I worked with who worked on a farm near the Canadian border. His family consisted of his parents and two brothers along with many chickens, turkeys, cows, and other assorted farm animals and pets. I went

to the farm to meet with the family and my young charge. On one occasion I came during the Spring of the year and the farm was bustling with new life, babies of all sorts imaginable. As we visited, there was considerable noise and commotion outside and it turned out that the baby chickens had gotten out of their cage and were running all about the yard. I spent the afternoon helping the three boys and their mother collect these little creatures. As I drove home that evening, I was heard to say in the isolation of my car, "Do I get paid enough to do this?" And of course the answer was "No." But I did it anyway and kind of enjoyed it.

Corrections and social work in rural North Dakota were like that. You have to make do; you have to be very flexible, and you have to be creative. And now as I grow older, enjoying my two sons, one daughter, one daughter-in-law, one son-in-law, and seven grandchildren, and now that the years to retirement are less than the years I have enjoyed this career, I feel satisfied and privileged to have served the children and families that I have come into contact with. They have enriched my life beyond measure and I know that I have sometimes been witness to tragic, spectacular, and life-altering events in their lives. Of course, like everyone else in this field, I see those children who make poor choices and decisions and continue to do so throughout my work with them and continue into the adult system. A long time ago I learned to accept that I could not force change. I offer support, services, and opportunities, and they choose. I never give up on a child and I always believe that they have the potential to change. It might not happen today, tomorrow, or next week, but it might happen 10 years down the road when something clicks and that former client of mine says to himself or herself, "Oh, that's what Susan was talking about. Now I get it!"

About a year ago I had the positive good fortune to run into the mother of a young man who I had worked with for a lengthy period of time. He was a very difficult and resistant young man with serious chemical addiction issues. To make it worse, whenever he was high or intoxicated his behavior became very obnoxious and dangerous. At any rate, when the case closed, he seemed in as much trouble as when he first came on my caseload about 12 years ago. For a time I heard information of his continued involvement in the adult legal system. When I visited with his mother, she shared that he was married, the father of a young son, living on the East Coast, had graduated from college, and was employed in a very good job as an engineer. He is no longer using drugs or alcohol. This is what gives me hope for every child and family.

Employment History and Events

After graduating from college, I was employed for about one year with this new and rather unique innovative program. I worked as the first Neighbor in the Bismarck Public School System in North Dakota, providing intensive in-home support, and teaching and modeling effective parenting and problem-solving techniques to client families. Referrals came through the school and this position was not part of the juvenile justice system. However, the program, together with some volunteer work with Parents Anonymous, was my first experience working with delinquent and unruly children. It seemed that the children having trouble in school and referred to the Neighbor's Program were also children involved in the juvenile justice system.

In the Spring of 1984, I took a position with the South Central Judicial District Juvenile Court in Bismarck, first as a probation officer and later as a Court Officer II. I continued in that position for over 7 years, providing supervision for a caseload of unruly and delinquent probationer-clients who usually resided in their homes. This position allowed me to expand my professional experience including completing assessments, doing referrals for services, having numerous collateral interagency contacts, conducting child custody studies, preparing petitions and stipulations, attending court hearings and testifying, serving on Child Protection and Permanency Planning Teams, and providing crisis intervention for children who came into contact with the juvenile court.

I came to my current home and position in Williston, North Dakota with the Division of Juvenile Services in the Fall of 1991 because of a family move and have continued in this position for over 14 years. I was very concerned that coming to Northwest North Dakota (a very rural setting) would mean that I would never work in my field again. Not so! Two weeks after my arrival, a position opened up with one Case Manager going on maternity leave and another going back to teaching. It was certainly an interesting experience, and little did I realize that I had entered the most challenging opportunity of my career. Today I am the only Case Manager in the Northwest Region of the state, covering four counties.

The juvenile court places legal custody of delinquent and or unruly children with the Division, and those children can be placed in their homes, foster homes, foster care facilities, or correctional facilities. I provide supervision and make decisions about services and placements. The difference between this position and working with the juvenile court is that the Division of Juvenile Services has legal custody of children and therefore has considerably more power in their lives as granted by the courts and of course more responsibility. Children come under the Division because they have committed a very serious crime or they have a long history with the juvenile court, and community services have not proved successful. As you may imagine, the children who are placed with the Division of Juvenile Services are usually the more troubled and chronic cases.

(continued)

Providing the above care involves the coordination of services offered to youthful offenders through community and residentially based services and always guided by the principles of least restrictive setting, accountability, community safety, and rehabilitation. This process requires close working relationships with the juvenile court, court services, human services, private service providers, placement facilities, and any other agencies providing services for my clients. I do a very thorough and complete assessment of each child, allowing for the development of an Individualized Treatment Plan based on needs and risks. This is reviewed with children and their parents, allowing for the provision of information and discussion. I recently spent several hours with a mother and her son reviewing and discussing a plan for placement of the young man out of his home. It was a difficult meeting, but it allowed this family the time they needed to work through a major life development. This process continues with providing needed services, arranging for the most appropriate placement setting, and then providing supervision of that placement through regular visits, telephone contacts with staff, Permanency Planning meetings, and case staffings to ensure the best possible service to each child. I also make arrangements for and monitor the provision of numerous services provided for children who continue in their homes or who are involved in an aftercare program. Examples are individual, group, and family therapy, tracking, drug and alcohol treatment and/or aftercare, random drug testing, educational services, parenting, mental health services, community service, and accountability conferences. I also provide crisis intervention and emergency services to children and families on my caseload. Sometimes a child needs to return to the juvenile court because he or she has new charges or a new extended court order is required. In this situation I will file an affidavit with the court requesting the required action, appear in court, and provide information and testimony.

Finally, I hope that I have not given you the impression that this career has always been wonderful and with no frustra-tions or difficulty. That certainly would not be an accurate picture. In my opinion, the people who provide direct service to children in the juvenile justice system are not paid enough. There usually is not enough money from state and local governments to provide the desperately needed services and programs for children, especially in rural areas. Several times over the years I have watched changes in political parties and budget priority shifts result in the loss of programs that my children and families need. I also find myself struggling with the need to complete paperwork and computer programs at the cost of less time for direct service to children and their families. I think that this is an unfortunate development and more and more a sign of the times, and I suspect something that will only become a greater problem in future years. However, I have never lost my love of the work that I do and the relationships that I share with the people I serve. Nothing feels as good as when I come out of a meeting with a child or family or professional and can feel in my bones that something really good just happened. Nothing is more exciting than closing a case and knowing that this child is better off than when he or she came on my caseload originally. These are the things that have kept me in this work for over 20 years.

Advice to Students

My advice is as follows:

1. First, get a good, solid education. Especially important are excellent communication skills and computer/technology skills. Your education is extremely important in helping you to be well prepared and provide the best service to clients.

2. Do volunteer work and take part in experiences with children and their families that assist you in knowing more about the people you will work with. Varied and different experiences give a new, fresh, and different perspective. It will also help you determine if this is really the kind of work you want to do. I have volunteered as a tutor in a grade

school, worked with a Parents Anonymous group, and my family and I have provided a foster home with the Casey Family Program for a young woman for 2½ years. I have found these activities to be valuable in helping me to better understand the experiences of the children and families I work with.

3. Always, always, always treat your clients fairly and with respect. Very often I hear from clients how they feel and how they have been mistreated by the system.

4. Learn early that you won't be every child's answer to their difficulties. Become as skilled as you are capable of, do the best that you can, and then accept that you cannot control the lives of all children that you serve. Find your reward and fulfillment from those that do make positive changes.

5. Continue your education throughout your career. The Division of Juvenile Services has offered me the opportunity to receive training in many areas, including drug and alcohol studies, mediation training, case management and supervision techniques, teen suicide and stress training, computer training, child protection issues, sexual offender issues, mental health issues, and Native American cultural issues. These opportunities have been invaluable in helping me to stay sharp, energized, connected with other professionals, and on top of new developments in our field.

6. I would advise students to be concerned with their personal safety. Be aware of the situations and circumstances that you find yourself in and don't take unnecessary or foolish chances.

7. Remember to reserve some time to take care of yourself. Reward yourself and learn to enjoy activities outside of your job. Balancing career, family, friends, and activities will allow you to maintain a positive attitude and stay motivated. I'm still working on this one.

8. Develop and maintain good working relationships with your agency staff and network with professionals in other agencies. I have found these relationships to be invaluable in getting my own job done.

THE DEINSTITUTIONALIZATION OF STATUS OFFENSES

The Juvenile Justice and Delinquency Prevention Act of 1974

The U.S. Congress passed the **Juvenile Justice and Delinquency Prevention Act of 1974 (JJDPA)** in response to a national concern about growing juvenile delinquency and youth crime (MacDonald and Chesney-Lind, 2001). This Act authorized the establishment of the **Office of Juvenile Justice and Delinquency Prevention (OJJDP),** which has been extremely helpful and influential in matters of disseminating information about juvenile offending and prevention and as a general data source. Box 2.2 is a history and summary of the JJDPA and its subsequent amendments.

Changes and Modifications in the JJDPA

In 1977 Congress modified the Act by declaring the juveniles should be separated by both sight and sound from adult offenders in detention and correctional facilities. Also in 1977, states were given five years to comply with the DSO mandate. Nonoffenders, such as dependent and neglected children, were also included. Congress relaxed certain JJDPA rules and gave states additional

BOX 2.2

HISTORY AND SUMMARY OF THE JUVENILE JUSTICE AND DELINQUENCY PREVENTION ACT OF 1974 AND ITS SUBSEQUENT AMENDMENTS

Fact Sheet

The Juvenile Justice and Delinquency Prevention Act of 1974 (JJDPA) provides the major source of federal funding to improve states' juvenile justice systems. The JJDPA was developed with a broad consensus that children should not have contact with adults in jails and other institutional settings and that status offenders should not be placed in secure detention. Under the JJDPA and its subsequent reauthorizations, in order to receive federal funds, states are required to maintain these core protections for children:

Deinstitutionalization of Status Offenders (DSO)

Status offenders may not be held in secure detention or confinement. There are, however, several exceptions to this rule, including allowing some status offenders to be detained for up to 24 hours. The DSO provision seeks to ensure that status offenders who have not committed criminal offenses are not held in secure juvenile facilities for extended periods of time or in secure adult facilities for any length of time. Status offenses are offenses that only apply to children, such as skipping school, running away, breaking curfew, and possession or use of alcohol. These children, instead, should receive community-based services, such as day treatment or residential home treatment, counseling, mentoring, alternative education, and job development support (Urban, 2005).

Adult Jail and Lock-Up Removal

Juveniles may not be detained in adult jails and lock-ups except for limited times before or after a court hearing (6 hours), in rural areas (24 hours plus weekends and holidays), or in unsafe travel conditions. This provision does not apply to children who are tried or convicted in adult criminal court of a felony-level offense. This provision is designed to protect children from psychologi-cal abuse, physical assault, and isolation. Children housed in adult jails and lock-ups have been found to be eight times more likely to commit suicide, five times more likely to be sexually assaulted, two times more likely to be assaulted by staff, and 50 percent more likely to be attacked with a weapon than children in juvenile facilities.

Sight and Sound Separation

When children are placed in an adult jail or lock-up, as in exceptions listed above, "sight and sound" contact with adults is prohibited. This provision seeks to prevent children from psychological abuse and physical assault. Under "sight and sound," children cannot be housed next to adult cells; share dining halls, recreation areas, or any other common spaces with adults; or be placed in any circumstances that could expose them to threats or abuse from adult offenders.

Disproportionate Minority Confinement (DMC)

States are required to assess and address the disproportionate confinement of minority juveniles in all secure facilities. Studies indicate that minority youth receive tougher sentences and are more likely to be incarcerated than non-minority youth for the same offenses. With minority children making up one-third of the youth population but two-thirds of children in confinement, this provision requires states to gather information and assess the reason for disproportionate minority confinement.

Of particular interest here is the fourth division, the State Relations and Assistance Division. This Division addresses directly the matter of removing juveniles, especially status offenders, from secure institutions (facilities similar to adult prisons), jails, and lock-ups. The second division, Research and Program Development, is concerned with examining how juvenile courts process juvenile offenders. Individual states and local jurisdictions are encouraged to devise ways of separating juvenile delinquents from status offenders and removing status offenders from the jurisdiction of juvenile courts. The Act suggests that status offenders should be processed by agencies and organizations other than juvenile courts, such as social or human services agencies and bureaus.

September 7, 1974: The JJDPA signed into law. It created a formula grant program; the Office of Juvenile Justice and Delinquency Prevention; the National Institute for Juvenile Justice and Delinquency Prevention; the Federal Coordinating Council; the National Advisory Committee; required each state to submit an annual plan for compliance; required each state to create an advisory group; established the separation requirement; and required that the state planning agency submit to the Law Enforcement Assistance Administration administrator an analysis of the plan's effectiveness.

October 5, 1974: The Departments of State, Justice, and Commerce, and Several Independent Agencies Act of 1975, which appropriated $25 million for fiscal year 1975 for the JJDPA was signed into law by the president.

July 10, 1975: Law Enforcement Assistance Administration issued guidelines for state receipt of formula grants; the DSO requirement provided that status offenders and non-status offenders shall not be placed in juvenile detention or correctional facilities, but must be placed in shelter facilities on a temporary or emergency basis; defined shelter facilities for status offenders; listed examples when a juvenile should be considered a status offender, a criminal-type offender, or a nonoffender; stated that the purpose of the separation requirement is to keep delinquents totally separate from adults, except for incidental contact.

October 7, 1975: Law Enforcement Assistance Administration of Legal Counsel Legal Option.

October 3, 1977: The Juvenile Justice Amendments of 1977 were signed into law; increased the amount of time within which a state must comply with the DSO requirement to three years; failure to reach full compliance with the DSO requirement

within three years made the state ineligible for funding, unless the state was found to be in substantial compliance; required a state to provide an annual report reviewing progress made on the DSO requirement, the number of accused status offenders and nonoffenders held in juvenile detention or correctional facilities did not include those held less than 24 hours following initial police contact or those held less than 24 hours following initial court contact; separation requirement expanded to include delinquents, status offenders, and nonoffenders.

August 16, 1978: The Law Enforcement Assistance Administration issued guidelines for the implementation of the 1977 amendments; each state was required to submit a report on its compliance with the DSO and the separation requirement; to demonstrate compliance the state must include information for both the baseline and the current reporting periods.

September 24, 1979: The Departments of State, Justice, and Commerce Act of 1980, which appropriated $100 million for fiscal year 1980 for the JJDPA, was signed into law by the president.

December 8, 1980: Juvenile Justice Amendments of 1980 were signed into law; amended the Act to require that states submit a three-year plan; established jail removal requirement and compliance provisions for the requirement; established the Office of Juvenile Justice and Delinquency Prevention as a separate entity; deleted the correctional institution or facility and added the definitions for secure detention facility and secure correctional facility; clarified that juveniles who are charged with or who have committed status offenses shall not be placed in secure detention facilities or secure correctional facilities; DSO provision is modified to exempt juveniles who commit offenses that constitute violations of valid court orders; the substantial compliance standard for the DSO requirement was modified; provided for an emphasis on dealing with learning disabled and handicapped juveniles, and on juveniles who commit serious crimes; renumbered and amended monitoring provision.

December 31, 1981: The OJJDP published final regulations, except for regulations

(continued)

concerning the valid court orders; set forth the DSO requirement's main provisions; set forth the separation requirement's main provisions; set forth the jail removal requirement's main provisions and exceptions to the requirement; indicated what substantial compliance was for each of the major provisions.

January 17, 1984: The OJJDP issued a position statement on the minimum requirements for the jail removal requirement; clarified the jail removal requirement's goals; set forth mandatory and recommended regulations if juveniles and adults are housed in one structure.

October 12, 1984: Juvenile Justice, Runaway Youth, and Missing Children's Act Amendments of 1984 of the Comprehensive Crime Control Act of 1984 was signed into law; established administrator of OJJDP as a presidential appointment; sought to provide for enhanced parental involvement and efforts to strengthen the family unit in addressing delinquency-related problems; jail removal requirement was amended to allow the OJJDP administrator, through 1989, to make exceptions to the requirement; added "valid court order" to the definition section of the JJDPA; amended to allow three additional years to achieve full compliance with the jail removal requirement if the state achieves substantial compliance.

June 20, 1985: The OJJDP published the final regulations on the jail removal requirement; adopted the requirements initially set forth on January 17, 1984; gave states until December 8, 1988, to achieve full compliance with the jail removal requirement; clarified the exceptions to the jail removal requirement; defined adult jail and adult lock-up.

November 2, 1988: The OJJDP revised the criteria for de minimis exceptions to full compliance with the jail removal requirement; issued a policy to aid in the determination of when a juvenile is held in nonsecure custody within a building that houses adults; defined secure detention and nonsecure detention.

November 18, 1988: The Juvenile Justice and Delinquency Prevention of the Anti-Drug Abuse Act of 1988 was signed into law; reauthorized juvenile justice act through fiscal year 1992; placed emphasis on the problem of overrepresentation of minority youth in juvenile justice system; amended the substantial compliance provision.

August 8, 1989: The OJJDP final regulations on jail removal requirement; amended jail removal requirement to provide an alternative way of substantial compliance; clarifies states' monitoring responsibilities.

November 4, 1992: The JJDPA amendments of 1992 were signed into law; reauthorized juvenile justice and delinquency prevention formula grant program through fiscal year 1996; established a number of new grant programs, including initiatives targeted at eliminating gender bias in treatment of juvenile delinquents; amended the separation requirement to require that detained or confined juveniles do not have contact with incarcerated adults; placed an emphasis on cooperation between federal, state, and local agencies in service delivery and program administration; emphasized delinquency prevention and diversion to services, including recreation programs, prevention and treatment in rural areas, prevention and treatment of hate crimes, family strengthening and involvement in treatment of delinquents; services for juveniles in custody; graduated sanctions and risk-need assessments; amended the DSO requirement to require that alien juveniles in custody also be deinstitutionalized; amended the separation requirement to prevent juveniles from having contact with part-time or full-time security staff or direct-care staff of a jail or lock-up for adults; amended the jail removal requirement to allow the administrator to promulgate regulations through 1997 making exceptions regarding the detention of juveniles; amended the substantial compliance provision with respect to the jail removal requirement. [*Source:* Adapted from Shay Bilchik (1995). *Unlocking the Doors for Status Offenders: The State of the States.* Washington, DC: Office of Juvenile Justice and Delinquency Prevention, pp. 50–60.]

May 10, 1999: Reauthorization of the Juvenile Justice and Delinquency Prevention Act through 2002.

October 1, 2003: Juvenile Justice and Delinquency Prevention Act of 2002 implemented and applicable through 2004.

2005: Block grants made available under the Juvenile Justice and Delinquency Prevention Act of 2002.

latitude regarding their placement options for status offenders and nonoffenders, including no placement.

In 1980 Congress recommended that states should refrain from detaining juveniles in jails and lock-ups. Explicit compliance with this recommendation by any state is complicated by several factors. First, many juveniles appear to be adults when arrested for various offenses. Second, the relatively easy access to false identification cards and driver's licenses makes a precise determination of one's age difficult. Sometimes it may take days or weeks in order for police to determine the identity and age of any particular youth being held in a jail or lock-up. Congress also directed that states should examine their secure confinement policies relating to minority juveniles and to determine reasons and justification for the disproportionately high rate of minority confinement. Congress also established an exception to DSO by declaring that juveniles who violate a valid court order can be placed in secure confinement for a period of time.

By 1992, Congress directed that any participating state would have up to 25 percent of its formula grant money withheld to the extent that the state was not in compliance with each of the JJDPA mandates. Thus, it is clear that state compliance with these provisions of the JJDPA was encouraged and obtained by providing grants-in-aid to various jurisdictions wanting to improve their juvenile justice systems and facilities. There has been almost universal compliance with the JJDPA mandate throughout the various state juvenile justice systems, and it has served as a significant catalyst for major reform initiatives (Leiber, 2002).

Deinstitutionalization of Status Offenses Defined

The most popular meaning of the deinstitutionalization of status offenses (DSO) means the removal of status offenders from juvenile secure institutions. However, the JJDPA has extended the meaning of DSO to include alternative ways of ensuring that status offenders are separated from delinquent offenders. Presently DSO occurs in three major ways: (1) decarceration; (2) diverting dependent and neglected children to social services; and (3) divestiture of jurisdiction.

Decarceration.   **Decarceration** means to remove status offenders from secure juvenile institutions, such as state industrial schools. Prior to the Juvenile Justice and Delinquency Prevention Act of 1974, it was common practice in most states to incarcerate both status and delinquent offenders together in reform schools or industrial schools (Roberts and Gabor, 2004). But more than a few people, scholars and the general public alike, questioned this practice. Why should truants, curfew violators, runaways, and difficult-to-control children be placed in prison-like facilities together with adjudicated juvenile murderers, rapists, burglars, thieves, robbers, arsonists, and other violent and property felony offenders? Qualitatively, there are substantial differences between status offenders and delinquent offenders. Do status offenders deserve to be treated the same as delinquent offenders for such drastically different offending behaviors? No.

Prevalent opinion suggests that causing status offenders to live and interact with delinquents in secure confinement, especially for prolonged periods of time, is definitely detrimental to status offenders. The mere exposure of status offenders to the criminogenic influence of and close association with hard-core delinquents adversely affects the social and psychological well-being of status offenders. The damage to a status offender's self-concept and -esteem is incalculable (Gaardner and Belknap, 2004). This particular problem has been acknowledged outside of the United States as well. Countries such as China have implemented similar reforms in their juvenile justice systems in recent years, in order to separate less serious juvenile offenders from more serious ones (Chen, 2000). Sensing the many problems associated with combining status offenders with delinquent offenders in secure institutions no doubt was a compelling factor leading to the passage of the JJDPA.

Subsequently, most states have implemented decarceration policies for status offenders. For instance, Pennsylvania does not place status offenders in secure facilities. However, in some predominantly rural states, such as Montana and North Dakota, some status offenders have continued to be disposed to secure institutions by juvenile court judges. One reason is that juvenile court judges view incarcerating these youths as an appropriate punishment and a potential cure for their status offending. Another reason is that these state legislatures have not devised alternative strategies for treating status offenders through other state agencies or services. A third reason is that often, facilities simply do not exist in rural areas to meet status offender needs and provide the social services they require. Thus, the only alternative for their treatment and punishment is to be locked up in secure juvenile facilities together with delinquent offenders.

In order to expedite the decarceration of status offenders from secure juvenile facilities, the federal government has made available substantial sums of money to the states for the purpose of establishing alternative social services. Usually states who agree to accept federal money in exchange for implementing DSO are given several years over which to implement these reforms in how status offenders are processed. Thus, a period of time is allocated in which to phase out the incarceration of status offenders and phase in the creation of alternative social service agencies designed to accommodate them and meet their needs. For instance, in Maryland, the Montrose Residential Training School was used to house a broad array of adjudicated juvenile offenders, including status offenders and delinquents, during the 1980s. In 1988 it was decided to close the facility. The closure was gradual and occurred over a period of time (Gottfredson and Barton, 1997).

Under certain conditions, however, states may incarcerate status offenders who are under some form of probationary supervision. For instance, a Texas juvenile, E.D., was on probation for a status offense (*In re E.D.*, 2004). During the term of E.D.'s probation, one or more probation conditions were violated. The juvenile court elected to confine E.D. to an institution for a period of time as punishment for the probation violation. The juvenile appealed, contending that as a status offender, he should not be placed in a secure facility. The appellate court disagreed and held that the juvenile court judge has broad discretionary powers to determine E.D.'s disposition, even including placement in a secure facility. The appellate court noted that secure placement of a status offender is warranted whenever the juvenile probation department (1) reviews the behavior of the youth and the circumstances under which the juvenile was brought before the court; (2) determined the reasons for the behavior that caused the youth to be brought before the court; and (3) determined that all dispositions, including treatment, other than placement in a secure detention facility or secure correctional facility, have been exhausted or are clearly inappropriate.

The juvenile court judge set forth an order that (1) it is in the child's best interests to be placed outside of his home; (2) reasonable efforts were made to prevent or eliminate the need for the child's removal from his home; and (3) the child, in his home, cannot be provided the quality of care and support that he needs to meet the conditions of probation. There was no suggestion in the record that the judge failed to comply with these three major requirements. Thus, even status offenders may suffer incarceration if they fail to obey court orders while on probation despite the deinstitutionalization initiative.

Diverting Dependent and Neglected Children to Social Services. A second type of DSO deals with **dependent and neglected children.** While the juvenile court continues to exercise jurisdiction over dependent and neglected youths, diversion programs have been established to receive these children directly from law enforcement officers, schools, parents, or even self-referrals. These diversion programs provide crisis intervention services for youths, and their aim is to return juveniles eventually to their homes. However, more serious offenders may need more elaborate services provided by shelter homes, group homes, or even foster homes (Fader et al., 2001).

Divestiture of Jurisdiction. The third type of deinstitutionalization is called **divestiture** of jurisdiction. Under divestiture, juvenile courts cannot detain, petition, adjudicate, or place youths on probation or in institutions for any status offense. However, several studies of DSO implementation policies reveal that there are gaps in coordinating interjurisdictional practices involving juveniles. Often, particular agencies continue to operate in their own philosophical contexts in contrast with, and sometimes in opposition to, legislative mandates for juvenile processing changes (Feld, 2000).

Potential Outcomes of DSO

Five potential outcomes of DSO are:

1. DSO has reduced the number of status offenders in secure confinement, especially in local facilities. Greater numbers of jurisdictions are adopting deinstitutionalization policies and the actual number of institutionalized status offenders is decreasing.

2. **Net-widening,** or pulling youths into the juvenile justice system who would not have been involved previously in the system, has increased as one result of DSO. Many state jurisdictions have drawn large numbers of status offenders into the net of the juvenile justice system following DSO. In past years, many status offenders would have been ignored by police or handled informally. But when specific community programs were established for status offenders, the net widened and many status offenders were placed in these programs regardless of whether they needed specific social services.

3. **Relabeling,** or defining youths as delinquent or as emotionally disturbed who, in the past, would have been defined and processed as status offenders, has occurred in certain jurisdictions following DSO. For instance, police officers can easily relabel juvenile curfew violators or loiterers as larceny or burglary suspects and detain these youths (Reynolds et al.,

1999). In many instances, juvenile court judges have resisted DSO reforms for similar reasons (e.g., loss of discretionary control and power over status offenders).

4. DSO has had little, if any, impact on recidivism rates among status offenders. More than a few jurisdictions report that removing status offenders from juvenile court jurisdiction or not institutionalizing them will decrease their recidivism (Gottfredson and Barton, 1997).

5. DSO has created several service delivery problems, including inadequate services, nonexistent services or facilities, or the general inability to provide services within a voluntary system. This is because there is so much variation among status offenders that it is difficult to establish standardized programming and services that will be effective for all of them.

Regardless of the relative merits of DSO and the ambiguity of research results concerning its short- and long-term effects, there is no doubt that DSO is widespread nationally and has become the prevailing juvenile justice policy. DSO has set in motion numerous programs in all jurisdictions to better serve the needs of a growing constituency of status offenders. This necessarily obligates growing numbers of agencies and organizations to contemplate new and innovative strategies—rehabilitative, therapeutic, and/or educational—to cope with these youths with diverse needs. Greater cooperation between the public, youth services, and community-based treatment programs is required to facilitate developing the best program policies and practices.

THE *UNIFORM CRIME REPORTS* AND *NATIONAL CRIME VICTIMIZATION SURVEY*

Two official sources of information about both adult and juvenile offenders are the *Uniform Crime Reports (UCR)* and the *National Crime Victimization Survey (NCVS)*.

Uniform Crime Reports

The **Uniform Crime Reports (UCR)** is published annually by the Federal Bureau of Investigation (FBI) in Washington, DC. The *UCR* is a compilation of arrests for different offenses according to several time intervals. Periodic reports of arrests are issued quarterly to interested law enforcement agencies. All rural and urban law enforcement agencies are requested on a voluntary basis to submit statistical information about 29 different offenses. Most of these agencies submit arrest information, and thus, the *UCR* represents over 15,000 law enforcement agencies throughout the United States.

Crime in the *UCR* is classified into two major categories, Part I and Part II offenses. Part I offenses are considered the most serious, and eight serious felonies are listed. These include murder and nonnegligent manslaughter, forcible rape, robbery, aggravated assault, burglary, larceny-theft, motor vehicle theft, and arson. Table 2.2 shows a listing of the eight major **Index Offenses** (Part I offenses) and their definition.

TABLE 2.2

Uniform Crime Report, Part I: Crimes and Their Definition

Crime	Definition
Murder and nonnegligent manslaughter	Willful (nonnegligent) killing of one human being by another
Forcible rape	Carnal knowledge of a female, forcibly and against her will; assaults or attempts to commit rape by force or threat of force are included
Robbery	Taking or attempting to take anything of value from the care, custody, or control of a person or persons by force or threat of force or violence and/or by putting the victim in fear
Aggravated assault	Unlawful attack by one person upon another for the purpose of inflicting severe or aggravated bodily injury
Burglary	Unlawful entry into a structure to commit a felony or theft
Larceny-theft	Unlawful taking, carrying, leading, or riding away of property from the possession or constructive possession of another, including shoplifting, pocket picking, purse snatching, and thefts of motor vehicle parts or accessories
Motor vehicle theft	Theft or attempted theft of a motor vehicle, including automobiles, trucks, buses, motorscooters, and snowmobiles
Arson	Any willful or malicious burning or attempt to burn, with or without intent to defraud, a dwelling house, public building, motor vehicle or aircraft, and the personal property of another

Source: U.S. Department of Justice, Federal Bureau of Investigation. *Crime in the United States* (Washington, DC: U.S. Government Printing Office, 1999). Updated 2005 by author.

Table 2.2 shows **index crimes** for 2004. The first eight offenses are major offenses classified as **felonies.** Felonies are violations of criminal laws that are punishable by terms of imprisonment of one year or longer in state or federal prisons or penitentiaries. These offenses are known as index offenses because they provide readers with a sample of key or index crimes that can be charted quarterly or annually, according to different jurisdictions and demographic and socioeconomic dimensions (e.g., city size, age, race, gender, urban–rural). Thus, the crime categories listed are not intended to be an exhaustive compilation. However, it is possible to scan these representative crime categories to obtain a general picture of crime trends across years or other desired time segments (Ulmer and Johnson, 2004).

The *UCR* also lists a second group of offenses known as Part II offenses. These include misdemeanors and status offenses. Offenses include embezzlement, stolen property, vandalism, carrying weapons, drug abuse violations, sex offenses, driving under the influence, liquor law violations, vagrancy, suspicion, curfew and loitering violations, runaways, and disorderly conduct (Chapple, Johnson, and Whitbeck, 2004; Victor, 2004). A **misdemeanor** is a violation of criminal laws that is punishable by an incarcerative term of less than one year in city or county jails. Status offenses listed, including runaway behavior, truancy, and violation of curfew, are not considered crimes, although they are reported together with criminal offenses to give a more complete picture of arrest activity throughout the United States (Shutt et al., 2004). The offenses listed are not an exhaustive compilation. Rather, a sample listing of crimes based on arrests is provided.

National Crime Victimization Survey

Compared with the *UCR,* the ***National Crime Victimization Survey (NCVS)*** is conducted annually by the United States Bureau of the Census. It is a random survey of approximately 60,000 dwellings, about 127,000 persons age 12 or over, and approximately 50,000 businesses. Subsamples of persons are questioned by interviewers who compile information about crime victims. Those interviewed are asked whether they have had different types of crimes committed against them during the past six months or year. Through statistical analysis, the amount of crime throughout the general population can be estimated (Lochner and Moretti, 2004).

The *NCVS* provides information about criminal victimizations and incidents. A **victimization** is the basic measure of the occurrence of a crime and is a specific criminal act that affects a single victim (Finkelhor and Jones, 2004). An **incident** is a specific criminal act that may involve one or more victims (Stucky, 2003). Because the *NCVS* reflects an amount of crime allegedly perpetrated against a large sample of victims, it is believed more accurate as a national crime estimate than the *UCR.* Thus, whenever comparisons of crime from the *UCR* are made against the *NCVS,* the *NCVS* reports from two to four times the amount of crime as indicated by law enforcement agency arrest figures in the *UCR.* But because of certain flaws inherent in both estimates of national crime, some observers believe both reports are underestimates of the true amount of crime in the United States (Bowers, Johnson, and Pease, 2004).

Strengths of These Measures

One strength of these indicators of crime in the United States is the sheer numbers of offenses reported. Few alternative sources of information about crime in the United States exhibit such voluminous reporting. Also, regional and seasonal reports of criminal activity are provided. The *UCR* also reports the proportion of different types of crime that are **cleared by arrest.** Cleared by arrest means that someone has been arrested and charged with a particular crime. Another favorable feature of both the *UCR* and *NCVS* is that numbers of arrests and reported crimes can be compared across years. Therefore, the *UCR* reports percentage increases or decreases in the amount of different types of crime for many different jurisdictions and over various time periods. And although the *NCVS* does not purport to survey all crime victims, the randomness inherent in the selection of the target respondents is such that generalizations about the U.S. population are considered reasonably valid (Tyler, Whitbeck, and Cauce, 2004).

A primary advantage of the *NCVS* over the *UCR* is that victims offer interviewers information about crimes committed against them. In many instances, these respondents disclose that they do not report these crimes to police. The reasons for not reporting crimes to police vary, although these victims often believe that the police cannot do much about their victimization anyway. Sometimes, rape victims are too embarrassed to report these incidents, or they may feel that they were partially to blame. Furthermore, in some of these cases, family members or close friends may be the perpetrators, and victims may be reluctant to press criminal charges.

Weaknesses of These Measures

Certain limitations of the *UCR* and *NCVS* are well documented. Focusing on the *UCR* first, we may cite some of the more important weaknesses of these statistics. For instance, *UCR* figures do not provide an annual per capita measure of crime frequency. Not all law enforcement agencies report crime to the FBI, and those that do may fail to report crime uniformly. Because law enforcement agencies are not compelled to submit annual information to the FBI, some agencies fail to report their arrest activity. Also, crimes of the same name vary in definition among jurisdictions. For instance, there are rapes in North Dakota, but there is no "rape" crime category. Rape is a form of "gross sexual imposition." And so is child sexual abuse (Vollman and Terry, 2005). This conceptual Tower of Babel contributes to inaccurate and/or incomplete crime reporting.

The *UCR* only reports arrests, not the actual amount of crime. When arrests are reported in the *UCR,* only the most serious offenses are often reported. Thus, if a robbery suspect is apprehended, she may possess burglary tools, a concealed weapon, and stolen property. She may have caused physical injuries to victims. All of these events are crimes, but only the robbery, the most serious offense, will be reported to the FBI. Therefore, there is much basis for the belief that these official reports of crime are at best underestimates. Arrest activity in the *UCR* may be attributable to fluctuations in police activity rather than actual fluctuations in criminal activity. Finally, although they only make up a fraction of national criminal activity, federal crimes are not reported in the *UCR.*

Both the *NCVS* and *UCR* overemphasize street crimes and underemphasize corporate crimes. Self-reported information contained in the *NCVS* is often unreliable. Sometimes victims interviewed may not be able to identify certain actions against them as crimes. For instance, date rapes may be reported as assaults. Also, persons may not be able to remember clearly certain criminal events. Fear of reprisals from criminals may compel some victims not to disclose their victimizations to interviewers. Some victimization data reported in the *NCVS* may be either exaggerated or more liberally reported. For various reasons, interviewees may lie to interviewers in disclosing details of crimes committed against them (Stucky, 2003).

Despite these criticisms, the *UCR* and *NCVS* provide valuable data for interested professionals. The fact that virtually all law enforcement agencies rely to some extent on these annual figures as valid indicators of criminal activity in the United States suggests that their utility in this regard is invaluable. Supplementing this information are other, more detailed, reports of selected offense activity. The U.S. Department of Justice Bureau of Justice Statistics publishes an incredible amount of information annually about different dimensions of crime and offender characteristics and behavior. This supplemental information, together with the data provided by the *UCR* and *NCVS,* may be combined to furnish us with a more complete picture of crime in the United States. Several alternative data sources are discussed in the following section.

OTHER SOURCES

One of the best compendiums of data specifically about juveniles and juvenile court adjudications is the **National Juvenile Court Data Archive.** While the federal government has collected data pertaining to juveniles since 1926, the data were dependent upon the voluntary completion of statistical forms by juvenile courts in a limited number of U.S. jurisdictions. The National Juvenile Court Data Archive contains over 800,000 annual automated case records of juveniles in various states. Numerous data sets are currently available to researchers and may be accessed for investigative purposes. These data sets are nonuniform, although they ordinarily contain information such as age at referral, gender, race, county of residence, offense(s) charged, date of referral, processing characteristics of the case (e.g., incarceration and manner of handling), and the case disposition (MacDonald, 2001).

However, in 1975 the Office of Juvenile Justice and Delinquency Prevention (OJJDP) assumed responsibility for acquiring court dispositional records and publishing periodic reports of juvenile offenses and adjudicatory outcomes. Today the OJJDP publishes periodic compilations of current juvenile offender data in a statistical briefing book, summarizing important delinquency statistics and trends. Also, every few years the OJJDP publishes a comprehensive summary of juvenile justice information in a national report on *Juvenile Offenders and Victims* (Office of Juvenile Justice and Delinquency Prevention, 2005).

Another compendium of offender characteristics of all ages is the ***Sourcebook of Criminal Justice Statistics*** published annually by the Hindelang Criminal Justice Research Center and supported by grants from the U.S. Department of Justice. This is perhaps the most comprehensive source that we have discussed, since it accesses numerous governmental documents and reports annually to keep readers abreast of the latest crime figures. Among other things, it describes justice system employment and spending, jail and prison management and prisoner issues, judicial misconduct and complaints, correctional officer characteristics, crime victim characteristics and victimization patterns, delinquent behavior patterns and trends, and considerable survey information. Literally hundreds of tables are presented that summarize much of the information reported by various private and governmental agencies. Useful annotated information is provided to supplement the tabular material (Eisner, 2002).

Statistics pertaining to juvenile offenders include juvenile admissions and discharges from public and private incarcerative facilities, average length of stay of juveniles in these facilities, a profile of juvenile custody facilities, demographic information about juveniles detained for lengthy terms, criminal history or prior records of juveniles, illegal drug and alcohol use among juveniles, waiver information, and offense patterns according to socioeconomic and demographic factors. Each annual sourcebook is somewhat different from those published in previous years, although much of the material in subsequent editions has been updated from previous years.

Self-Report Information

While these official sources of crime and delinquency are quite useful, a common criticism is that they tend to underestimate the amount of offense behaviors that actually occur in the United States (Lochner and Moretti, 2004). For many years, those interested in studying juvenile offense behaviors have frequently relied upon data derived from **self-reports.** The self-report is a data collection method involving an unofficial survey of youths or adults where the intent is to obtain information about specific types of behavior not ordinarily disclosed through traditional data collection methods, including questionnaires, interviews, polls, official agency reports, or sociodemographic summaries. This information is called **self-report information.** The exact origin of the use of self-reports is unknown. However, in 1943, Austin L. Porterfield investigated hidden delinquency, or delinquency neither detected by nor reported to police. He surveyed several hundred college students, asking them to disclose whether they had ever engaged in delinquent acts. While all of the students reported that they had previously engaged in delinquent acts, most also reported that they had not been caught by police or brought to the attention of the juvenile court (Porterfield, 1943).

In 1958, James Short and Ivan Nye became the first investigators to conduct the first self-report study of a delinquent population. They obtained self-report information from hundreds of delinquents in several Washington State training schools. They compared this information with self-report data from hundreds of students in three Washington State communities and three Midwestern towns. Their findings revealed that delinquency was widespread and not specific to any social class. Furthermore, both the seriousness and frequency of juvenile offending were key determinants of juvenile court treatment of youthful offenders and public policy relating to delinquents (Short and Nye, 1958).

Self-report surveys are believed to be more accurate and informative compared with official sources of crime and delinquency information. Before self-report surveys of such information are presented, it is helpful to become familiar with some of the more popular crime and delinquency information sources and their strengths and weaknesses.

The research applications of self-reports are both extensive and diverse. An inspection of research articles compiled by the *Criminal Justice Abstracts* in the years 1968–2005 by this author revealed that 284 articles utilized self-reports for different purposes. Two-thirds of the articles involved studies of juveniles, while article subject matter was dominated by the themes of drug/alcohol use, sex offenses, spousal abuse, status offending and delinquency, and early childhood sexual, psychological, or physical abuse.

Generally, self-report studies accomplish two important research objectives: (1) describing and understanding behavior and (2) predicting behavior. Self-report information provides considerable enriching details about persons under a variety of circumstances. Self-reports furnish important descriptive information about what people think and do. Such descriptions include how persons were treated as children and the events that were most significant to them as they grew to adulthood. The more that is learned about the significant occurrences in one's life, the better the predictive schemes to explain present, and to forecast future, behaviors. Self-reports, therefore, are an important source of information for descriptive and theoretical purposes. From a theoretical standpoint, self-reports represent one important means of theory verification.

Some of the popular self-report surveys conducted annually are the **National Youth Survey** and the **Monitoring the Future Survey** (Bachman and Peralta, 2001; Wright and Cullen, 2004). These large-scale surveys of high school students focus on particular behaviors. In addition, the Institute for Social Research at the University of Michigan annually solicits information from a national sample of 3,000 high school students. These informative reports are frequently cited in the research literature, which attests to the integrity, reliability, and validity of this information among noted juvenile justice professionals.

These national surveys involve administering confidential questionnaires and checklists to high school students. Students are asked to indicate which behaviors they have engaged in during the past six months or the previous year. Assuming that their responses are truthful, researchers believe that the results are a more accurate reflection of delinquent behaviors than are official sources, such as the *UCR* (Hennessy et al., 2001). Ordinarily, simple checklists are given to students and they are asked to identify those behaviors they have done, and not necessarily those for which they have been apprehended. Considered unofficial sources of information about delinquency and delinquency patterns, these self-disclosures are considered by many professionals to be more accurate than official sources (Demuth, 2004). An example of such a checklist is shown in Figure 2.6.

Self-reports enable researchers to determine whether there are changing offending patterns among juveniles over time. Substantial information exists that characterizes violent juvenile offenders and catalogs the many potential causal factors that are associated with violence, such as gang involvement (Curry, Decker, and Egley, 2002). Self-reported data about juvenile offenses sug-

FIGURE 2.6   A Hypothetical Checklist for Self-Report Disclosures of Delinquent or Criminal Conduct among High School Students.

"How often during the past six months have you committed the following offenses?" Check whichever best applies to you.

Offense	Frequency				
	0 times	1 time	2 times	3 times	4 or more times
Smoked marijuana	____	____	____	____	____
Stole something worth $50 or less	____	____	____	____	____
Got drunk on beer or wine	____	____	____	____	____
Got drunk on hard liquor	____	____	____	____	____
Used crack or cocaine	____	____	____	____	____

Source: Compiled by author.

gests that a sizeable gap exists between official reports of delinquent conduct and information disclosed through self-reports (Lochner and Moretti, 2004).

Self-reports reveal much more delinquency than is reported by either the *UCR* or *NCVS.* However, since *NCVS* information is also a form of self-disclosure, some investigators have found greater compatibility between delinquency self-reporting and the *NCVS* than between delinquency self-reporting and the *UCR,* which reports only arrest information. In any case, self-reports of delinquency or status offense conduct have caused researchers to refer to these undetected offending behaviors as **hidden delinquency.**

Some investigators question whether self-report information is reliable. Do youths tell the truth about their conduct, whatever the reported behavior? Some reported information is more easily refuted or confirmed by independent means. In the cases of illicit alcohol, tobacco, or drug use, independent tests may be conducted to determine the veracity of self-report information. In one school district, for instance, over 50 percent of all high school students interviewed disclosed through self-reports that they smoked. Subsequently, analyses of saliva specimens from these same students revealed that less than 10 percent of them tested positive for tobacco use. For several reasons unknown to the researchers, about half of these high schoolers reported that they used tobacco when most of them didn't use tobacco. Were they bragging? Was this peer pressure in action? In view of the evidence, this is the strong implication.

The relation between one's early childhood and the onset of status offending or delinquency has been heavily investigated. Typically, parent–child association and attachment are linked with delinquent conduct (Brank and Weisz, 2004). Samples of delinquents and nondelinquents are asked to provide self-reports of their early upbringing, including their perceived closeness with parents and the disciplinary methods used to sanction misconduct. Different themes are researched. For instance, the etiology of delinquency as related to different family processes according to race/ethnicity has been studied. Does a sample of inner-city high-risk youths reflect important differences in family processes according to race/ethnicity?

Information about runaways is almost exclusively gleaned from self-report studies. For example, it has been found that runaways compared with other types of status offenders have greater levels of family violence, rejection, and sexual abuse (Guerra, Asher, and DeRosier, 2004). Not unexpectedly, based on self-report experiences, runaways were from families where there was less parental monitoring of juvenile behavior, warmth, and supportiveness (Chapple, Johnson, and Whitbeck, 2004).

In a more general analysis of early childhood experiences involving adolescent maltreatment and its link with delinquency, self-reports were used by Ireland, Smith, and Thornberry (2002) to identify the frequency of delinquency and drug use among youths involved in the Rochester Youth Development Study. This was a multiwave panel study of adolescent development, involving youths starting at age 14 and interviewed every six months for nine consecutive waves. A general delinquency index included 32 offenses ranging from minor offenses like public disorder to robbery and assault with a deadly weapon. Over time, youths involved in the multiwave panel were separated according to the persistence and prevalence of their offending behavior. Childhood maltreatment was defined as a broad spectrum of aberrant behaviors that are harmful to children, including physical, sexual, neglect, and emotional, and that place children at risk for problem behaviors, including delinquency, during adolescence. A set of self-reported delinquency and drug use questions asked whether the respondents had committed particular offenses in the six-month interval between the last and current interview, and if so, the frequency of the behavior. The basic hypothesis postulated by these researchers was that exposure to any type of abusive condition disrupts the normal course of development and leads to maladaptive behaviors, including delinquency and drug use at later ages. It was expected that although different types of maltreatment may have effects of varying magnitude, the general expectation was that all types will generate negative behaviors. Mild support was found for the hypothesis tested, in that self-disclosed maltreatment during adolescence does increase the risk for delinquent behaviors in early adolescence.

School violence is an increasingly important topic of discussion among parents, school officials, and juvenile justice professionals. Although the media suggests that school violence is pervasive, the sensationalism attached to school shootings does not necessarily mean that school violence is increasing. For instance, a study of 3,364 high school seniors drawn from 113 public and 19 private schools across the United States revealed that between 1982 and 1988, school victimizations occurred at relatively low rates (Hanke, 1996). Boys were victimized more frequently than girls, and nonwhites were victimized more frequently than whites. Most victimizations were single occurrences, with dangerous weapons used in only limited instances. Verbal threats not involving injury or weapons were most commonly observed. These victimizations were noted through the use of self-reports, where juveniles were asked whether they had been victimized at school.

A frequently cited relation is between drug/alcohol abuse and delinquency. In Hillsborough County, Florida, the Juvenile Assessment Center was established as an intervention project to help at-risk youths and their families

Gangs are growing in the United States, and each gang develops its own identity. Juvenile violence is often linked with gang membership.

(Dembo, Pacheco, and Schmeidler, 1997). Self-reports of 114 project participants led researchers to conclude that a significant association exists between self-reported drug use and involvement in delinquent behavior. Self-reports of crime and delinquency are a valuable source of information to researchers. Research projects with exploratory, descriptive, and/or experimental study objectives benefit from the use of self-report data. Descriptions of different types of delinquents and the development of useful intervention strategies for delinquency prevention have been assisted greatly by the use of self-reports (Rhoades and Zambrano, 2005). The broad application of self-reports in virtually every facet of criminology and criminal justice suggests the long-term application of this data collection method (Eitle and Eitle, 2003).

VIOLENCE AND NONVIOLENCE: CAREER ESCALATION?

How much violent crime is committed by juveniles? Are juveniles likely to escalate to more serious offenses during their youthful years as they become more deeply involved in delinquent conduct? Are there certain kinds of juvenile offenders who are more or less susceptible to intervention programs and treatments as means of reducing or eliminating their propensity to engage in delinquent conduct? Are schools new battlezones for gang warfare and other forms of violence? Certainly the media have helped to heighten our awareness of the presence and violence of youth gangs in various cities. Startling information about extensive drug and alcohol use among juveniles is frequently broadcasted or reported (West, 2005). Is there currently an unstoppable juvenile crime wave prevalent throughout the United States?

School Violence

Violence among schoolchildren has received increased attention in recent years and is a serious problem in other countries as well as the United States (Kuntsche and Klingermann, 2004). The media suggest that school violence is pervasive. In Miami, Florida, for example, high school students have reported both serious and frequent victimization. In many of these victimizations, dangerous weapons such as firearms were used to effect the victimization (Thornton, 2005). But school violence is not restricted to schools in lower socioeconomic areas or where large numbers of at-risk youths are found. More affluent settings are increasingly sites of violence. On April 20, 1999, two youths entered Columbine High School in Littleton, Colorado, and proceeded to murder thirteen of their fellow students and a teacher. They used semi-automatic weapons and shotguns, together with an array of pipe bombs and other explosive devices. Surrounded by police, the two youths took their own lives rather than risk capture. This carnage came on the heels of similar mass murders committed by youths at elementary and secondary schools in Mississippi, Arkansas, and Oregon during 1998–1999 (Newman, 2004).

Surprisingly there are over 100 violent student deaths at elementary and secondary schools each year. A majority of these deaths do not receive national media coverage. For instance, in the first half of the 1998–1999 school year, about 135 children were killed at school, killed on school property, at a school-sponsored event, or on the way to or from school. Furthermore, teachers are also victims of crime at school. Between 1994 and 1998, for example, an average of 133,700 violent crimes and 217,400 thefts were committed by students against teachers each year. Teachers in urban school settings were more likely to be victims of violent crimes than were teachers in suburban or rural schools (Small and Tetrick, 2001:8).

Fortunately, most school violence is seldom fatal (Melde, 2005). In 2004 students ranging in age from 12 to 18 were victims of about 225,000 incidents of nonfatal serious violent crimes in their schools. There were 720,000 similar incidents involving this age group outside of school. During the period 2003–2004, 55 percent of all public schools reported either a serious violent crime, such as murder or rape, or less serious violent crimes (e.g., assault) to the police (Stoddard, Mueller, and Lawrence, 2005; Yalda, 2005).

A general response to school violence throughout the United States has led to the development of several aggressive policy changes (Chapin and Gleason, 2004). School systems are training their teachers and students how to react in ways that will rapidly contain potentially serious school violence. Special response police forces are being trained to be more effective in providing ancillary support for school administrators and staff. Intensive prevention training for all involved parties, after-school academic enrichment programs, enforcement of and punishment for firearms possession and drug use/sales on campus, and developing a standardized system of early detection and assessment of at-risk students are being implemented on a national basis (Bell, 2002; Tubman, Gil, and Wagner, 2004). Evidence of the successfulness of these initiatives is the dramatic reduction in school violence subsequent to 1996 and through 2005. One of the contributing factors to this decline in school violence has been the establishment of a zero tolerance policy in many school systems, which imposes more stringent penalties on youthful offenders who bring dangerous weapons to their schools.

At-Risk Youths and the Pittsburgh Youth Study

Who are **at-risk youths?** At-risk youths are often those who suffer from one or more disadvantages, such as lower socioeconomic status, dysfunctional family conditions, poor school performance, learning or language disabilities, negative peer influences, and/or have low self-esteem (Brownlie et al., 2004). It is difficult to forecast which youths will become delinquent and which ones won't. For many decades, researchers have attempted to profile so-called at-risk youths by assigning to them various characteristics that seem to be associated with hardcore delinquents. In 1986 and for the next decade, investigators conducted a longitudinal study of 1,517 inner-city boys from Pittsburgh, Pennsylvania. The Pittsburgh Youth Study (PYS) followed three samples of boys for over a decade to determine how and why boys became involved in delinquent and other problem behaviors (Browning and Loeber, 1999:1). Initially, boys were randomly selected from the first, fourth, and seventh grades and tracked over time.

Eventually three developmental pathways were defined that display progressively more serious problem behaviors. The first pathway, authority conflict, involves youths who exhibit stubbornness prior to age 12, and then they move on to defiance and avoidance of authority. The second pathway, covert, includes minor covert acts, such as lying, followed by property damage and

 **BOX 2.3**

CAREER SNAPSHOT

Susan Stenson Waild

Manager, Probation Services and Juvenile Justice Grants Juvenile Court Services, King County Superior Court

Statistics:

BA (sociology), University of California, Santa Barbara; MSW (social work), University of Washington

Work History and Background

Social work can be an excellent choice of study for students who are interested working in the field of juvenile probation and/or law. This is particularly true in Washington State where state law clearly defines three mandates when dealing with juvenile offenders: accountability, treatment, and community protection. To be successful in this field you must be able to balance these three distinct and different mandates. Skills taught in a university-level social work curriculum can establish a solid basis for future success in the field.

In the early 1970s, while obtaining my bachelor's degree majoring in sociology at the University of California (Santa Barbara), I came across an internship position at the Santa Barbara County Juvenile Probation Department. I have always found it fascinating how, given similar or dissimilar backgrounds, people live and why they make the choices they do. That, combined with my interest and love of kids, made juvenile probation a natural "draw" for me.

After becoming a familiar face around the Department, I was offered the chance to be an on-call worker at the local juvenile detention center. This meant working the unpopular shifts of swing, graveyard, or weekends. Even so, I jumped at this opportunity to learn the work of probation. Thus I began my first "professional" job, supervising juvenile detainees. This was an invaluable experience and I learned a lot. While attending to their individual needs, I also had to monitor the group and its dynamics. This was my first experience learning how

to balance competing needs, a necessary skill now used daily in my current work. The Administration was pleased with my work. I was reliable and, to get my foot in the door, willing to take any shift. It was a very positive experience for me and I learned from some wonderful staff.

Subsequently I was hired as full-time staff to work at La Morada, the Probation Department's group home for teenage girls. The girls residing at La Morada had been ordered by the local juvenile court judge to live at the group home and participate in treatment. Again, I learned from some of the best. One night there was a potential riot brewing at the group home. Although there were only 20 girls, they came from different backgrounds, communities, and socioeconomic groups. This was the beginning of the "gang era" and the girls were quickly becoming part of that phenomenon. When events like this happened, protocol dictated calling in extra staff to help diffuse the situation. Attempts at reasoning, intervention, and even trickery proved unsuccessful. We were unable to get the kids to disperse and go to bed. Finally, the director, Faith Ryan, was called. She walked in and immediately chastised the girls for having food on the new piano (a clear violation of a house rule) and sent them to bed. Being caught totally off guard they went to their rooms. I was furious! What was she doing? She hadn't gotten to the heart of the matter. She didn't attempt a treatment intervention. However, what I eventually realized was, in fact what

(continued)

she did do was diffuse a potentially violent situation. She was wise and skilled enough to know that 2:00 A.M. was not the time or place to deal with these types of issues. The next day the situation was addressed and sanctions were meted out based on each girl's participation and culpability.

Desiring to pursue social work as a career, obtaining my master's in Social Work became a necessary next stop for obtaining this goal. At the University of Washington School of Social Work, my focus of study was on administration and direct services, primarily working in group home–type settings. Upon graduation I was hired by Lutheran Social Services to work in their group care facilities. Initially I worked with younger boys but always came back to the teenage population. It seemed to be my natural "fit." In the late 1970s and early 1980s Washington State embarked on a full-scale revision of its juvenile code. As part of the revisions, judges no longer had the authority to order youth into group care. This change, in addition to funding reductions, resulted in the closure of many group homes statewide. Personally, I felt the strain and toll being on call 24/7, especially having a young child of my own.

Still desiring to work with adolescents, in 1985 I started working for the King County Superior Court Conference Committee (diversion) Program. This nationally recognized program provides first-time juveniles involved in minor offenses with an alternative to court. The youth appears before a panel of community volunteers who review the matter and then enter into an agreement with the youth. The agreement identifies sanctions (e.g., community service hours) with which the youth must comply as a consequence for his or her offense. The volunteers were amazing. They cared about the kids in their community. They wanted to help rather than just punish and they wanted be an active participant in addressing what they believed was a local neighborhood problem. Recruiting, training, and supervising this group was pure joy.

Up until 2000, with the agreement of the King County Superior Court, the Department of Youth Services, an executive branch department, administered juvenile probation and juvenile detention. In 2000, juvenile probation was returned to the administration of King County Superior Court. With the resulting change in leadership I was asked to take on the position of Probation Manager. It was a very difficult time of transition. In addition to changes in administration, due to budget constraints the department required downsizing. Programs were ending and others were beginning. There was a long list of labor grievances and labor contracts were up for renegotiation. There was a lot to do. Once again, a most amazing group of talented staff from all levels and branches of government came together and worked through these very difficult tasks. Each person provided a special area of skill and expertise, creating an incredible transition team. In a relative short period of time it became clear we all shared the same goal: to bring about stability in the department and create an environment that allowed staff to do their best work with kids and families.

During these administrative changes in King County another significant change was taking place at the state level. Based on an extensive study by the Washington State Institute for Public Policy, the state became more strategic in targeting juvenile justice program funding. Programs backed by research showing them to be cost effective at reducing juvenile recidivism received funding and funding was cut for other programs, including programs that we intuitively felt might work or believed intellectually should work. Additionally, the Washington State Risk Assessment tool was developed and instituted. This is a validated tool designed to assess a youth's risk to reoffend. In Washington State, every child who is formally charged with an offense receives an assessment. All staff are trained and certified in the use of the tool.

The focus on "proven programs" and implementation of the risk assessment tool significantly impacted my job as Probation Manager. First, it provided focus on where to direct probation resources. With research showing that for low-risk youth, probation contact actually increases a juvenile risk level, a low-level supervision unit was created. Low-risk kids are assigned to this unit where caseloads are larger than for regular supervision JPCs and contact less frequent.

Removing low-risk kids from the general supervision population allowed the shifting of resources (probation staff) for the moderate and high-risk youth, resulting in reduced probation caseloads. These youth also are eligible for the "proven programs." The positive outcomes from these changes are several: As intra-agency refocusing occurred, to increase capacity in the community for serving these youth, we also expanded our efforts in collaboration with other county and private agencies; our staff are better trained on assessing and engaging families and youth and are no longer seen as the probation "officer," the enforcer of the court order; and our judges have better information upon which to make decisions.

In addition to these programs, we have instituted a specialized juvenile drug court and are now piloting a treatment court for kids with co-occurring disorders (substance abuse and mental health). Most recently a family treatment court became operational, working with families with children in foster care due to a parent's substance abuse. I am blessed to work with such amazing people. They come from varied professional backgrounds, with lots of experience and a commitment to do good work.

This is an exciting time to be in the field of social work. More is being learned about youth and what works and what doesn't work. This is a significant change from the tradition of making program decisions based on intuition and personal logic. We are more attentive to the cultural backgrounds of the families served and their personal family dynamics. We are developing advocacy teams to help families build their own support systems so they can continue to function successfully after probation ends.

Social work, research, and the law are mutual catalysts. Each drives the other to be better. Each has a role in assisting the youth and protecting the community. This is not easy work. It is constantly changing. Professionals who choose this field need to be open and understand that working with children and families who are in need of our services is a painful business. No one comes to court because they are happy and things are going well. Most if not all are in crisis. As social workers, our job is to assess, develop, and then implement plans for getting beyond these issues and making their lives better.

Advice to Students

1. Get a degree.
2. Be humble. Do not expect to start at the top or to get where you want to be too quickly. You may need to start working "graveyard." Volunteer, take beginning but related jobs. Use each opportunity as a chance to become a better professional.
3. Bad things can happen to good people. People come to court in pain. Often others will blame you or be angry with you because you can't make it right. They often don't agree with your position. They may lash out or want to walk away from their child. You can't let them. You have to treat them ALL with respect and dignity.
4. You have to have a big heart with a big brain. While understanding their struggle you need to keep your boundaries straight and hold yourself to the highest professional standards. You are not their buddy. You are a role model, everyday, so be a good one.
5. While doing all of that, you need to keep balance in your life. You will do no one any good if you do not take care of yourself.
6. Look around you. You will be presented with great teachers from which to learn. Sometimes they will be coworkers, sometimes families and kids, and sometimes even your superiors. You can learn what to do and you can learn what not to do.
7. This is important work. You will touch many lives and you will be touched by many others.

Best of luck as you pursue this wonderful, challenging, and ultimately rewarding career opportunity.

moderately serious delinquency, and then serious delinquency. The third pathway, overt, starts with minor aggression followed by fighting and violence. Risk factors identified and associated with delinquency among the Pittsburgh youth include impulsivity; IQ; personality; forces in an individual's environment, including parents, siblings, and peers; and factors related to family, school, and neighborhood.

At-risk youth in the PYS tended to have greater impulsivity, lower IQ, a lower threshold for experiencing negative emotions, such as fear, anxiety, and anger, and were more inclined to be involved in thrill-seeking and acting without caution. Family risk factors included poor supervision by parents, family receipt of public assistance (welfare), and lower socioeconomic status. The greatest demographic variable associated with delinquency was having a broken family. Living in a bad neighborhood doubled the risk for delinquency.

These aggregate data are interesting, but they fail to enable researchers to forecast with accuracy which youths will become delinquent and which ones won't. Maybe this is too much to ask without more definitive criteria for identifying potential juvenile offenders. Nevertheless, a profile of at-risk youths has slowly been generated to the extent that various intervention programs can be attempted in certain jurisdictions. The theory is that if at-risk youth can be identified according to proven prior characteristics from delinquency research, then perhaps one or more interventions can be attempted to work with some or all of those youths who are at risk.

Juvenile courts have attempted various types of interventions involving at-risk youths. Since the mid-1970s, the National Council of Juvenile and Family Court Judges has sought to focus national attention on abused and neglected children (Brownlie et al., 2004). Youths placed in foster care and/or suffering from various forms of sexual or physical abuse in their families are considered at risk and in need of special treatment from various social services. It has been found, for instance, that a strategy for assisting at-risk youths is to educate family and juvenile court judges in ways to improve their court practices (Fields and McNamara, 2003). By 1999, the Permanency Planning for Children Department has established 17 Model Courts in 16 states. These Model Courts have implemented a number of programs to deal with at-risk youths and their families. Such programs can easily be replicated in other jurisdictions. For instance, court calendars are generated to ensure that judicial decision makers are assigned to specific dependency cases and will remain on those cases until the children involved achieve permanence, either by being safely reunited with their rehabilitative families or by being placed in permanent adoptive homes. Family group conferencing and mediation programs are also incorporated into several of these Model Court jurisdictions (Kontos, Brotherton, and Barrios, 2003). Proper handling of cases involving these types of at-risk youths tends to decrease the likelihood that placed youths will become delinquent in their future years.

Gang Violence

Juvenile justice professionals are interested in the increased incidence of gang formation and membership behavior (Kontos, Brotherton, and Barrios, 2003). The gang phenomenon seems widespread throughout the United States rather than localized in major city centers. **Gangs** are found in most jurisdictions and seem to organize along racial or ethnic lines, often for mutual protection against

Suspected gang members attract the attention of the police.

other gangs (Chapple and Hope, 2003; Valdez and Sifaneck, 2004). Various independent investigations of gang presence and activities have been undertaken in recent years, including Project GANGMILL, by the National Gang Crime Research Center in Chicago. This investigation studied 3,489 gang members in seven states and 22 correctional facilities (National Gang Crime Research Center, 2000:38). General findings from these investigations parallel other broader investigations of gangs in the United States conducted by various federal agencies.

The gang problem in the United States is increasing (Greene, Webb, and McDevitt, 2003). There has been a rapid proliferation of youth gangs in the United States since 1980, despite our best intervention and gang prevention efforts. In 1980, for instance, there were 2,000 gangs in 286 jurisdictions, with over 100,000 gang members. In 2005 there were more than 30,000 gangs in 5,200 jurisdictions, with over 1 million gang members (Office of Juvenile Justice and Delinquency Prevention, 2005). About 11 percent of all gang members are female. While definitive national trend data are unavailable concerning female gang members and the types of offenses they commit, independent investigations of selected jurisdictions suggest that the number of female gangs in the United States is increasing (Fields and McNamara, 2003).

In 1992 the Chicago City Council held hearings to identify strategies to combat youth violence attributable to gangs and gang membership. Subsequently the Gang Congregation Ordinance was passed. This ordinance authorized Chicago police officers to investigate youths on city streets, where the youths appeared to be loitering or congregating in groups. Furthermore, police were authorized to order such groups of youths to disperse (Regini, 1998:25–26). Similar ordinances were passed in other cities such as Los Angeles. This ordinance gave police officers considerable discretion to determine which youths were gang members and to intervene whenever they believed gangs were present. The intent of the ordinance was to discourage neighborhood gang activity and reduce gang-related violence. However, the American Civil Liberties Union and other interested rights organizations protested and sought injunctions against police from taking gang-busting actions in those cities where such ordinances were passed. In 1999 the U.S. Supreme Court held these ordinances to be unconstitutional. Among the reasons were the fact that the ordinances were unconstitutionally vague and failed to specify what behaviors were prohibited. Furthermore, no definitive criteria were established whereby gang members could be distinguished from non-gang members. More than a few police officers and police departments regarded this Supreme Court decision as a major setback in their efforts to combat gang violence (Chapple and Hope, 2003).

Kids Who Kill

Juveniles who commit homicide are relative rare (Fox and Zawitz, 1999:1). Of the 15,000 homicide offenders reported by the *UCR* in 2004, 900 (16 percent) of these involved juveniles under age 18 (Office of Juvenile Justice and Delinquency Prevention, 2005). Some juveniles have begun their careers of gang violence, including murder and attempted murder, as early as age 6. An increasing amount of youth violence, including homicide, is linked to gang membership (Flannery and Huff, 1999). There were 825 gang-related juvenile murders in 2004. Actually, gang-related murders declined from 1996 (858 murders) to 1999 (580 murders), but the number of murders increased again in 2004.

Apart from gang-related murders, many youths kill one or more of their family members, such as their mothers or fathers (Lennings, 2002). Studies of youths who kill their parents show that they are often severely physically or sexually abused, and that they are particularly sensitive to stressors in the home environment. Many juvenile murderers have chemical dependencies for which they require treatment. Juvenile murderers also exhibit greater psychotic and conduct disorder symptoms compared with other types of juvenile offenders (Mencken, Nolan, and Berbanu, 2004).

Some juvenile murders are sexually motivated and occur when victims threaten to tell others. But even something as specific as sexually motivated juvenile murder is poorly misunderstood by the public (Hensley et al., 2005). A wide variety of explanations is provided for explaining or rationalizing adolescent murders, although any excuse is rarely accepted as mitigating. One frequently cited reason for gang violence was that it was an expected part of gang initiation rites (Heide, 1999, 2003). Most often cited as mitigating factors in juvenile homicides are troubled family histories and social backgrounds; psychological disturbances; mental retardation; indigence; and substance abuse. Treatments often include psychotherapy, psychiatric hospitalization, institutional placement, and psychopharmacological agents (Johnson, 2005).

Juvenile Violence Trends

Violence committed by juveniles has increased during the last few decades. Between 1986 and 1996, the juvenile violent crime index soared. Subsequently there has been a mild decline in juvenile violence (Irwin, 2004; O'Shaughnessy, 2004). This decline in juvenile violence has not been substantial, less than 15 percent. However, this slight decline may be one indication that various youth crime intervention programs are working. One initiative is Project Safe Neighborhoods, a collaborative effort between probation, parole, and other community-based agencies and law enforcement to provide training and technical assistance relating to supervising juvenile offenders and preventing them from acquiring and using firearms (*APPA Perspectives,* 2004b:9; Bynum, 2005; Decker, 2005).

One concomitant of youth violence is access to firearms. Gun-related violence is both a criminal justice and a public health problem. In 2000 there were 8 murders per 100,000 U.S. residents. But in 2004, the murder rate had dropped to 3.4 per 100,000. This is the lowest murder rate in the United States since 1965. However, preliminary projections have disclosed that for 2004, the murder rate had increased by 3.1 percent (Office of Juvenile Justice and Delinquency Prevention, 2005). This increase excludes the September 11, 2001, World Trade Center loss of lives through terrorist acts.

The impact of gun violence is especially strong for juveniles and young adults. There were 1,500 murder victims under the age of 18 in 2004. This is nearly 50 percent lower than the peak year of 1993, when there were 2,900 juvenile deaths. About half of these deaths were from firearms. Various policies and laws have been implemented to intervene in gun-related violence (McDevitt, 2005). Sources of illegal guns are increasingly interrupted; penalties have been increased for illegal possession and carrying of guns; and persons who supply at-risk youths for violence (e.g., probationers, gang members, and drug traffickers) are being prosecuted more aggressively. Simultaneously, programs are in place to treat and deal with those youthful offenders who have mental disorders and/or substance abuse problems (Bowman, 2005).

Career Escalation

Do status offenders progress to more serious offending, such as juvenile delinquency? Do juvenile delinquents become adult offenders? This phenomenon is known as **career escalation.** Presently, there is little agreement among professionals that either status offenders or delinquents progress toward more serious offending as they get older (Zimring, 1998). This generalization applies to both male and female offenders. One problem is that different **pathways,** or developmental sequences over the term of one's adolescence, are associated with serious, chronic, and violent offenders (Kempf-Leonard, Tracy, and Howell, 2001). Thus, a single trajectory or pathway cannot be used as a general forecast of career escalation, whenever it occurs. Furthermore, comparative research on career escalation among delinquent youths suggests that situational factors, such as whether youths come from abusive families and where drug and/or alcohol dependencies are evident, are more significant predictors of future, more serious offending rather than the sheer onset of status of delinquent offending (Parry et al., 2004).

With little more information than whether youths commit particular status or delinquent acts at particular ages, long-term predictions of future career escalation among these juveniles are simply unwarranted (Zimring, 1998). Arrest rates for juvenile offenders change drastically within short-term cycles of three years, rather than long-term cycles of more than three years. Also, there are different varieties of juvenile violence (McGarrell, 2005). About half of all juvenile

BOX 2.4

INTERNATIONAL SNAPSHOT: JUVENILE JUSTICE IN POLAND

Poland gained its independence following World War I and subsequently made special provisions for its youth through its first Penal Code in 1932. The 1932 Penal Code established a few juvenile courts in some of its largest cities and defined juvenile delinquents as persons who committed an offense prior to their 17th birthday. Persons under age 13 were not accountable for their illegal actions. Educational measures were set in place for juveniles under age 13, which included verbal reprimands through close supervision by parents, guardians, or a probation officer to placement in an educational institution. The same educational measures could be imposed on those from age 13 to 17, provided that they were deemed not competent to understand the nature of the act they committed and direct their behavior accordingly. For those between ages 13 and 17 who did understand the nature of the act, they could be subject to placement in a house of correction. In all cases, decisions were made about juveniles based on the circumstances of the offense, the juvenile's character, and his or her life and environment. Under the 1932 Penal Code, youths could be institutionalized until age 21, although they might be granted early release through judicial discretion. Juvenile placements in institutions were controversial, in that some persons believed these placements to be specific penalties associated with retribution or punishment, in direct contradiction to the professed rehabilitative goals of educational measures. Others believed that institutions were good for juveniles in that they fulfilled preventive-educational goals. This controversy raged over the next several decades, through World War II, and into the 1960s, when the laws were changed dramatically and more juvenile courts were created.

The Code of Penal Procedure of 1969 was passed, largely for adult offenders. However, it included a provision for transferring juveniles to criminal courts if they were age 16 or older and had committed very serious offenses. But the Penal Code of 1932 remained in effect during this period as well. Eventually a major change in the treatment of offending juveniles occurred with the passage of the Juvenile Act of 1982. This act incorporated strong educational and social rehabilitation elements, including a wider variety of measures applied to juveniles and a more central role of family judges and family courts in all stages of juvenile processing.

The Preamble to the Juvenile Act of 1982 has as its main objectives:

1. to counteract the demoralization and delinquency of juveniles;
2. to create conditions for those who have come into conflict with the law or with the rules of acceptable social behavior, to return to normal life;
3. to strengthen the care and educational functions of the family and its sense of responsibility for the development of children.

The Juvenile Act provisions apply to:

1. juveniles age 13–17 who commit offenses and selected misdemeanors;
2. juveniles who are under 18 years of age and display signs of problem behavior.

Although demoralization is not defined explicitly, signs of it include prostitution, use of alcohol and drugs, running away from home, association with criminal groups, and systematic truancy of compulsory school attendance or vocational training. Any juvenile under age 13 who commits any of these acts indicates demoralization, although such persons cannot be punished. Punishable acts may be committed only by juveniles between the ages of 13 and 17. Under the Juvenile Act, punishments include educational, medical, and/or corrective measures. Educational and medical measures may be applied to any juvenile under age 18 and over age 13 who display serious problem behavior and commit offenses. Corrective measures, including institutionalization, are warranted for those age 13–17 if their demoralization and circumstances are such that educational measures have proved or are not likely to lead to rehabilitation. Corrective measures are the suspension and immediate placement of juveniles in houses of correction. These placements are for indeterminate terms until age 21.

A central role in juvenile proceedings is played by family court judges. Family courts have jurisdiction over cases including guardianship, the enforcement of compulsory treatment of alcoholics and drug addicts, and juvenile cases related to prevention of problem behavior of persons under age 18, as well as punishable acts of those between ages 13 and 17. Family judges oversee all stages of these proceedings, including the imposition of punishments. These judges make preliminary inquiries, conduct court proceedings, and oversee the execution of any measures imposed on juveniles. Judges may change the nature of any imposed measures on juveniles during the period under which such juveniles are under the judge's supervision. These judges also are very powerful and may either drop or continue proceedings at any time. The chief concern of such judges is child welfare, with an emphasis on bringing about favorable changes in personality and behavior, and ensuring the proper discharge by parents or guardians of their obligations related to juvenile supervision. Basic criteria used in the choice of proper measures to apply include the juvenile's personality, age, health, mental and physical development, character and behavior, the causes and degree of demoralization, and the environment and conditions of his or her upbringing. Any institutional placement is considered a last resort, like it is in the United States. Account must be taken of the circumstances and nature of the offense before institutional placement is imposed.

During the 1990s and beyond 2000, victim–offender mediation programs have become widespread throughout Poland. Therefore, restorative justice is becoming a popular alternative to family courts and the applications of remedial measures by judges. Despite this progressive alternative, the Polish media have sensitized the public to a great rise in juvenile offending, especially during the 1990s, whether it is real or artificial. One result of greater media attention on juvenile offenders is the perception that existing juvenile policies are too soft on juvenile offending, that such policies are far too liberal, and that existing punishments of juveniles are simply out of date and no longer effective. Juvenile offending is now defined as a dangerous phenomenon, particularly with the recent rise in violent offending. This situation has led to greater concern for juvenile legal rights and responsibilities, as well as a push for promoting the principle of greater proportionality of punishment, given the offense, as well as the right of juveniles to be adjudicated by impartial tribunals.

The Juvenile Act of 1982 is still in effect, although in 1995 family court judicial discretion was curtailed in matters involving prison sentences for those ages 16 and 17. Prior to 1995, family judges could execute a prison sentence including correctional treatments, conditionally suspend these sentences, or even dismiss these sentences. After 1995 a prison sentence for particular offenses must be imposed and correctional orders must be dropped. Furthermore, in 1997, the age limit of criminal responsibility was lowered from age 16 to 15 for exceptionally serious cases. Also, the maximum penalty for juveniles exceptionally tried was limited to two-thirds of the maximum penalty provided for adult offenders. As an example, juveniles might receive a maximum penalty of 25 years of imprisonment instead of a life sentence imposed on an adult for certain offenses.

In 2000 the Juvenile Act was further amended to adjust Polish juvenile laws to international standards, to strengthen victim's rights, and to provide more effective procedures for juvenile cases. Mediation was formalized as the result of this 2000 change. Family judges may now order mediation, with victim and offender agreement. These mediations may be carried out in in-

(continued)

stitutions or by trustworthy persons in the community acting as mediators. Less favorable for juveniles has been the implementation of policies to make more restrictive the treatment of serious offenders, where family judges are required to place such juveniles in houses of correction. A greater range of alternative treatments has also been established for more serious juveniles, where they may be sent to treatment institutions with restrictive educational supervision, to psychiatric hospitals, or to other appropriate health-care institutions. Early release from houses of correction is possible only after certain juveniles have completed a minimum of a one-year stay in these facilities. Despite all of these changes, however, the Polish Juvenile Act of 1982 and its welfare-oriented influence remains largely unchanged.

Between 1989 and 2005, juvenile offending rose until 1995, when it stabilized, and then it steadily declined commencing in 1996. Juvenile offending accounts for about 5 percent of all Polish crime. During the mid-1990s, juvenile offending accounted for about 16 percent of all Polish crime. The nature of juvenile offending is such that it rose during the early 1990s, peaked in the mid-1990s, and has declined since. In sheer numbers, however, the number of juvenile cases brought to family courts doubled between 1989 and 2005. In 2000 juveniles charged with offenses against life and health (robbery, murder, aggravated assault, rape) accounted for 1.6 percent of all crime, about one-fourth of the mid-1990 figure. Property offending by juveniles has followed a similar pattern between 1989 and 2005. Annual fluctuations in crimes by juveniles have tended to follow changing criminal policies toward juveniles as manifested by police reactions to juveniles committing offenses. Ideally police have no discretion and must report all juvenile contact to a family judge, although informally not all juvenile offenses are strictly reported.

Public prosecutors are only exceptionally involved in juvenile cases, and they may initiate and conduct investigations if juveniles were committing offenses in concert with one or more adults and if

their welfare does not preclude investigation. When prosecutors complete their investigations, a family court referral may be made, provided that a joint trial is essential. These proceedings are implemented against juveniles between age 13 and 17, although some proceedings have been instituted for 18-year-old offenders. The main objective of a preliminary inquiry is to determine whether there is problem behavior and a punishable act has been committed. Also, information about the juvenile's educational, health, and welfare situation is acquired. Some juveniles may be subject to family diagnostic consultative centers to be put under psychiatric observation for a period of 6 weeks or less. Family judges may discontinue an inquiry at any time. Or the family judge may order mediation, which is done on a voluntary basis between victims and youthful perpetrators.

Placements of youths in houses of corrections are last resorts, in most cases, if there is evidence that youths may flee the jurisdiction or destroy evidence, or if it is impossible to determine their identity. When preliminary inquiries have been concluded, family judges can refer cases to the school attended by the juvenile, refer the juvenile to community resources to receive further education, make medical referrals for some disturbed youths, or may refer youths to houses of corrections. Correctional proceedings occur in these instances to determine the propriety of correctional placements. These are rare occurrences. In correctional proceedings, juveniles may be represented by counsel.

Family courts may apply the following measures to all juveniles between age 13 and 17: (1) reprimand; (2) supervision by parents, guardians, youth officers, or other trustworthy persons; (3) assessing special conditions, such as restitution, apologies, educational training, and other therapies indicated, depending on the offense; (4) a ban on driving; (5) forfeiture of objects gained through commission of offenses; (6) placement in a youth probation center; (7) placement in a foster family; and/or (8) placement in a youth educational center or other suitable center providing vocational training. Medical measures may be applied to juveniles suffering from some mental disease or disorder, or from alcohol/drug addiction. Placement in a psychiatric hospital or suitable health-care institution may be imposed. Educational measures are applied for indeterminate periods, usually terminating on one's 18th birthday, or in rare cases, on one's 21st birthday. The vast majority of measures imposed are educational or medical, with less than 5 percent of all measures involving a house of correction. In 2005 the most common measure applied to juveniles was placement under the supervision of a probation officer for a short period or reprimand and supervision by parents. Mediation was also used extensively.

[*Sources:* Adapted from *The Statistical Yearbook of the Republic of Poland 2005;* Barbara Stando-Kawecka, "The Juvenile Justice System in Poland" (unpublished paper, 2005); European Society of Criminology, "Juvenile Justice in Poland" (proceedings, 2005).]

violence is gang related. This type of violence is quite different from the violence exhibited by youths who kill their parents or other youths out of anger or frustration. In fact, researchers have been aware of these different types of violence and their origins for several decades (Irwin, 2004).

Interest in career escalation among juveniles heightened during the 1970s and 1980s, when delinquency and crime increased appreciably (Wiesner and Windle, 2004). Statistical correlations between rising crime and delinquency rates and the amount of status and delinquent offending led to the tentative conclusion that career escalation was occurring. In retrospect, and after a closer examination of adult recidivists, a clear pattern of career escalation among juvenile offenders has not been revealed. More than any other factor, domestic violence and an abusive family environment seem to be critical determinants of whether certain youths from such families will become chronic and persistent offenders (Osgood and Anderson, 2004).

Institutionalized juveniles are permitted visits from family members in visiting rooms on weekends and holidays.

FEMALE VERSUS MALE DELINQUENCY: CATALOGING THE DIFFERENCES

In 2000, 24 percent of all juvenile arrests involved females. However, of the total number of juveniles held in either public or private juvenile secure facilities in 2004, approximately 10 percent of these detainees were female (American Correctional Association, 2005). Also, about 15 percent of all youths in juvenile community correctional programs were female (American Correctional Association, 2005). These figures indicate that female juvenile arrestees are committed to secure facilities at a lower rate than male juveniles, and that females are also returned to their communities more frequently after serving shorter secure confinement terms (Office of Juvenile Justice and Delinquency Prevention, 2005).

Profiling Female Juveniles

Are there significant differences between male and female juveniles concerning the nature of their offending? Yes. Female juveniles get into trouble more quietly. They tend to be involved to a greater degree in less serious types of offending, including runaway behavior, curfew violations, unruly behavior, larceny-theft, and drug abuse. In fact, the juvenile female offender of the 1990s and 2000s appears to be similar in demographic characteristics compared with female juvenile offenders of the 1980s. Survey data show that for many youthful female offenders, they have prior histories of being sexually or physically abused; they come from a single-parent home; and they lack appropriate social and work-related skills (Salazar et al., 2004).

Evidence indicates that growing numbers of female juveniles are entering the juvenile justice system annually, at younger ages, and for more violent offending (Siegel and Williams, 2003). Over 60 percent of all female juveniles charged with juvenile delinquency in 2003 were under age 16 (Sanger et al., 2004). Additionally, increasing numbers of female juveniles are being transferred to criminal courts for prosecution as adult offenders. Compared with 1988 figures, there were 400 female juveniles transferred to criminal court jurisdiction in 1997, up 37 percent (Scahill, 2000:1). Approximately 42 percent of these cases involved a violent offense as the most serious charge. Several important risk factors have been identified and associated with greater amounts of female offending (Sangster, 2002). Although every girl who gets into trouble with the juvenile justice system is unique, she is likely to share elements of the following profile with other female juvenile delinquents:

1. She's now 14 to 16 years old, although she may have started acting out a few years earlier.
2. She's poor and has grown up in a neighborhood with a high crime rate.
3. She's likely to belong to an ethnic minority group (50 percent of female juveniles in detention are black, 13 percent are Hispanic, and 34 percent are Caucasian).
4. She's had a history of poor academic performance and may be a high school dropout.
5. She's been a victim of physical, sexual, and/or emotional abuse or exploitation.

6. She has used and abused drugs and/or alcohol.

7. She has gone without attention for medical and mental health needs.

8. She feels that life is oppressive and lacks hope for the future (Office of Juvenile Justice and Delinquency Prevention, 2002:2).

Trends in Female Juvenile Offending

However, in recent years, the pattern of female delinquent offending compared with male delinquent offending has been changing. Between 1990 and 2000, there has been a substantial increase in the number of female juvenile arrestees compared with their male counterparts. In 1990, for instance, only 11 percent of all juvenile arrestees were female. But in 2000, this figure had risen to 24 percent. Furthermore, arrests of female juveniles for violent offenses increased during the 1990–2000 period. About 15 percent of all female arrestees in 2000 involved allegations of violent crimes. This figure compares with only 7 percent of all juvenile violent crime arrestees for 1990. One reason for this increase is the increased involvement of female juveniles in gangs (National Gang Investigator's Association, 2002).

The most common reason for female juveniles to join gangs is for protection, often from abusive sexual or physical encounters with their fathers at home (Turley, 2003). Another important reason is simple rebellion against parents (Bloom et al., 2002). For many female juvenile gang members, their membership gives them status among their peers and enables them to profit in illicit drug activities. It is difficult to estimate the numbers of females who are gang members. Conservatively about 10 percent of all juvenile gang members in the United States today are female, although estimates have ranged between 9 and 22 percent, depending on the survey conducted (Durst-Johnson, 2004). Although female gangs commit fewer violent crimes compared with male gangs, 38 percent of female youth gang offending involves violent crimes, while 37 percent of their offending involves drug offenses. Therefore, female youth gangs should be taken seriously (Sanger et al., 2004).

Is there a new breed of violent juvenile female offender emerging? No. Is female delinquency skyrocketing out of control? No. We don't know whether female juveniles are becoming more violent, although some evidence suggests that it is. We *do* know that juvenile courts are processing larger numbers of female juveniles, and that greater numbers of delinquency adjudications involve females (Siegel and Williams, 2003). We suspect that in past years, many juvenile court judges acted in a paternalistic manner toward female juveniles, and that often, their offenses were downgraded or downplayed in seriousness (Sangster, 2002). However, in more recent years, there has been more equitable treatment of female juveniles by the juvenile courts (Turley, 2003).

Myths and Misconceptions: Changing Views of Juvenile Females

Gelsthorpe (1987) indicates that there are four main themes guiding responses toward males and females in the juvenile justice system. First, males are more likely than females to offend at some point during their adolescence, although self-reports from female juveniles in a nationwide survey revealed that in 2000, 91 percent of them disclosed that they had committed at least one delinquent act (Office of Juvenile Justice and Delinquency Prevention, 2002). Females who offend during adolescence are often considered abnormal in some way. Second, much male offending is property-related, while it is assumed that female delinquency is predominantly sexual. Third, female delinquents seem to come from broken homes at a higher rate than their male counterparts. Therefore, their delinquency is often attributed to deficient family relationships (Rebellon, 2002). Fourth, female delinquents are characterized as having greater mental instability and nonrational behavior, whereas male juvenile offenders are characterized as rational and adventurous, simply testing the bounds of their adolescence. Most of this historical analysis of male and female juvenile differences is pure myth and misconceived. A similar analysis along political-legal lines has been made by Curran (1984). Curran examined the long-range impact of the women's movement in the United States during the period 1960–1980. A prevailing belief is that the women's movement brought about many changes in both the quality and quantity of female offenses during this period, as well as the way in which women were generally treated in both the criminal and juvenile justice systems. However, Curran disagrees with this view. Rather, he suggests that certain political and legal changes in the United States during the 1960–1980 period furnish a better explanation for how female juvenile offenders have been treated. Furthermore, changes in the rate of female delinquency are likely attributable to these same factors.

Two major events triggered the change from a liberal to a conservative approach to juvenile justice throughout the United States. First, states passed legislation in response to public perceptions of increased violent crime among juveniles. Second, status offenses were removed from the jurisdiction of juvenile courts in many jurisdictions. Greater priority was given to getting tough with juvenile offenders. Regarding female juveniles, Curran has identified three major political-legal periods: (1) the paternalistic period (1960–1967), during which female delinquents were dealt with more severely than boys by the juvenile courts "for their own good"; (2) a due process period (1968–1976), which reflected the impact of various legal decisions such as *In re Gault* (1967); and (3) a law-and-order phase (1977–1980), during which the court adjusted to the new conservatism of the late 1970s (Curran, 1984). Therefore, presumed changing rates in female juvenile offending were more attributable to changing policies in the treatment of female juveniles rather than actual increases in the rate of female criminality. However, as we have seen, the nature of female juvenile offending is definitely changing and increasing (Kakar, Friedemann, and Peck, 2002:57). While policy changes and juvenile court views toward female offenders have probably occurred during the 1980s and 1990s, increased female juvenile offending has been observed. At the very least, female delinquency is becoming increasingly similar to male delinquency in a number of respects, and court treatment of male and female juveniles is becoming more equalized (Siegel and Williams, 2003).

SUMMARY

Juveniles or infants are defined according to various ages, depending on individual jurisdictions. One way of defining juveniles is to use the maximum age limits over youths that are employed by juvenile courts. The most common maximum age for juvenile court jurisdiction is 17, although maximum age limits of 18, 16, and 15 are found in a small number of states. The federal government defines any juvenile as a person who has not reached age 18. Lower age limits over juveniles used by juvenile courts also vary, with some courts having no lower age limits. However, persons under the age of 7 are generally considered incapable of formulating criminal intent and are usually treated by one or more community agencies rather than processed by juvenile courts.

Delinquency is any act committed by a juvenile that would be a crime if an adult committed it. Any criminal act committed by someone who has not reached the age of majority would also define delinquency. Any offense committed by a juvenile that would not be a crime if an adult committed it is a status offense. Common status offenses include runaway behavior, curfew violation, incorrigibility, and truancy. There is considerable variation among status offenders of different types. Thus, generalizations about the characteristics of all runaways or truants are not warranted. Among the different types of status offenses, truancy and curfew violations are regarded as the most serious because they are viewed as undisciplined offenses. Such offenders are believed by some authorities to be more likely to persist in their offending or become chronic offenders and possibly engage in more serious criminal offending later.

Several policies have been established to differentiate between status and delinquent offenders and to separate them in various ways. The Juvenile Justice and Delinquency Prevention Act (JJDPA) of 1974 sought the removal of status offenders from secure institutions, where it used to be commonplace to house such offenders together with more hard-core delinquents. Thus, many states ultimately deinstitutionalized their status offenders (DSO), diverting such offenders to social service agencies in their communities for treatment rather than punishment. Another policy was for juvenile courts to divest themselves of their jurisdiction over status offenders. This practice has occurred in a majority of U.S. jurisdictions. One aim of separating status offenders from delinquent offenders is to minimize the adverse effects of labeling, where interaction with the juvenile justice system may lead status offenders to regard themselves as criminals. Through greater formalization of juvenile courts, many of the trappings of criminal courts are approximated, and it is easier for youths in these courts to identify with how criminal offenders are processed. Insulating status offenders from such criminogenic environments reduces the stigma associated with criminal conduct and reduces the likelihood of defining oneself as criminal or delinquent. The JJDPA has been renewed regularly since its inception in 1974. Individual states are not compelled to conform with JJDPA policies, but government financial incentives are substantial and most states have adopted these policies over the years.

The general meaning of the DSO has been broadly interpreted as decarceration of status offenders from institutions; diverting dependent and neglected children to social services; and divestiture of jurisdiction of juvenile courts over status offenders as has been observed. Several potential outcomes of DSO include a reduction of status offenders from secure confinement; greater net-widening as more youths have been pulled into the juvenile justice system through status offender–specific programming that has been established; relabeling of youths as delinquent or emotionally disturbed; failing to reduce the recidivism rate among status offenders; and creating a variety of service delivery problems because of the difficulty of establishing uniform programs to address the wide variation in status offender needs.

Several official and unofficial sources exist for measuring the nature and extent of delinquency and status offending. The *Uniform Crime Reports (UCR)* has been compiled by the Federal Bureau of Investigation for many years and published annually by the government. It classifies crimes into several serious index offenses, including murder and nonnegligent manslaughter, forcible rape, robbery, aggravated assault, burglary, larceny-theft, motor vehicle theft, and arson. These are felonies or violent or property crimes that are punishable by one or more years in prison. These offenses are also considered Part I offenses. A list of less serious offenses, mostly misdemeanors, is compiled under Part II offenses. Misdemeanors are crimes that are punishable by imprisonment of less than one year. Fines are also imposed on offenders by the courts for both felonies and misdemeanors. These offenses are tracked over different time periods by each jurisdiction according to different variables, including age, gender, race/ethnicity, and other factors.

Another measure of crime is the *National Crime Victimization Survey (NCVS)*. The *NCVS* is an annual survey of crime victims conducted by the U.S. Bureau of the Census. Over 125,000 persons are surveyed randomly, including 60,000 dwellings and 50,000 businesses. This compilation reports victimizations or specific criminal acts that affect a single victim. Incidents are also reported (Tyler and Johnson, 2004). These are crimes that may involve more than one victim. Both the *UCR* and *NCVS* are flawed in different respects. Not all law enforcement agencies report crimes in their jurisdictions on a regular basis, and not all crimes have the same definitions. Many victims of crime do not report these occurrences for various reasons. Although the *UCR* reports crimes that are cleared by arrests, these arrests do not necessarily mean that those arrested persons will eventually be convicted. These and other problems plague both official measures of crime. Other sources of crime and delinquency include the *National Juvenile Court Data Archive,* which contains over 800,000 automated annual case records of juveniles; the *Sourcebook of Criminal Justice Statistics,* which is a compilation of government document summaries and other useful information for law enforcement, prosecution and the courts, and corrections; the *National Youth Survey;* and the *Monitoring the Future Survey.*

Some information about delinquency and crime is provided through the use of self-reports. Self-reports involve a data collection method whereby persons disclose crimes or delinquent acts they have committed for which they have not been charged. Self-reports ordinarily disclose far greater crime figures than are reported by either the *UCR* or *NCVS.* Applied to delinquency, self-reports have mixed reliability. Some authorities consider this information reliable and indicative of hidden delinquency, thus suggesting that there is more delinquency committed annually than is officially reported. But often juveniles will brag about offenses they have never committed. The results and meaningfulness of self-report information are debatable.

Several types of delinquency have been tracked by authorities. Delinquency trends have been charted. Although delinquency escalated considerably during the period 1985–1995, evidence suggests that some delinquency has declined or has at least stabilized. Violent offending by juveniles attracted considerable media attention during the 1990s, although authorities believe that in recent years, youth violence has tapered off or declined. It is also uncertain whether less serious offenders, such as status offenders, progress to more serious types of offending, known as career escalation. Mixed findings from different empirical investigations have been reported. School violence, which has captured public attention to a greater degree in recent years, continues, although recent evidence from official reports suggests that it is declining. Better means of school violence prevention and youth supervision may be important factors that have affected school violence trends.

Attempts have been made by investigators to identify children at risk. At-risk youths are considered the most likely juveniles to engage in delinquent behavior. Thus, several useful interventions have targeted at-risk youths in their early years as types of delinquency prevention. At-risk youths are identified by their lower socioeconomic status, lower IQ, lower school achievement, learning disabilities, attention deficit disorders, and antisocial behaviors. Less fully developed cognitive abilities and poor social adjustment are associated with at-risk youth characteristics. Different intervention methods, such as out-of-home placements, special treatment programs, learning and counseling experiences, and other strategies have been applied in an effort to interrupt the pattern of at-risk factors that lead to delinquency and other forms of juvenile misconduct. Studies of different pathways or developmental sequences that lead to different types of offending have received considerable research attention in recent years with some degree of success.

Gangs and gang violence have also been studied. Although significant gang interventions have been attempted in recent years, no program seems to stem the growth of gangs and the violence such gangs exhibit. There were approximately 30,000 gangs in the United States in 2005 with over 1 million members. A growing proportion of gangs consist of female juveniles, and arrests of female juveniles have increased from 10 percent to 25 percent during the period 1995–2005. Females form and join gangs for many of the same reasons males form and join gangs. Gangs offer protection, recognition, and esteem, and ways of gaining status that are often unavailable to youths through their schools and other conventional organizations. Female gangs are rapidly approaching parity with their male gang counterparts by becoming increasingly violent and aggressive, and professional concern about female youth gangs has heightened. Although it is uncertain whether there is a new female crime wave, official figures suggest that greater attention should focus on female juvenile gang activities and more effective deterrence interventions.

QUESTIONS FOR REVIEW

1. What is juvenile delinquency? Why are juveniles defined according to different criteria from one jurisdiction to the next?

2. How do status offenders differ from delinquent offenders?

3. What are three types of status offenders and their characteristics? What is the significance of the Juvenile Justice and Delinquency Prevention Act of 1974 and what impact has it had on status offender processing in the juvenile courts?

4. What is meant by the deinstitutionalization of status offenses? What are three meanings of DSO? What are four different outcomes of DSO?

5. What is the *Uniform Crime Reports?* What type of information does it provide? How does it differ from the *National Crime Victimization Survey?*

6. What are some strengths and weaknesses of the *UCR* and *NCVS?* What are some other sources of information about delinquency and crime? How reliable are these sources?

7. What is self-report information? Is it more or less accurate compared with data reported by the *UCR* or *NCVS?* What are several problems accompanying self-report information?

8. Who are at-risk youths and why do they interest criminal justice professionals? Why are such youths targeted for interventions? What are pathways and why are they significant in relation to career escalation?

9. Why is there growing interest in female juvenile gangs? What are some general trends in female juvenile delinquency, and are these trends of interest to authorities?

10. What are some myths and misconceptions about female juveniles? How have these myths and misconceptions influenced social policies relevant to female delinquents? What are some general characteristics of female delinquents?

Internet Connections

Children Now
http://www.childrennow.org/

Children's Legal Protection Center
http://www.childprotect.org/

Children's Defense Fund
http://www.childrensdefense.org/

Drug War Chronicle
http://www.stopthedrugwar.org/index.shtml

National Council on Crime and Delinquency
http://www.nccd-crc.org/

National Organization for the Reform of Marijuana Laws
http://www.norml.org/

North Carolina Center for the Prevention of School Violence
http://www.nccjjdp.org/cpsv/

Office for the Victims of Crime
http://www.ovc.gov/

CHAPTER 3

Theories of Delinquency

Chapter Outline

Key Terms

anomie theory

anomie

atavism

biological determinism

bonding theory

Cesare Lombroso

classical school

classical theory

concentric zone hypothesis

conformity

consent decrees

containment theory

crime control model
cultural transmission theory
determinism
differential association theory
differential reinforcement theory
drift theory
due process model
ectomorphs
ego
endomorphs
hedonism
id
innovation
interstitial area
judicious nonintervention
just deserts/justice model

Juvenile Mentoring Program
  (JUMP)
labeling theory
labeling
libido
looking-glass self
medical model
mesomorphs
modes of adaptation
neutralization theory
noninterventionist model
positive school of criminology
positivism
primary deviation
psychoanalytic theory
psychological theories

radical nonintervention
rebellion
rehabilitation model
retreatism
ritualism
secondary deviation
social control theory
social learning theory
sociobiology
strain theory
subculture of delinquency
superego
theory
treatment model
Weed and Seed
zone of transition

Chapter Objectives

As the result of reading this chapter, the following objectives will be realized:

1. Understand alternative theories of juvenile conduct.
2. Differentiate between classical or biological theories and psychological theories of delinquency.
3. Understand several important sociological theories of juvenile delinquency.
4. Learn about several key psychological theories of juvenile delinquency.
5. Understand how to appreciate the importance of different theoretical explanations in terms of their successful use in forecasting delinquent behavior and creating intervention programs.

• *In Fort Lauderdale, Florida, Lionel Tate, age 12, allegedly used a professional wrestler body-slam technique to throw 6-year-old Tiffany Eunick to the floor, killing her. This happened on July 28, 1999. Tate weighed 170 pounds, while Tiffany weighed 48 pounds. Tate's defense argued that "horseplay" got out of hand and that the girl's death was an accident. Tate's mother, a Florida Highway Patrol trooper, told the judge that the girl's death was a "tragic accident." The defense contended that pro wrestling was to blame, a largely theatrical entertainment sport with persons in colorful costumes who promote violence without regard to the influence of pro wrestling on children. Even Tate himself said in a police interview that he picked up Tiffany and she accidentally hit her head on a coffee table. In another police interview, Tate said that he threw Tiffany into a stairway railing and a wall while trying to toss her onto a sofa. The prosecution countered these claims by noting that Tiffany's injuries were consistent with someone falling from a three-story building. She had a fractured skull, a lacerated liver, and more than 30 other injuries from being punched, kicked, stomped, and thrown. On January 25, 2001, Tate was convicted of first-degree murder and sentenced to life imprisonment. However, Tate's conviction was overturned by a court of appeals on technicalities in December 2003. Rather than retry him in 2004, the governor granted him clemency and he was released from prison, placed under one year of house arrest with electronic monitoring, and ordered to serve 10 years of probation.*

[*Source:* Adapted from Kari Sable Burns and the Associated Press, "Young Killers: Lionel Tate, 12 Years Old," January 20, 2005.]

• *In Moses Lake, Washington, on February 2, 1996, Barry Loukaitis, 14 years old, armed himself with two pistols, 78 rounds of ammunition, and a high-powered rifle and went to Frontier Junior High School. He entered the school and shot two students in the chest. He then shot a teacher who was writing on the blackboard to death. Next, he nearly amputated a girl's arm with another shot before he was wrestled to the floor by a teacher and several other students. Subsequently Loukaitis claimed that the musical group, Pearl Jam, and their song, "Jeremy," which was about a troubled youth, gave him the idea for the murder spree. He said that the song made him have mood swings. Before he commenced his murder spree, he wrote two poems. One poem, apparently written for his classmates in general, said "A sullen lifestyle gripped with pain/The feeling of murder, the heat of hate and the love of death." The other poem, directed at a student who had called him a "fag," said, " 'Murder': It's my first murder/I'm at the point of no return/ I look at his body on the floor/Killing a bastard that deserves to die/Ain't nuthin' like it in the world, But he sure did bleed a lot." Later, Loukaitis was tried and convicted as an adult on two counts of aggravated first-degree murder and sentenced to two mandatory life terms without the possibility of parole. His appeal for post-conviction relief was denied in November 1999.* [*Sources:* Adapted from the Associated Press, "Moses Lake Killer's Request for New Trial Denied," November 18, 1999; "Youth's Poems," *The Cincinnati Post*, November 10, 1998; Jeanne Zomes, "Free to Forgive," *Brio Magazine*, August 5, 2000.]

• *In 2004 in Carrollton, Georgia, a 12-year-old boy strangled to death an 8-year-old girl, Amy Yates. Under Georgia law, the boy cannot be tried as an adult. According to the Georgia juvenile court in Carrollton, children age 13 or older can be tried in criminal court as adults. In this boy's case, however, he must have his case adjudicated by a juvenile court judge. The maximum penalty the judge can impose is confinement in a secure juvenile facility for two years. Senator Bill Hamrick of Carrollton said of this situation, "Why is it that a person who commits murder can only serve two years in prison? It's something I had not come across in my legislative experience." In response, Judge Peggy Walker of Douglas County juvenile court said that judges should have more freedom in how they handle youth cases and that the state should provide more supportive services for youths under age 18. Walker said, "Legal scholars and child advocates are now taking the position that children should never be tried as adults." Any change in Georgia law would not occur until their next legislative session, and it would only affect future cases, according to Senator Hamrick. Hamrick said, "At what age do you draw the line? How much discretion should a juvenile court judge have?" The most likely outcome of the meetings would be a proposal to raise the possible penalty against children convicted of murder.* [*Source:* Adapted from the Associated Press, "Stiffer Sentences for Juvenile Murderers Discussed," December 14, 2004.]

• *In November 2004 in a lower-class suburb of Chicago, two 13-year-old girls decided to skip school and have some fun. They knew an old lady down the street who had previously been kind to them. They went to her door and she invited them in. As soon as the door was closed, they shoved the lady to the floor. While one of the girls sat on her, the other got a knife from the kitchen and began stabbing the woman repeatedly. Investigators later determined that there were 86 stab wounds from an autopsy that was performed. The girls were apprehended two days later in Indiana driving the woman's car. They possessed her purse, jewelry, and some credit cards. The prosecutor said that he would seek to have the girls tried as adults and that stiff penalties would be sought. He said that the girls were like animals, showed no remorse, and even bragged about all the blood to police while they were being transported back to their community for a hearing. A defense attorney countered by denying that the girls bragged about the murder. He said that the woman they killed had earlier made some offensive remarks critical of the girls' clothes and called them "cheap whores." He requested a psychiatric examination and stated that he would show that the girls came from single-parent homes, were economically disadvantaged, and were the victims of an unsupportive community.* [*Sources:* Adapted from the Associated Press, "Community and Economy Blamed for Female Teen Murders," April 12, 2005.]

INTRODUCTION

What would cause a 12-year-old youth to punch, kick, and body-slam a 6-year-old girl and neighborhood playmate to the floor and kill her? Why would he lie to police about the extensive injuries he inflicted on his 6-year-old victim? How do you explain away 30 serious body blows and bruises, a fractured skull, and a lacerated liver? Why would a 14-year-old boy arm himself with two pistols, a high-powered rifle, and a large quantity of ammunition, go to his school, kill a teacher, and shoot and kill or wound other students? Was name-calling to blame for two deaths? Why would a 12-year-old boy strangle to death an 8-year-old female neighbor? How could two 13-year-old girls rob and kill an old lady who had criticized their clothing and called them names? How could two 13-year-old girls inflict 86 stab wounds on an elderly, defenseless woman, and then steal her car, purse, jewelry, and other personal effects?

The troubling answer is we don't know for sure why these youths committed these crimes. Well, that's not entirely true. The boy who shot his teacher and several other students said some of those he shot had called him a "fag." The two girls said that the old woman had called them "cheap whores" because of the skimpy clothing they wore. The boy who body-slammed the 6-year-old girl to the floor said he was simply copying a wrestling move he had seen professional wrestlers do on television. Are revenge for name-calling and watching violent wrestling matches on television legitimate excuses for committing murders?

For many centuries, criminologists and others have sought to develop plausible and useful explanations for why people engage in deviant behavior and crime. During the twentieth century and beyond, a growing interest in delinquency and delinquent behavior has occurred. Why do juveniles commit crimes? What are the different forces that cause them to rob, steal, assault, rape, and kill?

This chapter describes several theories that have evolved over time to explain juvenile delinquency in various forms. Theories are tools that are useful in the development of explanations of relationships between variables, such as drugs and crime, peer pressure and gang violence, and family instability and antisocial behavior. Theories attempt to explain and predict how two or more variables are interrelated (Hoffmann, 2002). Because there are so many types of delinquent behavior to explain, no single theory has yet been developed to account for this behavior. Instead, numerous delinquency theories have been proposed, elaborated, and tested. Over time, some theories have been rejected, while other theories have become increasingly popular and regarded as useful. Rejected or less frequently used theories have lapsed into obscurity largely because they have lacked predictive utility. We cannot rely upon them to explain delinquency consistently or accurately. Some of these theories use concepts that are beyond scientific definition, and thus, they are untestable or unverifiable. Despite the fact that these theories vary in the amount of their predictive utility, each provides us with intuitive glimpses into the lives of juveniles and what motivates them to engage in different behaviors (Garbarino et al., 2002).

The chapter is divided into four general parts. The first part of the chapter presents a variety of theories grouped according to biological, psychological, and sociological themes. The biological theme explores delinquency as the result of internal or biological factors. Biological determinism is discussed, which posits that much of what juveniles do is rooted in genetics and predispositions to behave in given ways. Heredity is regarded as crucial in determining whether someone will acquire delinquent propensities. Biological theories include sociobiology, the *XYY* theory, low IQ, and a general linkage between body types and the types of behaviors associated with them (McGloin, Pratt, and Maahs, 2004). While these theories have been largely discounted over the years, several criminologists continue to pursue sociobiological factors and their possible contribution to criminality.

Psychological and sociological explanations of delinquency are also presented. Freud's psychoanalytic theory is described, which stresses the importance of early childhood experiences on one's behavior. Social learning theory is also discussed, with the view that there are different maturational stages that contribute to a youth's development and eventual demeanor. Sociological theories include the concentric zone hypothesis, which links delinquency with rapid urban changes, familial disruptions, and social instability. Delinquency is also viewed from a subcultural perspective, as a culture within a culture. Delinquents create and perpetuate their own social structure, status system, and reward mechanisms. The anomie theory of delinquency suggests that delinquents are innovators, discontent with conformity. Labeling theory is also discussed, where it is believed that associations with other delinquents and treatment as a delinquent by the system have adverse impacts on how youths define themselves. Bonding and strain theories are also discussed. Several other theories with sociological roots include containment theory, neutralization or drift theory, differential association, and cultural transmission. Each of these views is described.

The second part of the chapter looks at these theories in retrospect and examines the general question of which theory seems best at explaining delinquency. Different criteria are examined as bases for evaluating these theories and their usefulness for explaining various types of delinquent behavior. Many children who become delinquents are first considered children at risk. The factors that identify children at risk are listed and described.

The third part of this chapter examines several important models for dealing with juvenile offenders. Six models are described. These include the rehabilitation model, the treatment or medical model, the noninterventionist model, the due process model, the just-deserts or justice model, and the crime control model. These models typify how different actors in the juvenile justice system orient themselves toward delinquents and delinquency and help to explain their helping behaviors. These models are orienting mechanisms, often reflecting how different youth workers orient themselves toward their youthful clients, whether they are welfare workers, probation or parole officers, institutional corrections personnel, or community-based aftercare workers.

The chapter concludes with an examination of different interventions that have been and are continuing to be used in preventing or minimizing delinquency and the factors or social and psychological conditions that are associated with its occurrence. Most interventions reflect one or more theories of delinquency and can easily be associated with different prevention programs. Theories that drive particular programs will be identified to show the close relation between theory and practice. Thus, theories do not just attempt to explain behavior. They are often used to structure experiences and situations that can be applied in useful ways to hopefully deter youths from adopting delinquent behaviors in their early years or to assist juveniles in extracting themselves from strong delinquent influences such as gang membership or associations with chronic offenders (Moyer, 2001). Recidivism rates are frequently cited as evidence of the successfulness of these different interventions (Xiaoying, 2005). No intervention program is foolproof. Recidivism rates vary among programs, and some intervention programs work with certain types of juvenile offenders but not with others. It is also likely that some youths are insensitive to any type of existing intervention. But the juvenile justice system prides itself on not giving up on any child. A positive outlook persists among criminal justice professionals, and new and different interventions and strategies for combatting delinquency are continually being explored.

CLASSICAL AND BIOLOGICAL THEORIES

In this section, several classical and biological theories of criminality and delinquency are examined. These include (1) classical theory, (2) positivist theory or biological determinism, (3) sociobiology, and (4) the XYY theory.

Classical Theory

Classical theory is a criminological perspective indicating that people have free will to choose either criminal or conventional behavior. People choose to commit crime for reasons of greed or personal need. Crime can be controlled by criminal sanctions, which should be proportionate to the guilt of the perpetrator.

Philosophers have speculated about the causes of crime for centuries, and they have elaborated diverse explanations for criminal conduct. In the 1700s, criminologists devised several explanations for criminal behavior, which have persisted to the present day. Deeply rooted in the general principles of Christianity, the classical school of criminology originated with the work of Cesare Beccaria (1738–1794), *On Crimes and Punishments* (1764). Subsequent scholars who adopted perspectives about crime different from those of Beccaria labeled his views as classical, since they included an inherent conflict between good and evil and provided a standard against which other views of crime could be contrasted.

The **classical school** assumes that people are rational beings who exercise free will in choosing between good actions and evil ones. At the other end of the continuum is **determinism,** the view that a specific factor, variable, or event is a determinant of one's actions or behaviors. Determinism rejects the notion of free will and choice, relying instead on properties that cause human beings to behave one way or another. Within the classical context, however, societal progress and perpetuation are paramount, and individuals must each sacrifice a degree of their freedoms in order that all persons can pursue happiness and attain their respective goals. Evil actions operate adversely for societal progress and merit punishment. Because evil acts vary in their seriousness, the severity of punishments for those actions should be adjusted accordingly. Beccaria believed that punishments should be swift, certain, and just, where the penalties are appropriately adjusted to fit particular offenses. The primary purposes of punishment are deterrence and just deserts. In an ideal world, people will refrain from wrongdoing in order to avoid the pain of punishment. Furthermore, whatever punishment is imposed is equivalent or proportional in severity with the amount of social and physical damage caused by those found guilty of crimes. Fines and/or imprisonment were common penalties for those found guilty of property crimes and violent offenses (Moyer, 2001).

The origins of different sentencing schemes in the United States today can be traced to Beccaria's classical theory. Most states have mandatory sentences for specific offenses, including using a firearm during the commission of a felony. Also, most state statutes carry sentences of determinate lengths and/or fines that are roughly commensurate with crime severity.

Less than two decades after Beccaria outlined his philosophy of crime and punishment, Jeremy Bentham (1748–1832), an English philosopher, advanced a similar scheme in his book, *An Introduction to the Principles of Morals and Legislation* (1790). Bentham was known for his belief that **hedonism,** the pursuit of pleasure, was a primary motivator underlying much social and personal action. Simply, humans seek to acquire pleasure and avoid pain. Thus, in this pleasure–pain framework, Bentham formulated his views about the worth and intent of punishment. Like Beccaria, Bentham believed that punishments' objectives were to deter crime and to impose sanctions sufficient to outweigh any pleasures criminals might derive from the crimes they commit. Therefore, many would-be offenders might desist from crime because the threat of punishment would more than offset the projected pleasure derived from criminal actions. Those more persistent offenders would be subject to painful punishments adjusted according to the severity of their offenses (Gibson, 2002).

Under the prevailing common law of that period, those under the age of 7 were not held accountable for their actions or subject to the same kinds of punishments prescribed for adults. However, older youths eventually were vested with responsibilities for their own actions and were subject to similar adult punishments. One contemporary view of juvenile delinquents is that juveniles must accept responsibility for their actions. If they choose to ignore societal values and persist in violating the law, they must be held accountable for these offenses and punished accordingly.

In reality, the classical school of criminology is not so much an explanation of why crime or delinquency exists, but rather, it is a statement about how various offenses should be punished in order to frustrate criminal conduct. However, some elements of explanation are contained in classical thought. Bentham, for instance, would probably speculate that persistent criminal offenders are gamblers, in a sense, since they regard the calculated risk of being caught and punished for crimes as secondary to the pleasurable benefits derived from committing crimes. The pleasure of crime outweighs the pain of punishment. Beccaria might argue that criminals are comprised of those who have failed to inculcate societal values or respect for the common good.

 **BOX 3.1**

INTERNATIONAL SNAPSHOT: JUVENILE JUSTICE IN SPAIN

In 1992, Spain revised its juvenile justice laws for the first time since 1948, through the creation of the OL (organic law), which was revised again in 2000. The 1992 version of the OL implemented a model of responsibility, a dual framework seeking a balance between education and punishment for juvenile justice and consistent with a United Nations proposal for more international uniformity governing the treatment of juvenile offenders. Two objectives of the 1992 OL were deinstitutionalization and dejudicialization, seeking to place juveniles in more therapeutic and less legal frameworks for processing and treatment. Between 1992 and 2000, a movement in Spain was toward greater juvenile sanctions and a "get-tough" model of justice for juveniles. Due process gradually replaced individual justice and decisions made by authorities in a juvenile's best interests.

In 2000 all regulations for juveniles were compiled into the Juvenile Justice Regulations. Accordingly justice for juveniles is to be administered by a separate system within the general legal system with its own specific and specialized court. Jurisdiction of juvenile courts is determined by offender age and conduct, and thus it becomes a penal responsibility system. Legislative intent was to make juveniles responsible for their criminal acts, and at the same time, protect young adolescent persons against any arbitrariness throughout the decision-making process. Juvenile justice in Spain is primarily oriented toward those who commit acts defined as crimes according to the adult criminal law. Children who are in poverty, neglected or abused, or who are unruly fall within a different type of jurisdiction more similar to social welfare. The juvenile justice system applies to youths older than age 14 and younger than age 18; however, special provisions exist for treating those between age 18 and 21 as juveniles under some circumstances to enjoy the more lenient systemic benefits. A previous law used the 12–16 age range as the jurisdic-

tion of the juvenile court, but the 2000 revision changed that to the present range. Two groups of juveniles were identified by the 2000 OL regarding the consequences of their responsibility and measures to be applied to each group: for juveniles ages 14–15, measures would not last more than 2 years; for those ages 16–17, measures, even custody, could last up to 5 years. The OL intent is to give more criminal responsibility to older juveniles, and the gradualism inherent in such a distinction allows for a smoother transition from adolescence to adulthood and full adult criminal responsibility.

Juvenile delinquency data are derived from police records, the Prosecutor's Office, and the juvenile courts. In 2000, according to all official sources of juvenile arrests, the number of juvenile arrests rose dramatically. This rise in arrests was due to more specific articulations of law violations by juveniles under the new 2000 OL. Furthermore, a newly implemented data-gathering system provided more consistent and tangible evidence of juvenile arrests than in prior years. One result of more accurate disclosures of crime committed by juveniles is that violent juvenile offending increased from 1997–2002, slightly declining in 2003. Most other types of juvenile offending have followed this pattern. As of 2005, no self-report surveys of juvenile offending have been used. Presently Spain has no country-wide juvenile offense prevention strategies, other than to focus on the social conditions that contribute to criminality, to improve equality, and to make committing crimes unnecessary. Presently policies are stressed that promote juvenile rights and prevent social maladaptation. Regional governments accept responsibility for implementing these measures.

In the Spanish juvenile justice system, the role of prosecutor is central. Prosecutors investigate juvenile offenses and issue charges. Ultimately the juvenile court judge safeguards the rights of juveniles under investigation. The investigative process is slow, however, taking up to 10 months or longer between a crime's commission and a prosecutor's acknowledgment of it.

Police actions relating to juveniles are restricted and definitive. For those under age 14, they may be detained by police for up to 24 hours in order to determine their age and identity, and before accusing them of a crime. Juveniles under age 14 will be referred to a public entity such as a social welfare agency for temporary protection. Such agencies are responsible for initiating educational programming for very young offenders. While in police custody, juveniles must have the same constitutional rights as adults; police must use clear and understandable language according to the offender's age; written statements of accusations are given to parents or guardians, lawyers and prosecutors; and juveniles must be kept in special rooms separate from adults. In this respect, Spain is consistent with the policy in the United States articulated by the Juvenile Justice and Delinquency Prevention Act of 1974. A social team consisting of psychologists, educators, and social workers prepares a technical report about each juvenile, including their social history, family background, social and educational history, and any prior involvement with authorities. One's physical and mental health are assessed, and one or more interventions are recommended. Ultimately juvenile court judges are responsible for ordering one or more interventions for specific juveniles.

Under present law, juvenile court judges can continue to make decisions in a juvenile's best interests. First-offenders may have the proceedings against them dismissed by either prosecutors or judges. Their acts may be decriminalized and downgraded. Spain has adopted restorative justice as well, as mediation programs have proliferated throughout the country. Thus, mediation may be ordered by the judge, with the mutual consent of both victim and offender. Social services and community intervention teams are largely responsible for overseeing the mediation process. Half of all juvenile offense cases are dismissed by prosecutors before any official court action occurs.

If the prosecutor decides to go forward with a case, the juvenile's best interests are primary, and an informal hearing occurs, involving parents, the juvenile, the prosecutor, the social team, and the defense lawyer. Usually judicial action is based on the report from the social team, which is largely rehabilitative and educative. While this statement applies to most juveniles, in more serious juvenile cases the intervention must be proportional to the seriousness of the offense the juvenile committed. In the most serious cases, judges may order juveniles confined to a closed center for 1–5 years, without the possibility of modifying this measure for at least 1 year. Usually offenses deserving such punishments include terrorism, murder or homicide, and sexual assault. For the most serious offenses, juveniles may be placed in a closed center from 1–10 years, with up to 5 years of probation. Custody is imposed as a punishment for juveniles as a last resort, where all other interventions have failed. The main objective of custody is to provide a good and healthy environment in order to redirect a youth's antisocial behavior. Centers may be closed, half-open, open, or the juvenile may be placed in "therapeutic custody." This type of custody is reserved for youths with drug, alcohol, or psychotic problems, and the environment is hospital-like and treatment-centered.

Intermediate measures may be imposed, including weekend custody, community therapeutic treatment, and attendance at a day center. Weekend custody permits juveniles to live at home but perform educational tasks on weekends under official supervision. Therapeutic treatment means that juveniles must periodically attend a center to follow a specific plan to deal with their drug-related or psychiatric problems. Day centers are for the purpose of improving a youth's social competencies.

Community measures include probation, where youths are supervised by probation officers. These officers network with parents, community organizations, and other facilities to promote the youth's education and treatment. Skills, abilities, and

(continued)

attitudinal improvements are community measures objectives. Foster home placement, community service, and socioeducative measures are also included as a part of community measures. Other measures may include cautioning or deprivation of a li-

cense to drive a vehicle or to possess a gun or game license. Community interventions are imposed in about 25 percent of all cases, largely because of regional resource limitations.

[*Sources:* Adapted from Cristina Rechea Alberola and Esther Fernandez Molina, "Report of the Spanish Juvenile Justice System." Centre of Research in Criminology, University of Castilla–La Mancha, 2005; Centre of Research in Criminology, University of Castilla–La Mancha, 2005.]

This perspective has received attention from contemporary theorists such as Kohlberg (1981) who constructed a theory of moral development to account for both deviant and conforming behaviors. This theory is properly classified in a social learning context, and it is discussed briefly in the section on psychological theories presented below. Although Kohlberg's theory of moral development has been both supported and rejected by adherents and critics, some experts believe that his views may have intuitive value for furnishing insight into more aberrant modes of criminality. Furthermore, the theory may improve our understanding of a wide range of delinquent acts if integrated into a perspective that is sensitive to how varying social contexts shape individual inclinations.

Biological Theories

Determinism is strongly evident in biological theories of criminal and delinquent behavior. Generally, theories of determinism seek to associate criminal, delinquent, and deviant conduct with biological, biochemical, or genetic bases in a direct, causal relation. According to this view, juvenile delinquency is a selective phenomenon, in that it does not occur spontaneously. Delinquents are destined to become delinquent because of factors beyond their own control and/or because of the presence of certain internal factors, while nondelinquents are destined to be nondelinquent because of the presence of different internal factors. The idea that there are known, predisposing factors that cause delinquent behaviors conveniently shifts the responsibility for delinquent conduct from youths themselves to some internal or external source.

Although the attribution of criminality and delinquency to biological causes dates to pre-biblical times, such determinism, **biological determinism,** was given a degree of academic dignity in the work of an Italian physician and criminologist, **Cesare Lombroso** (1835–1909), during the 1860s (Gibson, 2002). Considered by many professionals to be the father of criminology, Lombroso was influenced by the work of Charles Darwin (1809–1882). Darwin's major writing, *The Origin of the Species,* was both revolutionary and evolutionary, arguing in part that human beings evolved from lower animal forms over thousands of years. Natural selection and survival of the fittest were key principles of Darwin's evolutionary theory. Lombroso was intrigued by these principles and applied them in his explanation of criminal conduct.

For Lombroso, criminals were products of heredity. Successive generations of human beings inherited not only physical features genetically from their ancestors, but they also inherited behavioral predispositions such as propensities toward criminal conduct or antisocial proclivities. Since heredity is more or less binding on future generations, it made sense to Lombroso and many of his disciples that certain physical characteristics would also be inexorably related to criminal behavior. Therefore, physical appearance would be a telling factor whether certain persons would be predisposed to criminality or other types of deviant behavior. This led Lombroso to conjecture extensively about criminal types and born criminals. Height, weight, hair and eye color, physiognomic features such as jaw sizes and angles and ear lobe shapes, finger lengths and hand sizes, and assorted other anatomical characteristics were painstakingly measured and charted by Lombroso. Samples of both willing and unwilling volunteers were obtained for his analyses, including populations of Italian prisoners and soldiers. Eventually, Lombroso concluded that many of the physiological characteristics shared by criminals were indicative of stunted evolutionary growth. Indeed, Lombroso considered criminals to be throwbacks typical of earlier evolutionary stages. This view of criminals is **atavism,** strongly suggestive of subhuman qualities.

Lombroso's views become known popularly as **positivism,** and the **positive school of criminology** originated (Yar and Penna, 2004). This view rejected the free will and choice doctrines espoused by Beccaria and other classical theorists. Rather, criminal conduct more likely emanated from biochemical and genetic factors peculiar to criminal types. Physical features of criminal types were describable, and inferences could be made about their inherited propensities toward various forms of criminal conduct. Lombroso made further refinements by concluding that certain physical features (e.g., sloping foreheads; compressed jaws; large earlobes; long, slender fingers; excessive facial and body hair) would tend to indicate the type of criminal behavior expected from those observed.

Although Lombroso limited his theoretical and empirical work primarily to adult criminals, his strong focus on the heredity factor was easily generalizable to juveniles. Thus, he simultaneously provided explanations for both criminal and delinquent conduct that relied almost exclusively on genetic factors. In later years, however, Lombroso changed his opinion about the key role played by genetics in promoting criminal behavior. His beliefs were changed, in part, as the result of extensive scientific studies of both juveniles and adults that disclosed little relation between physiological features and criminal behaviors. Also, the growth of other social sciences such as sociology and psychology led him to assign a more prominent role to one's social milieu as a prerequisite to criminal or delinquent conduct (Yar and Penna, 2004).

Despite the fact that specific biological features or characteristics could not be positively connected with specific types of criminal conduct, certain professionals in the early 1900s continued to regard biological determinism as a plausible explanation for criminality and delinquency. During the 1930s, Hooton (1939) and Kretschmer (1936) established physical typologies of criminals that were given some credence by the academic community. In the 1940s, William H. Sheldon (1949) provided what later became both a popular and an elaborate description of genetic types that seemingly manifested certain kinds of criminal characteristics. Sheldon defined three major categories of body types: (1) **mesomorphs,** or strong, athletic individuals; (2) **ectomorphs,** or thin, submissive beings; and (3) **endomorphs,** or fat persons. He assigned point valuations to each person observed and attempted to describe behaviors most typical of them. Mesomorphs were believed to typify those who manifested criminal or delinquent behaviors. Unfortunately, little consistency existed in his descriptions of those sharing these bodily characteristics. Particularly disturbing was the fact that many nondelinquents and noncriminals were classified as mesomorphs. His work was soundly criticized by other professionals who concluded that no relation between body type and criminality could be established positively (Sutherland, 1951).

Although Sheldon's work was widely criticized and subsequently discounted, some researchers continue to investigate the relation between biology and criminal propensities and regard such a connection as plausible. For instance, research conducted by Sheldon and Eleanor Glueck in 1950 targeted 1,000 white male youths, 500 of whom were delinquent and 500 of whom were nondelinquent (Glueck and Glueck, 1950). Mesomorphic characteristics similar to those described by Sheldon were found among 60 percent of the delinquents studied, while only 30 percent of the nondelinquents shared these characteristics. While the Gluecks interpreted their findings conservatively and never said that delinquency is caused by mesomorphic characteristics, they nevertheless described delinquents generally as more agitated and aggressive compared with nondelinquents. Over five decades later, we can look back at the Gluecks' study and argue, particularly in view of the rise in the incidence of juvenile gangs in many of the nation's larger cities, that more muscular youths are probably more likely to be gang members than less muscular youths. Furthermore, the fact that the Gluecks confined their analysis to white male juveniles means that they excluded from consideration several races and ethnic groups that have become increasingly conspicuous in American society and associated with certain forms of delinquency. Additionally, the Gluecks have been criticized on both methodological and statistical grounds (Laub, 1987).

Sociobiology.   In recent decades, several criminologists have reaffirmed the significance of the biological contribution to criminality and delinquency (Gebo, 2002). Genetic researchers and biologists have evolved **sociobiology,** or the study of the biological basis for social action (Wilson, 1975:16). While this new field is not necessarily biological determinism or positivism revisited, it nevertheless stimulates interest in and directs our attention toward the role of genetics in human behavior. Presently, it is believed that a connection exists, but we are unable to elaborate this connection.

The XYY Theory.   Closely associated in principle with the sociobiological explanation of criminality and delinquency is the **XYY theory.** This theory asserts that certain chromosomatic abnormalities may precipitate violence and/or criminal conduct. *X* chromosomes designate female characteristics and are regarded as passive, while *Y* chromosomes designate male characteristics and are regarded as aggressive. Normally, an *XX* chromosomatic combination produces a female, while the *XY* chromosomatic combination yields a male. Sometimes, an extra *Y* chromosome insinuates itself into the *XY* formula to produce an *XYY* type. The input from this additional aggressive chromosome is believed responsible, at least in some instances, for criminal behaviors among those observed to possess it. Unfortunately, this chromosomatic combination exists in less than 5 percent of the population, and thus it lacks sufficient predictive utility when considered on its own merits (Marsh and Katz, 1985).

Besides designating specific body types, physical features, and heredity as crucial manifestations or causes of delinquency and criminal behavior, other biological or physical causes have been advanced in previous years. Feeble-mindedness, mental illnesses, low intelligence, physical deformity including assorted stigmata, and glandular malfunction or imbalance have been variously described as concomitants of delinquency and criminality (Xiaoying, 2005). For instance, Walsh (1987) studied 256 delinquents in Toledo, Ohio, and Boise, Idaho. He examined their IQ levels and types of offenses committed. While he found that those delinquents with higher IQ levels tended not to engage in violent acts, he also found that those juveniles with lower IQ levels evidenced an inordinate amount of property crime, crime most likely to offer instant gratification to offenders. He argued accordingly that low IQ apparently predisposed delinquents to impulsive and spontaneous property crimes, while higher IQ disposed youths to commit crimes that required planning and offered deferred gratification. Presently, however, most professionals are not prepared to acknowledge IQ as a valid indicator of delinquent propensities (McGloin, Pratt, and Maahs, 2004).

Other Biologically Related Explanations.   Much research exists regarding the relation of criminal and delinquent behavior to physical deformities and glandular malfunctions. While these ideas that glandular malfunctions and physical defects are somehow causally related to various forms of deviant behavior are interesting, no consistent groundwork has been provided that empirically supports any of these notions. Regarding stigmata, for instance, Irving Goffman (1961) has observed that often, unusual behaviors are elicited from those possessing stigmata by defining audiences of others who regard such stigmata with repulsion. Thus, those with stigmas of one type or another, such as facial disfigurement, react to the reactions of others toward them, sometimes behaving as they believe others expect them to behave. It is not the stigma that causes deviant behavior, but rather, the reactions of stigmatized persons who respond to the reactions of others. No scientific continuity has been conclusively established between stigmata and criminality. Some relatively recent investigations have attempted to correlate antisocial and delinquent behavior with early exposure to lead and other toxicants. These investigations have also included examinations of delinquent youth exposed to marijuana use by one or both parents and determined by prenatal and postnatal exposures to the drug. Interestingly, a positive correlation has been drawn between prenatal exposure to certain drugs and toxicants from mothers and subsequent behavioral problems of children from their infant years through adolescence (Dietrich et al., 2001).

A key feature of many community-based juvenile correctional programs is counseling designed to assist juveniles to acquire more positive self-concepts and self-assurance. Sometimes, disfigurements or physical inadequacies might cause some of these youths to feel rejected by others or left out of group activities. Wilderness experiences and outdoors survival courses are designed, in part, to bolster one's confidence in the ability to set goals and accomplish them. If youths can cope with living in the wilderness, by learning camping, cooking, and other pioneer crafts, then they might assume that other problems can be overcome as well.

It is also the case that the ingestion of certain substances or drugs can and do interact with one's biological system to elicit different types of behaviors, some of which are deviant and delinquent (Tubman, Gil, and Wagner, 2004).

While it is impossible to tell for sure whether biological explanations of delinquent conduct have contributed to the establishment of such programs, it is clear that many individual and group activities involving youthful offenders are geared toward developing coping skills (Veress et al., 2004). And often, coping with one's own physical and/or psychological inadequacies is an essential part of growing out of the delinquent mode of conduct.

PSYCHOLOGICAL THEORIES

Theories that attribute criminal and delinquent behaviors to personality maladjustment or to some unusual cognitive condition are categorically known as **psychological theories.** These theories focus on the learning process, the process whereby humans acquire language, self-definitions, definitions of others, and assorted behavioral proprieties (Chapple, 2005). Because the precise mechanisms involved in the learning process are elusive and cannot be inspected or investigated directly, each psychological theory is inherently subjective and may be debated endlessly regarding its relative merits and explanatory effectiveness. In this section, two psychological explanations for delinquent conduct will be examined: (1) psychoanalytic theory and (2) social learning theory.

Psychoanalytic Theory

Some of the early pioneers of psychological theories of human behavior were Sigmund Freud, Karen Horney, and Carl Jung. These theorists conjectured about personality systems, how they are formed, and how personality and behavior are inexorably intertwined. The most popular psychologist historically was probably Sigmund Freud (1856–1939). At least Freud was one of the few early theorists who presented a very systematic explanatory scheme for personality emergence and development. Freud's investigations and writings eventually became widely known as **psychoanalytic theory.**

At the core of psychoanalytic theory, according to Freud, are three major personality components known respectively as the **id, ego,** and **superego.** The id is the uncontrolled "I want" component prevalent among all newborn infants. The desire of the id is for immediate gratification. Thus, infants typically exhibit little or no concern for others as they seek to acquire things they like or admire. As infants mature to young children, the id is suppressed to a degree by the ego, another personality component. The ego is a recognition of others and a respect of their rights and interests. Eventually, higher-level moral development occurs through the superego or conscience. When children begin to feel guilty when they have deprived others of something wrongfully, this is a manifestation of the superego in action, according to Freud. Eventually, a **libido** emerges, which is a basic drive for sexual stimulation and gratification. The onset of puberty is a common event signaling the importance of the libido. Again, the ego and superego function to keep the libido in check.

Deviant behavior generally and criminal behavior and delinquency specifically may be explained as the result of insufficient ego and superego development (Maruna, Matravers, and King, 2004). The id dominates and seeks activities that will fulfill the urges or needs it stimulates. Parent–child relations are often cited as primary in the normal development of the ego and superego. Therefore, if some children lack control over their impulses and desires, the blame is often placed at the parents' feet for their failure to inculcate these important inhibitors into the youth's personality system (Lord, Jiang, and Hurley, 2005).

Psychoanalytic theory stresses one's early childhood experiences as crucial for normal adult functioning to occur. Traumatic experiences may prevent proper ego or superego development. Adults may develop neuroses or psychoses that may be traceable to bizarre childhood events or other traumatic experiences. Investigations of juvenile rapists, for instance, have indicated that compared with nonrapists, rapists tended to exhibit higher rates of social isolation, physical problems, and problems with sexual identification. In fact, it may be useful to view juvenile rape as a violent, impulsive act committed by youths with a low level of ego integration.

Many treatment programs have been established that operate to improve a youth's cognitive development. In Albany, New York, for example, the Juvenile Sex Offender Project (JSOP) was established by the St. Anne Institute to meet the needs of juvenile sex offenders ages 10 to 19 (Lombardo and DiGiorgio-Miller, 1988). Interestingly, each candidate for treatment was selected only after a detailed assessment procedure, which examined psychosocial development, family processes, and past involvement with legal systems. Empathy for victims, an ego-related function, was stressed in the JSOP. The psychoanalytic approach continues to be widely used in treatment programs for errant adolescents. However, indications are that psychoanalytic theory is increasingly used together with other approaches that encourage systemic family therapy and a greater focus on one's psychosocial needs (Carswell et al., 2004).

Some male runaways turn to prostitution as a way of surviving on city streets.
http://pal.pearson.com/teams/View.do?action=7

Social Learning Theory

Social learning theory is somewhat different from psychoanalytic theory. Traumatic early childhood experiences may be important determinants of subsequent adult personality characteristics, but the primary factors influencing whether one conforms to or deviates from societal rules are those experiences youths have while learning from others such as their parents (Moseley, 2005). Adults in any institutional context (e.g., schools, churches, homes) provide role models for children to follow. Homes that are beset with violence and conflict between spouses are poor training grounds for children (Hagan, Boehnke, and Merkens, 2004). Children often learn to cope with their problems in ways that are labeled antisocial or hostile (Linning and Kearney, 2004) Even the punishments parents impose on children for disobeying them are translated into acceptable behaviors that children can direct toward their own peers (Chapple and Piquero, 2004).

In its most simplified form, social learning theory implies that children learn to do what they see significant others do, such as their parents (Talwar et al., 2004). Poor parental role models as a probable cause of poor adolescent adjustment and delinquent behavior have been emphasized (Lee, Akers, and Borg, 2004). The importance of the family in the early social development of children has been cited as influential in contributing to youth delinquency. Children who use violence to resolve disputes with other children likely have learned such behaviors in homes where violence is exhibited regularly by parents (Ingram et al., 2005). If delinquency is fostered through social learning, then, it seems, certain social learning intervention models might be useful for assisting youths to learn different, more acceptable behaviors (Talwar et al., 2004). In fact, provided that certain youths can be identified accurately who exhibit learning or developmental disabilities in school, teachers may modify their classroom curricula in ways that increase opportunities, skills, and rewards for these children (Wallace, Minor, and Wells, 2005).

Several researchers have examined the relation between delinquency and whether children are learning-disabled (Brownlie et al., 2004). Learning-disabled children suffer a double disadvantage, in a sense, since their learning disabilities have likely contributed to poor school performance and social adjustments. Such learning disabilities may impair their judgment regarding peer associations, and it is possible that they might have encounters with the law more frequently than other children. When they are evaluated at intake or later in juvenile court, their school records are "evidence" against them. Some persons may erroneously conclude that learning disabilities produce delinquent conduct, when, in fact, other factors are at work. Teachers themselves may become impatient with learning-disabled children, particularly if their conditions are unknown in advance. A lack of rewards from teachers may have deep emotional impacts for some learning-disabled children, thus creating a vicious cycle of failure for them.

These psychological theories stress one's early moral and cognitive development as influential in relation to one's later behaviors (Monroe, 2004). Many delinquency prevention programs have been designed as interventions in one's early years. Therefore, it is not unusual to see attempts by public agencies and professionals to intervene through early training or educational programs in schools. The California Office of Criminal Justice Planning, for example, designed a curriculum for children in grades K–4 about how to reduce their vulnerability to certain crimes. They were taught about personal safety, how to recognize child abuse situations, how to protect personal property from others, and certain types of responsible behaviors, including respecting the rights of others (California Office of Criminal Justice Planning, 1984).

Davidson (1987) has described the aims of different delinquency prevention programs that target young schoolchildren. One such program is Elan One, a program in Maine that emphasizes certain key elements, including acquiring feelings of interpersonal competence, understanding the impact of peer pressure, learning respect for authority, and receiving cognitive therapy to reinforce one's values and suggest future behavioral options. This particular program stresses individual learning. Other programs, such as Illinois's Ounce of Prevention program, attempt to involve the entire family in school-based interventions that assist youths and their families to learn more effective social skills (Zigler and Hall, 1987). Such familial support in one's early years serves to reinforce values believed important by program planners (Sturgeon, 2005).

Finally, the Perry Preschool project in Ypsilanti, Michigan, was an attempt to identify certain children who exhibited a strong likelihood of dropping out of school (Berrueta-Clement, et al., 1984). These youths at risk were targeted in their preschool years and placed in special education classes. Their special training was supplemented by weekly home visits. Compared with a birth cohort of youths not receiving such training, but who were also identified as high risks for failure, the experimental group of Perry preschoolers experienced less than half the rate of arrests. Furthermore, more of these youths stayed in school longer and tended to graduate, with some even obtaining graduate degrees. For some interventionists, then, exposure to special kinds of training in one's formative years does much to promote more socially and psychologically healthy school and home environments. The psychological school's impact here is quite apparent.

SOCIOLOGICAL THEORIES

It is worth noting that the theories advanced thus far have related deviant, criminal, and/or delinquent behaviors to factors almost exclusively within individuals (i.e., either their minds or bodies or both). These theories have been described elsewhere as inside notions (e.g., the positivist view, glandular malfunction, XYY theory, sociobiology, low IQ), primarily because they identify internal factors as causally important for explaining deviation of any kind (Walsh, 2000). While these inside notions have persisted over the years to provide plausible explanations for why criminals and delinquents commit their various offenses, other rival explanations have been advanced that shift certain causes of deviant conduct to factors outside of or external to individuals. Sociologists have encouraged strong consideration of social factors as major variables that can account for the emergence and persistence of delinquent conduct (Swain, Henry, and Baez, 2004).

It is perhaps most realistic to regard these different perspectives as mutually overlapping rather than as mutually exclusive. Thus, we might view social learning theory as predominantly a psychological theory with certain sociological elements. The biological factor may figure significantly into the delinquency equation, particularly when considering the matter of developmental disabilities of a physical nature in the social learning process. A pragmatic view will be adopted here, and we will regard any explanation as useful, provided that it is accompanied by some predictive utility.

Several sociological theories of juvenile delinquency are presented in this section. They include (1) the concentric zone hypothesis; (2) the subculture theory of delinquency; (3) the anomie theory of delinquency; (4) labeling theory; (5) bonding theory; and (6) Agnew's general strain theory.

The Concentric Zone Hypothesis and Delinquency

During the early 1900s, large cities such as Chicago were undergoing rapid expansion as one result of the great influx of laborers from farms and rural regions to city centers to find work. Urbanization emanated from the center of cities outward, and such expansion caused some of the older neighborhoods within the inner city to undergo dramatic transition. Sociologists at the University of Chicago and elsewhere studied the urban development of Chicago. Social scientists Ernest W. Burgess and Robert E. Park defined a series of concentric zones around Chicago, commencing with the core or "Loop" in downtown Chicago, and progressing outward away from the city center in a series of concentric rings. The outward ring or zone immediately adjacent to the central core was labeled by Burgess and Park as an **interstitial area** or **zone of transition.** This was the immediate periphery of downtown Chicago and was characterized by slums and urban renewal projects. This area was also typified by high delinquency and crime. These researchers believed that other cities might exhibit similar growth patterns and concentric zones similar to those identified in the Chicago area. Thus, the **concentric zone hypothesis** of urban growth originated, accompanied by descriptions of different social and demographic characteristics of those inhabiting each zone.

Concurrent with Burgess's and Park's efforts was an investigation of delinquency patterns in Chicago conducted by Clifford Shaw and Henry McKay (1972). These researchers studied the characteristics of delinquent youths in the zone of transition and compared the backgrounds of these youths with other youths inhabiting more stabilized neighborhoods in the zones further removed from the inner core of downtown Chicago. They based their subsequent findings and probable causes of delinquency on the records of nearly 25,000 delinquent youths in Cook County, Illinois, between 1900 and the early 1930s. Essentially, Shaw and McKay found that over the 30-year period, delinquency within the interstitial zone was widespread and tended to grow in a concomitant fashion with the growth of slums and deteriorating neighborhoods. For many of these youths, both of their parents worked in factories for long hours. Large numbers of juveniles roamed these Chicago streets with little or no adult supervision. Family stability was lacking, and many youths turned toward gang activities with other youths as a means of surviving, gaining recognition and status, and achieving certain material goals.

Compared with other zones, zones of transition were typically overcrowded, replete with families of lower socioeconomic status. No zones were completely free of delinquency, however. But in other zones, families were more affluent and stable, and accordingly, less delinquency was observed compared with delinquency within interstitial areas. Shaw and McKay explained delinquency in these transitional areas as likely attributable to a breakdown in

BOX 3.2

Tom Archer
Juvenile Probation Counselor, King County Superior Court, Juvenile Probation Services

Statistics:

B.A. (secondary education), Western Washington University

Background and Interests

I grew up in the greater Seattle area of Washington State and still live in the suburbs of Seattle in Renton, Washington. I've been married to the same amazing woman for over 27 years and have a beautiful daughter and son (ages 22 and 19). In 1968 I graduated from Shoreline High School where I participated in varsity basketball and track and went on to Western Washington State College (now university) in Bellingham, Washington, where I remained for 6 years (I enjoyed college life) and received a BA in secondary education with a minor in golf and pool.

In the fall of 1974 following 6 months of student teaching in the Kent School District and graduation, I accepted a position as a full-time teacher in a public middle school in Marysville, WA. I taught seventh grade there for one year and was nonrenewed along with 29 others after the district failed its eighth consecutive levy. Although I received a job offer in the district at the end of the summer of 1975, I decided to redirect my life. Although my year of teaching was successful and I enjoyed the students (especially the troubled ones), I did not enjoy teaching English and Social Studies in a group setting. Since I was still young and single I decided to be somewhat adventurous, get a real estate license, and seek my fortune. I was in (notice I didn't say sold) real estate for about a year and decided eating was something I enjoyed and so ironically went to work at a college friend's Italian restaurant in Seattle as a waiter for about a year. During that year a couple of

other friends were working at the King County Juvenile Court and encouraged me to apply.

In the Spring of 1976 I began working as an on-call child care worker (now called juvenile detention officer). At the time working on-call was the path to full-time employment with the juvenile court. Currently, King County detention does not have on-call officers. I enjoyed interacting with the detainees, playing basketball, pool, cards, etc. After all I was getting paid ($25 a shift) for participating in activities I enjoyed and staying in shape. The detainees were not that much younger than I was at the time. In November 1976 I was hired full time as a juvenile detention officer. I worked for 8+ years in detention in various living units and on all three shifts and also worked on an as-needed basis as a duty supervisor in detention. In March 1985 I was hired as a juvenile probation counselor (officer). For the majority of the almost 20 years in probation I have worked supervising a caseload of mostly felonious offenders. In Spring 2005 I was an interim supervisor for a unit of probation counselors. Furthermore, I have served on various interdepartmental work groups including my current participation on a policy and procedures committee that is drafting a new policy manual for the probation department. I also have served on the Maple Valley Communities that Care (MVCTC) committee since its inception about 9 years ago. MVCTC's goal is to create a safe and supportive environment for youth in the Greater Maple Valley Area by working collab-

(continued)

oratively with civic groups and community members to reduce and prevent violence and youth substance abuse. Communities That Care in general is a research-based strategy for involving neighborhoods in addressing the needs of youth. The program has been effectively implemented throughout the country.

Experiences

Throughout my career with the juvenile court I have had many memorable experiences working in detention and as a probation counselor. While working in detention a resident set his mattress on fire and then escaped from his room and somehow made his way onto the roof through a couple of doors that should have been locked. The escapee was seen by other residents running across the roof in his underwear. Remnants of his burnt hair were found along his escape route. He was finally apprehended some months later in New York and extradited back to Seattle on an armed robbery charge.

Another incident in detention involved a group of violent offenders in the Special Programs Unit on a graveyard shift. I was working the senior boys unit and received a call from the admissions/monitoring unit that something was going on in the Special Programs Unit where the most behaviorally disturbed youth were housed. I went downstairs and was the first backup on the scene. It was eerie; I could have heard a pin drop. As I cautiously made my way around the unit looking for staff, several youths' dorm doors were open and a number of the youth were not in their dorms. As I went down the hall further I found one staff unconscious on the floor in the hallway. As he came to, he explained that several youth had escaped and he had been choked unconscious. I found another staff locked in one of the youth's dorm rooms. The youth had sharpened toothbrushes to a point and used them as weapons. All of the youth, many of whom were serious, violent offenders, were eventually apprehended. Fortunately, no one was seriously hurt during the escape.

Another youth I had on probation used to regularly self-mutilate by smashing his forehead into heavy, sharp objects. Even more bizarre, he used to regularly insert foreign matter including a TV antenna and dry wall material up his genitals, which eventually required several surgeries. Sadly, he has been in prison for several years now and occasionally still calls to say hello. He is a very bright, articulate young man. You would never guess he is as mentally ill as he is by talking to him.

Once in a while I'll receive a call from or run into a former probationer who has turned his or her life around and become a productive member of society. Unfortunately, however, the majority of the calls I receive are from past probationers who have graduated to the adult system and are in jail or prison. Most of us who have been on the job for a while could write a book about all the detention and probation experiences we've had. The job is never boring and just when you think you've seen it all, something new happens.

Advice to Students

I believe some of the desired qualities to be a successful probation counselor include but are not limited to the following:

1. You need to care about and like people. If you can't find something good about everyone you meet, the job can become very frustrating and depressing.

2. You need to be an encourager of people. I've found that positive reinforcement goes the furthest in building professional relationships and affecting change in my clients. Most of my clients have been beaten down and told for years that they are no good. We accomplish very little if we reinforce that negative cycle.

3. You need to be organized. Meeting court deadlines for reports and managing a caseload of youth can be very difficult if you are not an organized person.

4. You need to be a patient, empathetic person. Metaphorically, I look at my clients as ice blocks that we carefully and strategically chip away at. Change does not happen overnight. After all, it has taken a lifetime for our clients to develop their bad habits and characteristics.

5. Developing a sense of humor is very important in maintaining a healthy attitude over the years. As probation counselors we are often exposed to a very negative, dysfunctional, sad, sick side of life. Without a sense of humor it is easy to focus too heavily on the dark side of the job.

Working as a juvenile correctional officer and juvenile probation counselor has and continues to be a very rewarding career. Additionally, my Christian faith has been instrumental in my ability to work with my clients and maintain an optimistic outlook and perspective. I truly believe that I am helping change in a positive way the lives of my clients. However, sometimes the influences we have are not immediately noticeable, but I have faith that my contribution is making a difference.

family unity and pervasive social disorganization. Interstitial areas lacked recreational facilities and schools and churches were run-down. As a result, youths literally played in the streets, with little or nothing to do to occupy their time other than to form gangs and commit delinquent acts. Because many of the same gangs formed at the turn of the century were still in existence in the early 1930s, Shaw and McKay believed that gang members perpetuated gang traditions and gang culture over time through cultural transmission.

One immediate effect of Shaw's and McKay's work was to divert explanations of delinquency away from biological explanations such as genetics and physical abnormalities to more sociological explanations (Ingram et al., 2005). The long-range influence of the pioneering work of Shaw and McKay is evident in contemporary studies seeking to link neighborhood characteristics with delinquent conduct (Liberman, Raudenbush, and Sampson, 2005). Generally, these studies have been supportive of Shaw's and McKay's work, although other factors closely associated with those residing in slum areas have also been

Easy access to firearms has contributed significantly to juvenile violence.

causally linked with delinquency. One of these factors is socioeconomic status (SES) (Dahlgren, 2005).

Studies investigating the relation between SES and delinquency have generally found more frequent and more violent types of juvenile conduct among youths of lower SES (Wolfgang and Ferracuti, 1967), while less frequent and less violent conduct has been exhibited by youths from families of upper SES (Liberman, Raudenbush, and Sampson, 2005). Some of this research also suggests that juveniles who are identified with lower SES seem more likely to do less well in school than other juveniles from higher SES.

It may be that students from families of lower SES may reflect different values and achievement orientations compared with youths from higher SES. This factor may figure significantly in the rate of juveniles' school successes or failures. School dropouts or underachievers may, in fact, turn toward other underachievers or dropouts for companionship, recognition, and prestige. Thus, a complex and vicious cycle is put into motion, with certain conditions and characteristics of lower SES leading to poor academic performance, growing antisocial behavior, and subsequent delinquent conduct. However, describing the concomitants of delinquents or their prominent characteristics does not necessarily pinpoint the true causal factors associated with their conduct in any predictive sense (Cauffman, Steinberg, and Piquero, 2005). After all, many lower SES youths adjust well to their academic work and refrain from delinquent activities (Swisher et al., 2004). Also, many seemingly well-adjusted and academically successful youths from higher SES may engage in certain forms of delinquent conduct.

Some research has associated having money or possessing monetary resources as being positively related to delinquent conduct. Thus, especially among higher SES youth, having money becomes a risk factor to criminal conduct in that it reduces family attachments, leads to increased dating, and increases illicit drug use (Ingram et al., 2005). It may be that efforts to facilitate adolescents' entrance into the adult world of earning, spending, credit, and financial obligation may produce unintended consequences, namely increased use of drugs and greater misbehavior. The attraction of purchasing wanted luxury items, such as clothes, CDs, cellular phones, and expensive cars, may be overwhelming when compared with the mere promise that delayed gratification somehow will improve one's life at some distant, uncertain point in the future. The proceeds from adolescents' employment and parental allowance may facilitate values and behaviors that divorce youths from the responsibility accompanying entrance into the adult world of economic relationships. In a sense, then, parents and employers may be the economic agents responsible for subsidizing adolescents' delinquent involvement and drug use (Wright et al., 2001:262).

The Subculture Theory of Delinquency

During the 1950s, sociologist Albert Cohen (1955) focused on and described a delinquent subculture or a **subculture of delinquency.** Delinquent subcultures exist, according to Cohen, within the greater societal culture. But these subcultures contain value systems and modes of achievement and gaining status and recognition apart from the mainstream culture (Davies and Pearson, 1999). Thus, if we are to understand why many juveniles behave as they do, we must pay attention to the patterns of their particular subculture.

The notion of a delinquent subculture is fairly easy to understand, especially in view of the earlier work of Shaw and McKay. While middle- and upper-class children learn and aspire to achieve lofty ambitions and educational goals and receive support for these aspirations from their parents as well as predominantly middle-class teachers, lower-class youths are at a distinct disadvantage at the outset. They are born into families where these aspirations and attainments may be alien and rejected. Their primary familial role models have not attained these high aims themselves. At school, these youths are often isolated socially from upper- and middle-class juveniles, and therefore, social attachments are formed with others similar to themselves. Perhaps these youths dress differently from other students, wear their hair in a certain style, or use coded language when talking to peers in front of other students. They acquire a culture unto themselves and one that is largely unknown to other students. In a sense, much of this cultural isolation is self-imposed. But it functions to give them a sense of fulfillment, of reward, of self-esteem and recognition apart from other reward systems. If these students cannot achieve one or more of the various standards set by middle-class society, then they create their own standards and prescribe the means to achieve those standards.

Cohen is quick to point out that delinquency is not a product of lower SES per se. Rather, children from lower SES are at greater risk than others of being susceptible to the rewards and opportunities a subculture of delinquency might offer in contrast with the system's middle-class reward structure. Several experiments have subsequently been implemented with delinquents, where these subcultures have been targeted and described, and where the norms of these subcultures have been used as intervening mechanisms to modify delinquent behaviors toward nondelinquent modes of action. The Provo Experiment was influenced, to a degree, by the work of Cohen (Empey and Rabow, 1961). Samples of delinquent youths in Provo, Utah, were identified in the late 1950s and given an opportunity to participate in group therapy sessions at Pine Hills, a large home in Provo that had been converted to an experimental laboratory.

In cooperation with juvenile court judges and other authorities, Pine Hills investigators commenced their intervention strategies assuming that juvenile participants (1) had limited access to success goals, (2) performed many of their delinquent activities in groups rather than alone, and (3) committed their delinquent acts for nonutilitarian objectives rather than for money (Empey and Rabow, 1961). These investigators believed that since the delinquents had acquired their delinquent values and conduct through their subculture of delinquency, they could unlearn these values and learn new values by the same means. Thus, groups of delinquents participated extensively in therapy directed at changing their behaviors through group processes. The investigators believed that their intervention efforts were largely successful and that the subcultural approach to delinquency prevention and behavioral change was fruitful.

A variation on the subcultural theme is the work of Wolfgang and Ferracuti (1967). Wolfgang and other associates investigated large numbers of Philadelphia boys in a study of birth cohorts. In that study, he found that approximately 6 percent of all boys accounted for over 50 percent of all delinquent conduct from the entire cohort of over 9,000 boys (Wolfgang, Figlio, and Sellin, 1972). These were chronic recidivists who were also violent offenders. Wolfgang has theorized that in many communities, there are subcultural norms of violence that attract youthful males. They regard violence as a normal part of their environment, they use violence, and respect the use of violence by others.

On the basis of evidence amassed by Wolfgang and Ferracuti, it appeared that predominantly lower-class and less-educated males formed a disproportionately large part of this subculture of delinquency. Where violence is accepted and respected, its use is considered normal and normative for the users. Remorse is an alien emotion to those using violence and who live with it constantly. Thus, it is socially ingrained as a subcultural value. This theme would suggest that violence and aggression are learned through socialization with others, even one's siblings.

The Anomie Theory of Delinquency

Anomie theory was used by the early French social scientist Emile Durkheim. Durkheim investigated many social and psychological phenomena including suicide and its causes. One precipitating factor leading to certain suicides, according to Durkheim, was anomie or normlessness (Maume and Lee, 2003). What Durkheim intended by the term was to portray a condition where people's lives, their values, and various social rules were disrupted and they found it difficult to cope with their changed life conditions. Thus, they would experience **anomie,** a type of helplessness, perhaps hopelessness (Heckert and Heckert, 2004). Most persons usually adapt to drastic changes in their lifestyles or patterns, but a few may opt for suicide since they lack the social and psychological means to cope with the strain of change (Konty, 2005).

Merton (1957) was intrigued by Durkheim's notion of anomie and how persons adapt to the strain of changing conditions. He devised a goals/means scheme as a way of describing different social actions that persons might use for making behavioral choices. Merton contended that society generally prescribes approved cultural goals for its members to seek (e.g., new homes, jobs, automobiles). Furthermore, appropriate, legitimate, or institutionalized means are prescribed for the purpose of attaining these goals. But not everyone is equally endowed with the desire to achieve societal goals nor are they necessarily committed to using the prescribed means to achieve these goals.

Merton described five different **modes of adaptation** that people might exhibit (Choi and Lo, 2002). These modes included (1) **conformity** (persons accept the goals of society and work toward their attainment using societally approved means), (2) **innovation** (persons accept the goals of society but use means to achieve goals other than those approved by society), (3) **ritualism** (persons reject goals but work toward less lofty goals by institutionally approved means), (4) **retreatism** (persons reject goals and reject the means to achieve goals—e.g., hermits, street people, or "bag ladies" typify those who retreat or escape from mainstream society and establish their own goals and means to achieve them), and (5) **rebellion** (persons seek to replace culturally approved goals and institutionalized means with new goals and means for others to follow).

Of these, the innovation mode characterizes juvenile delinquents, according to Merton. Juvenile delinquency is innovative in that youths accept culturally desirable goals, but they reject the legitimate means to achieve these goals. Instead, they adopt illegitimate means such as theft, burglary, or violence. Many youths may crave new clothes, automobiles, and other expensive material items. Since they may lack the money to pay for these items, one alternative is to steal them. This is regarded by Merton as one innovative response arising from a condition of anomie and the strain it emits.

Many intermediate punishment programs today are designed to assist youths in devising new strategies to cope with everyday life rather than to use crime or delinquent conduct to achieve their goals. VisionQuest, Homeward Bound, and various types of wilderness experiences incorporate adaptive experiences as integral features of these programs. Those youths with substantial energy are sometimes placed in camps or on ranches where they can act out some of their feelings and frustrations. These programs deliberately cater to youths who are innovative, but who lack a clear sense of direction. Subsequent empirical tests of Merton's theory of anomie have found the theory to have considerable predictive power in explaining drug use/abuse and other forms of deviance (Heckert and Heckert, 2004).

Labeling Theory

One of the more social sociological approaches to delinquent conduct is **labeling theory.** Labeling theory's primary proponent is Edwin Lemert (1951, 1967a, 1967b). Other social scientists have also been credited with originating this concept (Becker, 1963; Kitsuse, 1962). **Labeling** stresses the definitions people have of delinquent acts rather than delinquency itself. Applied to delinquent conduct, Lemert was concerned with two primary questions. These were: (1) What is the process whereby youths become labeled as delinquent? and (2) What is the influence of such labeling upon these youths' future behavior? Lemert assumed that no act is inherently delinquent, that all persons at different points in time conform to or deviate from the law, that persons become delinquent through social labeling or definition, that being apprehended by police begins the labeling process, that youths defined as delinquent will acquire self-definitions as delinquents, and finally, that those defining themselves as delinquent will seek to establish associations with others also defined as delinquent (Hart, 2005).

Not every youth who violates the law, regardless of the seriousness of the offense, will become a hardcore delinquent. Some infractions are relatively minor offenses. For example, experimenting with alcohol and getting drunk or trying certain drugs, joyriding, and petty theft may be one-time events never to be repeated (Parry et al., 2004; Schinke et al., 2004). However, "getting caught" enhances the likelihood that any particular youth will be brought into the juvenile justice system for processing and labeling. Youths who have adopted delinquent subcultures are often those who have attracted the attention of others, including the police, by engaging in wrongful acts or causing trouble. Wearing the symbols of gang membership such as jackets emblazoned with gang names helps to solidify one's self-definition of being delinquent.

Lemert suggested that juvenile deviation may be **primary deviation** or **secondary deviation.** Primary deviation occurs when youths spontaneously violate the law by engaging in occasional pranks. Law enforcement authorities may conclude that these pranks are not particularly serious. However, if juveniles persist in repeating their deviant and delinquent conduct, they may exhibit secondary deviation. Secondary deviation occurs whenever the deviant conduct becomes a part of one's behavior pattern or lifestyle. Thus, delinquency is viewed as a social label applied by others to those youths who have relative frequent contact with the juvenile justice system (Hart, 2005). The strength of such social labeling is such that juveniles themselves adopt such social labels and regard themselves as delinquent. This, too, is a vicious cycle of sorts, in that one phenomenon (social labeling by others of some youths as delinquent) reinforces the other (labeled youths acquiring self-definitions as delinquent and engaging in further delinquent conduct consistent with the delinquent label).

Lemert's labeling perspective has probably been the most influential theory relative to policy decisions by juvenile courts to divert youths away from the formal trappings of court proceedings (Hart, 2005). The sentiment is that if we can keep youths away from the juvenile justice system, they are less inclined to identify with it. Accordingly, they are less likely to define themselves as delinquent and engage in delinquent conduct. This theory is also more broadly applicable to adult first-offenders. Criminal courts often use diversion as a means of keeping first-offenders out of the system. This is done, in part, to give them another chance to conform to the law and not acquire a criminal record. Diversion doesn't always work for either adults or juveniles, but at least we can better appreciate why the different justice systems employ it to deal with at least some adult and juvenile offenders in the early stages of their processing by the system (Murrell, 2005).

Bonding Theory

Bonding theory or **social control theory** derives primarily from the work of Travis Hirschi (1969). This theory stresses processual aspects of youths becoming bonded or socially integrated into the norms of society. The greater the integration or bonding, particularly with parents and school teachers, the less likelihood that youths will engage in delinquent activity. Different dimensions of bonding include attachment (emotional linkages with those we respect and admire), commitment (enthusiasm or energy expended in a specific relationship), belief (moral definition of the rightness or wrongness of certain conduct), and involvement (intensity of attachment with those who engage in conventional conduct or espouse conventional values) (Warr, 2005).

Hirschi investigated large numbers of high school students in order to test his bonding theory. More academically successful students seemed to be bonded to conventional values and significant others such as teachers and school authorities compared with less successful students. Those students who apparently lack strong commitment to school and to education generally are more prone to become delinquent than those students with opposite dispositions. However, since Hirschi limited his research to students in high school settings, he has been criticized subsequently for not applying his bonding theory to juvenile samples in other, nonschool settings. Furthermore, Hirschi has failed to explain clearly the processual aspects of bonding. Also, since rejecting or accepting conventional values and significant others is a matter of degree, and because youths may have many attachments with both delinquent and nondelinquent juveniles, bonding theory has failed to predict accurately which youths will eventually become delinquent. This is regarded as a serious limitation (Chapple, 2005).

Agnew's General Strain Theory

Strain theory was developed from the theory of anomie described by Emile Durkheim and Robert Merton (Agnew, 2002). Anomie theory stresses the breakdown of societal restraints on individual conduct. Merton elaborated on this

BOX 3.3

CAREER SNAPSHOT

Alana Malloy
Assistant Teaching Parent, Presbyterian Hospitality House, Fairbanks, Alaska

Statistics:

B.A., M.A. (justice), University of Alaska–Fairbanks

Background and Interests

I currently work at Presbyterian Hospitality House (PHH) in Fairbanks, Alaska. PHH is a nonprofit residential treatment program designed to assist youth who are unable to remain in foster home placements or require a less restrictive alternative to incarceration. PHH operates five group homes and uses the internationally recognized Teaching Family Model as its treatment modality. Each home is run by professional staff called Teaching Parents. I work as the assistant to the live-in Teaching Parent couple of the gender-specific group home for girls. The average length of stay for a resident is about one year. This varies depending on their individual case plan, program progression, and completion. PHH's family-structured behavioral approach to treatment fosters self-awareness and understanding, and it promotes strength and stability through positive role modeling, which is the primary method of instruction. My job keeps me busy. What I like most about it is the challenge it still holds for me, even today.

As one of those graduating high school seniors, I was unsure of what to do next, but I did know that I wanted to be a part of something bigger than myself. I have always enjoyed working with kids, and studying the law is one of my fascinations. What better reason is there to go to college than to explore these interests academically and to find answers to my questions about career potential? I began college in 1999 and graduated in 2002 with a B.A. in justice. I was still unsure of what to do next, and so I headed off to law school. After a semester and a half in beautiful San Diego, California,

I soon realized that this avenue of study was too removed from the aspects of the law that truly intrigued me. I wanted to be outside and working one-on-one with people. More importantly, I wanted to see, as well as effect, change. I packed up and headed home to work on my master's degree in justice, and also to figure out my next step.

My work at PHH combines my love of the law with an opportunity to really affect kids' lives. When I go home at night after a long day of juggling crazy schedules for five very different youthful personalities, I have a feeling that I made a difference. One of the girls learned that caring for others does not have to involve abuse. Another girl learned how to call and check a flight reservation on her own. One girl learned how to grieve. Another girl is steadily preparing to return to her home village. Every day presents new challenges that are not exactly outlined in any rule book.

Experiences

At 21 years old, I walked into my first college course, unsure of anything other than that I wanted this degree. In three years, I walked back out with my bachelor's degree, and an idea. During the last summer before I graduated, I worked as a juvenile probation officer (JPO) in a rural Alaska village. This internship gave me the opportunity to try out one way I could put my justice degree to good use. I learned a lot that summer. The supportive staff went above and beyond to make sure that I got a chance to participate

(continued)

in every possible situation. I was able to get a glimpse of a JPO's world from the inside. With supervision, I carried a caseload of both formal and informal probationers. I flew out to various villages to conduct home visits and verify client compliance with probation conditions. I worked toward restorative justice alternatives with tribal councils, youth, and their families from several villages. I also assisted the Attorney General's Office in court hearings, a task that included individual case history preparation and recommendations to the court. I worked with the detention staff in supervising detainees, processing new intakes, and participating in several staff training seminars. I interacted further with the community when I attended numerous public awareness presentations on fetal alcohol spectrum disorder and HIV/AIDS awareness. Both of these are rising concerns for the Alaskan youth population. As a JPO intern, I was able to interact and assist youth in need, but I still did not impact them in as positive a way as I was capable. However, I was narrowing down what I wanted to do with my life.

Then I heard about PHH, an agency dedicated to living and working with troubled youth. I was hired as an assistant to work with a well-seasoned Teaching Parent couple who had believed enough in the Teaching Family Model and the youth that they had moved to Alaska from Kansas to carry out that mission. My initial training was detailed but brief. I soon found out that the *real* training came through experience. I now know that no two situations are the same, no two youths will perceive or react alike, and the challenge is to stay one step ahead.

Many of the youth I work with do not possess the basic social skills that could allow a dysfunctional person to pass as normal in today's society. Learning how to follow simple instructions, appropriate responses to routine criticism, control of social behavior under intense emotional states, and rational problem-solving behavior are among some of the skills that youth learn before graduating from this program. As tough as anyone thinks they had it growing up, the kids I work with have had it worst. They are a population of sexually,

emotionally, and physically abused teenage girls who suffer the ill effects of their parents' mistakes. This is not to say that they are not responsible for their actions. I am a strong believer in free will, but I also believe that circumstances put people in positions where they believe that they have limited choices. These kids and their families chose the wrong path.

Not only do I feel like I make a difference at the end of each day, but I also get to find out what qualities I appreciate in a career. At PHH, my responsibilities include direct supervision and driving the youths to various appointments; coordination and participation in recreational activities and community functions; and case management and treatment planning. I assist residents in continuing education, accessing community resources, and group and individual counseling. Every interaction with the girls is a chance for me to teach them. I do this job because I believe in the kids. I believe in the program. Most importantly, I have faith that they will teach these lessons to their children, and so the cycle of abuse will break and they will have new opportunities for success.

My job hasn't always been fun. Teenagers have tantrums that last for hours, intoxicated parents show up for a family visit whom I have turned away, and I often encounter a lack of tolerance from some in the community who would rather judge than understand the work I do. I never really considered myself a patient person before taking this job, but I have learned the fine art of fortitude. The end result and watching these kids grow in the program makes the struggle worth the process.

My favorite story to tell people is about Kristin. When I walked in the door of the group home one day, she was excited to talk to me. She had saved her money and had bought a new bike the week before. While riding it the previous day, she had fallen, scratched her knee, and ended up with a dark purple bruise. She woke up the next morning and saw the bruise, initially forgetting about the fall. She could not understand where the bruise had come from, and it had really scared her. It only took a minute to remember the bike accident, but the moment stuck with her. She told me that she knew there was no way she had gotten the bruise while at PHH because it was a safe place, but for a second, she was remembering how her life had been and the abuse she had endured. She admitted that although she didn't always like being in treatment, she understood that her life would be forever changed.

Advice to Students

The best advice I can give anyone interested in working with troubled youth is to be patient, both with the youth and with yourself. Also, seek out those internship opportunities before you decide on that career. I signed up to work at a rural probation office, serving the toughest population of youthful offenders in the state because I was also told

that if I could cut it there, I would be prepared for anything else that came my way. Even though I did not choose to continue working as a JPO, I would not have known that without participating in the internship. It may be a few months out of your life, but it allows you the time to see what it is really like and whether you want to continue in that field. My experience allowed me to further define what I expected from and for myself. Finally, taking child development and psychology classes while in college definitely helped me to gain a better understanding of the youth with whom I work. This academic foundation complimented my Teaching Family Model training and helps me extensively in the practical teaching situations I encounter daily.

breakdown by describing the emerging cultural imbalance between the goals and norms of individuals in society. The strain component is apparent since although many lower SES youths have adopted middle-class goals and aspirations, they may be unable to attain these goals because of their individual economic and cultural circumstances. This is a frustrating experience for many of these youths, and such frustration is manifested by the strain to achieve difficult goals or objectives. While middle-class youths also experience strain in their attempts to achieve middle-class goals, it is particularly aggravating for many lower-class youths, since they sometimes do not receive the necessary support from their families.

Robert Agnew views strain theory as cutting across all social classes. Strain theory is differentiated from control theory in that control theory is based on the premise that the breakdown of society frees individuals to commit delinquent acts. Control theory also suggests that the absence of significant relationships with nondeviant others means less social control from others over delinquent behavior. Strain theory is also differentiated from social learning theory, which stresses forces in groups that lead persons to view crime in positive ways. Social learning theory suggests that youths eventually find themselves in relationships with others who are deviant and delinquent, and these relationships are viewed as positive and rewarding. In contrast, strain theory focuses on the pressures that are placed on youths to commit delinquency. These pressures occur in the form of maltreatment by others, causing youths to become upset and turn to crime as a negative reaction.

Agnew believes that strain can be measured in different ways. One way is subjective, where investigators determine from delinquents whether they believe they dislike the way they have been treated by others. The objective method focuses on identifying particular experiences in groups that delinquents say they would dislike if they were subjected to such experiences. Thus, different components of potential strain for juveniles can be predetermined and identified. What are the major negative determinants of strain? One of these is the failure of youths to achieve positively valued stimuli. Youths want to have money, status (especially masculine status), and respect. When youths are blocked from attaining these things, strain is created. Autonomy is also highly valued. Autonomy is the power over oneself. In an effort to assert one's autonomy, some persons may be thwarted from achieving this desired state and turn to delinquency and crime to relieve strain and frustration. Thus, there are certain disjunctions in life, especially between aspirations and expectations. When someone achieves less than is expected, strain is experienced. This frustration to achieve whatever is desired may be judged to be the result of unfairness. When a youth expects to achieve a desired result and does not achieve it, the failure experience is an unjust one.

Another way of measuring strain is to examine potential losses of positively valued stimuli in one's life. The loss of significant others, broken relationships with friends or romantic partners, or the theft of a valued possession may create strain. Some youths react to these losses by turning to delinquency to retrieve what was lost, to prevent further loss, or to seek revenge against those perceived as causing the loss.

Yet another measure of strain consists of several negative stimuli in one's life, such as child abuse, neglect, adverse relations with parents or teachers or peers, negative school experiences, neighborhood problems, and homelessness (Pierce and Bozalek, 2004). Even parental unemployment, family deaths, and illnesses can contribute to increasing delinquent behavior in adolescents. Also, the external environment itself can create many negative feelings among youths, such as despair, defeatism, fear, and anger. Anger is especially significant as youths blame their negative circumstances and relationships on others. Those youths who experience repetitious incidents of stressful and frustrating experiences are more likely to engage in delinquent behaviors and hostile and aggressive actions (Whitaker, 2005).

Coping with strain is complex, according to Agnew. Cognitive, emotional, and behavioral coping strategies might include rationalizing, placing less importance on goals originally sought, and/or to accept the responsibility for one's failure to achieve goals. Positive stimuli rather than negative stimuli may be sought to counter the strain one experiences. Therefore, coping mechanisms may be either criminal or noncriminal. General strain theory includes constraints to nondelinquent behavior, as well as factors that may affect an individual's disposition to delinquent behavior. In this way, it is possible to predict the adaptations, delinquent or nondelinquent, that will be chosen.

One issue related to strain theory that Agnew addresses is that male and female delinquents adapt differently to strain. While this differential reaction has not been explained fully, it has been suggested that female juveniles may lack the confidence and self-esteem that may be conducive to committing delinquency. Females may in fact devise strategies that include avoidance and escape in an effort to reduce or eliminate strain. Furthermore, females may have stronger relational ties compared with males, and thus their strain-reduction efforts may be more successful. However, rising rates of female juvenile offending suggest that females may face strain in forms different from males. For instance, females often face sexual, emotional, and physical abuse to a greater degree than their male counterparts (Kinard, 2004). These are negative stimuli. Thus, female juvenile response to such negative stimuli may include acting out in delinquent ways. More research is needed in the study of male–female juvenile differences relative to strain theory and its gender-specific applications (Murrell, 2005).

EXTRANEOUS FACTORS

Obviously, many other explanations for delinquent conduct have been advanced by various theorists. Those selected for more in-depth coverage here are not necessarily the best theories to account for delinquency. Their inclusion is intended to describe some of the thinking about why juveniles might engage in delinquent conduct. Some of the other approaches that have been advocated include containment theory, neutralization or drift theory, differential association theory, and differential reinforcement theory.

Containment theory is associated with the work of sociologist Walter Reckless (1967). Reckless outlined a theoretical model consisting of pushes and pulls in relation to delinquency. By pushes he referred to internal personal factors, including hostility, anxiety, and discontent. By pulls he meant external social forces, including delinquent subcultures and significant others. The containment dimension of his theoretical scheme consisted of both outer and inner containments. Outer containments, according to Reckless, are social norms, folkways, mores, laws, and institutional arrangements that induce societal conformity. By inner containments, Reckless referred to individual or personal coping strategies to deal with stressful situations and conflict. These strategies might be a high tolerance for conflict or frustration and considerable ego strength. Thus, Reckless combined both psychological and social elements in referring to weak attachments of some youths to cultural norms, high anxiety levels, and low tolerance for personal stress. These persons are most inclined to delinquent conduct. A key factor in whether juveniles adopt delinquent behaviors is their level of self-esteem. Those with high levels of self-esteem seem most resistant to delinquent behaviors if they are exposed to such conduct while around their friends (Mueller and Hutchison-Wallace, 2005).

Neutralization theory or **drift theory** was originally outlined by David Matza (1964). Matza said that most juveniles spend their early years on a behavioral continuum ranging between unlimited freedom and total control or restraint. These persons drift toward one end of the continuum or the other, depending on their social and psychological circumstances. If youths have strong attachments with those who are delinquent, then they drift toward the unlimited freedom end of the continuum and perhaps engage in delinquent activities. However, Matza indicates that the behavioral issue is not clear-cut. Juveniles most likely have associations with normative culture, such as their parents or religious leaders, as well as the delinquent subculture, such as various delinquent youths. They may engage in delinquent conduct and regard their behavior as acceptable at the time they engage in it. Elaborate rationales for delinquent behavior may be invented by youths (e.g., society is unfair, victims deserve to be victims, nobody is hurt by our particular acts), and thus, they effectively neutralize the normative constraints of society that impinge upon them. Therefore, at least some delinquency results from rationalizations created by youths that render delinquent acts acceptable under the circumstances (Copes, 2003). Appropriate preventative therapy for such delinquents might be to undermine their rationales for delinquent behaviors through empathic

Youths teach other youths how to use weapons, including firearms, which are often involved in violent delinquent acts.

means. Also, activities that are geared toward strengthening family bonds are important, since greater attachments with one's parents tend to overwhelm the influence of one's associations with delinquent peers (Zimmermann and McGarrell, 2005).

Differential association theory was first advanced by Edwin Sutherland (1939). In some respects, it is an outgrowth of the **cultural transmission theory** described by Shaw and McKay in their investigations of juvenile offenders in Chicago. Sutherland described a socialization process (learning through contact with others) whereby juveniles would acquire delinquent behaviors manifested by others among their close associates. It would certainly be an oversimplification of Sutherland's views to claim that associating with other delinquents would cause certain juveniles to adopt similar delinquent behaviors. Sutherland's scheme was more complex and multifaceted than that (Monroe, 2004). He suggested that several interpersonal dimensions characterize relations between law violators and others who behave similarly. Sutherland said that differential association consists of the following elements: frequency, priority, duration, and intensity. Thus, engaging in frequent associations and long-lasting interactions with others who are delinquent, giving them priority as significant others, and cultivating strong emotional attachments with them will contribute in a significant way to a youth's propensity to commit delinquent acts.

Explicit in Sutherland's scheme is the phenomenon of attachments with others who are delinquent. Thus, this is at least one similarity differential association theory shares with containment theory and bonding. Sutherland sought to characterize relationships some juveniles have with delinquents as multidimensional relationships, and the association aspect was only one of several of these dimensions. Although Sutherland's work has been influential and has been widely quoted and utilized by criminologists, some experts have been critical of his theory on various grounds. He never fully articulated the true meaning of intensity, for instance. How intense should a relation be between a delinquent and a nondelinquent before making a difference and causing the nondelinquent to adopt delinquent patterns of behavior? How frequently should nondelinquents be in the company of delinquents before such contact becomes crucial and changes nondelinquent behavior? These and other similar questions were never fully addressed by Sutherland. Nevertheless, differential association has influenced certain correctional policies and treatment programs for both juveniles and adults (Monroe, 2004).

Much like labeling theory, differential association theory has encouraged minimizing contact between hardcore criminal offenders and first-offenders. The use of prison is often the last resort in certain cases, since it is believed that more prolonged contact with other criminals will only serve to intensify any criminal propensities first-offenders might exhibit. If they were diverted to some nonincarcerative option, they might not become recidivists and commit new crimes. The same principle applies to delinquent first-offenders and accounts for widespread use of noncustodial sanctions that seek to minimize a juvenile's contact with the juvenile justice system.

In 1966, Robert Burgess and Ronald Akers attempted to revise Sutherland's differential association theory and derived what they termed **differential reinforcement theory.** Differential reinforcement theory actually combines elements from labeling theory and a psychological phenomenon known as conditioning. Conditioning functions in the social learning process as persons are rewarded for engaging in certain desirable behaviors and refraining from certain undesirable behaviors. Juveniles perceive how others respond to their behaviors (negative reactions) and may be disposed to behave in ways that will maximize their rewards from others (Burgess and Akers, 1966).

Also, in some respects, Burgess and Akers have incorporated certain aspects of the **looking-glass self** concept originally devised by the theorist Charles Horton Cooley. Cooley theorized that people learned ways of conforming by paying attention to the reactions of others in response to their own behavior. Therefore, Cooley would argue that we imagine how others see us. We look for others' reactions to our behavior and make interpretations of these reactions as either good or bad reactions. If we define others' reactions as good, we will feel a degree of pride and likely persist in the behaviors. But, as Cooley indicated, if we interpret their reactions to our behaviors as bad, we might experience mortification. Given this latter reaction or at least our interpretation of it, we might change our behaviors to conform to what others might want and thereby elicit approval from them. While these ideas continue to interest us, they are difficult to conceptualize and investigate empirically. Akers and others have acknowledged such difficulties, although their work is insightful and underscores the reality of a multidimensional view of delinquent conduct.

AN EVALUATION OF EXPLANATIONS OF DELINQUENT CONDUCT

Assessing the importance or significance of theories of delinquency is difficult. First, almost all causes of delinquent conduct outlined by theorists continue to interest contemporary investigators. The most frequently discounted and consistently criticized views are biological ones, although as we have seen, sociobiology and genetic concomitants of delinquent conduct continue to raise questions about the role of heredity as a significant factor in explaining delinquency. Some evidence suggests that television and movie violence triggers aggressive and violent behavior among different youths, although blaming media violence for the actions of some youths fails to explain the absence of violence among those youths also exposed to it (Anderson et al., 2003). Other explanations rely on attention-deficit/hyperactivity disorder, or ADHD, to explain why some youths become delinquent or behave in abnormal ways (Cary, 2005).

Psychological explanations seem more plausible than biological ones, although the precise relation between the psyche and biological factors remains unknown. If we focus on psychological explanations of delinquency as important in fostering delinquent conduct, almost invariably we involve certain elements of one's social world in such explanations. Thus, one's mental processes are influenced in various ways by one's social experiences. Self-definitions, important to psychologists and learning theorists, are conceived largely in social contexts, in the presence of and through contact with others. It is not surprising, therefore, that the most fruitful explanations for delinquency are those that seek to blend the best parts of different theories that assess different dimensions of youths, their physique and intellectual abilities, personalities, and social experiences. Intellectual isolationism or complete reliance on either biological factors exclusively or psychological factors exclusively or sociological factors exclusively may simplify theory construction, but in the final analysis, such isolationism is unproductive (Osgood and Anderson, 2004). Certainly, each field has importance and makes a contribution toward explaining why some youths exhibit delinquent conduct and why others do not.

From a purely pragmatic approach in assessing the predictive and/or explanatory utility of each of these theories, we may examine contemporary interventionist efforts that seek to curb delinquency or prevent its recurrence. One way of determining which theories are most popular and/or influence policy and administrative decision making relative to juveniles is to identify the ways youthful offenders are treated by the juvenile justice system when they have been apprehended and adjudicated (Wallace, Minor, and Wells, 2005).

A preliminary screening of juvenile offenders may result in some being diverted from the juvenile justice system. One manifest purpose of such diversionary action is to reduce the potentially adverse influence of labeling on these youths. A long-term objective of diversion is to minimize recidivism among divertees. While some experts contend that the intended effects of diversion, such as a reduction in the degree of social stigmatization toward status offenders, are presently unclear, inconsistent, and insufficiently documented, other professionals endorse diversion programs and regard them as effective in preventing further delinquent conduct among first-offenders (Hartwell, 2004). In fact, the preponderance of evidence from a survey of available literature is that diversion, while not fully effective at preventing recidivism, nevertheless tends to reduce it substantially. This evidence is largely supportive of less aggressive intervention strategies for dealing with minor delinquent offenders until after they have committed at least two or three other offenses.

A promising idea is that minimizing formal involvement with the juvenile justice system is favorable for reducing participants' self-definitions as delinquent and avoiding the delinquent label. Thus, labeling theory seems to have been prominent in the promotion of diversionary programs. Furthermore, many divertees have been exposed to experiences that enhance or improve their self-reliance and independence. Many youths have learned to think out their problems rather than act them out unproductively or antisocially. When we examine the contents of these programs closely, it is fairly easy to detect aspects of bonding theory, containment theory, and differential reinforcement theory at work in the delinquency prevention process.

Besides using diversion per se with or without various programs, there are elements or overtones of other theoretical schemes that may be present in the particular treatments or experiences juveniles receive as they continue to be processed throughout the juvenile justice system. At the time of adjudication, for example, juvenile court judges may or may not impose special conditions to accompany a sentence of probation. Special conditions may refer to obligating juveniles to make restitution to victims, to perform public services, to participate in group or individual therapy, or to undergo medical treatment in cases of drug addiction or alcohol abuse (Patrick et al., 2004).

Learning to accept responsibility for one's actions, acquiring new coping skills to face crises and personal tragedy, improving one's educational attainment, and improving one's ego strength to resist the influence of one's delinquent peers are individually or collectively integral parts of various delinquency treatment programs, particularly where the psychological approach is strong (Carmona et al., 2004).

Program successes are often used as gauges of the successfulness of their underlying theoretical schemes. Since no program is 100 percent effective at preventing delinquency, it follows that no theoretical scheme devised thus far is fully effective. Yet, the wide variety of programs that are applied today to deal with different kinds of juvenile offenders indicates that most psychological and sociological approaches have some merit and contribute differentially to delinquency reduction (Jennings and Gunther, 2000). Policy decisions are made throughout the juvenile justice system and are often contingent upon the theoretical views adopted by politicians, law enforcement personnel, prosecutors and judges, and correctional officials at every stage of the justice process. We may appreciate most theoretical views because of their varying intuitive value and selectively apply particular approaches to accommodate different types of juvenile offenders.

Regarding theories of delinquency generally, their impact has been felt most strongly in the area of policymaking rather than in behavioral change or modification. Virtually every theory is connected in some respect to various types of experimental programs in different jurisdictions. The intent of most programs has been to change behaviors of participants. However, high rates of recidivism characterize all delinquency prevention innovations, regardless of their intensity or ingenuity. Policy decisions implemented at earlier points have long-range implications for present policies in correctional work. Probationers and parolees as well as inmates and divertees, adults and juveniles alike, are recipients or inheritors of previous policies layed in place by theorists who have attempted to convert their theories into practical experiences and action.

Current policy in juvenile justice favors the get-tough orientation, and programs are increasingly sponsored that heavily incorporate accountability and individual responsibility elements. At an earlier point in time, projects emphasizing rehabilitation and reintegration were rewarded more heavily through private grants and various types of government funding. No particular prevention or intervention or supervision program works best. Numerous contrasting perspectives about how policy should be shaped continue to vie for recognition among professionals and politicians. The theories that have been described here are indicative of the many factors that have shaped our present policies and practices. The influence of these diverse theories is reflected in a variety of models that have been and continue to be used by juvenile justice practitioners. Several of these models are presented in the following section.

MODELS FOR DEALING WITH JUVENILE OFFENDERS

Six models for dealing with juvenile offenders are described here. Each of these models is driven by a particular view of juvenile delinquency and what might cause it. The causes of delinquency are many and diverse, and thus not everyone agrees with any particular explanation. Therefore, not every expert dealing with juvenile offenders agrees that one particular model is most fruitful as a basis for delinquency intervention. Rather, these models serve as a guide to the different types of decisions that are made on behalf of or against specific juvenile offenders. Because each model includes aims or objectives that are related to a degree with the aims or objectives of other models, there is sometimes confusion about model identities. For example, professionals may use a particular model label to refer to orientations that are more properly included in the context of other models. Some professionals say that they do not use any particular model, but rather, they rely on their own intuition for exercising a particular juvenile intervention.

Additionally, some recently developed interventionist activities have combined the favorable features of one model with those of others. These hybrid models are difficult to categorize, although they are believed to be helpful in diverting youths to more productive and nondelinquent activities. One way of overcoming this confusion is to highlight those features of models that most directly reflect the models' aims. The models discussed include (1) the rehabilitation model; (2) the treatment or medical model; (3) the noninterventionist model; (4) the due process model; (5) the "just deserts"/justice model; and (6) the crime control model.

The Rehabilitation Model

Perhaps the most influential model that has benefited first-offender juveniles is the **rehabilitation model.** This model assumes that delinquency or delinquent conduct is the result of poor friendship or peer choices, poor social adjustments, the wrong educational priorities, and/or a general failure to envision realistic life goals and inculcate appropriate moral values (Haynie et al., 2005). In corrections, the rehabilitation model is associated with programs that change offender attitudes, personalities, or character (Weedon, 2002). These programs may be therapeutic, educational, or vocational. At the intake stage, however, there is little, if any, reliance on existing community-based programs or services that cater to certain juvenile needs. Intake officers who use the rehabilitation model in their decision-making activities will often attempt to impart different values and personal goals to juveniles through a type of informal teaching.

If a youth is being processed at the intake stage for theft, for example, the intake officer may emphasize the harmful effects of the theft for the owner from whom the merchandise was taken. Intake officers who meet with nonviolent first-offenders usually do not want to see these juveniles move further into the juvenile justice system. Therefore, these officers may attempt to get juvenile of-fenders to empathize with their victims and to understand the harm they have caused by their actions. While theft is a serious offense, it is less serious than aggravated assault, rape, armed robbery, or murder. Intake officers rely heavily on their personal experience and judgment in determining the best course of ac-tion to follow. When a juvenile is very young and has committed this single theft offense, this is an ideal situation where intake officers can exercise strate-gic discretion and temper their decisions with some leniency. But in the con-text of *parens patriae* and the rehabilitative framework guiding some of these officers, leniency does not mean outright tokenism or ineffective wrist-slapping. Doing nothing may send the wrong message to youths who have vio-lated the law. The same may be said of police officers who encounter youths on streets and engage in police cautioning or stationhouse adjustments as alterna-tive means of warning juveniles to refrain from future misconduct. Thus, it is believed that the informal intake hearing itself is sufficiently traumatic for most youths so that they will not be eager to reoffend subsequently. Advice, caution-ing, and warnings given under such circumstances are likely to be remembered. It is also important to involve one's family members in these intake confer-ences. If a youth who has committed a delinquent act can see that his or her be-havior has affected his or her family members, then the chances of recidivism may decline (Bowen et al., 2002).

The Treatment or Medical Model

The **treatment model** or **medical model** assumes that delinquent conduct is like a disease, the causes of which can be isolated and attacked. Cures may be ef-fected by administering appropriate remedies. The treatment model is very sim-ilar to the rehabilitation model. Indeed, some persons consider the treatment or medical model to be a subcategory of the rehabilitation model (Boyd and Myers, 2005). The aim of the treatment model is to provide conditional punish-ments for juveniles that are closely related to treatment. Intake officers have the authority to refer certain youths to select community-based agencies and ser-vices where they may receive the proper treatment. This treatment approach as-sumes that these intake officers have correctly diagnosed the illness and know best how to cure it (Davidson-Methot, 2004). Compliance with program require-ments that are nonobligatory for juveniles is enhanced merely by the possibility that the intake officer may later file a delinquency petition with the juvenile court against uncooperative youths.

In growing numbers of jurisdictions, social services are being utilized in-creasingly by juvenile courts and juvenile justice staff in order to treat various disorders exhibited by youthful offenders. Alcohol and drug dependencies characterize large numbers of arrested youths (O'Shaughnessy, 2004; Parry et al., 2004). Therefore, treatment programs are provided for these youths in order that they can learn about and deal with their alcohol or drug dependencies. Some youths need psychological counseling. Others require anger management training and courses to improve their interpersonal skills. In Idaho, for in-stance, the juvenile justice system was overhauled by the legislature in 1995. Added services included two detention centers staffed by juvenile probation of-ficers; an alternative school; psychological assessments of juveniles; treatment provisions by private agencies for juvenile sex offenders and drug/alcohol abusers; and mentoring provided by volunteers who also serve on diversion boards and youth court programs. Juvenile mentoring in both secure and nonsecure settings is receiving greater recognition (Rasmussen, 2004). The 1992 Reauthorization of the Juvenile Justice and Delinquency Prevention Act of 1974 has recognized mentoring as significant for addressing problems of school attendance and delinquent activity, and a **Juvenile Mentoring Program (JUMP)** has been established in various jurisdictions.

One drawback to the treatment model generally is that great variations exist among community agencies regarding the availability of certain services as remedies for particular kinds of juvenile problems. Also, the intake officer may incorrectly diagnose one's illness and prescribe inappropriate therapy. Certain types of deep-seated personality maladjustments cannot be detected through superficial informal intake proceedings (Boyd and Myers, 2005). Simply participating in some community-based service or treatment program may be insufficient to relieve particular juveniles of the original or core causes of their delinquent behaviors. Some juveniles may have incarcerated parents, and the effects of such circumstances have been unevenly studied (Engram, 2005). Nevertheless, intake screenings may lead to community-based agency referrals that eventually may or may not be productive. In most jurisdictions, these are conditional sanctions that may be administered by intake officers without judicial approval or intervention.

The Noninterventionist Model

As the name implies, the **noninterventionist model** means the absence of any direct intervention with certain juveniles who have been taken into custody. The noninterventionist model is best understood when considered in the context of labeling theory (Lemert, 1967a). Labeling theory stresses that direct and frequent contact with the juvenile justice system will cause those having contact with it to eventually define themselves as delinquent. This definition will prompt self-definers to commit additional delinquent acts, since such behaviors are expected of those defined or stigmatized as such by others. Labeling theory advocates the removal of nonserious juveniles and status offenders from the juvenile justice system, or at least from the criminalizing influence and trappings of the juvenile courtroom.

The noninterventionist model is strategically applied only to those juveniles who the intake officer believes are unlikely to reoffend if given a second chance, or who are clearly status offenders without qualification (e.g., drug- or alcohol-dependent, chronic or persistent offenders) (Boyd and Myers, 2005). Intake officers who elect to act in a noninterventionist fashion with certain types of offenders may simply function as a possible resource person for juveniles and their parents. In cases involving runaways, truants, or curfew violators, it becomes a judgment call whether to refer youths and/or their parents to certain community services or counseling. The noninterventionist model would encourage no action by intake officers in nonserious or status offender cases, except under the most compelling circumstances. Since not all runaways are alike, certain runaways may be more in need of intervention than others, for instance. Again, the aim of nonintervention is to assist youths in avoiding stigma and unfavorable labeling that might arise if they were to be involved more deeply within the juvenile justice system. Even minor referrals by intake officers might prompt adverse reactions from offenders so that future offending behavior would be regarded as a way of getting even with the system.

The noninterventionist model is popular today, particularly because it fits well with the deinstitutionalization of status offenses (DSO) movement that has occurred in most jurisdictions. DSO was designed to divest juvenile courts of their jurisdiction over status offenders and remove status offenders from secure custodial institutions. Therefore, the primary intent of DSO was to minimize the potentially adverse influence of labeling that might occur through incarceration or if juveniles appear before juvenile court judges in a courtroom atmosphere. Also, an intended function of DSO was to reduce the docket load for many juvenile court judges by transferring their jurisdiction over status offenders to community agencies and services. The noninterventionist strategy is significant here because it advocates doing nothing about certain juvenile dispositions. The works of Lemert (1967a) and Schur (1973) are relevant for the noninterventionist perspective. These have described **judicious nonintervention** and **radical nonintervention** as terms that might be applied to noninterventionist do-nothing policy.

Radical nonintervention counters traditional thinking about delinquency, which is to assume that the juvenile justice system merely needs to be improved. Radical nonintervention argues that many of the current approaches to delinquency are not only fundamentally unsound, but they are also harmful to youth whenever they are applied. Radical nonintervention assumes the following:

1. The delinquent is not basically different from the nondelinquent.
2. Most types of youthful misconduct are found within all socioeconomic strata.
3. The primary target for delinquency policy should be neither the individual nor the local community setting, but rather the delinquency-defining processes themselves.

Radical nonintervention implies that policies that accommodate society to the widest possible diversity of behaviors and attitudes rather than forcing as many individuals as possible to adjust to supposedly common societal standards are the best policies. Subsidiary policies would favor collective action programs instead of those that single out specific individuals, and voluntary programs instead of compulsory ones. However, some critics of nonintervention suggest that such nonintervention is defeatist. Thus, rather than adopt a do-no-harm stance, juvenile justice system officials should be more concerned with doing good with their various approaches and programs (Kilchling, 1995).

At the same time that some persons foster judicious nonintervention, others favor early intervention, especially for first-offenders and those who are 13 years old or younger at the time of their first police contact (Park, 2005). An Early Offender Program (EOP) was established in 1985 in Oakland County, Michigan, through the Probate Court (Howitt and Moore, 1991). The purpose of this program was to provide specialized, intensive, in-home interventions. Parents and youths would be visited in their homes by personnel working with the Probate Court. These personnel would assist the family through diverse and sometimes difficult interpersonal problems. Youths who were involved with drugs or had general chemical dependencies were assisted through community services as well as through home visits from counselors. Those youths with poor school adjustment received assistance from these counselors as well. This early in-home intervention proved quite valuable as a part of a general strategy to minimize recidivism among first-offenders. Although there was some recidivism, it was slight. Those tending to recidivate most often were previously involved with drugs and had numerous adjustment problems in their schools.

The Due Process Model

The notion of due process is an integral feature of the criminal justice system. Due process is the basic constitutional right to a fair trial, to have an opportunity to be heard, to be aware of matters that are pending, to a presumption of innocence until guilt is established beyond a reasonable doubt, to make an informed choice whether to acquiesce or contest, and to provide the reasons for such a choice before a judicial official (Brantingham and Brantingham, 2004). An important aspect of due process is that police officers must have probable cause to justify their arrests of suspected criminals. Therefore, one's constitutional rights are given considerable weight in comparison with any incriminating evidence obtained by police or others (Abatiello, 2005).

Intake officers who rely heavily on the **due process model** in their dealings with juveniles are concerned that the juveniles' rights are fully protected at every stage of juvenile justice processing (Toth, 2005). Therefore, these officers would pay particular attention to how evidence was gathered by police against certain juveniles, and whether the juvenile's constitutional rights were protected and police officers advised the juvenile of the right to counsel at the time of the arrest and/or subsequent interrogation. The higher priority given to due process in recent years is considered by some researchers to be a significant juvenile justice reform (Rehling, 2005). An intake officer's emphasis of due process requirements in juvenile offender processing stems, in part, from several important U.S. Supreme Court decisions during the 1960s and 1970s, although professional associations and other interests have strongly advocated a concern for greater protection of juvenile rights in recent years (Jordan and Freiburger, 2005).

Because of the interest certain intake officers might take in one's right to due process, some intake hearings may be more formally conducted than others. Legal variables, such as present offense, numbers of charges, and prior petitions, would be given greater weight in the context of due process. Many offender dispositions seem to be affected by nonlegal variables as well, including the youth's attitude, grades in school, race/ethnicity, and school status (Eitle, Stolzenberg, and D'Alessio, 2005). While mildly related to dispositions, gender, race, and social class are only moderately related to offender dispositions.

Extralegal variables include race ethnicity, gender, family solidarity, and socioeconomic status. Studies of juvenile court dispositions in different jurisdictions such as Utah and Pennsylvania reveal that minority offenders are dealt with more severely than white offenders. In Utah, it has been found that minority youths are more likely than white youths to be placed in custodial institutions or disposed to longer periods of probation (Jenson et al., 1995). In Pennsylvania, 4,683 official juvenile case records were examined (DeJong and Jackson, 1998). Black, white, and Hispanic youths were compared according to the severity of their dispositions following delinquency adjudications. Black youths tended to receive harsher dispositions compared with white or Hispanic youths. Furthermore, youths from single-parent families tended to be more harshly treated compared with other juvenile offenders, controlling for prior record and the nature of the present offense. Besides being treated differently compared with white offenders, black juveniles have been subjected to greater detrimental labeling by the juvenile justice system over time (Adams, Johnson, and Evans, 1998). Differential treatment according to one's gender has also occurred in more than a few jurisdictions (Lemmon, Austin, and Feldberg, 2005). Ideally, juvenile justice decision making should be free of the influence of these and other extralegal variables, according to the due process model.

The Just-Deserts/Justice Model

There is a strong rehabilitative orientation prevalent throughout the juvenile justice system, where the emphasis is on serving the best interests of offending youths and the delivery of individualized services to them on the basis of their needs. *Parens patriae* explains much of the origin of this emphasis in the United States. However, the changing nature of juvenile offending during the last several decades and a gradual transformation of public sentiment toward more punitive measures have prompted certain juvenile justice reforms that are aimed at holding youths increasingly accountable for their actions and punishing them accordingly (Rappaport, 2003).

The **just deserts/justice model** is punishment-centered and seemingly revenge-oriented, where the state's interest is to ensure that juveniles are punished in relation to the seriousness of the offenses they have committed. Furthermore, those who commit identical offenses should be punished identically. This introduces the element of fairness into the punishment prescribed. The usefulness of this get-tough approach in disposing of various juvenile cases is controversial and has both proponents and opponents (Henham, 2004). It is significant that such an approach represents a major shift of emphasis away from juvenile offenders and their individualized needs and more toward the nature and seriousness of their actions. Just deserts as an orientation has frequently been combined with the justice model or orientation. The justice orientation is the idea that punishments should be gauged to fit the seriousness of offenses committed. Therefore, juveniles who commit more serious acts should receive harsher punishments, treatments, or sentences than those juveniles who commit less serious acts. Besides promoting punishment in proportion to offending behavior, the justice model includes certain victim considerations, such as provisions for restitution or victim compensation by offending juveniles.

The Crime Control Model

The **crime control model** theorizes that one of the best ways of controlling juvenile delinquency is to incapacitate juvenile offenders, either through some secure incarceration or through an intensive supervision program operated by a community-based agency or organization (Eschholz, Mallard, and Flynn, 2004). Perhaps **consent decrees** may include provisions for the electronic monitoring of certain juvenile offenders in selected jurisdictions. These juveniles might be required to wear plastic bracelets or anklets that are devised to emit electronic signals and notify juvenile probation officers of an offender's whereabouts. Or juvenile offenders may be incarcerated in secure facilities for short- or long-term periods, depending on the seriousness of their offenses.

The crime control perspective causes intake officers to move certain chronic, persistent, and/or dangerous juvenile offenders further into the juvenile justice system. If they believe certain juveniles pose serious risks to others or are considered dangerous, these intake officers might decide that juveniles should be held in secure confinement pending a subsequent detention hearing. If juveniles who are chronic or persistent offenders are incapacitated, they cannot reoffend. Treatment and rehabilitation are subordinate to simple control and incapacitation. Intake officers who favor the crime control view have few illusions that the system can change certain juvenile offenders. Rather, the best course of action for them is secure incarceration for lengthy periods, considering the availability of space in existing juvenile secure confinement facilities. In this way, they are directly prevented from reoffending, since they are totally incapacitated. The cost-effectiveness of such incarceration of the most chronic and persistent juvenile offenders in relation to the monies lost resulting from thefts, burglaries, robberies, and other property crimes is difficult to calculate. Incarceration is costly, and immense overcrowding in existing juvenile secure confinement facilities already plagues most jurisdictions.

An alternative to incarceration for juveniles is to focus on those most susceptible to being influenced by the potential for incarceration if they continue to reoffend. More than a few intervention programs have emphasized the adverse implications for juveniles, such as incarceration, if they continue their delinquent behavior. Stressed is the unpleasantness of prison settings. Programs, such as Scared Straight, are intended to scare some juveniles into becoming more law-abiding. For instance, selected juvenile delinquents are brought to a prison where they are confronted by several inmates. The inmates talk about what it is like to be locked up and subjected to abuse from other inmates. The intent of programs such as this is to frighten juveniles so much with what it might be like to be incarcerated that they will not be inclined to reoffend in the future.

Crime control is also achieved to a degree through the establishment of after-school programs for youths considered at risk of becoming delinquent. It has been found that juveniles, particularly those who are unsupervised during after-school hours, are more inclined to commit delinquent acts compared with supervised youths. Thus, one method of crime control is to focus on those times when youths have the greatest opportunities to offend. Although unsupervised youths are more likely to commit delinquent acts at any time, their frequency of offending escalates especially during after-school hours (Gottfredson, Gottfredson, and Weisman, 2001:61–62). Sports events and other types of after-school activities that cause such youths to become more involved with other school peers are considered helpful at reducing the frequency of delinquency. However, other factors, such as urban ecological features (nearby malls, high schools, high unemployment areas), must be considered when devising particular types of after-school interventions.

DELINQUENCY PREVENTION PROGRAMS AND COMMUNITY INTERVENTIONS

Since the 1980s much has been done to establish delinquency prevention programs in various communities and to involve both citizens and the police in joint efforts to combat juvenile crime (Schaffner, 2005). Because of the great diversity of offending among juveniles, it has been necessary to devise specific types of programs to target certain juvenile offender populations. For instance, a significant amount of youth violence occurs in school settings. As a result, considerable resources have been allocated to address the problem of school violence and reduce its incidence (Patchin and Hinduja, 2005). At the same time that school violence is targeted for reduction, certain programs seek to heighten the accountability of offenders who are most prominently involved in school violence (Gerler, 2004). Programs that implement accountability principles include school-based probation, the Project Safe Neighborhoods program, and the Positive Adolescent Choices Training program, which provides skills training for high-risk youths between the ages of 12 and 16 (Decker, 2005).

Some programs are aimed at youthful sex offenders. Sex offender services and counseling are provided in various communities to assist those youths with these specific problems (Berenson and Underwood, 2001). Other programs target youths who engage in hate crimes (Steinberg, Brooks, and Remtulla, 2003). Such programs attempt to educate youths about the risks of gang membership as well as some of the personal and social reasons youths seek out gangs initially (Dahlgren, 2005). Even youths who are presently incarcerated in secure facilities are considered potential subjects for intervention programs. Therefore, various forms of assistance and services are made available to youthful inmates in juvenile industrial schools for their rehabilitation and reintegration.

The State of Washington has adopted a "best practices" approach in an effort to identify the most successful interventions that might be useful in reducing juvenile delinquency. The Washington State Legislature passed the Community Juvenile Accountability Act in 1997, which is designed to distribute resources and ensure that local governments are supported in their efforts to implement empirically validated programs. The goals of the Act are to demonstrate reductions in recidivism and crime rates of juvenile offenders in juvenile courts. The juvenile courts are required to (1) determine the level of risk for reoffending posed by juvenile offenders so that the courts may target more intensive efforts at higher-risk youth and not use scarce resources for lower-risk youth; (2) identify the targets of intervention to guide the rehabilitative effort; (3) develop a case management plan focused on intervention strategies that are linked to reductions in future criminal behavior by reducing risk factors and strengthening protective and competency factors; (4) identify and implement intervention strategies and programs with demonstrated outcomes in reducing juvenile crime; (5) monitor the youth's progress in reducing risk factors and increasing protective factors to know whether the case management strategy is effective; (6) reduce paperwork through the use of computerized assessment and monitoring software; and (7) provide juvenile court management with information on the progress made to reduce risk factors and increase protective factors by court programs and contracted service providers (Van Dieten, 2002:41). Washington officials believe that there are complex challenges and obstacles that frustrate their efforts to fulfill these objectives. Nevertheless, they believe that attempting to use those interventions with some demonstrated degrees of success will result in the wisest allocation of scarce juvenile justice resources for the state.

Many persons believe that effective intervention programs designed to prevent delinquent conduct should be started early in a youth's life, probably through school programs (Barnes, 2005; Crawley et al., 2005). School systems are logical conduits through which intervention programs can be channeled. A wide range of ages is targeted by various intervention programs. Some of these programs are described below.

The Weed and Seed Program.   The **Weed and Seed** Program is a federal initiative implemented in 1994 by the U.S. Department of Justice (Justice Research and Statistics Association, 2005). Also known as Operation Weed and Seed, the program is intended to prevent, control, and reduce violent crime, drug abuse, and gang activity in targeted high-crime neighborhoods throughout the United States. A two-pronged approach is used. Law enforcement agencies and prosecutors interact to weed out criminals who are leaders in violent crime and drug trafficking/abuse, and these agencies attempt to prevent criminals from returning to their targeted areas or neighborhoods. The seeding portion consists of bringing human services to these neighborhoods. Human services activities include prevention, intervention, treatment, and neighborhood revitalization (Barnes, 2005). A close interaction between community residents, prosecutors, and the police is sought in an effort to revitalize communities and promote public safety.

The Weed and Seed Program in action has been quite successful in various jurisdictions where it has been implemented. For instance, in Bridgeport, Connecticut, violent crime and drug trafficking were rampant during the early to mid-1990s. The weeding consisted of investigating and prosecuting over 100 members of the Latin Kings gang, one of the most violent drug gangs operating in the area. Twelve of the gang's leaders were convicted and sentenced to terms of life without the possibility of parole. The seeding process consisted of implementing truancy intervention, mentoring programs in the schools and communities, and a variety of after-school and weekend athletics programs for youths (U.S. Department of Justice, 2003).

The Perry Preschool Program.   The Perry Preschool Program provides high-level early childhood education to disadvantaged children in order to improve their later school life and performance. This intervention combats childhood poverty and school failure by promoting young children's intellectual, social, and physical development. By increasing academic success, the Perry Preschool Program is also able to improve employment opportunities and wages, as well as decrease crime, teenage pregnancy, and welfare use. School staff view children, ages 3 and 4, as active, self-initiated learners. Small classrooms of 20 children are conducted over a two-year period, 2.5 hours per day, five days per week, for seven months a year. The program consists of ongoing mentoring and sensitivity to the noneducational needs of disadvantaged children and their families, including providing meals and recommending other social service agencies. Program outcomes have been less delinquency, including less contact with the juvenile justice system, fewer arrests at age 19, and less involvement in serious fights, gang fights, causing injuries, and police contact. Also observed have been less antisocial behavior and misconduct during elementary school, higher academic achievement, fewer school dropouts, and greater economic independence (Center for the Study and Prevention of Violence, 2002).

The FAST Track Program.   The FAST Track Program is both a rural and an urban intervention for both boys and girls of varying ethnicities. It is a long-term, comprehensive program that is designed to prevent chronic and severe conduct problems for high-risk children. It originates from the view that antisocial behavior stems from multiple factors, including the school, home, and individual (McGee and Baker, 2002). FAST Track's goals are to increase communication and bonds between these three domains, improve children's social, cognitive, and problem-solving skills, improve peer relations, and ultimately decrease disruptive behavior at home and at school. FAST Track targets grades 1 through 6, but it is most intense during the first grade. It includes parent training, biweekly home visits to reinforce parenting skills, social skills training for involved youths, academic tutoring three times a week, and a curriculum is implemented that improves one's awareness skills, self-control, problem-solving skills, a positive peer climate, and teachers' classroom management skills. Program results have included better teacher–parent relations; improved interactions between parents and their children; better overall ratings by observers of a youth's classroom behavior; more appropriate discipline techniques; more maternal involvement in school activities; and greater liking of student peers by FAST Track students (Center for the Study and Prevention of Violence, 2002).

G.R.E.A.T. (Gang Resistance Education and Training).   The G.R.E.A.T. Program has been implemented in Phoenix, Arizona, between community leaders and educators and funded by the Bureau of Alcohol, Tobacco, and Firearms to intervene with gangs on a nationwide basis. This program uses police officers, who visit schools and interact with students on a regular basis over a specified time period. Classroom sessions consist of eight, one-hour periods where youths can learn to overcome peer pressure relative to drug use and joining delinquent gangs. The weekly topics are diverse, including cultural sensitivity and prejudice, crime, victims and rights, drugs and neighborhoods, diverse responsibilities, goal setting, and conflict resolution and need fulfillment. This program was designed and targeted for children in after-school hours. Parental involvement is encouraged, and police organizations sponsor summer activities to give local youths interesting alternative projects. Evidence suggests that this program is having significant results, in that participating students are acquiring more prosocial attitudes compared with non-G.R.E.A.T. students (Esbensen et al., 2001:87).

The Juvenile Mentoring Program (JUMP).   The Juvenile Mentoring Program is a federal program administered by the Office of Juvenile Justice and Delinquency Prevention. The three principal goals of this program are to (1) reduce juvenile delinquency and gang participation by at-risk youth; (2) improve academic performance of at-risk youth; and (3) reduce the school dropout rate for at-risk youth (Olivero, 2005). Mentoring is a one-on-one relation between a pair of unrelated individuals, one adult and one juvenile, which takes place on a regular basis over an extended period of time. It is almost always characterized by a special bond of mutual commitment and an emotional character of respect, loyalty, and identification. JUMP is designed to reduce juvenile delinquency and gang participation, improve academic performance, and reduce school dropout rates. To achieve these purposes, JUMP brings together caring, responsible adults and at-risk young people in need of positive role models. Mentors are college students, senior citizens, federal employees, businessmen, law enforcement and fire department personnel, and other interested private citizens.

Those treated range in age from 5 to 20. By 2002 JUMP was involved in attempting to keep more than 9,200 at-risk youths in 25 states in school and off the streets through one-on-one mentoring (Cain, 2002).

The CASASTART Program. The CASASTART Program targets high-risk youths, age 11–13, who are exposed to drugs and criminal activity. The program seeks to decrease individual, peer group, and family and neighborhood risk factors through case management services, after-school and summer activities, and increased police involvement. Eight core components of CASASTART include (1) community-enhanced policing/enhanced enforcement; (2) case management (13–18 families); (3) criminal/juvenile justice intervention; (4) family services, including parent programs, counseling, and organized parent–child activities; (5) after-school and summer activities for personal and social development, improving self-esteem, and studying one's cultural heritage; (6) education services, offering tutoring as well as work preparation opportunities; (7) mentoring through one-on-one relationships; and (8) incentives, both monetary and nonmonetary. CASASTART has reported lower rates of drug use among participants as well as more prosocial behavior (Center for the Study of Prevention and Violence, 2002).

Project Safe Neighborhoods. Project Safe Neighborhoods is a national initiative implemented to reduce violence attributable to firearms. It is also aimed at reducing gun violence among juveniles by deterring juveniles from gaining access to or possessing firearms. Under this initiative persons banned from possessing firearms include (1) convicted felons; (2) fugitives from justice; (3) aliens in the United States illegally; (4) mental defectives or persons committed at any time to a mental institution; (5) persons who have given up their U.S. citizenship; (6) persons dishonorably discharged from the armed forces; (7) anyone under court order to refrain from stalking, harassing, or threatening an intimate partner or other person; and (8) anyone convicted of a misdemeanor crime involving violence or threat with a deadly weapon (Project Safe Neighborhoods, 2005).

Partnerships are established between various agencies of the federal government and local law enforcement agencies, schools, and other organizations (Decker, 2005). Intelligence gathering includes crime mapping, identifying hot spots that are high-crime areas of communities, tracing, and ballistics technology. Local and regional training occurs relating to the proper use of firearms for interested persons (McDevitt, 2005). A deterrence message is delivered by different means, in order to deter local youths from possessing firearms. This initiative is aimed at gangs, who most frequently use firearms in their illegal activities (Bynum, 2005). Results thus far suggest that this initiative is having an impact on reducing the rate of firearms use among teens and particularly gangs (McGarrell, 2005).

These are only a few of the many programs operating throughout the United States involving police and interested citizens in proactive and positive roles, where they are taking an active interest in preventing delinquent conduct through interacting closely with youths. These programs will not make juvenile offenders desist from delinquent conduct, but it will make many of them aware of a positive side of police officers (Dahlgren, 2005). Furthermore, it will have the positive effect of helping police officers understand juveniles and their motives.

SUMMARY

Criminologists and criminal justicians are interested in explaining why people commit crime and delinquency. If these behaviors can be explained, then potentially useful interventions can be established to counter the variables that contribute to such conduct and minimize or prevent it. Establishing cause–effect relations between delinquency and different factors that seem associated with it is difficult. Most social scientists theorize about delinquency and approach it from a variety of frames of reference. Theories are explanatory and predictive tools. A formal definition of theory is an integrated body of assumptions, propositions, and definitions that are interrelated in such a way so as to explain and predict relationships between two or more variables. Assumptions and propositions are statements about the real world that have varying degrees of validity. Definitions consist of how different phenomena are conceptualized and measured for purposes of social research. Through social research, evidence is accumulated that suggests ways that different kinds of delinquency can be approached and reduced.

Theories about crime and delinquency have been classified into several broad areas. These include classical and biological theories, psychological theories, and sociological theories. Other theoretical classifications have been introduced, although these often represent blends of various existing theoretical perspectives. Classical theories assume that persons have free will to choose between good and evil, and that they weigh the advantages and disadvantages of committing crime to achieve their various goals. Classical theories contain possible biological elements, since persons were believed to commit crimes because of greed or personal needs. Whether these personal needs were in part biologically based was never articulated. Biological theories are rooted in the belief that a primary cause of delinquency and crime is one's biological makeup and genetic structure. Determinism is often used as an explanation for why delinquency and criminal acts are committed. Persons are predisposed to commit these acts because of their biological makeup. Determinism rejects free will and rational choice in whether one conforms to or deviates from society's rules. Hedonism, espoused as a major cause of deviant behavior by Jeremy Bentham, was the biologically based view that persons pursued pleasure and avoided pain. Criminal acts produced considerable pleasure for some persons, and thus they were compelled toward these acts in the quest to derive satisfaction from their commission.

Principal biological theories include biological determinism, where it was believed that human beings inherited physical traits from their ancestors. Some of these traits were related to criminal conduct, and thus there was a biological propensity to engage in such conduct that originated through heredity. Giving in to one's animal origins, some people would be destined to engage in criminal behavior without the will to resist. Early theorists such as Cesare Lombroso espoused doctrines that endorsed the profound influence of biochemical and genetic factors as determinants of criminal and delinquent behaviors. Some biological determinists attempted to link specific physical features with particular criminal activities, and thus different theories were spawned concerning the relation between different body types and crime. The work of William Sheldon led to the identification of ectomorphs, endomorphs, and mesomorphs as distinctive types of persons inclined to commit particular crimes. Such explanations of criminal behavior were largely discounted in later years.

Another biological theory is *XYY* theory, which suggests that particular chromosomatic patterns are responsible for criminal propensities and aggressive antisocial behavior. An extra male or *Y* chromosome sometimes occurs in an *XYY* configuration to create abnormally aggressive persons. The fact that some notorious criminals have had the *XYY* chromosomatic pattern merely served to underscore the importance of this aggressive chromosome and its influence on criminal conduct. However, studies of *XYY* chromosomatic patterns in criminal and noncriminal populations have not been impressive. There does not appear to be a greater representation of the *XYY* chromosomatic pattern among criminals compared with noncriminals. Thus, the predictive utility of such an explanation is questionable. Nevertheless, interest in biochemical explanations of criminal and delinquent conduct continue, largely in the work of sociobiologists. These persons continue to pursue possible relationships between genetics and social and/or psychological behaviors.

Psychological theories stress the importance of cognitive development in acquiring criminal and delinquent characteristics. One psychological theory is psychoanalytic theory suggested by Sigmund Freud. Freud identified several important personality components, including the id, ego, and superego. The id is essentially an uncontrolled dimension of one's personality, typical of newborn infants and young children who think only of themselves and instant gratification. As children grow and mature, ego and superego development occur, where the id is controlled or suppressed, and persons learn to respect others and their desires or wishes. Most persons cultivate a sense of propriety about right and wrong. Criminals and delinquents are those who have greater impulsivity and lack self-control to govern the id. Freud also identified the libido or a basic sex drive. Again, the ego and superego are mechanisms that keep the libido in check. Those who commit rape and other forms of sexual assault might be said to have low levels of libido control or less developed egos and superegos. Psychoanalytic theory has been modified and refined over the decades and is a prevalent theme in many intervention and treatment programs for contemporary criminals and delinquents.

Another psychological theory is social learning theory. A primary feature of social learning theory is the idea that different levels of learning occur at different stages in one's maturational development. Interruptions in one's cognitive development are interruptions in these social learning stages, and one result is that some youths fail to acquire high degrees of self-control and/or self-esteem. Several interventions have been devised to study cognitive development and are aimed at preventing interruptions in the stages of social learning believed to be critical in one's early formative years.

Sociological theories stress social environmental factors as they impact on one's behavior to produce criminal or delinquent conduct. One early sociological investigation occurred in Chicago, known as the concentric zone hypothesis. During the 1920s, Chicago was undergoing rapid industrialization and social change. Old downtown areas were being torn down and new housing and businesses were being constructed. These areas in transition, referred to as zones in transition or interstitial areas, were believed to have adverse effects on youths living in these areas. High delinquency rates were observed to occur in these interstitial areas compared with other areas of the city, thus lending credence to the idea that rapid social changes contribute to social disorganization, instability, and delinquency. Subsequent investigations of similar changes and improvements in other cities have failed to disclose similar patterns with any degree of consistency, however. Nevertheless, the impact of social disorganization on youths has continued to be studied.

In the 1950s Albert Cohen and others devised a theory about the subculture of delinquency. This theory posited that a delinquent subculture exists within the larger culture, complete with its own norms and status structure. This theory showed considerable promise as an explanatory tool and led to numerous experiments where delinquent subcultures were investigated. Interventions were attempted where delinquent subcultures were used to reverse the pattern of acquiring delinquent characteristics. Several theoretical offshoots of the delinquent subcultural perspective have been observed. At least one theory has evolved that highlights the strain between conventional or mainstream society and the subculture of delinquency. Different values come into conflict, and some youths have difficulty coping with this conflict, which produces strain. Thus, several strain theories have been devised to illustrate how delinquent patterns emerge and persist.

Another sociological theory is anomie. Initially suggested by Emile Durkheim, a French sociologist, and elaborated later by Robert K. Merton, anomie theory focuses on several modes of adaptation used by persons to achieve certain culturally approved goals. Modes of adaptation include conformity, where persons accept societal goals and the conventional means to achieve these goals; ritualism, where some persons reject certain societal goals but continue to use conventional means to achieve lesser or more modest goals; retreatism, where some persons reject both the culturally approved goals and the means to achieve them (e.g., homeless persons, street people, bag ladies); rebellion, where some persons replace culturally approved goals with their own objectives and use their own means to achieve these other goals; and innovation, where some persons achieve culturally approved goals but devise deviant and/or criminal means to achieve these goals. Delinquents are perceived as innovators in this anomie scenario.

Labeling theory is one of the more influential sociological theories to account for delinquent conduct. Labeling stresses the definitions people have of delinquent acts and how they come to define themselves as delinquent. It has been proposed that more than a few youths violate criminal laws at one time or another, however, many of these youths do not view these law violations as especially serious or believe that they will persist in such offending. Juvenile deviation can be classified as primary or secondary. Primary deviation is less serious, consisting of periodic pranks or acts juveniles may commit. These are often unique occurrences never to be repeated. Secondary deviation is more serious in that delinquency becomes habitual conduct and eventually reflects one's lifestyle. Youths engaged in secondary deviation are more likely to persist in their delinquent offending and progress to more serious types of criminal activity if this pattern of deviance is uninterrupted. Several policies have been implemented over the years in an effort to prevent youths from being labeled as delinquents or from engaging in repeated delinquent offending.

Another popular sociological theory is bonding or social control theory, which suggests that youths who bond successfully with school authorities and teachers, religious leaders, and family members will be less likely to engage in delinquent activities. However, some youths fail to bond successfully with significant others, and they become more susceptible to joining gangs and deviant groups with their own delinquent subcultures. Several other sociological theories have been posited, including containment theory, neutralization theory, differential association theory, and cultural transmission theory. Each of these theories focus on social forces that impact one's decision making and individual choices and social interactions at critical points in one's development.

Evaluating theories of delinquency is often based on the predictive utility of particular theoretical schemes and the frequency with which any particular theory is used in prevention programs or delinquency intervention activities. Particular explanations of delinquency have variable importance in terms of the amount of recidivism that is actually reduced resulting from a theory's application. However, many youths simply mature and grow out of their delinquency behaviors naturally. Therefore, it is difficult to determine when a particular theory is working or if normal maturational circumstances produce subsequent law-abiding behaviors as youths move into their adult years.

Several models for dealing with juvenile offenders have been identified. These models include rehabilitation, the treatment or medical model, the noninterventionist model, the due process model, the just deserts or justice model, and the crime control model. Each of these models reflects one's professional orientation toward delinquents as well as the particular strategies one adopts for helping them. Most personnel and agencies working with juveniles have a strong rehabilitative orientation geared toward providing juveniles with services that meet their needs and enable them to cope more successfully in their communities. The medical model identifies delinquency like a disease to be treated. For juveniles with alcohol or chemical dependencies, this model appears useful. Noninterventionist strategies suggest doing little or nothing with first-time offenders, since it is believed that any type of contact with the juvenile justice system will lead to adverse labeling. The due process, just deserts, and justice models emphasize one's legal rights and equal protection under the law. There is a strong legal emphasis underlying such approaches. The crime control model stresses close supervision of those offenders most likely to reoffend, or incarceration in a secure facility. This is not an especially popular strategy, since alternatives to incarceration are believed to be more conducive to one's rehabilitation and eventual societal reintegration.

Several delinquency prevention programs were presented. These are often in the form of community interventions designed to bring about changes in one's life. Targeted for interventions are at-risk youths, those with learning disabilities, persons with antisocial personalities, persons with drug or alcohol dependencies, or those who require more personalized guidance and supervision. Each year new interventions are proposed and some of the older intervention programs are abandoned or used less frequently. Usually, a particular theory or combination of theories of delinquency underlie these intervention programs to one degree or another.

QUESTIONS FOR REVIEW

1. What is meant by theory? What are some important components of theory? What are theories designed to do?
2. What is meant by biological determinism? How does biological determinism conflict with the classical school of criminology? Which theories are associated with determinism?
3. What are the major components of psychoanalytic theory? Describe the importance of one's formative years to psychoanalytic theory. In what respect is one's childhood regarded as one's "formative years"?

4. How does social learning theory differ from psychoanalytic theory?

5. How is cultural transmission theory related to the concentric zone hypothesis?

6. What is the role of socioeconomic status in juvenile delinquency? Who are at-risk youths? What are their characteristics?

7. What is meant by a delinquent subculture? How can we use information about a delinquent subculture to change delinquent behaviors in various communities?

8. What are some similarities and differences between Merton's theory of anomie and strain theory? In the theory of anomie, what mode of adaptation is most likely to be invoked by juvenile delinquents? What other modes of adaptation have been identified?

9. How are different theories of delinquent conduct evaluated? Which types of evaluation seem most useful?

10. What are four delinquency intervention programs? What is their relative successfulness in reducing delinquency?

INTERNET CONNECTIONS

Center for Policy Analysis
http://www.acenet.edu/AM/Template.cfm?Section=CPA

HandsNet
http://www.handsnet.org/

Human Rights and the Drug War
http://www.hr95.org/

Juvenile Justice Center
http://www.aba.net/crimjust/juvjus/home.html

Justice Policy Institute
http://www.justicepolicy.org/

Marijuana Policy Project
http://www.mpp.org/

National Center for Youth Law
http://www.youthlaw.org/

Chapter Outline

Key Terms

adjudication hearing
adjudication
adjudicatory hearing
adversarial proceedings
aftercare

aftercare
aggravating circumstances
arraignment
arrest
bail bond

bail
bench trials
beyond a reasonable doubt
booking
conditional dispositions

convictions
corrections
court reporters
courts of record
criminal informations
criminal justice process
criminal justice system
custodial dispositions
defendants
dispose
dispositions
exculpatory evidence
grand juries
hard time
inculpatory evidence
indictments
informations
initial appearance
intake hearings
intake officer
intake screenings

intake
intermediate punishments
jail removal initiative
jails
jury trials
jury
law enforcement officers
lock-ups
mistrial
mitigating circumstances
no bills
no true bills
nominal dispositions
nonsecure confinement
nonsecure custody
parole board
parole
petit juries
petitions
plea bargaining
plea bargains

police discretion
preliminary examination
preliminary hearing
preponderance of the evidence
presentments
pretrial detention
preventive detention
prisons
probable cause
probation
referrals
released on own recognizance
  (ROR)
restorative justice
screening
secure confinement
secure custody
sentencing hearing
standard of proof
taken into custody
true bills

Chapter Objectives

As the result of reading this chapter, you will accomplish the following objectives:

1. Understand the criminal justice system and how juvenile offenders are initially processed when taken into custody.
2. Understand the intake process for screening juveniles.
3. Learn about different prosecutorial options for pursuing cases against juveniles.
4. Acquire an understanding of the different types of juvenile court dispositions, including nominal, conditional, and custodial sanctions that may be applied.

• *Kerry R., 12, was babysitting a 4-year-old male child for a family in Fargo, North Dakota, in January 2005. She invited her friend, Becky R., 13, over for a few hours. The girls watched television and got bored. Becky R. suggested that they should "explore" the house. They prowled through the family's bedroom drawers, closets, and bathroom medicine cabinets and found several items of jewelry and some Valium. Becky R. gave Kerry R. several Valium pills and they washed them down with some vodka they had found in the family's liquor cabinet. At some point, the 4-year-old boy awakened and startled them. In anger, the two girls sodomized the boy with their fingers and some kitchen utensils. When the parents returned home, they found their son asleep in his bed. By that time, Becky R. had left, and Kerry R. was paid for her babysitting services. The next morning, the little boy's mother saw the boy's bed sheets, which were covered with blood. The boy had considerable rectal bleeding and was rushed to the emergency room where it was determined that he was probably sodomized by an object. The police took Kerry R. into custody where she subsequently admitted what she had done. Becky R.*

was also taken into custody, based on Kerry R.'s account. Both youths were turned over to juvenile authorities to decide what should happen to them. ["Charges Pending Against Female Teen Accused of Sodomizing 4-Year-Old," March 21, 2005.]

• *In Northumberland County, Pennsylvania, John F., a 15-year-old, was attending Shikellamy High School. But at some point, John F. became bored with school and decided to cut his classes. Joining some friends, John F. began to "hang out" with them at various places, usually abandoned buildings or unoccupied homes. His friends had some marijuana, and before too long, John F. was a full-fledged marijuana user. It wasn't long after that that he was introduced to cocaine and heroin by other friends who ran with the group. Together with alcohol and drugs, John F. managed to remain in a hazy daze, missing at least three months of school. Eventually he became involved with some of the other boys in theft and other crimes. He stole a car. He sold drugs. He would use his money from these sales to pay for more drugs and alcohol. Although John F. was apprehended by police on several occasions for being drunk and disorderly or for theft, the juvenile court would impose either nominal or conditional sanctions on him, such as verbal warnings or probation. None of these actions were effective at deterring him from further delinquency. On the most recent occasion in Fall 2003, John F. was caught by police again for a crime and eventually appeared before the same juvenile court judge. In frustration, the judge ordered John F. placed in CLANCY, an alternative out-of-home placement facility for troubled teens who are repeatedly in trouble with the law. CLANCY is an acronym for Coordinated Learning Alternatives for Northumberland County. Subsequently after 11 months of classes, counseling, and community service, John F. is now 17 and ready to return to his high school. John F. says, "I learned not to get in trouble because it doesn't pay. You can't get away with nothing."* [*Source:* Adapted from John Finnerty and the Center on Juvenile and Criminal Justice, "Program Gives Troubled Teens a Last Chance," January 19, 2005.]

• *On December 23, 2004, four boys ages 10, 13, 13, and 14 broke into Coconino High School in Flagstaff, Arizona. According to police reports, 16 classrooms were vandalized, including the gym and cafeteria. Rooms were ransacked, computer monitors were broken or destroyed, and animals in biology labs were killed, including a 15-year-old frog. Luckily for Coconino High School and the community, two of the boys were seen running from the school by police officers who happened to be driving by. One of the boys was chased down and soon the other boys were taken into custody. Subsequently the boys were turned over to Coconino County Juvenile Court Services. The Coconino County Attorney's Office charged all four boys with felony counts of burglary and aggravated criminal damage. The next step, according to Duane Shimpach, director of Coconino County Juvenile Court Services, is to make an assessment of each boy and make a recommendation to the juvenile court judge for a program for each individual. These assessments won't necessarily be the same for each boy, according to Shimpach. This is because each boy has individual needs different from the others. The possible alternatives include individual and/or family counseling, substance abuse treatment, if indicated, probation, restitution, community service, and even incarceration. Programs are based on a sliding-fee scale ability to pay. Much of what is done to youths in these situations involves education. Ideally, judges emphasize to youths the consequences of their actions, not only for themselves, but for others and the community at large. They need to be taught the consequences for delinquent or incorrigible behavior. The parents are obligated for some of the financial responsibility. Arizona caps parental financial responsibility for the acts of their juveniles at $10,000 per incident. In this case, damages were estimated to be between $30,000 and $50,000. According to Coconino County Superior Court Judge Charles Adams, an attempt is made to root out bad behavior and make the youths accountable to the law for what they've done. Juvenile justice must satisfy two factors: public protection and youth rehabilitation.* [*Source:* Adapted from Larry Hendricks and the *Arizona Daily Sun,* "Juvenile Justice: It's Not About the Punishment," January 9, 2005.]

INTRODUCTION

What should be done with 12- and 13-year-old children who sodomize a 4-year-old? What type of counseling should they receive? Should they be punished? What would be an appropriate punishment? How can juveniles be deterred from using drugs? How can school authorities recognize and deal with substance abuse among students? When juveniles are apprehended by police for stealing to support their drug use, what sort of treatment should they receive? How should they be punished? How should 10-, 13-, and 14-year-old felons be treated or punished for burglary, larceny, and aggravated criminal damage? Should their parents be held accountable? How should the juvenile justice system deal with these and other types of juvenile offenders?

This chapter is a general overview of the juvenile justice system. It is intended to provide a broad picture of the different components of juvenile justice. Later chapters will focus on each of these components in greater detail. The juvenile justice system consists of all of the processes involved whenever juveniles come into contact with law enforcement in some way, either through direct encounters with juveniles on the street, referrals from schools, neighbors, or parents, or any other means. Depending on one's offense seriousness, some juveniles may be treated as adults for purposes of a criminal prosecution. Although these situations involve about 1 percent of all juveniles who come into contact with the juvenile justice system annually, such treatment as adults means that the criminal justice system will become involved in their processing and subsequent case outcomes.

The first part of this chapter is a brief overview of all important stages of the criminal justice system. Just like the juvenile justice system, the criminal justice system consists of law enforcement, prosecution and the courts, and corrections. Criminal laws are passed by Congress and state legislative bodies. Different law enforcement agencies have the responsibility of ensuring that these laws are obeyed. Violations of criminal laws are investigated, usually by the police. Whenever crimes are detected or reported, investigations are undertaken to apprehend suspects. Persons believed responsible for committing crimes are arrested, booked, and are considered for bail in an initial appearance before a magistrate or other comparable official. Each of these stages of arrest, booking, and bail consideration are described. In many jurisdictions, persons are released on their own recognizance, where bail is not required. In more serious cases, bail may be high or it may be denied. Some more dangerous persons are held in pretrial detention until their case can be heard. Persons accused of crimes become defendants who are subsequently entitled to a preliminary hearing or are indicted by grand juries. The exclusive purpose of these different proceedings is to determine probable cause that a crime was committed and that one or more persons named as defendants committed the crime.

Where probable cause is established, either through a preliminary hearing or grand jury action, an arraignment is held later where a listing of charges is provided, a plea is entered, and a trial date is determined. Trials are either bench trials or jury trials. Bench trials are conducted exclusively by judges who determine one's guilt or innocence on the basis of the evidence presented. Jury trials are provided defendants who face substantial loss of liberty if convicted. During trials, both inculpatory and exculpatory evidence are presented to show one's guilt or innocence. Juries deliberate and decide the case. When juries find a defendant guilty of a crime, a sentencing hearing is conducted and a sentence is imposed. The convicted offender will either be placed on probation or incarcerated in a jail or prison. In many cases, persons sentenced to prison are subsequently paroled and supervised conditionally for a period of time. Those sentenced to probation, and even those who eventually are paroled, are supervised by probation and parole officers in their communities. Community-based corrections include varying levels of supervision, as well as various conditions, such as restitution, community service, electronic monitoring, day reporting, or home confinement. At virtually any stage of a criminal proceeding, defendants may plea bargain with prosecutors and avoid criminal trials by entering guilty pleas in exchange for sentencing leniency. In fact, plea bargaining accounts for over 90 percent of all criminal convictions. Agreements between defense counsel, defendants, prosecutors, and judges are normally required in such plea-bargained scenarios. These general steps in offender processing are described.

The next section of this chapter examines the juvenile justice system. There are numerous parallels between the criminal and juvenile justice systems. However, a somewhat different language applies when most juvenile offenders are processed. Usually juveniles are taken into custody rather than arrested. Compared with adult offenders, a juvenile's detention in a jail is relatively brief. Often, social services or welfare agencies supervise juveniles whose cases will eventually be heard before a juvenile court judge. Like their adult counterparts, some more dangerous juveniles may be held in pretrial detention. Their cases may be plea bargained in an effort to avoid a lengthy juvenile proceeding. Most juveniles who progress further into the juvenile justice system must proceed through intake, which is an informal proceeding normally conducted by a juvenile probation officer or intake officer. Intake is a screening mechanism where important decisions are made whether to move certain juveniles further into the juvenile justice system.

For those juveniles who are moved further into the system, prosecutors make decisions about which cases to pursue. Often these decisions are preceded by petitions from different parties requesting a formal juvenile court proceeding. When juveniles appear before a juvenile court judge, they face an adjudicatory proceeding and have their cases adjudicated. Juvenile court judges do not find them "guilty" in the criminal court sense, but rather, that the facts alleging their law violations are supported by the evidence presented. Juveniles are not sentenced. Rather, they are disposed. Juvenile court judges have a more limited range of punishment options compared with criminal court judges. Juvenile court judges may impose nominal, conditional, or custodial dispositions. Nominal dispositions are the equivalent of verbal warnings and symbolic wrist slaps. Conditional dispositions usually involve probation, which is the most frequently used punishment. Custodial dispositions, usually reserved for only the most chronic and serious juvenile offenders, involve placements in secure or nonsecure facilities. These procedures are defined and described.

The juvenile justice system has similar correctional provisions for their youthful offenders. A broad array of community-based punishments exists, including standard probation, intensive supervised probation, home confinement, electronic monitoring, community service, restitution, day reporting, various forms of aftercare, restorative justice, and several behavioral conditions, such as attending school and avoiding gang members or unsavory persons with prior delinquency histories. Both juvenile probationers and juvenile parolees are subject to supervision within their communities under different departments. These departments are usually established at the county level, although large cities have their own juvenile supervisory services and programs. Many juvenile corrections agencies are regulated by the state, with uniform provisions applying to all county or city juvenile corrections jurisdictions. A general description of these supervisory agencies and provisions is provided.

THE CRIMINAL JUSTICE SYSTEM

The **criminal justice system** or **criminal justice process** is an interrelated set of agencies and organizations designed to control criminal behavior, to detect crime, and to apprehend, process, prosecute, punish, or rehabilitate criminal offenders. Figure 4.1 is a diagram of the criminal justice system.

Figure 4.1 describes the criminal justice systems. Cases that fall within the jurisdiction of the juvenile justice system are diverted to it following arrests. Sending a case to juvenile court occurs either because of arrests by police officers or through referrals from various community agencies or organizations. Some cases that originate in juvenile courts may eventually be transferred to the jurisdiction of criminal courts (Burruss and Kempf-Leonard, 2002). Because some juveniles may be included within the jurisdiction of adult criminal courts, it is important that we should have a working familiarity with these courts and the criminal justice system. The following discussion is only a review of criminal justice system fundamentals otherwise covered extensively in introductory criminal justice courses.

The traditional elements of the criminal justice system include law enforcement agencies or law enforcement, prosecution and the courts, and **corrections,** although law-making bodies such as state legislatures and congress are sometimes included. The word *system* is misleading, in a sense, since the different criminal justice components are not as closely integrated and coordinated as a system would indicate. Some persons prefer to use process as a better way of depicting how arrested persons are treated during various phases of their processing. There is a criminal justice system and it exists as a system, although it is usually a loosely integrated one. For instance, law enforcement officers seldom ask prosecutors and the courts if they have arrested too many offenders for the system to handle. Also, prosecutors and the courts seldom ask jail and prison officials whether there is sufficient space to accommodate persons who are to be incarcerated for short or long periods. Below are descriptions of the various criminal justice system components.

Legislatures

Criminal laws originate largely as the result of legislative actions in most jurisdictions. Jurisdiction refers to the power of courts to hear cases, although we generally define a jurisdiction according to various political subdivisions, including townships, cities, counties, states, or federal districts. Thus, when criminals cross state or county lines, they leave the state or local jurisdictions where violations of the law occurred. Under certain circumstances, these jurisdictional boundaries may be crossed by pursuing authorities. At the federal level, any federal agency may enforce certain federal laws in any state, territory, or U.S. possession.

THE CRIMINAL JUSTICE SYSTEM

POLICE	COURTS			CORRECTIONS		
ENTRY INTO THE SYSTEM	PROSECUTION & PRETRIAL SERVICES	ADJUDICATION	SENTENCING & SANCTIONS	PROBATION	PRISON	PAROLE

FELONIES

MISDEMEANORS

CRIME

REPORTED & OBSERVED CRIME

UNRESOLVED OR NOT ARRESTED

INVESTIGATION

RELEASED WITHOUT PROSECUTION

ARREST

CHARGES FILED

DIVERSION BY LAW ENFORCEMENT, PROSECUTOR, OR COURT

UNSUCCESSFUL DIVERSION

OUT OF SYSTEM

INITIAL APPEARANCE

CHARGES DROPPED OR DISMISSED

PRELIMINARY HEARING

CHARGES DROPPED OR DISMISSED

BAIL OR DETENTION HEARING

REFUSAL TO INDICT

GRAND JURY

CHARGE DISMISSED

ARRAIGNMENT

INFORMATION

REDUCTION OF CHARGE

ARRAIGNMENT

CHARGES DISMISSED

INFORMATION

TRIAL

ACQUITTED

GUILTY PLEA

CONVICTED

TRIAL

ACQUITTED

GUILTY PLEA

CONVICTED

APPEAL

SENTENCING

INTERMEDIATE SANCTIONS

SENTENCING

PROBATION

CONVICTED

HABEAS CORPUS

REVOCATION

CAPITAL PUNISHMENT

PARDON & CLEMENCY

PRISON

REVOCATION

PAROLE

JAIL

REVOCATION

PROBATION

OUT OF SYSTEM

OUT OF SYSTEM

Legend:
DEFENDANT | JUDGE | LAWYER | OUT OF SYSTEM | DISTRICT ATTORNEY | CONVICT | LAW ENFORCEMENT

911

FIGURE 4.1 The Criminal Justice Systems.

The Congress of the United States passes criminal laws that are enforceable by various federal agencies, including the Federal Bureau of Investigation (FBI), Drug Enforcement Administration (DEA), and the Criminal Investigation Division (CID) of the Internal Revenue Service. State legislatures enact criminal laws that are enforced by state and local law enforcement officers. At the community level, city and county governments determine specific criminal laws, statutes, and ordinances that should be enforced, depending on the circumstances of the locality. Some local ordinances are especially geared to regulate juvenile conduct. Such ordinances include curfews, truancy laws, and incorrigibility provisions, where parents or guardians cannot control the behaviors of their children. Virtually all ordinances aimed at juveniles are status ordinances, since these ordinances are not applicable to adults. Whenever juveniles violate these ordinances or commit prohibited criminal offenses, they fall within the purview of law enforcement.

Law Enforcement

There were over 21,000 police and sheriff's departments in the United States in 2004. These law enforcement agencies employed over 1,200,000 full-time sworn officers with general **arrest** powers (Bureau of Justice Statistics, 2005). The most visible **law enforcement officers** are uniformed police officers in local and state governments. Federal officers, especially FBI agents, DEA personnel, and others may encounter juveniles who are involved in federal crimes, although most of the time their work is focused on apprehending adult offenders. Usually, federal agents who apprehend juveniles will deliver them to local authorities for processing. It is unusual for federal courts to prosecute juvenile offenders, despite the fact that juveniles may commit one or more federal crimes.

Law enforcement officers who are most likely to have direct contact with juveniles are city police and sheriff's deputies. These officers patrol city and county streets and general areas, and they may encounter juveniles acting suspiciously or in the act of committing offenses. They may respond to citizen reports of disturbances involving juveniles. In certain jurisdictions, special police forces are designated to deal with particular types of juvenile offenders.

Whenever juveniles are taken into custody by police officers, they may be taken to a local police station and questioned. **Police discretion** is very important, since officers may make on-the-spot decisions either to warn and release juveniles in their initial encounters with them on city streets or take them to a jail or police department for further questioning. Circumstances often dictate which course of action is followed. Juveniles loitering late at night near a store where a burglar alarm has been activated are likely targets for apprehension by police. The police have a right to be suspicious of these juveniles and to investigate the circumstances of their presence in the area until they are satisfied that the youths were not involved in a possible burglary. Community notification laws pertaining to sex offenses involving juveniles as perpetrators have also aroused the curiosity of police officers when they see certain youths prowling about late at night (Garfinkle, 2003).

Police discretion also influences where juveniles are taken if it is decided they should be detained. Extremely young juveniles may be taken directly to social service agencies where they can be reunited with their parents or

Taking youths into custody for alleged delinquent acts commences the juvenile justice process.

guardians. Many juveniles may not be involved in delinquent activity, but their youthful appearance may suggest to police the need for adult supervision and/or parental involvement. Many runaways may be taken to shelters where they can be fed and clothed. Many male and female juveniles appear older than they really are. They may lie to police and give them false names, addresses, and ages. Police officers have a right to detain these juveniles until their identity can be established and/or it can be learned whether they have violated any criminal laws.

Prosecution and the Courts

When criminal suspects and others are arrested by law enforcement officers, they are usually booked. **Booking** involves obtaining descriptive information from those arrested, including their names, addresses, occupations, next of kin, photographs, and fingerprints. Booking varies in formality among jurisdictions. Essentially, the booking process is a formality as well as an account or written report of the arrest or detention. Police may consult other law enforcement agencies through a computer network to determine whether those arrested have prior records. Interested agencies such as the Bureau of Justice Statistics within the U.S. Department of Justice collect this statistical information to profile those admitted to jails and prisons.

Figure 4.1 also shows other stages of processing in the criminal justice system subsequent to the arrest and booking of suspects. Note that one early discretionary action is to divert certain offenders directly to the juvenile justice system. For adult offenders, however, they will likely move forward to the **initial appearance** stage. The initial appearance of **defendants** or those charged

 **BOX 4.1**

Bonnie Farr
Chief Juvenile Probation Officer, Dougherty County Juvenile Court, Decatur, GA

Statistics:

Court Representative for the Juvenile Court of Independent Courts Association; Grant Coordinator; Deputy Clerk for the Judge of State Court

Background and Experiences

I graduated from high school in 1969. At that time I had no idea what I wanted to do. I was never crazy about school, and so I had no interest in going to college. I came from a home with two brothers and a sister. My father was an alcoholic. He worked different jobs but spent his money on liquor. My mother worked to support us. We lived in the housing projects for 6 years. My father died when I was 11 years old. After he died, we finally moved out of the projects into a house. Our family was not close, and education was not stressed. I did go to school and I was an average student.

I signed up to go to a technical school following high school graduation to take some business classes. I looked for a job all summer but couldn't find one. About a week before I was to start back to school, I was offered a job. My neighbor worked in the Clerk of Superior Courts office at the courthouse. They had an opening for a financing statement clerk. I was hired on a trial basis. If I could do the work, it would be a permanent position. I loved the job. It was very interesting. I especially loved the criminal part of it. My main job was recording financial statements, but when I got through with those, I helped out in other areas in the office. I knew that I wanted to work in this field. I worked for 3 years there. In that time, I got married and was expecting a baby. I was having complications with my pregnancy and so I had to quit work. I lost my position in the Clerk's Office but got a job in the Ordinary's Office, which was later named Probate Court when I was able to go back to work.

I did not like this work as much as the Clerk's Office. I left the Probate Court and went to work for the Judge of State Court. I was his secretary and was also appointed Deputy Clerk of the Court. I had one child at this time and he was having health problems, and so I had to quit work again. I worked at some part-time jobs with the Clerk's Office and Probate Court for a few years. I had another child during these years. I worked on a pilot project for the State of Georgia in which I entered information on court cases into a computer. I went to court to sit in on different cases. At the end of the project, the Clerk's Office adopted a new docket system, which was a part of the pilot project. I went back to work full time in 1985 for the Probate Court. Again, this was not where my main interest was. The Juvenile Court had an opening for a Probation Officer. I put in for the job and got it. I have been in the Juvenile Court for 14 years now. I have learned a lot about this job. I had been married to a youth director in church for 13 years, and so I had worked with youth and I had worked in the courts for years. This gave me considerable familiarity with the terminology and court procedures. The job qualifications called for a psychology degree, but because of my work experience, I was hired despite lacking this academic qualification.

With this job, there is always something going on. In our court, the probation officers are in charge of the court. We have court all day on Mondays and half days on Wednesdays, and we are in court for all

(continued)

cases. To me this is always interesting. You never know what will happen in court. We see a lot of crying, fighting, parents passing out, cursing, and even some comical cases. In one instance, an older boy had stolen a credit card and took a younger boy to the mall. He charged several things on the card, including a pair of shoes for the younger boy. At the hearing, the detective told the judge that she never recovered the shoes and wanted the judge to ask the boy where the shoes were. The judge asked him and he told the judge, "Right here," and pointed to his feet. He was wearing them. Needless to say, the detective made him give back the shoes. We had another case where a young girl was called to testify in the matter. The judge told her to come up and take the witness stand. She looked at him and asked, "Where do you want me to take it?"

Present Position and Activities

I am now the Chief Probation Officer for our court. I also serve as the Court Representative for the Juvenile Court of the Independent Courts Association. I work closely with the Boy's Club representatives for the programs they provide for us. I was Grant Coordinator for years. I served on the Detention Review Board at the RYDC. We attend training annually. I am probably the only Chief Probation Officer who does not have a college degree. I have worked many years to get where I am, but I do regret that I never went to college. There have been times when I was going to take psychology and criminal justice, but each time something would happen and I was unable to go. I do feel that it is important to further your education in whichever field you are interested in.

In working with the juveniles you will find that no matter what you do for some of them, they will never change. Not that they are bad, but their environment keeps them down. They have no support from anyone, and many come from families of criminals. Some kids come to court where the parents are both incarcerated. Most of the time there is no father around, and a grandparent is trying to raise the child. Also, in working with juveniles, you are the one person they

are always going to remember. Whether you make a good impression or a bad one, you will always make an impression on your child clients. In this work, you don't get a lot of pats on the back, and you may never know if you have made a difference in their lives. Some kids only need a little support from someone or someone who will listen to their side of things. Some kids like being on probation and locked up because they are getting attention from someone. Even though they went about it the wrong way, they are getting attention they never had from their families or influential others.

I had a brother and sister on probation years ago that kept getting into trouble because of problems in their home. The mother would call and tell me how bad they were and that I should do something about it, and that she wanted me to have the kids locked up. After talking with the kids by themselves, I found out that the mother was locking them in their rooms and not feeding them. She was especially cruel to the girl. She cut her hair off and made her go to school, which was very embarrassing to the child. I was finally able to get the Department of Family and Children Services to look into their home situation. They did not think that this was a case of deprivation. I found a placement for both children in a Baptist Children's Home. When they got there, they were caught eating out of the dumpsters. The workers said that they acted like they were starved. The girl did very well in the home, but her brother didn't. He was sent back home. The mother did not like the daughter being in the Children's Home because she thought that the daughter should be punished, and she thought that she was getting spoiled. Subsequently she made the girl come back home. The girl was not under any type of court order to attend the Home, and so there was nothing that I could do about this unfortunate situation. It was not long after that that the girl's father hit her in the head with a videotape. This time the Department of Family and Children's Services did remove the two children from the home. To make a long story short, these were not bad kids. They only got into trouble as their way of crying out for help.

You have to listen to what they tell you because even though we know they will often lie, they will also tell you the truth.

Advice to Students

We have hired probation officers over the years who did not care about their juvenile clients. They just wanted a job. I wish we had a perfect system and that we could have probation officers who want to be in this field and will take the necessary time to work with their youthful probationers. There is never going to be a perfect system, but if this is a field you choose to enter, you are needed. There are some probation officers who are very hard on their probationer-clients and talk down to them. I try not to handle my own probationers that way. I think that if I

talk respectfully to them, they will show respect for me. Most of the time this works. Over my years as a probation officer, I have only had a few kids that I have had to get ugly with. I will file a probation violation as fast as any other probation officer if any juvenile fails to comply with his or her court orders. I just don't think that yelling at them and telling them how bad they are will do any good. I have seen the same families coming through our court, and even if I don't remember each and every one of them, they remember me and actually act like they are glad to see me. In the end, you have to love what you are doing if you want to make a difference. You will not get rich in this type of work, but you will make a difference in the lives of some of the kids you deal with.

with crimes is before a magistrate or other court official, usually to advise defendants of the charges against them and to determine the amount of bail necessary to obtain their release. **Bail** or a **bail bond** is a surety in the form of money or property that may be posted by either a bonding company or others, including defendants themselves, to obtain their temporary release from custody and to ensure their subsequent appearance at trial.

Under the Eighth Amendment, only those entitled to bail may receive it. Bail is not an absolute right. Ordinarily, those not entitled to bail are either considered very dangerous to others or very likely to flee the jurisdiction to avoid prosecution for their crimes. Because of serious jail overcrowding problems and other considerations, bail is often waived in minor offense cases, and defendants are **released on** (their) **own recognizance (ROR).** These persons usually have ties within the community, are employed, and are not considered dangerous or likely to flee.

During the period following a defendant's initial appearance, prosecutors, representing the states' interests, must decide whether to bring formal charges against these persons. Evidence of criminal activity collected by police officers (e.g., eyewitness reports, confessions, weapons, fingerprints) is carefully examined, and consideration is given to the seriousness of the alleged criminal activity and prior record of the defendant, if any. If defendants are represented by counsel, interactions may occur between prosecutors and defense counsels where agreements are reached known as **plea bargains.** Plea bargains are preconviction agreements between defendants and the state whereby defendants enter guilty pleas to certain criminal charges in exchange for some state benefit such as sentencing leniency (Reddington, 2005). Probably over 90 percent of all criminal convictions are secured through **plea bargaining** in most U.S. jurisdictions at both the state and federal levels. In many instances, if the cases against certain defendants are weak, prosecutors may elect to drop the charges and excuse these defendants from further processing.

Depending on the circumstances, prosecutors may follow through with charges against defendants and take their cases to trial. Using this worst-case scenario (for the defendant), defendants who either do not plea bargain and plead not guilty will eventually be arraigned. An **arraignment** is a proceeding where (1) a list of specific charges is made available to defendants and their attorneys, (2) a formal plea to the charges is entered by the defendant, and (3) a trial date is established. Prior to being arraigned, however, those charged with especially serious crimes will be entitled to a **preliminary examination** or **preliminary hearing,** a proceeding where both the prosecutor and defense counsel may present some evidence against and on behalf of the defendant. Preliminary hearings establish whether **probable cause** exists. Probable cause is the determination or reasonable suspicion that a crime has been committed and the defendant likely committed it. These hearings are not trials and do not establish one's guilt or innocence. They are intended to determine probable cause, or whether sufficient evidence exists to proceed further.

The preliminary hearing is important also because it is an opportunity for judges and others to hear some of the evidence both in the defendant's favor and derogatory to the defendant. In some respects, as Figure 4.1 specifies, this is a preliminary testing of the evidence. Two types of evidence are exculpatory and inculpatory. **Exculpatory evidence** is anything that may help show the defendant's innocence. **Inculpatory evidence** is anything that may show defendant guilt. At this stage, prosecutors sometimes decide to withdraw charges against defendants. Also at this stage, the presiding magistrate may conclude that insufficient evidence exists against the defendant to proceed any further. Thus, the criminal charges either may be dropped or dismissed outright. Figure 4.1 shows this particular phase sandwiched between the initial appearance and arraignment.

Also note in Figure 4.1 that upward and downward branches of the process following the preliminary hearing include **informations.** A brief explanation of these branches is in order. First, informations, sometimes known as **criminal informations,** are formal charges against defendants brought by prosecutors acting on their own authority. Typically, informations may be brought against any defendant for minor crimes or misdemeanors. This is reflected by the lower branch stemming from preliminary hearings. However, if the crime is a felony, this follows the upper branch.

While preliminary hearings or preliminary examinations are used in most jurisdictions for an early test of the evidence against defendants for the purpose of establishing whether probable cause exists to proceed further, about half of all states and the federal government use grand juries to bring charges against defendants charged with serious offenses (Schmid, 2002). **Grand juries** are investigative bodies of citizens selected from residents of the jurisdiction. There is great variation among jurisdictions relating to the size and functions of grand juries. For example, federal grand juries consist of from 16 to 23 members and serve for 90-day or 120-day terms. Grand juries issue criminal charges against defendants known as **indictments** or **presentments.**

Indictments, also known as **true bills,** are the functional equivalent of criminal informations brought by prosecutors. Ordinarily, prosecutors present evidence to grand juries for their consideration. Defendants and their attorneys are barred from grand jury proceedings. When grand juries issue indictments, they are in effect saying, "We believe that probable cause has been established that a crime or crimes have been committed and John Doe (or the person or persons named in the indictment) probably committed the crimes." If the grand jury believes that insufficient evidence exists against defendants, they may issue **no bills** or **no true bills.** A no bill results in charges being dismissed against defendants, since probable cause that a crime was committed was not established.

The term **jury** is confusing to those unfamiliar with the criminal justice system. Because grand juries issue indictments or presentments against defendants, some persons believe immediately that those indicted must obviously be guilty of the crimes alleged, since a jury issued an indictment against them. This isn't so. Those juries charged with determining one's guilt beyond a reasonable doubt are known as **petit juries.** These petit juries, more commonly known as juries, are the citizens selected to hear evidence in trials. Thus, an important distinction exists between grand juries, who decide probable cause questions and whether further action should be taken against defendants, and petit juries, who decide the issue of guilt using the beyond a reasonable doubt standard in all criminal cases.

After a trial date is established from the point of arraignment, defendants may elect to have either **bench trials** or **jury trials,** depending on the seriousness of the crimes alleged. Bench trials are conducted exclusively by the judge who presides and determine's the defendant's guilt or innocence. Jury trials or trials by jury involve determinations of one's guilt or innocence by a jury of one's peers. These peers are selected by various methods from the community or jurisdiction where the trial occurs. All citizens charged with a crime are entitled to a jury trial as a matter of right under the U.S. Constitution, if the possible statutory incarcerative term accompanying the alleged offense is six months or longer (*Duncan v. Louisiana,* 1968). There are some exceptions to this provision, however.

Trials are adversarial proceedings where a defendant's guilt or innocence is established. Jury trials vary in size among jurisdictions. In some states, for instance, juries may consist of six jurors. Traditionally, jury size in the majority of states and in federal district courts in criminal trials is twelve jurors. In these jury trials, if jurors cannot agree on a verdict, the jury is considered deadlocked or hung, and a **mistrial** is declared. Most jurisdictions require that juries must be unanimous, regardless of their finding. However, in a few states such as Louisiana and Oregon where jury size is 12, majority verdicts of 9–3 or 10–2 are permitted (*Apodaca v. Oregon,* 1972; *Johnson v. Louisiana,* 1972).

When defendants are convicted of one or more crimes, their punishment is imposed in a **sentencing hearing.** Criminal court judges consider all circumstances and information available, and on the basis of their experience and judgment, together with statutory provisions mandated by legislatures, they impose sentences. Sentences do not necessarily involve incarceration. In many states, judges are permitted wide latitude in the sentences they impose on convicted offenders (Coyne and Entzeroth, 2001). Judges consider factors such as one's leadership role in the crime and whether physical injuries were inflicted on victims during the crime's commission. These circumstances are **aggravating circumstances** because they intensify the punishment convicted offenders receive (Bittle, 2001). Other factors are considered, including whether offenders furnished helpful information to police that enabled them to apprehend others connected with the crime. An offender's youthfulness would be considered as well. Whether offenders were mentally ill when they committed their crimes would also be important (Farr, 2000). These factors are considered **mitigating**

Many nonsecure facilities for juveniles emphasize vocational and educational training as a part of a youth's rehabilitation.

circumstances because they often result in less severe sentences imposed by judges (Ribeaud and Manzoni, 2004).

Because of serious prison and jail overcrowding problems in most jurisdictions, however, judges often impose **probation** as a punishment. Probation is a conditional nonincarcerative sentence, where the offender is under the management of probation department personnel or probation officers. Probation is most often used for first-offenders who have been convicted of minor crimes. However, evidence of its growing use in the United States annually for more serious crimes (e.g., felony probation) is well documented (Champion, 2005b). Regardless of whether convicted offenders receive probation or a sentence involving incarceration for designated terms, offenders move to the final component of the criminal justice process—corrections.

Corrections

Corrections consists of all agencies and personnel who deal with convicted offenders after court proceedings. As noted earlier, some convicted offenders may receive probation, or conditional sentences in lieu of incarceration. Other offenders may be confined in jails or prisons, again depending on the seriousness of their offenses, the jurisdiction where the conviction occurred, and the availability of jail or prison space. In 2004 there were over 2 million inmates in jails and prisons in the United States (Bureau of Justice Statistics, 2004).

Jails are short-term facilities and locally operated by city or county governments. A few jails are state-operated. Most jail functions include but are not limited to detaining those arrested for various offenses and who are awaiting trial; maintaining witnesses in protective custody pending their testimony in court; providing confinement for short-term, petty offenders serving sentences of less than 1 year; and accommodating overflow from state or federal prisons in instances where chronic prison overcrowding exists. Jails are not usually designed for long-term confinement of prisoners. They have few, if any, recreational facilities and few services.

Prisons are long-term facilities. Most prisons have recreational yards, hospitals, work programs, and a host of other facilities to accommodate inmates who are confined for lengthy periods. Prisons are usually reserved for more serious offenders who have received incarcerative sentences of one year or longer from judges. In many jurisdictions, inmates of prisons and jails may be released short of serving their full sentences. This is usually accomplished through **parole.** Parole is a conditional release from incarceration for a designated duration, usually the remainder of one's original sentence. A **parole board** determines an inmate's parole eligibility and whether early release from prison will be granted.

There are many correctional options available for judges to impose besides probation and incarceration. A vast array of **intermediate punishments** exists. Intermediate punishments are sanctions that exist somewhere between incarceration and probation on the continuum of criminal penalties. Intermediate punishments might include electronic monitoring, house arrest or home confinement, or community-based correctional alternatives such as halfway houses or intensive supervised probation or parole. Many of these options are available to juvenile as well as adult offenders.

The remainder of this chapter examines the juvenile justice system and provides an overview of how juveniles are processed by it. Later chapters provide more detailed coverage of each of these stages. We begin this discussion by identifying some important distinctions between juvenile and criminal courts.

SOME IMPORTANT DISTINCTIONS BETWEEN JUVENILE AND CRIMINAL COURTS

Some of the major differences between juvenile and criminal courts are indicated below. These generalizations are more or less valid in most jurisdictions in the United States.

1. Juvenile courts are civil proceedings exclusively designed for juveniles, whereas criminal courts are proceedings designed to try adults charged with crimes. In criminal courts, adults are targeted for criminal court actions, although some juveniles may be tried as adults in these same courts. The civil–criminal distinction is important because a civil adjudication of a juvenile court case does not result in a criminal record for the juvenile offender. In criminal courts, either a judge or jury finds a defendant guilty or not guilty. In the case of guilty verdicts, offenders are convicted and acquire criminal records. These **convictions** follow adult offenders for the rest of their lives. However, when juveniles are tried in juvenile courts, their juvenile court adjudications are sealed or expunged and generally forgotten, with exceptions, once they reach adulthood or the age of their majority.

2. Juvenile proceedings are more informal, whereas criminal proceedings are more formal. Attempts are made in many juvenile courts to avoid the formal trappings that characterize criminal proceedings. Juvenile court judges frequently address juveniles directly and casually. Formal rules of criminal procedure are not followed relating to the admissibility of evidence and testimony, and hearsay from various witnesses is considered together with hard factual information and evidence. Despite attempts by juvenile courts to minimize the formality of their proceedings, however, juvenile court procedures in recent years have become increasingly formalized. In some jurisdictions at least, it is difficult to distinguish criminal courts from juvenile courts in terms of their formality.

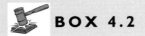

BOX 4.2

The juvenile justice system in Sierra Leone is loosely organized and has been adversely influenced by a 9-year civil war (1991–2000) that has destroyed or impaired important government structures and infrastructures. Because of this internal strife, many Sierra Leone youths have been displaced, orphaned, injured, and traumatized. Prior to the civil war, juvenile crime was not very high. During the 1990s all types of juvenile crime have increased. Much of the juvenile offending is related to the sex trade, where youths, both male and female, have turned to prostitution for survival. Theft, burglaries, and other property crimes have increased. There is little juvenile violence.

All actions in Sierra Leone concerning juveniles are based on the fundamental principle of doing what is in a child's best interest. This is consistent with the traditional view toward juveniles in the United States. The juvenile justice system is not extensive, and it is fragmented. The Ministry of Social Welfare, Gender and Children's Affairs, and the Ministry for Justice oversee different dimensions of the juvenile justice system, including making appointments of court officials and magistrates in the juvenile courts. Presently juvenile courts with magistrates exist in only three provinces and Freetown. These courts convene only on Tuesdays and Thursdays.

The Children and Young Persons Act of 1945 defined all persons under the age of 17 as being within the jurisdiction of juvenile court. Anyone who is age 17 or older is treated as an adult. Subsequently this provision was changed to be more consistent with international law, and today anyone under the age of 18 is considered a juvenile. Two further categories were established: (1) child and (2) young person. A child is anyone under the age of 14. A young person is anyone between the ages of 14 and 17. The age of criminal responsibility has been set at 10. Anyone under the age of 10 is not criminally responsible. It is believed that those age 10 or older can understand the differ-

ence between lies and truth, the criteria for criminal accountability. Children lack capacity below the age of 10 and are thus not responsible for any criminal act they may commit. Sierra Leone has the death penalty, although it is only applied to those age 18 and over. Juveniles under the age of 18 and who commit capital offenses may be given life imprisonment as a punishment. For all practical purposes, few life terms are ever imposed on juveniles. Juvenile courts do not have the jurisdiction to try homicide cases. Thus, if a 16-year-old is charged with homicide, the case is heard before the High Court in Sierra Leone. But because of poor record-keeping, children's ages are difficult to verify and determine.

Juvenile courts are presided over by a magistrate and two justices of the peace. These are attorney general appointments. Juvenile justice officials have little or no experience in juvenile matters; nevertheless, they have an interest in children's rights and furthering their interests. Furthermore, juvenile officials receive no special training to do their jobs. All juvenile proceedings are conducted in private, in order to safeguard the privacy of juveniles being adjudicated. Members of the press are also barred from juvenile proceedings. Most frequently the police act as prosecutors in bringing juvenile cases before the court and presenting these cases before magistrates. The police take a very proactive role in the prosecution of juvenile offenders. Ideally all juvenile matters are to be concluded without delay by a competent and impartial judicial body. Adjournments occur frequently, however, because many principals, including charged juveniles, fail to appear in court at their appointed times. For those children held in secure custody at the few secure facilities in the country, transportation is unreliable. The juvenile justice system lacks the resources to transport juveniles to and from court in limited numbers of vehicles. Although juvenile courts are held only on Tuesdays and Thursdays, a youth's attendance at a proceeding cannot be guaranteed at any particular time. The primary juvenile court is in Freetown, where two magistrates preside over all juvenile hearings.

Although juveniles are entitled to legal representation in court, free legal assistance is not always provided. This is because there has been a serious shortage of lawyers. In most cases, juveniles are not represented by counsel, despite the fact that most children come from poorer families or from broken homes. Only the wealthier children can afford legal representation. Since most children do not have attorneys, the court usually questions witnesses and the juveniles prosecuted. Juveniles charged with offenses are entitled to make statements in their own behalf. Parents or guardians are permitted to attend court, and magistrates may require their attendance, imposing fines on families for failure to attend. This is because it is believed that parents should bear some responsibility for their children's conduct. Furthermore, if the court imposes one or more measures, the family will likely be involved in assisting the court by ensuring the compliance of their children with these measures. In many cases, however, parents do not attend juvenile proceedings. This is because they cannot be found or have neglected or abandoned their children. Other reasons are that some parents believe that their children ought to be taught a severe lesson for violating the law. The official language of the court is English, although the court may appoint interpreters who speak Krio (a language of Sierra Leone). Also, juveniles have the right to appeal a court's decision in their behalf.

Throughout the provinces in Sierra Leone, juvenile justice is dispensed informally a great deal of the time. In most cases, victims and offenders will attempt to resolve disputes among themselves. This is because in many areas, there is simply no police presence. In some instances, corporal punishment known as "flogging" may be applied where a child has committed a crime or caused mischief. Cans or birch rods are used and are limited to 12 strokes applied to one's buttocks. Military punishments in areas controlled by militiamen may involve severe beatings as punishments for some youth.

Dispositions for juveniles found guilty of one or more offenses vary according to a youth's age. No child under age 14 shall be sentenced to imprisonment. For youths 14–17, imprisonment may be imposed in those cases where the court feels that other measures have been ineffective. But where juveniles are imprisoned, they are not permitted to associate with adult prisoners. Imprisonment involves locking up a juvenile in an adult detention center. The main adult detention center is in Freetown. Juveniles are to be separated from adults only as circumstances permit.

Deprivation of liberty for serious juveniles who have committed violent acts or are persistent offenders involve placement in either an approved school or a remand home. Approved schools were established following World War II and have aims of reforming and transforming delinquents into functioning members of society by equipping them with skill training programs—carpentry, tailoring, masonry, or some form of education. Youths sent to approved schools are usually for indeterminate periods until youths reach age 18. If a youth is age 16 when committed to an approved school, the youth must remain in the school until age 18. For children 10 years of age, they may be confined to an approved school until age 18 as well. Ideally, approved school placements are made only in those instances where the offenses by juveniles are such that adults would receive similar sentences if they committed such offenses. However, some juveniles have been placed in approved schools for 3 or more years for very minor offenses such as stealing a goat. Remand homes are essentially reform schools for delinquents, detention centers with few amenities, or treatment programs. The main remand home is located in Freetown. However, relatively few juveniles are ever placed in remand homes for lengthy periods.

Approved schools are limited. There are only two approved schools, consisting of two dormitories and an office. No space is provided for recreational activities. Because of a lack of resources, these schools cannot provide counseling, formal education, or the vocational training they were intended to provide. Fewer than 50 youths are accom-

(continued)

modated at approved schools. Remand homes are even worse. There is no recreation, and proper welfare facilities are lacking. Insufficient equipment in kitchens and other facilities make living difficult. At the Remand Home in Freetown, space is provided for up to 50 children, and some children under age 10 have been accommodated there despite policies to the contrary. These facilities are supposed to be secure, although it is easy for youths to escape from them whenever they wish. Children are locked up at night, but no toilets are provided. Thus, youths soil themselves and urinate and defecate on the floor, with cell disinfection occurring during daytime hours. Most children in the Remand Home have little or no contact with their families.

Alternative punishments not involving deprivation of liberty include (1) discharging the child or young person without making an order; (2) ordering the child or young person to be repatriated to his or her home; (3) ordering the child or young person placed in the care of a fit person or institution; (4) placement of a youth under the supervision of a probation officer; or (5) imposing a fine in conjunction with another punishment. If children are under age 14, parents will be ordered to pay fines imposed.

When children are placed under probation officer supervision, the probation officer is to see that the juvenile observes all probation conditions and help him or her find a job. In fact, most probation officers do not perform their duties effectively. This is because they lack or are not given any training in child psychology, sociology, or welfare; they are underpaid and lack incentives to do good work; and they lack transportation, such as motorcycles or motor vehicles, to visit children under their supervision. As a result, most children assigned to probation officers go unsupervised. Magistrates have few options under their present circumstances. If they allow children to return to their communities, the children go back into the same situations that brought them to the attention of authorities initially, and the process is repeated. This is the revolving-door phenomenon, and in Sierra Leone, it is very much in evidence.

One increasingly used method for dealing with juveniles is diversion, where formal judicial proceedings are circumvented. Diversion may include verbal warnings; community programs, which are limited; temporary supervision and guidance; restitution; and victim compensation. In this respect, police officers are the primary instruments through which diversion is implemented. This is largely through police cautioning or simple verbal warnings to stay out of trouble. However, the police force in Sierra Leone is fragmented and loosely organized, with vast corruption and numerous instances of misconduct.

The police of Sierra Leone are in a process of repair, restructuring, and retraining. There were approximately 10,000 officers in 2005. Some training is given to police regarding juveniles and how they ought to be treated. However, there is a great gap between what ideally should be done and what actually occurs. Widespread police corruption leads to child exploitation, where many children, especially females, are often sexually abused by police in exchange for lenient treatment on the streets in order to avoid being arrested or charged. Even at police stations, adjustments are made by police who accept sexual services from female youths age 12–20 in exchange for fines or other charges. Although it is against the law to have sexual intercourse with a child under the age of 12, it is commonly practiced since there are no minimum age limits on marriage. Most women who participate in the sex trade as prostitutes take drugs of some form and do not have access to education or health care. HIV/AIDS testing is nonexistent, since there is no medical assistance available. Therefore, it is believed there is no point in testing for the disease. Boys age 12–17 also engage in commercial sex activity, and there is a culture of silence surrounding this activity. Thus it is difficult for police to investigate thoroughly. Many children eventually come to Freetown, Sierra Leone's largest city. But not all of these children are orphaned. Many are accompanied by parents who turn their children out on the streets to beg for money.

Many proposals have been advanced to improve juvenile justice conditions. Greater resources need to be provided. Juveniles require greater legal assistance and representation. Conditions of approved schools and the remand home need to be improved. Various groups, including probation officers and the police, require extensive training and regulation in their dealings with juveniles. There is an absence of accurate data on juvenile crime in Sierra Leone. No one knows exactly the nature and extent of juvenile offending or what is being done about it. Furthermore, not many up-to-date programs, such as victim–offender mediation, have been attempted, because of scarce resources and a general lack of interest in such programs. Informal community methods have sufficed in this regard as acceptable punishments for juvenile offending.

[*Sources:* Adapted from Rachel Harvey, "Juvenile Justice in Sierra Leone: An Analysis of Legislation and Practice." Unpublished paper, 2000; "Sierra Leone Police and Prosecutors," Barrister Chambers of the Chief Justice, Sierra Leone, Unpublished paper, 2005.]

3. In 39 states, juveniles are not entitled to a trial by jury, unless the juvenile court judge approves. In all criminal proceedings, defendants are entitled to a trial by jury if they want one, and if the crime or crimes they are accused of committing carry incarcerative penalties of more than six months. Judicial approval is required for a jury trial for juveniles in most jurisdictions. This is one of the remaining legacies of the *parens patriae* doctrine in contemporary juvenile courts. Eleven states have legislative mandated jury trials for juveniles in juvenile courts if they are charged with certain types of offenses, if they are certain ages, and if they make a timely request for a jury trial.

4. Juvenile court and criminal court are **adversarial proceedings.** Juveniles may or may not wish to retain or be represented by counsel (*In re Gault,* 1967). In almost every juvenile court case, prosecutors allege various infractions or law violations against juveniles, and these charges may be rebutted by juveniles or others. If juveniles are represented by counsel, these defense attorneys are permitted to offer a defense to the allegations. Criminal courts are obligated to provide counsel for anyone charged with a crime, if defendants cannot afford to retain their own counsel (*Argersinger v. Hamlin,* 1972). Every state has provisions for providing defense attorneys to indigent juveniles who are adjudicated in juvenile court.

5. Criminal courts are **courts of record,** whereas transcripts of most juvenile proceedings are made only if the judge decides. **Court reporters** record all testimony presented in most criminal courts. All state criminal trial courts are courts of record, where either a tape-recorded transcript of proceedings is maintained, or a written record is kept. Thus, if trial court verdicts are appealed later by either the prosecution or defense, transcripts of these proceedings can be presented by either side as evidence of errors committed by the judge or other violations of one's due process rights. Original convictions may be reversed or they may be allowed to stand, depending on whatever the records disclose about the propriety of the proceedings. Juvenile courts are not courts of record. Thus, it is unlikely that in any given juvenile proceeding, a court reporter will keep a verbatim record of the proceedings. One factor that inhibits juvenile courts from being courts of record is the sheer expense of hiring court reporters for this work. Courts of record are expensive to maintain. Certainly in some of the more affluent jurisdictions, some juvenile court judges may enjoy the luxury of a court re-

porter to transcribe or record all court matters. But this is the exception rather than the rule. Furthermore, the U.S. Supreme Court has declared that juvenile courts are not obligated to be courts of record (*In re Gault,* 1967).

6. The **standard of proof** used for determining one's guilt in criminal proceedings is **beyond a reasonable doubt.** In juvenile courts, the less rigorous civil standard of **preponderance of the evidence** is used in most juvenile court matters. However, the U.S. Supreme Court has held that if any juvenile is in jeopardy of losing his or her liberty as the result of an adjudication by a juvenile court judge, then the evidentiary standard must be the criminal court standard of beyond a reasonable doubt (*In re Winship,* 1970). Losing liberty means to be locked up for any period of time, whether it is for one day, one month, or one or more years. Thus, juveniles who face charges in juvenile court where the possible punishment is confinement in a secure juvenile facility for any period of time are entitled to the beyond-a-reasonable-doubt criminal standard in determining their guilt. Therefore, it is expected of juvenile court judges that they will always apply this standard when adjudicating a juvenile's case and where one's loss of liberty is a possibility.

7. The range of penalties juvenile court judges may impose is limited, whereas in most criminal courts, the range of penalties may include life-without-parole sentences or the death penalty. The jurisdiction of juvenile court judges over youthful offenders typically ends when these juveniles reach adulthood. Some exceptions are that juvenile courts may retain jurisdiction over mentally ill youthful offenders indefinitely after they reach adulthood. In California, for instance, the Department of the Youth Authority supervises youthful offenders ranging in age from 11 to 25.

The purpose of this comparison is to show that criminal court actions are more serious and have harsher long-term consequences for offenders compared with juvenile court proceedings. Juvenile courts continue to be guided by a strong rehabilitative orientation in most jurisdictions, where the most frequently used punishments are either verbal reprimands or probationary dispositions. Secure confinement is viewed by most juvenile court judges as a last resort, and such a punishment is reserved for only the most serious youthful offenders, with exceptions. Probably less than 10 percent of all adjudicated delinquent offenders are incarcerated in secure juvenile facilities. However, in criminal courts, convicted offenders are more frequently jailed or imprisoned. Criminal courts also use probation as a punishment in about 60 percent of all criminal cases, especially for first-offenders or those who have committed less serious crimes. Although increasing numbers of juvenile courts are adopting more punitive sanctions similar to those of criminal courts, many youths continue to receive treatment-oriented punishments rather than incarceration in secure juvenile facilities.

AN OVERVIEW OF THE JUVENILE JUSTICE SYSTEM

The Ambiguity of Adolescence and Adulthood

Police have broad discretionary powers in their encounters with the public and dealing with street crime. Although some evidence suggests that police have shifted their policing priorities away from juveniles toward more serious adult offenders for various reasons (e.g., cases against juveniles are often dismissed or judges issue nothing more than verbal warnings to them and return them to the custody of their parents), police arrests and detentions of juveniles in local jails remains the major conduit of a juvenile's entry into the juvenile justice system.

Many juveniles are clearly juveniles. It is difficult to find youths age 13 or under who physically appear 18 or older. Yet, nearly 10 percent of all juveniles held for brief periods in adult jails annually are 13 years old or younger (Gilliard and Beck, 1998). For juveniles in the 14–17 age range, visual determination of one's juvenile or non-juvenile status is increasingly difficult. Thus, at least some justification exists for why police officers take many youthful offenders to jails initially for identification and questioning.

Other ways that juveniles can enter the juvenile justice system include referrals from or complaints by parents, neighbors, victims, and others (social work staff, probation officers) unrelated to law enforcement. Dependent or neglected children may be reported to police initially. Following up on these complaints, police officers may take youths into custody until arrangements for their care can be made. Or police officers may arrest youths for alleged crimes.

Being Taken Into Custody and Being Arrested

Being **taken into custody** and being arrested are different procedures. For law enforcement officers, whenever youths are taken into custody, they are not necessarily arrested, and they may not necessarily be arrested later. Being taken into custody means precisely what it says. Officers take certain youths into custody as a protective measure so that they can determine what is best for the juvenile. Some youths who are taken into custody might be those suffering from child sexual abuse or physical abuse inflicted by parents or others, runaways, or missing children (Ystgaard et al., 2004). Youths wandering the streets may also be taken into custody by police if they are suspected of being truant from school.

When youths are arrested, this is more serious police action. An arrest means that the juvenile is suspected of committing a crime. Charges may be filed against arrested youths once it is determined who should have jurisdiction over them. Police authorities may determine that the juvenile court has jurisdiction, depending on the age or youthfulness of the offender. Or authorities may decide that the criminal court has jurisdiction and the youthful-appearing offender should be charged as an adult (Alexander, 2000).

Juveniles in Jails

In 2004, there were 9,000 juveniles under the age of 18 being held in jails (Office of Juvenile Justice and Delinquency Prevention, 2005). About 89 percent of these juveniles were being held as adults. This represents about 1 percent of all jail inmates held in jails for 2004. This figure is misleading, however. It does not reflect the total number of juveniles who are brought to jails annually after they have been arrested or taken into custody by police. Many youths are jailed for short time periods, merely on suspicion, even though they haven't committed any obvious offenses. Short time periods are often two or three hours. Some states, such as Illinois, have passed laws preventing police officers from detaining juveniles in adult jails for more than six hours. Such laws reflect the **jail re-**

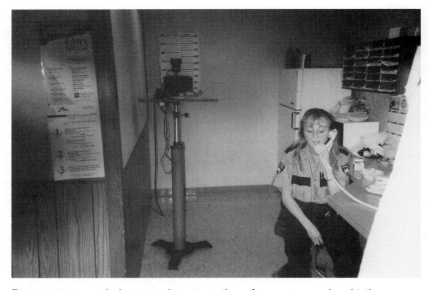

Fingerprinting and photographing juveniles often occurs at local jails, although such information is used primarily to identify youths and is subsequently destroyed.

moval initiative, whereby states are encouraged not to house juveniles in adult jails, even for short periods.

The Illinois policy preventing the police from detaining juveniles in jails except for limited periods is consistent with a major provision of the Juvenile Justice and Delinquency Prevention Act (JJDPA) of 1974. Although the JJDPA is not binding on any state, it does encourage law enforcement officials to treat juveniles differently from adult offenders if juveniles are taken to jails for brief periods. For instance, the JJDPA recommends that status offenders should be separated in jails by sight and sound from adult offenders. Furthermore, they should be held in nonsecure areas of jails for periods not exceeding six hours. They should not be restrained in any way with handcuffs or other restraint devices while detained. Their detention should only be as long as is necessary to identify them and reunite them with their parents, guardians, or a responsible adult from a public youth agency or family services.

Even more serious delinquent offenders brought to jails for processing should be subject to similar treatment by jail officials, according to JJDPA recommendations. Sight and sound separation and segregation from adult offenders is encouraged, although juveniles alleged to have committed delinquent offenses are subject to more restrictive detention provisions. The general intent of this aspect of the JJDPA is to minimize the adverse effects of labeling that might occur if juveniles were processed like adult offenders. Another factor is the recognition that most of these offenders will eventually be processed by the juvenile justice system, which is a civil entity. Any attributions of criminality arising from how juveniles are treated while they are in adult jails are considered incompatible with the rehabilitative ideals of the juvenile justice system and the civil outcomes or consequences ultimately experienced by most juvenile offenders. Thus, some of the JJDPA goals are to prevent juveniles from being influenced psychologically or physically by adults through jail contacts with them and to insulate juveniles from defining themselves as criminals, which might occur through criminal-like processing.

Despite new laws designed to minimize or eliminate holding juveniles in adult **jails** or **lock-ups,** even for short periods, juveniles continue to be held in jails for short time periods. In more than a few instances, these detentions are unavoidable. Many juveniles appear older to police officers than they really are. They carry fake IDs or no IDs, give false names when questioned, or refuse to give police any information about their true identities. It takes time to determine who they are and what responsible adult or guardian should be contacted. Many runaways are from different states, and it takes time for their parents or guardians to reunite with them. Some of these juveniles are very aggressive, assaultive, and obviously dangerous. They must be locked up or restrained, if only to protect others. Some are suicidal and need temporary protection from themselves.

The U.S. Supreme Court has authorized the **preventive detention** of juveniles in jails for brief periods without violating their constitutional rights, especially for those offenders who pose a danger to themselves or others (*Schall v. Martin,* 1984). In this particular case, a juvenile was detained by police on serious charges. He refused to give his name or other identification, and was deemed by those in charge to be dangerous, either to himself or to others. His preventive detention was upheld by the U.S. Supreme Court as not violating his constitutional right to due process. Prior to this Supreme Court ruling, however, many states had similar laws that permitted pretrial and preventive detention of both juvenile and adult suspects. Although **pretrial detention** presupposes a forthcoming trial of those detained and preventive detention does not, both terms are often used interchangeably or even combined, as in preventive pretrial detention (Brookbanks, 2002). If 1 percent of the 13 million admissions and releases to jails annually are juveniles, a reasonable estimate would be that at least 130,000 or more juveniles spend at least some time in jails annually, if only to determine their identity and release them into the custody of their parents or guardians after a few hours.

Referrals

Figure 4.2 is a diagram of the juvenile justice system. Although each jurisdiction in the United States has its own methods for processing juvenile offenders, Figure 4.2 is sufficiently general to encompass most of these processing methods. Focusing on the diagram in Figure 4.2, a majority of juvenile encounters with the juvenile justice system are through **referrals** from police officers (McClusky et al., 2004). Referrals are notifications made to juvenile court authorities that a juvenile requires the court's attention. Referrals may be made by anyone, such as concerned parents, school principals, teachers, neighbors, and others (Bryl et al., 2002). However, over 90 percent of all referrals to juvenile court are made by law enforcement officers. These referrals may be made for runaways; truants; curfew violators; unmanageable, unsupervised, or incorrigible children; children with drug or alcohol problems; or for any youth suspected of committing a crime (Burruss and Kempf-Leonard, 2002).

Each jurisdiction throughout the United States has its own policies relating to how referrals are handled (McCluskey et al., 2004). In Figure 4.2, following a police officer investigation, juveniles are either counseled and released to parents referred to community resources, cited and referred to juvenile intake, followed by a subsequent release to parents or transport to juvenile hall or shel-

THE JUVENILE JUSTICE SYSTEM

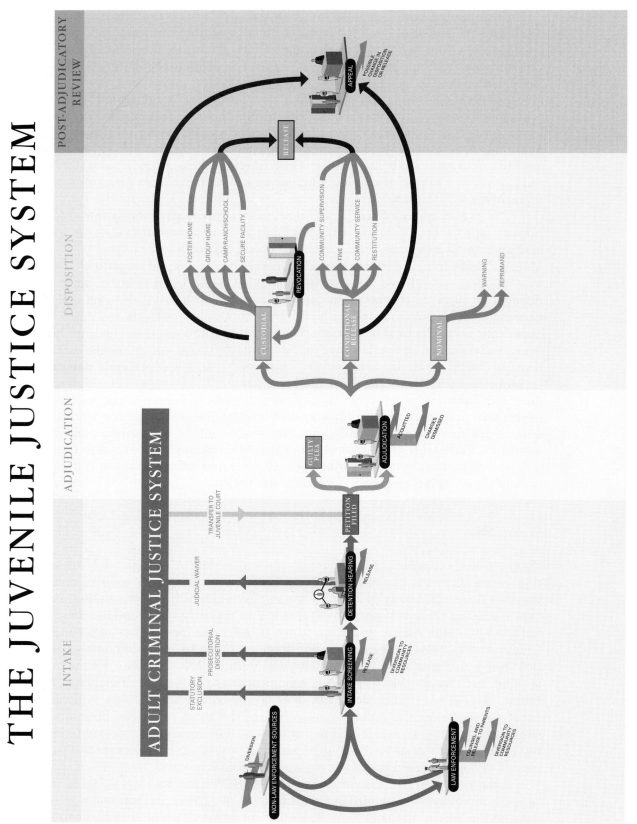

FIGURE 4.2 Diagram of the Juvenile Justice System.

Juveniles are frequently questioned by police on city streets, and police officers use situationally based discretion to take youths into custody or release them.

ter for further detention. Each of these actions is the result of police discretion. The nature of the discretionary action of police officers who take youths into custody for any reason is governed by what these officers have observed. If a youth has been loitering, especially in cities with curfew laws for juveniles, then the discretion of police officers might be to counsel the youth and turn him or her over to his or her parents without further action. In more than a few cases, youth are taken into custody and parents or guardians for these youths cannot be found. In these cases, police officers turn the youths over to community resources for further action. If particular youths have violated liquor laws or committed some minor infraction, they may be cited by police and referred to a juvenile probation officer for further action. Subsequently, most of these youths are returned to the custody of their parents or guardians. However, some youths are apprehended while committing serious crimes. Police officers will likely transport these youths to a juvenile hall or shelter to await further action by juvenile justice system personnel.

In New Mexico, for example, whenever a juvenile is referred to the juvenile justice system for any offense, the referral is first screened by the Juvenile Probation/Parole Office. Juvenile probation/parole officers (JPPOs) are assigned to initially screen a police report and file. This screening is performed, in part, to determine the accuracy of the report and if the information is correct. If the information is correct, then an intake process will commence, where the youth undergoes further screening by a JJPO assigned to the case by a supervisor (New Mexico Juvenile Justice Division, 2002). Figure 4.3 is a decision tree for the New Mexico Juvenile Justice Division and provides us with an overview of how their processing of juvenile offenders works.

Figure 4.3 shows that once a referral has been made to the Juvenile Probation/Parole Office, a decision is made whether to file **petitions** or to handle the

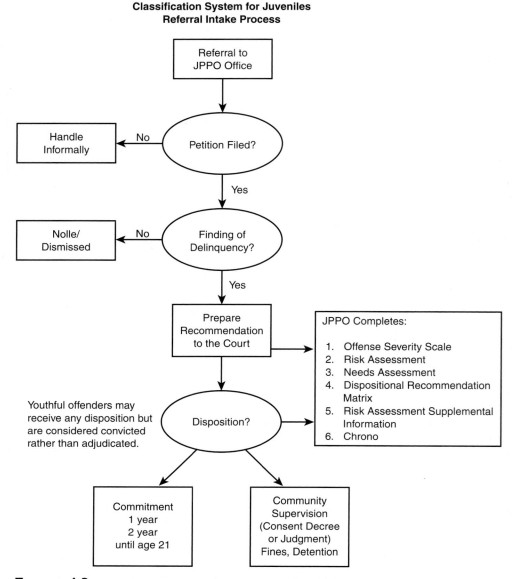

FIGURE 4.3 Decision Tree for the New Mexico Juvenile Justice Division.

case informally. About 50 percent of all juvenile cases are handled informally. Petitions are official documents filed in juvenile courts on the juvenile's behalf, specifying reasons for the youth's court appearance. These documents assert that juveniles fall within the categories of dependent or neglected, status offender, or delinquent, and the reasons for such assertions are usually provided. Filing a petition formally places the juvenile before the juvenile court judge in many jurisdictions. But juveniles may come before juvenile court judges in less formal ways. About 45 percent of the cases brought before the juvenile court each year are nonpetitioned cases. Less than 1 percent of these cases result in out-of-home placements, 30 percent receive probation, 50 percent are dismissed, and the remainder are diverted, downgraded, or result in verbal warnings (Champion, 2005b).

BOX 4.3

Jill A. Caldwell
Senior Court Officer, Glynn County Juvenile Court, Brunswick, GA

Statistics:

(criminal justice) South Georgia College

Background

I was born and raised in Claxton, Georgia. My grandfather was chief of police in Claxton and I had several uncles who were police officers. Law enforcement was instilled in me at an early age. I graduated from Claxton High School in 1972. In the fall of 1972, I moved to Douglas, Georgia, and attended South Georgia College. I made the decision to major in criminal justice. There were a couple of things that helped me make this decision. The first and most important was my interest and compassion for troubled children. The second was the fact that few women in my area were working in the criminal justice field. I was one of two women in my criminal justice class. Prior to finishing college, I was offered a job at the Glynn County Juvenile Court in Brunswick, Georgia. I took the job and never received my degree. For the past 29 years I have been working as a court officer with the Glynn County Juvenile Court.

My main job function is to provide supervision for children who are placed on probation by the court. I work closely with school administrators, mental health professionals, and other agencies to assist children in their rehabilitation. I am also the court coordinator for the Judicial Citizen's Review Panel. This is a program that operates under the Permanent Homes for Children in Georgia Program. The Judicial Citizen's Review Panel consists of a cross-section of volunteers from the community, appointed by the local juvenile court judge. The volunteers receive 15 hours of specialized training from the Council of Juvenile Court Judges' staff. Once their training is completed, they are sworn in as officers of the court. Their

goal is to ensure every child in foster care is safe, stable, and in a permanent home. I've been working with deprived children for many years, and it never gets any easier.

Perhaps the most difficult part of my job is being a member of the Child Fatality Review Committee. In the State of Georgia, all child deaths must be reviewed if the child is 17 or younger. I have reviewed many heart-breaking cases. For many years I was on call for one week out of every month. I provided intake and made detention decisions involving juveniles who were taken into custody by the police. If the child was detained, it was my responsibility to transport the child to the Regional Youth Detention Center, which was 65 miles away. I also served subpoenas for the juvenile court.

I look back on some of my responsibilities and see the danger in what I did. Subpoenas are now served by the Sheriff's Department, and children are transported by transport officers. In 1979 I was contacted by a 16-year-old male. He was a runaway, but he agreed to turn himself in if I would pick him up. Once I made contact with the child, he held me against my will. Approximately two hours later, when the ordeal was over, the police found a loaded gun on him. Fortunately, I came out of this incident unharmed. That was the last time I picked up a runaway. In 2002 I made a school visit involving one of my probationers who was disrupting class. The situation escalated to the point where the child picked up a pair of scissors and threatened to stab her teacher, the principal, and me. This child was later charged with aggra-
(continued)

vated assault and sentenced under the designated felony act. Her release date was May 2005. During the last two years, I've been supervising a 16-year-old male. This young man was one of the most pleasant children I have ever worked with. He had a heart of gold and a winning smile. I never would admit it, but he was my favorite probationer. The offenses he committed were never very serious until December 23, 2004. He was killed at 12:20 A.M. while driving a stolen vehicle. Needless to say, it was a sad Christmas.

Advice to Students

Criminal justice is an exciting profession. I promise you will never be bored but you will be frustrated, disappointed, and even heartbroken. Some people may tell you not to get too close to or involved with your clients. I believe just the opposite. So many children I have dealt with have few people, if any, who truly care about them. In order to be effective, you must take a sincere interest in the children. They will know if you really care or if it's just a job for you. The most important thing you need to know is that you can't save all of the children. There are those who don't want to be saved. Concentrate on the ones who want your help.

When individual cases are handled informally, JPPOs in New Mexico jurisdictions have several options. Whenever youths are determined to require special care, are needy or dependent, or are otherwise unsupervised by adults or guardians, JPPOs may refer them to a Juvenile Early Intervention Program (JEIP). The JEIP is a highly structured program for at-risk, nonadjudicated youths. Figure 4.4 shows a referral form used by New Mexico JPPOs to refer youths into this early intervention program.

Juveniles referred to the program will have been assessed to need services and/or supervision due to the nature of their current offense or situation, as well as their propensity for future misconduct as determined from a preliminary inquiry by the JPPO. The target group for the JEIP ranges in age from 10 to 12 at the time of the allegation against them. Status offenders, including truants, runaways, or curfew violators, may be referred to the JEIP. Both the juvenile and his or her family must agree to participate in the JEIP and to follow through with recommendations for additional services. The JEIP consists of eight weekly sessions, including an overall presentation of the program and expectations, choices, self-esteem including a parent's group, peer pressure, gangs, drug and alcohol issues with parents included, feelings, and a final session that includes a review and graduation ceremony. Following completion of the program, a 30-day follow-up is conducted by JPPOs.

Depending on the jurisdiction, however, the majority of alleged juvenile delinquents will be advanced further into the juvenile justice system. Some status offenders, especially recidivists, will also move further into the system. Some youths may be maintained in juvenile detention facilities temporarily to await further action. Other youths may be released to their parents' custody, but these youths may be required to reappear later to face further action. Most of these youths will subsequently be interviewed by an **intake officer** in a proceeding known as **intake.**

REFERRAL FORM

Date: _____ File #: _____ Cause # (if appl.): _____

Client's Name: _____ DOB: _____ Age: _____

Address: _____ Zip: _____ Phone #: _____

Ethnicity: _____ Gender: _____ SS#: _____

Referral Source: _____ Primary Language Spoken: _____

Guardian's Name: _____ Relationship: _____

Guardian's Legal Status: _____

Current Offense: _____

School: _____ Grade: _____ Reg. Ed. ____ Special Ed. _____

Client's Mental Health Issues (meds, if any): _____

_____

_____

_____

Guardian's Mental Health Issues (meds, if any): _____

_____

_____

_____

Directions to client's residence:

FIGURE 4.4   New Mexico Referral Form for Youth Early Intervention Program.

Intake

Intake varies in formality among jurisdictions (Mulford et al., 2004). Intake is a **screening** procedure usually conducted by a juvenile probation officer, where one or several courses of action are recommended. Some jurisdictions conduct **intake hearings** or **intake screenings,** where comments and opinions are solicited from significant others such as the police, parents, neighbors, or victims. In other jurisdictions, intake proceedings are quite informal, usually consisting of a dialogue between the juvenile and the intake officer. These are important proceedings, regardless of their degree of formality. Intake is a major screening stage in the juvenile justice process, where further action against juveniles may be contemplated or required. Intake officers hear complaints against juveniles and informally resolve the least serious cases, or they are more often juvenile probation officers who perform intake as a special assignment. In many small jurisdictions, juvenile probation officers may perform diverse functions, including intake, enforcement of truancy statutes, and juvenile placements (Gaarder, Rodriguez, and Zatz, 2004).

Intake officers also consider youths' attitudes, demeanor, age, offense seriousness, and a host of other factors. Has the juvenile had frequent prior contact with the juvenile justice system? If the offenses alleged are serious, what evidence exists against the offender? Should the offender be referred to certain community social service agencies, receive psychological counseling, receive vocational counseling and guidance, acquire educational or technical training and skills, be issued a verbal reprimand, be placed on some type of diversionary status, or be returned to parental custody? Interviews with parents and neighbors may be conducted as a part of an intake officer's information-gathering (Ray and Alarid, 2004). Although intake is supposed to be an informal proceeding, it is nevertheless an important stage in juvenile processing. The intake officer often acts in an advisory capacity, since he or she is the first contact children and their parents will have following an arrest or being taken into custody. Figure 4.5 is a form used by intake officers in some jurisdictions that provides both parents and children with an outline of their legal options in the case. Youths and their parents have a right to know the charge(s) against their children. Also it is indicated that the intake hearing is a preliminary inquiry and not a fact-finding session to determine one's guilt. Also, the intake officer advises that statements made by the child and/or parents may be used against them later in court if such action is warranted.

In most jurisdictions, intake results in one of five actions, depending on the discretion of intake officers: (1) dismissal of the case, with or without a verbal or written reprimand; (2) remand youths to the custody of their parents; (3) remand youths to the custody of their parents, with provisions for or referrals to counseling or special services; (4) divert youths to an alternative dispute resolution program, if one exists in the jurisdiction; (5) refer youths to the juvenile prosecutor for further action and possible filing of a delinquency petition (Mulford et al., 2004; Terry-McElrath and McBride, 2004). Many observers including juvenile court judges regard the intake process as a key opportunity to impose punishments, prescribe treatments, and issue threats or verbal warnings (McCluskey et al., 2004).

Returning to an examination of Figure 4.5, following an intake screening, some of the options available to intake officers noted above are indicated. Theoretically, at least, only the most serious juveniles will be referred to detention to await a subsequent juvenile court appearance. In order for a youth to be detained while awaiting a juvenile court appearance, a detention hearing is usually conducted. Most of the time, youths considered for such detention are either a danger to themselves or to others, or they are likely to flee the jurisdiction to avoid prosecution in juvenile court. Others may be released to the custody of their parents or they may be referred to one or more community resources. Usually these community resources are intended to meet the specific needs of particular juvenile offenders. Or the intake officer may release the juvenile to his or her parents prior to a subsequent juvenile court appearance. For serious cases, a petition is filed with the juvenile court. The juvenile court prosecutor further screens these petitions and decides which ones merit an appearance before the juvenile court judge. In Alaska, for example, a petition for adjudication of delinquency is used to bring delinquency cases before the juvenile court. An illustration of such a petition is shown in Figure 4.6.

Notice in Figure 4.6 that allegations are made concerning the delinquent acts committed by the juvenile. Furthermore, supporting information accompanies the petition, which presumably establishes probable cause and supports

IN THE MATTER OF: IN THE VIGO COURT
A CHILD ALLEGED TO BE A DELINQUENT CHILD

CAUSE NUMBER: JUVENILE DIVISION

INTAKE OFFICER'S ADVICE TO CHILD AND PARENT,GUARDIAN OR CUSTODIAN
(Indiana Code 31-6-4-7)

TO SAID CHILD AND HIS OR HER PARENT, GUARDIAN OR CUSTODIAN:
You are hereby advised that:

1.   You have the right to know the allegations against said child;

2.   The undersigned intake officer is conducting a preliminary inquiry to assist in
        determining whether a petition should be filed alleging that said child a delinquent child;

3   The undersigned intake officer will recommend whether to file a petition, informally
        adjust the case, refer the child to another agency, or dismiss the case;

4.   Said child has a right to remain silent; anything said child says may be used against said
        child in subsequent proceedings; said child has a right to consult with an attorney before
        he or she talks with the Intake Officer, and said child has a right to stop at any time and
        consult with an attorney, and to stop talking with the intake officer at any time; said child
        has a right to talk with his or her parents, guardian or custodian in private before he talks
        with the Intake Officer;

5.   If said child cannot afford an attorney, the Court will appoint one for him or her.

DATED THIS THE_____**DAY OF**_____**,2003**

_____
PROBATION OFFICER

By signing this paper you agree only that you have received this advice

_____
SIGNATURE OF CHILD

_____
SIGNATURE OF PARENT OR GUARDIAN

_____
SIGNATURE OF PARENT OR GUARDIAN

FIGURE 4.5   Intake Officer's Advice to Child and Parent, Guardian, or Custodian. (Vigo County, Indiana).

IN THE SUPERIOR COURT FOR THE STATE OF ALASKA

_____ JUDICIAL DISTRICT AT _____

In the matter of:)
)
)   CASE NO. _____CP
)
A minor under 18 years of age   )
Date of Birth: _____)

PETITION FOR ADJUDICATION OF DELINQUENCY

The petitioner requests that the above-named juvenile be adjudicated as a delinquent under A.S 47.12.020 and that an appropriate disposition be entered.

The petitioner alleges that:

Probable cause supporting the above allegation(s) is that:

The juvenile's address is _____.

The juvenile's father is: _____, whose address is

_____.

The juvenile's mother is: _____, whose address is

_____.

The juvenile's guardian/custodian/grandmother is _____, whose address is

_____.

06-9541 (Rev. 10/97) YC   PETITION FOR ADJUDICATION OF DELINQUENCY

2.b.1

FIGURE 4.6 Alaska Delinquency Petition.

In the Matter of: _____ Case No._____

Petitioner swears or affirms upon information and belief to the above statements.

_____   _____
        Date   PETITIONER (signature)

                                    _____
                                    PRINT NAME AND OCCUPATION/RELATIONSHIP

                                    _____
                                    ADDRESS AND PHONE NUMBER

SUBSCRIBED AND SWORN TO before me on _____.
                                              Date

    (SEAL)   _____
                                         CLERK/NOTARY PUBLIC

                                    My Commission Expires:_____

    CERTIFICATE OF SERVICE
I certify that on July 21,_____
a copy of this document was sent
to: _____

By:_____Notary

PETITION FOR ADJUDICATION OF DELINQUENCY
2.b.2

FIGURE 4.6   (Continued)

the facts alleged. The petitioner signs the petition under oath and avers that the statements made are true. Their occupation and relationship with the juvenile are also included, as well as their telephone number and address. It is up to the prosecutor to determine whether action should be taken on petitions filed. Figure 4.6 alleges delinquency, or one or more crimes committed by the named juvenile. Other petitions may allege status offending, such as truancy, runaway behavior, curfew violation, or violation of drug or liquor laws. These petitions are similar in form to Figure 4.6. Delinquency petitions throughout most U.S. jurisdictions resemble the Alaska delinquency petition. Regarding petitions filed with the juvenile court, not all petitions result in formal action by a juvenile court prosecutor. Like prosecutors in criminal court, juvenile court prosecutors prioritize cases they will prosecute. Such case prioritizing depends on the volume of petitions filed, the time estimated for the juvenile court judge to hear and act on these petitions, the sufficiency of evidence supporting these petitions, as well as an array of other factors.

Alternative Prosecutorial Actions

Cases referred to juvenile prosecutors for further action are usually, though not always, more serious cases. Exceptions might include those youths who are chronic recidivists or technical program violators and nonviolent property offenders (e.g., status offenders, vandalism, petty theft, public order offenders).

Juvenile court prosecutors have broad discretionary powers. They may cease prosecutions against alleged offenders or downgrade the offenses alleged from felonies to misdemeanors or from misdemeanors to status offenses. Much depends on the docket load or case activity of their own juvenile courts. In some instances, prosecutors may divert some of the more serious juvenile cases for processing by criminal courts. The least serious cases are disposed informally. Prosecutors either file petitions or act on petitions filed by others, such as intake officers, the police, school officials, or interested family and citizens.

ADJUDICATORY PROCEEDINGS

Jurisdictions vary considerably concerning their juvenile court proceedings. Increasingly, juvenile courts are emulating criminal courts in many respects. Most of the physical trappings of criminal courts are present, including the judge's bench, tables for the prosecution and defense, and a witness stand. Furthermore, there appears widespread interest in holding juveniles more accountable for their actions than was the case in past years (Morgan, 2003).

Besides the more formal atmosphere of juvenile courts, the procedure is becoming increasingly adversarial, where prosecutors and defense attorneys do battle against and on behalf of juveniles charged with various offenses. However, less than 50 percent of the juvenile offenders in most jurisdictions have the assistance of counsel, although they are entitled to counsel (Singer, 2003). Both alleged status offenders and those charged with crimes are entitled to be represented by counsel in their court cases. In most jurisdictions, juvenile court judges have almost absolute discretion in how their courts are conducted. Juvenile defendants alleged to have committed various crimes may or may not be granted a trial by jury if they request one. In 2004 only 11 states provided jury trials for juveniles in juvenile courts, and these jury trials were restricted to a narrow list of serious offenses.

After hearing the evidence presented by both sides in any juvenile proceeding, the judge decides or adjudicates the matter in an **adjudication hearing,** sometimes called an **adjudicatory hearing.** An **adjudication** is a judgment or action on the petition filed with the court by others. If the petition alleges delinquency on the part of certain juveniles, the judge determines whether the juveniles are delinquent or not delinquent. If the petition alleges that the juveniles involved are dependent, neglected, or otherwise in need of care by agencies or others, the judge decides the matter. If the adjudicatory hearing fails to yield supporting facts for the petition filed, then the case is dismissed and the youth exits the juvenile justice system. If the adjudicatory hearing supports the allegations in the petition, then the judge must **dispose** the juvenile according to a range of punishments (Cohn et al., 2002). An example of an adjudication form where action is taken by the juvenile court judge on facts alleged in a delinquency petition is illustrated in Figure 4.7.

In Figure 4.7, the adjudication form shows that a petition was filed with the court on a particular date, an adjudicatory hearing was conducted, and particular findings and conclusions are indicated. Notice in Figure 4.7 that juveniles may be adjudicated delinquent by the court, or they may be found in violation of one or more conditions of their probation, if they were originally disposed to probation by the juvenile court judge. This is because, like adult proceedings in criminal court, juvenile court judges retain jurisdiction over juveniles whenever they are placed on probation.

JUVENILE DISPOSITIONS

Disposing juveniles is the equivalent of sentencing adult offenders. When adult offenders are convicted of crimes, they are sentenced. When juveniles are adjudicated delinquent, they are disposed. At least twelve different **dispositions** or punishments are available to juvenile court judges, if the facts alleged in petitions are upheld. These dispositions are grouped according to: (1) nominal, (2) conditional, or (3) custodial options.

Nominal Dispositions

Nominal dispositions are either verbal warnings or stern reprimands and are the least punitive dispositional options. The nature of such verbal warnings or reprimands is a matter of judicial discretion. Release to the custody of parents or legal guardians completes the juvenile court action against the youth. Usually nominal dispositions are most often applied to low-risk first-offenders who are the least likely to recidivate and commit new offenses. The emphasis of nominal dispositions is upon rehabilitation and fostering a continuing positive, reintegrative relationship between the juvenile and his/her community (Altschuler and Armstrong, 2001).

IN THE SUPERIOR COURT FOR THE STATE OF ALASKA
AT _____

In the Matter of:)
)
)
)
)   CASE NO. _____ CP
A minor under 18 years of age.   )
)   ADJUDICATION UPON ADMISSION
Date of birth: _____   )

A petition was filed on _____ , 20 _____ , alleging that the
above-named juvenile is:

☐   a delinquent juvenile.

☐   a delinquent juvenile who has violated the conditions of his (probation) / (deferred
      institutional order) / (conduct agreement).

An adjudication hearing was held on the above petition on _____ .
20 ____ Present were:

The court has considered the allegation in the petition and evidence presented and makes the
following FINDINGS AND CONCLUSIONS:

1.   The court has jurisdiction over the parties and the subject matter of the proceedings.

2.   The child has knowingly and voluntarily admitted pursuant to Delinquency
      Rule 14(b)(4) that :

      ☐   all allegations in the petition are true.

      ☐   the following allegations in the petition are true:

THEREFORE, IT IS ADJUDGED that the above-named juvenile is:

☐   a delinquent juvenile.

☐   a delinquent juvenile who has violated the conditions of his (probation) / (deferred
      institutional order) / (conduct agreement).

Recommended on _____   Effective Date: _____

_____   _____ _____
      Superior Court Master   Superior Court Judge   Date

                                             _____
I certify that on _____   Type or Print Name
a copy of this adjudication was sent to:
      DHSS, Juvenile/Attorney, Parent/Guardian, Other: _____

Clerk: _____

CP-230 (5/88) (st.5)   Del.R. 14(b) (4)
ADJUDICATION UPON ADMISSION   AS 47.10.010

FIGURE 4.7   Adjudication Form.

Conditional Dispositions

All **conditional dispositions** are probationary options. The most frequently imposed disposition is probation. Youths are placed on probation and required to comply with certain conditions during a probationary period lasting from several months to several years. Conditional dispositions usually require offenders

Juvenile courts are increasingly suffering from overcrowded court dockets and a glut of cases to adjudicate.

to do something as a condition of probation. The nature of the conditions to be fulfilled depends on the needs of the offender and the nature of the offense committed. If youths have alcohol or drug dependencies, they may be required to undergo individual or group counseling and some type of therapy to cope with substance abuse. Juvenile murderers are often subjected to psychological counseling and clinical evaluation. In more than a few cases, polygraph tests may be administered contemporaneously with these evaluations, counseling, and assessments.

Property offenders may be required to make restitution to victims or to compensate the court in some way for the damage they have caused (Morgan, 2003). In a growing number of jurisdictions, **restorative justice** is practiced, where offenders and their victims are brought together for the purpose of mediation. Youths learn to accept responsibility for what they have done, and their accountability is heightened (Swanson, 2005). Many jurisdictions have gravitated toward a more balanced approach in sanctioning youths, where the emphasis is on restorative and victim-centered justice. The aim of this legislation is to (1) promote public safety and the protection of the community; (2) heighten accountability of youths toward victims and the community for offenses committed; and (3) increase competency and improve character development to assist youths in becoming responsible and productive members of society (Singer, 2003).

Offenders with behavioral disorders may require more intensive supervision while on probation (Abatiello, 2005). Those considered high risks for recidivism may be required to undergo electronic monitoring and house arrest as a part of their supervision by juvenile probation officers. These and other similar control strategies are a part of the growing area of community corrections and intermediate punishments, where greater emphasis is on community reintegration and rehabilitation (Rivers, 2005). During the 1990s there has been a gradual intensification of punishments for juveniles, including probation dispositions (Wilkerson, 2005). This emphasis on punishment is a reflection of state legislatures' tougher stance toward juveniles. Figure 4.8 is a conduct agreement form used by Alaska juvenile court judges whenever they place adjudicated juveniles on probation.

The terms and conditions of probation are outlined in Figure 4.8. Obeying the law, attending school, maintaining employment, reporting to the probation officer, attending vocational training or education courses, appearing at subsequent court hearings, refraining from using drugs and alcohol, and refraining from possessing dangerous weapons are standard probation conditions. Furthermore, the judge may add other conditions, such as mandatory counseling or therapy, depending on the particular needs exhibited by the offender and which are brought to the attention of the court.

Custodial Dispositions

Custodial dispositions are classified according to **nonsecure custody** or **nonsecure confinement** and **secure custody** or **secure confinement.** Nonsecure custody consists of placing certain juveniles into foster homes, group homes, camps, ranches, or schools. These are temporary measures often designed to lead to more permanent placement arrangements for juveniles later. Juveniles have freedom of movement, and they can generally participate in school and other youthful activities. If they are living in group homes or are on camp ranches, there are curfews to be observed. It is assumed that if they are in the care of others in foster homes or shelters, such curfews will be implicitly (if not explicitly) enforced.

The secure custodial option is considered by most juvenile court judges as the last resort for serious juvenile offenders. Some of the reasons for this include overcrowding in secure juvenile facilities, a general reluctance among judges to incarcerate youths because of adverse labeling effects, and the potential effectiveness of certain intermediate punishments through community-service agencies. Fewer than 10 percent of all juveniles processed by juvenile courts annually are subsequently placed in either nonsecure or secure facilities (Cohn et al., 2002).

JUVENILE CORRECTIONS

In 2004 there were over 50,000 juveniles in residential and nonresidential correctional programs other than probation (American Correctional Association, 2005). The range of juvenile corrections is almost as broad as programs for convicted adult offenders. In fact, since 1992 changes in juvenile court dispositions have been in the direction of increased incarceration of juveniles adjudicated delinquent for violent or other serious offenses without comparable attention to probation, community corrections, or other types of **aftercare** (Wilkerson, 2005).

Juveniles adjudicated delinquent may be placed on probation or in secure confinement, depending on juvenile court judge opinions and evaluations. Depending on juvenile probation officer caseloads in various jurisdictions, probation may be more or less intense, commensurate with intensive supervised

IN THE SUPERIOR COURT FOR THE STATE OF ALASKA

_____ JUDICIAL DISTRICT AT _____

In the Matter of:)
)
)   CASE NO. _____ CP
)
A minor under 18 years of age   )   ☐ **CONDUCT AGREEMENT**
Date of Birth: _____)   ☐ **CONDITIONS OF PROBATION**
                                                             OR DEFERRED INSTITUTIONAL
                                                             PLACEMENT

1.   I will obey all municipal, state and federal laws.

2.   I will remain in the placement designated by my Probation/Intake Officer and obey the curfew hours set by my parents, guardian, custodian or Probation/Intake Officer.

3.   I will notify my Probation/Intake Officer prior to changing my residence, employment or school.

4.   I will obey the rules and instructions set forth by my parents, guardian, custodian, and Probation/Intake Officer.

5.   I will attend school or vocational training when in session and conduct myself in accordance with school policy; otherwise, I will maintain steady employment.

6.   I will report as directed to my Probation/Intake Officer.

7.   I will appear at all scheduled court hearings.

8.   I will not ingest illegal drugs or alcohol, and will submit to random urinalysis as requested.

9.   I will not possess, have in my custody, handle, purchase or transport any firearm, knife, club or other type of weapon, ammunition or explosives. I will not carry any weapon on my person including pocket knives.

10. I will obey the following additional conditions: _____

_____

_____

_____

_____

_____

Page 1 of 2
06-9555 (10/97) YC
CONDUCT AGREEMENT/CONDITIONS OF PROBATION

Del.R. 12(c), 23 & 24
AS 47.12.120

3.q.1

FIGURE 4.8   Alaska Conduct Agreement Form for Adjudicated Juveniles.

In the Matter of: _____   Case No. _____CP

I (have read)(have had read to me) and understand these conditions. I agree to obey them and understand that any violation may result in my being detained or having my probation revoked.

_____   _____   _____   _____
Probation/Intake Officer   Date   Juvenile   Date

We have read and understand these conditions. We agree to require the juvenile to obey them and to report any violations. We understand that if we fail to report a violation which is known to us, action may be taken against us in court. We further understand that any violation by the juvenile may result in his/her detention. We agree to bring the juvenile before the court when directed.

_____   _____
Parent/Guardian/Custodian   Date

ORDER

The above juvenile is hereby released under the terms and conditions agreed to in this document.

Recommended on_____   Effective Date: _____
Date

_____   _____   _____
Superior Court Master   Superior Court Judge   Date

_____
Type or Print Name

I certify that on_____
a copy of this document was sent to:

    DHSS
    Juvenile/Attorney
    Parent/Guardian
    Placement Facility
    Other:_____

Clerk: _____

Page 2 of 2   Del.R. 12(c), 23 & 24
06-9555 (10/97) YC   AS 47.12.120
CONDUCT AGREEMENT/CONDITIONS OF PROBATION   3.q.2

FIGURE 4.8   (Continued)

probation for adults. One's placement in different types of probationary programs is dependent upon how the youth is originally classified. Interestingly, juvenile court judges have not consistently applied legal variables in their decision making about juvenile secure placements. More rational legal criteria for secure confinement decision making have been recommended (Altschuler and Armstrong, 2001).

Whether it is intensive, probation may be conditional and involve restitution to victims and/or community services. In 2004, there were over 475,000 juveniles on probation in various state jurisdictions (American Correctional Association, 2005). Juveniles may be placed in community-based residential programs or exposed to various therapies and treatments or training (Aloisi and LeBaroon, 2001).

Confinement in state industrial schools is the juvenile equivalent of incarceration in a state prison for adults. This type of confinement is considered **hard time** for many juveniles. The California Youth Authority operates various facilities to house growing numbers of juvenile offenders in secure confinement. Lengths of commitment vary for offenders, depending on the seriousness of their adjudication offenses (Bureau of Justice Statistics, 2005; Office of Juvenile Justice and Delinquency Prevention, 2005).

Juvenile Parole

When juveniles have served a portion of their incarcerative terms, they are paroled by a juvenile paroling authority to the supervision of an appropriate state or community agency (Haapanen and Britton, 2002). Such supervision may be in the form of intensive **aftercare** (Meisel, 2001). In 2001, there were 80,000 juveniles on parole in various state jurisdictions (American Correctional Association, 2005). In Utah, for instance, a nine-member board, the Utah Youth Parole Authority, makes early-release decisions over large numbers of incarcerated youths monthly. Operated by the Utah Division of Youth Corrections, this board conducted over 450 parole hearings in 2004 (American Correctional Association, 2005). Although the board appears to be guided by certain eligibility criteria, one's institutional behavior while confined is considered quite important as an indicator of one's future community reintegration.

One example of aftercare provisions for juvenile parolees is the Intensive Aftercare Demonstration Project (IAP), which was implemented in Golden, Colorado, in 1999 (Meisel, 2001). The IAP adhered to a reintegrative confinement concept in order to reduce recidivism among juvenile parolees at greatest risk of reoffending. Successful intensive case supervision often assumes that providers develop positive relationships with their clients. A sample of 97 juveniles was recruited from the Lookout Mountain Youth Services Center in Golden and randomly assigned to treatment and received intensive aftercare services, while other youths were subject to control conditions of traditional aftercare. The IAP clients reported having stronger relationships with their case managers and viewed them as being more supportive and responsive compared with those in the control group. IAP clients with former gang affiliations also reported less influence of their former gangs compared with clients in the control group. Overall, the IAP participants viewed their relationships with community resource persons the most favorably and exhibited considerably less recidivism in follow-ups compared with their control group counterparts. Thus quality aftercare programs are encouraged for juvenile parolees (Meisel, 2001).

SUMMARY

The criminal justice system is a vast network of agencies, organizations, and personnel that processes criminal offenders. The major components of it are law enforcement, prosecution and the courts, and institutional and community corrections. Criminal laws are passed by state legislatures and the U.S. Congress, and different law enforcement agencies enforce these laws. When one or more criminal laws are violated, these incidents are investigated and arrests of suspects made. Arrested persons are taken to police stations or jails, where they are booked. Booking is a process involving fingerprinting, photographing, and the collection of other important information about criminal suspects. Due process entitles arrestees to a presumption of innocence until their guilt is proven beyond a reasonable doubt in a court of law. However, certain procedures are followed that precede subsequent court action.

Arrestees become defendants who are subject to an initial appearance before a judicial figure, usually a magistrate. A determination is made whether bail should be granted. Bail is a surety used to guarantee a defendant's subsequent appearance at a trial. Bail is only available to those entitled to bail. Bail is denied under circumstances where persons pose a danger to the community or are likely to flee the jurisdiction to avoid prosecution. Persons may be released on their own recognizance, or ROR. At any stage during a defendant's processing, plea bargaining may occur. Plea bargaining is a preconviction agreement between the prosecutor and defense, with judicial approval, where some amount of leniency is extended toward defendants in exchange for a guilty plea. Plea bargaining accounts for over 90 percent of all criminal convictions.

Defendants are entitled to a preliminary hearing where probable cause is determined. This is a stage where it is determined whether a crime was committed and the defendant probably committed it. An alternative procedure used in about half of all states is a grand jury action, where indictments or presentments are issued. These are also known as true bills. Indictments are accusations based on probable cause, which grand juries determine. In many minor offense cases, prosecutors file criminal informations against criminal suspects. Informations are also accusations that must be proved beyond a reasonable doubt in court. Grand juries may issue no true bills and decide insufficient evidence exists against particular suspects. In other cases, grand juries either issue indictments, which are requested by prosecutors, or presentments, where the grand jury acts on its own in determining probable cause. Where indictments or presentments are issued, the case against the suspect proceeds to an arraignment before a judge, usually the judge who will eventually hear the case. Arraignments are critical stages and determine a finalized listing of charges against defendants. Defendants also enter a plea to the charges leveled against them, and a trial date is set.

Criminal trials may be either bench or jury trials. Bench trials are conducted by judges only without juries. Jury trials are held when requested by defendants and the possible incarcerative penalty upon conviction is beyond six months. Evidence is presented at one's trial, which may be both inculpatory or exculpatory. Inculpatory evidence shows one's guilt, while exculpatory evidence shows one's innocence. Petit juries, as distinguished from grand juries, deliberate once the evidence is presented, and determine whether a defendant is guilty or not guilty of the crime(s) alleged. A finding of guilt leads to the sentencing stage. In cases involving serious charges, formal sentencing hearings are scheduled 4–6 weeks beyond the trial's conclusion. This gives the probation department time to prepare presentence investigation reports about the convicted offender. These reports are useful for judges to consider when sentencing offenders. Sentences may be either incarcerative or nonincarcerative and are a part of the umbrella term *corrections.* Corrections may be community-based or institutional. Community-based corrections involves probation or some other conditional punishment. Institutional corrections involves confinement in a jail or prison for a period of time. Many offenders are sentenced to probation, which is mostly community based and involves supervision by a probation officer for a period of time as specified by the judge. Incarceration for varying periods is imposed by the judge in more serious cases. Once most offenders have served a portion of their original sentences, they may be paroled. Parole is a conditional release, again related closely with community supervision by parole agencies and parole officers. Successful completion of probation or parole programs concludes one's involvement with the criminal justice system.

The juvenile justice system parallels the criminal justice system in many respects, except that different terms are often used to describe stages similar to those experienced by criminal defendants during their processing. Juveniles suspected of committing delinquent acts are taken into custody. Some more serious juveniles are arrested. These persons are also taken to police stations or jails for brief periods, where they are identified and either reunited with parents or guardians or held in detention to await a juvenile court adjudicatory hearing. Juveniles enter the juvenile justice system in various ways. One common way is through a referral by police, school authorities, neighbors, or even one's parents. These referrals are made whenever it is suspected that juveniles have violated one or more laws. About half of all juvenile cases are petitioned. A petition is a formal document seeking a hearing for the juvenile in a juvenile court.

Before formal action is taken against any juvenile, a screening process occurs known as intake. Intake is usually conducted by an intake officer, who is either court-appointed or hired to conduct such screenings. Screening cases is intended to separate less serious cases from more serious ones. Intake officers have broad discretionary powers, and in many minor offense cases, they may conclude a case against a juvenile during the intake process. More serious juveniles are referred to juvenile court prosecutors who decide whether to seek an adjudicatory hearing before a juvenile court judge. An adjudicatory hearing is a formal court proceeding much like a criminal trial. Most adjudicatory hearings are the equivalent of bench trials, where juvenile court judges themselves hear and decide cases against juveniles. In some states, jury trials are provided for juveniles, especially in more serious cases. If the facts alleged in petitions are upheld or if the accusations against particular juveniles are found to be true, the judge declares the juvenile delinquent. The judge then imposes a disposition, similar to a criminal sentence. There are three broad categories of dispositions available to juvenile court judges. These include nominal dispositions, which most often are verbal warnings. Conditional dispositions, the ones most frequently chosen by these judges, involve probationary terms. Custodial dispositions are also imposed in about 25 percent of all juvenile cases. Custodial dispositions may involve nonsecure or secure confinement. Nonsecure confinement may be placement in foster care or some other type of out-of-home placement, wilderness experiences, or placement in a group home. Secure confinement is usually placement in an industrial school, which provides various types of educational or vocational training, counseling, and other useful treatments relevant for a youth's rehabilitation.

A wide range of punishment options is available to juvenile court judges that parallel the punishments available to criminal offenders. Community-based punishments may include probation, intensive supervised probation, home confinement, electronic monitoring, community service, restitution, fines, day reporting programs, halfway house placement, or other conditions. The most severe punishment, placement in a secure facility, is tantamount to imprisonment. Industrial schools are prison-like facilities with many of a prison's characteristics. Once juveniles have served a portion of their disposition in these facilities, they may be paroled. Juvenile parole is much like adult parole in that it is community-based and conditional. Once one's period of parole is completed, or whenever the probationary period ends for a juvenile under a nonincarcerative conditional disposition, one's interaction with the juvenile justice system ends.

QUESTIONS FOR REVIEW

1. What is the criminal justice system? What are its principal components?

2. What are booking and initial appearances? What are their functions?

3. What is a preliminary hearing? What is a grand jury? What are the functions of preliminary hearings and grand juries?

4. What are indictments, presentments, and criminal informations? What is an arraignment? What is determined at an arraignment?

5. What are some key differences between being arrested and being taken into custody? Which action is better for juvenile offenders and why?

6. What is a referral? Who can make referrals? What is a petition and what is its function?

7. What is an adjudicatory proceeding? How does intake influence whether adjudicatory proceedings will occur?

8. What are three kinds of juvenile dispositions? Which disposition is used most frequently by juvenile court judges?

9. What are several different kinds of juvenile corrections?

10. What is juvenile parole? How is parole a part of juvenile corrections?

INTERNET CONNECTIONS

Activism 2000 Youth Project
http://www.youthactivism.com

Aspen Youth Services
http://www.aspenyouth.com

Center on Juvenile and Criminal Justice
http://www.cjcj.org/

Children and Family Justice Center
http://www.law.northwestern.edu/depts/clinic/cfjc/programs/deathpenalty.htm

| **CHAPTER 5** | *The Legal Rights of Juveniles* |

Chapter Objectives

Key Terms

court unification
double jeopardy
family model

hands-off doctrine
litigation explosion

Miranda warning
traditional model

As the result of reading this chapter, you will realize the following objectives:

1. Understand the historical context within which juvenile rights were gradually acquired.
2. Learn about the hands-off doctrine as it once applied to juvenile cases.
3. Understand critical events in the emergence of juvenile rights.
4. Learn about key landmark cases advancing constitutional rights for juveniles charged with crimes.
5. Distinguish between criminal courts and juvenile courts in terms of the rights of offenders processed by each.
6. Understand the debate over whether the death penalty shall be applied to selected juvenile offenders who commit capital murder, including the pros and cons of this process.
7. Learn about several important death penalty cases involving juveniles.
8. Learn about court unification and some of the reasons for its implementation.

• *As a 15-year-old, David Dominguez, a Maryland high school freshman, stabbed two other freshmen, one of them several times in the back. Two Whitman High School youths, Andrew Klepper, 15, and Ryan Baird, 14, beat and sexually assaulted a young woman. John Lee Malvo, 17, admitted being the shooter in a rash of sniper shootings throughout various states, including Maryland. At least one of his victims was killed, 72-year-old Pascal Charlot, who was gunned down at random. Presently in Maryland, the maximum punishment juveniles can receive, no matter how serious or heinous their offense, is confinement in a secure juvenile facility until they are age 21, regardless of their age when they commit their crimes. Harsher punishments for these and similar offenders have been advocated. At the same time, a rights-oriented segment of society proclaims that all juveniles can be rehabilitated and should be given rehabilitative opportunities by being placed in educational and vocational programs with appropriate therapy and counseling. What is the best solution to youth violence?* [*Source:* Adapted from Edward Chan, "Should Juveniles Be Tried As Adults?" *Silver Chips Online,* December 19, 2002.]

• *Mississippi is attempting to revamp its juvenile justice system. A bill has been introduced into the Mississippi State Legislature aimed at establishing significant juvenile justice reforms. According to the bill's sponsors, Mississippi's juvenile justice system is doing an irresponsible job in handling juvenile offenders. Oversight of the state's training schools should be taken away from the Department of Human Services and a separate Department of Juvenile Justice should be created to perform this important function. The bill seeks to cap the number of youths incarcerated in training schools and establish a network of community-based programs as alternatives to state facilities. Described as "inhumane," Mississippi's industrial schools have allegedly hogtied and shackled youths to poles, made them exercise at odd hours, and forced them to eat their own vomit when they get sick from physical exertion. But the bill's opponents say that putting caps on industrial schools poses a safety risk. Clay County Judge Thomas Storey says, "You may have a crime spree. In rural counties, we don't have a place to put the children. If they need to go to training schools, we need to get them down there." Juvenile court judges are also pushing for provisions that will provide greater state funding for youth courts, which are seen as viable alternatives to juvenile courts in less serious juvenile offending cases. Some authorities are arguing for the development of a uniform juvenile court system throughout the state. But bills promoting this measure have been consistently defeated. What is the best way to ensure justice for juveniles?* [*Source:* Adapted from Shelia Byrd and the Associated Press, "Committee Passes Juvenile Justice Reform Bill," January 20, 2005.]

• *In 2005 Virginia was among several states reexamining the application of the death penalty for juveniles convicted of capital crimes. A Charlottesville, Virginia, high school sophomore, 16-year-old Brian Bills says that the state recognizes that at 16, he's not responsible enough to vote or drink alcohol, but he's old enough to be eligible for the death penalty. He says, "I think there's a fundamental flaw in this logic and it needs to be addressed." Bills isn't alone. A new coalition of 32 groups, including the Virginia Alliance to Abolish the Juvenile Death Penalty, Amnesty International, and numerous other religious, civil liberties, and child-advocacy organizations, has filed bills in both the Virginia House and Senate in a vigorous lobbying effort to ban the death penalty for juveniles in the state. Death penalty opponents say that children are not fully developed and that their brains don't function well enough to govern impulse control. They should not be held accountable as adults. They have bad judgment and are immature. They also argue that the death penalty is racist. Virginia has executed 21 juveniles, 19 of them black. Proponents of the death penalty say that if you do the crime, you ought to pay for it, even if it means the death penalty. Furthermore, a majority of the country favors the death penalty as a punishment for capital offenses. What should Virginia do? On March 1, 2005, the U.S. Supreme Court ruled in the case of Roper v. Simmons that it is unconstitutional to execute any juvenile who is or has been convicted of a capital offense that was committed if the youth was under age 18 when the crime was committed.* [*Source:* Adapted from Larry O'Dell and the Associated Press, "Activists Seek End to Juvenile Death Penalty." January 17, 2005; *Roper v. Simmons,* 543 U.S. _____ (2005).]

INTRODUCTION

One of the most controversial issues in the United States today is how to confront and deal with juvenile crime, especially violent crime. From its early origins, the juvenile justice system has been criticized in many ways for its treatment of juveniles under different circumstances. Juvenile institutions, previously referred to as reform schools, were considered mere depositories of juvenile waste, where juveniles were kept under Oliver Twist–like conditions. These juvenile warehouses were depicted in only the most unflattering terms. Juveniles purportedly received no rehabilitation, no services, no amenities, no counseling, no therapy, and no treatment. Media portrayals of juvenile facilities of every kind, even well beyond 2000, continue to be bleak. But as we will see in this and later chapters, these stereotypical views of juveniles and how they are treated no longer apply in most if not all jurisdictions. State-of-the-art facilities are provided and are the rule rather than the exception. Vocational and career counseling are provided in most of these facilities. Extensive educational opportunities abound. A vast array of social services exists in most jurisdictions to meet juvenile offender needs.

Against this backdrop of a new, improved, and decidedly more accurate portrayal of contemporary juvenile services and institutions, how should we judge this chapter's opening scenarios? How should youths, ranging in age from 14 to 17, be processed and treated, when they have committed murder, rape, aggravated assault, and other serious offenses? Can they be rehabilitated and should states attempt to rehabilitate them? Do they have a right to be rehabilitated? How can existing custodial institutions for juveniles that are described as "inhumane" be changed? What mechanisms, legal or otherwise, should be implemented to eliminate adverse treatment of juveniles under these and other similar conditions? When juveniles kill, especially in a deliberate, cold, calculating fashion, what sort of punishment should the states impose? Who should receive the death penalty, if the death penalty for specific crimes is prescribed?

This chapter explores the legal rights of juveniles. The chapter opens with a brief examination of a historical account of the emerging rights of juveniles in the United States. Since Colonial times and up until the mid-1960s, juveniles had no universally applicable legal entitlements. During the 1800s, for instance, juveniles were treated as chattel and counted as a part of one's farm property and animal holdings in periodic national censuses. Different states adopted unique policies applicable to juveniles and how they ought to be treated. As we have seen in previous chapters, Illinois led the states by establishing the first juvenile court in 1899. For the next 67 years, most juvenile courts, which had been established in all jurisdictions by the 1940s, acted much like social welfare agencies rather than legal apparatuses. Apart from unique enactments by particular state legislatures, juveniles enjoyed few if any legal rights commensurate with those of adults. Juvenile courts disposed of all manner of juvenile cases on the basis of what was in the child's best interests. These highly individualized and discriminatory decisions were far from uniform among jurisdictions, and juveniles and their families typically had little or no say in individual case outcomes. Juvenile court powers were and continue to be awesome. A major reason for such power is that the U.S. Supreme Court avoided hearing cases concerning juveniles. It practiced a "hands-off" policy, believing firmly that the juvenile court and juvenile justice agencies were in the best position to decide what was best for children. This hands-off policy is described and compared with a similar policy the high court had toward adult correctional decision making.

The second part of this chapter examines several landmark juvenile cases, which eventually were decided by the U.S. Supreme Court. The first three cases, *Kent v. United States* (1966), *In re Gault* (1967), and *In re Winship* (1970), are considered the "big three" legal cases that opened the floodgates of juvenile litigation before the U.S. Supreme Court. Once the *Kent* case had been decided in 1966, it became much easier for the U.S. Supreme Court to impose its vast precedent-setting powers on juvenile courts in all jurisdictions. Other important cases soon followed, including *McKeiver v. Pennsylvania* (1971), *Breed v. Jones* (1975), and *Schall v. Martin* (1984), were decided, granting various constitutional rights to juveniles. These cases pertained to waiver hearings for juveniles; cross-examining one's accuser and giving testimony in one's behalf; the right to counsel; the right to a notice of charges; the standard of proof required to support one's guilt; the right to a jury trial; the right against double jeopardy; and the issue of preventive detention. Several other cases are discussed involving other juvenile rights issues. A description of each of these cases is provided, together with the significance of the U.S. Supreme Court decision.

The chapter next explores the various implications of granting juveniles greater constitutional rights. The juvenile courts in all jurisdictions have gradually moved away from traditional approaches to juvenile offending and punishments and more toward due process and justice-oriented ones. Today the presence of attorneys in juvenile courts is more the rule rather than the exception. Attorneys represent their juvenile clients in a majority of juvenile courts in contemporary society. In fact, some states have mandated attorneys for all juveniles appearing in juvenile court, except under extraordinary circumstances. Although the U.S. Supreme Court refrained from granting jury trials to juveniles as a matter of right, as well as not requiring juvenile courts to be courts of record, several states presently grant jury trials to their juvenile offenders. Often, such jury trials are case-specific and depend on one's age and the nature of the delinquency charges. These and other issues are examined as the juvenile justice process has become increasingly legalistic and bureaucratized.

The chapter next focuses on the death penalty for juveniles. The death penalty itself is a very controversial subject. Although most surveys reveal strong public sentiment and support for the death penalty, particularly in the plurality of states that utilize it to punish the most serious offenders, the application of the death penalty to juveniles has generated both national and international protests. The history of the death penalty applied to juveniles is briefly explored. Several important cases decided by the U.S. Supreme Court are described, together with their implications for whether juveniles are executed for capital offenses. From 1989 to 2005, the legal standard for applying the death penalty to juveniles was the minimum age of 16. However, in March 2005, the U.S. Supreme Court ruled the application of the death penalty unconstitutional for any youth who committed a capital offense under the age of 18. This and other important cases are described. The discussion also includes a listing of key arguments both favoring and opposing the death penalty as it has been and is presently being applied.

The chapter concludes with an examination of court unification. So many changes have occurred in juvenile court organization and operation that some authorities believe that the two systems, the criminal and juvenile justice systems, should be merged. Thus, several proposals have been advanced that would result in a bifurcated type of court structure, with juvenile matters decided in one sector of such a unified court and adult matters concluded in another sector of it. Presently there is mixed support for court unification. There are numerous obstacles to overcome, including the fact that the juvenile court is largely a civil entity with little chance of changing. The civil nature of juvenile proceedings is such that juveniles in many jurisdictions continue to receive more lenient and protective treatment. Many juveniles are insulated from media coverage, and their identities are closely guarded and concealed. When these persons reach the age of accountability, depending on their jurisdiction, their cases are sealed, and they begin life as adults without the taint of a delinquent past. In a growing number of jurisdictions, however, these protections are gradually diminishing in favor of a get-tough policy toward juveniles, especially more violent ones. The implications of court unification for the future of juvenile courts and the juvenile justice system are explored.

ORIGINAL JUVENILE COURT JURISDICTION: *PARENS PATRIAE*

Until the mid-1960s, juvenile courts had considerable latitude in regulating the affairs of minors. This freedom to act in a child's behalf was rooted in the largely unchallenged doctrine of *parens patriae.* Whenever juveniles were apprehended by police officers for alleged crimes, they were eventually turned over to juvenile authorities or taken to a juvenile hall for further processing.

They were not advised of their right to an attorney, to have an attorney present during any interrogation, or to remain silent. They could be questioned by police at length, without parental notification or legal contact. In short, they had little, if any, protection against adult constitutional rights violations on the part of law enforcement officers and others. They had no access to due process because of their status or standing as juveniles (Rehling, 2005).

In the early years of juvenile courts, when juveniles appeared before juvenile court judges, they almost never had the opportunity to rebut evidence presented against them or to test the reliability of witnesses through cross-examination. This was rationalized at the time by asserting that juveniles did not understand the law and had to have it interpreted for them by others, principally juvenile court judges. Subsequent investigations of the knowledge youths have of their rights seems to confirm this assertion. These early adjudicatory proceedings were very informal. They were also conducted without defense counsel being present to advise their youthful clients. In one-sided affairs, facts were alleged by various accusers, often persons such as probation officers or police officers, and youthful defendants were not permitted to give testimony in their own behalf or cross-examine those giving testimony.

Prosecutors were seldom present in juvenile proceedings since they were largely nonadversarial, and juvenile court judges handled most cases informally, independently, and subjectively, depending on the youth's needs and the seriousness of the offense. If judges decided that secure confinement would best serve the interests of justice and the welfare of the juvenile, then the youth would be placed in a secure confinement facility (juvenile prison) for an indeterminate period. These decisions were seldom questioned or challenged. If they were challenged, higher courts would dismiss these challenges as frivolous or without merit.

The "Hands-Off" Doctrine

A major reason for the silent acceptance of juvenile court judges' decisions was that the U.S. Supreme Court had repeatedly demonstrated its reluctance to intervene in juvenile matters or question decisions made by juvenile court judges. In the case of *In re Gault* (1967), Justice Stewart typified the traditional orientation of former Supreme Courts by declaring:

> "The Court today uses an obscure Arizona case as a vehicle to impose upon thousands of juvenile courts throughout the Nation restrictions that the Constitution made applicable to adversary criminal trials. I believe the Court's decision is *wholly unsound* [emphasis mine] as a matter of constitutional law, and sadly unwise as a matter of judicial policy. . . . The inflexible restrictions that the Constitution so wisely made applicable to adversary criminal trials have no inevitable place in the proceedings of those public social agencies known as juvenile or family courts" (387 U.S. at 78–79).

The **hands-off doctrine** of the U.S. Supreme Court toward juvenile court matters was similar to their hands-off policy toward corrections (Gomez and Ganuza, 2002). In the case of *Ruffin v. Commonwealth* (1871), a Virginia judge declared that "prisoners have no more rights than slaves." Thus, during the next 70 years, prisoners were used as guinea pigs in various biological and chemical experiments, particularly in the testing of gases used on the front lines in Europe during World War I. Such tests of chemical agents on prisoners were conducted at the Michigan State Prison at Jackson. Some prisons mandated inmate sterilization, because it was believed that criminal behavior was hereditary. No committees for the protection of human subjects existed to protest these inmate treatments. Inmates had absolutely no rights, including mail privacy, visitation, or other privileges, other than those rights dispensed or withheld by prison authorities (Myers, 1973).

The U.S. Supreme Court commenced to change this state of affairs toward corrections in 1941 in the case of *Ex parte Hull* (1941). This case involved attempts by prisoners to petition the courts to hear various grievances or complaints. Prison superintendents and staff would routinely trash these petitions, contending that they were improperly prepared and hence, legally unacceptable. In the *Hull* decision, the Court held that no state or its officers could abridge inmates of their right to access the federal or state courts through their petitions. Once the *Hull* decision had been made, there was a proliferation of inmate rights cases in subsequent years known as a **litigation explosion.** Two decades later, a similar litigation explosion would occur. This time the subject matter would be juvenile rights (Anderson and Dyson, 2001).

In many respects, juveniles were treated like adult inmates in prisons. Youths had no legal standing and virtually no rights other than those extended by the courts. The right to a trial by jury, a basic right provided any defendant who might be incarcerated for six months or more by a criminal court conviction, did not exist for juveniles unless juvenile court judges permitted such trials. Most juvenile court judges abhor jury trials for their juveniles and refuse to permit them. Even today, juveniles do not have an absolute right to a trial by

Some more serious juveniles are sent to criminal court for processing as adults through judicial or discretionary waiver actions.

jury, with few exceptions through state statutes. Thus, juveniles may be deprived of their freedom for many years on the basis of a personal judicial decision.

Because of the informality of juvenile proceedings in most jurisdictions, there were frequent and obvious abuses of judicial discretion. These abuses occurred because of the absence of consistent guidelines whereby cases could be adjudicated. Juvenile probation officers might casually recommend to judges that particular juveniles "ought to do a few months" in an industrial school or other secure confinement facility, and the judge might be persuaded to adjudicate these cases accordingly.

However, several forces were at work simultaneously during the 1950s and 1960s that would eventually have the conjoint consequence of making juvenile courts more accountable for specific adjudications of youthful offenders. One of these forces was increased parental and general public recognition of and concern for the liberal license taken by juvenile courts in administering the affairs of juveniles. The abuse of judicial discretion was becoming increasingly apparent. Additionally, there was a growing disenchantment with and apathy for the rehabilitation ideal, although this disenchantment was not directed solely at juvenile courts (Anderson and Dyson, 2001).

The juvenile court as originally envisioned by Progressives was procedurally informal, characterized by individualized, offender-oriented dispositional practices. However, the contemporary juvenile court departs markedly from this Progressive ideal. Today, juvenile courts are increasingly criminalized, featuring an adversarial system and greater procedural formality. This formality effectively inhibits any individualized treatment these courts might contemplate, and it has increased the perfunctory nature of sentencing juveniles adjudicated as delinquent.

The transformation of juvenile courts into more formal proceedings as part of the national trend toward bureaucratization and as an institutional compromise between law and social welfare has occurred. Bureaucracy stresses a fixed hierarchy of authority, task specialization, individualized spheres of competence, impersonal social relationships between organizational actors, and impartial enforcement of abstract rules. Thus, in the context of bureaucracy, decision making is routinized rather than arbitrary. Personalities and social characteristics are irrelevant.

Applied to juvenile court proceedings, juvenile court decision making would most likely be a function of the nature and seriousness of offenses committed and the factual delinquent history of juvenile defendants. Emotional considerations in bureaucratic structures are nonexistent. The bureaucratic approach would be that juveniles should be held to a high standard of accountability for their actions. Furthermore, an individualized, treatment-oriented sanctioning system would be inconsistent with bureaucracy and violative of its general principles of impartiality. This type of system for juvenile justice seems consistent with the sentiments of a large portion of U.S. citizens and their belief that juvenile courts should get tough with juvenile offenders. Despite this due-process and bureaucratic emphasis, juvenile courts have continued to retain many of their seemingly haphazard characteristics. Sound policies have been established, but their implementation has remained inconsistent and problematic for many juvenile courts.

A major change from *parens patriae* state-based interests to a due-process juvenile justice model means that decision making about youthful offenders is increasingly rationalized, and the principle of just-deserts is fundamental. This means that less discretionary authority will be manifested by juvenile court judges, as they decide each case more on the basis of offense seriousness and prescribed punishments rather than according to individual factors or circumstances (Fader et al., 2001). Table 5.1 provides a general chronology of events relating to juvenile rights during the last 200 years.

During the mid-1960s and through the 1980s, significant achievements were made in the area of juvenile rights. Although the *parens patriae* philosophy continues to influence juvenile proceedings, the U.S. Supreme Court has vested youths with certain constitutional rights. These rights do not encompass all of the rights extended to adults who are charged with crimes. But those rights conveyed to juveniles thus far have had far-reaching implications for how juveniles are processed. The general result of these U.S. Supreme Court decisions has been to bring the juvenile court system under constitutional control. Several landmark cases involving juvenile rights are described in the following section.

LANDMARK CASES IN JUVENILE JUSTICE

Several significant changes have been made in the juvenile justice system and how youths are processed in recent decades. In this section, we examine several important rights bestowed upon juveniles by the U.S. Supreme Court during the period 1960–1990. Describing these rights will make clear those rights

TABLE 5.1

Chronological Summary of Major Events in Juvenile Justice

Year	Event
1791	Bill of Rights passed by U.S. Congress
1825	New York House of Refuge established
1828	Boston House of Refuge founded
1839	*Ex parte Crouse,* established right of juvenile court intervention in parent–child matters
1841	John Augustus initiates probation in Boston
1847	State institutions for juveniles opened in Boston and New York
1851	First adoption act in U.S. passed in Massachusetts
1853	New York Children's Aid Society established
1853	New York Juvenile Asylum created by Children's Aid Society
1855	Death penalty imposed on 10-year-old James Arcene in Arkansas for robbery and murder; earliest juvenile execution was Thomas Graunger, a 16-year-old, for sodomizing a cow in 1642
1866	Massachusetts statute passed giving juvenile court power to intervene and take custody of juveniles under age 16 whose parents are unfit
1868	Fourteenth Amendment passed by U.S. Congress, establishing right to due process and equal protection under the law
1870	*People ex rel. O'Connell v. Turner* case holding that reform school commitments of youths could not be made on the basis of simple misfortune or vagrancy; limited institutionalization of youths to those who committed crimes; denied confinement of youths who were not afforded legal due process
1874–1875	Massachusetts established first Children's Tribunal to deal with youthful offenders

TABLE 5.1

Chronological Summary of Major Events in Juvenile Justice *(cont.)*

Year	Event
1881	Michigan commences child protection with the Michigan Public Acts of 1881
1884	*Reynolds v. Howe* case gives state authority to place neglected children in institutions
1886	First child neglect case is heard in Massachusetts
1889	Indiana established children's guardians to have jurisdiction over neglected and dependent children
1890	Children's Aid Society of Pennsylvania, a foster home for juvenile delinquents used as an alternative to reform schools, is established
1891	Minnesota Supreme Court establishes doctrine of parental immunity
1897	*Ex parte Becknell* case reverses disposition of juvenile who has not been given a fair trial
1899	Hull House established in Chicago by Jane Addams to assist unsupervised children of immigrant parents
1899	Compulsory School Act, Colorado; statutory regulation of truants
1899	Illinois Act to Regulate the Treatment and Control of Dependent, Neglected, and Delinquent Children; first juvenile court established in United States
1900	Case law begins to deal with children's protective statutes
1901	Juvenile court established in Denver, Colorado
1906	Massachusetts passes act providing for treatment of children not as criminals but as children in need of guidance and aid
1907	Separate juvenile court with original jurisdiction in juvenile matters established in Denver, Colorado
1908	*Ex parte Sharpe* defines more clearly power of juvenile court to include *parens patriae*
1910	Compulsory school acts passed in different state jurisdictions
1912	Creation of U.S. Children's Bureau, charged with compiling statistical information about juvenile offenders; existed from 1912 to 1940
1918	Chicago slums studied by Shaw and McKay; delinquency related to urban environment and transitional neighborhoods
1924	Federal Probation Act passed
1930	Children's Charter
1938	Federal Juvenile Court Act passed
1954	*Brown v. Board of Education* school desegregation decision
1959	Standard Family Court Act of National Council on Crime and Delinquency establishes that juvenile hearings are to be informally conducted
1966	*Kent v. United States* case established juveniles' right to a hearing before transfer to criminal court, right to assistance of counsel during police interrogations, right to reports and records relating to transfer decision, and right to reasons given by the judge for the transfer
1967	*In re Gault* case established juvenile's right to an attorney, right to notice of charges, right to confront and cross-examine witnesses, and right against self-incrimination
1968	*Ginsberg v. New York* establishes that it is unlawful to sell pornography to a minor
1969	*Tinker v. Des Moines Independent Community School District* establishes that the First Amendment applies to juveniles and protects their constitutional right to free speech
1970	*In re Winship* case established juveniles' right to criminal court standard of "beyond a reasonable doubt" where loss of freedom is a possible penalty
1971	*McKeiver v. Pennsylvania* case established that juveniles' right to a trial by jury is not absolute
1971	26th Amendment to Constitution is passed granting the right to vote to 18 year olds
1972	*Wisconsin v. Yoder* case gives parents the right to impose their religion on their children
1972	Marvin Wolfgang publishes *Delinquency in a Birth Cohort*

TABLE 5.1

Chronological Summary of Major Events in Juvenile Justice *(cont.)*

Year	Event
1973	*In re Snyder* gives minors the right to bring legal proceedings against their parents
1973	*San Antonio Independent School District v. Rodriguez* establishes that differences in education based on wealth are not necessarily discriminatory
1974	Juvenile Justice and Delinquency Prevention Act, intended to deinstitutionalize status offenders, separate delinquents from status offenders generally, and divest juvenile court judges of their jurisdiction over status offenders
1974	Office of Juvenile Justice and Delinquency Prevention, instrumental in promoting deinstitutionalization of status offenders
1974	Federal Child Abuse Prevention Act
1974	Buckley Amendment to Education Act of 1974, the Family Education Rights and Privacy Act; students have right to see their own files with parental consent
1975	*Goss v. Lopez* case establishes that a student facing school suspension has right to due process, prior notice, and an open hearing
1975	*Breed v. Jones* case established that double jeopardy exists if juvenile is adjudicated as delinquent in juvenile court on a given charge and tried for same offense later in criminal court; prohibits double jeopardy
1977	Report of the Committee on the Judiciary, especially concerning the rights of the unborn and the right of 18-year-olds to vote
1977	Juvenile Justice Amendment of 1977
1977	*Ingraham v. Wright* case establishes that corporal punishment is permissible in public schools and is not a violation of the Eighth Amendment
1977	American Bar Association, Standards on Juvenile Justice
1977	Washington State amends its sentencing policies
1979	*Fare v. Michael C.* case established "totality of circumstances" standard for evaluating propriety of custodial interrogations of juveniles by police without parents or attorneys present; defines *Miranda* rights of minors
1980	National concern over child abuse and neglect
1982	*Eddings v. Oklahoma* case established that death penalty applied to juveniles is not cruel and unusual punishment per se
1982	Efforts to decarcerate status offenders escalate
1984	*Schall v. Martin* case established the constitutionality of the preventive detention of juveniles
1985	*New Jersey v. T.L.O.* case established lesser standard of search and seizure on school property; searches and seizures permissible without probable cause or warrant
1985	Wilson and Herrnstein publish *Crime and Human Nature,* focusing attention on the biological causes of delinquency
1985	United Nations General Assembly adopts "Standard Minimum Rules for the Administration of Juvenile Justice"
1986	*Woods v. Clusen* case established right of juveniles against aggressive police interrogation tactics by failing to observe juvenile's constitutional rights and provide for fundamental fairness
1986	Juvenile offenders waived to criminal court are executed, focusing attention on the death penalty administered to children
1987	Conservative trends result in 10,000 juvenile waivers to criminal courts
1988	Reemergence of nationwide gang problem
1988	*Thompson v. Oklahoma* case established that death penalty applied to juveniles convicted of murder who were under age 16 at time of murder is cruel and unusual punishment

TABLE 5.1	

Chronological Summary of Major Events in Juvenile Justice *(cont.)*

Year	Event
1989	*Stanford v. Kentucky* and *Wilkins v. Missouri* cases established that the death penalty is not cruel and unusual punishment applied to juveniles convicted of murder who were ages 16 or 17 at the time the murder was committed
1990	*Maryland v. Craig* allows child abuse victims to testify on closed-circuit television in courts
1991	Juvenile violence rate hits all-time high of 430 acts per 100,000 adolescents
1995	Reported child abuse cases exceed 3 million
1996	Michigan parents criminally convicted for failing to supervise delinquent son
1997	Juvenile crime rates begin to remain stable in United States.
1998	School shooting in Jonesboro, Arkansas, leaves five killed, raises questions about children and access to firearms
1999	School shoootings on rise; Littleton, Colorado, high school scene of mass murders of 15 persons by two students who then commit suicide; public policies implemented about safeguarding school systems from similar incidents in future
2000	*Santa Fe Independent School District v. Jane Doe* case bans student-led prayer at sporting events, further defining separation of church and state in school settings
2002	U.S. Supreme Court strikes down federal law banning computer-generated images of minors engaging in sex, thereby allowing virtual kiddie porn to be sold freely over the Internet
2004	40-year follow-up of Perry Preschool Project; fewer lifetime arrests and other social benefits accrue to participants
2005	*Roper v. Simmons* case determines that execution of persons who are under age 18 at time they commit capital crimes is prohibited by Eighth and Fourteenth Amendments; overturned *Stanford v. Kentucky* and *Wilkins v. Missouri* decided in 1989

juveniles did not have until the landmark cases associated with them were decided. Then, a comparison is made of juvenile rights and those rights enjoyed by adults charged with crimes in criminal courts. Despite sweeping juvenile reforms and major legal gains, there are still several important differences between the rights of juveniles and adults when both are charged with crimes (Wilkerson, 2005).

Currently, juvenile courts are largely punishment-centered, with the justice and just-deserts models influencing court decision making. Interests of youths are secondary, while community interests are seemingly served by juvenile court actions. Juveniles are being given greater responsibility for their actions, and they are increasingly expected to be held accountable for their wrongdoing (Feld, 2001).

Each of the cases presented below represents attempts by juveniles to secure rights ordinarily extended to adults. Given these cases, juveniles have fared well with the U.S. Supreme Court in past years. While juveniles still do not enjoy the full range of rights extended to adult offenders who are tried in criminal courts, juveniles have acquired due-process privileges that were not available to them prior to the 1960s. The first three cases presented, *Kent v. United States, In re Gault,* and *In re Winship,* comprise the "big three" of juvenile cases involving their legal rights. The remaining cases address specific rights issues, such as the right against double jeopardy, jury trials as a matter of right in juvenile courts, preventive detention, and the standards that should govern searches of students and seizures of contraband on school property.

Kent v. United States (1966)

Regarded as the first major juvenile rights case to preface further juvenile court reforms, *Kent v. United States* (1966) established the universal precedents of (1) requiring waiver hearings before juveniles can be transferred to the jurisdiction of a criminal court (excepting legislative automatic waivers as discussed in this and other chapters, although reverse waiver hearings must be conducted at the juvenile's request), and (2) juveniles are entitled to consult with counsel prior to and during such hearings (Grisso, 1998).

The facts in the case are that in 1959, Morris A. Kent, Jr., a 14-year-old in the District of Columbia, was apprehended as the result of several housebreakings and attempted purse snatchings. He was placed on probation in the custody of his mother. In 1961, an intruder entered the apartment of a woman, took her wallet, and raped her. Fingerprints at the crime scene were later identified as those of Morris Kent, who was fingerprinted when apprehended for housebreaking in 1959. On September 5, 1961, Kent, now age 16, was taken into custody by police, interrogated for seven hours, and admitted the offense as well as volunteering information about other housebreakings, robberies, and rapes. Although the records are unclear about when Kent's mother became aware of Kent's arrest, she did obtain counsel for Kent shortly after 2:00 P.M. the following day. She and her attorney conferred with the Social Service Director of the Juvenile Court and learned there was a possibility Kent would be waived to criminal court. Kent's attorney advised the Director of his intention to oppose the waiver.

Kent was detained in a receiving home for one week. During that period, there was no arraignment and no determination by a judicial officer of probable cause for Kent's arrest. His attorney filed a motion with the juvenile court opposing the waiver as well as a request to inspect records relating to Kent's previous offenses. Also, a psychiatric examination of Kent was arranged by Kent's attorney. Kent's attorney argued that because his client was "a victim of severe psychopathology," it would be in Kent's best interests to remain within juvenile court jurisdiction where he could receive adequate treatment in a hospital and would be a suitable subject for rehabilitation.

Typical of juvenile court judges at the time, the juvenile court judge failed to rule on any of Kent's attorney's motions. He also failed to confer with Kent's attorney and/or parents. In a somewhat arrogant manner, the juvenile court judge declared that "after full investigation, I do hereby waive" jurisdiction of Kent and direct that he be "held for trial for [the alleged] offenses under the regular procedure of the U.S. District Court for the District of Columbia." He offered no findings, nor did he recite any reason for the waiver or make mention of Kent's attorney's motions. Kent was later found guilty of six counts of housebreaking by a federal jury, although the jury found him "not guilty by reason of insanity" on the rape charge. Because of District of Columbia law, it was mandatory that Kent be transferred to a mental institution until such time as his sanity is restored. On each of the housebreaking counts, Kent's sentence was 5–15 years, or a total of 30–90 years in prison. His mental institution commitment would be counted as time served against the 30- to 90-year sentence.

Kent's conviction was reversed by a vote of 5–4. This is significant, because it signified a subtle shift in Supreme Court sentiment relating to juvenile rights. The majority held that Kent's rights to due process and to the effective assistance of counsel were violated when he was denied a formal hearing on the waiver and his attorneys' motions were ignored. It is also significant that the Supreme Court stressed the phrase "critically important" when referring to the absence of counsel and waiver hearing, respectively. In adult cases, critical stages are those that relate to the defendant's potential loss of freedoms (i.e., incarceration). Because of the *Kent* decision, waiver hearings are now critical stages. Regarding the effective assistance of counsel, this was also regarded by the Court as a "critically important" decision. They observed that "the right to representation by counsel is not a formality. It is not a grudging gesture to a ritualistic requirement. It is of the essence of justice. . . . Appointment of counsel without affording an opportunity for a hearing on a 'critically important' decision is tantamount to a denial of counsel" (383 U.S. at 561).

In re Gault (1967)

In re Gault (1967) is perhaps the most noteworthy of all landmark juvenile rights cases. Certainly it is considered the most ambitious. In a 7–2 vote, the U.S. Supreme Court articulated the following rights for all juveniles: (1) the right to a notice of charges; (2) the right to counsel; (3) the right to confront and cross-examine witnesses; and (4) the right to invoke the privilege against self-incrimination. The petitioner, Gault, requested the Court to rule favorably on two additional rights sought: (1) the right to a transcript of the proceedings and (2) the right to appellate review. The Court elected not to rule on either of these rights.

The facts in the case are that Gerald Francis Gault, a 15-year-old, and a friend, Ronald Lewis, were taken into custody by the Sheriff of Gila County, Arizona, on the morning of June 8, 1964. At the time, Gault was on probation as the result of "being in the company of another" who had stolen a wallet from a lady's purse," a judgment entered February 25, 1964. A verbal complaint had been filed by a neighbor of Gault, Mrs. Cook, alleging that Gault had called her and made lewd and indecent remarks. [With some levity, the Supreme Court said that "It will suffice for purposes of this opinion to say that the remarks or questions put to her were of the irritatingly offensive, adolescent, sex variety" (387 U.S. at 4)]. When Gault was picked up, his mother and father were at work. Indeed, they did not learn where their son was until much later that evening. Gault was being held at the Children's Detention Home.

Gault's parents proceeded to the Home. Officer Flagg, the deputy probation officer and superintendent of the Children's Detention Home where Gault was being detained, advised Gault's parents that a hearing would be held in Juvenile Court at 3:00 P.M. the following day. Flagg filed a petition with the court on the hearing day, June 9. This petition was entirely formal, stating only that "said minor is under the age of 18 years, and is in need of the protection of this Honorable Court; [and that] said minor is a delinquent minor." It prayed for a hearing and an order regarding the "care and custody of said minor." No factual basis was provided for the petition, and Gault's parents were not provided with a copy of it in advance of the hearing.

On June 9, the hearing was held, with only Gault, his mother and older brother, Probation Officers Flagg and Henderson, and the juvenile court judge present. The original complainant, Mrs. Cook, was not there. No one was sworn at the hearing, no transcript was made of it, and no memorandum of the substance of the proceedings was prepared. The testimony consisted largely of allegations by Officer Flagg about Gault's behavior and prior juvenile record. A subsequent hearing was scheduled for June 15. On June 15, another hearing was held, with all above present, including Ronald Lewis and his father, and Gerald's father. What actually transpired is unknown, although there are conflicting recollections from all parties who were there. Mrs. Gault asked why Mrs. Cook was not present. Judge McGhee said "she didn't have to be present at that hearing." Furthermore, the judge did not speak to Mrs. Cook or communicate with her at any time. Flagg spoke with her once by telephone on June 9. Officially, the charge against Gault was "lewd telephone calls." When the hearing was concluded, the judge committed Gault as a juvenile delinquent to the Arizona State Industrial School "for a period of his minority" (until age 21). (Parenthetically, if an adult had made an obscene telephone call, he would have received a $50 fine and no more than 60 days in jail. In Gerald Gault's case, he was facing nearly six years in a juvenile prison for the same offense.)

A **habeas corpus** hearing was held on August 17, and Judge McGhee was cross-examined regarding his actions. After "hemming and hawing," the judge declared that Gault had "disturbed the peace" and was "habitually involved in immoral matters." Regarding the judge's reference to Gault's alleged "habitual immorality," the judge made vague references to an incident two years earlier when Gault had been accused of stealing someone's baseball glove and had lied to police by denying that he had taken it. The judge also recalled, again vaguely, that Gault had testified some months earlier about making "silly calls, or funny calls, or something like that."

After exhausting their appeals in Arizona state courts, the Gaults appealed to the U.S. Supreme Court. Needless to say, the Court was appalled that Gault's case had been handled in such a cavalier and unconstitutional manner. They reversed the Arizona Supreme Court, holding that Gault did, indeed, have the right to an attorney, the right to confront his accuser (Mrs. Cook) and to cross-examine her, the right against self-incrimination, and the right to have notice of the charges filed against him. Perhaps Justice Black summed up the current juvenile court situation in the United States when he said, "This holding strikes a well-nigh fatal blow to much that is *unique* [emphasis mine] about the juvenile courts in this Nation."

In re Winship (1970)

In re Winship was a less complex case compared with *Gault.* But it established an important precedent in juvenile courts relating to the standard of proof used in establishing defendant guilt. The U.S. Supreme Court held that "beyond a reasonable doubt," a standard ordinarily used in adult criminal courts, was henceforth to be used by juvenile court judges and others in establishing a youth's delinquency. Formerly, the standard used was the civil application of "preponderance of the evidence."

The facts in the *Winship* case are that Samuel Winship was a 12-year-old charged with larceny in New York City. He purportedly entered a locker and stole $112 from a woman's pocketbook. Under Section 712 of the New York Family Court Act, a juvenile delinquent was defined as "a person over seven and less than sixteen years of age who does any act, which, if done by an adult, would constitute a crime." Interestingly, the juvenile court judge in the case acknowledged that the proof to be presented by the prosecution might be insufficient to establish the guilt of Winship beyond a reasonable doubt, although he did indicate that the New York Family Court Act provided that "any determination at the conclusion of [an adjudicatory hearing] that a [juvenile] did an act or acts must be based on a preponderance of the evidence" standard (397 U.S. at 360). Winship was adjudicated as a delinquent and ordered to a training school for 18 months, subject to annual extensions of his commitment until his 18th birthday. Appeals to New York courts were unsuccessful.

The U.S. Supreme Court heard Winship's case and, in a 6–3 vote, reversed the New York Family Court ruling. A statement by Justice Brennan succinctly states the case for the beyond-a-reasonable-doubt standard:

> "In sum, the constitutional safeguard of proof beyond a reasonable doubt is as much required during the adjudicatory stage of a delinquency proceeding as are those constitutional safeguards applied in *Gault*—notice of charges, right to counsel, the rights of confrontation and examination, and the privilege of self-incrimination. We therefore hold, in agreement with Chief Justice Fuld in dissent in the Court of Appeals, that where a 12-year-old child is charged with an act of stealing which renders him liable to confinement for as long as six years, then, as a matter of due process, the case against him must be proved beyond a reasonable doubt" (397 U.S. at 368).

McKeiver v. Pennsylvania (1971)

The *McKeiver* case was important because the U.S. Supreme Court held that juveniles are not entitled to a jury trial as a matter of right. (It should be noted that as of 1990, 12 states legislatively mandated jury trials for juveniles in juvenile courts if they so requested such trials, depending on the seriousness of the offense(s) alleged.) The facts are that in May 1968, Joseph McKeiver, age 16, was charged with robbery, larceny, and receiving stolen goods. Although he was represented by counsel at his adjudicatory hearing and requested a trial by jury to ascertain his guilt or innocence, Judge Theodore S. Gutowicz of the Court of Common Pleas, Family Division, Juvenile Branch, of Philadelphia, denied the request. McKeiver was subsequently adjudicated delinquent. On subsequent appeal to the U.S. Supreme Court, McKeiver's adjudication was upheld. Again, of interest to criminal justice analysts, the remarks of a U.S. Supreme Court Justice are insightful. Justice Blackmun indicated: "If the formalities of the criminal adjudicative process are to be superimposed upon the juvenile court system, there is little need for its separate existence. Perhaps that ultimate disillusionment will come one day, but for the moment, we are disinclined to give impetus to it" (403 U.S. at 551).

Throughout the opinion delivered in the *McKeiver* case, it is apparent that the Supreme Court was sensitive to the problems associated with juvenile court procedure. Since criminal courts were already bogged down with formalities and lengthy protocol that frequently led to excessive court delays, it was not unreasonable for the Court to rule against perpetuating such formalities in juvenile courts. But we must recognize that in this instance, the Court merely ruled that it is not the constitutional right of juveniles to have the right to a jury trial upon their request. This proclamation had no effect on individual states that wished to enact or preserve such a method of adjudicating juveniles as delinquent or not delinquent. Therefore, about a fourth of the states today have legislative provisions for jury trials in juvenile courts. See the discussion below on the 2005 status of jury trials for juveniles.

Breed v. Jones (1975)

The *Breed v. Jones* case raised the significant constitutional issue of **double jeopardy.** Double jeopardy means being tried for the same crime twice. The Fifth Amendment provides us with the protection against double jeopardy. Thus, if someone is charged with a crime and acquitted, they cannot be tried again for that same offense. This would violate their Fifth Amendment right against double jeopardy. In *Breed v. Jones,* the U.S. Supreme Court concluded that after a juvenile has been adjudicated delinquent for a particular offense, the youth cannot be tried again as an adult in criminal court for that same offense.

The facts of the case are that on February 8, 1971, in Los Angeles, Gary Steven Jones, 17 years old, was armed with a deadly weapon and allegedly committed robbery. Jones was subsequently apprehended and an adjudicatory hearing was held on March 1. A petition was filed against Jones. After testimony was taken from Jones and witnesses, the Juvenile Court found that the allegations in the petition were true and sustained the petition. A dispositional hearing date was set for March 15. At that time, Jones was declared "not . . . amenable to the care, treatment and training program available through the facilities of the juvenile court" under a California statute. Jones was then transferred by judicial waiver to a California criminal court where he could be tried as an adult. In a later criminal trial, Jones was convicted of robbery and committed for an indeterminate period to the California Youth Authority. The California Supreme Court upheld the conviction.

When Jones appealed the decision in 1971, the U.S. Supreme Court reversed the robbery conviction. Chief Justice Warren Burger delivered the Court opinion: "We hold that the prosecution of [Jones] in Superior Court, after an adjudicatory proceeding in Juvenile Court, violated the Double Jeopardy Clause of the Fifth Amendment, as applied to the States through the Fourteenth Amendment." The Court ordered Jones's release outright or a remand to juvenile court for disposition. In a lengthy opinion, Justice Burger targeted double jeopardy as (1) being adjudicated as delinquent on specific charges in a juvenile court, and (2) subsequently being tried and convicted on those same charges in criminal court. Within the context of fundamental fairness, such action could not be tolerated.

Schall v. Martin (1984)

In the *Schall* case, the U.S. Supreme Court issued juveniles a minor setback regarding the state's right to hold them in preventive detention pending a subsequent adjudication. The Court said that the preventive detention of juveniles by states is constitutional, if judges perceive these youths to pose a danger to the community or an otherwise serious risk if released short of an adjudicatory hearing. This decision was significant, in part, because many persons advocated the separation of juveniles and adults in jails, those facilities most often

TABLE 5.2

Comparison of Juvenile and Adult Rights Relating to Delinquency and Crime

Right	Adults	Juveniles
1. "Beyond a reasonable doubt" standard used in court	Yes	Yes
2. Right against double jeopardy	Yes	Yes
3. Right to assistance of counsel	Yes	Yes
4. Right to notice of charges	Yes	Yes
5. Right to a transcript of court proceedings	Yes	No
6. Right against self-incrimination	Yes	Yes
7. Right to trial by jury	Yes	No in most states
8. Right to defense counsel in court proceedings	Yes	No
9. Right to due process	Yes	No[a]
10. Right to bail	Yes	No, with exceptions
11. Right to cross-examine witnesses	Yes	Yes
12. Right of confrontation	Yes	Yes
13. Standards relating to searches and seizures:		
a. "Probable cause" and warrants required for searches and seizures	Yes, with exceptions	No
b. "Reasonable suspicion" required for searches and seizures without warrant	No	Yes
14. Right to hearing prior to transfer to criminal court or to a reverse waiver hearing in states with automatic transfer provisions	N/A	Yes
15. Right to a speedy trial	Yes	No
16. Right to *habeas corpus* relief in correctional settings	Yes	No
17. Right to rehabilitation	No	No
18. Criminal evidentiary standards	Yes	Yes
19. Right to hearing for parole or probation revocation	Yes	No
20. Bifurcated trial, death penalty cases	Yes	Yes
21. Right to discovery	Yes	Limited
22. Fingerprinting, photographing at booking	Yes	No, with exceptions
23. Right to appeal	Yes	Limited
24. Waivers of rights:		
a. Adults	Knowingly, intelligently	
b. Juveniles	Totality of circumstances	
25. Right to hearing for parole or probation revocation	Yes	No, with exceptions
26. "Equal protection" clause of 14th Amendment applicable	Yes	No, with exceptions
27. Right to court-appointed attorney if indigent	Yes	No, with exceptions
28. Transcript required of criminal/delinquency trial proceedings	Yes	No, with exceptions
29. Pretrial detention permitted	Yes	Yes
30. Plea bargaining	Yes, with exceptions	No, with exceptions
31. Burden of proof borne by prosecution	Yes	No, with exceptions[b]
32. Public access to trials	Yes	Limited
33. Conviction/adjudication results in criminal record	Yes	No

[a]Minimal, not full, due-process safeguards assured.
[b]Burden of proof is borne by prosecutor in 23 state juvenile courts; the remainder make no provision or mention of who bears the burden of proof.
Source: Compiled by author.

used for preventive detention. Also, the preventive detention of adults was not ordinarily practiced at that time. [Since then, the preventive detention of adults who are deemed to pose societal risks has been upheld by the U.S. Supreme Court (*United States v. Salerno,* 1987).]

The facts are that 14-year-old Gregory Martin was arrested at 11:30 P.M. on December 13, 1977, in New York City. He was charged with first-degree robbery, second-degree assault, and criminal possession of a weapon. Martin lied to police at the time, giving a false name and address. Between the time of his arrest and December 29 when a fact-finding hearing was held, Martin was detained (a total of 15 days). His confinement was based largely on the false information he had supplied to police and the seriousness of the charges pending against him. Subsequently, he was adjudicated a delinquent and placed on two years' probation. Later, his attorney filed an appeal, contesting his preventive detention as violative of the Due Process Clause of the Fourteenth Amendment. The U.S. Supreme Court eventually heard the case and upheld the detention as constitutional. Table 5.2 summarizes some of the major rights available to juveniles and compares these rights with selected rights enjoyed by adults in criminal proceedings.

IMPLICATIONS OF MORE CONSTITUTIONAL RIGHTS FOR JUVENILES

Some of the major implications of more constitutional rights for juveniles include: (1) more equitable treatment through less disparity in dispositions among juvenile judges; (2) greater certainty of punishment through the new justice orientation; (3) less informality in dispositions and less individualized rehabilitative treatments; (4) greater likelihood of acquiring a juvenile offender record, since procedures from intake through adjudication are increasingly codified; and (5) greater likelihood of being transferred to criminal courts through waivers, since the most serious cases will move forward more frequently to juvenile courts.

Almost all juvenile courts in the United States are civil courts. When juveniles are adjudicated delinquent by these courts, they do not acquire criminal records. Once youths reach the age of majority or adulthood, their juvenile records are expunged, forgotten, or sealed. They begin a fresh life as adults without a prior record of delinquency or criminal activity. This works to their advantage. However, the jurisdiction of juvenile courts in various states is changing. As we will see in subsequent chapters, the powers of juvenile court judges are being extended. Increasingly it is possible for these judges to impose both juvenile and adult penalties on youths adjudicated delinquent. These dual sanctions are both innovative and controversial (Bilchik, 1996). Furthermore, many states are lowering the age at which a juvenile may be tried as an adult in criminal court. In a deadly school shooting in Arkansas, for instance, the two shooters were 13 and 14 years of age, respectively. The 14-year-old was subsequently tried as an adult in criminal court. However, the 13-year-old was adjudicated in juvenile court where the harshness of penalties was severely limited. This was because the law as it was applied then meant that he could not be tried as an adult in criminal court, regardless of the heinousness of his actions. Only those age 14 or older could be tried as adults. As a result, the Arkansas legislature lowered the minimum age at which a juvenile could be tried as an adult in criminal court. Thus, if in the future, a 13-year-old juvenile committed

The Juvenile Justice and Delinquency Prevention Act of 1974 mandated the removal of juveniles from jails in all U.S. jurisdictions.

murder in Arkansas, the juvenile could be prosecuted as an adult offender in criminal court (Associated Press, 2001).

For the majority of jurisdictions as of 2005, while most juveniles remain within juvenile court jurisdiction, they are subject to harsher penalties as juveniles than might otherwise be the case if they were treated as adults. For instance, the case of *Gault* reported earlier in this chapter saw a boy disposed to nearly six years in a state industrial school for allegedly making an obscene telephone call, a low-level misdemeanor. For offenses such as this, adults would not be incarcerated. Rather, they would be fined a nominal amount. Currently, juvenile court judges have considerable power to influence a juvenile's liberty to the limits of one's infant status. Even now in most jurisdictions, if juvenile court judges wish, they may dispose youths to long-term secure confinement far beyond incarcerative terms for sentenced adults who have been convicted of similar offenses. This unfairness is a carry-over from the *parens patriae* years of juvenile courts.

The Juvenile's Right to Waive Rights

With all of the legal rights extended to juveniles since 1966, there are more than a few occasions when juveniles may waive various rights, such as the right to counsel, at one or more critical stages of their juvenile justice system processing. For instance, a 1968 case decided following the *In re Gault* decision was *West v. United States* (1968). In the *West* case, a juvenile had waived his right to counsel, as well as several other important rights that had been extended to juveniles through the *Gault* case. A nine-point standard for analysis was established by the 5th Circuit Court of Appeals when the *West* disposition was imposed and an appeal followed. The nine-point standard was devised in order for judges to determine whether *any* juvenile is capable of understanding and waiving one or more of their constitutional rights. These nine points are:

1. Age
2. Education
3. Knowledge of the substance of the charge, and the nature of the right to remain silent and the right to an attorney
4. Whether the accused is allowed contact with parents, guardian, attorney, or other interested adult
5. Whether the interrogation occurred before or after indictment
6. Methods used in interrogation
7. Length of interrogation
8. Whether the accused refused to voluntarily give statements on prior occasions, and
9. Whether the accused had repudiated an extrajudicial statement at a later date.

While these nine points are interesting and relevant, the fact that they were articulated by the 5th Circuit Court of Appeals meant that they were not binding on federal district courts in other circuits. For that matter, since these were rights conveyed through a federal circuit, they were not binding on any particular state jurisdiction, even a state within the territory of the 5th Circuit Court of Appeals.

Subsequently a totality of circumstances test, determined in the case of *Fare v. Michael C.* (1979), was established by the U.S. Supreme Court and it has resulted in mixed decisions among appellate courts. For instance, in *Woods v. Clusen* (1986), the 7th Circuit Court of Appeals ruled that a 16½-year-old's confession was inadmissible because the juvenile had been taken from his home at 7:30 A.M., handcuffed, stripped, forced to wear institutional clothing but no shoes or socks, showed pictures of the crime scene, and intimidated and interrogated for many hours. These police tactics were criticized by the court and the investigators were reprimanded for their failure to uphold and respect the offender's constitutional rights and provide fundamental fairness.

Research by Grisso (1998), for instance, shows that juveniles have little grasp of their constitutional rights. Grisso studied a large sample of juveniles and found that only 10 percent of them chose not to waive their rights where serious charges were alleged. Grisso found that they (1) demonstrated less comprehension than adults of their *Miranda* rights; (2) had less understanding of the wording of the **Miranda warning;** (3) misunderstood their right to counsel; and (4) did not understand their right to remain silent, believing that they could later be punished if they failed to tell about their criminal activities (*Miranda v. Arizona,* 1966).

Another study was conducted to determine the degree of compliance of state juvenile codes with the actual rights juveniles have been extended by U.S. Supreme Court decisions (Caeti, Hemmens, and Burton, 1996). A content analysis was used to examine all state statutes pertaining to legal counsel for juveniles. Among other things, the investigators wanted to determine whether there were statutory guarantees of a juvenile defendant's right to counsel; whether judicial discretion is permitted in the actual appointment of counsel for indigent juveniles; whether strict rights waivers were included; and whether defense counsel was mandated for all critical stages of juvenile justice processing.

First, these researchers found that all states, with the exception of Hawaii, Massachusetts, Michigan, Mississippi, Missouri, New Hampshire, North Car-

Attorneys for juveniles are increasingly used in most U.S. jurisdictions.

olina, North Dakota, Rhode Island, South Carolina, South Dakota, and West Virginia, had a specific juvenile statute identifying the juvenile's right to legal counsel. Table 5.3 shows a distribution of the states according to this and other legal rights of juveniles regarding defense counsel appointments and waivers of the right to counsel. Only about half of all states have vested juvenile court judges with the discretion to appoint counsel for juveniles, while even fewer states provide strict rights waiver requirements and mandatory defense counsel appointments.

Subsequently, the researchers divided the states according to which ones were least and most protective of juveniles. They divided all states according to five categories. These are shown in Table 5.4. The first category in Table 5.4 shows six states where no specific statute exists guaranteeing juveniles the right to counsel.

The authors correctly indicate that despite the fact that these states do not have specific statutes addressing a youth's right to counsel, the case of *In re Gault* is applicable to all states and ensures a juvenile's right to counsel at critical stages of their processing. Thus, there may not be a need to articulate this right as a legislated statute. The second category contains those states where minimal statements exist concerning a child's right to counsel at specific stages. They use Indiana as such a state where a statute says that "a child charged with a delinquent act is also entitled to be represented by counsel" (Caeti, Hemmens, and Burton, 1996:627). The third category contains states where statutory language extends the right to counsel to all juveniles at all stages or every stage of proceedings against them. The fourth category contains those states that provide counsel for juveniles beyond the stages articulated by *Gault.* These researchers cite Arkansas as a state where strict criteria are applicable in the event a juvenile wishes to waive certain constitutional rights. In the fifth and final category, states are shown where the right to counsel is extended, even to juveniles who do not face the prospect of secure confinement or any loss of freedom. Therefore, Table 5.4 is actually a continuum of the degree of statutory

TABLE 5.3

Right to Counsel for Juveniles by State

Conditions under Which the Right to Counsel is Invoked[a]

State	Specific Juvenile Statute	Discretionary Appointment	Strict Waiver Requirements	Mandatory Appointment
Alabama	X	X		
Alaska	X			
Arizona	X	X		
Arkansas	X	X	X	
California	X	X		X
Colorado	X	X	X	
Connecticut	X	X	X	
Delaware				
Florida	X			
Georgia	X	X		
Hawaii				
Idaho	X	X		
Illinois	X	X		X
Indiana	X	X		
Iowa	X	X	X	
Kansas	X	X		X
Kentucky	X			
Louisiana	X		X	X
Maine	X			
Maryland	X	X	X	
Massachusetts		X	X	X
Michigan				
Minnesota	X			
Mississippi				
Missouri				
Montana	X	X	X	
Nebraska	X			
Nevada	X			
New Hampshire				
New Jersey	X		X	
New Mexico	X	X	X	X
New York	X			
North Carolina		X		X
North Dakota		X		
Ohio	X	X	X	
Oklahoma	X	X	X	
Oregon	X	X		
Pennsylvania	X	X	X	
Rhode Island		X		
South Carolina		X		
South Dakota		X	X	
Tennessee	X	X		
Texas	X	X	X	X
Utah	X	X		

TABLE 5.3

Right to Counsel for Juveniles by State (cont.)

Conditions under Which the Right to Counsel is Invoked[a]

State	Specific Juvenile Statute	Discretionary Appointment	Strict Waiver Requirements	Mandatory Appointment
Vermont	x	x		
Virginia	x	x	x	
Washington	x			
West Virginia		x		
Wisconsin	x	x		
Wyoming	x			

[a]Six states—Delaware, Hawaii, Michigan, Missouri, and New Hampshire—do not have statutory references to a juvanila's right to legal counsel in their state legal codes.
Source: Caeti, Hemmens, and Burton, 1996:622–623. Reprinted with permission of the *American Journal of Criminal Law* and the authors. Updated 2005 by author.

TABLE 5.4

Degree of Statutory Protection[a]

Category 1	Category 2	Category 3	Category 4	Category 5
Delaware	Alaska	Arizona	Alabama	California
Hawaii	District of Columbia	Colorado	Arkansas	Illinois
Michigan	Florida	District of Columbia	Connecticut	Kansas
Mississippi	Indiana	Georgia	Georgia	Louisiana
Missouri	Kentucky	Idaho	Iowa	New Mexico
New	Maine	Maryland	Montana	North Carolina
Hampshire	Minnesota	Massachusetts	Ohio	Texas
	Missouri	New Jersey	Oklahoma	
	Nebraska	North Dakota	Pennsylvania	
	Nevada	Ohio	Virginia	
	New York	Oregon	Wisconsin	
	North Dakota	Pennsylvania	Wyoming	
	Rhode Island	South Dakota		
	South Carolina	Tennessee		
	South Dakota	Utah		
	Tennessee	Vermont		
	Washington	Virginia		
	West Virginia	Washington		
		Wisconsin		

[a]Category 1 is least protective: category 5 is most protective.
Source: Caeti, Hemmens, and Burton, 1996:626. Reproduced with permission of the *American Journal of Criminal Law* and the authors. Updated 2005 by author.

protection provided juveniles by various states, ranging from least protective to most protective (Caeti, Hemmens, and Burton, 1996).

The Continued Leniency of Juvenile Court Adjudications and Dispositions

Juvenile court actions continue to be fairly lenient. The sanction of choice among juvenile court judges is probation. Even those offenders who appear multiple times before the same judge are likely to continue to receive probation for their persistent offending. However, the many juvenile justice reforms that have occurred during the 1980s and 1990s have caused some persons to see little difference between how adults are processed by criminal courts and how juveniles are processed by juvenile courts (Feld, 1993a). However, despite the increased criminalization of juvenile courts, there are significant differences that serve to differentiate criminal courts and criminal processing from how youths are treated or processed by the juvenile justice system.

Perhaps the most important implication for juveniles is that in most cases, juvenile court adjudications do not result in criminal records. These courts continue to exercise civil authority. Once juveniles reach adulthood, their juvenile records are routinely expunged and forgotten, with some exceptions. But having one's case adjudicated by a juvenile court operates to a youth's disadvantage in some respects. For instance, the rules governing the admissibility of evidence or testimony are relaxed considerably compared with the rules governing similar admissions in criminal courts. Thus, it is easier in juvenile courts to admit inculpatory evidence and testimony than in criminal courtrooms.

Further, cases against juveniles do not need to be as convincing as cases against criminal defendants. Lower standards of proof are operative relative to search and seizure and the degree of probable cause required. Schoolchildren are particularly vulnerable in this regard, in view of *New Jersey v. T.L.O.* (1985). In this case, a 14-year-old girl was caught smoking a cigarette in the school bathroom, violating school rules. When confronted by the principal, she denied that she had been smoking. The principal examined her purse and discovered a pack of cigarettes, some rolling papers, money, marijuana, and other drug materials. This information was turned over to police, who charged the girl with delinquency. She was convicted. The girl's attorney sought to exclude the seized evidence because it was believed to be in violation of her Fourth Amendment right against unreasonable searches and seizures. The U.S. Supreme Court heard the case and ruled in favor of school officials, declaring that they only need reasonable suspicion, not probable cause, in order to search students and their possessions while on school property. When students enter their schools, they are subject to a lower standard than that applied to adult suspects when suspected of wrongdoing or carrying illegal contraband in violation of school rules.

Adversely, juveniles do not always receive jury trials if they request them (Sanborn, 1993). Less than a fourth of all states permit jury trials for juveniles by statute. In all other states, jury trials are available to juveniles only if judges permit them. In most cases, therefore, the judgment of the juvenile court is final, for all practical purposes. Appeals of decisions by juvenile court judges are relatively rare. Long-term dispositions of incarceration may be imposed by juvenile court judges at will, without serious challenge. Current profiles of long-term detainees in secure juvenile facilities suggests that judges impose dispositions of secure confinement frequently. Furthermore, a majority of these long-term detainees are less serious property offenders with some chronicity in their rate of reoffending.

An Update on Jury Trials for Juvenile Delinquents

The National Center for Juvenile Justice has investigated various state jurisdictions to determine their present status concerning jury trials and other formal procedures for juveniles. The categories created by this investigation included the following: (1) states providing no right to a jury trial for juvenile delinquents under any circumstances; (2) states providing a right to a jury trial for juvenile delinquents under any circumstances; (3) states not providing a jury trial for juvenile delinquents except under specified circumstances; (4) states providing the right to a jury trial for juvenile delinquents under specified circumstances; and (5) states with statutes allowing juvenile delinquents with a right to jury trial to waive that right.

1. *States Not Providing Jury Trials for Juvenile Delinquents Under Any Circumstances:* Alabama; Arizona; Arkansas; California; District of Columbia; Georgia; Hawaii; Indiana; Kentucky; Louisiana; Maryland; Mississippi; Nevada; New Jersey; North Dakota; Ohio; Oregon; Pennsylvania; South Carolina; Tennessee; Utah; Vermont; and Washington.

2. *States Providing Jury Trials for Juvenile Delinquents Under Any Circumstance:* Alaska; Massachusetts; Michigan; West Virginia.

3. *States Not Providing Jury Trials for Juvenile Delinquents, Except Under Specified Circumstances:* Colorado: All hearings, including adjudicatory hearings, shall be heard without a jury; juvenile not entitled to a trial by jury when petition alleges a delinquent act that is a class 2 or class 3 misdemeanor, a petty offense, a violation of a municipal or county ordinance, or a violation of a court order if, prior to the trial and with the approval of the court, the district attorney has waived in writing the right to seek a commitment to the department of human services or a sentence to the county jail.

   District of Columbia: Probation revocation hearings heard without a jury.

   Florida: Adjudicatory hearings heard without a jury.

   Louisiana: Adjudicatory hearings heard without a jury.

   Maine: Adjudicatory hearing heard without a jury.

   Montana: Hearing on whether juvenile should be transferred to adult criminal court heard without a jury; probation revocation proceeding heard without a jury.

   Nebraska: Adjudicatory hearing heard without a jury.

   New Mexico: Probation revocation proceedings heard without a jury.

   North Carolina: Adjudicatory hearing heard without a jury.

   Texas: Detention hearing heard without a jury; hearing to consider transfer of child for criminal proceedings and hearing to consider waiver of jurisdiction held without a jury; disposition hearing heard without a jury, unless child in jeopardy of a determinate sentence; hearing to modify a disposition heard without a jury, unless child in jeopardy of a sentence for a determinate term.

Wisconsin: No right to a jury trial in a waiver hearing.

Wyoming: Probation revocation hearing heard without a jury; transfer hearing heard without a jury.

4. *States Where Juvenile Delinquent Has a Right to a Jury Trial Under Specified Circumstances:* Arkansas: If amount of restitution ordered by the court exceeds $10,000, juvenile has right to jury trial on all issues of liability and damages.

Colorado: No right to a jury trial unless otherwise provided by this title; juvenile may demand a jury trial, unless the petition alleges a delinquent act that is a class 2 or class 3 misdemeanor, a petty offense, a violation of a municipal or county ordinance, or a violation of a court order if, prior to the trial and with the approval of the court, the district attorney has waived in writing the right to seek a commitment to the department of human services or a sentence to the county jail; any juvenile alleged to be an aggravated juvenile offender (defined in statute) has the right to a jury trial.

Idaho: Any juvenile age 14–18 alleged to have committed a violent offense (defined in statute) or a controlled substance offense has the right to a jury trial.

Illinois: Any habitual juvenile offender (defined in statute) has the right to a jury trial.

Kansas: Any juvenile alleged to have committed an act that would be a felony if committed by an adult has the right to a jury trial.

Minnesota: Child who is prosecuted as an extended jurisdiction juvenile has the right to a jury trial on the issue of guilt.

Montana: Any juvenile who contests the offenses alleged in the petition has the right to a jury trial.

New Mexico: Jury trial on issues of alleged delinquent acts may be demanded when the offenses alleged would be triable by a jury if committed by an adult.

Oklahoma: Child has right to a jury trial in adjudicatory hearing.

Rhode Island: Child has right to jury when court finds child is subject to certification to adult court.

Texas: Child has right to jury trial at adjudicatory hearing; child has right to a jury trial at disposition hearing only if child is in jeopardy of a determinate sentence; child has right to a jury trial at a hearing to modify the disposition only if the child is in jeopardy of a determinate sentence on the issues of the violation of the court's orders and the sentence.

Virginia: If juvenile indicted, juvenile has the right to a jury trial; if found guilty of capital murder, court fixes sentence with intervention of a jury; where appeal is taken by child on a finding that he or she is delinquent and the alleged delinquent act would be a felony if done by adult, the child is entitled to a jury.

Wyoming: Juvenile has right to jury trial at adjudicatory hearing.

5. *States Providing Right to a Jury Trial for Juvenile Delinquents Where Juvenile Delinquents Can Waive Their Right to a Jury Trial:*

Colorado: Unless a jury is demanded, it shall be deemed waived.

Illinois: Minor can demand in open court and with advice of counsel, a trial by the court without a jury.

Massachusetts: Child can file written waiver and consent to be tried by the court without a jury; this waiver cannot be received unless the child is represented by counsel or has filed, through his parent or guardian, a written waiver of counsel.

Montana: In the absence of a demand, a jury trial is waived.

Oklahoma: Child has right to waive jury trial.

Texas: Trial shall be by jury unless jury is waived.

Wyoming: Failure of party to demand a jury no later than 10 days after the party is advised of his right, is a waiver of this right.

Source: Compiled by author, 2005.

Gelber (1990) has speculated what the juvenile court might be like during the first several decades of the 21st century. He envisions a court, conceivably renamed the Juvenile Services Consortium, with two tiers. The first tier will be devoted to adjudicating offenders under age 14. These offenders will always receive rehabilitative sanctions, such as probation or placement in conditional, community-based correctional programs. The second tier consists of those age 14–18. For these juveniles, jury trials will be available and these offenders will be subject to the same incarcerative sanctions that can be imposed by criminal courts.

Gelber's two-tiered juvenile court projection for the 21st century may not be far off the mark in relation to societal expectations for such courts in future years. The public mood seems to be in favor of deserts-based sentencing and toward due process for juvenile offenders. The two-tiered nature of Gelber's projected court organization would seemingly achieve this get-tough result, although provisions would remain for treatment-centered rehabilitative sanctions for younger offenders. In a sense, this two-tiered court projection seems to be nothing more than lowering the age jurisdiction of criminal courts from age 18 to 14. However, Gelber's intent is to preserve the jurisdictional integrity of the juvenile justice system in relation to the criminal justice system. In any case, this would be an effective compromise between those favoring the traditional rehabilitative posture of juvenile courts and those favoring a shift to more punitive court policies and practices.

THE DEATH PENALTY FOR JUVENILES

In 2004, there were 3,374 prisoners on death row awaiting the penalty of death. There were 440 death row inmates age 19 or younger, which accounted for approximately 13 percent of all death row inmates (Bonczar and Snell, 2004:1). Between 1642 and 2004 there were over 325 executions of youths in the United States when they were under age 18 when committing capital crimes.

The first documented execution of a juvenile occurred in 1642. Thomas Graunger, a 16-year-old, was convicted of bestiality. He was caught sodomizing

Court avoided the issue. The Justices did not say it was cruel and unusual punishment, but they also did not say that it wasn't. What they said was that the youthfulness of the offender is a mitigating factor of great weight that may be considered. Therefore, all jurisdictions where death penalties are imposed were left to draw their own conclusions and interpretations of U.S. Supreme Court remarks about death penalty cases.

Reasons for Supporting the Death Penalty

The primary reasons for supporting the death penalty in certain capital cases are three-fold: (1) retribution; (2) deterrence; and (3) just-deserts.

1. The death penalty is retribution. Retribution is defended largely on the basis of the philosophical just-desert rationale. Offenders should be executed because they did not respect the lives of others. Death is the just-desert for someone who inflicted death on someone else. Retribution is often regarded as the primary purpose of the death penalty.

2. The death penalty deters others from committing murder. The deterrence function of the death penalty is frequently questioned as well. An examination of homicide rates in Illinois during a 48-year period (1933–1980) was conducted. It revealed that average homicide rates for three different periods did not fluctuate noticeably. These periods included (1) times when the death penalty was allowed; (2) years when the death penalty was allowed but no executions were performed; and (3) years when the death penalty was abolished (Bonczar and Snell, 2004:3). Persons favoring the abolition of the death penalty argue that no criminal act ever justifies capital punishment (Boots, Heide, and Cochran, 2004).

3. The death penalty is a just desert for commission of a capital offense. The "just-deserts" philosophy is that the death penalty is just punishment for someone who has committed murder. The U.S. Supreme Court has indirectly validated this reasoning by refusing to declare the death penalty cruel and unusual punishment (Cochran, Boots, and Heide, 2003; Steinberg and Scott, 2003).

Reasons for Opposing the Death Penalty

Some of the reasons persons use to oppose the death penalty are that (1) it is barbaric; (2) it may be applied in error to someone who is not actually guilty of a capital offense; (3) it is nothing more than sheer revenge; (4) it is more costly than life imprisonment; (5) it is applied arbitrarily; (6) it does not deter others from committing murder; and (7) most persons in the United States are opposed to the death penalty.

1. The death penalty is barbaric. Belbot et al. (2004) say that the death penalty is barbaric and violates international law. There are other avenues whereby convicted capital offenders can be punished. The United States is one of the few civilized countries of the modern world that still uses the death penalty. Portraits of persons condemned to death include accounts

of their past lives by close friends and family members who oppose capital punishment in their cases. Even statements from various family members of victims express opposition to the death penalty because of its alleged barbarism.

2. The death penalty is unfair and may be applied erroneously. Some convicted offenders are wrongly convicted. Evidence subsequently discovered has led to freeing several persons who were formerly on death row awaiting execution. The American Civil Liberties Union and Amnesty International are strong death penalty opponents. This reason is one of their strongest arguments against its application. Thus, this view proposes an outright ban on the death penalty because of the mere possibility that some persons sentenced to death are actually innocent and should not be executed (Bohm and Vogel, 2004; Vogel and Vogel, 2003).

3. The death penalty is nothing more than revenge. Some observers argue that by condoning the death penalty, the U.S. Supreme Court has sanctioned vengeance, which is an unacceptable justification for imposing capital punishment. For persons who are retarded or intellectually disabled, it is likely that they cannot reach the level of culpability necessary to trigger the need for the death penalty. They cannot engage in cold calculus to weigh committing the crime against the potential death penalty used to punish it (Frantzen, 2005).

4. The death penalty is more costly than life-without-parole sentences. Many opponents of capital punishment grasp the cost factor to show that executing prisoners under death sentences is more costly over time than imprisoning them for life (Belbot et al., 2004). However, a key reason for the high cost of executing prisoners is that they have been entitled to file endless appeals and delay the imposition of their death sentences (Lofquist, 2002; Stolzenberg and D'Alessio, 2004). In 1996, Congress acted to limit the number of appeals inmates on death rows could file. Thus, it is expected in future years that the length of time between conviction and imposition of the death penalty will be greatly abbreviated. This shorter period of time will decrease the expense of death penalty appeals and undermine this particular argument.

5. The death penalty is still applied arbitrarily despite efforts by legislatures and Congress to make its application more equitable. Although bifurcated trials have decreased the racial bias in death penalty applications, disproportionality of death sentences according to race and ethnicity have not been completely eliminated. While some persons argue that some races and ethnic categories have higher rates of capital murder and thus are disproportionately represented on death row, other persons say that the death penalty continues to be applied in a discriminatory manner in many jurisdictions (Mallicoat and Radelet, 2004).

6. The death penalty does not deter others from committing murder. The literature strongly supports the idea that the death penalty apparently has no discernable deterrent effect. Persons will commit murder anyway, even knowing that there is a chance they may be caught eventually and executed for the crime. An examination of crime statistics and comparisons of those jurisdictions where the death penalty is applied and jurisdictions where it isn't applied show few, if any, differences in capital murder

 **BOX 5.2**

 **CAREER SNAPSHOT**

William Hitchcock
Juvenile Court Judge, Alaska Court System, Anchorage, Alaska

Statistics:

B.A. (political science), Whitman College (1967); J.D., University of Oregon School of Law (1975)

Background

When I was growing up in the 1950s and 1960s, young people were expected to decide fairly early whether they were going to select college and a professional career path, or something else such as a career in the military. I knew from junior high that I wanted to pursue a college education and professional career. I thought I would go into a scientific field because of the obsession with science that was created by *Sputnik* and the dawn of the space race. I pursued physics and math until in high school it became apparent that I had no aptitude for anything that complicated. I was better at acting in plays and being in debate, so I was on my way to becoming a liberal arts major. The field of law soon became my ambition, so I majored in Political Science and began law school immediately after getting my undergraduate degree.

I lost my draft deferment just as my second year of law school began, meaning I would have to enter the military. This was in 1969, when the Vietnam War was underway. I enlisted in the U.S. Air Force, where I became a personnel specialist at Elmendorf Air Force Base in Anchorage, Alaska. I landed a unique opportunity there to run an ombudsman program that aimed at improving the quality of life for airmen and their families.

After concluding my four-year tour of duty in the Air Force, I returned to the University of Oregon School of Law to resume my second year. After graduation, I returned to Anchorage and snagged a job as a law clerk for the Alaska Court System. Soon I was elevated to the position of court master, a judicial position hearing divorce and other uncontested routine civil matters, eventually

growing into handling delinquency and child protection matters as well. In other states, this kind of position may be called a "referee," "court commissioner," or "magistrate." These terms are basically meant to describe a judicial position with limited powers.

In the mid-1980s the Alaska Court System divested itself of the function of juvenile intake for delinquency cases, and the administrative function of case management became my responsibility. This period of time also saw the beginning of tremendous growth in the number of child protection cases coming to the court. By the early 1990s, juvenile crime waves were sweeping more delinquency cases into court as well. I became much more involved in the administration and management of Children's Court at this time.

The 1980s also marked the beginning of my involvement with the National Council of Juvenile and Family Court Judges, which had a significant impact on my career. I became aware of the importance of becoming educated in understanding the behavioral and societal issues underpinning our children's caseload. I also began to see that judges handling these matters needed to be involved in system improvement efforts, and that they could do so without violating the boundaries of judicial ethics. My first real endeavor in that area was to lead the implementation of a new process called citizen foster care review, whereby citizens from the community would become trained and tasked with reviewing abuse/neglect cases and holding systems accountable for

(continued)

performance. That led to my being appointed to the Board of Directors of the National Association of Foster Care Reviewers and a nearly 10-year stint in a volunteer capacity with citizen review nationally.

Over the past ten years, I have undertaken a number of other initiatives designed to improve the handling of children's cases. I developed an interagency network of juvenile justice agencies and providers in Anchorage, which meets regularly to exchange information and promote collaborative projects and processes. I was also involved in the design and implementation of a domestic violence coordinating council, which remains active. In 2001 I facilitated the planning of a proposal that led to a multiyear grant called Reclaiming Futures, aiming to create an effective community care system for substance-abusing juveniles.

Like everyone else who deals with juveniles, I have had my share of interesting cases. The saddest are the cases of young children who come from abusive homes and who cannot bond with normal caretakers. Many of these kids also suffer the further victimization of having their foster or adoptive home placements fail as well. I have seen delinquency cases in which kids acting out their rage have done wanton and malicious destruction of property, even killing pets in the course of burglarizing or vandalizing a home. However, I still believe that the majority of the kids who commit crimes have a core of positive assets that can be tapped into and developed so that they may be redirected into productive lifestyles.

Among the more difficult cases are those presented by kids who have been fetally affected by alcohol (FAS). I think we see more of these kids than those in other states because of the high rates of alcoholism in Alaska. I remember a kid who became involved in the juvenile justice system from a very young age. He could not internalize or learn anything because of his FAS, and always seemed to be stuck in a continuing cycle of failure. He was an example of the difficulties of applying the traditional justice system to kids who can't learn anything from generic behavioral modification programs. It's the same for kids with mental health needs. It's kids like these who are driving the inter-est in problem-solving courts, such as drug courts, or mental health courts. This trend is changing the way traditional courts operate and forcing us to address what causes kids to get involved in crime in the first place.

What do I like about my work? The power of a judge to influence the way the case may move is appealing. But only part of that power is exerted in the courtroom. I'm a big believer in being engaged in the community—in being involved in local activities and initiatives, and taking a leadership role in efforts to make our justice system more responsive to the community. I believe the time spent on these efforts is as important as the time I spend wearing the robe and working in the courtroom. I believe in leading from in front of the bench as well as behind the bench.

Advice to Students

A lot of people who go into law do so because they think they can make a lot of money. But others go into the field because they want to change society for the better. There's not as much money if you go in the direction of public service, and a lot of people don't stay in those kinds of jobs because they can make more money elsewhere. But I believe public service work is just as rewarding because you can make a difference.

To anyone who goes into this work I would say two things. First, if you want a long-term career in helping people, you need to stay current in understanding what the literature and research tells us about human behavior. The traditional view of our judicial work is that one simply needs to know the law and how it applies in particular cases. Judges and helping professionals alike need to understand the dynamics and implications of child abuse, of bonding and attachment, and of the impact of domestic violence, to name a few.

Second, don't ever forget that you need to take something away for yourself. Working with child abuse and delinquency can be very stressful, so you need to recognize your achievements and celebrate your victories. Don't get caught up in crises and gloss over your achievements. Every individual who touches these cases can make a difference in the lives of children and their families.

cases. Thus, the argument is that if capital punishment fails to deter capital murder, then it should be abolished (Boots, Heide, and Cochran, 2004; Young, 2004).

7. Most persons in the United States are against the death penalty. Bedau (1992) has suggested that there is a growing lack of public support for the death penalty in the United States. However, several national surveys show that over 75 percent of those interviewed support the death penalty and its application (Bohm and Vogel, 2004; Mallicoat and Radelet, 2004). Certainly a knowledge of the death penalty and its deterrent and retributive effects makes a difference in whether persons support or oppose its use. Growing violent street crimes, especially resulting in the deaths of innocent victims, do nothing but trigger pro–capital punishment reactions from an increasingly frightened public (Stolzenberg and D'Alessio, 2004).

All of the arguments that function as either pros or cons relative to the death penalty also apply directly to the issue of juvenile executions. However, the nature of juvenile justice reforms is such that a strong belief persists that substantial efforts must be made by juvenile courts and corrections to rehabilitate juveniles rather than incarcerate or execute them. In those states where executions are conducted, where should the line be drawn concerning the minimum age at which someone becomes liable, accountable, and subject to the death penalty?

U.S. SUPREME COURT DEATH PENALTY CASES

Several U.S. Supreme Court cases have been decided in recent years involving questions of executions of juveniles. These cases have been especially significant in providing a legal foundation for such executions. These include *Eddings v. Oklahoma* (1982), *Thompson v. Oklahoma* (1988), *Stanford v. Kentucky* (1989), *Wilkins v. Missouri* (1989), and *Roper v. Simmons* (2005). As a prelude to discussing these cases, it should be noted that until 1988, 16 states had minimum-age provisions for juvenile executions (under age 18), where the range in minimum age was from 10 (Indiana) to 17 (Georgia, New Hampshire, and Texas). When the *Thompson v. Oklahoma* case was decided in 1988, the minimum age for juvenile executions in all states was raised to 16. The following year, the U.S. Supreme Court upheld death sentences of a 16-year-old and a 17-year-old.

Eddings v. Oklahoma (1982)

On April 4, 1977, Monty Lee Eddings and several other companions ran away from their Missouri homes. In a car owned by Eddings's older brother, they drove, without direction or purpose, eventually reaching the Oklahoma Turnpike. Eddings had several firearms in the car, including several rifles, which he had stolen from his father. At one point, Eddings lost control of the car and was stopped by an Oklahoma State Highway Patrol officer. When the officer approached the car, Eddings stuck a shotgun out of the window and killed the officer outright. When Eddings was subsequently apprehended, he was waived to

BOX 5.3

INTERNATIONAL SNAPSHOT: JUVENILE JUSTICE IN GERMANY

The juvenile justice system in Germany was officially recognized in 1922 with the passage of the Juvenile Welfare Act (JWA) and the 1923 Juvenile Justice Act (JJA). These acts dealt respectively with juveniles in need of care and justice. A new juvenile penal law was not created. Rather, the JJA consisted of a specific system of sanctions applied to youths and specific procedural rules for the juvenile court and its proceedings. Status offenses were not encompassed by the JJA. Punishable crimes for juveniles were the same for adults. However, the JJA created the possibility of educational measures for juvenile offenders besides punishment. The age of criminal responsibility was raised from 12 to 14 under the JJA. Educational measures were broadly interpreted and no precise definition of education was ever provided. Subsequently with the Nazi regime gaining power during the 1930s, education by punishment of a repressive nature was instituted.

Under the JWA of 1922, the *parens patriae* doctrine was practiced much like it was in the United States prior to juveniles acquiring substantial legal rights. In 1990 the JWA was replaced by modern social welfare provisions, where juvenile welfare boards functioned to provide help or offers to help juveniles in need of intervention. Several major changes in the treatment of juvenile offenders occurred since the 1970s, and the secure confinement of youths was drastically reduced in favor of more community-based sanctions.

In contemporary German society, minimum intervention is stressed. Sanctions are ideally subject to the principle of proportionality, and juvenile court sanctions are considered last resorts. Primary sanctions of the juvenile court are either educational or disciplinary measures. Most petty offenses are dismissed without sanction. For more serious law violations, police are strictly bound to report all serious juvenile offending to the public prosecutor. There is no tolerance for police cautioning or discretion in serious juvenile matters.

However, in 1990 reforms were implemented by modifications made in the JJA. Diversion and mediation became major options in lieu of official juvenile court sanctions. The 1990 reforms have emphasized the discharge of juvenile and young adult offenders because of the petty nature of crimes committed or because of other social and/or educational interventions that have occurred. Victim–offender reconciliation or mediation is the functional equivalent of educational measures, and there are no restrictions of such policies because of the nature of offending. Even most felony offenses can be diverted provided that offenders have repaired the damage or made some sort of apology to victims.

Four levels of diversion include: (1) diversion without any sanction; (2) diversion with education; (3) diversion with intervention, such as verbal warnings and/or community service, mediation, participation in training courses, or reparations or restitution to victims; and (4) imposition of one or more of the first three levels after the youth has undergone some form of educational measure such as mediation. During the 1990s and 2000s, recidivism rates resulting from diversion have been under 30 percent.

Juvenile court sanctions are structured according to the principle of minimum intervention; youth prison sentences are considered a last resort. Community service, special care orders, social training courses, and other directives are ordered by the court, including preventing dangerous situations, such as forbidding juveniles to associate with certain persons or going to places likely to compromise their safety and welfare. Separate juvenile prisons have been established apart from adult facilities. The minimum length of youth imprisonment is 6 months; the maximum imprisonment length for the most serious offenses is 10 years, for juveniles age 14–17. For some juveniles age 18–20, the maximum penalty is also 10 years. A major precondition of youth imprisonment is dangerous tendencies of the offender and the inappropriateness or ineffectiveness of community sanctions. Youth imprisonment sentences of up to 2 years may be suspended, depending on individual circumstances. About 5 percent of all adjudicated youths are placed in detention centers or prison, and for short periods such as 6 months or less. About 70 percent of all youth prison sentences are suspended. For those whose sentences are suspended, they are placed on probation for various periods. Probationers have been quite successful in becoming rehabilitated. Germany uses shock incarceration in some cases, where juveniles will be sentenced to lengthy periods of confinement, only to be removed from prison after a few months and resentenced to probation.

All juvenile court proceedings are closed to the public and media to avoid stigma and adverse labeling. Juvenile trials are conducted for more serious offenders, and social court assistants and a social worker with the community youth welfare department are required to attend. They are responsible for preparing a social report about the personal background of the juvenile and to assist judges in determining the most appropriate sanctions. Pretrial detention of juveniles, especially those age 14–15, are limited. Residential care in a juvenile home is preferred over pretrial detention. Once a juvenile's case has been decided, juveniles are entitled to a single appeal. The appeal must not be made solely to receive another educational measure, but rather, to review certain legal questions. The appeals process is swift in order to streamline the justice system. This is so the educational measures can be implemented more quickly. Furthermore, the length of pretrial detention of juveniles is not taken into account when a juvenile is serving a prison sentence of six months or less. Juveniles under age 14 are considered less accountable under the law and are dealt with by social welfare agencies, who supervise their treatment and provide various therapeutic interventions. Foster home placements and medical treatments are options.

Juvenile delinquency trends in Germany were not studied systematically until 1984. Then more adequate records were kept annually to chart juvenile offense trends. During the 1990s juvenile offending increased, although it has leveled off and become more stable since 2000. A larger amount of juvenile violence compared with other countries has been observed among German juveniles. One reason is that there has been a large influx of young migrants and ethnic minorities into German culture. Minority youths are overrepresented in violent offending, especially Turkish minority youths, who through self-reports disclose that their violent offending is twice as high as German juveniles. Also, a large contingent of Russian children show some adjustment problems, largely because of language deficiencies and other problems. Their subsequent involvement in youth violence and placement in prisons creates a more explosive prison subculture.

The minority youth problem does not exist in all regions of Germany, however, and thus generalizations about German delinquency trends are limited in various respects. It has also been speculated that the rise in juvenile violent offending is attributable to greater sensitivity to juvenile violence and more formal reporting of it compared with past years. Generally, despite rising violent crime, especially robbery and serious bodily injury (aggravated assault), most juveniles and young adults are not violent offenders. About 70 percent of all juvenile offending involves property offending.

Victim–offender reconciliation projects and mediation have been growing since the mid-1980s. By the late 1990s over 60 percent of all youth welfare agencies reported mediation programs in progress with successful results in most cases. Mediation has been regarded as the most promising alternative to more repressive traditional sanctions. Also, community sanctions including social training courses have been instituted. These social training courses are group-centered educational measures targeting day-to-day living problems. The aim of such programming is to improve social competence and skills required in private and professional life. Social training courses are organized as regular meetings twice a week, often in combination with intensive week

(continued)

end arrangements including outdoor experiences. Community service orders have also become popular juvenile court sanctions. These sanctions are considered both educational and constructive.

A get-tough movement exists in contemporary German society, where some persons are pushing to lower the age of criminal responsibility from 14 to 12. Harsher punishments, including more definite confinement of more serious juveniles, ought to be implemented. The argument is that juveniles should be held accountable and be responsible like adults for the crimes they commit. They should also be treated accordingly. These ideas are currently being debated.

[*Sources:* Adapted from Frieder Dunkel, "Juvenile Justice in Germany: Between Welfare and Justice" University of Greifswald, Germany (Unpublished paper), March 2004; "Jugendstrafvollzug in Deutschland," Unpublished paper, 2005; "Diversion im Jugendstrafverfahren der Bundesrepublik Deutschland," Unpublished paper, 2005.]

criminal court on a prosecutorial motion. Efforts by Eddings and his attorney to oppose the waiver failed.

In a subsequent bifurcated trial, several aggravating circumstances were introduced and alleged, while several mitigating circumstances, including Eddings's youthfulness, mental state, and potential for treatment, were considered by the trial judge. However, the judge did not consider Eddings's "unhappy upbringing and emotional disturbance" as significant mitigating factors to offset the aggravating ones. Eddings's attorney filed an appeal, which eventually reached the U.S. Supreme Court. Although the Oklahoma Court of Criminal Appeals reversed the trial judge's ruling, the U.S. Supreme Court reversed the Oklahoma Court of Criminal Appeals. The reversal pivoted on whether the trial judge erred by refusing to consider the "unhappy upbringing and emotionally disturbed state" of Eddings. The trial judge had previously acknowledged the youthfulness of Eddings as a mitigating factor. The *fact* of Eddings's age, 16, was significant, precisely because the majority of Justices did not consider it as significant. Rather, they focused on the issue of introduction of mitigating circumstances specifically outlined in Eddings's appeal. Oklahoma was now in the position of lawfully imposing the death penalty on a juvenile who was 16 years old at the time he committed murder.

Thompson v. Oklahoma (1988)

In the case of William Wayne Thompson, he was convicted of murdering his former brother-in-law, Charles Keene. Keene had been suspected of abusing Thompson's sister. In the evening hours of January 22–23, 1983, Thompson and three older companions left his mother's house, saying "We're going to kill Charles." Facts disclose that later that early morning, Charles Keene was beaten to death by Thompson and his associates with fists and hand-held weapons, including a length of pipe. Thompson later told others, "We killed him. I shot him in the head and cut his throat in the river." Thompson's accomplices told police shortly after their arrest that Thompson had shot Keene twice in the head, and then cut his body in several places (e.g., throat, chest, and abdomen), so that, according to Thompson, "the fish could eat his body." When Keene's body was recovered on February 18, 1983, the medical examiner indicated that

Keene had been shot twice in the head, had been beaten, and that his throat, chest, and abdomen had been cut.

Since Thompson was 15 years old at the time of the murder, juvenile officials transferred his case to criminal court. This transfer was supported, in part, by an Oklahoma statutory provision indicating that there was "prosecutive merit" in pursuing the case against Thompson. Again, the subject of the defendant's youthfulness was introduced as a mitigating factor (among other factors), together with aggravating factors such as the "especially heinous, atrocious, and cruel" manner in which Keene had been murdered. Thompson was convicted of first-degree murder and sentenced to death.

Thompson filed an appeal, which eventually reached the U.S. Supreme Court. The Court examined Thompson's case at length, and in a vigorously debated opinion, it overturned Thompson's death sentence, indicated in its conclusory dicta that

> "petitioner's counsel and various *amici curiae* have asked us to 'draw the line' that would prohibit the execution of any person who was under the age of 18 at the time of the offense. Our task, today, however, is to decide the case before us; we do so by concluding that the Eighth and Fourteenth Amendments prohibit the execution of a person who was under 16 years of age at the time of his or her offense" (108 S.Ct. at 2700).

Accordingly, Thompson's death penalty was reversed. Officially, this Supreme Court action effectively drew a temporary line of 16 years of age as a minimum for exacting the death penalty in capital cases. This "line" awaited subsequent challenges, however.

Stanford v. Kentucky (1989)

Kevin Stanford was 17 years old when, on January 17, 1981, he and an accomplice repeatedly raped and sodomized and eventually shot to death 20-year-old Baerbel Poore in Jefferson County, Kentucky. This occurred during a robbery of a gas station where Poore worked as an attendant. Stanford later told police, "I had to shoot her [since] she lived next door to me and she would recognize me . . . I guess we could have tied her up or something or beat [her up] . . . and tell her if she tells, we would kill her . . ." A corrections officer who interviewed Stanford said that after Stanford made that disclosure, "he [Stanford] started laughing." The jury in Stanford's case found him guilty of first-degree murder and the judge sentenced him to death. The U.S. Supreme Court eventually heard his appeal, and in an opinion that addressed the "minimum age for the death penalty" issue, decided both this case and the case of Heath Wilkins in the paragraphs to follow. Subsequently in December 2003, the governor of Kentucky commuted Stanford's death sentence to life imprisonment without parole, with the proclamation that "we ought not to be executing people who, legally, were children" (*Lexington Herald Leader,* December 9, 2003:B3).

Wilkins v. Missouri (1989)

Heath Wilkins, a 16-year-old at the time of the crime, stabbed to death Nancy Allen Moore, a 26-year-old mother of two who was working behind the counter of a convenience store in Avondale, Missouri. On July 27, 1985, Wilkins and his accomplice, Patrick Stevens, entered the convenience store to rob it, agreeing with Wilkins's plan that they would kill "whoever was behind the counter" because "a dead person can't talk." When they entered the store, they stabbed Moore, who fell to the floor. When Stevens had difficulty opening the cash register, Moore, mortally wounded, offered to help him. Wilkins stabbed her three more times in the chest, two of the knife wounds penetrating Moore's heart. Moore began to beg for her life, whereupon Wilkins stabbed her four more times in the neck, opening up her carotid artery. She died shortly thereafter. Stevens and Wilkins netted $450 in cash and checks, some liquor, cigarettes, and rolling papers from the robbery/murder. Wilkins was convicted of first-degree murder and the judge sentenced him to death.

The U.S. Supreme Court heard both the *Stanford* case and the *Wilkins* case simultaneously, since the singular issue was whether the death penalty was considered cruel and inhumane as it pertained to 16 and 17-year-olds. At that time, not all states had achieved consensus about applying the death penalty to persons under the age of 18 as a punishment for capital crimes. Although several Justices dissented from the majority view, the U.S. Supreme Court upheld the death sentences of Stanford and Wilkins, concluding that "we discern neither a historical nor a modern societal consensus forbidding the imposition of capital punishment on any person who murders at 16 or 17 years of age. Accordingly, we conclude that such punishment does not offend the Eighth Amendment's prohibition against cruel and unusual punishment" (109 S.Ct. at 2980). Thus, this crucial opinion underscored age 16 as the minimum age at which the death penalty may be administered. But this age standard would be changed 16 years later in the case of *Roper v. Simmons* (2005).

Roper v. Simmons (2005)

In March 2005 the U.S. Supreme Court revisited the issue of administering the death penalty to juveniles under the age of 18. Despite their decisions in the cases of *Wilkins v. Missouri* (1989) and *Stanford v. Kentucky* (1989), evolving community standards between 1989 and 2005, public opinion surveys concerning the application of the death penalty to juveniles, as well as United Nations sentiment and pressure, created a sociopolitical climate that placed the United States almost alone in its stance toward the application of the death penalty to persons under the age of 18. The case heard and decided was *Roper v. Simmons* (2005).

The facts of the case are as follows. In 1993 in Fenton, Missouri, Christopher Simmons, 17, told two other youths, Charles Benjamin, 15, and John Tessmer, 16, that he wanted to murder someone. Simmons said that he wanted to commit burglary by breaking and entering and then commit murder, tying up a victim and then throwing the victim from a bridge. Simmons assured Benjamin and Tessmer that they could "get away with it because they were minors." At 2:00 A.M. one morning, Simmons, Benjamin, and Tessmer met to carry out a burglary and murder, but Tessmer left before they started out to do their deeds. Simmons and Benjamin went to the home of Shirley Crook, a woman who had previously been involved in an auto accident with Simmons. They entered her home through an open window and she awakened. She recognized Simmons who bound her with duct tape, including placing duct tape over her eyes and mouth. They took her to a railroad trestle spanning the Meramec River, tied her hands and feet with wire, and then covered her entire face with duct tape. Next, they threw her from the trestle into the river where she drowned. Simmons later bragged to others that he had killed a woman because "the bitch had seen my face." Fishermen in the river found Crook's body and investigating detectives linked her death with Simmons, who was taken into custody for questioning. Simmons gave a videotaped confession, describing his heinous actions to police. He was subsequently convicted of first-degree murder and sentenced to death. Aggravating factors included the especially heinous nature of the murder; committing the murder for money; and attempting to conceal the crime by disposing of Crook's body into the river. His acts were described as wantonly vile, horrible, and inhuman. Mitigation included that Simmons had no prior juvenile record.

He appealed his conviction to the Missouri Supreme Court, alleging incompetence of counsel, since he had a difficult home environment, had poor school attendance and performance, abused alcohol and drugs, and exhibited dramatic changes in behavior, suggested an altered mental state. The Missouri Supreme Court affirmed his conviction and death sentence. A second appeal was subsequently filed, alleging that it was a violation of his Eighth and Fourteenth Amendment rights for the state to execute him, since he was under 18 and a juvenile at the time he committed the crime. The Missouri Supreme Court set aside his death sentence and resentenced him to life imprisonment without the possibility of parole or release except by act of the governor. Prosecutors appealed and the U.S. Supreme Court heard the case.

In a precedent-setting action, the U.S. Supreme Court in a 5–4 decision affirmed the Missouri Supreme Court, effectively overturning their earlier decisions in the cases of *Stanford v. Kentucky* (1989) and *Wilkins v. Missouri* (1989), where the ages of 16 and 17, respectively, were approved for lawful executions. The U.S. Supreme Court declared that it is unconstitutional to execute juveniles under the age of 18 at the time they committed a capital offense. In its lengthy opinion, the Court noted United Nations provisions against executing persons under the age of 18; the fact that the United States was among a very limited number of countries that continued to execute juveniles under age 18; and evolving community standards that increasingly opposed executing juveniles. The Court alluded to a "national consensus" against the death penalty for juveniles, although evidence presented to support such a view of national sentiment was sketchy.

It is quite likely that this U.S. Supreme Court decision was influenced to some extent by international sentiment and an emerging sociopolitical climate that opposed executing juveniles under the age of 18 for any reason. The decision brought the United States into line with most other world nations. The Court supported its decision with alternative rationales other than political ones, however. The Court observed that juveniles are not fully formed adults; that they have an underdeveloped sense of responsibility; that they lack maturity; that they are more vulnerable or susceptible to negative influences and outside pressures, including peer pressure; and that they have less control over their own environment. Furthermore, the Court said that the character of juveniles is not as well formed as that of adults, and that their personality traits are more transitory and less fixed. Thus the court recognized the diminished culpability of juveniles in capital cases. The Court also observed that retribution and deterrence fail to justify imposing the death penalty on juvenile offenders. Table 5.5 shows the minimum age allowable or authorized by statute for juveniles in those states with death penalties.

TABLE 5.5

Minimum Age Authorized for Capital Punishment of Juveniles, 2005

Age 18	None Specified
Alabama	Arizona
Arkansas	Idaho
California	Louisiana
Colorado	Montana
Connecticut	Pennsylvania
Delaware	South Carolina
Federal System	South Dakota
Florida	
Georgia	
Illinois	
Indiana	
Kansas	
Kentucky	
Maryland	
Mississippi	
Missouri	
Nebraska	
Nevada	
New Hampshire	
New Jersey	
New Mexico	
New York	
North Carolina	
Ohio	
Oklahoma	
Oregon	
Tennessee	
Texas	
Utah	
Virginia	
Washington	
Wyoming	

Source: Compiled by author 2005.

Recognizing that some persons may take issue with their decision to raise the legal age at which youthful offenders may be executed, the U.S. Supreme Court noted that drawing the line at 18 years of age is subject to the objections always raised against categorical rules. The qualities that distinguish juveniles from adults do not disappear when an individual turns 18. By the same token, some under age 18 already have attained a level of maturity some adults will never reach. But for the reasons the Court has noted, a line must be drawn. The age of 18 is the point where society draws the line for many purposes between childhood and adulthood. The Court therefore concludes that 18 is the age at which the line for death eligibility ought to rest.

Because of this U.S. Supreme Court decision, it is likely that all juveniles who were convicted for capital crimes and sentenced to death when they were under 18 at the time their crimes were committed will have their death sentences set aside. Much U.S. Supreme Court decision making is not retroactively applicable to previous decisions by other courts. But this decision will profoundly affect the status of all persons on death rows in the United States who were under age 18 when they committed their crimes. Also affected are those youths under age 18 who are presently undergoing capital murder trials where the death penalty is sought. This decision effectively eliminates the death penalty for these juveniles as a prosecutorial option. No doubt most if not all states with capital murder statutes for juveniles under the age of 18 will commute these sentences either to life imprisonment or to life without the possibility of parole. In almost every state, the governor exercises the power to grant clemency, pardons, and other more lenient actions relative to juveniles convicted of capital crimes.

In 2005 there were 72 juveniles on death row in U.S. state prisons (Death Penalty Information Center, 2005). Because of the declining frequency with which juveniles have been executed in recent years, the death penalty issue as it applies to juveniles does not seem as strong as it once was. There will always be many persons in society who will oppose the death penalty for any reason (Bohm and Vogel, 2004; Vogel and Vogel, 2003). But with the 2005 U.S. Supreme Court decision of *Roper v. Simmons,* it is doubtful that future major changes will be made concerning death penalty policy toward youthful offenders age 18 or over, since the United States is now aligned with United Nations policy. While public sentiment is not always easy to measure, there seems to be strong sentiment for harsher penalties meted out to juveniles (Hood, 2002). This doesn't necessarily mean the death penalty or life imprisonment, but it does mean tighter laws and enforcement of those laws where juveniles are concerned.

PUBLIC SENTIMENT ABOUT THE DEATH PENALTY FOR JUVENILES

Views of criminologists are not that different from the views held by the general public about juvenile delinquency and what should be done to prevent or punish it (Hood, 2002). Victor Streib (1987:189) has summarized succinctly a commonly expressed solution that "our society must be willing to devote enormous resources to a search for the causes and cures of violent juvenile crime, just as we have done in the search for the causes and cures of such killer diseases as cancer. And we must not demand a complete cure in a short time, since no one knows how long it will take." Obviously, we have not cured cancer. We are even further away from discovering the etiology of delinquent behavior in all of its diverse forms and finding one or more satisfactory cures for it.

Early identification of at-risk youths who have suffered some type of child abuse from their parents has been linked with subsequent youth violence (Aarons, Powell, and Browne, 2004). Family dysfunction has been linked with assault behavior manifested by youths who have witnessed it compared with those who have not witnessed it (Ballif-Spanvil et al., 2004). Explanations for youth violence are varied and complex. So far, we do not have a good grasp of the specific factors that produce violent behavior among adolescents. We can say, for instance, that in certain instances, childhood victimization has increased the overall risk of violent offending among affected juveniles. But we are not yet in a position to say which juveniles will commit specific violent types of offenses in their future years (Olivero, 2005).

UNIFICATION OF CRIMINAL AND JUVENILE COURTS

Presently, there are several different types of courts in every U.S. jurisdiction. Usually, these courts have general, original, and concurrent jurisdiction, meaning that some courts share adjudicatory responsibilities involving the same subject matter. In Arkansas, for example, chancery courts have jurisdiction over juvenile delinquency cases, although separate county courts may also hear cases involving juveniles. In Colorado, district courts have general jurisdiction over criminal and civil matters, probate matters, and juvenile cases. However, there are specific juvenile courts in Colorado that hear juvenile cases as well. Tennessee county courts, circuit courts, and juvenile courts have concurrent jurisdiction over delinquency and other types of juvenile cases (e.g., children in need of supervision, child custody cases).

Court unification is a general proposal that seeks to centralize and integrate the diverse functions of all courts of general, concurrent, and exclusive jurisdiction into a more simplified and uncomplicated scheme. One way of viewing court unification is that it is ultimately intended to abolish concurrent jurisdiction wherever it is currently shared among various courts in a common jurisdiction, although no presently advocated court unification model has been shown to be superior to others proposed. Thus, there are different ways of achieving unification, although not everyone agrees about which method is best (Lahey, Christenson, and Rossi, 2000). One example of court unification is Pennsylvania.

Prior to 1969, Pennsylvania had two appellate courts and numerous local courts that functioned independently of one another (Yeager, Herb, and Lemmon, 1989). Even the Pennsylvania Supreme Court lacked full and explicit administrative and supervisory authority over the entire judicial system. As the result of the Pennsylvania Constitutional Convention of 1967–1968, a new Judiciary Article, Article V of the Pennsylvania Constitution, was framed. Vast changes were made in court organization and operations. A Family Division was established to deal exclusively with all juvenile matters. A 10-year follow-up evaluation of Pennsylvania's court unification concluded that the present court organization is vastly superior to the pre-1969 court organization. Efficiency and economy were two objectives sought by these court changes. Both aims were achieved.

Earlier studies of jurisdictions representing various degrees of unification have been conducted to assess whether there is necessarily greater economy, coordination, and speed associated with maintaining records and processing cases (Henderson et al., 1984). Georgia, Iowa, Colorado, New Jersey, and Connecticut were examined. Data were collected from records maintained by state administrative officials and local trial courts, and interviews were conducted with key court personnel. A total of 103 courts were selected for analysis, including 20 courts of general jurisdiction, 69 courts of limited jurisdiction, and 15 juvenile courts. More centralized organizational schemes only partially fulfilled the expectations of these researchers. Henderson et al. (1984) report that under centralization, poorer areas were likely to do better financially, although courts in well-off areas faced tighter budget restrictions. Greater uniformity of operations was observed in most jurisdictions. Furthermore, centralization of court organization tended to highlight problems in previously neglected areas, including family and juvenile services. Their findings relating to differences in the effectiveness and efficiency of case processing in trial courts in both decentralized and centralized systems were inconclusive, however.

Implications of Court Unification for Juveniles

For juveniles, court unification poses potentially threatening consequences. For example, in those jurisdictions where considerable fragmentation exists in the processing of juvenile cases or where concurrent jurisdiction distributes juvenile matters among several different courts, juveniles, especially habitual offenders, may be able to benefit because of a general lack of centralization in record-keeping. Thus, juveniles may be adjudicated delinquent in one juvenile court jurisdiction, but this record of adjudication may not be communicated to other courts in adjacent jurisdictions. In time, it is likely that a national record-keeping network will exist, where all juvenile courts may access information from other jurisdictions. Currently, however, the confidentiality of record-keeping is a structural constraint that inhibits the development of such extensive record-sharing. However, as has been reported in earlier chapters, one major change in juvenile justice record-keeping has been the creation of various state repositories of juvenile information that can be shared among interested agencies. This is considered a part of the get-tough movement and is intended to hold juveniles more accountable for their offending by giving authorities in different jurisdictions greater access to their prior offense records (Torbet et al., 1996).

Those who favor a separate and distinct juvenile justice system apart from the criminal justice system contend that the primary goal of juvenile courts should be individualized treatment, with therapy and rehabilitation as dominant factors (Dwyer and McNally, 1987). However, other voices encourage perpetuating a separate juvenile justice system that not only is designed to treat and prevent delinquency, but is also designed to hold juveniles strictly accountable for their actions (Torbet et al., 1996). Thus, it is suggested that less use be made of secure confinement, and greater use be made of probation and parole, with the primary objectives of offering restitution to victims, compensating communities and courts for the time taken to process cases, and performing community services to learn valuable lessons (Maloney, Romig, and Armstrong, 1988).

Getting Tough and Court Unification

There is no question that the get-tough movement is still in force and is pervasive throughout the juvenile justice system. One indication of this is the increased use of waivers or transfers, as more juveniles are shifted to the jurisdiction of criminal courts (Glick, 1998). We have seen certain implications of juveniles as they enter criminal courts for processing, although some of these implications are not entirely unfavorable. Increasing numbers of juvenile court judges are soliciting the involvement of members of the community in voluntary capacities to assist in monitoring adjudicated youths. Greater responsibilities are shifting toward parents in many jurisdictions, particularly when their children commit crimes against property.

Public policy currently favors protecting juveniles as much as possible from the stigmatization of courts and criminal labeling, including the large-scale removal of youths from jails and prisons. Accordingly, recommendations from the public include greater use of nonsecure facilities and programs as opposed to confinement in secure facilities. Especially manifest is the concern for very young offenders. More children under age 12 are entering the juvenile justice system annually (Butts and Snyder, 1997). Clearly, effective programs and procedures for processing such youths need to be in place and operative. Encouragement for greater use of community-based services and treatment programs, special education services, and school-based, early intervention programs is apparent.

There is increasing bureaucratization of juvenile courts, indicated in part by greater formality of juvenile case processing. Juvenile proceedings are increasingly adversarial proceedings similar to criminal courts. Almost all of the criminal court trappings are found in juvenile courts (Feld, 2001). Most juvenile courts are not courts of record, and much informality exists regarding calling witnesses and offering testimony. Federal and state rules of evidence are relaxed considerably and do not attach directly to juvenile civil proceedings.

Juvenile courts are sometimes classified according to a **traditional model** or **family model** and due process distinction. Traditional courts perpetuate the doctrine of *parens patriae,* and juvenile court judges retain a good deal of discretion in adjudicating offenders. They rely more heavily on confinement as a punishment. The due-process juvenile courtroom relies more heavily on preadjudicatory interactions between defense counsels and prosecutors, and nonjudicial handling of cases is more the rule rather than the exception. More frequently used in such courts are nonsecure facilities, community-based programs, probation, and diversion with conditions.

Politicizing Juvenile Punishments

The political approach to punishing juveniles is to rely heavily on the sentiments expressed by voting constituencies. State legislators are at the helm of juvenile justice reforms currently, and several organizations are in strategic positions to offer their guidance and assistance in formulating new juvenile policies. The American Bar Association, the American Legislative Exchange Council, and the Institute of Judicial Administration have provided legislators with model penal codes and proposed juvenile court revisions to introduce consistency throughout an inconsistent juvenile justice system. The federally funded Juvenile Justice Reform Project has reviewed existing juvenile codes and statutes in all 50 states and conducted an extensive national opinion survey of child-serving professionals (Rossum, Koller, and Manfredi, 1987). Two model juvenile justice acts have been proposed—the Model Delinquency Act and the Model Disobedient Children's Act. Among other things, these acts respectively distinguish between delinquent and status offenders and make provisions for their alternative care, treatment, and punishment. Both acts are designed to hold juveniles responsible for their acts and to hold the system accountable for its treatment of these youths as well.

It is doubtful whether these codes are functional and in the best interests of those youths served. Some persons say that these codes will weaken the current protection extended to dependent children or children in need of supervision. Furthermore, a serious erosion of judicial discretion may occur, accompanied by increased use of pretrial detention for juveniles where serious crimes are alleged. Also, status offenders may be jailed for violating court orders. It is difficult to devise a code of accountability founded on the principle of just-deserts and nevertheless performs certain traditional treatment functions in the old context of *parens patriae.* Additionally, codes of any kind promote a degree of blind conformity or compliance with rules for the sake of compliance. With greater codification of juvenile procedures, less latitude exists for judges and others to make concessions and impose individualized dispositions where appropriate. The very idea of individualized dispositions, while appealing to just-deserts interests, invites abuse through discriminatory treatment on racial, ethnic, gender, and socioeconomic grounds.

SUMMARY

For over a century since the United States was formed, juveniles had little or no legal standing. Matters were decided on their behalf or in their best interests by others, usually by chancellors or local officials. The advent of the first juvenile court in Illinois in 1899 was the first official recognition of juveniles. Prior to juvenile courts, the doctrine governing juveniles and matters relevant for them was *parens patriae,* a philosophy established during the 1500s in England. The King of England was figuratively the father of the country and hence responsible for all juveniles. He appointed chancellors to make decisions in his stead, however, throughout various English counties or shires. English influence on American treatment of juveniles was and continues to be profound. Although altered significantly by the U.S. Supreme Court during the 1960s and 1970s, the *parens patriae* doctrine, a strong manifestation of the traditionalism of juvenile justice, continues.

The U.S. Supreme Court refrained from becoming involved in juvenile matters for many decades, largely as the result of a hands-off doctrine, which expressed the view that those in the best position to determine a youth's interests and destiny were juvenile courts and youth welfare agencies. This hands-off doctrine was similar to that found in corrections, where a decree by a Virginia judge in *Ruffin v. Commonwealth* in 1871 was that prisoners have no more rights than slaves. However, this hands-off doctrine as it applied to corrections eventually eroded in the case of *Ex parte Hull* (1941) where the U.S. Supreme Court declared that no one can abridge a prisoner's right to access the courts with one or more appeals. This decision opened up the floodgates of inmate litigation, and today the courts are inundated with appeals from all types of prisoners seeking various types of relief.

Although several states had gradually acknowledged juvenile rights, no substantial constitutional rights were available to juveniles for the better half of the twentieth century. In 1966, however, a precedent-setting case, *Kent v. United States,* was decided in a 5–4 U.S. Supreme Court decision, where it was declared that juveniles have a right to a hearing prior to being transferred to a criminal court for prosecution as an adult. While this right was not especially significant since juvenile court judges could continue to transfer youths even after granting them hearings on the issue, the case meant that the U.S. Supreme Court was amenable to hearing cases involving other juvenile rights. Two cases immediately followed. These were *In re Gault* (1967) and *In re Winship* (1970). The *Gault* case involved a charge against an Arizona juvenile for making obscene telephone calls. In a one-sided proceeding, Gault was adjudicated delinquent and sent to the Arizona State Industrial School for a 5½-year period. The case was appealed and the decision was eventually reversed. Gault won the rights to a notice of charges against him, to confront and cross-examine his accuser, the right against self-incrimination and to give testimony in his own behalf, and the right to an attorney. In the *Winship* case, the civil standard of proof necessary to confine youths in secure facilities, preponderance of the evidence, was changed to the criminal standard of beyond a reasonable doubt. The *Kent, Gault,* and *Winship* cases are considered the Big Three juvenile cases that set a pattern of gradually accruing rights for juveniles. Other significant U.S. Supreme Court cases were *McKeiver v. Pennsylvania* (1971), where a juvenile's automatic right to a jury trial was denied; *Breed v. Jones* (1975), where it was decided that juveniles could not be adjudicated delinquent and convicted in criminal court of the same offense without violating one's right against double jeopardy; and *Schall v. Martin* (1984), which authorized the preventive detention of certain juveniles because of the societal risks they might pose if released.

Several implications of obtaining greater rights for juveniles include more equitable treatment for juveniles through less juvenile court disparity; greater certainty of punishment through greater emphasis on due process and justice; greater likelihood of juveniles acquiring juvenile records; and a greater likelihood of having one's case moved from the jurisdiction of juvenile courts to criminal courts. Presently any juvenile is entitled to representation by counsel, whether privately acquired or publicly appointed. The extent of attorney involvement in juvenile cases has systematically increased over the years, and greater formalization has been observed to occur in most types of juvenile justice system proceedings. In 11 states, jury trials for juveniles are a matter of right under certain kinds of conditions. In the other states, jury trials are held at the discretion of juvenile court judges. Despite the fact that juveniles have acquired many of the rights presently enjoyed by criminal defendants and juvenile proceedings have become more formalized, most juvenile courts continue to exercise a high degree of leniency when adjudicating juvenile cases and imposing particular dispositions. In fact, juvenile court judges are encouraged to exercise leniency toward juveniles in virtually all jurisdictions, and secure confinement of certain juveniles is only to be used as a last resort.

A very controversial issue relating to juveniles is the age at which they can be executed for committing capital crimes. Until 2005, juveniles age 16 or over could be executed for capital offenses in most of the jurisdictions with death penalties. The first documented execution of a juvenile was in 1642, and the youngest juvenile ever executed was 10 years old. A contemporary view of the death penalty in the United States and how it has been applied to juveniles shows, for instance, that James Roach, a South Carolina 17-year-old, was convicted in 1977 of a double murder and subsequently sentenced to death and electrocuted. In 1982, the U.S. Supreme Court heard the case of *Eddings v. Ok-*

lahoma, where a 16-year-old boy shot and killed an Oklahoma State Trooper. Eddings was convicted in an Oklahoma court and sentenced to death. His conviction and sentence were upheld by the U.S. Supreme Court. In 1988 the case of *Thompson v. Oklahoma* was decided by the U.S. Supreme Court, where 15-year-old William Thompson was found guilty of murder and sentenced to death. In this particular case, the U.S. Supreme Court overturned Thompson's death sentence and held that it was a violation of the Eighth Amendment prohibition against cruel and unusual punishment to execute a youth who was under age 16 at the time a capital crime was committed.

In 1989, two landmark death penalty cases were decided. These were *Wilkins v. Missouri* and *Stanford v. Kentucky.* These cases involved a 16-year-old and a 17-year-old, respectively. Both crimes were especially heinous. The U.S. Supreme Court upheld the death sentences in both cases, and the age of 16 was firmly established as the minimum age where a juvenile could be legally executed in the United States for committing a capital crime. In 2005, over 70 youths were on U.S. death rows awaiting execution. However, in March 2005 the U.S. Supreme Court heard the case of *Roper v. Simmons,* a Missouri case involving a 17-year-old who had been convicted of murder and sentenced to death. In a precedent-setting decision, the U.S. Supreme Court declared that executions of juveniles under the age of 18 at the time they committed capital murder were unconstitutional. The *Stanford* and *Wilkins* cases were no longer applicable with the higher age standard articulated. All juveniles on death row at the time of this decision had their sentences commuted to life, either with or without the possibility of parole. This newer standard comports with most other United Nations members where juveniles are defined as those under age 18 and executions of such persons are prohibited.

The death penalty is controversial for a variety of reasons. Opponents of the death penalty say that it is barbaric; it is not a deterrent to others who contemplate committing murder; most persons in the United States are against the death penalty anyway; it is more costly to execute someone than to keep them imprisoned for life; it is arbitrarily applied in ways that suggest racial, ethnic, and socioeconomic biases; it is nothing more than revenge, which is wrong; and it is unfair and applied erroneously, where some persons convicted of murder are sentenced to death and subsequently found to be innocent of the offense. Those supporting the death penalty claim that it is retribution; it deters others from committing murder; and it is a just and fitting punishment. Public sentiment is reflected in numerous surveys of public opinion. This opinion consistently reveals that a majority of those polled favor the death penalty rather than oppose it. However, polls about the use of the death penalty in juvenile cases show far less support for its use.

Because juveniles have acquired and are acquiring greater rights commensurate with those of adult criminal offenders, some experts have proposed court unification, or a general-purpose court where both juvenile and criminal cases may be heard. Arguments both for and against court unification have been advanced. Proponents of court unification point to the similarities between juvenile and criminal courts and to the fact that juveniles would enjoy the same rights as adults in trial proceedings. Also more serious juveniles would be subject to harsher punishments beyond the jurisdiction of juvenile courts. Opponents of court unification argue that it is virtually impossible to blend the civil focus of the juvenile court with the goals and structure of criminal courts. Furthermore, individualized rehabilitative measures, traditional characteristics of juvenile courts, would be undermined through court unification. Presently public policy favors maintaining separate court systems for adults and juveniles. This situation is unlikely to change in the near future.

QUESTIONS FOR REVIEW

1. How has the get-tough movement influenced juvenile rights?

2. What is the hands-off doctrine? What corrections case seemed to establish this doctrine in corrections? What case undermined this doctrine? What is the significance of the hands-off doctrine for juvenile cases appealed to the U.S. Supreme Court? What juvenile case was precedent-setting by eliminating the hands-off doctrine?

3. What was the significance of (a) *Kent v. United States* and (b) *In re Gault?*

4. What is the standard of proof currently used in juvenile courts, where a juvenile's liberty is in jeopardy? What case was significant in evolving this standard of proof?

5. What is the case of *Breed v. Jones* and its significance for juvenile rights?

6. What is the minimum age for seeking the death penalty against a juvenile who has allegedly committed capital murder? What are some distinctions between the cases of *Wilkins v. Missouri* and *Stanford v. Kentucky* on the one hand and *Roper v. Simmons* on the other?

7. What are three arguments for and three arguments against the death penalty?

8. What was the significance of the case of *Thompson v. Oklahoma* and whether juveniles could be executed for committing capital crimes?

9. What is meant by court unification? What are some implications of court unification for juvenile offenders?

10. What are some problems with establishing court unification in the United States?

INTERNET CONNECTIONS

Justice Project
http://www.ccjr.policy.net/

Moratorium 2000
http://www.transfigpittsford.org/moratorium_2000.htm

Office of Juvenile Justice and Delinquency Prevention
http://www.ojjdp.ncjrs.org/

Youth Defense Counsels
http://www.juveniledefense.com

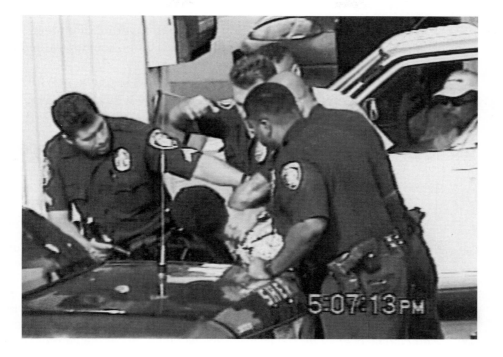

CHAPTER 6 | *Juveniles and the Police*

Chapter Outline

Chapter Objectives
Introduction
Police Discretion: Use and Abuse
   The Diffuseness of Police
      Officer Roles
   Juvenile Gang Units in Police
      Departments
   Proactive Restorative Policing
   Youth Gangs, Minority
      Status, and Gender
   Myths and Truths About
      Gangs
   Female Gangs
   Juvenile Response to Police
      Officer Contacts

Arrests of Juveniles
   Juvenile–Adult Distinctions
   The Ambiguity of Juvenile
      Arrests
   Booking, Fingerprinting, and
      Photographing Juvenile
      Suspects
   Interrogations of Juvenile
      Suspects
   Expungement and Sealing
      Policies
Status Offenders and Juvenile
   Delinquents
Divestiture and Its Implications:
   Net-Widening

Relabeling Status Offenses as
   Delinquent Offenses
Protecting Status Offenders
   from Themselves
Parens Patriae versus Due
   Process
Gender Stereotyping and DSO
Race and Ethnicity
Redefining Delinquency
Summary
Questions for Review
Internet Connections

Key Terms

automatic transfer laws
beats
children in need of supervision
   (CHINS)
community policing
corporate gangs
criminogenic environment

discretionary powers
expungement orders
National Youth Gang Survey
   (NYGS)
proactive units
reactive units
restorative policing

scavenger gangs
sealing records of juveniles
situationally based discretion
stationhouse adjustments
territorial gangs
totality of circumstances
youth squads

Chapter Objectives

As the result of reading this chapter, you will have accomplished the following objectives:

1. Learn about police discretion relative to juvenile offenders.
2. Assess the importance of youth squads in police departments that interdict delinquent conduct.
3. Understand differential response of youths to contacts with police.
4. Understand the ambiguity associated with juvenile arrests.
5. Understand how police officers distinguish between and process status and delinquent offenders.
6. Learn about several important delinquency intervention programs within communities and their effectiveness.

• *It happened in Sweetwater, Florida. Officer Allen B. St. Germain's personal watercraft turned up missing. An investigation revealed that an 18-year-old juvenile, Peter Daniel, had knowledge of the theft. Officer St. Germain and Sgt. George I. Alvarez escorted the youth to another suspect's house, and subsequently, they returned to the police station. Daniel was in bad shape. His spleen and liver were lacerated, requiring emergency surgery. Later Daniel said that the officers had beaten him severely and that after the beating, they ignored his requests for medical help. According to Daniel, the officers hit and kicked him repeatedly, accusing him and another suspect of stealing the officer's watercraft. Another officer at the station intervened when he saw Daniel and said that he looked gray and near death. Subsequently the two officers were arrested and charged with aggravated assault.* [*Source:* Adapted from the Associated Press, "Two Police Officers Are Charged with Beating Teen." June 18, 2004.]

• *It happened in Donora, Pennsylvania, in a neighborhood known as a "trouble area." Early in the evening of August 16, 2004, a white police officer observed three black teenagers enter a convenience store and walk back outside. He approached them and ordered them to leave the area. Next, he pulled out his Mace and sprayed the teens in their faces, placing all three under arrest for failing to disperse and disorderly conduct. Subsequently the boys were released and the charges were dropped. It turned out that the boys had just finished football practice and had stopped by the store for a soda. One of the youths was a high school honor student. None of the youths had ever been in trouble with the law. An adult eyewitness said that the officer had not been provoked and that the youths were not being disorderly in any way. Furthermore, the officer used unnecessary force when taking the youths into custody. The Superintendent of Police, Jim Brice, was interviewed and defended the police officer's actions. Brice said, "He [the officer] told me he asked the kids to leave three or four times and they basically said, 'No.' Then, as he was attempting to arrest them, they struggled and he was alone." Mayor John Lignelli said of the eyewitness, "He said he witnessed some of the incident, but he was blocks away. How much could he have seen?" The conduct of the officer was under investigation.* [*Source:* Adapted from Jeff Oliver, "Police Abuse Alleged." *Valley Independent*, August 24, 2004.]

• *The party in Mequon, Wisconsin, being given at the home of a teacher from Brookfield Central High School for her daughter's 18th birthday on the night of January 24, 2004, was going a little late and was a little loud. A neighbor complained about the noise. Police officers were dispatched to the scene. What happened after that is anyone's guess.*

According to the teacher, Anna Annina, 44, she heard loud pounding on her front door and opened it. Police officers yelling that they had a search warrant rushed in with handcuffs, threatened to shoot her 1-year-old barking dog, and pepper-sprayed a young woman. Annina's daughter was kicked in the head by one of the officers. Fifteen youths were ticketed by police at the party for underage drinking. Annina was handcuffed tightly and taken to the police station where she was charged with disorderly conduct. The police version is that they went to the home to investigate allegations by neighbors of underage drinking. They say that Annina opened the front door when they knocked politely and then tried to shut it. They forced their way into the home because of suspicious circumstances and discovered numerous juveniles consuming alcoholic beverages. They took appropriate action from there. The case was being investigated. [Source: Adapted from Mike Johnson, "Brookfield Teacher's Husband Files Complaint in Drinking Party Case." Journal-Sentinel, March 8, 2004.]

• Colerain, Ohio, police officers say they aren't targeting minority juveniles with a new curfew ordinance. When the curfew went into effect in July 2003 until November 2003, 104 juveniles were apprehended by police for being on city streets after curfew. The curfew ordinance makes it illegal for anyone younger than 18 to be in a public place or privately owned business after midnight. Of the 104 juveniles taken into custody, 20 were arrested, mostly for drug violations. The 104 juveniles comprised 58 white males, 25 white females, and 21 black males. Some residents have worried that the ordinance would be used as a form of racial profiling. [Source: Adapted from Reid Forgrave, "Curfew Statistics Alleviate Race Fears." Cincinnati Inquirer, December 12, 2003.]

INTRODUCTION

Since the nineteenth century, there has been a pervasive and persistent tension between juveniles and the police. It is not necessarily the case that juveniles are targeted by the police for discrimination or mistreatment, but rather, police contacts with juveniles in the course of their normal patrol routines are inevitable. The opening scenarios in this chapter depict some of the types of police–juvenile encounters that have occurred and continue to occur. A juvenile is apparently "roughed up" by police officers while in their custody. Minority teenagers are confronted by police and ordered to leave the area. The teen responses escalate the situation to a full-fledged conflict, where officers use Mace and physical force to manhandle the youths into custody. A party given for teens disturbs neighbors and police officers are summoned. After assessing the situation, the officers make arrests and issue citations to many youths for underage drinking and other illicit conduct. An adult is arrested, handcuffed, and roughly hauled away. Curfews for juveniles in various cities are established, and the police are expected to enforce these curfew laws. The result is numerous arrests of juveniles and accusations of racism and discrimination.

This chapter describes various interactions between the police and juveniles. The chapter begins with an examination of police discretionary powers and how the exercise of this discretion is both used and abused. Police departments are increasingly sensitive to the issue of how juveniles should be treated. Many larger police agencies today have established juvenile units whose exclusive function is to investigate juvenile offending whenever it occurs. At the same time, police departments have also implemented various community policing policies designed to improve their relationships with community residents, including juveniles. These policies and related activities generated as a result of them will be described and examined.

The chapter next explores juvenile gangs, their formation and growth, and how the police respond to gangs and gang problems. Since youth gangs almost always form along racial and/or ethnic lines, police–gang interactions have led to accusations of racial discrimination and mistreatment. Contemporaneous with juvenile gang formation and growth have evolved numerous myths and misconceptions about who gang members are and what they do. These myths and misconceptions are listed and described. Over the years different authorities have classified and categorized various types of gangs according to their structure, organization, and operation. Some of these classification schemes are described and discussed. Female juveniles have also formed gangs, and these gangs seem to be increasing in greater proportion to their male juvenile counterparts. Female gang formation and growth is also described.

The next section of this chapter describes several types of responses by juveniles to their contacts with the police. Several important factors are considered as dimensions affecting the nature of this contact. Socioeconomic status, race/ethnicity, and gender all play important roles in how different juvenile–police encounters occur as well as the resulting outcomes of these encounters. The criminal justice literature is replete with evidence supporting the idea that the juvenile justice system exhibits substantial racism, and the police treatment of juveniles in most jurisdictions fuels professional views that more than a little discrimination exists relating to juvenile–police encounters. This discrimination is not always race/ethnicity-based, however. Socioeconomic and gender factors are also operative in influencing outcomes of police–juvenile contacts. These factors are discussed in some detail.

The chapter next explores the nature of decision making relative to juvenile arrests. Arresting juveniles is complicated by the fact that it is not always easy for police officers to know the ages of youths they encounter and how these youths ought to be processed. Many juveniles possess false identification information or no information whatsoever, thus making it impossible for police officers to know with certainty who they have arrested and how such persons should be processed. Thus, some ambiguity exists in more than a few juvenile–police encounters. Many juveniles are booked, photographed, fingerprinted, and otherwise subjected to many of the procedures associated with adult offender processing. Even when it is known that juveniles have been taken into custody, it is often customary for authorities to book juveniles similar to adults, at least for the limited purpose of identifying them and placing them with parents, guardians, or social service agencies. These procedures are described.

Juveniles are also subject to questioning by police, especially if they are apprehended relative to offenses in which they are involved. Some caselaw has evolved concerning interrogations of juvenile suspects, and the nature and scope of such caselaw will be examined. The fact that many juveniles are processed in ways similar to adults at police agencies does not mean that juveniles acquire criminal records. Even if a record is maintained by the police agency of the juvenile arrest, it is subsequently sealed or expunged when the juvenile reaches his or her age of majority or adulthood. Again, these practices stem from the fact that the juvenile justice system is a civil entity rather than a criminal one. A distinction is also made between status and delinquent offenders as well. The Juvenile Justice and Delinquency Prevention Act of 1974 and its subsequent revisions and renewals have guided and governed police department policies and officer conduct toward juveniles who have engaged in a wide range of offending behavior. Status offenders are routinely transferred to social service agencies for processing rather than formal handling in jails or police departments. Different provisions for the treatment of delinquent offenders exist. These policies are listed and described.

In a majority of U.S. jurisdictions, juvenile courts have divested themselves of jurisdiction over status offenders. Despite divestiture, some police officers have continued to interact with status offenders as though they were delinquents. Status offending may be relabeled by police as delinquency, and police officers act accordingly. The influence of race, ethnicity, socioeconomic status, and gender on such police behaviors toward juvenile status offenders has not gone unnoticed. The implications of divestiture of jurisdiction over status offenders are discussed in some detail.

POLICE DISCRETION: USE AND ABUSE

Police officers make up the front line or first line of defense in the prevention and/or control of street crime committed by juveniles, although the effectiveness of this line in crime control continues to be questioned (Myers, 2004). Police officers are vested with considerable **discretionary powers,** depending on the circumstances, ranging from verbal warnings in confrontations with the public to the application of deadly force (*Tennessee v. Garner,* 1985). Police discretion is the range of behavioral choices police officers have within the limits of their power. Beyond the formal training police officers receive from law enforcement agency training academies, police discretion is influenced by many other factors, including the situation, as well as the race, ethnicity, gender, socioeconomic status, and age of those confronted. Many of those stopped by police, questioned, and subsequently arrested and detained in jails or other lock-up facilities, even for short periods, are juveniles (Eitle, Stolzenberg, and D'Alessio, 2005).

The Diffuseness of Police Officer Roles

The public tends to define the police role diffusely, where police are expected to address a wide variety of human problems. The nature of this police intervention is that the police will intervene in various situations and ensure that matters do not get worse. Thus, police training in various jurisdictions is geared to reflect this broad public expectation of the police role (Shafer, Carter, and Katz-Bannister, 2004). Training manuals for police officers include numerous examples of field situations, including how to deal with domestic disturbances, traffic violations, narcotics, civil disorders, vice, drunkenness, federal offenses, and juveniles (Myers, 2004).

Much of this **situationally based discretion** in confronting crime in the streets and the public is covert. Most of what transpires in the interaction between police officers and suspects is known only to these actors. Thus, it is often difficult to enforce consistently high standards of accountability for police to observe in their diverse public encounters (Poyser, 2004). In short, police officers make on-the-spot decisions about whether to move beyond simple verbal warnings or reprimands to more formal actions against those stopped and questioned on suspicion. Considering the circumstances or situation, law enforcement officers may be more or less aggressive.

Contributing to the diffuseness of police officer roles in communities is a relatively recent phenomenon known as **community policing.** Community policing is a major policing reform that broadens the police mission from a narrow focus on crime to a mandate that encourages the police to explore creative solutions for a host of community concerns, including crime, fear of crime, disorder, and neighborhood decay. It rests on the belief that only by working together will people and the police be able to improve the quality of life in the community, with the police not only as enforcers, but also as advisors, facilitators, and supporters of new community-based police-supervised initiatives (Brandl and Bartow, 2004).

One immediate effect of community policing in many neighborhoods is to place greater discretionary power in the hands of police officers, whether they are on foot or in cruisers. An implicit consequence of community policing is to create better relations between the police department and the community, in order for community residents to place greater trust in the police rather than to fear them (Myers, 2004). In communities where such discretion power shifts occur through planning, police officers may be expected by higher-ups to take a greater interest in youths, even where petty infractions are involved. Police officers may be punished for failing to take seriously minor infractions and for not intervening when necessary. Thus, they are in a dilemma about whether to get involved in the activities of minor offenders. In more sensitive settings where ethnicity may play an important role, law enforcement officers may be criticized unfairly by citizens for simply doing their jobs.

For many police officers, stopping and detaining juveniles is not a particularly popular activity (Shafer, Carter, and Katz-Bannister, 2004). One reason is that juvenile court judges are inclined to be quite lenient with juvenile first-offenders or minor offenders. Many juvenile courts consider youths chronic offenders only after they have been adjudicated as delinquents five or six times. Thus, the considerable time police officers spend by taking youths into custody and filling out extensive paperwork seems like so much wasted time when these youths are released later with only verbal warnings from judges. There are also additional regulations governing how juveniles should be processed and detained when brought to jails following their encounters with police officers (Schulenberg, 2003). These increasingly complex procedures for juvenile offender processing discourage police–juvenile interaction except under the most serious circumstances and where serious crimes have been committed (Mastrofski, 2004).

Nevertheless, police officers in every jurisdiction encounter large numbers of juveniles annually during their patrols or **beats.** Because of the informal nature of many of these police officer/juvenile encounters, the *UCR* and other official sources for arrest information fail to disclose the true incidence of all juvenile contacts with the law (Thurman and Zhao, 2004). In 2004 there were over 2 million juvenile arrests, about half of which were petitioned to juvenile courts for further action. Furthermore, self-reports from juveniles in elementary schools and high schools suggest considerably greater delinquent activity as well as contacts with police that do not necessarily result in arrests or being taken into custody for brief periods (Office of Juvenile Justice and Delinquency Prevention, 2005).

Juvenile Gang Units in Police Departments

In the early years of police–juvenile encounters, police departments operated under a type of siege mentality. In Los Angeles, for example, the zoot suit riots of 1943 involved a 10-day attack by civilians on alleged Mexican American youth gang members. Extraordinarily repressive police policies were implemented at that time, and police–juvenile relations were strained for many decades (Mauro, 2005). Subsequently, police departments throughout the nation, particularly larger municipal police departments with 200 or more officers, established specialized juvenile units as a part of their organizational structure to deal with different types of offenders. Even relatively small departments in remote geographical areas have at least one juvenile officer who deals exclusively with juvenile affairs. Despite this specialization, however, every police officer who encounters juveniles while policing becomes a juvenile officer temporarily. Not all of the police activities in these juvenile units have been directed at gang violence or violent offenses committed by juveniles, however. Those targeted for active police intervention and assistance have included truants; runaways and missing children; property offenders and those who commit vehicular theft; curfew violators; and school-related offenses (Thurman and Zhao, 2004).

Police interest in gangs is most often focused on prevention rather than retaliation (Mauro, 2005). Prevention measures by police include profiling gang members; methods used by gangs to recruit new members; neighborhood roots that spawn and perpetuate gang activity; the influence and presence of gang members in prison settings; providing materials and strategies for parents and school authorities to use for coping with gang activities; and examining gang structure (Katz, Webb, and Decker, 2005).

By 1997, all 51 jurisdictions in the United States had made extensive changes in their laws concerning juveniles who commit violent or serious crimes (Torbet and Szymanski, 1998). In turn, these legislative changes have

There is always an uneasy tension between police and juveniles in many communities, especially when juveniles exhibit suspicious behavior.

caused numerous police departments to implement programs that will achieve certain delinquency prevention objectives contemplated by these changes (West, 2005). Many of these programs involve the establishment of gang units (Katz, 2003).

Actually, the activities of juvenile units or **youth squads** are largely directed toward delinquency prevention (Santana, 2005). These units tend to be **reactive units,** in that they respond to public requests for intervention and assistance whenever offenses committed by juveniles are reported. That is, these officers react to calls from others about crimes that have already been committed or are in progress. Gang fights or break-ins involving youths would activate these juvenile units. In contrast, police officers who patrol city streets are most often **proactive units** involved in contacts with juveniles who may or may not be offenders and/or law violators. These officers are almost constantly on the lookout for suspicious activities (Katz, 2003). They monitor the streets and investigate potentially troublesome situations.

Proactive Restorative Policing

In Bethlehem, Pennsylvania, a Police Family Group Conference Project (FGC) was established in the mid-1990s and coordinated by the Bethlehem Police Department (McCold and Wachtel, 1998). First-time moderately serious juvenile offenders were randomly assigned either to formal adjudication in juvenile court or to a diversionary **restorative policing** process involving family group conference. Police-based family group conferencing uses trained police officers to facilitate meetings attended by juvenile offenders, their victims, and their families and/or friends to discuss the harm caused by the offender's action and to create an agreement to repair the harm. Data were obtained and analyzed for 80 FGC participants, 180 victims, and 169 parents. These data were compared with control groups with similar characteristics. The FGC participation rate was 42 percent; 100 percent of the conferences produced an agreement on restorative actions; and 94 percent of all offenders were in full compliance with the agreements. The FGC seemed to produce lower rearrest rates among participants, and perceptions of fairness were as high as 96 percent for all participants. Researchers concluded that the Bethlehem Police Department was able to reduce recidivism substantially among FGC participants while avoiding net-widening. It was also demonstrated that police officers were able to conduct FGCs successfully, and without special training. Thus the potential for applying FGCs in other jurisdictions was demonstrated.

Youth Gangs, Minority Status, and Gender

Types and Numbers of Gangs.   The increased visibility of delinquent gangs organized along ethnic and racial lines in many cities and the violence such gangs manifest have caused police departments to establish task forces of special police officers who do nothing but monitor and investigate gang activities (Santana, 2005). Some writers have classified these gangs as **scavenger gangs, territorial gangs,** and **corporate gangs** (Shelden, Tracy, and Brown, 2001). Scavenger gangs form primarily as a means of socializing and for mutual protection. Territorial gangs are organized for the purpose of preserving a fixed

 **BOX 6.1**

INTERNATIONAL SNAPSHOT: JUVENILE JUSTICE IN NIGERIA

Historically, Nigeria was a colony of the British Colonial government until 1960. Until that time, the Nigerian criminal justice system was an instrument of repressive British legal and social powers and institutions designed to take control of deprived and destitute natives, including children, so that they did not constitute a threat or nuisance to the British social order. However, when Nigerian independence occurred, a form of neocolonialism replaced the earlier British colonialism, without a significant change in the repressive legal and penal powers of the new Nigerian government. The present Nigerian legal system is an arena for struggle among competing groups with diverse views of social order. Nigeria is presently a federation of 30 states. National constitutions of 1979 and 1991 provided for a National Assembly. State governors were appointed to oversee each of the 30 states. Individual federal and state courts exist, including one supreme court.

The juvenile justice system has not changed much since the colonial era. The goals of juvenile justice administration are to: (1) increase awareness of civil society and political authorities about the experience and treatment of juvenile offenders; (2) sensitize police, prison officials, social and community development workers, educationists, and others about the conditions and needs of juvenile offenders; (3) encourage the development of a comprehensive socioeconomic policy that meets the aspirations and needs of children and young people in the country; (4) encourage the use of noncustodial measures in dealing with juvenile offenders; and (5) sensitize the public about the need to promote and defend the rights of children and young persons, including juvenile offenders. These objectives are a part of a broad scholarly program to educate the Nigerian public and government about how youths ought to be processed and treated.

Juvenile delinquency in Nigeria is the violation of criminal codes by young persons. There is no official definition of a juvenile or delinquency. Furthermore, the terms *child juvenile,* and *young person* are used interchangeably, thus creating some confusion about specific punishments and/or treatments as well as court jurisdiction. The Children and Young Act was passed in 1945 and revised several times through 1955. It defined a child as any person under the age of 14. Young persons were defined as persons who have attained the age of 14. The law did not define a juvenile. However, other indicators suggest that the term refers to persons under the age of 17.

Juvenile delinquency is defined in a way similar to the U.S. definition. Thus, any offense committed by a juvenile that would be a crime if an adult committed it would be delinquency. Other types of offenses are analogous to the U.S. interpretation of status offenses and are labeled as such. These offenses include truancy from school, running away from home, drinking alcohol in public, and associating with disreputable persons such as prostitutes and criminals. There is very little juvenile violence. Most juvenile offending is property crime, including theft and burglary. Very young offenders, children, are often given educational measures and selected community treatments. Because the police exercise considerable discretion in juvenile matters, accurate information about the number of juveniles who violate the law does not exist. Over 60 percent of all cases that should become a part of police records are simply not recorded; rather, they are disposed of by informal means, such as verbal warnings and reprimands, or police leniency, especially for more wealthy youths.

The ages of criminal responsibility are based in part on English common law. Persons under the age of 7 are not presumed accountable for crimes they may commit. From ages 7–11, these persons are considered children. Juveniles are persons 12–16

(continued)

years of age. Offenses of both children and juveniles are handled by ad hoc juvenile courts, which are informally administered. These are presided over by a county magistrate, a layman, and a laywoman.

Because delinquency and juveniles have been broadly defined or diffuse, this creates some confusion about specific treatments or punishments that should be imposed on different age categories of offenders. Juveniles are subject to a wide variety of legal restrictions and differential treatment within the juvenile justice system. Law enforcement officers and juvenile judicial officers thus have broad discretionary powers when dealing with young persons and children, including discriminatory actions against different youths. Delinquency has been attributed to conditions of drift, maladjustment, pathology, disturbance, moral depravity, and unruly behavior. Discrimination is rooted in the differences in Nigerian social classes, where the rich enjoy greater access to legal rights and the poor do not. These socioeconomic distinctions are invisible and not formally recognized. Because official records of crime and delinquency are only incidentally maintained by the Nigerian government, it is difficult to delineate trends in offending or offense patterns. No records of victimization by ethnicity, gender, or age exist to determine with confidence the relation between victims and offenders. Prison reports give some information, however, that suggest offenders are mostly younger males.

Ideally the juvenile justice system is guided by a philosophy of concern, care, and reformation. Young offenders are deemed to be immature and should not be treated like adult offenders. Rather, delinquents are viewed as misguided and therefore rescued through treatment, reformation, and rehabilitation programs in correctional institutions. However, the juvenile justice system is a track within the adult criminal justice system. Adult and juvenile tracks have been formally recognized.

The principals in Nigerian criminal justice administration are the police, courts, and prisons. The Nigerian police were nationalized in legislation in 1979 and 1999 so that now, there is only the Nigerian Police Force (NPF). The NPF has wide functions and power. These functions are to prevent, investigate, and detect crimes; apprehend offenders; protect life and property; preserve law and order; enforce all laws and regulations with which they are directly charged; and to perform military duties. The Children and Young Persons Act was revised to assign law enforcement duties to the police. Juvenile welfare units were created and managed in major divisional police offices. However, these units have not been fully developed, staffed, or trained. The quality of services delivered to detained juveniles is poor.

The judicial system of Nigeria is quite fragmented. The rights of accused persons, including juveniles, are limited. Public defenders are appointed the accused, although jury trials for accused persons are virtually nonexistent. Charges against suspects, including juveniles, are brought by police who make reports to the office of the Director of Public Prosecution (DPP). The DPP evaluates evidence and decides whether to drop or pursue cases against suspects. There is no plea bargaining in Nigeria. Minor cases are resolved through civil means in lower state courts by presiding magistrates. One's mental capacity may be evaluated upon judicial order. Interestingly, police actions may be taken prior to trial to avoid one. Police may dismiss a case because of insufficient evidence; they may warn and discharge a suspect who has no prior criminal record; or they may refer the case to a juvenile court or simply discharge a suspect who is less than 17 years old. There is no reliable information about the proportion of cases that is dismissed or how many result in trial for different age groups. Pretrial detention can be ordered for juveniles in need of protection or if juveniles are unruly.

Nigerian prisons are primarily overcrowded human warehouses and do not have adequate programs to rehabilitate or educate imprisoned offenders, youthful or otherwise. Prisons are primarily punitive and repressive. Although reformation is prescribed, it is only incidental. Some more violent and older juveniles are confined in prisons, while younger offenders may be detained in borstals, approved schools, and remand homes.

Juvenile justice is haphazard at best. Individual states deal with juveniles at the community level for the most part, with the exception of the most serious older juvenile offenders. In rural areas, shaming is used as a method of social control. Some use of restorative justice occurs between victims and their victimizers. Mediation seems to be used increasingly as a means of repairing the harm done to victims by juvenile offenders.

Judges determine penalties in all cases. Sentences are imposed shortly after a determination of one's guilt has been made. Justice is swift. Although psychiatrists, social workers, and other relevant personnel work closely with the court in all juvenile matters, they have no influence in the sentencing process. There are no predispositional reports delivered to judges to influence their decision making. The range of punishments includes fines; verbal warnings; probation; corporal punishments; community service; imprisonment for indeterminate periods; house arrest; and a variety of other community-based alternatives. There is no parole in Nigeria. The death penalty is imposed for capital crimes including murder, armed robbery, treason, and currency offenses. Executions are by firing squad in public.

[*Sources:* Tamuno Chukwuma, "Juveniles in Nigeria," Unpublished paper, 2005; Obi N.I. Ebbe, "Facts About Nigeria," Unpublished paper, 2005; Oliver Chukwu, "Nigerian Juvenile Delinquency," Unpublished paper, 2005.]

amount of territory, such as several city blocks. They maintain control over these geographical areas and repel efforts by other gangs to invade their territory or turf. The most violent gangs are corporate gangs (Hughes and Short, 2005). These types of gangs emulate organized crime syndicates. While all types of gangs pose dangers to the public, corporate gangs are more profit-motivated and rely on illicit activities such as drug trafficking to further their profit interests (Katz, Webb, and Decker, 2005). Thus corporate gangs are more dangerous than scavenger or territorial gangs. Corporate gangs use excessive violence including murder to carry out their goals. Often, innocent bystanders are gunned down as victims of gang retaliation against rival gangs and gang members (Duran, 2005).

Less conventional gangs, such as the Skinheads, have been targeted by some youth gang bureaus and other police agencies within departments. For example, Skinheads claimed at least 100,000 members worldwide in 2004. They have a cumulative record of gang violence involving weapons. And it is not always cities with large populations where police gang units are deployed. In Alabama, for instance, law enforcement agencies in 46 cities with populations of 10,000 or more have reported substantial gang activities in their jurisdictions (Thomas, Holzer, and Wall, 2004). Alabama officials report that their gang visibility is comparable to that reported by larger cities, especially concerning the amount of female involvement or participation in gangs, the trappings of gang culture, and other critical gang elements. Officials in other jurisdictions have reported similar gang presence and activity (Santana, 2005).

In 1995, the National Youth Gang Center (NYGC) conducted an extensive survey, which became known as the **National Youth Gang Survey (NYGS)** (Wilson, 2001:xiii). Subsequently, the NYGS has been conducted annually to track gang activities and describe critical gang components and characteristics. At least nine types of gangs were identified in the original survey: (1) juvenile gangs; (2) street gangs; (3) taggers; (4) drug gangs; (5) satanic groups; (6) posses;

(7) crews; (8) stoners; and (9) terrorist groups. Traditionally, gangs were formed by racial, ethnic, or religious groups. Gangs of today are based on needs to identify with a group (Greenleaf, 2005). However, not all gangs today are limited to youths. Increasing numbers of youth gangs have adults as members. One estimate is that in 2005 there were over 29,000 gangs with a membership in excess of 1 million members (Mauro, 2005; Santana, 2005).

Myths and Truths About Gangs

Joan Moore (1993:28–29) has described several stereotypes of gangs that are not true. These include:

1. Gangs are exclusively males who are violent, addicted to drugs and alcohol, sexually hyperactive, unpredictable, and confrontational.
2. They are either all African American or all Hispanic.
3. They thrive in inner-city neighborhoods where they dominate, intimidate, and prey upon innocent citizens.
4. They all deal heavily in drugs, especially crack cocaine.
5. All gangs are alike.
6. There is no good in gangs, it is all bad.
7. Gangs are basically criminal enterprises and youths start gangs in order to collectively commit crimes.

Findings that challenge these erroneous and stereotypical gang characteristics are:

1. Gangs, drugs, and violence appear to apply more to adult drug and criminal gangs than to youth gangs.
2. The connection between gangs, drugs, and violence is not as strong as it has been believed.
3. More young adult males than juveniles are involved in most criminal youth gangs, and they appear to be disproportionately involved in serious and violent crimes.
4. It is not as difficult for adolescents to resist gang pressures as was commonly believed. Youths can refuse to join gangs without reprisals.
5. Gang members can usually leave their gangs without serious consequences.
6. Modern gangs make less use of gang symbols and rites than gangs of the past.
7. Modern youth gangs are based less on territory than in the past.
8. More adolescents were gang members than in past years.
9. More gangs are in suburban areas, small towns, and rural areas than in the past.
10. There is more gang presence in the schools than in the 1980s and 1990s.
11. White gang members are more prevalent in adolescent gangs than in the past.
12. Females are more prevalent in adolescent gangs than previously reported.
13. Gangs in rural and sparsely populated areas are quite different from city gangs. (Wilson, 2001:49–50).

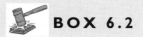

BOX 6.2

David L. Reeves
Team Leader for the Juvenile Justice Team, Department of Children's Services, Knox County Region, Knoxville, TN

Statistics:

B.A. (psychology), University of Tennessee; M.P.H. (public health, planning and administration),University of Tennessee.

Background and Interests

In 2005 I had spent 21 years working with juveniles. Eighteen of these years have been spent as a case manager (Knoxville Group Home/West View Center) and as Director of the Oak Ridge Group Home. I have spent nearly a year in my present position. I began my career with the Department of Human Services, and after 2 years of Child Protective Services work, the last work exclusively dealing with allegations of child sexual abuse, I felt that perhaps it was time for a change. A new friend I had met through my eventual wife had just been promoted to the Director of the Knoxville Group Home, then under the Department of Corrections. He recruited me to come and take his former position as counselor at the group home. He didn't have to recruit me very hard. I was a counselor there and then at the West View Center, which was the newly reinvented Knoxville Group Home, for approximately 7 years.

Then I was promoted to the Director at Oak Ridge Group Home. I remained there for the past 12 years until June 2004. However, the building we were located in was leased and was originally constructed in 1944 during World War II at the time Oak Ridge was established. A financial decision was made to close the facility, as it was believed to be no longer an appropriate or cost-effective facility for housing juveniles. The quality of the program, which I felt was very high, was not taken into consideration in the final decision. I thoroughly enjoyed most of my time in community residential programs as counselor and then director. My stories come from my time spent in these residential programs.

Interesting Experiences

"Suicide Attempt"—At the Oak Ridge Group Home, a Youth Services Officer (YSO) who was too authoritative with the kids was summoned to one child's bedroom by another child who told him that the child in question had hanged himself. The YSO, "Ben," had been particularly hard on "Bob" that evening. Ben raced to the bedroom to discover Bob hanging from his bunk bed post. After an initial panic when Ben collected himself enough to check the status of the child, Bob broke into laughter. When Ben turned to the doorway, there were six or seven of the other boys all laughing hysterically. Yes, it was a classic group home set-up.

"The Punch"—Each Christmas at the former Knoxville Group Home, a tradition had been established of having two punch bowls for the Christmas party. One bowl was for the students and the other was for the staff. The idea was that the staff punch bowl would be spiked. It wasn't, of course. Then the staff would "accidentally" leave the punch bowl unguarded as the evening wore on. The boys would always observe this, always help themselves, and invariably one or more would get "drunk." We'd watch them stagger up the stairs to bed, "drunkenly" thinking that they'd gotten one over on the stupid staff. We'd always wait until the following day to tell them what was not in the staff punch.

"The Drug Test"—"Dan" was a kid who was initially as defiant/oppositional as anyone we'd ever had the pleasure of having at the Oak Ridge Group Home. He also entered the program with a significant *(continued)* alcohol/drug problem. Finally he was able to earn weekend passes. We routinely conducted drug and alcohol screens of these kids after each weekend pass. After his second pass and while he was urinating, one of the officers noticed Dan doing a lot of fumbling around. He allowed Dan to finish urinating and then searched him. An empty test tube was discovered that he had concealed in his underwear. This held someone else's fake "clean" sample of urine of course. We made him retake the drug screen with his own urine. Yep, the fake sample turned out to test positive for THC and cocaine, and Dan's own real sample was clean! He probably had good reason to believe it wouldn't be, but nonetheless, for his efforts, Dan was given an extra 30 days in the program, just as though his own sample had been dirty. What a genius. One of his "buddies" had set him up.

"Another 'Dan' Story"—Initially Dan was very demanding and argumentative. He also had a terrible temper, which he was more than willing to display whenever things didn't go to suit him, which was frequently. He tried, usually successfully, to push staff buttons and relished the subsequent arguments. However, Dan got a counselor who probably should be nominated for sainthood. This is not to say that Dan never got to him, but it was rare, and more often than not, Dan's games would backfire. One day he asked his counselor if he could leave one day early for a pass for the coming weekend and if he could go to the mall right then. Now, Dan should have known the answer to both questions would probably be "No," but he was spoiling for a confrontation. His counselor, who was preparing lunch at the time of the inquisition, never broke stride from his lunchtime duties as he

calmly replied, "No, and No." For a few seconds, Dan was speechless, as he was still relatively new and not used to the word, "No." Then he asked (and the request became part of the group home folklore), "Can't I at least have one of my ways?" A Dan classic!

Advice to Students

As you can see, I feel that humor is an essential ingredient to successful casework. We try to laugh with our kids, not at them. But sometimes, that's hard to do. On a more serious note, I feel that what we offer the juveniles in our care is the opportunity to change. We can give them all the counseling in the world; we can empathize or sympathize; we can temporarily keep them in an environment that is drug-free; we can force them to go to school for the period of their confinement; but it is ultimately up to them to make real changes in their lifestyles.

We provide the opportunity for that change. They must be willing to take advantage of it. Some do and some don't. You must be able to accept the cold hard fact when beginning this type of work that you will never have a 100 percent success rate, and you shouldn't expect it. Once in a while, the exceptional young person will come along who you can observe actually change through his or her daily efforts. Such was the case with Dan, who I mentioned in the previous stories. Eventually he made the correct choices to help himself. We watched him mature and begin thinking more clearly and rationally over nearly a year that we had him in our program. His personality evolved and he went from being a terror to an actual joy to be around. That was truly rewarding!

The fact of racial and ethnic disproportionality in the juvenile justice system is underscored by a study undertaken by Darlene Conley in 1994. The juvenile justice system of a western state was investigated. Juvenile courts in six counties were selected as the target for her research. A representative sample of 1,777 juvenile cases was drawn, together with 170 in-depth interviews with court personnel, community leaders, defense attorneys, prosecutors, law enforcement officers, parents, youths, and others. The study also included 65 hours of participant observation covering court proceedings and plea bargaining involving adjudicated juveniles. Focus group interviews with juveniles were also conducted. It was found that blacks were twice as likely than whites to be arrested; five times more likely to be referred to juvenile court; five times more likely to be detained; three times more likely to be charged; 2.5 times more likely to be adjudicated delinquent; and 11 times more likely to be placed in secure confinement for a lengthy period. Hispanics were also overrepresented in the same counties, although they were not processed as extensively as blacks. Similar findings relative to dissimilar treatment of minority juveniles have been reported elsewhere (Myers, 2004).

Female Gangs

How prevalent are female gangs in the United States? Do female gangs commit similar types of offenses compared with male gangs? In 2005 it was estimated that there were over 100,000 female gang members in the United States, accounting for about 10 percent of all gang membership (Mauro, 2005). Contemporary descriptions of female gang members suggest that they typically lack a formal education; have violent experiences at their schools; have seriously dysfunctional family lives; and have social problems including poverty, substance abuse, and gang violence (Johnson, 2005; Turley, 2003). Interviews with a sample of Texas female gang members indicated that they often join gangs to achieve power and protection, engendering respect from others based on fear, and they often resort to more serious criminal conduct. Often, membership in female gangs is contingent upon one's ethnic or racial status. Family disintegration and community deterioration often lead female gang members to create their own subculture where recognition can more easily be attained. Another factor is the lack of appropriate intervention, diversion, and treatment alternatives available to female juveniles compared with their male counterparts. With the presence of such gender inequities, young female involvement in delinquent behavior is more easily explained (Johnson, 2005).

Jill Rosenbaum (1996) studied 70 female gang members who had earlier been committed to the California Youth Authority in 1990. She studied a sample of 70 girls with known gang affiliations. Almost all the girls studied by Rosenbaum had records of violent offending. The girls averaged four arrests, and 62 percent of their commitment offenses were committed with other female gang members. Rosenbaum found that many of these girls joined gangs initially to satisfy needs that they could not satisfy from their home environments. Gang affiliation gave these girls loyalty to friends, fun, and excitement. Furthermore, many of these female gang members were of minority status and resented the white, blond "California girl" image that is often unattainable by minority girls. Thus, female gang criminality, at least in Southern California, appeared to be similar to male gang criminality in both the level and nature of violence. Offense similarities between female and male gang members have been reported in other jurisdictions (Santana, 2005).

Profiling of female gang members has been limited, in part because of inaccessibility by researchers (Chesney-Lind and Hagedorn, 1999; Dubowitz, Pitts, and Black, 2004). However, interviews have been conducted with female gang members who are or have been incarcerated in juvenile facilities. A large-scale study was conducted by the National Gang Crime Research Center. Data were gathered from 17 states and 85 correctional facilities, including boot camps and juvenile institutions. The sample comprised 10,166 offenders of whom 4,140 were self-reported gang members. Over 1,000 of these gang members were fe-male. On the basis of reported information, females were more likely than males to have been sexually abused; to have grown up in a father-only house-hold; to have stopped committing violent crimes if they were juveniles tried as adults; and to have joined gangs while incarcerated. Female gang members compared with male gang members were less likely to have fired a gun at a po-lice officer, to have held rank or any leadership position in a gang, and to have engaged in physical fights with other rival gang members while incarcerated. The implication from this research is that at least for these females studied, they were generally less violent in their offending compared with their male counterparts, although violence differences between male and female gang members are gradually diminishing (National Gang Crime Research Center, 2000). However, the research is persuasive in that the nature and seriousness of female offending is increasingly matching male offending patterns and fre-quency. It is too early to make sweeping generalizations about female delin-quents and whether they are becoming more violent (Kelly, 2005). More attention needs to be directed toward understanding their interpersonal behav-iors as well as certain institutionalized patterns of a patriarchal society (Dubowitz, Pitts, and Black, 2004).

Juvenile Response to Police Officer Contacts

Police officers who observe juveniles in pairs or larger groupings, particularly in areas known to be gang-dominated, may assume that these youths are gang-related, and this observation may heighten police officer interest in and activity against them (St. Cyr, 2003; Stuart-Ryter, 2002). The nature of this heightened interest and activity may be more frequent stopping and questioning certain ju-veniles on the basis of their appearance and geographical location and whether they are minority youths. The precise impact of police–gang interactions is un-clear, although in some jurisdictions, proactive policing against gang members has created sufficient conflict necessary to unify and perpetuate some gangs.

While some investigators question whether police officers discriminate against certain youths or single them out for stopping and questioning on the basis of racial or ethnic factors, other researchers have found patterns of police behavior that appear discriminatory on racial or ethnic grounds (Sun and Payne, 2004). At least in some jurisdictions, minority youth stops, arrest rates, and detentions are at least three times as high as those for white youths.

However, much police officer activity is centered in high-crime areas, which also tend to be areas inhabited by large numbers of persons of lower so-cioeconomic statuses (SES). And those areas with larger numbers of persons in the lower socioeconomic statuses are also those that contain larger concentra-tions of minorities (Greenleaf, 2005). Thus, some selectivity regulates where po-lice officers will concentrate their patrol efforts as well as those youths they target for questioning and those they choose to ignore. Some observers believe that this opens the door to allegations of police officer harassment against cer-tain classes of juvenile offenders on the basis of subjectively determined stereo-typical features such as a youth's appearance (Sun and Payne, 2004).

Interestingly, how youths behave toward police officers whenever juve-niles are stopped and questioned by them seems to make an important differ-ence about what the officers will eventually do. The appearance and demeanor

BOX 6.3

CAREER SNAPSHOT

Nancy B. Jones
Parole Officer, Amarillo District Parole, Texas Youth Commission

Statistics:

B.S. (general studies), West Texas A & M University; M.A. (political science), West Texas A & M University; Alpha Phi Sigma.

Background and Experience

In 1986 I began working for the Swisher County Attorney, who had jurisdiction over several courts, among those being the juvenile court. In the capacity of legal assistant, I witnessed many frustrated parents who needed special guidance with the court system and many who needed parenting skills, and also youth who needed special guidance to make the transition to adulthood. In 1987 it became clear that if I wanted to be of some practical help to these people, I would need to get my degree, and so I decided to finish my education, which was commenced in 1967.

I continued to work for the county attorney, and in 1994 I did an internship with the juvenile probation department in Swisher/Hale Counties. It was during this time that I decided I could be of more help by working directly with troubled youth in the capacity of a probation officer. Also at this time I was very idealistic, and I felt that I could improve the system.

I was eventually hired by the Deaf Smith County Juvenile Probation Department as a probation officer in March 1996. I worked in that position until 2000, when I was hired by the Texas Youth Commission as a parole officer for Potter/Randall Counties, which cover the Amarillo and Canyon areas.

While working in Hereford for Deaf Smith County, I had my first experience with a depressed agricultural community, with many unemployed migrant workers. Most of the youth on probation were from these same migrant workers. Many of these youth were gang-oriented, and easily three-fourths of these youths were involved with drugs. At one time, there were 15 documented rival gangs. These youth were not oriented to going to school, and the families, if there was any interest from the family system, had no control, or professed to have no control, over their youths. Many of the parents were members of gangs, and were proud that their kids were carrying on the tradition.

Like most small communities, there were and still are limited resources for the county and juvenile board to take advantage of to help these youths, even with the help of the TJPC. However, the juvenile department was very proactive and used every resource to provide these youths with better options. We had a very close relationship with the schools, and we were allowed free access to them. We provided programs in the lower grades, where the students were still open to positive discussions about the drugs and gang culture. We had several programs, such as Scared Straight, where the Texas Department of Criminal Justice (TDCJ) women's unit in Amarillo allowed us to take young girls into the unit to show them what a life of crime was truly like. It certainly made a believer of me. We also had a program geared toward the girls gaining respect for themselves. We also took advantage of the Title IV-E Program, which allowed lower-income youths, who didn't have a positive environment, to go to a placement, and see what their lives could be like. This program allowed parents to take part in the progress their children made, and pro-

(continued)

vided them with a different perspective on how much better their children's life could be.

After going to the Texas Youth Commission (TYC) in Amarillo, I found out there was an urgent need to develop a program geared toward helping the youth transition back into the family and community successfully, and to rebuild TYC's image in the community. Programs needed to be developed to help with the transition of youths from total confinement to semi-total freedom. The trick here is that the TYC supervises youth from the age of 10 to 21, with many of these young people coming out as young adults. Also in supervising youth, there is a fine line between the youths and their parents, who mostly resent TYC and anyone associated with it, because they're a part of the establishment.

Fortunately, I made the acquaintance of a social worker who had been where these kids had been and wanted to help provide these youths with other alternatives. His organization was associated with the Amarillo Council on Alcoholism, and it could provide some much-needed counseling for drug abuse, anger management, social skills, job skills, and gang intervention, not to mention mental health needs. The program being developed will continue the Resocialization Program in TYC facilities. With youth, there is no single, all-encompassing curriculum that will provide all of the needs for each child, but the curriculum must be kept within the designed guidelines.

Like probation, the TYC has specifically outlined the way youth are to be supervised. These rules are not just for the protection of youth rights, but also for the protection of the supervising officer. If rules are followed and documented, any grievance made, and there will be grievances, can be justified.

Advice to Students

Many people go into probation or parole because it seems like a good place to start, or they may even be laboring under the misconception of being able to "make a difference." My suggestion is to define why one wants to supervise youth. If one doesn't like

this type of youth and think they are all "punks," then probably this is not the profession for you. If you feel that these youths are all misunderstood, who haven't had a chance, and you want to give them the opportunities they missed, you will probably get discouraged, and you will decide that this is not the profession for you. However, if you have a strong sense of right and wrong, and if you want to provide troubled youths with a positive support system that they need to continue in positive ways, while providing safety for the community, and also realizing that the successes will be few and far between, then this could be the profession for you.

Things to remember:

1. These youths are street-wise. They know what you want to hear, and if they detect any weakness, they will exploit it.
2. These youth are dangerous. No one should ever feel so comfortable with them, to feel you could take them home with you.
3. Do not think for one minute that they won't misconstrue everything you say and use it against you at another time.
4. Remember that most of these youths are gang-oriented, and they use drugs, a very dangerous combination.
5. You can't change someone who doesn't want to change.
6. Failures happen. Remember, "Your failure is not my failure, Your success is not my success. Your failure is your failure, and Your success is your success."
7. When someone succeeds, you know you've helped to make a difference in one's life.
8. You may represent the only person who cares, and so never belittle what you do.

It takes patience. These youth took years getting the way they are, and they can't be changed in a short time. This is an important profession that provides a much-needed resource for these kids. If you choose it, be good at it, and be smart at it.

of youths stopped by police officers and their subsequent actions seems to indicate that youths who are poorly dressed and/or behave defiantly and belligerently toward police are more likely to be harassed, possibly arrested (Schulenberg, 2003). Related research is consistent with these early findings and suggests that cooperative, neatly dressed youths stand a better chance of avoiding being stopped, questioned, or arrested by police (Shelden, Tracy, and Brown, 2001).

In fact, some police officers insist that a youth's demeanor when responding to police questioning on the street is crucial to whether the youth will be taken into custody, even if temporarily. Therefore, if youths do not display the proper amount of deference toward police officers whenever those youths are stopped and questioned, the youths stand a good chance of being taken to the police station for further questioning (Reynolds, Seydlitz, and Jenkins, 2000). Interestingly, youths also may be too polite and arouse the suspicions of police officers. Thus, there is an elusive range of politeness that minimizes a youth's chances of being taken into custody. It is possible to be too polite or not polite enough so that police officers are sufficiently aggravated or motivated to act.

Despite statutory safeguards about detaining youths in adult jails for long periods and the division of labor relating to youthful offender processing in any jurisdiction, police officers are free to do pretty much whatever they want relative to juveniles they question and who are either acting suspiciously or belligerently. If any pretext exists for assuming that certain youths have been or are engaging in delinquent acts, they are subject to temporary detention by police officers. In many instances, these detention decisions by police are purely arbitrary (Schulenberg, 2003).

The following is a listing of discretionary actions that may be taken by police officers when encountering youths on the street:

1. Police officers may ignore the behaviors of youths they observe in the absence of citizen complaints. The most frequent types of encounters police officers have with juveniles do not stem from complaints filed by others. Rather, police officers observe youths under a wide variety of circumstances. The situation and circumstances are important, since youths walking down a street in pairs during daylight hours would not attract the same kind of attention as pairs of youths walking the streets late at night. Depending on what the officers regard as serious behaviors, if youths are on skateboards on the sidewalks of the main street of a local community, they may or may not be posing risks to other pedestrians. If youths are playing ball on a vacant lot near other homes in a neighborhood, they may or may not be disturbing others. Police action in each case is probably unwarranted.

2. Police officers may act passively on someone's complaint about juvenile behaviors. If a store owner complains that youths are jeopardizing the safety of store customers by riding their skateboards down crowded city streets, police officers may respond by directing youths to other streets for their skateboarding. If neighbors complain that youths are making too much noise playing in a nearby vacant lot, police officers may appear and advise youths to play elsewhere. The intent of police officers in these situations is two-fold. First, they want citizens to know they are there doing something. Second, they want citizens to know action has been taken and

the problem no longer exists. Police officers continue to view the behaviors they observe as not especially serious. In these instances, police warnings are ordinarily sufficient to satisfy complainants. Since complaints were made by complainants, dispositions of those complaints are usually logged officially. Police officers may or may not choose to name those youths warned. Rather, they may file a generalized report briefly describing their action taken. A sample complaint form is shown in Figure 6.1.

3. Police officers may take youths into custody and release them to parents or guardians without incident. Those youths who may be acting suspiciously or who are in places where their presence might indicate an intent to do something unlawful (e.g., the youths who were in the uninhabited house to crash after their party) are likely to be taken into custody for more extensive questioning. In many instances, these **stationhouse adjustments** may result in their release to parents with warnings from police about refraining from suspicious conduct in the future. While these actions are official in the sense that police officers actually took youths into custody for a brief period and made records of these temporary detentions, they do not result in official action or intervention by intake officers or juvenile courts.

4. Police officers may take youths into custody and refer them officially to community service agencies for assistance or treatment. Sometimes youths appear to police to be under the influence of drugs or alcohol when they are stopped and questioned. Other youths may not have parents or guardians responsible for their conduct. They may be classified by police officers as runaways. In these cases, police officers arrange for various community services to take custody of these juveniles for treatment or assistance. These youths will be under agency care until arrangements can be made for their placement with relatives or in foster homes. Those youths with chemical dependencies may undergo medical treatment and therapy. In either case, juvenile courts are avoided. In growing numbers of jurisdictions, drug courts are being established to deal with juveniles with alcohol or chemical dependencies (Whiteacre, 2004).

5. Police officers may take youths into custody, file specific charges against them, and refer them to juvenile intake where they may or may not be detained. Only a small percentage of all juveniles detained by police will subsequently be charged with offenses. Conservatively, probably less than 10 percent of all juveniles who have contact with police officers annually engage in serious violent or property offenses. Therefore, many youths are taken into custody for minor infractions, and their referrals to juvenile intake may or may not result in short- or long-term confinement. The discretion shifts from police officers to intake officers whether to process certain juveniles further into the juvenile justice system. Those juveniles who are deemed dangerous, violent, or persistent-nonviolent are most likely to be subject to detention until adjudication by a juvenile court. Police officers may respond to citizen complaints or actually observe juveniles engaging in illegal conduct. Their likelihood of taking these youths into custody for such wrongdoings alleged or observed is increased accordingly (McCluskey et al., 2004).

6. Police officers may take youths into custody, file criminal charges against them, and statutorily place them in jails pending their initial appearance, a preliminary hearing, and a subsequent trial. Some juveniles may be

COMPLAINT
IN THE JUVENILE COURT OF
DOUGHERTY COUNTY, GEORGIA

State F.F. #   Case #   File #

Name: (last, F, M)	Age:
AKA:	DOB:

Race: Lives		Res.: _____
Sex: With:		Bus.: _____

Child's (Name)   (Phone)
Address:
(Street)   (Apt.#)   (City)   (County)   (State)   (Zip)

Mother's   Res.: _____
Name: Phone: Bus.: _____
(Include Mother's Maiden Name in Parenthesis)

Mother's
Address:
(Street)   (Apt.#)   (City)   (County)   (State)   (Zip)

Father's   Res.: _____
Name: Phone: Bus.: _____

Father's
Address:
(Street)   (Apt.#)   (City)   (County)   (State)   (Zip)

Legal   Res.: _____
Custodian: Phone: Bus.: _____

Custodian's
Address
(Street)   (Apt.#)   (City)   (County)   (State)   (Zip)

Complaint:
(Code Section)   (Misd./Fel.)   (Date of Offense)

Complaint:
(Code Section)   (Misd./Fel.)   (Date of Offense)

Complaint:
(Code Section)   (Misd./Fel.)   (Date of Offense)

Taken Into Custody: Yes ( ) No ( )
By Whom:

Placement of   (Name)   (Agency)   Date: _____
Deprived Child   Time: _____

Person Notified   Date: _____
By: Via   Time: _____

Detained: Yes ( ) No ( )   Place   Date: _____
Authorized By: Detained   Time: _____

Released To: Date: _____
Relation: Time: _____

Co-Perpetrators:
(Names and Ages)

Co-Perpetrators:
(Names and Ages)

Victim's Name: Phone #: _____
Victim's Address:

Victim's Name: Phone #: _____
Victim's Address:

JUVENILE COURT # 41 (A&M)

FIGURE 6.1 Complaint Against Juvenile
(*Source:* Dougherty County, GA).

Police officers investigate reports of suspicious activities in neighborhoods and conduct stops and frisks of loitering juveniles.

classified as adults for the purpose of transferring them to criminal courts where they might receive harsher punishments. Jurisdictions such as Illinois, Washington, DC, New York, and California are a few of the many places where **automatic transfer laws** exist and where some juveniles are automatically placed within the power of criminal courts rather than juvenile courts. Therefore, police officers *must* act in accordance with certain statutory provisions when handling certain juvenile offenders, whenever they effect arrests of youthful suspects. Often, they have no choice in the matter. Changing get-tough policies toward violent or serious juvenile offenders are making it more difficult for police to be lenient when confronting juveniles on city streets (Torbet et al., 1996).

Therefore, police discretion is exercised the most during the normal course of police patrols. Those youths who stand the best chance of being targeted for special police attention include minorities who are acting suspiciously and live in high-crime neighborhoods known as gang territories. Also increasing the likelihood of being taken into custody is the demeanor or behaviors exhibited by youths, whether they are polite or impolite to police officers. Short of any illicit conduct actually observed by or reported to police officers, a youth's appearance and behaviors are key considerations in whether they will be harassed and/or detained temporarily by police. However, comparatively few youths are actually arrested in relation to the actual number of police officer/juvenile encounters on city streets.

ARRESTS OF JUVENILES

Police officers need little, if any, provocation to bring juveniles into custody (Schulenberg, 2003; Thurman and Zhao, 2004). Arrests of juveniles are, by degree, more serious than acts of bringing them into custody. Since any juvenile may be taken into custody for suspicious behavior or on any other pretext, all types of juveniles may be detained at police headquarters or at a sheriff's station, department, or jail temporarily. Suspected runaways, truants, or curfew violators may be taken into custody for their own welfare or protection, not necessarily for the purpose of facing subsequent offenses. It is standard policy in most jurisdictions, considering the sophistication of available social services, for police officers and jailers to turn over juveniles to the appropriate agencies as soon as possible after these youths have been apprehended or taken into custody (Katz, 2003).

Before police officers turn juveniles over to intake officials or juvenile probation officers for further processing, they ordinarily complete an arrest report, noting the youth's name; address; parent's or guardian's name and address; offenses alleged; circumstances; whether other juveniles were involved and apprehended; the juvenile's prior record, if any; height; weight; age; and other classificatory information. If immediate action against the juvenile is warranted, the police officer may complete and file an application for filing of a juvenile court petition. An affidavit and application used by San Diego County, California, is shown in Figure 6.2.

Except in unusual circumstances and where youths are especially violent and pose a danger to others or themselves, they will be released to the custody of their parents or guardians following a brief detention and booking. In some instances, juveniles fail to appear later at their scheduled appointments with either the juvenile court or intake officers. When such persons fail to appear for scheduled proceedings against them, juvenile court judges issue orders for their immediate apprehension and detention. Figure 6.3 shows an apprehend and detain order for Dougherty County, Georgia. Parents may become involved as well, since it is their responsibility to insure that their children appear at any scheduled proceedings against them by the juvenile court.

Juvenile–Adult Distinctions

According to the Juvenile Justice and Delinquency Prevention Act of 1974 and its subsequent amendments, juveniles must be separated from adults, both by sight and sound, and treated as juveniles as soon as possible following their

Delinquency among juvenile females may be increasing.

Affidavit and Application for Filing of Juvenile Court Petition
(Welfare and Institutions Code Section 653)

I,_____
     Officer's/Citizen's Name

_____hereby state that
Officer's Agency & Duty Station or Citizen's Address

_____a   minor,   DOB_____

_____is within San Diego County   _____resides within San Diego County
_____was within San Diego County   _____committed an offense described within sec-
                                               tions 601/602 within San Diego County

and that said minor comes within the provisions of sections 601/602 of the Welfare and Institutions Code
of the State of California as evidenced by the case reports dated _____ and consisting of _____
pages, which are attached hereto and incorporated by reference herein. On the basis of this information,
the undersigned requests that a Juvenile Court Petition be filed on the above named minor for the
offense(s) of
_____
         (State the name of the offense and the appropriate statutory authority)

I declare under penalty of perjury that the facts set forth in this affidavit and its attachments are true
and correct to the best of my knowledge.

Dated: _____   Signed:_____

Companions referred_____

Companions not referred_____

REPORT OF ACTION AND ENDORSEMENT

The following action was taken on this application: _____
                                                              (JDA No. or Misd. No.)

_____Petition requested under section(s)_____
_____D.A. reject
_____Referred to Traffic Court
_____Referral recorded and handled informally**

_____Active delinquent ward (602 W&I)/Offense reported to Juvenile Court**
_____6 Months' Probation Supervision (654 W&I)**

**Reasons(s):
_____Active to another jurisdiction   _____Family moving
_____Active dependent ward (300 W&I)   _____Referred to community agency
_____Minor offense   _____PC 26 problem
_____No prior referral   _____Administrative exception
_____No prior arrests (2 yr. period)   _____Minor cannot be located
_____Transient   _____Parents handling appropriately
_____Restitution paid/property recovered   _____Low maturity/intellectual level

Other reasons/Additional information (if any):_____
_____
_____

_____   _____   _____   _____
  (Date)   (Please Print)   (Deputy Probation Officer)   (Phone No.)

Prob. 419 (8-87)   Dist: White-Ref. Agency   Canary-Prob. Clerk   Pink-Prob. File

FIGURE 6.2   Affidavit and Application.

apprehension. If juveniles are brought into custody and charged with offenses
that might be either felonies or misdemeanors if committed by adults, they may
be clearly distinguishable as juveniles. It would be difficult to conclude that an
8-, 9-, or 10-year-old could pass for 18 or older. But many juveniles who are
taken into custody may or may not be under age 18. Their appearance is decep-

JUVENILE COURT
OF
DOUGHERTY COUNTY, GEORGIA

APPREHEND & DETAIN ORDER

STATE OF GEORGIA, DOUGHERTY COUNTY:

In the interest of:
       DOB:
      Address:
            Albany, GA 31701

To any Sheriff, Deputy Sheriff, or any peace officer of said State or subdivision thereof,

GREETINGS:

Complaint being made before me this 2nd day of December, 2004, by , Intake Officer, with the Dougherty County Juvenile Court (431-2162), that:

Said child failed to appear for Court for pending charges of Disorderly Conduct, Simple Battery and Unruly Child.

You are therefore commanded to take into custody said child bring and detain him in the **Albany RYDC** pending a hearing before me to be dealt with as the law directs.

WITNESS MY HAND AND OFFICIAL SIGNATURE, AS JUDGE.

This 2nd day of December, 2004.

                                         _____
                                         Herbie Solomon, Judge
                                         Richard W. Brooker, Associate Judge
                                         Juvenile Court of Dougherty County

Executed by: _____
      Date: _____

FIGURE 6.3 Apprehend and Detain Order
(Dougherty County, GA).

tive, and if they deliberately wish to conceal information about their identity or age from officers, it is relatively easy for them to do so. This is a common occurrence, since many juveniles are afraid that police will notify their parents. Fear of parental reaction may sometimes be more compelling than the fear youths may have of police officers and possible confinement in a jail.

Because juveniles generally have less understanding of the law compared with adults, especially those who make careers out of crime, they may believe that they will fare better if officers believe that they are adults and not juvenile offenders (Brandl and Bartow, 2004; Mastrofski, 2004; Thurman and Zhao, 2004). Perhaps there is a chance they might be released after spending a few hours or even a day or two confined in a jail cell. However, if they are identified positively as juveniles, then parents will invariably be notified of their arrest. But these youths often underestimate the resources police have at their disposal to verify information received from those booked after arrests. With proper identification, adults are ordinarily entitled to make bail and obtain early temporary release from jail. If fake IDs are used by these juveniles, however, this phony information is easily detected and arouses police officer suspicions and interest in these youths. They will likely be detained as long as it takes to establish their true identities and ages. Furnishing police officers with false information is a rapid way to be placed in preventive detention for an indefinite period. And police officers are entitled to use preventive detention lawfully in such cases (*Schall v. Martin,* 1984).

The Ambiguity of Juvenile Arrests

Little uniformity exists among jurisdictions about how an arrest is defined. There is even greater ambiguity about what constitutes a juvenile arrest (McDowall, Loftin, and Wiersema, 2000). An arrest is the legal detainment of a person to answer for criminal charges or (infrequently at present) civil demands (Black, 1990). Available evidence suggests that increasing numbers of police departments are proactively changing their police–juvenile policies so that decision making regarding juvenile processing will be more rational and effective (Brandl and Bartow, 2004; Poyser, 2004).

Early research by Klein, Rosenzweig, and Bates (1975) focused on juvenile arrest procedures followed by 49 suburban and urban police departments in a large metropolitan county. Over 250 police chiefs and juvenile officers and their supervisors were surveyed, some of whom participated in follow-up, in-depth interviews about juvenile arrests and processing. Among police chiefs, for example, fewer than 50 percent were in agreement that booking juvenile suspects was the equivalent of arresting them. Furthermore, respondents variously believed that arrests involved simple police contact with juveniles and cautioning behavior. Others believed that taking youths into custody and releasing them to parents constituted an arrest. Less than half of those surveyed appeared thoroughly familiar with juvenile rights under the law and the different restrictions applicable to their processing by police officers. Record-keeping and other activities related to juvenile processing by police have not changed much in subsequent years (Bilchik, 1998).

Booking, Fingerprinting, and Photographing Juvenile Suspects

Under the Juvenile Justice and Delinquency Prevention Act of 1974, its subsequent revisions, and recommendations from the National Advisory Committee on Criminal Justice Standards and Goals in 1976, significant restrictions were placed on law enforcement agencies concerning how juveniles should be processed and the nature and types of records that may be maintained relating to such processing. Under the 1974 Act, for instance, status offenders were separated from delinquent offenders through deinstitutionalization or DSO. According to the 1974 Act, status offenders should not be taken to jails for temporary detention. Rather, they should be taken to social service agencies for less formal dispositions. One intent of the Act was to minimize the adverse impact and labeling influence associated with jails (Decker, 2005; Miller, 2001). While DSO is fairly common in most jurisdictions, police officer discretion causes a significant proportion of status offenders to be processed as delinquent anyway. Thus, some status offenders fall through the cracks and continue to be placed in U.S. jails annually, even though such housing is only for a few hours.

Since most juveniles are under the jurisdiction of juvenile courts, extensions of civil authority, procedural safeguards for juveniles are in place to prescribe conduct for both police and jail officers in their dealings with juveniles. For example, it is common practice for jail officers to photograph and fingerprint adult offenders. This is basic booking procedure. However, juveniles are often processed differently at the point of booking. Most jurisdictions have restricted photographing and fingerprinting juveniles for purposes related solely to their identification and eventual placement with parents or guardians. Fingerprinting is also useful if property crimes have been committed and fingerprints have been left at crime scenes.

Interrogations of Juvenile Suspects

Until 1966, custodial interrogations of criminal suspects by police were largely unregulated. Many of these custodial interrogations involved police brutality against particular suspects who were believed guilty of certain crimes. Suspects were denied access to defense counsel, and they were interrogated for many hours at a time, often without food, water, or rest. More than a few suspects confessed to crimes they didn't commit simply to end these brutal interrogations. However, in 1966 the U.S. Supreme Court heard the case of *Miranda v. Arizona.* Miranda was arrested on suspicion of rape and kidnapping. He was not permitted to talk to an attorney, nor was he advised of his right to one. He was interrogated by police for several hours, eventually confessing and signing a written confession. He was convicted. Miranda appealed, contending that his right to due process had been violated because he had not first been advised of his right to remain silent and to have an attorney present during a custodial interrogation. The U.S. Supreme Court agreed and set forth what later became known as the Miranda warning. This monumental decision provided that confessions made by suspects who were not notified of their due-process rights cannot be admitted as evidence. Suspects must be advised of certain rights before they are questioned by police; these rights include the right to remain silent, the right to counsel, the right to free counsel if suspects cannot afford one, and the right to terminate questioning at any time.

When the Miranda warning became official policy for police officers when arresting criminal suspects, the warning and accompanying constitutional safeguards were not believed by police to be applicable to juveniles. Thus, law enforcement officers continued to question youths about crimes during several post-Miranda years. Since it is generally accepted that a juvenile's understanding of the law is poor, it might be further assumed that juveniles might be more easily manipulated by law enforcement authorities (Rehling, 2005).

A decision to protect juveniles from themselves by making incriminating Fifth Amendment–type statements was made by the U.S. Supreme Court in

1979. In that year, the U.S. Supreme Court decided the case of *Fare v. Michael C.* Michael C. was a juvenile charged with murder. During a preliminary interrogation, Michael C. was alone with police officers and detectives. Neither his parents nor an attorney were present. Michael C. asked to see his probation officer, but the interrogating detectives denied this request, since a probation officer is not an attorney and cannot be permitted to function as defense counsel under these circumstances. Subsequently, Michael C. waived his right to counsel and answered police questions. He was convicted of murder and appealed, alleging that his right to counsel was violated when he asked to see his probation officer and his request had been denied by the investigating officers. The court considered Michael C.'s case and determined that Michael C. had, indeed, made an intelligent, understanding, and voluntary waiver of his rights. The standard devised by the U.S. Supreme Court was the **totality of circumstances** test, which was essentially a standard they had adopted earlier in a criminal case involving an adult offender. Thus, the U.S. Supreme Court said that juvenile rights waivers should not be based on one sole characteristic or procedure, but rather, on all of the relevant circumstances of the case.

This case involved a juvenile who waived his constitutional right to be questioned by police about his involvement in a crime. The Court ruled that the totality of circumstances test should govern whether juveniles intelligently and knowingly waive their right to be questioned by police about crimes, and whether it is necessary first to obtain parental consent. Undoubtedly this decision had led many states to enact statutes that specifically render inadmissible any admissions juveniles might make to police in the absence of parental guidance or consent (Johnson, 2002).

Expungement and Sealing Policies

Historically, once photographs and fingerprints have been taken, they have been destroyed as soon as possible following their use by police (Torbet et al., 1996:xiv). If such records exist in police department files after juveniles have reached the age of their majority, they may have their records expunged or sealed through **expungement orders.** Expungement orders are usually issued from judges to police departments and juvenile agencies to destroy any file material relating to one's juvenile offense history. Policies relating to records expungements vary among jurisdictions. Expunging one's juvenile record, sometimes known as **sealing records of juveniles,** is a means of preserving and insuring confidentiality of information that might otherwise prove harmful to adults if disclosed to others such as employers.

Theoretically, sealing of records is intended as a rehabilitative device, although not all juvenile justice professionals believe that sealing one's records and enforcing the confidentiality about one's juvenile past through expungement is always beneficial to the general public. State policies about police fingerprinting of juvenile suspects are diverse and inconsistent among jurisdictions. Furthermore, there continues to be considerable disagreement about how such fingerprint and related information should be used by either juvenile or criminal courts in their subsequent processing of youthful offenders. In 2004, 47 states permit fingerprinting of juveniles, while 46 states allowed photographing of them for law enforcement purposes.

By 2004, many jurisdictions extended the time interval for sealing or expunging one's juvenile record. Most states have increased the number of years that must pass before one's juvenile record can be expunged. Thus, one's juvenile record may not be expunged for several years after a person has become an adult. In fact, by 2004, 25 states specified that if any juvenile has committed a violent or other serious felony, his or her juvenile record cannot be sealed or expunged. Indications are that more states will adopt similar policies in the immediate future. Figure 6.4 shows an order to seal a juvenile's records used by the juvenile court in Glynn County, Georgia.

IN THE JUVENILE COURT OF GLYNN COUNTY
STATE OF GEORGIA

IN THE INTEREST OF:

—
—
—
—
—
—

ORDER SEALING RECORDS

The above-named Petitioner having come before this Court with his/her application to seal his/her records, and it having been shown to the satisfaction of the Court that the Petitioner has been rehabilitated and that he/she has not been charged with any crime during the period of time between his/her termination of probation and the filing of this application and it being further found that the **District Attorney's Office, Glynn County Police Department, Glynn County Sheriff's Office and the Brunswick City Police Department** were apprised of the Application for Sealing Records and they agree to a waiver of Hearing on the same as evidenced by Exhibit "A".

It is **ORDERED** that the records of   are sealed and all index references to the Petitioner shall be deleted. The Court, the Petitioner, law enforcement officers and all departments shall reply that no record exists with respect to the Petitioner upon inquiry in any matter.

IT IS FURTHER ORDERED that a copy of this **ORDER** shall be transmitted forthwith to the **District Attorney's Office, Glynn County Police Department, Glynn County Sheriff's Office and the Brunswick City Police Department**.

Inspection of the Petitioner's sealed files and records may hereafter be permitted only upon **Order of this Court**.

This the

_____
George M. Rountree, Judge

FIGURE 6.4   Order Sealing Records
(*Source:* Glynn County, GA).

By 2004, 34 states had mandated open proceedings and the release of juvenile records to the public, particularly where serious offenses are involved. Furthermore, many states now expose juvenile court records to school officials or require that schools be notified whenever a juvenile is taken into custody for a crime of violence or when a deadly weapon is used. Another widely adopted policy change is that 44 states have lowered the age at which juvenile court records may be made available to the public. Also, these states have established statewide repositories of information about violent and serious juveniles (Office of Juvenile Justice and Delinquency Prevention, 2005).

STATUS OFFENDERS AND JUVENILE DELINQUENTS

One of the more controversial issues in juvenile justice is how status offenders should be classified and managed. The fact that status offenders are labeled as status offenders contributes significantly to this controversy (Hil and McMahon, 2001). Such a label implies that all status offenders are somehow alike and should be treated similarly in all jurisdictions. But this implication is about as valid as assuming that all juvenile delinquents are alike and should be treated similarly. If we think about the etiology of runaway behavior compared with the respective etiologies of curfew violation, truancy, incorrigibility, liquor law violation, and sex offenses, it is likely that different sets of explanatory factors account for each type of deviant conduct (Hoge, 2001). Thus, different treatments, remedies, or solutions would be required for dealing with each effectively.

In 1974, the Juvenile Justice and Delinquency Prevention Act acknowledged some major differences between status offenders and delinquents by mandating that status offenders should not be institutionalized as though they had committed crimes. Rather, they should be diverted away from the trappings of juvenile courts that seemingly criminalize their behaviors. By managing status offenders less formally and dealing with their behaviors largely through counseling and assistance provided through community-based services, it was reasoned that they would be less likely to define themselves as delinquent and that others would be less likely to define them as delinquent as well. The long-range implication of such differential treatment is that status offenders will not be inclined to progress or escalate to more serious types of offenses compared with those more serious delinquent offenders who are exposed to the **criminogenic environment** of the juvenile courtroom (Austin, 2003).

Between the time the 1974 Act was implemented and individual states adopted policies to desinstitutionalize status offenders, there was a 95 percent reduction in the number of status offenders who are placed in some type of secure confinement (U.S. General Accounting Office, 1996b). However, a portion of those detained consisted of status offenders who violated court orders, or one or more conditions imposed by juvenile court judges at the time of their status offender adjudications. Status offenders tend to exhibit less recidivism compared with those referred to juvenile court for delinquent acts. Furthermore, the earlier juveniles are referred to juvenile court, for whatever reason, the more likely they will be to reoffend and reappear in juvenile courts (Snyder, Sickmund, and Poe-Yamagata, 1996). Therefore, diversionary procedures employed by police officers at their discretion when confronting extremely youthful offenders or those who are not doing anything particularly unlawful would seem to be justified on the basis of existing research evidence (Hoge, 2001).

But deinstitutionalizing status offenders is seen by some persons as tantamount to relinquishing juvenile court control over them, and not all persons favor this particular maneuver. A strong undercurrent of *parens patriae* persists, especially pertaining to those status offenders who need supervision and guidance from caring adults (Souweine and Khashu, 2001). Retaining control over status offenders is one means whereby the juvenile court can compel them to receive needed assistance and/or appropriate treatment (Hoge, 2001). But disagreement exists about the most effective forms of intervention to be provided status offenders. One problem experienced by more than a few juvenile justice systems is inadequate resources for status offenders and others require less drastic interventions as alternatives to incarceration.

DIVESTITURE AND ITS IMPLICATIONS: NET-WIDENING

Divestiture means that juvenile courts relinquish their jurisdiction or authority over certain types of offenders, such as status offenders. Thus, if a juvenile court in Kansas or Colorado were to divest itself of authority over status offenders or children in need of supervision, then those processing status offenders, such as police officers, would probably take such offenders to social service agencies or other community organizations designed to deal with these youths. Under divestiture provisions, status offenses are simply removed from the jurisdiction of juvenile courts. Various community agencies and social service organizations take over the responsibility for ensuring that status offenders will receive proper assistance and treatment. Referrals to juvenile court, incarceration, and the imposition of formal sanctions are no longer justified on the basis that one is a status offender and should suffer this processing and these punishments.

Relabeling Status Offenses as Delinquent Offenses

Because of police discretion, curfew violation, runaway behavior, and truancy can easily be reinterpreted or relabeled as attempted burglary or attempted larceny. Hanging out or common loitering may be defined by police as behaviors associated with casing homes, businesses, and automobiles as future targets for burglary and theft. And these acts are sufficiently serious and provocative to bring more juveniles into the juvenile justice system, thereby widening the net. Widening the net occurs whenever juveniles are brought into the juvenile justice system who would ordinarily have been dealt with by police differently prior to divestiture. Prior to divestiture, many status offenders would have received wrist-slaps and verbal warnings by police instead of being taken into custody. However, when police officers resort to relabeling status offenses as conceivably criminal actions, greater rather than fewer numbers of juveniles will be netted into the juvenile justice system in the post-divestiture period than was the case in the pre-divestiture period. Sometimes such relabeling occurs because of police attitudes about youths or personal idiosyncrasies that cannot be legislated away or controlled by police departments. Police discretion is very individualized.

In the Washington cities of Yakima and Seattle, police officers were not particularly receptive to the idea that their discretion in certain juvenile matters was abolished by legislative mandate in the late 1970s. In effect, the police officers in these cities literally created a fictitious juvenile delinquency wave in the post-divestiture period, where the rate of delinquency appeared to double overnight. Such an artificial wave was easily accomplished, since these front-line officers merely defined juvenile behaviors differently according to their unchecked discretion. A similar phenomenon occurred in Connecticut during approximately the same period (Logan and Rausch, 1985). The primary implication of their actions seems to be that they perceived divestiture as a criticism of their integrity and discretionary quality in dealing with juvenile matters rather than as a positive move to assist certain youths in avoiding the delinquency label (Lieb, Fish, and Crosby, 1994).

An ambitious DSO provision was implemented in California on a state-wide basis. Again, like Washington, DSO did not necessarily deliver what was intended by deinstitutionalization and divestiture. For example, a study of San Bernardino County by Krause and McShane (1994) examined 123 youths who had had previous involvement with the juvenile justice system and 493 youths who had no prior involvement with it. Both groups of juveniles consisted of nonserious youths who were largely from dysfunctional families. Prior to DSO many of these youths would simply be diverted from the juvenile justice system and subjected to family counseling outside of any custodial setting. However, following DSO in San Bernardino County, many of the youths who normally would have been given diversion and family counseling were relabeled, placed in custody in juvenile hall, and placed outside their parents' homes in foster care or group homes. Krause and McShane strongly recommended that San Bernardino County juvenile authorities should seriously reexamine their institutionalization criteria and invoke more effective screening mechanisms to avoid the practice of detaining for prolonged periods those youths who deserve to be diverted instead.

Protecting Status Offenders from Themselves

Many runaways and truants may have certain mental health or educational needs that can only be met through mandatory participation in a mental health therapy program or educational intervention (Kingree, Braithwaite, and Woodring, 2001). Court intervention may be necessary to ensure that juveniles take advantage of these services. Informal dispositions of status offense cases may not have the legal coercion of a juvenile court order. Thus, one's participation in various assistance programs is either voluntary or strongly recommended. However, agency response in accommodating youths with various problems seems selective and discriminatory. Often, those youths most in need of certain agency services are turned away as unqualified. Thus, status offender referrals to certain agencies may be unproductive, particularly if the status offenders are psychotic, violent, or drug/alcohol dependent (Escarcega et al., 2004).

Parens Patriae versus Due Process

The *parens patriae* philosophy is in increasing conflict with the due-process orientation that typifies most juvenile court procedures today (Lamb, Weinberger, and DeCuir, 2002; Myers, 2003). Status offenders represent a juvenile offender class clearly in the middle of this conflict (Sanborn, 2001). Reducing admissions of status offenders to various detention centers and treatment facilities may result in a reversal of the hardening effect of custodial confinement on these youths.

Gender Stereotyping and DSO

A continuing problem of DSO in any jurisdiction is how male and female status offenders are differentially treated by juvenile court judges (Chapple, Johnson, and Whitbeck, 2004; Harris and Dagadakis, 2004). For instance, in a survey of 87 juvenile probation officers in a large metropolitan county of a southwestern state, it has been found that female juveniles tend to receive relatively punitive protection from juvenile court judges (Reese and Curtis, 1991). In fact, this differential treatment of females by juvenile courts seems fairly routinized and institutionalized. DSO has failed to change how juvenile court judges dispose of female status offense cases compared with how cases were disposed prior to DSO. It has been suggested that judicial stereotyping of female status offenders is such that many judges act to protect females from the system and society by placing them in restrictive circumstances such as secure confinement, even if their offenses do not warrant such placement (Sanborn, 2001). Thus, a double standard continues to be applied, despite the best intentions of DSO (Lundman, 2004).

Race and Ethnicity

Do police officers and juvenile court judges stereotype status offenders on other factors besides gender? Some jurisdictions report that disproportionately high numbers of black youths are represented in their juvenile justice system. In Georgia, for instance, a youth's race has had a direct impact on disposition decision making, as well as at the law enforcement, intake, and adjudication decision points (Brooks and Jeon, 2001). Closely related to the race variable was socioeconomic status. Thus, race and socioeconomic status operated in this instance to predict correctly more adverse consequences for youths who were black compared with other youths who had committed similar offenses, had similar delinquency histories, but were white.

Presently, juvenile justice policy statements have been made declaring differential treatment on the basis of race/ethnicity, gender, and socioeconomic status to be illegal, immoral, and inadvisable (Ribeaud and Manzoni, 2004). Such extralegal factors should have no place in determining one's chances in the juvenile justice system, whether one is a delinquent or a status offender (Eitle, Stolzenberg, and D'Alessio, 2005).

REDEFINING DELINQUENCY

Police officers might consider taking a more proactive role as interventionists in the lives of juvenile offenders encountered on the street. For instance, Trojanowicz and Bucqueroux (1990:238) say that "young people do not launch long-term criminal careers with a daring bank robbery, an elaborate kidnapping scheme, or a million-dollar dope deal. Yet the traditional police delivery system does not want officers 'wasting' much time tracking down the kid who may have thrown rocks through a few windows at school. Narcotics officers on their way to bust Mr. Big at the dope house cruise right by those fleet-footed 10-year-old lookouts. And a call about a botched attempt by a youngster to hotwire a car would not be much of a priority, especially where far more serious crimes occur every day." These criminologists indicate that officers should be encouraged to intervene and to take these petty offenses and juvenile infractions seriously. It is possible for police officers to identify those youngsters most at risk in particular neighborhoods and perhaps do something to assist them to refrain from future lives of crime.

But the nature of systems is such that the actions of particular parts of the system may not function properly or be permitted to function properly in relation to other systemic parts. This was especially the case when divestiture of jurisdiction was implemented in Yakima and Seattle during the 1980s and status offenders were removed from the jurisdiction of the juvenile courts. Whether or not Yakima or Seattle police officers were justified in doing so, they intervened in the lives of numerous status offenders after divestiture was enacted and relabeled status offenses as delinquent offenses. This intervention was contrary to the spirit of intervention explicitly outlined by Trojanowicz and Bucqueroux in their description of police actions under community policing policies. More status offenders and petty offenders on the streets of Yakima and Seattle were taken to jails and juvenile halls following divestiture than in previous years. This is quite different from officers acting as interventionists in positive ways and doing things for youths rather than against them.

There are obvious gaps between different contact points in the juvenile justice system. It is one thing to legislate change and remove status offenders from the jurisdiction of juvenile court judges and police officers. It is quite another thing to expect that juvenile court judges and police officers will automatically relinquish their powers over status offenders. While many juvenile court judges and police officers won't admit it to others, they do not like having their discretionary powers limited or undermined by legislatures.

Some observers have recommended that police departments should have separate units to interface with juveniles and manage them. This has already been accomplished in many of the larger city police departments throughout the United States. However, many smaller police departments and sheriff's offices simply lack the staff or facilities to accommodate such special youth units. These luxuries are usually enjoyed only by larger departments. Smaller departments must be content with individual officers who assume responsibilities for managing juvenile offenders and perform related tasks. Most of initial contacts with juveniles who roam the streets in various cities are usually made by patrolling uniformed police officers (Greenleaf, 2005).

Police officers will continue to exhibit interest in those juveniles who violate criminal laws. Offense seriousness and the totality of circumstances will usually dictate their reactions in street encounters with these youths (Duran, 2005). But most juveniles who are the subjects of police-initiated contacts have committed no crimes. These may be status offenders or those reported to police as **children in need of supervision (CHINS)** (Souweine and Khashu, 2001). The wise use of discretion by police officers is especially crucial in dealing with status offenders. Fine lines may be drawn by academicians and others to distinguish between offender arrests and temporary detentions resulting from being taken into custody, but the bottom line is usually a record of the contact being entered in a juvenile file. One buffer between police actions against status offenders and less serious delinquents is to divert certain juveniles to alternative and informal mechanisms where their cases can be disposed of with minimal visibility.

SUMMARY

Law enforcement is a crucial link between juveniles and the juvenile justice system. A majority of juvenile court referrals are made by police officers and agencies, largely as the result of street contacts between juveniles and the police. Presently there is some amount of tension between juveniles and the police, particularly with the growing pervasiveness and proliferation of gangs and gang activities. The relationship between the police and juveniles is considered diffuse, since police officers are able to exercise much situationally based discretion. Police officers have generally regarded contact with juveniles on the streets unfavorably, since the juvenile justice system deals with a majority of juvenile cases with great leniency. Thus, for many officers, law enforcement efforts involving juveniles seem wasted, since prosecutors and juvenile court judges are probably going to downgrade the offenses charged against youthful offenders, and many of these youths will escape what police consider to be significant punishment and accountability. Furthermore, most juvenile offending involves minor delinquent conduct. Police officers therefore regard crime fighting and real police work as catching criminals rather than processing juveniles, who often must be treated differently anyway.

Most large police departments in the United States have gang units, which are largely reactive. These youth squads are oriented toward delinquency prevention and respond to reports of delinquent activity whenever it occurs, especially if it appears to be gang related. Front-line police officers are more proactive in their anti-gang efforts, and they seek to regulate juvenile conduct by their increased visibility throughout the community through community policing.

Studies of youth gangs are abundant, and several types of youth gangs have been identified. Many gangs are known as scavenger gangs, whose activities are largely socializing and mutual protection from other gangs. Territorial gangs are more organized and profess to control certain areas of a city, usually several city blocks known as their territory or turf. By far the most violent of all types of gangs are corporate gangs, whose principal activities consist of trafficking in illegal drugs, such as methamphetamine and Ecstasy, and firearms (Carlson et al., 2004). In 2005 there were approximately 30,000 gangs in the United States with over 1 million members.

There are several myths and misconceptions about gangs. It is believed, for instance, that gangs are mostly male, consist of blacks and Hispanics, thrive in inner cities, deal heavily in drugs, and engage in criminal enterprises of various kinds. While some gangs exhibit some or all of these characteristics, many of these generalizations have been discounted by gang research. Today more gangs committing violent acts tend to be older; gangs appear less concerned with territories in communities; more gangs exist in suburban areas than in past years; greater numbers of gang members are females, and the rate of female gang membership is growing annually; and modern gangs rely less on gang symbols and rites compared with past gangs. Gang members are younger each year, and rural- and urban-based gangs differ considerably. The relation between gangs, drugs, and violence is not as strong as it once was. Female juveniles make up about 10 percent of all U.S. youth gangs presently, and this proportionate distribution seems to be growing. Female gangs are also achieving some parity with their male gang counterparts, especially by engaging in violence and other delinquent activities (Johnson, 2005).

Responses by juveniles to police officer contacts are sketchy. Because of extensive police officer discretion, often juveniles do not know how to behave when confronted by police, even if these youths have done nothing wrong. Being too polite or not polite enough is sufficient to arouse police suspicions. Police officers need relatively little if any justification to interfere in juvenile activities, regardless of their innocence or seriousness. Police officers have a variety of discretionary actions they may take when confronting juveniles on the street. They can ignore youths; they may act passively on citizen complaints about juveniles; officers may take some youths into custody for a few hours and release them later through stationhouse adjustments; they may take youths into custody and refer them to some social service agency or to juvenile court authorities; or they may arrest youths and charge them with various offenses.

Juvenile arrests usually involve processing juveniles as though they were adult offenders. Juvenile arrests are qualitatively different from being taken into custody, which is largely a protective action and typical of juvenile court traditionalism. Whenever juveniles are arrested, these situations may or may not be clear-cut. Many arrested juveniles have false identifications or no identification. In these situations, police officers and jail personnel need time to find out who these youths are and reunite them with their parents, guardians, or place them in some protective agency or social service organization. More serious youths may be photographed, fingerprinted, and booked like criminal offenders. Juvenile suspects may also be interrogated, subject to the totality of circumstances under which they were arrested. The Miranda warning is applicable to virtually every juvenile arrest situation. When juveniles become adults, their records in most jurisdictions are sealed through expungement orders. However, a growing number of jurisdictions are retaining these records for longer periods, and this information may be used later if these youths commit new crimes as adults.

Status offenders are treated quite different from juvenile delinquents. As we have seen in earlier chapters, every effort is made by most jurisdictions to separate status offenders from delinquent offenders because of the potentially adverse effects of labeling. A majority of juvenile courts have divested themselves of jurisdiction over status offenders in recent years, although this has not prevented police officers from relabeling status offending as delinquency under certain circumstances. Relabeling and net-widening are possible as the result of police discretionary powers. A tension presently exists between the *parens patriae* traditional philosophy, which emphasizes rehabilitation and reintegration, and due process, which emphasizes just deserts and justice. Thus far, this tension has not diminished.

Several important factors have been linked with how juveniles are treated by the police and the juvenile justice system generally. Gender, socioeconomic status, race, and ethnicity continue to be extralegal factors that are used by different actors throughout the juvenile justice system to make decisions and impose sanctions. Presently there are mixed opinions about whether the juvenile justice system discriminates in significant ways against juveniles of different ethnicities, races, genders, or socioeconomic statuses.

QUESTIONS FOR REVIEW

1. What is situationally based police discretion? How is such discretion used and abused?

2. How are police officer roles considered diffuse regarding interactions with juveniles?

3. What are youth squads and gang units? What are their functions?

4. What is proactive restorative policing? What are some of its characteristics?

5. What are several myths and truths about juvenile gangs and their membership?

6. What proportion of gangs in the United States are female gangs? What are some general characteristics of female gang members?

7. What are four different discretionary actions police officers may take in relation to juveniles they encounter?

8. Why are arrests of juveniles sometimes considered ambiguous?

9. Under what circumstances can police officers book, fingerprint, and photograph juvenile suspects?

10. What is meant by expungement or sealing juvenile records? How does divestiture of jurisdiction lead to net widening?

INTERNET CONNECTIONS

Bibliography on Gang Culture
http://www.streetgangs.com/bibliography/gangbib.html

Federal Gang Violence Act
http://www.feinstein.senate.gov/booklets/gangs.pdf#search='federal%gang%20violence%20act'

Fight Crime, Invest in Kids
http://www.fightcrime.org/

Inner City Struggle
http://www.schoolsnotjails.com/

Juvenile Law Center
http://www.jlc.org/index.php

National Criminal Justice Reference Service
http://www.virlib.ncjrs.org/JuvenileJustice.asp

National Youth Violence Prevention Resource Center
http://www.safeyouth.org/scripts/teens/gangs.asp

REALJUSTICE
http://www.realjustice.org/

Urban Institute
http://www.urban.org/

Youth Gangs in the Schools
http://ncjrs.org/html/ojjdp/jjbul2000_8_2/contents.html

CHAPTER 7 | *Intake and Preadjudicatory Processing*

Chapter Outline

Key Terms

assessment centers
due-process
extralegal factors
Interagency Agreement Plan

legal factors
recidivism
socioeconomic status (SES)

Stop Assaultive Children (SAC)
   Program
strategic leniency

Chapter Objectives

As the result of reading this chapter, you should realize the following objectives:

1. Understand the intake process.
2. Learn about the roles of juvenile intake officers and the screening decisions they make.
3. Understand different models for dealing with juvenile offenders.
4. Distinguish between and learn about several important legal and extralegal factors that affect how juveniles are processed and treated within the juvenile justice system.
5. Describe several preliminary options available for juvenile offenders in lieu of formal juvenile court processing.

• *The number of female juvenile offenders throughout the United States has increased gradually between 1995 and 2005. In 2003, for instance, girls made up about 30 percent of all juvenile arrests, up from 19 percent in 1990. In Arizona in 2003, there were 16,000 girls in the juvenile justice system, about half of them runaways. Many female juveniles in trouble with the law are placed in detention for a time and then in some type of institution or group home. When they finally are released from these places, they have acquired very little in the way of adaptive skills and coping mechanisms to transition into adulthood and make it in society. It has been estimated that 80 percent of all institutionalized girls have had a history of trauma, with at least one time in a psychiatric hospital, and most likely for a suicide attempt. One of the biggest frustrations reported by girls is too much dead time in detention with no access to mental health services. Many girls have communication issues and don't know how to develop relationships with others. One example is Beth Collett, 21, of Tempe, Arizona. She spent her teen years being transferred from one shelter or group home to another, after reporting family sex abuse. She lived in over a dozen homes between the ages of 16 and 18, each time with new counselors and new rules. She felt like she was being punished for being sexually abused. She cut and burned herself repeatedly. Although she never drank alcohol or took drugs, she took mandatory drug tests once every week while institutionalized. She also had extensive counseling aimed at girls who drank alcohol and abused drugs. She thought that this was a total waste of services. Boys represent the majority of youths in the juvenile justice system and behavior management programs, which use consequences and rewards, are better suited for them. Opportunities for girls in the system are limited. The Florence Crittenton 40-bed girl's facility in Phoenix is one attempt to provide more gender-specific services for female juveniles. Collett was able to finish her high school coursework while at the Florence Crittenton group home, and a few years ago she got her own apartment and began attending a local community college. Collett says she would have preferred a regular home instead of a facility or institution during her formative years in the system. Presently Arizona is implementing an Interagency Girls Initiative aimed at helping girls to live in noninstitutionalized places and providing them with more gender-specific programming for transitioning into society. How many other states have deficiencies in their resources available for their female juveniles?* [Source: Adapted from Monica Mendoza, "Needs of Troubled Girls Get New Attention," *Arizona Republic*, January 4, 2005.]

• *Georgia was one of the first states to implement a vast network of boot camp programs for its juvenile offenders. After over a decade of experimentation with them,*

Georgia officials phased out most of them by 2000. In lieu of boot camps, the Georgia juvenile justice system substituted a secure confinement option and gave juvenile court judges broad discretionary powers to lock up youths for 90 days in detention centers or other secure facilities throughout the state. This option grew out of 1994 legislation that empowered the juvenile courts to get tough with even the most minor offenders. At least one juvenile court judge, O. Wayne Ellerbee, likes the present system because he sees it as an opportunity for him to remove young offenders from bad influences, including family and friends. He believes that it helps to get children out of adverse environments in order to modify their behavior and teach them that there's a different way of life. However, another juvenile court judge, John Worcester-Holland, asks what is the point of sending kids off for 90 days? He doesn't think that 90-day stays in secure confinement are therapeutic, and that they aren't very effective at providing needed services. Some critics have observed that many children are being locked up for 90 days for violating curfew or skipping school. They wind up being celled with hard-core juvenile felons in one of Georgia's secure facilities for youths. Pete Colbenson, the Executive Director of the Children and Youth Coordinating Council, says that there have been armed robbers sent to these facilities and placed side by side with shoplifters. The 90-day program is open to any juvenile offender coming into juvenile court. A $10 million infusion of funds into local Georgia juvenile services seeks to strengthen local community programs and rely more on probation rather than incarceration. This money would mean about $200,000 per juvenile court at the county level. The proposed program would provide swift punishment for youthful offenders who violate probation, and the sanctions would get more serious with each violation. While the need for greater programming exists, many juvenile court judges believe that too little money is being made available to establish effective local programs. One juvenile court judge, Bill Tribble, says that he would like to set up mental health, sexual abuse treatment, and other programs for youngsters in his court, but he can't imagine how to do that with $200,000. Thus the new plan is receiving mixed reactions from Georgia juvenile court judges, with opponents of the plan claiming that it's just another way of abrogating responsibility for troubled children. [*Source:* "Juvenile Justice: No Lock Up for Minor Offenders," *Access North Georgia*, November 29, 2004.]

• *Drug use among teens is on the decline in the United States, down by as much as 10 percent. This is a good statistic. However, evidence suggests that teens have simply shifted gears from using marijuana, Ecstasy, methamphetamines, and cocaine to greater use of inhalants, such as glue and ordinary cleaning products that emit toxic fumes. Between 2002 and 2004, inhalant abuse among middle school children has increased by 44 percent, according to the Partnership for a Drug-Free America. Most disturbing is the fact that there is greater inhalant use among sixth graders than among eighth graders. Approximately one-fourth of all eighth graders, about 1 million youths, have reported experimenting with inhalants at least once. Commonly known among teens as sniffing, inhaling, or huffing, inhalant abuse is the deliberate inhalation of fumes from common products found in homes or offices in schools to get high. Inhalant abuse can cause brain damage and can lead to death, even in the trial stage. Steve Pasierb, president and CEO of the Partnership, says that there are two major concerns: (1) more kids are using inhalants to get high, and (2) fewer kids are seeing risk in this behavior, which suggests that more kids will experiment in the future. The Partnership for a Drug-Free America and the Alliance for Consumer Education are discussing ways to help educate parents about the dangers of inhalant abuse by building awareness through new prevention efforts. The National Inhalant Prevention Coalition, based in Austin, Texas, sees this problem on a national scale as well. It's Director Harvey Weiss says, "We must talk about the very real threats of inhalants with our children; to do nothing about this now invites needless tragedies." To what extent should the juvenile court participate in such inhalant education initiatives? To what extent is juvenile offending related to this new form of getting high among youths?* [*Source:* Adapted from "More Pre-Teens Abusing Inhalants." *Join Together*, June 1, 2004.]

INTRODUCTION

What mechanisms exist for processing juveniles who come into contact with the juvenile justice system? Approximately 2 million juveniles a year come into contact with police, school authorities, and others who often petition to have their cases heard before the juvenile court. About half of these cases are screened and no further action is taken. Who performs these screening tasks? What criteria are used to determine which juveniles should advance further into the juvenile justice system and which ones should not?

Each of the scenarios at the opening of this chapter describes different youths and programs designed to deal with their particular problems. Many youths are addicted to drugs or abuse alcohol or other substances. Many youths have psychological issues and have suffered different forms of abuse from relatives and others. Some youths are suicidal and/or suffer from one or more problems that often require extensive counseling and therapy. Many juveniles lack discipline and are considered ungovernable or incorrigible, either by their teachers or parents. Easy access to drugs as well as common household products that have unintended uses by teens for getting "high" bring many youths to the attention of school authorities, parents, guardians, and/or the police. A wide variety of interventions and therapeutic programs has been created to deal with diverse juvenile problems.

This chapter describes the intake process. Intake is an important stage of juvenile offender processing. It is usually considered the first screening point where important decisions are made about juveniles and whether they should be drawn further into the juvenile justice system. The intake process is examined, as well as a description provided of persons known as intake officers who perform these screening chores. Some states, such as Florida, use assessment centers as a part of the preliminary screening process, in an effort to classify and categorize different types of juvenile offenders. Less serious offenders are treated by various community agencies and social services, whereas more serious offenders are moved further into the system for processing and an eventual appearance before the juvenile court.

Because juveniles have acquired many of the same constitutional rights enjoyed by adult offenders charged with crimes, the intake process itself has been affected in various ways. Although intake continues to be largely an informal enterprise, some amount of formality has occurred as the presence of defense counsels for juveniles has increased in these and subsequent juvenile proceedings. Due process has become the dominant theme governing juvenile offender processing, and this extends to intake as well as later stages where juveniles are subsequently adjudicated and disposed. The formalization of the intake process is described. It is important to recognize that juvenile cases are increasingly plea bargained in much the same way as criminal cases are plea bargained. Plea bargaining in criminal courts accounts for over 90 percent of all convictions. It is unknown at this time precisely how much plea bargaining occurs throughout the juvenile justice system, although the literature suggests that it is equally pervasive compared with criminal processing. The intake process has sometimes been compared with plea bargaining, since intake officers often negotiate with parents or guardians in less serious juvenile matters. The discretionary powers of intake officers are examined and the parallels between the intake process and plea bargaining are described.

The chapter next describes an assortment of both legal and extralegal factors that influence how juvenile offenders are treated. Legal factors are binding elements and must be considered in all juvenile decision making. These factors include the seriousness of the offense; the type of crime committed; the nature of evidence, whether it is exculpatory, inculpatory, or both; the prior record of the juvenile; and one's age. A similar set of extralegal factors exists that influences how juveniles are treated by the juvenile justice system. These factors are not considered binding on juvenile justice authorities, but they have noticeable impacts on juvenile offender processing. These factors include one's age, which doubles as both a legal and an extralegal factor; gender; race/ethnicity; and the socioeconomic status of juveniles. It is clear that extralegal factors shouldn't influence juvenile treatments, their adjudications, and subsequent dispositions, but these factors nevertheless play important informal roles in how offenders are processed.

Much of the decision making about juveniles is highly subjective. Police officers often make subjective judgments about which juveniles to arrest and which ones to release with verbal warnings or reprimands. Intake officers make decisions based on one's appearance, the type of attorney representing a juvenile, and the demeanor of the parents or the youths themselves. Juvenile court judges are in the most powerful position in that it is impossible to know whether their decision making is race-based, gender-biased, or influenced by socioeconomic factors. Arrest, intake processing, adjudication records, and dispositions of juvenile offenders suggest that one or more extralegal factors are given considerable weight in juvenile affairs. While these factors should have no place in the decision-making behaviors of juvenile court judges and others, it is obvious that many such decisions are based on one's race, ethnicity, gender, and socioeconomic status. These factors and their influence on the lives of juveniles are almost always covert and impossible to control or eliminate from the discretionary process of judicial decision making. Each of these factors is explored in some detail, and research is presented to indicate the presence of such factors in judicial decision making as well as at other points in juvenile offender processing and treatment.

WHAT IS INTAKE?

Intake or an intake screening is the second major step in the juvenile justice process. Intake is a more or less informally conducted screening procedure whereby intake probation officers or other juvenile court functionaries decide whether detained juveniles should be (1) unconditionally released from the juvenile justice system; (2) released to parents or guardians subject to a subsequent juvenile court appearance; (3) released or referred to one or more community-based services or resources; (4) placed in secure confinement subject to a subsequent juvenile court appearance; or (5) waived or transferred to the jurisdiction of criminal courts. Many jurisdictions are currently reevaluating the intake process and whether it should be modified (Toth, 2005).

Intake usually occurs in the office of a juvenile probation officer away from the formal juvenile court area. The juvenile probation officer, or intake officer, schedules an appointment with the juvenile and the juvenile's parents to consider the allegations made against the juvenile. The meeting is informal. An attorney representing the juvenile's interests may attend, although the primary purpose of the intake hearing is to screen juveniles and determine which ones are deserving of further attention from the juvenile justice system. Juvenile probation officers are vested with limited powers, but they do not have full adjudicatory authority possessed by juvenile court judges. For especially petty offending, intake officers can divert a case to social services, or they can recommend a full-fledged juvenile prosecution.

The Discretionary Powers of Intake Officers

The pivotal role played by intake probation officers cannot be underestimated. While police officers are often guided by rules and regulations that require specific actions such as taking juveniles into custody when certain events are observed or reported, the guidelines governing intake actions and decision making are less clear-cut. In most jurisdictions, intake proceedings are not open to the public, involve few participants, and do not presume the existence of the full range of a juvenile's constitutional rights. This is not meant to imply that juveniles may not exercise one or more of their constitutional rights during an intake hearing or proceeding, but rather, the informal nature of many intake proceedings is such that one's constitutional rights are not usually the primary issue. The primary formality of these proceedings consists of information compiled by intake officers during their interviews with juvenile arrestees. The long-range effects of intake decision making are often serious and have profound implications for juvenile offenders once they reach adulthood (Toth, 2005).

Intake officers must often rely on their own powers of observation, feelings, and past experiences rather than a list of specific decision-making criteria in order to determine what they believe is best for each juvenile. Each juvenile's case is different from all others, despite the fact that several types of offenses occur with great frequency (e.g., shoplifting and theft, burglary, and other property crimes). Some juveniles have lengthy records of delinquent conduct, while others are first-time offenders. Many jurisdictions have standard forms completed by probation officers during intake interviews. One of these forms is a Social History Report, illustrated in Figure 7.1.

Sometimes intake officers will have access to several alternative indicators of a juvenile's behavior, both past and future, through the administration of paper-and-pencil instruments that purportedly measure one's risk or likelihood of reoffending. Armed with this information, intake officers attempt to make important decisions about what should be done with and for juveniles who appear before them.

Various studies of intake officers have been conducted in an effort to determine the successfulness of their actions in influencing the lives of those they screen. For instance, during the period 1986–1987, 81 juvenile male offenders were court-referred to Lakeside Center, a residential treatment center in St. Louis, Missouri. Previously these juveniles had been rated and evaluated by intake officers. The officers reviewed social and referral history information, and they conducted an admission interview with each youth. The intake officers rated these juveniles as "good," "fair," or "poor" in terms of their prognosis for whether each juvenile would reoffend. Later, after the juveniles had attended the Lakeside Center for a period of time, a majority successfully completed the program, while 27 percent failed to complete it. Those who completed the program were far less likely to reoffend later when follow-ups were conducted. However, specific juveniles who were rated earlier by intake officers as having

Social History Report

Routing Information	Case Identification

TO: _____ CASE NAME: _____

FROM: _____ DATE: _____ SERIAL: _____ STATUS: _____

AREA: _____ OFFICE: _____ BIRTH DATE: _____ SEX: ___ RACE: _____

REPORT REQUESTED BY: _____ JPC ASSIGNED CASE: _____

1. IDENTIFYING DATA
   a. Youth's birthplace:
   b. Youth's birth status:
   c. Other names used:
   d. Youth's address at time of commitment:
   e. With whom living at time of commitment:
   f. Family's relationship to youth:
   g. Legal guardian:
   h. Social security number: Youth: Father: Mother:

2. PERSONS AND AGENCIES INTERVIEWED

3. AGENCIES THAT HAVE WORKED WITH YOUTH AND FAMILY

4. DELINQUENCY HISTORY (USE ONLY AS SUPPLEMENTAL TO COURT REPORT. IDENTIFY ANY PARTICULAR CHRONIC AND/OR PECULIAR PROBLEMS.)

5. DEVELOPMENTAL HISTORY
   a. Early history (Use only when obvious value in detailing youth's problems.)
   b. Medical history (Detail only if pertinent.)
   c. Description of youth (How parents perceive youth, attitudes, and behavior patterns.)

6. FAMILY HISTORY—REVISED
   a. Marital history and youth's previous living situations
   b. Father
   c. Mother
   d. Siblings
   e. Family income
   f. Parents' perception of problem
   g. Impression of family functioning
      (1) How parents relate to youth
      (2) Parents' concept of discipline
      (3) Evaluation of parent role (how they should/do perform as parents)
      (4) JPC's impression of performance and evaluation (identify strengths and weaknesses)
      (5) Family's financial resources, including benefits, veterans, social security, welfare, etc., medical/hospital insurance (Note: Income is reported elsewhere—preadmission history.)

7. COMMUNITY INFORMATION
   a. Placement possibilities, including own home. (Note attitudes, family structural compatibility, and other placement considerations.)
   b. Community attitudes toward placement
      (1) Neighbors
      (2) School officials

8. SCHOOL AND VOCATIONAL HISTORY
   a. School performance
      (1) Last school attended and grade completed
      (2) Level of scholastic performance
   b. Vocational history
      (1) Part-time or full-time jobs held
      (2) Performance evaluation

9. IMPRESSIONS AND RECOMMENDATIONS
   a. Overall evaluation by JPC
   b. Family's willingness to become involved and cooperate
   c. Problem list (JPC's perception of specific problems)
   d. Strengths and assets of family and youth which can be used in dealing with problems.

FIGURE 7.1 Social History Report.

a "fair" or "poor" prognosis reoffended at a much higher rate compared with those rated by these officers as "good." Researchers concluded that intake officer assessments of the future conduct of juveniles they screened were highly reliable, especially when accompanied by an independent risk assessment device to measure their propensity to reoffend (Sawicki, Schaeffer, and Thies, 1999).

The process of intake is far from uniform throughout all U.S. jurisdictions. Often, intake officers do not believe that a comprehensive assessment of all juveniles is necessary at the point of intake (Toth, 2005). Juvenile probation office policies may not be clearly articulated, thus causing some confusion among intake officers about how intake screenings should be conducted and which variables should be considered most crucial in intake decision making. A wide variety of early interventions suggests a lack of consistency among jurisdictions and how effectively intake officers perform their jobs (Castellano and Ferguson, 1998; Glaser et al., 2001).

Florida Assessment Centers

In Florida, juvenile **assessment centers** have been established as processing points for juveniles who have been taken into custody or arrested (Dembo and Schmeidler, 2003). These centers provide comprehensive screenings and assessments of youths to match various available services to client needs; to promote interagency coordination; and to generate data relevant to resource investment and treatment outcomes. Florida intake officers conduct clinical screenings, recommend confinement, make provisions for youth custody and supervision, arrange transportation, and track juveniles as they move throughout the juvenile justice system.

The U.S. Supreme Court has rejected attempts by various interests to extend the full range of **due-process** guarantees for juveniles to intake proceedings, largely because of the informal nature of them. Thus, there are numerous interjurisdictional variations concerning the intake process and the extent to which one's constitutional rights are safeguarded or protected (Salekin, Larrea, and Ziegler, 2002). Generally, these proceedings are conducted informally, without court reporters and other personnel who are normally equated with formal court decorum. A casually dressed, folksy juvenile probation officer sits at a desk with the juvenile accused of some infraction or crime, or who is alleged to be in need of some special supervision or care. One or both parents may be present at this informal hearing, although it is not unusual for parents or guardians to be absent from such proceedings. Victims may or may not attend, again depending on the jurisdiction.

The Increasing Formalization of Intake

Intake is such an important stage of a juvenile's processing that it must be scrupulously monitored so that fairness and equitable treatment of juveniles by intake officers is preserved. Both legal and extralegal factors have been found to influence intake decision making in various jurisdictions. For instance, a study of the intake process in Iowa provides information about intake proceedings, suggesting that extralegal factors are often at work to influence intake officer decision making. Leiber (1995) investigated a random sample of referrals to juvenile courts in Iowa during the period 1980–1991. Included in his study were 3,437 white juveniles, 2,784 black juveniles, and 350 Hispanic juveniles. Agency records provided detailed information about how the cases were disposed and processed at different stages, commencing with intake. Leiber found that the ultimate case outcome was influenced mostly by legal factors, such as offense seriousness, prior record of offending, and one's age. However, he found compelling evidence of discrimination in offender processing at the

BOX 7.1

INTERNATIONAL SNAPSHOT: JUVENILE JUSTICE IN SOUTH KOREA

South Korea has been described as a centralized nation-state with a tripartite system of government, including administration, legislation, and judicature. The entire system of government, including prosecution, the courts, and prisons, is the responsibility of the central government. The first modern criminal laws in South Korea were adopted in 1905. Following World War II, the Criminal Law of 1953 was enacted and the Criminal Procedure Law of 1954 was passed. These laws have undergone broad revisions up to the present, and continuing plans for revision exist. In recent years several measures have been taken to protect South Korean youth. The Youth Protection Law was passed in 1999, which was designed to prevent child labor exploitation and prostitution. South Korea also made education compulsory for all children through age 15. High-quality health care was also instituted for children.

Crimes in South Korea are distinguished according to violent and property crimes. Each type of crime has a prescribed punishment. Property crimes include theft, fraud, embezzlement, breach of trust, and damage. Violent crimes include injury, assault and battery, and rape. In recent years specific drug laws have been passed under the Narcotics Act to control the distribution of different types of drugs, including heroin, cocaine, cannabis, and methamphetamines. Selling, producing, cultivating, manufacturing, smuggling, possessing, or using any or all of these drugs are considered serious violations of the law with serious penalties imposed upon conviction. Considering South Korea's population, the crime rates for various offenses are relatively low. There are fewer than 2 murders per 100,000 per year, and fewer than 15 rapes per 100,000 per year. Theft is a primary offense, with nearly 200 per 100,000 per year. Because of the Narcotics Act, the trafficking in illegal drugs has been curtailed significantly. Fewer than 5,000 persons per year are charged with drug offenses.

The age of criminal responsibility in South Korea is 14. Persons ages 14–20 are considered juveniles and are under the jurisdiction of the Juvenile Law. Although South Korea has capital punishment, the death penalty is not applied to offenders under the age of 18. When persons ages 14–20 are convicted of one or more crimes, indeterminate sentences are imposed at the discretion of family court judges. Indeterminate sentences of up to 5 years are imposed for less serious offenses, while sentences of up to 10 years are imposed for more serious offenses. Juvenile offenses are heard and decided by the Family Court, which is located in Seoul.

Two types of judicial proceedings are possible as actions to be taken against juveniles who violate the law. These are (1) criminal and (2) protective. Criminal proceedings are conducted in the District Court, while protective proceedings are conducted in the Family Court. The dispositions of juvenile protection cases are handled by single judges of the Family Court within the Juvenile Department. The primary approach to juvenile delinquency in South Korea is realistic guidance and prevention rather than punishment. Thus, protective types of dispositions overwhelm punishment-centered dispositions in the ordinary course of carrying forth cases against juvenile offenders ages 14–20.

Active intervention programs in juvenile cases were commenced in the late 1970s. More accurate and formalized record-keeping was initiated during this period as well concerning the nature and extent of juvenile offending. When official records were initiated, annual trends disclosed a general increase in different types of juvenile delinquency during the 1980s up until the mid-1990s. Subsequently, most types of delinquency stabilized and declined. From 1997 to 2004, for instance, the numbers of juveniles under age 18 declined substantially. Interestingly, the numbers and proportionate distribution of persons age 18–19 committing delinquent acts increased during this same period. Furthermore, the rate of female delinquency doubled during 1997–2004. The nature of juvenile offending shows that 37 percent of the delinquency has been violent offending (primarily assaults), property crimes accounting for 25 percent, traffic offenses 32 percent, and murder, robbery, and rape 2 percent. Juvenile drug use has been relatively low. In fact, between 1997 and 2004, drug use and trafficking among juveniles declined by 75 percent.

Prosecutions of juvenile cases are initiated by police investigations of crimes where juveniles are involved. Prosecutors consider police reports and send cases either to the District Court or to the Family Court. The District Court processes more serious types of juvenile offending. Less serious cases in Family Court usually result in fines or some type of protective disposition. Prosecutors exercise a great deal of discretion in all types of juvenile cases. Suspensions of proceedings against juveniles can occur, depending on the individual circumstances of each case.

Usually when suspensions of cases occur, these are conditional dispositions where the juvenile will submit to the supervision of a volunteer supervisor. It is believed that such supervisory protection is more beneficial to juveniles than placement in a correctional institution. For drug offenders requiring some form of medical assistance, therapy, or education, offenders may be placed under probation officer supervision for an indeterminate period. The primary criterion for determining whether to suspend prosecution is the judgment of the prosecutor that the offender is not likely to recidivate. Enabling prosecutors to make such decisions are risk assessments and social inquiry reports from welfare workers, teachers, work supervisors, and even statements from victims. Juveniles receiving such treatment enter into agreements with prosecutors by signing a written pledge that he or she will start a new life and observe all program conditions. Periods of supervision vary according to the prosecutor's judgment of one's likelihood of recidivating. Those considered higher risks are placed on

one-year probationary terms, while those considered low risks are placed on 6-month terms. Suspension is subject to revocation if the juvenile violates one or more stipulations of the signed agreement. When the suspension system was implemented in 1981, there were 4,070 suspension cases. In 2001 there were 143,600 suspension cases. Suspension actions are considered successful at curbing juvenile recidivism.

Probation for juveniles is used increasingly as opposed to placement in custodial institutions. Probation and parole generally were initiated in South Korea in 1982. For juveniles this development was intended as a means of adjusting the juvenile's social environment and dealing more effectively with juveniles exhibiting antisocial behavior. By 1989 there were 12 probation and parole offices and 6 branch offices operating throughout South Korea, with many services offered to juvenile offenders. These offices have subsequently proliferated. Presently placement of juveniles under the care of probation officers includes (1) short-term probation; (2) probation; (3) placement under the care and custody of a child welfare institution; (4) commitment to a hospital or sanitarium; (5) short-term transfer to a juvenile training school; and (6) transfer to a juvenile training school.

Probation requirements generally include supervision by probation officers while staying at home and going to school, community service orders, and participating in required treatments as ordered by the Family Court. Community service orders for juveniles age 16 or over shall not exceed 50 hours for short-term probation and 200 hours for ordinary probation. Community service orders include (1) activities for ecological conservation such as sweeping up rubbish; (2) services at botanical gardens; (3) services at libraries; (4) services at historical sites such as guiding visitors; (5) services at judicial or correctional institutions such as directing traffic or assisting in crime prevention; and (6) services at institutions for the handicapped, the elderly, or the disabled. Attendance orders imposed by the Family Court may include participating in (1) a drug abuse prevention program; (2) a traffic

(continued)

school; (3) a sexual assault prevention program; and/or (4) a domestic violence prevention program. The recidivism rate of those on probation performing community service orders or fulfilling attendance orders is less than 10 percent. Community service aims to provide offenders with a sense of fulfillment and satisfaction; permit the offender an opportunity for repentance and restitution; foster good work ethics; recover self-esteem; and assist in helping offenders return to society as law-abiding citizens.

Juvenile training schools are also constructive enterprises. Established in 1942, such schools initially emphasized supervision. Presently, these schools are heavily educational, offering a wide variety of vocational, technical, and educational training programs to enable juveniles to acquire useful skills. Under the Juvenile Training School Act of 1999, numerous educational reforms were implemented. One interesting feature of these schools, primarily located in Seoul, is the inclusion of small houses that can accommodate parents who make weekend visits. It is believed beneficial to have parents of youths confined in such training schools visit them on-site as a part of their growth and social development.

[*Sources:* Hak Eui Kim, "Juvenile Delinquency in Korea." Unpublished paper, 2005; "Republic of Korea," U.S. Department of State, Washington, DC, 2004; "Republic of Korea," Country Reports by the Bureau of Democracy, Human Rights, and Labor, 2005.]

intake stage. Black juveniles tended to receive a larger proportion of recommendations from intake officers for further proceedings in the juvenile justice system. Black juveniles were also far less likely than whites and Hispanics to receive diversion or other lenient outcomes from the intake proceeding.

Often, these disparities in processing juveniles at the intake stage are attributable to the subjective impressions of intake officers. While most of these officers are perhaps well-intentioned in their individualization of juvenile treatment, there is some general bias inherent in such individualization. This bias occurs most likely as the result of gender, race/ethnic, and socioeconomic factors (Escarcega et al., 2004). Adding fuel to the charge that the intake process is often discriminatory according to race/ethnicity, gender, and socioeconomic status, a study of 1,256 youths was undertaken in Fairfax County, Virginia, in the early 1990s (Williams and Cohen, 1993). It was determined that disproportionately more black youths were processed at the point of intake compared with youths of other races/ethnicities. While secure confinement was almost always used for those juveniles where serious offenses were alleged, disproportionately more minority offenders were placed in secure confinement, even controlling for type of offense and prior juvenile record. Furthermore, blacks were less likely than whites to receive lenient dispositions and treatment. Disproportionately lower numbers of blacks were likely to have hearings compared with whites, and more minorities used public defenders. Thus, minorities, especially black males, received adverse treatment at the early stages of their processing.

Regardless of whether any particular jurisdiction exhibits differential, preferential, or discriminatory treatment toward juvenile offenders at *any* stage of their processing, there are those who believe that increased defense attorney involvement for at least the most serious juveniles is a necessity (Burruss and Kempf-Leonard, 2002). The primary reason for the presence of defense attorney involvement in the early stages of a juvenile's processing is to ensure that the juvenile's **due-process** rights are observed. If there are extralegal factors at work and that somehow influence an intake officer's view of a particular juvenile's case, then the impact of these extralegal factors can be diffused or at least minimized by the presence of someone who knows the law—a defense attorney. During the 1980s where data were available from reporting states, the amount of attorney use in juvenile proceedings increased substantially (Champion, 2005b). Specific states involved in a 10-year examination of juvenile attorney use trends were California, Montana, Nebraska, North Dakota, and Pennsylvania. Attorney use increased systematically during this decade.

The increased presence of counsel in juvenile proceedings at virtually any stage may have both positive and negative effects (Feld, 2001). An attorney's presence can preserve due process. Intake officers and other juvenile court actors, including judges, are inclined to apply juvenile law more precisely than under circumstances where defense counsel are not present to represent youthful offenders (Pierce and Brodsky, 2002). Where defense counsel are not present, however, the law might be relaxed to the point where some juveniles' rights are ignored or trivialized. But an attorney's presence in juvenile proceedings criminalizes these proceedings to a degree. The fact of needing an attorney for one's defense in juvenile court is suggestive of criminal proceedings ensuring a criminal defendant's right to due process. In circumstances where defense counsel and prosecutors argue the facts of particular cases, juveniles cannot help but be influenced by this adversarial event (Juvenile Justice Center, 2001).

This experience is sometimes so traumatic that juveniles come to identify with criminals who go through essentially the same process. Many persons believe that youths who identify with criminals will eventually label themselves as criminal or delinquent, and thus they will be harmed from the experience. This is consistent with labeling theory, where self-definitions of particular types of persons are acquired by others, such as juveniles identifying with criminals on the basis of how they, the juveniles themselves, are treated and defined by others. To the extent that labeling theory adversely influences youths who are either first-offenders or have only committed minor infractions including status offenses, then some thought ought to be given to maintaining a degree of informality in intake proceedings. Nevertheless, it is important to emphasize a youth's accountability at all stages of juvenile justice processing (Escarcega et al., 2004; Myers, 2003).

The Need for Greater Accountability

More than a few persons seek greater accountability from those who work with juvenile offenders from intake through adjudication and disposition (Feld, 2001). Presently there is much variation among juvenile justice systems throughout the United States. Different types of family courts attempt to apply juvenile law in resolving a wide assortment of familial disputes and juvenile matters. Juvenile courts are increasingly seeking new methods and techniques, such as expanded intake functions and nonadversarial resolution of disputes, not only to create smoother case processing for juvenile courts, but also to provide more efficient, just, and enforceable social solutions to diverse juvenile problems. Accountability for judicial power requires that the court act comprehensively in providing social services either directly or by way of referral. This accountability involves not only the enforcement of dispositional orders requiring the parties and families to respond, but also the agencies and service providers to function effectively and the court to hold itself responsible for its case processing and management systems. This is a significant shift from the traditional treatment of juveniles by courts under the doctrine of *parens patriae* (Sanborn, 2001, 2005).

INTAKE PROCEEDINGS: WHERE DO WE GO FROM HERE?

Intake Compared with Plea Bargaining

A parallel has been drawn between what goes on in juvenile intake hearings and criminal plea bargaining (Dougherty, 1988). In plea bargaining, prosecutors and defense attorneys will negotiate a guilty plea and a punishment that are acceptable to both parties. Ordinarily, plea bargaining occurs before any formal disposition or trial. Thus, the accused waives certain constitutional rights, including the right to a trial by jury, the right to confront and cross-examine witnesses, and the right against self-incrimination (Terry-McElrath and McBride, 2004). A plea bargain is an admission of guilt to one or more criminal charges, and it is anticipated by those entering guilty pleas that leniency will be extended to them in exchange for their guilty pleas. The theory is that the accused will save the state considerable time and expense otherwise allocated to trials as well as the important prosecutorial burden of proving the defendant's guilt beyond a reasonable doubt. Although some jurisdictions prohibit plea bargaining (e.g., Alaska and selected counties throughout the United States), the U.S. Supreme Court has ruled that plea bargaining is constitutional in any jurisdiction that wishes to use it (*Brady v. United States,* 1970).

For many cases, this exchange is a reasonable one. In adult cases, crime for crime, other factors being reasonably equal, convicted offenders who plea bargain receive more lenient treatment compared with those who subject the state to the time and expense of jury trials (Champion, 2005b). Plea bargaining is favored by those who believe that it accelerates the criminal justice process.

During intake hearings, intake probation officers have almost unlimited discretion regarding specific outcomes for youths, especially those where minor offending is alleged. Apart from certain state-mandated hearings that must precede formal adjudicatory proceedings by juvenile court judges, no constitutional provisions require states to conduct such hearings. Intake officers seldom hear legal arguments or evaluate the sufficiency of evidence on behalf of or against youths sitting before them. These proceedings, which most often are informally conducted, usually result in adjustments, where intake officers adjust disputes or allegations informally. Thus, it may not be in the child's best interests for parents to hire attorneys to represent their children at this early and critical screening stage.

Intake officers are in the business of behavioral prediction. They must make important predictions about what they believe will be the future conduct of each juvenile, depending on their decision. Sometimes personality tests are administered to certain youths in order to determine their degree of social or psychological adjustment or aptitude. Those considered dangerous, either to themselves or to others, are detained at youth centers or other juvenile custodial facilities, until a detention hearing is conducted. Florida Juvenile

Assessment Centers administer a battery of tests to juveniles during intake, including clinical screenings by psychiatric professionals (Dembo et al., 2000b). For sex offenders in some jurisdictions, other psychological assessments are made and inventories administered, such as the Tennessee Self-Concept Scale, Beck Depression Inventory, the Rape-Myth Acceptance Scale, the Adversarial Sexual Attitudes Scale, the Assessing Environments Scale, the Buss–Durkee Hostility Inventory, and the Youth Self-Report (Worling, 1995). On the basis of these and other criteria, decisions are made by intake officers about whether additional steps are necessary in juvenile offender processing.

Intake officers may decide to refer juveniles to community-based services or agencies where they can receive needed treatment in cases such as alcohol or drug dependency. They may decide that certain juveniles should be detained in secure facilities to await a subsequent adjudication of their cases by juvenile court judges (Sanborn, 2001). Therefore, any action they take, other than outright dismissal of charges, that requires juveniles to fulfill certain conditions (e.g., attend special classes or receive therapy from some community agency or mental health facility) is based on their presumption that the juvenile is guilty of the acts alleged by complainants.

If parents or guardians or the juveniles themselves insist that the intervention of an attorney is necessary during such informal proceedings, this effectively eliminates the informality and places certain constraints on intake officers. The coercive nature of their position is such that they may compel youths to receive therapy, make restitution, or comply with any number of other conditions to avoid further involvement in the juvenile justice process. It is relatively easy to file petitions against juveniles and compel them to face juvenile court judges.

There are some adverse consequences of plea bargaining for juveniles, however. If juveniles admit to their crimes, they may be treated more severely than juveniles who denied committing their crimes (Ruback and Vardaman, 1997). For instance, researchers studied 2,043 adjudication decisions in 16 Georgia counties. Compared with juveniles who denied committing a crime but were adjudicated delinquent anyway, those youths who admitted their crimes to juvenile court judges received harsher dispositions in terms of longer terms of probation, longer incarcerative dispositions, and a greater proportion of more severe dispositions generally. Investigators found that race had no effect on judicial decision making. This study suggests that juvenile plea bargaining may not work the same way as it usually does for adults.

Parens Patriae Perpetuated

Some evidence indicates that intake probation officers in many jurisdictions are perpetuating the *parens patriae* philosophy. For example, a study of intake probation officers in a southwestern United States metropolitan jurisdiction revealed that probation officers believed that they were the primary source of their juvenile clients' understanding of their legal rights, although these same probation officers did not themselves appear to have a sound grasp or understanding of these same juvenile rights (Lawrence, 1984). In this same jurisdiction, juveniles believed that they clearly understood their legal rights. However, interview data from them suggested that in general, they tended to have a very poor understanding of their rights. Emerging from this study was a general recommendation that probation officers who perform intake functions should receive more training and preparation for these important roles.

Juvenile court judges have been criticized for ineffective decision making about the conditions of one's probation and the social and community services they should receive. In more than a few instances, judges are limited primarily because there are limited social services available in their communities. Thus, even if judges wanted to maximize their effectiveness in placing youths in treatment programs that could help them, their actions would be frustrated by an absence of such programs (Lamb, Weinberger, and DeCuir, 2002; Ribeaud and Manzoni, 2004).

Studies of intake dispositions in several jurisdictions have found that most intake dispositions tend to be influenced by extralegal factors, such as family, school, and employment (Wordes, Bynum, and Corley, 1994). The preoccupation of intake probation officers in this jurisdiction with social adjustment factors rather than legalistic ones reflected a strong paternalistic orientation in dispositional decision making. Many intake officers dispose of cases according to what they perceived to be in the best interests of the children involved, rather than according to legalistic criteria, such as witness credibility, tangible evidence, and one's prior offending record (Holsinger and Latessa, 1999).

Intake probation officers are not inundated exclusively with cases that require fine judgment calls and discretionary hair-splitting. Many youths appearing before intake officers are hard-core offenders and recidivists who have previously been there. Also, evidentiary information presented by arresting officers is overwhelming in many cases, and a large portion of these cases tend to be rather serious. Therefore, intake officers will send many of these juveniles to juvenile court and/or arrange for a detention hearing so that they may be confined for their own safety as well as for the safety of others. Increasingly, serious juvenile offenders will be referred to juvenile prosecutors with recommendations that these juveniles should be transferred to the jurisdiction of criminal courts. The theory for this measure is that juveniles who are transferred to criminal courts will be amenable to more severe punishments normally meted out to adult offenders. However, it is questionable at present whether those who are transferred to criminal courts actually receive punishments that are more severe than they would otherwise receive if their cases were adjudicated in juvenile courts (Champion, 2005b).

Thus, intake is a screening mechanism designed to separate the more serious cases from the less serious ones as juveniles are processed by the system. Intake officers perform classificatory functions, where they attempt to classify informally large numbers of juveniles according to abstract criteria. Clearly, intake is not an infallible process. Much depends on the particular experience and training of individual intake probation officers, juvenile court caseloads, and the nature of cases subject to intake decision making.

The discretionary powers of intake probation officers are in some ways equivalent to prosecutors in criminal courts. Intake officers may direct cases further into the system, they may defer certain cases pending some fulfillment of conditions, or they may abandon cases altogether and dismiss them from further processing. This powerful discretion can be used in both positive and negative ways, however. In response to a growing demand for juvenile justice reforms, numerous juvenile court judges have urged that more objective criteria be used for evaluating youthful offenders in the early stages of their processing, particularly at intake (Sanborn, 2001, 2005).

LEGAL FACTORS: CRIME SERIOUSNESS, TYPE OF CRIME COMMITTED, EVIDENCE, AND PRIOR RECORD

A distinction is made between **legal factors** and **extralegal factors** that relate to intake decision making, as well as at other stages of the juvenile justice process. Legal factors relate to purely factual information about the offenses alleged, such as crime seriousness, the type of crime committed, any inculpatory (incriminating) or exculpatory (exonerating) evidence against offending juveniles, and the existence or absence of prior juvenile records or delinquency adjudications (Ribeaud and Manzoni, 2004). Extralegal factors include, but are not limited to, juvenile offender attitudes, school grades and standing, gender, race or ethnicity, socioeconomic status, and age. Age also functions as a legal factor for certain types of offenses. Specific legal variables examined here include (1) offense seriousness; (2) type of crime committed; (3) inculpatory or exculpatory evidence; and (4) prior record.

Offense Seriousness

Offense or crime seriousness pertains to whether bodily harm was inflicted or death resulted from the youth's act. Those offenses considered serious include forcible rape, aggravated assault, robbery, and homicide. These are crimes against persons or violent crimes. By degree, they are more serious than the conglomerate of property offenses, including vehicular theft, larceny, and burglary. In recent years, drug use has escalated among youths and adults in the United States and is considered one of the most serious of the nation's crime problems. One general deterrent in every jurisdiction has been the imposition of stiff sentences and fines on those who sell drugs to others, and lesser punishments imposed on those who possess drugs for personal use. All large cities in the United States today have numerous youth gangs, many of which are involved rather heavily in drug trafficking (Wilson, 2001). One result of such widespread drug trafficking among youths is the provision in most juvenile courts for more stringent penalties to be imposed for drug sales and possession. Thus, crimes don't always have to be violent in order to be considered serious.

Type of Crime Committed

Another key factor in screening cases for possible subsequent processing by the juvenile justice system is the type of crime or offense committed (Holsinger and Latessa, 1999). Is the offense property-related or violent? Was the act either a felony or a misdemeanor? Were there victims with apparent injuries? Did the youths act alone or in concert with others, and what was the nature of their role in the offense? Were they initiators or leaders, and did they encourage or incite others to offend? Intake officers are more likely to refer cases to juvenile prosecutors where juveniles are older (i.e., 16 years of age and over), and where the offenses alleged are especially serious, compared with referring younger, petty first-offenders to prosecutors for additional processing.

Regarding juvenile justice policy, greater leniency with many offenders, particularly first-offenders, is often accompanied by less recidivism (Chapple, Johnson, and Whitbeck, 2004). Shay Bilchik says that greater intrusion into the juvenile justice system characterizes more serious offenders, probably meaning

 **BOX 7.2**

Stephen Vilhelmsen
Juvenile Probation Officer, 31st District Court Service Unit, Virginia Department of Juvenile Justice, Woodbridge, VA

Statistics:

B.S. (criminal justice administration), Park University; M.S. (public administration), Central Michigan University

Background and Interests

I was born in Hollywood, California, to Danish immigrant parents. English was a second language to me and when I began school I was enrolled in ESL classes; I was the only blonde kid in the class! I experienced some common difficulties during my adolescence; my parents divorced and I found myself being misdirected by negative influences. This period had a significant effect on my life; I developed a desire to give something back to the community by helping misguided youth. I enrolled in a community college to work toward a criminal justice degree, in the back of my mind hoping to someday work with juveniles.

While attending the community college I worked on an urchin boat and did salvage diving to cover my expenses. A friend's relative suggested I should look into the military, as this had always been an interest of mine. I joined the Army and received training as a military policeman. While in the Army I continued my education, always with the intention of pursuing employment as a police officer working with juveniles. After my experiences growing up I wanted the chance to work with and try to change the lives of other young people. I had three very fulfilling years in the army as a military policeman. I was stationed in Washington, DC, and I was involved in vice presidential and dignitary security. Upon my separation from the Army, I went to Georgetown University as a campus police officer. I later went to work for the Washington, DC Metro Transit Police, then to the Alexandria, Virginia police department. Along the way I finished my degree in criminal justice and set my sights on becoming a juvenile proba-

tion officer. I worked at a juvenile detention center in Woodbridge, Virginia, and then was hired by the court service unit in Warrenton, Virginia, as a juvenile probation officer. In the years to come I complete my master's degree.

My current post is in Prince William County, with about 300,000 residents. In Virginia juvenile probation officers are responsible for intake, investigation, probation, and parole. We work for the Juvenile and Domestic Relations Court, so we also handle adult domestic relations matters. I have been a member of our statewide parole advisory committee. I have specialized in parole and sex offender cases. About three years ago we were awarded a grant to serve juvenile sex offenders. Our Sex Offender Program adheres to a "best practices" model developed by Dr. Jonathan Hunter. He provided our staff training, and we have continued to seek further professional development. I especially admire the work of the Association for the Treatment of Sexual Abusers (ATSA) and the Family Violence and Sexual Abuse Institute (FVSAI). I have also been employed with the county's Office of Criminal Justice Services, where I provide case management and investigative services. For 10 years I have been an adjunct faculty member at the Northern Virginia Community College where I teach Juvenile Justice, Administration of Justice, and Corrections courses.

Before working with sex offenders I worked with all kinds of youth; one was Jesse. He was 16 years old when I met him. He was from East St. Louis. When Jesse was 10 years old his mother's boyfriend beat

Jesse's little brother to death. Jesse tried to stop him, and for that the man stabbed Jesse three times in the belly. Jesse entered foster care. After a year he began to "act out," he got caught shoplifting. Later Jesse was arrested for burglary and robbery. Jesse served time in Missouri, and then was sent to live with an aunt and uncle here in Virginia. When people tell me that jails need to be tough, I tell them the story of Jesse. I tell people that nothing in jail could be worse for Jesse than his own home had been. I helped Jesse get into a job training and placement program. He saved money and got an apartment. Some other workers and I gave Jesse some household items for his new apartment. When I closed Jesse's case he told me that he felt that he had something good in his life and it looked as though things might turn out alright for Jesse.

more chronic, persistent, dangerous, or habitual offenders—precisely the category of youthful offenders who are more likely to reoffend anyway (Bilchik, 1996). Perhaps the term **strategic leniency** is appropriate. The implication is that at least some punishment, properly administered, appears to have therapeutic value for many juvenile offenders compared with no punishment. For more violent or chronic, persistent offenders, however, leniency may be unwarranted (Chapple, Johnson, and Whitbeck, 2004).

Inculpatory or Exculpatory Evidence

Offense seriousness and type of crime are considered quite influential at intake hearings, but some attention is also given by intake officers to the evidence police officers and others have acquired to show the offender's guilt. Direct evidence, such as eyewitness accounts of the youth's behavior, tangible objects such as weapons, and the totality of circumstances give the intake officer a reasonably good idea of where the case would end eventually if it reached the adjudicatory stage in a juvenile court.

Also, intake officers can consider exculpatory evidence or materials and testimony from others informally that provide alibis for juveniles or mitigate the seriousness of their offenses. Evidentiary factors are important in establishing one's guilt or innocence, but referrals of juveniles by police officers to intake usually is indicative of the fact that the officers were persuaded to act in accordance with the situation they confronted. It is extraordinary for officers to pursue juvenile cases to the intake stage purely on the basis of whim, although some officers do so as a means of punishing certain juvenile offenders with poor attitudes. Most intake officers screen the least serious cases quickly at intake or provide dispositions for juveniles other than formal ones.

Prior Record

Intake officers use prior records of delinquency adjudications and factor this data into their decisions. In other jurisdictions, even jurisdictions in other countries such as Canada, prior records strongly suggest that prior treatments and/or punishments were apparently ineffective at curbing offender recidivism (Peterson, Ruck, and Koegl, 2001). It would be logical to suspect that intake officers would deal more harshly with those having prior records of delinquency adjudications. One's prior record of juvenile offenses would suggest persistence and chronicity, perhaps a rejection of and resistance to prior attempts at intervention and treatment. And in some of these cases, harsher punishments and dispositions have been observed (Kurlychek and Johnson, 2004). However, this is not a blanket generalization designed to cover all offense categories. Some offense categories have greater priority over others for many intake officers (Fader et al., 2001).

Also, the previous disposition of a particular juvenile's case seems to be a good predictor of subsequent case dispositions for that same offender. For instance, dispositions for prior offenses seem very similar to new dispositions for these very same offenses, regardless of the type or seriousness of the offense. Thus, if a juvenile has formerly been adjudicated delinquent on a burglary charge and probation for 6 months was imposed as the punishment, a new burglary charge against that same juvenile will likely result in the same probationary punishment for 6 months (Butts and Sanborn, 1999).

EXTRALEGAL FACTORS: AGE, GENDER, RACE/ETHNICITY, AND SOCIOECONOMIC STATUS OF JUVENILE OFFENDERS

Most intake officers have vested interests in the decisions they make during screening hearings. They want to be fair to all juveniles, but at the same time, they are interested in individualizing their decision making according to each juvenile case. This means that they must balance their interests and objectives to achieve multiple goals, some of which may be in conflict. Furthermore, in recent years, greater pressure has been exerted on all juvenile justice components to implement those policies and procedures that will increase offender accountability at all stages of processing. Thus, a balanced approach has been suggested (Seyko, 2001). Three major goals of the balanced approach for probation officers serving in various capacities in relation to their clients include: (1) protecting the community; (2) imposing accountability for offenses; and (3) equipping juvenile offenders with competencies to live productively and responsibly in the community.

Ideally, each of these goals is equal. These researchers say that such balanced objectives have been used by probation officers in Deschutes County, Oregon; Austin, Texas; and the Menominee Indian Reservation in Wisconsin. Individuality in decision making, where all three goals can be assessed for each juvenile offender, is sought. However, these three goals may have variable importance to probation officers performing intake functions in other jurisdictions. Depending on their orientation, some intake officers may emphasize their community protection function, while others may emphasize juvenile offender accountability. Those officers with rehabilitative interests would tend to promote educational programs that would enable youths to operate productively in their respective communities.

In the context of attempting to achieve these three objectives and balance them, several extralegal characteristics of juvenile offenders have emerged to influence adversely the equality of treatment these youths may receive from probation officers at intake: (1) age; (2) gender; (3) race/ethnicity; and (4) socioeconomic status.

Age

Age is both a legal and an extralegal factor in the juvenile justice system. Age is legally relevant in decisions about waivers to criminal court jurisdiction. Waivers of juveniles under the age of 16 to criminal courts are relatively rare, for example (Champion and Mays, 1991). Also, age has extralegal relevance. Older youths perhaps are assumed to be more responsible for their actions compared with younger youths, and they are often treated accordingly. Also, arrest data show that the peak ages of criminality lie between the 16th and 20th birthdays (Office of Juvenile Justice and Delinquency Prevention, 2005). Perhaps some intake officers believe that more aggressiveness in their decision making should be directed against older juveniles than against the younger ones.

However, the earlier the onset of a juvenile's contact with the juvenile justice system and police, the more serious the problem (Mazerole et al., 2000). Thus, younger offenders rather than older offenders are often treated with greater interest and attention. This is supported by the array of risk assessment instruments used by both juvenile and adult corrections departments throughout the United States today (Jones et al., 2001). Almost every one of these instruments uses age as an important component in arriving at one's degree of risk or dangerousness. The younger the offender, the greater weight is assigned. This means that if youths become involved with delinquent acts at earlier ages, then greater weight is given and one's dangerousness score increases (Champion, 1994). This evidences the seriousness with which age is regarded as a predictor of chronic and persistent recidivism, whether property or violent offending is involved.

For many intake officers, the age factor appears to function in much the same fashion in influencing their intake decision making as it does when prosecutors assess the seriousness of identical offenses committed by both youths and adult offenders (Lee, 1995; Leiber and Stairs, 1999). For an assortment of nonrational reasons, armed robbery is not as serious for some prosecutors when committed by a 12-year-old as it is when it is committed by a 21-year-old. Applied to intake decision making, probation officers may regard certain serious offenses as less serious when committed by those age 13 and under, while 14-year-olds and older youths may have those same offenses judged as more serious. There are no precise age divisions that separate younger from older youthful offenders when one's age is functioning as an extralegal factor (Toth, 2005).

Gender

Generally, traditional patterns of female delinquency have persisted over the years. Because there are so few female juvenile offenders compared with their male counterparts, the influence of gender on intake decision making and at other stages of the juvenile justice process has not been investigated extensively. Juvenile females make up approximately 14 percent of the juvenile incarcerative population in the United States annually (American Correctional Association, 2005). Females are only slightly more represented proportionately among those on probation or involved in assorted public and private aftercare services. Explanations for gender differences in their comparative rate of offending have ranged from different socialization experiences to different testosterone levels and genetic compositions (DeZolt, Schmidt, and Gilcher, 1996).

Differential treatment of males and females in both the juvenile and criminal justice systems is well documented. However, some of the traditional reasons given for such differential treatment, especially about female juveniles and their delinquency patterns, appear to be misconceived or have no basis in fact. Selected assessments of the impact of gender on intake decision making show that it is only moderately related to dispositions, consistent with intake guidelines in selected jurisdictions such as Arizona and Florida (University of New Mexico, 1996). Investigations of other jurisdictions as well as analyses of national figures show generally that female juveniles seem to be detained less often than male juveniles, and/or they are returned to the community at a greater rate than males, and/or they are committed to secure confinement at a much lower rate than males (Hodges and Kim, 2000).

Within the just-deserts, justice, or crime control frameworks, the attention of those interested in the juvenile justice system is focused on the act more than on the juveniles committing the act or their physical or social characteristics. Thus, gender differences leading to differential treatment of offenders who behave similarly would not be acceptable. However, the differential treatment of male and female juveniles in the United States and other countries persists.

A strong contributing factor is the paternalistic view of juvenile court judges and others in the juvenile justice system that has persisted over time in the aftermath and influence of *parens patriae.* Differences between the arrest rates of female and male juveniles and the proportion of females to males who are subsequently adjudicated as delinquent suggests that the case attrition rate for females is significantly higher at intake than it is for male juveniles (Rowe, Vazsonyi, and Flannery, 1995). Specific studies of intake decision making have disclosed, however, that gender exerts only an indirect impact on such decision making by officers (Hsieh, 1993). Paradoxically, female juveniles with prior referrals to juvenile court seem to be treated more harshly than male offenders with prior referrals, especially for committing one of several index violent offenses. Based on his analysis of the juvenile court careers of 69,504 juvenile offenders in Arizona and Utah, Snyder (1988) calculated probabilities of being referred to juvenile court for an index violent offense, where both male and female juveniles had similar numbers of prior court referrals. He found that males with eight prior referrals were more than three times as likely to be referred to juvenile court for an index violent offense than a male with only one previous referral, and more than twice as likely as a male with two prior referrals. However, females with eight prior referrals were six times as likely to be referred to juvenile court for an index violent offense compared with females who had only one prior referral, and three times as likely to be referred compared with females with two prior referrals (Snyder, 1988:44–45). There were negligible differences between male and female juvenile offenders relating to referrals for property crimes.

Thus, it would seem that first-offender females are more likely to experience favorable differential treatment from the juvenile justice system compared with those females with records of prior referrals (Triplett and Myers, 1995). In Howard Snyder's study, for instance, the great differential referral rate between male and female juveniles may have been the result of a backlash phenomenon, where females were being unduly penalized later for the greater leniency extended toward them earlier by juvenile justice authorities.

In some intervention projects designed to decrease or eliminate female gang delinquency, researchers have attempted to undermine the normative group functions served by gangs (Wang, 2000). In one intervention project known as the Tabula Rosa Intervention Project for Delinquent Gang-Involved Females in Ohio, a sample of female gang members was targeted for intervention. The nature of the intervention consisted of several components. These were (1) an educational component; (2) a wellness component; and (3) a job skills and vocational component. Many female gang members lacked formal education and coping skills. Also, they lacked various skills that would make them employable. Each participant was obligated to develop specific goals within each of these components and to strive to achieve them with interventionist assistance. The objective of the intervention was to interrupt the influence of gang membership and to divert these girls' interests in more productive directions. Early results of the intervention program for the participating females were regarded as successful (DeZolt, Schmidt, and Gilcher, 1996).

Race and Ethnicity

More important as predictors of decision making at virtually every stage of the juvenile justice process are race and ethnicity. Race and ethnicity appear to be significant predictor variables in arrest and detention discretion as well as referrals (Schafer, 1998). For instance, Bishop and Frazier (1996) have found clear evidence of racial disparities in juvenile justice processing at the point of intake and at other stages. Generally, the effect of race was disadvantageous to those juveniles processed. They studied 161,369 youths processed by the Florida Department of Health and Rehabilitative Services in 1987. Furthermore, they interviewed 34 juvenile justice officials. Most affected by racial factors were delinquent offenders compared with status offenders. Blacks, Hispanics, and other minorities tended to be advanced further into the juvenile justice system by intake officers. However, white status offenders were penalized more harshly than minority status offenders. In fact, white status offenders were more likely to be incarcerated more often than minority status offenders. Thus, at least for Florida during the year examined, racial factors were at work in different ways to influence how youths were processed, either as delinquents or status offenders.

Minority overrepresentation throughout the juvenile justice process has been reported in a study of North Carolina juveniles. Data were obtained from case files of all juveniles processed through intake during 1993 in 10 North Carolina counties (Dean, Hirschel, and Brame, 1996). While black juveniles accounted for substantially less than half of the delinquency in these counties, half of the juveniles referred to intake were black. Interestingly, blacks comprised only about one-fourth of the entire juvenile population for these counties. Furthermore, half of those adjudicated delinquent were black, while two-thirds of those committed to secure confinement were black. The use of other control variables failed to reveal any other critical operating factor besides race in this disproportionate offender processing. Absent any other reason for such disparate treatment of these juveniles, we may conclude that at least in this study, race was a crucial intervening variable influencing juvenile case outcomes, even though it is an extralegal factor.

Socioeconomic Status

Closely related to racial and ethnic factors as extralegal considerations in intake decision making is the **socioeconomic status (SES)** of juvenile offenders. It has been found that generally, the poor as well as racial and ethnic minorities are disenfranchised by the juvenile justice system at various stages. This is true not only of juvenile courts in the United States but also in those of other countries (Vestergaard, 2004). One explanation for this alleged disenfranchisement is more limited access to economic resources among the poor and minorities.

More restricted economic resources reduces the quality of legal defenses that may be accessed by the socioeconomically disadvantaged. Greater reliance on public defenders is observed among the poor compared with those who are financially advantaged (Leiber and Stairs, 1999).

A greater proportion of the socioeconomically disadvantaged tend to acquiesce and quietly accept systemic sanctions that accompany charges of wrongdoing rather than acquire counsel and contest the charges formally in court. But not all investigators believe that the relation between SES and delinquency is necessarily strong or negative. For instance, Leona Lee (1995) studied 3,520 youths who were charged with delinquent offenses between 1977 and 1986 and had 10 or fewer referrals. She found that intake disposition was determined primarily by the type of prior disposition rather than by the seriousness of the current offense or the socioeconomic background of juveniles.

PRELIMINARY DECISION MAKING: DIVERSION AND OTHER OPTIONS

Diverting Certain Juveniles from the System

A long-range interest of most, if not all, intake officers is minimizing recidivism among those diverted from the system at the time of an intake hearing. **Recidivism** is also a commonly used measure of program effectiveness in both adult and juvenile offender treatment and sanctioning schemes (Hodges and Kim, 2000). Because of the fragmented nature of the juvenile justice systems throughout the United States, it is extremely difficult to compile reliable, accurate information about the extent of juvenile delinquent recidivism. However, criminal justice practitioners estimate that the rate of recidivism among juveniles is similar to that for adult criminal offenders (Smith and Aloisi, 1999). In a government-sponsored study of 272,111 former state prison inmates released in 1994, for instance, inmates were tracked for 3 years. Sixty-seven percent were rearrested for a new crime within this 3 year period, while 46.9 percent were reconvicted for a new offense (Langan and Levin, 2002:1). For those inmates age 17 or younger who were released, 82.1 percent were rearrested within 3 years, while 55.7 percent were reconvicted for a new offense. To the extent that juvenile recidivism figures parallel these findings, the problem of juvenile offender recidivism is a potentially serious one.

Intake officer interest in the type of offense committed is triggered not only by the seriousness of the act itself and what should be done about it, but by evidence from various jurisdictions that suggests that recidivism rates vary substantially for different types of juvenile offenders. For example, studies of violent and nonviolent and chronic and nonchronic juvenile recidivists suggest that greater proportions of chronic offenders repeat violent offenses than nonchronic offenders. However, chronic offenders also commit subsequent nonviolent acts as well as violent ones. Despite increasing juvenile violence, it remains the case that only a small proportion of youths accounts for a majority of the violent crimes committed (Irwin, 2004).

How Should We Deal with Chronic Violent Offenders?

Closely associated with recidivism among chronic violent offenders in certain jurisdictions are predictor variables such as whether the delinquent has delinquent siblings and/or significant others as associates, whether the delinquent

Dangerous juveniles are locked up in secure detention facilities for varying periods, depending on the seriousness of their offending.

has school problems, and whether the acts committed were misdemeanors or felonies (U.S. General Accounting Office, 1995a). Some jurisdictions such as San Diego County, California, attempt to divert and process informally nonserious and first-offenders through an **Interagency Agreement Plan.** This plan seems to be modestly successful at reducing recidivism (Pennell, Curtis, and Scheck, 1990). For more serious offenders designated as chronic, violent, aggressive, or persistent, various types of mandatory group therapy have been regarded as successful interventions in past years (Hodges and Kim, 2000).

In growing numbers of jurisdictions, chronic violent or serious offenders and other aggressive youths have been targeted for priority processing at intake and other stages. Harsher measures, including rapid identification of youths, expedited hearings, close monitoring of their cases, and their segregation from other, less serious offenders, have been employed by different Hawaiian juvenile justice units as a means of crime control. Continuous counseling, placement in long-term secure confinement facilities, extended court jurisdiction, and the revelation of these youths' identities to the public seem effective at curbing recidivism among these hardcore offenders. Several constitutional issues that must be resolved concerning identities of juvenile offenders and the publication of information about them have been made available to others.

The Inadequacy of Treatment and Community Services

Also, many jurisdictions are hard-pressed to provide adequate treatment facilities and interventions that contain the ingredients for effectiveness. Some programs might have security without a jail-like atmosphere, close coordination

BOX 7.3

Tamara M. Carter
Juvenile Probation Officer, Vigo County, Terre Haute, IN

Statistics:

B.S.W. (social work), Indiana State University

Background

July 7, 1985, became a day that changed my life. I became a juvenile probation officer in Vigo County, Terre Haute, Indiana. Twenty years later, I am still here and amazed. I am a 1982 graduate of Indiana State University, with a Bachelor of Social Work degree. I had enrolled with the intention of majoring in dietetics, but Chemistry 104 told me to leave! Social work became my new major. The day of graduation, I went back to my hometown of Bloomington, Indiana. With a degree in hand (which came a month later in the mail), I was ready for the world. Then tragedy struck. My father died one month after graduation. We were truly devastated but our faith and the prayers of others got us through. This put my job seeking on hold for a while. My family was more important.

Before I had moved back to Terre Haute, I had interviewed for a position as a social worker at a nursing home. I had interviewed very well. Then the topic of salary came up. I told them that I wanted $10,000 a year. I did not get the job. My request was too high and more than minimum wage. I had a college degree! What a reality check.

Fast forward to 1985. The first day was quite interesting as a probation officer. My office had a window and I was able to see some of the kids who were being brought in handcuffed. This was an eye-opener. Many looked sad and scared, but a few acted like it was no bother. I found out later that they were the "regulars" and they knew the routine. After a while, it did not bother me as much. In fact, if I saw them coming up the walk or knew they were on their way, I'd meet them at the door. They hated that!

The building we worked in had been the "colored orphanage." It had housed both boys and girls since the 1920s through the 1960s. I have met many people who were reared there and/or had family members there. For them, it had a lot of good and sad memories.

After becoming a juvenile center, the probation department, court, kitchen, and detention were housed in the same building. Male detainees were held on one side downstairs and the females were confined on the other side. The building sat on a hill out in the country. Many kids talked about being transported there and how scary it seemed. Imagine driving up a hill handcuffed in a police car late at night. The moon is shining through the trees, the building is old red brick, it looks dark and cold, and you are going to be placed in a cell in the basement, and . . . your parents are going to be called. Whew, what an eery feeling! For a lot of the kids, it was their first and last time in this facility.

That building holds a lot of memories for me. I met a lot of children and their parents. I was so amazed at the lack of parental knowledge and boundaries that they had. When I had first started, I was just a few years older than some of the kids, but the parents seemed to listen to probation at one time or another. I was truly a part of the family. Sad to say, but I am now seeing their children. Just recently I placed a young lady on informal probation for another probation officer and found out that I had both of her parents when they were younger.

In 2001 we moved into our new building. The Court and Probation Department are in one building and the Detention Center is in the other one, although we are connected by a hallway. It is a much nicer building and it is in the city limits. Many of our families do not have transportation and/or little money. They are able to ride the city bus or walk.

In 20 years of working, I have seen a lot of changes in the kids and their families. The biggest change is respect. They have very little. In the past, 10 to 15 years ago, even if the kids were involved with our system, they still showed more respect toward their parents. For some, they would have rather stayed at the center rather than face their parents. Today, many show no respect for their parents, teachers, the court, or even themselves. This is so sad. I know that you cannot group all young people together, but because it does exist, it makes you stop and wonder about the future.

As a probation officer, I have had the opportunity to supervise many college students. Many were from Indiana State University and social work majors. I have had a few criminology and psychology majors too. The length of internship, one semester or two, determines how soon they are able to work on their own. By the time they finish, they have met with the kids and their families, made decisions for the outcome, school visits, referrals, and of course, paperwork!

Advice to Students

I try to stress that each day is different just as each situation is different. You cannot look at the offense on paper and make a good decision until you get the full report and background about the child and his or her family. There will be times that you will have to make decisions quickly. You will not have time to think about the theory, open-ended questions. If you have learned anything, it'll come to you as you are working.

Do not prejudge because of what is written down. One intern stated, "Well, there is no father and they are poor. What do you expect?" First of all, she never said that again! Then I showed her my caseload, and those who had two parents in the home outnumbered the single-parent households. The father had just died and the mother was starting over. By the way, the intern graduated, earned her M.S.W., and is an outstanding social worker in her field. Students, while in your internship, be excited, willing to listen and learn. There are so many areas that a social work degree can take you and for you to do some good. Dietetics is a great field, but my social work degree has given me so much more experience and joy than I could ever imagine.

and cooperation between the community and the criminal justice system, paraprofessional staffs, and provisions for remedial education and job training for these youths. But existing limited budgets and other priorities in many jurisdictions prevent the development of such sophisticated interventions. Yet another view is that interventions should be aimed at modifying one's social and psychological environment that fostered such violence and chronicity originally (Crawley et al., 2005; Supancic, 2005).

Intake officers are also influenced by existing services and programs, especially in their decisions about violent offenders. In Tucson, Arizona, for example, a **Stop Assaultive Children (SAC) Program** was created in the late 1980s, designed especially for those youths who have committed family violence (Zaslaw, 1989). In SAC, the child is usually detained or locked up in a juvenile detention center for one day, and release from detention is contingent upon the youth's attendance at school, abiding by a curfew, refraining from committing future delinquent acts or violence, and an agreement by the youth to be interviewed by the intake officer. Children in SAC are ordered to reappear within two weeks, at which time their prosecution is deferred for three months, provided that they are accepted into SAC. Each of the SAC participants must sign a contract acknowledging responsibility for their acts, agreeing further to participate in counseling and/or volunteer work, or to make a donation to a domestic violence service or agency. If the contract is unfulfilled for any reason, the juvenile is subsequently prosecuted.

Parents are also obligated to sign the contract and to enforce its conditions. The primary result of the successful completion of the SAC program is a dismissal of all charges against the juvenile. Involving parents in various juvenile violence interventions is not a new concept. In many jurisdictions today, parents are held liable for their youths' actions (Brank and Weisz, 2004). Zaslaw (1989) reports favorably that the SAC program has had a recidivism rate of only 9.6 percent compared with a recidivism rate of 48.7 percent among a control group of assaultive delinquent nonprogram participants in the same jurisdiction. But while Tucson may be able to operate such programs successfully, other jurisdictions may not be as fortunate, or intake officers elsewhere may believe their own plans for intervention are more effective.

Getting Tough with Persistent Offenders

For persistent offenders and otherwise hardcore violent recidivists, even for some violent first-offenders, the strategy employed at intake may be a waiver of jurisdiction to criminal courts (Champion, 2005b; McNeill and Batchelor, 2004). Some jurisdictions, such as New York, Washington, and Illinois, have automatic transfer laws that compel juvenile authorities to send certain types of juvenile offenders in a particular age range (normally 16 or 17 years of age) directly to criminal court to be processed as adults. The manifest intent of such waivers to criminal court is for harsher punishments to be imposed on these youthful offenders beyond those that can ordinarily be administered within the power of juvenile court judges.

The get-tough movement clearly has incarceration in mind for those youths who have been adjudicated delinquent for violent offenses. Anything less than secure confinement for such youths adjudicated for aggravated assault, rape, robbery, or homicide is considered as too lenient. However, some juvenile justice observers argue that there is presently too much incarceration, that incarceration is overdone, and that many youths can remain in their communities under close supervision, participating in productive self-improvement and rehabilitative programs (Benda, 1999).

Is There Too Much Juvenile Incarceration?

Several alternatives to confinement have been investigated in Delaware (Brandau, 1992). In 1987 the Delaware Plan was established, whereby certain community programs were established as alternatives to incarcerating certain types of delinquent offenders. Brandau found that over time, a sample of 363 youths adjudicated for various serious delinquency offenses were assigned randomly to either reform school, placed on probation, or sent to the Delaware Bay Marine Institute (DBMI). The DBMI was a community-based program designed to equip certain youths with coping skills and other useful experiences. Legal, social, and demographic variables were controlled, and all youths were evaluated according to whether they were more likely to be assigned to the reform school following their delinquency adjudications. Subsequently, recidivism information was compiled for all youths to determine the influence of the different experiences on them. Youths in the DBMI program had recidivism rates similar to those placed on straight probation and those placed in reform schools. This finding is significant because it shows in this instance, at least, that the DBMI program was about as effective as incarceration or probation for decreasing one's likelihood of recidivating. Since incarcerating juveniles is more expensive than placing them on probation or in the DBMI program, it is suggested that nonincarcerative community-based alternatives should be used more frequently, even for serious offenders.

Some criminologists argue that secure confinement is overused in many instances where juveniles have been adjudicated (Kreisel et al., 2005). Surveys of incarcerated youth suggest that many do not need to be incarcerated. Over a third of all youths in state training schools probably belong in less secure settings. In more than a few jurisdictions, juvenile court judges may be exercising a rather heavy hand when meting out punishments and disposing of cases through secure custody rather than imposing alternative community-based punishments (Xiaoying, 2005). Increasingly emphasized, particularly as a cost-cutting measure, is focusing attention on methods or interventions that will reduce the recidivism rates of previously committed youth (Kreisel et al., 2005).

ASSESSMENT OF GUARDIANSHIP

While most cases that are furthered to the intake stage of the juvenile justice process involve some type of juvenile offending, criminal or otherwise, intake officers are often confronted with cases that require assessments of a youth's parents or guardians and the general sociocultural environment. Ordinarily, children in need of supervision (CHINS), including unruly or incorrigible youths, dependent and/or neglected youths, and abused children, are channeled by police officers to certain community agencies for special services and placement. Departments of Health and Human Services, social welfare agencies, and family crisis or intervention centers are frequently contacted and receive youths for further processing. However, if some youths in need of supervision are eventually subject to intake screenings, probation officers must evaluate the nature of one's needs and the seriousness of the situation before a disposition of the case is made. Beyond the broad classification of CHINS, many youths may have chemical dependencies that precipitated their delinquent conduct and require medical attention rather than punishment.

Examples of such youths include youthful male and female prostitutes who originally may have been runaways and/or incorrigible, alcohol- or drug-dependent youths who have turned to burglary and petty theft to support their dependencies, psychologically disturbed or mentally retarded juveniles, and sexually exploited children. If the facts disclosed at intake enable probation officers to make the strong presumption that certain youths should be diverted to human services shelters or community welfare agencies for treatment or temporary management, then this conditional disposition can be made of the case. This decision is often predicated upon the belief that a strong connection exists between the child's delinquency and physical, psychological, or sexual abuse received from adults or significant others (Ystgaard et al., 2004). Thus, it is imperative that early interventions be attempted with those considered to be at the greatest risk of chronic offending (McNeill and Batchelor, 2004).

SUMMARY

Once juveniles have been taken into custody or arrested by police for whatever reason, most jurisdictions process youths through intake. Intake is a preliminary screening stage for deciding which juveniles should be moved further into the juvenile justice system. Intake is performed either by persons hired for this specific purpose, or by juvenile probation officers who have been appointed to perform the intake function. Some jurisdictions, such as Florida, use assessment centers as screening mechanisms that operate in much the same way as intake. Many juveniles who enter the juvenile justice system are first-time offenders who have been charged with petty offenses. In these cases, intake officers have broad discretionary powers.

Intake officers may decide whether detained juveniles should be unconditionally released from the juvenile justice system; they may determine whether youths should be placed in the supervision of their parents or guardians; they may release youths temporarily pending a subsequent court appearance before a juvenile court judge; some youths may be referred to one or more community-based social services or counseling; some youths may be recommended for temporary detention pending an adjudicatory hearing; and/or some youths may be recommended for transfer to criminal court. One's parents and/or attorney may attend these proceedings and assist in the decision-making process.

There is little uniformity among jurisdictions relating to the intake process. Not all intake officers have the same discretionary powers. The nature of intake proceedings varies as well, especially as defense counsels have increased their involvement in juvenile matters. One important consequence of greater attorney involvement in juvenile affairs, largely through the greater rights acquired by juveniles through U.S. Supreme Court action or state court precedents, is greater formalization of the intake process. Formerly, when defense counsels were rarely involved with juvenile proceedings during intake, intake officers could be more informal with juveniles and their families. Their decisions were made for particular juveniles on a case-by-case basis. Although this informality would be considered inconsistent with due process today since it is inherently discriminatory, it nevertheless worked often to the juvenile's advantage, largely because intake officer decision making was lenient and mostly nominal, involving verbal warnings. With the greater intrusion of defense counsels, however, intake officers have become more concerned about complying with due process and making decisions broadly applicable to all juveniles, regardless of their individual circumstances. It seems unusual that the presence of defense counsel in juvenile matters at such an early stage of juvenile processing would tend to jeopardize their opportunities for lenient treatment. But this is precisely what seems to have been the outcome.

Some authorities have compared intake with plea bargaining. This is because informal negotiations may transpire between defense counsels and intake officers where agreements are made and strategies devised that enable many juveniles to avoid further contact with the juvenile justice system. Parents or guardians are frequently an integral part of this process, since they must agree to certain plea bargain–like terms as well that involve their youths. In spite of the greater formality of the intake process and defense counsel involvement, much individualization of case processing continues, as intake officers attempt to prescribe treatment strategies on a case-by-case basis that suit particular juvenile offenders. Like juvenile court judges, intake officers in many jurisdictions tend to perpetuate the *parens patriae* philosophy through their individualized decision making.

When decisions are made about juveniles, several factors influence these decisions. These factors are considered either legal or extralegal. Legal factors are usually objective criteria articulated by legislatures that must be scrupulously observed in juvenile decision making. Several legal variables crucial to decisions made about juvenile offenders include offense seriousness; type of crime committed; the presence or absence of inculpatory or exculpatory factors; prior record; and age. Offense seriousness may involve bodily injuries to one or more victims, or it may involve an offense against property. The type of crime committed often determines how juveniles are classified and suggests particular dispositions in delinquency adjudications. The presence of inculpatory evidence shows one's guilt or degree of involvement in the offenses alleged. Exculpatory evidence shows one's innocence. Both types of factors are given degrees of weight in determining whether delinquency allegations are subsequently supported in court. One's prior record is indicative of recidivism, which works to a youth's disadvantage. A youth's age is critical in determining whether particular punishments are imposed and also as a basis for evaluating one's culpability in the alleged offense. One's age may be a factor in determining whether the death penalty should be sought in a capital case or whether a youth should be transferred to criminal court for prosecution as an adult.

Extralegal factors are those that should not affect how juveniles are treated within the juvenile justice system. Nevertheless, it has been found that often, they are determinants of the type of treatment one receives. Extralegal factors include age, gender, race/ethnicity, and socioeconomic status. Age functions in a dual capacity. It is both a legal and an extralegal factor. Older juveniles are viewed as more accountable than more youthful offenders. However, as we will see in later chapters, the earlier the onset of delinquency, the more this age factor is weighted in determining the seriousness of the offense and the likelihood of reoffending. Persons who are extremely young may escape the juvenile justice system entirely, where social service agencies and other services will treat these youths rather than punish them because they are not considered accountable under the law.

One's gender functions in decision making as well. Often, female juveniles are adversely affected by decisions made by traditional juvenile court judges, who decide that these persons deserve confinement in a secure facility or in some other protected setting to preserve their virtue. Male offenders do not receive similar consideration under most circumstances. Male juveniles are more likely to be punished more severely than female juveniles for violent offending, however. Again, traditionalism and paternalism act in different ways to alter how juveniles are treated by juvenile court judges and other actors in the system. Race, ethnicity, and socioeconomic status work either directly or indirectly to influence one's life chances in the juvenile justice system. The evidence about the influence of race and ethnicity as it pertains to the differential treatment of juvenile offenders is mixed. Generally criminal justice professionals believe that racism and ethnic biases are exhibited in different ways throughout the juvenile justice system, either through more severe dispositions, or longer terms of confinement or probation or parole, or through more abrasive contacts with police officers on city streets. Socioeconomic status differences impact juveniles in less obvious ways. Those in the lower socioeconomic statuses are often represented by public defenders who are less motivated to work hard for their youthful clients. While this generalization doesn't apply to all public defenders, there is sufficient information available to show that the quality of one's representation is measured according to what one can afford. Less affluent youths also are more susceptible to harsher punishments or longer periods of confinement in secure or nonsecure facilities, or more lengthy probation or parole periods.

Preliminary decision making about youthful offenders may involve diversion, where a juvenile's case is temporarily removed from the juvenile justice system. Divertees are placed on a type of probation, although it is not known as such formally. They must complete several requirements for a period of time. The successful completion of diversion may be an expungement of one's juvenile record. Some juveniles are persistent offenders who may be either serious or nonserious. How should less serious offenders who chronically offend be treated? There are no easy answers to this question. More serious offenders may be incarcerated in secure facilities, although more than a few authorities believe that there is already too much juvenile incarceration. The tension between rehabilitation and lenient treatment on the one hand and the get-tough movement on the other persists.

QUESTIONS FOR REVIEW

1. What is the intake process? Who performs the intake officer role? What are the duties of intake officers?

2. How much discretion does an intake officer have? In what respects is intake compared with plea bargaining?

3. What is an assessment center? What are some general features of the Florida Assessment Center? What are some of its functions?

4. How has intake become increasingly formalized? How does the growing presence of defense counsels in juvenile matters increase intake formality?

5. How has the doctrine of *parens patriae* influenced the intake process?

6. What are several legal factors and how do they influence intake decision making?

7. What are several extralegal factors that influence decision making about juvenile offenders? Should extralegal factors be considered in any particular juvenile's case? Why or why not?

8. What types of juvenile offenders should be diverted from the juvenile justice system? Why?

9. Who are chronic and violent juvenile offenders? How should they be treated by the juvenile justice system?

10. Do we use incarceration too much for punishing juvenile offenders? Under what circumstances should incarceration be used? Which factors should determine whether a particular juvenile should be confined to an industrial school?

INTERNET CONNECTIONS

National Council on Juvenile and Family Court Judges
http://www.ncjfcj.org/

Peacefire.org
http://www.peacefire.org/

Safe and Responsive Schools Project
http://www.nasponline.org/publications/cq297safeschools.html

Teens, Crime, and the Community
http://www.nationaltcc.org/

Unusual Suspects Theatre Company
http://www.theunusualsuspects.org/index.html

CHAPTER 8 | *Prosecutorial Decision Making in Juvenile Justice*

Chapter Outline

Key Terms

Barker balancing test
confidentiality privilege

statute of limitations
with prejudice

without prejudice

Chapter Objectives

As the result of reading this chapter, you will realize the following objectives:

1. Understand the importance of defense counsels for juveniles charged with crimes.
2. Learn about the changing prosecutorial role relative to juvenile offenders.
3. Learn about important procedural safeguards to protect the privacy of juveniles, including rules governing photographing and fingerprinting juveniles, and making juvenile records accessible to the public.
4. Learn about the time restrictions governing juvenile offender processing.
5. Understand the speedy trial rights for juvenile offenders.
6. Understand the growing formality of juvenile offender processing and the greater adversarial nature of juvenile court proceedings.
7. Understand the importance of plea bargaining in juvenile cases.

• In Dayton, Nevada, Storey County District Attorney Howard Swafford filed third-degree felony arson charges against two 13-year-olds who allegedly started a fire in American Ravine that burned a Lyon County fire engine and threatened the lives of two volunteer firefighters near Silver City. One juvenile pleaded guilty in exchange for leniency and agreed to testify against the other teens. The juveniles are to be charged as adults and stand trial in the First District Court in Carson City. If convicted, the youths could be sentenced to 1–4 years in prison. Defense counsels for the two youths opposed the motion to have their clients tried as adults. In juvenile court, the youths could receive probation, confinement in a school for juvenile offenders for several years, or be ordered to perform community service. The parents of the boys are responsible for $10,000 in damages caused by them. [*Source:* Adapted from Laura Tennant, "Juveniles Charged with Felony Arson: Lyon Also Expects to Press Charges." *Reno Gazette-Journal,* August 29, 2003.]

• Ricky Mitchell was a 15-year-old New York juvenile suspected of committing armed robbery. Police officers went to Mitchell's high school and brought him to the police station for a lineup. Before the lineup, a detective called Mitchell's mother, who said that she was unable to attend, that she had a baby who needed her attention, and that Ricky had a lawyer. She asked the detective if he wanted the attorney's number. The detective advised Mrs. Mitchell that he was aware that Ricky was already represented by counsel in another matter pending before the court unrelated to the robbery. However, the detective did not attempt to contact Ricky's attorney or make it possible for him to attend the lineup. The lineup was held and Ricky was identified as the robber by an eyewitness. Ricky was tried in juvenile court for two counts of robbery in the first degree and in a jury trial, he was found guilty of these offenses. A motion by his attorney during the trial to suppress the lineup identification was denied. Ricky's attorney appealed on his behalf, contending that Ricky was denied the right to counsel during the lineup. An appellate court later upheld Ricky's robbery convictions, holding that there is no automatic entitlement to counsel in preaccusatory, investigatory lineups, including the context of juvenile delinquency proceedings. If a parent of an accused requests that counsel be present, then the police would be prevented from holding a lineup until the attorney appears. In this case, Ricky Mitchell's mother did not request an attorney for her son; she merely advised officers that he was represented by counsel in another unrelated matter. The suggestion that "counsel might be desired," or a query whether counsel should be obtained, is not considered a specific request for the presence of counsel at a lineup for a juvenile. [*Source: The People v. Ricky Mitchell,* _____NY2d_____, May 4, 2004.]

• *In the Spring of 2004 in New Haven, Connecticut, several unknown persons went on a shooting spree. The shootings began on early Sunday morning, with two persons being shot during a 15-minute period in the Newhallville section of New Haven. A third person was shot at on Congress Avenue later that afternoon but was uninjured. On Monday morning, three men were shot in the southern part of the city. A stolen car used in the shootings was recovered the following day. Bullet casings were found in the car and weapons were identified. Subsequently five persons were arrested in a car theft ring. Three adults and two juveniles were arrested on a variety of violent charges. The charges for both juveniles include five counts of 1st-degree assault; five counts of conspiracy to commit first-degree assault; criminal attempt to commit assault; six counts of unlawful discharge; carrying a concealed weapon without a permit; larceny in the first degree; and two counts of larceny in the second degree. They are being held on $5 million bonds. New Haven Police Chief Francisco Ortiz said the two juveniles face a long list of charges and speculated that the district attorney may charge them as adults.* [*Source:* Adapted from the Associated Press, "Police Arrest Two Adults in New Haven Shootings; Third, Two Juveniles to Face Charges." February 22, 2005.]

INTRODUCTION

A 13-year-old youth commits felony arson in the company of two other youths of the same age. He plea bargains for lenient treatment in exchange for his testimony against the other two youths who face being charged as adults so that they can stand trial in a criminal court. A 15-year-old youth is charged with armed robbery after being identified by an eyewitness. His attorney objects, contending that the boy was subjected to a police lineup without benefit of counsel when it was specifically requested. The objection is dismissed. Two juveniles are charged in a drive-by shooting, where they accompanied several adults who were operating a carjacking and car theft ring in a large city. Serious charges, including first-degree assault, carrying a concealed weapon, and larceny have been filed against them. How should the youths involved in these situations be treated? How much discretionary power should prosecutors have in deciding how and where these youths should be charged?

This chapter examines the role of juvenile court prosecutors. Like prosecutors in criminal courts, juvenile court prosecutors enjoy considerable discretionary powers in deciding whether to pursue particular charges against juvenile suspects. The chapter begins with an examination of the transformation of the prosecutorial role, especially the changes in this role resulting from the greater rights extended to juveniles by the U.S. Supreme Court. One of the rights extended to juveniles that has directly affected prosecutors is the standard of proof that must be used if prosecutors seek to incarcerate youthful offenders. The criminal standard of "beyond a reasonable doubt" has raised the bar concerning what prosecutors must prove in juvenile courts to make solid cases against juveniles charged with serious offenses.

Furthermore, juvenile court proceedings are usually open proceedings today, and greater public scrutiny occurs about what goes on during these proceedings. A third factor is the pervasive presence of defense counsels in over 90 percent of all juvenile cases. Juvenile court prosecutors must adhere to many of the same standards applicable to criminal court prosecutors in carrying forth proceedings against juvenile defendants. A fourth factor is that each state jurisdiction has imposed very rigorous time lines for conducting juvenile prosecutions. These time lines have created greater pressures on juvenile court prosecutors to move more quickly against youths suspected of crimes. These restrictions greatly limit evidence-gathering by investigators and others and developing solid prosecutable cases against charged youths. The changing role of juvenile court prosecutors is described.

The chapter next examines the advocacy role of public defenders and defense counsels generally who represent youthful clients in juvenile courts. The extensive presence of legal counsel for juveniles means that juvenile courts and the entire juvenile process must comport more fully with procedures and rules similar to those found in criminal courts. While juveniles are not entitled to speedy trials like adults, the time lines associated with scheduling juvenile court adjudicatory proceedings and other stages of juvenile defendant processing are accelerated and in fact are more immediate. One result is that juvenile case processing proceeds at a far more rapid rate than criminal cases. There are several reasons for accelerating the juvenile justice process, and these reasons are examined and explained.

Defense counsels are available for any juvenile defendant as a matter of right. There has been increased attorney use by juveniles over the most recent 30 years, and this upward trend continues. Defense counsels for juveniles do appear to make a difference in the outcomes of adjudicatory proceedings, and these differences are described. Defense counsels as advocates for juveniles also seek outcomes most favorable to their clients. Thus, defense counsels play a proactive role in seeking plea bargain arrangements with juvenile justice prosecutors. The nature and influence of the defense counsel role in plea bargaining are described. Working closely with some defense counsels are *guardians ad litem,* or special guardians appointed by the juvenile court to assist in ensuring that a juvenile's rights are observed. Parents are also involved to varying degrees in seeing to the legal needs of their children. The respective roles of *guardians ad litem* and parents are examined as they pertain to youthful defendants.

THE CHANGING PROSECUTORIAL ROLE IN JUVENILE MATTERS

Juvenile court prosecutors have had to make several adjustments in their orientation toward and treatment of juvenile defendants during the last several decades. As juveniles acquire more legal rights, prosecutors must be increasingly sensitive to these rights and constitutional safeguards and ensure that they are not violated. Constitutional rights violations can and will be challenged in the event of unfavorable juvenile court adjudications and/or sentences (Wilson and Petersilia, 2002).

For example, the standard of proof in juvenile proceedings, as well as the introduction of evidence against youths, are currently different compared with pre-*Gault* years. Defense counsel may now aggressively challenge the quality of evidence against youths and how it was obtained, the accuracy of confessions or other incriminating utterances made by youths while in custody and under interrogation, the veracity of witnesses, and whether juveniles understand the rights they are asked to waive by law enforcement officers and others. Competency hearings may be required before certain juveniles are subjected to an adjudicatory hearing (Burnett, Noblin, and Prosser, 2004; Rehling, 2005).

Modifying Prosecutorial Roles by Changing the Standard of Proof in Juvenile Proceedings

Regarding the standard of proof in juvenile courts prior to 1970, it was customary to use the preponderance of the evidence standard in determining whether a juvenile was delinquent. This was a far less stringent standard compared with criminal court proceedings, where the standard of proof used to determine a defendant's guilt is "beyond a reasonable doubt." On the basis of using the preponderance of evidence standard, juvenile court judges could find juveniles delinquent and order them incarcerated in industrial schools or detention facilities for more or less long periods. Thus, a loss of a juvenile's liberty rested on a finding by the juvenile court judge based on a relatively weak civil evidentiary standard.

However, the case of *In re Winship* (1970) resulted in the U.S. Supreme Court decision to require the beyond-a-reasonable-doubt standard in all juvenile court cases where the juvenile was in danger of losing his or her liberty. Although every juvenile court jurisdiction continues to use the preponderance of evidence standard for certain juvenile proceedings currently, these jurisdictions are required to use the criminal standard of beyond a reasonable doubt whenever an adjudication of delinquency can result in confinement or a loss of liberty.

Juveniles have benefited in at least one respect as the result of these new rights and standards of proof. These changed conditions have forced law enforcement officers, prosecutors, and judges to be more careful and discriminating when charging juveniles with certain offenses. However, changing the technical ground rules for proceeding against juveniles has not necessarily resulted in substantial changes in police officer discretion, prosecutorial discretion, or judicial discretion. Juveniles remain second-class citizens, in a sense, since they continue to be subject to street-level justice by police officers. Nevertheless, juveniles are entitled to almost all constitutional protections. This includes determining their competency to be adjudicated if this issue arises (Burnett, Noblin, and Prosser, 2004).

Despite the increased bureaucratization of juvenile courts, these courts continue to exhibit some of the traditionalism of the pre-*Gault* years. This means that relatively little change has occurred in the nature of juvenile adjudications. Juvenile court judges, with the exception of those few jurisdictions that provide jury trials for serious juvenile cases, continue to make adjudicatory decisions as they did prior to *In re Winship* (1970). Regardless of new evidentiary standards and proof of guilt requirements, these judges continue to exercise their individual discretion and decide whether one's guilt or delinquency has been established beyond a reasonable doubt. The fact is that nearly 80 percent of all states do not provide jury trials for juveniles in juvenile courts. Therefore, bench trials are used where the judge decides each case. We don't know how many judges are or are not complying with the beyond-a-reasonable-doubt standard, since these judges are exclusively the finders of fact. In one respect, at least, the *In re Winship* case was a somewhat hollow victory for juveniles in jeopardy of losing their liberty. The beyond-a-reasonable-doubt standard was established, but its use is dependent upon the subjective judgments of juvenile court judges.

For juvenile court prosecutors, changing the standard of proof to beyond a reasonable doubt made their cases harder to prove, even under bench trial conditions compared with jury trial conditions. Thus, the stage was set for greater use of plea bargaining in juvenile cases, especially when the evidence was weak and not particularly compelling. One important reason for weak evidence in juvenile cases is that in many jurisdictions, police officers do not regard juvenile offending as serious as adult offending. Therefore, evidence-gathering procedures relating to delinquent acts may not be as aggressive as evidence-gathering procedures relating to serious adult crimes. Lackluster evidence-gathering by police in juvenile delinquency cases may be explained by the fact that juvenile courts have exhibited extraordinary leniency toward juveniles, even where serious crimes were alleged and the evidence was strong. It is discouraging for police officers to see their best evidence-gathering efforts wasted when a juvenile court judge disposes an adjudicated juvenile delinquent to probation or some other lenient punishment.

For the most part, however, juvenile court prosecutors have adapted well to their changing roles as the juvenile court has gradually transformed (Massachusetts Statistical Analysis Center, 2001). The due process emphasis has prompted many prosecutors to prioritize their prosecutorial discretion according to one's offense history and crime seriousness. Nevertheless, this priority shift has not caused prosecutors to ignore potentially mitigating factors in individual juvenile cases, such as undue exposure to violence and domestic abuse (Jacobson, 2000).

Eliminating the Confidentiality of Juvenile Court Proceedings and Record-Keeping

Enhancing the accountability of juvenile courts is greater public access to them under the provisions of the First Amendment. This also applies to interjurisdictional requests for juvenile information among the states (Musser, 2001). During the 1990s, considerable changes have occurred regarding the confidentiality of juvenile court matters as well as juvenile records. Table 8.1 shows a summary of confidentiality provisions of the various states for 2005.

In 2005, for instance, 30 states had provisions for open hearings in juvenile or family court proceedings. Only eight states did not provide for the release of the names of those juveniles charged with serious offenses. Only two states did not permit court record releases to interested parties. In fact, all states currently make available juvenile court records to any party showing a legitimate interest. In such cases, information is ordinarily obtained through a court order. Fingerprinting and photographing of juveniles is conducted routinely in most states. Half the states require registration of all juvenile offenders when they enter new jurisdictions. Also, most states presently have state repositories of juvenile records and other relevant information about juvenile offending. Seventeen states prohibited sealing or expunging juvenile court records after certain dates, such as one's age of majority or adulthood. Therefore, juveniles today are considerably more likely to have their offenses known to the public. Open-records policies are increasingly favored by the public and juvenile justice professionals (Chambliss, Dohrn, and Drizin, 2000).

Kansas is an example of a state that made substantial changes in its confidentiality provisions governing juvenile offenders. The juvenile crime rate rose nationwide during the 1990s, and Kansas juvenile crime escalated accordingly during this same time interval. In an effort to hold juveniles more accountable

TABLE 8.1

Summary of Confidentiality Provisions Relating to Serious and Violent Juvenile Offenders, 2005

State	Open Hearing	Release of Name	Release of Court Record[a]	Statewide Repository[b]	Finger-printing	Photo-graphing	Offender Registration	Seal/Expunge Records Prohibited
Totals:	30	42	48	44	47	46	39	25
Alabama			•	•	•	•	•	
Alaska	•	•	•	•	•	•	•	•
Arizona	•	•	•	•	•	•	•	
Arkansas		•	•	•	•	•	•	
California	•	•	•	•	•	•	•	•
Colorado	•	•	•	•	•	•	•	
Connecticut								
Delaware	•	•	•	•	•	•	•	•
Dist. of Columbia			•		•	•		
Florida	•	•	•	•	•	•	•	•
Georgia	•	•	•	•	•	•	•	•
Hawaii	•	•	•	•	•	•	•	
Idaho	•	•	•	•	•	•	•	
Illinois		•	•	•	•	•	•	
Indiana	•	•	•	•	•	•	•	
Iowa	•	•	•	•	•	•	•	•
Kansas	•	•	•	•	•	•	•	•
Kentucky		•	•	•	•	•	•	
Louisiana	•	•	•	•	•	•	•	
Maine	•	•	•				•	
Maryland	•		•	•	•	•	•	
Massachusetts	•	•	•	•	•	•	•	
Michigan	•	•	•	•	•	•	•	•
Minnesota	•	•	•	•	•	•	•	•
Mississippi		•	•	•	•	•	•	
Missouri	•	•	•	•	•	•	•	
Montana	•	•	•	•	•	•	•	•
Nebraska		•	•	•	•			
Nevada	•	•	•	•	•	•	•	•
New Hampshire		•	•				•	
New Jersey		•	•	•	•	•	•	
New Mexico	•			•				
New York			•		•	•	•	
North Carolina			•		•	•	•	•
North Dakota		•		•	•	•	•	
Ohio			•	•	•	•	•	
Oklahoma	•	•	•	•	•	•	•	•
Oregon		•	•	•	•	•	•	•
Pennsylvania	•	•	•	•	•	•	•	
Rhode Island		•	•	•			•	
South Carolina					•	•	•	•
South Dakota	•	•	•	•	•	•	•	
Tennessee		•	•	•	•	•	•	

TABLE 8.1 (CONTINUED)

Summary of Confidentiality Provisions Relating to Serious and Violent Juvenile Offenders, 2005

State	Open Hearing	Release of Name	Release of Court Record[a]	Statewide Repository[b]	Finger-printing	Photo-graphing	Offender Registration	Seal/Expunge Records Prohibited
Texas	•	•	•	•	•	•	•	•
Utah	•	•	•	•	•	•	•	•
Vermont					•	•		
Virginia	•	•	•	•	•	•	•	•
Washington	•	•	•	•	•	•	•	•
West Virginia		•	•		•			•
Wisconsin	•	•	•	•			•	
Wyoming		•	•	•	•	•	•	•

Legend: • indicates the provision(s) allowed by each state as of the end of the 1997 legislative session.

[a]In this category, • indicates a provision for juvenile court records to be specifically released to at least one of the following parties: the public, the victims(s), the school(s), the prosecutor, law enforcement, or social agency; however, all states allow records to be released to any party who can show a legitimate interest, typically by court order.

[b]In this category, • indicates a provision for fingerprints to be part of a separate juvenile or adult criminal history repository.

Source: Patricia Torbet and Linda Szymanski, *State Legislative Responses to Violent Juvenile Crime: 1996–1997 Update.* Washington, DC.: U.S. Department of Justice, 1998:10.

Updated 2005 by author.

for their actions, the Kansas State Legislature demanded a more open juvenile justice system. Several measures to enhance accountability were established:

1. Parents of offenders younger than age 18 now may be assessed the cost of certain services, such as probation and out-of-home placement services; juvenile offenders age 18 and older can be assessed the costs.

2. Courts now may order families to attend counseling together.

3. Parents' health insurance policies now may be accessed to pay for their child's care while in state custody. Kansas previously paid for drug treatment and medical care expenses for juvenile offenders because most insurance policies did not cover these costs while a juvenile offender was in state custody.

4. Hearings for juvenile offenders age 16 and older are open to the public.

5. Official file records for juvenile offenders are open to the public (Musser, 2001:112–113).

The Kansas law now states that the official file shall be open for public inspection as to any juvenile 14 or more years of age at the time any act is alleged to have been committed or as to any juvenile less than 14 years of age at the time any act is alleged to have been committed except if the judge determines that opening the official file for public inspection is not in the best interest of such juvenile who is less than 14 years of age. Not all records are open. Personal history files, including reports and information the court receives, are privileged and only may be seen by the parties' attorneys and juvenile intake and assessment staff, or by order of a district court judge. Between 1995 and 2001, the Office of Juvenile Justice and Delinquency Prevention has noted that more states have made substantial changes with juvenile records, such as greater identification of juveniles, while others are considering making juvenile records available to the public (Musser, 2001:113). This means that the **confidentiality privilege** that juveniles have enjoyed for many decades is rapidly disappearing.

Open Juvenile Proceedings and Changing Judicial Conduct

The greater formality of juvenile proceedings as well as their openness to others may restrict the discretion of juvenile court judges, although this limitation is not particularly an undesirable one. Juvenile court judges have been known to make decisions that only incidentally related to one's alleged offense. For instance, Emerson (1969:88–89) reported that a juvenile court judge once ordered physical examinations for two 15-year-old girls who had been arrested for shoplifting (clothes) in a department store. Among other things, he wished to determine whether they had been sexually active. His motives were patently unclear, since knowing whether or not the girls had been sexually active is wholly unrelated to shoplifting. Nevertheless, the physicals were conducted, although it is unknown what the judge did with this information or how it was used in their adjudications and dispositions. Today, it is doubtful that many juvenile court judges would be able to get away with irrelevant and demeaning requests such as the one described by Emerson. The presence of a defense counsel representing the juvenile's interests and promoting due process would tend to deter judges from such conduct.

The Prosecution Decision Beyond 2000

The juvenile justice system has been notoriously slow in its case processing of juvenile offenders. In fact, delays in filing charges against juveniles and the eventual adjudicatory hearing are chronic in many jurisdictions. Juveniles arrested for various types of offenses may wait a year or longer in some jurisdictions before their cases are heard by juvenile court judges. Juvenile court prosecutors may delay filing charges against particular juveniles for a variety of reasons. Competency decisions must be made in certain cases where a youth's mental state is an issue (Burnett, Noblin, and Prosser, 2004). The most obvious reasons for delays—court caseload backlogs, crowded court dockets, insufficient prosecutorial staff, too much paperwork—are not always valid reasons. In many instances, the actors themselves are at fault. In short, prosecutors and judges may simply be plodding along at a slow pace, because of their own personal dispositions and work habits. It has been illustrated that in many jurisdictions where prosecutors and judges have aggressively tackled their caseload problems and forced functionaries to work faster, juvenile caseload processing has been greatly accelerated. Thus, the time between a juvenile's arrest and disposition has been greatly shortened because of individual decision making and not because of any organizational constraints or overwork (Butts and Halemba, 1996:73–91).

Another factor contributing to juvenile court delays is the sizeable increase in juvenile court caseloads. Many of these cases involve serious and

 **BOX 8.1**

INTERNATIONAL SNAPSHOT: JUVENILE JUSTICE IN BELIZE

Belize was established as a British Caribbean colony in 1950. During the next 30 years, Great Britain and Guatemala engaged in continuing discussions and conferences about the future and control of Belize. During this same period, the people of Belize sought independence from Great Britain and separation from all claims of territorial rights by Guatemala. Belize finally gained independence in 1981. When Belize was first established, its population was approximately 60,000. By 1970, it had doubled to 120,000. The 1991 census showed 200,000 persons living in Belize. By 2000 this figure had exceeded 250,000. The major economy of Belize consists of sugar, citrus, grain, and livestock production; tourism; and business.

Relatively little information is available about the nature and amount of juvenile delinquency in Belize, although the majority of juvenile offending consists of property crimes. As early as 1936 recognition was given to the problem of juvenile offending. Following Belize's creation in 1950, a Juvenile Offender Act was subsequently passed in 1958 and has undergone extensive revision and modification through 2003.

Juvenile offenders are under the broad jurisdiction of the Ministry of Human Development, Women and Children and Civil Society. The mission of the Ministry is to empower people by promoting, developing, and coordinating programs within the framework of a human development agenda that will enable Belizeans to become self-sufficient based on the principles of social justice, equality, and participation, thereby contributing to the process of national development.

Within the Ministry is the Department of Human Services. This department is the primary public sector agency with distinct offices and oversees a broad range of community projects; the administration of a social safety net, income support (social assistance), care of the elderly, programs for families and children, and disability services. It is headquartered in Belize City. Two divisions include the Family Services Division and Human Services.

The Family Services Division provides services to children and families, including child protection, foster care and adoptive services, local contact for missing and abducted children, education on parenting, and child advocacy relating to child rights. The division recognizes and respects the family as the first and best resource for children. Its programs are dedicated to strengthen and support families with children. Its services include family counseling and support; investigations of child abuse and neglect; placing children in protective custody or foster care; and parent empowerment through conducting classes on parenting skills.

Foster care services is a substitute family for all ages and sizes of children who need a safe and loving home. Families are prepared for the legal process of adoption. Parent empowerment encompasses skills and educational courses designed to enable families to fulfill their responsibilities for the care and protection of children. There are several child care centers for neglected, abused, and dependent children who are made wards of the court. The Human Services Division provides financial and other forms of assistance, such as assistance with groceries, clothing, school books, medical treatment, and social services.

Belize juveniles are (1) young persons who are age 16 or older and under age 18 or (2) children, defined as any person under the age of 16. Under the Juvenile Court Act of 2003, a juvenile court will hear cases involving children or young persons in separate rooms and on different days and times from those when other courts are sitting. Any person under the age of 18 and who appears before the juvenile court shall be under that court's jurisdiction. Physical separation from adult criminal offenders is mandated by the juvenile court. Whenever the juvenile court convenes, no one other than members and officers of the court and the parties to the case and their counsel will be allowed to attend. Newspaper agencies are excluded from these proceedings, and

(continued)

no person shall publish the names, addresses, schools, or photographs of a child or young person appearing in juvenile court. Thus, a strong confidentiality privilege exists to insulate youths from the adverse effects of delinquency labeling. Juvenile courts may order the pretrial detention of any alleged serious juvenile offender if the offender is charged with homicide or if such a person poses a threat to others. Bail is made available to those youths entitled to bail. Bail is denied under special circumstances if there is possible danger posed to others.

When juveniles are adjudicated in juvenile court, the juvenile court judge determines the disposition or measures to be imposed without consulting with the parents. For serious offenses, such as violent crimes, youths may be entitled to either a trial by the court or by a jury at their request. The law is explained to them as well as their options under the law. They may be represented by counsel. They may make statements in their own behalf, call witnesses, and cross-examine witnesses against them. Subsequently if the child or young person admits to the offense or if the judge determines that the offense was committed by the child or young person, mitigating and aggravating circumstances, if any, are identified.

Before exacting a particular measure, the judge will obtain a report from the Family Services Division concerning the youth's general conduct, home surroundings, school record, and medical history. A disposition is made in the best interests of the child or young person, and measures are imposed that might include educational programming or placement in detention. No child is subject to imprisonment. Fines may be imposed, and parents or guardians or counsel may appeal judicial decisions. No young person shall be imprisoned if it is determined that he or she can be suitably dealt with in any other way, whether by proba-

tion, fine, committal to a place of temporary detention or certified institution, or otherwise.

Juveniles qualify for custodial sentences if (1) they have a history of failure to respond to noncustodial penalties and are unwilling or unable to respond to them; (2) only a custodial sentence would be adequate to protect the public from serious harm or damage from him or her; or (3) the nature, gravity, or prevalence of the offense was such that a noncustodial sentence would not be appropriate. Children or young persons may be placed in detention under special circumstances as a last resort, where other measures and methods have failed to rehabilitate them.

The juvenile court has jurisdiction over what might be termed in the United States as status offenders, including those found begging; wandering about without a home and without a useful purpose or visible means of subsistence; orphans or destitute persons; youths in the care of parents or guardians who commit crimes or have drunken habits; or are offspring of one or both parents who have engaged in gross indecency.

A finding of guilt by a juvenile court may result in the following dispositions: (1) dismissal of the charge; (2) discharging offenders on their own recognizance; (3) releasing offenders on probation; (4) committing offenders to the care of a relative or other fit person; (5) sending offenders to certified institutions; (6) ordering parents or guardians to pay fines, damages, or costs; (7) ordering parents or guardians of the offender to give security for his or her good behavior; (8) committing the offender to a place of detention; (9) sentencing the offender to community service; or (10) dealing with a case in any manner in which it may be legally dealt with. The duration of sentences is indeterminate and dependent upon the successfulness of treatments, therapies, or interventions imposed.

[*Sources:* "Belize on the World Stage," Unpublished paper, Cubola Productions, 2005; "Functions of the Belize Judiciary," Unpublished paper, The Judicial System of Belize, 2005; *Juvenile Offenders Act,* Government of Belize, Revised Edition, 2003.]

violent offenses, as well as an ever-expanding number of drug offenses. In fact, the number of juvenile court cases involving drug offenses more than doubled between 1993 and 2000 (Stahl, 2001:1). For instance, drug offense cases accounted for 11 percent of all delinquency cases in 2000, compared with only 8 percent of all cases in 1993. The proportionate female juvenile involvement in drug cases increased from 14 to 16 percent between 1993 and 2000 as well. These types of cases take more time to resolve, simply because of their greater complexity. The juvenile courts have simply failed to keep pace with the growth of juvenile crime over the last few decades.

In 34 states in 2004, juvenile court prosecutors were at liberty to file charges against juvenile offenders whenever they decided (Office of Juvenile Justice and Delinquency Prevention, 2005). No binding legislative provisions were applicable to these actors to force them to act promptly and bring a youth's case before the juvenile court. In the meantime, 20 states have established time limits that cannot be exceeded between the time of a juvenile's court referral and the filing of charges by prosecutors. Table 8.2 shows various time limits imposed by various states for juvenile court adjudication and disposition of cases. For instance, in Minnesota, juvenile court prosecutors must file charges against juveniles within 30 days of their referral to juvenile court by police, if such juveniles are placed in secure confinement. These same prosecutors must file charges against undetained juveniles within 60 days following the juvenile's referral to juvenile court by police. In Maryland, prosecutors have 60 days to file charges against either detained or undetained juveniles following their court referrals. And in Georgia and Ohio, prosecutors must file charges within 10 days, if juveniles are being detained. A failure to file charges against juveniles in these jurisdictions within the time periods specified results in a dismissal of their cases **with prejudice,** meaning that the prosecutors cannot refile charges again at a later date against the same offenders (Butts and Sanborn, 1999).

Time Standards in Juvenile Court for Prosecutors and Other Actors

Establishing time standards for accomplishing various procedures within the juvenile justice process are not new. As early as 1971, various organizations were at work to encourage the juvenile justice system to process cases more quickly. It was believed at the time that only legislatively created time standards would cause police, intake officers, prosecutors, and judges to take faster action in processing juvenile offenders.

Butts (1996b:544–547) notes, for instance, that the Joint Commission on Juvenile Justice Standards led the way in 1971 with early time standards for juvenile processing. A product of the Institute of Judicial Administration (IJA) and the American Bar Association (ABA), the IJA/ABA Project convened periodically over the next several years and issued 27 different volumes during the years 1977–1980. The standards promulgated by the IJA/ABA Project were intended as guidelines for juvenile courts and the juvenile justice system generally. The Commission formed through the IJA/ABA Project was guided by the principle that juvenile court cases should always be processed without unnecessary delay (Butts, 1996a:545).

TABLE 8.2

Time Limits (in Days) for Juvenile Court Adjudication and Disposition Hearings, in Cases *Not* Involving Proceedings for Transfer to Criminal Court[a]

State	Court Referral	Start of Adjudication Deadline — Filing of Charges (det/not det)	Preliminary Hearing (det/not det)	Detention Admission	Detention Hearing	Start of Disposition Deadline — Filing of Charges (det/not det)	Adjudication (det/not det)
Alaska							Immed.[b]
Arizona			30/60				30/45
Arkansas					14		14/—
California	30	30[b]		15			
Delaware				30[c]			
Florida		21/90[c]					15/—
Georgia		10/60					30/—
Illinois		120[b,c]		10[c]			
Iowa		60[b,d]					ASAP[b]
Louisiana			30/90				30[b]
Maryland		60[b]		30			30[b]
Massachusetts	60						
Michigan		180[b]		63			35/—
Minnesota		30/60					15[c]/45[c]
Mississippi		90/—		21			14/—
Montana							ASAP[b]
Nebraska		180/—				180[c]	
New Hampshire		21/30					21/30
New Jersey				30			30/60
New Mexico							20/—
New York			14/60				10/50
North Dakota		30[b]		14			
Ohio		10/—					Immed.[b]
Oregon	56			28			28[c]
Pennsylvania		10/—					20/—
Rhode Island				7			
South Carolina		40[b]					
Tennessee		—/90		30			15/90
Texas		10/—					
Vermont		15/—					30[b]
Virginia		—/120		21			30/—
Washington		30[b]/60[b]					14/21
Wisconsin			20[e]/30[e]			10[e]/30[e]	10/30
Wyoming					60		

[a]Twenty states did not have time limits for adjudication as of 1993: AL, AK, CO, CT, DC, HI, ID, IN, KS, KY, ME, MO, MT, NV, NM, NC, OK, SD, UT, and WV. Twenty-six states did not have time limits for dispositions: AL, CA, CO, CT, DE, DC, HI, ID, IL, IN, KS, KY, ME, MA, MO, NV, NC, ND, OK, RI, SC, SD, TX, UT, WV, and WY.
[b]Statute did not distinguish detention status.
[c]Extensions are possible.
[d]If statutory right to speedy trial is waived.
[e]Statute-specified time from "plea hearing."
Source: Butts, 1996b: 557–558. Data source: analysis by the National Center for Juvenile Justice. Reprinted by permission of the American Journal of Criminal Law and the authors. Updated 2005 by author.

BOX 8.2

Ian J. McDonough
Supervisor, Intensive Supervision Unit, Kootenai County Juvenile Probation, ID

Statistics:

B.A. (criminal justice and sociology, political science), Washington State University; POST-Certified, Idaho; graduate, Washington State Security Worker's Academy; 2002 Line Worker of the Year—Idaho Juvenile Justice Association

Background and Interests

I was born and raised in Tacoma, Washington, where I attended Bellarmine Preparatory High School. Because I did not have a career in mind when I graduated from high school, I took a job as an airplane refueler at the Seattle/Tacoma International Airport. Although this job was interesting, I wanted a change, and so I decided to take some classes at Tacoma Community College. One of the classes I took was an entry-level criminal justice class. I enjoyed the subject matter and was an active participant in class discussions. Eventually I began speaking with the professor of this class regarding my interest in a career in law enforcement. I was very intrigued when he began discussing the job duties of a parole/probation officer and I was impressed with the diversity of responsibilities involved in this position.

I attended Washington State University and majored in criminal justice and sociology, with a minor in political science. While attending college I accepted a job working with developmentally delayed young adults. I always felt that I had a knack for dealing with young people, and my experiences in this job confirmed it. I began focusing more on occupations that involved working with juveniles. After graduating from Washington State University, I had difficulty finding an entry-level opportunity in a probation department. I was advised by many that I would increase my employment chances as a probation officer either by working in a related field first to gain more experience or by doing volunteer work. I ended up accepting a job at the Region I Juvenile Detention Center in Kootenai County, Idaho. After a few years at the detention center, I was hired by Kootenai County Juvenile Probation as a probation officer assistant. Several months later, I was offered the position of probation officer and I have been with Kootenai County Juvenile Probation ever since. I enjoy my job and the people I work with very much. Several months ago, I was promoted to supervising probation officer of the Intensive Supervision Unit.

Work Experiences

The profession of "juvenile probation officer" can be very exciting and rewarding. Although it is not necessarily a high-paying profession, I have found that you can earn a good salary. The working environment has changed even in my short time in this line of work. With the introduction of gangs, the increase of methamphetamine use, along with other changes in our society, the job has become increasingly hazardous. I have been threatened by probationers and parents, and unfortunately I have been involved in physical altercations on the job. When I first started as a probation officer, I would see probationers involved in offenses such as battery, petit theft, and status offenses. Although these offenses are still prevalent, we are seeing an increase in the severity of offenses committed by our offenders, including murder, arson, rape, drug trafficking, and much more. Our department's case management philosophy is based on the balanced approach components of public safety, accountability, and competency development. Often one component of the balanced approach outweighs another, and the probation officer has to adapt to each case independently.

(continued)

When I began my career as a probation officer in Kootenai County, I started in our Standard Unit. Many of the probationers on my caseload were entry-level into the juvenile justice system. The caseloads were higher in this unit and I averaged about 70 cases. I would see each probationer an average of once every two weeks. A few years ago I moved to the Intensive Unit. The juveniles placed on the Intensive Unit tend to have had a longer stay in our justice system. Many of their offenses have escalated, and the probationers require more contact from their probation officer. A lot of the probationers on the Intensive Unit have been (or are) committed to the Department of Juvenile Corrections, where they are placed in secure facilities an average of eight or nine months (some for several years) before reentering our community.

What I like most about my job is the varying responsibilities that encompass being a probation officer. I spend half my time in the office and the other half in the field. Office duties generally involve answering/making telephone calls, entering information into our database, and preparing/writing reports for court proceedings. Field work consists of home visits, school visits, court proceedings, and much more. I also conduct a variety of collateral contacts to make sure that my probationers are attending and participating in counseling, community service projects, and other commitments. We are also expected to work closely with the judges, prosecutors, and police officers.

The duties of a probation officer can be exciting, stressful, and monotonous at times. You must be able to work in an autonomous setting and make good decisions in a split second. I believe many attributes that make up a good probation officer can be learned over time, but I do believe that you need to be able to work/communicate effectively with people from the very beginning. I believe that it is equally important that you are able to work with people in a respectful manner, even when that respect is not reciprocated by your clients and their families.

When working in this field, you see sadness, anger, depression, and dysfunction every day. I have seen many probation officers burn out because they were unable to cope with these working conditions. If you want to make a long career out of this profession, I think that it is important to have a good sense of humor and the ability to keep things in perspective. Having a good relationship with my co-workers and being able to laugh at myself and with others has helped me through many stressful times.

Advice to Students

If you are currently trying to obtain employment as a parole/probation officer, then (1) be open to volunteering within a department—the investment of your time could pay off; and (2) be open to working in a field related to parole/probation; I am not saying that obtaining a job as a parole/probation officer directly out of college cannot happen, but it can be difficult.

Once you obtain employment as a parole/probation officer: (1) always return your telephone calls; (2) be consistent; (3) when developing case plans, make sure expectations are realistic for your probationers; (4) document everything—although some information may not seem important when you first hear it, it could be extremely important several months later when you are at a court hearing; (5) be confident, not arrogant; (6) network with other agencies; and (7) be organized.

The IJA/ABA standards relating to processing juveniles were as follows (Butts, 1996a:546):

Time	Action
2 hours	Between police referral and the decision to detain
24 hours	Between detention and a petition justifying further detention
15 days	Between police referral and adjudication (if youth is detained)
30 days	Between police referral and adjudication (if youth is not detained)

| 15 days | Between adjudication and final disposition (if youth is detained) |
| 30 days | Between adjudication and final disposition (if youth is not detained) |

Notice that in these time guidelines, law enforcement officers are not given much time to detain youths once they have been taken into custody. Once police officers have referred a youth to juvenile court, only 2 hours is recommended in order for a decision to be made about detaining the youth. If a youth is detained, then only 24 hours are allowed between the start of one's detention and filing a petition to justify further detention. And depending on whether youths are detained or undetained, the time limits recommended are either 15 or 30 days, respectively, between detention and adjudication. These guidelines are rather rigorous compared with the traditional sluggishness of juvenile offender processing. Table 8.2 shows that only a handful of states thus far have adopted these or more rigorous standards for filing charges against juveniles (e.g., Georgia, Ohio, Pennsylvania, Texas, and Vermont).

Butts (1996b:547) also notes that similar time limits for juvenile processing were recommended contemporaneously by the National Advisory Committee for Juvenile Justice and Delinquency Prevention in 1980. These limits are shown below (Butts, 1996b:546–547):

Time	**Action**
24 hours	Between police referral and the report of intake decision (if youth is detained)
30 days	Between police referral and the report of intake decision (if youth is not detained)
24 hours	Between detention and detention hearing
2 days	Between intake report and the filing of a petition by the prosecutor (if detained)
5 days	Between intake report and the filing of a petition by the prosecutor (if not detained)
5 days	Between filing of the petition and the initial arraignment hearing
15 days	Between filing of the petition and adjudication (if detained)
30 days	Between filing of the petition and adjudication (if not detained)
15 days	Between adjudication and final disposition

Again, the National Advisory Committee gave little latitude to juvenile court prosecutors in dispatching juvenile cases. In this particular arrangement of scenarios, however, the intake stage was addressed, and rather strongly. Not only were prosecutors obligated to file petitions against specified juveniles more quickly following intake, but intake officers were required to make their assessments of juveniles and file reports of these assessments within a 2-day period. One major difference in the National Advisory Committee recommendations and guidelines was the fact that if certain actors in the juvenile justice system did not comply with these time standards, then cases against certain juveniles could be dismissed, but **without prejudice.** This meant that juvenile court prosecutors could resurrect the original charges and refile them with the juvenile court at a later date. Thus, no particularly compelling constraints were placed on either intake officers or prosecutors to act in a timely manner, according to this second set of standards. However, we must recognize that neither the

Many juveniles are taken to local sheriff's departments or police stations and held until they can be placed with parents or guardians.

IJA/ABA time guidelines nor the National Advisory Committee guidelines are binding on any state jurisdiction. They are set forth as strongly recommended guidelines for juvenile court officials to follow.

Why Should the Juvenile Justice Process Be Accelerated?

Several compelling arguments are made for why juvenile justice should be applied quickly. Butts (1996b:525–526) makes compelling arguments that adolescence is a critical period wherein youths undergo many changes. Maturational factors seem especially accelerated, while one's personality and response to peer pressures are modified and enhanced in diverse ways. A month may seem like a year to most adolescents. Secure confinement of 24 hours is a serious deprivation of one's freedom. When some juvenile cases undergo protracted delays of up to a year or longer, it is difficult for many youths to accept their subsequent punishment for something they did long ago. More than a few juveniles have grown out of delinquency by the time their cases come before the juvenile court, and they wonder why they are now being punished for something they did when they were younger.

Studies of juvenile justice system delays disclose that the size of a jurisdiction plays an important part in how fast juvenile cases are concluded. In 1985, for example, the median number of days it took to process juvenile cases in a large sample of U.S. county jurisdictions was about 44 days. By 1994, the median processing time in these same counties was 92 days (Butts and Halemba, 1996:131). For smaller jurisdictions with fewer and presumably less serious cases to process, case processing time ranged from 34 to 83 days in 1994, while larger counties took from 59 to 110 days to complete juvenile case processing.

These juvenile justice processing delays parallel criminal court processing of adult defendants. We might be inclined to accept these long juvenile justice delays if the cases processed were sufficiently serious to warrant more court time. However, only about 17 percent of all cases handled by both small and large county jurisdictions involved serious or person offenses in 1994 (Butts and Halemba, 1996:129).

Therefore, it has been recommended that juvenile justice case processing time should be decreased so as to move the disposition closer to the time when the offense was committed. Juveniles should be able to relate whatever happens to them in court later to the offense they committed earlier. In more than a few instances, juveniles awaiting trial on one charge have had subsequent opportunities to reoffend. When they are arrested for new offenses before being adjudicated for earlier offenses, their cognitive development may inhibit their understanding of the process and their disposition (Butts, 1996b:525).

Shine and Price (1992) provide two important reasons for why juvenile cases should be processed quickly. These reasons are:

1. In order to maximize the impact upon the juvenile that he or she has been caught in a criminal act, that he or she will be held accountable for what he or she has done, and that there will be consequences for this action, it is important that the case be resolved quickly. If the case continues too long, the impact of the message is diluted, either because the juvenile has been subsequently arrested for other offenses and loses track of just what it is that he or she is being prosecuted for or because the juvenile has not engaged in any further delinquent acts and feels that any consequences for the past offense are unfair.

2. If there are victims, then unwarranted delays in juvenile case processing are unfair and damaging to victims. Many victims suffer some type of financial loss or physical injury. Expenses are incurred. Faster resolutions of juvenile court cases can lead to more rapid compensation and victim restitution plans imposed by the court. Such compensation of victim restitution can do much to alleviate any continued suffering victims may endure.

PUBLIC DEFENDERS FOR JUVENILES

Greater procedural formality in the juvenile justice system has occurred with respect to the appointment of public defenders for juveniles who are indigent. Every juvenile court jurisdiction provides public defenders for juveniles and their families who cannot afford to appoint private counsel, especially in more serious cases where incarceration in secure confinement facilities is a strong possibility. Formerly, defense counsels for juveniles often were the juvenile's probation officer or a social caseworker with a vested interest in the case. It is not entirely clear how these officers and workers were able to separate their law enforcement and defense functions to avoid allegations of conflicts of interest. But little interest in the quality of defense of juvenile cases was exhibited by the public in previous years anyway. While some persons believe that juveniles are now insulated to some extent from the whims of juvenile court prosecutors and judges, others suspect that defense attorneys have in some instances made it more difficult for juveniles to receive fair treatment (Juvenile Justice Center, 2001).

During intake, it has been found that the presence of attorneys, who represent juveniles' interests and attempt to protect them so that their full range of constitutional rights are observed at each stage of the juvenile justice process, actually detract from the informal nature of intake. Intake officers change these proceedings into formal hearings, and recommendations for subsequent dispositions might be more severe than if defense attorneys were not present. In fact, intake officers have openly discouraged juveniles and their parents from availing themselves of an attorneys' services at this stage, since their presence hampers informal adjustments of cases and limits a youth's informal compliance with informal probationary conditions. In some cases, intake officers consider themselves the primary source of a youth's understanding of legal rights, although a recommendation that these officers receive more training and preparation in law and juvenile rights suggests that their own understanding of the law merits improvement.

In a growing number of instances, many cases are being diverted to victim–offender mediation, where various nonprofit, private organizations receive referrals from juvenile courts. The intent of such victim–offender mediation is to reach a resolution of differences between victims and offenders without subjecting offenders to juvenile court and its adverse labeling impact. In those communities with mediation programs, there is support from community residents. Financial support in the form of grants is provided by local, state, and federal grants. Mediators may be interested citizens, retired judges, community leaders, or even intake officers who undertake these tasks during nonworking hours (Lightfoot and Umbreit, 2004).

Despite these alternatives to juvenile court action, it is true that juvenile court proceedings have become increasingly formalized. Furthermore, public access to these proceedings in most jurisdictions is increasing. Thus, the presence of defense counsel, an adversarial scenario, a trial-like atmosphere where witnesses testify for and against juvenile defendants, and adherence to Rules of Procedure for Juvenile Courts are clear indicators of greater formalization, bureaucratization, and criminalization, as Feld (2001) has suggested.

Two problems have been highlighted relating to the use of public defenders in juvenile courts. These problems include the limited resources and growing caseloads of public defenders for juveniles in many jurisdictions. A study examined the access to counsel in selected states and local juvenile delinquency proceedings (U.S. General Accounting Office, 1995b). Data sources were relevant state statutes, state administrative procedures, and case law in 15 states; National Council on Juvenile Justice statistics for three states; national surveys of county prosecutors and public defenders; telephone interviews with selected state and local judges in eight states; and site visits to juvenile justice officials in four states. Statutes guaranteeing a juvenile's right to counsel were found in all 15 states examined. Overall, the rate of defense counsel representation for juveniles varied from 65 percent in Nebraska to 97 percent in California. Representation by offense category varied, as did the overall impact of representation on case outcomes. In most cases where juveniles were not represented by counsel, juveniles were less likely to receive out-of-home placements, such as a disposition to an industrial school. This shouldn't be interpreted to mean that defense counsel cause more juveniles to receive out-of-home placements. Rather, a better explanation is that defense counsel were not used in the least serious cases, those that didn't merit placement in an institution anyway. Prosecutors and juvenile justice officials were generally pleased with the quality of counsel provided to juveniles, apart from their concerns about scarce resources and growing caseloads (U.S. General Accounting Office, 1995b).

THE SPEEDY TRIAL RIGHTS OF JUVENILES

Juveniles have no federal constitutional right to a speedy trial (Butts and Sanborn, 1999). The U.S. Supreme Court has not decided any juvenile case that would entitle a juvenile to a speedy trial commensurate with adults in criminal courts. Criminal defendants are assured a speedy trial through the Sixth Amendment and the leading 1972 case of *Barker v. Wingo* (see Box 8.3). This case led to the establishment of the **Barker balancing test.** Each state and the federal government has established speedy trial procedures that establish time standards between different events, such as between the time of arrest and initial appearance, between one's initial appearance and arraignment, and between one's arraignment and trial. The federal government uses a 100-day standard. New Mexico is perhaps the most liberal, providing a 180-day period. Many states have adopted the federal standard.

For juveniles, standards vary among jurisdictions between comparable stages of juvenile justice processing, such as between arrest and intake, between intake and prosecutorial decision making and case filing, between case filing and adjudication, and between adjudication and disposition. However, some state legislatures have provided time standards that proscribe different maximum time limits between each of these events. As of 1993, for instance, 30 states provided some form of time limit for adjudications following arrests. Twenty-six states did not have time limits between adjudications and dispositions of juveniles. And only a handful of state courts have recognized some form of speedy trial rights for accused juveniles (Butts, 1996b:553, 558).

Jeffrey Butts (1996b:554) recommends that youths facing adjudication for delinquent offenses should be vested with the same speedy trial rights as adults. Thus, a federal constitutional right to a speedy trial for juvenile defendants would send the message that efficient case processing is an essential element in the overall effectiveness of the juvenile justice system. Often, juvenile court actors themselves can greatly enhance juvenile case processing by their own behaviors. Juvenile court judges are particularly powerful entities, and their decision making can be far-reaching, extending back to the time of juvenile arrests and intake proceedings, as well as forward to prosecutorial filings, adjudicatory proceedings, and disposition hearings.

It seems that the longer juveniles remain within the juvenile justice system, the more adverse the consequences for their subsequent recidivism and seriousness of offending. One reason juvenile case processing has been sluggish is that the doctrine of *parens patriae* has been pervasive, suggesting rehabilitation over other themes, such as punishment, crime control, or due process. According to the *parens patriae* concept, juvenile courts need a certain amount of time to provide for the needs of youths drawn into the system. If insufficient time is allocated for rehabilitation, then rehabilitation will not occur. However, the U.S. Supreme Court has characterized the doctrine of *parens patriae* as "murky" and of "dubious historical relevance" in the case of *In re Gault* (1967). The U.S. Supreme Court also declared in *Gault* that juveniles do not need to give up their due process rights under the Fourteenth Amendment in order to

BOX 8.3

DO JUVENILES HAVE A RIGHT TO A SPEEDY TRIAL?

The Case of Barker v. Wingo. Barker and another person were alleged to have shot an elderly couple in July 1958. They were arrested later and a grand jury indicted them in September 1958. Kentucky prosecutors sought 16 continuances to prolong the trial of Barker. Barker's companion, Manning, was subjected to five different trials, where a hung jury was found except in the fifth trial, where Manning was convicted. Then, Barker's trial was scheduled. During these five trials, Barker made no attempt to protest or to encourage a trial on his own behalf. After scheduling and postponing Barker's trial for various reasons, his trial was finally held in October 1963 when he was convicted. He appealed, alleging a violation of his right to a speedy trial. The U.S. Supreme Court heard the case and declared that since from every apparent factor, Barker did not want a speedy trial, he was not entitled to one. The case significance is that if you want a speedy trial, you must assert your privilege to have one. Defendants must assert their desire to have a speedy trial in order for the speedy trial provision to be invoked and for Amendment rights to be enforceable. In Barker's case, the U.S. Supreme Court said that Barker was not deprived of his due process right to a speedy trial, largely because the defendant did not desire one (at 2195).

The present standard, known as the Barker balancing test, consists of four factors. These are:

1. The length of the delay between charging the defendant and the defendant's trial

2. The reason for the delay

3. The defendant's assertion of his or her due-process right to a speedy trial

4. The existence of prejudice to the defendant by prosecutorial and/or judicial actions.

Source: Barker v. Wingo, 407 U.S. 514, 92 S.Ct. 2182 (1972).

derive juvenile justice system benefits because of their status as juvenile offenders, such as the greater concern for their well-being supposedly inherent in juvenile court proceedings. Instead, the U.S. Supreme Court suggested the due process principles of fairness, impartiality, and orderliness were of paramount importance in contrast with the *parens patriae* philosophy. Essentially the U.S. Supreme Court has acted to bring the juvenile court system under constitutional control.

Examinations of juvenile court prosecutorial opinions about the effectiveness of juvenile court processing indicate that in at least some jurisdictions, such as Illinois, prosecutors perceive juvenile courts to be relatively ineffective at rehabilitating juveniles (Ellsworth, Kinsella, and Massin, 1992). These prosecutors believe that probation services are most vital to a youth's rehabilitation, and that specific community programs and services intended to prevent delinquency are either inadequate, nonexistent, or ineffective. Specific sectors of the community were targeted as most important by these prosecutors. They believe that greater juvenile court intervention should occur in school matters. All things considered, however, these prosecutors believe that their rehabilitative impact in specific juvenile cases becomes less effective as their involvement in such cases increases. Again, this suggests moving youths through the system more quickly to minimize their exposure to the process.

THE ADVOCACY ROLE OF DEFENSE ATTORNEYS

For especially serious juvenile offender cases, defense attorneys are increasingly useful and necessary as a means of safeguarding juvenile rights and holding the juvenile justice system more accountable regarding its treatment of juvenile offenders. For instance, it is important for defense counsel to advise their clients about the **statute of limitations** associated with various offenses, where the government can bring charges within specified time periods following the crime's occurrence. Some crimes, like murder, have no statute of limitations, and thus, there is an indefinite period of time when the state can bring charges against a potential defendant. Widespread abuse of discretion by various actors throughout all stages of the juvenile justice process is well documented. The intrusion of defense attorneys into the juvenile justice process, under a new due-process framework, is anticipated as a logical consequence of the rights juveniles have obtained from the U.S. Supreme Court (Burruss and Kempf-Leonard, 2002).

Attorneys for Juveniles as a Matter of Right

Although juveniles are entitled to the services of attorneys at all stages of juvenile proceedings, some investigators have shown that about half of all youths processed in the juvenile justice system are not represented by counsel (Feld, 2001). Shortly after the *Gault* decision in 1967, the Minnesota legislature mandated the assistance of counsel for all juveniles in delinquency proceedings. It was believed that making provisions for defense counsel would maximize the equitable treatment of youths by Minnesota juvenile courts. However, Feld's (1988) analysis of 17,195 cases involving adjudications of delinquency in 1986 found that only about half of all juveniles adjudicated delinquent in these Minnesota juvenile courts had attorneys to represent them.

Analyzing adjudication data from an earlier period in five other jurisdictions besides Minnesota, Feld (1988) discovered similar figures. Roughly half of all juveniles adjudicated delinquent in these state juvenile courts had legal representation at the time of their adjudications. It is unclear whether the juveniles who did not have defense counsel also did not request defense counsel. It would have been inconsistent with *Gault* as well as unconstitutional if these juveniles had requested defense counsel and been denied it in those jurisdictions. But Feld may have provided at least two plausible explanations for this finding. He found that juveniles who were represented by attorneys in each of these jurisdictions, and who were also adjudicated as delinquent, tended to receive harsher sentences and dispositions from juvenile court judges compared with those juveniles who did not have defense counsel to represent them. Thus, it would seem that the presence of defense counsel in juvenile courts, at least in those jurisdictions examined by Feld, actually aggravated the dispositional outcome rather than mitigated it. An alternative explanation is that the more serious offenders in those jurisdictions were more likely to acquire counsel. Thus, they would logically receive harsher sentences compared with less serious offenders, if they were ultimately adjudicated as delinquents.

Subsequent to Feld's research, the presence of defense counsel in juvenile proceedings has escalated dramatically. Although there continue to be regional variations in the proportionate representation of juveniles by defense counsel,

especially rural areas contrasted with urban areas, the overall trend has been toward increased attorney representation. With the presence of defense counsel
in juvenile proceedings becoming increasingly commonplace, it is also likely
that the adverse impact of defense attorneys on the outcomes of these proceedings has lessened accordingly (Burruss and Kempf-Leonard, 2002).

Defense Counsel and Ensuring Due-Process Rights for Juveniles

The manifest function of defense attorneys in juvenile courts is to ensure that
due process is fulfilled by all participants. Defense attorneys are the primary
advocates of fairness for juveniles who are charged with crimes or other types
of offenses. Minors, particularly very young youths, are more susceptible to the
persuasiveness of adults. Law enforcement officers, intake officers, and prosecutors might extract incriminating evidence from juveniles in much the same
way as police officers and prosecutors might extract inculpatory information
from suspects in criminal cases, provided that certain constitutional safeguards
were not in place. For adults, a major constitutional safeguard is the Miranda
warning, which, among other things, advises those arrested for crimes of their
right to an attorney, their right to terminate police interrogations whenever they
wish and remain silent, their right to have their attorneys present during questioning, and the right to have an attorney appointed for them if they cannot afford one (Sanborn, 2001).

Some persons believe that the U.S. Supreme Court has always supported
the *parens patriae* nature of juvenile courts, and that their purportedly liberal
decisions about juvenile constitutional guarantees have been intended only to
provide minimal procedural protections. Nevertheless, the possibilities of incarceration in secure juvenile incarcerative facilities and/or transfer to criminal
court jurisdiction where harsher penalties may be administered are sufficient to
warrant the intervention of defense counsel in many juvenile cases (Feld,
2001). At the very least, defense counsel may prevent some youths from being
railroaded into accepting unnecessary conditional interventions from intake officers or juvenile court judges. It is not the intention of defense attorneys to aggravate matters and cause their juvenile clients to receive harsher punishments
than they would normally receive from the same judges if defense counsel
weren't present. But it is a curious paradox that those seeking justice and due
process and who exercise their rights for these aims are often penalized for exercising these rights.

In many respects, this paradox is similar to the disparity in sentencing
among those who have similar criminal histories and are convicted for the same
offenses, but who receive widely disparate sentences depending on whether
their convictions are obtained through plea bargaining or a jury verdict in a
criminal trial. There is no particular reason for judges to impose harsher punishments on convicted offenders who exercise their right to a jury trial
compared with those who enter into plea agreements and plead guilty, but differential punishments are frequently administered. One explanation, an extralegal and nonlegal one, is that the extra punishment is the penalty for obligating
the state to prove its case against the defendant in open court. Being aware of
this type of sentencing disparity, many defense attorneys counsel their clients,
especially where there is strong inculpatory evidence, to plead guilty to lesser
charges and accept a lesser penalty to avoid more severe punishments that

judges almost certainly will impose upon conviction through a trial. It would appear from the available evidence that juvenile court judges may be guilty of the same behavior when relating to juvenile clients who are represented by counsel and those who are not. For the present, anyway, being represented by counsel in juvenile court seems more of a liability than an asset (Burruss and Kempf-Leonard, 2002).

Are Attorneys Being Used More Frequently by Juvenile Defendants?

Yes. At least a survey of five states during the 1980–1995 period (California, Montana, Nebraska, North Dakota, and Pennsylvania) found that attorney use by juvenile offenders increased systematically across these years (Champion, 1999). Attorney use varies by jurisdiction, however. In the mid-1990s, over 90 percent of all California juvenile cases involved either private or publicly appointed defense counsel. However, in states such as Nebraska and North Dakota, attorney use by juveniles occurred in about 60 percent of the cases.

It may seem that whenever youths invoke their right to an attorney, it would be under circumstances where the offenses alleged are serious or violent. While it is true that attorney use was more prevalent in these states where serious and violent offenses were alleged, it is also true that attorney use increased during the 10-year period for status offenders and those charged with public order, property, and drug offenses as well. The primary implication of this research is that juvenile courts are experiencing greater defense attorney involvement each year. If these states are representative of all U.S. jurisdictions, then the formalization of juvenile courtrooms is definitely increasing with greater involvement of defense counsel in juvenile cases.

Do Defense Counsel for Juveniles Make a Difference in Their Case Dispositions?

The use of defense counsel by juveniles results in mixed outcomes. In some instances, because of the greater formality of the proceeding because defense counsel are present, outcomes occur that may be unfavorable to juvenile defendants. For instance, if an intake officer would be inclined to divert a particular case from the juvenile justice system because of his or her judgment that the youth will probably not reoffend, this diversion decision may not be made if an attorney is present to represent the juvenile's interests. The intake officer may feel that a higher authority should decide the case. The defense counsel may be intimidating. In an otherwise attorney-free environment, the intake officer would act differently. Thus, different actions by different actors in the system may be anticipated, depending on the presence or absence of an attorney.

In cases adjudicated before juvenile court judges, a defense counsel's presence seems to work for the juvenile's benefit. Judicial discretion is affected to the extent that stricter or less strict adherence to juvenile laws is affected. There seems to be a tendency for juvenile court judges to be more lenient with juveniles who are represented by defense counsel compared with those juvenile defendants who are not represented by defense counsel. This leniency manifests itself in various ways. For instance, juvenile court judges may impose probation more often than incarceration where juveniles are represented by counsel. Represented juveniles who are disposed to a secure facility for a period of months may serve shorter incarcerative terms compared with those juveniles sent to these same secure facilities but who were not represented by counsel. More frequent granting of juvenile parole occurs among those youths represented by counsel compared with those youths not represented by counsel.

Defense Counsel as *Guardians Ad Litem*

In some juvenile cases, child abuse has been alleged. Thus, defense counsel perform additional responsibilities as they attempt to ensure that the best interests of their clients are served in ways that will protect children from parents who abuse them (Keilitz et al., 1997; Minnesota Office of the Legislative Auditor, 1995). *Guardians ad litem* are special guardians appointed by the court in which a particular litigation is pending to represent a youth, ward, or unborn person in that particular litigation (Black, 1990:706). Most juvenile court jurisdictions have *guardian ad litem* programs, where interested persons serve in this capacity. In some cases, defense counsel for youths perform the dual role of defense counsel and the youth's *guardian ad litem. Guardians ad litem* are supposed to work in ways that will benefit those they represent, and such guardians provide legal protection from others. Defense counsel working as *guardians ad litem* may act to further the child's best interests, despite a child's contrary requests or demands. Thus, this is a different type of nonadversarial role performed by some defense counsel (Eltringham and Aldridge, 2000).

Juvenile Offender Plea Bargaining and the Role of Defense Counsel

Often, we think that plea bargaining occurs only within the criminal justice system. The fact is that juveniles enter into plea agreements with juvenile court prosecutors with great frequency (Sanborn, 2001). Sanborn says that plea bargaining is an invaluable tool with which to eliminate case backlogs that might occur in some of the larger juvenile courts. Sanborn gathered data from 100 juvenile court officers in 1988. Specifically, Sanborn wanted to know whether plea bargaining was consistent with the guiding doctrine of *parens patriae* that characterized juvenile courts at that time. Most of those surveyed believed that plea bargaining was used solely to help those youths in need of social services or other forms of assistance. Defense counsel entering into plea agreements with juvenile court prosecutors wanted the least restrictive option imposed on their juvenile clients. Most frequently sought by defense counsel were charge reductions against their clients by prosecutors. Defense counsel were interested in reducing the stigma of a serious, negative juvenile court profile of their youthful clients by seeking reduced charges from prosecutors. Prosecutors would benefit in that plea agreements would speed up case processing and save them time from having to prove critical elements of crimes against juvenile defendants. Both actors, prosecutors and defense attorneys, sought personal goals instead of pursuing some type of *parens patriae* objective. The former were interested in concluding adjudications with sanctions, while the latter were interested in protecting their clients from more serious charges that could influence their future lives.

The degree to which *parens patriae* is alive and well depends on how much a particular court has accepted and furthered the due-process renovation created by *Gault* (Sanborn, 2001). If fairness is to be realized in the adjudicatory hearing of juveniles, judges and defense attorneys should know the rules of criminal procedure and evidence, and they must be made aware that adjudications are serious for youths. Defense lawyers should also be reminded that appellate review is both a necessary and valuable weapon, although few juvenile court decisions are ever appealed. However, one continuing and troublesome aspect of plea bargaining in the juvenile justice system is that admissions of guilt are elicited from juveniles without benefit of a trial (Burruss and Kempf-Leonard, 2002).

Parental Intrusion in Juvenile Courts Is Often More Damaging Than Attorney Involvement

The impact of the parents of juveniles who appear in juvenile courts has been investigated (Pierce and Brodsky, 2002). The attitudes and opinions of various juvenile justice actors, such as judges, prosecutors, defense attorneys, and probation officers have been investigated. In more than a few instances, parents of processed juveniles tend to make matters for their children worse by their own actions. Some parents threaten intake officers, prosecutors, and/or judges. Many of those surveyed viewed the interventions of parents in juvenile proceedings as primarily negative. Some of their negative behaviors might be due to a basic misunderstanding of the due-process rights of their children. Other parents may feel that the juvenile court is not a formally contrived proceeding with legal powers. As some parents attempt to intervene and circumvent procedural matters before the juvenile court, all actors, including defense counsel, become exasperated and tend to impose harsher sanctions than would otherwise be imposed if the parents were not there. However, parental involvement in juvenile matters is often required according to court or procedural rules.

It is clear from juvenile justice trends observed in most states thus far that defense counsel are increasingly present during all stages of juvenile processing (Bradley, 2005). This increased involvement of defense counsel is intended to ensure that a juvenile's constitutional rights are observed. Another intention of counsel is to ensure the best dispositional outcome for their youthful clients. This usually means some form of lenient treatment from the system. We have seen that attorney involvement does preserve one's rights at different processing stages; however, it is not yet clear whether a defense counsel's presence is totally beneficial to juvenile clients at all times. Too much formalization may cause various actors (e.g., intake officers, prosecutors, judges) to act differently when others are present who can monitor their actions. The traditional view of juvenile courts is that whatever is done to and for the juvenile will be in the youth's best interests. Sometimes, this means making one type of decision for one offender and a different type of decision for another offender, even when the offenders share similar background characteristics and have committed similar offenses.

Extralegal factors, such as race/ethnicity, socioeconomic status, gender, age, and a youth's demeanor all contribute to decision making at different processing stages (Kurlychek and Johnson, 2004). Ideally, these criteria should not be considered when making decisions about juvenile offenders. But sometimes judges and others will respond and make decisions about some youths based on these and other variables (Dimmick, 2005). In many cases, these decisions are favorable for the youths involved, but outsiders may perceive this differential treatment to be inherently unequal treatment. Thus, questions arise about one's equal protection rights as set forth in the Fourteenth Amendment. Therefore, judges and others may tend to deal with some offenders more severely, simply to preserve due process. And this greater harshness is sometimes the result of a defense attorney's presence.

Consider the following scenario. Two 12-year-old youths have been taken into custody for theft. One boy stole some candy from a grocery store, while the other boy stole some pencils from a convenience store. Both boys have no prior juvenile records. One boy is Hispanic, while the other is Asian. The intake officer, who is black, sees both boys and their families, with no defense counsel present. The Hispanic boy utters various obscenities at the intake officer. The Asian boy sits calmly and responds politely to questions asked. The intake officer might be inclined to recommend further juvenile justice processing for the Hispanic juvenile, while he might be inclined to divert the Asian juvenile from the system. Is this decision motivated by prejudice? Or is the decision motivated by the attitude or demeanor displayed by each youth? If, in fact, these different decisions are made, the Hispanic boy is adversely affected by the intake officer's decision. But the Asian boy benefits from the informal handling of his case by the intake officer.

Now let's consider these same scenarios, but in each case, we will place in the room defense counsel for both youths. Whether the defense counsel are privately retained or publicly appointed, they are interested in justice for their respective clients. Because of the presence of an attorney in each of the cases, the intake officer decides to apply standard decision-making criteria. Both of these boys have committed theft, at least a misdemeanor if an adult committed these acts. Thus, the intake officer moves both boys further into the system, so that a juvenile court prosecutor can take over from there. In the Hispanic boy's case, the presence of his defense counsel merely gave credence to the intake officer's decision to move the boy further into the system. The boy's demeanor or attitude didn't help matters, but the intake officer is merely following the rules. The letter of the law is applied. In the Asian youth's situation, the intake officer moves the boy further into the system, even though he believes this decision is *not* in the boy's best interests. But the intake officer is treating both boys equally, thus ensuring their due-process and equal protection rights under the Fourteenth Amendment. The presence of defense counsel explains the consistency of the intake officer's conduct in both cases.

Some get-tough observers may say, so what? The boys stole something of value and they must learn not to steal. If we excuse the Asian boy from the system without punishing him, he will learn contempt for the system because the system is lenient and tolerates theft. The due-process view is that both boys need to be punished equally, because they have equal background characteristics and have committed commensurate offenses. Should they be punished equally? At the other end of the spectrum are those who wish to preserve the *parens patriae* concept of juvenile courts. Doing things that are in a youth's best interest may involve making decisions that may be inherently discriminatory. Should we punish one's demeanor or attitude, which varies greatly from youth to youth, or should we punish the same delinquent acts in the same ways? This

Dining areas in juvenile facilities resemble high school lunch rooms.

hypothetical example shows both the good and bad stemming from greater attorney involvement in juvenile proceedings at any stage.

SUMMARY

Juvenile court prosecutors have considerable discretionary powers. They can decide to drop cases against certain juveniles and pursue other cases vigorously. They can meet with and plea bargain cases with defense attorneys and their youthful clients. They can recommend particular punishments to juvenile court judges. One consequence of the acquisition of greater rights by juveniles is that the power of prosecutors has increased considerably. At the same time, these prosecutors have gradually been held to a higher standard in determining whether to prosecute juvenile offenders. If it is the intent of a juvenile court prosecutor to seek secure confinement of particular juveniles, they must now prove their cases against these juveniles beyond a reasonable doubt instead of on the basis of the preponderance of evidence. Using the criminal court standard in juvenile court proceedings has done much to change the prosecutorial role.

The changing nature of the prosecutorial role has also been attributable in part to the greater openness of juvenile court proceedings. Greater prosecutorial accountability is expected, particularly as a greater proportion of juvenile cases involve defense counsel representation to ensure that a juvenile's constitutional rights are protected.

Although juveniles do not enjoy the right to a speedy trial like criminal defendants in criminal courts, the time lines governing their processing are strict and greatly abbreviated compared with criminal court processing standards. The acceleration of the juvenile justice process is due in large part to the belief by many authorities that juveniles have a different concept of time compared with adults. Thus, it is crucial that the time between arrest and adjudication should be brief. The closer one's punishment is to the offense, it is believed that juveniles will experience greater accountability and associate their illegal actions with the punishments they will eventually receive. Ensuring a juvenile's right to rapid case processing is the appointment of public defenders or counsels to safeguard a youth's constitutional rights.

Today juveniles are entitled to defense counsels as a matter of right. These counsels may be either privately retained or court-appointed, depending on the socioeconomic circumstances of one's family. Defense counsels are the principal advocates for juveniles and ensure that their constitutional rights are observed. However, under certain circumstances and at different stages of proceedings against juveniles, the very presence of defense counsels may adversely affect case dispositions. Juvenile court judges may feel compelled to deal harshly with particular offenders, even though certain extralegal factors may exist that might warrant more lenient treatment. A concern for due process may override the concern for individualized justice and leniency otherwise contemplated by juvenile court judges. Like intake officers, juvenile court judges as well as prosecutors may feel duty-bound to observe due process to the letter rather than exercise individualized decision making for particular juveniles. Despite the discrimination inherent in treating all juveniles individually, sometimes unequal treatment by judges and other juvenile court actors may be better for certain juveniles than for others. But the presence of defense counsels prevents such individualized and potentially beneficial actions.

The rate of attorney use by juveniles has increased steadily in the United States for the past 25 years. There is every indication that this trend will continue. In a majority of juvenile court scenarios, the presence of defense counsel is not negatively viewed. Rather, over time this has become an accepted and common occurrence. Defense counsels have learned to engage in plea bargaining with prosecutors in many cases, and formal and more costly court actions have been avoided. As is the case with adult criminal defendants, juveniles who engage in plea bargaining enjoy greater leniency from juvenile court judges in most cases. This phenomenon is known as strategic leniency, and it occurs in most jurisdictions. However, some factors are beyond the control of the attorney and his or her youthful client. Sometimes parental intrusions in juvenile proceedings create adverse conditions for juveniles and the ultimate treatment they receive from the juvenile court. Under certain conditions where parents or guardians are deemed unsuitable to supervise particular juveniles, *guardians ad litem* are appointed by the court to promote and protect a child's interests.

QUESTIONS FOR REVIEW

1. How are juvenile courts becoming increasingly adversarial proceedings? How has the prosecutorial role in juvenile courts changed in recent years?
2. How has the standard of proof, beyond a reasonable doubt, modified the prosecutorial role?
3. Should confidentiality of juvenile records be maintained? Why or why not?
4. What are some reasons for removing confidentiality surrounding juvenile records and opening juvenile courts to the general public?
5. What kinds of time standards govern prosecutorial decision making in the juvenile justice system? Are these time standards uniform for all jurisdictions?
6. What are some reasons for accelerating juvenile case processing?
7. Under what circumstances are public defenders appointed for juveniles? Do different types of defense counsel, public or private, make a difference in juvenile proceedings? If yes, why? If no, why not?

8. Do juvenile offenders have the right to a speedy trial? In what ways do more accelerated time lines for concluding juvenile cases parallel the speedy trial provisions of criminal courts?

9. What is the significance of the *Barker v. Wingo* case? Does the *Barker* case have any influence on juvenile matters? Why or why not?

10. How do defense counsels ensure that a juvenile's due-process rights are preserved? What are *guardians ad litem* and what are their functions?

INTERNET CONNECTIONS

Action without Borders
http://www.idealist.org/

Help My Teen
http://www.helpmyteen.com/

Victim–Offender Mediation Association
http://igc.org/voma

What Happens in Juvenile Court
http://www.falsely-accused.net/what_happens_in_juvenile_court.htm

Youth Law Center
http://www.ylc.com/

CHAPTER 9

Classification and Preliminary Treatment: Waivers and Other Alternatives

Chapter Outline

Key Terms

acceptance of responsibility
blended sentencing
capital punishment
certification
concurrent jurisdiction
contempt of court
criminal–exclusive blend
criminal–inclusive blend
death penalty
demand waiver
direct file
Discretionary waivers
judicial waivers

juvenile court records
juvenile–contiguous blend
juvenile–exclusive blend
juvenile–inclusive blend
legislative waiver
life-without-parole
mandatory waiver
once an adult/always an adult
   provision
placed
placement
presumptive waiver
reverse waiver

reverse waiver actions
reverse waiver hearings
statutory exclusion
sustained petitions
transfer hearings
waiver
waiver hearing
waiver motion

Chapter Objectives

As the result of reading this chapter, you will have accomplished the following objectives:

1. Distinguish between different types of offenses in terms of their seriousness.
2. Understand the criminal justice and juvenile justice system responses to juvenile violence.
3. Understand the get-tough movement and the policies advocated toward violent juveniles.
4. Understand the meaning of juvenile transfers, waivers, and certifications.
5. Understand different types of waiver actions and their implications for juvenile offenders.
6. Learn about the ages at which juveniles may be transferred to criminal court for processing.
7. Understand the importance of waiver hearings for juveniles.
8. Become familiar with important case law governing juvenile transfers or waivers.
9. Understand blended sentencing statutes as emerging optional punishments for juveniles who commit serious crimes.

• *It happened in Mesa, Arizona. Rafael G. was 13 years old and a ninth-grader at a local high school. He was also a gang wanna-be. He frequently skipped school and went to a local arcade where he played video games in a nearby mall with several older gang members. School officials notified Rafael G.'s parents who brought Rafael G. to a parent–school counselor conference to discuss Rafael G.'s absences from classes. Rafael G. promised he would attend school. But after a few weeks of attending school, he began to absent himself from campus and hang out with his friends at the arcade. One day they went to a home a few miles from the mall and smoked marijuana and drank wine. Rafael G. got drunk and became sick. He vomited and later he passed out on a sofa. When he didn't return home and his parents found out that he wasn't in school, they were frantic and contacted the police. Early the next morning, the police spotted Rafael G. walking along a sidewalk toward his home. Again, Rafael G. and his parents met with school authorities, including the school principal. Rafael G. signed an agreement to attend his classes. But the absences continued. One afternoon, Rafael G. was riding in a stolen car with some of his gang friends when police officers stopped them and took them into custody. Rafael G. was turned over to the custody of his parents. Later he appeared before the juvenile court judge where the judge issued an order for Rafael G. to attend school. Rafael G. continued to be absent from school despite the judge's order, and an arrest warrant was issued for contempt of court, a misdemeanor. Rafael G. again appeared before the juvenile court judge, who adjudicated Rafael delinquent on the contempt charge. This time, Rafael G. was placed under the authority of a juvenile probation officer and subjected to intensive supervision. One of his probation conditions was that he attend school and observe a curfew. The very first day following school, Rafael G. went out with his friends again and didn't come home until 10:00 P.M., well beyond his curfew. The juvenile probation officer was at his home at the time and filed a report with the juvenile court the following day, noting the curfew violation. This time, the juvenile court judge ordered Rafael G. placed in juvenile detention for 30 days. [Source: Adapted from William Geary and the Associated Press, "Truant Gets 30 Days for Contempt of Court," June 16, 2005.]*

• Two California high school football players at Antioch High School and Deer Valley High School, Brandon McMullen and Jack Soberal, both 17, were charged with raping several intoxicated girls during an after-game party. Allegedly, one girl was locked in a bedroom and told, "You're not leaving this room until you have oral sex with us." The prosecutor in the case, Contra Costa County Deputy District Attorney Brian Welch, filed felony charges against the youths and charged them as adults under California Proposition 21, which gives prosecutors the discretion to file charges against juveniles age 14 or older in adult court if the offenses alleged are sex crimes or violent felonies. At least seven girls have come forward as witnesses against the two youths. If convicted, the football players could be sentenced to life imprisonment. The boys were being held on $1 million bond.

• In another case in Honesdale, Pennsylvania, two Mepham High School football players, a 16-year-old and a 17-year-old, were charged with several sex crimes, including sodomizing three junior varsity players with broomsticks, pine cones, and golf balls in a hazing ritual during a preseason training camp. Wayne County District Attorney Mark Zimmer filed a petition to have the youths tried as adults in criminal court. However, Wayne County Presiding Judge Robert J. Conway denied the ruling and declared that the youths' cases would be heard in juvenile court instead. A third football player, 15 years old, pleaded guilty and was scheduled to testify against the other two players. Families of the victims said, "We want them in adult court so that there will be some punishment." These same families feared that the boys would receive only probation as a punishment. In criminal court, convictions for sex offenses such as these carry mandatory minimum incarcerative terms, while in juvenile court, there are no mandatory dispositions, and juvenile court judges have broad discretionary powers. [Sources: Adapted from Charlie Goodyear, "Antioch Youths Face Life for Rape Under New Law: Football Players to Be Tried as Adults." San Francisco Chronicle, September 15, 2000; adapted from Karla Schuster, "Staying in Youth Court: PA Judge Ignores Public Pleas in Ruling in Mepham Case." Newsday, November 13, 2003; adapted from the Associated Press, "Family in Football Sex Attack Wish Trial Was Under New York Law," November 13, 2003.]

• Two South Carolina teens, Hobart Drake Jr., 15, and Jeremy Avery, 14, were charged in the death of a Sumter County deacon and will be tried as adults. The boys are accused of stabbing to death Master Sergeant Timothy Maggard, 42, who was found on a dirt road. Authorities allege the boys attempted to carjack Maggard, and stabbed him 22 times. Maggard is survived by his wife, daughter, and son. He was a church deacon at

Wedgefield Baptist Church. Judge George McFadden who ruled that the boys will be tried as adults said that the murder was premeditated and violent, and that based on their past record, they both pose a threat to society.

• In a second case, Chad Pruchnitzky, 16, and James Moore III, 15, set fire to a residence and killed Anna Lazabeck, 85, of North Braddock, Pennsylvania. Under Pennsylvania statutes, the boys were automatically charged as adults with second-degree murder, although a defense motion was granted to have the case sent to juvenile court for adjudication and disposition. In criminal court, second-degree murder carries a mandatory life term. However, juvenile court judges have considerable discretion and can impose probation or some other conditional punishment if the circumstances merit such leniency.

• In a third case in Everett, Washington, two teens, Joshua David Goldman, 17, and Jenson Hugh Hankins, 16, were charged with the premeditated murder of 16-year-old John Daniel Jasmer. They lured him from his home by telling him they were going out to buy some marijuana. They took Jasmer into the woods and stabbed him to death. Then they emptied his pockets, took $110, and buried him in a shallow grave. They burned their clothes and knives in another location to conceal the crime. A judge ruled that the two juveniles would be tried in criminal court as adults with first-degree murder. Under Washington law, convictions would mean life imprisonment for the youths. [*Sources:* Adapted from Megan Hughes, "Teens Charged with Deacon's Murder To Be Tried as Adults." *World Now,* February 21, 2003; adapted from Robert Baird, "Firefighter Accused of Murder To Be Tried in Juvenile Court." *Pittsburgh Tribune-Review,* February 7, 2002; CNET News, "2 Teens Charged as Adults in Classmate's Slaying." *Seattle Times,* September 3, 2003.]

INTRODUCTION

The seriousness of juvenile offending ranges from truancy, runaway behavior, and breaking curfew to rapes and murders. The juvenile justice system attempts to classify these offenses in different ways. On the basis of these classifications, strategies are implemented that are designed to treat and/or punish the offenders in ways that will rehabilitate them, cause them to accept responsibility for their actions, compensate victims for their losses, and in many other ways provide a therapeutic milieu for most youths. Many juveniles are chronic recidivists, regardless of the seriousness of the offenses they commit. As the opening scenarios in this chapter indicate, some youths have trouble attending school or complying with court-ordered rules. Other youths engage in very serious offending, including rape or sodomy. Yet other youths rob and/or kill. No single theory explains this range of juvenile offending. No single strategy seems to work best with all offenders. Juvenile authorities in all jurisdictions attempt to use their personal skills, experimental programs, and a wide variety of interventions to help the juveniles being supervised in different ways. Every professional who has worked with youths has reported successful experiences as well as failures and frustrations.

This chapter examines how juveniles are classified by juvenile justice systems in most jurisdictions. When juveniles first come into contact with this system, they are ordinarily separated according to the seriousness of their offense. Presently virtually all jurisdictions distinguish between status and delinquent offenders and have procedures in place for dealing with each type of offender.

In more than a few jurisdictions, status offenders have been insulated from juvenile court jurisdiction. Juvenile courts have divested themselves of jurisdiction over such juveniles, and other mechanisms in the community are used to process, treat, and supervise these types of offenders. For delinquents, juvenile courts act to deal with these juveniles in ways that will make them more accountable for their actions. Many juvenile court judges continue to individualize their decision making relating to all juveniles, in the belief that individualized attention to the diverse needs and situations of these offenders works better than the blanket application of uniform rules without regard to one's personal circumstances. Some youths commit offenses that are so serious that the juvenile courts are not equipped to deal with them effectively. Juvenile court judges may or may not be given choices concerning the ultimate outcomes of these cases.

The next part of this chapter examines the waiver or transfer process, which is a mechanism used to transfer jurisdiction over certain juveniles from juvenile courts to criminal courts. Different jurisdictions refer to this process in different ways. All waiver proceedings are subject to a hearing to determine one's suitability for transfer. While waivers and transfers are common terms to label this process of changing the jurisdiction over these juveniles, certification is also used. The certification process is a means whereby youths are certified as adults for the purpose of being prosecuted as adults in criminal courts. This section describes the nature and use of waivers or transfers, including the rationale for why such mechanisms are used. Certain types of offenders are targeted for transfers or waivers, and these types of offenders are profiled. But the transfer process is imperfect. Many juveniles are transferred to criminal courts for processing who do not necessarily fit the ideal profile of juveniles targeted for transfers. A description of transferred juveniles is provided, and several rationales are provided to explain how many of these persons eventually are processed by criminal courts.

Several types of waivers or transfers have been distinguished. The next section examines these different types of waivers, which include judicial waivers, direct file, statutory exclusion, and demand waivers. Judicial waivers may be discretionary, mandatory, or presumptive. Other types of waivers are prosecutor-initiated, as is the case with direct-file actions. State legislatures also provide that some offenses should be removed from the jurisdiction of juvenile courts. Thus, under statutory exclusion, the juvenile court is barred from hearing particular kinds of cases, particularly the most serious ones. Nevertheless, some juveniles and their attorneys may initiate reverse waiver actions, to reassign these automatic or legislative waivers back to juvenile courts for adjudication. In some instances, juveniles themselves may demand to have their cases brought before the criminal court and removed from juvenile court jurisdiction. Although such demand waiver actions are rare, they have occurred. Several other options exist in various jurisdictions relating to how juveniles are treated by either the juvenile or criminal justice system. All of these waiver procedures are explained and described.

The chapter next explains the implications of waiver actions for juveniles. These implications include some of the more important reasons for why treatment of a juvenile as an adult may be advantageous to particular juveniles, or why it may be advantageous to keep the case within juvenile court jurisdiction. At least one positive outcome resulting from a youth's transfer to criminal court is that the youth is entitled to a jury trial as a matter of right, and the full range of rights enjoyed by adult offenders are extended to all transferred juveniles. Thus, there are several pros and cons relating to transfers, and these are described in some detail. In most jurisdictions, there are also time standards that govern the transfer process. These time standards are defined and explained.

The chapter concludes with an examination of blended sentencing statutes. In a growing number of jurisdictions, juvenile and criminal courts are devising mechanisms to deal more effectively with juvenile offenders in ways that circumvent the cumbersome transfer or waiver process. Blended sentencing statutes enable both juvenile and criminal court judges to impose both juvenile and adult punishments on particular juvenile offenders simultaneously, depending on the jurisdiction and the particular blended sentencing statutes that the jurisdiction has adopted. Several variations of blended sentencing statutes are described, and several examples are provided concerning how these proceedings may be applied.

SERIOUSNESS OF THE OFFENSE AND WAIVER DECISION MAKING

Seriousness of the Offense

Investigations of the nature and seriousness of violent juvenile offending have been conducted by several researchers (Crews and Montgomery, 2001). Some researchers have concluded that today's juveniles do not commit more acts of violence than did juveniles in previous generations, but more juveniles are violent (Kurlychek and Johnson, 2004). However, in a comparison of mid-1990s juvenile offending with the nature and type of juvenile offending in 1980, it was found that about the same proportion of youths commit serious violent offenses in 1994 as they did in 1980 (Carmona et al., 2004; Casella, 2001). However, the violent acts committed in the 1990s are more lethal, with larger proportions of these violent acts likely to result in either serious injury or death. It has been found that the peak years of committing violent acts among juveniles are between the ages of 15 and 16. Also, the major causes of juvenile violence tend to be poor family relations, socioeconomically disadvantaged neighborhoods, poor school adjustments, peer pressure, greater availability of firearms, and greater dependence on alcohol or drugs (Bowman, 2005).

Separating Status Offenders from Delinquent Offenders

One of the first steps taken to separate juveniles into different offending categories was the deinstitutionalization of status offenses, or DSO. Also including divestiture, this major juvenile justice system reform was calculated to remove the least serious and noncriminal offenders from the jurisdiction of juvenile courts in every jurisdiction. Presumably and ideally, after DSO has occurred, only those juveniles who are charged with felonies and/or misdemeanors—delinquents—will be brought into the juvenile justice process and formally adjudicated in juvenile courts. These courts would also retain supervisory control over children in need of supervision, abused children, or neglected children (Arthur, 2004). In reality, events have not turned out as legislators had originally anticipated or intended. Many status offenders continue to filter into the juvenile justice system in most jurisdictions (Feld, 2001).

"Hanging out" suggests an absence of productive activities and recreational outlets for juveniles in many communities.

When DSO occurred on a large scale throughout the United States during the late 1970s, several jurisdictions made policy decisions about how both non-serious and serious offenders would henceforth be treated by their juvenile justice systems. In West Virginia, for instance, the Supreme Court of Appeals ruled in 1977 that an adjudicated delinquent was constitutionally entitled to receive the least restrictive alternative treatment consistent with his or her rehabilitative needs (*State ex rel. Harris v. Calendine* [1977]). While this decision didn't eliminate institutionalizing more serious or violent juveniles, it did encourage juvenile court judges to consider seriously various alternatives to incarceration as punishments for youthful offenders. Relating to DSO, the Court also prohibited the commingling of adjudicated status offenders and adjudicated delinquent offenders in secure, prison-like facilities (Costello, 2003). Again, the court didn't necessarily rule out the secure confinement, long-term or otherwise, of status offenders as a possible sanction by juvenile court judges, despite encouragement by the Court for judges first to attempt to apply nonincarcerative sanctions before imposing incarcerative penalties.

These mixed messages sent by the West Virginia Supreme Court of Appeals did little, if anything, to restrict the discretionary powers of juvenile court judges. The Court's emphasis on rehabilitation and alternative treatments to be considered by juvenile court judges reinforced the traditional concept of juvenile courts as rehabilitative rather than punitive sanctioning bodies. However, the Court's ruling led to a substantial overhaul of the West Virginia juvenile code as well as a substantial drop in the incarcerated juvenile offender population in state-operated correctional facilities.

Juvenile Court Adjudications for Status Offenders

In many jurisdictions, DSO has reduced the volume of juvenile court cases over the years, but it has not prevented juvenile courts from continuing to adjudicate large numbers of status offenders annually (Costello, 2003). A comprehensive study of U.S. juvenile courts between 1990 and 1997 shows systematic

 **BOX 9.1**

INTERNATIONAL SNAPSHOT: JUVENILE JUSTICE IN GREECE

The Greek government has been concerned with the formal development and welfare of its youth for over a century. In 1950 the Penal Code and the Code of Penal Procedure was implemented, which set forth the principles whereby criminal justice in Greece would be administered. The influence of German, Swiss, and Italian penal and criminological theories on these codes and procedures is acknowledged. Furthermore, these codes reflect prior and subsequent revisions of the justice system to reflect changing societal conditions and policies.

Under the original Greek Penal Code of 1950, provisions were made for juveniles and designed to promote assistance to, and re-education and therapy for, young offenders ages 13–17. Children 12 and under were treated by educational and therapeutic measures only. For those ages 13–17, the court adopted the idea that judges must consider, in view of the circumstances of the criminal acts committed and the personality of the juvenile, if educational or therapeutic measures would be sufficient to deter further offending. If these measures were deemed insufficient, then certain youths would be given a penal sanction and incarcerated. At the same time, the Code of Penal Procedure established juvenile courts, probation services for juveniles, the Society for the Protection of Minors, and centers for the re-education of juvenile delinquents and their compulsory primary education. However, no centers were established to conduct investigations of the personalities of juveniles.

Since the 1980s changing socioeconomic factors, urbanization, industrialization, and vast internal migration, together with political and economic changes in Eastern Europe, drug trafficking, and weakened Greek family structure and community solidarity and control made it clear to the Greek government that revisions of the Penal Code relative to juvenile offenders were required. Thus in 2003 Act 3189 was adopted and incorporated into the Penal Code. Additions were also made to the Code

of Penal Procedure, strengthening the protection of juvenile victims and establishing units for the care of at-risk youths. Today the Greek government utilizes restorative justice, community-based services and other alternatives as a part of a comprehensive therapeutic program in dealing with juvenile offenders and their families.

Greek delinquency is difficult to assess, in part because of the absence of self-report surveys. Information for the past 30 years suggests that juvenile delinquency in Greece is increasing. Recent evidence suggests that this trend has changed, however. It is significant to note that delinquency among those ages 7–12 has been scarce, and no serious upward trends in offending have been detected. The most prevalent juvenile offense is theft. During the period 1999–2003, the incidence of theft among juveniles has declined. Traffic violations have increased, however. Drug use among juveniles, although high in 1999, declined considerably through 2003. Juvenile offending appeared to peak in 2001 and has declined somewhat in recent years. Males commit over 90 percent of all juvenile offenses.

In recent years major changes have occurred regarding the definition of juveniles and the measures used to deal with their behavior. The guiding philosophy of these changing provisions has been the respect of individual rights and interests of minors, and the prevention of delinquent behavior by means of adequate primarily noncustodial measures of assistance, education, and treatment. The 7–17 age bracket has been deemed dysfunctional. Case law defined the minimum age of criminal accountability to be 6 years and 1 day, while the end of minority status was age 17. These minimums and maximums were changed to new age limits of one's 8th and 18th birthday, respectively.

Another revision abolished the term "criminal" as applied to minors. Furthermore, the terms "child" and "adolescent" are no longer used for two reasons: the term child covered ages 0–18 under a United

(continued)

Nations provision and was confusing, and maturity varies considerably among individuals. Thus, the new provisions refer to ages only rather than to adolescent labels.

Under the new rules, juveniles ages 8–13 are not penally liable. Those 13–18 are penally liable in exceptional cases. Amendments to these rules provide that children of less than 8 years of age who violate the penal law are now under the jurisdiction of welfare services, while youths above age 17 but under 18 are under the jurisdiction of the juvenile court. None of these persons are referred to the criminal courts and they cannot be sentenced to adult penal sanctions. Because of court delays in processing, however, juvenile courts may have jurisdiction over some youths who turn age 18 while waiting to be adjudicated.

One of the major reasons for rejecting penal sanctions for those under age 18 is because of the adverse stigmatization of convicted persons. In lieu of penal measures, mediation and restorative justice have been instituted for a majority of youths under age 18. Thus, the victim–offender mediation intervention has proved quite successful for avoiding formal prosecutions. Noncustodial measures have also been increased, including foster family placement and community service. Noninstitutional treatment has become the rule rather than the exception. Indeterminate sentences have been abolished as well.

Considerable attention has been devoted to crime victims. Measures implemented have been designed to compensate victims as an educational action imposed on adjudicated juveniles. Also various measures have been implemented to protect child victims of certain offenses such as trafficking in human beings and crimes against sexual freedom. Presently under existing mediation provisions, offenders now take an active role in their treatment and vest them with a feeling of responsibility for their own development. Special provisions have been established for children of migrant families and other minorities in an effort to assist them and meet their special needs. The post of ombudsman has been created as an important step in assisting such youths.

For minors 8–18, educational measures for various offenses and imposed by the juvenile court include the following: (1) a reprimand or verbal warning administered by the juvenile court judge during the hearing; (2) placing the minor under the responsible supervision or custody of parents or guardians (parents may also be sanctioned if they fail to deter their children from prostitution or other law-breaking conduct); (3) placing the minor under the responsible supervision and care of a foster family; (4) placing the minor under the responsible supervision of a society for the protection of minors, an institution for the education of minors, or in the care of a probation officer; and (5) mediation between the minor and victims through probation officer intervention (mediation societies or individual mediators do not exist, and these tasks are performed by probation officers who work for the Ministry of Justice).

Alternative measures may also be imposed by the juvenile court. These include (1) payment of compensation to victims or reparations for damages; (2) community service by the minor to contribute to the welfare of the community; (3) participation of the minor in social or psychological programs in public, municipal, or private services; (4) professional or other training, where such training would develop a minor's personality, improve his or her vocational skills, and divert him or her from further delinquent activity; (5) traffic education; (6) intensive probation supervision; and (7) placing the minor in a public, municipal, or private educational institution.

Therapeutic measures that may be imposed by the juvenile court are designed for those youths who are alcoholics or drug users or have mental retardation or difficulties, or are lacking in moral and ethical values. Such educative measures include participation in an open or day care therapeutic program, or placement in a therapeutic or other adequate closed institution. These measures are ordered after diagnosis and advice by a team of physicians, psychiatrists, psychologists, and social workers. Diagnostic teams are used in lieu of diagnostic centers, which are quite expensive to operate and are thus scarce.

Detention in special institutions is reserved for only the most serious youths. This penal sanction is used as a last resort and is necessary to prevent persons ages 13–18 from reoffending. Two detention centers currently operating in Greece include one in Avlona and one in Volos. The capacity of these facilities is designed to accommodate approximately 375 juveniles. The primary aim of these special institutions is educational, and they attempt to promote social reintegration of detainees.

Special attention has been given by the Greek government to human trafficking, including child prostitution. These are considered offenses against sexual self-determination. Child pornography is also encompassed. Measures of assistance in these cases include medical, psychological, legal, educational, and protective.

A recent bill has focused on Units for the Care of Youngsters. These are considered at-risk children, offenders, drug addicts, delinquents with psychological or mental problems, and victims. The main characteristics of the bill feature (1) emphasizing the physical and psychological well-being as well as the fulfillment of the best interests and welfare of youths; (2) safeguarding the rights of youths served; (3) setting up open, semi-open, or closed institutions, hospitality homes for victims, youths at risk and released delinquents, outpatient therapeutic services for diagnosis and treatment; (4) provision for a global scheme of a sufficient number of interrelated and integrated facilities for both males and females 8 to 21 years old to be located in different parts of the country; (5) licensing and supervision by the Ministry of Justice for the above categories and operating under the auspices of the local government; and (6) annual evaluations of both old and new units.

The new legislation for juvenile justice is consistent with the principle of protecting children and ensuring the observance of their legal rights. Most measures are noncustodial in nature. Particular attention is devoted to victims and seeing to their wellness and healing. Diversion and mediation are emphasized to avoid the adverse effects of labeling from interacting with a criminal-like court apparatus and accompanying penal processing. Also emphasized is greater training for personnel who work with juveniles to maximize the quality of care and treatment juveniles receive.

[*Sources:* Adapted from Calliope D. Spinellis and Aglaia Tsitsoura, "Juvenile Justice in Greece," University of Athens, Unpublished paper, 2005; "Criminal and Juvenile Justice Trends," Greece Ministry of Justice, 2005.]

increases in the absolute numbers of status offenders adjudicated across all status offense categories (National Center for Juvenile Justice, 2001). In 1997 an estimated 158,500 status offense cases were formally processed by juvenile courts through referrals and subsequent status offender petitions. These represent about a fifth of all status offense cases that came to the attention of juvenile courts (850,000) in 2004. Proportionately, status offense cases processed formally by juvenile courts comprised only 14 percent of the entire delinquency and status offense court caseload. In 2004, juvenile courts formally processed approximately 26,000 runaway cases; 45,000 truancy cases; 24,200 ungovernability cases; 42,800 status liquor law violation cases; and 34,000 other miscellaneous status offense cases. Thus, truancy and liquor law violations were most often referred to juvenile courts for some type of action. About half of these referrals were made by police officers. About 54 percent of all of these cases were adjudicated as status offenders (Office of Juvenile Justice and Delinquency Prevention, 2005). Among those status offense cases that were not adjudicated, 67 percent were dismissed, 23 resulted in informal sanctions other than probation or out-of-home placement (e.g., fines, community service, restitution, or referrals to other community agencies for services), 10 percent resulted in informal probation, and less than 1 percent resulted in placement. **Placement** refers to out-of-home placement, such as a group home or foster care. Seldom does placement mean secure confinement for status offenders in a state industrial school or reform school. Thus, juveniles who are subjected to these dispositional options are considered **placed.**

Formal adjudications become an official part of a juvenile's record. For offenders who are nonadjudicated, a formal decision is not rendered; rather, an informal declaration is made by the judge to dispose of these cases with minimal intrusion into the families and lives of those affected by the court decision.

The Use of Contempt Power to Incarcerate Nondelinquent Youths

While most adjudicated status offenders are not sent to industrial schools or directed to alternative out-of-home placements, it is the case that juvenile court judges wield considerable power to make status offenders comply with routine court directives. Truants may be ordered by the judge to attend school. Incorrigible youths may be ordered to obey their parents and remain law-abiding. Runaways may be ordered to participate in group counseling. Those youths with alcohol or drug dependencies may be ordered to attend individual counseling and alcohol/drug education sessions on a regular basis. If certain status offenders fail to obey these judicial directives in any way, they are at risk of being cited for **contempt of court.** A contempt-of-court citation is a misdemeanor, and juvenile court judges can use their contempt power to incarcerate any status offenders who do not comply with their orders. This judicial contempt power is unlimited (Virginia Commission on Youth, 1998).

Some observers believe that the use of contempt power by juvenile court judges is an abuse of judicial discretion. This is because some juvenile court judges hold juveniles accountable for their actions and consider them like adults in terms of their understanding of the law. Also, contempt power allows judges to circumvent and suspend procedural protections provided under state juvenile court acts. Furthermore, incarcerating status offenders as a punishment for contempt of court is inconsistent with legislative priorities. Thus, citing and incarcerating status offenders for contempt has created a dual system in which judges are free to uphold protective provisions of the act or ignore them in favor of punishment by invoking contempt power. Therefore, status offenders are not fully insulated from incarceration as a punishment, despite the prevalence of DSO throughout the United States.

Delinquent Offenders and Juvenile Court Dispositions

Assuming that for the majority of jurisdictions, juvenile courts have effectively weeded out the bulk of the nonserious, nondelinquent cases, the remainder should theoretically consist of those charged with delinquent offenses or acts that would be criminal if adults committed them. In 2004 there were approximately 70 million youths in the United States under the age of 18. Juvenile courts in the United States processed about 2.2 million delinquency cases (about 3 percent of all youths) in 2004 (Office of Juvenile Justice and Delinquency Prevention, 2005). This number represents a 50 percent increase over the number of delinquency cases handled in 1993. About 60 percent of all cases processed in 2004 were handled formally, where a petition was filed requesting an adjudicatory hearing. Furthermore, about 60 percent of these formally processed cases resulted in delinquency adjudications. About half of all adjudicated delinquents received probation or some other conditional release. About 30 percent of those adjudicated delinquent were ordered placed in a residential facility, such as a group home or a foster home. Approximately 12 percent of all adjudicated delinquency cases resulted in placement in secure detention facilities, such as industrial schools. The juvenile courts waived jurisdiction and transferred youths to criminal courts in 1 percent of all formally handled cases (Office of Juvenile Justice and Delinquency Prevention, 2005).

Between 1972 and 2004, several interesting trends have occurred with respect to juveniles who have been arrested or taken into police custody. In 1972, for instance, 50.8 percent of all juveniles taken into police custody were referred to juvenile courts, whereas 48 percent of these cases were handled within the department and subsequently released. However, during the next 32 years, the percentage of referrals to juvenile court systematically increased so that by 2004, 65 percent of all juveniles taken into custody by police were referred to juvenile court. Only 18 percent were handled within police departments and released through stationhouse adjustments (Office of Juvenile Justice and Delinquency Prevention, 2005). The remainder of youths in the custody of police were referred to social service agencies for further processing. Many of these referrals were status offenders.

Less than 1 percent of all juvenile cases are transferred annually from the jurisdiction of juvenile courts to the jurisdiction of criminal courts (Office of Juvenile Justice and Delinquency Prevention, 2005). By yearend 2004, 48 state jurisdictions and the District of Columbia gave juvenile court judges the power to waive their jurisdiction over certain juveniles so that they could be transferred to criminal court. However, in 2004 all states had some type of mechanism in place so that specific juvenile offenders could be treated as adults for the purpose of a prosecution in criminal courts (Jordan and Freiburger, 2005).

Transfers, Waivers, and Certifications

What are Transfers?   Transfers refer to changing the jurisdiction over certain juvenile offenders to another jurisdiction, usually from juvenile court jurisdiction to criminal court jurisdiction. Transfers are also known as waivers, referring to a **waiver** or change of jurisdiction from the authority of juvenile court judges to criminal court judges. Prosecutors or juvenile court judges decide that in some cases, juveniles should be waived or transferred to the jurisdiction of criminal courts. Presumably, those cases that are waived or transferred are the most serious cases, involving violent or serious offenses, such as homicide, aggravated assault, forcible rape, robbery, or drug-dealing activities (Brown, 2005). These jurisdictions conduct **transfer hearings.**

In some jurisdictions, such as Texas and Utah, juveniles are waived or transferred to criminal courts through a process known as **certification** (Texas Youth Commission, 2005). A certification is a formal procedure whereby the state declares the juvenile to be an adult for the purpose of a criminal prosecution in a

BOX 9.2

Nick Kalogris
Home County Case Manager, Juvenile Justice,
Department of Children's Services, Knoxville, TN

Statistics:

B.A. (sociology), Rider University, Lawrenceville, New Jersey

Background and Experience

I grew up outside Philadelphia and went to college in New Jersey. I majored in sociology and minored in psychology. When I graduated, I worked for a tree company for 2 years and did some house painting for a living. I moved to Knoxville, Tennessee, when I was offered a job as a social worker at a center for the mentally retarded. I did that for 6 years and was offered a job with the Department of Corrections to be a counselor at a group home for juvenile delinquents in the state's custody. After several years, I became the Director of the Knoxville Group Home. We had 10–12 residents ranging in age from 14 to 19. Eventually we were split away from the Department of Corrections and became part of a new department, Youth Development. As a result, I was given the opportunity to write and create a residential "Step Down" program for juveniles coming out of our institutions to transition back into the community. We had a staff of 12 that included a teacher, two counselors, a steward, a secretary, and seven Youth Service Officers (YSOs). Our boys could go to in-house school and earn credits or a GED and could work in the community and save their paychecks to help them to become independent when they completed their program commitments. We also had several students attend a junior college and trade school. The program lasted 6–9 months. Every day was a new challenge as the students we served were committed for everything up to and including murder. For the most part, our students were proud to work for businesses in the area where they could be judged on their merits and not on their previous reputations. Many of our boys experienced their first academic successes at the program and many achieved their GEDs. It was very satisfying for us to see a boy leave with his education and a health bankbook. Eventually the Department of Youth Development combined with the Department of Human Services to become the current Department of Children's Services. I enjoyed my many years as director of the program but I reached the point where my administrative duties were taking me away from directly working with the youth we served. I asked for and received a transfer to the field after about 20 years with residential services. Now I'm a Home County Case Manager and I supervise custody and probation cases. I much prefer working directly with our youth and their families and was lucky to be allowed to roll back, as they say. If I find a creative opportunity to help our clients prepare for adulthood, I'll reenter the supervision ranks; but for now, I'm quite happy with my role.

Interesting Experiences

"Genius of Escape and Master of Disguise"—"Ronald" went AWOL from the group home. Word had it that he was headed out West. Several days later, we were notified by West Virginia that Ronald had been apprehended and would be flown back to Knoxville. The circumstances were that Ronald was hitchhiking and was picked up by a truck driver. The gentleman asked where Ronald was from and Ronald told him he had run away from a state group home in Tennessee. The driver happened to be traveling through the county where his brother was the sheriff. The driver called his brother, the sheriff, via CB radio and delivered Ronald to the county jail where he was taken into custody. When we were notified of the date and time of Ronald's flight, we were also told that Ronald had dyed his hair from dark brown to black. At the airport, we knew Ronald would be the last one off of the plane. As his counselor and I waited, we decided to pretend we didn't recognize Ronald because of his "disguise." He came out of the tunnel looking like a bowling pin with an Elvis wig. He walked up to where we were seated and said, "Hi, guys." I asked who he was, and he said, "It's me, Ronald!" The counselor replied that he couldn't be Ronald as our Ronald had brown hair. I asked him what he did with the real Ronald. Ronald spent the next few minutes trying to establish his identity, while we acted dubious. Finally we allowed him to convince us of who he really was and we put the cuffs on him and brought him back to the group home. He was later awarded "Worst AWOL" at our next group meeting. He was very proud.

Advice and Insights

My biggest insight has always been, but for the grace of God go I. Pure luck and the intervention of my track coach is all that seems to have separated these kids's situations from my own. When I trained new staff, my first words were, "If these guys tell you the sun rises in the East, you'd better double check." You have to be able to tolerate getting lied to and not taking it personally. Empathy is fine; sympathy is not. "Firm and fair" is a good motto. Have fun with the kids, as they'll be glad to have fun at your expense. Kids want guidelines and rules even though they complain. It's a scary world otherwise. Whatever you say you're going to do, good or unpleasant, stand by your word. Don't debate a teenager in front of his peers, and never embarrass a kid. You are an adult and not a friend. You don't get paid to be a friend. When you make a mistake, then apologize for it. Finally, as often as you'll get deceived, cursed, and yelled at, these kids are watching you, as you're the only stability they may have. Understand and respect them.

criminal court (Sanborn, 2003). The results of certifications are the same as for waivers or transfers. Thus, certifications, waivers, and transfers result in juvenile offenders being subject to the jurisdiction of criminal courts where they can be prosecuted as though they were adult offenders. A 14-year-old murderer, for instance, might be transferred to criminal court for a criminal prosecution on the murder charge. In criminal court, the juvenile, now being treated as though he were an adult, can be convicted of the murder and sentenced to a prison term for one or more years. If the juvenile is charged with capital murder, is age 18 or older, and lives in a state where the death penalty is administered to those convicted of capital murder, then he or she can potentially receive the death penalty as the maximum punishment for that offense, provided there is a capital murder conviction. Or criminal court judges might impose life-without-parole sentences on these convicted 18-year-olds. Imposing life-without-parole sentences or the death penalty are *not* within the jurisdiction of juvenile court judges. Their jurisdiction ends when an offender becomes an adult. Thus, a delinquency adjudication on capital murder charges in juvenile court might result in a juvenile being placed in the state industrial school until he is age 18 or 21, depending on whichever is the age of majority or adulthood.

The actual numbers of juveniles waived to the jurisdiction of criminal courts annually has fluctuated between 6,700 in 1988 to 11,700 in 1994. Waivers declined by 1997 to 8,400 juveniles. However, from 1997 through 2004, the use of waivers has gradually increased and fluctuated between 11,000–13,000 juveniles per year (Office of Juvenile Justice and Delinquency

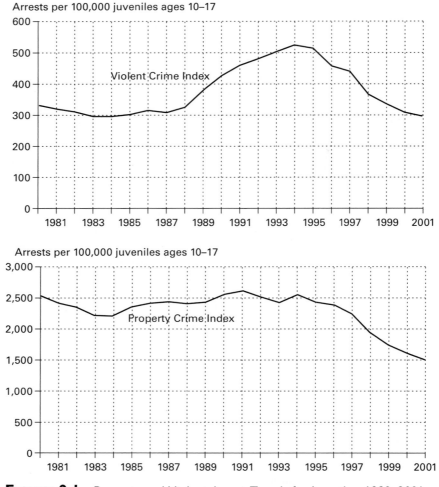

FIGURE 9.1 Property and Violent Arrest Trends for Juveniles, 1980–2001
(*Source:* Snyder, 2003:5).

Prevention, 2005). Available figures relating to juvenile arrest trends for both violent and property offenses during the period 1980–2001 are shown in Figure 9.1. It should be noted that both violent and juvenile offending, as measured by arrest figures, seemed to peak during the mid-1990s, although both property and violent offending systematically declined in subsequent years, at least through 2001.

The Rationale for Using Transfers, Waivers, or Certifications.   The basic rationale underlying the use of waivers is that the most serious juvenile offenders will be transferred to the jurisdiction of criminal courts where the harshest punishments, including capital punishment, may be imposed as sanctions (Brown, 2005). Since juvenile courts lack the jurisdiction and decision-making power to impose anything harsher than secure confinement dispositions of limited duration in industrial or reform schools, it would seem that the waiver would be an ideal way to impose the most severe punishments on those juveniles who commit the most violent acts. A list of reasons for using transfers, waivers, or certifications are as follows:

1. To make it possible for harsher punishments to be imposed.
2. To provide just-deserts and proportionately severe punishments on those juveniles who deserve such punishments by their more violent actions.
3. To foster fairness in administering punishments according to one's serious offending.
4. To hold serious or violent offenders more accountable for what they have done.
5. To show other juveniles who contemplate committing serious offenses that the system works and that harsh punishments can be expected if serious offenses are committed.
6. To provide a deterrent to decrease juvenile violence.
7. To overcome the traditional leniency of juvenile courts and provide more realistic sanctions.
8. To make youths realize the seriousness of their offending and induce remorse and **acceptance of responsibility.**

Ideal Offender Characteristics for Justifying Transfers to Criminal Courts. Those designated for transfer or waiver by various participants in the juvenile justice process should exhibit certain consistent characteristics (Brown, 2005; Kurlychek and Johnson, 2004). Age, offense seriousness, and prior record (including previous referrals to juvenile court, intake proceedings and dispositions, or juvenile court delinquency adjudications) are some of these characteristics (Toth, 2005).

Juvenile offenders most in need of processing by criminal courts should be chronic, persistent, and violent offenders. Person offenses, such as rape, murder, robbery, and aggravated assault, should top the list of those who merit transfer from the jurisdiction of juvenile courts to criminal courts for criminal prosecutions (Terry-McElrath and McBride, 2004). Because of the therapeutic environment generated by juvenile courts and their emphasis on rehabilitation, treatment, and reform, less serious property and drug offenders, a largely nonviolent class, might benefit more from juvenile court processing. Therefore, we would expect to see almost all transferred cases to criminal court typified by person or violent offenders, clearly the most serious and dangerous juvenile offender class (Brown, 2005).

Actual Characteristics of Transferred Juveniles.   Are the most serious juveniles actually transferred to criminal courts for processing? No. In 1998, transfers of violent juvenile offenders increased to 43 percent, and property offenders represented 37 percent of those transferred. Drugs and public order offenses accounted for the remaining 19 percent. By 2004, however, violent offenders represented only 36 percent of all transferred youths. Those juveniles charged with various drug offenses represented 16 percent of all transferred youths. Those charged with public order offenses represented 8 percent of those transferred. Therefore, if we combine the nonviolent categories of property offending, drug offending, and public order offending, they account for 60 percent of all transferred youths in 2004. Clearly the most violent person offenders are not being targeted for transfer to criminal courts. Juvenile court judges ought to be concerned about these alarming figures (Office of Juvenile Justice and Delinquency Prevention, 2005). It should be noted that the abrupt increase in transfers of juveniles charged with various drug crimes in the early 1990s probably reflects various federal and state initiatives to prosecute drug offenders more aggressively and subject them to more severe punishments. Some idea of the types of offenders who enter the juvenile justice system annually may be gleaned from arrest figures. Table 9.1 shows the numbers and percentage of juvenile arrests for 2001 (Snyder, 2003:3). In 2001, 96,500 juveniles were arrested for violent offenses, most of which were aggravated assault. About 6,000 arrests were for forcible rape and manslaughter, while about 25,600 arrests were for robbery. While the youths involved in these violent crime arrests represented the most likely persons to be targeted for transfers, such persons did not get transferred to criminal courts most frequently.

Despite earlier references to more extensive and violent female juvenile offending, female juveniles transferred to criminal court increased from 5 percent in 1998 to 9 percent in 2004. It is also significant to note that youths under age 16 are being transferred to a greater degree in 2004 compared with 1998. In 1998, for instance, only 13 percent of those transferred to criminal court were under age 16. In 2004, however, this figure had grown to 19 percent. This is likely reflective of the get-tough movement reaction toward more violent crimes committed by younger youths. Regarding race/ethnicity, the percentage of white youths transferred to criminal courts increased from 55 percent in 1998 to 62 percent in 2004, whereas the percentage of black youths declined from 50 percent to 42 percent during the same time interval (Office of Juvenile Justice and Delinquency Prevention, 2005). The disproportionate representation of blacks transferred to criminal courts has drawn criticism from various observers (Moak and Wallace, 2003; Redding, 2003).

Youngest Ages at Which Juveniles Can be Transferred to Criminal Court. Table 9.2 shows the youngest ages at which juveniles could be transferred or waived to criminal courts in all U.S. jurisdictions in 2004 (Office of Juvenile Justice and Delinquency Prevention, 2005).

In 2004, 14 states and all federal districts had no specified age for transferring juveniles to criminal courts for processing. Two states, Vermont and Wisconsin, specified age 10 as the minimum age at which a juvenile could be waived. Colorado, Missouri, Montana, and Oregon established age 12 as the earliest age for a juvenile waiver. Eighteen states used age 14 as the youngest transfer age, while the District of Columbia set the minimum transfer age at 15, and one state, Hawaii, used the minimum transfer age of 16. Thus, since 1987 a majority of states reduced substantially the age at which juveniles could be tried as adults in criminal courts.

Some idea of the aggressiveness of state governments and public policies directed toward getting tough toward violent juvenile offending is provided by Table 9.3. Table 9.3 shows the various states that have modified or enacted changes in their transfer provisions for juveniles during the 1996–2005 period.

Under judicial waiver modifications, four states have lowered the age limit at which juveniles can be transferred to criminal court. One example of a significant age modification is Missouri, where the minimum age for juvenile transfers was lowered from 14 to 12 for any felony. In the case of Texas, the minimum transfer age was lowered from 15 to 10. Virginia lowered the transfer age from 15 to 14. Table 9.3 also shows that other modifications were made to get tough toward juvenile offenders. Ten states added crimes to the list of those qualifying youths for transfer to criminal courts. In six states, the age of criminal accountability was lowered, while 24 states authorized additional crimes to

TABLE 9.1

Juvenile Arrests 2001

Most Serious Offense	2001 Estimated Number of Juvenile Arrests	Percent of Total Juvenile Arrests		Percent Change		
		Female	Under Age 15	1992–2001	1997–2001	2000–2001
Total	2,273,500	28%	32%	−3%	−20%	−4%
Crime Index total	587,900	29	37	−31	−28	−5
Violent Crime Index	96,500	18	33	−21	−21	−2
Murder and nonnegligent manslaughter	1,400	10	12	−62	−47	−2
Forcible rape	4,600	1	38	−24	−14	−1
Robbery	25,600	9	24	−32	−35	−4
Aggravated assault	64,900	23	37	−14	−13	−1
Property Crime Index	491,400	31	38	−32	−29	−6
Burglary	90,300	12	38	−40	−30	−6
Larceny-theft	343,600	39	39	−27	−30	−6
Motor vehicle theft	48,200	17	25	−51	−26	−2
Arson	9,300	12	64	−7	−9	8
Nonindex						
Other assaults	239,000	32	43	30	−2	2
Forgery and counterfeiting	5,800	36	11	−27	−26	−8
Fraud	8,900	33	16	−5	−18	−9
Embezzlement	1,800	44	7	152	24	−10
Stolen property (buying, receiving, possessing)	26,800	17	27	−45	−37	−6
Vandalism	105,300	13	44	−29	−22	−7
Weapons (carrying, possessing, etc.)	37,500	11	34	−35	−26	0
Prostitution and commercialized vice	1,400	69	15	−8	−5	15
Sex offense (except forcible rape and prostitution)	18,000	8	54	−10	6	1
Drug abuse violations	202,500	15	17	121	−7	0
Gambling	1,400	3	13	−53	−47	−17
Offenses against the family and children	9,600	37	37	109	−11	6
Driving under the influence	20,300	18	5	35	5	−3
Liquor law violations	138,100	32	10	21	−9	−11
Drunkenness	20,400	21	13	4	−21	−10
Disorderly conduct	171,700	30	40	34	−21	1
Vagrancy	2,300	19	25	−37	−24	−10
All other offenses (except traffic)	397,200	26	28	27	−13	−3
Suspicion	1,300	36	33	−53	−42	9
Curfew and loitering	142,900	31	28	34	−29	−13

Source: Crime in the United States 2001, Washington, DC: U.S. Government Printing Office, 2003; Howard N. Snyder, *Juvenile Arrests 2001*, Washington, DC: Office of Justice Programs, 2003.

TABLE 9.2

Minimum Age for Transferring Juveniles to Adult Court

Minimum Age	States
None	Arizona, Florida, Georgia, Indiana, Maine, Maryland, Nebraska, Nevada, New Hampshire, Oklahoma, Pennsylvania, Rhode Island, South Carolina, South Dakota, Tennessee, Washington, West Virginia
10	Vermont, Wisconsin
12	Colorado, Missouri, Montana, Oregon
13	Illinois, Mississippi, New York, North Carolina, Wyoming
14	Alabama, Arkansas, California, Connecticut, Iowa, Kansas, Kentucky, Louisiana, Massachusetts, Michigan, Minnesota, New Jersey, New Mexico, North Dakota, Ohio, Texas, Utah, Virginia
15	District of Columbia
16	Hawaii

Compiled by author 2005.

TABLE 9.3

States Modifying or Enacting Transfer Provisions, 1996–2005

Type of Transfer Provision	Action Taken (Number of States)	States Making Changes	Examples
Discretionary Waiver	Added crimes (7 states)	DE, KY, LA, MT, NV, RI, WA	Kentucky: 1996 provision permits the juvenile court to transfer a juvenile to criminal court if 14 years old and charged with a felony with a firearm.
	Lowered age limit (4 states)	CO, DE, HI, VA	Hawaii: 1997 provision adds language that allows waiver of a minor at any age (previously 16) if charged with first- or second-degree murder (or attempts) and there is no evidence that the person is committable to an institution for the mentally defective or mentally ill.
	Added or modified prior record provisions (4 states)	FL, HI, IN, KY	Florida: 1997 legislation requires that if the juvenile is 14 at the time of a fourth felony, and certain conditions apply, the State's attorney must ask the court to transfer him or her and certify the child as an adult or must pro-

TABLE 9.3

States Modifying or Enacting Transfer Provisions, 1996–2005 (cont.)

Type of Transfer Provision	Action Taken (Number of States)	States Making Changes	Examples
			vide written reasons for not making such a request.
Presumptive Waiver	Enacted provisions (2 states)	KS, UT	Kansas: 1996 legislation shifts the burden of proof to the child to rebut the presumption that the child is an adult.
Direct File	Enacted or modified (8 states)	AR, AZ, CO, FL, GA, MA, MT, OK	Colorado: 1996 legislation adds vehicular homicide, vehicular assault, and felonious arson to direct file statute.
Statutory Exclusion	Enacted provision (2 states)	AZ, MA	Arizona: 1997 legislation establishes exclusion for 15- to 17-year-olds charged with certain violent felonies.
	Added crimes (12 states)	AL, AK, DE, GA, IL, IN, OK, OR, SC, SD, UT, WA	Georgia: 1997 legislation adds crime of battery if victim is a teacher or other school personnel to list of designated felonies.
	Lowered age limit (1 state)	DE	Delaware: 1996 legislation lowers from 16 to 15 the age for which the offense of possession of a firearm during the commission of a felony is automatically prosecuted in criminal court.
	Added lesser-included offense (1 state)	IN	Indiana: 1997 legislation lists exclusion offenses, including any offense that may be joined with the listed offenses.

Source: Patricia Torbet and Linda Szymanski, *State Legislative Responses to Violent Juvenile Crime: 1996–1997 Update.* Washington, DC: U.S. Department of Justice, 1998:5. Updated 2005 by author.

be included that would automatically direct that the criminal court would have jurisdiction rather than the juvenile court.

Waiver Decision Making

Organizational and political factors are at work to influence the upward trend in the use of transfers. Politicians wish to present a get-tough facade to the public by citing waiver statistics and showing their increased use is the political response to the rise in serious youth crime. Despite political rhetoric, there has been a general increase in the use of waivers, although from 1998–2004, at least, the number of waivers has remained fairly constant (Office of Juvenile Justice and Delinquency Prevention, 2005).

Several types of waivers are used by different jurisdictions for transferring jurisdiction over juveniles from juvenile to criminal courts. One of these is the automatic transfer or automatic waiver, which several jurisdictions currently employ. This means that if youthful offenders are within a particular age range, such as age 16 or 17, and if they are charged with specific types of offenses (usually murder, robbery, rape, aggravated assault, and other violent crimes), they will be transferred automatically to criminal courts. These types of waivers, also known as legislative waivers because they were mandated by legislative bodies in various states and carry the weight of statutory authority, involve no discretionary action among prosecutors or judges. For other types of waivers, the decision-making process is largely discretionary (Flory and Hutchinson-Wallace, 2005).

Because of the discretionary nature of the waiver process, large numbers of the wrong types of juveniles are transferred to criminal courts. The wrong types of juveniles are wrong because they are not those originally targeted by juvenile justice professionals and reformers to be the primary candidates for transfers. The primary targets of waivers are intended to be the most serious, violent, and dangerous juveniles who also are the most likely to deserve more serious sanctions that criminal courts can impose. But there is a serious credibility gap between the types of juveniles who are actually transferred each year and those who should be transferred. In 1994, for instance, we have already seen that nearly half (45 percent) of all youths transferred to criminal court were charged with property or public order offenses. These types of offenses include theft, burglary, petty larceny, and disturbing the peace. Only 44 percent of those transferred in 1994 were charged with person offenses or violent crimes. If transfers, waivers, or certifications were applied as they should be applied, 100 percent of those transferred annually would be serious, violent offenders. Juvenile courts would handle all of the other cases (Jordan and Freiburger, 2005). Table 9.4 shows some of the characteristics of juveniles waived to criminal courts for the years 1989, 1994, and 1998, respectively. Although this information is somewhat dated, it nevertheless gives a fairly accurate and current portrayal of the characteristics of youths who continue to be transferred to criminal courts by juvenile court judges and others. It is very difficult to obtain accurate information about juvenile transfers for any given year. One reason is the traditional nature of juvenile courts. However, the information shown in Table 9.4 seems to be consistent with random reports and descriptions of transferred youths in selected jurisdictions in subsequent years.

Why Do Property and Public Order Offenders Get Transferred to Criminal Court?

An interested public wants to know why juvenile courts would send property offenders or public order offenders to criminal courts for processing. After all, these are the least serious offenders compared with those committing aggravated assault, attempted murder, homicide, forcible rape, and armed robbery. Studies of juvenile court judges disclose that often, persistent nonserious offenders are transferred from juvenile courts because juvenile court judges are tired of seeing these same offenders in their courts. They believe that if such persistent offenders are sent to criminal courts, this will be a better deterrent to their future offending (McNeill and Batchelor, 2004). What these judges do not understand is that criminal court prosecutors and judges often tend to downplay the significance of these small-time offenders. At least half of these nonserious property offenders will have their cases dismissed, diverted, or downgraded (Champion, 2005b). Another 40 percent will enter plea bargains and receive probation from criminal court judges. Most criminal court judges do not want to put 14-year-old property offenders or public order offenders in

---

TABLE 9.4

The Characteristics of Waived Cases Changed between 1989 and 1998

	1989	*1994*	*1998*
Total cases waived	8,000	12,100	8,100
Most serious offense			
Person	28%	43%	36%
Property	48	37	40
Drug	16	11	16
Public order	7	8	8
Gender			
Male	95%	95%	93%
Female	5	5	7
Age (years) at time of referral			
Under 16	11%	13%	13%
16 or older	89	87	87
Race/ethnicity			
White	49%	51%	55%
Black	50	45	42
Other	2	4	3
Predisposition detention			
Detained	59%	56%	50%
Not detained	41	44	50

Note: Detail may not equal 100% due to rounding.
Source: Charles M. Puzzanchma (2001). *Delinquency Cases Waived to Criminal Court, 1989–1998.* Washington, DC: U.S. Department of Justice.

adult prisons, where chronic overcrowding and the potential for sexual exploitation are pervasive. Thus, only about 10 percent of those nonserious offenders who are transferred annually will be placed in confinement for a term of months or years. About 90 percent will return to their neighborhoods and continue to reoffend (Champion and Mays, 1991).

A list of some of the factors cited by juvenile court judges that result in the transfer of nonserious property, public order, or drug offenders to criminal court are:

1. Although property offenders aren't especially serious or violent, their persistence in offending causes juvenile court judges to tire of their frequent appearances; transfers of these offenders to criminal court will "teach them a lesson."

2. Some jurisdictions mandate transfers to criminal court of those offenders who exceed some previously determined maximum of juvenile court adjudications; these may include property or public order offenders.

3. Individual differences among juvenile court judges will dictate which juveniles are transferred, despite the seriousness of their offense; if the judge doesn't like a particular youth's attitude, the youth will be transferred.

4. Any kind of drug offense should be dealt with by criminal courts; thus, a simple "possession of a controlled substance" charge (e.g., prescription medicine) may be sufficient to qualify a juvenile for a criminal court transfer.

5. What is a serious or violent offense in one juvenile court jurisdiction may not be considered serious or violent in another jurisdiction; thus, different standards are applied to the same types of juveniles in different jurisdictions.

Some idea of what happens to youths following their arrest and detention by law enforcement officers may be gleaned from an examination of Table 9.5,

TABLE 9.5

Percent Distribution of Juveniles Taken Into Police Custody By Method of Disposition, United States, 1972–2000[a]

	Referred to Juvenile Court Jurisdiction	Handled Within Department and Released	Referred to Criminal or Adult Court	Referred to Other Police Agency	Referred to Welfare Agency
1972	50.8%	45.0%	1.3%	1.6%	1.3%
1973	49.5	45.2	1.5	2.3	1.4
1974	47.0	44.4	3.7	2.4	2.5
1975	52.7	41.6	2.3	1.9	1.4
1976	53.4	39.0	4.4	1.7	1.6
1977	53.2	38.1	3.9	1.8	3.0
1978	55.9	36.6	3.8	1.8	1.9
1979	57.3	34.6	4.8	1.7	1.6
1980	58.1	33.8	4.8	1.7	1.6
1981	58.0	33.8	5.1	1.6	1.5
1982	58.9	32.5	5.4	1.5	1.6
1983	57.5	32.8	4.8	1.7	3.1
1984	60.0	31.5	5.2	1.3	2.0
1985	61.8	30.7	4.4	1.2	1.9
1986	61.7	29.9	5.5	1.1	1.8
1987	62.0	30.3	5.2	1.0	1.4
1988	63.1	29.1	4.7	1.1	1.9
1989	63.9	28.7	4.5	1.2	1.7
1990	64.5	28.3	4.5	1.1	1.6
1991	64.2	28.1	5.0	1.0	1.7
1992	62.5	30.1	4.7	1.1	1.7
1993	67.3	25.6	4.8	0.9	1.5
1994	63.2	29.5	4.7	1.0	1.7
1995	65.7	28.4	3.3	0.9	1.7
1996	68.6	23.3	6.2	0.9	0.9
1997	66.9	24.6	6.6	0.8	1.1
1998	69.2	22.2	6.8	0.9	1.0
1999	69.2	22.5	6.4	1.0	0.8
2000	70.8	20.3	7.0	1.1	0.8

Note: See *Notes*, tables 4.1 and 4.2. These data include all offenses except traffic and neglect cases.

[a] Because of rounding, percents may not add to 100.

Source: U.S. Department of Justice. Federal Bureau of Investigation, *Crime in the United States, 1972*, p. 116; *1973*, p. 119; *1974*, p. 177; *1975*, p. 177; *1976*, p. 220; *1977*, p. 219; *1978*, p. 228; *1979*, p. 230; *1980*, p. 258; *1981*, p. 233; *1982*, p. 242; *1983*, p. 245; *1984*, p. 238; *1985*, p. 240; *1986*, p. 240; *1987*, p. 225; *1988*, p. 229; *1989*, p. 233; *1990*, p. 235; *1991*, p. 278; *1992*, p. 282; *1993*, p. 282; *1994*, p. 282; *1995*, p. 265; *1996*, p. 271; *1997*, p. 279; *1998*, p. 267; *1999*, p. 269; *2000*, p. 273 (Washington, DC: USGPO).

which shows the percent distribution of juveniles taken into police custody by method of disposition for 1972–2000. Again, although this material is somewhat dated, there appears to be several trends. First, over the years, greater proportions of youths are being referred to juvenile court jurisdiction. In 2000 over 70 percent of all youths taken into police custody were referred to the juvenile court for further action. At the same time, the proportionate numbers of youths who were detained and released by police decreased from 45 percent in 1972 to 20 percent in 2000. It is especially interesting to note that criminal court referrals of youths rose from 1.3 percent in 1972 to 7 percent in 2000. These adult court referrals are somewhat misleading, however. While law enforcement officers may be referring more youths to adult court, prosecutors have the ultimate decision-making authority in charging decisions in most jurisdictions. Given the fact that approximately 1 percent of all youths referred each year to juvenile court are actually transferred or waived to criminal courts annually, it would seem that much of this initial police action is overly optimistic concerning a criminal court resolution of these referred juvenile cases.

It is questionable whether waivers have functioned as effective deterrents to future juvenile offending (Herring, 2005). For example, a study of waived youths in Idaho between 1976 and 1986 found that numerous youths were transferred to criminal courts for processing. These youths ranged in age from 14 to 18. Once processed, a majority of these youths continued to reoffend in later years. This was attributed to prosecutorial leniency, whereby more serious offenses charged against juveniles were downgraded to less serious ones before being concluded with diversion or probation (Jensen and Metsger, 1994). Also cited were the facts that juveniles don't always know that when they commit certain acts, they will be transferred to criminal court; and one's youthfulness often functions as a mitigating factor, causing charge reductions or dismissals.

In some jurisdictions where gang presence is strong, local task forces have targeted gangs for harsher treatment, including the greater likelihood of being transferred to criminal court. A study of 38 state jurisdictions disclosed, however, that most prosecutors had no specific plans relating to dealing with gang members when they were transferred to criminal courts. Furthermore, specialized gang prosecution units were rare (5 percent), even though it was believed that tougher juvenile laws would help combat the gang problem (Knox, Martin, and Tromanhauser, 1995). Most jurisdictions continue to experiment with various strategies that will target the most serious offenders for criminal prosecutions (Sanborn, 2005).

TYPES OF WAIVERS

There are four types of waiver actions. These include (1) judicial waivers; (2) direct file; (3) statutory exclusion; and (4) demand waivers.

Judicial Waivers

The largest numbers of waivers from juvenile to criminal court annually come about as the result of direct judicial action. **Judicial waivers** give the juvenile court judge the authority to decide whether to waive jurisdiction and transfer the case to criminal court (Myers, 2001). There are three kinds of judicial waivers: (1) discretionary; (2) mandatory; and (3) presumptive.

Discretionary waivers. **Discretionary waivers** empower the judge to waive jurisdiction over the juvenile and transfer the case to criminal court. Because of this type of waiver, judicial waivers are sometimes known as discretionary waivers. This is because the judge may or may not decide to waive particular youths to criminal courts for processing (Robinson, 1991).

Mandatory waivers. In the case of a **mandatory waiver,** the juvenile court judge *must* waive jurisdiction over the juvenile to criminal court if probable cause exists that the juvenile committed the alleged offense.

Presumptive waivers. Under the **presumptive waiver** scenario, judges still decide to transfer youths to criminal courts. However, the burden of proof concerning a transfer decision is shifted from the state to the juvenile. It requires that certain juveniles shall be waived to criminal court unless they can prove that they are suited for juvenile rehabilitation. In this respect, at least, they are similar to mandatory waivers. Defense counsels who wish to keep their juvenile clients within the jurisdiction of the juvenile court have a relatively difficult time arguing that their clients deserve a juvenile court adjudicatory hearing instead of prosecution in criminal court.

Table 9.6 shows the minimum ages for judicial waivers among the states and the District of Columbia for 2004. Judicial waivers are often criticized

TABLE 9.6

Minimum Ages for Judicial Waivers, by Offense Category, 2004

Judicial Waiver Offense and Minimum Age Criteria, 2004

States	Minimum Age for Judicial Waiver	Any Criminal Offense	Certain Felonies	Capital Crimes	Murder	Certain Person Offenses	Certain Property Offenses	Certain Drug Offenses	Certain Weapon Offenses
Alabama	14	14							
Alaska	NS*	NS				NS			
Arizona	NS		NS						
Arkansas	14		14	14	14	14			14
California	14	16	16		14	14	14	14	
Colorado	12		12		12	12			
Connecticut	14		14	14	14				
Delaware	NS	NS	15[a]		NS	NS	16[b]	16[b]	
District of Columbia	NS	15	15		15	15	15		NS
Florida	14	14							
Georgia	13	15		13	14[c]	14[c]	15[b]		
Hawaii	NS		14		NS	NS			
Idaho	NS	14	NS		NS	NS	NS	NS	
Illinois	13	13	15						
Indiana	NS	14	NS[b]		10			16	
Iowa	14	14	15						
Kansas	10	10	14			14		14	

TABLE 9.6

Minimum Ages for Judicial Waivers, by Offense Category, 2004 (cont.)

Judicial Waiver Offense and Minimum Age Criteria, 2004

States	Minimum Age for Judicial Waiver	Any Criminal Offense	Certain Felonies	Capital Crimes	Murder	Certain Person Offenses	Certain Property Offenses	Certain Drug Offenses	Certain Weapon Offenses
Kentucky	14		14	14					
Louisiana	14				14	14			
Maine	NS		NS		NS				
Maryland	NS	15		NS					
Michigan	14	14							
Minnesota	14		14						
Mississippi	13	13							
Missouri	12		12						
Montana	NS	NS							
Nevada	14	14	14			14			
New Hampshire	13		15		13	13		15	
New Jersey	14	14[b]			14	14	14	14	14
North Carolina	13		13	13					
North Dakota	14	16	14[b]		14	14		14	
Ohio	14		14		14	14	16		
Oklahoma	NS		NS						
Oregon	NS		15		NS	NS	15		
Pennsylvania	14		14		15	15			
Rhode Island	NS		16	NS	17	17			
South Carolina	NS	16	14		NS	NS		14	14
South Dakota	NS		NS						
Tennessee	NS	16			NS	NS			
Texas	14		14	14				14	
Utah	14		14			16	16		16
Vermont	10				10	10	10		
Virginia	14		14		14	14			
Washington	NS	NS							
West Virginia	NS		NS		NS	NS	NS	NS	
Wisconsin	14	15	14		14	14	14	14	
Wyoming	13	13							

Examples: Alabama allows waiver for any delinquency (criminal) offense involving a juvenile age 14 or older. Arizona allows waiver for any juvenile charged with a felony. New Jersey allows waiver for juveniles age 14 or older who are charged with murder or certain person, property, drug, or weapon offenses. In New Jersey, juveniles age 14 or older who have prior adjudications or convictions for certain offenses can be waived regardless of the current offense.

Note: Ages in minimum age column may not apply to all offense restrictions but represent the youngest possible age at which a juvenile may be judicially waived to criminal court.

*"NS" indicates that in at least one of the offense restrictions indicated, no minimum age is specified.

[a]Only if committed while escaping from specified juvenile facilities.

[b]Requires prior adjudication(s) or conviction(s), which may be required to have been for the same or a more serious offense type.

[c]Only if committed while in custody.

Source: Adapted from Snyder. H., and Sickmund, M. 1999. *Juvenile Offenders and Victims: 1999 National Report.* Washington, DC: U.S. Department of Justice. Office of Justice Programs, Office of Juvenile Justice and Delinquency Prevention. Updated 2005 by author.

because of their subjectivity. Two different youths charged with identical offenses may appear at different times before the same judge. On the basis of impressions formed about the youths, the judge may decide to transfer one youth to criminal court and adjudicate the other youth in juvenile court. Obviously, the intrusion of extralegal factors into this important action generates a degree of unfairness and inequality. A youth's appearance and attitude emerge as significant factors that will either make or break the offender in the eyes of the judge. These socioeconomic and behavioral criteria often overshadow the seriousness or pettiness of offenses alleged. In the context of this particular type of transfer, it is easy to see how some persistent, nonviolent offenders may suffer waiver to criminal court. This is an easy way for the judge to get rid of them.

Although judges have this discretionary power in most jurisdictions, youths are still entitled to a hearing where they can protest the waiver action (Mears, 2003; Myers, 2003). While it is true that the criminal court poses risks to juveniles in terms of potentially harsher penalties, it is also true that being tried as an adult entitles youths to all of the adult constitutional safeguards, including the right to a trial by jury. In a later section of this chapter, we examine closely this and other options that may be of benefit to certain juveniles. Thus, some juveniles may not want to fight waiver or transfer actions, largely because they may be treated more leniently by criminal courts.

Direct File

Whenever offenders are screened at intake and referred to the juvenile court for possible prosecution, prosecutors in various jurisdictions will conduct further screenings of these youths (Massachusetts Statistical Analysis Center, 2001). They determine which cases merit further action and formal adjudication by judges. Not all cases sent to prosecutors by intake officers automatically result in subsequent formal juvenile court action. Prosecutors may decline to prosecute certain cases, particularly if there are problems with witnesses who are either missing or who refuse to testify, if there are evidentiary issues, or if there are overloaded juvenile court dockets. A relatively small proportion of cases may warrant waivers to criminal courts (Toth, 2005). Table 9.7 shows the states that had direct file or concurrent jurisdiction provisions in 2004.

Under **direct file,** the prosecutor has the sole authority to decide whether any given juvenile case will be heard in criminal court or juvenile court. Essentially, the prosecutor decides which court should have jurisdiction over the juvenile (Feld, 2001). Prosecutors with direct file power are said to have **concurrent jurisdiction.** This is another name for direct file. In Florida, for example, prosecutors have concurrent jurisdiction. They may file extremely serious charges (e.g., murder, rape, aggravated assault, robbery) against youths in criminal courts and present cases to grand juries for indictment action. Or prosecutors may decide to file the same cases in the juvenile court (D'Angelo and Brown, 2005).

Statutory Exclusion

Statutory exclusion means that certain juvenile offenders are automatically excluded from the juvenile court's original jurisdiction (Ziedenberg et al., 2001). Legislatures of various states declare a particular list of offenses to be excluded

TABLE 9.7

States with Concurrent Jurisdiction and Direct File Provisions, by Offense, 2004

Concurrent Jurisdiction Offense and Minimum Age Criteria, 2004

States	Minimum Age for Concurrent Jurisdiction	Any Criminal Offense	Certain Felonies	Capital Crimes	Murder	Certain Offenses			
						Person Offenses	Property Offenses	Drug Offenses	Weapon Offenses
Arizona	14		14						
Arkansas	14		14	14	14	14			14
Colorado	14		14		14	14	14		14
District of Columbia	16				16	16	16		
Florida	NS*	16ᵃ	16	NSᵇ	14	14	14		14
Georgia	NS			NS					
Louisiana	15				15	15	15	15	
Massachusetts	14		14			14			14
Michigan	14		14		14	14	14	14	
Montana	12				12	12	16	16	16
Nebraska	NS	16ᶜ	NS						
Oklahoma	15				15	15	15	16	16
Vermont	16	16							
Virginia	14				14	14			
Wyoming	14	17	14						

Examples: In Arizona, prosecutors have discretion to file directly in criminal court those cases involving juveniles age 14 or older charged with certain felonies (defined in State statutes). In Florida, prosecutors may "direct file" cases involving juveniles age 16 or older charged with a misdemeanor (if they have a prior adjudication) or a felony offense and those age 14 or older charged with murder or certain person, property, or weapon offenses; no minimum age is specified for cases in which a grand jury indicts a juvenile for a capital offense.

Note: Ages in minimum age column may not apply to all offense restrictions but represent the youngest possible age at which a juvenile's case may be filed directly in criminal court.

*"NS" indicates that in at least one of the offense restrictions indicated, no minimum age is specified.

ᵃApplies to misdemeanors and requires prior adjudication(s), which may be required to have been for the same or a more serious offense type.

ᵇRequires grand jury indictment.

ᶜApplies to misdemeanors.

Source: Adapted from Snyder. H., and Sickmund, M. 1999. *Juvenile Offenders and Victims: 1999 National Report.* Washington, DC: U.S. Department of Justice, Office of Justice Programs, Office of Juvenile Justice and Delinquency Prevention. Updated 2005 by author.

from the jurisdiction of juvenile courts. Added to this list of excluded offenses is a particular age range. Thus, in Illinois, if a 16-year-old juvenile is charged with murder, rape, or aggravated assault, this particular juvenile is automatically excluded from the jurisdiction of the juvenile court. Instead, the case will be heard in criminal court (Snyder, Sickmund, and Poe-Yamagata, 2000). In 2004, 30 states had statutory exclusion provisions and excluded certain types of offenders from juvenile court jurisdiction (Office of Juvenile Justice and Delinquency Prevention, 2005). Because state legislatures created statutory exclusion provisions, this waiver action is sometimes known as a **legislative waiver** (Myers, 2001). And because these provisions mandate the automatic waiver of juveniles to criminal court, they are also known as automatic waivers. States with statutory exclusion provisions by minimum age for 2004 are shown in Table 9.8.

TABLE 9.8

States with Statutory Exclusion by Offense and Minimum Age, 2004

Statutory Exclusion Offense and Minimum Age Criteria, 2004

States	Minimum Age for Concurrent Jurisdiction	Any Criminal Offense	Certain Felonies	Capital Crimes	Murder	Certain Offenses			
						Person Offenses	Property Offenses	Drug Offenses	Weapon Offenses
Alabama	16		16	16				16	
Alaska	16					16	16		
Arizona	15		15[a]		15	15			
Delaware	15		15						
Florida	NS*	NS[a]				NS			
Georgia	13				13	13			
Idaho	14				14	14	14	14	
Illinois	13		15[b]		13	15		15	15
Indiana	16		16		16	16		16	16
Iowa	16		16					16	16
Louisiana	15				15	15			
Maryland	14			14	16	16			16
Massachusetts	14				14				
Minnesota	16				16				
Mississippi	13		13	13					
Montana	17				17	17	17	17	17
Nevada	NS	NS[a]			NS	16[a]			
New Mexico	15				15[c]				
New York	13				13	14	14		
Oklahoma	13				13				
Oregon	15				15	15			
Pennsylvania	NS				NS	15			
South Carolina	16		16						
South Dakota	16		16						
Utah	16		16[d]		16				
Vermont	14				14	14	14		
Washington	16				16	16	16		
Wisconsin	NS				10	NS[e]			

Examples: In Delaware, Juveniles age 15 or older charged with certain felonies must be tried in criminal court. In Arizona, juveniles age 15 or older must be tried in criminal court if they are charged with murder or certain person offenses or if they have prior felony adjudications and are charged with a felony.

Note: Ages in minimum age column may not apply to all offense restrictions but represent the youngest possible age at which a juvenile's case may be excluded from juvenile court.

*"NS" indicates that in at least one of the offense restrictions indicated, no minimum age is specified.

[a]Requires prior adjudication(s), or conviction(s), which may be required to have been for the same or a more serious offense type.

[b]Only escape or bail violation while subject to prosecution in criminal court.

[c]Requires grand jury indictment.

[d]Requires prior commitment in a secure facility.

[e]Only if charged while confined or on probation or parole.

Source: Adapted from Snyder, H., and Sickmund, M. 1999. *Juvenile Offenders and Victims: 1999 National Report.* Washington, DC: U.S. Department of Justice, Office of Justice Programs, Office of Juvenile Justice and Delinquency Prevention. Updated 2005 by author.

Demand Waivers

Under certain conditions and in selected jurisdictions, juveniles may submit motions for **demand waiver** actions. Demand waiver actions are requests or motions filed by juveniles and their attorneys to have their cases transferred from juvenile courts to criminal courts. Why would juveniles want to have their cases transferred to criminal courts?

One reason is that most U.S. jurisdictions do not provide jury trials for juveniles in juvenile courts as a matter of right (*McKeiver v. Pennsylvania,* 1971). However, about a fifth of the states have established provisions for jury trials for juveniles at their request and depending on the nature of the charges against them. In the remainder of the states, jury trials for juveniles are granted only at the discretion of the juvenile court judge. Most juvenile court judges are not inclined to grant jury trials to juveniles. Thus, if juveniles are (1) in a jurisdiction where they are not entitled to a jury trial even if they request one from the juvenile court judge; (2) face serious charges; and (3) believe that their cases would receive greater impartiality from a jury in a criminal courtroom, they may seek a demand waiver in order to have their cases transferred to criminal court. Florida permits demand waivers as one of several waiver options (Office of Juvenile Justice and Delinquency Prevention, 2005).

Other Types of Waivers

Reverse Waivers.   **A reverse waiver** is an action by the criminal court to transfer direct file or statutory exclusion cases from criminal court back to juvenile court, usually at the recommendation of the prosecutor (Bilchik, 1996:4). Typically, juveniles who would be involved in these reverse waiver hearings would be those who were automatically sent to criminal court because of statutory exclusion. Thus, criminal court judges can send at least some of these juveniles back to the jurisdiction of the juvenile court. Reverse waiver actions may also be instigated by defense counsels on behalf of their clients.

Once An Adult/Always An Adult.   The **once an adult/always an adult provision** is perhaps the most serious and long-lasting for affected juvenile offenders. This provision means that once juveniles have been convicted in criminal court, they are forever after considered adults for the purpose of criminal prosecutions. For instance, suppose a 12-year-old is transferred to criminal court in Vermont and then convicted of a crime. Subsequently at age 15, if the same juvenile commits another crime, such as vehicular theft, he would be subject to prosecution in criminal court. Thus, the fact of a criminal court conviction means that the juvenile permanently loses his access to the juvenile court. In 2004, two-thirds of all states had once an adult/always an adult provisions (Office of Juvenile Justice and Delinquency Prevention, 2005).

Interestingly, the once an adult/always an adult provision is not as ominous as it appears. It requires that particular jurisdictions keep track of each juvenile offender previously convicted of a crime. This record-keeping is not particularly sophisticated in different jurisdictions. Some juveniles may simply move away from the jurisdiction where they were originally convicted. Fourteen-year-old juveniles who are convicted of a crime in California may move to North Dakota or Vermont, where they may be treated as first-offenders in those juvenile courts. How are North Dakota and Vermont juvenile courts

 **BOX 9.3**

Deborah E. Kesler
Chief Juvenile Probation Officer, Vigo County, Terre Haute, IN

Statistics:

B.S.W. (social work), Indiana State University

Background and Experiences

When I enrolled in the fall semester at Indiana State University in 1977, I really had no idea what I wanted to do with my life. I just knew I was supposed to go to college. I ended up in the School of Social Work still wondering what I was going to do with my degree. It was in the fall semester of my senior year that the light came on. I was assigned to an internship at the Vigo County Juvenile Center and was to shadow one of the probation officers there by the name of Monte Tosser. To this day I am grateful to Monte, for he was so interested in his job and the clientele, that I couldn't help being enthused also. It took one week for me to realize that this was what I wanted for a professional career. I loved the challenge of working with the probationers and their families. There were so many aspects to deal within just one case and I enjoyed the networking that needed to be done in an attempt to be successful with that one child. One part of the job that I had no idea I would become interested in was law. To sit in court and watch all that went on between children, their parents, the judge, and attorneys was very exciting for me. I liked the fact that I was learning a part of the legal system that was specialized and not known to everyone, just those that worked within it.

I graduated from Indiana State University in May 1981 and took a position with Big Brother/Big Sister of Vigo County and settled into adult living. After 18 months with Big Brother/Big Sister, I received a telephone call from Monte, my internship supervisor, asking if I was still interested in juvenile probation. The juvenile court and staff were very politically connected at that time, and the newly elected judge was coming into office and "cleaning house" at the juvenile center. Monte said he couldn't promise anything, but the Chief Probation Officer had remembered me and suggested that I apply for one of the three positions. I was thrilled at the possibility of becoming a probation officer and submitted my resume. I was granted an interview with the Circuit Court Judge and after waiting three hours in his waiting room, I was escorted in to meet with him. The interview lasted 15 minutes and I left feeling that the judge had not been impressed with me and that I had blown my shot at getting my dream job. To my surprise, I was called several days later by the chief and offered the last position! The judge had told the chief that he had chosen two of the three new officers and she could decide who the third officer would be. Because I had shown such an interest and worked hard during my internship, I was hired. I had obtained my career goal at the age of 23. To this day, I tell my interns this story to emphasize the importance of their performance during their internship and how it may affect them long after the job is done.

I have been at the Vigo County Juvenile Justice Center since January 1983. I began as a line officer and was promoted to Chief Juvenile Probation Officer in May 1989. Certainly a lot has changed throughout my years here, both good and bad. My staff has grown from four probation officers to seven, but so has the number of juveniles we work with. I logged in 1,443 reports my staff dealt with in 2004, as opposed to 809 reports in 1984, and we now average 60–70 juveniles on probation. We have a new facility, which was built in 2001, replacing a facility that was renovated and opened as the juvenile center in 1964. A full-time magistrate replaced the part-time referee in 1996. We have two alternative high schools in addition to the three regular high schools, along with two specialized classrooms located in our mental health facility. We have a Community Corrections Program strictly for juveniles, and several programs through our mental health facilities are now offered for youthful offenders. Our community network system is growing with new programs and new positions, but so is our target population.

I enjoy the challenges that my job brings every day and no two days are ever alike. In order to be successful in this field, you need to be able to get along with all walks of life and never attempt to force your morals on anyone. I work hard to have my probationers see that there is a better way to live and that they have the capabilities to live that way, the way without drugs, violence, or constant drama. I have gotten close to several of the children I have worked with and some still call for advice or just to check in. I recently saw one of the girls I worked with when I first started in the department. Joy (not her real name) is now 34 years old with three children of her own working as a server in a nice restaurant. She told me after several bad relationships with men that she has married a good guy who works hard to take care of her family, treats her well, and does not use any drugs or alcohol. She has just enrolled at Indiana State University majoring in criminal justice and is doing very well. This was a single girl who I thought despised me and never listened to anything I said. I had heard she was a single mother working as an exotic dancer in another city. She has really turned things around and, to my surprise, told me I had truly influenced her life and that I had inspired her to study criminal justice, and that she hopes to work with kids. To have a former probationer tell me that makes all the bad days in my office worth it.

I also have another ex-probationer who is in her late 30s who calls whenever she needs help or advice. She was one of the toughest girls I had ever worked with. The first report I received on Ann (not her real name) was for battery where she had spit on the victim 25 times along with punching her in the face. She comes from a family of alcoholics and her father was well known by police for fighting in the local bars. Ann and I were together from the time she was 13. Her thoughts were certainly not like mine, and they got her into lots of trouble in the community and school. She was the type of child that nobody wanted around. I finally had her sent to a residential placement facility 3 hours from home. I traveled there several Sundays to visit her and check on her progress. She later told me that my husband and I were the only visitors she ever had, and that her parents had tried to come up once, but they had gotten drunk on the way and arrived at the facility intoxicated. They were made to leave and never attempted another trip. Ann has not fared as well as Joy, unfortunately, but she always feels comfortable to call whenever she needs me and I'm happy that we have a relationship that she is comfortable with. She was recently arrested for prostitution and called me, although she was obviously embarrassed with the situation. She was uncomfortable with the police wanting to "wire her up" to arrest other prostitutes. I arranged to meet her at the police station to help with the situation, but she never showed up. She later came to my office and left a note saying that she was sorry she had stood me up and she would call later, signing the note, "Love ya, Ann." Ann knows that I will advise and suggest without judgment. She knows what I want for her life, but she also knows I won't give up on her for all of her poor decisions.

My department works hard to help each child see the best in himself or herself. Of all the juveniles that I have worked with over the years, I can honestly say that only a very small percentage have made it impossible for me to find good qualities in them. Although I have my days, I still very much enjoy my job and am so thankful that I was sent to the Juvenile Center to complete my internship for my major all those years ago. I work with many competent, caring professionals throughout my community who also inspire me to do my very best every day. Two of the highlights of my career have been receiving the "Juvenile Probation Officer of the Year" award from the Indiana Correctional Association in 1999, and the Law Enforcement Commendation Award from the Sons of the American Revolution in 2000.

Advice to Students

The field of probation plays a very important part in the criminal justice system. It is a fast-moving job that takes lots of energy and patience. I am often invited by professors at Indiana State University to speak to their classes about my job, and one piece of advice I always give is to pace yourself. We work with many sad, unfortunate families and situations. It is easy to become immersed in the various cases and children, but probation officers have to safeguard themselves from that or you risk burnout. I am sure that this profession has lost many wonderful officers simply because they let the job overtake them. Don't cheat yourself out of reaching your potential in this profession. I make sure that when I am home, I am centered on my life there and my family. It's a time to reenergize yourself for the next day and all of the challenges that come with the territory.

Laws are always changing, as well as policies, programming, and techniques to deal with delinquents and the situations they find themselves in. Professionals need to always be ready to learn and change their approach. If you decide you know all there is to know about your selected profession, you will not be effective with your clients. You need to be open to new ideas, new programs, and new techniques. You will only benefit from attending conferences, reading

periodicals, and keeping up on changes in the law.

Acknowledge that you are human and you will make mistakes. The key is to realize the mistake and correct it. You also have to be able to say you're wrong, apologize, and move on. In just one case, there are so many decisions to make along with people, situations, and details to remember, it is difficult to know it all. Probationers and their families expect you to know and remember all about their case and you won't. Whenever you have a detail wrong, admit it and move on. Don't beat yourself up for words or advice that does not come out right. I have gone home wishing I had used more patience on the phone or worded instructions differently. I think through the situation and how I might have handled it more successfully. Be ready to apologize if need be, and have a more patient attitude ready for the next frustrating situation that will land on your office doorstep.

Be confident in your abilities and enjoy yourself. This is a job that can eat you alive if you let it. Don't let law officials or attorneys tell you how to do your job. You can learn from them, but do what you think is best for the child and situation. Don't let probationers or families intimidate you. Often the type of clientele you will deal with is used to this technique to get the results he or she wants. Make sure all involved know you are in charge, that input is welcomed, but that you will make the decision you feel most comfortable with. I always encourage my staff to make recommendations to the court that they feel comfortable with, no matter how the prosecutor, defense, or even the judge might feel about those recommendations. It's always a good feeling to arrive at the end of the day and feel that you did your best. I wish you all the best with whatever career choice you make.

supposed to know that a particular 14-year-old has a criminal conviction in California? Information-sharing among juvenile courts throughout the United States is very limited or nonexistent. Thus, the intent of the once an adult/always an adult provision can often be defeated simply by relocating and moving to another jurisdiction. This is true also of juvenile court jurisdictions within the same state. In California, for instance, a state with the once an adult/always an adult provision, if a juvenile has been transferred to a criminal court for prosecution in Long Beach, California, and moves to Bellflower, Carson, Paramount, or Pomona, other California cities, it is very likely that the juvenile courts in those cities will be unaware of the fact that the juvenile was treated as an adult for purposes of a criminal prosecution in Long Beach. Such is the state of the art regarding juvenile record information-sharing among California juvenile courts. The fact is that most states have a combination of various transfer or waiver provisions.

The most popular type of waiver action is the judicial waiver, where 46 states and the District of Columbia had judicial waiver provisions in 2004 (Office of Juvenile Justice and Delinquency Prevention, 2005). Over half of all states (30) had statutory exclusion provisions in 2004. Reverse waivers, which result from automatic or legislative waivers, were used in 25 states in 2004. Also, 33 states enacted had the once an adult/always an adult provision. Fifteen states had concurrent jurisdiction or direct file provisions. A summary of the juvenile transfer provisions for all states for 2004 is shown in Table 9.9.

TABLE 9.9

Juvenile Transfer Provisions for All States, 2004

State	Judicial Waiver			Concurrent Jurisdiction	Statutory Exclusion	Reverse Waiver	Once an Adult Always an Adult
	Discretionary	Presumptive	Mandatary				
Total Number of States	46	15	14	15	28	23	31
Alabama	•				•		•
Alaska	•	•			•		
Arizona	•	•		•	•	•	•
Arkansas	•			•		•	
California	•	•					•
Colorado	•	•		•		•	
Connecticut			•			•	
Delaware	•		•		•	•	•
District of Columbia	•	•		•			•
Florida	•			•	•		•
Georgia	•		•	•	•	•	
Hawaii	•						•
Idaho	•				•		•
Illinois	•	•	•		•		
Indiana	•		•		•		•
Iowa	•				•	•	•
Kansas	•	•					•
Kentucky	•			•		•	
Louisiana	•		•	•	•		
Maine	•						•
Maryland	•				•	•	
Massachusetts				•	•		
Michigan	•			•			•

(continued)

TABLE 9.9

Juvenile Transfer Provisions for All States, 2004 (cont.)

State	Judicial Waiver			Concurrent Jurisdiction	Statutory Exclusion	Reverse Waiver	Once an Adult Always an Adult
	Discretionary	Presumptive	Mandatory				
Minnesota	•	•			•		•
Mississippi	•				•	•	•
Missouri	•						•
Montana	•			•	•		
Nebraska				•		•	
Nevada	•	•			•	•	•
New Hampshire	•	•					•
New Jersey	•	•					
New Mexico					•		
New York					•	•	
North Carolina	•		•				
North Dakota	•	•	•				•
Ohio	•		•				•
Oklahoma	•			•	•	•	•
Oregon	•				•	•	•
Pennsylvania	•	•			•	•	•
Rhode Island	•	•	•				•
South Carolina	•		•		•	•	
South Dakota	•				•	•	•
Tennessee	•					•	
Texas	•						•
Utah	•	•			•		
Vermont	•			•	•	•	
Virginia	•		•	•		•	•
Washington	•				•		•
West Virginia	•		•				
Wisconsin	•				•	•	•
Wyoming	•			•		•	

Note: In States with a combination of transfer mechanisms, the exclusion, mandatory waiver, or concurrent jurisdiction provisions generally target the oldest juveniles and/or those charged with the most serious offenses, while those charged with relatively less serious offenses and/or younger juveniles may be eligible for discretionary waiver.

Source: Adapted from Snyder, H., and Sickmund, M. 1999. *Juvenile Offenders and Victims: 1999 National Report,* Washington, DC: U.S. Department of Justice. Office of Justice Programs, Office of Juvenile Justice and Delinquency Prevention. Updated 2005 by author.

WAIVER AND REVERSE WAIVER HEARINGS

Waiver Hearings

All juveniles who are waived to criminal court for processing are entitled to a hearing on the waiver if they request one (Massachusetts Statistical Analysis Center, 2001). A **waiver hearing** is a formal proceeding designed to determine whether the waiver action taken by the judge or prosecutor is the correct action, and that the juvenile should be transferred to criminal court. Waiver hearings are normally conducted before the juvenile court judge. Waiver hearings are initiated through a **waiver motion,** where the prosecutor usually requests the judge to send the case to criminal court. These hearings are to some extent evidentiary, since a case must be made for why criminal courts should have jurisdiction in any specific instance. Usually, juveniles with lengthy prior records, several previous referrals, and/or one or more previous adjudications as delinquent are more susceptible to being transferred. While the offenses alleged are most often crimes, it is not always the case that the crimes are the most serious ones. Depending on the jurisdiction, the seriousness of crimes associated with transferred cases varies. As has been shown by previous research, large numbers of cases involving property crimes are transferred to criminal courts for processing. In some instances, chronic, persistent, or habitual status offenders have been transferred, particularly if they have violated specific court orders to attend school, participate in therapeutic programs, perform community service work, make restitution, or engage in some other constructive enterprise.

If waivers are to be fully effective, then only those most serious offenders should be targeted for transfer. Transferring less serious and petty offenders accomplishes little in the way of enhanced punishments for these offenders. Criminal courts often regard transfers of such cases as nuisances, and it is not uncommon to see the widespread use of probation or diversion here. Criminal court prosecutors may ***nolle prosequi*** many of these cases before they reach the trial stage. These are plea agreement hearings that require judicial approval before guilty pleas are accepted.

Reverse Waiver Hearings

In those jurisdictions with direct file or statutory exclusion provisions, juveniles and their attorneys may contest these waiver actions through **reverse waiver hearings** or **reverse waiver actions.** Reverse waiver hearings are conducted before criminal court judges to determine whether to send the juvenile's case back to juvenile court. For both waiver and reverse waiver hearings, defense counsel and the prosecution attempt to make a case for their desired action. In many respects, these hearings are similar to preliminary hearings or preliminary examinations conducted within the criminal justice framework. Some evidence and testimony are permitted, and arguments for both sides are heard. Once all arguments have been presented and each side has had a chance to rebut the opponents' arguments, the judge decides the matter.

Time Standards Governing Waiver Decisions

Although only less than 1 percent of all juveniles processed by the juvenile justice system annually are transferred to criminal courts for processing as adults, only nine states had time limits governing transfer provisions for juveniles as of 1993 (Butts, 1996b:559). These states included Arizona, Indiana, Iowa, Maryland, Massachusetts, Michigan, Minnesota, New Mexico, and Virginia. Table 9.10 shows the time limits that govern juvenile court handling of delinquency cases considered for transfer to criminal court.

Table 9.10 shows that for Maryland, as an example, a 30-day maximum time limit between one's detention and the transfer hearing. If the transfer hearing results in a denial of the transfer, then there is a 30-day maximum between

TABLE 9.10

Time Limits (in Days) for Juvenile Court Adjudication and Disposition Hearings, in Cases Not Involving Proceedings for Transfer to Criminal Court[a]

State	Court Referral	Start of Adjudication Deadline — Filing of Charges (det/not det)	Preliminary Hearing (det/not det)	Detention Admission	Detention Hearing	Start of Disposition Deadline — Filing of Charges (det/not det)	Adjudication (det/not det)
Alaska							Immed.[b]
Arizona			30/60				30/45
Arkansas					14		14/—
California	30	30[b]		15			
Delaware				30[c]			
Florida		21/90[c]					15/—
Georgia		10/60					30/—
Illinois		120[b,c]		10[c]			
Iowa		60[b,d]					ASAP[b]
Louisiana			30/90				30[b]
Maryland		60[b]		30			30[b]
Massachusetts	60						
Michigan		180[b]		63			35/—
Minnesota		30/60					15[c]/45[c]
Mississippi		90/—		21			14/—
Montana							ASAP[b]
Nebraska		180/—				180[c]	
New Hampshire		21/30					21/30
New Jersey				30			30/60
New Mexico							20/—
New York			14/60				10/50
North Dakota		30[b]		14			
Ohio		10/—					Immed.[b]
Oregon	56			28			28[c]
Pennsylvania		10/—					20/—
Rhode Island				7			
South Carolina		40[b]					
Tennessee		—/90		30			15/90
Texas		10/—					
Vermont		15/—					30[b]
Virginia		—/120		21			30/—
Washington		30[b]/60[b]					14/21
Wisconsin			20[e]/30[e]			10[e]/30[e]	10/30
Wyoming					60		

[a]Twenty states did not have time limits for adjudication as of 1993: AL, AK, CO, CT, DC, HI, ID, IN, KS, KY, ME, MO, MT, NV, NM, NC, OK, SD, UT, and WV. Twenty-six states did not have time limits for dispositions: AL, CA, CO, CT, DE, DC, HI, ID, IL, IN, KS, KY, ME, MA, MO, NV, NC, ND, OK, RI, SC, SD, TX, UT, WV, and WY.
[b]Statute did not distinguish detention status.
[c]Extensions are possible.
[d]If statutory right to speedy trial is waived.
[e]Statute-specified time from "plea hearing."
Source: Butts, 1996b: 557–558. Data source: analysis by the National Center for Juvenile Justice. Reprinted by permission, of the American Journal of Criminal Law and the authors. Updated 2005 by author.

the denial of the transfer and the juvenile court adjudication. In contrast, Minnesota provides only a one-day maximum between placing youths in adult jails and filing transfer motions by juvenile court prosecutors. New Mexico's provisions are similar to those of Maryland.

IMPLICATIONS OF WAIVER HEARINGS FOR JUVENILES

Those juveniles who contest or fight their transfers to criminal courts or attempt to obtain a reverse waiver wish to remain within the juvenile justice system, be treated as juveniles, and be adjudicated by juvenile court judges. But not all juveniles who are the subject of transfer are eager to contest the transfer. There are several important implications for youths, depending on the nature of their offenses, their prior records, and the potential penalties the respective courts may impose. Under the right circumstances, having one's case transferred to criminal court may offer juvenile defendants considerable advantages not normally enjoyed if their cases were to remain in the juvenile court. In the following discussion, some of the major advantages or disadvantages of being transferred are examined.

Positive Benefits Resulting from Juvenile Court Adjudications

Among the positive benefits of having one's case heard in juvenile court are that:

1. Juvenile court proceedings are civil, not criminal; thus, juveniles do not acquire criminal records;
2. Juveniles are less likely to receive sentences of incarceration;
3. Compared with criminal court judges, juvenile court judges have considerably more discretion in influencing a youth's life chances prior to or at the time of adjudication;
4. Juvenile courts are traditionally more lenient than criminal courts;
5. There is considerably more public sympathy extended to those who are processed in the juvenile justice system, despite the general public advocacy for a greater get-tough policy;
6. Compared with criminal courts, juvenile courts do not have as elaborate an information-exchange apparatus to determine whether certain juveniles have been adjudicated delinquent by juvenile courts in other jurisdictions; and
7. Life imprisonment and the death penalty lie beyond the jurisdiction of juvenile judges, and they cannot impose these harsh sentences.

First, since juvenile courts are civil bodies, records of juvenile adjudications are suppressed, expunged, or otherwise deleted when these adjudicated juveniles reach adulthood. Also, juvenile court judges often act compassionately, by sentencing youthful offenders to probation, by issuing verbal warnings or reprimands, or by imposing nonincarcerative, nonfine alternatives as sanctions.

A fourth advantage is that juvenile courts are traditionally noted for their lenient treatment of juveniles. This seems to be more a function of the influence of priorities in dealing with juvenile offenders rather than some immovable policy that might impose standard punishments of incarceration as penalties. For example, a national conference of juvenile justice researchers in New Orleans, Louisiana, recommended that juvenile courts should emphasize three general goals in their adjudication decisions: (1) protection of the community; (2) imposing accountability; and (3) helping juveniles and equipping them to live productively and responsibly in the community (Maloney, Romig, and Armstrong, 1988). This balanced approach is largely constructive, in that it heavily emphasizes those skills that lead to the rehabilitation of youthful offenders. And in the minds of many citizens, rehabilitation is equated with leniency. Increasingly used, however, are residential placement facilities in various jurisdictions, where the rate of recidivism among juveniles is relatively low compared with those offenders with more extensive histories of delinquent conduct.

A fifth advantage of juvenile court processing is that sympathy for youths who commit offenses is easier to extend in sentencing. Many juveniles get into trouble because of sociocultural circumstances. Individualized treatment may be necessary, perhaps administered through appropriate community-based facilities, in order to promote greater respect for the law as well as to provide needed services. Mandatory diversion policies have received some public support in various jurisdictions, especially where less serious youthful offenders are involved and they are charged with nonviolent, petty crimes. Many of these juveniles may not require intensive supervised probation or incarceration, but rather, they require responsible supervision to guide them toward and assist them in various services and treatment-oriented agencies (Beyer, Grisso, and Young, 1997).

Juvenile courts do not ordinarily exchange information with most other juvenile courts in a massive national communication network. Local control over youthful offenders accomplishes only this limited objective—local control. Thus juveniles might migrate to other jurisdictions and offend repeatedly, where getting caught in those alternative jurisdictions would not be treated as recidivism in the original jurisdiction. This is beneficial for juveniles, who might seek to commit numerous offenses in a broad range of contiguous jurisdictions. The probability that their acts in one jurisdiction would come to the attention of juvenile officials in their own jurisdiction is often remote.

Furthermore, juveniles in certain jurisdictions may reappear before the same juvenile court judge frequently. Multiple adjudications for serious offenses do not mean automatically that these youths will be placed in juvenile detention or transferred to criminal court (Feld, 2003). Even those who reappear before the same juvenile court judge may be adjudicated repeatedly without significant effect. In one investigation, it was found that a sample of serious juvenile offenders had been adjudicated in the same jurisdiction an average of 10 times (Snyder, Sickmund, and Poe-Yamagata, 1996). Thus, juvenile court judges may give juveniles the "benefit of the doubt" and impose nondetention alternatives. Nondetention alternatives as sentences are influenced significantly by the degree of overcrowding in secure juvenile facilities. Thus, leniency displayed by juvenile court judges may really be due to necessity rather than because of some personal belief that incarceration should be avoided.

Finally, it is beyond the jurisdiction of juvenile court judges to impose life imprisonment and/or the death penalty, despite the potential for jury trials in some juvenile court jurisdictions (Sanborn, 1993). Thus, if offenders come before a juvenile court judge for processing and have committed especially aggravated violent or capital offenses, the juvenile court judge's options are limited. Incarceration in a juvenile facility, possibly for a prolonged period, is the most powerful sanction available to these judges. However, if waiver actions are successful, the road is paved for the possible application of such punishments in criminal courts.

Unfavorable Implications of Juvenile Court Adjudications

Juvenile courts are not perfect, however, and they may be disadvantageous to many youthful offenders. Some of their major limitations are that:

1. Juvenile court judges have the power to administer lengthy sentences of incarceration, not only for serious and dangerous offenders, but for status offenders as well;

2. In most states, juvenile courts are not required to provide juveniles with a trial by jury;

3. Because of their wide discretion in handling juveniles, judges may over-penalize a large number of those appearing before them on various charges; and

4. Juveniles do not enjoy the same range of constitutional rights as adults in criminal courts.

Adverse to juveniles, juvenile court judges may impose short- or long-term secure confinement on offenders, regardless of the nonseriousness or pettiness of their offenses. The case of *In re Gault* (1967) makes it abundantly clear that juvenile court judges can impose lengthy custodial dispositions for youths adjudicated delinquent for relative minor offending. For committing the same offense, an adult would have been fined $50 and may have served up to 30 days in a local jail. As we learned in Gault's case, the disposition to an industrial school for nearly 6 years was excessive and there were constitutional irregularities. This unusual incarcerative sentence was subsequently overturned by the U.S. Supreme Court on several important constitutional grounds. However, juvenile court judges continue to have broad discretionary powers and may impose similar sentences, provided that the constitutional guarantees ensured by the *Gault* decision are present in any subsequent case.

The case of *Gault* is not an isolated instance of disposing of youths who have committed petty offenses with long periods of secure confinement. For instance, in Hennepin County, Minnesota, 330 transfer motions between 1986 and 1992 were studied by Podkopacz, Rasmussen, and Feld (1996). These researchers found that when juveniles were transferred to criminal courts for various crimes, those charged with violent offenses tended to serve longer prison terms than the periods of incarceration imposed on juveniles who committed the same types of offenses, but who had their cases adjudicated in juvenile courts. However, juvenile court judges typically imposed *longer* incarcerative sentences on property offenders compared with how criminal courts sentenced convicted juvenile property offenders who had been transferred to criminal court jurisdiction. Thus, these researchers question existing juvenile court policies about the nature and types of dispositions imposed on adjudicated juvenile offenders. Presently, there is great diversity among juvenile court judges in different states about the nature and types of dispositions they impose on juveniles adjudicated for similar offenses.

Another disadvantage of juvenile courts is that granting any juvenile a jury trial is mostly at the discretion of prosecutors and juvenile court judges. If the judge approves, the juvenile may receive a jury trial in selected jurisdictions, if a jury trial is requested. This practice typifies juvenile courts in 38 states. In the remaining states, juveniles may request and receive trials under certain circumstances. In other words, the state legislatures of at least 12 states have made it possible for juveniles to receive jury trials upon request, although the circumstances for such jury trial requests parallel closely the jury trial requests of defendants in criminal courts. Again, we must consider the civil–criminal distinction that adheres respectively to juvenile and criminal court proceedings. Jury trials in juvenile courts retain the civil connotation, without juveniles acquiring criminal records. However, jury trials in adult criminal courts, upon the defendant's conviction, result in the offender's acquisition of a criminal record.

A third limitation of juvenile proceedings is that the wide discretion enjoyed by most juvenile court judges is often abused. This abuse is largely in the form of excessive leniency, and it doesn't occur exclusively at the adjudicatory stage of juvenile processing. Because of this leniency and wide discretionary power, many juvenile courts have drawn criticisms from both the public and juvenile justice professionals. A common criticism is that juvenile courts neglect the accountability issue through the excessive use of probation or diversion (Nieto, 1998).

Another criticism of these courts is that juveniles do not enjoy the full range of constitutional rights that apply to adults in criminal courts (Snyder, Sickmund, and Poe-Yamagata, 2000). In many jurisdictions, transcripts of proceedings are not made or retained for juveniles where serious charges are alleged, unless special arrangements are made beforehand. Thus, when juveniles in these jurisdictions appeal their adjudications to higher courts, they may or may not have the written record to rely upon when lodging appeals with appellate courts.

DEFENSE AND PROSECUTORIAL CONSIDERATIONS RELATING TO WAIVERS

Juvenile Trial Options: Interstate Variations

Juveniles are only infrequently given a jury trial if their cases are adjudicated by juvenile courts. Table 9.11 shows the interstate variation in jury trials for juveniles in juvenile courts in 2004. In nearly 80 percent of all state juvenile courts, jury trials for juveniles are denied. There is a great deal of variation among jurisdictions relating to trying and disposing of juvenile offenders (Klug, 2001).

Implications of Criminal Court Processing

When juveniles are waived to criminal court, then the full range of constitutional guarantees for adults also attaches for them (Sanborn, 2005). We have already examined the advantages of permitting or petitioning the juvenile court to retain jurisdiction in certain cases. An absence of a criminal record, limited punishments, extensive leniency, and a greater variety of discretionary options on the part of juvenile court judges make juvenile courts an attractive adjudicatory medium, if the juvenile has a choice. Of course, even if the crimes alleged are serious, leniency may assume the form of a dismissal of charges, charge reductions, warnings, and other nonadjudicatory penalties.

TABLE 9.11

Interstate Variation in Jury Trials for Juveniles, 2004

Provision	States
Jury trial granted upon request by juvenile	Alaska, California, Kansas, Massachusetts, Michigan, Minnesota, New Mexico, Oklahoma, Texas, West Virginia, Wisconsin, Wyoming
Juvenile denied right to trial by jury	Alabama, Florida, Georgia, Hawaii, Indiana, Iowa, Louisiana, Maine, Maryland, Mississippi, Nebraska, Nevada, New Jersey, North Carolina, North Dakota, Ohio, Oregon, Pennsylvania, South Carolina, Tennessee, Utah, Vermont, Washington
No mention	Alaska, Arizona, California, Connecticut, Colorado, Idaho, Illinois, Missouri, New Hampshire, New Mexico, New York, Virginia
By court order	South Dakota

Source: Patricia Torbet and Linda Szymanski, *State Legislative Responses to Violent Juvenile Crime: 1996–1997 Update.* Washington, DC: U.S. Department of Justice, 1998. Updated 2005 by author.

The primary implications for juveniles of being processed through the criminal justice system are several, and they are quite important. First, depending on the seriousness of the offenses alleged, a jury trial may be a matter of right. Second, periods of lengthy incarceration in minimum, medium, and maximum security facilities with adults becomes a real possibility (Escarcega et al., 2004). Third, criminal courts in a majority of state jurisdictions may impose the death penalty in capital cases. A sensitive subject with most citizens is whether juveniles should receive the death penalty if convicted of capital crimes. In recent years, the U.S. Supreme Court has addressed this issue specifically and ruled that in those states where the death penalty is imposed, the death penalty may be imposed as a punishment on any juvenile who was age 18 or older at the time the capital offense was committed (*Roper v. Simmons,* 2005).

Jury Trials as a Matter of Right for Serious Offenses

A primary benefit of a transfer to criminal court is the absolute right to a jury trial. This is conditional, however, and depends on the minimum incarcerative period associated with one or more criminal charges filed against defendants. In only 12 state jurisdictions, juveniles have a jury trial right granted through legislative action (Office of Juvenile Justice and Delinquency Prevention, 2005). However, when juveniles reach criminal courts, certain constitutional provisions apply to them as well as to adults. First, anyone charged with a crime where the possible sentence is 6 months' incarceration or more, with exceptions, is entitled to a jury trial if one is requested (*Baldwin v. New York,* 1970). Therefore, jury trials are not discretionary matters for judges to decide. Any defendant who may be subject to more than 6 months' incarceration in a jail or prison as the prescribed statutory punishment associated with the criminal offenses alleged may request and receive a jury trial from any U.S. judge, in either state or federal courts.

Juveniles who are charged with particularly serious crimes, and where several aggravating circumstances are apparent, stand a good chance of receiving favorable treatment from juries. Aggravating circumstances include a victim's death or the infliction of serious bodily injuries, committing an offense while on bail for another offense or on probation or parole, use of extreme cruelty in the commission of the crime, use of a dangerous weapon in the commission of a crime, a prior record, and leadership in the commission of offenses alleged. However, mitigating circumstances, those factors that tend to lessen the severity of sentencing, include duress or extreme provocation, mental incapacitation, motivation to provide necessities, youthfulness or old age, and no previous criminal record.

Among the several aggravating and mitigating circumstances listed above, having a prior record or being a first offender becomes an important consideration. Youths who are transferred to criminal courts sometimes do not have previous criminal records. This doesn't mean that they haven't committed earlier crimes, but rather, that their records are **juvenile court records.** Juveniles may have **sustained petitions,** where the facts alleged against them have been determined to be true by the juvenile court judge. However, this adjudication hearing is a civil proceeding. As such, technically, these youths do not bring prior criminal records into the criminal courtroom. This is a favorable factor for juveniles to consider when deciding whether to challenge transfers or have their automatic waivers reversed. However, changes in state laws regarding the confidentiality of juvenile court records have been made so that greater access to such records is available to others, and for longer periods beyond one's adulthood. Increasingly, one's juvenile past may affect one's criminal court trial outcome and sentencing.

Another important factor relative to having access to a jury trial is that prosecutors often try to avoid them, opting for a simple plea bargain agreement instead. Plea bargaining or plea negotiating is a preconviction bargain between the state and the defendant where the defendant enters a guilty plea in exchange for leniency in the form of reduced charges or less harsh treatment at the time of sentencing. It is well known that plea bargaining in the United States accounts for approximately 90 percent of all criminal convictions. But plea bargaining also involves an admission of guilt without benefit of a trial. For this reason, plea bargaining is often criticized.

Jury trials are costly and the results of jury deliberations are unpredictable. If prosecutors can obtain guilty pleas from transferred juveniles, they assist the state and themselves, both in terms of the costs of prosecution and avoidance of jury whims in youthful offender cases. Also, plea bargaining in transferred juvenile cases often results in convictions on lesser charges, specifically charges that would not have prompted the transfer or waiver from juvenile courts initially. However, this is a bit ironic, since it suggests that the criminal justice system is inadvertently sabotaging the primary purpose of juvenile transfers through plea bargaining arrangements that are otherwise commonplace for adult criminals. Furthermore, when prosecutors decide to file charges, sufficient evidence should exist to increase the chances of a successful prosecution. Also, the charges alleged should be serious ones. But many transferred juveniles are not necessarily the most serious youthful offenders, and the standard of evidence in juvenile courts is sometimes not as rigorous as it is in criminal courts. Thus, many transferred juvenile cases fail from the outset and are dismissed by the prosecutors themselves, often because of inadequate or poor evidence.

Closely associated with prosecutorial reluctance to prosecute many of these transferred juveniles is the fact that a majority of those transferred are charged with property crimes. While these cases may stand out from other cases coming before juvenile court judges, prosecutors and criminal court judges might regard them as insignificant. Thus, juveniles enter the adult system from juvenile courts, where their offenses set them apart from most other juvenile offenders. But alongside adults in criminal courts, they become one of many property offenders who face criminal processing. Their youthful age works in their behalf to improve the chances of having their cases dismissed or of being acquitted by juries. Most prosecutors wish to reserve jury trials for only the most serious offenders. Therefore, their general inclination is to treat youthful property offenders with greater leniency, unless they elect to *nolle prosequi* outright.

The Potential for Capital Punishment

The most important implication for juveniles transferred to criminal courts is the potential imposition of the **death penalty** upon their conviction for a capital crime. About two-thirds of the states use **capital punishment** for prescribed offenses that are especially aggravated. For youths who are age 18 or older at the time they committed a capital offense and who live in a state that has the death penalty, they are in jeopardy of being sentenced to death (*Roper v. Simmons,* 2005).

An alternative to the death penalty applied to juveniles is the life-without-parole option. In 2004, 43 states had **life-without-parole** provisions for capital murder statutes, including aggravated homicide as well as for habitual or career offenders (Bureau of Justice Statistics, 2005). Thus, it is possible for youths to be sentenced to life without the possibility of parole if they are convicted of a capital offense in a state with or without the death penalty (Moon et al., 2000).

One way of decreasing the incidence of youth violence is to promote gun awareness and the hazards of possessing deadly firearms.

In these instances, juveniles take their chances in criminal courts, often not knowing what outcome can be expected.

BLENDED SENTENCING STATUTES

In recent years, many states have legislatively redefined the juvenile court's purpose and role by diminishing the role of rehabilitation and heightening the importance of public safety, punishment, and accountability in the juvenile justice system (Torbet et al., 2000). One of the most dramatic changes in the dispositional/sentencing options available to juvenile court judges is **blended sentencing.** Blended sentencing statutes represent a dramatic change in dispositional/sentencing options available to judges. Blended sentencing refers to the imposition of juvenile and/or adult correctional sanctions on serious and violent juvenile offenders who have been adjudicated in juvenile court or convicted in criminal court. Blended sentencing options are usually based on age or on a combination of age and offense (Redding, 2000).

There are five blended sentencing models. Figure 9.2 shows these five models. These include (1) juvenile–exclusive blend; (2) juvenile–inclusive blend; (3) juvenile–contiguous blend; (4) criminal–exclusive blend; and (5) criminal–inclusive blend.

The Juvenile-Exclusive Blend

The **juvenile–exclusive blend** involves a disposition by the juvenile court judge, which is either a disposition to the juvenile correctional system or to the adult correctional system, but not both. Thus, a judge might order a juvenile adjudicated delinquent for aggravated assault to serve 3 years in a juvenile industrial school; or the judge may order the adjudicated delinquent to serve 3 years in a prison for adults. The judge cannot impose *both* types of punishment under this model, however. In 2004, only one state, New Mexico, provided such a sentencing option for its juvenile court judges.

The Juvenile-Inclusive Blend

The **juvenile–inclusive blend** involves a disposition by the juvenile court judge, which is both a juvenile correctional sanction and an adult correctional sanction. In cases such as this, suppose the judge had adjudicated a 15-year-old juvenile delinquent on a charge of vehicular theft. The judge might impose a disposition of 2 years in a juvenile industrial school or reform school. Furthermore, the judge might impose a sentence of 3 additional years in an adult penitentiary. However, the second sentence to the adult prison would typically be suspended, unless the juvenile violated one or more conditions of his or her original disposition and any conditions accompanying the disposition. Usually, this suspension period would run until the youth reaches age 18 or 21. If the offender were to commit a new offense or violate one or more program conditions, he or she would immediately be placed in the adult prison to serve the second sentence originally imposed.

Court	Type of Sanction	Description	Examples
		Juvenile–Exclusive Blend: The juvenile court has original jurisdiction and responsibility for adjudication of the case. The juvenile court has the authority to impose a sanction involving either the juvenile or adult correctional systems.	New Mexico
		Juvenile–Inclusive Blend: The juvenile court has original jurisdiction and responsibility for adjudication of the case. The juvenile court has the authority to impose a sanction involving both the juvenile and adult correctional systems. In most instances, the adult sanction is suspended unless there is a violation, at which point it is invoked.	Connecticut Minnesota Montana
		Juvenile–Contiguous Blend: The juvenile court has original jurisdiction and responsibility for adjudication of the case. The juvenile court has the authority to impose a sanction that would be in force beyond the age of its extended jurisdiction. At that point, various procedures are invoked to determine if the remainder of that sanction should be imposed in the adult correctional system.	Colorado (1) Massachusetts Rhode Island South Carolina Texas
		Criminal–Exclusive Blend: The criminal court tries the case. The criminal court has the authority to impose a sanction involving either the juvenile or adult correctional systems.	California Colorado (2) Florida Idaho Michigan Virginia
		Criminal–Inclusive Blend: The criminal court tries the case. The criminal court has the authority to impose a sanction involving both the juvenile and adult correctional systems. In most instances, the adult sanction is suspended unless there is a violation, at which point it is invoked.	Arkansas Missouri

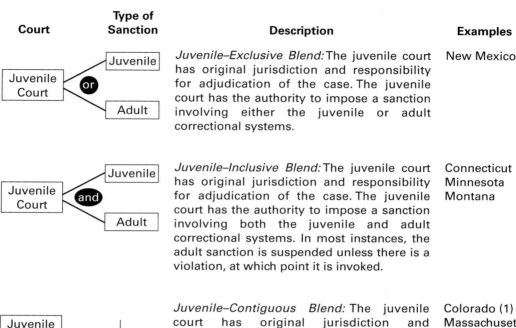

FIGURE 9.2 "Models of 'Blended Sentencing' Statutes" (*Source:* Bilchik, 1996:13).

The Juvenile–Contiguous Blend

The **juvenile–contiguous blend** involves a disposition by a juvenile court judge that may extend beyond the jurisdictional age limit of the offender. When the age limit of the juvenile court jurisdiction is reached, various procedures may be invoked to transfer the case to the jurisdiction of adult corrections. States with this juvenile–contiguous blend include Colorado, Massachusetts, Rhode

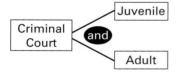

Island, South Carolina, and Texas. In 1987 the Texas legislature enacted a determinate sentencing law that is an example of the juvenile–contiguous blended sentencing model, whereby for certain offenses the juvenile court may impose a sentence that may remain in effect beyond its extended jurisdiction (Redding, 2000). In Texas, for example, a 15-year-old youth who has been adjudicated delinquent on a murder charge can be given a determinate sentence of from 1 to 30 years. At the time of the disposition in juvenile court, the youth is sent to the Texas Youth Commission and incarcerated in one of its facilities (similar to reform or industrial schools). By the time the youth reaches age 17½, the juvenile court must conduct a hearing to determine whether the youth should be sent to the Texas Department of Corrections to serve some or all of the remaining sentence. At this hearing, the youth may present evidence in his or her favor to show why he or she has become rehabilitated and no longer should be confined. However, evidence of institutional misconduct may be presented by the prosecutor to show why the youth should be incarcerated for more years in a Texas prison. This hearing functions as an incentive for the youth to behave and try to improve his or her behavior while confined in the juvenile facility. This particular sentencing blend seems most effective at punishing serious and violent offenders while providing them with a final chance to access certain provided Texas rehabilitative programs.

On February 16, 1997, a 12-year-old Austin, Texas, girl was convicted and sentenced by a juvenile court judge to 25 years' imprisonment. She had beaten a 2½ year-old toddler, Jayla Belton, to death in her grandmother's unlicensed day care center. In May 1996, she had been found guilty of the toddler's murder and given a 40-year sentence. Her first conviction was thrown out, however, since the court found that she was not adequately defended. In her first conviction when she was age 11, the girl could have been released by age 16 or transferred to an adult prison, where she would serve out the remaining years of her original sentence. Prosecutors said that the girl kicked and beat Jayla Belton because she was angry about being left to babysit the toddler. The child died of a ruptured liver. In the sentencing scheme used by the judge, the girl's case would be reviewed before she became an adult. If her conduct while confined as a juvenile is poor, then there is a good likelihood that the results of a hearing will result in the girl being transferred to the Texas Department of Corrections to serve more time for her crime as an adult (Associated Press, 1997:A2).

In 1995 the Texas legislature expanded the number of offenses that qualify for the most severe sentences, and it added an additional crime in 1997. The Texas legislature also established a seven-level system of progressive sanctions to be used by juvenile court judges, with determinate sentences acquiring the status of the most severe tier (Torbet and Szymanski, 1998:7).

The Criminal–Exclusive Blend

The **criminal–exclusive blend** involves a decision by a criminal court judge to impose either a juvenile court sanction or a criminal court sanction, but not both. For example, a criminal court judge may hear the case of a 15-year-old youth who has been transferred to criminal court on a rape charge. The youth is convicted in a jury trial in criminal court. At this point, the judge has two options: the judge can sentence the offender to a prison term in an adult correctional facility, or the judge can impose an incarcerative sentence for the youth to serve in a juvenile facility. The judge may believe that the 15-year-old would be better off in a juvenile industrial school rather than an adult prison. The judge may impose a sentence of adult incarceration, but he or she may be inclined to place the youth in a facility where there are other youths in the offender's age range.

The Criminal–Inclusive Blend

The **criminal–inclusive blend** involves a decision by the criminal court judge to impose both a juvenile penalty and a criminal sentence simultaneously. Again, as in the juvenile court–inclusive blend model, the latter criminal sentence may be suspended depending on the good conduct of the juvenile during the juvenile punishment phase. For example, suppose a 13-year-old boy has been convicted of attempted murder. The boy participated in a drive-by shooting and is a gang member. The criminal court judge sentences the youth to a term of 5 years in a juvenile facility, such as an industrial school. At the same time, the judge imposes a sentence of 20 years on the youth to be spent in an adult correctional facility, following the 5-year sentence in the juvenile facility. However, the adult portion of the sentence may be suspended, depending on whether the juvenile behaves or misbehaves during his 5-year industrial school incarceration. There is an additional twist to this blend. If the juvenile violates one or more conditions of his confinement in the juvenile facility, the judge has the power to revoke that sentence and invoke the sentence of incarceration in an adult facility. Thus, a powerful incentive is provided for the youth to show evidence that rehabilitation has occurred. It is to the youth's advantage to behave well while confined, since a more ominous sentence of confinement with adult offenders may be imposed at any time. Furthermore, with good behavior, the youth can be free of the system following the period of juvenile confinement; the adult portion of the sentence is suspended if the youth deserves such leniency. One state that has the revocation power and ability to place youths in adult correctional facilities is Arkansas, although this power is rarely used by criminal court judges (Redding, 2000).

Blended sentencing statutes are intended to provide both juvenile and criminal court judges with a greater range of dispositional and/or sentencing options. In the 1980s and earlier, juvenile courts were notoriously lenient on juvenile offenders. Dispositions of juvenile court judges were mostly nominal or conditional, which usually meant verbal warnings and/or probation. While probation continues to be the sanction of choice in a majority of juvenile courts following delinquency adjudications, many states have armed their juvenile and criminal court judges with greater sanctioning powers. Thus, it is now possible in states, such as Colorado, Arkansas, and Missouri, for juvenile court judges to impose sanctions that extend well beyond their original jurisdictional authority. Juvenile court judges in New Mexico, for instance, can place certain juveniles in either adult or juvenile correctional facilities. Criminal court judges in Florida, Idaho, Michigan, or Missouri can place those convicted of crimes in either juvenile or adult correctional facilities, depending on the jurisdiction. These are broader and more powerful dispositional and sentencing options to hold youthful offenders more accountable for the serious offenses they commit (Torbet et al., 2000).

Jury Trials as a Matter of Right in All Juvenile Court Blended Sentencing Proceedings

When juveniles are tried as adults in criminal court, they are entitled to the full range of constitutional rights extended to criminal defendants, including the right to a jury trial. This same provision exists whenever juveniles are tried in juvenile courts, and where the juvenile is subject to the application of blended sentencing statutes. All states with either the juvenile–inclusive blend, the juvenile–exclusive blend, or the juvenile–contiguous blend must grant juvenile defendants the right to a jury trial in juvenile court upon request.

If the jury verdict is "guilty," then the juvenile court judge has the right under one of these blended sentencing statutes, depending on the state jurisdiction, to impose both a juvenile penalty and a criminal penalty, or either a juvenile penalty or a criminal penalty but not both. Thus, juvenile court judges may exercise considerable discretion relating to dispositions and sentencing. If the juvenile court judge is in a state where both juvenile and criminal penalties may be imposed, such as Michigan, he or she may impose both types of penalties on a convicted juvenile or he or she may impose the juvenile penalty but not the criminal penalty. This aspect of blended sentencing is totally discretionary with the judge.

One of the positive aspects of blended sentencing statutes is that the use of transfers or waivers and subsequent waiver hearings are rendered obsolete. By statute, juveniles in one state or another with blended sentencing statutes are either in juvenile or criminal court where the court can exercise one or both types of juvenile and adult sanctions.

Surprisingly, some judges have resisted applying blended sentencing statutes in their jurisdictions, even when they have been authorized to use them. In Michigan, for instance, one juvenile court judge chided the Michigan legislature for passing a blended sentencing statute. When sentencing a juvenile offender who had been convicted of a heinous, premeditated murder, the judge sentenced the juvenile only to the juvenile punishment and did not impose the criminal punishment. He took it upon himself to chastise the Michigan legislature for its abuse of authority in changing the sentencing laws governing youthful offenders.

It is unfortunate that some judges have chosen to view these blended sentencing statutes as somehow incongruous with how juvenile sanctions ought to be imposed. They have overlooked a very important fact that applies to virtually all of these statutes. If a criminal penalty is imposed together with a juvenile penalty, the criminal penalty may be set aside at a later date, provided that the juvenile shows evidence of rehabilitation while confined as a juvenile in an institution.

Suppose a 12-year-old is convicted of murder in Michigan, through a jury trial in juvenile court. Suppose the judge were to impose both a juvenile penalty, such as confinement in a secure juvenile facility until the juvenile reaches the age of his or her majority or 21. Further suppose that in addition to this penalty, the judge imposes a sentence of 30 years to life on the juvenile, such sentence to commence upon completion of the juvenile punishment and institutionalization. Provisions are in place in all jurisdictions for a mandatory review of one's juvenile record prior to the age of their majority. Usually, a hearing is set for 6 months prior to a juvenile reaching adulthood. The hearing is for the purpose of determining whether the adult portion of the punishment should be imposed. This hearing provides a committee with a unique opportunity to review a youth's prior institutional conduct and determine whether the adult sentence should be set aside. If the juvenile's conduct has been favorable, then it is compelling for the committee to set aside the original adult sentence. The juvenile will be free of the system once he or she becomes an adult. However, suppose that the juvenile has behaved poorly while confined in a juvenile facility. He or she has repeatedly fought with others, been disruptive, and has been resistant to any rehabilitative efforts to improve his or her educational level or receive useful counseling, therapy, or vocational/educational training. For cases such as these, the committee reviewing the juveniles' prior institutional record may be inclined to allow the adult portion of the penalty to resume when the juvenile reaches adulthood. The juvenile will commence a 30-years-to-life sentence upon reaching the age of his or her majority.

The primary positive implication for juveniles sentenced under such blended sentencing statutes is that it provides them with a strong incentive to behave well and to participate in needed counseling, training, or other activities that will improve their skills and psychological and social development. If they know that poor behavior will jeopardize their chances of being released upon reaching adulthood, then they will be motivated to behave in a law-abiding and productive fashion for the period of their confinement in the juvenile facility. The juvenile court judge who fails to recognize the motivational value of these blended sentencing statutes seriously undermines a significant juvenile justice reform.

Judicial resistance to change regarding juvenile sentencing was not anticipated, although Bilchik (1996) has written about his observations and the reactions of both juvenile court and criminal court personnel in those jurisdictions where blended sentencing statutes have been implemented. Bilchik says that there are a number of considerations with respect to the shift toward offense-based sentencing patterns for serious and violent juvenile offenders. Because many of the sentencing options for serious and violent juvenile offenders in juvenile court put the juvenile at risk of an adult sentence or allow that such adjudications will be used in future prosecutions, the right to counsel is a critical concern and has been successfully used to challenge the use of juvenile adjudications in criminal court.

Blended sentencing options demonstrate the ambivalence of what to do about serious and violent juvenile offenders. The creation of middle ground disposition/sentencing and correctional options demonstrates a lack of resolve on two fronts: (1) coming to closure on (i.e., removing) certain juveniles for whom the juvenile justice system is inadequate, or (2) bolstering the resolve and resources of the juvenile justice system to adequately address the needs of these very difficult young offenders. Blended sentencing creates confusing options for all system actors, including offenders, judges, prosecutors, and corrections administrators. Contact with juvenile and criminal justice personnel across the country revealed that confusion exists about these statutes and the rules and regulations governing them, especially with respect to the juvenile's status during case processing and subsequent placement. This has repercussions on the definition of a juvenile with regard to compliance with the Juvenile Justice and Delinquency Prevention Act mandates (Redding, 2000). Perhaps in time, the good stemming from the application of these blended sentencing statutes by growing numbers of states will outweigh the negative perceptions of it by various system actors (Torbet et al., 2000).

SUMMARY

Distinguishing between different types of offenders is an integral part of juvenile offender processing. Not all juvenile offenders have committed equally serious offenses. Status offenders and delinquent offenders are clearly different in the seriousness of their offending. Among delinquents, some offenders are violent while most are property offenders and nonviolent. Most status offenders today are dealt with in a lenient manner, with more than a few of these types of offenders placed in group homes or foster care because of their own home environments, which are often unstable or fragmented. However, some of these status offenders refuse to comply with juvenile court orders to stay in school, obey their parents, or engage in other court-ordered treatments and run the risk of being held in contempt. Contempt of court is a misdemeanor that escalates the seriousness of their offending.

When more serious delinquent offenders are screened by intake officers and juvenile court prosecutors, a decision may be made to process some of these offenders as adults and send them to criminal courts. These decisions are known variously in different jurisdictions as waivers, transfers, or certifications, and about 1 percent of all juveniles each year who come into contact with the juvenile justice system are transferred to criminal courts for adult offender processing. All juveniles who are eventually waived to criminal court are entitled to a hearing on the waiver if they request one. The rationale for using waivers is to provide for harsher penalties for more serious offenses; to hold offenders more accountable because of the more serious offenses they commit; to promote greater fairness and just-deserts in punishments according to offense seriousness; to provide a broader range of penalties that fit these crimes in terms of proportionality of the seriousness of them; to overcome the traditional leniency of juvenile courts; to promote deterrence for other juveniles who might contemplate committing serious offenses; and to encourage youthful offenders to accept responsibility for their actions.

Ideally only the most serious juvenile offenders are considered for transfer to criminal courts. These transfers would include violent offenders, such as accused murderers, rapists, persons who have committed aggravated assault, arson, robbery, and other violent acts. In reality, only about 40 percent of all transferred persons each year are violent offenders. About 15–20 percent are charged with various drug offenses, while the remaining 40 percent consist of property offenders who have been charged with burglary, larceny, vehicular theft, and other property crimes. One reason for such larger numbers of property and drug offenders being transferred to criminal courts is that individual juvenile court judges waive them because of the chronicity of their offending. Many less serious offenders are repeat offenders, appearing before the same judge numerous times. The judge believes that a criminal court can send a stronger message to such persons by deterring them from further offending. Sometimes judges must send certain juveniles to criminal court because of an excessive number of previous, less serious delinquency adjudications. Some judges are more concerned than others about those juveniles who engage in drug use, and thus a waiver action is warranted. Also, depending on the jurisdiction, different standards are applied, meaning that some acts considered more serious in one jurisdiction might not be of the same degree of seriousness in other jurisdictions.

Types of waivers include judicial waivers, where the judge is the primary authority making the transfer decision. Judges can use discretionary waivers, where they decide which juveniles should be waived. Mandatory waivers are also used by judges, but they are compelled by law to waive certain types of juveniles to criminal court. Presumptive waivers are also judicial actions, but the burden of proof concerning whether the waiver occurs shifts to the juvenile to show whether or not such a waiver action should be taken by the judge. Other types of waivers include direct file and statutory exclusion. Under direct file, prosecutors decide whether to pursue cases against juveniles in either juvenile court or criminal court. Under statutory exclusion, also known as automatic or legislative waivers, some types of offenses are excluded from the jurisdiction of juvenile courts and end up in criminal courts directly. Since all juveniles are entitled to a hearing on any waiver action, even automatic waivers, such waiver actions are called reverse waivers, since a juvenile's interest might be to remove the case from the criminal court and have it returned to the juvenile court for an adjudication. Another type of waiver is a demand waiver, where a juvenile may ask the juvenile court to waive him or her to the jurisdiction of the criminal court. And in a few jurisdictions, there are once an adult/always an adult provisions where juveniles who have been transferred to criminal court once are subsequently considered adults for criminal prosecutions if they continue to reoffend as juveniles and until they reach the age of their majority.

Waiver hearings are made by a motion, and it is up to the judge to decide whether the waiver should be granted. In reverse waiver actions, criminal court judges decide whether the case should be sent to the juvenile court for adjudication. There are stringent time standards governing the use of waiver actions and the hearings held to determine their legitimacy for each juvenile. Hearings are proceedings where the relative merits of the transfer are discussed by the prosecutor and defense counsel. The presiding judge makes the final determination.

There are both positive and negative implications of waivers for juveniles. If a juvenile's case remains in the juvenile court, there is a good chance that lenient treatment will be extended as a consequence of a subsequent delinquency adjudication. However, some juvenile court judges can impose secure confinement for extraordinarily long periods, and thus this potential incarcerative sanction should not be overlooked. Juvenile court adjudications do not result in criminal records for adjudicated delinquents. Often these records are expunged when one becomes an adult. Juvenile courts do not have as broad a range of punishments compared with criminal courts. The death penalty and life-without-parole dispositions are not within juvenile court jurisdiction. There is also a great deal of public sympathy extended to juveniles processed in juvenile courts, and often these offenders receive individualized treatments in the form of counseling, vocational and educational training, and a number of other services. One disadvantage is that most juvenile courts do not provide juveniles with jury trials as a matter of right. Their fate rests with the judgment of juvenile court judges, whose rulings can at times be harsh. Also, juveniles do not have the same range of constitutional rights enjoyed by adults in criminal courts.

If juveniles are waived to criminal courts, they are susceptible to more severe punishments. The death penalty is possible to administer to anyone age 18 or older in those jurisdictions with death penalties for capital offenses. Life-without-the-possibility-of-parole punishments can also be imposed. But juveniles have the full range of constitutional rights as adults, and they are entitled to a trial by jury on request for most types of offenses they have been charged with committing. One advantage of juveniles being prosecuted as adults is that their age becomes a mitigating factor in most court actions, and defense counsels often use their age to encourage jury sympathy. Many juveniles transferred to criminal courts therefore receive greater leniency anyway. The outcomes of transfers are also different from those expected by many citizens. About half of all youths transferred to criminal courts each year either have their cases dismissed or downgraded to less serious charges. Plea bargains result in probation or diversion. Another 35 percent of these juveniles will eventually receive probation from criminal courts anyway. Only about 10–15 percent of all juveniles convicted of crimes in criminal courts annually will do time in a jail or prison.

During the past 20 years, significant modifications have occurred in how juveniles are processed, especially those juveniles who have committed more serious offenses. Blended sentencing statutes have been created in many states, where it has been made possible for either juvenile or criminal courts to impose either juvenile court punishments, criminal court punishments, or both. Blended sentencing statutes for juvenile courts include the juvenile–inclusive blend, where a juvenile court judge can impose both a juvenile and an adult punishment. Under the juvenile–exclusive blend, the judge may impose either a juvenile punishment or an adult punishment, but not both. A juvenile–contiguous blend is a third type of juvenile blended sentencing statute, where the judge may impose a disposition that extends beyond the age of one's majority or adulthood. Criminal court judges may also exercise blended sentencing statutes for their youthful offenders. These judges may use the criminal–inclusive blend, where both juvenile and criminal penalties may be imposed simultaneously. Or these judges may impose a criminal–exclusive blend, where either a juvenile disposition or a criminal sentence may be imposed, but not both. There is considerable and growing support for blended sentencing statutes, since they provide greater flexibility compared with sometimes cumbersome transfer or waiver actions. Also, blended sentencing statutes that impose both juvenile and criminal penalties offer incentives to juveniles to participate in rehabilitative programs as juveniles. If they participate in such programming successfully while doing their time as juveniles, then a committee has the discretionary power to relieve them of the adult portion of their original sentence.

QUESTIONS FOR REVIEW

1. What are the implications of offense seriousness for the use of waivers in the juvenile justice system?
2. What is the rationale for distinguishing between status offenders and delinquent offenders in juvenile justice system processing?
3. What is contempt power used by juvenile court judges? How does the use of contempt power by juvenile court judges influence status offenders?
4. What are several types of judicial waivers? What is the rationale for using transfers?
5. What are some of the ideal characteristics of youths targeted for transfers to criminal courts? What are the actual characteristics of youths who are transferred to criminal courts?
6. What is meant by the once an adult/always an adult provision? What implications does this policy have for affected youths?

7. What are some contrasts between direct file, legislative waivers, and demand waivers?

8. Under what circumstances are juveniles entitled to hearings on transfer decisions?

9. What are some favorable and unfavorable implications for juveniles if their cases are heard in juvenile courts instead of criminal courts? What are some positive and negative implications for juveniles if they have their cases heard in criminal courts?

10. What are five different types of blended sentencing statutes? What are some positive benefits of blended sentencing statutes for serious and violent juvenile offenders?

INTERNET CONNECTIONS

Criminal Justice Consortium
http://www.bapd.org/gcrium-1.htm

Criminal Justice Policy Foundation
http://www.cjpf.org/

CURE-NY
http://www.users.bestweb.net~cureny/cure-ny.htm

NetAction
http://www.netaction.org/

Open Society Institute
http://www.soros.org/crime/

CHAPTER 10 | *The Adjudicatory Process: Dispositional Alternatives*

Chapter Outline

Chapter Objectives
Introduction
The Nature of the Offense
First-Offender or Repeat
 Offender?
  Is the First-
   Offender/Repeat-
   Offender Distinction
   Relevant? Race, Ethnicity,
   and Socioeconomic
   Status Revisited
Aggravating and Mitigating
 Circumstances

Aggravating Circumstances
Mitigating Circumstances
Juvenile Risk Assessments and
 Predictions of Dangerousness
  Dangerousness and Risk
  Needs Assessment and Its
   Measurement
  Selective Incapacitation
  Common Elements of Risk
   Assessment Instruments
  The Functions of
   Classification

Risk Prediction from Arizona
 and Florida
Needs Assessments
Predisposition Reports
 The Predisposition Report
  and Its Preparation
 Victim-Impact Statements in
  Predisposition Reports
Summary
Questions for Review
Internet Connections

Key Terms

actuarial prediction
anamnestic prediction
classification
clinical prediction
dangerousness
false negatives
false positives
first-offender
flat time

needs assessment
overrides
prediction
predictors of dangerousness and
 risk
predisposition reports
presentence investigation
 reports (PSIs)
repeat offender

risk/needs assessment instruments
risk
selective incapacitation
victim-impact statement
Violent Juvenile Offender
 Programs (VJOP)

392

Chapter Objectives

As the result of reading this chapter, you will realize the following objectives:

1. Differentiate between first offenders and repeat offenders.
2. Understand the differences between aggravating and mitigating circumstances.
3. Learn about juvenile dangerousness and risk, as well as how these phenomena can be assessed.
4. Learn about selective incapacitation and how it is used in juvenile cases.
5. Learn about anamnestic, actuarial, and clinical prediction, and how each is used to forecast juvenile offender dangerousness.
6. Examine several risk instruments, their applications and limitations.
7. Understand the importance of victim impact statements in dispositional hearings for juvenile offenders.
8. Learn about predispositional reports, who prepares them, and how they are used for sanctioning juveniles.

• *It happened in New Jersey on July 6, 2003. Matthew Lovett, 18, and two 14-year-old companions, Cody Jackson and Christopher Olson, gathered up numerous guns, swords, and thousands of bullets and set off on what they thought was going to be a major crime spree. They had planned to hijack a car first. Next, they were going to drive around and find three specific teens to kill. Finally, they were just going to drive around and kill people at random. They approached a motorist with the intent of taking away his car, but when he spotted them approaching, he sped off quickly. On foot, the youths decided to go back home. In the meantime, the motorist called police and reported that several youths had pulled a gun on him at a traffic light. He gave police officers a general description of the boys and their last reported location. The teens were taken into custody within a few blocks of Lovett's home. All three youths were charged as adults for carjacking, attempted carjacking, and weapons and conspiracy offenses. Attorneys were appointed for these youths, and Lovett pleaded guilty to carjacking. He still faced the weapons and conspiracy charges. The other two youths also pleaded guilty. Jackson is now serving a 5-year prison sentence for carjacking, and Olson is serving 4 years for a weapons offense. Lovett could be sentenced up to 50 years if convicted on all counts. The families of each boy wrote letters of apology to the judge. Lovett's father further explained that his son had become withdrawn since the death of his mother 10 years earlier. [Source: CBS News, "Gun-Toting N.J. Teen Gets 10 Years," April 8, 2004.]*

• *An Illinois 14-year-old boy faced murder and aggravated sexual assault charges in criminal court resulting from feeding a toxic cleaning solution to his 14-month-old niece after the infant scratched him. The boy, Henry J., was ordered to stand trial in criminal court after he appeared before the juvenile court judge. The judge said at the time of the waiver that there probably would be no hope of rehabilitation because of this brutal and vicious act. Henry J. could face confinement in a juvenile facility until age 17, at which time he would be placed in a prison for the rest of his life without the possibility of parole. If the case remained in juvenile court, then Henry J. would face confinement in a secure juvenile facility until he turned 21 years of age. Henry J. was babysitting his 14-month-old niece and his 3-year-old nephew. He said that the infant scratched him while he was holding her, and so he made her drink some of the cleaning solution from a bottle. She immediately choked on the substance and died. The prosecutor's office added that there was also evidence of sexual assault, although Henry J. denied this allegation. A defense attorney appointed for Henry J. said that a preliminary private psychiatric examination of Henry J. showed that he was mildly retarded and probably was not competent enough to understand the nature and consequences of his acts. He believed that there were other mitigating circumstances to warrant some form of leniency from the judge.* [*Source:* Adapted from the Associated Press, "Boy Feeds Infant Cleaning Fluid," February 26, 2005.]

• *Danny Z. is a 16-year-old Detroit gang member. He has numerous prior arrests for all types of offenses, ranging from shoplifting to aggravated assault and arson. He has been placed on probation seven times by several juvenile courts in the greater Detroit area. On two occasions, Danny Z. was confined to a secure juvenile facility for 90 days. Danny Z. does not go to school and lives with his uncle, who is addicted to crack cocaine. Recently Danny Z. and three other youths were picked up by police for attempted murder, after they were identified by eyewitnesses in a drive-by shooting outside a popular suburban night club. Four persons were wounded in the attack, although there were no fatalities. All four youths are members of the same Detroit gang and denied any involvement in the drive-by shooting. However, police executed a search warrant of Danny Z.'s premises and located the semi-automatic weapon that was used in the drive-by shooting. Danny Z. now faces four attempted murder charges. Danny Z.'s attorney has cited numerous circumstances, such as Danny Z.'s unstable home life, a drug-dependent uncle, an unsupportive school environment, and the pressures from other gang members as factors that contributed to Danny Z.'s involvement in the shooting. The other gang members arrested with Danny Z. are ages 13, 14, and 15, respectively. Danny Z. is reputedly a leading member of the gang and thus he is considered the principal defendant in the drive-by shooting incident. He denies being a gang leader. He quit attending school when he was 12 years old and has been involved in a life of delinquency ever since. His first known contact with the Detroit juvenile justice system was at the age of 8 when he was taken into custody for carrying a concealed weapon.* [*Source:* Adapted from the Associated Press, "Teen Drive-By Shooters Prosecuted as Adults," December 12, 2004.]

INTRODUCTION

Two 14-year-olds and an 18-year-old arm themselves with an arsenal of weapons, including thousands of rounds of bullets. They prepare themselves for carjacking and murder. Their first attempt at a carjacking goes awry, they get discouraged, and decide to go home. On the way home they get stopped and arrested by police. All three youths are charged as adults and face a variety of serious criminal charges. Another 14-year-old feeds his niece a toxic substance because he became angry when she scratched him. The niece died and the boy was charged with murder. In another city, a youth who has been placed on probation at least seven times by the juvenile court participates in a drive-by shooting where several persons were wounded. What can the juvenile justice system do for these youths? What mechanisms can be implemented within the community to provide treatments or therapies that might prove useful in rehabilitating them or decreasing their propensity to recidivate? Were any of these acts by these juveniles predictable and could they have been prevented?

This chapter examines the adjudicatory process, focusing on the consideration of factors that influence youthful offender dispositions. The first part of the chapter describes the nature of offenses charged and whether youths are first-offenders or repeat offenders. Offense seriousness is a primary consideration, together with one's age, one's association with others when the offense was committed, the nature of one's participation in the offense, and a variety of other legal and extralegal factors. As is the case with adult offenders, juveniles are assessed and disposed according to an evaluation of both aggravating and mitigating factors, or factors that intensify or lessen one's culpability in the offense as well as one's punishment.

Several important aggravating factors are listed and described. Did the juvenile have a prior delinquent record? Did the juvenile play a leadership role in the commission of one or more delinquent acts? Were there injuries to one or more victims? Was the juvenile on probation or parole when the delinquent act was committed? These and other aggravating circumstances are examined. Other factors, known as mitigating factors, are also listed and described. These factors tend to minimize the seriousness of the offenses committed. The facts that no serious injuries to victims occurred or that no intent to inflict serious bodily injury on victims mitigate the offense. Did the juvenile act under duress or extreme provocation? Was there an absence of a juvenile record? Did the youth cooperate with authorities to apprehend others involved in the offense? Were there psychological or social problems that influenced the youth's delinquent conduct? These and other factors are considered as lessening the severity of the adjudication offense.

About half of all juvenile courts during the 1980s had devised measures of risk or dangerousness as well as assessments of youthful client needs. By 2005 almost every juvenile court had devised such instrumentation. The next part of this chapter examines the concepts of dangerousness, risk, and needs assessment as these terms apply to evaluations of juveniles. While these instruments are not designed to be stand-alone measures to determine one's subsequent disposition in the juvenile justice system, they nevertheless function in various ways to provide different actors in the system with a sense of the nature and extent of services required to meet individual needs as well as the degree and type of supervision required for each offender.

Risk and needs assessments are conducted by both juvenile probation and parole personnel. These instruments identify critical problem areas that may require individualized interventions and services. A wide variety of community services is available to all juvenile offenders according to the types of problems and needs disclosed. The nature and degree of supervision may range from cursory contact with juvenile probation officers to full incapacitation in a secure facility for a period of time. These decisions about particular offenders involve predictions of future behaviors, and the instrumentation devised by different juvenile agencies attempts to forecast one's future risk posed. Several important elements of risk assessment instruments are listed and described.

Several types of risk prediction are listed and defined. These include actuarial, anamnestic, and clinical prediction. It will be evident that no prediction method is foolproof, and that errors in prediction occur. Some offenders are predicted to be dangerous and turn out not to be dangerous. These are known as false positives. Other offenders are predicted not to be dangerous but turn out to be dangerous. These are known as false negatives. There will always be false positives and false negatives in the juvenile justice system, despite the fact that this instrumentation is constantly being revised and improved. Partially on the basis of these prediction methods, each juvenile offender is classified and categorized. The diverse functions of classification are discussed. In the course of classifying juvenile offenders, selective incapacitation occurs, where some offenders are placed in secure confinement and others are placed in their communities with various restrictions. The issue of selective incapacitation is examined.

The chapter next explores several instruments devised by different states to assess one's risk and needs. Examples are provided, and hypothetical calculations are made to illustrate how assessments of juveniles are made. The contents of these instruments are listed and explained. Also described are the individual weighting criteria for items included on these instruments and how they are used to measure one's potential for recidivism. Some instruments are comprised of items that measure exclusively the risks posed by juveniles, while others are exclusively needs-oriented. It is not uncommon to find instruments where these items have been blended in various ways so that authorities can appraise both one's risk and individual needs simultaneously.

One of the most critical documents in juvenile offender processing is the predispositional report. The chapter concludes with a detailed presentation and analysis of such reports and how they are used in the juvenile justice process. Similar to presentence investigation reports prepared by probation officers for criminal offenders, predispositional reports furnish similar information about youths. This information is used by juvenile court judges, by juvenile probation agencies and officers who supervise youths, and by youth paroling authorities. Plans are often devised for one's aftercare based on the contents of these reports. Probation programs are tailored to meet the needs of individual offenders, and juvenile probation and parole officers are able to glean much valuable information from them concerning how their clients should be supervised and treated. A sample of a detailed predispositional report is provided. Additionally, victim-impact statements are often appended to these reports, where there have been victim injuries, deaths, and/or economic losses. Juvenile court judges and others may impose restitution, fines, community service, and other requirements for youths to follow that are influenced by such statements.

THE NATURE OF THE OFFENSE

In 2004 it is estimated that there were 2.2 million arrests of youths under age 18 (Office of Juvenile Justice and Delinquency Prevention, 2005). About 1.7 million cases were sent to the juvenile justice system for processing. About half of these cases were processed formally. Of the 820,000 petitioned cases that were handled formally, 485,000 juveniles were adjudicated. Of these, about 135,000 were placed in secure institutions, such as industrial schools. About 13,000 cases were recommended for transfer to criminal courts (Office of Juvenile Justice and Delinquency Prevention, 2005). Of all arrests of youths under age 18 in 2004, approximately 480,000 were for violent or person offenses, such as aggravated assault, rape, and murder.

During the period 1986–1996, violent crime by juveniles increased by nearly 70 percent nationally. This dramatic increase in juvenile violence has drawn greater public attention to juveniles and to how juvenile courts deal with them. Violence by juveniles is growing at uneven rates among state jurisdictions (Irwin, 2004). In Hawaii, juvenile arrests for serious crimes of violence increased by over 200 percent during the period 1986–1996 (Chesney-Lind et al., 1998). But more recent figures suggest that juvenile violence is decreasing in most jurisdictions. The incidence of violence among younger juveniles has leveled off during the late 1990s and through 2004, declining slightly for offense-specific categories (Office of Juvenile Justice and Delinquency Prevention, 2005).

Adjudicated juveniles are subject to a limited range of juvenile court penalties, from verbal warnings and reprimands to secure confinement in a state industrial school. Delinquent acts involving physical harm to others or the threat of physical harm are considered violent offenses, in contrast with the larger category of property offenses that encompasses vehicular theft, petty larceny, or burglary. Intake officers perform the initial screening function by sending forward only the more serious offenders or those who the intake officers believe should have their cases adjudicated by juvenile court judges.

Juvenile court prosecutors screen those cases further by deciding which cases have the most prosecutive merit. Prosecutors are influenced by numerous factors whether to prosecute juveniles formally. Age, offense seriousness, and one's previous record often convince prosecutors to move forward with selected cases, whereas they may divert less serious cases to informal arbitration through alternative dispute resolution (Moak and Wallace, 2000).

One important consideration is the willingness of juveniles to compensate victims for their monetary losses through a program of restitution. Juries comprised of one's peers may impose restitution as a condition of diversion, and a youth's satisfactory completion of such a diversion program will likely avoid the scars of a formal delinquency adjudication. Juvenile courts continue to view their roles as largely rehabilitative, and judges seek to assist youths in avoiding any negative consequences of secure confinement (Bilchik, 1996). Various interventions are believed beneficial to juveniles in lieu of formal adjudicatory actions in juvenile courts.

In many jurisdictions, secure confinement is the last resort for judges when disposing serious juvenile offenders (Torbet et al., 2000). This reluctance to incarcerate juveniles has prompted criticisms that juvenile courts are soft on crime and that present juvenile crime control policies are insufficiently stringent. Some jurisdictions, such as New York, have established juvenile offender laws designed to transfer the most serious juvenile offenders from juvenile court to criminal court. However, such laws have proved ineffective at deterring juvenile violence (Irwin, 2004).

Nevertheless, growing rates of violence among juveniles during the early 1990s, especially for offenses such as first-degree sexual assault, aggravated robbery, and homicide, and the increasing influence of the get-tough movement in juvenile courts caused juvenile court judges to impose harsher dispositions for those juveniles who committed more serious offenses. Thus, the nature of the offenses alleged, together with inculpatory evidence against youths charged, weighed heavily in favor of moving certain more serious offenders into the system toward formal adjudication. Even though juvenile violence has tapered off and even decreased in most jurisdictions, the get-tough initiatives spawned by early 1990s juvenile violence continue. The rise of youth gangs in large U.S. cities, together with greater involvement in illicit drug trafficking, has done much to place more youths at risk regarding possible incarceration in secure facilities (Durst-Johnson, 2004).

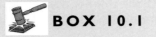

BOX 10.1

Matt Friesen
Program Manager, Colorado Division of Youth Services, Northeast Region

Statistics:

B.S. (criminal justice), University of Nebraska–Lincoln; M.S. (criminal justice), University of Nebraska–Omaha

Background

I started working in the juvenile justice field in 1992 after completing a bachelor's degree in criminal justice. I worked in a small juvenile detention center in Lincoln, Nebraska, while attending graduate school on my weekends, which for me were Wednesdays and Thursdays. I can't remember exactly why I decided to pursue a degree in criminal justice, but there I was, standing in the detention center listening to some kid threatening to assault the staff member who was training me. The learning curve in these jobs is typically pretty steep, and you will get tested early and often by staff as well as the clientele.

Doing direct care (e.g., guard, staff positions) is probably the best way to get started in the field. I can remember my friends in graduate school who had not done any direct care, talking about those "troubled youth" and thinking to myself, "That troubled youth threw a chair at me last night." I worked in juvenile detention for about 2 years before a pilot program was initiated through the Separate Juvenile Court of Lancaster County, Nebraska, which involved pretrial release of youth in the overcrowded detention facility. This new opportunity gave me a different view of delinquency and crime from a community perspective, and I quickly learned how important it is to network and develop relationships with people in the community to assist in getting the job done. What I mean by this is getting to know the schools and school personnel, treatment providers, law enforcement, and the neighborhoods very well in the effort both to assist and contain the offenders you work with.

In working with youth, you typically need the help of many people as much as they need you to help them with their youths. After a year or so in probation, I moved to Colorado to work in a pretrial program in the first Judicial District doing assessments and pretrial recommendations for the court. It was great to experience a completely different juvenile justice system, and although the economy was great, so was business in the corrections field with an exponential growth in delinquency filings, so many positions with the Division of Youth Corrections became available. You will recall from the old juvenile justice filter how cases go out at the decision to arrest, file, diversion, probation, and so on; well, with a greater number of arrests and filings, so came a greater number of youth to the end of the filter, which in Colorado is the Division of Youth Corrections (DYC). I have definitely enjoyed my work with the DYC as a client manager and parole officer. Once again, the importance of networking at every level of the job is the key to success, and it has given me the opportunity to meet people from all over Colorado and the country.

As a client manager/parole officer, I have a great deal of discretion and autonomy in what I do and how I do it. Parole officers must decide when a parolee presents too high of a risk to the community to safely maintain on parole and when to utilize the contacts they have established in the community to try to get them back into compliance. I used to be under the impression that a parole violation meant that your parole would be revoked. Far from it, the decision for me would be based on nearly every conversation I had with a client over the past two years in the institution and what their behavior looked like prior to them being sentenced to the DYC. Simply put, if you ran away from home, hung out with gang members, used drugs, and hurt people before you were sentenced to DYC, and I saw the same pattern on parole, I would try to stop you before we got to the "hurt people" stage.

The job is challenging when you go from meeting with a client with severe mental health needs to arresting a potentially dangerous parole violator. I have literally gone from a day enrolling a parolee in school, and the next day I was in a remote rural county filing search warrants in an effort to locate a parole absconder. You have to be able to switch hats and change gears at a moment's notice and sometimes without any warning. I have also always taken time to become a part of activities such as rock climbing or snowshoeing with clients. This gives both you and them a chance to interact in a completely different environment and is enlightening for each of you.

Finally now as a program manager or parole officer supervisor, I have the opportunity to try and shape policy and the direction of programs that we offer for the youth and families we work with in Colorado. I think that the best advice I can offer anyone getting started in the field is to take the time to understand how what you do fits into the bigger picture. This is true whether you go into law enforcement, social services, probation, or wherever you may land. Understanding your job completely and then how that job interacts with the rest of the justice system will give you the big-picture perspective that will allow you to succeed in whatever you do. Furthermore, do *not* blow off your research methods and statistics classes. The future of what we do will be guided not by those frustrating anecdotal case presentations, but rather by an analysis of trends, numbers, and facts. Too often the issue perceived is not entirely accurate, and once we look deeper into the issue, we find that the answer is very much different. This information comes from a collection of data from many sources and much to my surprise, it is often contrary to what we thought to be true initially. This would be a very basic example. Many professionals would argue that we were getting more mental health clients in the past few years, and that they were getting much worse in their presenting behaviors. A review of the entire regional caseload indicated that we had relatively very few clients with severe mental health needs in contradiction to the perception. I hope you enjoy whatever you choose to do in this field as much as I do, and good luck!

FIRST-OFFENDER OR REPEAT OFFENDER?

Is a juvenile a **first-offender** or a **repeat offender?** First-offenders have no prior record of delinquency, and it is presumed that their current offense is their first offense. Repeat offenders have prior delinquency or criminal records, either delinquency adjudications or criminal convictions or both. This is a key question raised by prosecutors when examining one's file to determine whether to prosecute the case in court (Risler, Sutphen, and Shields, 2000). The overwhelming tendency among prosecutors is either to divert petty first-offenders to some conditional program or dismiss these cases outright. Many diversionary programs involve restitution or victim compensation in some form. Contracts are arranged between youths and their victims, whereby youths reimburse victims, either partially or completely, for their financial losses. These programs often involve mediators who are responsible for securing agreements between juvenile offenders and their victims. Known as alternative dispute resolution, these mediation programs are believed to be fairly widespread and effective (Smith and Lombardo, 2002).

Evidence suggests that prior offenders, even chronic and violent offenders, stand good chances of receiving some nonincarcerative sanction, if they are eventually adjudicated as delinquent (Risler, Sutphen, and Shields, 2000). However, chronic juvenile offenders compared with first-offenders also have a greater chance of pursuing criminal careers as adults (Lee, 1996). Currently, no uniform policies exist among jurisdictions about how chronic offenders should be identified. Because of poor record-keeping and the lack of interjurisdictional record-sharing, many youthful offenders are continually diverted from formal juvenile court processing, despite their chronic recidivism. Some jurisdictions measure whether formal action against juveniles should be taken on the basis of the number of times they have been arrested. After four arrests, youths in some jurisdictions may be considered serious enough to have petitions filed against them as delinquents. During the 1990s, however, the compilation and centralization of state delinquency figures has increased, as well as the openness and availability of this information to the public sector.

Despite the relatively greater seriousness of violent offenses compared with property offenses, property offenders account for nearly two-thirds of all petitioned juveniles annually in most juvenile courts (Champion, 2005b). Substantial numbers of status offenders continue to be processed by the juvenile justice system as well. Thus, it is unclear who is being targeted by get-tough policies nationwide. Ideally, only those most serious chronic and violent juveniles should be targeted for the harshest juvenile court penalties. However, an overwhelming majority of long-term detainees in public and private secure facilities are property offenders, again by a substantial margin of 2 to 1 (Office of Juvenile Justice and Delinquency Prevention, 2005). One implication of this finding is that those most likely to be targeted for juvenile court action are persistent or chronic and nonviolent property offenders. They are considered the most troublesome in several respects. They clog juvenile court dockets again and again, and they sluggishly abandon their pattern of delinquent conduct. Furthermore, they consume valuable juvenile court time, which costs taxpayers considerable money.

The strong rehabilitative and reintegrative principles upon which the juvenile courts have operated for most of the twentieth century continue to influence how violent juvenile offenders are treated. For instance, various reintegrative programs have been described that are designed especially for violent juvenile offenders, called **Violent Juvenile Offender Programs (VJOP).** These programs provide several positive interventions and treatments (Fagan, 1990). Instead of long-term incarceration in secure confinement, many violent juvenile offenders are placed in community-based secure facilities, where they remain for short periods before being reintegrated into their communities. Transitional residential programs include sustained intensive supervision as youths are gradually given freedoms and responsibilities.

The VJOP is based on a theoretical model integrating strain, control, and learning theories. Four program dimensions include:

1. Social networking: the strengthening of personal bonds (attitudes, commitment, and beliefs) through positive experiences with family members, schools, the workplace, or nondelinquent peers.
2. Provision of opportunities for youths: the strengthening of social bonds (attachment and involvement) through achievement and successful participation in school, workplace, and family activities.

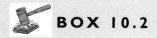

BOX 10.2

Compared with the United States, Russia had the second largest imprisonment rate in the world in 2000. Furthermore, juveniles in Russia are imprisoned nearly 12 times higher than those of other countries where alternative measures for their treatment and rehabilitation exist. Most of the juvenile incarcerations in Russia are for less serious offenses, property crimes, rather than for more serious ones, such as for murder, attempted murder, rape, robbery, or assault.

Russia is a federative state. The sources of law in Russia include the Russian constitution, federal constitutional law, federal laws, and the laws of subjects of federation. Administrative bodies issue acts that must comply with the laws. Criminal procedure law is under the exclusive jurisdiction of federal bodies. The system of Russian courts is governed by the Justice Ministry of Russia, which has territorial branches throughout the federation. Judges are independent and make their decisions according to the rule of law and the Criminal Code. All crimes are listed in the Criminal Code. Crime is classified into two categories: (1) major offenses, such as rape, kidnapping, treason, espionage, crimes against the justice system, serious violent crimes, and murder; and (2) minor offenses, such as offenses against property, hooliganism, and offenses against public order. This distinction is used to determine the nature and length of sentences. Russian record-keeping related to crime and juvenile offending is regionalized and unreliable. It is conceded by Russian authorities that actual unreported victimizations are far greater than official crime statistics disclose. Reported crimes are investigated, with a 50 percent investigative success rate.

The age of criminal responsibility in Russia is 16. Persons over 14 will bear responsibility only for murder, major bodily injury, rape, kidnapping, larceny, robbery, burglary, stealing firearms and drugs, malicious hooliganism, and train catastrophe. Educational or reform measures instead of punishment may be imposed on persons under the age of 18 who committed a crime.

Russian police are militia under the general jurisdiction of the Ministry of Internal Affairs. Their tasks are to protect life, physical health, rights, and freedoms of citizens; protect property; and protect the interests of the state and society from criminal and other unlawful infringements. Militia have prevention and suppression tasks, expose criminal offenses that require preliminary investigation; conduct searches of persons who have escaped from bodies of inquiry; and investigate missing persons. Special detachments of militia are created for cities in excess of 300,000, and watching units of 8–12 officers are established for towns of 50,000 or larger. There is usually one officer for each 50 cases investigated, and one juvenile delinquency inspector for every 4,000–5,000 persons under age 16. Militia may use force in any law enforcement activity, including the use of several types of defense equipment. They have broad discretionary powers of arrest in all criminal matters.

Where juveniles under age 16 are involved, cases may be transferred to a comrade's court or to a juvenile commission. Official reprimands may be issued, and offenders may be released on bail. If the juvenile is deemed not mentally fit, compulsory medical or psychological treatment may be prescribed for any person under age 18. Judges who hear juvenile matters require no special training. They must be citizens of Russia, have a certificate of higher education, pass an appropriate qualifying examination, and have a good reputation. They must be 25 years of age or older to be on a people's court or juvenile commission. Whenever juvenile commissions decide measures to be imposed on juvenile offenders found guilty of one or more offenses, it is done by majority vote.

The range of penalties for all types of offenders, including juveniles, includes imprisonment, fines, reforming works without imprisonment, publicity, dismissal from office, deprivation of the right to hold certain positions or perform certain activities; *(continued)* restitution for financial damage; and additional punishments, including the confiscation of property and deprivation of special military or other ranks. The death penalty may be administered to anyone age 18 or older. Execution is by firing squad.

Imprisonment is a common punishment. In 1994 there were 600,000 persons imprisoned, of which 21,600 were women and 19,100 were juveniles. In 2004 this figure doubled. Over half of all persons imprisoned were convicted of violent crimes, and half are either alcoholics or have drug abuse problems. These figures are estimates, since no reliable imprisonment figures are compiled by Russian authorities on a consistent basis. No special training is required to work as prison guards. All prisoners must work at different tasks, although this obligation depends on available work. About a third of all prisoners have no work to do and thus are warehoused with little or no productive work or rehabilitative activity. Juvenile prisoners are required to complete secondary education programs. Other prisoners must comply with 8-year secondary education standards. Those over age 40 may choose to study at their own discretion.

During the period 1990–2005, rights groups throughout Europe and elsewhere have focused on the rights of Russian juveniles, promoting their opportunities for happiness, love, and understanding. The United Nations has declared that all youths should be reared and treated in the spirit of peace, dignity, tolerance, freedom, equality, and solidarity. Because of their special immaturity, juveniles ought to have safeguards and care, including legal protection. The United Nations has further declared that all children should have decisions made on the basis of whatever is in their best interests.

International officials have declared that juveniles who are detained under arrest should be presumed innocent until proved guilty. Detention should be avoided to the extent possible and limited to exceptional circumstances. Untried detainees should be held separate from convicted juveniles. Thus, some attempt is made to avoid adverse labeling effects. Juveniles who are to be sentenced should be thoroughly evaluated to determine their social, economic, and psychological circumstances. Their sub-

sequent classification and placement should be proportional to the offenses they have committed, and measures should be imposed to meet their individual needs. Juveniles should be separated from adults under all detention or imprisonment conditions. Open detention facilities are encouraged. Vocational and educational training for juveniles are stressed, and all international standards relative to juvenile labor should be observed. Although these international recommendations have been encouraged, it is unknown the degree to which Russian authorities acknowledge or adhere to them in any strict sense.

Responses from Russian officials to international bodies such as the United Nations and the European Court of Human Rights and Criminal Procedure have been limited and vague. In 1999 the Minister of Labor, Sergei Kalashnikov, declared that he had personally visited many facilities where juveniles were being detained and did not see drastic violations of children's rights. No guarantees were forthcoming from any official Russian source that children's rights would be rigorously protected. No mechanisms have been articulated for protecting the rights of minors. However, Russia has indicated that over 500 educational institutions for children have been established where psychological, educational, medical, and social assistance of different forms are being provided. Furthermore, there are prosecutor's offices that oversee the observation of children's rights, particularly of those juveniles in custody for various terms. Nevertheless, it has been acknowledged that it is impossible for these prosecutor's offices to detect and correct any and all instances of child abuse that may occur within these institutions. In 2004, there were estimates of at least 250,000 children without the care of parents; 60,000 children placed in children's homes or other institutions; and over 100,000 children placed in foster care. Child welfare agencies have been created to monitor the rights and legal interests of these children, although resources for carrying out these monitoring tasks are limited.

It has also been estimated that approximately 70–80 percent of all institutionalized children have been diagnosed incorrectly for medical and psychological maladies requiring treatment. Less than 10 percent of all teachers have special qualifications for dealing with special needs children. Thus, a large portion of mentally disabled children are subsequently discharged from institutions without having received any type of meaningful assistance or treatment. Presently in Russia there is a critical shortage of special schools and rehabilitation programs, such that many youths who advance beyond age 14 continue their law-breaking activities. The government response is largely repressive rather than preventive. Teenagers in Russia were serving sentences of up to 2 years, while some of the more serious youthful offenders were serving terms of 5 or more years.

Statistical information about incarcerated offenders is sparse. A very complex and cumbersome system presently exists that results in juvenile incarcerations until adulthood, where the welfare of children is lost in the bureaucracy and necessary treatments and measures for particular juveniles are simply not provided. Children in most institutions are treated poorly, and in many cases, these children are physically abused. They lack the necessary social, educational, and vocational skills to function in society. Russian orphans and youthful indigents have limited prospects for effective and useful placements, treatments, or services.

Penitentiaries in Russia hold nearly 100,000 juveniles ranging in age from 11 to 18. Pretrial detention facilities are called SIZOs. These administrative detention centers are used to hold youths awaiting trial. Ideally, youths should be held no longer than 3 days in SIZOs, although much longer detention periods have occurred. IVS cells are worse than SIZOs. IVS cells are preliminary detention cells and are the equivalent of U.S. holding tanks for vagrants and drunks. Terms of pretrial detention of juveniles are excessively long, ranging from 6 months to 3 years. Children's cells in SIZOs hold 4–12 inmates. Ideally juveniles are permitted 2 hours a day for exercise. Arrest is applied unreasonably often. Juveniles who develop diseases in SIZOs often go untreated for lengthy periods.

Most youthful offenders cannot afford to hire skilled defense lawyers. They do not know or understand their rights or the meaning of legal proceedings. Violence in SIZOs is rampant. An informal code of conduct exists among juvenile inmates. Juveniles who are sexually abused by other inmates are considered disgraced boys. Incarcerated girls are often raped with various objects. The prison administration is largely unresponsive to prisoner complaints, and often, psychological tortures of different types are applied. As punishments for complaining, juveniles may be denied work, continued education, books and newspapers, visits from their relatives, and other measures. SIZO administrators are aware of these problems but ignore them with little or no accountability.

In 2000 Russian authorities appeared amenable to implementing restorative justice in lieu of incarceration, although this practice has been limited to particular geographic areas. A few restorative justice centers have been established in some of the larger Russian cities, such as Moscow, with promising results. The major problem is educating officials to implement restorative justice, mediation, and victim–offender reconciliation successfully. It is promising that a growing number of concerned Russian officials and academics are pursuing restorative justice and other reintegrative and rehabilitative measures for the purpose of improving juvenile justice.

[*Sources:* Adapted from Center for Human Rights, "Russian NGOs' 'Alternative Answer,'" Unpublished paper, September 19, 1999; Convention on the Rights of the Child, "Concluding Observations of the Committee on the Rights of the Child," United Nations, Unpublished paper, October 11, 1999; Alexander Severance, "Old Habits Die Hard: Alexandr Nikitin, the European Court of Human Rights, and Criminal Procedure in the Russian Federation," Unpublished paper, 2005; Bureau of Democracy, Human Rights, and Labor, "Russia: Country Reports on Human Rights Practices 2003," Unpublished paper, 2005; Centre for Legal and Judicial Reform "Transition from the System of Correction to Restorative Justice, the Situation in Society" Unpublished paper, 2005; Moscow Center for Prison Reform, "Juvenile SIZO Prisoners," Unpublished paper, 1998.]

3. Social learning: the process by which personal and social bonds are strengthened and reinforced; strategies include rewards and sanctions for attainment of goals or for contingent behaviors.

4. Goal-oriented behaviors: the linking of specific behaviors to each client's needs and abilities, including problem behaviors and special intervention needs (e.g., substance abuse treatment or psychotherapy) (Fagan, 1990:240).

Violent juvenile offenders who have participated in these programs seem less inclined to recidivate. He believes that "carefully implemented and well-managed intervention programs," those that involve "early reintegration activities preceding release from secure care and intensive supervision in the community, with emphasis on gradual reentry and development of social skills to avoid criminal behavior" do much to "avert the abrupt return to criminality after release from the program" of these youths. Those youths exposed to more conventional and longer secure confinement and treatment appear to recidivate at greater rates and to persist in their delinquent behaviors (Fagan, 1990:258). Therefore, it is difficult to formulate specific guidelines about how violent juvenile offenders ought to be handled in their juvenile court processing. Currently, competing philosophies of rehabilitation and just-deserts recommend polarities in treatments, ranging from total diversion to total secure confinement.

Is the First-Offender/Repeat-Offender Distinction Relevant? Race, Ethnicity, and Socioeconomic Status Revisited

Juvenile courts are supposed to be objective in their adjudicatory hearings and imposition of sanctions. Legal variables, such as prior record and the seriousness of the current offense, are supposed to be defining criteria for a system of graduated sanctions. Indeed, investigations of selected juvenile courts reveal

Juveniles enjoy almost all of the legal rights afforded adult offenders, including the right to due process.

that current offense seriousness and prior record are the most important variables in determining the dispositions of repeat delinquents. But juvenile courts in virtually every jurisdiction have drawn criticism that adjudications and dispositions are more a function of race, ethnicity, and socioeconomic status than of offense seriousness and prior record (Kowalski and Caputo, 1999). This is because of the disproportionately high representation of minorities in juvenile arrests, adjudications, and incarcerative dispositions (Eitle, Stolzenberg, and D'Alessio, 2005).

In many jurisdictions, white juveniles stand a better chance than blacks or Hispanics of not being detained following their arraignment. White juveniles also have a better chance of avoiding incarceration compared with blacks and Hispanics if they are adjudicated delinquent (Bradley, 2005; Brooks and Jeon, 2001; Feld, 2001). This charge against juvenile justice systems in the United States has led to a federal mandate to document the existence and nature of minority overrepresentation and to devise strategies to reduce such overrepresentation. One strategy designed to overcome the prejudicial effects of race, ethnicity, and social class is to establish objective criteria for juvenile justice decision making (Eitle, Stolzenberg, and D'Alessio, 2005).

Several objective criteria might be applied to decision making at various points throughout the juvenile justice system. These criteria are found in most state criminal codes and describe various conditions or circumstances that are more or less influential regarding juvenile offender dispositions, regardless of their seriousness. Some of these objective criteria include aggravating and mitigating circumstances.

AGGRAVATING AND MITIGATING CIRCUMSTANCES

Playing an important part in determining how far any particular juvenile moves into the juvenile justice system are various aggravating and mitigating circumstances accompanying their acts. In the early stages of intake and prosecutorial decision making, aggravating and mitigating circumstances are often informally considered, and much depends on the amount of detail furnished by police officers about the delinquent events. Aggravating circumstances are usually those actions on the part of juveniles that tend to intensify the seriousness of their acts. Accordingly, where aggravating circumstances exist, one's subsequent punishment might be intensified. At the other end of the spectrum are mitigating circumstances, or those factors that might weigh in the juvenile's favor. These circumstances might lessen the seriousness of the act as well as the severity of punishment imposed by juvenile court judges (Coyne and Entzeroth, 2001). Lists of aggravating and mitigating circumstances are presented below.

Aggravating Circumstances

Aggravating circumstances applicable both to juveniles and adults include:

1. Death or serious bodily injury to one or more victims. The most serious juvenile offenders are those who cause death or serious bodily injury to their victims. Homicide and aggravated assault are those offenses that most directly involve death or serious physical harm to others, although it

is possible to inflict serious bodily injury or inflict deep emotional scars through armed robbery and even some property crimes, including burglary (Silver, 2002). The harshest option available to juvenile court judges is direct commitment to secure confinement, such as an industrial school or reform school.

2. An offense committed while the offender is awaiting other delinquency charges. Are juveniles awaiting an intake hearing after being arrested for previous offenses? Many juveniles commit new delinquent acts between the time they are arrested for other offenses and the date of their intake hearing. These offenders are probably good candidates for temporary confinement in secure holding facilities until their cases can be heard by intake officers and delinquency petitions can be filed.

3. An offense committed while the offender is on probation, parole, or work release. Offenders with prior adjudications and who are currently serving their sentences may reoffend during these conditional periods. Usually, a condition of diversionary and probatory programs is that youths refrain from further delinquent activity. Thus, they may be in violation of a program condition. Probation, parole, and work release program violations are separate offenses that are accompanied by harsher penalties. In effect, these are incidents of contempt of court, since they involve violations of direct court-ordered conditional activities. The probation, parole, or work release conditional programs have usually been granted to certain offenders because they have been deemed trustworthy by officials. Therefore, violations of the court's trust are especially serious, and it becomes less likely that these juveniles will be extended such privileges in the future (Kowalski and Caputo, 1999).

4. Previous offenses for which the offender has been punished. Having a prior record is a strong indicator of one's chronicity and potential for future offending behavior. Juvenile court judges may be less inclined to be lenient in sentencing those with prior records, especially where serious delinquent acts have been committed. For example, repeat sex offenders are often treated more harshly by juvenile court judges, because of their suspected high rate of relapse. Thus, whether or not the belief that a high rate of relapse among sex offenders is justified, the mere fact of being a sex offender becomes an unofficial aggravating factor for many juvenile court judges.

5. Leadership in the commission of the delinquent at involving two or more offenders. Especially in gang-related activities, one's leadership role is an aggravating circumstance. Are certain youths gang leaders? Do they incite others to commit delinquent acts? Gang leaders are often targeted for the harshest punishments, since they are most visible to their peers and serve as examples of how the system deals with juvenile offenders. Those playing minor roles in gang-related activity might be treated more leniently by judges.

6. A violent offense involving more than one victim. As the number of victims increases as the result of any delinquent conduct, the potential for physical harm and death rapidly escalates. Robberies of convenience stores and other places where large numbers of customers might be are likely to involve multiple victims. The number of victims or potential victims aggravates the initial delinquent conduct.

7. Extreme cruelty during the commission of the offense. Maiming victims or torturing them during the commission of delinquent acts is considered extreme cruelty and worthy of enhanced punishments by juvenile court judges.

8. Use of a dangerous weapon in the commission of the offense, with high risk to human life. The second and third leading causes of death among juveniles under age 21 are homicides and suicides, and most of these events include the use of firearms (Metts, 2005). Using firearms to commit delinquent acts increases greatly the potential harm to victims of such acts. Many states currently have mandatory **flat time** or hard time associated with using firearms during the commission of felonies. This means that if someone uses a dangerous weapon during the commission of a crime, a mandatory sentence enhancement is included, which may be an additional 2- to 5-year sentence in addition to the initial punishment, which might be a 10-year sentence for armed robbery (Roberts, Nuffield, and Hann, 2000).

Mitigating Circumstances

Mitigating circumstances include the following:

1. No serious bodily injury resulting from the offense. Petty property offenders who do not endanger lives or injure others may have their sentences mitigated as a result. Interestingly, however, property offenders account for a majority of long-term juvenile detainees in industrial schools or secure juvenile facilities.

2. No attempt to inflict serious bodily injury on anyone. Those juveniles who commit theft or burglary usually wish to avoid confrontations with their victims. While some juveniles prepare for such contingencies and therefore pose bodily threats to others, most youthful offenders committing such acts run away from the crime scene if discovered. This is evidence of their desire to avoid inflicting serious bodily harm on their victims.

3. Duress or extreme provocation. A compelling defense used in criminal court cases is that offenders were under duress at the time they committed their crimes. They may have been forced to act in certain ways by others. Under certain circumstances, youths may plead that they were coerced or were acting under duress when committing delinquent acts in concert with others. Gang membership and gang violence may be precipitated to a degree because of duress. Youths may join gangs for self-protection and to avoid being assaulted by other gang members.

4. Circumstances that justify the conduct. Any circumstance that might justify one's conduct is a mitigating factor. If youths act to protect themselves or others from physical harm, then judges may find these circumstances strong enough to justify whatever conduct was exhibited.

5. Mental incapacitation or physical condition that significantly reduced the offender's culpability in the offense. This factor specifies conditions that relate to drug or alcohol dependencies or to mental retardation or mental illness. If youths are suffering from some form of mental illness or are

retarded, or if they are alcohol- or drug-dependent, this may limit their capacity to understand the law and interfere with their ability to comply with it (Everle and Maiuro, 2001).

6. Cooperation with authorities in apprehending other participants in the act or making restitution to the victims for losses they suffered. Those youths who assist police in apprehending others involved in delinquent acts are credited with these positive deeds. Also, juveniles who make restitution to victims or compensate them in part or in whole for their financial losses stand a good chance of having their cases mitigated through such restitution and good works.

7. No prior record of delinquency. First-offender juveniles, particular those under age 16, are especially targeted for more lenient treatment compared with recidivists.

8. One's youthfulness. The younger the juvenile, the greater the mitigation. Under common law, for instance, persons who commit crimes and who are under the age of 7 are presumed incapable of formulating criminal intent. However, those who are 8, 9, 10, 11, and 12 years of age are entitled to some mitigation as well, in the opinions of some observers. Not being a fully formed adult renders a juvenile less mature and capable of sound decision making. One line of thought is that it is simply more difficult for juveniles to understand the law and comply with it. Thus, one's youthfulness should be weighed against any aggravating circumstances that might exist.

These lists of aggravating and mitigating circumstances are not exhaustive. Other factors may affect the judicial decision. At each stage of the juvenile justice process, interested officials want to know whether certain offenders will recidivate if they receive leniency. No one knows for sure whether certain offenders will recidivate more frequently than other offenders, although certain factors correlate highly with recidivism. In the following section, we examine several ways of assessing a juvenile's dangerousness or risk to the community. Such assessments are crucial in many jurisdictions in influencing prosecutorial and judicial decision making.

JUVENILE RISK ASSESSMENTS AND PREDICTIONS OF DANGEROUSNESS

Risk assessment is an element of a classification system and traditionally means the process of determining the probability that an individual will repeat unlawful or destructive behavior. Risk **prediction** takes several forms, including the prediction of violent behavior, predictions of new offenses (recidivism), and the prediction of technical program violations associated with probation and parole. Most states have some semblance of risk assessment of juvenile offenders, but only about half of the states have formal risk assessment instruments (Benda, Corwyn, and Toombs, 2001).

Dangerousness and Risk

The concepts of **dangerousness** and **risk** are often used interchangeably. Dangerousness and risk both convey propensities to cause harm to others or oneself. What is the likelihood that any particular offender will be violent toward others?

Does an offender pose any risk to public safety? What is the likelihood that any particular offender will commit suicide or attempt it? Risk (or dangerousness) instruments are screening devices intended to distinguish between different types of offenders for purposes of determining initial institutional classification, security placement and inmate management, early release eligibility, and the level of supervision required under conditions of probation or parole. These instruments contain information believed useful in forecasting future delinquent conduct or criminality (Salekin, Rogers, and Ustad, 2001). This information is collectively referred to as **predictors of dangerousness and risk.** Most state jurisdictions and the federal government regard these measures that forecast future criminality or delinquency as **risk/needs assessment instruments** rather than dangerousness instruments (Mitchell et al., 2000). There is considerable variability among states regarding the format and content of such measures.

Needs Assessment and Its Measurement

Needs assessment instruments are instruments that measure an offender's personal/social skills, health well-being and emotional stability, educational level and vocational strengths and weaknesses, alcohol/drug dependencies, mental ability, and other relevant life factors, and which highlight those areas for which services are available and could or should be provided (Benda, Corwyn, and Toombs, 2001).

Attempts to forecast juvenile dangerousness/risk and needs are important, because many actors in the juvenile justice system use these predictions or forecasts as the basis for their decision making (Risler, Sutphen, and Shields, 2000). Intake officers who initially screen youthful offenders try to decide which offenders are most deserving of leniency and which should be pushed further into the system for formal processing. Prosecutors want to know which juveniles are most receptive to diversion and amenable to change (Miner, 2002). Thus, they can ensure that only the most serious and chronic offenders will be processed, while the remaining youths will have another chance to live reasonably normal lives in their communities without juvenile justice system supervision (Siegel and Williams, 2003). And judges want to know which youths will likely reoffend if returned to their communities through probation or some other nonincarcerative option. Some juvenile offenders may be penalized purely on the basis of their likelihood of future offending. Others may receive leniency because they are considered good probation or parole risks and unlikely to reoffend. Thus, some juveniles are selectively incapacitated. **Selective incapacitation** is confining those who are predicted to pose a risk to others, usually on the basis of their prior record and/or risk score on some risk instrument (Escarcega et al., 2004; Feld, 2001).

Selective Incapacitation

False Positives and False Negatives.   There are at least two major dangers inherent in risk or dangerousness predictions. First, youths who are identified as likely recidivists may receive harsher treatment compared with those who are considered unlikely to reoffend. In fact, many of those youths considered as good risks for probation or diversion may eventually turn out to be dangerous, although predictions of their future conduct gave assurances to the contrary.

Second, those youths who receive harsher punishment and longer confinement because they are believed to be dangerous may not, in fact, be dangerous. Therefore, we risk overpenalizing those who will not be dangerous in the future, although our forecasts suggest they will be dangerous. We also risk underpenalizing those believed by our forecasts not to be dangerous, although a portion will eventually turn out to be dangerous and kill or seriously injure others (Vincent et al., 2003).

These two scenarios depict **false positives** and **false negatives.** False positives are those persons predicted to be dangerous in the future but who turn out not to be dangerous. False negatives are those persons predicted not to be dangerous in the future but turn out to be dangerous anyway. False positives are those who are unduly punished because of our predictions, while false negatives are those who do not receive needed punishment or future supervision (Nafekh, 2002). For adult criminals, attempts to forecast criminal behaviors have led to recommendations for selective incapacitation in many jurisdictions. Selective incapacitation involves incarcerating or detaining those persons believed to be likely recidivists on the basis of various behavioral and attitudinal criteria. The theory behind selective incapacitation is that if high-risk offenders can be targeted and controlled through long-term confinement, then their circulation will be limited as well as the potential crimes they might commit (Auerhahn, 2003, 2004).

Selective incapacitation is controversial. Samuel Walker (2001) raises five general questions about the usefulness and desirability of selective incapacitation in dealing with offenders in general. They are:

1. Can we correctly estimate the amount of crime reduction?
2. Can we accurately identify chronic offenders and predict their future behavior?
3. Can we afford the monetary costs of implementing selective incapacitation should it involve massive new detention center construction?
4. Can we implement a policy of consistent selective incapacitation without violating constitutional rights?
5. What will be the side effects?

Basically, incapacitation is a strategy for crime control involving the physical isolation of offenders from their communities, usually through incarceration, to prevent them from committing future crimes (Auerhahn, 2002). But Walker's questions are quite important, since there are some important implications of selective incapacitation for youthful offenders. The major harm is penalizing certain youths for acts they haven't yet committed (Miner, 2002; Nafekh, 2002). Can we legitimately punish anyone in the United States for suspected future criminality or delinquency? Whatever one's personal feelings in this regard, the answer is that such punishments are imposed each time parole boards deny parole requests or probation recommendations are rejected in favor of incarceration.

Visher (1987:514–515) describes two types of incapacitation: collective and selective. Under collective incapacitation, crime reduction would be accomplished through traditional offense-based sentencing and incarcerative policies, such as mandatory minimum sentences. Under selective incapacitation, however, those offenders predicted to pose the greatest risk of future

Electronic monitoring centers for juveniles on home confinement are headquartered in probation offices, jails, police stations, and other public facilities.

crimes would become prime candidates for incarceration and for longer prison sentences. A major problem throughout both the criminal justice system and the juvenile justice system is that no universally acceptable implementation policies have been adopted in most jurisdictions supporting the use of such incapacitation strategies. Furthermore, there are serious problems with many of these instruments because they cannot distinguish adequately between risks posed by male and female juvenile offenders (Loucks and Zamble, 1999).

The quality of risk assessment devices is such at present that we cannot depend on them as absolutely perfect indicators of one's future conduct (Champion, 1994). One problem is that many risk assessment instruments are almost exclusively tested on adult offenders rather than juvenile offenders. Also, follow-up periods for assessments of predictive effectiveness are often relatively short, thus preventing researchers from validating the predictive utility of these scales over time. Despite the continuing controversy surrounding the application of risk prediction measures and the criticisms by some researchers that such predictions are either impossible or inappropriate, such predictions continue to be made. Furthermore, several researchers are cautiously optimistic about the predictive utility of the assessment instruments they have devised and used (e.g., Auerhahn, 2003, 2004).

Generally, risk assessment measures are one of the three following categories: (1) anamnestic prediction; (2) actuarial prediction; and (3) clinical prediction.

Anamnestic prediction. Anamnestic prediction uses past sets of circumstances to predict future behaviors. If the current circumstances are similar to past circumstances, where previous offense behaviors were observed, then it is probable that youths will exhibit future offending (Heyman et al., 2002).

Actuarial prediction. Actuarial prediction is an aggregate predictive tool. Those youthful offenders who are being considered for diversion, probation, or parole are compared with former offenders who have similar characteristics (Campbell, 2003). Performances and records of previous conduct in view of diversion, probation, or parole decisions serve as the basis for profiling the high-risk recidivist (Janus and Prentk, 2003). Certain youths may exhibit characteristics similar to previous juveniles who became recidivists. The expectation is that current youths will likely recidivate as well (Banks et al., 2004).

Clinical prediction. Clinical prediction involves professional assessments of diagnostic examinations and test results. The professional training of probation officers, prosecutors, and judges, as they experience working with youthful offenders directly, enables them to forecast probable behaviors of their present clients (Douglas and Kropp, 2002). Clinical prediction involves administration of psychological tools and personality assessment devices. Certain background and behavioral characteristics are assessed as well. Some persons consider clinical prediction to be superior to actuarial and anamnestic prediction, although there is little support for this claim. In fact, actuarial prediction, the simplest prediction form, is either equal to or better than clinical prediction under a variety of circumstances.

Common Elements of Risk Assessment Instruments

Most risk assessment measures for juvenile offenders contain several common elements (Park, 2005). Adapting these common elements to youthful offender scenarios, the following elements seem prevalent:

1. Age at first adjudication
2. Prior delinquent behavior (a combined measure of the number and severity of priors)
3. Number of prior commitments to juvenile facilities
4. Drug/chemical abuse
5. Alcohol abuse
6. Family relationships (parental control)
7. School problems
8. Peer relationships

For each of the elements above, some evidence has been found to establish a definite association between these and a youth's recidivism potential (Glaser, Calhoun, and Petrocelli, 2002). These associations are not always strong, but in an actuarial prediction sense, they provide a basis for assuming that each of these elements has some causal value. The earlier the age of first adjudication and/or contact with the juvenile justice system, the greater the risk of recidivism (Janus and Prentk, 2003). Poor school performance, family problems and a lack of parental control, drug and/or alcohol dependencies, prior commitments to juvenile facilities, and a prior history of juvenile offending are individually and collectively linked with recidivism (Glaser, Calhoun, and Petrocelli, 2002).

For example, the California Youth Authority includes the following variables and response weights as a means of assessing one's risk level:

1. Age at first police contact:
   9 = score 6 points
   10 = score 5 points
   11 = score 4 points
   12 = score 3 points

13 = score 2 points
14 = score 1 point
15 = score 0 points

2. Number of prior police contacts (number):
   (score actual number)

3. Aggression and/or purse snatching:
   score "yes" = 1, "no" = 0

4. Petty theft:
   score "yes" = 1, "no" = 0

5. Use of alcohol or glue:
   score "yes" = 1, "no" = 0

6. Usually three or more others involved in delinquent act:
   score "yes" = 1, "no" = 0

7. Family on welfare:
   score "yes" = 1, "no" = 0

8. Father main support in family:
   score "no" = 1, "yes" = 0

9. Intact family:
   score "no" = 1, "yes" = 0

10. Number of siblings:
    3 = score 1 point
    4 = score 2 points
    5+ = score 3 points

11. Father has criminal record:
    score "yes" = 1, "no" = 0

12. Mother has criminal record:
    score "yes" = 1, "no" = 0

13. Low family supervision:
    score "yes" = 1, "no" = 0

14. Mother rejects:
    score "yes" = 1, "no" = 0

15. Father rejects:
    score "yes" = 1, "no" = 0

16. Parents wanted youth committed:
    score "no" = 1, "yes" = 0

17. Verbal IQ:
    equal to or less than 69 = 4
    70–79 = 3
    80–89 = 2
    90–99 = 1
    100+ = 0

18. Grade level:
    at grade level = 1
    1 year retarded = 2
    2 years retarded = 3
    3 years retarded = 4
    4+ years retarded = 5

19. Negative school attitude:
    score 0–3

20. School disciplinary problems:
    score "yes" = 1, "no" = 0

On the basis of the score obtained, youths might be assigned the following risk levels:

Risk Level Score	Degree of Risk
0–22	Low
21–31	Medium
32+	High

Adapted from the California Youth Authority, 2001.

Youths who receive scores of 0–22 are considered low risks, while those with scores of 32 or higher are considered high risks. California Youth Authority officials believe that while these scores do not necessarily indicate that all youths with higher scores will be recidivists and all those with lower scores will be nonrecidivists, there does appear to be some indication that these categorizations are generally valid ones. Thus, these classifications might be used to segregate more serious offenders from less serious ones in secure confinement facilities. Or such scores might be useful in forecasts of future performance in diversion or probationary programs.

When measures or indices such as these are examined critically, it is interesting to note how such important life-influencing decisions are reduced to six or seven predictive criteria. In the case of the instrumentation devised by the California Youth Authority, decisions about youths made by this organization are supplemented with several other important **classification** criteria, such as personality assessment tools, youth interviews, and professional impressions.

The Functions of Classification

1. Classification systems enable authorities to make decisions about appropriate offender program placements.
2. Classification systems help to identify one's needs and the provision of effective services in specialized treatment programs.
3. Classification assists in determining one's custody level if confined in either prisons or jails.
4. Classification helps to adjust one's custody level during confinement, considering behavioral improvement and evidence of rehabilitation.
5. While confined, inmates may be targeted for particular services and/or programs to meet their needs.
6. Classification may be used for offender management and deterrence relative to program or prison rules and requirements.
7. Classification schemes are useful for policy decision making and administrative planning relevant for jail and prison construction, the nature and number of facilities required, and the types of services to be made available within such facilities.
8. Classification systems enable parole boards to make better early-release decisions about eligible offenders.

9. Community corrections agencies can utilize classification schemes to determine those parolees who qualify for participation and those who don't qualify.

10. Classification systems enable assessments of risk and dangerousness to be made generally in anticipation of the type of supervision best suited for particular offenders.

11. Classification schemes assist in decision making relevant for community crime control, the nature of penalties to be imposed, and the determination of punishment.

12. Classification may enable authorities to determine whether selective incapacitation is desirable for particular offenders or offender groupings.

For most states, the following general applications are made of risk assessment instruments at different client-processing stages:

1. To promote better program planning through optimum budgeting and deployment of resources.

2. To target high-risk and high-need offenders for particular custody levels, programs, and services without endangering the safety of others.

3. To apply fair and appropriate sanctions to particular classes of offenders and raise their level of accountability.

4. To provide mechanisms for evaluating services and programs as well as service and program improvements over time.

5. To maximize public safety as well as public understanding of the diverse functions of corrections by making decision making more open and comprehensible to both citizens and offender-clients.

Several important and desirable characteristics of such predictive models are:

1. The model should be predictively valid.

2. The model should reflect reality.

3. The model should be designed for a dynamic system and not remain fixed over time.

4. The model should serve practical purposes.

5. The model should not be a substitute for good thinking and responsible judgment.

6. The model should be both qualitative and quantitative (Rans, 1984:50).

The state of Washington has a Juvenile Rehabilitation Administration (JRA), an agency charged with the custody and treatment of committed youths. During the mid-1990s, the JRA created a juvenile rehabilitation model that utilizes assessment tools designed to specify appropriate treatment programming for juvenile offenders. The mission of the JRA is to teach offenders accountability, provide preventative and rehabilitative programming and public protection, and reduce repetitive criminal behavior using the least restrictive setting necessary. Under this model, the JRA evaluates committed offenders' risks to the community, articulates competency-based treatment outcomes, and assesses youths' sustained treatment progress while incarcerated. The goal of this model is to effectively move youths through a continuum of care, from structured residential settings through community parole (Schmidt et al., 1998:104–105). Thus, Washington authorities have devised initial security classification assessment tools and an assessment of community risk. Furthermore, community placement eligibility criteria have been established, together with a variety of rehabilitative treatment programs. Core treatment programming includes substance abuse education, work, vocational and life skills, problem solving, constructive response to frustration, and victim empathy/restoration. Specialized treatment programming is provided for sex offenders, mentally ill offenders, and substance abusers. Similar treatment programs are found in other jurisdictions (Smith et al., 2004).

Risk Prediction from Arizona and Florida

Below are two different risk prediction instruments devised by Arizona and Florida. As a simple exercise, read the following scenarios involving several hypothetical delinquents. Next, read through the particular risk prediction instruments, paying attention to their instructions for score determinations. Then, complete each instrument and determine the total score for each juvenile. It will be apparent that this task is easier for some instruments than for others. You will need to do several things when you compute scores for each of these juvenile offenders. You will need to keep track of their ages, how many formal and informal delinquency or status offender adjudications they have acquired, and whether they have escaped or attempted escape from a secure juvenile facility. In some of the instruments, you will need to determine whether they are drug- or alcohol-dependent. A brief solution will be provided at the end of these three scenarios.

Scenario 1: Arizona and Jerry J.   Jerry J. lives in Phoenix, Arizona. He is 14 years old. Jerry J. is a member of the Scorpions, a Phoenix juvenile gang. He has been a gang member for three years and has participated in several drive-by shootings, none of which has resulted in fatalities to intended victims. Jerry J. is known to the police. When Jerry J. was 11 years old, he was taken into custody for assaulting another student in his school. This was the result of a referral by the school principal. An intake officer adjusted the case and returned Jerry J. to the custody of his parents. Two months later, Jerry J. was taken into custody again, this time for beating another student with a lead pipe and causing serious bodily injuries. Again, the school principal referred Jerry J. to juvenile authorities for processing, and a delinquency petition was filed. This time, the juvenile court judge heard Jerry J.'s case and adjudicated Jerry J. delinquent on the assault charge. Jerry J. was disposed to probation for one year.

While on probation, Jerry J. joined the Scorpions and was involved in at least three convenience store thefts and five crack cocaine sales. During the last crack cocaine sale, an undercover police officer posing as a crack cocaine customer arrested Jerry J. and two of his gang companions and took them to the police station for processing. Jerry J. appeared again before the same juvenile court judge after a police referral. This time, the judge adjudicated Jerry J. delinquent on the drug charge and disposed him to an 18-month probationary term. In the meantime, a routine drug screen at the local jail where Jerry J. was being detained in preventive detention revealed that he tested positive for cocaine and alcohol use. Under questioning, Jerry J. admitted to using drugs occasionally, as well as consuming alcohol at gang meetings. When Jerry J. was 12 years old and still on probation, he was taken into custody by police following a burglary report at a local drug store. When officers apprehended Jerry J., he was crawling out of a back window of the drug store with several bottles of Percodan, a prescription pain reliever. Officers confiscated a loaded .22-caliber pistol, which Jerry J. was carrying in his jacket pocket. Officers filed a delinquency petition with the juvenile court, alleging several law violations, including burglary, theft, and carrying a concealed firearm. Jerry J.'s probation officer also referred Jerry J. to the juvenile court and recommended that Jerry J.'s probation program be revoked, since he was in clear violation of his probation program requirements. The juvenile court judge adjudicated Jerry J. delinquent on the firearms charge as well as on the burglary and theft charges. He also revoked Jerry J.'s probation after a two-stage hearing where substantial evidence was presented of Jerry J.'s guilt. Jerry J. was disposed to 6 months' intensive supervised probation with electronic monitoring.

Subsequently, Jerry J. has been adjudicated delinquent three more times. Police officers filed petitions with the juvenile court on all three occasions. Two of these delinquency adjudications were for felonies (aggravated assault and selling one kilo of cocaine). For the aggravated assault offense, the juvenile court judge disposed Jerry J. to the Arizona State Industrial school, a secure-custody facility, for a term of 6 months. The judge also revoked Jerry J.'s probation program. A predispositional report filed by the juvenile probation officer disclosed that Jerry J. has frequently been truant from school and has had serious behavioral problems when in school. He has had difficulty relating with other youths. Two weeks ago, Jerry J. was taken into custody and charged with arson, a felony. He and two Scorpion gang members were observed by three eyewitnesses setting fire to the occupied home of a rival gang member. Fortunately, no one was injured in the resulting fire. The juvenile court judge has just adjudicated Jerry J. delinquent on the arson charge and has committed him to the Arizona State Industrial School for 2 years.

Using the Arizona Department of Juvenile Corrections (ADJC) Risk Assessment form illustrated in Figure 10.1, determine Jerry J.'s total risk score. What is Jerry J.'s risk category? What is Jerry J.'s most serious commitment offense? What is Jerry J.'s most serious prior adjudicated offense?

Scenario 2: Florida and Mary M. Mary M. is 15 years old. She lives in Tampa, Florida, and is a sophomore in high school. Recently a juvenile court judge adjudicated Mary M. delinquent for stealing a neighbor's car and joyriding. She drove the car into another state, where she wrecked it. She was accompanied by two other girls, who were subsequently identified as members of a female gang from Tampa. Mary M. has admitted that she, too, is a member of that same gang. The auto theft charge is a third-degree felony. The judge has disposed her to 2 years' probation, together with mandatory psychological and substance-abuse counseling, since she had been using marijuana at the time of her arrest. She is currently receiving both psychological counseling and treatment for her substance abuse. The marijuana possession was a second-degree misdemeanor, although this charge was subsequently dropped pursuant to a plea bargain with the juvenile court prosecutor. A predispositional report prepared by a juvenile probation officer for the juvenile court disclosed the following background factors for Mary M. She began her career of delinquency

ADJC RISK ASSESSMENT

YOUTH NAME _____ K# _____   DATE OF ASSESSMENT _____

COMMITTING COUNTY _____   DATE OF ADMISSION _____ DOB _____

R1   **Number of Referrals**   (__)   SCORE
      1 to 4 0
      5 or More ....+1   _____

R2   **Number of Adjudications**   (__)
      1 or 2 ....-1
      3 or 4 0
      5 or More ....+1   _____

R3   **Age at First Juvenile Referral** (__)
      12 yrs 5 mos. or Younger...................................+1
      12 yrs 6 mos. or Older...................................... 0   _____

R4   **Petition Offense History (check applicable below and add for score)**
      A.(__) 2 or More Assaultive Offenses...................+1
      B.(__) 2 or More Drug Offenses...........................+2
      C.(__) 3 or More Property Offenses......................+1
      D.(__) Weapons Offense or use in above.............+1   _____

                    R 4 Sub Total   _____

R5   **Petitions for Felony Offenses**   (__)
      0 to 2... 0
      3 or More...+1   _____

R6   **Affiliation with a Delinquent Gang**
      No..0
      Yes..+1   _____

R7   **Enrolled in School with no Serious Truancy or Behavioral Problems**
      No.. 0
      Yes...-1   _____

R8   **Known Use of Alcohol or Drugs**
      No..-1
      Yes.. 0   _____

                    TOTAL RISK SCORE   _____

RISK CATEGORY (CHECK ONE)		
[ ] LOW(1 or Less)	[ ] MEDIUM (2-4)	[ ] HIGH (5+)

_____
Signature of Staff Completing Assessment Instrument

CURRENT COMMITMENT TYPE (CHECK ONE):   [ ] NEW COMMIT   [ ]ADJC REVOCATION

MOST SERIOUS COMMITMENT OFFENSE:

OFFENSE DESCRIPTION   ARS CODE   F/M CLASS   SUBCLASS   DATE
_____   _____   _____   _____   ____

MOST SERIOUS PRIOR ADJUDICATED OFFENSE:

OFFENSE DESCRIPTION   ARS CODE   F/M CLASS   SUBCLASS   DATE
_____   _____   _____   _____   ____

CLASS: 1,2,3,4,5,6 OR 9 = NOT APPLICABLE
F=FELONY   M=MISDEMEANOR   V=VIOLATION PROB. OR PAROLE   O=OTHER

FIGURE 10.1   The Arizona Department of Juvenile Corrections Risk Assessment Instrument

when she was 12 years of age. At that time, she shoplifted some cosmetics from a local department store. When she was confronted by a store security officer, Mary M. assaulted the officer by pushing her into a display counter. The glass broke and the officer sustained severe lacerations. Mary M. was charged with theft and aggravated assault. The theft was related to a gang initiation. The juvenile court judge adjudicated her delinquent on both charges and ordered her committed to the Florida Industrial School, a secure facility, for a term of 6 months. Mary M. and another inmate escaped from this facility one evening, although they were apprehended 3 days later and returned to custody. Over the next few months, Mary M. tried to escape from the facility on at least four different occasions. The juvenile court judge adjudicated her delinquent on an escape charge, and the term of her confinement in the Florida Industrial School was extended to one year. Mary M. was subsequently released from secure confinement at age 13, and she returned to school. Over the next 2 years, Mary M. was involved in several minor incidents involving low-level misdemeanors. In one instance, she was placed on diversion by the prosecutor, with judicial approval. A part of her diversion was performing 200 hours of community service as well as observance of a curfew. Her juvenile probation officer caught her violating curfew on at least three occasions, and filed an affidavit with the juvenile court. The juvenile court judge verbally reprimanded Mary M. on this occasion, but he did not impose other sanctions.

An interview with Mary M.'s parents revealed that Mary M. is incorrigible. The parents say that they have no control over Mary M.'s actions. However, Mary M.'s siblings, a younger brother and a sister, report that their parents, who have physical altercations frequently in front of them and use drugs themselves, are seldom home to monitor them and their sister, Mary M. A counselor has concluded independently that the family has a history of domestic violence, and that the home is quite unstable. Mary M.'s mother has been committed to a psychiatric institution in previous years for depression as well as schizophrenia. The mother is currently on medication for the purpose of managing her depression. Mary M.'s father has a previous conviction for receiving stolen property, a second-degree misdemeanor. He has also been previously convicted of sexual battery and served 6 months in the county jail for this crime. In fact, at the present time, the Florida Department of Human Services is conducting an investigation of Mary M.'s family on charges of alleged child neglect.

Mary M. herself has no obvious developmental disabilities or prior mental illnesses and appears to be in good physical health. However, because of the history of her family, it has been recommended that she should have a psychological assessment to determine her present mental state. Mary M. is currently unemployed and has no marketable skills. Thus, she would be unable to obtain and/or sustain employment if she were expected to work. It has been recommended that she take several vocational/technical courses to improve her skill level. Her peer relations are poor, and she is socially immature and withdrawn. She is easily led by others, as evidenced by the ease with which she was recruited into her gang. Most of Mary M.'s close peers are other gang members. Although she is currently enrolled in school, she has poor attendance. During periods when she has attended school, she has been compliant and not disruptive. According to her teachers, Mary M. reads well and has no obvious learning disabilities. But it has been determined that Mary M. has used marijuana frequently with her gang friends. Mary's home situation has been cited by the juvenile probation officer as a substantial mitigating circumstance, and she recommends a 5-point reduction in Mary M.'s risk score. The probation supervisor, who oversees risk assessment instrument preparation and administration, concurs with this recommendation and has chosen not to override it.

Figure 10.2 shows the Florida Department of Juvenile Justice Supervision Risk Classification Instrument. Notice that it consists of two parts. The first part is a risk assessment scale. The second part is a needs assessment scale.

FLORIDA DEPARTMENT OF JUVENILE JUSTICE
SUPERVISION RISK CLASSIFICATION INSTRUMENT

Youth's Name: Sharon H Test   Court Docket #: _____
Juvenile Probation Officer: _____   Unit: _____
Date Completed: _____   DJJID: 532950   Referral ID: 1507938

RISK ASSESSMENT	

A.   INSTANT OFFENSE (most serious) ....
- Capital or life felony — 32 points
- 1st degree felony (violent) — 20 points
- 1st degree felony/2nd degree felony (violent) — 18 points
- 2nd degree felony/3rd degree felony (violent) — 15 points
- 3rd degree felony — 7 points
- 1st degree misdemeanor (violent) — 5 points
- 1st degree misdemeanor — 3 points
- 2nd degree misdemeanor — 1 point

B.   PRIOR HISTORY (highest applicable score)
- Meets the criteria for Level 10 placement — 7 points
- Has met the definition of a SHO/IRT with this offense — 6 points
- Two or more prior non-related felonies resulting in adjudication or withheld adjudication — 3 points
- One felony or two or more non-related misdemeanors resulting in adjudication or withheld adjudication — 2 points
- One prior misdemeanor resulting in adj. or withheld adj. — 1 point

C.   OTHER SCORING FACTORS (combined score) ....
- Current legal status CC/F (2 pts) - committed (4 pts)
- Previous completed CC/F (2 pts) committed (4pts)
- Previous technical violation (1 point. per affidavit)
- Youth 12 years old/under at time of 1st charge (1pt)
- Substance use/abuse involved (1 pt.)
- History of escape or absconding (1pt.)
- Current or previous JASP/community arb. (2 pts each)
- Other previous or current diversion (1 pt. each)
- Domestic violence involved (youth as perpetrator) (2 pts each)
- Gang related offense (2 pt.)

D.   A+B+C = SUBTOTAL   0
Mitigating (maximum 5 pts.).................................(-)   ____
Justification ____

Aggravating-consider pending offenses (max 5) ......(+)   ____
Justification ____

TOTAL: A+B+C – mitigation + aggravating =   0

TOTAL RISK SCORE ____ 0   **TOTAL NEEDS SCORE** ____ 0

CLASSIFICATION DECISION (see matrix on page 3):
☐ Diversion ☐ Minimum ☐ General ☐ Intensive
☐ Level 2   ☐ Level 4   ☐ Level 6   ☐ Level 8/10

OVERRIDE CLASSIFICATION DECISION (if applicable):
☐ Diversion ☐ Minimum ☐ General ☐ Intensive
☐ Level 2   ☐ Level 4   ☐ Level 6   ☐ Level 8/10
OVERRIDE JUSTIFICATION: ____

JPO Initials _____   Date: _____
Supervisor Initials _____   Date: _____

NEEDS ASSESSMENT		

FAMILY RELATIONSHIPS (score total points)   0
A.   ....
- Parents unable/unwilling to control youth — 3 pts. ____
- Parent cooperative, some control — 1 pt. ____
- Youth in unstable independent living situation — 2 pts. ____
- Family history of domestic violence — 2 pts. ____
- Family history of abuse/neglect — 2 pts. ____
- Parent or sibling with criminal history — 1 pt. ____
- Parent with mental illness — 2 pts. ____
- Parent with substance abuse — 2 pts. ____
- Out of home dependency placement — 2 pts. ____
- Current abuse/neglect investigation — 3 pts. ____
- Youth is a parent — 3 pts. ____

B.   PEER RELATIONSHIPS (score total pts)   0
- Socially immature — 1 pt. ____
- Socially withdrawn — 1 pt. ____
- Easily led by others — 1 pt. ____
- Exploits or aggressive to others — 2 pts. ____
- Peers have delinquent history or gang involvement — 3 pts. ____

C.   SIGNIFICANT ADULT RELATIONS (score highest)   0
- Authority figure relationships are inconsistent — 1 pt. ____
- Youth unavailable/unwilling to positively relate to adult authority figures — 2 pts. ____

D.   EDUCATIONAL (score total pts.)   0
- Poor attendance/not enrolled (under 16) — 3 pts. ____
- Disruptive school behavior — 2 pts. ____
- Literacy problems — 2 pts. ____
- Learning disability — 2 pts. ____
- Withdrawn/expelled/suspended — 3 pts. ____
- Enrolled and failing — 2 pts. ____

E.   YOUTH'S EMPLOYMENT (score total pts)   0
(youth over 16, not in school or youth with monetary needs)
- Currently developing marketable skills/no school — 1 pt. ____
- Needs to develop marketable skills — 2 pts. ____
- Currently unemployed — 2 pts. ____

F.   DEVELOPMENTAL DISABILITY (score highest)   0
- Known dev. disability/no current services — 3 pts. ____
- Known dev. disability/with current services — 2 pts. ____
- Disability suspected/no diagnosis — 2 pts. ____

G.   PHYSICAL HEALTH & HYGIENE (score total pts.)   0
- Medical or dental referral needed — 1 pt. ____
- Health or hygiene education needed — 1 pt. ____
- Handicap or illness limits functioning — 3 pts. ____

H.   MENTAL HEALTH (score total pts.)   0
- Assessment needed — 2 pts. ____
- Prior history of mental health problems — 2 pts. ____
- Currently in treatment — 2 pts. ____
- Assessment indicates treatment needs/no current services — 3 pts. ____

I.   SUBSTANCE ABUSE (score total pts.)   0
- Assessment needed — 2 pts. ____
- Occasional user — 1 pt. ____
- Frequent user — 3 pts. ____
- Assessment indicates treatment needs/no services — 3 pts. ____
- Receiving treatment services — 2 pts. ____

TOTAL NEEDS SCORE   0

April, 1998   Case Management: Intake   DJJ/IS Form 4
                            Page 1 of 3

FIGURE 10.2   Florida Department of Juvenile Justice Supervision Risk Classification Instrument

Figure 10.2 illustrates the Florida Department of Juvenile Justice Classification Matrix. This matrix is used to determine the level of a youth's placement in the Florida Department of Juvenile Justice based on a combination of one's needs assessment score and risk assessment score. Using the information in the scenario above, determine Mary M.'s risk assessment and needs assessment scores. Next, place Mary M. in the Classification Matrix according to the scores you have calculated.

Calculating the ADJC Risk Score for Jerry J.   Before determining Jerry J.'s score on the Arizona Risk Assessment instrument, familiarize yourself with the

FLORIDA DEPARTMENT OF JUVENILE JUSTICE
CLASSIFICATION MATRIX

NEEDS	RISK			
	LOW 0 10	MODERATE 11 17	HIGH 18 24	VERY HIGH 25 32
LOW 0 : : : : 15	Diversion	Minimum Supervision General Supervision	Minimum Supervision General Intensive Supervision	Level 4 Level 6 Level 8/10
MODERATE 16 : : : 30	Diversion	Minimum Supervision General Supervision	Intensive Level 2	Level 4 Level 6 Level 8/10
HIGH 31 : : : : 45	Diversion Minimum Supervision	General Supervision	Intensive Level 2 Level 4	Level 6 Level 8/10
VERY HIGH 46+ : : : :	Diversion Minimum Supervision	General Supervision Intensive Supervision	Level 2 Level 4 Level 6	Level 8/10

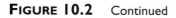

FIGURE 10.2   Continued

instrument's contents. There are eight categories: (1) number of referrals; (2) number of adjudications; (3) age at first juvenile referral; (4) petition offense history; (5) petitions for felony offenses; (6) affiliation with a delinquent gang; (7) enrolled in school with no serious truancy or behavioral problems; and (8) known use of alcohol or drugs.

First, let's count the number of times Jerry J. has been referred to juvenile court on various charges. We can count *both* referrals *and* delinquency petitions filed against Jerry J., because both actions are intended to bring juveniles before the juvenile court. Delinquency petitions are only filed in about half of all juvenile cases that reach the juvenile courts annually throughout the United States. The other types of cases are nonpetitioned cases. In Jerry J.'s case, he was referred by the school principal on two occasions, with a delinquency petition filed on the second occasion. Jerry J. was referred again to juvenile court by police officers for selling crack cocaine. Later, Jerry J. was referred to the juvenile court for burglary, theft, and carrying a concealed weapon. Jerry J.'s probation officer also referred him to the juvenile court because of a probation violation. Subsequently, Jerry J. was referred to juvenile court three more times, all resulting in delinquency adjudications. Two of these offenses were felonies: aggravated assault and selling cocaine. Finally, Jerry J. was most recently referred to the juvenile court for arson and adjudicated delinquent on that charge. Therefore, there are at least nine referrals of Jerry J. to juvenile court. Since this is "5 or more," we will give Jerry J. a +1 for "R1," as shown in Figure 10.1.

Next, we determine the number of Jerry J.'s adjudications. He was adjudicated delinquent on the school assault charge; the drug charge; the firearms, burglary, and theft charges; three additional adjudications for offenses, including aggravated assault and selling cocaine; and for arson. This adds up to seven delinquency adjudications. For "R2," this is "5 or more," and therefore, we score R2 with a +1.

Jerry J.'s age at his first juvenile court referral was 11. For "R3," this is 12 years, 5 months or younger," and therefore we score Jerry J. a +1.

Jerry J.'s petition offense history includes "2 or more assaultive offenses." We score this portion of the risk instrument with a +1. Jerry J. also has "2 or more drug offenses," and therefore, we assign him a +2. Although Jerry J. has participated in several thefts, as mentioned in the scenario, we should count only what police and other authorities actually know about Jerry J. and which types of offenses resulted in petitions filed with the juvenile court. He has a burglary and a theft charge for which petitions have been filed. Since this is not "3 or more property offenses," we do not assign Jerry J. a score. However, we can give Jerry J. a +1 for "weapons offense or use in above." Thus, for the R4 Petition Offense History score, Jerry J. should receive a "4."

R5 is "Petitions for Felony Offenses," and Jerry J. has at least three or more of these. Therefore, we assign him a +1 for R5.

R6 is easy to score. Is Jerry J. a gang member? Yes. Therefore, he receives a +1 for R6.

R7 is also easy to score. Jerry J. has been enrolled in school in the past, but he has serious truancy problems. We must assign him a "0" for R7.

Finally, for R8, Jerry J. is known for his use of alcohol and drugs. We must assign him a "0" for R8.

Summing R1 through R8, we have 1 + 1 + 1 + 4 + 1 + 1+ 0 + 0 = 9. Jerry J.'s total risk assessment score is 9. According to the ADJC Risk Assessment instrument, the Risk Category where we would place Jerry J. is "High" (5+ points).

Notice that there are other items to fill in on this form. One space is for "Most Serious Commitment Offense." We are not in a position to know how Arizona rates the seriousness of aggravated assault in relation to arson. But these are the two offenses resulting in Jerry J.'s commitment to the Arizona State Industrial School. If "arson" were the more serious offense, then we would list this in the first space for "Most Serious Commitment Offense," with an appropriate code and date. It would be a felony. For the "Most Serious Prior Adjudicated Offense," we would have to list "aggravated assault" as the offense, which is also a felony. We would also enter a code for this offense, as well as the date of the adjudication.

Without the accompanying Arizona Department of Juvenile Corrections instruction manual for this instrument, we don't know how Jerry J.'s score of "9" will be used. In all likelihood, it will relate to his placement in the secure facility and the intensity of supervision he will receive while confined. He is definitely a risk to others and must be monitored carefully. However, this score is only one of many criteria that are used in placement and level-of-custody decision making.

It should be noted that if Jerry J. is alternatively considered for admission into a community-based program by the juvenile court judge instead of placement in a secure facility, another form is used by the Arizona Department of Juvenile Corrections. This form is very similar to the form shown in Figure 10.1 and is illustrated in Figure 10.3.

In Figure 10.3, this is a reassessment form, and it serves to give us an impression of how much Jerry J. has improved his behavior since being admitted into the community-based program. In this form, attention is focused on one's peer relationships within a 30–90 day period; whether there have been problems with school or work adjustment within a similar time interval; and whether the client has had problems adjusting to supervision or compliance with program requirements within the most recent 30–90 day period.

In Jerry J.'s case, if he were placed in a community program instead of being incarcerated, he would be evaluated within a 30–90 day period following his community program placement. If he had improved his behavior, there is a good possibility that his risk level (or risk category) could be reduced. This possible risk category reduction may have implications for how closely or loosely Jerry J. is supervised in his community-based program. It is also indicative of whether he is becoming rehabilitated and reintegrated.

Calculating the Florida Risk Assessment Score for Mary M. The Florida Department of Juvenile Justice Risk Classification Instrument, Figure 10.2, is divided into two parts. One part is "Risk Assessment," while the other is "Needs Assessment." Again, when determining the score for any juvenile, we must first familiarize ourselves with the instrument's contents before computing a risk score. There are three categories (A, B, and C), which refer to (1) the instant offense, (2) prior history, and (3) "other scoring factors."

For category A, "Instant Offense," Mary M. has recently been adjudicated delinquent on an auto theft charge, which is a third-degree felony. According to this risk assessment scale, a third-degree felony rates a score of 7 points.

For category B, we are to assign Mary M. the "highest applicable score." This means that we are not supposed to add or sum the scores for all categories that fit Mary M. Given her delinquency history since age 12, including her escape from a secure facility, an assault on a store security officer, and gang membership, she probably meets the criteria for "Level 10 placement." According to Florida officials, the risk score derived from this instrument at the time of a youth's arrest is used to make an appropriate recommendation to the state attorney's office (Friedenauer, 2002:1). Let's assume that Mary M. qualifies for Level 10 placement, and therefore we will assign her a "7."

Category C is additive in that we are to consider a number of factors, each associated with specific points. These factors include current legal status (presently committed to a secure facility), previous completed commitment (to

ADJC RISK REASSESSMENT
FOR YOUTH IN COMMUNITY PROGRAMS

YOUTH NAME _____ K# _____ DOB _____ DATE OF REASSESSMENT _____

For items 1 - 4 use initial Risk Assessment information

RE 1. **Age At First Referral**   (___)   **SCORE**
  12 Years or Less ....+1
  13 Years or Older 0   _____

RE 2. **Number of Prior Referrals**   (___)
  4 or Less 0
  5 or More ....+1   _____

RE 3. **Prior Petition Offense History**
  A (___) 3 or More Property ....+1
  B (___) 2 or More Assaultive Offenses ....+1
  C (___) 2 or More Drug Offenses ....+2
  D (___) Weapons Offense...+1   _____

                        RE 3 SUBTOTAL   _____

RE 4. **Prior Petitions For Felony Offenses**   (___)
  2 or Less 0
  3 or More ....+1   _____

Score All Following Items for Last 30/90 Days.

RE 5. **Referrals To Court or For Revocation Hearing (Last 30/90 days)**
      None ....-1
      One ....+1
      Two or More...+2

RE 6. **Use of Alcohol or Other Drugs (Last 30/90 Days)**
  No... 0
  Yes..+1   _____
  Check type (if any)   _____ Alcohol   _____ Marijuana   _____ Other Drug

RE 7. **Peer Relationships (Last 30/90 Days)**
  No Problems 0
  Associates with Delinquent Peers ....+1   _____
  Associates with Gang Members ....+2

RE 8. **School or Work Adjustment (Last 30/90 Days)** _____ **Where**
  No Problems or Minor Problems.......................................0
  Some Attendance /Behavior Problems ....+1   _____
  Serious Work or School Attendance/Behavior Problems...................+2

RE 9. **Adjustment to Supervision/Compliance with Plan (Last 30/90 Days)**
  No Problems ....-1
  Minor Problems..0
  Serious Compliance Problems with Plan ....+1   _____

                              TOTAL SCORE   _____

RISK CATEGORY (CIRCLE ONE)

| LOW (5 or Less) = LEVEL III | MEDIUM (6 - 10) = LEVEL II | HIGH (11 or HIGHER) = LEVEL I |

Assigned Supervision Level_____   Override Y/N   Reason _____
                                                                     _____
                                                                     _____

Parole Officer's Signature _____ Date _____
Supervisor's Signature _____ Date _____

FIGURE 10.3 ADJC Risk Reassessment for Youth in Community Programs

a secure facility), previous technical violation (in connection with a probation or parole program or diversion), age at time of first charge, substance use/abuse involvement, history of escape or absconding, current or previous community arbitration (alternative dispute resolution), other previous or current diversion, and a gang-related offense. For each category that applies to Mary M., we should assign a score. Subsequently we will sum the individual scores to determine the combined score for "C."

Currently Mary M. is on probation. However, she has had a previous commitment to the Florida Industrial School. We assign her 4 points for this category. She has a technical violation, violating curfew while on probation, and an affidavit has been filed in connection with this violation. Therefore, Mary M. receives 1 point for this category.

Mary M. began her career of delinquency at age 12. Therefore, she receives 1 point for this category. She is a substance abuser, and therefore she receives 1 point for this category. She has a history of escape from the secure facility where she was placed, and this entitles her to 1 point. She has never participated in alternative dispute resolution, and therefore she receives no points for this category. However, she has been placed on diversion once in the past, and she receives 1 point for this category. Although there is domestic violence in Mary M.'s home, Mary M. has never been the perpetrator. Therefore, she receives no points for this category. Finally, she has had at least one gang-related offense, shoplifting. We assign her 2 points for this category. There are ten categories as subparts of "C," and we sum the various subparts as follows: 0 + 4 + 1 + 1 + 1 + 1 + 0 + 1 + 0 + 2 = 11 points. Mary M.'s score for "C" is 11.

Summing her scores for categories A, B, and C, we have 7 + 7 + 11 = 25 points. Notice that for "D," adjustments may be made for the presence of aggravating or mitigating circumstances. Anyone completing this risk assessment might choose to focus on Mary M.'s violent acts, such as pushing the store security officer. They might also focus on Mary M.'s escape from the Florida Industrial School and subsequent attempts to escape. These factors might be considered as aggravating. However, substantial evidence exists that might constitute mitigating circumstances. Mary M.'s home life is a disaster. She has a dysfunctional family where frequent physical altercations and drug use are evident. Background information about Mary M. from school officials suggest that but for her gang affiliation, Mary M. is a compliant and reasonably intelligent student. In the present scenario, the juvenile probation officer has recommended a 5-point reduction for Mary M., given her home circumstances. The probation supervisor has concurred with this recommendation. Therefore, there will probably be a 5-point reduction in Mary M.'s final score. This would be 25 − 5 = 20 points. Thus, Mary M.'s final risk assessment score would be 20.

One final word about the Florida risk reassessment device is in order. At the very bottom of the risk assessment instrument shown in Figure 10.2, a classification decision is illustrated. But immediately below this classification decision is an override classification decision. **Overrides** are decisions by someone in authority and with pertinent expertise to change whatever classification is yielded from the original risk score that has been computed. For instance, Mary M.'s score of 20 can be overridden for one or more reasons. The nature of the override is either to increase or decrease the resulting score or classification decision.

No risk assessment instrument captures every single facet of one's existence or circumstances. If there are circumstances or facts that are relevant to cases such as Mary M.'s, then the original classification decision may be overridden. For instance, Mary M. may have been coerced into committing burglaries and thefts by her other gang members. Duress might be a mitigating circumstance that is otherwise undetected through conventional measurement methods. Or Mary M. may be emotionally immature for her age. Factors such as these may be detected through interviews with juvenile clients. Perhaps information is yielded through other means, such as reports from school or church officials. In any case, any particular score assigned to a juvenile client may be overridden. It may be raised or lowered, provided that a reasonable justification is articulated to account for the change.

Needs Assessments

Besides measuring a juvenile's potential risk or dangerousness, it is important for juvenile justice practitioners to know what types of problems afflict particular youths. Many youths enter the juvenile justice system who are drug- or alcohol-dependent, or who have psychological problems, suffer from maladjustments in their homes or schools, or who are impaired physically in some respect. Therefore, practitioners must assess juveniles who are processed to determine their respective needs. Sometimes scales are combined to obtain information about *both* risk and needs. These risk/needs assessment instruments enable those conducting such assessments to obtain both types of information from youths in one test administration. Not all juveniles need the same community services. There are diverse community resources available to meet a wide variety of needs exhibited by the youth who enter the juvenile justice system. Some juveniles require minimal intervention, while other youths need extensive treatments and services. Whether youths are confined in secure facilities or allowed to attend their schools and remain with their families in their communities, different provisions often must be made to individualize their needs. Needs assessment instruments are used to determine which specific services and treatments ought to be provided each youth.

For example, in the example of the Florida Risk Classification Instrument described above and our hypothetical case of Mary M., Figure 10.2 contained a "needs assessment" component as well as a "risk assessment" component. We calculated the risk assessment component. In the next section, we compute Mary M.'s needs assessment score based on the scenario information provided above.

Computing Mary M.'s Florida Needs Assessment Score.   Again, we should familiarize ourselves with the needs assessment instrument, the second part of the Risk Classification Instrument as shown in Figure 10.2. There are nine areas covered, including family relationships, peer relationships, significant adult relations, educational factors, youth's employment, developmental disability (if any), physical health and hygiene, mental health, and substance abuse. Some of these areas contain additive components, meaning that we must assign points to juveniles such as Mary M. if certain subparts of these areas pertain to his or her circumstances.

For Part A, Family Relationships, we know from the above scenario about Mary M. that her parents cannot control her. We also know that she lives in an unstable family environment with a family history of domestic violence, abuse, and/or neglect, and that one parent has a criminal history. We also know that the parents use drugs. Furthermore, there is an ongoing investigation of this allegedly abusive environment being conducted by the Florida Department of Human Services. Mary M. herself is not a parent. There are 11 subparts for Part A. We would score these subparts sequentially as follows: 3 + 0 + 2 + 2 + 2 + 1 + 2 + 2 + 0 + 3 + 0 = 17 points. The Part A calculation is determined as follows:

Parents unable/unwilling to control youth? Yes.	3 points
Parent cooperative, some control? No.	0 points
Youth in unstable independent living situation? Yes.	2 points
Family history of domestic violence? Yes.	2 points
Family history of abuse/neglect? Yes.	2 points

Parent or sibling with criminal history? Yes.	1 point
Parent with mental illness? Yes.	2 points
Parent with substance abuse? Yes.	2 points
Out of home dependency placement? No.	0 points
Current abuse/neglect investigation? Yes.	3 points
Youth is a parent? No.	0 points

Part B has five subparts: socially immature, socially withdrawn, easily led by others, exploits or aggressive to others, and peers have delinquent history or gang involvement. We would score these subparts as follows: 1 + 1 + 1 + 0 + 3 = 6 points. The Part B calculation is determined as follows:

Socially immature? Yes.	1 point
Socially withdrawn? Yes.	1 point
Easily led by others? Yes.	1 point
Exploits or aggressive to others? No.	0 points
Peers have delinquent history or gang involvement? Yes.	3 points

Part C deals with significant adult relations. We can assign Mary M. 1 point for "authority figure relationships are inconsistent," although we have no data to suggest that Mary M. is unavailable/unwilling to positively relate to adult authority figures. Thus, for Part C, Mary M.'s score would be 1 point.

For Part D (educational), there are six components: poor attendance/not enrolled, disruptive school behavior, literacy problems, learning disability, withdrawn/expelled/suspended, enrolled and failing. Mary M. has poor attendance at school, although she is not disruptive and has no literacy or learning disability problems. She has not withdrawn from school, nor has she been expelled or suspended. She is not failing her classes, despite her truancy. We would give her 3 points for poor attendance, but "0" points for the other subparts. Her score for Part D, therefore, would be 3 points.

For Part E (youth's employment), since Mary M. is not "over 16," these subparts are not relevant for her. She receives a "0" for Part E.

For Part F (developmental disability), Mary M. has no known developmental disabilities. Therefore, she will receive a "0" for this part.

For Part G (physical health and hygiene), Mary M. is in good physical health. She needs no health or hygiene education, and no obvious handicaps or illnesses limit her functioning. Therefore, she receives a "0" for Part G.

For Part H (mental health), there are three subparts: assessment needed; prior history of mental health problems, currently in treatment; and assessment indicates treatment needs/no current services. Mary M. will receive 3 points because of the recommended mental health assessment. Furthermore, she is currently receiving psychological counseling for her substance abuse problems. She receives 2 points for this subpart. Otherwise, no other points apply to Mary M. Part H, therefore, is scored as 3 + 2 = 5 points.

Finally for Part I (substance abuse), an assessment of her substance abuse problem is needed, and she is a frequent user of marijuana. Although a substance abuse assessment is recommended and will likely be conducted, Mary M. is currently receiving mandatory substance-abuse counseling/treatment.

We would score Part I as follows: $2 + 0 + 3 + 0 + 2 = 7$ points. This score accrues as follows:

Assessment needed? Yes.	2 points
Occasional user? No.	0 points
Frequent user? Yes.	3 points
Assessment indicates treatment needs/no services? No (not yet, anyway).	0 points
Receiving treatment services? Yes.	2 points

If we sum the various parts, we would have the following cumulative score:

Part	Points
A	17
B	6
C	1
D	3
E	0
F	0
G	0
H	5
I	7

Total = 39 points

Mary M.'s total needs score is 39 points.

Together with this needs assessment score of 39, we can use Mary M.'s risk score of 20 and determine where Mary M. should be placed in the Florida Department of Juvenile Justice Classification Matrix illustrated in Figure 10.2. This matrix cross-tabulates one's risk and needs scores, with one's risk score across the top and one's needs score down the left-hand side. Where these scores intersect in the body of the table defines the suggested nature of supervision Mary M. should receive by Florida juvenile corrections officials. Where a needs score of 39 (High) intersects with a risk score of 20 (High), a square is indicated with "Intensive," "Level 2," and "Level 4." Since we have no interpretive booklet from the Florida Department of Juvenile Justice, we don't know what these different levels mean, although we can glean that the levels range from 2 to 10, with "2" being the lowest level and "10" being the highest level. "Intensive" would suggest to us that Mary M. should receive intensive supervision, regardless of the program, community or institutional, where she is ultimately placed. We know from Mary M.'s scenario that the juvenile court judge disposed Mary M. to 2 years' probation, with mandatory psychological and substance-abuse counseling. No doubt there were other conditions, such as community service and/or restitution. This is because she stole a neighbor's car and wrecked it. Some compensation to the neighbor for the loss of the car will be provided. Mary M. will be expected to make some restitution for the car loss.

It should be emphasized that juvenile justice officials do not depend entirely on risk/needs instruments for their information about youth needs. Interviews with youths and their families are often conducted (Virginia Department of Criminal Justice Services, 2000). Intake officers acquire extensive information about a youth's background. If certain youths are recidivists and have extensive juvenile records, some indication of their needs will already be on file. Thus, we will know what interventions have been applied in the past and whether these interventions have helped in any way. If not, then we might try alternative interventions and programs. Furthermore, the needs of male juvenile offenders often differ from the needs of female juvenile offenders. These gender differences are important and should be taken into consideration whenever assessment instruments are devised. Another source of information about youths and their needs comes from juvenile probation officers. These court officials compile information about a youth's background and furnish this material to juvenile court judges (Glaser, Calhoun, and Petrocelli, 2002). Subsequently, dispositions are individualized according to the probation officer's report. This is known as a predisposition report.

PREDISPOSITION REPORTS

Assisting juvenile court judges in their decision making relating to sentencing juvenile offenders during adjudicatory proceedings are predisposition reports that are often filed by juvenile probation officers, especially in serious cases. Predisposition reports contain background information about juveniles, the facts relating to their delinquent acts, and possibly probation officer recommendations for particular dispositions. They serve the function of assisting judges to make more informed sentencing decisions. They also serve as needs assessment devices, where probation officers and other juvenile authorities can determine high-need areas for certain youths and channel them to specific community-based organizations and agencies for particular treatments and services.

The Predisposition Report and Its Preparation

Juvenile court judges in many jurisdictions order the preparation of **predisposition reports,** which are the functional equivalent of presentence investigation reports for adults. Predisposition reports are intended to furnish judges with background information about juveniles to make a more informed sentencing decision (Myers, 2001). They also function to assist probation officers and others to target high-need areas for youths and specific services or agencies for individualized referrals. Trester (1981:89–90) has summarized four important reasons for why predisposition reports should be prepared:

1. These reports provide juvenile court judges with a more complete picture of juvenile offenders and their offenses, including the existence of any aggravating or mitigating circumstances.
2. These reports can assist the court in tailoring the disposition of the case to an offender's needs.
3. These reports may lead to the identification of positive factors that would indicate the likelihood of rehabilitation.
4. These reports provide judges with the offender's treatment history, which might indicate the effectiveness or ineffectiveness of previous dispositions, and suggest the need for alternative dispositions.

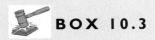

BOX 10.3

Sheley J. Beck

Administrator, Kootenai County Juvenile Probation, Coeur d'Alene, ID

Statistics:

B.A. (sociology), University of Central Oklahoma; M.A. (criminal justice management and administration), University of Central Oklahoma; Instructor, Idaho Juvenile Probation Peace Officer Standards and Training Academy

Background

When I started college, I didn't have any idea what I wanted to pursue for a career. I enjoyed the sociology classes and I found them thought-provoking, and so I ended up going in that direction with my studies. When I finished my B.A., I immediately started work on my M.A., mostly because I found the coursework interesting and I wasn't necessarily ready to go into the working field. As I was nearing graduation, I saw a job announcement for a juvenile probation officer. I thought it sounded intriguing and so I applied. Surprisingly, I got the position. Keep in mind that I haven't even done an internship anywhere, and so I had absolutely no idea what I was getting myself into. That was nearly 15 years ago when they handed me my first caseload, and I was as green as they come! I've been fortunate though to have worked for really good people, and to have great co-workers to learn from. I've also been fortunate to have the benefit of ongoing training in the field.

Work Experiences

I've worked as a juvenile probation officer and then as a supervisor for both Standard Supervision and Intensive Supervision. I also spent a year as the Pre-Sentence Investigator for our department. Just a few months ago, our administrator retired, and I was promoted to that position. I don't have a caseload now, and I find that I miss the contact with the juveniles, although I'm enjoying this new challenge. I am now learning more about budgets, policy and procedure, and grants, which is all new to me. I am still co-facilitating a girls group, and that keeps me in touch with some of the juveniles.

Looking back, I realize that I always had an interest in working with adolescents, and so I was probably somewhat drawn to this field. The juveniles have so much energy, and you've just got to laugh sometimes at what they say and do! You must possess a sense of humor to work in this field. Youth work can be challenging and very rewarding, but at the same time, it can be disappointing and frustrating. Sometimes the same youth comes through our door many times, and you've got to be creative to find new ways to work that case. The good news is that most of our youth *don't* come through the door more than once, and so we are making an important impact. The probation officer must always be aware of services available in the community that may benefit the youth. Probation officers must also be diligent about their duties relating to community protection, and they must never forget that there is a victim involved as well.

A majority of the youth suffer from substance abuse issues. We also see a large number that have mental health issues, or that have been victimized themselves. In addition, it's concerning how many of the youth come from homes where the parental figures suffer from these same types of issues. Sometimes the parents themselves are on probation or parole, or sometimes we find ourselves having to make referrals to Child Protection. Through all of this, it's critical that probation officers maintain good working relationships with the family and with the other agencies that they will be involved with. It's vitally important that we treat the juveniles and their families with respect and dignity, and that we model appropriate behavior.

It's easy to focus on all of the problems or challenges with the family or situation. It's important, however, to focus on the strengths and to build from there. It also feels better as a probation officer to approach the casework from this angle. I have been taught to catch your probationer doing something right, and then let them know it! I've also been taught to be fair but firm, and that admonition seems to work well. The rewards in this position can sometimes seem like they are few and far between. I have come to realize that even though we may not see the immediate results of our efforts, I've found many times that we just plant that seed for change, and that change will materialize somewhere down the road.

I want to comment that I've come to realize how important it is to maintain your own mental stamina to work in this field. It is sometimes physically dangerous, but with all of the difficult cases, some people could overlook that it can be mentally depressing and difficult. One other caution I want to mention is to be aware of the amount of pa-

perwork a probation officer does, and that can itself be overwhelming. This can place a further burden on an already busy probation officer.

Advice to Students

I learned somewhere along the way some of the following useful ideas. Remember the serenity of prayer. When I was in school I had this vision that you'd just get all of these great resources to these families, and all would be well. However, nobody ever told me that sometimes, the family doesn't want help, or it just isn't ready for it. Also, remember that you don't have to solve their problems, but perhaps you should explore options with them and then they can be responsible for their own choices. I've always felt that a probation officer falls somewhere between a social worker and a law enforcement officer, which is quite a wide spectrum. You will have to wear different hats, depending on the day and circumstance, and so be flexible. There is never a dull day, and that's probably a lot of the attraction for me. You won't become financially wealthy in this line of work, but you can make a decent living, and the work itself can be rewarding. When a youth comes to you and says, "Thank you," it makes the job worth it.

It is important to recognize that predisposition reports are not required by judges in all jurisdictions. By the same token, legislative mandates obligate officials in other jurisdictions to prepare them for all juveniles to be adjudicated. Also, there are no specific formats universally acceptable in these report preparations. An example of a predispositional report from New Mexico is shown in Box 10.4.

Rogers (1990:44) indicates that predisposition reports contain insightful information about youths that can be helpful to juvenile court judges prior to sentencing. Six social aspects of a person's life are crucial for investigations, analysis, and treatment. These include: (1) personal health, physical and emotional; (2) family and home situation; (3) recreational activities and use of leisure time; (4) peer group relationships (types of companions); (5) education; and (6) work experience. According to the National Advisory Commission on Criminal Justice Standards and Goals (1976), predisposition reports have been recommended in all cases where the offenders are minors. In actual practice, however, predisposition reports are only prepared at the request of juvenile court judges. No systematic pattern typifies such report preparation in most U.S. jurisdictions.

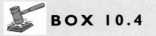 **BOX 10.4**

SAMPLE PREDISPOSITIONAL REPORT FROM NEW MEXICO

CHILDREN, YOUTH AND FAMILIES DEPARTMENT
JUVENILE JUSTICE DIVISION

IDENTIFYING INFORMATION*
*Fictitious names because of New Mexico confidentiality provisions

NAME: Mary Allen
DOB: October 15, 1988
SSN: n/a
ADDRESS: 301 1st St.
Las Cruces, NM
PHONE NUMBER: (444)555-1212
P/G/C: Parents
RELIGIOUS PREF: unknown
PRIMARY LANGUAGE SPOKEN: English

AKA: n/a

COURT INFORMATION

COMPLETED BY: Ann Ames
DATE COMPLETED: October 10, 2002
CASE NUMBER: 123456
CAUSE NUMBER: 7890
JUDGE: Hon. Mark Jones
COUNTY: McNabb
DEFENSE ATTY: Charles Barkin
CCA: unknown

FINAL DISPOSITION: No contest plea
FINAL DISPOSITION DATE: Pending

I. REFERRAL INFORMATION

Current Offense: On 1-02-2002 at 3:40 AM, Mary Allen was taken (by her parents) to the hospital after she was bleeding profusely. Doctors there notified Mary Allen's parents that it was apparent that she had just given birth to a baby. The location of the baby was unknown at the time and doctors suspected that Mary Allen had possibly killed the baby. Police were notified and searched her room where they found a full-term baby (deceased) in a trash can in Mary Allen's bedroom. Mary Allen allegedly told police that she did not know she was pregnant, but gave birth to the baby, by herself, on 12-30-01. An autopsy report indicates that the baby girl, who was found with the umbilical cord still attached and wrapped around her neck, was alive at birth and died of asphyxiation. Mary Allen was arrested on 1-11-02 and booked into McNabb County Jail, Juvenile Unit, at approximately 6:00 PM.

Number of Co-Offenders: 0

Victim Impact Mailed: ☐ Yes   ☐ No   ☐ N/A   Response: ☐ Yes   ☐ No

Victim Requests Restoration:

On 1-13-02, a petition was filed charging Mary Allen with Count 1: Child Abuse (intentionally caused) (death), or in the alternative: Child Abuse (negligently caused) (death), or in the alternative: Child Abuse (negligently permitted) (death) and Count 2: Tampering with Evidence. Mary Allen's parents were able to post the ten percent cash deposit of $10,000 bond and Mary Allen was released home on January 14, 2002. A forensic evaluation was ordered at this time.

On September 22, 2002, Mary Allen entered into a plea agreement with the Children's Court Attorney. Mary Allen pleaded No Contest to Alternative Count 1: Child Abuse (negligently permitted) (death). In exchange for the plea, the remaining counts in the petition were dismissed and the state agreed to handle the case in a juvenile setting. There was no agreement as to the disposition in the matter and a Predispositional Report was ordered.

Victim Impact Summary: A victim impact statement is not applicable in this case. It should be noted, however, that Mary Allen has given two names for the father of her child. Initially, Mary Allen told investigators that she had sexual intercourse with Walter Brooks and that the condom broke. She said she had taken a pregnancy test at Planned Parenthood with negative results. During this officer's conversation with Mary Allen, however, she indicated that the father is John Johnson. She said that Johnson denied that he is the father and that they do not have any contact with each other.

Chronological report attached: ☐ Yes   ☐ No

Currently on Probation/Parole: ☐ Yes   ☐ No   Location:

Prior Supervision:

Cause No.	Begin Date	Type	Length	Expiration	Release Date	Release Type
N/A	10-13-00	Informal supervision	3 months	1-12-01	1-12-01	Now supervising under conditional release.

Comments: Mary Allen was placed on Informal Supervision after her first referral to the probation department in October 2000. Mary Allen was referred to Juvenile Probation for a citation she had received for criminal trespass. Mary Allen and her two sisters were cited as a group of teens who were caught loitering at Grady's, a restaurant and popular hangout for youth. Mary Allen came to see this officer at least one time every week, without fail. Mary Allen turned in weekly grade checks from school and attendance was verified.

Prior Commitment to Correctional Facility:

Cause No.	Commit Date	Type	Length	Expiration	Dis.Date	Dis.Type
N/A	N/A	N/A	N/A	N/A	N/A	N/A

Comments: Mary Allen has had no prior commitments to correctional facilities.

Prior Youthful Offender: ☐ Yes ☐ No
Outstanding Restitution: ☐ Yes ☐ No   Amount: $0.00
Outstanding Community Service: ☐ Yes ☐ No   Hours: 0

II. SOCIAL, EDUCATIONAL, AND SUBSTANCE ABUSE HISTORY

(*Please include information on siblings, dependents, employment, parents' marital status, primary language spoken in home, current school status, special expectations, truancy, behavior problems, gang activity, weapons, extracurricular activities, alcohol, marijuana, and other drug use.*)

A. Social

Mary Allen is the youngest of three daughters born to Martin and Jane Allen. Jean Allen is 19 years old, married, and living with her husband, William Smith, 21, and their infant son, Frederick. Olivia Allen (18), lives in the family home along with Mary Allen. The family lives in a rented house in the northeast heights of Las Cruces, and have for the past four years. The home is a three-bedroom home, which appears cluttered but clean. The front and back yards seem moderately maintained and the *(continued)* inside is well furnished. The ashes of Mary Allen's (deceased baby) sit on the fireplace mantel in an urn the shape of an angel. Baby Allen was cremated on 1-28-02, after the Office of Medical Investigators released the body. For weeks after the incident, the mailbox outside the house and the cars belonging to the family and friends were decorated with tiny pink ribbons in remembrance of the baby. Mary Allen has moved out of the bedroom that she resided in at the time of the incident. Mary Allen's parents have moved into that room and report that Mary Allen is unable (emotionally) to go in there. Mary Allen is currently working at Best Industries, as of May 1, 2002. Mary Allen previously worked at McDonald's but lost her job shortly after the events of this case came to light. Mary Allen had to take 4 months off of work after the incident. She was an emotional wreck, making her "dysfunctional" and therefore unable to complete her job as expected. Taking this time off paid its toll on the family as well, and Martin Allen was forced to work even more at his job of 11 years. Martin Allen said that he had to "keep the family going" in a time when it seemed everything was falling apart. Mary Allen is currently working with her father at Best Industries where she is working in the mail room. Mary Allen is currently considered a part-time employee, although she works 7.5 hours/day. Mary Allen has been there for 3 months and currently makes $6.50/hour. The remainder of her day is spent on her home schooling. Mary Allen spends much of her weekends babysitting her 5-month-old nephew, Frederick.

Mary Allen attended Las Cruces Elementary School where her mother was the President of the P.T.A. Both Mrs. Allen and her father report that Mary Allen was a good student and did fine in elementary school. Once in middle school, Mary Allen attended Craig Middle School. She and her family lived in the south valley and Mary Allen said she was one of the very few blonde-haired, blue-eyed girls there. Mary Allen reported that she did fine in school, but had problems with peers because of her race. The family eventually moved and Mary Allen began attending Burgess Middle School. Mary Allen reported no problems at

Burgess. Once in high school, Mary Allen began attending informal student parties and that she was very much into marijuana her ninth-grade year. Mary Allen became involved with a boyfriend who proved to be a bad influence on her. After her ditching classes became a habit, Mary Allen was referred to a truancy officer and ordered to complete community service. Mary Allen reportedly got back on track after her parents placed her on more structure and restriction. By the time this incident took place, Mary Allen was seemingly doing much better. Mary Allen was in the midterm of her sophomore year when this incident occurred and did not return following her arrest in January 2002. Mary Allen plans to continue with her home-schooling until graduation. Incidentally, Mary Allen has done very well in this program and is now classified as a junior, ahead of her schedule in a mainstream educational setting. Mary Allen's sister, Olivia, left her school after the incident as well when the publicity brought adverse reactions from her peers. Olivia, however, has since returned to the school and is reportedly not having any problems there. Jean Allen graduated from school before any of these circumstances arose.

As mentioned earlier, Mary Allen was referred to the probation department on one other occasion. In July 2000, police officers working a tac-plan in the Northeast Heights cited Mary Allen and her sisters for trespassing at a local restaurant. Officers were working in an effort to reduce the number of young people loitering in the various parking lots. Mary Allen and her sisters were at Grady's when the three of them were cited. Mary Allen came in to see this officer for her Preliminary Inquiry on 10-13-00 and was placed on informal supervision. Mary Allen made weekly visits with this officer, called in regularly, and turned in school reports as requested. There does not appear to be any other legal history with the family, however it has been reported that things have been tense at home.

There does not appear to be any physical evidence in the home; however, it has been reported that there is tension and that marital conflict is present. According to the

Forensic Evaluation, dated 1-20-01, there were frequent fights about issues relating to the three daughters, money, and the father's drinking. Martin Allen has been said to have a "long-standing alcohol abuse Hell." Counseling was offered initially to help cope with the surrounding offense and any issues exacerbated by it; however, Martin Allen advised that he does not need any more counseling. Martin Allen reports that he will support Mary Allen throughout her counseling, but that he has no intention of continuing himself. Martin Allen reported that he does not believe the incident should be "dwelled on" and that "you have to go on, or it will tear you up." It was unclear if Martin Allen would participate in further counseling or not.

Initially, Martin Allen sought counseling services for his family through the Employee Assistance Program, which his employer provides. This program only allowed for five visits and the family quickly exhausted that service. Dr. Martha Ames, a private psychologist, was recommended and Mary Allen has been seeing her for some

time now. Mary Allen sees Dr. Ames every two weeks, but no other family member attends. Mary Allen's sessions are on average one hour at a time. Mary Allen reports that she likes Dr. Ames and feels comfortable in working with her.

Mary Allen has admitted to using substances in the past such as marijuana and acid. It is this officer's understanding that Mary Allen used acid on an experimental basis only and that marijuana was her drug of choice while in the ninth grade. It is also this officer's understanding that Mary Allen has not used any marijuana since June 2001. It is a concern, however, that Mary Allen admits to using alcohol on New Year's Eve 2000. This apparently took place at the house with her parents present, along with other friends drinking as well. It is of concern that Mary Allen's parents would allow minors to drink in their home. This was not typical, however, according to Mary Allen, but rather something of a celebration of the upcoming new year. Mary Allen advised her parents allow drinking on special occasions only.

B. Education/Employment

Diploma:
    ☐ HS Diploma   ☐ GED Certificate
    Graduation date: Pending   GED Date: N/A
Special Education:
    ☐ Eligible for Sp.Ed.   ☐ Ineligible for Sp.Ed.   ☐ May require Sp.Ed.
    Qualifications for Sp.Ed: N/A
    Level: N/A   Effective Date: N/A

C. School History

School Name	Type	Program	Prog. Type	Grade/Sp.Ed.	Start Date Stat.
Hardcourt Learning Direct	Home School	Mail/correspondence school	Regular Education	10	03/01/02

Comments: As mentioned earlier, Mary Allen is doing well in school and is now classified as a junior in high school. Mary Allen mails in her schoolwork and completes the assignments that she is provided

through the Hardcourt Learning Direct Program. Mary Allen has goals of completing her high school education and eventually obtaining a degree in Auto Mechanics.

(continued)

D. Mental Health/Substance Use History

Treatment:

☐ Prior Treatment ☐ Prior Treatment Outpatient   Date of Last Psych. Eval: 4-17-01
  Outpatient

Substance Use:

☐ Alcohol   Frequency: Special Occasions
☐ Marijuana   Frequency: Daily in the past
☐ Drugs   Frequency: Experimental
☐ Solvents   Frequency:
Date Updated: 11-7-01

Comments: Please refer to Section II above for details.

III. JPPO OVERVIEW RECOMMENDATION

(Include core services, P/G/C and client's view of needs, issues and strengths, treatment/residential placement, JPPO areas of concern, and community-based service required if removal of client from home is recommended.)

Mary Allen appeared to be very nervous about the outcome of this case. Mary Allen acknowledged that she would like to continue working and complete her education. Mary Allen described herself as a very caring person who is "good minded" and prides herself in her good grades and employment history. Mary Allen's father was equally complimentary in his description of Mary Allen. Martin Allen described Mary Allen as a hard worker, energetic, focused, and good with chores at home, never having to be reminded to do them. The only negative issue that Mary Allen and her father could pinpoint was her need to stay on track with school. Nothing was mentioned in regards to counseling or the deep issues associated with the death of her child.

It is difficult to ascertain what Mary Allen's thoughts are about the incident itself. It is unfortunate that she was able to plead No Contest in that she now can keep her side of the story to herself. It has been very difficult to assess the situation given that much of the very important information will never have to be given by Mary Allen. It impedes treatment as well by not having to talk about the incident or specific actions in the matter as long as that is the case. Mary Allen's own state of mind is at risk. As Dr. Ames described it, Mary Allen has been greatly limited in her ability to work with other students, as she has not been permitted to talk about the offense. Dr. Ames has been hampered in her ability to investigate with Mary Allen and her family the causes of the offense and to directly address them. When weighing the distinction between retribution, safety of the public, and the best interest of the child, it is difficult to suggest that incarceration is the most appropriate outcome. Mary Allen has been afforded the opportunity to show that she can comply with the structure and rules that the probation department can provide and she has done that. Incarcerating her at this point would serve no purpose other than punishment and this could impede the treatment process even further. Dr. Ames feels that Mary Allen does not lack the capacity for empathy and the concern for others. Furthermore, it is this officer's understanding that Mary Allen does not pose a threat to anyone. The amount of denial in this case is insurmountable and the plea agreement encourages it. It is imperative that Mary Allen be allowed to engage in therapy to the point that she can talk about the incident and work, with her parents, to move past this and begin the lengthy process of intensive therapy. It is equally important that Mary Allen's family engage in therapy. According to the Forensic Evaluation, a likely factor in Mary Allen's situation is the stress in the family characterized by parental alcohol abuse, depression, and chronic marital conflict. The results of these family problems affected the whole family. Mary Allen, it has been reported, is deficient in coping skills, judgment, problem solving, and decision making. Mary Allen, according to the Forensic, appears to be "overwhelmed by especially stressful circumstances, and to ill-judged behavior at such times." Mary Allen, it reports, "does not seem to be a girl with antisocial or prominent aggressive tendencies, or characteristic tendencies toward remorseless use of others." Given these findings, it would seem appropriate to think that with support and supervision, and with intense therapy to recognize these contributing factors, Mary Allen would seem to be a low risk for repeat offenses and danger to others.

It is this officer's recommendation that Mary Allen be given a term of probation, for an extended period of time, to be determined by the court, but that addresses these crucial elements. It is highly recommended that Mary Allen be monitored closely to determine her progress and participation. It is also recommended that Mary Allen's parents be made party to the petition and moni-

tored for their compliance in therapy as well. A referral to the JIPS program could also be made to address what could be a rocky transition from intense publicity of this case back to more routine circumstances. It is also recommended that Mary Allen continue with intense psychotherapy and address specifics of the incident. The probation department would ideally work with the therapist in maintaining compliance and progress. Incarceration at this point would serve no other purpose than to address punishment and retribution. These issues could be served in the context of probation supervision just as well, while allowing Mary Allen to obtain the therapy that she desperately needs. Periodic Judicial Reviews could be used to further monitor compliance and progress. Community service is advised and possible options with meaningful results could be explored through the context of therapy.

IV. CLINICAL SOCIAL WORKER COMMENTS

(Must be completed for mandatory referrals and court order)

Please refer to Forensic Evaluation dated 1-20-02.

_____
Clinical Social Worker

Respectfully Submitted,   Approved:

_____   _____
Jane Clark, JPPO   Chief JPPO/Supervisor

Rogers (1990:46) lists the following characteristics that were included in 100 percent of all of the cases he has examined: (1) gender; (2) ethnic status; (3) age at first juvenile court appearance; (4) source of first referral to juvenile court; (5) reason(s) for referral; (6) formal court disposition; (7) youth's initial placement by court; (8) miscellaneous court orders and conditions; (9) type of counsel retained; (10) initial plea; (11) number of prior offenses; (12) age and time of initial offense; (13) number of offenses after first hearing; (14) youth's total offense number; (15) number of companions, first offense; (16) number of detentions; and (17) number of out-of-home placements.

Not all juvenile courts require the preparation of predisposition reports. They take much time to prepare, and their diagnostic information is often limited, since juvenile justice system budgets in many jurisdictions are restricted. In many respects, these reports are comparable to **presentence investigation reports (PSIs)** filed by probation officers in criminal courts for various convicted adult offenders. Unfortunately, there is no consistent pattern regarding the use of such predisposition reports and their preparation among jurisdictions (Rogers and Williams, 1995).

In recent years, various juvenile justice reforms have been implemented in many juvenile courts. Some of these reforms have been mandated by U.S. Supreme Court decisions regarding more extensive rights of juvenile offenders. Greater uniformity in handling and less disparity in sentencing are desirable outcomes in the aftermath of extensive informal juvenile processing that characterized the juvenile courts of previous decades. Nevertheless, there continues to exist a great deal of individualism exhibited among juvenile court judges in different jurisdictions and how the various laws and decisions pertaining to juveniles should be interpreted.

Victim-Impact Statements in Predisposition Reports

Predisposition reports may or may not contain a **victim-impact statement.** Presentence investigation reports or PSIs that are prepared for adults who are convicted of crimes in criminal courts are the adult equivalents to predisposition reports. It is more common to see such victim-impact statements in PSI reports, although some predisposition reports contain them in certain jurisdictions (Herman and Wasserman, 2001). These statements are often prepared by victims themselves and appended to the report before the judge sees it. They are intended to provide judges with a sense of the physical harm and monetary damage victims have sustained, and thus, they are often aggravating factors that weigh heavily against the juvenile to be sentenced (Edwards, 2001).

Since 1992, however, there has been a trend among state legislatures to increase the rights of victims of juvenile crime (Herman and Wasserman, 2001). By 1996, 22 state legislatures had enacted legislation addressing the victims of juvenile crime (Erez and Laster, 1999). This state legislation addresses the role of victims in various ways, including:

1. Including victims of juvenile crime in the victim's bill of rights
2. Notifying the victim upon release of the offender from custody
3. Increasing opportunities for victims to be heard in juvenile court proceedings
4. Expanding victim services to victims of juvenile crime
5. Establishing the authority for victims to be notified of significant hearings (e.g., bail disposition)
6. Providing for release of the name and address of the offender and the offender's parents to the victim upon request
7. Enhancing sentences if the victim is elderly or handicapped (Torbet et al., 1996:48). States enacting such legislation include Alabama, Alaska, Arizona, California, Connecticut, Florida, Georgia, Idaho, Iowa, Louisiana, Minnesota, Montana, New Mexico, North Dakota, Pennsylvania, South Dakota, Texas, Utah, Virginia, and Wyoming.

A strong consideration when enacting this legislation is the matter of restitution to victims. Restitution is increasingly regarded as an essential component of fairness in meting out dispositions for juvenile offenders. Offender accountability is heightened as restitution is incorporated into the disposition, especially if there was some type of property loss, damage, physical injury, or death. In reality, however, many states continue to haggle over how reparations will be imposed on either the youths or families or both.

Some states have incorporated into their juvenile statutes high dollar limits relating to parental liability whenever their children destroy the property of others or cause serious physical injuries. The theory is that if parents are held accountable, they will hold their own children accountable. Thus, reparations assessed against parents for the wrongdoing of their children is an indirect way of preventing delinquency, or so some state legislatures have contemplated. Another accountability measure is to include victim-impact statements to these reports. This makes judges aware of the true nature and extent of victim injuries and/or financial losses suffered because of the juvenile perpetrator. These statements are not obligatory, but they do assist judges in determining which dispositions should be imposed (Carr, Logio, and Maier, 2003; Meredith and Paquette, 2001).

SUMMARY

Dispositions of juvenile offenders following the conclusion of an adjudicatory hearing consist of several options available to juvenile court judges, ranging from nominal to custodial sanctions, with or without conditions. First, judges must determine whether the youth is a first-offender or a repeat offender. Juveniles who have just experienced their first contact with the juvenile justice system are usually treated more leniently compared with those who have appeared in juvenile courts frequently in the past. Those receiving harsher sanctions have usually been adjudicated of more serious violent offenses.

Even those adjudicated of more serious violent offenses still may receive judicial leniency, however. This is because of the strong juvenile court emphasis on rehabilitation and reintegration. The Violent Juvenile Offender Program (VORP), for example, seeks to provide social networking with various community agencies for violent youths. Also, these youths are provided with learning opportunities, vocational and educational opportunities, and other services that seek to meet their particular needs and deter them from future violent offending. Dispositional options also appear related in some instances to extralegal factors, such as gender, race, ethnicity, and/or socioeconomic status, although the literature relating to this issue is inconsistent. No doubt there are jurisdictional variations observed concerning the importance of these extralegal phenomena and how they impact upon dispositions for certain juveniles imposed by juvenile courts.

Juvenile court judges consider both aggravating and mitigating circumstances whenever deciding which dispositions are best to impose in individual cases. Aggravating circumstances are any factors that make one's offense more serious. All states and the federal government have articulated statutory aggravating factors that may be cited in sentencing decisions of adults convicted in criminal courts. Similar factors have been delineated in most juvenile courts. Aggravating factors include whether death or serious bodily injury occurred as the result of a juvenile's actions; whether the offense was committed while the juvenile was awaiting a future juvenile court adjudicatory hearing on another matter; whether the offense was committed while the juvenile was on probation or parole for another offense; whether the offender had a prior juvenile record; whether the juvenile was a leader in the commission of the offense if more than one juvenile was involved; whether the offense involved more than one victim; whether extreme cruelty was inflicted on the victim if the adjudication offense was a violent one; and whether a dangerous weapon was used in the commission of the offense.

Mitigating factors are also considered. These factors decrease the seriousness of one's offense or mitigate it. Thus, the following mitigating factors are usually set forth in most state and federal statutes: no bodily injury or death occurred to victims; no attempt was made by the juvenile to inflict serious bodily injury on anyone; the act was committed under extreme duress or provocation; whether circumstances existed that justified the offense; whether the juvenile was suffering from some mental disease or defect, or some other psychological condition that would otherwise impair his or her judgment in understanding the nature and consequences of his or her actions; whether the youth cooperated with law enforcement authorities to apprehend others involved in the offense; an absence of a prior juvenile record; and one's youthfulness. Other aggravating and mitigating factors may be cited by juvenile court judges as nonstatutory ones, if there is justification or support for them in reports filed by police officers or from probation officer investigations and recommendations to the court by prosecutors.

Most states today have constructed measures to assess one's dangerousness or risk posed to society. All states have developed such instruments for adult offenders, while juvenile courts and correctional services are rapidly constructing similar instrumentation. Risk assessment is the attempt by any agency to forecast the risk one might pose if released or if placed in a particular therapeutic program. The greater the risk posed, the greater the supervision required. Some juveniles are deemed to pose such a great risk that secure confinement is the most promising option, although most juvenile courts seek to avoid secure confinement for their juveniles if at all possible. Secure confinement is usually viewed as a last resort. One important objective of making risk assessments is to intensively supervise or confine those offenders who need more intensive supervision or incarceration. This phenomenon is known as selective incapacitation.

Needs assessments are also made. These are often paper-and-pencil instruments that are administered to disclose one's particular circumstances and needs that may indicate the usefulness of particular interventions or social services. Juveniles may lack self-esteem, have less education and low reading ability or comprehension, or may have social and emotional issues or problems. Treatments may be indicated, including group or individual counseling or a variety of other therapies. Almost every risk and needs instrument is flawed in one respect or another. Some instruments disclose that certain juveniles pose great risk when in fact they are not dangerous at all. Sometimes certain needs are disclosed by instrumentation that are not especially significant for particular juveniles. When these instruments are used in the decision-making process by juvenile court judges, probation departments, and parole boards, decisions about juveniles may be inaccurate. Some juveniles may be incarcerated who should not be incarcerated. At the same time, some juveniles may receive nonincarcerative dispositions when incarceration is what they require. Persons believed to be dangerous but are not actually dangerous are called false positives. Those who are considered nondangerous but turn out to be dangerous anyway are called false negatives. Authorities attempt to minimize the incidence of false positives and false negatives in their instrumentation. But despite a jurisdiction's best efforts, false positives and false negatives are almost always affected by the flaws of instrumentation and by the criteria used in making decisions about adjudicated juveniles.

Three general types of prediction have been identified. These are actuarial prediction, anamnestic prediction, and clinical prediction. Actuarial prediction, the most popular type of prediction, uses descriptive criteria of persons who have recidivated in the past in an effort to identify those most likely to fail in the future. Juveniles whose characteristics most resemble youths who have failed in their probation or parole programs are often rejected for probation or parole, or these options are delayed for a time. Also, youths whose characteristics are consistent with those who have been successful on probation or parole will likely be granted entry into these particular conditional programs. Anamnestic prediction uses projected future situational circumstances and compares these circumstances with the circumstances that existed when a juvenile initially came into contact with the court. Where circumstances have changed considerably for the better, predictions are made that project one's likely success on probation or parole. Prospective probationers or parolees who are likely to lapse into routines similar to those from which they emerged when they were arrested initially may be denied entry into probation or parole programs. Where the projected circumstances are greatly improved, probation or parole are more likely to be granted.

Clinical prediction involves a behavioral forecast by a psychiatrist or psychologist. An intensive examination of a particular youth characterizes such individualized predictions, where professionals make their best estimates about a youth's success chances if placed on probation or parole. Clinical prediction, the most expensive type of prediction, is considered superior to other types of prediction, because of the intensive examinations of juveniles by qualified professionals. Nevertheless, studies comparing the effectiveness of all prediction schemes show that they exhibit little differences in their overall effectiveness at predicting one's future behaviors successfully. Thus, actuarial prediction and anamnestic prediction, the least expensive types of prediction, are about the same in the predictive utility as clinical prediction. Some jurisdictions may show certain types of prediction superior over others under particular circumstances, however.

Risk instrumentation varies greatly among jurisdictions. However, most risk instruments share several common elements. Criteria usually found on risk or dangerousness instruments include one's age, prior record of delinquent or status offending, number of prior commitments to juvenile facilities, escapes from those facilities, drug or chemical dependencies, alcohol abuse, family relationships and stability or instability, school adjustment problems and academic performance, and peer relationships. These different criteria are weighted and raw scores are determined for each juvenile. Depending on one's score, a juvenile is considered more or less of a risk compared with other youths who have responded to the same instrument.

Risk instruments serve various purposes. The major purpose is classification. Classification enables authorities to place youths in programs that are deemed most suitable for them in terms of the risk they pose and the needs they reflect. Classification also suggests where such youths might be placed if secure confinement of them is warranted. The nature of one's supervision depends on how an offender is classified, as well as the services one should receive while on probation or parole, or in secure confinement. Generally classification attempts to maximize the service delivery systems available to juveniles in various communities as well as to suggest programs that might be developed to better serve their needs. Authorities involved in instrument development believe that the classification potential of risk/needs instruments can be enhanced if the instrument's validity can be improved, if it is considered dynamic and amenable to changing social conditions, if it serves practical purposes, and if it reflects reality.

Assisting in the proper categorization and placement of juveniles and their ultimate dispositions are predisposition reports. These reports are similar to adult presentence investigation reports in that they contain much descriptive information about juveniles, their personal characteristics and circumstances, and other variables. A listing of variables contained in such reports includes information about gender, ethnic status, age at first juvenile court appearance, the reason(s) for referral, the formal court disposition, the youth's initial placement by the court, the plea, number of prior offenses, age at time of first offense commission, number of companions involved when first offense occurred, number of out-of-home placements, number of detentions, the conditions and requirements of previous dispositions, and the type of counsel retained. Predisposition reports are usually prepared by juvenile probation officers at the order of juvenile court judges. They assist judges in their decision making since the juvenile probation officer often makes a dispositional recommendation based on the report's contents. An optional appendage to these reports is a victim-impact statement, where one or more persons were victimized by a youth's offense. Victim-impact statements describe how one or more victims were affected by the youth's offense. Increasingly juvenile court judges are considering victim input in deciding particular dispositions for adjudicated juveniles. While such statements are not binding on juvenile courts, they nevertheless may be persuasive, favoring one disposition over another in judicial decision making.

QUESTIONS FOR REVIEW

1. How do first-offenders and repeat offenders differ? How does being a first-offender as opposed to a repeat offender make a difference in how one's dangerousness or risk is assessed?

2. What are aggravating circumstances? What are several types of aggravating circumstances? How might these circumstances affect judicial decision making in a juvenile's disposition?

3. What are four mitigating circumstances? How do judges use these mitigating circumstances to lessen one's punishment?

4. What are some major differences between risk instruments and needs assessments?

5. What is meant by selective incapacitation? How is it used? What are false positives and false negatives? How do such designations occur?

6. What are three types of prediction? Which ones are most effective and why?

7. What is a predisposition report? Who prepares this report? How are such reports used for determining a juvenile's disposition?

8. What is a victim-impact statement? How is it used to modify the severity of one's disposition?

9. What are Violent Juvenile Offender Programs? What are their functions?

10. What are some moral and ethical questions that have been raised about selective incapacitation? Is selective incapacitation successful? Why or why not?

INTERNET CONNECTIONS

Families and Corrections Network
http://www.fcnetwork.org/

Human Services and Community Development
http://www.handsnet.org/

Keeping Youth Safe
http://www.preventviolence.org/

National Center on Education, Disability, and Juvenile Justice
http://www.edjj.org/

CHAPTER 11 | *Nominal Sanctions: Warnings, Diversion, and Alternative Dispute Resolution*

Chapter Outline

Chapter Objectives
Introduction
Nominal Dispositions Defined
Diversion
    Functions and Dysfunctions
      of Diversion
Diversion Programs for Juveniles
    Youth Service Bureaus
    Youth Services/Diversion
      and Community Service
      Programs, Inc.

The Diversion Plus Program
See Our Side (SOS) Program
The Community Board
    Program
Implications of Diversion
    Programs for Juveniles
Teen Courts
    The Use of Teen Courts
    The Anchorage Youth Court
    Teen Court Variations
    The Successfulness of Teen
      Courts

Day Reporting Centers
    Goals and Functions of Day
      Reporting Centers
    Some Examples of Day
      Reporting Centers
Alternative Dispute Resolution
Summary
Questions for Review
Internet Connections

Key Terms

28
Adult Judge Model
alternative dispute resolution
  (ADR)
Anchorage Youth Court
citizen action model
community organization model
Community Service Programs,
  Inc. (CSP, Inc.)

cooperating agencies model
day reporting centers
Diversion Plus Program
diversion
mediation
mediator
Peer Jury Model
Reparative Probation Program
See Our Side (SOS) Program

street outreach model
systems modification model
teen courts
tribunal
Youth Judge Model
Youth Service Bureaus (YSBs)
Youth Services/Diversion
  (YS/D) Program

Chapter Objectives

As the result of reading this chapter, you will accomplish the following objectives:

1. Understand what is meant by nominal dispositions.
2. Learn about several important juvenile dispositions, including diversion and alternative dispute resolution, as well as their functions and dysfunctions.
3. Understand what is meant by teen courts and why teen courts are important in delinquent offender processing.
4. Learn about day treatment centers and how they operate in communities as important services for juveniles.

• *Are school punishments more severe than those imposed by juvenile courts? Ask Ysatis Jones, a 15-year-old sophomore at Clay-Chalkville High School in Birmingham, Alabama, and she'll tell you. Jones was suspended from school on December 3, 2003, and required to serve a 15-day sentence in the school district's alternative school, a place for more persistent truants and chronic offenders who engage in bullying behavior, assault, and other forms of aggressiveness and incorrigibility. What did Jones do? She was caught at a drinking fountain during lunch break taking an ibuprofin pill, Motrin, for menstrual cramps. The school has a zero tolerance policy for "possession of an authorized prescription and over-the-counter medication." These are considered "major drug offenses." The intent of zero tolerance is simple: to reduce certain crimes by making them automatically punishable. But their simplicity may be why they fail and are opposed by many parents. Rachel Jones, Ysatis's mother, retained counsel, attorney Sam Wiggins, declared that there is a "shocking disparity" between the student's offense and the punishment. He filed an injunction in court against the school. Judge Houston Brown issued an injunction on January 21, 2004, entitling Ysatis to attend school while the case was scheduled for a hearing. In the meantime, school board attorney Carl Johnson defended the school's policy and said that there is no "shocking disparity" between the offense and penalty, and certainly not one that would warrant judicial intervention. State law allows judges to revise the policies of school boards relating to student punishments in certain cases. Rachel Jones thinks that each case, including her daughter's case, needs to be considered individually. And Alabama is not alone in heavy-handed zero tolerance policies. In Indiana, a female middle school student was arrested by police after writing a note simply threatening to bring a gun to school. A Tennessee juvenile was suspended from his high school because of suspicion of engaging in sexual intercourse with a female student. In Pennsylvania, a student was suspended from a middle school on suspicion of smoking. And in Wyoming, a school punished several students who had attended a off-campus weekend party where it was alleged that alcohol was served. The students were suspended anyway, despite their denials that they drank alcohol and the fact that the party was not on school grounds. Are these punishments fair? Should juvenile courts intervene?* [*Sources:* Adapted from "Zeroing in on Zero Tolerance." *Times Leader,* May 17, 2004; adapted from Chanda Temple "Judge Asked to Review Motrin Decision—Lawyer Says Court Can Revise School Board's Punishment." *The Birmingham News,* May 15, 2004.]

• *The prosecutor argued the defendant's guilt. The defense counsel pleaded for leniency. In the end, the jury deliberated and found Albert M. guilty of theft. Punishment was swiftly dispensed. Albert M. would be required to perform 40 hours of community service and make restitution for the property he had pilfered from a student locker at his high school. A judge upheld the ruling and punishment. Three months later, Albert*

M. was a jury member listening to charges leveled against another high schooler. All of this happened in a California youth court. Teen courts or youth courts are being used increasingly as alternatives to juvenile court in disposing of less serious juvenile cases. Aimed at minor and first-time offenders, youth courts use other teens, one's peers, to perform the roles of prosecutor, defense counsel, and other court officers. The courts are conducted in after-school hours, usually in empty classrooms or in a gymnasium. The proceedings require juveniles accused of delinquent acts to admit them and agree to accept any punishments imposed by the court. The punishments are almost always restitution, community service, or some other form through which an offending juvenile can be held accountable and understand that his or her delinquency will have consequences. Do these informal proceedings undermine formal juvenile court decision making? Will juveniles who offend take their punishments seriously? [*Source:* Adapted from the Associated Press, "Teen Courts Take Bite Out of Delinquency," July 1, 2005.]

• *In Douglas County, Minnesota, and throughout other parts of the country, first-time teen offenders have been allowed the option of teen court, a community-based program that allows some offenders to clear their juvenile records in exchange for admitting to their crime and completing conditions imposed on them by a jury of their peers. Also known as peer court or youth court, Douglas County has processed over 140 cases since 2003. Appearances in Douglas County Teen Court are a little different from traditional juvenile court proceedings. "The jurors really bring a personal touch to the deliberations," says Konstance Hill, progam director. "What are you involved in after school? Who are your friends and what kind of influence do they have on you? How have your parents reacted to your situation? What were you thinking when you did this?" The offenders going through teen court don't usually think of themselves as juvenile offenders. Most of them are just kids who made foolish mistakes, and once they realize that they can and will get caught, they don't reoffend. The teen court allows them to maintain their self-esteem but also shows them there are serious consequences. The jurors, other teens and one's peers from school, really try to determine which consequences would effect the best change in the offender. All jurors and other participants go through a 3-hour training program, volunteer to sit in on actual adult court cases, and diligently try to match the punishment with the offense and the offender. Examples of conditions imposed by teen courts include enrolling in educational classes, writing essays, attending school on a regular basis, riding the bus to help monitor safety, honoring curfews, avoiding contact with negative peers, getting a job, journaling, joining an extracurricular activity, and even attending student counseling. Another option is subsequently serving as a juror sitting in judgment of other offenders. Hill says that "It really gives them a new perspective on their offense. It is eye-opening to see how others have gotten themselves into situations, trouble, and how it affects them, their families, their friends, and the community at large." Douglas County Teen Court is a community effort. A total of 90 teens have been trained as jurors since 2003 and each case is overseen by a volunteer attorney who also acts as a teen court judge.* [*Source:* Adapted from Lori White, "A Jury of Their Peers." *Echo Express*, February 16, 2005.]

INTRODUCTION

Should taking Motrin for menstrual cramps result in a 15-day school suspension and mandatory attendance at an alternative school for chronic truants, school bullies, and those written up for fighting? Should a note written by a student threatening to bring a gun to school merit a police investigation? Should students be suspended from school on mere suspicion of smoking, having sexual intercourse, or drinking alcohol on a weekend at an off-campus party? Should teens be allowed to sit in judgment of and prescribe punishments for other teens accused of committing various minor infractions? Under what circumstances should the juvenile court become involved, if at all, in these and other types of minor rule violations and zero-tolerance policies? When should juvenile court judges issue verbal reprimands instead of imposing probation or confinement?

This chapter examines a broad range of dispositional options available to juvenile courts known as nominal sanctions, diversion, and alternative dispute resolution. These types of sanctions or dispositions are applied only for those juveniles considered to pose the least amount of risk to others or are considered low-risk first-offenders unlikely to recidivate. An array of less formal options exists for juvenile court judges to administer that are far less intrusive in one's life compared with juvenile probation or confinement.

The first part of the chapter defines nominal dispositions. Nominal dispositions are typically verbal warnings issued by judges in lieu of any formal adjudication for either status offending or delinquency. It has been found that verbal warnings or reprimands are often sufficient deterrents to future misconduct by most juveniles who enter the juvenile justice system.

In an effort to insulate youthful offenders from the trappings of juvenile courts and their criminal-like appearance, many juveniles are diverted from the juvenile justice system through deferred prosecution and diversion. Diversion is defined and discussed. There are many types of diversion programs. One shared feature of these programs is that they attempt to provide constructive interventions in the lives of youths that will hold them accountable for their actions without the formality of juvenile court processing. However, although diversion means a temporary cessation of legal action against particular juveniles, it does not always excuse them from complying with various diversion program requirements. Juveniles placed in diversion programs are usually expected to do various things to demonstrate that they understand the seriousness and consequences of their actions. Different types of diversion programs are described, together with their general functions and dysfunctions for juveniles. Some of the programs discussed include the Diversion Plus Program, the PINS Diversion Program, and the Community Board Program. The implications of diversion programs for juveniles are examined.

A growing and promising method of sanctioning juveniles outside of formal juvenile court settings is the use of teen courts, youth courts, or peer courts. These courts are known by different names in many jurisdictions, although their operations and results are fairly uniform and effective. In 2005 there were over 1,000 teen courts in the United States, with plans for establishing more of these courts in larger numbers of jurisdictions. Teen courts are comprised of one's peers who sit as a jury to decide one's punishment. Secure confinement is not an optional sanction. Youths who have committed minor offenses and admit their guilt beforehand qualify to participate in teen courts, where their fate rests with others like them. Overseeing the teen court process are seasoned judges, some retired, or other persons with extensive legal knowledge. Their presence is intended to ensure that proper legal protocol is followed. But the punishments meted out by peer juries are almost exclusively oriented toward community service and restitution. Teen courts are described in detail, including their respective strengths, weaknesses, and applications. Several teen courts are illustrated to show how the youth court process functions.

The next section of this chapter describes day reporting centers. Located in one's community, day reporting centers offer an extensive array of services and assistance to youths. The goals and functions of day reporting centers are described. Several examples of day reporting centers are given, together with an estimate of their successfulness in treating and supervising less serious juveniles.

The chapter concludes with an examination of alternative dispute resolution and restorative justice. These types of programs are known collectively as victim–offender mediation programs. They are designed to bring together both victims and offenders and engage them in positive interaction experiences. Restorative justice is an old concept and is found in the historical anecdotal information of Native Americans, Canadian tribes, and Australian aborigine societies. Restorative justice is defined, and several examples are provided of its use as an alternative to processing juvenile offenders. Mediation programs are intended to unite victims and their youthful victimizers for constructive purposes. These programs offer youths the opportunity to face their victims and accept responsibility for their actions. Victims confront offenders as well, and they can verbalize how they have been harmed by the offender's actions. Amicable solutions are often arranged by mediators who seek to restore to victims whatever they have lost. In the context of restorative justice, healing occurs through offender understanding of the consequences of their actions for others. At the same time, victims learn much about offenders and their actions. The functions, uses, and operations of victim–offender mediation programs are examined.

NOMINAL DISPOSITIONS DEFINED

Nominal dispositions are verbal and/or written warnings issued to low-risk juvenile offenders, often first-offenders, for the purpose of alerting them to the seriousness of their acts and their potential for receiving severe conditional punishments should they ever reoffend. These sanctions are the least punitive alternatives. Nominal dispositions may be imposed by police officers in their encounters with juveniles. These verbal warnings or reprimands are often in the form of stationhouse adjustments, where youths are taken into custody and released to their parents later, without a record being made of the incident.

Juvenile court judges are encouraged in most states to utilize the least restrictive sanctions after adjudicating juveniles as delinquents, status offenders, or CHINS. The use of incarceration as a sanction is within the judicial powers of juvenile courts, although these courts are obliged and encouraged to seek other options as sanctions. Some persons believe that secure confinement as a disposition is overused, and that public safety is better served to the extent that most juveniles can remain at home within their communities, where a more therapeutic milieu exists for them to become rehabilitated (Weatherburn and Baker, 2001). One community-based option in Delaware is the Delaware Bay Marine Institute (DBMI), a program that emphasizes sea-related activities and underwater skills. While the results of this research were inconclusive, the fact remains that there are viable alternatives to incarcerating juveniles that may work as good or better than simply incarcerating them (Brandau, 1992). For some persons, even better alternatives include doing little or nothing other than issuing certain juveniles verbal warnings or reprimands.

For example, intake officers may also use nominal dispositions against certain juveniles, if it is perceived that they merit only verbal warnings instead of more punitive sanctions. If petitions against certain juveniles are filed, depending on the circumstances, judges may find them to be delinquent as alleged in these petitions. However, these adjudications do not automatically bind judges to implement conditional or custodial sanctions. Thus, judges may simply issue warnings to adjudicated juveniles. These warnings are serious, especially after a finding that the juvenile is delinquent. Juveniles with prior records face tougher sentencing options later if they reoffend in the same juvenile court jurisdiction and reappear before the same judges. Actually, various juvenile court actors engage in the process of attempting to forecast a youth's behavior if certain actions are taken or not taken. Some persons have created decision trees to operationalize this process. Ashford and LeCroy (1988) suggest the decision tree shown in Figure 11.1.

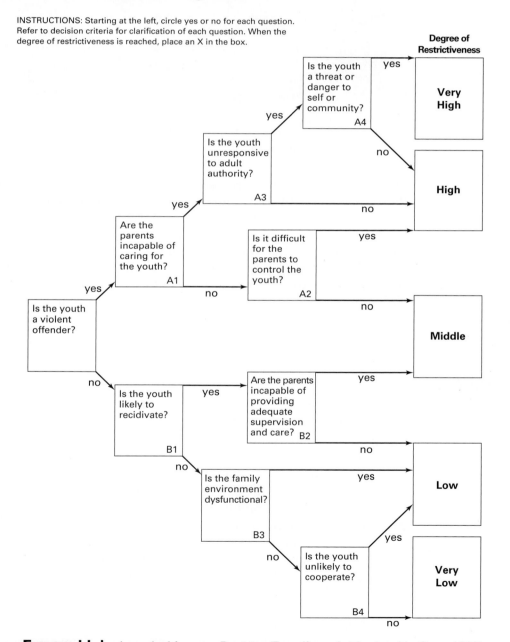

FIGURE 11.1 Juvenile Aftercare Decision Tree (from Ashford and LeCroy, 1988)

Proactive policing seeks to bring police officers into more frequent contact with juveniles on city streets to improve interpersonal relations and serve as a visible deterrent to delinquency.

This juvenile aftercare decision tree begins with the question of whether the youth is violent. Depending on the answer to this question, either "yes" or "no," the tree branches two different ways where other questions are posed. Notice that if the answers to successive questions are "yes," the degree of restrictiveness recommended to the juvenile court increases. The more "no" answers suggest less restrictiveness. This tree merely conceptualizes court thinking, particularly following an adjudication. However, actors may utilize similar decision trees much earlier in the system. For instance, intake officers and prosecutors may contemplate seriously the use of **diversion** for some youths (Hassett, 2002).

DIVERSION

The Juvenile Justice and Delinquency Prevention Act of 1974 and its subsequent amendments was intended, in part, to deinstitutionalize status offenders and remove them from the jurisdiction of juvenile courts. Another provision of this Act was to ensure that all other adjudicated delinquent offenders would receive the least punitive sentencing options from juvenile court judges in relation to their adjudication offenses. In fact, the National Advisory Committee for Juvenile Justice and Delinquency Prevention declared in 1980 that juvenile court judges should select the least restrictive sentencing alternatives, given the nature of the offense, the age, interests, and needs of the juvenile offender, and the circumstances of the conduct. Thus, judicial actions that appear too lenient are the result of either federal mandates or national recommendations (American Bar Association, 2001).

Diversion is not new. It is regarded as a form of deferred prosecution where offenders, especially low-risk ones, can have a chance to prove themselves as law-abiding persons. An early instance of diversion was created by Conrad Printzlien, New York's first chief probation officer. Printzlien was concerned that many youths were stigmatized by rapid prosecution and conviction, and thus he set out to find an alternative to unnecessary and unwarranted incarceration of juveniles (Rackmill, 1996). The result was the Brooklyn Plan, a deferred prosecution program that provided a way to distinguish situational offenders from more serious chronic and persistent juvenile delinquents. Between 1936 and 1946, 250 youths were handled as divertees. The program proved successful at decreasing recidivism among divertees and eventually was operated in other cities besides New York.

According to some persons, a primary, intended consequence of diversion is to remove large numbers of relatively minor offenders from juvenile court processing as quickly as possible (Weatherburn and Baker, 2001). However, other professionals caution that one unintended consequence of diversion is the development of a wider, stronger, and different net (Campbell and Lerew, 2002). This means in the simplest terms that those youngsters diverted from the formal juvenile justice system are captured in nets formed by the community-based agencies. Thus, if we view social control in its broadest terms, this means that more, not fewer, children will fall under some form of social control through diversionary programs.

Some authorities say that diversion of offenders should be aimed at the client population that would otherwise have received formal dispositions if diversion had not occurred (Gavazzi et al., 2000). This client population consists of youths who have committed delinquent acts and not simply status offenses. However, some critics say that status offenders may escalate to more serious offenses if left untreated by the system. Therefore, intervention of some sort is necessary to prevent this escalation of offense seriousness. Status offenders do not necessarily progress to more serious offenses. Sometimes, their apparent involvement in more serious offenses is a function of relabeling of the same acts differently by police (LoGalbo and Callahan, 2001). On other occasions, status offenders may be upgraded to misdemeanants by juvenile court judges if they fail to obey valid court orders. If a status offender is ordered to attend school and doesn't, this provides the judicial grounds for issuing a contempt of court citation, a misdemeanor. Not everyone favors this particular use of juvenile court contempt power, especially against status offenders. Regardless of whether they are status offenders or have committed serious delinquent acts, divertees often exhibit some recidivism. Therefore, it is true that at least some of these divertees do progress to more serious offenses, as some critics allege.

Functions and Dysfunctions of Diversion

Diversion has certain logistical benefits and functions. First, it decreases the caseload of juvenile court prosecutors by shuffling less serious cases to probation departments. Of course, this increases the supervisory responsibilities of probation departments who must manage larger numbers of divertees in addition to juvenile probationers. Another function of diversion is that it seems to reduce recidivism in those jurisdictions where it has been used (Hassett, 2002). Another intended consequence of diversion is to reduce the degree of juvenile institutionalization or placement in either secure or nonsecure incarcerative facilities. A fourth function is that diversion is potentially useful as a long-range

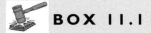

BOX 11.1

Katherine Theresa Sumey
Clinical Associate, Community Cares Alternative Project, Jail Diversion, Southcentral Counseling Center, Anchorage, AK

Statistics:

A.A.S. (human services, families and youth), University of Alaska, Anchorage; B.A. (justice, psychology), University of Alaska–Anchorage; M.A. (criminal justice management and administration), University of Alaska–Fairbanks.

Background and Education

I was a lifelong Alaskan, intrigued by the criminal justice system since a child. My father was an Alaska State Trooper in the 1970s and 1980s, and my earliest memories are filled with visions of the wide-brimmed hats and shined shoes of the trooper uniform. Growing up, dad provided a foundation that influenced my decision to choose a career path in the criminal justice field. My mother also helped shape my choices—as a nurse, she instilled the importance of helping others in times of need, being relentlessly compassionate, and working hard throughout life no matter what the challenges.

My undergraduate education at the University of Alaska–Anchorage included pursuing an associate degree in human services. During this time I did my practicum/internship with Youth Probation. I continued my education and earned my bachelor's degree in justice and am currently midway through a master's program in Criminal Justice and Administration through the University of Alaska–Fairbanks. I have a strong desire to influence social change and believe that this can be achieved through active involvement with the criminal justice system. Expanded knowledge of justice processes can only assist in helping to create a more efficient and effective justice system and work to solve some of the longstanding problems that contribute to our overloaded courts and bulging prison system.

The practicum with Youth Probation was my first real professional position. I worked alongside a seasoned probation officer for about a one-year period supervising delinquent youths. During this period I interviewed youths on probation and helped prepare predisposition reports for the court, making recommendations for treatment and placement of delinquent youths. Placement sometimes included being retained in the youth detainment center, in foster care or group homes, in substance abuse treatment centers, on electronic monitoring, in specialized treatment centers out of state, and with their family of origin.

It was important to maintain contact and establish rapport not only with youths but also with families, as they hold a significant role in the success (or demise) of the troubled youths. I remember a young probationer, only just old enough to fall under juvenile probation jurisdiction but whose family had years of contact with family and youth services with the children having periods of removal from the home. Substance abuse was a severe problem contributing to the dysfunction and chaos of the family, and during the initial interview, one parent made a half-hearted statement about it being "time" to quit drinking. Another youth was on the electronic monitoring program and required to be in his home but wanted to get high. He accomplished this task by finding cleaning supplies under the kitchen sink and making a concoction to get high. I once worked with a young gentleman who had an early psychotic breakdown and was diagnosed with schizophrenia as a teen. He was on "forced" psychotropic medication as a part of his treatment and was the first of many psychotic persons to tell me he would not continue to take medication to control his illness. Some of the juveniles we supervised were sex offenders, committing crimes against others their age and upon children. These youths were provided specialized group homes and foster care to help treat these inappropriate and damaging behaviors, some of these behaviors continuing to occur while they were in treatment. It was no surprise to learn that all of the youths who were abusers had been sexually abused by a family member, neighbor, or other trusted individual earlier in their life.

Most of the youths on supervision at least tried, whether showing some motivation and even remorse for the delinquent behavior at least at some point during their probationary period. I was most impressed with a young man who was on probation for manslaughter. He appeared truly remorseful about the crime he had been involved in and took his probation requirements quite seriously. He was a hard worker, made every scheduled appointment, and his plans for the future included serving his country.

Work Experiences

My first professional paid position after Youth Probation was working as a job coach and then employment specialist with the community mental health center. Here I assisted mentally ill and disabled adults in achieving their vocational and educational goals. I helped consumers with prevocational skill-building activities such as practicing interview questions and developing resumes, and then assisted with on-site training for successful placement in competitive work environments. This work provided valuable insight into the challenges of working with individuals with disabilities and their struggles and successes in the workforce.

I continued employment with the mental health center working within a multidisciplinary team for about 3 years, providing intensive case management services for consumers with chronic and persistent mental illness. Here I learned a ton about people. I provided intensive case management and group skill development services, to include assisting with many individuals who were involved with the criminal justice system (e.g., on probation or parole, frequent arrests, involvement with mental health court). During this position I developed substance abuse, trauma treatment, and crisis intervention skills, which I continue to apply in my current position.

I currently work as a part of a research project providing intensive services to adults who are diverted from jail into mental health services. Anchorage was chosen as one of 17 sites nationwide to participate in this 3 year federally funded research project. Locally much cooperation is required from partnering agencies to make this program a reality, such as cooperation with corrections, the municipal prosecutor, and the mental health center. I work on the treatment end of things, providing direct services to clients who we assess and divert from the jail the same day after they are arrested. If inmates meet appropriate diagnostic and legal criteria, as well as consideration of previous criminal history, an agreement is made with the municipal prosecutor to hold the charges if the participant complies with treatment recommendations. I go into the jail and I work to help a person obtain immediate shelter, food, and clothing, and then I continue to assist them with linkages to medication resources, substance abuse treatment, housing programs, entitlement programs such as Social Security and public assistance, and other identified areas where one might need assistance.

One of my greatest challenges in my current position is working with teens who are transitioning into adulthood. Young adults who are experiencing depression may really be having a tough time navigating through their formative years. More difficult is the young adult who has a psychotic breakdown as a teen, has recompensated on psychotropic medication, or is still struggling with facing having to take medication to control mood, delusional thinking, and hallucinations. There is a halt in the maturation of the youth as they are preoccupied with new sensations and may in some ways lose this period of life. More

(continued)

often than not, persons turn to drugs and alcohol to help self-medicate the pain, depression, or psychosis—in some ways, "using" helps things to seem normal again.

With both adults and youths I've worked with, substance abuse is prevalent. With dually diagnosed mental health clients, it is really the *expectation* and not the exception that substance use contributes to some of the problems in their lives. Juveniles and adults can be quite successful in cleaning up when they are detained/incarcerated, in a structured-living situation, or in a substance abuse treatment facility. It can be frustrating to see someone doing so well, and then once they are out of the structure, they quickly revert to using and engaging in self-destructive behaviors. I've learned the importance of seeking supervision when feeling these frustrations and acknowledging that a person may have to have a number of relapses and contacts with the criminal justice system before they "get it" and change their behavior.

Youth Courts

As a teenager, I was involved with the Anchorage Youth Court. Back then, this was a new program in Anchorage that trained youths in the community to judge their peers who were diverted from juvenile intake to this informal court. Youths were eligible for court participation if they committed low-level crimes (e.g., shoplifting, truancy, minor consumption, curfew violations). Youth courts have expanded since the mid-1980s and now they are connected throughout Alaska through the United Youth Courts of Alaska, with courts operating all over the state. This year my 12-year-old daughter completed the training to pass the bar exam to become a youth "lawyer." Youth courts operate from the restorative justice philosophy in which the attempt is made to repair the harm violators have done to the community. I learned about restorative justice interventions applied in the Anchorage Youth Court from helping my daughter study for her bar exam—youths may be assigned community service work, anger management, writing letters of apology, writing drug or alcohol assessment essays, fire prevention, anti-theft, learn weapons safety, attend victim impact classes, view adult proceedings, and make restitution to one or more victims.

I am now involved as a parent, which equates with giving rides to bar associate meetings, providing pep talks to promote continued interest, and clarifying and teaching from my own experience/education. I am looking forward to supporting and participating in upcoming events, including selling raffle tickets and auctions to support the organization, participation in a Sourdough Cook-Off at Fur Rondy activities at the start of the world-famous Iditarod, and a golf tournament at the beginning of the summer.

Advice to Students

My advice to students would be as follows:

1. One of the greatest ways to get an idea if you want to work in a given field is to do an internship placement. Even if you do not choose right away to be a youth probation officer, a law enforcement officer, or correctional officer, depending on the internship you do, you will gain valuable experience. You will have hands-on experience of what it is like to work with a specific population, which will only aid you in your future endeavors.

2. Seek out positive mentors. I cannot stress more the importance of seeking positive mentors to guide you in your professional and personal growth. I truly value the wealth of knowledge my Youth Probation field instructor provided during the year practicum. She was a positive mentor, a strong influence in helping me gain the strength and confidence needed to continue in a traditionally male-dominated field. Seek mentors in different arenas, whether it is a friend, school mate, teacher, coworker, or supervisor; surround yourself with positive influences. One of my mentors now is my martial arts instructor; he has been very supportive as he sees me focus and improve with my self-defense skills.

3. Continue to set and evaluate your goals. Once you set a goal, such as entering a degree program or internship, evaluate how you are doing in the program. Is it working for you? Do you need to make changes? If it is working, then follow through to fruition.

4. Continue your education. Whether it be formal education from a university, continuing education classes, workshops, or conferences, try and soak it in as much as you can. Seek supportive employers/supervisors who will encourage education and training to promote your personal and professional growth.

crime prevention measure. Finally, diversion reduces certain youth risks, such as suicide attempts as the result of being confined in adult jails or lock-ups for short periods. The stress and anxiety generated as the result of even short-term confinement for certain juveniles, including their propensity to commit suicide, has been described. At least for some youths, diversion assists in avoiding the stresses of confinement or prosecution (LoGalbo and Callahan, 2001).

One of the dysfunctions of diversion is that it may widen the net by including some youths who otherwise would have received stationhouse adjustments by police or warnings from juvenile court judges. Much of this net widening occurs through changes in police discretion and relabeling of juvenile behaviors as more serious, however. Another dysfunction is that some affected youths may acquire beliefs about the juvenile justice system that it is lenient and will tolerate relatively minor law-breaking. The fact that many juvenile offenders are not disposed to secure confinement until their fourth or fifth delinquency adjudications would provide support for these beliefs.

A key problem with applying diversion on a large-scale basis is that not all status offenders or low-level delinquent offenders are suitable as divertees. We cannot say that all status offenders are alike, or that all minor delinquent offenders share the same characteristics. In order for diversion programs to maximize their effectiveness, they should target offenders most amenable to having minimal contact with the juvenile justice system. Ideally we ought to be able to identify certain youths who are at risk of becoming more serious delinquent offenders or dangerous adult criminals. This means that it is necessary to identify particular factors that qualify certain youths as being at risk (Bernat, 2005). Thus, diversion could be selectively applied, depending on whether certain youths possess more risk characteristics than others. Net-widening would be minimized and the sheer operating costs would be reduced substantially (Kennedy, 2005).

DIVERSION PROGRAMS FOR JUVENILES

Youth Service Bureaus

Diversion programs have operated in the United States for many years. In the early 1960s, **Youth Service Bureaus (YSBs)** were established in numerous jurisdictions in order to accomplish diversion's several objectives. While we still cannot identify precisely those youths considered delinquency-prone or at risk, YSBs were created, in part, as places within communities where delinquent-prone youths could be referred by parents, schools, and law enforcement agencies (Norman, 1970). Actually, YSBs were forerunners of our contemporary community-based correctional programs, since they were intended to solicit volunteers from among community residents and to mobilize a variety of resources that could assist in a youth's treatment. The nature of treatments for youths, within the YSB concept, originally included referrals to a variety of community services, educational experiences, and individual or group counseling. YSB organizers attempted to compile lists of existing community services, agencies, organizations, and sponsors who could cooperatively coordinate these resources in the most productive ways to benefit affected juveniles (Romig, 1978).

Five model YSB programs have been described. These are (1) the cooperating agencies model; (2) the community organization model; (3) the citizen action model; (4) the street outreach model; and (5) the systems modification model.

The Cooperating Agencies Model.   The **cooperating agencies model** consists of several different community-based agencies and organizations. Each organization or agency furnishes at least one paid full-time worker to the YSB program. As a team, these workers attempt to involve citizens and youth by bringing in interested professionals and others to work with juveniles who might have poor self-concepts or social adjustment problems.

The Community Organization Model.   The **community organization model** utilizes community citizens who work on a strictly voluntary basis. They are encouraged to form a board of directors who will assist them in coordinating diverse community services in ways that can benefit those juveniles serviced. Such organizations would provide temporary shelter for runaways or those youths who are experiencing family difficulties or school problems. Thus, these agencies would function to accommodate those who need emergency treatment or assistance.

The Citizen Action Model.   As the name implies, citizen involvement in the **citizen action model** is intensified. Community volunteers are attracted from various types of youth services. Each youth referred to these organizations is regarded as a case, and case conferences are held to determine the best treatment approaches to assist youths in solving their problems.

The Street Outreach Model.   The **street outreach model** provides for the establishment of neighborhood centers in business areas, where group and individual therapy may be administered to troubled youths. The accessibility of such centers in business districts is an attractive feature, since it caters to assisting juvenile transients who are roaming those same streets constantly.

The Systems Modification Model.   The **systems modification model** has led to the establishment of community-based facilities that function in relation with other agencies, schools, churches, and institutions to help these other organizations become more effective in supplying the needed youth services (Norman, 1970:15–19).

Youth service bureaus may contribute to the net-widening problem, because they include many youths who might otherwise have avoided prolonged contact with the juvenile justice system. Nevertheless, they have established common patterns that many community-based organizations have found useful as program guides over the years. In retrospect, youth service bureaus failed to live up to their goals relative to effective treatment and services for low-risk offenders. This is particularly true regarding offense-specific crimes such as drug offenses.

Generally, diversion programs operate in pretty much the same ways for juveniles as they operate for adult offenders. Diversion in the juvenile justice system has the primary objective of avoiding labeling and the stigma associated with involvement in juvenile court (LoGalbo and Callahan, 2001). Diversion may be either unconditional or conditional. Unconditional diversion simply means that the divertee will attend school, behave, and not reappear before the juvenile court for a specified period. Conditional diversion may require juveniles to attend lectures, individual or group psychotherapy, drug or alcohol treatment centers, police department–conducted DUI classes, and/or vocational or educational classes or programs. Successful completion of the diversion program means dismissal of the case. These programs are of variable lengths, but most run for periods of 6 months to a year (Campbell and Lerew, 2002).

Youth Services/Diversion and Community Service Programs, Inc.

In Orange County, California, the **Youth Services/Diversion (YS/D) Program** and **Community Service Programs, Inc. (CSP, Inc.)** were established in the early 1990s to fulfill two goals. These goals are to teach client responsibility and reduce family dysfunction (Polan, 1994). Family dysfunction has been linked with youth violence in selected studies (Ballif-Spanvil et al., 2004). Samples of youths from Orange County were selected and subjected to several experimental interventions. Family counseling sessions were established on a regular basis for diverted youths from juvenile court. Youths themselves participated in several self-help programs designed to enhance their self-esteem and confidence. Not all youths and their families completed the project. Those who dropped out were compared with those who finished the program requirements. Evidence suggests that most of those who successfully completed their programs fared better over time by exhibiting reduced recidivism compared with those who dropped out. Some persons suggest that the program is cost-effective and can conceivably be implemented on a large scale in other jurisdictions. One of the most positive benefits of this program accrued to juveniles whose self-concepts and general psychological well-being were improved.

The Diversion Plus Program

An alternative to formal court processing for status and less serious delinquent offenders is the **Diversion Plus Program.** This program was established in Lexington, Kentucky, in July 1991 and operated until November 1992 (Kammer, Minor, and Wells, 1997:52). Besides reducing recidivism among its clients, the goal of the program was to promote conformity to the law without causing stigmatization. Eligibility requirements were that youths had to be (1) between the ages of 11 and 18; (2) charged with a status or less serious delinquent offense; and (3) free of any prior record of delinquency.

The entire program consisted of eight separate sessions during a 2-month period, Monday through Friday, from 6:00 P.M. to 9:00 P.M. Group size was limited to 12 persons. The first sessions were designed to orient clients and teach them to work as a group. A variety of exercises were used to promote interpersonal trust and cooperation. Needs of program participants were assessed initially and one-on-one counseling and small group interaction emphasizing active learning occurred through hands-on projects. Each session emphasized a core curriculum emphasizing building self-esteem and self-control, improvement in decision-making processes, independent living skills, career exploration, substance abuse prevention, recreation, and team challenges. After learning about a particular topic (e.g., independent living), participants used the knowledge acquired to complete specific tasks (e.g., budgeting money). A point system was used to encourage compliance with compliance requirements. Points could be earned for participating and completing requirements, and points could be lost for noncompliance. Persons could use their points at the end of the program to purchase items in an auction during the final evening. Also, a $100 gift certificate was given to the person earning the most points.

During the Diversion Plus Program, there were 94 participants. Half were female, and the average age was 14.5 years. Subsequently 81 clients graduated from the program. Most of the 13 nongraduates terminated the program because of noncompliance. A follow-up showed that 63 percent of the graduates were subsequently rearrested for various charges. Interestingly, the rearrests of status offenders most often involved delinquent offenses. This finding shows for this sample at least that some offense escalation occurred. However, the escalation was from status offending to minor delinquent offending. No strong pattern of escalation to felonious offenses was detected. Thus it cannot be said presently that high levels of program involvement and completion are sufficient to ensure low recidivism. However, the investigators conjectured that had this program not been available, more youths would have penetrated the juvenile justice system further with perhaps more serious types of offending (Kammer, Minor, and Wells, 1997:54).

See Our Side (SOS) Program

In Prince George's County, Maryland, a program was established in 1983 called the **See Our Side (SOS) Program** (Mitchell and Williams, 1986:70). SOS is referred to by its directors as a juvenile aversion program, and dissociates itself from shock programs such as Scared Straight. Basically, SOS seeks to educate juveniles about the realities of life in prison through discussions and hands-on experience and attempts to show them the types of behaviors that can lead to incarceration. Clients coming to SOS are referrals from various sources, including juvenile court, public and private schools, churches, professional counseling agencies, and police and fire departments. Youths served by SOS range in age from 12 to 18, and they do not have to be adjudicated as delinquent in order to be eligible for participation. SOS helps any youth who might benefit from such participation.

SOS consists of four, 3-hour phases. These are described below.

Phase I: Staff orientation and group counseling session where staff attempt to facilitate discussion and ease tension among the youthful clients; characteristics of jails are discussed, including age and gender breakdowns, race, and types of juvenile behavior that might result in jailing for short periods.

Phase II: A tour of a prison facility.

Phase III: Three inmates discuss with youths what life is like behind bars; inmates who assist in the program are selected on the basis of their emotional maturity, communication skills, and warden recommendations.

Phase IV: Two evaluations are made—the first is an evaluation of SOS sessions by the juveniles; a recidivism evaluation is also conducted for each youth after a one-year lapse from the time they participated in SOS; relative program successfulness can therefore be gauged.

An evaluation of the program by SOS officials in 1985 found that SOS served 327 youths during the first year of operation, and that a total of 38 sessions were held. Recidivism of program participants was about 22 percent. Again, this low recidivism rate is favorable. Subsequent evaluations of the SOS program showed that the average rate of client recidivism dropped to only 16 percent. The cost of the program was negligible. During the first year, the program cost was only $280, or about 86 cents per youth served.

Programs similar to SOS are operated in other states. In Tennessee, for instance, the Davidson County (Nashville) Sheriff's Department operates D.E.P.U.T.Y., which stands for Developing, Educating, and Promoting Unity among Tennessee Youth (*American Jails,* 1998:98). The program is designed to give young people a look inside a jail without actually being arrested. The program will teach children that jail is not a place they want to be. The program is available to any interested organization, such as Boys and Girls Clubs and scouting groups. Sheriff Gayle Ray shows videos of inmates sharing their personal stories, where they explain when they started to go wrong in their own lives and how alcohol, drugs, and crime lead to a lifetime of problems. Sheriff Ray says, "We are expecting a great deal out of the D.E.P.U.T.Y. program. Children need to know that there's nothing exciting about jail. We want them to unite together and decide to make the right choices—the choices that will keep them out of the jail system."

The Community Board Program

One innovation introduced by the Vermont juvenile courts is the **Reparative Probation Program,** which is a civil **mediation** mechanism. This program involves first- and second-time juvenile offenders who have been charged with minor offenses, often property offenses, where damage to or loss of property was sustained by one or more victims. The Community Board Program uses volunteers to meet with both offenders and their victims as an alternative to a full juvenile court adjudicatory hearing (Karp, 2001). Mediation is conducted wherein a mutually satisfactory solution is arranged by the **mediator.**

One of the positive aspects of this program is that victims can meet and confront their attackers. Victims may become involved and empowered. Their face-to-face encounters with youths who victimized them enable victims to tell them of the harm they caused. In a selective way, the mediation program was successful. That is, some types of juveniles directly benefited from their confrontation experience. This type of mediation program doesn't seem to work well with particularly youthful offenders. Older juveniles have higher maturity levels and are more responsive to mediation (Karp, 2001).

IMPLICATIONS OF DIVERSION PROGRAMS FOR JUVENILES

One result of the Juvenile Justice and Delinquency Prevention Act of 1974 was to deinstitutionalize status offenders and remove them from the jurisdiction of juvenile courts. This has been done in some jurisdictions, but not in all of them. One result is that there is much variation among jurisdictions about how juvenile offenders are processed and treated (Potter and Kakar, 2002). In recent years, however, an increasing number of juvenile courts have imposed dispositions according to offender needs as well as according to what is just and deserved. Better classifications of offenders need to be devised. Additional information is needed about offender characteristics, their backgrounds, and specific circumstances in order that proper punishments and treatments can be imposed by juvenile court judges. For diversion programs to be successful, they must be targeted at the most successful juvenile candidates. Most frequently, these are low-risk first-offenders or juveniles who are quite young.

Some diversion programs include some rather stringent conditions and may even involve participation in intervention projects designed to remedy certain manifested problems. For example, a sample of 39 juvenile sex offenders was assigned to the Behavioral Studies Program of the Pines Treatment Center in Portsmouth, Virginia (Hunter and Goodwin, 1992). All participants received a minimum of 6 months of verbal satiation, in addition to individual, group, and family counseling and other therapies. Youths were also exposed to psychophysiological assessments of changes in their penile circumference by various testing procedures. The result was that deviant sexual arousal was decreased significantly and that the youths had favorably responded to therapy designed to treat their deviant conduct. However, not all divertees are subjected to these or similar experiences.

Juvenile courts have come under attack in recent years as the result of what the public considers excessive judicial leniency in dealing with youthful offenders. Often, juvenile cases are dismissed. This occurs not only during formal adjudicatory proceedings by juvenile court judges, but also by intake officers in earlier screenings of offenders. Thus, it is unreasonable to identify any specific part of the juvenile justice process as unusually lenient in juvenile case processing. All phases of the system seem to be influenced by the rehabilitative philosophy. And for many people, rehabilitation is equated with leniency (Campbell and Retzlaff, 2000).

In addition to charges of being too lenient with offenders and dismissing or diverting their cases, the juvenile court has been targeted for other criticisms. Critics say that the juvenile court has failed to distinguish adequately between less serious and more serious offenders; it has often ignored the victims of juvenile violence; it has often failed to correct or rehabilitate juveniles in a manner consistent with its manifest purposes; it has been unconcerned or complacent about juvenile offenders and how they should be punished; it has confined children at times in adult jails; it has failed often to protect juveniles' rights; its services have been too thinly spread; and it has been too resistant to self-examination and suggestions for improvement. But one criticism of these criticisms is that collectively, they do not especially apply to any single juvenile court at a particular point in time. Rather, they are loosely distributed and shared by many juvenile courts. By the same token, there are many juvenile courts operating with few serious flaws.

Music instruction and other types of classes are offered in many juvenile correctional institutions as a part of a youth's vocational and educational training.

The goals of diversion can be achieved more effectively, according to some authorities, if divertees are obligated to accept responsibility for their actions through restitution or community service. When youths must do something constructive and repay victims for damages to property, they learn valuable lessons concerning their actions and how they affect others. Sometimes diversion coupled with other program elements has been termed creative diversion and is used throughout the United States in diverse jurisdictions.

TEEN COURTS

Increasing numbers of jurisdictions are using **teen courts** as an alternative to juvenile court for determining one's guilt and punishment (Butts and Buck, 2002). Teen courts are informal jury proceedings, where jurors consist of teenagers who hear and decide minor cases. First-offender cases, where status offenses or misdemeanors have been committed, are given priority in a different type of court setting involving one's peers as judges. Judges may divert minor cases to these teen courts. Adults function only as presiding judges, and these persons are often retired judges or lawyers who perform such services voluntarily and in their spare time. The focus of teen courts is on therapeutic jurisprudence, with a strong emphasis on rehabilitation. One objective of such courts is to teach empathy to offenders. Victims are encouraged to take an active role in these courts. Youths become actively involved as advisory juries (Peterson, 2005).

Teen courts are also known as youth courts, peer courts, and student courts (Preston and Roots, 2004). In 1997 there were 78 active teen courts. By 2005 there were 1,019 youth court programs operating in juvenile justice systems, schools, and community-based organizations throughout the United States, with an anticipated 2,000 youth courts being established over the next few years (Peterson, 2005). The American Probation and Parole Association has recognized the significance

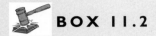

BOX 11.2

RESOLUTION BY AMERICAN PROBATION AND PAROLE ASSOCIATION IN SUPPORT OF YOUTH COURTS

In 2004, the American Probation and Parole Association adopted the following resolution in support of youth courts:

Whereas, Youth courts, also known as teen courts, peer courts, and student courts, are one of the fastest growing crime intervention and prevention programs in the nation.

Whereas, Youth volunteers under the supervision of adult volunteers, act as judges, jurors, clerks, bailiffs, and counsel for youth who are charged with minor delinquent and status offenses, problem behaviors or minor infractions of school rules, and who consent to participate in the program.

Whereas, Youth courts engage the community in a partnership with the juvenile justice system, youth programs, schools, attorneys, judges, and police departments working together to form and expand diversionary programs responding to juvenile crime and problem behavior.

Whereas, Youth courts increase the awareness of delinquency issues and problem behavior on a local level and mobilize community members, including youth, to take an active civil role in addressing the problem. Youth courts exemplify the practices of empowering youth through involvement in developing community solutions to problems, teaching decision-making, and applying leadership skills.

Whereas, Youth courts design effective program services and sentencing options that hold youth accountable, repair the harm to the victim and the community and contribute to public safety.

Whereas, Youth courts promote attitudes, activities, and behaviors that create and maintain safe and vital communities where crime and delinquency cannot flourish; and youth court practices provide a foundation for crime prevention and community justice initiatives, as well as embrace the principles of restorative justice. And

Therefore, be it resolved, That the American Probation and Parole Association hereby recognizes the importance of youth courts to our communities and recommends that probation, parole, and community supervision agencies support and assist in the formation and expansion of diversionary programs, known as youth courts.

Source: "Resolution in Support of Youth Courts." *APPA Perspectives* **28**:8 (2004a).

and contributions of teen courts by establishing September as National Youth Court Month to highlight the activities of youth courts and their contributions to the youth justice system (*APPA Perspectives,* 2004a:8).

The Use of Teen Courts

Among the first cities to establish teen courts were Seattle, Washington, and Denver, Colorado (Rasmussen, 2004). Subsequently, teen courts have been established in many other jurisdictions, including Odessa, Texas. In Odessa, for instance, juveniles are referred to teen courts for Class C misdemeanors and minor traffic violations. Defendants range in age from 10 to 16. Traffic citation cases result in teen court referrals by municipal judges, who give youths the option of paying their fines or having their cases heard by the teen court. If youths select the teen court for adjudication, then they do not acquire a juvenile record. The teen court listens to all evidence and decides the matter (Peterson, 2005).

Teen court dispositions are always related closely to community service as well as jury service (Butts et al., 2002; Karp, 2001, 2004). Thus, juveniles who are found guilty by teen courts may, in fact, serve on such juries in the future, as one of their conditional punishments (Rasmussen, 2004). Or they may be required to perform up to 22 hours of community service, such as working at an animal shelter, library, or nursing home; picking up trash in parks or ball fields; or working with various community agencies. The teen court program in Odessa has been very successful. Prior to using teen courts, the recidivism rate for all juvenile offenders in the city was between 50 and 60 percent. However, teen court adjudications all but eliminated this recidivism figure. Interestingly, juveniles who are tried by the teen court often develop an interest in the legal system. Teen courts place a high priority on educating young people about their responsibilities of being individuals, family members, and citizens (Roberts, 2003). As a part of one's diversion, conditional options such as restitution, fines, or community service may be imposed in those cases where property damage was incurred as the result of the juvenile's behavior (Chapman, 2005b). Juvenile court judges must exercise considerable discretion and impose dispositions that best meet the juvenile's needs and circumstances.

Constructive dispositions are the objective of teen courts in Kentucky. In September, October, and November 1992, teen jurors in a Kentucky teen court heard case details in nine different cases (Williamson, Chalk, and Knepper, 1993). Referrals to teen court were made from the regular juvenile court, a division of the state's district court. If juveniles are found guilty by the teen court, then the court imposes constructive dispositions involving community service hours. It should be noted that these teen courts do not determine one's guilt or innocence—rather, they convene and recommend appropriate dispositions. Teenagers act as prosecutors, defense attorneys, clerks, bailiffs, jury forepersons, and jurors as they carry out roles similar to their counterparts in criminal courts. The Kentucky teen court variety is interesting because accused and judged teens are themselves recruited subsequently to serve as teen jurors. Thus, all defendants are assigned to jury duty following their teen court appearances. When this study was conducted, no youth had been returned to the teen court for noncompliance. Perhaps seeing how the process works from the other side, as jurors, made these teenagers understand the seriousness of what they had done themselves as victimizers in the past. A detailed example of the workings of a teen court is the Anchorage, Alaska Youth Court.

The Anchorage Youth Court

By 2005, there were over 1,000 teen courts established in most states (Peterson, 2005). These courts are not always known as teen courts. In Anchorage, Alaska, for instance, a teen court program was established in 1989 and exists today as the **Anchorage Youth Court.** Subsequently 14 other youth courts have been established in various Alaska cities and modeled after the Anchorage Youth Court (AYC) (Anchorage Youth Court, 2005). Funding for youth courts in Alaska varies. AYC receives one-third of its funds from federal block grants, United Way, and program fees, one-third from fundraising and donations, and one-third from the Anchorage Assembly. The AYC targets first-time offenders

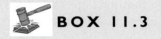 **BOX 11.3**

INTERNATIONAL SNAPSHOT: JUVENILE JUSTICE IN PAKISTAN

Pakistan ratified a United Nations ordinance in 1990 and implemented the Juvenile Justice System Ordinance (JJO) in 2000. The Pakistan Penal Code, closely connected with Islamic law, governs all offenses. Juvenile justice is an area of criminal law applicable to persons not old enough to be held accountable for criminal acts. The main goal of the juvenile justice system in Pakistan is rehabilitation rather than punishment. State police powers are oriented toward ensuring the safety and welfare of children.

The Penal Code prescribes that the age of criminal responsibility is 12, while children between ages 7 and 12 are criminally responsible if they have attained sufficient maturity of understanding to judge the consequences of their conduct. For all practical purposes, children age 7 or older are eligible for the full range of penalties under the Penal Code, including death and life imprisonment.

A large majority of children currently incarcerated in Pakistan's prisons are detained on charges of murder, dangerous weapons possession, theft, prohibition, and zina (sexual acts outside of marriage). The Zina Ordinance defines the age of majority as 16 for females and 18 for males. Pakistan has a statutory rape law, where girls as young as 12 have been prosecuted for having sexual intercourse. Typical punishments include whipping, amputation, and death by stoning. Punishments for minors include fines, imprisonment for up to 5 years, or up to 30 lashes with a whip.

Under the JJO, the primary thrust of juvenile justice should be the furtherance of rehabilitation and community reintegration. Children should be separated from adult offenders while awaiting trial or being kept in detention, and they should have the right to counsel. Timely processing of their cases is encouraged. Release on probation with educational or other treatment measures is recommended, including vocational training and other necessary services.

Under the JJO, every child under the age of 18 shall have counsel and receive a notice of charges against him or her. Children facing trial who have physical or mental impairments requiring treatment should receive such treatment as is deemed necessary by the court. Children suffering from mental illness should be hospitalized and treated until documentary evidence is produced of their successful recovery. Children under the age of 15 shall not suffer preventive detention except under extraordinary circumstances. However, many female juveniles are still unable to enjoy the status of juvenile offenders.

The JJO provides that children charged with crimes should be brought before a court within 24 hours of their arrest and suffer from minimal detention. However, Pakistan lacks resources to comply fully with this JJO mandate, and therefore, many children are kept in overcrowded cells in detention facilities for many months while their trial proceedings are scheduled. Few if any educational or recreational opportunities are provided youths who are kept in police custody. In reality about 90 percent of all juveniles charged with bailable crimes have remained in jail because of lack of funds to pay lawyer's fees or a lack of knowledge about legal assistance mechanisms available from the government.

Pakistan official crime figures are notoriously unreliable. Much of this information is estimated by academics and other professionals from incidental research. As of 2004, approximately 2,500 juveniles were awaiting trial out of a total juvenile prisoner population of 3,061. This is actually a decline from the 4,000 juvenile prisoners in Pakistani prisons in 2000. Pakistan has only one juvenile court in Karachi, and thus, juvenile justice moves very slowly. The JJO has provided for the establishment of other juvenile courts, although these bodies have only developed slowly and crudely. New juvenile rights have been articulated by the Pakistani government, although the implementation of these rights has occurred very slowly if at all. Children's rights advocates claim that the legislation relating to juveniles has failed to ensure juvenile justice largely because of poor communication and a general lack of awareness among officials in remote areas of Pakistan. Several civil society organizations have been working with those involved in juvenile justice work to train them through workshops and other training mediums. However, nothing significant has been accomplished with the police, the judiciary, and the probation department according to these organizations. This is because of a general lack of coordination between different agencies in various cities and towns.

Most juveniles charged with crimes are maintained for lengthy periods in unsanitary conditions. These conditions expose them to diseases and other health problems. The reformation of youthful offenders is a neglected area, and no rehabilitation centers exist for those youths released from incarceration. There are three separate juvenile secure custody facilities and two borstal (juvenile offender) institutions in different provinces. In all other areas of Pakistan, juveniles are kept in prisons with adults, but in special juvenile cells. One promising step has been taken by the Pakistani government. There are fewer lengthy major punishments for minor offenses committed by juveniles. Furthermore, the government has implemented measures to establish shelter homes with rehabilitative services to provide for some of the needs of children without families or who have been abandoned by their families.

Despite these positive steps toward ensuring the rights and proper treatment of juveniles, there are still flagrant violations of juvenile rights that occur. Often, there is a distinction made between youths who are rich and poor. Few if any rich juveniles are in Pakistani prisons. Also, rich children seldom suffer punishments for minor offenses. Poor children, however, are cruelly treated for minor offending such as stealing an apple or sleeping on the street at night, which is considered vagrancy and a punishable offense. When such juveniles are jailed, often for indeterminate periods, they emerge from confinement more often as hardened criminals rather than rehabilitated youths. They are largely at the mercy of jail authorities who routinely exploit them physically, psychologically, and sexually.

One major problem with juvenile detentions is that the staff overseeing these youthful detainees is often untrained. Prisoners are herded into overcrowded, unsanitary facilities. Washing and sanitary facilities are poor and privacy is lacking. Access to medical and dental treatment is severely lacking. Juvenile detainees also lack information about the rules in force in their prison settings. No educational or vocational opportunities are provided youths while under detention or imprisonment.

Pakistan generally recognizes the need to alleviate the social and economic exclusion of children. It is believed important to provide them with educational opportunities, and to end gender and socioeconomic discrimination. Community-based initiatives are acknowledged as important and their eventual development is contemplated. Also, more adequate parenting skills are being promoted. But scarce resources make the implementation of these worthy objectives difficult. However, some critics have suggested that the claim of insufficient resources is merely a convenient way of ignoring an important problem that could be remedied with sufficient resolve.

[*Sources:* Rabeea Anwar, "Juvenile Justice in Pakistan," Multi-Sol Networks, Unpublished paper, 2005; IRIN News Organization, "Pakistan: Child Advocacy Groups Press for Reform of Justice System," Unpublished paper, 2005; "India/Pakistan: Juvenile Justice Tramples on Children," *Asia Times,* February 18, 2000; Society for the Protection of the Rights of the Child, "Issues: Juvenile Justice," Unpublished paper, February 11, 2005; Society for the Protection of the Rights of the Child, "Child Rights in Pakistan," Unpublished paper, February 11, 2005.]

and makes extensive use of volunteers from the community. The protocol of the AYC is outlined below.

Intake and No Contest Pleas. At the intake stage, a decision is made whether to recommend a youth for AYC. Not all youths are eligible. Youths with extensive juvenile records or who are charged with extremely serious felonious offenses are usually prohibited from participating in AYC. For low-risk, first-time juveniles, however, they may be offered the opportunity to enter "no-contest" pleas and attend AYC for sentencing. A no-contest plea means that the youth admits to the offense and avoids formal adjudication by a juvenile court judge. An appointment date is scheduled for the youth's subsequent appearance before the AYC for sentencing. The AYC utilizes volunteers from grades 7–12 who serve in different capacities. Thus, youths who volunteer may serve as prosecutors, defense counsels, judges, clerks, bailiffs, and jurors for youths who have committed misdemeanors and minor felonies. There are three AYC juvenile judges who hear each case and impose a punishment or sentence. Offenders and their parents are given a detailed list of instructions about when to appear, where, and how to behave while the AYC progresses. These instructions pertain to a courtroom dress code, courtroom decorum, courtroom attendance, and client contact. Also covered in detail is a list of consequences for not following AYC courtroom guidelines. If youths scheduled for AYC fail to appear, such nonappearances will be taken into account at a subsequent rescheduled sentencing hearing. The conduct of all participants, including judges, is also governed. An ethics committee has sanctioning power over all court officers who fail to appear for AYC duty. All AYC sessions are tape-recorded. Thus, the AYC is like a court of record in the event a dispute arises later over what was said or if any evidence presented is questioned.

The Sentencing Options. The following sentencing options are available to impose on any defendant: (1) AYC classes, including anger management class; defensive driving class; property and theft crimes class; skills for life class; "Start Smart" and "Stay Smart" classes; victim impact class; and weapons safety class; (2) apology letter to family; (3) apology letter to victim; (4) community work service; (5) diversity awareness; (6) drug/alcohol assessment; (7) essay; (8) fire prevention program; (9) jail tour; (10) juvenile anti-shoplifting program; parent–adolescent mediation; restitution; and victim–offender mediation.

No-Contest Script. A no-contest script is presented to the defendant, the prosecutor, defense counsel, and the judges. This script is shown in Figure 11.2.

The AYC no-contest script outlines the entire protocol for the AYC proceeding. The defendant is advised that one or more persons have been appointed to defend him or her. Prosecutors are named. Although AYC uses three-judge panels, sometimes two-judge panels are permitted, with defendant approval. The charging document is read, outlining all charges against the defendant as well as the defendant's admissions to all offenses alleged. The defendant is asked whether the facts outlined in the charging document are true and enters a no-contest plea.

Prosecution and Defense Sentencing Recommendations. Both the prosecution and defense have the opportunity to examine the case, the facts, and circumstances and make a recommendation to the AYC judges. Both prosecutors and defense counsels are provided with prep lists, which outline their specific duties and options. These prep lists are quite specific, and defense counsels go over them with their clients to make sure all procedures are understood fully. Both sides also have access to the list of sentencing options noted earlier in this

ANCHORAGE YOUTH COURT NO-CONTEST SCRIPT

1.   "This is the case of State of Alaska versus __[defendant's name]__; case number 04-_[case #]___. Is the defendant present in the courtroom?"

2.   "Mr./Ms. _[defendant's last name]_, the record reflects your true name as _____, spelled _____. Is this information correct?
    a.   [*If YES*] "Then let the record stand."
    b.   [*If NO*] "Please spell your name for the court." . . . "Let the record stand corrected."

3.   "You have the right to have an Anchorage Youth Court attorney and (one has/two have) been appointed to represent you."
    a.   "At this time, will defense counsel please identify themselves."
    b.   "Will the prosecutors please identify themselves."

4.   [*If there are only 2 judges present, state:*] "For the record, there are only 2 AYC judges present. You have the right to have your sentence decided by 3 AYC judges. Please confer with your attorney and decide whether you agree to proceed with 2 judges or want to reschedule for a time when 3 judges are available." [*If the defendant wants to reschedule, recess the case.*]

5.   "You entered into Anchorage Youth Court by signing an agreement at Juvenile Intake."
    a.   "Please look at a copy of this agreement in your attorney's case file."
    b.   "Did you read and understand this agreement prior to signing it?"
    c.   "Did you knowingly and willingly sign this agreement of your own free will?"
    d.   "The charge(s) in the agreement is/are _____." [*Read the charge(s) from the McLaughlin Agreement, NOT the charging document.*]
    e.   "Do you understand that you pled no contest to (this charge/these charges) at Juvenile Intake?"
    f.   "Defense counsel, are you satisfied that the defendant knowingly and willingly signed the agreement with a full understanding of its content and the jurisdiction of Anchorage Youth Court, and that this was his/her own free will?"

6.   "_[Defendant's name]_, having knowingly, willingly and voluntarily signed the agreement with Anchorage Youth Court and agreeing to plead no contest at Juvenile Intake to the charge(s) of _____, it is hereby ordered that the agreement between _[defendant's name]_ and the Anchorage Youth Court is made a part of the record of this proceeding."

7.   "Mr./Ms. _[defendant's last name]_, please rise for the reading of the charging document. Count I . . ." [*Read the charging document.*] "Mr./Ms. _[defendants' last name]_, do you agree that (this is/these are) the same charge(s) you pled no contest to at Juvenile Intake?"

8.   [*If the charge in the charging document is different from what the defendant pled no contest to at Juvenile Intake, look in the file for a "Change of Charge" form. If there is a "Change of Charge" form, state:* "The charge has been changed from _____ to _____. The effect of this change is [from the "Change of Charge" form]_____. Do you understand this change and do you agree to plead no contest to ____[the new charge]___?" [*If the defendant says no, recess court and call the legal advisor.*]]

9.   "Will the prosecution team please present to the court the probable cause statement, the elements of the charge(s) and the evidence you would bring against the defendant if this case went to trial."

FIGURE 11.2   Anchorage Youth Court No-Contest Script.

(continued)

section. This listing is detailed also, and it describes the nature of each sentencing option. In the process of considering the case, both sides examine the Anchorage Youth Court Sentencing Matrix, which includes a listing of both aggravating and mitigating factors. These are shown in Figure 11.3.

    Figure 11.3 not only lists aggravating and mitigating factors that may be considered by both sides, but it also lists a sentencing matrix for calculating

10. "Mr./Ms. __[defendant's last name]__, do you understand the case the prosecution has against you?" [*If the defendant says no, ask defense counsel what the defendant doesn't understand so that you can explain it.*]

11. "Since the defendant has pled no contest, we will go immediately into a sentencing hearing."
    a. "Will the prosecution team please present its sentencing recommendation, including any aggravating and mitigating factors, <u>any recommendation from the probation officer</u> and <u>any statement written by the victim</u>."
    b. "Will the defense team please present its sentencing recommendation. This includes information about the defendant, any mitigating factors and information from the probation officer reports."
    c. [*Ask any questions needed for clarification.*]

12. [*If a sentencing agreement has been presented,*
    a. "Mr./Ms. __[defendant's last name]__, do you understand the sentencing agreement?"
    b. "Did you voluntarily sign this agreement?"
    c. "Were any promises made to you which are not included in the agreement?"
    d. "Do you understand that, if we follow this agreement, you do <u>not</u> have a right to appeal the sentence?"]

13. "Mr./Ms. __[defendant's last name]__, at this time you have the right to address the court on your own behalf. This is purely optional and we will not hold it against you if you choose not to do so. Keep in mind that your words are the last thing we will hear before deliberating your sentence. Would you like to take advantage of this opportunity?" [*If you return to the courtroom for any reason prior to reading the sentence, repeat this step, allowing the defendant to have the last word.*]

14. "We will now adjourn to chambers for deliberation of sentence. Court is in recess."

15. [*The judges' decision must be unanimous. Completely fill out the sentencing order prior to returning to the courtroom. Give the sentence and reasons behind it. Be sure to state what aggravating and mitigating factors you accepted and why.*] "You have the right to immediately move for reconsideration of this sentence. You also have the right to file a written appeal within 5 working days. Please consult with your attorneys now and then us know whether you accept this sentence or seek immediate reconsideration of the sentence."

16. [*If the defendant moves for reconsideration, listen to the argument and give the prosecution a chance to respond. you do <u>not</u> have to allow unlimited responses to responses. You do <u>not</u> have to allow the defendant to address the court again. You do not have to adjourn to chambers to decide a motion for reconsideration, but you may and you should if your deliberation will take more than a minute or if you disagree among yourselves. <u>If you change the sentencing order, initial the changes.</u> A defendant <u>still</u> has the right to appeal even if he/she moves for reconsideration.*]

Hand the sentencing order to the clerk or bailiff before leaving the courtroom.

12/30/03   C:\MyDocuments\AYC Cases\Case File Forms\AYC-judge_script

FIGURE 11.2   Continued

community work service (CWS) hours. Every youth processed by AYC performs a certain number of CWSs determined by the seriousness of the offense and the presence or absence of aggravating and mitigating circumstances.

Figures 11.4 and 11.5, respectively, show the defense's and prosecution's sentencing recommendations. These recommendations take into account any and all aggravating and mitigating factors from both the defense's and prosecution's point of view.

It is not unusual for the defense and prosecution to disagree about which aggravating or mitigating factors should be counted or how much community

ANCHORAGE YOUTH COURT SENTENCING MATRIX

Class B felony and all firearm offenses	*48 CWS hours*
Class C felony	*40 CWS hours*
Class A misdemeanor	32 CWS hours
Class B misdemeanor	24 CWS hours
Theft of $15 or less	12 CWS hours

Add 5 hours for an official misdemeanor prior. Add 10 hours for an official felony prior.
Add 10% for each aggravating factor. Subtract 10% for each mitigating factor.
Matrix and the listed factors are suggested, not mandatory guidelines.

AGGRAVATING FACTORS

1. A person suffered physical injury as a result of defendant's conduct.
2. The defendant was the leader of a group which committed the crime.
3. The defendant possessed a dangerous instrument during the commission of the crime.
4. The defendant committed an assault offense against someone physically weaker.
5. The defendant's conduct created a risk of injury to three or more persons.
6. The defendant has committed an unreported a crime (misdemeanor or felony level crime) in the past
7. The offense has more that one victim. (A company, store or business only counts as one victim).
8. The conduct was the most serious type of offense within its class, approaching the next most serious class of offense. (**Example:** theft of $49 in merchandise, is the most serious in its class, since theft in the fourth degree is defined as theft of less that $50. The crime is close to the next class, theft in the third degree).
    If the crime is theft in the second degree, the AYC guidelines for determining "most serious" are from $500-$3000, regardless of the official definition of theft in the second degree.
9. The crime was committed against someone:
    within the defendant's household (someone who regularly resides in the house);
    who s/he is related to;
    who lives in the neighborhood; or
    to whom s/he owes a duty, has a special relationship with, or who has specifically entrusted him/her.
        (E.g. robbing a family the defendant baby-sits for).
10. The defendant targeted the victim because of the victim's race, religion or other discriminatory factor.
11. The defendant was 16 years or older at the time of the crime.
12. The defendant was accompanied by, or influenced, one or more persons younger than s/he during the c ommission of the crime.
13. If the crime is burglary or criminal trespass, the building was occupied.
14. The crime was committed at night (between sunset and sunrise) or, in the summer months, between the hours of 9 p.m. and 6 am.
15. The defendant used drugs and/or alcohol before committing the crime, or possessed drugs and/or alcohol, or committed the crime in order to buy drugs and/or alcohol, or if a theft crime, stole something which was illegal for the defendant to possess (e.g. cigarettes).

MITIGATING FACTORS

1. The defendant has no history of trouble, reported or unreported, with the authorities or police
2. The defendant fully admitted upon initial confrontation by police, parents, school, authorities or anyone the defendant could reasonably anticipate would promptly inform authorities.
3. The crime was principally committed by another person.
4. The defendant was accompanied, influenced or pressured by an older person to commit the crime.
5. The defendant was **less than** 15 years of age at the time of the crime.
6. In an assault case, the defendant was provoked by the victim.
7. The conduct was among the least serious in its class. (Example: theft of $52 in merchandise, is the least serious in its class, since theft in the third degree is defined as a theft between $50 and $500. The crime is close to the next lower class, theft in the fourth degree).
8. The defendant made restitution to a victim before the defendant knew the crime had been reported to authorities.
9. The defendant assisted authorities to discover the identity and role of others who participated in the crime.

Revised 7/10/2002

FIGURE 11.3   Anchorage Youth Court Sentencing Matrix.

(continued)

work service hours should be performed. Both sides can recommend that the defendant should write an essay of a specified length, make restitution, attend one or more classes as needed, and engage in other activities.

Probation Officer's Recommendation, Victim-Impact Statement, and Recommendation to Judges.   A juvenile probation officer may prepare the equivalent of a predispositional report for any particular juvenile and make a

HOW TO DETERMINE COMMUNITY WORK SERVICE HOURS

The following guideline explains how to determine community work service hours in each case. These are only <u>GUIDELINES</u>. The attorneys may deviate from the guidelines as the individual case requires.

AYC SENTENCING GUIDELINE PROCEDURES

The intent of the AYC guideline is to establish some degree of uniformity in sentencing offenders who commit similar crimes to similar sentences. However, sentencing must be an individualized process. No two crimes are ever the same. No two offenders are ever the same. The sentencing judges have the ultimate duty to balance the factors, the impact on the victim, the need to express community condemnation, and impose a fair and just sentence. Justice rarely can be achieved by rigid application of mathematical formulae. The intent of these guidelines is to **establish a range** within which sentencing judges may balance the variables that may be present in a case. The benchmark will be expressed in terms of hours of community work service.

A.   Duties of attorneys.
At the sentencing hearing, the prosecution and defense will present their sentencing recommendations to the court, including the amount of community work service (CWS) hours.

The prosecution team must also present to the judges the aggravating factors that it believes apply to the case. (The prosecution team may present mitigating factors that it finds, if it is advantageous to do so.) The defense team must present mitigating factors that it believes apply to the case. The written list of aggravating and mitigating factors is **not an exclusive list**. If the attorneys believe that factors which are not listed should be considered, they are free to bring them to the court's attention. The attorneys may present witnesses during the sentencing hearing, if they choose.

Finally, the prosecution and defense teams should present any McLaughlin Juvenile Intake probation officer recommendations   and argue the merits of the recommendations.   (Probation officer recommendations are not binding on the court).

B.   Court Procedures.
The sentencing court shall first determine the applicable benchmark sentence for the given crime by referring to the sentencing matrix. The court shall next determine the number of aggravating and mitigating factors only if they are supported by **clear and convincing evidence**.

1.   How To Determine Aggravating and Mitigating Factors.
The court shall determine the number of aggravating and mitigating factors which apply to the case by subtracting the mitigating factors from the aggravating factors. Should the result of this subtraction yield a net number of aggravating factors, the court may, but need not, aggravate the sentence by 10%, expressed in number of CWS hours, for each net aggravating factor. Should the result of subtraction yield a net number of mitigating factors, the court may, but need not, mitigate the sentence by 10% for each net mitigating factor. In no case should the sentence be adjusted by more than 50% from the benchmark sentence as a result of aggravating or mitigating factor adjustment.
<u>EXAMPLE:</u> Assume that a defendant is to be sentenced for a crime for which the benchmark is 40 CWS hours. The court finds three aggravating factors and one mitigating factor. The result is two net aggravating factors. The court may, but need not, aggravate the sentence by 20%. Therefore, the court may, but need not, sentence the defendant to a total of 48 hours. However, the precise sentence is within the discretion of the sentencing judges.
In each case, whether to aggravate or mitigate a sentence from the benchmark sentence is within the discretion of the sentencing judges.
In each case, the sentencing judges shall announce whether the sentencing court has found aggravating or mitigating factors, and what those factors are. In addition, the court shall announce

FIGURE 11.3   Continued

recommendation. A probation officer's recommendation may be given considerable weight, or it may be discounted. All of this information is considered by the judges, who ultimately decide the nature and amount of punishment to impose.

One or more victims are likely involved. Their opinions are solicited in written form. Figure 11.6 is a form letter sent to one or more victims of the whether the finding of such factors has provided the court with reason to depart from a benchmark sentence.

The judges may, but need not, subtract hours for classes or court viewing. No hours may be subtracted for an essay or letter of apology. **Full monetary restitution must be ordered in all appropriate cases.**

2.   More Than One Count.

In the event that the defendant is charged with more than one count, the judges should determine whether the counts are related to the same crime or two or more crimes. If the two counts are related to the same crime, 100% of the CWS hours for the most serious count is used, and only 50% of the CWS hours for the second and subsequent related counts are used. For example, if a person is charged with a class A misdemeanor and a class B misdemeanor from related crimes, the hours counted would be 32 for class A misdemeanor and class B misdemeanor only 12 (usually it is counted at 24 hours). If, however, the defendant is charged with two or more counts which are not related, 100% of the hours for each count is used. An example of related crimes would be a vehicle tampering and a theft from the same vehicle, or a burglary of a house and a theft from the same house. The crimes are not related, for example, if a person vandalized a vehicle and a few hours later shoplifted some candy.

3.   Upper Limit Of Hours.

The cap for actual CWS hours served is 150. In order for a defendant to be sentenced to more than 100 hours, special circumstances must be found. More than 100 hours should be reserved for the most serious cases.

4.   Theft Of $15 Or Less.

If the crime charged is a theft of $15 or less, the benchmark used is 12 CWS hours. Theft is defined as a charge of theft in the fourth degree or concealment of merchandise. If the 12 hour benchmark is used, the judges should assign a JASP class (or adult sentencing, arraignment, or jail tour if the defendant has already been to JASP), and an essay. If it is appropriate, the judges may sentence the defendant to write an apology letter to the defendant's family. With the 12 CWS hours, the mitigating factor of "least serious in the class" does **not** apply, since that factor was taken into account when the benchmark was reduced. Mitigators or aggravators are calculated as one hour each.

5.   Suspended Hours.

Judges may use suspended CWS hours in a sentence. The CWS hours suspended would **not** be served by the defendant, but would show the defendant what they could have been sentenced for the crime. The suspended CWS hours will be taken into consideration by the McLaughlin probation officer in the future if the defendant ever commits another crime. Actual hours to be served may not exceed the cap of 150.

6.   Optional Sentences.

Judges may sentence a defendant to an "optional" sentence if drug screening or counseling is appropriate. "Optional" means that the defendant has the choice whether to serve the whole amount of CWS hours or serve a lesser amount and present proof of counseling or drug screening. Counseling may only be requested or ordered upon the recommendation of a probation officer.

7.   Prior Record

If a defendant has an official prior record as recorded by Juvenile Intake, the community work service **base rate** will raise in the following manner.

One **misdemeanor** prior add **5** hours of community work service.
One **felony** prior add **10** hours of community work service.
Each prior recorded by Juvenile Intake will be added **separately**.

FIGURE 11.3   Continued

(continued)

defendant. This letter advises the victim(s) that the defendant has agreed to participate in AYC and will appear at some future date.

Information about the crime and damage or injuries to the victim(s) is solicited. Thus, victims have an opportunity to verbalize how the crime committed by the defendant affected them. An open-ended form is attached to the letter, and it is recommended that the material be returned to the AYC at the

Example: A defendant commits a class B misdemeanor, normally 24 hours of community work service. One prior misdemeanor reported by Juvenile Intake will increase the community work service hours by 5 hours. The <u>new</u> base rate is 29 hours.

Example: a defendant commits a class B misdemeanor, normally 24 hours of community work service. One prior felony reported by Juvenile Intake will increase the community work service hours by 10 hours. The <u>new</u> base rate is 34 hours.

The amount of community work service added for each aggravating or mitigating factor will be based on the total amount after the hours for a prior record have been added. The normal 10% for each aggravating and mitigating factor is figured on the **new** hour number.

<u>These guidelines DO NOT apply to informal priors</u>. For example: a mother may report that the defendant was suspended from school for fighting, or that the defendant was caught shoplifting but was let go with just a warning. Informal priors may **still** be counted as an aggravating factor separate from the prior record as recorded by Juvenile Intake.

Benchmark Community Work Service Hours	10%	20%	30%	40%
12	1.2	2.4	3.6	4.8
17	1.7	3.4	5.1	6.8
22	2.2	4.4	6.6	8.8
24	2.4	4.8	7.2	9.6
29	2.9	5.8	8.7	11.6
32	3.2	6.4	9.6	12.8
34	3.4	6.8	10.2	13.6
37	3.7	7.4	11.1	14.8
40	4	8	12	16
42	4.2	8.4	12.6	16.8
45	4.5	9	13.5	18
48	4.8	9.6	14.4	19.2
50	5	10	15	20
53	5.3	10.6	15.9	21.2
55	5.5	11	16.5	22
58	5.8	11.6	17.4	23.2
60	6	12	18	24

3/22/04

FIGURE 11.3   Continued

<u>Calculation</u>

1.   Community Work Service Hours:

    a.   Class of crime from charging document (A misd., etc.)   _____

    b.   Benchmark CWS hours for this class of crime: _____

    c.   Does the defendant have any formal prior charges on his/her record? If yes, add 5 CWS hours for each prior misdemeanor; 10 CWS hours for each prior felony. If no, add 0.   _____

    d.   Subtotal of CWS hours prior to mitigators   _____

    e.   Review the list of mitigators. How many apply?   _____
       List them:
       1. _____
       2. _____
       3. _____
       4. _____
       5. _____

    f.   To the CWS subtotal in subpart d, subtract 10% for each mitigator from the CWS subtotal in subpart d. The resulting number is the number of CWS hours you recommend. [DO NO FORGET: DEFENSE DOES <u>NOT</u> INCLUDE AGGRAVATORS.]   _____

2.   Essay. How old is the defendant? Is there any evidence that the defendant has learning disabilities? Ask for an essay between 1000 and 1500 words.   _____ wd essay

3.   Restitution. Is restitution necessary? If the amount is known, state it: _____. If the amount is not known, ask that it be determined by the sentencing coordinator.

4.   Classes. JASP / weapons class / anger management class / VOA drug & alcohol assessment, etc.   _____

5.   Other sentencing options. Do any other sentencing options make sense in this case? Jail tour, etc.   _____

FIGURE 11.4   Defense's Sentencing Recommendation.

(continued)

victim's earliest opportunity. Victims may indicate how the crime affected them; whether financial losses were sustained; and whether any other comments should be considered by AYC judges. This information is delivered to the AYC for their consideration.

Oral Arguments to the AYC.   Both the prosecution and defense make oral arguments that essentially reflect what their written recommendations to the court contain. Similar to criminal court plea bargain agreements, prosecutors must outline the factual basis for the crime admitted by the defendant. In short, they must show the AYC judges what they would have presented as evidence of defendant guilt. This portion of the proceeding is scripted to a degree and is illustrated in Figure 11.7.

<u>Recommendation to Judges</u>

1. We found _____ mitigators.

    a.   The mitigators are: 1. _____
                               2. _____
                               3. _____
                               4. _____
                               5. _____

    This results in a recommendation of _____ community work service hours.

2. We recommend a _____ word essay.

3. *[If restitution if needed]*, we recommend restitution [in the amount of $_____]/ an amount to be determined by the sentencing coordinator].

4. We recommend that the defendant attend _____ *[appropriate class such as JASP]* _____.

5. *[If any other sentencing recommendations, state them and the reason for the recommendation.]* _____
    _____
    _____

To summarize, we recommend: _____ CWS hours,
                                   a _____ word essay
                                   [restitution of $ _____/an amount to be determined by the sentencing coordinator]
                                   the _____ class

                                   _____
                                   _____

Thank you, your honors.

FIGURE 11.4   Continued

Defendant's Statement to the AYC.   Defendants are permitted to address the AYC judges on their own behalf. This is their right, and they may or may not choose to exercise it. It is important to note that like criminal defendants, youthful offenders may take this opportunity to accept responsibility for their crime(s), to show remorse, and to perhaps argue for leniency. However, AYC judges admonish them that their words are the last thing these judges will hear before they deliberate and determine the sentence. As an integral part of the defense prep document, defense counsels can advise their clients that they may want to tell judges that they are sorry; what they've done to make things right; how they are going to win back the trust of the people they have harmed; and what they will do differently if they are in a similar situation in the future.

Judicial Adjournment and Sentence Determination.   AYC judges retire to their chambers where they deliberate and eventually produce a sentencing document. The sentencing document is a unanimous decision by the judges outlining the sentencing order and the reasons for it. The aggravating and mitigating factors considered by the judges are listed, and a rationale is given for why

Calculation

1. Community Work Service Hours:

    a. Class of crime from charging document (A misd., etc.)   _____

    b. Benchmark CWS hours for this class of crime: _____

    c. Does the defendant have any formal prior charges
        on his/her record? If yes, add 5 CWS hours for each
        prior misdemeanor; 10 CWS hours for each prior
        felony. If no, add 0.   _____

    d. Subtotal of CWS hours prior to aggravators & mitigators   _____

    e. Review the list of aggravators. How many apply?   _____
        List them: 1. _____
                      2. _____
                      3. _____
                      4. _____
                      5. _____

    f. Review the list of mitigators. How many apply?   _____
        List them: 1. _____
                      2. _____
                      3. _____
                      4. _____
                      5. _____

    g. Subtract the number of mitigators from the number of   _____
        aggravators. If the result is a positive number, add 10%
        for each net aggravator to the CWS subtotal in subpart d.
        If the result is a negative number, subtract 10% for each
        net mitigator from the CWS subtotal in subpart d. The
        resulting number is the number of CWS hours you
        recommend.   _____

2. Essay. How old is the defendant? Is there any evidence that the defendant has learning
    disabilities? Ask for an essay between 500 and 1500 words.   _____ wd essay

3. Restitution. Is restitution necessary? If the amount is known, state it: _____.
    If the amount is not known, ask that it be determined by the sentencing coordinator.

4. Classes. JASP / weapons class / anger management class / VOA drug & alcohol
    assessment, etc.   _____

5. Other sentencing options. Do any other sentencing options make sense in this case?
    Jail tour, etc.   _____

3/22/04

FIGURE 11.5 Prosecution's Sentencing Recommendation.

these factors were considered important. At that time, they must advise the defendant that he or she has the right to a reconsideration of the sentence by filing a written appeal within 5 working days. They are then asked to consult with their attorneys and determine whether the sentence is accepted or whether they will file an appeal. In a limited number of cases, judges may revise their original sentencing recommendations, but even these reconsidered sentences may

Recommendation to Judges

1.   *If there is recommendation from the probation officer, read the recommendation to the judges. If there is a victim impact statement, read the victim impact statement to the judges. If there is neither a probation officer recommendation nor a victim impact statement, tell the judges:* "There is no recommendation from the probation officer and there is no victim impact statement."

2.   *If the defendant has a formal prior:* "The defendant has __number__ formal prior(s)." *State the charge and the date(s) of the offenses. Inform the judges whether the prior(s) is/are misdemeanors or felonies and how many hours you added for the prior(s).*

2.   We found _____ aggravators and _____ mitigators.

      a.   The aggravators are: 1. _____
                                       2. _____
                                       3. _____
                                     4. _____
                                     5. _____

      b.   The mitigators are: 1. _____
                                         2. _____
                                       3. _____
                                     4. _____
                                   5. _____

This results in a recommendation of _____ community work service hours. These community work service hours will allow the defendant to pay back his/her debt to society.

3.   We recommend a _____ word essay. The essay will allow the defendant to reflect on what he/she has learned through this experience.

4.   *[If restitution if needed]*, we recommend restitution [in the amount of $_____]/ an amount to be determined by the sentencing coordinator] to compensate the victim for _____

5.   We recommend that the defendant attend _____ *[appropriate class such as JASP]* _____ _____ so the defendant can learn _____ _____

6.   *[If any other sentencing recommendations, state them and the reason for the recommendation.]* _____ _____ _____

To summarize, we recommend: _____ CWS hours,
                                   a _____ word essay
                                   [restitution of $ _____/an amount to be determined by the sentencing coordinator]
                                   the _____ class
                                   _____
                                   _____

Thank you, your honors.

FIGURE 11.5   Continued

be appealed. In most cases, however, defendants agree to the AYC judicial sentencing terms.

The Successfulness of the AYC.   As is the case with many intervention programs, effectiveness is measured by recidivism. For the AYC, a low recidivism rate of 11 percent has been exhibited by those processed. This means that there is nearly a 90 percent success rate, and that most sentenced offenders will not

A̶Y̶C

Anchorage Youth Court
PO Box 102735
Anchorage, AK 99510
Phone: (907) 274-5986 • Fax: (907) 272-0491
Email: ayc@alaska.net

Dear (victim name),   February 1, 2005

APD Case # 04-__ was referred to McLaughlin Juvenile Intake regarding a case in which you were a victim. The juvenile defendant has agreed to attend Anchorage Youth Court for sentencing as a consequence of his/her crime.

The attached form is your opportunity to explain the effect of the crime to the Anchorage Youth Court judges who will sentence the defendant. You may fill out the form if you wish but are under no obligation to do so. If your property was damaged or you were injured and incurred medical bills as a result of this crime, please provide details on the form and attach any receipts. If full or partial restitution is ordered, you will be contacted when the money order is collected from the defendant.

Defendants usually appear in Anchorage Youth Court within a couple of weeks of the crime occurring. For the Anchorage Youth Court judges to consider your comments, we must receive the completed form by _____. You may bring the completed form to our office at 838 W. 4th Avenue, mail it to us as P.O. Box 102735, or fax it to us at 272-0491.

Anchorage Youth Court is a non-profit 501(c)(3) educational organization which trains youth in grades 7-12 to represent and judge their peers in actual criminal cases. Members volunteer to serve as prosecuting and defense attorneys, judges, clerks, bailiffs and jurors for juvenile offenders who have committed misdemeanors and minor felonies. 89% of the defendants who complete the program do not commit another crime.

The sentencing options used at Anchorage Youth Court include community work service, a mandatory essay, educational classes about specific crimes, viewing an adult sentencing hearing or jail tour, and restitution for property damage or medical bills for physical injury. Anchorage Youth Court holds the defendant himself/herself responsible for earning the money to pay for the Anchorage Youth Court service fee ($50), educational class fee(s) ($30-$125) and any restitution amount.

If you have any questions, please call me at 274-5986.

Sincerely,

_____

Denise Wike, AYC Legal Advisor

"A New Generation for Justice"

FIGURE 11.6   Letter and Victim Impact Statement.

commit future crimes. A majority of youth or teen courts in the United States have reported similar success results, which attests to their growing popularity.

Teen Court Variations

Several variations of teen courts have been described (Butts and Buck, 2002). Four courtroom models of teen courts include (1) adult judge; (2) youth judge; (3) peer jury; and (4) tribunal.

Anchorage Youth Court
PO Box 102735
Anchorage, AK. 99510
Phone: (907) 274-5986 • Fax: (907) 272-0491

Please return this form to Anchorage Youth Court by 3:00 p.m.

Anchorage Police Department Case # 04-   AYC Case # 04-

1. How did the crime affect you and/or your family?

2. Did you or your family have any financial loss because of this crime?
   If so, describe any loss not covered by insurance and attach copies of receipts for repairing or replacing the damaged items, or your medical bills.

3. Please add any other comments you want the judges to hear.

_____   _____
Signature   Date

If you wish to be contacted after the sentence is complete, please provide a phone number: _____

"A New Generation for Justice"

FIGURE 11.7 Evidence of Offense and Victim Impact.

Adult Judge Teen Court Model.   Adult judge teen courts use adult judges to preside over all actions. The judge is responsible for managing all courtroom dynamics. Generally a youth volunteer acting as the prosecutor presents each case against a juvenile to a jury comprised of one's peers. This is similar to a prosecutor in the adult system presenting a case against a defendant in a grand jury action. A juvenile defense counsel offers mitigating evidence, if any, which the jury may consider. The jury is permitted to ask the youthful defendant any question in an effort to determine why the offense was committed and any circumstances surrounding its occurrence. Subsequently, the jury deliberates and determines the most fitting punishment. This is a recommendation only. The suitability of the recommended punishment, which is most often some form of community service and/or victim compensation or restitution, is decided by the judge. About half of all teen courts in the United States use the adult judge model.

Youth Judge Model.   The youth judge variation of teen courts uses a juvenile judge instead of an adult judge. Youths are used as prosecutors and defense counsel as well. This teen court variation functions much like the adult judge teen court model. Again, a sentence is recommended by a jury, and the appropriateness of the sentence is determined by the juvenile judge. About a third of all teen courts use this model.

Peer Jury Model.   In the peer jury model, an adult judge presides, while a jury hears the case against the defendant. There are no youth prosecutors or defense counsels present. After hearing the case, which is usually determined through jury questioning of the defendant directly, the jury deliberates and decides the sentence, which the judge must approve.

Tribunal Model.   Under the tribunal model, one or more youths act as judges, while other youths are designated as prosecutors and defense counsels. The prosecution and defense present their side of the case against the youthful defendant to the judges, who subsequently deliberate and return with a sentence. All sentences may be appealed. Again, the sentences usually involve restitution or some form of victim compensation, community service, or a combination of punishments depending on the circumstances. This tribunal model is the one featured in the Anchorage Youth Court example earlier.

Each of these models is summarized below:

	Judge	**Youth Attorneys**	**Jury/Role of Jury**
Adult Judge Model	Adult	Yes	Recommend sentence
Youth Judge Model	Youth	Yes	Recommend sentence
Peer Jury Model	Adult	No	Questions defendant, recommends sentence
Tribunal	Youths (1–3)	Yes	No jury present

The Successfulness of Teen Courts

The growing popularity of teen courts as alternatives to formal juvenile court actions attests to their successfulness in sanctioning first-time low-risk youthful offenders (Patrick et al., 2004). Being judged by one's peers seems to be an effective method of imposing sanctions. Youths who function as judges, prosecutors, and defense counsels usually receive a certain number of hours of training to perform these important roles (Carrington and Schulenberg, 2004). In New York, for instance, an average of 16–20 hours of training is required of youth court juvenile officials (Butts and Buck, 2002). In some instances, written tests are administered following one's training. These are the equivalent of bar exams for youths, to ensure that they understand some basic or fundamental legal principles.

Several national youth court guidelines have been articulated. These guidelines have been developed for (1) program planning and community mobilization; (2) program staffing and funding; (3) legal issues; (4) identified respondent population and referral process; (5) volunteer recruitment and sentencing options; (6) volunteer training; (7) youth court operations and case management; and (8) program evaluation.

Recidivism rates of teen courts have not been studied consistently throughout all jurisdictions. However, available information suggests that the recidivism rates among youthful defendants who have gone through the teen court process are very low, less than 20 percent. One positive consequence that is reported in many jurisdictions is that processed youth emerge with a greater appreciation for the law, a greater understanding of it, and a greater respect for authority figures. They appear to be more law-abiding compared with youths adjudicated in more traditional ways through juvenile courts (Butts and Buck, 2002). A majority of states have adopted teen court models of one type or another, and many are in the process of considering legislation to establish them (Chapman, 2005).

States vary in terms of the eligibility age limits and types of offenses that youth courts may consider. Mostly first-offense, low-level misdemeanors or status offenses are included. More serious offenses are usually passed along to the juvenile court beyond the intake stage. The accountability of participating youths is heightened considerably inasmuch as youths must admit guilt before participating in teen courts (Butts and Buck, 2002). Furthermore, they must waive their confidentiality rights in most jurisdictions.

DAY REPORTING CENTERS

Goals and Functions of Day Reporting Centers

Some jurisdictions have day treatment program centers, following a day treatment model. **Day reporting centers** were established first in England in 1974 to provide intensive supervision for offenders who would otherwise be incarcerated (Roy, 2004). Offenders in England day treatment centers typically lived at home while remaining under the supervision of a correctional administrator. Inmates would either work or attend school, regularly participate in treatment programming, devote at least 4 hours a week to community service, and observe a strict curfew.

A variation on day treatment programs in England has been attempted in the United States for juvenile offenders (Craddock and Graham, 2001). The first American day reporting centers were established in Connecticut and Massachusetts in the mid-1980s. During that period, there were 13 day treatment centers operating. By 2004, there were over 400 day treatment centers in 36 states (Office of Juvenile Justice and Delinquency Prevention, 2005).

Day treatment programs are presently operated in most state jurisdictions throughout the United States (Illinois Department of Corrections, 2000). Both male and female clients benefit from day treatment services. Since the mid-1970s these programs have helped to expand the continuum of services available to at-risk and delinquent youths. These programs have been developed through the collaborative efforts of educators, judiciary, and social service professionals and provide an effective alternative to out-of-home placements. Many day treatment programs are operated on a year-round basis, offering community-based nonresidential services to at-risk and delinquent youths.

These centers offer offenders a variety of treatments and services. Offenders report to these centers frequently, usually once or twice a day, and treatment and services are provided on site in most instances. For more serious types of problems or illnesses, personnel at these centers will refer clients to the appropriate community services where they can receive necessary specialized treatments. The types of services provided by 60 percent or more of these day reporting centers include the acquisition of job-seeking skills, drug abuse education, group counseling, job placement services, education, drug treatment, life skills training, individual counseling, transitional housing, and recreation and leisure activities (Smith et al., 2004).

The goals of day treatment centers are to provide access to treatment and services, to reduce prison and jail overcrowding, protect the public, and build political support. Eligibility requirements are that offenders should be low-risk delinquents or criminals, with a good chance of succeeding while free in the community. Those with serious and violent prior records are usually excluded. Surveillance of day reporting center clients consists of on-site contacts and off-site contacts. On-site contacts average 18 hours per week, where clients must be at these day reporting centers for treatment and special programming during the most intensive phases. Off-site surveillance includes site visits to one's home or dwelling, telephonic contact, and visits to one's place of work or school. Although day reporting centers have failure rates among their clientele of about 50 percent, these failure rates are still better than traditional probation programs, where recidivism is as high as 65–70 percent (Illinois Department of Corrections, 2000).

Not all day treatment programs are operated for low-risk offenders. In some jurisdictions, such as Wisconsin, day reporting centers are operated as intermediate sanctions for more serious offenders (Craddock and Graham, 2001). Furthermore, some of these day treatment programs are offense-specific, such as day treatment for drug offenders. In Boston, for example, the Metropolitan Day Treatment Center has been operating since 1987 as a residential, transitional facility for inmates released early from local jails. Most of these inmates have had former drug problems and need special assistance in remaining drug free (McDevitt, Domino, and Baum, 1997). Also, some day reporting centers are operated almost exclusively for DWI offenders. In Arizona, for instance, a day reporting center functions to reduce recidivism among those convicted of driving while intoxicated (Jones and Lacey, 1999). Additionally, some day reporting centers operate almost exclusively for technical probation and parole violators.

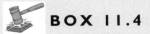 **BOX 11.4**

Al Parker
Juvenile Probation and Parole Officer, Division of Juvenile Corrections, Rhode Island Department of Children, Youth, and Families

Statistics:

B.A. (psychology), Barrington College; M.A. (rehabilitative counseling), Rhode Island College

Background and Experience

I have been working in probation and parole for the past 30 years. For the last 15 years I have been a supervisor of juvenile probation for the northern third of Rhode Island. Upon graduation from college, my first work experience was as a child care worker at Bradley Hospital, a facility for highly emotionally disturbed children. This was the most difficult job I ever performed. Two years later I took a job working for St. Mary's Home for Children. I worked with a group of mildly emotionally disturbed children. These two jobs gave me my initial insight into the needs and backgrounds of troubled youths.

My first work experience in corrections was with the Rhode Island Youth Service Bureau, a prevention program for predelinquent youth. After 2 years, it became clear to me that the program's future was tenuous at best, given the lack of appreciation and focus of the current administration. Later I took a job as an adult probation counselor. I did this work for 11 years, and I was the only probation counselor covering the 5th Division District Court most of that time. I was largely in charge of misdemeanants. The numbers were high and the level of my involvement with each case was necessarily low, although I developed a great deal of compassion for these youths. I was tough with them, insisting on their compliance with court orders, but I remained positive and supportive of their attempts to bring about positive changes in their lives.

By 1980 I conducted a study of all closed probation cases for that year. Of those placed on probation, 20 percent were rearrested; the average age was 27; 54 percent were unemployed; 78 percent had no skills; the average educational level was the 9th grade; the average weekly income was $62 (with 46 percent having no income); and 37 percent admitted to having substance abuse problems. It was more likely the case that 70 percent or more of these probationers had problems with substance abuse. With the number of relapses exceeding 20, I saw much of their problems with the court resembled a revolving door. Most of these probationers were trapped in poverty, and the only way out of this situation was to acquire an education and/or vocational skills for better employment possibilities.

In 1988 I accepted a juvenile probation officer position where I hoped to work with smaller caseloads and with clients where I could have a greater and more positive impact on their lives. Two years later I became Supervisor of Juvenile Probation in the same community where I had worked in adult probation. I would frequently remark to judges, "By the grace of God, if you or I had the same parents, would we be any different?" Typically, there were not many supportive or positive role models for these youths to emulate.

Juvenile Probation Population

My present supervisory work encompasses three of the state's five poverty areas. We use risk/needs tools to assess a youth's risk of recidivating. On the basis of our risk measures, these clients break down into low risk

(19 percent), medium risk (48 percent), high risk (19 percent), and intense risk (14 percent). Almost 70 percent of this caseload does not pose a significant danger of recidivating. Most of these clients are likely to complete their probation programs without incident. But the remaining 30 percent are the ones deserving of our greatest effort, time, and resources, in order to meet their needs and to ensure public safety. Only 16 percent of these youths come from two-parent families. About 14 percent are out-of-home placements, whereas 15 percent are previous runaways; 42 percent were suspended from school; 34 percent are special education clients; 15 percent have indicated substance abuse problems at the intake stage; 61 percent have some difficulty with their peers; 10 percent come from abusive families or where neglect charges have been brought against their parents; and 10 percent have been incarcerated during the most recent 3-year period.

In order to define the major forces driving their negative behavior, we conduct an in-depth social intake investigation. From these findings a triage begins. Needs areas are identified and plans are devised with appropriate services prescribed to deal with their specific issues. Referrals are made to local community vendors who provide needed services.

One of the most prevalent characteristics of these youths and their home environments is that only 16 percent come from two-parent families. Most of these youths are being reared in single-parent families, where one parent, usually the mother, is responsible for fulfilling all of their emotional and financial needs. These mothers struggle to meet these demands. Another problem is the lack of clear, fair, and consistent limits being set by parents. Often there are threats made but little consistency exists in the way of a follow-through. A clear understanding between right and wrong is nonexistent. As one result, these youths learn to have little or no respect for authority.

As probation counselors, we are viewed like the parents. We are often ignored by our clients, but soon after meeting with them, we draw lines in the sand and establish consequences. The youths often continue to ignore us with their negative behavior. But then we begin to apply sanctions that eventually get their attention and compliance. The most important sanction we have is to violate them and their program. This is done through a Violation of Probation petition. Our true goal is not to incarcerate these youths; rather, we want to get across the idea that negative behaviors have negative consequences and changes in behaviors must be made. We cannot just be hammers in their lives. We must engage them constructively so that they will learn to listen to us and consider alternative and positive behaviors that are rewarded. We change our strategies depending on the nature and personalities of our clients. We might act very differently with a youth who is passive-aggressive as opposed to a youth who is acting out. We must look beyond the immediate negative behaviors they're exhibiting and acknowledge their particular strengths. Usually, you will find that they lack a supportive environment from their families, who are often involved in criminal behavior themselves. Many parents are substance abusers and neglect their kids. They are definitely not positive role models. Thus, we, together with their teachers, are probably their only source of positive reinforcement as role models, offering them any meaningful support.

Therefore, there are numerous issues associated with their education. There are numerous youth who have special educational needs or are suspended or expelled from their schools. Often, schools don't want to accept these youths through reentry. Or if the youths are accepted back, they continue to be suspended. These repetitive suspensions demoralize school counselors and teachers. Juvenile probation counselors have a significant role to perform as advocates for these youth. It is not an easy job. There is a vicious cycle in effect. As these youths are suspended from school, they fail to acquire the education and training necessary to get good jobs and function well as adults. They are structuring themselves to fail in the future. Most of them do fail. Many of them turn to substance abuse or alcohol. We eventually supervise them and work

(continued)

with them in diverse ways to meet their needs. We do all we can to break the vicious cycle they are in and have helped to create.

How Do We Know When We Are Successful?

When you examine the criteria for success in our jobs, you look at recidivism figures. If youths continue to recidivate, they will eventually be placed in secure facilities. But placement in a secure facility may be a necessary step in their learning process. When they emerge from a correctional institution, they receive some support from juvenile parole counselors, who attempt to help them to become reintegrated into their communities. A great deal of effort goes into breaking the vicious cycle of poverty through helping them acquire an education or vocational training.

The counselors I have supervised function at a very high level and work hard to engage their clients in productive work. But some youths do not respond to their positive efforts and are incarcerated for a period. Following their incarceration, they return to us and find that our counselors continue to accept them and try to provide positive experiences for them. This action shows them that we care what happens to them. In many cases, I have seen previously incarcerated youths turn their lives around with the assistance of my juvenile probation counselors. It's a good feeling to know that we have had such a positive impact on at least some of their lives.

How Will I Know Whether This Is the Profession for Me?

My own clients gave me a picture one Christmas entitled "Passion." I keep it on a wall in front of my desk. It is a picture of a golf course with green and orange hues and an ocean sunset. It is a striking picture. Beneath the picture is written, "There are many things in life that will catch your eye, but only a few that will catch your heart. . . pursue those." That's a great litmus test for those who are considering going into this profession. Those who function at a high level in this job have both compassion for their clients and the passion to make a dif-

ference in youths' lives. There are no throwaway lives in their view. And they work hard to develop their craft of engaging clients to make a positive impact in their lives.

This profession will not bring you lots of accolades or cheers from the public. Your clients will not embrace you. Your effect on your clients may not be seen immediately or ever. Yet your role and the impact you have is very important. The following story illustrates this fact. This is the story of "John."

About 4 years ago I received a telephone call from someone who wanted to know if I knew an older probation counselor, William Kenney. He said he'd called the local police department, but nobody knew of Kenney. But the police department referred him to me. I knew William Kenney, who had worked with me as a probation counselor many years ago and had retired. He was always a real gentleman and a credit to his profession. His success was measured in part by the amount of respect he engendered from his clients. This person, John, wanted to contact Kenney, saying that Kenney had been his previous probation officer and that John wanted to thank him for the impact that Kenney had had in his life.

As you might suspect, this doesn't often occur in probation work. John explained that he had been put up for adoption by his biological mother when he was very young. He was adopted by a loving family and had a great life. However, his adoptive father had a heart attack and died. This was traumatic. John became lost with no clear direction in life. One morning when his mother went to work, he pretended that he was going to school. However, he went back into the home and drank some alcohol from a liquor cabinet. He got drunk and eventually got into trouble with police from a larceny he committed. Later he was adjudicated delinquent and placed on probation. He was undisciplined and unruly. But his probation officer, Kenney, pushed him to set goals. Kenney advised him to join the military, where he could find the discipline he needed in life. He went into the service and later used the G.I. Bill to get an education from Louisiana State University. Later he transferred to UCLA where he eventually graduated. He became a reporter for the *Los Angeles Times.* He went on to relate many of his accomplishments.

In order to assist me in helping to connect him with William Kenney, I asked him to fax me his credentials and other identifying information. When it arrived I was overwhelmed. On the front of the stationery, it said, "Ambassador of the United States of America." He had sent his resume. It went on to describe his positions as CEO and President of the Voice of America, CEO and President of King World Public Television, CEO and President of the Corporation of Public Broadcasters, a *Los Angeles Times* reporter, a television news anchor, a wire service reporter, and a bank vice president. He'd authored hundreds of magazine and newspaper articles, and had received numerous journalism awards, two Golden Mike awards, and three Emmys. In his references, he'd listed a Supreme Court Justice. One of his sons is presently a high-profile news personality for a major television network. And John wanted to thank his juvenile probation counselor for what he had done in his life.

I have often wondered, what would have happened to this man if Kenney had not intervened? And how many millions of people would have missed being affected and touched by his work and the work of his son? This man was on probation in 1956. And it took 45 years for his probation counselor to know of the profound influence he had had on John's life. I dropped off a copy of John's resume to Bill Kenney and he was as overwhelmed as I was. The power of one! It reminds me of the Chinese student standing in front of a seemingly unmovable tank, blocking that tank's travel, and ultimately altering its path. We all have the power to make a positive impact on the lives of others. We cannot always predict what our influence will be on those we supervise and assist. In my own case, I have learned some very important lessons from my own mentor, Mrs. Alfred "Billie" Gammon. Thank God for that Chinese student, the Bill Kenneys, and the Billie Gammons of this world who urge us to set goals that we initially think are beyond our grasp. The power of one! It begins with you.

Some Examples of Day Reporting Centers

The Moore County Day Reporting Center.   The Moore County (North Carolina) Day Reporting Center is a state-funded program that involves youths ages 7–16 who have been adjudicated delinquent or undisciplined. The juveniles come to the center every day after school hours to receive various services. Particularly targeted are youths who are nonviolent, who have a substance abuse history, and who need to develop living skills (Dubowitz, Pitts, and Black, 2004).

Participation in the day reporting center is approved, provided that clients meet the following eligibility requirements:

1. A Moore County resident
2. Not charged with a serious or violent crime
3. Have an approved residence
4. Have access to a telephone
5. Agree to abide by the conditions of the contract with the day reporting center
6. Meet the requirements for intermediate punishment under the Structured Sentencing Act of 1994.

Youths who come to the center acquire valuable employment skills; participate in general education development (GED) classes; undergo life skills training; participate in random drug testing; have access to a variety of mental health services, including group or individual counseling; participate in vocational rehabilitation programs; participate in health education courses; and undergo cognitive-behavioral interventions. The cognitive-behavioral interventions program is a 36-session program designed to change a person's thought processes to more law-abiding orientations. Numerous youths have been assisted by this day reporting program. The recidivism rate is quite low, less than 30 percent (Moore County Government, 2002).

The Englewood Evening Reporting Center.   Some day reporting centers are operated during evening hours. This is true of the Englewood Evening Reporting Center, operated between the hours of 4:00 P.M. and 8:00 P.M. weekdays in Englewood, Illinois, a Chicago suburb. The Englewood center is an alternative detention site to serve local juvenile offenders who would otherwise be ordered held in the Juvenile Temporary Detention Center. The center was opened in 1995. Subsequently, the center has received numerous state awards for the services it provides participating Illinois youth.

A part of the court's Juvenile Alternative Detention initiative, evening reporting centers such as the Englewood center are community-based facilities that operate through partnerships between sponsoring social service organizations and the court. Under the program, the juvenile court judge can order nonviolent juvenile offenders awaiting disposition on a warrant or probation violation to report to the evening reporting center as an alternative to being held in detention. Youths are required to report to the center between the hours of 4:00 P.M. and 8:00 P.M. daily. At these centers, they meet with professional staff who consist of educational specialists, recreational specialists, and three group workers who provide programs, activities, and workshops for a maximum of 25 youths. Transportation to and from the Englewood center and an evening meal are provided.

Day reporting centers offer many amenities for youths who participate in vocational and educational training as well as receive counseling and job placement assistance.

Chief Judge Donald P. O'Connell of the Cook County Court has said that "The purpose of the Circuit Court's support for establishing evening reporting centers is two-fold. First, we are helping at-risk kids avoid the possibility of being rearrested and sent to detention centers by getting them off the street and offering them positive, structured programming. We are able to do this through a low staff-to-client ratio of five to one, which ensures the personal attention simply not possible at the detention center." The expectation is that stronger, safer neighborhoods are fostered by reducing the likelihood of criminal activity, and by providing various jobs to community residents.

The average daily cost per client at the Englewood center is $33 per day, which is significantly less than the $100 per day it would cost to hold the juvenile in detention facilities. Funding is provided by the Cook County Court. The Englewood center is operated by Reach Out and Touch Someone, Inc. and Treatment Alternatives for Safer Communities (TASC), Aunt Martha's Youth Service Center, and the Circuit Court of Cook County Juvenile Department's Probation and Court Service Division. This particular evening reporting center is in a community that has one of the highest rates of juvenile arrests and referrals to detention (Cook County Court, 2002).

The Day Reporting Center for Juvenile Firearms Offenses. In McLean County, Illinois, a day reporting center is operated for juveniles who have possessed firearms during the commission of delinquent acts. It is called the Day Reporting Center for Juvenile Firearms Offenses. The purpose of this program is to provide the juvenile court with meaningful sanctions for juveniles possessing firearms. Three components of the program include mandatory public service, public health education addressing the risks of firearms and their possession, and psychological evaluation and appropriate referrals.

Community service is a mandatory component of the program. The purpose of community service is to assist the juvenile in learning how to assume responsibility for him- or herself and for the community in which he or she lives. Service to the local public will enable the youth to form attachments and commitments that promote civility and safety within the community. Mandatory public health education is designed to instill in the juvenile participants more complete understanding of the personal and public health risks associated with the unlawful use of firearms. And an exhaustive psychological evaluation is required prior to a juvenile's acceptance into the program. All files are meticulously maintained during the juvenile's participation. Referrals to psychological and/or counseling services are made where appropriate.

Each juvenile spends between one and 60 days in the program. Juveniles receive tutoring, especially those in need of assistance with schoolwork. Tutoring time can also be used for the completion of homework. The main goal of this portion of the program is to teach the juvenile how to use his or her study time effectively. Group therapy is also included. Group therapy includes presentations by informed authorities on positive peer relationships, drug education, handgun education, esteem building, and understanding of the juvenile court system. Individual therapy is sometimes conducted on a one-to-one basis, depending on the youth's needs. Basic life skills are imparted in an instructional component of the program, which includes personal hygiene, meal planning, preparation, and cleanup. The goal of this part of the program is to heighten the juvenile's awareness of him- or herself and family members. The program runs Monday through Friday, after normal school hours. Juveniles are expected to attend school and keep up with their studies.

There is strong parental input in this day reporting center. The parent's role in rehabilitating the juvenile is large, as they can reinforce the program's message. Parents are responsible for transporting their children to the program, and they have an opportunity to become integrated into the actual program. Program officials maintain daily case notes on each juvenile in the program. Attainment of and progress toward the juvenile's goals would also be noted. When the juvenile successfully completes the program, a full report of the juvenile's progress is made to the court. The cost of maintaining each child in the day reporting program is $50 per day, compared with $92 per day if the juvenile were placed in secure detention in the McLean County Juvenile Detention Center. The recidivism rate of youths who have successfully completed the program is about 25 percent (McLean County Court Services, 2002).

The Pre-Dispositional Supervision Program.   The Pre-Dispositional Supervision (PDS) Program is operated in Geary County, Kansas, through the local community corrections office. The original purpose of the program was to reduce juvenile crime and recidivism. Local law enforcement officials in Geary County believed that the juvenile crime rate was directly related to the high incidence of substance abuse among its youth. Therefore, early assessments and treatments of juveniles arrested for drug-related offenses were believed to be an effective means of decreasing the crime rate.

The predispositional nature of the program is such that juvenile court judges in Geary County are provided with additional information about a youth's suitability for probation prior to disposition. Prior to the program, juvenile court judges were often unaware of a particular juvenile offender's needs and other problems, including behavioral/emotional problems. The predispositional day reporting program operating in Geary County commenced operations in September 1996.

Eligible offenders are restricted to adjudicated youths who have not as yet been disposed (sentenced) by juvenile court judges. Prior to the dispositional hearing, the court can order the juvenile detained or released on bond. As a condition of the bond, the court can order the juvenile to predispositional supervision. The local community corrections department offers predispositional supervision. Juvenile offenders must report to the community corrections day reporting center for an assessment. The day reporting staff conducts a needs assessment as well as a substance abuse assessment, including a urinalysis. Services are provided as needed. A local provider supplies substance abuse assessment and treatment.

The juvenile offender must report to the day reporting center from 8:30 A.M. to 5:00 P.M. daily. During this time, the juvenile participates in academic sessions, job skills training, social skills training, anger management, conflict resolution, and community service for a maximum of 20 hours. All predispositional-ordered youth meet in one classroom and are supervised by two staff members. The staff may utilize electronic monitoring for noncompliant youths. Curfews are generally ordered from 6:00 P.M. to 6:00 A.M., and clients are randomly monitored by the community corrections surveillance officers.

The maximum capacity is 30 clients at any given time, based on staff and space limitations. The average length of supervision varies between 30 and 60 days. The staff consists of the director and a life skills instructor. The typical length of time clients remain in the predispositional program is 4 weeks, and the average cost of this experience is $155 per offender. The expenditures include staffing, alcohol and drug evaluations, urinalyses, electronic monitoring, books, and software. The successfulness of this program is reflected by the low 6 percent rate of recidivism among all clientele (Geary County Community Corrections, 2002).

ALTERNATIVE DISPUTE RESOLUTION

In most U.S. jurisdictions, youths are subject to **alternative dispute resolution (ADR)** or mediation to resolve school problems (Sinclair, 2005; Swanson, 2005). The mediation process allows people to resolve conflicts in a nonthreatening and nonpunitive atmosphere. Mediators are third-party neutrals who help people in a dispute to express their points of view, identify their needs, clarify issues, explore solutions, and negotiate satisfactory agreements (Deukmedjian, 2003; Lemon, 2001; London, 2003).

Mediation centers generally train students in different grade levels to serve as mediators to intervene in school-based disputes among students (Holterman, 2001). Several common components of these centers include: (1) a conflict resolution curriculum that can be taught either in academic or residential settings; (2) a mediation program that trains residents and staff to help resolve conflicts among themselves; and (3) a reintegration component involving parents and residents developing terms of daily living for when the residents return home. The rationale for such programming is that by giving students a model for positive expression and conflict resolution, it can teach them alternatives to violent and self-destructive behavior (Abramson, 2003). By using these skills within the institutional setting, students can be assisted to interact successfully with their peers and adults. A voluntary program, this mediation effort has seemingly reduced juvenile deviance in the jurisdiction. Thus, it may be viewed as an early intervention for preventing juvenile delinquency (Braithwaite, 2002; Holterman, 2001).

Victim–offender mediation is now established as an important and growing part of alternative dispute resolution (Lightfoot and Umbreit, 2004). For juveniles who have committed property offenses, it is often beneficial for them to face their victims and learn how they have been affected by their losses. It is believed that their accountability is heightened, and that they are more inclined to accept responsibility for whatever they have done (Gregorie, 2005).

Some victim–offender mediation sessions may involve all parties, including family members, the child's attorney, social service agencies, and others involved in the case. The goal is to work toward an agreement and a restitution plan that everyone approves. This agreement is submitted to the juvenile court judge for approval. It is believed that the family-centered nature of the mediation process provides the social support youths need for long-term behavioral change associated with the mediation. No single victim–offender mediation model is workable in all situations, however. Individual factors and circumstances must be considered in order to configure the best mediation plan (Lightfoot and Umbreit, 2004).

South Carolina has been operating juvenile arbitration programs since 1983. One such program is the Lexington County Juvenile Arbitration Program.

Some of the conditions of this program include waiving rights to legal representation and permitting impartial arbitrators to make a determination of guilt at the beginning of the hearing. The juvenile admits guilt and the hearing proceeds to a mutually satisfactory conclusion between the offender and victim. If the juvenile does not admit guilt, then the arbitration proceedings are terminated and the juvenile is sent to the juvenile court. Arbitrators are chosen from the community on the basis of their skill and expertise, and they are given over 20 hours of arbitration training prior to conducting arbitration sessions. During 1995–1996, for instance, 370 juveniles were referred to the Lexington County Juvenile Arbitration Program, with a success rate of 94 percent. Total hours of community service generated by these sessions were 4,666, while the restitution amount collected was $5,038. The future of juvenile arbitration in South Carolina is bright and is designed to promote successful prevention/intervention strategies for at-risk juvenile offenders (Alford, 1998:28, 34).

The prevailing correctional philosophy applied to juvenile corrections today as well as to programs for adults is punishment/control rather than treatment/rehabilitation (Sinclair, 2005). But like adults, not all juvenile offenders are the same according to their emotional needs, offense seriousness, educational levels, vocational skills, and honesty. Therefore, it is difficult for judges to prescribe meaningful, categorical punishments for aggregates of youthful offenders facing similar charges. Even if specific predictor variables could be identified, they are not always foolproof for effective program placement decision making (Gregorie, 2005).

SUMMARY

About half of all juveniles who enter the juvenile justice system annually are often low-risk first-time offenders. Many of these youths receive one or more nominal dispositions, which frequently consist of verbal warnings or reprimands from juvenile court judges. The use of nominal sanctions reduces a youth's interaction with the juvenile court and lessens the likelihood that they will reoffend. Nominal sanctions are usually used in cases where youths are especially young and more sensitive and responsive to verbal reprimands.

For many first-time offenders, judges may use diversion as a means of keeping these youths out of the formal trappings of the juvenile justice system. Diversion is a preadjudication agreement in the form of a deferred prosecution, whereby many youths will be required to obey several diversion program requirements, which often mandate that they attend school, stay out of trouble, avoid gang members and others likely to be delinquent, and otherwise be good citizens during the period of their diversion. Later these youths are brought back into court and their progress in their diversion program is evaluated. A prosecutorial recommendation usually follows to drop the charges and dismiss the case. One's record is often expunged as a result. A general outcome of diversion has been to reduce recidivism among these youths for whom harsher punishments may have been unsuitable. Not everyone qualifies for diversion, and judges must exercise their best judgment in determining who and who does not receive it. Diversion reduces the caseload of juvenile courts. At the same time, it increases the supervisory responsibilities of probation departments, who often oversee divertees. But it does seem to reduce recidivism of those placed on diversion in those jurisdictions where it is used. Thus it is regarded as a delinquency prevention measure. One potentially adverse consequence is that it may widen the net by including certain youths who would otherwise not be processed in any way by the juvenile court if the diversion option did not exist.

Several types of diversion programs exist. An early type of diversion program was in the form of a youth service bureau (YSB), which was community based. YSBs originally included referrals to a variety of community-based services, educational experiences, and individual and/or group counseling. Volunteers and others in their respective communities would contribute their efforts in assisting youths entering these YSBs. Different variations of YSBs include the cooperating agencies model, where a team of workers is formed from different organizations and agencies to assist youths with poor self-concepts or social adjustment problems. The community organization model involves community residents who work with youths strictly on a voluntary basis. Temporary shelters are provided for runaway youths, and those experiencing family problems or school difficulties may receive volunteer assistance. The citizen action model uses case conferencing to assist certain youths who are having difficulties in their lives. The street outreach model uses neighborhood centers in business areas to provide group and individual therapies for troubled youths. This program is especially designed for transient youths who have become separated from their families or guardians. The systems modification model is an integration of schools, churches, and other agencies that collaborate to provide necessary services to children in need.

In California, two diversion programs are the Youth Services/Diversion Program (YS/D) and the Community Services Program, Inc. (CSP, Inc). Both programs were established in the early 1990s to fulfill the goals of teaching youths responsibilities and reduce family dysfunctions. These goals were implemented through family counseling sessions and several types of self-help programs. Reduced recidivism rates were observed. Another program is the Diversion Plus Program (DPP). The DPP was established in Lexington, Kentucky, in 1991 and operated for about 2 years. One objective of the program was to reduce stigmatization of youths by helping them avoid interaction with juvenile courts. Those ages 11–18 who were charged with a status offense or a low-level delinquent offense were eligible for inclusion. Groups of 12 persons would meet for eight sessions during a 2-month period, usually for 3 hours at night. One-on-one counseling was also provided. Each session focused on a core curriculum topic emphasizing improving self-esteem, self-control, decision-making skills, career exploration, substance abuse prevention, recreation, and independent living skills. Nearly 100 participants were involved in the program, which had modest success rates.

Other diversion programs include the PINS Diversion Program, the See Our Side (SOS) Program, and the Community Board Program. The PINS program, located in New York, focused on status offenders, children in need of supervision, and cases where dismissals were contemplated. Youth counselors worked with these juveniles by providing individual and group counseling, and out-of-home placements were used to establish health social environments. The SOS program, located in Maryland, was described as a juvenile aversion program. Objectives included helping youths to see what their delinquent behaviors could lead to if continued and consisted of four 3-hour phases. Youths toured a prison, discussed their problems with selected inmates who related their own experiences, and engaged in discussions that described jails and prisons and the nature and types of incarceration. Recidivism rates were quite low among participants. Subsequently other jurisdictions established similar programs with equivalent success levels. The Community Board Program, based in San Francisco, is a civil mediation program. It uses volunteers who act as mediators between victims and juvenile offenders. Clients are first- and second-time low-risk property offenders who have caused damages to one's property and possessions. Youths are required to engage in discussions with their victims and learn about the damages they have caused as well as the consequences suffered by their victims. The program seemed less effective for particularly young youths, since it was often difficult for them to understand and empathize with their victims.

Overall, diversion programs seem to be effective at reducing recidivism among low-risk youths who have first-time encounters with the juvenile justice system. Adverse labeling is avoided, and youths acquire greater self-esteem, individual coping skills, and have better school adjustment following their diversion experiences. Courts are devising better classification methods annually to determine those youths most inclined to be responsive to involvement in diversion programs, and success rates among youths involved in these programs are improving. However, citizens regard diversion as an indication of leniency, which reinforces their impression of juvenile courts and the juvenile justice system generally. More credibility is associated with those diversion programs incorporating elements of restitution, heightened accountability, and community service, with some attention given to victims and the losses they have incurred.

Teen courts are used increasingly as an alternative to formal juvenile court action. Teen courts, peer courts, or youth courts consist of youths who function as prosecutors, defense counsels, and juries and judge other youths who have committed minor offenses. Teen courts, originally established in Washington and Oregon, have proliferated such that by 2005, there were over 1,000 teen courts operating in different U.S. jurisdictions. Teen courts are considered effective because one's peers impose punishments rather than adults. Although adult judges and lawyers oversee teen court proceedings, the dispositions imposed on teen offenders are imposed by one's peers. These punishments almost always involve some form of community service and restitution. Eventually, youths who have been on the receiving end of teen court justice, teen defendants, become members of future teen courts as jurors in helping others decide new cases and impose appropriate punishments. Teen court effectiveness at reducing recidivism among affected youths is especially strong. One example of a teen court is the Orange County Peer Court in California. Youths found guilty of their offenses are punished through required essay-writing, attending drug and alcohol counseling programs, attending school regularly, obeying curfews, interviews with victims, seeking employment, and avoiding negative peer relationships. The general purpose of teen courts is rehabilitation.

Another nominal option is the use of day reporting centers, which provide day treatments to youthful clients in their own neighborhoods. Juvenile offenders report to these centers once or twice a day, where they receive various treatments and assistance, including job placement services, individual counseling, life skills training, drug abuse education, education, drug treatment, and some amount of recreation. The goals of day reporting centers are reducing prison and jail overcrowding, protecting the public, providing youths access to necessary services, and building public support for their operations. Eligibility requirements are that youths should be low-risk offenders with a good chance of remaining delinquency-free. Youths in day reporting programs average 18 hours of face-to-face contact with officials weekly. Off-site surveillance includes home visits, telephonic contact, and visits at one's work or school.

Another option that avoids formal juvenile court processing is alternative dispute resolution, or ADR. ADR is a mediation program where victims and youthful offenders can meet and resolve their conflicts. Parental and community involvement in ADR programs improves their effectiveness. Not all youths are suited for victim–offender reconciliation encounters, but where youths have met with victims and worked out equitable solutions, which often involve restitution, results have been favorable. A similar ADR alternative is restorative justice, which focuses on the healing process for both youthful offenders and their victims. All participating parties must agree to the conditions worked out by mediators, and the program may be terminated at any time by either party. However, most ADR sessions are successful and result in reduced recidivism rates among participating youths.

QUESTIONS FOR REVIEW

1. How are nominal dispositions distinguished from conditional and custodial dispositions? What are some variations of nominal dispositions? How effective are they at reducing recidivism of disposed juveniles?

2. What is diversion? What are some of the eligibility requirements of prospective divertees?

3. What are some of the functions and dysfunctions of diversion?

4. What are youth service bureaus? What are four types of youth service bureaus? Have they been successful at accomplishing their goals? Why or why not?

5. How does the Diversion Plus Program compare with the See Our Side Program? What are the basic components of each?

6. What is meant by the PINS Diversion Program? Is it effective? Why or why not?

7. What are teen courts? What types of juvenile offenders are the best types of clients for teen courts? How do teen courts function? What are the success rates of teen courts for reducing youth recidivism?

8. What are day reporting centers? What are some of their goals and functions?

9. What are two examples of day reporting centers? What are some of their characteristics and which types of juveniles are served by them?

10. What is meant by alternative dispute resolution? Do you think it is an effective way of settling disputes between victims and youthful offenders? Why or why not?

INTERNET CONNECTIONS

CompassPoint Nonprofit Services
http://www.compasspoint.org/

DrugSense
http://www.drugsense.org/

Empowerment Resources
http://www.empowermentresources.com/

Georgia Alliance for Children
http://www.gac.org/

Idaho Youth Ranch
http://www.youthranch.org/

Institute for Global Communications
http://igc.org/iga/gateway/index.html

Nonprofit Consultants ONTAP
http://www.ontap.org/

Nonprofit GENIE
http://www.genie.org/

Redcliff Ascent Wilderness Treatment Program
http://www.redcliffascent.com/

Vera Institute of Justice
http://www.vera.org/

CHAPTER 12 | *Juvenile Probation and Community-Based Corrections*

Chapter Outline

Key Terms

American Correctional
   Association (ACA)
balanced approach
case supervision planning
caseloads
community corrections acts
community service
conditional probation
conditional probation
conventional model with
   geographic considerations
conventional model
creative sentencing
electronic monitoring signalling
   devices

electronic monitoring
fines
home confinement
home incarceration
house arrest
Intensive Aftercare Program
   (IAP)
intensive probation supervision
   (IPS)
intensive supervision program
juvenile intensive supervised
   probation (JISP)
juvenile probation camps (JPCs)
numbers game model
Ohio experience

recidivism rate
recidivists
restitution
Sexual Offender Treatment
   Program (SOT)
SpeakerID Program
special conditions of probation
specialized caseloads model
standard probation
tagging
unconditional probation
unconditional standard probation
victim compensation
victim–offender mediation

Chapter Objectives

As the result of reading this chapter, you will realize the following objectives:

1. Understand what is meant by juvenile probation and parole, as well as the extent to which these sanctions are used in juvenile cases.
2. Become familiar with several important types of probation programs for juveniles.
3. Learn about different dispositional options as conditions of probation, including restitution, fines, community service, and victim compensation.
4. Understand what is meant by home confinement and electronic monitoring for juveniles and how often such options are used in their conditional supervision.
5. Understand what is meant by intermediate punishments for juveniles.
6. Learn about several important intensive supervised probation programs for juveniles, including their weaknesses and strengths.

• *Stephen Barth, 16, was riding a metro bus in Seattle when police officers stopped and boarded the bus. As they approached Barth, he dropped the marijuana cigarette he was smoking on the bus floor and stuck the bag of weed he was carrying between the seats. Police moved rapidly toward him, drew out their handcuffs, and placed him under arrest. But it wasn't the marijuana they were after. Since the age of 14, Barth had become a regular cocaine user. He began committing burglaries and robberies to pay for his drug habit. He robbed a lot of people. His description was well known to police, and eventually he was identified by one of his former victims, who called police officers and reported his whereabouts. Barth later appeared before a juvenile court judge in King County. Barth was facing a possible 3-year term in the juvenile detention center. The judge knew Barth's offenses were serious, but at the same time, the judge knew that confinement in a secure facility may not be in Barth's best interests. Therefore, he adjudicated Barth delinquent and placed him on probation, but with several important conditions. Barth was required to wear an electronic tracking bracelet on his wrist, the size of a cigarette lighter, and be under house arrest for 60 days. He would have to at-*

tend school and be on time every day, be back home by 3:30 P.M., and be within range of his home telephone until the next morning, when the process would be repeated. If he wasn't within range of his telephone after 3:30, his noncompliance would be reported and someone would visit his home to investigate. Counselors and a probation officer dropped by random times to check up on him. His mother made regular reports to the juvenile probation office and could call juvenile authorities for help if Barth started hanging around with the wrong friends. Now Barth no longer wears the electronic bracelet. He's doing a year of probation. He does well in school. He is even thinking of eventually going to law school. His mother says, "People are proud of him. Stephen Barth says that being forced to go to school and come home after school instead of running wild gave him the time he needed for his studies." "School used to be a struggle. I hated it. Now it's a lot easier," Barth said. [*Source:* Adapted from Chris McGann, "Electronic Monitors Help Juvenile Offenders Get Back on Track." *Seattle Post-Intelligencer Reporter*, December 25, 2003.]

• *S.S. is a 15-year-old Corsicana, Texas, juvenile. He never knew his father. His mother lived with an unemployed man who was involved in drug trafficking and is now in prison. S.S. was sexually abused by homosexual friends and his mother. In his earlier years, S.S. had lived with his mother in Illinois. They moved many times. S.S. didn't do well in school. He was accused of vandalism at the apartment complex where his mother lived. Later he moved in with his grandmother and uncle in Corsicana. Shortly after arriving in Corsicana, he was put in charge of babysitting his 2-year-old cousin. The babysitting turned into a disaster. S.S. sexually assaulted the toddler and beat him on the head, causing a severe head injury requiring emergency surgery. S.S. was later declared delinquent for aggravated sexual assault. The juvenile court judge placed S.S. on probation for 2 years, with the first 9 months to be spent in a residential treatment facility for sex offenders. Following his sex offender treatment, S.S. was placed on probation in the supervision of his mother, who had returned to Texas. The probation officer believed that the mother could provide S.S. with suitable supervision, and that she could provide the necessary support S.S. needed. She also provided the court with the names of two juvenile justice centers near her home and a phone book listing the numbers of counselors she had called to inquire about sexual abuse and family counseling.*

• *In another development, the Texas Youth Commission has implemented a juvenile intensive supervision program (ISP) called Project Spotlight. Project Spotlight is a program targeted toward young offenders who possess the highest risk factors and have committed crimes against a person, gun-related offenses, or are failing under supervision. The program has operated since 1999 and has served over 400 offenders in seven counties. The program uses teams of probation and law enforcement officers to provide community supervision between 3:00–11:00 P.M. Participants are required to receive three to five face-to-face contacts per week. ISPs such as Project Spotlight provide services as an intermediate sanctions alternative to youths who require a higher level of control than youth receiving standard probation services. ISP requires strict and frequent reporting to a probation officer who carries a limited caseload and must include additional conditions for rehabilitation or deterrence, such as community service, restitution, and curfews.* [*Sources:* Adapted from *In the Matter of S.S.*, No. 10-03-00270-CV, Tex.App., 2004; adapted from the Texas Youth Commission, *TJPC/TYC Coordinated Strategic Plan 2004–2005*. Austin, TX: Austin Youth Commission, August 2004.]

• *Brandon Robinson, a 16-year-old Penn Hills, Pennsylvania, youth, was charged in early June 2004 with criminal homicide in the death of a 14-year-old girl, Karis Adams. Robinson is alleged to have been riding in a car with another person, Eugene Cooper, 20, when shots were fired into another car in which Adams was riding. Adams died of head wounds. Initially Robinson was charged as an adult, but his attorney had the case moved back to juvenile court. He was placed on house arrest and required to wear an electronic bracelet in order that his movements could be monitored and until his juvenile court adjudicatory hearing could be held. According to the juvenile court, in cases like this in which the charges are serious but not serious enough to hold the youth in Shuman Juvenile Detention Center, house arrest is imposed and supervised by a juvenile probation officer.*

• In late January 2005 a 13-year-old girl in Seattle, Washington, was charged with killing a baby. Subsequently she was released into the custody of her parents pending an adjudicatory hearing and placed under house arrest. She can eat what she wants, watch television, and live, more or less, like any other teenager. She has been on good behavior for several months while her case is pending.

• Down the street lives Curtis, also 13 years old. In Fall 2004 Curtis burglarized a home, stole a Sony PlayStation, poured bleach across the carpet, and generally vandalized the place. Later, Curtis ran away from home between court dates and stole money from a collection jar because he was hungry. Subsequently Curtis was ordered by the juvenile court to wear an electronic monitoring device and required to remain at his home with a telephone nearby. For nearly 2 months, Curtis has been behaving well.

• In Chicago six evening reporting centers are being operated by the Westside Association. These centers provide several community-based alternatives for minors who would otherwise be placed in detention for probation violations. These centers are operated between the hours of 3:00 P.M. and 9:00 P.M., hours when working parents are not at home and kids are most likely to get into trouble. Offering a range of educational and recreational opportunities, these centers offer transportation, an evening meal, and informal counseling. Meaningful relationships are established between different youths and select adults who really care about them. Some 10,000 youths have been served by these evening reporting centers. [Sources: Adapted from the Associated Press, "Penn Hills Youth Charged in Shooting Death of Girl Was Awaiting Trial: Teen Was Confined at Home," June 4, 2004; adapted from Claudia Rowe, "Home Detention Slashes Jailings: Electronic Monitoring of Kids Saves $1 Million Yearly." Seattle Post-Intelligencer Reporter, January 28, 2005; adapted from The Annie E. Casey Foundation, Detention Alternative "Jewels." Baltimore, 2005.]

• On December 11, 2002, E.T., a 16-year-old Texas youth was granted a deferred adjudication for being a minor in possession of tobacco and for failing to identify himself. He was ordered to pay a fine, perform 12 hours of community service, attend school counseling, and attend a preparatory class for the high school equivalency examination. On April 2, 2003, a justice of the peace found that E.T. had violated the court order and sent E.T. to juvenile court for contempt of court. On August 13, 2003, E.T. was charged with delinquent conduct in three counts of contempt of court. He was placed on probation for 18 months and placed him outside of his home in the custody of his probation officer. The court said that placement with the probation officer was in the best interests of E.T.'s health, safety, morals, and education. The judge also declared that his own home could not provide the quality of care and level of support and supervision that he needs to meet the conditions of his probation. [Source: Adapted from In the Matter of E.T., No. 04-03-00796-CV, Tex.App., 2004].

INTRODUCTION

Despite a youth's extensive juvenile record, juvenile court judges may sometimes believe that a probationary disposition is warranted. An extensive probation term, such as that imposed on Stephen Barth in the first scenario above, may be warranted based on the particular facts of the case. One's situation or personal circumstances may suggest that probation as a punishment would better serve one's best interests rather than incarceration in a secure facility. Some youths may require more intensive supervision and monitoring than others. Certain youthful sex offenders may be ordered to attend sex therapy courses and individual or group counseling. Often these youths have been the victims of sexual or physical abuse themselves. Yet other youths who have committed or participated in murders may be placed in their communities subject to certain behavioral conditions, such as house arrest and/or electronic monitoring. Many youths must comply with other behavioral requirements of their probationary sentences, such as having to attend school and earn a G.E.D., participate in educational/vocational programming, take anger management courses, receive counseling or other forms of therapy, make restitution to victims, perform community service, or engage in other constructive activities.

This chapter describes juvenile probation and a variety of other community-based programs. Probation is the most frequently used sanction by juvenile court judges. Over two-thirds of all youths adjudicated delinquent are placed on probation annually. As was seen in the chapter opening scenarios, probation is extended as a dispositional option to all types of offenders, regardless of the seriousness of their offending. Juvenile court judges have considerable discretion in deciding who or who does not receive probation. Such is the individualized nature of juvenile court decision making.

The chapter opens with a definition of standard probation. All probation is conditional, although there are several common features among most juvenile court jurisdictions that describe standard probation. These features are described. Next, standard probation with conditions is discussed. Juvenile courts are empowered to include additional requirements in probation orders. Often these additional requirements include community service, restitution, home confinement, and electronic monitoring, or youths may be required to engage in other activities, including school attendance, vocational/educational training, or counseling. Several advantages and disadvantages of probation are described, including how the successfulness of different types of probation programs is measured.

The next section describes juvenile intensive supervised probation, or JISP. JISP is an intermediate punishment. Intermediate punishments range between standard probation and secure confinement. The goals of intermediate punishment programs, all of which are community based, are listed and described. Not all juveniles are eligible for participation in JISPs. Therefore, this section describes the eligibility requirements for those chosen to participate in such community programming. Several JISP programs are featured, including their specific characteristics and behavioral requirements expected of participating clients. The strengths and weaknesses of JISP programs are also discussed.

Supervising youths more or less intensely are juvenile probation officers or POs. These POs are assigned different caseloads, depending on their jurisdiction and the total number of juvenile offenders. Increasing numbers of juvenile probation departments are adopting the balanced approach, which seeks to ensure public safety, heighten offender accountability, and individualize one's needs. Juvenile POs are more effective with particular clients to the extent that they can relate with them more closely and learn about their particular needs. The relation between juvenile POs and their clients is explored.

Enabling legislation in most jurisdictions has established various community corrections agencies and services over the years. Through community corrections acts in different cities and counties, a wide variety of services has been established to meet offender needs more effectively. Different types of community corrections initiatives are highlighted, together with their purposes, goals, strengths, weaknesses, and effectiveness.

The next section of this chapter examines electronic monitoring programs and home confinement. As our technology has improved, so has our ability to supervise offenders more effectively in different ways. Electronic monitoring has become a commonly used supervisory tool in most adult and juvenile probation and parole departments since the mid-1980s. Different types of electronic monitoring programs exist, and these programs are defined and explained. Frequently used in collaboration with electronic monitoring is home confinement or house arrest. Together, these monitoring and supervisory methods have been very effective in verifying an offender's whereabouts at particular times. The functions, advantages, disadvantages, and usefulness of both electronic monitoring and home confinement are examined and discussed.

The chapter concludes with an examination of various conditions that frequently accompany probation programs of any kind. These conditions include fines, victim compensation or restitution, victim–offender mediation, and community service. Each condition is imposed on a case-by-case basis, depending on the nature of one's offense and suitability for such punishments and behavioral requirements. All of these conditions are intended to heighten offender accountability and ensure that the ends of juvenile justice are fulfilled. Evaluations of these sanctions will be made in terms of offender recidivism and other criteria.

STANDARD PROBATION FOR JUVENILES

Standard Probation Defined

Standard juvenile probation is fairly simple to understand and is considered a routine disposition for most juvenile court judges. Of all dispositional options available to juvenile court judges, standard probation is the one most frequently used. The first probation law was enacted in Massachusetts in 1878, although probation was used much earlier. John Augustus invented probation in Boston in 1841. **Standard probation** is either a conditional or unconditional nonincarcerative disposition for a specified period following an adjudication of delinquency (Steiner, Roberts, and Hemmens, 2003).

There are several types of standard probation programs. Like their diversion program counterparts, probation programs for juveniles are either **unconditional probation** or **conditional probation.** Again, there are many similarities between probation programs devised for adults and those structured for juvenile offenders (Campbell and Schmidt, 2000). **Unconditional standard probation,** another term for unconditional probation, basically involves complete freedom of movement for juveniles within their communities, perhaps accompanied by periodic reports by telephone or mail with a probation officer (PO) or the probation department. Because a PO's caseload is often large, with several hundred juvenile clients who must be managed, individualized attention cannot be given to most juveniles on standard probation. The period of unsupervised probation varies among jurisdictions depending on offense seriousness and other circumstances (Shearer, 2002).

Conditional probation programs may include optional conditions and program requirements, such as performing a certain number of hours of public or community service, providing restitution to victims, payment of fines, employment, and/or participation in specific vocational, educational, or therapeutic programs. It is crucial to any probation program that an effective classification system is in place so that juvenile court judges can dispose offenders accordingly. It is common practice for conditional probation programs to contain special conditions and provisions that address different youth needs. These special conditions are usually added by the juvenile court judge on the basis of information provided by juvenile POs (Knupfer, 2001).

The terms of standard probation are outlined in Figure 12.1. Although these terms may be accompanied by special conditions, known as **special conditions of probation,** more often than not, no special conditions are attached. Thus, youths disposed to standard probation experience little change in their social routines. Whenever special conditions of probation are attached, they usually mean additional work for probation officers. Some of these conditions might include medical treatments for drug or alcohol dependencies, individual or group therapy or counseling, or participation in a driver's safety course. In some instances involving theft, burglary, or vandalism, restitution provisions may be included, where youths must repay victims for their financial losses. Most standard probation programs in the United States require little, if any, direct contact with the probation office. Logistically, this works out well for probation officers, who are frequently overworked and have enormous client caseloads of 300 or more youths. However, greater caseloads means less individualized attention devoted to youths by POs, and some of these youths require more supervision than others while on standard probation. Item 12 of the juvenile probation form used by Orange County, California, as shown in Figure 12.1, specifies which, if any, special conditions apply for particular juveniles.

Community service orders are increasingly used, although in some states, juvenile probation departments have found it difficult to find personnel to supervise youthful probationers (Bond-Maupin, Maupin, and Leisenring, 2002). For instance, a North Dakota delinquent was ordered to perform 200 hours of community service. The community had about 500 residents, and the work ordered involved park maintenance and general cleanup duties. However, the youth never performed any of this community service, since the probation department did not have the money to pay a juvenile probation officer to monitor the youth for the full 200 hours. Despite these occasional limitations, most probation program conditions today are geared toward heightening offender accountability by having him or her do something constructive (Decker, 2000). In a growing number of jurisdictions, drug courts are being established to deal more effectively with youthful substance abusers (Rodriguez and Webb, 2004).

Parental Responsibilities for a Juvenile's Delinquent Conduct. In more than a few instances, parents of juveniles can be held financially liable for the actions of their delinquent children. For instance, D.D.H. was a Texas juvenile who committed burglary and larceny (*Matter of D.D.H.,* 2004). Following

INSTRUCTIONS:
1. Original to Probation Files
2. Pink to Parents
3. Blue to Minor
4. Goldenrod to Division Officer

**ORANGE COUNTY PROBATION DEPARTMENT
INFORMAL PROBATION AGREEMENT**

The authority for undertaking a plan of informal probation which may include the use of a crisis resolution home or shelter-care facility is contained in Section 654 of the Welfare and Institutions Code, which is printed in full on the reverse side of this form. Before signing this agreement, please read it and resolve any questions about it with the deputy probation officer.

Minor's Initials   **GENERAL RULES AND REQUIREMENTS**

_____ 1. You are to report in person and submit written reports to your probation officer as directed.

_____ 2. You are to obey all laws, including traffic rules and regulations. You are not to operate a motor vehicle in any street or highway until properly licensed and insured. You are to report to your probation officer any arrests or law violations immediately.

_____ 3. You are to obey the curfew law of the city or county in which you live or any special curfew imposed by the Court or the probation officer, specifically: _____

_____ 4. You are not to leave the State of California or change your residence without first getting permission from your probation officer. Prior to change of residence, you are to notify your probation officer of the new address. You are not to live with anyone except your parents or approved guardian without specific permission of your probation officer.

_____ 5. You are to attend school every day, every class, as prescribed by law, and obey all school regulations. Suspension from school and/or truancies/tardiness could result in action being taken by the Probation Department. You are to notify your probation officer by 10:00 a.m. on any school day that you are absent from school. If you are home from school because of illness or suspension, you are not to leave your home that day or night except to keep a doctor's appointment.

_____ 6. You are not to use or possess any intoxicants, alcohol, narcotics, other controlled substances, related paraphernalia, poisons, or illegal drugs; including marijuana. You are not to be with anyone who is using or possessing any illegal intoxicants, narcotics or drugs. Do not inhale or attempt to inhale or consume any substance of any type or nature, such as paint, glue, plant material or any aerosol product. You are not to inject anything into your body unless directed so by a medical doctor.

_____ 7. You are not to frequent any places of business disapproved by your probation officer, parents or guardians, specifically: _____

_____ 8. You are not to associate with individuals disapproved by your probation officer, parents or guardians, specifically: ____

_____ 9. You may be required to participate in any program outlined in Section 654 W&I Code.

_____ 10. You are to seek and maintain counseling if and as directed by the probation officer.

_____ 11. You are not to have any weapons of any description, including firearms, numchucks or martial arts weaponry, and knives of any kind, in your possession while you are on probation, or involve self in activities in which weapons are used, i.e., hunting, target shooting.

_____ 12. You are ordered to obey the following additional terms of probation:

Probation supervision will expire on _____ unless you fail to abide by the above terms and conditions of your probation resulting in court action.

I have personally initialed, read and understand the above rules and requirements of informal probation that apply in my particular case as explained to me by the probation officer. I understand that my failure to comply with the initialed items could result in the petition, that is pending in my case, being filed with the District Attorney.

SIGNED: _____ DATE: _____
(minor)

SIGNED: _____ DATE: _____
(parent)

SIGNED: _____ DATE: _____
(parent)

MICHAEL SHUMACHER
Chief Probation Officer

BY: _____ DATE: _____
(Deputy Probation Officer)

FIGURE 12.1 Orange County Probation Department Informal Probation Agreement.

D.D.H.'s apprehension and adjudication, the court determined that the damages accruing to the victim amount to $5,400, which included $4,500 to repair the property at the point where the burglary occurred, as well as $900 for unrecovered stolen property resulting from the burglary. The juvenile court judge ordered D.D.H.'s parents to pay $5,000 restitution to the victim for their son's delinquent acts as a special condition of the youth's probation orders. Although the parents appealed, a Texas appellate court upheld the juvenile court judge's restitution orders for the parents of the youth.

Juvenile Probationer Recidivism. In view of the fact that little or no monitoring of juvenile conduct exists in many state probation agencies, standard probation has fairly high rates of recidivism, ranging from 40 to 75 percent. Even certain youth camps operated in various California counties, where some degree of supervision over youths exists, have reported recidivism rates as high as 76 percent among their youthful clientele (Palmer, 1994). Therefore, it is often difficult to forecast which juveniles will have the greatest likelihood of reoffending, regardless of the program we are examining (Steen, 2001).

Ron Corbett (2000:28) has recommended the following steps toward a reformed type of juvenile probation:

1. Let research drive policy. All too often, the field becomes enthralled in the latest fad and rushes to adopt it. Any and all new initiatives should include an evaluation component. Smart programs should be developed, especially programs that emphasize restitution.

2. Emphasize early intervention. Interventions occurring in one's early years are far more effective than those attempted when one is in his or her midteen years.

3. Emphasize the paying of just debts. Just deserts and justice should be emphasized in part to change the coddling image persons presently have of juvenile courts. Restitution and community service do much to heighten offender accountability, and they can easily be integrated into one's probation or parole program.

4. Make probation character building. Many delinquents lack character, or good habits of thought and action, as well as self-control. Programs that include psychoeducational strategies are better at character-building than those that are strictly punishment-centered.

5. Prioritize violence prevention. Juvenile probation must focus on efforts to suppress violent behavior. Programs that are educational in nature are more profitable in the long run compared with punishment-centered programs. These educational programs are geared to enable youths to learn how to cope more effectively with their environment. Such programs would include anger management training, acquiring skills (social and emotional), improving moral reasoning, and instilling heightened self-esteem (Corbett, 2000:28–29; Mayzer, Gray, and Maxwell, 2004).

Mission-Driven Probation versus Outcome-Focused Probation. More effective juvenile probation appears to be both mission-driven and outcome-focused (Texas Juvenile Probation Commission, 2002). Good juvenile probation is outcome-focused. Both for individual offenders and for entire juvenile probation officer caseloads, outcome-focused probation systematically measures the tangible results of its interventions, compares those results to its goals, and makes itself publicly accountable for any differences. Organizations tend to become whatever they measure. Departments must measure more than their failures (recidivism) and the sanctions they have imposed (Taxman, 2005). Outcome measures assess whether goals have been achieved. They provide evidence of the degree to which probation supervision goals have or have not been achieved, in essence measuring the department's performance in meeting system goals. Long-term outcomes measure the degree to which probation supervision has impacted youthful offenders after their release, in terms of changing their thinking, behaviors, and attitudes (Parker, 2005).

Mission-driven juvenile probation is that the work of probation must be directed at achieving clearly articulated and widely shared goals (Brown and Ygnacio, 2002). Getting there requires a commitment to a strategic planning or focus group process that gives a representative cross-section of staff a chance to define their values about the juvenile justice system and juvenile probation in particular, and to translate them into action and results. Such an effort will increase staff buy-in and provide a basis for continuous feedback, evaluation, and improvement at the policy program and individual employee levels. Mission statements provide an organizational compass that points in the direction of an agreed-upon destination, and they are central to the operations and activities of any organization. What does juvenile probation stand for in the community? What is it attempting to accomplish? Ultimately, mission statements should be broken down into individual goals that are directed at protecting the public, holding the juvenile accountable for repairing harm caused to victims and the community, and engaging offenders in rehabilitative activities designed to address their most pressing problems and needs (Torbet and Griffin, 2002:22–23).

The Youth-to-Victim Restitution Project

One factor associated with significant reductions in recidivism is restitution. Programs that use restitution and enforce it seem to have lower recidivism rates associated with their youthful clientele. This is because offenders are required to repay victims for damages they inflict and take some responsibility for their actions. Restitution is a powerful deterrent to further offending. At least a financial connection is made between what the youthful offenders did and how

Juvenile probation offices are places where youths can report weekly or monthly and keep probation officers apprised of their progress.

much it will cost to compensate victims for their losses. Therefore, these tangible punishments were considered most effective as delinquency deterrents (Taxman, 2005).

Juvenile Probation Camps

In the early 1980s, California experimented with several types of **juvenile probation camps (JPCs)** (Thomas, Holzer, and Wall, 2002; Watson et al., 2003). These camps were county-operated and included physical activities, community contacts, and academic training. These nonincarcerative camps were designed as dispositional alternatives to secure custody for youthful offenders. Eligibility requirements included first-offender status and nonviolent behaviors. Counselors worked with youth who were carefully screened before entering the program. Groups of youths were deliberately small in order to maximize individualized attention for each youth. Older juveniles who participated in these probation camps had lower rates of recidivism compared with younger youths. Overall, the camps were viewed as successful in minimizing recidivism and maximizing rehabilitation of participants. One reason for the lower rates of recidivism among youthful clients was greater direct supervision by camp personnel. This circumstance is not unlike that found in communities where various methods of formal social control, including police and probation officer surveillance, are employed to supervise juvenile probationers and parolees (Altschuler and Armstrong, 2001; Thomas, Holzer, and Wall, 2002).

The Intensive Aftercare Program

Between 1988 and 1990, the **Intensive Aftercare Program (IAP)** was designed in Philadelphia and targeted serious youthful offenders (Altschuler and Armstrong, 2001). A sample of 46 youths committed to the Bensalem Youth Development Center was compared with a control group of 46 youths who received traditional aftercare probation services. While the IAP participants exhibited lower rates of recidivism compared with those subject to conventional aftercare probation, the differences were not significant. It was reported, however, that IAP officers believed that their interventions with IAP youth were both rapid and positive. Thus, some officials believed that they were able to assist some of these IAP participants from incurring subsequent rearrests. The successfulness of IAP in any particular jurisdiction often depends on the nature and quality of supervision received by clients (Meisel, 2001).

The Sexual Offender Treatment Program

Not all specialized programs for juvenile probationers are successful. For example, an assessment was made of the **Sexual Offender Treatment Program (SOT)** established by a juvenile probation department of a large Midwestern U.S. metropolitan county in January 1988 (Lab, Shields, and Schondel, 1993). The program consisted of 20 peer-group meetings with a psychosocioeducational intervention focus, supplemented by individual family counseling sessions with youths who had been adjudicated delinquent for assorted sex offenses. Subsequently, an experimental program was conducted for 46 youths referred to the SOT program and compared with a control group of 109 youths assigned to nonsexually specific interventions during the same period. Data sources included juvenile court and program records. Essentially, youths handled by the SOT program fared no better than youths processed through normal, nonoffense-specific programming. Thus, these researchers concluded that simply knowing one's symptoms and problems and designing specific interventions for those problems are not always workable. Additional study is needed to identify appropriate treatment factors that might make a difference in reducing their recidivism rates for sexual offending (Craig, Browne, and Stringer, 2003; Parton and Day, 2002; Ward, Laws, and Hudson, 2003).

THE SUCCESSFULNESS OF STANDARD JUVENILE PROBATION

The successfulness of standard juvenile probation as well as other probation and parole programs is measured according to the **recidivism rate** accompanying these program alternatives. Recidivism is measured various ways, including rearrests, reconvictions, new adjudications, return to secure confinement, movement from standard probation to intensive supervised probation, and simple probation program condition violations, such as drug use or alcohol and curfew violation (Taxman, 2005). **Recidivists** are persons who commit new crimes or delinquent acts after having been convicted or adjudicated for previous offenses (Stalans et al., 2004).

The most popular meaning of recidivism is a new adjudication as delinquent for reoffending (Craissati and Beech, 2004). It is generally the case that, with exceptions, intensive supervision programs have less recidivism associated with them than standard probation. Over the years, a recidivism standard of 30 percent has been established among researchers as the cutting point between a successful probation program and an unsuccessful one (Holtfreter, Reisig, and Morash, 2004). Programs with recidivism rates of 30 percent or less are considered successful, while those programs with more than 30 percent recidivism are not particularly successful. This figure is arbitrary, although it is most often used as a success standard (Rodriguez and Webb, 2004). No program presently has zero percent recidivism.

Probation and Recidivism

Standard probation, which means little or no direct and regular supervision of offenders by probation officers, has a fairly high rate of recidivism among the various state jurisdictions. Recidivism rates for juveniles on standard probation range from 30 percent to 70 percent, depending on the nature of their offenses and prior records (Bates et al., 2004; Stalans et al., 2004).

The following elements appear to be predictive of future criminal activity and reoffending by juveniles: (1) one's age at first adjudication; (2) a prior criminal record (a combined measure of the number and severity of priors); (3) the number of prior commitments to juvenile facilities; (4) drug/chemical abuse; (5) alcohol abuse; (6) family relationships (parental control); (7) school problems; and (8) peer relationships (Baird, 1985:36).

Christopher Baird (1985) recommends that needs assessments should be individualized, based on the juvenile's past record and other pertinent characteristics, including the present adjudication offense. The level of supervision should vary according to the degree of risk posed to the public by the juvenile. While Baird furnishes no weighting procedure for each of the risk factors listed above so that judges can use these criteria effectively at the sentencing stage, he does describe a supervisory scheme that acts as a guide for juvenile probation and aftercare. This scheme would be applied based on the perceived risk of each juvenile offender. Baird's scheme would include the following:

Regular Supervision
1. Four face-to-face contacts per month with youth.
2. Two face-to-face contacts per month with parents.
3. One face-to-face contact per month with placement staff.
4. One contact with school officials.

Intensive Supervision
1. Six face-to-face contacts per month with youth.
2. Three face-to-face contacts per month with parents.
3. One face-to-face contact per month with placement staff.
4. Two contacts with school officials.

Alternative Care Cases
1. One face-to-face contact per month with youth.
2. Four contacts with agency staff (one must be face-to-face).
3. One contact every 2 months with parents.

An assignment to any one of these supervision levels should be based on both risk and needs assessments. Baird (1985:38) says that often, agencies make categorical assignments of juveniles to one level of supervision or another, primarily by referring to the highest level of supervision suggested by two or more scales used. Each juvenile probation agency prefers specific predictive devices, and some agencies use a combination of them. Again, no scale is foolproof, and the matter of false positives and false negatives arises, as some juveniles receive more supervision than they really require, while others receive less than they need.

At the beginning of the twentieth century, when probation began to be used for juvenile supervision, a report was issued entitled "Juvenile Courts and Probation" in 1914 (Flexner and Baldwin, 1914). Writing 7 years following the establishment of the National Probation Association in 1907, Flexner and Baldwin described three important aspects of probation as it applied to juvenile offenders:

1. The period of probation should always be indeterminate because judges cannot possibly fix the period of treatment in advance.
2. To be effective, probation work must be performed by full-time, professionally trained probation officers.
3. Probation is not a judicial function (Hurst, 1990:17).

It is interesting to see how Flexner and Baldwin discounted the value of the judiciary in fixing one's term of probation and performing supervisory functions. They were adamant in the belief that only professional probation officers

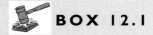

BOX 12.1

Carrie A. Bellamy
Juvenile Probation Officer
Community Control Supervision, Huron County Juvenile Court, Norwalk, OH

Statistics:

Bachelor of Criminal Justice (forensic psychology, minor in corrections), Tiffin University, Ohio; Ohio Peace Officer Academy (corrections)

Background

I am a 1997 graduate of Tiffin University where I majored in Forensic Psychology and minored in Corrections. I have always been interested in law enforcement, crime, and why criminals do what they do. During the summers when I wasn't attending Tiffin University pursuing my degree I started out working as a security officer at a local Radisson Inn where I had my first experiences dealing with irate, intoxicated, and just overall difficult people at times. I worked along with the local police department at times when there was a guest in violation of hotel policy or even the law (e.g., drugs, domestic violence, vandalism). In my senior year at Tiffin University I had the opportunity to do an internship with the Sandusky Police Department. I had the chance to experience different aspects of the department. I got to spend time with the Detective Bureau and the Drug Task Force where I rode along on a drug bust. I went on routine patrol with the officers, spent a few days sitting in dispatch, and also worked closely with the DARE officer and went to many of the area schools and helped present the DARE program to the kids. I was also a mentor in the Big Brothers/Big Sisters Program—ROY (Reach Our Youth) of Huron County. The more work I did with youth, the more rewarding I found it to be and that's when I decided I wanted to have a career in working with juveniles.

Shortly after I graduated from Tiffin University, after applying to numerous jobs, I got hired as a correction's officer at the newly built Huron County Correctional Facility. I went through the Ohio Peace Officers Training for Corrections in 1997 and started out as a booking officer in the jail, where I was responsible for processing inmates coming into the jail. I continued working as a booking officer until 1999 when I was promoted to Corporal, Shift Supervisor. As a Cpl. I was in charge of overseeing the overall operation of the facility during my shifts. I continued to work at the jail up until April 2000 when I had heard that there was a juvenile probation officer position at the Huron County Juvenile Court available. Finally, my chance to work with juveniles was here. I applied, got hired, and have been working with the court going on 5 years now. I work with both male and female juveniles and their ages vary. I have worked with kids as young as 7 years old to as old as 19 years old. The level of offenses that the juveniles commit also varies, from unruly to felony level offenses. I would say that the average caseload over the past 5 years has been about 40 juveniles under my supervision at one time. Case management is important when working with such a large caseload. In working with juveniles you have to have patience and understanding as well as an understanding of appropriate consequences to inappropriate behaviors or actions.

Work Experiences

With almost 8 years of experience I can honestly say that no two days of working in the criminal justice field have been the same for me. You're constantly working with different people under different circumstances for different reasons. I have gained so much experience in just the hands-on of the different kinds of jobs that I have had up to this point in my career. I have found working with juveniles especially rewarding for me. I like to help them see the bad choices they have made and help them recognize the different things they can do to avoid making those bad choices again. At times the job can be frustrating, especially when you have a juvenile that continues to act out and violate laws or break rules and you can't understand or figure out why. Many of the juveniles I deal with just need the right guidance and some additional resources to help them move on and out of the system. It is my hope that the juveniles I have worked with these past 5 years have learned from me and the Juvenile Court half as much as I have learned from them. If you take the time and really listen and try to relate to the person you are serving then you have a better chance of reaching them and helping them deal with the issues that are causing them to make the choices they do. Not everyone can work in the community corrections field, it takes a very unique, open-minded, patient, and dedicated person to be able to perform the duties in the juvenile justice field.

Advice to Students

If you're considering going into the juvenile justice field I would suggest to you to talk to others in the field and do an internship in the area you're interested in. Flexibility and understanding are important when you're working with juveniles. The role of the Juvenile Court is to do what is in the best interest of the child/juvenile. At times I have to recommend sanctions such as detention or possibly even placing a juvenile in a foster home due to conditions in their home or because of other issues going on in their home. It's hard at times to see the way the juveniles and families react to the court's decisions. The system is trying to help juveniles and their families but sometimes the families see it as if the system is punishing them. When you work with juveniles you are also working with the parents and others in the household and that can be very challenging at times. Hands-on experience in the field is the best way to test yourself to see if you're able to do the job, so if you have the chance to do an internship or something similar then I would strongly recommend doing so.

should engage in such supervisory tasks, and that the judicial function should be minimal. The strong treatment orientation of probation is apparent as well, suggesting their belief that probationer treatment programs should be tailored to fit the probationer's needs. Furthermore, they underscored the power originally assigned to probation officers and the leverage that probation officers could exert upon their clients, including possible probation revocation action if program infractions occurred.

An effective probation program is one where probation officers (POs) have an awareness of the juvenile offender's needs and weaknesses. One problem in many existing probation programs is that POs find it hard to establish rapport between themselves and their juvenile clients. A high degree of mistrust exists, in large part because of the age differential between the PO and offender.

Some POs have suggested an approach normally practiced by psychological counselors in developing rapport between themselves and their clients. It has been suggested, for instance, that each PO should (1) thoroughly review the youth's case, including family and juvenile interviews and other background information; (2) engage in introspection and attempt to discover his or her own reactions to adolescents and responses to verbal exchanges; (3) attempt to cultivate a relationship of acceptance rather than rejection and punitiveness; (4) react favorably to a "critical incident," where the juvenile may "screw up" and expect reprimand or punishment but where acceptance and understanding are reflected instead; and (5) follow-through with continued support, which bolsters juvenile confidence in the PO (Sweet, 1985:90). When juveniles fail to comply with one or more terms of their standard probation, they run the risk of being in contempt of court, since the juvenile court originally imposed their probation orders. In Dougherty County, Georgia, for example, a PO may believe that a juvenile court judge should review a particular juvenile's behavior where it is believed that he or she has not been in compliance with the terms of the probation orders. A motion is made for a judicial review of the juvenile to determine whether the allegations against him or her are true. Figure 12.3 shows a motion for judicial review, where one or more particulars are noted that indicate what the PO believes are probation violations. The motion also contains a notice of a hearing where these allegations may be aired. Figure 12.4 shows the actual judicial review, where the judge's findings are articulated.

As the result of the judicial review if the allegations are supported, the judge will make a determination about what should be done to the juvenile as punishment for noncompliance. Judges have an array of options, including intensifying one's supervision by POs, imposing restitution, community service, fines, or participation in one or more kinds of counseling programs. Or the judge can simply continue the youth's probation with a verbal reprimand or warning.

Some juveniles are unreachable through any kind of effective exchange. Chronic offenders, hardcore offenders, or psychologically disturbed juveniles frequently reject any attempts by authorities to understand them or assist them in any task (Carlson et al., 2004; Carswell et al., 2004). If some youths are chemically dependent, the fact of substance abuse may interfere with effective interventions of any kind (Dowden, 2003). Where standard probation is not feasible, an **intensive supervision program** is required for certain types of offenders.

INTERMEDIATE PUNISHMENTS FOR JUVENILE OFFENDERS

Intermediate Punishments Defined

Intermediate punishments are community-based sanctions that range from **intensive probation supervision (IPS)** to nonsecure custodial programs. These programs include more intensive monitoring or management of juvenile behaviors through more intensive supervision. They may include home confinement, electronic monitoring, or both. Other community-based services are included, where the goal is to maintain fairly close supervision over youthful offenders (Sims and Shi, 1999). The most successful ISP programs seem to be those that emphasize the social structural causes of delinquency and use greater community participation and agency networking rather than focus on individual youths' problems. Cognitive-behavioral interventions and participatory problem-solving activities are used as a part of probation department programs designed to reduce offender recidivism and promote long-term law-abiding behaviors (Robertson, Grimes, and Rogers, 2001).

Intermediate punishment programs are presently operated in all states for both juvenile and adult offenders. They are sometimes referred to as **creative sentencing,** since they are somewhere between standard probationary dispositions and traditional incarcerative terms that might be imposed by judges. These alternatives to incarceration are regarded as positive interventions for a majority of today's youth who are brought to the attention of the juvenile justice system (Trulson, Triplett, and Snell, 2001; Warchol, 2000).

**IN THE JUVENILE COURT
OF
DOUGHERTY COUNTY, GEORGIA**

In The Interest Of:

_____

Name   Race/Sex   DOB

File Number: _____

Referral Number/s: _____

_____

MOTION FOR JUDICIAL REVIEW

Now comes _____ and moves the Court to judicially review the
          Name

probation status of the above-named juvenile.

Movant is of the opinion and belief that the juvenile and or parent are not cooperating with the

juvenile's case manager and are not complying with the Court's Order of probation dated

_____ in the following particulars:

1. _____
2. _____
3. _____
4. _____
5. _____

This _____ day of _____, 20___.

_____

Signature of Movant

NOTICE OF HEARING

The within and foregoing motion filed and said matter to come on for a review in the Juvenile

Court of Dougherty County, Georgia, on _____ at _____ a.m. / p.m.,

all interested parties should be present in Court to show cause, if any, why the conditions of

probation have not been complied with, or why the conditions should not be enforced.

This _____ day of _____, 20___.

shared files\probation\motion for judicial review

FIGURE 12.3   Motion for Judicial Review.
(*Source:* Dougherty County, GA)

IN THE JUVENILE COURT
OF
DOUGHERTY COUNTY, GEORGIA

Judicial Review

In The Interest Of:

_____

DOB: _____   **Age:** _____

Hearing Date: _____
File Number: _____

Issue/s:
1. _____
_____
2. _____
_____
3. _____
_____

Juvenile's comments and explanations:_____
_____
_____
_____
_____
_____
_____

Judge's findings:_____
_____
_____
_____
_____
_____
_____
_____
_____
_____
_____

shared files\probation\judicial review form

FIGURE 12.4 Judicial Review.
(*Source:* Dougherty County, GA)

The Goals of Intermediate Punishment Programs

There is considerable variation among intermediate punishment programs, although they tend to exhibit similar goals or objectives. These include, but are not limited to:

1. Provision of less expensive sanctions compared with secure confinement.
2. Achievement of lower rates of recidivism compared with standard probation.

3. Greater emphasis on reintegration into communities as the primary correctional goal.

4. Provision of a greater range of community services and organizations in a cooperative effort to assist youthful offenders.

5. Minimization of the adverse influence of labeling that might stem from secure confinement.

6. Improvement in personal educational and vocational skills of individual offenders, together with acquisition of better self-concepts and greater acceptance of responsibility for one's actions.

Classification Criteria for Placement in ISP Programs

One problem for juvenile court judges is deciding which juveniles should be assigned to which programs. This is a classification problem, and the level of accuracy associated with juvenile risk prediction instruments is about as poor as adult risk prediction devices. This problem is considered one of correction's greatest challenges (Trulson, Triplett, and Snell, 2001; Warchol, 2000). Nevertheless, judges attempt to make secure or nonsecure confinement decisions on the basis of the following elements:

1. Classification based on risk of continued criminal activity and the offender's need for services.

2. A case management classification system designed to help probation and parole officers develop effective case plans and select appropriate casework strategies.

3. A management information system designed to enhance planning, monitoring, evaluation, and accountability.

4. A workload deployment system that allows agencies to effectively and efficiently allocate their limited resources (Baird, 1985:34).

Chronic recidivists and serious offenders are most often designated for secure confinement. However, an increasing number of community-based programs are being designed to supervise such offenders closely and offer them needed services and treatments. It is helpful to review briefly some of the issues relating to the effectiveness of such instrumentation (Latessa, 2005). Depending on the scores received by various juvenile clients when classified, they may or may not be entitled to assignment to intensive supervised probation or to a community-based program. Theoretically, those youthful offenders who are considered dangerous and violent are poor candidates for inclusion, because it is predicted that they might harm themselves or others, including agency staff or probation officers. Also, those considered not dangerous would be predicted to be good candidates as program clients. However, the flaws of our instrumentation do not always discriminate effectively.

JUVENILE INTENSIVE SUPERVISED PROBATION

Intensive supervised probation (ISP) programs, also known as **juvenile intensive supervised probation (JISP),** have become increasingly popular for managing nonincarcerated offender populations. JISP will be used to describe the programs developed in different jurisdictions, regardless whether the JISP or JIPS designation is used by individual programs. Since the mid-1960s, these programs have been aimed primarily at supervising adult offenders closely, and in recent years, JISP programs have been designed for juvenile offenders as well. Intensive supervised probation is a highly structured and conditional supervision program for either adult or juvenile offenders that serves as an alternative to incarceration and provides for an acceptable level of public safety. For administrators of secure facilities for juveniles, community-based options such as ISP are desirable, since overcrowding is reduced (Parker, 2005).

Juvenile court judges impose intensive supervised probation for those juveniles who are believed to be in need of greater monitoring or supervision by POs. Because POs who supervise these youths must meet with and monitor them frequently, their caseloads are reduced substantially. Thus JISP is more expensive than traditional standard probation. Figure 12.5 shows an order for intensive probation supervision used by the juvenile court in Dougherty County, Georgia. It is important to note that the juvenile and the parents must sign this order, signifying their intent to comply with it. A violation of one or more of these intensive supervision conditions may result in a judicial review at the request of the supervising PO.

Characteristics of JISP Programs

JISP programs for juveniles have been developed and are currently operating in about half of all U.S. jurisdictions. It is important to note that many of these JISP programs are operated on a countywide or citywide basis, rather than on a statewide basis. Thus, it is difficult to find a state jurisdiction with a uniform policy and program information about JISPs that apply to all local agencies within the state. One example of a JISP program operated by a county is the Johnson County (Kansas) Department of Corrections. The JISP conditions and guidelines for Johnson County are provided below.

The Johnson County, Kansas Juvenile Intensive Supervision Program. The court grants probation for a set period of time with the specific conditions of such supervision are outlined in the "Probation Plan"or Conditional Release Contract. Each client must abide by the written rules and regulations of the program, which will be reviewed by the Intensive Supervision Officer (ISO) assigned.

There are levels in the Intensive Supervision Program. Listed below are some of the minimum requirements of each level:

Level I
1. 30 days in length
2. Three face-to-face contacts with ISO per week
3. Four random urinalyses/breath analyses per month as directed by the ISO
4. Twenty hours of community service
5. Curfew as directed

Level II
1. Sixty days in length
2. Two face-to-face contacts with ISO per week

ORDER FOR INTENSIVE SUPERVISION

IN THE JUVENILE COURT OF
«COUNTYNAME» COUNTY, GEORGIA

In the interest of   *   FILE #:   «juvenileFilenbr»
                        *   CASE #:   «CASENUMBER»
                        *   SEX: «JUVENILESEX»
                        *   DOB: «JUVENILEDOB»

«JUVENILENAMEALL»   *
A child under 17 years of age

A petition having been filed and a hearing regarding the allegations contained therein having been held, the Court hereby finds as follows:

1.

The filing of a petition and all proceedings therein, including the hearing, has been held in compliance with the Juvenile Court Code.

2.

Testimony was received (and the child admitted) the allegations as set forth in the complaint (petition).

3.

Based upon said testimony (and admission) the Court hereby finds that the child is hereby adjudicated delinquent (and unruly).

4.

The Court then held its dispositional hearing immediately thereafter with the consent of all parties and hereby finds that said youth is in need of INTENSIVE SUPERVISION, treatment, and rehabilitation, but that commitment is not necessary at this time and the child is therefore placed in the INTENSIVE SUPERVISION PROGRAM until released by order of the Court.

5.

Said child is subject to the terms and conditions of the INTENSIVE SUPERVISION PROGRAM which are attached hereto and made a part hereof.

SO ORDERED this «FORMALDATE».

«HEARINGOFFICERTITLE»

«HEARINGOFFICER»,

«COUNTYNAME» County Juvenile Court

FIGURE 12.5 Order for Intensive Supervision.
(*Source:* Dougherty County, GA)

3. Three random urinalyses/breath analyses per month as directed by ISO
4. Curfew as directed

Level III

1. Sixty days in length
2. One face-to-face contact with ISO per week
3. Two random urinalyses/breath analyses per month as directed by ISO
4. Curfew as directed

JUVENILE COURT OF DOUGHERTY COUNTY, GEORGIA

ORDER OF DISPOSITION

IN THE INTEREST OF:

«NAME», «RACESEX», DOB: «DOB», File #: «FileNumber»

Case Number/s: «Case_Numbers»

WHEREAS, a hearing having been held in this Court on **«CourtDate»**, with the following persons being present, including for said child «PresentInCourt».

«NAME» is hereby placed on probation in his/her home for an «PeriodofProbation» beginning **«CourtDate»**.

It is the **Order of this Court** that the probationer comply with the following conditions of probation:

1. Obey all Federal, State and City laws/ordinances.
2. Be at home by **«CurfewTime»**, unless special permission is granted by Probation Officer of the Juvenile Court or child is accompanied by parent or parents.
3. Do not associate with anyone currently on probation or who uses or possesses illegal drugs.
4. Obey the reasonable and lawful commands of your parents.
5. Attend school regularly, obey school authorities and maintain passing grades.
6. Meet with your Probation Officer, **«ProbationOfficer»,** at times specified by the Probation Officer.
7. Notify your Probation Officer before making any change in your present address.
8. Submit to random urinalysis testing as scheduled by your Probation Officer.
9. Failure to obey any of the terms of your supervision could result in your detention in the Regional Youth Development Center.
10. The Court reserves the right to modify or review this order.
11. «Condition11»
12. «Condition12»
13. «Condition13»
14. «Condition14»
15. «Condition15»
16. «Condition16»
17. «Condition17»
18. «Condition18»

I have had read and explained to me by my Probation Officer these Conditions of Probation and understand that they are intended to develop my personal responsibility.

SO ORDERED, this «HearingDay1st2ndetc» day of «HearingMonth», «year».

_____   _____
             Child   **Probation Officer**

_____   _____
         Parent/Guardian   **«JudgeName», Judge**

shared files\brooker\orders\probation\probation-juvenile court-merge

FIGURE 12.5   Continued

Level IV

1. No specified minimum length
2. One face-to-face contact with ISO per week for the first 30 days
3. One face-to-face contact every other week after a minimum of 30 days
4. One random urinalysis/breath analysis per month as directed by ISO

ISOs are also required to have frequent contact with those individuals who play a significant role in your life, such as family, friends, treatment providers, sponsors, etc.

A face-to-face contact may include:

1. Visits to the probation office
2. Visits at employment sites
3. Home visits
4. Meetings at other designated places

The curfew is monitored on a random basis.

Compliance with the previously stated requirements, and any other requirements, will allow the individual to progress through the Intensive Supervision Program (Johnson County Department of Corrections, 2002).

Similar to their adult ISP program counterparts, juvenile intensive supervised probation (JISP) programs are ideally designed for secure incarceration-bound youths and are considered as acceptable alternatives to incarceration. According to Armstrong (1988:342), this is what JISP programs were always meant to be. Armstrong differentiates JISP programs from other forms of standard probation by citing obvious differences in the amount of officer/client contact during the course of the probationary period. For example, standard probation is considered no more than two face-to-face officer/client contacts per month. He says that JISP programs might differ from standard probation according to the following face-to-face criteria: (1) two or three times per week versus once per month; (2) once per week versus twice per month; or (3) four times per week versus once per week (the latter figure being unusually high for standard probation contact).

The brokerage nature of probation officer dispositions toward their work is evident in the different types of services provided by the different JISP programs investigated by Armstrong (1988). For example, of the 55 programs he examined (92 percent of his total program sample), he found that the following range of services, skills, and resources were mentioned as being brokered by POs in different jurisdictions: (1) mental health counseling; (2) drug and alcohol counseling; (3) academic achievement and aptitude testing; (4) vocational and employment training; (5) individual, group, and family counseling; (6) job search and placement programs; (7) alternative education programs; (8) foster grandparents programs; and (9) Big Brother/Big Sister programs.

Although not all ISP programs are alike, many juvenile ISP programs share certain similarities, such as the following: (1) recognition of the shortcomings of traditional responses to serious and/or chronic offenders (e.g., incarceration or out-of-home placement); (2) severe resource constraints within jurisdictions that compel many probation departments to adopt agencywide classification and workload deployment systems for targeting a disproportionate share of resources for the most problematic juvenile offenders; (3) programs hope to reduce the incidence of incarceration in juvenile secure confinement facilities and reduce overcrowding; (4) programs tend to include aggressive supervision and control elements as a part of the get-tough movement; and (5) all programs have a vested interest in rehabilitation of youthful offenders (Armstrong, 1991).

From these analyses of ISP program content generally, we can glean the following as basic characteristics of ISP programs:

1. Low officer/client caseloads (i.e., 30 or fewer probationers)
2. High levels of offender accountability (e.g., victim restitution, community service, payment of fines, partial defrayment of program expenses)
3. High levels of offender responsibility
4. High levels of offender control (home confinement, electronic monitoring, frequent face-to-face visits by POs)
5. Frequent checks for arrests, drug and/or alcohol use, and employment/ school attendance (drug/alcohol screening, coordination with police departments and juvenile halls, teachers, family) (Fagan and Reinarman, 1991).

The Ohio Experience

A comprehensive description of a juvenile intensive supervised probation program is the **Ohio experience** (Wiebush, 1990). Three different Ohio counties were compared that used different ISP programs for their juvenile offenders, as well as the Ohio Department of Youth Services (ODYS). The different counties include Delaware County (predominantly rural), Lucas County (Toledo), and Cuyahoga County (Cleveland). The ODYS is state-operated and manages the most serious offenders, since these are exclusively felony offenders on parole from secure confinement. In each of the county jurisdictions, most of the offenders are incarceration-bound, with the exception of the Lucas County juveniles who are disposed to ISP after having their original dispositions of secure confinement reversed by juvenile court judges. Tables 12.1 and 12.2 show the basic parameters of the different Ohio programs as well as the program sizes and staffing patterns.

Table 12.1 shows the different types of agencies involved, the particular program models used by each, and the types of juvenile offender/clients served. Each of the programs uses risk scores for client inclusion, with the exception of the Lucas County program. Table 12.2 shows that all four programs follow a four-phase plan, where the intensity of supervision and surveillance over offenders is gradually reduced after particular time intervals. The ODYS program elects to reevaluate juveniles at 3-, 5-, and 7-month intervals, through the use of a risk assessment device, rather than to graduate them to new phases automatically.

The Delaware JISP program targets those juveniles with a high propensity to recidivate as well as more serious felony offenders who are incarceration-bound. Youths begin the program with a 5-day incarceration, followed by 2 weeks of house arrest. Later, they must observe curfews, attend school and complete schoolwork satisfactorily, report daily to the probation office, and submit to periodic urinalysis. Each youth's progress is monitored by intensive counselors and surveillance staff 16 hours a day, 7 days a week. Wiebush says that although the Delaware program has a rather strict approach, it embodies rehabilitation as a primary program objective. The Delaware program has about a 40 percent recidivism rate, which is high, although it is better than the 75 percent rate of recidivism among the general juvenile court population of high-risk offenders elsewhere in Ohio jurisdictions.

In Lucas County, program officials select clients from those already serving incarcerative terms and are considered high-risk offenders. Lucas County

TABLE 12.1

Basic Parameters of the Ohio Programs: Models, Goals, and Client Selection

	Jurisdiction			
Characteristic	*Delaware*	*Lucas*	*Cuyahoga*	*ODYS*
Agency type	County probation	County probation	County probation	State parole
Program model	Probation enhancement and alternative incarceration	Alternative to incarceration	Probation enhancement	Probation enhancement
Program goals	Reduced recidivism	Reduced recidivism	Reduced recidivism	Reduced recidivism
	Reduced commitments	Reduced commitments		Reduced recommitment
	Reduced overhead placement		Reduced overhead placement	
Primary client selection criterion	High-risk score	Post-commitment status	High-risk score	High-risk score
Additional criteria	Chronic felony offenders; high	Excluded offenses = use of weapon, victim injury, drug trafficking	Status offenders excluded	Metro area resident; 2 + violent offenders included automatically
Philosophy, supervision emphasis	All stress "balanced" approach—relatively equal emphasis on public safety and rehabilitation			

Source: Richard G. Wiebush, "Programmatic Variations in Intensive Supervision for Juveniles: The Ohio Experience," *Perspectives* 14:28 (1990). Reprinted by permission, American Probation and Parole Association and Richard G. Wiebush.

officials wished to use this particular selection method, since they wanted to avoid any appearance of net widening that their JISP program might reflect. Drawing from those already incarcerated seemed the best strategy in this case. The Lucas program is similar to the Delaware program in its treatment and control approaches. However, the Lucas program obligates offenders to perform up to 100 hours of community service as a program condition. House arrest, curfew, and other Delaware program requirements are also found in the Lucas program. The successfulness of the Lucas program has not been evaluated fully, although it reduced institutional commitments by about 110 percent between 1986 and 1987.

The Cuyahoga County program (Cleveland) was one of the first of several ISP programs in Ohio's metropolitan jurisdictions. It is perhaps the largest county program, with 1,500 clients at any given time, as well as six juvenile court judges and 72 supervisory personnel. One innovation of the Cuyahoga program was the development of a team approach to client surveillance and management. This program, like the other county programs, performs certain broker functions by referring its clients to an assortment of community-based services and treatments during the program duration. Currently, there are six

---

TABLE 12.2

ISP Program Size and Staffing Patterns

	Jurisdiction			
Characteristic	Delaware	Lucas	Cuyahoga	ODYS
Total agency caseload[a]	225	500	1500	1500
ISP caseload	17	60	360[b]	525
ISP staff/youth ratio (probation/ parole officers)	1:17	1:15	1:30	1:13
Surveillance staff/youth ratio	2:17	2.5:60	3:60	2:39
Team configuration	Court administrator	1 unit supervisor	1 team leader	3 ISP Pos
	1 ISP PO	4 ISP Pos	2 ISP Pos	2 surveillance staff (part-time)
	2 surveillance staff (part-time)	2 surveillance staff (full-time)	3 surveillance staff (full-time)	
	Student interns	2 surveillance staff (part-time)		
	Family advocates	3 comm. service staff (part-time)		
Number of teams	1	1	6	1-3 per region, 14 total
Coverage	7 days; 14 hours/day	7 days; 14 hours/day	7 days; 24 hours/day	7 days; 14 hours/day

[a] Caseload = cases under supervision at any one time.
[b] Projected figure for summer 1989.
Source: Richard G. Wiebush, "Programmatic Variations in Intensive Supervision for Juveniles: The Ohio Experience," Perspectives 14:29 (1990). Reprinted by permission, American Probation and Parole Association and Richard G. Wiebush.

teams of surveillance officers who each serve about 60 youths. These teams are comprised of a team leader, two counselors, and three surveillance staff. The nature of contact standards for this and the other three programs are shown in Table 12.3.

The ODYS program operates the state's nine training schools in addition to supervising the 3,000 youths each year who are released on parole. ODYS has 93 youth counselors to staff seven regional offices. ODYS commenced JISP in February 1988 and supervised those high-risk offenders with a predicted future recidivism rate of 75 percent or higher. Since these clients were all prior felony offenders with lengthy adjudication records, they were considered the most serious group to be supervised compared with the other programs. Accordingly, the ODYS supervision and surveillance structure exhibited the greatest degree of offender monitoring. The team approach has been used by ODYS, with teams consisting of three youth counselors and two surveillance staff.

TABLE 12.3

Contact Standards by Type and Phase

Type of Contact[a]	Jurisdiction[b]			
	Delaware	Lucas	Cuyahoga	ODYS[c]
Phase I				
PO, direct with youth	5/week	2/week	1/week	6.5/month
Family, direct	n.s.	4/month	n.s.	2/month
Surveillance	11/week	14/week	17/week	4/week
Duration (minimum)	21 days	30 days	30 days	90 days
Phase II				
PO, direct with youth	5/week	2/week	1/week	4–6/month
Family, direct	n.s.	2/month	n.s.	2/month
Surveillance	11/week	10/week	8/week	4/week
Duration	28 days	50 days	75 days	60 days
Phase III				
PO, direct with youth	3/week	1/week	1/week	2–6/month
Family, direct	n.s.	2/month	n.s.	1/month
Surveillance	0–11/week	7/week	5/week	2–4/week
Duration	70 days	50 days	75 days	60 days
Phase IV				
PO, direct with youth	1–3/week	2/month	As needed	2–6/month
Family, direct	n.s.	1/month	n.s.	1/month
Surveillance	None	5/week	3/week	2–4/week
Duration	By contract	26 days	75 days	60 days

[a]Surveillance includes direct and telephone contacts.
[b]n.s., not specified.
[c]Ohio Department of Youth Services does not use phase system to govern youth movement through the program. Youths are classified at three, five, and seven months, based on reassessment of risk.
Source: Richard G. Wiebush, "Programmatic Variations in Intensive Supervision for Juveniles: The Ohio Experience," *Perspectives* 14:30 (1990). Reprinted with permission. American Probation and Parole Association and Richard G. Wiebush.

Because of geographical considerations, some variations have been observed among teams regarding the numbers of offenders supervised as well as the intensity of their supervision or surveillance. Basically, the ODYS program incorporated many of the program conditions that were included in the various county programs. These conditions or components have been divided into control components and treatment components and are shown respectively in Tables 12.4 and 12.5.

Since its creation, the JISP program operated by ODYS has exhibited a drop in its recidivism rate. On the basis of a comparison of the first year of its operation with recidivism figures for its clients from the previous year, the ODYS program had a 34 percent reduction in its rate of recidivism. Furthermore, a 39 percent reduction in parole revocations occurred. This is significant, considering the high-risk nature of the offender population being managed.

Wiebush notes that all of these programs have required enormous investments of time and energy by high-quality staff. Furthermore, each program has illustrated how best to utilize existing community resources to further its objectives and best serve juvenile clients in need. However, Wiebush says that what is good for Ohio probationers and parolees may not necessarily be suitable for

TABLE 12.4

Program Components: Control Elements[a]

	Jurisdiction			
Component	Delaware	Lucas	Cuyahoga	ODYS
Surveillance	x	x	x	x
Curfew	x	x	x	x
Front-end detention	x	—[b]	—	—
House arrest	x	x	x	o
Prior permission	x	—	—	—
Electronic surveillance	—	—	o	—
Urinalysis	o	x	o	o
Daily sanctioning (phase system)	x	x	x	—
Hourly school reports	x	x	x	—
Formal graduated sanction schedule	—	x	—	x

[a] x = Mandatory component; — = component not available; o = component optional, varies by youth.
[b]Most Lucas ISP youth do have front-end detention, but it is not mandated.
Source: Richard G. Wiebush, "Programmatic Variations in Intensive Supervision for Juveniles," *Perspectives* 14:31 (1990). Reprinted with permission, American Probation and Parole Association and Richard G. Wiebush.

those offenders of other jurisdictions. Nevertheless, these programs function as potential models after which programs in other jurisdictions may be patterned.

Other programs designed for both male and female juvenile offenders have been described (Vollman and Terry, 2005). The Youth Center in Beloit, Kansas, is the state's only institutional facility for female juvenile offenders. The em-

TABLE 12.5

Program Components: Treatment Elements[a]

	Jurisdiction			
Component	Delaware	Lucas	Cuyahoga	ODYS
Individualized contracts'	x	x	x	x
Individual counseling (non-PO)	o	o	o	o
Family counseling or family conferences	o	x	o	o
Group counseling	x	x	o	o
In-home family services	x	—	x	—
Community sponsors, advocates	—	—	—	—
Alternative education	o	o	o	o
Job training	o	o	o	o
Substance abuse counseling	o	o	o	o
School attendance (or work)	x	x	x	x
Community service	o	x	o	o
Restitution	o	o	o	o

[a] x = Mandatory component; — = component not available; o = component optional, varies by youth.
Source: Richard G. Wiebush, "Programmatic Variations in Intensive Supervision for Juveniles," *Perspectives* 14:32 (1990). Reprinted with permission, American Probation and Parole Association and Richard G. Wiebush.

phasis of treatment programs at the Youth Center is assisting these female youths in dealing with problems of sexual abuse, which many of these offenders have experienced. Besides treatment, the females are exposed to vocational and educational experiences designed to prepare them for useful lives once they are released. Another program described by Mardon (1991) is the Fort Smallwood Marine Institute near Baltimore, Maryland. This program was established in 1988. Between 1988 and 1991, approximately 225 delinquent youths have been treated successfully.

Similar programs described by Mardon include the Eckerd Youth Challenge Program, which is a community-based alternative to placing adjudicated youths in training schools. Youths are housed in residences at this site, and they participate in programs designed to improve their interpersonal and living skills. Experiential and action-oriented phases of this program include activities such as hikes, canoe trips, and community service projects.

STRENGTHS AND WEAKNESSES OF JISP PROGRAMS

A strength of JISP programs is that they are substantially less expensive compared with the costs of incarcerating juvenile offenders. For instance, the Texas Youth Commission reports that juvenile incarceration represents the most expensive criminal justice option, averaging $124 as the daily expenditure per juvenile (Texas Youth Commission, 2005). Alternatively, juvenile probation programs manage youths at the rate of $10.50 per day. Various ISP programs in Texas average $30 per day per juvenile.

Another strength is that JISP programs generally report lower rates of recidivism compared with standardized probation and other, more conventional nonincarcerative options. One reason is that JISP clients are more closely monitored and thus are given less opportunity to reoffend. Another reason is that prospective clients for JISP programs are more closely screened. More serious offenders are usually excluded, which increases the success rates of included clients (Gordon and Malmsjo, 2005).

A weakness of most JISP programs is that local demands and needs vary to such an extent among jurisdictions that after 25 years, we have yet to devise a standard definition of what is meant by intensive supervised probation (Corbett, 2000). Thus, the dominant themes of current JISP programs appear to be (1) those that are designed as front-end alternatives to secure confinement, (2) those that combine incarceration with some degree of community supervision (shock probation), and (3) those that follow secure confinement.

Terminating One's Probation Program

At some point, almost all juveniles placed on standard probation or JISP will complete their programs, more or less successfully. Those who don't complete them will have other dispositions imposed, such as secure confinement or placement in some alternative setting, such as a group home, foster care, boot camp, or wilderness experience. Again judges are most often responsible for issuing orders terminating one's probation program. In Dougherty County, Georgia, for example, an order for termination of probation is issued by the juvenile

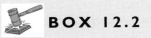

BOX 12.2

Dean J. Conder
Colorado Juvenile Parole Board, Representative of the Colorado Department of Labor and Employment

Statistics:

B.S. (political science), University of Southern Colorado; M.S. (legal administration), University of Denver College of Law; Paralegal Certificate, Denver Paralegal Institute

Background

I grew up in Walsenburg, a small town in southern Colorado then mostly supported by mining and agriculture. My father, of whom I am extremely proud, had what many folks thought to be the best job in town—the president of the local bank. With a natural gift for numbers, he started as a teller and worked his way up to be president and later Chairman of the Board before his retirement. My father was born during the Great Depression and knew very well the value of hard work and common sense. Luckily, these values were passed along to my brother and me. He emphasized education from an early age and by the time I got to high school, there was no doubt in my mind that I wanted to go to college.

I worked at a grocery store during high school and college, which at first piqued an interest in business. I struggled my first few years of college mostly due to my lack of maturity. I transferred to a new college and was lucky to be influenced by two professors who helped me discover my true interest in political science. Not party politics, but public policy and what was termed in elementary school as civics. With this interest in constitutional law but not a very marketable degree in political science, I went to school to become a paralegal, which was actually my first step into the area of criminal justice. I returned to school a few years later and received a Master of Science degree in Legal Administration.

Work Experiences

With my new skills of legal research and writing, I was hired by the Colorado Department of Corrections to run a prison law library. Before this time, my only familiarity

with a correctional institution was what I saw in the movies. Boy, was I surprised to find out that these fictional accounts were indeed mostly fiction.

I spent the next 10 years working in various prison facilities, including an infirmary unit, providing access to the courts for inmates. While doing this job, I supervised inmate workers and civilian paralegals at other facilities. Providing legal help to inmates placed me in an awkward situation. I was being paid to assist inmates in their legal matters, which meant that at times, I was being paid to help the inmates sue the department based on the conditions of their confinement. The inmates looked to me for help, and some of the unprofessional correctional officers took my helping an inmate sue the department as an insult. As I look back on that situation, I realize that the problem was not mine but that of the unprofessional correctional officers.

The opportunity arose for me to transfer agencies, and I took a job with the Colorado Department of Labor and Employment. My new job focused on tax matters, but when the department appointed a new director, he, realizing my experience in the criminal justice system, nominated me to the governor for appointment to the Colorado Juvenile Parole Board. Under Colorado law, the makeup of the Juvenile Parole Board is required to have a representative from four different departments of the state and five citizen members. As such, I started my endeavor as a juvenile parole board member.

Juvenile Parole Board Experiences

Colorado is somewhat unique in that we are one of only a handful of states that have a juvenile parole board. It functions basically like an adult offender parole board, in that members of the board decide whether a particular youth should be allowed back into the community. Panel hearings consist of two of the nine members and are conducted wherein the juvenile, the case manager, program staff, and others including the youth's parents or guardians, are interviewed by the two members. Based on the information in the file (usually containing among other items the police report, a diagnostic summary, and program progress reports) and the testimony, the two board members vote whether to parole the youth. The more serious offenses require a hearing and a vote of all nine members.

As is obvious, it is extremely difficult to forecast an individual's future behavior. And so, we (board members) must rely on the professional opinions of program staff and counselors. This being said, however, the most important function that we can provide in the area of public safety is to provide an independent "baloney detector." I do not mean to imply that experienced program staff cannot recognize when a youth is trying to manipulate them and others, but the nature of their jobs is to focus on the aspects of therapy and counseling. This is demonstrated by a discouraging part of the job when we conduct parole violation hearings. A youth, who we have seen several months prior and had the full support and confidence of the program staff, will be brought before us for violating conditions of his or her parole. And so, fully recognizing that setbacks are a part of the rehabilitative process, and while the youth demonstrated enough positive change to garner the support of others, those types of cases show that past performance is not always indicative of future results, and it remains exceedingly difficult to predict an individual's future behavior.

I find the most difficult part in assessing a youth's progress is remembering that they are in fact juveniles, and by definition, immature. When reading about their offenses and their progress report, it is sometimes easy to forget that they are young, immature kids, and to unfairly hold their age against them. With adults it is easier to say that they should have known better, but with juveniles, that convenience is simply not there. Thus, we must look for causes beyond immaturity. The problem of immaturity, however, can also be the cure, absent other causes and circumstances, in that there is the hope that some of these troubled youth will simply outgrow their antisocial behaviors.

Research will show that the three most prevalent risk factors to juvenile criminality are family condition, substance abuse, and criminally minded friends. As a juvenile parole board member, I believe that we must look at these areas and determine if the offender has received adequate counseling and training in these critical areas. For example, many offenders come from homes where chaos and even criminality are the norm. It becomes difficult, if not outright detrimental, to return an offender on parole to such a situation without the necessary family counseling and therapy. The "system" almost requires that the youths become the adults and set the limits of not only their behavior, but also that of their parents.

While the work we do on the juvenile parole board can at times be disheartening, there are also many times that we have the honor to validate proud success. As one would suspect, many of the youths that come before us are from homes where one or both parents are absent, if not physically, certainly psychologically. When these misguided youths enter the youth corrections system, they encounter parental controls (provided by the system) for the first time. These controls naturally involve punishments and rewards, with rewards coming for positive changes in behavior. Like all things in life, those things that are worked for and earned are those that are savored most. And so, as they work hard on various issues, attend school, do chores and the like, they progress through the system. And at the end of the system is the Juvenile Parole Board. Those dedicated to change and that have demonstrated positive growth are rightfully proud of their accomplishments and approach the board, as the final arbiter of their success, seeking validation. What better way to reinforce the positive changes and provide them with motivation for continued success than to have a formal hearing where they can boast of their success, at the end of which we get to say, "Job well done!"

DOUGHERTY COUNTY JUVENILE COURT
Room 302
225 Pine Avenue
Albany, Georgia 31701

In the Interest of

Date of Birth: **Sex:**   **Race:**

ORDER

TERMINATION OF PROBATION

It appearing to the Court that the above-named juvenile, having been placed on probation under the supervision of the Court, has made satisfactory adjustment while on probation. It is further Ordered and Decreed that said child is hereby dismissed from probation and the Jurisdiction of this Court terminated.

ORDERED AND DECREED THIS
The _____ day of _____ 2004

_____

Judge/Associate Judge

Dougherty County Juvenile Court

FIGURE 12.6   Termination of Probation.
(*Source:* Dougherty County, GA)

court judge. This form is shown in Figure 12.6. Bonnie Farr, a juvenile probation officer for the Dougherty County Juvenile Court, has provided a form her department uses for these types of actions. Figure 12.7 shows a request for termination filed by Officer Farr. She has the option of including any relevant comments for the judge's consideration that are often favorable for the probationer.

On her form, she notes when the probation was imposed; the nature of the adjudication offense; the fact that the juvenile has completed all of the terms required by the original probation orders; the fact that the youth is attending school or some vocational program; and whether the youth paid a fine or made

Request for Termination

Date:

Childs Name:
Age:

Probation Officer: Bonnie Farr

Date of Probation:

Offense:

The above named juvenile is   years of age and has completed all conditions of probation as ordered by the Court. I am requesting to terminate from probation.

This juvenile is attending

This juvenile has paid a

This juvenile has completed

Probation Officer's Comments:

FIGURE 12.7   Request for Termination of Probation.

restitution to one or more victims. Her recommendation for the youth's termination from probation is usually granted by the juvenile court judge unless there are compelling reasons for not doing so.

CASE SUPERVISION PLANNING

Caseload Assignments

A popular strategy for assigning caseloads to probation officers that is used extensively by probation departments is the numbers-game reshuffling of **caseloads,** where reduced caseloads for POs are given to improve officer/client interpersonal contact. Reduced caseloads for POs arguably should intensify their supervision as well as their supervisory quality in relation to client/offenders (Worrall et al., 2004). Several recent studies have experimented with varying degrees of officer/client contact and recidivism rates. PO caseload reductions were mandated by one of the recommendations of the Task Force on Corrections appointed by the President's Commission on Law Enforcement and the Administration of Justice in 1967 (Sturgeon, 2005).

Models of Case Supervision Planning

Case supervision planning makes more sense if we consider several alternative case assignment strategies that are presently used by different probation departments (Gowen, 2001). The most popular model is the **conventional model,** which is the random assignment of probationers to POs on the basis of one's present caseload in relation to others. This is much like the **numbers game model,** where total probationers are divided by the total POs in a given department, and each PO is allocated an equal share of the supervisory task. Thus, POs may supervise both very dangerous and nondangerous probationers. Another model is the **conventional model with geographic considerations.** Simply, this is assigning probationers to POs who live in a common geographic area. The intent is to shorten PO travel between clients. Again, little or no consideration is given to an offender's needs or dangerousness in relation to PO skills. The **specialized caseloads model** is the model used for case supervision planning, where offender assignments are made on the basis of client risks and needs and PO skills and interests in dealing with those offender risks and needs. Some POs may have special training and education in psychology or social work or chemical dependency. Thus, if certain clients have psychological problems or chemical dependencies, it is believed that these POs with special skills and education might be more effective in relating to them (Sturgeon, 2005).

THE BALANCED APPROACH

Some of the problems of JISP have been attributable to different caseload assignment models or to other organizational peculiarities and conflicting organizational goals that interfere with the performance of juvenile PO roles. One solution is referred to as the **balanced approach** (Seyko, 2001). The balanced approach to juvenile probation is neither a wholly punitive nor rehabilitative formulation, but rather is a more broad-based, constructive approach. It operates on the assumption that decision making must take into consideration the converging interests of all involved parties in the juvenile justice process, including offenders, victims, the community-at-large, and the system itself. No party to the decision making should benefit at the expense of another party; rather, a balancing of interests should be sought. The balanced approach, therefore, simultaneously emphasizes community protection, offender accountability, individualization of treatments, and competency assessment and development (Abatiello, 2005).

The balanced approach obligates community leaders and juvenile justice system actors to consider their individual juvenile codes and determine whether a balance exists between offender needs and community interests (Seyko, 2001). Punitive provisions of these codes should address victim needs as well as the needs of juvenile offenders, to the extent that restitution and victim compensation are a part of improving an offender's accountability and acceptance of responsibility. The fairness of the juvenile justice system should be assessed by key community leaders, and a mission statement should be drafted that has the broad support of diverse community organizations. Training programs can be created through the close coordination of chief probation officers in different jurisdictions, where offender needs may be targeted and addressed.

All facets of the community and the juvenile justice process should be involved, including juvenile court judges. The high level of community involvement will help to ensure a positive juvenile probation program that will maximize a youth's rehabilitative benefits (Ayers-Schlosser, 2005).

Some ISP programs fail because they often neglect to address many of the problems that include those suggested by the balanced approach. Some of the reasons for why case supervision planning is often unsuccessful are:

1. Purpose: the purposes of case supervision planning have not been thought out carefully.

2. Perceptual differences: offenders often change only when they find it necessary to change; not because we want them to change.

3. Resistance: we don't always recognize that resistance to change is normal; sometimes we prematurely shift emphasis to an enforcement orientation and rules of probation; case planning starts to look more like the probation order whenever this occurs.

4. Expectation: desired change is sought too quickly; we sometimes expect too much from offenders or expect unrealistic changes to be made.

5. Focus: there is a tendency to focus on lesser problems in order to gain "success."

6. Involvement: we often fail to involve offenders in the case planning process.

7. Stereotyping: case supervision planning is equated with treatment and rehabilitation, and thus, it is often rejected without an adequate consideration of its strengths.

8. Getting too close: sometimes POs are perceived as getting too close to offenders.

9. Perceptions of accountability: nonspecific case plans cannot be criticized by supervisors.

10. Use of resources: there is a tendency to "burn out" community resources by referring involuntary offenders, those who are not ready to work on their problems.

11. Measurement: probation successes or failures are not measured according to some case plan, but rather, according to arrests, convictions, or numbers of technical violations; how should success be evaluated or measured?

12. Management: there is a general lack of understanding or support for case supervision planning by management; POs are considered exclusively officers of the court, and judges don't particularly expect offenders to change because of officer "treatments," only that someone shares the blame or accountability whenever offenders commit new crimes or violate one or more of their probationary conditions.

13. Training: staff members have not been adequately trained in the development, implementation, and evaluation of case plans (Ellsworth, 1988: 29–30).

The principles of JISP programs are sound. Basically, implementation problems of one type or another have hindered their successfulness in various jurisdictions (Jones, 1990). It is apparent that juvenile probation services will need to coordinate their activities and align their departmental and individual

Drug education programs are sponsored by many local police departments, where police officers visit schools and explain the harmful effects of various substances for youths.

PO performance objectives with those of community-based agencies that are a part of the referral network of services and treatments in order to maximize goal attainment. Consistent with the balanced approach to managing offenders, it has been recommended that in order for ISP programs to maximize their effectiveness, they should be individualized to a high degree, so that a proper balance of punishment/deterrence and rehabilitation/community protection may be attained (Ayers-Schlosser, 2005). Public safety remains a key goal of any community-based program responsible for serious and violent juvenile offenders (Kennedy, 2005). An offender's constitutional rights should be recognized, but at the same time, accountability to victims and the community must be ensured. In the next section, we examine several specific ISP programs that are considered community-based alternatives in contrast with state- or locally operated public programs.

COMMUNITY-BASED ALTERNATIVES

Community Corrections Acts

Community-based corrections agencies and organizations are not new. Originally, these programs were intended to alleviate prison and jail overcrowding by establishing community-based organizations that could accommodate some of the overflow of prison-bound offenders (Nuffield, 2003). However, corrections officials soon realized that the potential of such programs was great for offender rehabilitation and reintegration, and that juveniles as well as adult offenders could profit from involvement in them. Many states subsequently passed **community corrections acts** that were aimed at funding local government units to create community facilities that could provide services and other resources to juveniles (Clear and Dammer, 2003). Minnesota passed the Community Corrections Act (CCA) in the early 1970s, for example. In 1979 the state undertook a comprehensive examination of the CCA in order to evaluate its effectiveness (Minnesota Crime Control Planning Board, 1981).

The evaluation results indicated that the objectives of Minnesota's CCA were all met. In planning and administration, CCA participation led to the emergence of new organizational structures and activities. The improvement was most apparent in the functions of training and budgeting. There were 11 CCA areas established for juvenile offenders. Considerable attention was devoted to programming for juvenile clients. A primary objective of Minnesota's CCA was to retain more juvenile offenders in their communities. In 9 out of 11 CCA areas, this goal was achieved. One potentially disturbing finding reported in this evaluation was that juvenile arrest rates were somewhat higher in the CCA areas compared with non-CCA areas. Officials associated with the evaluation were quick to point out that this did not mean that the CCA had a negative effect on public protection from juvenile offenders. Rather, the fact of larger concentrations of juvenile delinquents in given CCA areas explained the higher arrest rates compared with other areas. Statistically accounting for these disproportionate differences, it was concluded that public protection was maintained in ways similar to non-CCA areas, and that individual safety was not compromised despite the higher juvenile arrest rates.

The overall objective of community corrections agencies is to develop and deliver front-end solutions and alternative sanctions in lieu of state incarceration (Burrell, 2005). In 1984, the **American Correctional Association (ACA)** Task Force on Community Corrections Legislation recommended that community corrections acts should not target violent offenders. Rather, the states should be selective about who meets their program requirements. It was recommended that (1) states should continue to house violent juvenile offenders in secure facilities; (2) judges and prosecutors should continue to explore various punishment options in lieu of incarceration; and (3) local communities should develop programs with additional funding from state appropriations (Huskey, 1984:45). The ACA Task Force identified the following elements as essential to the success of any community corrections act:

1. There should be restrictions on funding high-cost capital projects as well as conventional probation services.

2. Local communities should participate on a voluntary basis and may withdraw at any time.

3. Advisory boards should submit annual criminal justice plans to local governments.

4. There should be a logical formula in place for allocating community corrections funds.

5. Incarceration-bound juveniles should be targeted, rather than adding additional punishments for those who otherwise would remain in their communities (in short, avoid "net-widening").

6. Financial subsidies should be provided to local government and community-based corrections agencies.

7. Local advisory boards in each community should function to assess program needs and effectiveness, and to propose improvements in the local

BOX 12.3

INTERNATIONAL SNAPSHOT: JUVENILE JUSTICE IN FRANCE

French laws concerning juveniles have evolved from pre–World War II penal provisions. In fact, contemporary juvenile measures continue to be influenced largely by a juvenile ordinance of 1945. This ordinance espoused several principles, including a specialized jurisdiction for youthful offenders, mitigated responsibility due to one's age, and priority given to educational rather than enforcement or punishment measures. However, subsequent modifications of this law, particularly in 2002, were more consistent with equivalent "get-tough" measures implemented in the United States to deal with more serious juvenile offenders who commit violent crimes.

The French media have described juvenile delinquency as increasing in recent years. Furthermore, it has been reported that delinquents are becoming younger and more violent. These assertions are largely speculations based on limited statistical information, but they have been influential in modifying contemporary juvenile justice policies. One favorable indicator of French juvenile offense trends is self-report information that has been collected more or less systematically since the early 1990s. Self-report information is yielded about the risk factors associated with delinquency, profiles of perpetrators, and the criminal processing of juvenile defendants and consequences of legal actions. Another source of information about juvenile offending is from monitoring boards such as the National French Delinquency Monitoring Board, established by the Interior Ministry in 2003. Preceding the results of such self-report disclosures, official documents revealed that juvenile delinquency in France rose about 20 percent between 1977 and 1992, and it increased by 80 percent between 1992 and 2001. This information has been made available by the French police and the judicial system.

As of 2002 the age of criminal responsibility in France is 13. Juvenile sanctions may be applied to youths up to age 18. There is an exception in juvenile law allowing officials to impose educational sanctions or measures on juveniles under the age of 13, by only under extraordinary circumstances.

Juvenile justice in France is largely oriented toward crime prevention. French-style prevention encompasses educational and social dimensions, however, that are aimed at preserving public safety. Unfortunately, France has failed to devise methods to detect or identify early at-risk factors that contribute to delinquency of youth. Terms such as antisocial behavior are vaguely defined, and it is unknown precisely what actions should be taken against children considered to be at risk or antisocial. One promising development has been the creation of parent centers and Local Security Contracts, with the overall objective of assisting parents at being parents or referring them to other agencies, particularly psychiatric facilities, where they can gain valuable information and insight into the motives of their children and their law-breaking behaviors. Local Security Contracts consist of community-based initiatives and extracurricular and general recreational activities, proposed mainly for youths in the most troubled neighborhoods and organized in the context of urban policy.

Prior to the 1980s, France utilized prevention clubs, which were primarily street contacts with youths by specialized educators who attempted to build individualized relationships with certain youths. These prevention clubs were much like Big Brother/Big Sister organizations in operation throughout the United States. But the prevention clubs were not particularly successful at preventing increases in delinquency. One reason was that delinquency was repeated continuously and among children of younger ages.

New forms of social prevention beyond 2000 include recommended actions from the Bonnemaison Report, which was set forth within the City Councils for Crime Prevention. Campaigns were implemented to bring together a broad range of agents including educators, social workers, police, municipal services, and businesses. These would also include school monitoring, national education relay services, and police recreational centers. Although school monitoring is not explicitly linked with preventing delinquency, it is still closely connected with work to distance youths from delinquency and to preserve public order. The ultimate aim is to bring together and coordinate educational and social agents and other professionals in public health and social integration to identify youths who have dropped out of school and/or who are in danger of dropping out, and to propose educational and integrative solutions.

This program consists of local partnerships that have the basic principle of developing educational responses rather than law-enforcement oriented ones, and to build a network in which all agents including the national educational system are on an equal footing. Tutoring and the widespread use of volunteers in different communities, local community residents, and members of the city council, as well as elected parent representatives, participate in this therapeutic-like milieu to assist youths and encourage them to remain in the formal educational process (Rivers, 2005).

Relay services for school dropouts or potential dropouts are geared to providing temporary solutions and services. Many students have been socially marginalized. Thus, services are oriented toward reintegrating these youths with their teachers, families, and others significant in their lives. Youths in these situations are viewed as someone in need of help to situate themselves as students. Thus the process is developmental, as these students work toward acquiring adult-like adaptive skills to prepare them for law-abiding behaviors as adults.

The police have also become involved in delinquency prevention by establishing and operating recreational, sports, or cultural activities for youths. Projects are organized, such as summer prevention campaigns, now called "City Life Holidays," coordinated with the Ministry of Youth and Sports, and are run by the national police service.

Actual enforcement of the law by police is carefully regulated. Police have little discretionary powers. When minors are arrested, they cannot be held in police custody without the agreement of the prosecutor's office. To avoid police custody, prosecutors often ask police to invite minors back for voluntary questioning. Prosecutors decide whether to pursue cases against any juvenile. In less serious cases involving juvenile first-offenders, prosecutors can simply propose a settlement, which concludes the case. The settlement may be restitution, if property is damaged or stolen, or community service.

Minors under the age of 13 cannot be held in police custody, with some exceptions. If a minor age 10–13 has committed or attempted to commit a serious felony or an offense punishable by at least 5 years of imprisonment, they may be held in the custody of a judicial police officer with prior agreement of the prosecutor or examining magistrate or under the protection of a juvenile court judge. The period of detention cannot exceed 12 hours. However, this period may be extended for an additional 12 hours maximum under exceptional conditions. The youth's parents are notified whenever their children are in custody. All youths under 16 years of age must be examined by a physician. When custody begins, the juvenile can request to speak with an attorney and be informed of this right. Police custody of a minor age 13–16 cannot be extended if the offense is punishable by a sentence of less than 5 years' imprisonment. All police custody of minors is controlled by prosecutors. This control varies according to the particular court. Therefore, there is a close working relationship between the police and prosecutors.

Prosecutors have considerable discretion relating to minors and their ultimate dispositions. Educational measures or criminal sanctions or both may be recommended and imposed with judicial approval. Some courts in France have special prosecutors for juveniles while others do not. Prosecutors may recommend mediation justice, which is of the form of victim–offender reconciliation, or restorative justice as it is

(continued)

known in the United States (Lightfoot and Umbreit, 2004). This measure seeks to compensate victims for their losses and serve the best interests of the community. Judges prefer special prosecutors with unique experience in working with juveniles, because it is believed that such prosecutors know what is best for particular children charged with various offenses. Prosecutors also have the right to report children and their families to social services for various types of interventions. Such prosecutorial actions might occur if juveniles are caught by police late at night wandering the streets without any particular purpose.

The use of probation for minors age 13–18 is increasing. Laws established in 2002 stipulated obligations of minors on probation. They must submit themselves to measures of protection, assistance, supervision, and education implemented by the Judicial Youth Protection Office, or by a licensed private facility. Or they must respect the conditions for placement in an educational center, in particular a closed educational center, for up to 6 months. This placement may be renewed for an additional 6 months.

Pretrial detention of minors is an exceptional measure. Two ways are provided for detaining minors prior to trial. First, minors under age 16 can be held if under suspicion for committing a crime punishable by imprisonment for 3 or more years. Second, they may be placed in a closed educational center. Pretrial detention of minors is subject to various forms of control, including (1) by rules of procedure themselves that limit detention according to offense seriousness and offender's age; (2) by the jail's incarceration commission for minors; (3) by educators of the Judicial Youth Protection Office who follow detained minors and report to the magistrates; (4) by the lawyers who handle applications for release; and (5) by the judge. Social and educational services are provided during these detention periods for all juveniles. Investigations are

conducted by interdisciplinary teams who work with offenders to determine their individualized needs and requisite services.

Sentencing sanctions for juveniles has three dimensions. First, the youth court magistrate can judge a case much like a bench trial in the United States. Educational measures can be ordered. Or the case can be sent to juvenile court. Second, the juvenile court is comprised of a juvenile court magistrate who presides and two assessors (nonprofessional magistrates). This court judges a variety of serious and nonserious offenses and can order educational and penalty measures. Third, the Juvenile Azize Court hears minors ages 16–18. These courts are comprised of three professional magistrates and a jury of citizens. This court can impose educational measures, fines, and/or prison sentences.

If juveniles are placed in secure imprisonment, these are largely secure educational centers for the short- or long-term detention of juveniles who are delinquent or seriously marginalized, or are in danger of recidivism. Working in sessions in groups of 5–7 youths for 3 to 6-month periods, these secure educational centers attempt to create new lives for juveniles by transforming them into law-abiding functional adults. Emergency placement centers attempt similar objectives, but for shorter periods. Finally, youths may be placed in closed educational centers. These are reserved for youths ages 13–18. Youths are placed under supervision and detention for a period of 6 months. Closed means that the threat of incarceration exists if the youth attempts to escape from the center. The parents of juveniles can also be sanctioned by juvenile court judges if they fail to appear. Sanctions usually are in the form of fines.

[*Sources:* Anne Wyvekens, "The French Juvenile Justice System: Working Group on Juvenile Justice." Ministry of Justice, Unpublished paper, 2005. "La Delinquance des Jeunes." Ministry of Justice, Unpublished paper, 2005.]

Campus-like residential accommodations are provided for some youths in many correctional centers.

juvenile justice system and educate the general public about the benefits of intermediate punishments.

8. A performance factor should be implemented to ensure that funds are used to achieve specific goals of the act.

Shawnee County (KS) Community Corrections. A good example of a contemporary view of community corrections acts in action within specific cities and counties is the Shawnee County, Kansas, community corrections program (Shawnee County Department of Community Corrections, 2002:1). Originally in Kansas, a Community Corrections Act (CCA) was passed in 1978, and Shawnee County was one of the first counties to join in the CCA and begin programming. At first there were only nine counties involved. In 1989 Kansas mandated that all counties should have community corrections services. In 1994 juvenile services were included. And in 1996–1997, juvenile offender services were transferred from the Kansas Department of Corrections to the Juvenile Justice Authority (JJA).

One original purpose of the Kansas CCA was the diversion of prison-bound offenders from institutions to community-based intermediate sanction programs. With the changes brought about by the implementation of sentencing guidelines, offenders are formally sentenced to probation pursuant to the guidelines' computation of sentence. In 2002 the Department of Community Corrections supervised chronic or violent offenders within the community. Effective community-based programming involves intensive supervision of these clients, together with solution-focused case management services that assist offenders in becoming productive members of society.

When Shawnee County Community Corrections (SCCC) was established, it was one of three units within the Shawnee County Department of Corrections. The Department of Corrections included the jail, a juvenile detention center, and community corrections. In 2000, community corrections became a separate department. Presently the mission of the SCCC is to (1) provide highly structured community supervision to felony offenders; (2) hold offenders accountable to their victims and to the community; and (3) improve the offenders' ability to live productively and lawfully.

The juvenile community corrections program is a state and local partnership. It is designed to (1) promote public safety; (2) hold juvenile offenders accountable for their behavior; and (3) improve the ability of youth to live productively and responsibly in their communities. In this respect, the juvenile program reflects the basic elements of the balanced approach.

Program goals are attained in the following manner. For the goal of public safety, manageable caseloads are maintained, allowing staff to closely supervise offenders in the community. For the goal of enforcing court-ordered sanctions, supervision plans are devised that meet the requirements of the court and provide structure, which will improve the offender's ability to successfully complete the terms of his or her probation program. For the aim of restoring losses to crime victims, payment of restitution by offenders is overseen, including the collection of court costs and supervision of community service work. Finally, for the aim of assisting offenders to change their behaviors, offender participation in services provided by community corrections or community resources is enforced through close offender monitoring to ensure their compliance. Services include drug treatment, job search and maintenance skills, literacy enhancement, and life skills.

Several supervisory options are available, depending on the juvenile offender's needs. For example, a juvenile intensive supervised probation program includes intensive monitoring and provides an intermediate sanction between standard probation and placement in a juvenile correctional facility for adjudicated juvenile offenders. The juvenile offender community case management program consists of services provided for juvenile offenders who have been placed by the court in the care and custody of the JJA. The court may order out-of-home placement for certain juvenile offenders after all other reasonable efforts have been made to address the problems that caused their illegal behavior. Case management services are provided to assist juveniles and their caregivers to find resources that will meet their needs. Finally, the juvenile conditional release supervision program provides monitoring of juveniles who have been released from one of four JJA-operated juvenile correctional facilities and returned to the community. Community corrections officers monitor these juveniles so that they comply with the conditions of their release. These officers also assist juveniles in accomplishing their aftercare plans.

The juvenile justice process followed in Shawnee County is as follows:

Arrest

Juvenile Detention Center (if danger to self or others during court process)

Adjudication (court determines juvenile committed offense; juvenile is adjudicated a delinquent offender)

Sentencing alternatives:

1. Place juvenile offender in parent's custody (to follow terms and conditions of the court, including making restitution).
2. Place juvenile offender on probation through court services for a fixed period (to follow terms and conditions of the court, including making restitution).

3. Place juvenile offender on intensive supervised probation for a fixed period through community corrections (to follow terms and conditions of the court, including making restitution; reporting to ISO as required; submit to drug screens; use no alcohol or illegal drugs; follow mental health or drug treatment plan; perform community service work—20 hours; attend school; employment, if not enrolled in school; no firearms; other conditions as ordered by the court).

4. Place juvenile offender in custody of JJA (case management through community corrections) once reasonable efforts have been met for juveniles requiring more services (supervision plan may include similar items as intensive supervised probation and may require placement out of the home).

5. Commit juvenile offender to a juvenile correctional facility (incarceration).

6. Conditional release supervision (follow conditional release requirements; similar requirements as outlined under intensive supervised probation).

On any given day in Topeka and the Shawnee area, there are about 465 juvenile misdemeanor or felony offenders on probation supervised by court services. Approximately 35 juvenile misdemeanor or felony offenders are on intensive supervised probation, while 90 juvenile misdemeanor or felony offenders are on community case management supervision. About 15 juvenile offenders are on conditional release and are supervised by community corrections, while 40 juvenile offenders are in a state juvenile correctional facility supervised by community corrections for reintegration planning. Overall, 645 juveniles from Shawnee County are on some type of supervision for a criminal offense. Shawnee County has approximately 165,000 people.

Approximately 2,915 adults and juveniles are in the county criminal or juvenile justice system each day. This figure does not include ex-offenders or alleged offenders. The cost of having an offender on intensive supervised probation is about $2,650 a year compared with $18,775 per year in a Kansas correctional facility. All offenders are screened and evaluated according to their risk to reoffend. A risk assessment form is the instrument used for this evaluation. The higher one's score, the more intense their supervision. Offenders are reassessed at different time intervals in order to allow for progress in their individual programs. This reassessment may reduce the intensity of their future supervision if they are doing well. Besides frequent meetings with each offender, the intensive supervision officer will have contact with the offenders' employers, counselors, teachers, families, and law enforcement agencies. Random drug/alcohol screens are also conducted (Shawnee County Department of Community Corrections, 2002:1–4). The successfulness of this community corrections program has been assessed in recent years. Between 1999 and 2002, the amount of recidivism among juvenile clients has been approximately 12 percent. This low recidivism rate suggests that at least in Shawnee County, Kansas, the community corrections program is fulfilling its diverse objectives.

In the following section, we examine three increasingly important intermediate punishments that seem to be working well with adult and juvenile offenders alike. These include (1) electronic monitoring; (2) home confinement; and (3) shock probation.

ELECTRONIC MONITORING

Electronic Monitoring Defined

Electronic monitoring or **tagging** is the use of telemetry devices to verify that an offender is at a specified location during specified times. Electronic monitoring is also a system of home confinement aimed at monitoring, controlling, and modifying the behavior of defendants or offenders. The offender wears an electronic bracelet/anklet or other electronic device in accordance with conditions set by the courts. The tagged person is monitored by computer for 24 hours a day and is supervised by a private company or a combination of a company and the criminal justice authority, usually a probation department. The person must remain in the home under surveillance, unless authorized to leave for employment, school, participation in community treatment programs, or similar activities. Electronic monitoring tends to be used for less serious, nonviolent offenders who are identified by a risk formula.

Electronic Monitoring Origins.   Electronic monitoring devices were first used in 1964 as an alternative to incarcerating certain mental patients and parolees (Harig, 2001). Subsequently, electronic monitoring was extended to include monitoring office work, employee testing for security clearances, and many other applications. Other countries are currently experimenting with electronic monitoring. For instance, England and Germany use electronic monitoring for managing certain adult and youthful offenders (Haverkamp, 2002; Nellis, 2004).

Second Judicial District Judge Jack Love of New Mexico is credited with implementing a pilot electronic monitoring project in 1983 for persons convicted of drunk driving and certain white-collar offenses, such as embezzlement (Houk, 1984). Subsequent to its use for probationers, the New Mexico State Supreme Court approved the program, since it required the voluntariness and consent of probationers as a condition of their probation programs. Judge Love directed that certain probationers should wear either anklets or bracelets that emitted electronic signals that could be intercepted by their probation officers who conducted surveillance operations. After a short period of such judicial experimentation, other jurisdictions decided to conduct their own experiments for offender monitoring with electronic devices. Eventually, experiments were underway, not only for probationers, but for parolees and inmates of jails and prisons.

How Much Electronic Monitoring Is There in the United States?

Accurate statistical information about the extent and use of electronic monitoring in the United States for either juveniles or adults is difficult to obtain. Most of this information is based on estimated usage rather than actual usage (Gainey and Payne, 2003). Some of this information is derived from sales figures reported by firms that manufacture electronic monitoring equipment, such as BI, Inc. Sales figures are often misleading, since jurisdictions that order electronic monitoring equipment may replace older equipment, or they may only use some of this equipment rather than all of it at any given time. The numbers of electronically monitored clients fluctuate daily, and there are great variations in the amount of time clients spend being monitored. However, the amount of time spent on electronic monitoring averages about 12–15 weeks. Other information is obtained from those jurisdictions interested enough in reporting such information (King and Gibbs, 2003).

Contemporary surveys that seek accurate information about electronic monitoring usage throughout the United States only obtain such information from about 25 percent of the jurisdictions canvassed (Seiter and West, 2003). Considering all of these limitations, virtually every report about electronic monitoring shows that its frequency is increasing annually. For instance, in 1997 a report was issued showing that 31,236 probationers and parolees were being electronically monitored (Schmidt, 1998:11). In 1998, over 95,000 clients were being electronically monitored. By 2004 over 150,000 persons were on electronic monitoring and/or house arrest (Office of Juvenile Justice and Delinquency Prevention, 2005). Over 25,000 youths were involved in electronic monitoring programs by 2004 (American Correctional Association, 2005). The average cost of using this equipment in different probation and parole departments ranges from $5–$25 per day, depending on the intensity of the surveillance by POs. This is at least half of the cost of maintaining a juvenile or adult under some type of detention per day.

Types of Signalling Devices

There are at least four types of **electronic monitoring signalling devices.** First, a continuous-signal device consists of a miniature transmitter that is strapped to the probationer's wrist. The transmitter broadcasts an encoded signal that is received by a receiver-dialer in the offender's home. The signal is relayed to a central receiver over the telephone lines. A second type of monitor is the programmed contact device, which is similar to the continuous-signal device. However, in this case, a central computer from the probation office is programmed to call the offender's home at random hours to verify the probationer's whereabouts. Offenders must answer their telephones, insert the wristlet-transmitter into the telephone device, and their voices and signal emissions are verified by computer (Cadigan, 2001).

A third monitor is a cellular device. This is a transmitter worn by offenders and emits a radio signal that may be received by a local area monitoring system. Up to 25 probationers may be monitored at once with such a system. The fourth type of monitor is the continuous signalling transmitter, which is also worn by the offender. These also send out continuous signals, which may be intercepted by portable receiving units in the possession of probation officers. These are quite popular, since POs may conduct drive-bys and verify whether offenders are at home during curfew hours when they are supposed to be.

These wristlet anklet transmitters are certainly not tamper-proof. They are similar in plastic construction to the wristlet ID tags given patients at the time of hospital admissions. However, these electronic devices are somewhat more sturdy. Nevertheless, the plastic is such that it is easy to remove. It is easily seen whether the device has been tampered with (e.g., stretched, burned, mutilated), since it is impossible to reattach without special equipment in the possession of the probation department. If tampering has occurred and probationers have attempted to defeat the intent of the device, they may be subject to probation revocation. This offense may be punished by incarceration.

Types of Offenders on Electronic Monitoring

The types of offenders placed on electronic monitoring are selected because of their low likelihood of reoffending and the fact that their crimes are less serious, usually property offenses. Thus, there is a certain amount of creaming that occurs, where those most likely to succeed are selected. This is one reason why electronic monitoring exhibits low recidivism rates among its clientele in numerous jurisdictions. However, in recent years, electronic monitoring has been extended to include more violent types of juvenile offenders, such as violent juvenile parolees (Finn and Muirhead-Steves, 2002). One reason is that juvenile correctional facilities are increasingly overcrowded to the point where more dangerous juveniles must be released short of serving their full terms. The public is increasingly concerned about community safety. One result is the greater use of electronic monitoring equipment for such offenders to verify their whereabouts and exert a minimum amount of behavioral control.

Gradually, the use of electronic monitoring devices was extended to include both low- and high-risk juvenile offenders. In Knoxville, Tennessee, for example, electronic monitoring is used to a limited degree with juvenile probationers, but only as a last resort. Thus, juvenile offenders who have failed in other types of probation programs or community-based agencies are placed in an electronic monitoring program prior to being placed in secure confinement. If they do not comply with their electronic monitoring program conditions, they will be sent to secure confinement at one of the state's several public and private secure confinement facilities (Knox County Juvenile Services, 2002).

Electronic monitoring is used in most jurisdictions for both adult and juvenile offenders (Cohn, 2000). Electronic monitoring should not be viewed as a panacea for every low-risk offender, however. Some selectivity is necessary to ensure that persons who do not require electronic monitoring are not monitored, thus increasing the cost-effectiveness of the program.

When the alternative to electronic monitoring is jail, most offenders, juveniles or otherwise, prefer electronic monitoring to confinement in a jail cell (Gainey and Payne, 2003). There are significant punitive dimensions of electronic monitoring, including both physical and psychological. One's presence is required in a particular place at a particular time, and computer checks of one's whereabouts are frequent enough to cause some clients stress. Being confined to one's house as a punishment is more serious than it sounds. Many electronically monitored clients point out that the electronic monitoring program is in many ways equivalent to a jail sentence and is very much a punishment (Gowen, 2001).

The SpeakerID Program

Some jurisdictions, such as the Dane County, Wisconsin Sheriff's Office, have implemented a **SpeakerID Program** (Listug, 1996:85). SpeakerID is a voice verification monitoring system allowing law enforcement and criminal justice agencies to monitor low-risk offenders under probation or house arrest. Implemented in October 1994, the SpeakerID program is a completely automated system that calls clients at their authorized locations at random times. Prior to using SpeakerID, the Dane County Sheriff's Office used traditional ankle bracelets and wristlets as described earlier. The SpeakerID system started out with only 8–12 offenders. In 1996 there were between 30 and 35 offenders participating in this system. When offenders answer their telephones, they are asked specific questions. Voice matches are verified perfectly, and thus there is little likelihood that any particular offender can fool the system with a previously recorded tape or some other device. Because of the automated nature of the system, SpeakerID is cost-effective. Apart from initial startup costs, the SpeakerID system costs about $3 per day per monitored offender. This compares very favorably with jail and prison costs of $40 and $49 per prisoner per day in Wisconsin jails and prisons.

Some Criticisms of Electronic Monitoring

Some limitations of electronic monitoring programs are that they are quite expensive to implement initially. The direct costs associated with their purchase or lease are seemingly prohibitive to local jurisdictions that are used to incarcerating juveniles and defraying their maintenance costs over an extended period. However, once a given jurisdiction has installed such equipment, it eventually pays for itself and functions to reduce overall incarcerative expenses that otherwise would have been incurred had these same youths been placed in secure confinement.

Also, electronic monitoring programs require some training on the part of the users. While those using such systems do not need to be computer geniuses, some computer training is helpful. Electronic monitoring is a delinquency deterrent for many offenders (Johnston, 2000). However, it is not foolproof. In spite of the fact that they may be easily tampered with, electronic wristlets and anklets only help to verify an offender's whereabouts. They do not provide television images of these persons and whatever they may be doing. One federal probation officer has reported that one of his federal probationers on electronic monitoring was running a successful stolen property business out of his own home. Thus, he was able to continue his criminal activity unabated, despite the home confinement constraints imposed by electronics.

Electronic monitoring has also been criticized as possibly violative of the Fourth Amendment search-and-seizure provision, where, it is alleged by some critics, electronic eavesdropping might be conducted within one's home or bedroom. This argument is without serious constitutional merit, since the primary function of such monitoring is to verify an offender's whereabouts. Some sophisticated types of monitoring systems are equipped with closed-circuit television transmissions, such as those advertised by the Bell Telephone Company as viewer-phones of the future. But even if such monitoring were so equipped, this additional feature would only intrude where offenders wished it to intrude, such as their living rooms or kitchens.

The fact is that many offenders may be inexpensively tracked through these monitoring systems and their whereabouts can be verified without time-consuming face-to-face checks (Cohn, 2000). For instance, a single juvenile probation officer may conduct drive-bys of client residences during evening hours and receive their transmitted signals with a portable unit. This silent means of detection is intended only to enforce one program element, namely, observance of curfews. Other checks, such as those conducted for illegal drug or alcohol use, must be verified directly, through proper testing and expert confirmation. Electronic monitoring is increasingly used in tandem with another sentencing option—home confinement.

Summarizing the arguments for and against electronic monitoring, proponents of electronic monitoring say that it (1) assists offenders in avoiding the criminogenic atmosphere of prisons or jails and helps reintegrate them into their communities; (2) permits offenders to retain jobs and support families; (3) assists probation officers in their monitoring activities and has potential for easing their caseload responsibilities; (4) gives judges and other officials considerable flexibility in sentencing offenders; (5) has the potential of reducing the recidivism rate more than existing probationary alternatives; (6) is potentially useful for decreasing jail and prison populations; (7) is more cost-effective in relation to incarceration; and (8) allows for pretrial release monitoring as well as for special treatment cases such as substance abusers, the mentally retarded, women who are pregnant, and juveniles.

Those against electronic monitoring say that (1) some potential exists for race, ethnic, or socioeconomic bias by requiring offenders to have telephones or to pay for expensive monitoring equipment and/or fees (ironically, some jurisdictions report that many offenders enjoy better living conditions in jail or prison custody compared with their residences outside of prison); (2) public safety may be compromised through the failure of these programs to guarantee that offenders will go straight and not endanger citizens by committing new offenses while free in the community; (3) it may be too coercive, and it may be unrealistic for officials to expect full offender compliance with such a stringent system; (4) little consistent information exists about the impact of electronic monitoring on recidivism rates compared with other probationary alternatives; (5) persons frequently selected for participation are persons who probably don't need to be monitored anyway; (6) technological problems exist, making electronic monitoring somewhat unreliable; (7) it may result in widening the net by being prescribed for offenders who otherwise would receive less costly standard probation; (8) it raises right to privacy, civil liberties, and other constitutional issues such as Fourth Amendment search-and-seizure concerns; (9) much of the public interprets this option as going easy on offenders and perceives electronic monitoring as a nonpunitive alternative; and (10) the costs of electronic monitoring may be more than published estimates.

HOME CONFINEMENT OR HOUSE ARREST

The use of one's home as the principal place of confinement is not new. In biblical times, St. Paul was sentenced in Rome to house arrest for 2 years, where he performed tent maker services for others. **Home confinement** is a program of intermediate punishment involving the use of the offender's residence for mandatory incarceration during evening hours after a curfew and on weekends (Cadigan, 2001).

Florida introduced the contemporary use of home confinement in 1983 (Boone, 1996). At that time, corrections officials considered the use of homes as incarcerative facilities as acceptable alternatives to prisons or jails for certain low-risk offenders. Home confinement was a very inexpensive way of maintaining supervisory control over those offenders who were deemed not in need of costly incarceration. When Florida began its home confinement program, it was established under the Correctional Reform Act of 1983. This Act

provided that the home could be used as a form of intensive supervised custody in the community. This highly individualized program is intended primarily to restrict offender movement within the community, home, or nonresidential placement, together with specific sanctions such as curfew, payment of fines, community service, and other requirements. When Florida started to use home confinement as a punishment, prison costs averaged $30 per inmate per day, while home confinement required an expenditure of about $3.00 per offender per day. In the late 1990s prison maintenance costs per prisoner were in excess of $75 per day in most jurisdictions, while home confinement costs stabilized at about $5 per day (Tonry, 1997). Although Florida officials consider **home incarceration** or **house arrest** punitive, some persons disagree. They believe that incarceration should be in a jail or prison, if it is meaningful incarceration (Landreville, 1999).

Functions and Goals of Home Confinement Programs

The functions and goals of home confinement programs include the following:

1. To continue the offender's punishment while permitting the offender to live in his or her dwelling under general or close supervision.
2. To enable offenders to perform jobs in their communities to support themselves and their families.
3. To reduce jail and prison overcrowding.
4. To maximize public safety by ensuring that only the most qualified clients enter home confinement programs and are properly supervised.
5. To reduce the costs of offender supervision.
6. To promote rehabilitation and reintegration by permitting offenders to live under appropriate supervision within their communities.

In many jurisdictions, including U.S. federal probation, home confinement is used together with electronic monitoring (Administrative Office of the U.S. Courts, 2001). The National Juvenile Detention Association has significantly encouraged different jurisdictions to adopt home confinement and other nonincarcerative alternatives as ways of dealing with low-risk juvenile offenders. Executive Director Earl Dunlop says that "the vast majority of kids do not need to be locked up. Our emphasis is upon detention services, the process—home prevention, electronic monitoring, staff supervision—not detention services, the place" (*Corrections Today,* 1999a:20).

Relatively little is known about the extent to which home confinement is used as a sentencing alternative for juvenile offenders. Since probation is so widely used as the sanction of choice except for the most chronic recidivists, home confinement is most often applied as an accompanying condition of electronic monitoring (Bowers, 2000). However, this type of sentencing may be redundant, since curfew for juvenile offenders means home confinement anyway, especially during evening hours. As a day disposition, home confinement for juveniles would probably be counterproductive, since juveniles are often obligated to finish their schooling as a probation program condition. Again, since school hours are during the daytime, it would not make sense to deprive juveniles of school opportunities through some type of home confinement.

Home confinement is also useful for certain types of offenders who are drug- or alcohol-dependent. Probation officers can visit the homes of certain drug-dependent clients and perform instant checks to determine whether they have used alcohol or drugs in the recent past. While access to drugs or alcohol is relatively easy when a client is confined to his or her home, the threat of a random drug/alcohol test by a PO is often a sufficient deterrent (Latessa and Allen, 1999). Needs assessments for certain offenders can determine which services they require, and they are relatively mobile to seek these services with probation department approval (Gowen, 2001).

Advantages and Disadvantages of Home Confinement

Among the advantages of home confinement are that (1) it is cost effective; (2) it has social benefits; (3) it is responsive to local citizen and offender needs; and (4) it is easily implemented and is timely in view of jail and prison overcrowding. Some of the disadvantages of home confinement are: (1) house arrest may actually widen the net of social control; (2) it may narrow the net of social control by not being a sufficiently severe sentence; (3) it focuses primarily on offender surveillance; (4) it is intrusive and possibly illegal; (5) race and class bias may enter into participant selection; and (6) it may compromise public safety. Some of these advantages and disadvantages are addressed at length below as issues concerning home confinement where electronic monitoring is also used.

OTHER ISP PROGRAM CONDITIONS

Briefly reviewing judicial dispositional options, at one end of the sentencing spectrum, they may adjudicate youths as delinquent, impose nominal sanctions, and take no further action other than to record the event. Therefore, if the same juveniles reappear before the same judge in the future, sterner measures may be taken in imposing new dispositions. Or the judge may divert juveniles to particular community agencies for special treatment. Juveniles with psychological problems or who are emotionally disturbed, sex offenders, or those with drug and/or alcohol dependencies may be targeted for special community treatments. At the other end of the spectrum of punishments are the most drastic alternatives of custodial sanctions, ranging from the placement of juveniles in nonsecure foster homes and camp ranches, or secure facilities, such as reform schools and industrial schools. These nonsecure and secure forms of placement and/or incarceration are usually reserved for the most serious offenders (Latessa and Allen, 1999).

In many jurisdictions, such as Dougherty County, Georgia, a PO assigned to a juvenile's case will conduct a home evaluation prior to judicial actions imposing electronic monitoring, home confinement, or any other alternative condition. In Dougherty County, POs conduct home evaluations and report the results of these evaluations to juvenile court judges who can then make a more informed decision about the most appropriate disposition to impose. Figure 12.9 is an example of a home evaluation report that might be prepared. This document contains much valuable information about one's neighborhood; neighbors; gang presence, if any; family status; legal history of the family; the

HOME EVALUATION REPORT

Sending State:_____ Receiving State:_____

Juvenile's Name:_____ DOB:_____

Placement Investigated:

Parent/Guardian:_____
Address:_____
Work Phone: _____ Home Phone #: _____

HOME/NEIGHBORHOOD/PEERS (Physical description, criminal/gang
activity,etc.):_____
_____
_____
_____

FAMILY STATUS (composition, interactions, at-risk family members, attitude):
_____
_____
_____

LEGAL HISTORY OF FAMILY (current charges, probation or parole status):
_____
_____

PROPOSED PLAN (school/employment, court ordered conditions,
_____
_____
_____

OTHER COMMENTS
_____
_____
_____
_____
_____

Probation
Officer:_____

FIGURE 12.9   Home Evaluation Report.
(*Source:* Dougherty County, GA)

proposed plan for the juvenile; and any other comments believed important to
include by the investigating PO.

Also helpful in juvenile court judge decision making are regular reports
filed by POs in different jurisdictions, outlining the sociodemographic characteristics of youths under supervision, their numbers, number of terminations,
transfers, commitments, court-ordered fines and their payment or nonpayment,
and other factors. In some instances, psychological evaluations have been ordered. Some juveniles have been ordered to boot camps, or to counseling, or to
participation in youth clubs or other activities. Community service orders have

MONTH OF _____2005

BONNIE FARR

I.   **TOTAL NUMBER OF JUVENILES RECEIVED FOR SUPERVISION_____**

   Number of White Males_____   Number of Black Males_____
   Number of White Females_____   Number of Black Females_____

2.   **TOTAL NUMBER OF NEW PROBATIONERS THAT REPORTED IN FOR THAT MONTH:____**

   Number of White Males_____ Number of Black Males_____
   Number of White Females_____ Number of Black Females_____

3.   **TOTAL NUMBER OF JUVENILES REQUIRING INTENSIVE SUPERVISION_____**

   Number of White Males_____ Number of Black Males_____
   Number of White Females_____ Number of Black Females_____

4.   **TOTAL NUMBER OF JUVENILES THAT REPORTED IN FOR THE MONTH_____**

   Number of White Males_____ Number of Black Males_____
   Number of White Females_____ Number of Black Females_____

5.   **TOTAL NUMBER OF JUVENILES TERMINATED, TRANSFERRED, COMMITTED OR CLOSED DURING THE MONTH_____**

   Number of White Males_____ Number of Black Males_____
   Number of White Females_____ Number of Black Females_____

6.   **TOTAL NUMBER OF JUVENILES BEING SUPERVISED AT THE END OF THE MONTH____**

   Number of White Males_____ Number of Black Males_____
   Number of White Females_____ Number of Black Females_____

I.   **TOTAL NUMBER OF JUVENILES THAT OWE SUPERVISION FEES: _____**

   Number of White Males_____ Number of Black Males_____
   Number of White Females_____ Number of Black Females_____

2.   **TOTAL NUMBER OF JUVENILES THAT OWE RESTITUTION & FINES_____**

   Number of White Males_____ Number of Black Males_____
   Number of White Females_____ Number of Black Females_____

3.   **TOTAL NUMBER OF JUVENILES THAT WERE ORDERED PSYCHOL. EVALUATIONS _____**

FIGURE 12.10 Dougherty Juvenile Probation Officer Report.
(*Source:* Dougherty County, GA)

been issued as well. Regular documentation of this and other relevant information enables judges to see whether their dispositional orders are effective or in need of modification. Figure 12.10 shows a juvenile probation officer monthly report used by the Dougherty County Juvenile Court in Georgia.

Probation is the most commonly used sentencing option. Probation is either unconditional or conditional. This chapter has examined several conditional intermediate punishments, including intensive probation supervision

NAMES:_____
_____

DOUGHERTY JUVENILE PROBATION OFFICER MONTHLY REPORT
PAGE 2

4. **TOTAL NUMBER OF JUVENILES OVER 17 YEARS OF AGE BEING SUPERVISED_____**

Number of White Males_____ Number of Black Males_____
Number of White Females_____ Number of Black Females_____

_____
_____

l. **TOTAL NUMBER OF JUVENILES THAT ARE IN BOYS CLUB PROGRAM_____**

Number of White Males_____ Number of Black Males_____
Number of White Females_____ Number of Black Females_____

2. **TOTAL NUMBER OF JUVENILES THAT ARE IN A COUNSELING PROGRAM:_____**

Number of White Males_____ Number of Black Males_____
Number of White Females_____ Number of Black Females_____

3. **TOTAL NUMBER OF JUVENILES THAT ARE IN JAG PROGRAM_____**

Number of White Males_____ Number of Black Males_____
Number of White Females_____ Number of Black Females_____

4. **TOTAL NUMBER OF JUVENILES THAT ARE IN BOOT CAMP OR WAITING TO GO_____**

Number of White Males_____ Number of Black Males_____
Number of White Females_____ Number of Black Females_____

5. **TOTAL NUMBER OF JUVENILES RELEASED FROM BOOT CAMP DURING MONTH_____**

Names:_____
_____

TOTAL NUMBER OF JUVENILES THAT WERE ORDERED TO COMPLETE COMMUNITY SERVICE HOURS_____

Number of White Males_____   Number of Black Males_____
Number of White Females_____   Number of Black Females_____

FIGURE 12.10 Continued

and community-based programs. A youth's assignment to any of these programs may or may not include conditions. Apart from the more intensive monitoring and supervision by POs, juveniles may be expected to comply with one or more conditions, including restitution, if financial loss was suffered by one or more victims in cases of vandalism, property damage, or physical injury. Also, fines may be imposed. Or the judge may specify some form of community service. All of these conditions may be an integral part of a juvenile's probation program. Violation of or failure to comply with one or more of these conditions may result in a probation revocation action. Probation officers function as the link between juvenile offenders and the courts regarding a youth's compliance with these program conditions.

Restitution, Fines, Victim Compensation, and Victim–Offender Mediation

Restitution. An increasingly important feature of probation programs is **restitution** (O'Mahony, 2000). Several models of restitution have been described. These include:

1. The financial/community service model, which stresses the offender's financial accountability and community service to pay for damages;
2. The victim/offender mediation model, which focuses on victim–offender reconciliation; and
3. The victim/reparations model, where juveniles compensate their victims directly for their offenses (Schneider and Schneider, 1985).

The potential significance of restitution, coupled with probation, is that it suggests a reduction in recidivism among juvenile offenders. In a restitution program in Atlanta, Georgia, for example, 258 juvenile offenders participated in several experimental treatment programs, where one of the programs included restitution. The restitution offender group had a 26 percent reduction in recidivism compared with other juveniles where restitution was not included as a condition (Schneider and Schneider, 1985). But other observers caution that if restitution is not properly implemented by the court or carefully supervised, it serves little deterrent purpose (London, 2003).

Fines and Victim Compensation. Beyond reductions in recidivism, restitution, payment of **fines,** and **victim compensation** also increase offender accountability. Given the present philosophical direction of juvenile courts, this condition is consistent with enhancing a youth's acceptance of responsibility for wrongful actions committed against others and the financial harm it has caused (Arthur, 2000). Many of these programs include restitution as a part of their program requirements. Restitution orders may be imposed by juvenile court judges with or without accompanying dispositions of secure confinement (Abramson, 2003).

Victim–Offender Mediation. There is growing interest in programs for juvenile offenders that heighten their accountability, especially toward their victims. Since 1980, there has been growing awareness of and interest in **victim–offender mediation** as a means of resolving disputes between the juvenile perpetrator and his or her victim. Victim–offender mediation is bringing together victims, offenders, and other members of the community to hold offenders accountable not only for their crimes but for the harm they caused to victims (Sinclair, 2005). These programs provide an opportunity for crime victims and offenders to meet face-to-face to talk about the impact of the crime on their lives and to develop a plan for repairing the harm. Most of these programs work with juvenile offenders, although a growing number are involving adult offenders (Gregorie, 2005). Sometimes referred to as restorative justice, victim–offender mediation was quite prevalent throughout the world in 2004, with over 1,500 programs in 22 countries (Lightfoot and Umbreit, 2004). In 2005, there were 700 victim–offender mediation programs in the United States. One unique feature of such programs is that they are dialogue-driven rather than settlement-driven. While not all victims are totally satisfied with the outcomes of such programs, most report being satisfied with having the opportunity of sharing their stories and their pain resulting from the crime event. Many juveniles report being surprised at learning about the impact their actions had on various victims they confront.

Community Service

Associated with restitution orders is **community service.** Community service may be performed in different ways, ranging from cutting courthouse lawns and cleaning up public parks to painting homes for the elderly or repairing fences on private farms. Youths typically earn wages for this service, and these wages are usually donated to a victim compensation fund. The different types of community service activities are limited only by the imagination of the juvenile court and community leaders. Similar to restitution, community service orders are intended to increase offender accountability and individual responsibility (Sinclair, 2005).

SUMMARY

The most frequently used disposition by juvenile court judges is probation. Probation is a conditional nonincarcerative punishment where probationers are supervised by juvenile probation officers for various periods. Standard probation includes conditions such as reporting to probation officers in person at regular times and submitting written reports; obeying all laws; observing curfew; attending school; avoiding alcohol and drugs; not frequenting places where delinquent juveniles may be present or having any association with them; seeking counseling if directed by the court; not possessing firearms or any dangerous weapons; and participating in designated programs required by juvenile court judges. While all types of probation are conditional, some probation programs include special conditions of probation, such as attending DWI school; participating in individual or group counseling or therapies; making restitution to victims; and/or performing community service. Other conditions may be added as needed on a case-by-case basis, since these special conditions are individualized depending on offender needs. This type of probation is called probation with special conditions.

Over two-thirds of all juveniles who are adjudicated by juvenile courts receive probation of one type or another. Probation is intended to be rehabilitative and reintegrative, since offenders are permitted to reside in their communities while completing their program requirements. Heightened accountability is emphasized for juvenile probationers, and this accountability is improved by imposing restitution requirements and compulsory hours of community service, depending on offense seriousness. Restitution is often program-related, and programs such as the Youth-to-Victim Restitution Project and the Second Chance Program are examples of ways in which one's accountability and acceptance of responsibility may be heightened.

Some programs, such as juvenile probation camps and intensive aftercare programs, have been used in past years to provide youths with physical activities, improve community contact, and improve academic training. These programs have often involved compulsory participation in vocational and educational training, individual and group counseling, and character-building activities. Some programs have been offense-specific, such as the Sexual Offender Treatment (SOT) Program, which was established in a large Midwestern city during the late 1980s. Operating with a psychosocioeducational intervention focus, the program included family members of youths in counseling sessions as a means of making this program more effective at reducing recidivism rates among youthful sex offenders. The successfulness of this program was low and it was eventually discontinued.

The successfulness of any probation program is frequently evaluated according to the amount of recidivism demonstrated. Juvenile recidivists are those previously adjudicated of offenses and who enter the juvenile justice system again later for new offending. Recidivism rates of juvenile offenders in most probation programs are the same as they are for adult offenders, or from 65–70 percent. Closely associated with greater recidivism rates are one's age at one's first adjudication; having a prior delinquency record; prior commitments to juvenile facilities; drug or alcohol dependency; school problems; family discipline problems; and poor peer relationships. Risk and needs assessments are often used to determine individual offender needs and prescribe specific treatments to improve one's chances of remaining delinquency-free. It has been found that more frequent contact with one's juvenile probation officer is often associated with lower recidivism rates. Thus, some youthful offenders are designated by the courts for intensive supervised probation for a period of time.

A broad class of intermediate punishments for juveniles has been identified. Intermediate punishments include any sanctions that lie between standard probation and secure confinement. All of these punishments are community-based and involve close supervision by juvenile probation officers. Sometimes referred to as creative sentencing, intermediate punishments have several goals. These include providing less costly sanctions compared with secure confinement; achieving lower recidivism rates compared with standard probation programs; providing a greater range of community services for juvenile clients; minimizing the adverse effects of labeling by reducing one's contact with the juvenile justice system; improving one's personal educational and vocational skills, which help to improve one's self-concept; and greater acceptance of responsibility.

Juvenile intensive supervised programs (JISPs) are an integral part of intermediate punishments, which may include electronic monitoring, house arrest, and other requirements. Eligibility requirements for entry into JISPs vary among jurisdictions, but chronic recidivists and more serious offenders are usually designed for such programming. Although JISPs are more costly to operate than standard probation because of far lower officer-to-client ratios, about half of all states had adopted them by 2005. JISP characteristics include frequent face-to-face contact; frequent drug/alcohol checks; performing specified hours of community service; and observance of curfew. Most JISPs, such as the Johnson County, Kansas Juvenile Intensive Supervision Program, promote one or more of the following: mental health counseling; drug/alcohol counseling; academic achievement and aptitude testing; vocational and employment training; individual, group, and family counseling; job and employment training; alternative educational programming; foster home placement; and Big Brother/Big Sister programs. JISP effectiveness depends on those factors that tend to heighten offender accountability by creating high offender responsibility; promote greater offender control throughout the duration of their programs; low officer-to-client caseloads (30 or fewer probationers per officer); and frequent curfew, drug and alcohol, school, and employment checks. The Ohio Experience is one comprehensive JISP that seeks to heighten offender accountability, ensure public safety, and individualize sanctions that meet client needs. These objectives are achieved in part through the use of home confinement, electronic monitoring, and intensive supervision and client surveillance.

Strengths and weaknesses of JISPs include that they are more expensive to operate compared with standard probation programs, although they are far less expensive compared with the use of secure confinement. Also, demonstrated lower rates of recidivism suggest that greater offender monitoring ensures greater compliance with program goals. Some youths have special needs that are beyond the skill levels of their supervising POs. It is generally conceded that the overall goals of JISPs are sound. Usually more successful JISPs are those that emphasize a balanced approach, which is based on achieving three fundamental goals: an emphasis on improving community protection through close offender surveillance and supervision; using activities and engaging youths in programs that heighten their accountability; and individualizing treatments delivered to juveniles with special problems.

Caseloads of POs have been studied extensively. An early study of caseloads, the San Francisco Project, concluded tentatively that "close" PO supervision had little or no effect on recidivism rates among probationers compared with "general" PO supervision. However, low caseloads consisted of 20 offenders per PO, while 40 offenders per PO were defined as high caseloads. In fact, both 20 and 40 clients per juvenile PO are considered quite low, and thus the results of the San Francisco Project were flawed in this important respect. More credibility would have been attained had these caseload differences been more realistic compared with actual PO supervisory responsibilities, where high caseloads are 75 or more clients, and low caseloads are 30 or fewer clients. If this study were to be repeated under these more significant caseload distinctions, the results might be quite different. Subsequent research has supported the idea that lower caseloads do trigger lower rates of recidivism among juvenile clients in most jurisdictions, however.

Several caseload assignment models have been suggested as different forms of case supervision planning. The conventional model of case supervision planning uses random assignment to equalize the distribution of juvenile clients among a jurisdiction's PO workforce. The numbers-game model involves dividing the total number of juvenile clients by the total number of POs in a given agency and dividing supervisory responsibilities accordingly. The conventional model with geographic considerations is like the conventional model, except in this instance, consideration is given to grouping juvenile offenders in particular geographic areas and making caseload assignments on this basis, thus saving POs considerable time in traveling from one client to the next for face-to-face visits. A fourth caseload assignment type is the specialized caseloads model, where offender assignments are made on the basis of a PO's special skills. If certain POs have psychology backgrounds and have worked with special-needs offenders in the past, they may be assigned to youths with special needs or particular psychological problems. It is believed that this specialized supervisory model maximizes PO skills in any agency.

Each community has evolved different community-based programs based on the nature and types of juvenile offenders. These initiatives have usually been established through community corrections acts, or infusions of funds into community programs to develop necessary organizations, agencies, and/or services. Once community-based agencies have been established and demonstrated high success levels with clients, it is anticipated that the community will invest additional and continuing resources into such programs to maintain supervisory effectiveness over clients and minimize their potential for recidivism. Developing community correctional services means that youths can remain in their communities and receive necessary services and treatments, thus furthering their rehabilitation and reintegration. Programs in various jurisdictions, such as the Shawnee County, Kansas, community corrections program, have experienced high success rates with their youthful clients. In this program, many secure confinement-bound offenders have been diverted to community programs, which has reduced substantially treatment and supervision costs. In this program, the goals are to promote public safety, hold youths accountable for their behavior, and improve a youth's ability to live productively in the community by providing educational, vocational, and counseling services. The balanced approach is apparent in this program.

Other types of intermediate punishment programs have been implemented in different jurisdictions. The Boston Offender Project (BOP) was implemented in 1981. It sought to intervene with violent juveniles by developing specialized treatments and delivering comprehensive services. Violent juveniles would be placed in secure confinement for a short period, and then they would be released into community programming matching their particular needs. Diagnostic assessments disclosed the nature of these needs, and treatments for individual offenders were tailored accordingly. The BOP was considered a shock probation program similar to shock probation programs for adult offenders. During the community phase, clients were tracked according to their psychological and vocational development, as well as according to their medical needs. BOP counselors were highly skilled and trained to deliver needed services to clients. Low rates of recidivism were observed among BOP clientele who eventually left the program after successfully completing its requirements.

Another program is Project New Pride, which was established in Denver, Colorado, in the early 1970s. New Pride blends educational experiences, counseling, employment, and cultural education activities for youths between ages 14–17 committing more serious crimes. The aims of New Pride are to reintegrate offenders into their communities and reduce recidivism rates among clients. The project emphasizes schooling, employment counseling, and family closeness. Employment counseling services are offered, together with job placement, school tutoring, and vocational training. Recidivism rates among participating clients have been less than 20 percent over the years. Most successful community programs help prepare youths for increased responsibility and community freedom; increase a youth's involvement in useful community activities; work with youths and their families, peers, schools, and employers in an effort to identify those qualities necessary for one's successful adaptation and reintegration; develop new resources and support systems where needed; and monitor and test youths and their communities concerning their ability to interact productively.

An increasingly used supervisory tool in many probation departments is electronic monitoring (EM). This is the use of telemetry devices, which are affixed to one's ankle or wrist and emit electronic signals to verify one's whereabouts at particular times. EM does not control one's behavior. Rather, it assists juvenile POs in ascertaining a youth's whereabouts and verifying their compliance with curfews and other court-ordered placement requirements. Numbers of youths on EM are difficult to determine because of lack of access to records from various probation departments. Estimates from companies that market such equipment suggest that as many as 20,000 or more youths may be on EM at any given time. EM exists in several different forms. There are continuous signalling devices, programmed contact devices, devices that use cellular services; and continuous signalling transmitters that can be intercepted by juvenile POs who can drive by one's residence and verify one's whereabouts at particular times. Some jurisdictions use EM as a last resort before placing youths in secure confinement. But most departments are using EM increasingly because it supplements conventional surveillance and supervisory practices by juvenile POs and is far less costly than confinement for offender control. Another variation of EM is SpeakerID, which verifies one's voice when a youth is telephoned from a central location.

Criticisms of EM include that it is not tamper-proof, although it is not intended to be. It requires some training on the part of those who use it, although this training is minimal. Startup costs of EM are high, but once a jurisdiction has used it for a year or longer, the cost-effectiveness of EM is much better than secure confinement. EM is potentially intrusive and thus may violate certain rights to privacy, although those on EM sign agreements authorizing its use and waive such rights. EM permits offenders the opportunity of working at their jobs or attending schools; participating in individual or group counseling without significant restriction; gives judges greater flexibility in the punishments they impose; decreases prison and jail overcrowding; and is far less costly than incarceration. Some potential exists for socioeconomic or racial/ethnic discrimination, because EM sometimes requires that offenders must have telephones and not all of them can afford them. Also, no guarantees can be made that public safety will be improved, since EM cannot regulate one's conduct, although that is not an EM function.

Home confinement or house arrest is another supervisory option for juvenile POs. Often used in conjunction with EM, house arrest uses one's home as one's principal place of confinement. While this option may not sound like much of a punishment, it is considered a burdensome option for many youths who have previously taken their community freedom for granted. The goals of home confinement are to enable offenders to remain in their communities and attend school or jobs at regular times; reduce the cost of offender supervision; promote rehabilitation and reintegration; reduce jail and prison overcrowding; and maximize public safety by using one's home as a place of confinement where compliance can be strictly enforced.

Other JISP conditions may include restitution, which emphasizes repayments to victims especially for their economic losses resulting from one's delinquency. Several restitution models include the financial/community service model, the victim/offender mediation model, and the victim/reparations model. Fines and victim compensation may also be used to assess court costs and other expenses associated with offender processing and supervision. Victim–offender mediation, such as alternative dispute resolution (ADR), may also be used. Community service in different forms may also be imposed. Making youthful offenders pay for their actions and do something to restore to victims whatever economic losses they have sustained dramatically improves their accountability and heightens their responsibility. Heightening accountability and one's responsibility are effective in reducing one's potential for recidivism.

QUESTIONS FOR REVIEW

1. What is standard probation? What are some of its characteristics? What are some of the conditions of standard probation?

2. How does standard probation differ from probation with special conditions? What are some of the types of special conditions usually included in such probation orders?

3. What are juvenile probation camps? What is meant by intensive aftercare? Are such alternative sanctions effective at reducing recidivism? Why or why not?

4. What are intermediate punishments? How do intermediate punishments differ from standard probation?

5. What are some goals of intermediate punishments? What are some of the criteria for placement in intensive supervised probation programs?

6. What is the Ohio Experience? What are some of its prominent characteristics?

7. What is case supervision planning? Is there an ideal caseload for probation/parole officers?

8. What is meant by the balanced approach? What are some of its important elements? Is it successful in dealing with delinquent offenders? Why or why not?

9. What are home confinement and electronic monitoring? Are home confinement and electronic monitoring used together in many jurisdictions? Who are the juvenile clients who are disposed to electronic monitoring and/or home confinement? What are the goals and functions of these respective programs?

10. What is victim–offender mediation? What sorts of juveniles are eligible for participating in such mediation? How successful are such programs at resolving disputes between juveniles and their victims?

INTERNET CONNECTIONS

American Jail Association
http://www.corrections.com/aja/index.shtml

Corrections Connection
http://www.corrections.com/

The Fortune Society
http://www.fortunesociety.org/

Intensive Aftercare for High Risk Juveniles
http://www.nicic.org/Library/012231

Network for Good
http://www.networkforgood.org/

Sentencing Project
http://www.sentencingproject.org/

ServiceLeader
http://www.serviceleader.org/new/

CHAPTER 13	*Juvenile Corrections: Custodial Sanctions and Parole*

Chapter Outline

Key Terms

About Face
Army Model
boot camps
combination sentences
commitment placements
detention centers
detention hearing
foster homes
group homes
halfway houses
IMPACT
industrial schools

Intensive Motivational Program of
  Alternative Correctional
  Treatment
intermittent sentences
jail as a condition of probation
juvenile offender laws
long-term detention
minimum due-process rights
mixed sentences
parole revocation hearing
parole revocation

parolees
privatization
probation revocation hearing
Regimented Inmate Discipline
  Program (RID)
shock incarceration
shock parole
shock probation
short-term confinement
split sentences
wilderness experiments

Chapter Objectives

As the result of reading this chapter, you will realize the following objectives:

1. Understand the different components and goals of juvenile corrections.
2. Differentiate between nonsecure and secure confinement, as well as examine some of the programs associated with nonsecure treatment of juvenile offenders.
3. Learn about various types of custodial facilities for juveniles and their relative successfulness in fostering juvenile rehabilitation and reintegration.
4. Learn about several important correctional issues as they apply to juvenile offenders.
5. Learn about juvenile parole and the characteristics of parole programs.
6. Understand the process of juvenile probation and parole revocation.
7. Learn about some of the leading U.S. Supreme Court cases that apply to juvenile probation and parole as well as the revocation process.

• *The California Youth Authority (CYA), created by the Youth Corrections Act of 1941, is one of the worst and most punitive secure institutional systems in the country. Thousands of California juvenile offenders are confined in these facilities annually. Incidents of correctional officer brutality, juvenile inmate-on-inmate violence, and deplorable living conditions are abundant. Shariffe Vaughn, age 21, was an inmate at the CYA for his role in a burglary committed with two other teens. During that time, he was gassed about 20 times for different reasons. When he was 17 years old, he was sent to the CYA and placed in a cramped dormitory building where 80 youths were housed, two to a bunk. Within a day, a fight broke out and Mace canisters were shot into the dormitory by CYA officers. The rule was that if any inmate left his bunk, he would be subject to harsh punishments. Vaughn tried to protect himself from the gas by covering his face with a towel and hunkering down on the floor next to his bunk. But it is hard to breathe in that chemical fog. Gas-masked guards entered the dorm and tried to identify and isolate those fighting. Vaughn said, "The staff will grab you for no reason and start hitting you. The gas burns your eyes, you can't see, you can't breathe, and you've got snot and buggers coming out of your nose. Some of my skin peeled off later from the gas." The gas is intended to be used outdoors to break up riots, but the guards at the CYA routinely use it indoors. Sometimes gas is used as a punishment. Vaughn says that life at the CYA for youths is a lose–lose situation. "They set it up so you get add-ons to your sentence for rule violations, such as missing classes. They lock up units for any reason, and you can't go to class. Then you get more time on your sentence because you missed class." As a result, Vaughn maxed out his sentence and left the CYA at age 21. During that time, he was relocated in four different CYA facilities. Frequently he was locked down in a cell for 23 hours a day, and as a result, he never got to attend any rehabilitative classes or receive counseling. He saw a lot of instances of prisoner abuse by guards. One youth held in a cell across from him had medication forced on him by several officers. "They went into his cell, four or five of them, grabbed him, beat the crap out of him, then tied his arms down and put a needle in him," he said. While there have been numerous lawsuits filed against the CYA, conditions haven't improved much. Rape, sexual assault, and sexual harassment are common. Governor Arnold Schwarzenegger and Walter Allen, the head of CYA, announced several reforms designed to improve conditions at all of the CYA facilities. But with California's budget crunch, the money may simply not be there. [Source: Adapted from Stephen James, "CYA Goes to Reform School." Sacramento News & Review, December 30, 2004.]*

• *The Missouri Division of Youth Services (MDYS) had one of the worst juvenile corrections departments in the United States in 1965. Today the MDYS has one of the best systems. The MDYS refers to its wards (i.e., wards of the court, juvenile offenders) as "kids." The kids live in small units in one of 32 residential facilities around the state. Family visits are encouraged, and the kids are assigned as close to home as possible. There are no guards or cells. The kids and staff wear street clothes and jewelry, sleep in regular beds with their own comforters, and live in housing units with artwork on the walls and vases with flowers. The environment is considered treatment-centered 24 hours a day. Recidivism rates among MDYS clients are about 34 percent compared with juveniles institutionalized in other states, such as California, where recidivism rates are 74 percent. The MDYS deliberately structures juveniles into groups of 10–12 offenders each. In each group, 3–4 members are about to be released, and so they provide positive role models for those serving longer terms. Some of the kids are rival gang members, but authorities have emphasized the pro-rehabilitation and pro-treatment ethic. Peer influence is promoted, and violence is prohibited. The MDYS doesn't allow "hurting" behavior. All the "gang stuff" and violence is left at the door. Part of the improved performance of the MDYS is the fact that all staff have college degrees and are considered youth specialists. Uneducated and uncooperative guards have been weeded out and terminated. Also used are the same tactics gangs use, such as support among the youths. Except at the MDYS, these tactics are turned into positive experiences. There is very, very close monitoring by the staff. There is a staff–client ratio of 1 to 8, whereas California has a 1 to 25 staff–client ratio. Staff supervision is intense; at least two staff members are around each group of kids 24 hours a day. The MDYS uses eyes-on supervision, where you never let the kids out of your sight, because if you don't have a safe environment, you can't get a good treatment environment. Constant supervision has reduced or eliminated other problems, such as inmate suicides or suicide attempts. During a typical day, each kid will attend school, they will eat their meals together, exercise, and do an evening check-in session, where the kids describe how their day went. There are also counseling sessions and pullout groups for kids who have special needs, such as drug, alcohol, and sex-offender treatment. Is this kind of individualized treatment possible in other states or systems? [Source: Adapted from Stephen James and the Sacramento News & Review, "CYA Goes to Reform School," December 30, 2004.]*

Correctional Snapshots in Four Jurisdictions:

1. *"Take six adolescents, cram them into a room originally constructed for one, mix a short temper, and the result could be explosive," says Kevin Ryan, child advocate and critic of the Camden County Youth Center (CCYC) in Blackwood, New Jersey. Ryan is investigating overcrowding in detention centers throughout the state. On that day in March 2004, there were 95 offenders being held in the 37-bed facility. Mary T. Previte, the administrator of the CCYC, says that judges do not have suitable*

alternative placements. "The lock-ups become the answer. Not a good answer, but they become an answer," Previte says.

2. *In Red Bluff, California, an investigation was launched into allegations of child abuse and other problems occurring at the Tehama County Juvenile Justice Center (TCJJC). Former counselor Barry Clausen alleges that several unidentified staff have mentally and physically abused several juveniles. There are also construction problems that have led to an unhealthy environment. A hostile working environment exists for staff, and there are inadequate staff resting facilities. Clausen claims to have seen a staff member order another guard to pepper spray a boy who was handcuffed. Another employee provoked a girl into "going off" so that she could be put in 24-hour lockdown. An unidentified spokesman for the TCJJC said that there are times when the staff are tired, kids push buttons, and overworked people react. Sometimes kids are slapped. Some air conditioners leak. Sewers sometimes back up, creating health hazards. These things happen. But many of these things that happen are beyond staff control.*

3. *One in four juvenile inmates in Florida juvenile secure facilities is a girl, marking a sharp increase in the number of juvenile females in these facilities. Between 1993 and 2003, the number of girls placed in the state's institutions for violent crimes rose 24 percent. In 2004 there were 1,914 girls under age 16 being held for violent offenses. Many girls in Florida's juvenile institutions have histories of sexual abuse and have begun sexual activity at an early age. Their abuse usually leads to depression and eating disorders. They often run away from home and get into trouble with petty offenses, such as shoplifting. Many violate their probation and go deeper into the system. They have low self-esteem. Some programs, like the PACE Center for Girls in Jacksonville, a nationally known day program for at-risk girls, attempts to assist girls in need before they reach the institutionalization stage. Florida corrections officials acknowledge that they have their hands full attempting to meet the needs of a growing population of teen female offenders.*

4. *In Fairbanks, Alaska, the Fairbanks Youth Facility is expanding its physical plant by adding a gymnasium and two classrooms. These expansions are expected to assist the facility by improving its ability to provide educational and physical activities needed to promote discipline, teamwork, a sense of belonging, trust in others, and self-confidence. Alaska Senator Pete Kelly says, "Our children have to be able to go to school, regardless of whether they are incarcerated. The facility opened in 1981 with 20 beds and an exclusively male clientele. Now it has been greatly expanded, offering a variety of rehabilitative, educational, and indoor/outdoor recreational facilities. Kelly adds, "We've got to get some more equipment. I'd like to get a climbing wall."* [*Sources:* Adapted from Bernie Mixon, "Overcrowding Plagues Camco Youth Center." *Cherry Hill Courier Post,* March 10, 2004; adapted from Cheryl Brinkley, "Tehama County Probes Alleged Child Abuse in Juvenile Hall." *Red Bluff Daily News,* December 22, 2004; adapted from *South Florida Sun-Sentinel,* "Female Inmates Increasing in Florida's Juvenile System," November 29, 2004; adapted from Amanda Bohman, "Detention Center's Facilities Expanded." *Fairbanks Daily News-Miner,* June 4, 2004.]

INTRODUCTION

Few persons if anyone ever said that doing time in a juvenile facility was easy. Vaguely reminiscent of an old 1940s movie of the big house and gloomy penitentiaries, the California Youth Authority seems disturbingly in step with the stereotypical portrayals of prison life. Except that the prisoners are juveniles, not adults. Are sexual and other forms of physical assault commonplace occurrences at the California Youth Authority and other custodial institutions for juveniles throughout the United States? Judging from the abundance of lawsuits filed against this and other correctional systems for juveniles, one might think so. But what about secure juvenile facilities where violence is rare? In Missouri, a totally different picture of life behind bars for juveniles is painted by criminal justice professionals and correctional experts. Examinations of secure custody situations in other jurisdictions throughout the United States offer a mixed picture of how life is for juvenile inmates as well as how it is supposed to be. Many facilities for juveniles appear to be achieving positive results. Yet other facilities seem to be warehousing violence, an allegation that is all too frequently leveled at adult institutions.

This chapter examines juvenile corrections, particularly institutional corrections. The first section describes various goals of juvenile corrections, including deterrence, rehabilitation, reintegration, prevention, punishment and retribution, isolation, and control. Each of these goals is sought by all types of juvenile institutions, particularly rehabilitation and reintegration. Thus, the individualization and tradition of juvenile court philosophy is carried forth to some extent into the institutionalization of juvenile offenders. But whether these positive goals are achieved depends on the jurisdiction and the institution. These goals are discussed.

Custodial alternatives are discussed in the following section. The institutionalization of juvenile offenders may be either nonsecure or secure. Nonsecure custody options for juveniles include foster home placements, group homes, halfway houses, camps, ranches, experience programs, and wilderness projects. The goals of these nonsecure options are examined, together with an evaluation of their respective effectiveness for rehabilitating and reintegrating youthful offenders. Several programs are featured as examples of how these options function and how certain goals are achieved.

The next section of this chapter focuses on secure confinement and its different variations. Secure confinement encompasses any type of program where youths are placed and cannot leave for any reason. For some youths, shock probation is used. Shock probation is the temporary placement of youths in secure custody, and then the sudden removal of these youths from custody and placement in a community program of some kind. Ordinarily, youths don't know they are being subjected to shock probation until it actually occurs. Temporary stays in secure confinement of 30, 60, 90, or 120 days have a profound effect on many juvenile offenders. When many of these offenders are suddenly released from secure confinement and redisposed or "resentenced" to community corrections, where they are permitted to move about freely in their communities, the mere fact that they have been incarcerated provides them with the motivation to remain law-abiding and avoid further incarceration.

Other youths, especially those with disciplinary problems, are placed in boot camps, or military-like facilities with many rules and regulations. Thus, boot camps are defined, as well as a discussion of their characteristics, primary goals and rationale, and a profile of boot camp clientele. Several boot camps currently operating in different jurisdictions will be described. Not everyone believes that boot camps are effective and accomplish their intended objectives, which include improving one's self-concept, self-sufficiency, discipline, and law-abiding behavior. The controversy over the use of boot camps is presented and the pros and cons of boot camps are discussed.

Several persistent problems associated with nonsecure and secure confinement are also examined. Many facilities designed to accommodate juveniles are outdated and in need of remodeling and other improvements. Furthermore, some evidence suggests that many of the personnel who staff these facilities are poorly trained and receive little or no instruction on how best to supervise juveniles in their charge. Some facilities are designed for short-term confinement of juvenile offenders, while other facilities are designed for long-term incarceration of them. These different types of facilities are examined and discussed. Several criticisms associated with incarcerating juveniles are presented.

The next section of this chapter examines juvenile parole. Many states have juvenile parole boards that function in ways similar to parole boards for adults. Juvenile parole is defined and the purposes of juvenile parole are discussed. General juvenile parole policies in various state jurisdictions are discussed, and juvenile parolees are profiled. Parole decision making for juvenile offenders is at least as complex as it is for deciding which adults should be paroled. Some of the criteria for deciding which juveniles to parole are listed and described.

The next section of this chapter examines the juvenile probation and parole revocation process. Presently no case law exists from the U.S. Supreme Court concerning the rights of juvenile probationers and parolees pertaining to conditions under which their respective programs may be revoked. However, juvenile court judges and parole boards are guided by nonbinding U.S. Supreme Court decisions about adult probation and parole revocation. Many of the states have adopted policies for revoking juvenile probation and parole that follow adult probation and parole revocation policies. Several key U.S. Supreme Court probation and parole revocation cases are presented. A sampling of state cases involving juvenile probation and parole revocation actions are described. Several important issues are addressed upon which juvenile probation and parole revocation actions are based.

The chapter concludes with an examination of selected issues in juvenile corrections. One important issue pertains to whether juvenile corrections should be privatized. Should the private sector operate juvenile facilities, especially secure facilities? Another issue is how should juvenile offenders be classified? Despite the remarkable improvements that have been made in correctional instrumentation, little evidence exists that suggests that juveniles are classified accurately and/or receive appropriate treatments/punishments. Is there too much or too little use of secure confinement for juveniles? How can authorities distinguish clearly between those juveniles who deserve to be locked up from those who don't deserve such a punishment? A third issue pertains to detaining juveniles, even for brief periods, in adult lock-ups or jails. Every year, attempts are made to avoid juvenile incarcerations in adult facilities. But every year, a certain proportion of those incarcerated in adult jails are juveniles. There are several reasons for these incarcerations. These issues are examined in some detail.

GOALS OF JUVENILE CORRECTIONS

Various goals of juvenile corrections include (1) deterrence; (2) rehabilitation and reintegration; (3) prevention; (4) punishment and retribution; and (5) isolation and control. These goals may at times appear to be in conflict. For instance, some jurisdictions stress delinquency prevention through keeping juveniles away from the juvenile justice system through diversion and warnings. However, other jurisdictions get tough with juveniles by providing more certain and stringent penalties for their offenses. A middle ground stresses both discipline and reform (Escarcega et al., 2004).

Deterrence

Significant deterrent elements of juvenile correctional programs include clearly stated rules and formal sanctions, anti-criminal modeling and reinforcement, and a high degree of empathy and trust between the juvenile client and staff (Robinson and Darley, 1995). Traditional counseling, institutionalization, and diversion, which are integral features of many community corrections programs, are considered largely ineffective (Burrell, 2005). A natural intervention may occur apart from any particular program designed to deter. As youths grow older, their offending tends to reach a plateau and then declines. Thus, many youths simply outgrow delinquency as they become older.

Rehabilitation and Reintegration

Various juvenile correctional programs stress internalizing responsibilities for one's actions, while other programs attempt to inculcate youths with social and motor skills. Other programs attempt to diagnose and treat youths who are emotionally disturbed. Alternative medical and social therapies are often used. Group homes are becoming increasingly popular as alternatives to incarceration, since a broader array of services can be extended to juveniles with special needs.

Prevention

Delinquency prevention seems to be a function of many factors (Altschuler and Armstrong, 2001). It is believed that the threat of incarceration in a secure facility, even for a brief period, might prevent many juveniles from committing delinquent acts. However, like many adults, the idea of such a punishment doesn't seem to be much of a deterrent.

Punishment and Retribution

Some persons want to see youths, especially violent ones, punished rather than rehabilitated (Mears, 2001). One major impact of the get-tough-on-crime policy adopted by many jurisdictions is that the juvenile justice system seems to be diverting a larger portion of its serious offenders to criminal courts where they may conceivably receive harsher punishments (Wilson and Petersilia, 2002). This may be one reaction to widespread allegations that the juvenile courts are too lenient in their sentencing of violent offenders, or that the punishment options available to juvenile court judges are not sufficiently severe. For those juveniles who remain within the juvenile justice system for processing, secure confinement for longer periods seems to be the court's primary response to citizen allegations of excessive leniency.

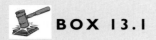 **BOX 13.1**

Al Lick
Director, Division of Juvenile Services, ND

Statistics:

B.S. (education), Dickinson State University

Background

I attended Bismarck State College and graduated from Dickinson State University with a B.S. degree in education. Originally I planned to be a junior high school teacher and basketball coach. I taught for 7 years but then a career change resulted in my involvement with state government.

Initially my early work experience in state government had a great deal to do with adult corrections and a little time providing services for troubled adolescents. After another career move, I knew that I wanted very much to return to working with young people. That opportunity was afforded me in a short period of time, when I became the first Director of Juvenile Services in the State of North Dakota.

Some of my initial efforts in developing a system of care and treatment were directed at the following:

1. Development of laws to allow the implementation of a comprehensive juvenile corrections system.

2. Pulling together a partial community system and developing the remaining community offices throughout the state.

3. Implementation of a risk/needs assessment in order to provide quality services.

4. Development of a continuum of services from most restrictive to least restrictive without endangering public safety.

5. Policies and procedures for proactive, positive case management of juvenile offenders.

6. Providing a positive work environment where employees and juveniles are safe.

7. Implementation of a training program that is comprehensive and ongoing. That program needs to provide for both community and institutional staff.

8. Designate a treatment program that can be used by the total system, both in the community and correctional facility.

9. Development of measurement devices to track the positive and negative results of the system. If you are not constantly improving, you are regressing as a system.

10. Development of many more details that need to be in place for a new agency.

Experiences

Working in juvenile corrections is very satisfying. The vast majority of troubled adolescents with whom we deal have made some very poor decisions in their younger years. Our job is to provide them with the skills to break that cycle of poor decision making. What cannot be lost in the rehabilitation process is the responsibility to maintain public safety when making decisions relative to levels of confinement.

There is a very basic premise we operate under, and that is "Nothing positive can take place in a young person's life until you get behavior under control." In addition to that basic premise, we feel strongly that young people need structure, accountability, and positive relationships as they make their personal journey through juvenile corrections.

Through the years, methods of treatment philosophies, public sentiment about troubled adolescents, standards of accountability for juveniles, and measurement of success in the field have changed greatly. The good systems rehabilitate juvenile offenders while always maintaining a great balance between public safety and treatment.

Characteristics of Good Corrections Personnel

You must be sure you enjoy being around young, troubled adolescents and the many journeys their lives will take. This is not a glamorous career, and you must be able to take satisfaction in the small successes of your clients. You certainly are not going to accumulate large sums of money working in this field. Therefore, the inner satisfaction you receive from being a part of seeing your clients succeed must be high. A well-balanced lifestyle and a good sense of humor are also very important personnel characteristics in the field of corrections. If you are unsure that juvenile correctional work is your career, you have many opportunities to test your interests. You could be a volunteer, an intern, a Big Brother/Big Sister, or work in a part-time temporary position as you complete your degree. That hands-on experience sometimes is a good indicator if this is the field in which you wish to spend your working career.

Isolation and Control

Apprehension and incarceration of juvenile offenders, especially chronic recidivists, is believed important to isolating them and limiting their opportunities to reoffend (Steen, 2001). In principle, this philosophy is similar to selective incapacitation. However, the average length of juvenile incarcerative terms in public facilities in the United States is less than 10 months (Office of Juvenile Justice and Delinquency Prevention, 2005). Thus, incarceration by itself may be of limited value in controlling the amount of juvenile delinquency (Lobley, Smith, and Stern, 2001).

CURRENT JUVENILE CUSTODIAL ALTERNATIVES

The custodial options available to juvenile court judges are of two general types: nonsecure and secure. Nonsecure custodial facilities are those that permit youths freedom of movement within the community. Youths are generally free to leave the premises of their facilities, although they are compelled to observe various rules, such as curfew, avoidance of alcoholic beverages and drugs, and participation in specific programs that are tailored to their particular needs. These types of nonsecure facilities include foster homes, group homes and halfway houses, and camps, ranches, experience programs, and wilderness projects (Peterson, Ruck, and Koegl, 2001; Platt, 2001).

Secure custodial facilities are the juvenile counterpart to adult prisons or penitentiaries. Such institutions are known by different names among the states. For example, secure, long-term secure confinement facilities might be called youth centers or youth facilities (Alaska, California, Colorado, District of Columbia, Illinois, Kansas, Maine, Missouri), juvenile institutions (Arkansas), schools (California, Connecticut, New Mexico), schools for boys (Delaware),

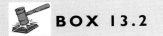

BOX 13.2

**INTERNATIONAL SNAPSHOT:
JUVENILE JUSTICE IN IRELAND**

The Republic of Ireland had approximately 4 million people in 2002. Since the 1980s the Irish juvenile justice system has undergone substantial transformation. Recent developments in Irish juvenile justice are best understood by paying attention to the early roots of juvenile justice that date back to the early twentieth century. In the early 1900s Ireland had no juvenile justice system. Many of the provisions pertaining to youthful offenders were very traditional and relied heavily on parental interventions rather than government-initiated responses. Juveniles were not clearly defined as a class, and juvenile offenses were also ambiguous. Few if any provisions existed for accommodating youthful offenders, particularly female ones. There were no community-based alternatives to meet the needs of youths, and many of their social, medical, psychological, and educational problems remained unsolved. The state of theories about delinquency was such that no particular theory was especially influential in implementing useful interventions that would explain delinquency or reduce it significantly. Explanations for juvenile conduct were limited to dysfunctional family conditions and/or poor school performance.

Throughout much of the twentieth century, Irish reforms pertaining to delinquency and youthful offending were few or nonexistent. However, during the 1970s and 1980s, greater attention was focused on the growing problem of juvenile crime and violence. Academicians began to focus their attention more on factors associated with rising rates of delinquency in Ireland, from about 1980 to the present. Gradually, factors such as personality, temperament, academic ability, and personal history were cited increasingly as variables playing an increasingly important role in defining youths who were either delinquent or at risk. A summary of motives for juvenile crime includes factors such as material gain, low self-esteem, prestige gained among peers who seek pure excitement and reward deviant behavior, socioeconomic deprivation, and a pervasive and strong delinquent subculture.

Poverty and harsh living conditions have caused families to become dysfunctional. Delinquent behavior has been fostered also by the inability of parents to provide constructive social environments for their children. The stresses of earning a living when economic conditions are severely limiting have undermined family ef-

Secure facilities for juveniles are equipped with sinks, commodes, and other fixtures that are intended to minimize tampering.

forts to foster prosocial behaviors among their children and contribute positively to their sound moral development. Youths have become stigmatized as a result, marginalized by socioeconomic deprivation and poor school performance. Thus, they are increasingly psychologically amenable to both crime and drug addiction, which offer rewards and escape from boredom and a lack of self-esteem. A growing gang presence has contributed to growing juvenile violence and general youth offending (Irwin, 2004).

During the 1980s and 1990s, greater drug use among juveniles occurred, which contributed to the growing delinquency rate. Presently drug use by juveniles in Ireland is a prevalent phenomenon that is targeted the most by official governmental intervention programs. The fact that recidivism rates among delinquents are high is further cause for concern and explains the nature and development of intervention programs designed to deal with drug dependencies. In response to growing delinquency and illicit drug use, the Ministerial Task Force on Measures to Reduce the Demand for Drugs was established together with a National Anti-Poverty Strategy during the period 1996–1997. These initiatives helped to stimulate a more realistic approach toward drug problems and provide for more effective governmental funding designed to prevent or minimize these important problems.

At about the same time, police agencies in Ireland became more proactive through the establishment of community activist/vigilante antidrug movements in different towns and cities. This movement used mass public protest, citizen street patrols, and evictions of drug dealers from different dwellings in communities to rid drug-infested areas of those contributing to the growing drug problem. Methadone treatment programs were also established during the 1990s to treat those in need of drug abuse assistance and addictions. Centers were also established to create greater recreational and sports opportunities for youths, and to educate and train them in various ways. The Ireland Department of Education also focused more attention on school dropouts, by attempting various interven-

tions to break the cycle of educational disadvantage and social exclusion. Head Start–type programs were established, and after-school homework clubs were created by different schools to assist youths who had trouble completing their classroom assignments. Presently there are at least 60 outreach centers that offer full-time services to those ages 15–18 who have dropped out of school. Services of these outreach centers include personal development, skills training, and preparation for work in the community.

The Irish juvenile justice system is closely patterned after the juvenile justice system of England. The common law age of 7 is the minimum age of criminal responsibility in Ireland. However, those under the age of 15 cannot be imprisoned. But some of these youths ages 7–15 can be sent to reformatories or industrial schools, which are now called special schools. The primary jurisdiction to deal with children or young persons is vested in the District Court, which is the equivalent to the Magistrate's Court in England. The District Court is presided over by a professional judge who can deal summarily with children and youths charged with indictable offenses other than homicide. When dealing with juvenile cases, the District Court must sit and decide these cases at different times compared with adult proceedings. The primary exception is in Dublin, which has a Children's Court. This Dublin court deals exclusively with youths under age 15 and has the same sanctioning powers as the District Courts in other Irish jurisdictions.

Judges may impose a wide variety of sanctions on juveniles. Youths may be committed to the care of a relative or other fit person, or a fine may be imposed. Court costs and damages to victims may also be assessed. Thus, victim compensation is a frequently used sanction. Children who are 15 years of age may be sent to prison, although this occurrence is rare. Usually these persons are designated as unruly or depraved and incapable of being helped by traditional educational measures. Ireland has an inconsistent and unreliable system for keeping track of delinquency and delin-

(continued)

quency trends. Thus, it is difficult if not impossible for academics and others to chart Ireland offense trends with any precision.

Ireland does have pretrial diversion, however. This pre-prosecution diversion scheme is aimed specifically at juveniles under the age of 18. This is the Juvenile Liaison Scheme and is run by the Garda Siochana. It involves a formal or informal caution and a period of supervision. Acceptance by the scheme is conditional on the offender admitting to the offense and the consent of the offender's family. In 1997, for instance, there were 12,000 referrals resulting in diversion. The use of diversion has escalated dramatically beyond 2000, although accurate figures about how much diversion is presently used are unavailable.

One official source of crime and delinquency figures is police statistics. Police provide national statistical information about persons convicted or against whom charges were proved or orders were initiated without conviction. There were approximately 16,000 such persons in 1997. That same year, there were about 91,000 reported offenses. Of the 16,000 persons against which criminal proceedings were commenced, about 10 percent of these were under 17 years of age. About 7 percent of these were female. About 45 percent of these cases under 17 years of age resulted in diversion.

The successfulness of diversion is measured by the amount of recidivism among those placed in diversion programs. Recidivism among those placed in diversion has been less than 15 percent, thus attesting to the successfulness of this program. Diversion also may include community service orders. Other sanctions are dispositions of probation for indeterminate periods. Some youths are placed in hostels to receive services resulting for diagnoses performed by specialists at these hostels.

The Juvenile Liaison Office has reported a breakdown of the criminal activity among those youths serviced by the office and its subordinate organizations. These offenses include larceny (27 percent), criminal damage (16 percent), burglary (12 percent), public order offending (7 percent),

vehicle offenses (8 percent), alcohol offenses (9 percent), and other miscellaneous offenses (27 percent). Less than 3 percent of all cases involved drug offenses.

Some indication of the failure of Ireland's progressive policies toward juveniles is the extent to which youths under age 21 are incarcerated in prisons. Proportionately compared with the rest of the industrialized countries throughout the world, Ireland has the largest proportion of youths under age 21 in prison for a variety of offenses. This means that they have been declared unruly and depraved by the courts. Irish prisons are typically overcrowded, drug-infested settings, and they are extremely unsuitable for youths who need to be in more therapeutic and rehabilitative environments for their own social and educational progress and welfare. About a third of all inmates in Irish prisons are under age 21. This is twice the incarceration rate of similar offenders in English prisons. The Probation and Welfare Service supervises relatively few offenders by comparison.

One of the more important problems facing Ireland is the lack of foster care for children in need of such placement. Hostels are limited and cannot possibly accommodate all of the youths who deserve such accommodations. There are simply not enough families in Ireland willing to make commitments to receive into their homes children who deserve close supervision and familial attention.

Juvenile justice reformers are continually pushing for new initiatives and changes in juvenile laws. One proposal is to raise the age of criminal responsibility from 7 to 10. Presently children are any persons under the age of 18 years unless the context otherwise requires. Other proposals are to limit police interviewing of youthful offenders. Greater emphasis is encouraged on family conferences. More restrictions on juveniles are encouraged, such as the greater use of curfews, especially in the larger cities. Another initiative is a proposal to hold parents accountable financially for any property damage their children may cause. Some of these measures have been hotly debated, and their feasibility and effectiveness have been challenged. It is important to note that presently, there is considerable interest in the Irish juvenile justice system. Vast resources are presently being devoted to improving different services for juveniles in Ireland. Restorative justice and victim–offender reconciliation projects of various kinds have been conducted in various Irish cities, and their use is growing as a viable alternative to formal court action. Thus, growing partnerships between the juvenile court and community-based services and organizations are viewed as a positive trend toward significant improvement in Ireland's juvenile justice system.

[*Sources:* Adapted from Paul O'Mahony, "Children, Young People, and Crime in Britain and Ireland," Unpublished paper, 2004; National Crime Forum, "Juvenile Justice in Ireland," Unpublished paper, 2005; Dublin Stationery Office, "Juvenile Justice Reforms," Unpublished paper, 2005.]

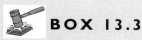 **BOX 13.3**

 **CAREER SNAPSHOT**

Jennine Hall
Senior Juvenile Parole Officer, CO

Statistics:

B.A. (psychology), University of Northern Colorado; M.S.W. (child, family, and adolescent), Denver University; Ph.D. candidate (human rehabilitative psychology), University of Northern Colorado

Background

As an undergraduate at the University of Northern Colorado, I was unsure what career path I wanted. After studying abroad in Plymouth, England, for one year, I returned to the states with a newfound passion for working with people and psychology. I enjoyed learning about human behavior and after graduation, I gained employment working with individuals who were dually diagnosed. As a case manager for this population, I learned about mental illness and became aware of the many providers and community programs in Denver, Colorado. Eventually I decided to go back to school and obtain my master's degree in social work.

Graduate school was a wonderful experience both professionally and personally. I met other professionals in the human services field and found the classroom instruction fascinating and challenging. After graduation, I decided to change my career path and began working with adolescents. I received a position in Boulder County as a parole tracker. As a tracker, I was able to learn more about the juvenile justice system and worked with several different juvenile parole officers, assisting them in supervising their parolees in the community while on parole. The job was exciting, fast paced, and there were different challenges every day. I enjoyed engaging kids and working in their communities assisting them in learning skills to help in their transition back into the community. After 2 years in this position, I applied for and received a position as a Colorado State Juvenile Parole Officer. I have been in this position for 7 years and I am still learning new things every day. I have enjoyed every case that I have had, although some have been more challenging than others. Recently I became a student again and a Ph.D. candidate at the University of Northern Colorado. I hope to continue working with youth in the juvenile justice system and complete research that leads to the continued development of service delivery in this field.

Work Experiences

Although I have been a parole officer for the last 7 years and have said goodbye to many youths, I still remember each one of them and the first day we met like it was yesterday. Regardless of the case, each youth has left an imprint on my memory. One of the greatest rewards in this job is the simple experience of watching someone grow into adulthood. As I reflect back on my experiences as a parole officer, a youth named "Lee" has been my most memorable case to date.

Lee was adjudicated delinquent for participating in a violent gang fight. He repeatedly struck a rival gang member with a baseball bat on the downtown streets of Denver. Witnesses reported that the attack was violent and that Lee could have killed his victim if a passerby had not intervened. I first met Lee in detention after he had been disposed to 2 years in the juvenile correctional system. I was surprised at first, since Lee was extremely small for his age, 14, and was unable to understand English. He seemed primitive and childlike in his behaviors, and it was difficult to comprehend that this small boy committed such a heinous and violent crime. Later, I learned that Lee and his family, who were originally from Vietnam, fled to Cambodia to reside in a Cambodian refugee camp where he had grown up for much of his early childhood. The family had suffered and survived unspeakable horrors before coming to the United States where they have been for the past 5 years. As a part of their relocation, they were given a subsidy to reside in a housing project located in West Denver. This project was known for its high crime and Asian gang activity. Once the family resettled, Lee's mother began working long hours at an Asian market, unable to supervise Lee adequately. Lee became susceptible to the gangs in this area and was "jumped" into the Tiny Rascals at the young age of 10. The Tiny Rascal gang is a Cambodian gang in Denver known for their fierce protection over the west side projects and their violent attacks against rival gang members. His fellow gang members named Lee "Wacko" as the result of his willingness to do anything, regardless of the risk, on behalf of the gang.

As the parole officer on this case, I was instantly overwhelmed with the language barrier and cultural differences. I had not worked with any individuals with refugee status, and I had no idea how properly to assess future case planning with this youth. Little did I know at the time that this was the beginning of an incredible journey with this youth and his family.

Slowly, as Lee learned more about American culture, I, too, learned more about Vietnamese culture. He learned in one year not only how to speak English fluently, but also Spanish. He often would study vocabulary words out of the dictionary and then impress me with his ability to use them properly during our staffing. I often joked with my co-workers that in just 2 years, Lee had learned how to speak English better than me! Lee was a proud high school graduate just this past year. This was a tremendous accomplishment for him, as 4 years earlier, he could barely read or write in English as well as his native language.

Initially I was struck by how small Lee was for his age. I later learned that Lee had been malnourished for the majority of his life due to poor living conditions in Vietnam and Cambodia. As a result, he was significantly smaller and his physical development had been stunted. In 2 years, not only did Lee grow intellectually but physically as well. Currently he is 5'6" and is the tallest person in his family.

Perhaps one of the most striking accomplishments of this youth was his ability to communicate through art. While in treatment Lee worked with an art therapist extensively. This enabled him to process a lot of trauma that he suffered while growing up in Vietnam and Cambodia. Initially Lee's paintings were primitive and dark. Often they were very surreal and told stories of abuse, death, and starvation. As Lee progressed in his treatment, his paintings changed. Eventually his art beautifully depicted the lush and colorful Vietnam countryside. Lee's art had become so enchanting that he was invited to participate in a Ft. Collins, Colorado, art show. At this art show, Lee displayed 10 pieces that he had skillfully worked on for a year. Every piece sold, and Lee was left with a sizeable fortune for the first time in his life. I later found out that Lee donated all of the money that he made that night to a local charity. When I asked him about this, he simply replied to me, "It seemed like the right thing to do." As Lee worked on his own victimization, he began to understand how his own action had harmed others. Today Lee still resides in Denver with his family. I am happy to report that he is working full time in construction and has never returned to the gang that still persists in his neighborhood. I am the proud owner of one of his paintings and have it prominently displayed in my office to remind me of our incredible journey.

Advice to Students

When I first began this job 7 years ago, I was the youngest female working in this position in Colorado. Caucasian males in the mid-40s held a majority of parole officer positions. Over the past 5 years this situation has changed dramatically, and the field has opened to include a wide variety of ethnicities, races, and more female officers. It re-

mains a competitive field, and having an undergraduate degree in a related field will only get you through the door. Graduate degrees, as well as practical experience working with adolescents, separate those who desire to work in the field and those who actually do. If you hope to become a juvenile parole officer in the future, focus on your education and get as much experience as you can. Do whatever it takes to be a competitive candidate in this field.

Do you have passion for working with kids? Do you love their tenacious, sharp wit, resourceful and dramatic personalities? Are you willing to accept that you will never be an "expert" and will constantly be challenged by this population? Will you be able to consider the possible risk they might present to the community while cautiously providing them with opportunities to succeed? Can you be a parole officer, mentor, advocate, educator, and social worker, all on the same day and perhaps on the same case? Are you flexible and able to think outside of the box? If so, then a job in the juvenile justice system might just be the right choice for you.

training schools or centers (Florida, Indiana, Iowa, Oregon), youth development centers (Georgia, Nebraska), youth services centers (Idaho), secure centers (New York), industry schools (New York), and youth development centers (Tennessee). This listing is not intended to be comprehensive, but it illustrates the variety of designations states use to refer to their long-term, secure confinement facilities.

NONSECURE CONFINEMENT

Nonsecure confinement involves placing certain youths in (1) foster homes; (2) group homes and halfway houses; and (3) camps, ranches, experience programs, and wilderness projects.

Foster Homes

If the juvenile's natural parents are considered unfit, or if the juvenile is abandoned or orphaned, **foster homes** are often used for temporary placement. Those youths placed in foster homes are not necessarily law violators. They may be children in need of supervision (CHINS) (Arthur, 2004). Foster home placement provides youths with a substitute family. A stable family environment is believed by the courts to be beneficial in many cases where youths have no consistent adult supervision or are unmanageable or unruly in their own households. In 2004, approximately 22,000 youths were under the supervision of foster homes in state-operated public placement programs (American Correctional Association, 2005; Office of Juvenile Justice and Delinquency Prevention, 2005).

Foster home placements are useful in many cases where youths have been apprehended for status offenses (Baker, Schneiderman, and Parker, 2001). Most families who accept youths into their homes have been investigated by state or local authorities in advance to determine their fitness as foster parents. Socioeconomic factors and home stability are considered important for child placements. Foster parents often typify middle-aged, middle-class citizens with above-average educational backgrounds. Despite these positive features, it is unlikely that foster homes are able to provide the high intensity of adult supervision required by more hardcore juvenile offenders. Furthermore, it is unlikely that these parents can furnish the quality of special treatments that might prove effective in the youth's possible rehabilitation or societal reintegration. Most foster parents simply are not trained as counselors, social workers, or psychologists. For many nonserious youths, however, a home environment, particularly a stable one, has certain therapeutic benefits (Baker, Schneiderman, and Parker, 2001).

Group Homes and Halfway Houses

Another nonsecure option for juvenile court judges is the assignment of juveniles to **group homes** and **halfway houses.** Placing youths in group homes is considered an intermediate option available to juvenile court judges. Group homes or halfway houses are community-based operations that may be either publicly or privately administered (Minor, Wells, and Jones, 2004). The notion of a halfway house is frequently used to refer to community homes used by adult parolees recently released from prison. These halfway houses provide a temporary base of operations for parolees as they seek employment and readjustment within their communities (Masters, 2004). Therefore, they are perceived as transitional residences halfway between incarceration and full freedom of life "on the outside." To many ex-inmates, exposure to unregulated community life is a traumatic transition from the rigidity of prison culture. Many ex-inmates need time to readjust. The rules of halfway houses provide limited structure as well as freedom of access to the outside during the transitory stage.

Usually, group homes will have counselors or residents to act as parental figures for youths in groups of 10–20. Certain group homes, referred to as family group homes, are actually family-operated, and thus, they are in a sense an extension of foster homes for larger numbers of youths. In group homes, nonsecure supervision of juvenile clients is practiced. About 7,500 youths were in group homes during 2004 (American Correctional Association, 2005).

No model or ideal group home exists in the nation to be emulated by all jurisdictions, and what works well for youths in some communities may not be effective in other jurisdictions (Masters, 2004). However, most successful group homes have strong structural components, where all residents are obligated to participate in relevant program components, where predictable consequences

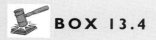 

BOX 13.4

Herbert C. Covey
Vice-Chair, Colorado State Juvenile Parole Board

Statistics:

B.A. (sociology), Colorado State University; M.A. (sociology), University of Nebraska at Omaha; Ph.D. (sociology), University of Colorado at Boulder

Background

I serve as the Vice-Chair of the State Juvenile Parole Board and a part-time instructor at the University of Colorado teaching a class on juvenile delinquency. My main occupation is being a field administrator with the Colorado Department of Human Services. I provide management support to nine county departments of social services and five agencies working with aging populations. My serving on the Board is a part-time activity.

Before I joined the Board, I had a conversation with an officemate regarding his service on the Board and how I could not imagine how he could do it given the responsibility and stress of making such important life-altering decisions. I recall stating, "I don't know how you do it." Two years later, I replaced him and have served over 10 years on the Board. It has been one of the richest experiences I have had in my life.

I was asked to serve on the Board because Colorado law required my employer, the Department of Human Services, to have a representative. In addition, I had coauthored a book on youth street gangs and was teaching a juvenile delinquency class. To become a member of the Board, the candidate must apply, be appointed by the governor, be approved by the Senate Judiciary Committee, and then confirmed by the full Senate. I remember my confirmation hearing as being more interesting than stressful. The Committee essentially wanted to know how I would respond to pressure from juvenile corrections to parole youths that I felt were not ready. In other words, would I succumb to pressure to parole youths for the purpose of

freeing up beds in state facilities. For me, the answer was an obvious "no," community safety should come first. A second set of questions focused on my values relative to parole. I stated that after safety, the best interests of the youth and family should be considered. I also added that the sentiments of the victims have to be considered. Too often after trial, victims are excluded from the judicial process. Finally, I indicated that it was better to send out youth with transitional services than to simply let them burn and turn them loose to the community.

I was attracted to the Board because I view parole hearings as being an important rite of passage for youth and their families. I wanted to be part of that important passage. For many youth, the parole hearing is similar to a graduation ceremony for their return to the community. For others, it is a wakeup call when they are denied parole and returned to facilities to work on their issues. Finally, I believe that if someone needed to take the responsibility of making parole decisions, it might as well be me because I deeply care about youth, families, victims, and communities.

Work Experiences

There are many pros and a few cons to serving on the Board. One pro is that I have served on many committees, work groups, and boards, none of which comes close to offering the kinds of rich experiences I have had serving on the Juvenile Parole Board. It has been my ticket to the "reality of it all." Over the course of about one hour, I get to delve into the human experience in ways not available to most other people. In my 10 years of service, I can honestly say that I have just about seen and heard it all. In saying this, I realize that my next hearing will offer new experiences and little about it will be routine. It can be very humbling at times. A second pro is that although little can occur in a one-hour hearing to turn a youth's life around, sometimes I get a sense that a youth may have been influenced in a positive direction. By being tough, supportive, honest, emphatic, holding the youth accountable, and otherwise appropriately addressing each case, I believe I am playing an important role in the system.

I cannot really think of many cons to serving on the Board. If anything, I consider it a privilege to serve the citizens of Colorado. It does take a considerable amount of personal time preparing for hearings. I believe sometimes it is very difficult to not dwell on specific hearings and what life courses youth have taken. I find myself being haunted by some of the human tragedies that are sometimes summarized over the course of a hearing for the victims as well as the families, and offenders. There are also many success stories to counterbalance the negative.

As to the basic question of predicting how well youth do on parole, one must take into account that a one-hour parole hearing is not likely to tell a Board member enough about the youth to be 100 percent sure how well the individual will do on parole. The old adage, "you can't judge a book by its cover," is also true for youth. Board members learn that they cannot stereotype youth and predict with 100 percent accuracy how they will behave on parole. Each parole candidate has to be considered on a case-by-case basis.

This is not to suggest that it is total guesswork. I learned early that prior behavior is a good predictor of future behavior. If a youth has a lengthy history of serious offending and started at an early age, then the risk of reoffending increases. Property offenders are more likely to reoffend than violent offenders. If a youth does well in rehabilitation programs, shows victim empathy, has a positive attitude, has positive peers in the community, has bonded with positive adult role

models, takes accountability for actions, has developed tools to keep from relapsing, and has good support systems, the chances for success on parole are better. If the youth returns to the same crime-infested neighborhood, begins associating with negative peers, and other systems such as school and family have not changed, then the chances are higher the youth will not succeed on parole.

I have many positive memories of parolees and parole hearings. For instance, one sex offender attempted to reoffend within 2 weeks of being paroled. Because all the family members had been trained by a multisystemic therapist, he was caught early in his offense cycle and never reoffended. In another hearing, I witnessed a mother of a physical assault victim heal her anger by seeing the offending youth show genuine remorse for what he had done and had changed for the better. Without that hearing, she would have never healed her anger. Once, we revoked parole of a drug-using youth because he was not complying with parole and we thought he was a danger to himself. He reeked of drugs and had an enabling and argumentative mother. After she called us every name in the book, the revoked youth attempted suicide 2 weeks later. After much work by youth corrections and an insightful client manager, I later paroled a dramatically changed youth who successfully completed parole and finished college. I'd like to think the Board played a role in turning this youth around.

Advice to Students

As a Board member, I come into contact with many professionals working with youth offenders. I believe the common characteristics of those who are successful are that they really care about helping youth, have the ability to accept failure and success with grace, are forthright with youth and families, and get to know their cases in detail. They never become friends with their clients but are sources of authority and direction. I also offer that being able to work as a member of a multidisciplinary team is important. Many of today's delinquent youth have multiple and confounding issues, such as mental health and substance abuse, and this requires team-work to address. If you do not have these qualities, along with dedication, then you need to find something else to do with your life. If you possess these qualities and want a meaningful career, this is a great area to pursue.

My advice to students interested in parole and aftercare services, or parole boards, is to contact people working in these areas and conduct informational interviews on how they developed their careers. Students should ask them what they like and dislike about their jobs and why they do what they do? How do they deal with parole successes and failures? What do they believe works and does not work for what types of youth?

Many professionals are willing to share their thoughts and help students.

I am convinced considerable time and resources in the juvenile justice system are wasted by well-intentioned people who apply ineffective treatments to youth based on feelings and emotions rather than evidence-based practice. Students will do well to become familiar with what research evidence shows works rather than the latest fad or what their feelings suggest. Evidence of effectiveness should drive treatment decisions, not program marketing or false assumptions about effectiveness. While our interventions may not always work for all youth, we want to at least ensure that our efforts are not making them worse.

for rule violations are rigorously enforced, and where constant monitoring by staff workers occurs (Kadish et al., 2001). Thus, juveniles have the best of both worlds—they can live in a home-like environment and visit with family and friends in a home setting. Yet, they must comply with strict rules governing curfew, program participation, and other court-imposed conditions. In an examination of nine facilities located in five counties in southwestern Pennsylvania, for example, all of the facilities operated under the principles of community-based treatment and relied on behavior modification as the major program. Little victimization occurred, especially where supervision was fairly intensive.

Privately or publicly operated, group homes require juvenile clients to observe the rights of others, participate in various vocational or educational training programs, attend school, participate in therapy or receive prescribed medical treatment, and observe curfew. Urinalyses or other tests may be conducted randomly as checks to see whether juveniles are taking drugs or consuming alcohol contrary to group home policy. If one or more program violations occur, group home officials may report these infractions to juvenile court judges who retain dispositional control over the youths. Assignment to a group home or any other type of confinement is usually for a determinate period.

Positively, group homes provide youths with the companionship of other juveniles. Problem-sharing often occurs through planned group discussions, where the subjects might include peer relations in school to suicide prevention. Staff are available to assist youths to secure employment, work certain difficult school problems, and absorb emotional burdens arising from difficult interpersonal relationships. However, these homes are sometimes staffed by community volunteers with little training or experience with a youth's problems. There are certain risks and legal liabilities that may be incurred as the result of well-intentioned but bad advice or inadequate assistance (Minor, Wells, and Jones, 2004). Currently, there are limited regulations among states for how group homes are established and operated. Training programs for group home staff are scarce in most jurisdictions, and few standards exist relating to staff preparation and qualifications. Therefore, considerable variation exists among group homes relating to the quality of services they can extend to the juveniles they serve (Corwin, 2005).

One way that group homes can improve their effectiveness is for staff workers and home administrators to develop associations with various community interests. Kearon (1990) has made several recommendations, including the following:

1. Develop a network in every community of voluntary service delivery systems, such as day treatment, nonsecure shelter and group homes, and small, nonsecure institutional care centers.
2. Increase staffing levels in these systems.
3. For the most disturbed and abused youth, who will inevitably escape from a nonsecure setting, establish perimeter-secure facilities.
4. Ensure that authorities intervene with youths at crucial entry points such as bus and railway terminals.
5. Educate youths in facilities about AIDS and at-risk behavior and make voluntary testing available, and provide these services as outreach centers to youths still on the streets.

Depending on how youths are screened, some youths are more suited than others for placement under conditions where supervision may be minimal. For instance, the Texas Youth Commission operated Independent Living, where selected youths were placed away from home, such as in an apartment, and possibly received some temporary financial support from the Commission (Texas Youth Commission, 1990). Some Independent Living youths engaged in new delinquent offenses, but their recidivism rate was low (9 percent). Rearrests where no charges were subsequently placed against youths also yielded a successful result for Independent Living participants. Compared with standard juvenile parolees who had a 52 percent rearrest rate, Independent Living participants had a rearrest rate of only 33 percent. One factor cited by Texas authorities was the additional trust and confidence in these youths by the Texas Youth Commission, as well as living and financial support while these youths attended school or looked for work.

Missouri Division of Youth Services Aftercare Program.   Professionals in the field agree that the ultimate measure of success for residential or institutional treatment programs is the assurance that youths exiting such facilities maintain positive gains and refrain from reoffending or engaging in otherwise problematic behaviors upon return to the community (Glover and Bumby, 2001:68). The Missouri Division of Youth Services has taken some aggressive steps to ensure that youths who go through their juvenile justice system are not simply released and forgotten once they have been punished. The Missouri Division of Youth Services is a subpart of the Department of Social Services. Missouri's approach to juvenile justice includes a balanced focus on rehabilitation and community safety. Thus, Missouri has established various regionally based treatment programs that are designed to serve youths and their families close to home.

Each of these facilities is small, ranging in size from 10–30 beds. Youths are placed in these facilities in groups of 10 in order to provide greater individualized attention to them and their respective needs. A consistent, safe, caring, and structured environment is provided (Glover and Bumby, 2001:69). The services and approaches the Department of Youth Services (DYS) provides include:

1. A continuum of security and programming, ranging from community-based and nonresidential programs, such as alternative living and day treatment, to residential programs, including group homes and moderate and secure care placements.

2. Comprehensive, standardized needs and risk assessments that enhance classification and placement decisions and facilitate development of individualized treatment plans.

3. An emphasis on individualized psychosocial, educational, and vocational needs.

4. Community-based partnerships for job placement and alternative education.

5. Incorporation of treatment outcome exploration, quality assurance, and program reviews to evaluate efficacy and improve service delivery.

6. Demonstrated investment and commitment toward collaboration with local juvenile courts in early intervention and prevention efforts through the provision of more than $6 million for diversionary programs.

7. A singular case management system in which a service coordinator follows each youth throughout his or her tenure with the DYS (Glover and Bumby, 2001:69).

The ultimate goal of the Missouri program is to successfully reintegrate delinquent youths into their communities. The system does this by ensuring that comprehensive and appropriate transitional and aftercare services are delivered. The Missouri aftercare program consists of an indefinite period of time where youths remain on PO caseloads but have already transitioned into the community. The range of services offered to youths includes family therapy, drug and alcohol counseling, general equivalency diploma (GED) preparation, community service, sex offender groups, mentoring services, and college and vocational programming. POs work with individual youths to make sure that they work on meeting program expectations, maintain curfew if imposed, attend school, and perform other responsibilities, such as restitution to victims or community service. The Missouri program includes extensive day treatment programming and a jobs program to assist those youths in need of work in finding it. Considerable emphasis is placed on family therapy, where entire families are involved in one's rehabilitation and reintegration. While not all youths who go through the Missouri program complete it successfully, the results thus far are quite favorable. Recidivism rates are lower compared with traditional probation programming, and many youths report successful transition experiences and moral improvement (Glover and Bumby, 2001:75).

Camps, Ranches, Experience Programs, and Wilderness Projects

Camps, ranches, or camp ranches are nonsecure facilities that are sometimes referred to as **wilderness experiments** or experience programs (MacKenzie and Wilson, 2001). A less expensive alternative to the incarceration of juvenile offenders, even those considered chronic, is participation in experience programs (Gover and MacKenzie, 2000). Experience programs include a wide array of

Many nonsecure programs for juveniles are located in remote areas and country settings where survival skills and other types of training are conducted.

outdoor programs designed to improve a juvenile's self-worth, self-concept, pride, and trust in others (Tarolla et al., 2002).

Three Springs Wilderness School. In Trenton, Alabama, a wilderness-based residential treatment program was established in the late 1980s (McCord, 1995). Screening juveniles was accomplished through interviews with residential counselors and administration of the Minnesota Multiphasic Personality Inventory (MMPI), a widely used personality assessment device. The MMPI results helped to profile and select 46 juvenile participants. These juveniles were clustered into three groups, according to their MMPI scores. One group was labeled "nonconformist." Those in this group exhibited the following characteristics: anger, resentment, passivity–aggressivity, immaturity, and narcissism. A second group, labeled "party animal," tended to exhibit hedonism, extroversion, rule-avoidance, and defiance toward authority. The third group, "emotionally disturbed," were primarily distressed. According to the different characteristics exhibited by these three groups, specialized treatments were configured to fit those with particular needs. The results of the treatment experiences were considered positive by staff researchers, indicating that the MMPI might be a useful tool as a means of differentiating between juveniles and their individual needs in subsequent wilderness experiments. These data have received independent support from other research under different treatment conditions (Swenson and Kennedy, 1995). In this latter research, scales were used for youth selection, including the Child Behavior Checklist, the Multidimensional Measure of Children's Perceptions of Control, the Perceived Contingency Behavioral Domain Scale, and the Piers–Harris Self-Concept Scale.

APPEL Program. In Williamson County, Texas, a wilderness challenge program was created in 1988 (Harris et al., 1993). This program involved weekly 2-hour meetings, two one-day sessions, and two half-day sessions held over a 12-week period. Unlike many of the programs designed for juveniles, the

APPEL program was designed to complement other correctional services, particularly those offered by various community supervision agencies. The challenge curriculum has an articulated mission that addresses the documented, underlying problems of a large proportion of youthful community corrections clients. These wilderness treatments are relatively low in cost and can easily be adopted by community corrections agencies.

SECURE CONFINEMENT: VARIATIONS

Shock Probation

Shock probation is an intermediate punishment where offenders are initially disposed to incarcerative terms; after a period of time, between 90 and 180 days, youths are removed from secure confinement and obligated to serve the remainder of their disposition on probation. The actual term "shock probation" was coined by Ohio authorities in 1964. Shock probation is also known as **shock parole,** because it technically involves a release from jail or prison after serving some amount of time in incarceration (MacKenzie and Wilson, 2001).

Sometimes, shock probation is used synonymously with **combination sentences** or **split sentences.** Other terms, such as **intermittent sentences, mixed sentences,** or **jail as a condition of probation,** are also used interchangeably with shock probation, although they have somewhat different meanings. Combination sentences or split sentences occur whenever judges sentence offenders to a term, a portion of which includes incarceration and a term of which includes probation. Mixed sentences occur whenever offenders have been convicted of two or more offenses and judges sentence them to separate sentences for each conviction offense. Intermittent sentences occur whenever judges sentence offenders to terms such as weekend confinement only. Jail as a condition of probation is a sentence that prescribes a specified amount of jail incarceration prior to serving the remainder of the sentence on probation (Gover and MacKenzie, 2003).

Technically, shock probation is none of these. Youths disposed to shock probation don't know they have received such dispositions. The judge disposes them to incarceration. The youths have no way of knowing that within three or four months, they will be yanked out of incarceration, brought before the same judge, and disposed to probation. This new probationary disposition is contingent upon their good behavior while they are incarcerated. Thus, they are shocked or traumatized by their incarceration. When they are redisposed to probation later, they should be sufficiently shocked to avoid further offending. But recidivism figures suggest it doesn't always work that way.

Shock probation is a misnomer in a sense. If we recall that probation is a disposition in lieu of incarceration, then it seems peculiar to incarcerate these offenders first, and then release them later and call them probationers. This practice is more accurately shock parole, since these are previously incarcerated offenders who are resentenced to a supervised release program. But also since a parole board does not grant them parole, we are uncertain about what they should be called other than shock probationers. In any case, the intended effect of incarceration is to scare offenders sufficiently so that they refrain from reoffending. Simply, their incarcerative experiences are so shocking that they don't want to face further incarceration.

Boot Camps

The juvenile version of shock probation or **shock incarceration** is perhaps best exemplified by juvenile **boot camps** (Parent, 2003). Also known as the **Army Model,** boot camp programs are patterned after basic training for new military recruits. Juvenile offenders are given a taste of hard military life, and such regimented activities and structure for up to 180 days are often sufficient to shock them into giving up their lives of delinquency or crime and staying out of jail (Gover and MacKenzie, 2003). Boot camp programs in various states have been established, including the Regimented Inmate Discipline program in Mississippi, the **About Face** program in Louisiana, and the shock incarceration program in Georgia. These are paramilitary-type programs that emphasize strict military discipline and physical training.

What Are Boot Camps?   Boot camps are highly regimented, military-like, short-term correctional programs (90–180 days) where offenders are provided with strict discipline, physical training, and hard labor resembling some aspects of military basic training; when successfully completed, boot camps provide for transfers of participants to community-based facilities for nonsecure supervision. By 1993, boot camps had been formally established in over half of the states (Florida Office of Program Policy Analysis, 1995). In 1995, there were 35 federal and state boot camps being operated, with a total of 9,304 inmate-clients. Of these, there were 626 females. Of the 9,304 inmate-clients, 455 were juvenile offenders distributed throughout nine locally operated programs (Bourque, Han, and Hill, 1996:3). By 2004 there were over 100 residential boot camps for adjudicated juveniles operating in 35 states (Office of Juvenile Justice and Delinquency Prevention, 2005). Many jurisdictions throughout the United States issue boot camp orders for juveniles who are believed to be unruly and in need of discipline. In Glynn County, Georgia, for instance, boot camp orders are issued by juvenile court judges. Figure 13.1 shows a short-term boot camp order for those juveniles targeted for involvement in such programming.

Boot camp programs emphasize discipline, obedience, and integrity as primary goals.

IN THE JUVENILE COURT OF GLYNN COUNTY
STATE OF GEORGIA

IN THE INTEREST OF: CASE #:_____

_____

A Child

ORDER
SHORT TERM/ BOOT CAMP PROGRAM

Petition(s) having been filed in this Court and after hearing evidence , this Court has determined that the above named child is subject to the jurisdiction and protection of this Court as provided by law; and

After hearing evidence, the Court finds that the child committed the act(s) alleged in said petition(s), to wit:

_____

_____

_____and that said child is hereby found to be in a state of delinquency/unruliness and in need of treatment or rehabilitation.

It is Ordered that said child be and is hereby detained by the Department of Juvenile Justice for care, supervision, and planning as provided by O.C.G.A. Section 15-11-35(b) and 49-4A-8, and that the child be detained for a period of _____days.

THE CHILD WILL/WILL NOT BE GIVEN CREDIT FOR THE TIME SPENT IN DETENTION BOTH PRIOR TO ADJUDICATION AND WHILE AWAITING ENTRY INTO THE PROGRAM.

SAID CHILD SHALL NOT BE GRANTED CREDIT FOR ANY TIME SPENT IN DISCIPLINARY ISOLATION OR DETENTION, FOR REFUSING TO PARTICIPATE IN THE PROGRAM, OR FOR FAILURE TO ABIDE BY THE RULES OF THE FACILITY.

The department of Juvenile Justice is authorized to provide such emergency psychological evaluation or treatment, medical treatment, hospitalization, or surgery as is considered necessary by competent medical authorities for said child. The Department of Juvenile Justice is authorized to apprehend such child if such child shall have escaped from a facility or institution operated or under the supervision of the Department.

CONSIDERED, ORDERED AND ADJUDGED this the _____day of_____,_____.

_____
George M. Rountree, Judge
Juvenile Court of Glynn County

FIGURE 13.1 Short-Term Boot Camp Program Order
(*Source:* Glynn County, GA)

Some persons regard boot camps as the latest correctional reform (Styve et al., 2000). Other professionals are skeptical about their success potential (Zachariah, 2002). Much depends on how particular boot camps are operated and for how long. Boot camp programs are operated for as short a time as 30 days or as long as 180 days. While boot camps were officially established in 1983 by the Georgia Department of Corrections Special Alternative Incarceration (SAI), the general idea for boot camps originated some time earlier in the late 1970s, also in Georgia (MacKenzie et al., 2001).

The Rationale for Boot Camps.   Boot camps have been established as an alternative to long-term traditional incarceration. Austin, Jones, and Bolyard (1993:1) outline a brief rationale for boot camps:

1. A substantial number of youthful first-time offenders now incarcerated will respond to a short but intensive period of confinement followed by a longer period of intensive community supervision.

2. These youthful offenders will benefit from a military-type atmosphere that instills a sense of self-discipline and physical conditioning that was lacking in their lives.

3. These same youths need exposure to relevant education, vocational training, drug treatment, and general counseling services to develop more positive and law-abiding values and become better prepared to secure legitimate future employment.

4. The costs involved will be less than a traditional criminal justice sanction that imprisons the offender for a substantially longer period of time.

Boot Camp Goals.   Boot camps have several general goals. These goals include: (1) rehabilitation/reintegration; (2) discipline; (3) deterrence; (4) ease prison/jail overcrowding; and (5) vocational, educational, and rehabilitative services.

1. *To Provide Rehabilitation and Reintegration.* In 1986, the Orleans (Louisiana) Parish Prison System established a boot camp program called About Face (Caldas, 1990). This program sought to improve one's sense of purpose, self-discipline, self-control, and self-confidence through physical conditioning, educational programs, and social skills training, all within the framework of strict military discipline. One early criticism of this Louisiana program was the amount of inexperience among boot camp staff. Over time, however, this criticism was minimized (MacKenzie and Shaw, 1993:463–466).

2. *To Provide Discipline.* Boot camps are designed to improve one's discipline. Certain boot camps, especially those aimed at younger offenders, must deal with adjudicated juvenile offenders who usually resist authority and refuse to listen or learn in traditional classroom or treatment environments (MacKenzie and Wilson, 2001). Physical conditioning and structure are most frequently stressed in these programs. But most boot camp programs also include educational elements pertaining to literacy, academic and vocational education, intensive value clarification, and resocialization (Styve et al., 2000).

3. *To Promote Deterrence.* The sudden immersion of convicted offenders into a military-like atmosphere is a frightening experience for many participants. The rigorous approach to formal rules and authority was a challenging dimension of boot camp programs for most participants (Shaw and MacKenzie, 1992). Mack (1992:63–65) reports that of the many clients who have participated in the Rikers Boot Camp High Impact Incarceration Program (HIIP), only 23 percent have recidivated compared with 28 percent of those released from traditional incarceration. While these recidivism rate differences are not substantial, the direction of the difference says something about the potential deterrent value of boot camp programs.

4. *To Ease Prison and Jail Overcrowding.* Boot camps are believed to have a long-term impact on jail and prison overcrowding. Theoretically, this is possible because of the low recidivism rates among boot camp participants. The short-term nature of confinement in boot camp programs with the participant's subsequent return to the community helps to ease the overcrowding problem in correctional settings. It is believed that boot camp experiences are significant in creating more positive attitudes among participants (Gover and MacKenzie, 2003).

5. *To Provide Vocational and Rehabilitative Services.* An integral feature of most boot camp programs is the inclusion of some form of educational and/or vocational training. A New York Shock Incarceration program makes it possible for participants to work on GED diplomas and provides elementary educational instruction (New York State Department of Correctional Services, 1992). Educational training is also a key feature of **IMPACT, or Intensive Motivational Program of Alternative Correctional Treatment,** in Louisiana jurisdictions. As an alternative to traditional incarceration, boot camps do much to promote greater social and educational adjustment for clients reentering their communities.

Profiling Boot Camp Participants. Who can participate in boot camps or shock incarceration programs? Participants may or may not be able to enter or withdraw from boot camps voluntarily. It depends on the particular program. Most boot camp participants are prison-bound youthful offenders convicted of less serious, nonviolent crimes, and who have never been previously incarcerated (Zachariah, 2002).

Participants may either be referred to these programs by judges or corrections departments or they may volunteer. They may or may not be accepted, and if they complete their programs successfully, they may or may not be released under supervision into their communities. Screening of boot camp participants is extremely important. For instance, a boot camp program in California, LEAD, sponsored by the California Youth Authority, conducted screenings for 365 eligible juveniles during 1992–1993. Only 180 were admitted into the LEAD program, while only 107 graduated successfully and were granted parole after 4 months (Bottcher and Isorena, 1994).

Representative Boot Camps. Several boot camps described below are indicative of the general nature of boot camps in the various states that have them.

The Camp Monterey Shock Incarceration Facility. New York State has a major boot camp project with the following features:

a. Accommodates 250 participants in a minimum-security institution;
b. Has 131 staff (83 custody positions);
c. Participants are screened and must meet statutory criteria; three-fourths volunteer; one-third of applicants rejected;
d. Inmates form platoons and live in open dormitories;
e. Successful program completion leads to parole board releases to an intensive probation supervision program called "aftershock";
f. Physical training, drill, 8 hours daily of hard labor;

Boot camps emphasize exercise and other tasks as a means of instilling discipline and greater self-esteem among participating youths.

g. Inmates must participate in therapeutic community meetings, compulsory adult basic education courses, mandatory individual counseling, and mandatory recreation;
h. All must attend alcohol and substance abuse treatment; and
i. Job seeking skills training and reentry planning.

The Oklahoma Regimented Inmate Discipline Program (RID). Oklahoma has a **Regimented Inmate Discipline Program (RID)** with the following features:

a. 145-bed facility at the Lexington Assessment and Reception Center; also houses 600 long-term general population inmates as medium security;
b. Offenders screened according to statutory criteria and may volunteer;
c. Inmates live in single or double-bunk cells;
d. Strict discipline, drill, physical training; housekeeping and institutional maintenance;
e. Six hours daily in educational/vocational programs;
f. Drug abuse programs, individual and group counseling; and
g. Subsequently, participants are resentenced by judges to intensive supervised probation or "community custody," perhaps commencing at a halfway house.

The Georgia Special Alternative Program (SAI). This program includes the following characteristics:

a. Program for male offenders;
b. Judges control selection process and SAI is a "condition of probation"; if successful, boot camp graduates are released, since judges do not ordinarily resentence them to probation;

   c. Program includes physical training, drill, hard work; two exercise and drill periods daily, with 8-hour hard labor periods in between;

   d. Participants perform limited community services;

   e. Little emphasis on counseling or treatment;

   f. Inmates do receive drug abuse education and information about sexually transmitted diseases; and

   g. Inmates are double-bunked in two 25-cell units at Dodge, and at Burris, 100 inmates are single-bunked in four 25-cell units (MacKenzie, Shaw, and Gowdy, 1993).

Because many of these boot camp programs have been established since about the late 1980s and early 1990s, extensive evaluation research about general boot camp program effectiveness has not been abundant (Zachariah, 2002). However, indications from available research are that boot camps generally are effective at reducing recidivism among participants. Currently, some states, such as Georgia, report relatively high rates of recidivism among boot camp clientele, whereas New York and Oklahoma have much lower recidivism rates. Besides reducing recidivism, boot camps might also be effective at saving taxpayers money over time. For various states, operating boot camps is considerably cheaper than using traditional incarceration for particular offenders. In some instances, the cost savings is considerable.

Industrial Schools and Other Juvenile Institutions

In the 1950s, 1960s, and earlier, particularly troublesome youths were sent to reform schools. These were prison-like facilities with few amenities. Juveniles were assigned various menial tasks, and educational opportunities were limited. Some more affluent jurisdictions with reform schools offered various types of counseling and vocational and educational programs. But for most youths sent to reform schools, their prospects for learning useful skills and emerging as law-abiding young adults were bleak. If anything, many youths emerged from these institutions as more hardcore offenders than when they entered. More than a few youths went on to commit crimes as adults.

During the period 1950–1970, a concerted effort was made by the Federal Bureau of Investigation and other agencies to intervene in various ways to interrupt those social patterns believed responsible for generating youthful offenders or delinquents. Many interventions were attempted, and some of these interventions were mentioned earlier in Chapter 3. J. Edgar Hoover, the Director of the FBI during that period, was a firm believer in delinquency interventions and their relationship to general adult crime prevention. The FBI would send teachers and professors useful teaching materials, articles, and other information that could be used in educational programs to advise and inform. Much of this information was descriptive and informed readers about ongoing interventions in various jurisdictions and their successfulness. In turn, these federal efforts prompted many communities throughout the United States to develop strategies for dealing with delinquent offenders. Different types of treatments and punishments were the subject of experimentation for selected groups of juveniles.

Today there is a wide variety of intervention programs for juveniles operating in virtually every major city and most communities. These programs generally emphasize vocational training, acquisition of social and coping skills and education, substance abuse counseling, mental health counseling, and a wide variety of other activities. But it is clear that almost all of these interventions have been limited in their effectiveness for deterring youths from committing delinquent offenses. The growing influence of gangs, the greater use of drugs and other substances, and pervasive family disunity and fragmentation have combined with other factors, such as higher unemployment rates, hard economic times, and pressures for higher standards in education, to frustrate the most well-intentioned intervention programs.

Delinquency and violent youthful offending appeared to peak during the mid-1990s, although there continues to be an unacceptable level of violent offending among juveniles today. Citizen response to such violence, much of it gang-related, has been to get tough with juveniles. The get-tough movement generally equates with incarceration or institutionalization as the harshest measure to apply as a juvenile punishment for delinquency.

As we have seen, locking up juveniles is generally an unpopular response to juvenile offending. In many jurisdictions, it is considered as a last resort. In Tennessee, for instance, juvenile corrections personnel will place juveniles on electronic monitoring and/or home confinement for 30, 60, or 90 days to see if they can remain law-abiding. If they cannot, then this is often considered as the last measure to be taken before incarceration of these juveniles is ordered.

Today institutionalized juveniles in all states are held in facilities most frequently known as **industrial schools.** The use of the term "reform school" has been abandoned. Also, no juvenile facility is called a prison, even though most secure juvenile facilities are prison-like in their construction and operation. Industrial schools are not new. The term has been used for over 60 years in different jurisdictions. In the 1950s, for instance, the Utah State Industrial School was the juvenile prison and also the place where most hardcore juvenile offenders were sent by juvenile court judges. In the 1960s the Arizona State Industrial School was where Gerald Gault was housed for allegedly making obscene telephone calls (*In re Gault,* 1967). Industrial schools now exist in most states and are operated either publicly or privately or both (Sickmund, 2004). Youths sent to industrial schools are considered **commitment placements,** where they are held for longer terms compared with youths placed in detention.

Numbers and Types of Juveniles Held in Secure Facilities.

There are few precise figures about how many juveniles are held in secure facilities each year. Given the rate of discharges and admissions, the numbers are fluid from one day to the next. However, it is apparent from available information that the number of confined youths in secure facilities is growing each year. Between 1991 and 1999, for instance, the number of youths committed to secure facilities almost doubled from 58,000 to nearly 110,000 (Sickmund, 2004:4). In 2001 it was reported that 127,251 youths were assigned beds in 3,580 secure facilities nationwide (Office of Juvenile Justice and Delinquency Prevention, 2004:2). At the time of this writing, more recent information was unavailable to report. However, extrapolating from previous information and trends suggests that there might have been as many as 150,000 youths in secure confinement by 2005.

Youths are committed either to short- or long-term detention or secure confinement, depending on the particular stage of juvenile offender processing. Prior to a formal adjudicatory hearing, juveniles may be detained in custody of juvenile authorities pending the outcome of a subsequent adjudicatory hearing.

ORDER FOR DETENTION

IN THE JUVENILE COURT OF GLYNN COUNTY, GEORGIA

IN THE MATTER OF:	CASE NO.:
	SEX:
	DOB:
A CHILD	AGE:

WHEREAS a complaint has been made to the Court concerning the above-named child and the Court finding from information brought before it that it is necessary for the protection of said child and/or society that he or she be detained.

It is therefore ordered that said child be detained in the custody of the Court until further order of the Court or until released by a person duly authorized by the Court.

Said child is being detained pursuant to Official Code of Georgia Ann. 15-11-46 for the following reason(s):

( ) to protect the person or property of others or of the child;

( ) the child may abscond or be removed from the justification of the Court;

( ) because he has no parent, guardian or legal custodian or other person able to provide supervision and care for him and return him to the Court when required;

( ) an order for his detention or shelter care has been made by the Court pursuant to the Juvenile Proceedings Code.

It   is   further   ordered   that   the   place   of   detention   shall   be   the

_____

ORDERED AND ADJUDGED, this the _____ day of _____, 2004.

_____
George M. Rountree, Judge

FIGURE 13.2   Order for Detention
(*Source:* Glynn County, GA)

Figure 13.2 shows an order for detention for Glynn County, Georgia. The reasons for detention are outlined. These usually pertain to protecting others from the juvenile; protecting the juvenile from him- or herself while awaiting a formal adjudicatory hearing; the absence of parents or legal guardians; or some other valid reason.

Typically, reported figures reflect all youths under age 21 who are housed in either public or private secure facilities; who have been adjudicated delinquent by the juvenile court; who are in residential placement because of that offense; and who have been assigned a bed by a given date. Table 13.1 shows the number of offenders being held in both public and private secure facilities in 1999 according to their offense.

TABLE 13.1

Juveniles in Secure Residential Facilities in 1999 By Offense

Most serious offense	Juvenile offenders in residential placement on October 27, 1999					
	All facilities		Public facilities		Private facilities	
	Number	Percent	Number	Percent	Number	Percent
Total juvenile offenders	108,931	100%	77,158	100%	31,599	100%
Delinquency	104,237	96	75,537	98	28,536	90
Person	38,005	35	28,056	36	9,897	31
Criminal homicide	1,514	1	1,368	2	141	<1
Sexual assault	7,511	7	5,154	7	2,352	7
Robbery	8,212	8	6,825	9	1,386	4
Aggravated assault	9,984	9	7,848	10	2,124	7
Simple assault	7,448	7	4,479	6	2,949	9
Other person	3,336	3	2,385	3	948	3
Property	31,817	29	22,725	29	9,051	29
Burglary	12,222	11	9,069	12	3,141	10
Theft	6,944	6	4,791	6	2,148	7
Auto theft	6,225	6	4,164	5	2,040	6
Arson	1,126	1	843	1	282	1
Other property	5,300	5	3,855	5	1,437	5
Drug	9,882	9	6,819	9	3,054	10
Drug trafficking	3,106	3	2,298	3	807	3
Other drug	6,776	6	4,521	6	2,247	7
Public order	10,487	10	7,380	10	3,087	10
Weapons	4,023	4	3,162	4	858	3
Other public order	6,464	6	4,215	5	2,229	7
Technical violation*	14,046	13	10,557	14	3,447	11
Violent Crime Index[†]	27,221	25	21,192	27	6,003	19
Property Crime Index[‡]	26,517	24	18,870	24	7,614	24
Status offense	4,694	4	1,623	2	3,063	10

Source: Melissa Sickmund, *Juveniles in Corrections*. Washington, DC: U.S. Department of Justice, Office of Justice Programs, 2004:6.

An inspection of Table 13.1 shows that 108,931 juveniles were being held in secure facilities in 1999. Of these, about 35 percent (38,005) were being housed for person or violent offenses, 29 percent were being housed for property offenses, and 9 percent were being confined for drug offenses. Interestingly, about 27 percent of these youths were being held in secure confinement for public order and status offenses, such as weapons charges, runaway behavior, intoxication, truancy, and technical violations (Sickmund, 2004:6). Thus, it is not true that a majority of youths who are incarcerated in secure facilities are violent or person offenders. Two-thirds of those committed are nonviolent property, drug, public order, or status offenders. Figure 13.3 shows an order of commitment used by Glynn County, Georgia, for juveniles who are to be placed for long terms in secure confinement. It is interesting to note in these commitment orders that the reasons for commitment are related closely to the need for the youth's rehabilitation or treatment under close supervision. The length of

ORDER OF COMMITMENT

IN THE JUVENILE COURT OF GLYNN COUNTY, GEORGIA

In the interest of: **CASE NO.**

                                                            SEX:
                                                            DOB: **AGE:**

Petition(s) having been filed in this court and after hearing evidence in this court, this court has determined that the above-named child is subject to the jurisdiction and protection of this court as provided by law; and

After hearing evidence or upon the recommendation of the judge, no appeal having been timely filed, the court finds that the child committed the act(s) alleged in said petition(s), to wit:

_____

And that said child is hereby found to be in a state of: (place an "X" in appropriate space).

_____ delinquency and in need of treatment of rehabilitation.

_____ unruliness and in need of treatment, rehabilitation, or supervision. The court also finds that the child is not amenable to treatment or rehabilitation pursuant to O.C.G.A. §15-11-66(a)(1)(3).

The Court also finds that reasonable efforts have been made to prevent the unnecessary removal of the child from the child's home, and that removal is in the best interest of the child at this time.

It is further ordered that said child be and hereby is committed to the Department of Juvenile Justice, for care, supervision and planning as provided in O.C.G.A. §49-4A-8. The undersigned judge hereby recommends that the child be:

COMMITTED TO THE DEPARTMENT OF JUVENILE JUSTICE

The said Department of Juvenile Justice is authorized to provide such medical treatment, hospitalization and/or surgery as is considered necessary by competent medical authorities for said child.

It is further ordered that said child be released into the custody of _____ _____. Detained in the _____ pending placement by the Department of Juvenile Justice.

Considered, Ordered and Adjudged this the _____ day of _____, 2004.

                                    _____
                                    George M. Rountree, Judge
                                    Juvenile Court of Glynn County

FIGURE 13.3 Order of Commitment
(*Source:* Glynn County, Georgia)

any particular commitment varies according to one's offense or the nature of the unruly behavior.

Table 13.2 shows the numbers of youths committed to secure facilities in 1999 by state as well as the rate of their incarceration per 100,000 youths. California led all states with 19,072 youths being committed to secure confinement. Texas was second with 7,954 youths in secure confinement. Other states with large numbers of incarcerated youths (4,000 or more) included Florida, Ohio,

TABLE 13.2

Numbers of Youths in Secure Confinement By State and Rate of Incarceration per 100,000 Youths

State of offense	Juvenile offenders in residential placement on October 27, 1999 Number	Rate	State of offense	Juvenile offenders in residential placement on October 27, 1999 Number	Rate
U.S. total	108,931	371	Upper age 17 (continued)		
Upper age 17			Oklahoma	1,123	273
Alabama	1,589	333	Oregon	1,549	404
Alaska	382	419	Pennsylvania	3,819	285
Arizona	1,901	334	Rhode Island	310	284
Arkansas	705	234	South Dakota	603	632
California	19,072	514	Tennessee	1,534	256
Colorado	1,979	407	Utah	985	320
Delaware	347	431	Vermont	67	96
Dist. of Columbia	259	704	Virginia	3,085	415
Florida	6,813	427	Washington	2,094	307
Hawaii	118	96	West Virginia	388	202
Idaho	360	220	Wyoming	310	488
Indiana	2,650	384	Upper age 16		
Iowa	1,017	296	Georgia	3,729	475
Kansas	1,254	383	Illinois	3,885	322
Kentucky	1,188	270	Louisiana	2,745	580
Maine	242	167	Massachusetts	1,188	206
Maryland	1,579	269	Michigan	4,324	417
Minnesota	1,760	290	Missouri	1,161	205
Mississippi	784	229	New Hampshire	216	167
Montana	246	220	South Carolina	1,650	441
Nebraska	720	342	Texas	7,954	370
Nevada	789	378	Wisconsin	1,924	338
New Jersey	2,386	273	Upper age 15		
New Mexico	855	378	Connecticut	1,466	513
North Dakota	235	297	New York	4,813	334
Ohio	4,531	345	North Carolina	1,429	221

Source: Melissa Sickmund, *Juveniles in Corrections.* Washington, DC: U.S. Department of Justice Programs, 2004:7.

Michigan, and New York (Sickmund, 2004:7). Despite having the largest number of youths incarcerated, California did not have the highest rate of incarceration. The District of Columbia led all jurisdictions with 704 youths per 100,000 held in secure confinement. South Dakota had a rate of 632 youths per 100,000 in secure confinement. Those states with the lowest rates of youth confinement were Hawaii and Vermont, each with 96 youths per 100,000 in secure commitment (Sickmund, 2004:7).

PERSISTENT PROBLEMS OF NONSECURE AND SECURE CONFINEMENT

Secure juvenile incarcerative facilities in the United States are known by various names. Furthermore, not all of these secure confinement facilities are alike. While many institutions provide only custodial services for chronic or more serious juvenile offenders, other incarcerative facilities offer an array of services and treatments, depending on the diverse needs of the juveniles confined, such as mental health services (Merianos, 2005). Clarifying the mission and goals of corrections agencies helps staff to do a better job supervising youthful clientele. Institutional rules tend to be couched in a more meaningful context, and incarcerated youth are able to cope more effectively with their confinement (King, 2005).

Architectural Improvements and Officer Training Reforms

In recent years, however, numerous improvements have been made generally in the overall quality of juvenile secure confinement facilities throughout the United States. Evidence of improvement in juvenile corrections is the massive efforts made by authorities in numerous jurisdictions to design and build more adequately equipped juvenile facilities that minimize youthful inmate problems of idle time and overcrowding. Private interests, including the Corrections Corporation of America, have assisted as well in providing more modern designs and plant operations for secure juvenile facilities in various states such as California and Tennessee (Mendel, 2001).

Both male and female correctional officers are targeted for additional training to cope with inmate problems. Formerly, it has been alleged by some critics that female correctional officers tend to lack the same degree of authority of their male officer counterparts when dealing with inmates. However, programs such as on-the-job training and self-improvement courses sponsored and conducted by the American Correctional Association have done much to improve correctional officer credibility and performance (Mitchell et al., 2000). According to ACA standards, correctional officers should have at least 160 hours of orientation and training during their first year of employment. Certification is awarded after satisfactorily completing the ACA training course (American Correctional Association, 2005; Jurich, Casper, and Hull, 2001).

Juvenile Detention Resource Centers

The U.S. Department of Justice's Office of Juvenile Justice and Delinquency Prevention (OJJDP) promulgated specific guidelines for all juvenile detention facilities in the early 1980s. These guidelines were published as *Guidelines for the Development of Policies and Procedures for Juvenile Detention Facilities*. The goal of the OJJDP was to establish national juvenile detention resource centers around the United States in various jurisdictions that would provide information, technical assistance, and training to juvenile detention professionals who wished to participate (King, 2005). The ultimate aim of these juvenile detention centers was to provide juveniles with better and more adequate services and assistance (Teske, 2005).

Such **detention centers** have done much to improve juvenile incarceration standards throughout the nation. The ACA has been actively involved in assisting different jurisdictions in their efforts to establish juvenile detention resource centers and operate them successfully (Russell, 2001). The educational dimension of such centers can assist in transmitting knowledge about communicable diseases, such as AIDS, and inform adolescents about the risks of sexual misconduct. Other positive contributions of these centers might be to assist youths in managing their anger and providing them with opportunities to improve their general mental health (Butts and Adams, 2001).

Short- and Long-Term Facilities

Secure juvenile confinement facilities in the United States are either short term or long term. Short-term confinement facilities are designed to accommodate juveniles on a temporary basis. These juveniles are either awaiting a later juvenile court adjudication, subsequent foster home or group home placement, or a transfer to criminal court. Whether a juvenile is held for a period of time in detention depends on the outcome of a **detention hearing,** where the appropriateness of the detention is determined.

Sometimes youths will be placed in short-term confinement because their identity is unknown and it is desirable that they should not be confined in adult lock-ups or jails. Other youths are violent and must be detained temporarily until more appropriate placements may be made. The designations short term and long term may range from a few days to several years, although the average duration of **long-term detention** across all offender categories nationally is about 6–7 months. The average short-term incarceration in public facilities for juveniles is about 30 days (Office of Juvenile Justice and Delinquency Prevention, 2005).

Some **short-term confinement** is preventive detention or pretrial detention, where juveniles are awaiting formal adjudicatory proceedings. While some authorities question the legality of jailing juveniles or holding them in detention centers prior to their cases being heard by juvenile court judges, the U.S. Supreme Court has upheld the constitutionality of pretrial or preventive detention of juveniles, especially dangerous ones, in the case of Schall v. Martin (1984). One objective of pretrial detention is to prevent certain dangerous juveniles from committing new pretrial crimes (King, 2005). Juvenile court judges must make a determination of whether certain juveniles should be held in pretrial detention or released into the custody of parents or guardians. While their discretion is not perfect, many juvenile court judges exercise good judgment in determining which juveniles should be temporarily detained. It is often difficult to determine the future behaviors of adjudicated youths, especially in probation or parole contexts (Xiaoying, 2005).

Dormitory rooms with minimum amenites characterize many overcrowded secure facilities for juveniles.

Some Criticisms of Incarcerating Juveniles

There are numerous proponents and opponents of juvenile secure confinement of any kind. Those favoring incarceration cite the disruption of one's lifestyle and separation from other delinquent youths as a positive dimension. For example, youths who have been involved with delinquent gangs or friends who engage in frequent law-breaking would probably benefit from incarceration, since these unfavorable associations would be interrupted or terminate (Fried and Reppucci, 2001). Of course, juveniles can always return to their old ways when released from incarceration. There is nothing the juvenile justice system can do to prevent these reunions. But at least the existing pattern of interaction that contributed to the delinquent behavior initially is temporarily interrupted.

Another argument favoring incarceration of juveniles is that long-term secure confinement is a deserved punishment for their actions. This is consistent with the just-deserts philosophy that seems to typify contemporary thinking about juvenile punishment. There is a noticeable trend away from thinking about the best interests of youths and toward thinking about ways to make them more accountable for their actions. This shift has prompted debate among juvenile justice scholars about the true functions of juvenile courts and the ultimate aims of the sanctions they impose (King, 2005).

Opponents to long-term secure confinement of juveniles believe, among other things, that there are possibly adverse labeling effects from confinement with other offenders. Thus, juveniles might acquire labels of themselves as juvenile delinquents and persist in reoffending when released from incarceration later. However, it might be maintained that if they are incarcerated, they know they are delinquents anyway. Will they necessarily acquire stronger self-definitions of delinquents beyond those they already possess? In some respects, it is status-enhancing for youthful offenders to have been confined in some joint or juvenile secure confinement facility, so that they may brag to others about their experiences later. No doubt, confinement of any kind will add at least one dimension to one's reputation as a delinquent offender among other offenders in the community.

Most of the successful incarcerative programs for juveniles have built-in educational and vocational components, many of which are voluntary (Houchins, 2001). It seems to make a difference whether confined juveniles are forced to take vocational or educational courses or whether they can enroll in such programs on a voluntary basis (Kadish et al., 2001). For example, a literacy program in the South Carolina Department of Youth Services was investigated in 1990–1991. The sample consisted of 415 participants enrolled in the General Educational Development (G.E.D.) program. While few differences were exhibited between those forced to enroll in this program and those who voluntarily entered it, the volunteers seemed to make a better adjustment in a subsequent follow-up program evaluation (U.S. General Accounting Office, 1996a). Providing needed psychological and medical services also seems to make a difference in those institutions managing hardcore offenders.

In recent years, organizations such as the American Correctional Association have promulgated standards for juvenile correctional facilities that provide educational and vocational goals for juvenile inmates of these institutions. Presently educational programming is mandatory for all juvenile offenders, and educational programs in juvenile correctional facilities are required to follow the same laws and practices as their public school counterparts. These standards also are applicable to privately operated secure juvenile facilities (Corwin, 2005:83).

Juvenile facilities may seek accreditation from various organizations such as the Correctional Education Association (CEA). In October 2004 the Standards Commission of the CEA approved a set of standards for accrediting correctional educational programs in juvenile facilities. Actually CEA began accrediting juvenile corrections educational programming in 1988. Both adult and juvenile institutions are now subject to CEA accreditation and the standards established by it. The accreditation process is a dynamic one, with constant improvements and assessment plans being devised. These improvements speak well of continuing to improve juvenile rehabilitation, particularly rehabilitation associated with educational and vocational training goals (Corwin, 2005).

In the state of Washington, for example, juveniles as young as age 14 may be sent to the Department of Corrections (Fleming and Winkler, 1999:132). However, separate housing units are provided for more youthful offenders before they are placed in the general inmate population. Washington officials have established a number of successful multidisciplinary, psychological, and case management programs to treat incarcerated youths. Juveniles are exposed to an offense cycle group, where they are taught to think critically about their crimes and what led up to their behaviors. They also receive anger management training, victim awareness experience, social skills, assertiveness skills, problem-solving activities, and cognitive-behavioral awareness. They are compelled to follow a mandatory dress code and maintain a healthy regimen of exercise. Whether these youths want this training and exposure or not, they must have it. These services are believed beneficial to one's law-abiding behavior in future years.

Other arguments suggest that the effects of imprisonment on a juvenile's self-image and propensity to commit new offenses are negligible (Fried and Reppucci, 2001). Thus, incarceration as a punishment may be the primary result, without any tangible, long-range benefits such as self-improvement or reduction in recidivism. At least there does not appear to be any consistent or reliable evidence that detaining juveniles automatically causes them to escalate to more serious offenses or to become adult criminals. According to some analysts, the peak ages of juvenile criminality fall between the 16th and 20th birthdays, with participation rates falling off rapidly. Thus, incarceration for a fixed period may naturally ease the delinquency rate, at least for some of the more chronic offenders. Some opponents note that racial, ethnic, and gender factors are more operative in secure confinement decisions than legal factors (King, 2005; Merianos, 2005).

Disproportionate Minority Confinement

Considerable attention has been directed in recent years toward the issue of disproportionate minority confinement, especially in secure juvenile facilities (Pope, Lovell, and Hsia, 2002:1). A far greater proportionate number of arrests of juveniles, for instance, involves racial and ethnic minorities. In 2001, the racial composition of the 10- to 17-year-old population in the United States was 78 percent white, 17 percent black, 4 percent Asian/Pacific Islander, and 1 percent American Indian (Snyder, 2003:9). However, that same year, of all juvenile arrests for violent crimes, 55 percent of the arrestees were white youths, while

43 percent were black and 2 percent other. For juvenile property offending in 2001, 68 percent of all arrests involved white youths, blacks accounted for 28 percent, and 4 percent consisted of Asians and others. Thus, at the point of entry into the juvenile justice system, disproportionately larger numbers of minority youths were arrested compared with white juveniles.

It is beyond the scope of this book to explore the many reasons or explanations for such disproportionate representations of minorities in these arrest figures. Interestingly, arrest figures for adult offenders mirror those of youthful offenders each year. One plausible explanation, however, is that minority youths are often from the lower socioeconomic levels, and thus, they generally have more limited opportunities for success in school and other activities. Thus, the mere fact of socioeconomic deprivation might account for more frequent property crime among such youths, such as burglary, larceny, and vehicular theft. Violent crimes such as robbery, which are related closely to socioeconomic factors, might also reflect disproportionate numbers of minority offenders. In fact, in 2001, 58 percent of all youths arrested for robbery were black.

Is there pervasive racism throughout law enforcement in cities and towns? Do police officers single out minority youths for arrests and overlook crimes committed by white youths? There have been numerous investigations of the impact of race and minority status generally on the likelihood of arrest. While most of these studies are inconclusive, an indirect bias has been detected in more than a few investigations indicating that nonwhite juveniles are more likely to be arrested compared with white juveniles when the victim is white rather than nonwhite (Pope and Snyder, 2003:6). However, no direct evidence presently exists to show that police arrests of juveniles are race-based or biased. Essentially, what the research literature suggests is that whenever youths commit violent crimes and police are aware of these acts, the juveniles will be arrested whether they are white or nonwhite (Snyder, 2003).

Carl Pope, Rick Lovell, and Heidi Hsia (2002) conducted a study that analyzed 34 research investigations pertaining to different stages of juvenile processing, paying particular attention to the influence of racial and ethnic factors. After substantial analysis of the findings from these studies, the researchers concluded that a youth's racial status tended to make a difference at different stages of offender processing. This generalization seems warranted, especially when the secure confinement rates of youths are examined.

Available figures for secure confinement of youths for 1999 reveal that of all youths placed in secure facilities that year, 63 percent were minorities. Approximately 40 percent of all incarcerated youths were black, while 19 percent were Hispanic (Sickmund, 2004:9). A breakdown of minority status and type of offense among those youths who were incarcerated in 1999 is shown in Table 13.3.

An inspection of Table 13.3 shows that black juveniles made up 65 percent of all youths confined for drug trafficking and 55 percent of those confined for robbery. Black youths were confined to a disproportionately higher degree compared with whites for all offense categories except sexual assault, simple assault, burglary, theft, and status offending. White youths were confined to the greatest degree for sexual assault (52 percent) and status offenses (54 percent). Hispanic youths made up 18 percent of all confined juveniles (Sickmund, 2004:9). Thus, despite the fact that 55 percent of all youths arrested are white, only about 38 percent of these youths are subsequently incarcerated in secure facilities.

TABLE 13.3

Race/Ethnicity and Type of Offense among Incarcerated Youths, 1999

| | Racial/ethnic profile of juvenile offenders in residential placement, 1999 | | | | | |
Most serious offense	Total	White	Black	Hispanic	American Indian	Asian
Total	100%	38%	39%	18%	2%	2%
Delinquency	100	37	40	19	2	2
Criminal homicide	100	23	44	24	3	6
Sexual assault	100	52	31	13	2	1
Robbery	100	19	55	22	1	3
Aggravated assault	100	29	40	25	2	3
Simple assault	100	43	37	15	2	1
Burglary	100	43	34	18	2	2
Theft	100	43	38	15	2	1
Auto theft	100	36	38	21	2	3
Drug trafficking	100	16	65	18	0	1
Other drug	100	30	47	20	1	1
Weapons	100	26	42	27	1	4
Technical violation*	100	39	39	18	2	2
Status	100	54	31	10	2	1

| | Offense profile of juvenile offenders in residential placement, 1999 | | | | | |
Most serious offense	Total	White	Black	Hispanic	American Indian	Asian
Total	100%	100%	100%	100%	100%	100%
Delinquency	96	94	97	98	95	98
Criminal homicide	1	1	2	2	2	4
Sexual assault	7	10	5	5	7	3
Robbery	8	4	11	9	4	11
Aggravated assault	9	7	9	13	10	15
Simple assault	7	8	6	6	8	5
Burglary	11	13	10	11	13	12
Theft	6	7	6	5	6	5
Auto theft	6	5	6	6	7	8
Drug trafficking	3	1	5	3	1	1
Other drug	6	5	7	7	5	4
Weapons	4	3	4	5	2	7
Technical violation*	13	13	13	13	14	10
Status	4	6	3	2	5	2

Source: Melissa Sickmund, *Juveniles in Corrections.* Washington, DC: U.S. Department of Justice, Office of Justice Programs, 2004:9.

It is clear that various events transpire between one's arrest and subsequent disposition in juvenile court. Both legal and extralegal factors are at work to influence decision making at various stages of the juvenile justice process. Ideally, only legal factors should be relevant to all decision making, but there is compelling evidence showing that extralegal factors are operating as well. The pervasiveness of the disproportionality of minority confinement in the United States is underscored further by the fact that minorities make up the majority of those confined in secure institutions in most states (Sickmund, 2004:10). And in those states with greater white than nonwhite secure juvenile confinement, most of these jurisdictions have far fewer minority juveniles. Only eight states had minority 10–17 populations of less than 30 percent. In West Virginia, for instance, minority youths make up about 5 percent of the 10–17 population, yet minority youths in that state make up 18 percent of those in secure confinement. Do West Virginia minorities rate confinement in secure facilities three to four times greater than white youths who commit similar offenses? No clear-cut answers to this question have been forthcoming. And West Virginia does not stand alone as a state with low proportionate numbers of minority youths in the general population but with three to four times that proportion in secure confinement.

Presently the issue of race/ethnicity and differential juvenile justice processing is unresolved. Clear evidence of racial and ethnic bias exists and is reported in more than few studies. No single stage of the juvenile justice process can be singled out as especially discriminatory, however. It may be that white youths use private counsel to defend them to a greater degree, whereas minority youths may have to rely more on public defenders. Therefore, the plea bargaining prospects of minorities might be adversely affected because of the general quality of their defense counsels. Do private counsels do a better job generally in representing their clients compared with public defenders or publicly appointed counsel for indigents? Probably. This particular differential has been explored extensively, but with mixed results in the research literature (Champion, 2005a).

It is likely that one's lower socioeconomic status becomes a contributing factor to the quality of defense one receives as well as how one is treated by the juvenile justice system. And the relation between socioeconomic status and race/ethnicity is fairly strong. Therefore, in view of these associations and other related factors, we can understand why there is disproportionality in minority confinement in the United States. It is unknown at present precisely which factors influence this disproportionality. Furthermore, if such factors could be identified, it is unknown precisely what could be done to rectify any problems of disproportionality attributable to racial or ethnic factors. This obvious problem continues to be examined and explored, and alternative explanations are tested by many investigators.

Example of Residential Failure

Not all residential programs for juveniles are successful. One such program was operated for a brief period in Kane County, Illinois, under the direction of the Court Services Department. The Kane County Youth Home was established and designed to house up to nine male delinquents, age 13–17, and who had been previously adjudicated delinquent and deemed in need of intensive services that could not be provided otherwise on an outpatient basis (Kearney, 1994). The program failed because the essential balance between safety and trust could not be achieved. Staff workers could not be hired, trained, or evaluated primarily as residential treatment workers. The program director, court service hierarchy, and child care workers' theory and philosophy of change contrasted dramatically with the therapists' philosophy. Thus, the program philosophy itself was self-contradictory. Through no fault of their own, the youths served by the program were destined to "fail," simply because the administrators and practitioners could not agree on which philosophy should govern the youths' treatment. Kearney has observed that in order to be successful, such programs should have the following three essential components: (1) they must have a consistent philosophy of management shared by all participants; (2) peroses should be hired and trained according to that philosophy; and (3) administration of the program should be consonant with the program philosophy, including any changes introduced into program operations. Thus, the program itself was probably workable. However, staff disagreements about how best to implement the program led to its demise.

Example of Program Success

Kent State University's Department of Criminal Justice established a Juvenile Justice Assistants Program in December 1990 (Babb and Kratcoski, 1994). The goals of the program were to maximize the community-based treatment potential for unruly, delinquent, or victimized youths. To ensure the effectiveness of this program, program coordinators screened prospective employees in recruitment, training, and placement over a one-year period. About 45 juvenile justice assistants were hired and devoted a minimum of 200 hours to juvenile courts and justice agencies in a five-county area.

During the first 18 months of the program, 69 assistants were assigned to placement agencies for further training, together with service to the agency and its clients. Ultimately, more than 11,400 hours of training and service had been completed in approximately 25 agencies. Students involved in the program were able to assist numerous clientele during this same period. Thus, a successful internship/field experience was converted into a meaningful assistance program with juvenile justice assistants. A director oversaw the project and ensured that all program goals were consistent and implemented evenly. Any staff–client problems were dealt with immediately. Equitable solutions were found. The study yielded little recidivism among participating clientele during a follow-up period.

JUVENILE PAROLE

Juvenile Parole Defined

Parole for juveniles is similar to parole for adult offenders. Those juveniles who have been detained in various institutions for long periods may be released prior to serving their full sentences. Generally, parole is a conditional supervised release from incarceration granted to youths who have served a portion of their original sentences (Williams, 2003). They are known as **parolees.**

Purposes of Parole for Juveniles

The general purposes of parole are:

1. To reward good behavior while youths have been detained
2. To alleviate overcrowding

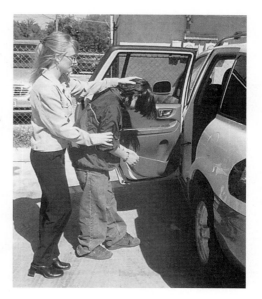

Juvenile parole officers have the authority to take parole violators into custody and have them reappear before parole boards for possible revocation actions.

3. To permit youths to become reintegrated back into their communities and enhance their rehabilitation potential

4. To deter youths from future offending by ensuring their continued supervision under juvenile parole officers

Some authorities also believe that the prospect of earning parole might induce greater compliance to institutional rules among incarcerated youths (Haapanen and Britton, 2002). Also, parole is seen by some persons as a continuation of the juvenile's punishment, since parole programs are most often conditional in nature (e.g., observance of curfew, school attendance, staying out of trouble, periodic drug and alcohol urinalyses, participation in counseling programs, and vocational and educational training). Many juvenile justice professionals agree that early-release decision making should not necessarily be automatic. Rather, releases should be based on a well-defined mission, strategy, and a matching continuum of care, which might also include assorted aftercare enhancements. Considerable attention must also be given to community safety as well as offender rehabilitation (Parker, 2005).

A standard parole agreement from the Minnesota Department of Corrections for juveniles is shown in Figure 13.4. Notice that this agreement specifies that the particular juvenile must remain in the legal custody and control of the Commissioner of Corrections "subject to the rules, regulations, and conditions of this parole as set forth on the reverse side of this agreement." While the reverse side of this agreement is not shown here, it provides sufficient space for the juvenile parole board to specify one or more program conditions, such as mandatory attendance at vocational/educational training schools, therapy or counseling, community service, restitution orders, or fine payments and maintenance fees. The parole plan is actually a continuation of the youth's punishment.

Often, the public thinks that if the youth is free from custody, he or she is completely unrestricted. This is not true. Both probation and parole are considered punishments. The behavioral conditions specified under either parole or probation may be very restrictive. Also, it is ordinarily the case that juvenile

Minnesota Department of Corrections

JUVENILE PAROLE AGREEMENT

WHEREAS, it appears to the Commissioner of Corrections that

_____
(NAME)

❏ presently in custody at _____, and

❏ presently on parole, and

WHEREAS, the said Commissioner, after careful consideration, believes that parole at

this time is in the best interests of this said individual and the public.

Now, THEREFORE, be it known that the Commissioner of Corrections, under authority

vested by law,   ❏ grants parole to,
                  ❏ continues parole for,   _____
                                                              (NAME)

and does authorize his/her release from the institution with the parole plan which has been

approved. Upon being paroled and released he/she shall be and remain in legal custody and

under the control of the Commissioner of Corrections subject to the rules, regulations, and

conditions of this parole as set forth on the reverse side of this agreement.

Signed this_____day of_____19_____.

**COMMISSIONER OF CORRECTIONS
BY:**

_____
(HEARING OFFICER)

DISTRIBUTION: ❏ New Parole Agreement
Original—Central Office
2nd Copy—Parolee   ❏ Restructured Parole Agreement
3rd Copy—Agent
4th Copy—Inst. File
CR-00100-03

FIGURE 13.4   Minnesota Juvenile Parole Agreement

probation/parole officers to have unlimited access to the premises where the youth is located. This intrusion by parole officers is unrestricted so that if youths are using drugs or are in possession of illegal contraband, it can be detected by surprise, through an unannounced visit from an officer at any time of the day or night.

How Many Juveniles Are on Parole?

The American Correctional Association (2005) estimates that over 28,000 juveniles were in nonsecure, state-operated halfway houses and other community-based facilities in 2004. Also, there were over 100,000 youths in secure institutions and training schools. It has been estimated that approximately 8,000 youths were under other forms of state-controlled supervision as parolees, although no precise figures are available.

Characteristics of Juvenile Parolees

Selected studies of juvenile parolees indicate that a majority are male, black, and between 17 and 19 years of age (Office of Juvenile Justice and Delinquency Prevention, 2005). Some jurisdictions, such as New York, have **juvenile offender laws.** These laws define 13-, 14-, 15-, and 16-year-olds as adults under certain conditions, whenever they are charged with committing specified felonies. They may be tried as adults and convicted. When they are subsequently released from institutionalization, they are placed under adult parole supervision. Many other jurisdictions do not have such Juvenile Offender Laws but have waiver or transfer provisions for particularly serious juvenile offenders. Juvenile parolees share many of the same programs used to supervise youthful probationers. Intensive supervised probation programs are used for both probationers and parolees in many jurisdictions. Furthermore, juvenile parole officers often perform dual roles as juvenile parole officers as they supervise both types of offenders.

Juvenile Parole Policy

Between November 1987 and November 1988, Ashford and LeCroy (1993:186) undertook an investigation of the various state juvenile parole programs and provisions. They sent letters and questionnaires to all state juvenile jurisdictions, soliciting any available information on their juvenile paroling policies. Their response rate was 94 percent, with 47 of the 50 states responding. One interesting result of their survey was the development of a typology of juvenile parole. Ashford and LeCroy discovered eight different kinds of juvenile parole used more or less frequently among the states. These were listed as follows:

1. Determinate parole (length of parole is linked closely with the period of commitment specified by the court; paroling authorities cannot extend confinement period of juvenile beyond original commitment length prescribed by judge; juvenile can be released short of serving the full sentence).
2. Determinate parole set by administrative agency (parole release date is set immediately following youth's arrival at secure facility).
3. Presumptive minimum with limits on the extension of the supervision period for a fixed or determinate length of time (minimum confinement period is specified, and youth must be paroled after that date unless there is a showing of bad conduct).
4. Presumptive minimum with limits on the extension of supervision for an indeterminate period (parole should terminate after fixed period of time; parole period is indeterminate, where PO has discretion to extend parole

period with justification; parole length can extend until youth reaches age of majority and leaves juvenile court jurisdiction).

5. Presumptive minimum with discretionary extension of supervision for an indeterminate period (same as #4 except PO has discretion to extend parole length of juvenile with no explicit upper age limit; lacks explicit standards limiting the extension of parole).

6. Indeterminate parole with a specified maximum and a discretionary minimum length of supervision (follows Model Juvenile Court Act of 1968, providing limits for confinement but allows parole board authority to specify length of confinement and period of supervised release within these limits).

7. Indeterminate parole with legal minimum and maximum periods of supervision (parole board is vested with vast power to parole youths at any time with minimum and maximum confinement periods; more liberal than #1 and #2 above).

8. Indeterminate or purely discretionary parole (length of parole unspecified; may maintain youths on parole until youths reach the age of majority; at this time, parole is discontinued; may release youths from parole at any time during this period) (Ashford and LeCroy, 1993:187–191).

The most popular parole type is #8; the least popular is #1.

Deciding Who Should Be Paroled

The decision to parole particular juveniles is left to different agencies and bodies, depending on the jurisdiction. In most state jurisdictions, the dispositions imposed are indeterminate (Archwamety and Katsiyannis, 2000). In 32 states, early-release decisions are left up to the particular juvenile correction agency, whereas six states use parole boards exclusively, and five other states depend on the original sentencing judge's decision. Only a few states had determinate sentencing schemes for youthful offenders, and therefore, their early release would be established by statute in much the same way as it is for adult offenders.

In New Jersey, for instance, a seven-member parole board appointed by the governor grants early release to both adult and juvenile inmates. In Utah, a Youth Parole Authority exists, which is a part-time board consisting of three citizens and four staff members from the Utah Division of Youth Corrections. Ideally, paroling authorities utilize objective, decision-making criteria in determining which youths should be released short of serving their full incarcerative terms. Often discrepancies exist between what the paroling authority actually does and what it is supposed to do. Thus, some criticisms have been to the effect that the primary early-release criteria are related to one's former institutional behavior rather than to other factors, such as one's prospects for successful adaptation to community life, employment, and participation in educational or vocational programs (Cavender and Knepper, 1992).

Many parole boards for both adults and juveniles are comprised of persons who make subjective judgments about inmates on the basis of many factors beyond so-called objective criteria. Predispositional reports prepared by juvenile probation officers, records of institutional behavior, a youth's appearance and demeanor during the parole hearing, and the presence of witnesses or victims may exert unknown impacts on individual parole board members. Parole decision making is not an exact science. Where elements of subjectivity intrude into the decision-making process, a juvenile's rights are seemingly undermined. Thus, parole board decision-making profiles in various jurisdictions may exhibit evidence of early-release disparities attributable to racial, ethnic, gender, or socioeconomic factors.

RECIDIVISM AND PAROLE REVOCATION

Parole revocation is the termination of one's parole program, usually for one or more program violations. When one's parole is terminated, regardless of who does the terminating, there are several possible outcomes. One is that the offender will be returned to secure confinement. This is the most severe result. A less harsh alternative is that offenders will be shifted to a different kind of parole program. For instance, if a juvenile is assigned to a halfway house as a part of the parole program, the rules of the halfway house must be observed. If one or more rules are violated, such as failing to observe curfew, failing drug or alcohol urinalyses, or committing new offenses, a report is filed with the court or the juvenile corrections authority for possible revocation action. If it is decided later that one's parole should be terminated, the result may be to place the offender under house arrest or home confinement, coupled with electronic monitoring. Thus, the juvenile would be required to wear an electronic wristlet or anklet and remain on the premises for specified periods. Other program conditions would be applied as well. The fact is that one is not automatically returned to incarceration following a **parole revocation hearing.**

Usually, if a return to incarceration is not indicated, the options available to judges, parole boards, or others are limited only by the array of supervisory resources in the given jurisdiction. These options ordinarily involve more intensive supervision or monitoring of offender behaviors. Severe overcrowding in many juvenile incarcerative facilities discourages revocation action that would return large numbers of offenders to industrial schools or youth centers.

The Colorado Juvenile Parole Board.

The process of parole revocation for juveniles is not as clear-cut as it is for adult offenders. The U.S. Supreme Court has not ruled thus far concerning how juvenile parole revocation actions should be completed. Furthermore, very little is known about the actual numbers of juveniles who are paroled annually. Reliable statistical information about the extent of juvenile parole revocation throughout the United States simply does not exist.

Prior to several significant U.S. Supreme Court decisions, either parole or probation revocation could be accomplished for adult offenders on the basis of reports filed by probation or parole officers that offenders were in violation of one or more conditions of their programs. Criminal court judges, those ordinarily in charge of determining whether to terminate one's probationary status, could decide this issue on the basis of available evidence against offenders. For adult parolees, former decision making relative to terminating their parole could be made by parole boards without much fanfare from offenders. In short, parole officers and others might simply present evidence that one or more infractions or violations of probation or parole conditions had been committed. These infractions, then, could form the basis for revoking probation or parole as well as a justification for these decisions.

A probationer's or parolee's right to due process in any probation or parole revocation action was largely ignored prior to 1967. Thus, technical violations, such as failing to submit monthly reports, violating curfew, filing a falsified report, or drinking alcoholic beverages "to excess," might result in an unfavorable recommendation from one's PO that the probation or parole program should be terminated. Popular television shows sometimes portray parole officers as threatening their clients with parole revocation: "Do this or else I'll have you back in the joint!", meaning a return to prison for adult offenders. Currently, it is not so easy to accomplish either type of revocation.

For adult parolees as well as for adult probationers, revocations for either probation or parole are currently two-stage proceedings. The landmark cases that have directly affected parolees and probationers and their rights are: *Mempa v. Rhay* (1967), *Morrissey v. Brewer* (1972), and *Gagnon v. Scarpelli* (1973). While these landmark cases pertain to adult probationers and parolees, they have significance for juvenile probationers and parolees. The significance is that juvenile justice policies are often formulated or influenced on the basis of U.S. Supreme Court decisions about the rights of inmates, parolees, or probationers, and the procedures involved in their processing throughout the criminal justice system. Thus, these cases are not binding on juvenile court judges or juvenile paroling authorities. But they provide a legal basis for specific actions in pertinent juvenile cases, if the juvenile justice system chooses to recognize them as precedent-setting.

Mempa v. Rhay (1967)

Jerry Mempa was convicted in criminal court of "joyriding" in a stolen vehicle on June 17, 1959, in Spokane, Washington. The judge placed him on probation for 2 years. A few months later, Mempa was involved in a burglary on September 15, 1959. The county prosecutor in Spokane requested that Mempa's probation be revoked. Mempa admitted that he committed the burglary to police. At a **probation revocation hearing** conducted later, the sole testimony about his involvement in the burglary came from his probation officer, who obtained his factual information largely from police reports. Mempa, an indigent, was not permitted to offer statements on his own behalf, nor was he provided counsel, nor was he asked if he wanted counsel, nor was he permitted to cross-examine the probation officer about the officer's incriminating statements. The judge revoked Mempa's probation and sentenced him to 10 years in the Washington State Penitentiary.

A short time later, Mempa filed a writ of *habeas corpus,* which essentially challenges the fact of his confinement and the nature of it. He alleged that he had been denied the right to counsel in his probation revocation hearing, and thus, he claimed his due-process rights had been violated in part. The Washington Supreme Court denied his petition, but the U.S. Supreme Court elected to hear it on appeal. The U.S. Supreme Court overturned the Washington Supreme Court and ruled in Mempa's favor. Specifically, the U.S. Supreme Court said that Mempa was entitled to an attorney but was denied one. Furthermore, and perhaps most important, the Court declared that a probation revocation hearing is a "critical stage" that falls within the due-process provisions of the Fourteenth Amendment. Critical stages refer to any stages of the criminal justice process where a defendant is in jeopardy. If defendants are accused of crimes, or arraigned, or prosecuted, their due-process rights "attach" or become relevant. Thus, they are entitled to attorneys at any of these critical stages, since they are in jeopardy of losing their freedom. This ruling did not mean that Mempa would be entirely free from further court action. However, it did provide for a rehearing, and his 10-year sentence in the Washington State Penitentiary was set aside.

Morrissey v. Brewer (1972)

In 1967, John Morrissey was convicted in an Iowa court for falsely drawing checks. He was sentenced to "not more than 7 years" in the Iowa State Prison. Subsequently, he was paroled in June 1968. Seven months later, his parole

Juvenile parolees must report regularly to local parole offices where they may be tested for drugs or other substances.

officer learned that Morrissey had bought an automobile under an assumed name and operated it without permission, had obtained credit cards giving false information, and had given false information to an insurance company when he became involved in an automobile accident. Furthermore, Morrissey had given his PO a false address for his residence. After interviewing Morrissey, Morrissey's PO filed a report recommending that Morrissey's parole be revoked. The parole violations involved all of the infractions and false information noted above. In his own defense, Morrissey claimed to be "sick" and had been prevented from maintaining continuous contact with his PO during the car-buying, credit-card accumulating, and automobile accident period. The PO countered by alleging that Morrissey was "continually violating the rules." The Iowa Parole Board revoked Morrissey's parole and he was returned to the Iowa State Prison to serve the remainder of his sentence.

During his parole revocation hearing, he was not represented by counsel, nor was he permitted to testify in his own behalf, nor was he permitted to cross-examine witnesses against him, nor was he advised in writing of the charges against him, nor was there any disclosure of the evidence against him. Furthermore, the Iowa Parole Board gave no reasons to Morrissey for their revocation action. Morrissey appealed to the Iowa Supreme Court who rejected his appeal. The U.S. Supreme Court decided to hear his appeal, however, and overturned the Iowa Supreme Court and Iowa Parole Board actions. The Court did not specifically address the issue of whether Morrissey should have been represented by counsel, but it did establish the foundation for a two-stage parole revocation proceeding. The first or preliminary stage or hearing would be conducted at the time of arrest or confinement, and its purpose would be to determine whether probable cause exists that the parolee actually committed the alleged parole violations. The second stage or hearing would be more involved and designed to establish the parolee's guilt or innocence concerning the alleged violations. Currently, all parolees in all states must be extended the following rights relating to **minimum due-process rights:**

1. The right to have written notice of the alleged violations of parole conditions.
2. The right to have disclosed to the parolee any evidence of the alleged violation.
3. The right of the parolee to be heard in person and to present exculpatory evidence as well as witnesses in his behalf.
4. The right to confront and cross-examine adverse witnesses, unless cause exists why they should not be cross-examined.
5. The right to a judgment by a neutral and detached body, such as the parole board itself.
6. The right to a written statement of the reasons for the parole revocation.

Thus, the primary significance of the *Morrissey* case was that it established minimum due-process rights for all parolees and created a two-stage proceeding where alleged infractions of parole conditions could be examined objectively and where a full hearing could be conducted to determine the most appropriate offender disposition.

Gagnon v. Scarpelli (1973)

Because the matter of representation by counsel was not specifically addressed in the *Morrissey* case, the U.S. Supreme Court heard yet another parolee's case concerning a parole revocation action and where court-appointed counsel had not been provided. Gerald Scarpelli was convicted of robbery in July 1965 in a Wisconsin court. At his sentencing on August 5, 1965, Scarpelli was sentenced to 15 years in prison, but the judge suspended the sentence and placed him on probation for 7 years. Believe it or not, the following day, August 6, 1965, Gerald Scarpelli was arrested and charged with burglary. The judge immediately revoked his probation and ordered Scarpelli placed in the Wisconsin State Reformatory for a 15-year term.

At this point, Scarpelli's case becomes a little complicated. During his early stay in prison, Scarpelli filed a *habeas corpus* petition with the court, alleging that his due-process rights were violated when his probation was revoked. He was not represented by counsel and he was not permitted a hearing. However, Scarpelli was paroled from prison in 1968. Nevertheless, the U.S. Supreme Court acted on his original *habeas corpus* petition filed earlier and ruled in his favor. The U.S. Supreme Court held that Scarpelli was indeed denied the right to counsel and had not been given a hearing in the probation revocation action. While this might seem to be a hollow victory, since Scarpelli was already free on parole, the case had profound significance on both subsequent parole and probation revocation actions. The U.S. Supreme Court, referring to the *Morrissey* case that it had heard the previous year (1972), said that "a probation revocation, like parole revocation, is not a stage of a criminal prosecution, but does result in loss of liberty. . . . We hold that a probationer, like a parolee, is entitled to a preliminary hearing and a final revocation hearing in the conditions specified in *Morrissey v. Brewer*."

The significance of the *Scarpelli* case is that it equated probation with parole regarding revocation hearings. While the Court did not say that all probationers and parolees have a right to be represented by counsel in all probation and parole revocation hearings, it did say that counsel should be provided in cases where the parolee or probationer makes a timely claim contesting the allegations. This U.S. Supreme Court decision has been liberally interpreted by the courts and parole boards in all jurisdictions. Thus, while no constitutional basis currently exists for providing counsel in *all* probation or parole revocation proceedings, most of these proceedings usually involve defense counsel if legitimate requests are made in advance by probationers or parolees.

Some persons are understandably perplexed by the seemingly excessive time interval that lapses between when questioned events occur, such as probation revocation actions that may be unconstitutionally conducted, and when the U.S. Supreme Court gets around to hearing such petitions or claims and deciding cases. It is not unusual for these time intervals to be 5 or 6 years, or even longer. The wheels of justice move slowly, especially the wheels of U.S. Supreme Court actions. Interestingly, of the more than 3,500 cases that are presented to the U.S. Supreme Court annually for hearing, only about 150–175 cases are heard where decisions are written. Four or more Justices must agree to hear any specific case, and even then, their convening time may expire before certain cases are heard. It is beyond the scope of this text to discuss the process by which U.S. Supreme Court cases are initiated and processed, but this short discussion serves to explain the apparent slowness in rendering significant opinions in landmark cases.

For juveniles, these three cases are important because they provide juvenile courts and juvenile paroling authorities within juvenile corrections with certain guidelines to follow. These guidelines are not mandatory or binding, since these U.S. Supreme Court rulings pertain to adults rather than to juveniles. However, the law is not always abundantly clear regarding its application in a wide variety of different cases. While it may be anticipated that the U.S. Supreme Court will eventually address probation and parole revocation issues that pertain to juvenile offenders, we can only use adult guidelines for the present.

Currently, probation and parole revocation proceedings for juveniles differ widely among jurisdictions. Knepper and Cavender (1990), for instance, indicate that in a Western state they examined, informal hearings were conducted by a juvenile parole board outside of the presence of juveniles. In such informal settings, decisions about parole revocations were made. Subsequently, juveniles were brought before the board and advised in a more formal hearing of the rightness of the board's decision about the revocation action taken. This is strongly indicative of the continuation of *parens patriae* in juvenile matters. In other jurisdictions, explicit criteria exist for determining court or parole board actions relating to juvenile parolees who violate program rules or commit new offenses. Statutory constraints may or may not be in place to regulate judicial or parole board decision making in these situations. Again, the cases of *Morrissey, Scarpelli,* and *Mempa* are not binding on juvenile probation or parole revocation actions in any state jurisdiction.

EXAMPLES OF PROBATION AND PAROLE REVOCATION FOR JUVENILES

Since there is no federal law governing juvenile probation or parole revocation, we must examine state statutes and decisions to determine the types of situations and circumstances where the probation or parole programs of juveniles have been revoked. This will give us some indication of what practices are prevalent among the states, as well as the grounds used in such revocation actions.

Juvenile Probation and Parole Revocation Cases

Several cases have been reported involving revocations of juvenile probation and parole. These are reported below. There are considerably more juvenile probation revocation cases reported than parole revocation cases, the former outnumbering the latter by as much as 20 to 1. Thus, most of the cases below are probation revocation cases. It is important to note, however, that the same grounds used to revoke one's probation program are also used to revoke one's parole program. Thus, for all practical purposes, each jurisdiction can use these grounds almost interchangeably, whether it is for probation or parole revocation actions.

Are oral pronouncements of standard probation conditions by the juvenile court judge necessary to make them enforceable? No.

D.P.B. v. State (2004). D.P.B. is a Florida juvenile who was adjudicated delinquent. One of the standard conditions of D.P.B.'s probation was that he should live and remain at liberty without violating the law and that he refrain from conduct prescribed by statute. Following D.P.B.'s adjudicatory hearing and disposition of probation, the court failed to provide D.P.B. with a copy of the formal written probation orders. Subsequently, D.P.B. violated one or more probation conditions and the juvenile court moved to revoke his probation. D.P.B. countered by arguing that the judge failed to orally advise him of the statutory conditions contained in the probation orders that he never received. Thus, according to D.P.B., his due-process rights had been violated. The appellate court disagreed and held that the judge was not obligated to articulate verbally the statutory language of D.P.B.'s standard probation orders, which D.P.B. had been required to read and sign prior to the probation disposition. Under the Florida Juvenile Code, increased punishment was available for juveniles who violated one or more conditions of their probation. The juvenile was on constructive notice that a new criminal charge could result in the revocation of his probation supervision.

Can new probation violations result in more restrictive probation conditions and a longer probationary term within the maximum limits of one's original statutory probation requirements? Yes.

John L. v. Superior Court (2004). John L. is a California juvenile and gang member who was adjudicated delinquent on various charges. During his probationary term, John L. committed new probation violations. The juvenile court conducted a probation revocation hearing, and on the basis of a preponderance of the evidence, John L.'s probationary term was extended to the maximum term and the nature of his probation supervision was intensified. John L. contested the court's decision to intensify his probation supervision and extend his probationary term, arguing that the "beyond a reasonable doubt" standard should be used. He also alleged that his due-process rights were violated because of the judge's decision. The appellate court disagreed and allowed the juvenile court judge's ruling to stand. Under current California juvenile law, if a probation violation occurs, the violator could at most receive more restrictive placement within the original maximum term. In John L.'s case, the court held that the preponderance of evidence standard was sufficient to establish John L.'s guilt for the probation violations. Furthermore, new criminal charges are treated like probation violations and the judge may impose appropriate punishments within the limits of one's original probationary term.

Can juvenile courts authorize parents to disapprove of certain associates of an adjudicated juvenile as a probation condition? Yes.

In re Byron B. (2004). Byron B. is a California juvenile who was placed under probation supervision for stealing. One of the conditions of Byron B.'s probation prohibited him from associating with anyone disapproved by a parent or by the probation officer. Byron B. objected and claimed that this condition was invalid. The appellate court disagreed. The court reviewed the statute, which read that a probation condition is unreasonable if it (1) has no relationship to the crime of which the juvenile was adjudicated; (2) relates to conduct that is not itself criminal; and (3) requires or forbids conduct that is not reasonably related to future criminality. The appellate court upheld the judicial order because it was not unreasonable, overbroad, or void for vagueness.

Can the preponderance-of-evidence standard be used to revoke a juvenile's probation? Yes.

In re Devon A.A. (2004).   Devon A.A. is a New York juvenile who was adjudicated delinquent on various charges. As a part of his probation conditions, Devon A.A. was ordered to attend school regularly and obey school rules. Furthermore, Devon A.A. was required to meet with a tutor for regular tutoring sessions. Subsequently, Devon A.A.'s tutor reported that Devon A.A. missed several tutoring sessions, was late for others, and even threatened the tutor that he would do something to her house or dogs because he became upset with her. The tutor also said that Devon A.A. also left tutoring sessions early without permission. The probation officer sought to have Devon A.A.'s probation revoked. On a review of the record, it was disclosed that Devon A.A. had originally read and signed a copy of the conditions of probation outlining the school attendance and tutoring sessions. Even Devon A.A. admitted to missing at least four tutoring sessions. On the basis of preponderance of the evidence, Devon A.A.'s probation was revoked. Devon A.A. appealed, contending that the beyond-a-reasonable-doubt standard should have been used. The appellate court disagreed and upheld the judge's revocation order based on the preponderance-of-evidence standard.

Can juveniles who agree to have their probationary terms extended withdraw their consent to have their probationary terms terminated? Yes.

In re Juvenile (2004).   A New Hampshire juvenile was adjudicated delinquent and disposed to probation for a specified term. Following the expiration of this probationary term, the juvenile court inquired of the juvenile whether he would agree to have his probationary term extended for additional treatment and other conditions to be fulfilled. The juvenile agreed. After a few weeks, however, the juvenile withdrew his consent to have the probationary term extended, but the judge refused to terminate the extension. The juvenile appealed. The appellate court reversed the juvenile court judge, holding that where a juvenile voluntarily consents to have his or her probationary term extended, that consent may be withdrawn at any time without any further penalty.

Can a juvenile's probation be revoked because of the juvenile's failure to follow a judge's verbal (rather than written) order to attend vocational school training? No.

Matter of Appeal in Maricopa County (1996).   A juvenile was verbally ordered by a judge to attend Valley Vocational School in Arizona as a condition of his probation. No written order requiring such attendance was provided, however. Later, evidence was presented to the juvenile court that the juvenile had failed to attend the Valley Vocational School. The judge brought the youth before him and revoked his probation. The youth appealed, contending that there had been no written order requiring his attendance at the vocational school. In this case, the appellate court in Arizona reversed the juvenile court judge's revocation order. They concluded that probation revocation for juveniles is an area where the adult criminal requirement regarding written notice of the terms of probation upon which revocation is based must appropriately be applied in juvenile cases as a matter of due process and general fairness. The appeals court noted that although there had been a verbal order from the judge to require the youth's attendance at the vocational school, it was not sufficiently important, since a written order was issued to revoke one's probation. The court said, "If an order is important enough to warrant a revocation petition, the order first must be reduced to writing and given to [the] probationer."

Can a juvenile court judge order a continuation of sex offender therapy for a juvenile following a favorable recommendation for the termination of one's probation after a successful term of therapy? No.

In re M.O.R. (2004). M.O.R. is a District of Columbia juvenile who was placed on probation after he admitted to two counts of simple sexual assault. One of his probation conditions was that he participate in a sex offender counseling program. During the period of his probation supervision, the probation officer reported M.O.R.'s progress to the juvenile court. These reports were consistently favorable for the juvenile. Toward the end of M.O.R.'s probationary period, a review was conducted wherein the probation officer recommended that M.O.R.'s probation should be allowed to expire since M.O.R. had responded positively to the counseling program. However, the judge denied the probation termination and continued it based on a therapist's report that M.O.R.'s disorder could not be cured. Thus, the stage was set for continued counseling and treatment without end. M.O.R. appealed and the appellate court reversed the juvenile court, thus terminating M.O.R.'s probation program. Under D.C. law, the Director of Social Services is granted the sole authority to decide whether to seek an extension of a probationary period. Any child who is subject to an extension must receive proper notice and a hearing to determine such an extension is warranted. The juvenile court has the authority to review and decide whether to continue a dispositional order if the recommendation by the Director is to continue probation. However, if the Director decides not to seek an extension of one's probation, the juvenile court may inquire about but not review the Director's reasons for not doing so. The decision to not seek an extension of probation is solely with the Director, not the juvenile court.

If juveniles are not given the opportunity to present evidence in their own behalf prior to a probation revocation hearing, can their probation be revoked anyway? No.

In re Casey V.V. (2004). Casey V.V. is a New York juvenile who was adjudicated delinquent on various charges. During Casey V.V.'s probationary term, one or more probation condition violations were alleged and a hearing was held. Casey V.V. attempted to introduce exculpatory evidence in the hearing but was denied this opportunity, and his probation was summarily revoked. Casey V.V. appealed and the appellate court reversed the juvenile court probation revocation order. All parties must be given the opportunity to be heard, including the probationer, Casey V.V. Since he was denied the right to be heard, this violated his right to due process and the revocation order was set aside.

Can weekend detention be ordered by juvenile court judges for juveniles who violate diversion conditions prior to a formal disposition for delinquency? Yes.

State v. Steven B. (2004). Steven B. was a New Mexico juvenile who was adjudicated delinquent but placed on diversion pending completion of a diversion program requiring completion of school and other conditions. The actual disposition was deferred pending the successful completion of Grade Court, an educational course of study. Steven B. subsequently violated a condition of the "Grade Court" and the juvenile court judge placed Steven B. in weekend detention as a punishment. Steven B. appealed, arguing that detention was excessive and not consistent with rehabilitation. Furthermore, no formal disposition had been entered yet, and thus the detention was a violation of his due-process rights. The appellate court disagreed and upheld the judge's detention orders. The New Mexico juvenile code authorizes judges to detain children who are adjudicated but not yet disposed and who fail to comply with conditions of release. The court found that the juvenile court had the authority to order detention under this statutory provision.

Can a juvenile's probation program be revoked if the juvenile court judge fails to state in writing the specific reasons for revoking the probation program and the specific nature of the program infractions? No.

A.D. v. State (2001). A.D., a juvenile, was adjudicated delinquent for fighting at school. He was placed on probation and ordered to obey the law, conduct himself properly, to cooperate with probation services, to comply with electronic monitoring, and not to leave the county of his residence. Subsequently, a juvenile PO filed a complaint seeking to revoke A.D.'s aftercare status, claiming that A.D. had violated the terms of his aftercare by assaulting a school employee, by being absent from class without authorization, and by using profane language. A juvenile court judge ordered A.D.'s probation revoked, stating that A.D. had caused chaos at the high school and was completely unamenable to treatment. An Alabama appellate court set aside the juvenile court judge's revocation order, holding that in Alabama, a court must provide a written order stating the evidence relied upon and the reasons for revoking probation. Because the juvenile court failed to state the specific reason for revoking A.D.'s aftercare status, and because it did not set out the evidence it relied upon, the matter had to be remanded.

Can juveniles have their probation revoked for associating with persons disapproved by their probation officer without knowing who these disapproved persons are? No.

In re Sheena K. (2004). Sheena K. is a California juvenile who was placed on probation with the order to avoid associating with any disapproved persons at the discretion of the probation officer. However, Sheena K. was not advised as to which persons she should avoid associating with. Subsequently she associated with one or more persons deemed disapproved by the probation officer and the officer sought Sheena K.'s probation program revocation. Sheena K. appealed, arguing that the condition imposed was unconstitutionally vague. The appellate court agreed and reversed Sheena K.'s probation revocation. The appellate court noted that although the condition prohibited the juvenile from associating with any person disapproved by the probation officer, the condition failed to include the requirement that the juvenile know which persons are disapproved. Under these circumstances, the court held that the condition was unconstitutional.

Can a juvenile court judge extend the term of a youth's probation beyond an original period of probation pursuant to an adjudication of delinquency and a probation disposition? Yes.

In re A.N.A. (2004). A.N.A., a Texas juvenile probationer, violated one or more terms of his original probation orders. The judge had placed A.N.A. on a 12-month probationary term according to A.N.A.'s original conditional disposition. Based on the probation violations, a modification order was entered to re-dispose A.N.A. to an additional probationary term. In the meantime, the 12-month probationary term for A.N.A. expired. Subsequently, the juvenile court judge imposed an additional 12-month probationary period on A.N.A. and A.N.A. appealed. The Texas appeals court upheld the 12-month probationary extension ordered by the juvenile court judge, because the order to modify A.N.A.'s probation had been entered prior to the expiration of A.N.A.'s original probationary term, and A.N.A. had been found guilty of violating the original probationary terms.

Can a juvenile be placed in secure confinement without supporting evidence from the juvenile court judge if standard probation is the conventional disposition absent any circumstances to the contrary? No.

A.W. v. State (2003).   A.W. is a Florida juvenile who was adjudicated delinquent on one or more charges. Under prevailing dispositional guidelines, standard probation was called for. But in A.W.'s case, the judge imposed a term of secure confinement. A.W. appealed, arguing that no evidence had been presented or articulated by the judge to warrant the more restrictive disposition. The appellate court reversed the juvenile court judge and agreed with A.W. The court noted that while juvenile courts are not required to articulate the characteristics of the restrictiveness level for any juvenile, there still must be some evidence in the record to support the juvenile court's disposition and departure from whatever is customary or prevalent. In this case, neither the juvenile court's findings nor the record support A.W.'s commitment to the high-risk residential facility.

Can a juvenile's record be expunged following the completion of a probationary disposition, even if the adjudication offense is a felony? Yes.

State v. Sanchez (2004).   Sanchez was an Arizona juvenile who was adjudicated delinquent on a serious felony charge. Although secure confinement was recommended, the judge placed Sanchez on probation. When the probationary term was completed, Sanchez moved to have his record of the felony offense expunged and the state opposed this motion. The expungement order was entered and the state appealed. An appellate court upheld the juvenile court judge and permitted the expungement order. If the juvenile successfully completes the terms and conditions of probation, the court may set aside the judgment of guilt, dismiss the information or indictment, expunge the juvenile's record, and order the juvenile to be released from all penalties and disabilities resulting from the adjudication.

Can an oral admission by a probationer that he visited his probation officer once in 18 months be grounds for revoking his probation? Yes.

J.W. v. State (2004).   J.W. was a Florida juvenile who was placed on probation. As one condition of J.W.'s probation, he was required to meet with his probation officer once a month. Following an 18-month period, J.W.'s probation officer sought to revoke J.W.'s probation for failure to abide by the original probation conditions since he only appeared at the probation office once. J.W. countered by contending that he was never asked by the probation officer to appear at the probation office monthly. Rather, J.W. showed up once during the 18-month period to "check in" with the probation officer. The admission on J.W.'s part during the probation revocation hearing was a sufficient self-admission that J.W. had failed to comply with his original probation orders. His probation was revoked and an appellate court upheld the revocation order.

Written orders for probationers to appear monthly and meet with the probation officers must be obeyed explicitly.

Can juveniles be placed in out-of-state facilities if those same facilities do not exist in the originating state? Yes.

State v. Steven H. (2004).   Steven H. was a West Virginia juvenile who was adjudicated as a status offender and ordered committed to an out-of-home institution. Since there was no institution in West Virginia to house Steven H., he was sent to a comparable facility in neighboring Virginia. He appealed, contending that the juvenile court had no authority to send him out of state to another facility. The appellate court upheld the judge's ruling of placing Steven H. out of state in Virginia. The appellate court noted that (1) there was a specific finding that institutional care was in the juvenile's best interests; (2) the institutional care would not produce undue hardship for Steven H.; and (3) there was evidence that all reasonable efforts had been made to provide appropriate services for Steven H. prior to the out-of-state placement order.

Can juvenile court judges impose restitution orders on juvenile probationers as compensation for offenses for which they were not adjudicated delinquent? Yes.

Com. v. Palmer P. (2004).   Palmer P. was a Massachusetts juvenile who was charged with burglary and larceny. Subsequently Palmer P. was adjudicated delinquent on the burglary or "breaking and entering" charge, although he was acquitted of the larceny charge. However, the juvenile court judge imposed a restitution order requiring Palmer P. to make restitution for property stolen as the result of the burglary. Palmer P. appealed, contending that he should not be required to make restitution if he had been acquitted of the larceny. However, the appellate court disagreed and upheld the juvenile court judge's restitution orders. The court held that juveniles may be ordered to pay restitution even where they are acquitted of the charge in question, so long as the restitution is significantly related to their adjudication offense, in this case, burglary. In the present case, Palmer P.'s burglary or breaking and entering facilitated the taking of the victim's property. Thus, restitution was warranted as a part of Palmer P.'s disposition and conditions of probation.

Can juvenile parole boards terminate a juvenile's commitment to an institution and grant parole despite a judge's order to continue the juvenile's commitment for a period of time until the juvenile is age 21? No.

In re Ruben D. (2001).   Ruben D., a juvenile, was committed to an industrial school for a period of years. From time to time, the juvenile court judge would review Ruben D.'s institutional behavior and progress. On the basis of these reports, the judge would decide to extend Ruben D.'s commitment to the institution for additional one-year periods. Following one such order by the juvenile court judge, which extended Ruben D.'s commitment to the institution for one more year, the juvenile parole board convened and acknowledged that Ruben D.'s original commitment order had expired. The parole board did not acknowledge the extension of the commitment order by the juvenile court judge. Ruben D. appealed, contending that he should be paroled because of the juvenile parole board acknowledgment that his commitment term had expired. The appellate court upheld the juvenile court judge's authority to extend Ruben D.'s commitment by one-year periods until Ruben D. reached 21 years of age. The order that extended the commitment of Ruben D. was affirmed.

Can a juvenile have his parole program revoked for violating an implied rather than written order requiring him to participate in a particular aftercare program following his release from commitment? No.

K.G. v. State (2000).   K.G., a female juvenile, was adjudicated delinquent and committed to a juvenile secure facility. Subsequently K.G. was paroled. The parole board implied that it would be a good idea for K.G. to participate in a particular aftercare program involving treatment for substance abuse, which was a problem K.G. had prior to being committed initially. K.G. did not participate in the particular aftercare program and the parole board sought to revoke her parole program. K.G. appealed, contending that there were no specific orders requiring her to participate in the aftercare program following the completion of the term of commitment. The appellate court reversed the parole board, holding that there was nothing showing that K.G. had been properly transferred to the aftercare program following the term of commitment. In order for a violation of one's parole program to be upheld, a valid written order by the parole board must have been violated. Since no written orders had been violated, K.G. was reinstated into her parole program.

SELECTED ISSUES IN JUVENILE CORRECTIONS

Investigations of the rate of secure confinement of juveniles during the past two centuries have disclosed that the rate of juvenile institutionalization has increased, especially during the most recent decades (Office of Juvenile Justice and Delinquency Prevention, 2005). Many of those youths detained for fairly long periods of 30 days or longer are less serious misdemeanants and status offenders. For this and other reasons, juvenile corrections has been under attack from various sectors for years. This attack comes from many quarters, and it coincides with a general attack on the criminal justice system for its apparent failure to stem the increasing wave of crime in the United States. Sentencing reforms, correctional reforms, experiments with probation and parole alternatives, and a host of other options have been attempted in an apparent effort to cure or control delinquents and criminals.

In 1985, the United Nations and National Council of Juvenile and Family Court Judges adopted policy statements about the juvenile justice system that bear directly on juvenile corrections. The issues to be discussed in this final section may be better understood in the context of these statements. Several recommendations have been made by Dwyer and McNally (1987:50–51). These are that:

1. Primary dispositions of juvenile courts should be to have a flexible range for restricting freedom with the primary goal focused on the restoration to full liberty rather than let the punishment fit the crime; that no case dispositions should be of a mandatory nature, but rather, they should be left to the discretion of the judge based on predetermined dispositional guidelines; that in no case should a juvenile under 18 years of age be subject to capital punishment.

2. Individualized treatment of juveniles should be continued, including the development of medical, psychiatric, and educational programs that range from least to most restrictive, according to individual need.

3. While being held accountable, chronic, serious juvenile offenders should be retained within the jurisdiction of the juvenile court. As a resource, specialized programs and facilities need to be developed that focus on restorations rather than punishment.

4. Policymakers, reformers, and researchers should continue to strive for a greater understanding as to the causes and most desired response to juvenile crime; research should be broad-based rather than limited to management, control, and punishment strategies.

5. Where the juvenile court judge believes that the juvenile under consideration is nonamenable to the services of the court and based on the youth's present charges, past record in court, and his or her age and mental status, the judge may waive jurisdiction; that in all juvenile cases the court of original jurisdiction be that of the juvenile court; that the discretion to waive be left to the juvenile court judge; that the proportionality of punishment would be appropriate with these cases, but the most high-risk offenders should be treated in small, but secure, facilities.

Each of the issues discussed below are affected directly by these recommendations and policy statements. While these statements are not obligatory for any jurisdiction, they do suggest opinions and positions of a relevant segment of concerned citizens—juvenile court judges and juvenile corrections personnel. These issues include (1) the privatization of juvenile corrections; (2) the classification of juvenile offenders; and (3) juveniles held in adult jails and lock-ups.

The Privatization of Juvenile Corrections

Juvenile corrections has many of the same problems as adult corrections. Chronic overcrowding in secure confinement facilities is extensive among jurisdictions. Existing facilities in many states are deteriorating rapidly. Furthermore, there are disproportionate representations of black, Hispanic, and Native American youths (American Correctional Association, 2005). With the current emphasis on more punitive juvenile sentencing policies, it is unlikely that significant improvements in the quality of juvenile incarcerative facilities will be implemented in the near future. **Privatization** is believed by some authorities to be one solution to overcrowded publicly operated facilities. Privatization is the establishment and operation of correctional services and institutions by nongovernmental interests, including private corporations and businesspersons (Armstrong, 2001).

Nonsecure and secure facilities are both publicly and privately operated. Florida is one of several states experimenting with various forms of private juvenile secure confinement. Historically, Florida sought to rehabilitate youths through incarceration, including placement of serious offenders in reform or training schools (Rivers, Dembo, and Anwyl, 1998). The first school for male juveniles opened in Florida in 1900, and by 1972, four schools were operating in various jurisdictions throughout the state. But because of serious institutional overcrowding and the ineffectiveness of program treatments, Florida officials decided to shift their incarcerative priorities to the development of less secure, community-based facilities (Pingree, 1984:60). Florida's objectives are to (1) reduce the number of juveniles actually placed in secure confinement facilities, and (2) to provide juveniles with a broader base of community options that will be instrumental in helping them to acquire vocational training and education. Much emphasis is placed on assisting youths with psychological problems as well. Thus, trained counselors work closely with Florida juvenile offenders to meet their psychological and social needs more effectively. The Florida model has served as an example for other jurisdictions in later years.

Several important issues relating to the privatization of corrections, for both adult and juvenile offenders, have been outlined (Robbins, 1986:29). These are:

1. What standards will govern the operation of the institution?
2. Who will monitor the implementation of the standards?
3. Will the public still have access to the facility?
4. What recourse will members of the public have if they do not approve of how the institution is operated?
5. Who will be responsible for maintaining security and using force at the institution?
6. Who will be responsible for maintaining security if the private personnel go on strike?
7. Where will the responsibility for [incarcerative] disciplinary procedures lie?
8. Will the company be able to refuse to accept certain inmates, such as those with AIDS?
9. What options will be available to the government if the corporation substantially raises its fees?
10. What safeguards will prevent a private contractor from making a low initial bid to obtain a contract, and then raising the price after the government is no longer immediately able to reassume the task of operating the facility?
11. What will happen if the company declares bankruptcy?
12. What safeguards will prevent private vendors, after gaining a foothold in the corrections field, from lobbying for philosophical changes for their greater profit?
13. What options will the public have if they do not approve of how the institution is operated?

Currently, juvenile corrections has a large share of the privatization business. The Corrections Corporation of America (CCA), headquartered in Nashville, Tennessee, currently operates numerous facilities for both adults and juveniles throughout the United States. The CCA began operating several juvenile facilities in Tennessee in 1985, although there have been continuing debates and controversies over the years about the effectiveness of private corrections for the state (Kyle, 1998:88, 158). Other private interests are increasingly entering these correctional areas to provide services and supervisory tasks, often at less cost to taxpayers than government-operated facilities.

Favorably for privatization, private interests can often cut the red tape associated with secure confinement operations. The private sector can work cooperatively with the public sector in providing the best of both worlds for offenders. Private-sector operations can reward employees more quickly for excellent service performed, and new operational ideas may be implemented more quickly in private operations compared with government organizations.

Furthermore, many of those involved in private corrections operations have formerly been employed in administrative and staff capacities in public corrections agencies and institutions. Thus, they possess experience to do the job and do it well.

The profit issue is often raised by opponents of privatization of corrections. In turn, this profit motive may inspire private interests to keep inmates confined for longer periods to maximize profits. However, it is apparent that the current state of chronic overcrowding in both adult and juvenile incarcerative facilities will continue, regardless of whether these institutions are privately or publicly operated. Also, if private interests can make a profit while providing quality services to inmates at less cost to government, this seems to be a compelling argument in favor of greater privatization.

The Classification of Juvenile Offenders

Classification of any offender is made difficult by the fact that the state-of-the-art is such in predictions of risk and dangerousness that little future behavior can be accurately forecasted. This holds for juveniles as well as adults. We know that status offenders may or may not escalate to more serious offenses, with the prevailing sentiment favoring or implying nonescalation (Crowe, 2000). Fully effective classification schemes have not yet been devised, although we know that on the basis of descriptions of existing aggregates of offenders, factors such as gender, age, nature of offense, seriousness of offense, race or ethnicity, and socioeconomic status are more or less correlated.

The flaws of various classification schemes are made more apparent when program failures are detected in large numbers. Juvenile court judges make the wrong judgments and decisions about juvenile placements. Intake officers make similar errors of classification when conducting initial screenings of juveniles. The issue of false positives and false negatives is raised here, because some youths may be unfairly penalized for what authorities believe are valid predictive criteria of future dangerousness. By the same token, some youths are underpenalized, because it is believed, wrongly, that they will not pose risks or commit serious offenses in the future. But these same offenders do pose risks.

Guarino-Ghezzi (1989:112–114) has suggested that a systematic classification model can be devised by incorporating objective predictors of an offender's risk of recidivism into the intake assessment. She believes that an objective risk classification procedure can accomplish the following objectives:

1. Increase control over juvenile offenders who are placed in community settings
2. Increase agency accountability for placement decisions
3. Increase consistency in decision making
4. Direct allocation of scarce resources
5. Increase support for budget requests

Guarino-Ghezzi (1989:116) says that with few exceptions, administrative control factors are often given low priority whenever classification models are designed. But she encourages their adoption, since they are crucial in influencing how private vendors will react toward youths (in a privatization context, for instance), how youths will adjust to their programs, determining which youths are most likely to cause behavioral problems and assault staff, and whether gang involvement is indicated (possibly requiring a youth's separation from other gang members upon arrival at a new facility). Some results of more effective classification schemes include greater staff accountability, greater staff and inmate safety, and more effective programming relative to individual offenders and their needs.

Juveniles Held in Adult Jails or Lock-Ups

The most apparent problems with celling juveniles in adult lock-ups or jails are that (1) youths are subject to potential sexual assault from older inmates and (2) youths are often traumatized by the jailing experience (Kerle, 1998). This latter problem leads to another problem that is even more serious—jail suicides. Juveniles are especially suicide-prone during the first 24 hours of their incarceration in jails. Thus, it is little consolation that states such as Illinois pass laws prohibiting a juvenile's confinement in adult jails for periods longer than 6 hours.

Currently, there are organized movements in many jurisdictions to mandate the permanent removal of juveniles from adult jails, even on temporary bases. Civil rights suits as well as class action claims are being filed by and on behalf of many juveniles currently detained in adult facilities (Howell and Krisberg, 1998). In the Iowa case of *Hendrickson v. Griggs* (1987), a federal district judge, Donald E. O'Brien, ruled that the Juvenile Justice and Delinquency Prevention Act could be used as the basis for a lawsuit seeking the permanent removal of juveniles from adult jails. Much remains to be done to rectify a situation that seems more within the purview of the juvenile justice system rather than within the criminal justice system.

SUMMARY

Most juvenile court judges consider secure confinement for adjudicated juveniles as a last resort. These judges are admonished to select the least restrictive alternative when disposing of juvenile cases. While not all juvenile court judges follow this admonition, most do. Despite juvenile justice policy that encourages reductions in the use of secure confinement for youths as a punishment, several million youths are admitted to or released from correctional supervision in the United States annually.

Juvenile corrections encompasses all the agencies, personnel, organizations, and institutions that supervise youthful offenders, even for short periods. These agencies, personnel, and organizations include community corrections as well as institutional corrections. Both juvenile probationers and parolees, as well as divertees and other youths, are under the general supervisory control of one or more community corrections agencies. Many of the same problems that plague adult institutions, such as chronic overcrowding, poor rehabilitative conditions, less well-trained personnel, and other problems, also typify juvenile corrections among the states. In 2005 there were over 400,000 youths under some form of correctional supervision, with about a fourth or 100,000 of these youths incarcerated in secure facilities. Just as the adult numbers on probation, parole, and in institutional corrections has been growing steadily each year, so have the numbers of youths subjected to similar punishments.

The goals of juvenile corrections include deterrence, rehabilitation and reintegration, prevention, punishment and retribution, and isolation and control. Presently we don't know how much of a deterrent juvenile corrections poses for most juvenile offenders. The fact that it is used in only a fraction of all juvenile cases suggests that many juveniles processed by the juvenile justice system believe that they will not receive liberty-threatening sanctions. Clearly major goals of rehabilitation and reintegration are sought by all juvenile authorities. Many youths have low self-esteem and educational levels. Many of them are antisocial and act out. Different strategies are continually being devised to provide the necessary services for such persons and help them improve their law-abiding conduct.

A great deal of effort is devoted to delinquency prevention, especially interventions that target youths in their early and formative years. Some interventions have involved preschool children and have had modest success levels with low recidivism rates. At the same time, the get-tough movement has prompted juvenile authorities to deal more harshly with certain offenders, especially violent ones. Thus a strong focus is on isolation and control, especially of the most violent and chronic juveniles who recidivate frequently.

Institutional corrections for juveniles consists of either nonsecure or secure facilities. Nonsecure facilities include foster home placement, halfway houses, group homes, placement in camps and ranches, and wilderness experiences. An integral feature of these nonsecure options is to provide youths with experiences that will enable them to cope more effectively in their communities, in their schools, and other places where they may be found. Foster homes are frequently used, especially where one's own family lacks stability and is fragmented. Foster parents attempt to provide love and a supportive environment for affected youths. Group homes and halfway houses are also placement options available to judges, where certain youths can benefit from living with others like them and receive various forms of assistance.

Camps, ranches, experience programs, and wilderness experiences usually involve outdoor activities in an attempt to provide youths with skills that make them self-sufficient and less dependent upon adverse influences, such as other delinquents and gang members. Many different kinds of wilderness experiences are provided for youths in most jurisdictions. One of the primary problems faced by camp personnel is selecting the right youths for participation in these experiences. Not all youths fit easily into these types of programs, and many of them lack patience and other qualities that would otherwise assist smoothly in their rehabilitation. Some examples of wilderness experiences include Homeward Bound and VisionQuest, both of which have demonstrably high success levels among their youthful clients.

Some youths are exposed to shock incarceration or shock probation, where they are confined in a secure facility for a period of time. Then, they are suddenly removed from these facilities and placed on probation. The intent of authorities is to shock these juveniles with the realities of incarceration and make them less inclined to recidivate. Such programming is not always effective. One strategy that has gained momentum during the 1990s and beyond is the boot camp experience. Boot camps are highly regimented, military-like facilities that use strict discipline, hard work, and physical training to give unmanageable youths greater structure in their lives. Boot camps are operated for different periods, such as 90 or 180 days. They are offered for both male and female juveniles who lack discipline. Boot camps include educational and vocational experiences to make it possible for youths to improve themselves in different ways. Boot camps, many of which follow the Army model, have goals that include rehabilitation and reintegration; reductions in prison/jail overcrowding; provision of discipline; promoting deterrence; and providing educational and vocational training. Most youths who participate in boot camps are prison-bound offenders who are carefully screened and scrutinized for inclusion.

Secure confinement for juveniles consists of industrial schools and detention centers for both long-term and short-term confinement for those most likely to require it. Short-term detentions of juveniles average 30 days, while long-term confinement is about 180 days. Those youths adjudicated for the most serious offenses, such as murder, aggravated assault, rape, or robbery, usually serve terms that average 2 years. While these periods of short- and long-term confinement do not seem overly penalizing for many critics of the juvenile justice system, it is likely the case that youths have a different concept of time compared with adults. A 30-day period of detention may seem like a lifetime to a 14-year-old. Secure confinement facilities are increasingly privatized, and privatization generally has been responsible for many needed improvements in staffing and important services for youthful inmates.

At the other end of the juvenile correctional system is juvenile parole. Increasing numbers of youths are subjected to early release under adult-like parole programs. Colorado and other states operate sophisticated juvenile parole programs and seek to rehabilitate and reintegrate offenders beyond their periods of incarceration. The goals and purposes of juvenile parole are to alleviate industrial school and detention center overcrowding; permit youths to become reintegrated into their communities; reward good conduct while youths are in confinement; and deter youths from future offending by exercising a high degree of parolee control. No precise figures are available to indicate the extent to which juvenile parole is used in the United States, although probably at least 10,000 youths or more are under some form of parole supervision among jurisdictions. Decisions about who should be paroled are made by juvenile parole board members who use criteria similar to those used for adult offenders.

For both juvenile probationers and parolees, respectively, the juvenile court and parole boards maintain a loose form of jurisdictional control over these youths. When one or more program requirements are violated, however, certain youths may have their probation or parole programs revoked. Interestingly there is little if any U.S. Supreme Court case law concerning the conditions under which juvenile probation or parole can be revoked. However, juvenile court judges and parole boards in different states follow several important adult cases, which have been decided since the late 1960s. U.S. Supreme Court cases decided for adult probationers and parolees are not in any way binding on juvenile authorities. However, individual states often adopt revocation policies for their juveniles that closely parallel the same criteria used in adult probation/parole revocation cases. Juvenile probation and parole revocation are influenced to some extent by *Mempa v. Rhay* (1967)*, Morrissey v. Brewer* (1972), and *Gagnon v. Scarpelli* (1973). These adult cases have defined probation and parole revocation hearings and proceedings as critical stages where adults are in jeopardy of losing their liberty. These cases have bestowed upon adults minimum due-process rights, including the right to a notice of charges, the right to an attorney, and the right against self-incrimination. Several state-level cases involving probation and parole revocation proceedings for juveniles were examined.

Several juvenile corrections issues were discussed, including the privatization of juvenile corrections; the classification of juveniles; and the issue of holding juveniles in adult jails or lock-ups. The privatization issue is controversial since so many persons are critical of those seeking to profit from incarcerating offenders, including juveniles. While the profit motive is apparent in privatization, it is not necessarily a bad thing. Under the theory of agency, persons who carry out different supervisory and administrative functions in private juvenile facilities receive considerable training commensurate with their counterparts in the public correctional sector. Another issue involves the classification of juvenile offenders according to different criteria. As we have seen in previous chapters, our prediction instrumentation is flawed in different ways. But most states are improving their classification schemes for juveniles so that appropriate and individualized treatments may be prescribed. Finally, the jail removal initiative has been in effect for over two decades, as authorities seek to remove juveniles from jail and prison settings. These efforts have not been completely successful for a variety of reasons. Many youths look older than they really are, and phony identifications contribute to difficulties among jail personnel deciding who is or is not a juvenile.

QUESTIONS FOR REVIEW

1. What are five goals of juvenile corrections? How effectively are these goals achieved?
2. What are foster homes? How do they differ from group homes?
3. What are halfway houses? What are their functions and goals?
4. What are wilderness experiences and what are their functions?
5. What is meant by shock probation? What are several different types of shock probation? What are some major differences between each?
6. What is a boot camp? What are some specific goals and features of boot camps? Are they effective? Why or why not?
7. What are some major differences between short- and long-term secure juvenile facilities?
8. What is meant by juvenile parole? How much juvenile parole is there? Is juvenile parole successful? Why or why not?
9. What are three key adult probation and parole revocation cases that have guided state juvenile probation and parole revocation decision making?
10. What are three examples of probation and parole revocation cases for juveniles?

INTERNET CONNECTIONS

American Correctional Association
http://www.aca.org/

Boot Camps
http://www.boot-camps-info.com

Boot Camp Information
http://www.ncjrs.org/txtfiles/evalboot.txt

Close Cheltenham Now!
http://www.closecheltenham.org/

Corrections Connection
http://www.corrections.com

Debt to Society
http://www.motherjones.com/prisons/

Engaged Zen Foundation
http://www.engaged-zen.org/

Families Against Mandatory Minimums
http://www.famm.org/index2.htm

Federal Bureau of Prisons
http://www.bop.gov/

Fortune Society
http://www.fortunesociety.org/

Howard League
http://www.howardleague.org/

John Howard Association
http://www.johnhowardassociation.org/

Juvenile Boot Camps
http://www.juvenile-boot-camps.com/?source=overture

National Coalition to Abolish the Death Penalty
http://www.ncadp.org/

National Institute of Corrections
http://www.nicic.org/

Other Side of the Wall
http://www.prisonwall.org/

Penal Reform International
http://www.penalreform.org/

Prison Activist Resource Center
http://www.prisonactivist.org/

Stop Prisoner Rape
http://www.spr.org/index.html

Teen Boot Camps
http://www.teenbootcamps.com/resources/BootCamps.html

UNICOR Federal Prison Industries, Inc.
http://unicor.gov/index.cfm

Glossary

About Face Georgia boot camp program. *See also* **Boot Camps**.

Acceptance of responsibility Genuine admission or acknowledgment of wrongdoing; in federal presentence investigation reports, for example, convicted offenders may write an explanation and apology for the crime(s) they committed; a provision that may be considered in deciding whether leniency should be extended to offenders during the sentencing phase of their processing.

Act to Regulate the Treatment and Control of Dependent, Neglected, and Delinquent Children Delinquency act passed by Illinois legislature in 1899; established first juvenile court among states.

Actuarial justice The traditional orientation of juvenile justice, rehabilitation and individualized treatment, has been supplanted by the goal of efficient offender processing.

Actuarial prediction Projection of future inmate behavior based on a class of offenders similar to those considered for parole.

Addams, Jane Established Hull House in Chicago during 1880s; assisted wayward and homeless youths.

Adjudication Judgment or action on a petition filed with the juvenile court by others.

Adjudication hearing Formal proceeding involving a prosecuting attorney and a defense attorney where evidence is presented and the juvenile's guilt or innocence is determined by the juvenile judge; about one-fifth of all jurisdictions permit jury trials for juveniles under certain circumstances, with or without judicial approval.

Adversarial proceedings Opponent-driven court litigation, where one side opposes the other; prosecution seeks to convict or find defendants guilty, while defense counsel seeks to defend their clients and seek their acquittal.

Aftercare Describes a wide variety of programs and services available to both adult and juvenile probationers and parolees; includes halfway houses, psychological counseling services, community-based correctional agencies, employment assistance, and medical treatment for offenders or ex-offenders.

Age of majority Chronological date when one reaches adulthood, usually either age 18 or 21; when juveniles are no longer under the jurisdiction of the juvenile courts but rather, the criminal courts; also age of consent.

Aggravating circumstances Factors that may enhance the severity of one's sentence; these include brutality of act, whether serious bodily injury or death occurred to a victim during crime commission, and whether offender was on probation or parole when crime was committed.

Alternative dispute resolution (ADR) Procedure whereby a criminal case is redefined as a civil one and the case is decided by an impartial arbiter, where both parties agree to amicable settlement; criminal court is not used for resolving such matters; usually reserved for minor offenses; court-approved mediation programs where civilians are selected from community to help resolve minor delinquency, status offense, and abuse/neglect cases without formal judicial hearings.

American Correctional Association (ACA) Established in 1870 to disseminate information about correctional programs and correctional training; designed to foster professionalism throughout correctional community.

Anamnestic prediction Projection of inmate behavior according to past circumstances.

Anomie Condition of feelings of helplessness and normlessness.

Anomie theory Robert Merton's theory, influenced by Emile Durkheim, alleging that persons acquire desires for culturally approved goals to strive to achieve, but they adopt innovative, sometimes deviant, means to achieve these goals (e.g., someone may desire a nice home but lack or reject the institutionalized means), instead using bank robbery, an innovative mean, to obtain money to realize the culturally approved goal. Implies normlessness.

Appearance One's apparent socioeconomic status on the basis of one's clothing and general demeanor; unreliable criterion of socioeconomic status.

Army Model *See* **Boot Camps.**

Arraignment Following booking, a critical stage of the criminal justice process where defendants are asked to enter a plea to criminal charges, a trial date is established, and a formal list of charges is provided.

Arrest Taking persons into custody and restraining them until they can be brought before court to answer the charges against them.

Assessment centers Organizations selecting entry-level officers for correctional work; assessment centers hire correctional officers and probation or parole officers.

Assumptions Statements of fact about the real world or events; examples of assumptions might be "All societies have laws" or "The greater the deviant conduct, the greater the group pressure on the deviant to conform to group norms."

Atavism Positivist school of thought arguing that a biological condition renders a person incapable of living within the social constraints of a society; according to Cesare Lombroso, the physical characteristics that distinguish born criminals from the general population and are evolutionary throwbacks to animals or primitive people.

At-risk youths Any juveniles who are considered more susceptible to the influence of gangs and delinquent peers; tend to be characterized as having less developed reading skills, greater immaturity, lower socioeconomic status, parental dysfunction, and who are otherwise disadvantaged by their socioeconomic and environmental circumstances.

Automatic transfer laws Jurisdictional laws that provide for automatic waivers of juveniles to criminal court for processing; legislatively prescribed directive to transfer juveniles of specified ages who have committed especially serious offenses to jurisdiction of criminal courts.

Bail Surety provided by defendants or others to guarantee their subsequent appearance in court to face criminal charges; bail is available to anyone entitled to bail; bail is denied when suspects are considered dangerous or likely to flee.

Bail bond Written guarantee, often accompanied by money or other securities, that the person charged with an offense will remain within the court's jurisdiction to face trial at a time in the future.

Balanced approach Probation orientation that simultaneously emphasizes community protection, offender accountability, individualization of treatments, and competency assessment and development.

Banishment Sanction used to punish offenders by barring them from a specified number of miles from settlements or towns; often a capital punishment, since those banished could not obtain food or water to survive the isolation.

Barker balancing test Speedy trial standard, where delays are considered in terms of the reason, length, existence of prejudice against the defendant by the prosecutor, and the assertion of the defendant's speedy trial rights [from the case of *Barker v. Wingo,* 407 U.S. 514 (1972)].

Beats Patrol areas assigned to police officers in neighborhoods.

Beccaria, Cesare (1738–1794) Developed classical school of criminology; considered "father of classical criminology"; wrote *Essays on Crimes and Punishments;* believed corporal punishment unjust and ineffective; believed that crime could be prevented by plain legal codes specifying prohibited behaviors and punishments; promoted "just-deserts" philosophy; also endorsed a *utilitarianism* approach to criminal conduct and its punishment by suggesting that useful, purposeful, and reasonable punishments ought to be formulated and applied; also viewed criminal conduct as pleasurable to criminals, and that they sought pleasure and avoided pain; thus, pain might function as a deterrent to criminal behavior.

Bench trials Proceedings where guilt or innocence of defendant is determined by a judge rather than a jury.

Beyond a reasonable doubt Evidentiary standard used in criminal courts to establish guilt or innocence of criminal defendant.

Big Brothers/Big Sisters Program Federation of over 500 agencies to serve children and adolescents; adults relate on a one-to-one basis with youths to promote their self-esteem and self-sufficiency; utilizes volunteers who attempt to instill responsibility, excellence, and leadership among assisted youths.

Biological determinism View in criminology holding that criminal behavior has physiological basis; genes, foods and food additives, hormones, and inheritance are all believed to play a role in determining individual behavior; one's genetic makeup causes certain behaviors to become manifest, such as criminality.

Blended sentencing Any type of sentencing procedure where either a criminal or juvenile court judge can impose *both* juvenile and/or adult incarcerative penalties.

Bonding theory A key concept in a number of theoretical formulations. Emile Durkheim's notion that deviant behavior is controlled to the degree that group members feel morally bound to one another, are committed to common goals and share a collective conscience; in social control theory, the elements of attachment, commitment, involvement, and belief; explanation of criminal behavior implying that criminality is the result of a loosening of bonds or attachments with society; builds on differential association theory. Primarily designed to account for juvenile delinquency.

Booking Process of making a written report of arrest, including name and address of arrested persons, the alleged crimes, arresting officers, place and, time of arrest, physical description of suspect, photographs (sometimes called "mug shots"), and fingerprints.

Boot camps Also known as the Army Model, boot camp programs are patterned after basic training for new military recruits. Juvenile offenders are given a taste of hard military life, and such regimented activities and structure for up to 180 days are often sufficient to "shock" them into giving up their lives of delinquency or crime and staying out of jail.

Boston Offender Project (BOP) Experimental program in Boston, targeted for violent juveniles; program goals include reducing recidivism, enhancing public protection by increasing accountability for major violators, and improving the likelihood of successful reintegration of juveniles into society by focusing on these offenders' academic and vocational skills.

Bridewell Workhouse Sixteenth-century London jail (sometimes gaol) established in 1557; known for providing cheap labor to business and mercantile interests; jailers and sheriffs profited from prisoner exploitation.

Bullying Prevention Program Targets bullies in elementary, middle, and high schools; vests school authorities with intervention powers to establish class rules for disciplining bullies and bullying behavior through student committees.

Capital punishment Imposition of the death penalty for the most serious crimes; may be administered by electrocution, lethal injection, gas, hanging, or shooting.

Career escalation Moving as a juvenile offender to progressively more serious offenses as new offenses are committed; committing new violent offenses after adjudications for property offenses would be career escalation; committing progressively more serious offenses.

CASASTART Program Targets high-risk youths who are exposed to drugs and delinquent activity; decreases risk factors by greater community involvement.

Caseloads Number of cases a probation or parole officer is assigned according to some standard such as a week, month, or year; caseloads vary among jurisdictions.

Case supervision planning A means whereby a probation or parole department makes assignments of probationers or parolees to probation officers or parole officers.

Certification Similar to waivers or transfers; in some jurisdictions, juveniles are certified or designated as adults for the purpose of pursuing criminal prosecution against them.

Chancellors Civil servants who acted on behalf of the King of England during the Middle Ages; chancellors held court and settled property disputes, trespass cases, minor property offenses, thievery, vagrancy, and public drunkenness.

Chancery Courts Court of equity rooted in early English common law where civil disputes are resolved; also responsible for juvenile matters and adjudicating family matters such as divorce; has jurisdiction over contract disputes, property boundary claims, and exchanges of goods disputes.

Child savers, Child-saving movement Organized effort during early 1800s in the United States, comprised primarily of upper- and middle-class interests who sought to provide assistance to wayward youths; assistance was often food and shelter, although social, educational, and religious values were introduced to children later in compulsory schooling.

Children at risk *See* **At-risk youths.**

Children in need of supervision (CHINS) Any children determined by the juvenile court and other agencies to be in need of community care or supervision.

Children's tribunals Informal court mechanisms originating in Massachusetts to deal with children charged with crimes apart from system of criminal courts for adults.

Chronic offenders Habitual offenders; repeat offenders; persistent offenders; youths who commit frequent delinquent acts.

Citizen action model Youth Service Bureau model using community volunteers to actively intervene and assist in the lives of delinquency-prone youths.

Civil tribunals *See* **Children's tribunals.**

Classical school Line of thought that assumes that people are rational beings who choose between good and evil.

Classical theory A criminological perspective indicating that people have free will to choose either criminal or conventional behavior; people choose to commit crime for reasons of greed or personal need; crime can be controlled by criminal sanctions, which should be proportionate to the guilt of the perpetrator.

Classification Means used by prisons and probation/parole agencies to separate offenders according to offense seriousness, type of offense, and other criteria; no classification system has been demonstrably successful at effective prisoner or client placements.

Cleared by arrest Term used by FBI in the *Uniform Crime Reports* to indicate that someone has been arrested for a reported crime; does not necessarily mean that the crime has been solved or that the actual criminals who committed the crime have been apprehended or convicted.

Clinical prediction Forecast of inmate behavior based on professional's expert training and working directly with offenders.

Combination sentences Occurs whenever judges sentence offenders to a term, a portion of which includes incarceration and a term of which includes probation.

Commitment placement Confinement in a secure juvenile facility, usually for a term such as one year or longer.

Common law Authority based on court decrees and judgments, which recognize, affirm, and enforce certain usages and customs of the people; laws determined by judges in accordance with their rulings.

Community Board Program Civil mediation mechanism utilizing volunteers to mediate between victims and offenders.

Community corrections acts Enabling legislation by individual states to fund local government units to provide community facilities, services, and resources to juveniles who are considered at risk of becoming delinquent or who are already delinquent and need treatment/services.

Community organization model Youth Services Bureau model that uses citizens on a voluntary basis to assist delinquency-prone youth.

Community policing Major police reform that broadens the police mission from a narrow focus on crime to a mandate that encourages the police to explore creative solutions for a host of community concerns, including crime, fear of crime, disorder, and neighborhood decay; rests on belief that only by working together will citizens and police be able to improve the quality of life in their communities, with the police not only as enforcers, but also as advisors, facilitators, and supporters of new community-based police-supervised initiatives; activities conducted by law enforcement officers to enhance public relations between police and the community; foot patrols and other "back-to-the-people" patrol strategies are considered integral elements of community policing.

Community reintegration model Operating theory whereby offender who has been incarcerated is able to live in community under some supervision and gradually adjust to life outside of prison or jail.

Community service Any activity imposed on a probationer or parolee involving work in one's neighborhood or city, performed in part to repay victims and the city for injuries or damages caused by one's unlawful actions.

Community Service Program, Inc. (CSP, Inc.) Established in Orange County, California; designed to instill self-confidence in youths, reduce parental and familial dysfunction, and establish self-reliance and esteem through family counseling therapy and sessions.

Compulsory School Act Passed in 1899 by Colorado, this act targeted those youths who were habitually absent from school; it encompassed youths who wandered the streets during school hours; originally designed to enforce truancy laws; erroneously regarded as first juvenile court act, which was actually passed in Illinois in 1899.

Concentric zone hypothesis Series of rings originating from a city center, such as Chicago, and emanating outward, forming various zones characterized by different socioeconomic conditions; believed to contain areas of high delinquency and crime.

Concurrent jurisdiction Power to file charges against juveniles in either criminal courts or juvenile courts.

Conditional dispositions Results of a delinquency adjudication that obligate youths to comply with one or more conditions of a probation program, such as restitution, community service, work study, therapy, educational participation, or victim compensation.

Conditional probation Program where divertee is involved in some degree of local monitoring by probation officers or personnel affiliated with local probation departments.

Confidentiality privilege Right between defendant and his or her attorney where certain information cannot be disclosed to prosecutors or others because of the attorney–client relation; for juveniles, records have been maintained under secure circumstances with limited access, and only then accessed by those in authority with a clear law enforcement purpose.

Conformity Robert K. Merton's mode of adaptation characterized by persons who accept institutionalized means to achieve culturally approved goals.

Consent decrees Formal agreements that involve children, their parents, and the juvenile court, where youths are placed under the court's supervision without an official finding of delinquency, with judicial approval.

Containment theory Explanation elaborated by Walter Reckless and others that positive self-image enables persons otherwise disposed toward criminal behavior to avoid criminal conduct and conform to societal values. Every person is a part of an external structure and has a protective internal structure providing defense, protection, and/or insulation against one's peers, such as delinquents.

Contempt of court Any citation by a judge against anyone in court who disrupts the proceedings or does anything to interfere with judicial decrees or pronouncements.

Conventional model Caseload assignment model where probation or parole officers are assigned clients randomly.

Conventional model with geographic considerations Similar to conventional model; caseload assignment model is based on the travel time required for POs to meet with offender-clients regularly.

Convictions Judgments of a court, based on a jury or judicial verdict, or on the guilty pleas of defendants, that the defendants are guilty of the offenses alleged.

Cooperating agencies model Youth Service Bureau model where several agencies act as a team to provide delinquency-prone youths with needed services.

C.O.P.Y. Kids (Community Opportunities Program for Youth) Spokane, Washington, program for disadvantaged youth commenced in 1992; youth participated in arts and crafts and learned valuable work skills.

Corporate gangs juvenile gangs emulate organized crime; profit-motivated gangs that rely on illicit activities, such as drug trafficking, to further their profit interests.

Corrections Aggregate of programs, services, facilities, and organizations responsible for the management of people who have been accused or convicted of criminal offenses.

Court of record Any court where a written record is kept of court proceedings.

Court reporters Court officials who keep a written word-for-word and/or tape-recorded record of court proceedings.

Court unification Proposal that seeks to centralize and integrate the diverse functions of all courts of general, concurrent, and exclusive jurisdiction into a more simplified and uncomplicated scheme.

Courts Public judiciary bodies that apply the law to controversies and oversee the administration of justice.

Courts of equity *See* **Chancery courts.**

Creative sentencing Broad class of punishments as alternatives to incarceration that are designed to fit the particular crimes; may involve community service, restitution, fines, becoming involved in educational or vocational training programs, or becoming affiliated with other "good works" activity.

Crime control model Criminal justice program that emphasizes containment of dangerous offenders and societal protection; a way of controlling delinquency by incapacitating juvenile offenders, through some secure detention or through intensive supervision programs operated by community-based agencies.

Criminal-exclusive blend Form of sentencing by a criminal court judge where either juvenile or adult sentences of incarceration can be imposed, but not both.

Criminal-inclusive blend Form of sentencing by a criminal court judge where both juvenile and adult sentences can be imposed simultaneously.

Criminal informations Charges filed by prosecutors directly against defendants; usually involve minor crimes.

Criminal justice Interdisciplinary field studying nature and operations of organizations providing justice services to society; consists of lawmaking bodies including state legislatures and Congress and local, state, and federal agencies that try to enforce the law.

Criminal justice professional Anyone interested in studying the criminal justice system; may have a Ph.D. or master's degree in criminal justice or a related field; may be a practitioner, such as a police officer, corrections officer, probation or parole officer, prosecutor, or judge.

Criminal justice system, criminal justice process Interrelated set of agencies and organizations designed to control criminal behavior, to detect crime, and to apprehend, process, prosecute, punish, and/or rehabilitate criminal offenders.

Criminogenic environment Setting where juveniles may feel like criminals or may acquire the characteristics or labels of criminals; settings include courtrooms and prisons.

Criminology Study of crime, the science of crime and criminal behavior, the forms of criminal behavior, the causes of crime, the definition of criminality, and the societal reaction to crime.

Cultural transmission theory Explanation emphasizing transmission of criminal behavior through socialization. Views delinquency as socially learned behavior transmitted from one generation to the next in disorganized urban areas.

Curfew violators Youths who violate laws and ordinances of communities prohibiting youths on the streets after certain evening hours, such as 10:00 P.M.; curfew itself is a delinquency prevention strategy.

Custodial dispositions Either nonsecure or secure options resulting from a delinquency adjudication; juveniles may be placed in foster homes, group homes, community-based correctional facilities, or secure detention facilities that are either publicly or privately operated.

Dangerousness Defined differently in several jurisdictions; prior record of violent offenses; potential to commit future violent crimes if released; propensity to inflict injury; predicted risk of convicted offender or prison or jail inmate; likelihood of inflicting harm upon others.

D.A.R.E. (Drug Abuse Resistance Education) Intervention program sponsored and implemented by the Los Angeles Police Department; utilizes officers familiar with drugs

and drug laws who visit schools in their precincts and speak to youths about how to say "no" to drugs; children are taught how to recognize illegal drugs, different types of drugs, and their adverse effects.

Day reporting centers Established in England in 1974 to provide intensive supervision for low-risk offenders who lived in neighborhoods; continued in various U.S. jurisdictions today to manage treatment programs, supervise fee collection, and other responsibilities, such as drug testing and counseling.

Death penalty Sentence that terminates the life of an offender, either through lethal gas, electrocution, lethal injection, hanging, or by firing squad.

Decarceration Type of deinstitutionalization where juveniles charged with status offenses are still under court jurisdiction and subject to filing of petitions; detention of youths is prohibited; youths may be removed from their homes and placed in nonsecure facilities, put on probation, required to attend treatment or service programs, and subjected to other behavioral restraints.

Defendants Anyone charged with one or more crimes.

Defense attorneys Advocates for juvenile defendants; represent the interests and defend the rights of juveniles in either juvenile or criminal courts.

Deinstitutionalization of status offenses (DSO) Eliminating status offenses from broad category of delinquent acts and removing juveniles from or precluding their confinement in juvenile correctional facilities; the process of removing status offenses from jurisdiction of juvenile court so that status offenders cannot be subject to secure confinement.

Delinquency Act committed by an infant of not more than a specified age who has violated criminal laws or engages in disobedient, indecent, or immoral conduct, and is in need of treatment, rehabilitation, or supervision; status acquired through an adjudicatory proceeding by juvenile court.

Delinquent child Infant of not more than a specified age who has violated criminal laws or engages in disobedient, indecent, or immoral conduct, and is in need of treatment, rehabilitation, or supervision.

Demand waiver Requests by juveniles to have their cases transferred from juvenile courts to criminal courts.

Dependent and neglected children Youths considered by social services or the juvenile court to be in need of some type of adult supervision.

Detention Confining youths for short terms in secure facilities, usually to await a juvenile court adjudicatory hearing or some other proceeding; some youths are placed in secure settings for short terms as a punishment for delinquent offending.

Detention centers Juvenile secure facilities used for serious and violent juveniles who are awaiting an adjudication hearing.

Detention hearing Judicial or quasi-judicial proceeding held to determine whether or not it is appropriate to continue to hold or detain a juvenile in a shelter facility.

Determinism Concept holding that persons do not have a free will but rather are subject to the influence of various forces over which they have little or no control.

Dickerson's Rangers Antidrug program in the San Fernando Valley of Southern California; targets children ages 7–13, and it operates in various city parks and recreational centers; children meet weekly and discuss drug abuse in their schools and communities; police officers advise them how to resist overtures made by drug dealers or their peers who might use drugs; field trips are also sponsored that include speakers whose specialties include drug abuse and illicit drug prevention.

Differential association theory Edwin Sutherland's theory of deviance and criminality through associations with others who are deviant or criminal; theory includes dimensions of frequency, duration, priority, and intensity; persons become criminal or delinquent because of a preponderance of learned definitions that are favorable to violating the law over learned definitions unfavorable to it.

Differential reinforcement theory Explanation that combines elements of labeling theory and a psychological phenomenon known as conditioning; persons are rewarded for engaging in desirable behavior and punished for deviant conduct.

Direct file Prosecutorial waiver of jurisdiction to a criminal court; an action taken against a juvenile who has committed an especially serious offense, where that juvenile's case is transferred to criminal court for the purpose of a criminal prosecution.

Discretionary powers Relating to the police role, police discretion is the distribution of non-negotiable coercive force employed in accordance with the dictates of an intuitive grasp of situational exigencies; police have authority to use force to enforce the law, if, in the officer's opinion, the situation demands it.

Discretionary waivers Transfers of juveniles to criminal courts by judges, at their discretion or in their judgment; also known as **judicial waivers.**

Dispose To decide the punishment to be imposed on a juvenile following an adjudication hearing.

Dispositions Punishments resulting from a delinquency adjudication; may be nominal, conditional, or custodial.

Diversion Official halting or suspension of legal proceedings against criminal defendants after a recorded justice system entry, and possible referral of those persons to treatment or care programs administered by a nonjustice or private agency. *See also* **Pretrial release.**

Diversion Plus Program Established in Lexington, Kentucky, in 1991, designed to reduce recidivism and promote conformity to the law without stigmatization; youths targeted included first-offenders, low-risk delinquent offenders, and any youth without a prior juvenile record; consists of a series of weekly meetings and self-help sessions, stressing self-esteem and self-control, substance abuse prevention, and independent living; one-on-one counseling and small group interaction.

Divestiture Strategy for deinstitutionalizing status offenders, where juvenile courts cannot detain, petition, adjudicate, or place youths on probation for any status offense; according to legislatively created statutes, juvenile court does not accept most, if not all, status offense cases.

Double jeopardy Subjecting persons to prosecution more than once in the same jurisdiction for the same offense, usually without new or vital evidence. Prohibited by the Fifth Amendment.

Drift theory David Matza's term denoting a state of limbo in which youths move in and out of delinquency and in which their lifestyles embrace both conventional and deviant values.

Due process Basic constitutional right to a fair trial, presumption of innocence until guilt is proven beyond a reasonable doubt, the opportunity to be heard, to be aware of a matter that is pending, to make an informed choice whether to acquiesce or contest, and to provide the reasons for such a choice before a judicial official.

Due process model Treatment model based on one's constitutional right to a fair trial, to have an opportunity to be heard, to be aware of matters that are pending, to a presumption of innocence until guilt has been established beyond a reasonable doubt, to make an informed choice whether to acquiesce or contest, and to provide the reasons for such a choice before a judicial officer.

Ectomorphs Body type described by Sheldon; persons are thin, sensitive, delicate.

Electronic monitoring Use of electronic devices that emit electronic signals; these devices, anklets or wristlets, are worn by offenders, probationers, and parolees; the purpose of such monitoring is to monitor an offender's presence in a given environment where the offender is required to remain or to verify the offender's whereabouts.

Electronic monitoring signalling devices Apparatuses worn about the wrist or leg that are designed to monitor an offender's presence in a given environment where the offender is required to remain.

Endomorphs Body type described by Sheldon; persons are fat, soft, plump, jolly.

Exculpatory evidence Information considered beneficial to defendants, tending to show their innocence.

Expungement orders Deletion of one's arrest record from official sources; in most jurisdictions, juvenile delinquency records are expunged when one reaches the age of majority or adulthood.

Extralegal factors Characteristics influencing intake decisions, such as juvenile offender attitudes, school grades and standing, gender, race, ethnicity, socioeconomic status, and age.

Faith in Families Multisystematic Therapy Program (MST) Operated by the Henry and Rilla White Foundation in Bronson, Florida; attempts to modify youth behaviors by working with their interpersonal environment, including family, therapists, and peer groups; subjects taught include self-control, anger management, self-reflectiveness, and problem-solving skills.

False negatives Offenders predicted to be dangerous who turn out not to be dangerous.

False positives Offenders predicted not to be dangerous who turn out to be dangerous.

Family model Established under the Juvenile Law of 1948, it exists in all Japanese jurisdictions and hears any matters pertaining to juvenile delinquency, child abuse and neglect, and child custody matters; both status offenders and delinquents appear before Family Court judges; similar to juvenile court judges in U.S. jurisdictions, Family Court judges have considerable discretionary authority; decide cases within the *parens patriae* context.

FAST Track Program Rural and urban intervention program targeting girls and boys of many ethnicities; designed to provide severe and chronic misconduct problems for high-risk children.

Felonies Crimes punishable by imprisonment for a term of one or more years; major crimes; any index offense.

Fines Financial penalties imposed at time of sentencing convicted offenders; most criminal statutes contain provisions for the imposition of monetary penalties as sentencing options.

First-offender Criminals who have no previous criminal records; these persons may have committed crimes, but they have only been caught for the instant offense.

Flat time Frequently known as hard time, meaning the actual amount of time one must serve while incarcerated.

Foster homes Temporary placement of youths in need of supervision or control; usually families volunteer to act as foster parents and maintain placed youths for short-term care.

Friends for the Love of Reading Project Self-help program and offshoot of District of Columbia Book Buddies Program designed to assist youths with poor reading abilities to improve their reading skills; involves parents and volunteers on a one-to-one basis with youths.

Gangs Groups who form an allegiance for a common purpose and engage in unlawful or criminal activity; any group gathered together on a continuing basis to engage in or commit antisocial behavior.

Gemeinschaft Term created by Ferdinand Tonnies, a social theorist, to describe small, traditional communities where informal punishments were used to punish those who violated community laws.

Gesellschaft Term created by Ferdinand Tonnies, a social theorist, to describe more formalized, larger communities and cities that relied on written documents and laws to regulate social conduct.

Get-tough movement General orientation toward criminals and juvenile delinquents that favors the maximum penalties and punishments for crime and delinquency; any action toward strengthening sentencing provisions or dispositions involving adults or juveniles.

Graffiti Removal Initiative Program Community program designed as a condition of probation in cases of vandalism, where youths must remove graffiti from public buildings or houses; used in conjunction with other program conditions.

Grand juries Investigative bodies whose numbers vary among states; duties include determining probable cause regarding commission of a crime and returning formal charges against suspects. *See* **True Bill and No Bill.**

G.R.E.A.T. (Gang Resistance Education and Training) Established in Phoenix, Arizona; police officers visit schools and help youths understand how to cope with peer pressure to commit delinquent acts; topics of educational programs include victim rights, drugs and neighborhoods, conflict resolution, and need fulfillment.

Group homes Also known as group centers or foster homes, these are facilities for juveniles that provide limited supervision and support; juveniles live in home-like environment with other juveniles and participate in therapeutic programs and counseling; considered nonsecure custodial.

Guardians ad litem Special authorities appointed by the court in which particular litigation is pending to represent a youth, ward, or unborn person in that particular litigation.

Habeas corpus Writ meaning "produce the body"; used by prisoners to challenge the nature and length of their confinement.

Halfway houses Nonconfining residential facilities intended to provide alternative to incarceration as a period of readjustment of offenders to the community after confinement.

Hands-off doctrine Policy practiced by the federal courts, where official court policy was not to intervene in matters relating to adult corrections; belief that correctional superintendents and wardens and departments of corrections are in best position to make decisions about welfare of inmates; applied to juvenile corrections and juvenile courts similarly.

Hard time Also known as flat time, actual amount of secure confinement juveniles must serve as the result of a custodial disposition from a juvenile court judge.

Hedonism Jeremy Bentham's term indicating that people avoid pain and pursue pleasure.

Hidden delinquency Infractions reported by surveys of high school youths; considered "hidden" because it most often is undetected by police officers; disclosed delinquency through self-report surveys.

Home confinement Program intended to house offenders in their own homes with or without electronic devices; reduces prison overcrowding and prisoner costs; intermediate punishment involving the use of offender residences for mandatory incarceration during evening hours after a curfew and on weekends.

Home incarceration *See* **Home Confinement**.

Homeward Bound Established in Massachusetts in 1970; designed to provide juveniles with mature responsibilities through the acquisition of survival skills and wilderness experiences. A 6-week training program subjected 32 youths to endurance training, physical fitness, and performing community service.

Hospital of Saint Michael Custodial institution established at request of Pope in Rome in 1704; provided for unruly youths and others who violated the law; youths were assigned tasks, including semi-skilled and skilled labor, which enabled them to get jobs when released.

House arrest *See* **Home Confinement**.

Houses of refuge Workhouses, the first of which was established in 1824 as a means of separating juveniles from the adult correctional process.

Id Sigmund Freud's term to depict that part of personality concerned with individual gratification; the "I want" part of a person, formed in one's early years.

Illinois Juvenile Court Act Legislation passed by Illinois legislature in 1899 providing for the first juvenile court and treatment programs for various types of juvenile offenders.

IMPACT (Intensive Motivational Program of Alternative Correctional Treatment Boot camp program operated in New York; incorporates educational training with strict physical and behavioral requirements.

Incident Specific criminal act involving one crime and one or more victims.

Inculpatory evidence Information considered adverse to defendants or tending to show their guilt.

Indentured servants, indentured servant system Voluntary slave pattern where persons without money for passage from England entered into a contract with merchants or businessmen, usually for 7 years, wherein merchants would pay for their voyage fare to the American colonies from England in exchange for their labor.

Index crimes Any violations of the law listed by the *Uniform Crime Reports* under **Index Offenses** (e.g., homicide, rape, aggravated assault, robbery, burglary, larceny, arson).

Index Offenses Specific felonies used by the Federal Bureau of Investigation in the *Uniform Crime Reports* to chart crime trends; there are eight index offenses listed prior to 1988 (includes aggravated assault, larceny, burglary, vehicular theft, arson, robbery, forcible rape, murder).

Indictments Charges or written accusations found and presented by a grand jury that a particular defendant probably committed a crime.

Industrial schools Institutions that resemble prisons; secure facilities where some juveniles are held for up to one year or longer; such institutions usually have different types of programming to aid in the rehabilitation and reintegration of youthful offenders, consisting of vocational and educational courses or programs, counseling for different types of youth needs, and other services; these facilities are largely self-contained like prisons, and they offer a limited range of medical and health services.

Infants Legal term applicable to juveniles who have not attained the age of majority; in most states, age of majority is 18.

Informations Sometimes called criminal informations; written accusations made by a public prosecutor against a person for some criminal offense, without an indictment; usually restricted to minor crimes or misdemeanors.

Initial appearance Formal proceeding during which the judge advises defendants of the charges against them.

Innovation Robert K. Merton's mode of adaptation where persons reject institutionalized means to achieve culturally approved goals; instead, they engage in illegal acts, considered innovative, to achieve their goals.

Intake Critical phase where a determination is made by a juvenile probation officer or other official whether to release juveniles to their parent's custody, detain juveniles in formal detention facilities for a later court appearance, or release them to parents pending a later court appearance.

Intake hearings, intake screenings Proceedings where a juvenile official, such as a juvenile probation officer, conducts an interview with a youth charged with a delinquent or status offense.

Intake officer Juvenile probation officer who conducts screenings and preliminary interviews with alleged juvenile delinquents or status offenders and their families.

Intensive Aftercare Program (IAP) Philadelphia-based intervention for serious youthful offenders involving intensive counseling and training for acquiring self-help skills; recidivism of participants greatly reduced during study period of 1980–1990.

Intensive probation supervision (IPS) *See* **Intensive supervised probation.**

Intensive supervised probation (ISP) Controlled probation overseen by probation officer; involves close monitoring of offender activities by various means (also known as "intensive probation supervision," or IPS).

Intensive supervision program Offender supervision program with the following characteristics: (1) low officer/client caseloads (i.e., 30 or fewer probationers); (2) high levels of offender accountability (e.g., victim restitution, community service, payment of fines, partial defrayment of program ex-

penses); (3) high levels of offender responsibility; (4) high levels of offender control (home confinement, electronic monitoring, frequent face-to-face visits by POs); (5) frequent checks for arrests, drug and/or alcohol use, and employment/school attendance (drug/alcohol screening, coordination with police departments and juvenile halls, teachers, family).

Interagency Agreement Plan Early intervention plan instituted in San Diego County, California, in 1982 for the purpose of reducing delinquency; graduated sanctions used for repeat offenders; youths held accountable for their actions; gradual increase of services and punishments for repeat offenders.

Intermediate punishments Sanctions existing somewhere between incarceration and probation on a continuum of criminal penalties; may include home incarceration and electronic monitoring.

Intermittent sentences Occur whenever judges sentence offenders to terms such as weekend confinement only.

Interstitial area In concentric zone hypothesis, area nearest the center of a city undergoing change, such as urban renewal; characterized by high rates of crime.

Jail as a condition of probation Sentence where judge imposes some jail time to be served before probation commences; also known as shock probation.

Jail removal initiative Action sponsored by the Office of Juvenile Justice and Delinquency Prevention and the Juvenile Justice and Delinquency Prevention Act of 1974 to deinstitutionalize juveniles from secure facilities, such as jails.

Jails City or county operated and financed facilities to contain those offenders who are serving short sentences; jails also house more serious prisoners from state or federal prisons through contracts to alleviate overcrowding; jails also house pretrial detainees, witnesses, juveniles, vagrants, and others.

Judicial waivers Decision by juvenile judge to waive juvenile to jurisdiction of criminal court.

Judicious nonintervention Similar to a "do nothing" policy of delinquency nonintervention.

Jurisdiction Power of a court to hear and determine a particular type of case; also refers to territory within which court may exercise authority, such as a city, county, or state.

Jury *See* **Petit jury.**

Jury trials Proceeding where guilt or innocence of defendant is determined by jury instead of by the judge.

Just-deserts/justice model Stresses offender accountability as a means to punish youthful offenders; uses victim compensation plans, restitution, and community services as ways of making offenders pay for their offenses; philosophy that emphasizes punishment as a primary objective of sentencing, fixed sentences, abolition of parole, and an abandonment of the rehabilitative ideal; rehabilitation is functional to the extent that offenders join rehabilitative programs voluntarily.

Juvenile court records Formal or informal statement concerning an adjudication hearing involving sustained allegations against a juvenile; a written document of one's prior delinquency or status offending.

Juvenile courts Formal proceeding with jurisdiction over juveniles, juvenile delinquents, status offenders, dependent or neglected children, children in need of supervision, or infants.

Juvenile delinquency Violation of the law by a person prior to his or her 18th birthday; any illegal behavior committed by someone within a given age range punishable by juvenile court jurisdiction; whatever the juvenile court believes should be brought within its jurisdiction; violation of any state or local law or ordinance by anyone who has not as yet achieved the age of their majority.

Juvenile delinquents Infant of not more than a specified age who has violated criminal laws or engages in disobedient, indecent, or immoral conduct, and is in need of treatment, rehabilitation, or supervision.

Juvenile–contiguous blend Form of sentencing by a juvenile court judge where the judge can impose a disposition beyond the normal jurisdictional range for juvenile offenders; for example, a judge may impose a 30-year term on a 14-year-old offender, but the juvenile is entitled to a hearing when he or she reaches the age of majority to determine whether the remainder of the sentence shall be served.

Juvenile–exclusive blend Sentencing form where a juvenile court judge can impose either adult or juvenile incarceration as a disposition and sentence but not both.

Juvenile–inclusive blend Form of sentencing where a juvenile court judge can impose *both* adult and juvenile incarceration simultaneously.

Juvenile intensive supervised probation (JISP) Ohio-operated program for youthful offenders, including home confinement, electronic monitoring, and other intensive probation supervision methods.

Juvenile Justice and Delinquency Prevention Act of 1974 (JJDPA) Legislation recommending various alternatives to incarcerating youths, including deinstitutionalization of status offending, removal of youths from secure confinement, and other rehabilitative treatments.

Juvenile justice system Stages through which juveniles are processed, sentenced, and corrected after arrests for juvenile delinquency.

Juvenile Mentoring Program (JUMP) Federally funded program administered by the Office of Juvenile Justice and Delinquency Prevention; promotes bonding between an adult and a juvenile relating on a one-to-one basis over time; designed to improve school performance and decrease gang participation and delinquency.

Juvenile offender laws Regulations providing for automatic transfer of juveniles of certain ages to criminal courts for processing, provided they have committed especially serious crimes.

Juvenile offenders Any infant or child who has violated juvenile laws.

Juvenile Probation Camps (JPCs) California county-operated camps for delinquent youth placed on probation in early 1980s;

including physical activities, community contacts, and academic training.

Juveniles Persons who have not reached the age of majority or adulthood.

Labeling Process whereby persons acquire self-definitions that are deviant or criminal; process occurs through labels applied to them by others.

Labeling theory Explanation of deviant conduct attributed to Edwin Lemert whereby persons acquire self-definitions that are deviant or criminal; persons perceive themselves as deviant or criminal through labels applied to them by others; the more people are involved in the criminal justice system, the more they acquire self-definitions consistent with the criminal label.

Law enforcement agencies, law enforcement Any organization whose purpose is to enforce criminal laws; the activities of various public and private agencies at local, state, and federal levels that are designed to ensure compliance with formal rules of society that regulate social conduct.

Law enforcement officers Any persons sworn to uphold and enforce local, state, or federal laws.

Legal factors Variables influencing the intake decision relating to the factual information about delinquent acts; crime seriousness, type of crime committed, prior record of delinquency adjudications, and evidence of inculpatory or exculpatory nature.

Legislative waiver Provision that compels juvenile court to remand certain youths to criminal courts because of specific offenses that have been committed or alleged.

Libido Sigmund Freud's term describing the sex drive he believed innate in everyone.

Life-without-parole Penalty imposed as maximum punishment in states that do not have the death penalty; provides for permanent incarceration of offenders in prisons, without parole eligibility; early release may be attained through accumulation of good time credits.

Litigation explosion Rapid escalation of case filings before appellate courts, often based on a landmark case extending rights to particular segments of the population, such as jail or prison inmates or juveniles.

Lock-ups Short-term confinement facility; usually a small jail where drunks and disorderly persons are held for brief periods.

Lombroso, Cesare (1835–1909) School of thought linking criminal behavior with abnormal, unusual physical characteristics.

Long-term detention Period of incarceration of juvenile offenders in secure facilities that averages 180 days in the United States.

Looking-glass self Concept originated by Charles Horton Cooley where persons learn appropriate ways of behaving by paying attention to how others view and react to them.

Mandatory waiver Automatic transfer of certain juveniles to criminal court on the basis of (1) their age and (2) the seriousness of their offense; for example, a 17-year-old in Illinois who allegedly committed homicide would be subject to mandatory transfer to criminal court for the purpose of a criminal prosecution.

Mediation A process whereby a third party intervenes between a perpetrator and a victim to work out a noncriminal or civil resolution to a problem that might otherwise result in a delinquency adjudication or criminal conviction.

Mediator Third-party arbiter in alternative dispute resolution.

Medical model Known as the treatment model, this model considers criminal behavior as an illness to be treated; delinquency is also a disease subject to treatment.

Mesomorphs Body type described by Sheldon; persons are strong, muscular, aggressive, tough.

Midwestern Prevention Project Multifaceted program for adolescent drug abuse prevention; targets middle and late adolescents; assists youths to recognize pressures to use drugs and to avoid such pressures.

Minimum due-process rights *See* **Due process.**

Miranda warning Sanction given to suspects by police officers advising suspects of their legal rights to counsel, to refuse to answer questions, to avoid self-incrimination, and other privileges.

Misdemeanor Crime punishable by confinement in city or county jail for a period of less than one year; a lesser offense.

Mistrial Trial ending before defendant's guilt or innocence can be established; usually results from hung jury where jurors are unable to reach agreement on one's guilt or innocence; also occurs because of substantial irregularities in trial conduct.

Mitigating circumstances Factors that lessen the severity of the crime and/or sentence; such factors include old age, cooperation with police in apprehending other offenders, and lack of intent to inflict injury.

Mixed sentences Punishments imposed whenever offenders have been convicted of two or more offenses and judges sentence them to separate sentences for each conviction offense.

Mode of adaptation A way that persons who occupy a particular social position adjust to cultural goals and the institutionalized means to reach those goals.

Monitoring the Future Survey Study of 3,000 high school students annually by the Institute for Social Research at the University of Michigan; attempts to discover hidden delinquency not ordinarily disclosed by published public reports.

National Crime Victimization Survey (NCVS) Published in cooperation with the United States Bureau of the Census, a random survey of 60,000 households, including 127,000 persons 12 years of age or older; includes 50,000 businesses; measures crime committed against specific victims interviewed and not necessarily reported to law enforcement officers.

National Juvenile Court Data Archive Compendium of national statistical information and databases about juvenile delinquency available through the National Center for Juvenile Justice, under the sponsorship of the Office of Juvenile Justice and Delinquency Prevention; involves acquisition of court dispositional records and publishing periodic reports of juvenile offenses and adjudicatory outcomes from different jurisdictions.

National Youth Survey Study of large numbers of youths annually or at other intervals to assess hidden delinquency among high school students.

National Youth Gang Survey (NYGS) Conducted annually since 1995, purpose of survey is to identify and describe critical gang components and characteristics.

Needs assessment *See* **Risk/needs assessment instruments.**

Net-widening Pulling juveniles into juvenile justice system who would not otherwise be involved in delinquent activity; applies to many status offenders (also known as "widening the net").

Neutralization theory Explanation holds that delinquents experience guilt when involved in delinquent activities and that they respect leaders of the legitimate social order; their delinquency is episodic rather than chronic, and they adhere to conventional values while "drifting" into periods of illegal behavior; in order to drift, the delinquent must first neutralize legal and moral values.

New York House of Refuge Established in New York City in 1825 by the Society for the Prevention of Pauperism; school managed largely status offenders; compulsory education provided; strict prison-like regimen was considered detrimental to youthful clientele.

No bill, no true bill Decision issued by grand jury indicating no basis exists for charges against defendant; charges are usually dropped or dismissed later by judge.

Nolle prosequi Decision by prosecution to decline to pursue criminal case against defendant.

Nominal dispositions Adjudicatory disposition resulting in lenient penalties such as warnings and/or probation.

Noninterventionist model Philosophy of juvenile delinquent treatment meaning the absence of any direct intervention with certain juveniles who have been taken into custody.

Nonsecure custody, nonsecure confinement Custodial disposition where a juvenile is placed in a group home, foster care, or other arrangement where he or she is permitted to leave with permission of parents, guardians, or supervisors.

Numbers-game model Caseload assignment model for probation or parole officers where total number of offender/clients is divided by number of officers.

Office of Juvenile Justice and Delinquency Prevention (OJJDP) Agency established by Congress under the Juvenile Justice and Delinquency Prevention Act of 1974; designed to remove status offenders from jurisdiction of juvenile courts and dispose of their cases less formally.

Ohio Experience Program for juvenile delinquents in various Ohio counties where home confinement, electronic monitoring and other forms of intensive supervised probation are used; emphasis is on public safety, offender accountability, and offender rehabilitation.

Once an adult/always an adult provision Ruling that once a juvenile has been transferred to criminal court to be prosecuted as an adult, regardless of the criminal court outcome, the juvenile can never be subject to the jurisdiction of juvenile courts in the future; in short, the juvenile, once transferred, will always be treated as an adult if future crimes are committed, even though the youth is still not of adult age.

Orange County Peer Court Established in Orange County, California, teen court consists of high school students who volunteer for different court positions, including prosecutors, defense counsel, and jurors; intent is to vest youths with responsibility and accountability in deciding whether other youths charged with delinquency or status offenses are guilty or innocent through jury process; judge presides, together with community volunteers.

Overrides Actions by an authority in an institution or agency that overrules a score or assessment made of a client or inmate; raw scores, assessments, or recommendations can be overruled; function of override is to upgrade seriousness of offense status or downgrade seriousness of offense status, thus changing the level of custody at which one is maintained in secure confinement; may also affect the type and nature of community programming for particular offenders.

Parens patriae Literally "parent of the country" and refers to doctrine where state oversees the welfare of youth; originally established by the King of England and administered through chancellors.

Parole Status of offenders conditionally released from a confinement facility prior to expiration of their sentences, placed under supervision of a parole agency.

Parole board Committee of persons who determine whether or not prisoners should be released prior to serving their full terms prescribed by original sentences in court.

Parolees Offender who has served some time in jail or prison, but has been released prior to serving entire sentence imposed upon conviction.

Parole revocation Two-stage proceeding that may result of a parolee's reincarceration in jail or prison; first stage is a preliminary hearing to determine whether parolee violated any specific parole condition; second stage is to determine whether parole should be cancelled and the offender reincarcerated.

Parole revocation hearing Formal proceeding where a parole board decides whether a parolee's parole program should be terminated or changed because of one or more program infractions.

PATHS Program Promoting Alternative THinking Strategies program; aimed to promote emotional and social competencies and to reduce aggression and related emotional and behavioral problems among elementary school children.

Pathways Developmental sequences over the course of one's adolescence that are associated with serious, chronic, and violent offenders.

Perry Preschool Program Provides high-level early childhood education to disadvantaged children in order to improve their later school life and performance.

Petitions Official documents filed in juvenile courts on juvenile's behalf, specifying reasons for the youth's court appearance; document asserts that juveniles fall within the categories of dependent or neglected, status offender, or delinquent, and the reasons for such assertions are usually provided.

Petit juries Traditional jury that hears evidence of crime in jury trial and decides a defendant's guilt or innocence.

Philadelphia Society for Alleviating the Miseries of Public Prisons Philanthropic society established by the Quakers in Pennsylvania in 1787; attempted to establish prison reforms to improve living conditions of inmates; brought food, clothing, and religious instruction to inmates.

PINS Diversion Program New York program established in 1987 to divert youths in need of supervision to out-of-home placements, such as foster care.

Pittsburgh Youth Study (PYS) Longitudinal investigation of 1,517 inner-city boys between 1986 and 1996; studied factors involved in what caused delinquency among some youths and why others did not become delinquent.

Placed Judicial disposition where juvenile is disposed to a group or foster home, or other type of out-of-home care; also includes secure confinement in an industrial school or comparable facility.

Placement One of several optional dispositions available to juvenile court judges following formal or informal proceedings against juveniles where either delinquent or status offenses have been alleged; adjudication proceedings yield a court decision about whether facts alleged in petition are true; if so, a disposition is imposed, which may be placement in a foster or group home, wilderness experience, camp, ranch, or secure institution.

Plea bargains, plea bargaining Preconviction agreement between the defendant and the state whereby the defendant pleads guilty with the expectation of either a reduction in the charges, a promise of sentencing leniency, or some other government concession short of the maximum penalties that could be imposed under the law.

Police discretion Range of behavioral choices available to police officers within the limits of their power.

Poor Laws Regulations in English Middle Ages designed to punish debtors by imprisoning them until they could pay their debts; imprisonment was for life, or until someone could pay the debtor's debts for them.

Positive school of criminology School of criminological thought emphasizing analysis of criminal behaviors through empirical indicators such as physical features compared with biochemical explanations. Postulates that human behavior is a product of social, biological, psychological, or economic forces. Also known as "Italian School."

Positivism Branch of social science that uses the scientific method of the natural sciences and that suggests that human behavior is a product of social, biological, psychological, or economic factors.

Prediction Assessment of some expected future behavior of a person, including criminal acts, arrests, or convictions.

Predictors of dangerousness and risk Assessment devices that attempt to forecast one's potential for violence or risk to others; any factors that are used in such instruments.

Predisposition reports Documents prepared by a juvenile intake officer for a juvenile judge; purpose of report is to furnish the judge with background about juveniles to make a more informed sentencing decision; similar to PSI report.

Preliminary hearing, preliminary examination Proceeding where both prosecutor and defense counsel present some evidence against and on behalf of defendants; proceeding to determine whether probable cause exists to believe that a crime was committed and that the particular defendant committed the crime.

Preponderance of the evidence Standard used in civil courts to determine defendant or plaintiff liability.

Presentence investigation reports (PSI) Inquiry conducted about a convicted defendant at the request of the judge; purpose of inquiry is to determine worthiness of defendant for parole or sentencing leniency.

Presentments Charge brought against a defendant by grand jury acting on its own authority.

Presumptive waiver Requirement that shifts the burden to the juvenile for defending against their transfer to criminal court by showing that they are capable of being rehabilitated; following automatic or legislative waiver, juveniles can challenge the waiver in a hearing where they must demonstrate to the court's satisfaction their capability of becoming reformed.

Pretrial detention Holding delinquent or criminal suspects in incarcerative facilities pending their forthcoming adjudicatory hearing or trial.

Prevention/control model Attempts to repress or prevent delinquency by using early intervention strategies, including wilderness programs and elementary school interventions.

Preventive detention Constitutional right of police to detain suspects prior to trial without bail, where suspects are likely to flee from the jurisdiction or pose serious risks to others.

Primary deviation Part of labeling process whenever youths engage in occasional pranks and not especially serious violations of the law.

Prisons Incarcerative facilities designed to house long-term serious offenders; operated by state or federal government; houses inmates for terms longer than one year.

Privatization Trend in prison and jail management and correctional operations generally where private interests are becoming increasingly involved in the management and operations of correctional institutions.

Proactive units Police officer youth squads assigned special duties of aggressively patrolling high-delinquency areas in an effort to deter gangs from operating.

Probable cause Reasonable belief that a crime has been committed and that person accused of crime committed it.

Probation Sentence not involving confinement that imposes conditions and retains authority in sentencing court to modify conditions of sentence or resentence offender for probation violations.

Probation revocation hearing Proceeding wherein it is determined whether to revoke a probationer's probation program because of one or more violations.

Project New Pride One of the most popular probation programs established in Denver, Colorado, in 1973; a blend of education, counseling, employment, and cultural education directed at those more serious offenders between the ages of 14 and 17; juveniles eligible for the New Pride program must have at least two prior convictions for serious misdemeanors and/or felonies; goals include (1) reintegrating participants into their communities through school participation or employment, and (2) reducing recidivism rates among offenders.

Project Outward Bound *See* **Wilderness experiments.**

Propositions Statements about the real world that lack the high degree of certainty associated with assumptions; examples of propositions are, "Burnout among probation officers may be mitigated or lessened through job enlargement and giving officers greater input in organizational decision making" or "Two-officer patrol units are less susceptible to misconduct and corruption than one-officer patrol units."

Prosecution and the courts Organizations that pursue cases against criminal suspects and determine whether they are guilty or innocent of crimes alleged.

Prosecutors Court officials who commence civil and criminal proceedings against defendants. Prosecuting defendants represent state or government interest.

Psychoanalytic theory Sigmund Freud's theory of personality formation through the id, ego, and superego at various stages of childhood. Maintains that early life experiences influence adult behavior.

Psychological theories Explanations linking criminal behavior with mental states or conditions, antisocial personality traits, and early psychological moral development.

Radical nonintervention Similar to a "do nothing" policy of delinquency nonintervention.

Reactive units Police youth squad units that respond to calls for service whenever gangs are terrorizing neighborhoods.

Reality therapy model Equivalent of shock probation, where short incarcerative sentences are believed to provide "shock" value for juvenile offenders and scare them from reoffending behaviors.

Rebellion Mode of adaptation suggested by Robert K. Merton where persons reject institutional means to achieve culturally approved goals and created their own goals and means to use and seek.

Recidivism New crime committed by an offender who has served time or was placed on probation for previous offense; tendency to repeat crimes.

Recidivism rate Proportion of offenders who, when released from probation or parole, commit further crimes.

Recidivists Offenders who have committed previous offenses.

Reeve Chief law enforcement officer of English counties, known as **shires.**

Referrals Any citation of a juvenile to juvenile court by a law enforcement officer, interested citizen, family member, or school official; usually based on law violations, delinquency, or unruly conduct.

Reform schools Different types of vocational institutions designed to both punish and rehabilitate youthful offenders; operated much like prisons as total institutions.

Regimented Inmate Discipline Program (RID) Oklahoma Department of Corrections program operated in Lexington, Oklahoma, for juveniles; program stresses military-type discipline and accountability; facilities are secure and privately operated.

Rehabilitation model Concept of youth management similar to medical model, where juvenile delinquents are believed to be suffering from social and psychological handicaps; provides experiences to build self-concept; experiences stress educational and social remedies.

Relabeling Redefinition of juvenile behaviors as more or less serious than previously defined; an example would be police officers who relabel or redefine certain juvenile behaviors, such as curfew violation, as loitering for purposes of committing a felony, such as burglary or robbery; relabeling is associated with political jurisdictions that have deinstitutionalized status offenders or have divested juvenile courts of their authority over specific types of juvenile offenders; as one result, police officers lose power, or their discretionary authority, to warn such juveniles or take them into custody; new laws may mandate removing such juveniles to community social services rather than to jails; in retaliation, some officers may relabel status behaviors as criminal ones, in order to preserve their discretionary authority over juveniles.

Released on own recognizance (ROR) Arrangement where a defendant is able to be set free temporarily to await a later trial without having to post a bail bond; persons released on ROR are usually well known or have strong ties to the community and have not been charged with serious crimes.

Repeat offender Any juvenile or adult with a prior record of delinquency or criminality.

Restitution Stipulation by court that offenders must compensate victims for their financial losses resulting from crime; compensation for psychological, physical, or financial loss by victim; may be imposed as a part of an incarcerative sentence.

Restorative justice Mediation between victims and offenders whereby offenders accept responsibility for their actions and agree to reimburse victims for their losses; may involve community service and other penalties agreeable to both parties in a form of arbitration with a neutral third party acting as arbiter.

Restorative policing Police-based family group conferencing uses police, victims, youths, and their families to discuss the harm caused by the youth and creates an agreement to repair the harm; similar to restorative justice.

Retreatism Mode of adaptation suggested by Robert K. Merton where persons reject culturally approved goals and institutionalized means and do little or nothing to achieve; homeless persons, bag ladies, vagrants, and others sometimes fit the retreatist profile.

Reverse waiver Motion to transfer juvenile's case from criminal court to juvenile court following a legislative or automatic waiver action.

Reverse waiver hearings, reverse waiver actions Formal proceedings to contest automatic transfer of juveniles to jurisdiction of criminal courts; used in jurisdictions with automatic transfer laws.

Risk Potential likelihood for someone to engage in further delinquency or criminality.

Risk/needs assessment instruments Predictive device intended to forecast offender propensity to commit new offenses or recidivate.

Ritualism Mode of adaptation suggested by Robert K. Merton where persons reject culturally approved goals but work toward lesser goals through institutionalized means.

Runaways Juveniles who leaves their homes for long-term periods without parental consent or supervision; unruly youths who cannot be controlled or managed by parents or guardians.

San Francisco Project Compared recidivism rates of probationers supervised by POs with caseloads of 20 and 40, respectively, and found no significant differences in recidivism rates of probationers were reported between "intensive" and "ideal" caseload scenarios.

Scared Straight Juvenile delinquency prevention program that sought to frighten samples of hardcore delinquent youths by having them confront inmates in a Rahway,

New Jersey, prison; inmates would yell at and belittle them, calling them names, cursing, and yelling; inmates would tell them about sexual assaults and other prison unpleasantries in an attempt to get them to refrain from reoffending.

Scavenger gangs Groups formed primarily as a means of socializing and for mutual protection.

Screening Procedure used by prosecutor to define which cases have prosecutive merit and which ones do not; some screening bureaus are made up of police and lawyers with trial experience.

Sealing records of juveniles *See* **Expungement orders.**

Second Chance Program Probation program operated in Iowa in early 1990s to provide delinquent youths with opportunities to acquire skills, vocational and educational training, pre-employment training, and job placement services.

Secondary deviation Part of labeling theory that suggests that violations of the law become a part of one's normal behavior rather than just occasional pranks.

Secure custody, secure confinement Incarceration of juvenile offender in a facility that restricts movement in community; similar to adult penal facility involving total incarceration.

See Our Side (SOS) Program Juvenile aversion program in Prince George's County, Maryland, designed to prevent delinquency.

Selective incapacitation Incarcerating individuals who show a high likelihood of repeating their previous offenses; based on forecasts of potential for recidivism; includes but not limited to dangerousness.

Self-reports, self-report information Surveys of youths (or adults) based on disclosures these persons might make about the types of offenses they have committed and how frequently they have committed them; considered more accurate than official estimates.

Sentencing hearing Formal proceeding where convicted offender receives a punishment by the court.

Sexual Offender Treatment Program (SOT) Treatment program for juvenile offenders adjudicated delinquent on sex charges; includes psychosocialeducational interventions, therapies, and counseling.

Shires Early English counties.

Shock incarceration *See* **Shock probation.**

Shock parole *See* **Shock probation.**

Shock probation Intermediate punishment where offenders are initially sentenced to terms of secure detention; after a period of time, between 90 and 180 days, youths are removed from detention and sentenced to serve the remainder of their sentences on probation; the term was coined by Ohio authorities in 1964.

Short-term confinement Placement in any incarcerative institution for either adults or juveniles where the period of confinement is less than one year; jails are considered short-term facilities.

Situationally based discretion Confronting crime in the streets on the basis of immediate situational factors, time of night, presence of weapons, numbers of offenders; requires extensive personal judgments by police officers.

Smart sentencing *See* **Creative sentencing.**

Social control theory Explanation of criminal behavior that focuses on control mechanisms, techniques, and strategies for regulating human behavior, leading to conformity or obedience to society's rules, and that posits that deviance results when social controls are weakened or break down so that individuals are not motivated to conform to them.

Social learning theory Applied to criminal behavior, theory stressing importance of learning through modeling others who are criminal; criminal behavior is a function of copying or learning criminal conduct from others.

Society for the Prevention of Pauperism Philanthropic society that established first public reformatory in New York in 1825, the New York House of Refuge.

Sociobiology Scientific study of causal relation between genetic structure and social behavior.

Socioeconomic status (SES) Station or level of economic attainment one enjoys through work; acquisition of wealth; the divisions between various levels of society according to material goods acquired.

Sociological theories Explanations of criminal conduct that emphasize social conditions that bear upon the individual as the causes of criminal behavior.

Solitary confinement Segregation of prisoners into individual cells; originally used at the Walnut Street Jail in Philadelphia in 1790.

Sourcebook of Criminal Justice Statistics Compendium of statistical information about juvenile and adult offenders, court facts, statistics, and trends, probation and parole figures, and considerable additional information; published annually by the Hindelang Criminal Justice Research Center at the University of Albany, SUNY; funded by a grant from the U.S. Department of Justice, Bureau of Justice Statistics.

SpeakerID Program Electronic voice verification system used as a part of electronic monitoring to verify the identity of the person called by the probation or parole agency.

Special conditions of probation Extra requirements written into a standard probation agreement, including possible vocational or educational training, counseling, drug or alcohol treatment, attendance at meetings, restitution, and community service.

Specialized caseloads model Case assignment method based on POs' unique skills and knowledge relative to offender drug or alcohol problems; some POs are assigned particular clients with unique problems that require more than average PO expertise.

Split sentences *See* **Combination sentences.**

Standard of proof Norms used by courts to determine validity of claims or allegations of wrongdoing against offenders; civil standards of proof are "clear and convincing evidence" and "preponderance of evidence," while criminal standard is "beyond a reasonable doubt."

Standard probation Probationers conform to all terms of their probation program, but their contact with probation officers is minimal; often, their contact is by telephone or letter once or twice a month.

Stationhouse adjustments Decisions made by police officers about certain juveniles taken into custody and brought to police stations for processing and investigation; adjustments often result in verbal reprimands and release to custody of parents.

Status offenders Anyone committing a status offense, including runaway behavior, truancy, curfew violation, or loitering.

Status offenses Violation of statute or ordinance by minor, which, if committed by an adult, would not be considered either a felony or a misdemeanor; also any acts committed by juveniles that would (1) bring them to the attention of juvenile courts and (2) not be crimes if committed by adults.

Statute of limitations Maximum time period within which a prosecution can be brought against a defendant for a particular offense; many criminal statutes have 3- or 6-year statute of limitations periods; there is no statute of limitations on homicide charges.

Statutory exclusion Provisions that automatically exclude certain juveniles and offenses from the jurisdiction of the juvenile courts, for example, murder, aggravated rape, armed robbery.

Stigmas, stigmatize, stigmatization Social process whereby offenders acquire undesirable characteristics as the result of imprisonment or court appearances; undesirable criminal or delinquent labels are assigned those who are processed through the criminal and juvenile justice systems.

Stop Assaultive Children (SAC) Program Activity started in Phoenix, Arizona, in late 1980s and designed for those youths who have committed serious family violence; children are detained in a juvenile facility for a short time, and their release is contingent upon being law-abiding, observing curfew, and other conditions; their prosecution is deferred; must participate in counseling; may include volunteer work.

Strain theory A criminological theory positing that a gap between culturally approved goals and legitimate means of achieving them causes frustration, which leads to criminal behavior.

Strategic leniency Less harsh dispositions meted out to certain offenders believed to be nonviolent and least likely to reoffend.

Street outreach model Youth Service Bureau model establishing neighborhood centers for youths who are delinquency-prone, where youths can have things to do other than hang out on the streets.

Subculture of delinquency A culture within a culture where the use of violence in certain social situations is commonplace and normative; Marvin Wolfgang and Franco Ferracuti devised this concept to depict a set of norms apart from mainstream conventional society, in which the theme of violence is pervasive and dominant. Learned through socialization with others as an alternative lifestyle.

Superego Sigmund Freud's label for the part of personality concerned with moral values.

Sustained petitions Adjudication resulting in a finding that the facts alleged in a petition are true; a finding that the juvenile committed the offenses alleged, which resulted in an adjudication and disposition.

Sweat shops Exploitative businesses and industries that employed child labor and demanded long work hours for low pay.

Systems modification model Youth Service Bureau model involving the establishment of community-based facilities for delinquency-prone youths; associations of churches, schools, and neighborhood businesses organizing to assist youths.

Tagging Being equipped with an electronic wristlet or anklet for the purpose of monitoring one's whereabouts.

Taken into custody For juveniles, not technically an arrest; law enforcement officers may pick up juvenile hitchhikers or runaways and take them into custody, meaning that the juveniles are taken to a care facility where their parents or legal guardians can be located.

Teen courts Tribunals consisting of teenagers who judge other teenagers charged with minor offenses; much like regular juries in criminal courts, where juvenile prosecutors and defense counsel argue cases against specific juvenile offenders; juries decide punishment with judicial approval.

Territorial gangs Groups of youths organized to defend a fixed amount of territory, such as several city blocks.

Theory A set of propositions from which a large number of new observations can be deduced. An integrated body of definitions, assumptions, and propositions related in such a way to explain and predict relations between two or more variables.

Totality of circumstances Sometimes used as the standard whereby offender guilt is determined or where search-and-seizure warrants may be obtained; officers consider an entire set of circumstances surrounding an apparently illegal event and act accordingly.

Traditional model Juvenile court proceedings characterized by less formal adjudications and greater use of detention.

Transfer hearings Proceeding to determine whether juveniles should be certified as adults for purposes of being subjected to jurisdiction of adult criminal courts where more severe penalties may be imposed.

Transfers Proceedings where juveniles are remanded to the jurisdiction of criminal courts; also known as certifications and waivers.

Transportation Early British practice of sending undesirables, misfits, and convicted offenders to remote territories and islands controlled by England.

Treatment model *See* **Medical model.**

Truants Juveniles who are habitually absent from school without excuse.

True bills Indictments or charges against defendants brought by grand juries after considering inculpatory evidence presented by a prosecutor.

Unconditional probation, unconditional standard probation Form of conditional release without special restrictions or requirements placed on offender's behavior other than standard probation agreement terms; no formal controls operate to control or monitor divertee's behavior.

Uniform Crime Reports (UCR) Official source of crime information published by Federal Bureau of Investigation annually; accepts information from reporting law enforcement agencies about criminal arrests; classifies crimes according to various index criteria; tabulates information about offender age, gender, race, and other attributes.

Victim compensation Financial restitution payable to victims by either the state or convicted offenders.

Victim-impact statement Appendage to a predisposition report or presentence investigation report that addresses the effect of the defendant's actions against victims or anyone harmed by the crime or delinquent act; usually compiled by the victim.

Victim–offender mediation Third-party intervention mechanism whereby perpetrator and victim work out a civil solution to an otherwise criminal or delinquent action.

Victimization Basic measure of the occurrence of a crime. A specific criminal act affecting a specific victim.

Violent Juvenile Offender Programs (VJOP) Procedures designed to provide positive interventions and treatments; reintegrative programs, including transitional residential programs for those youths who have been subject to long-term detention; provides for social networking, provision of educational opportunities for youths, social learning, and goal-oriented behavioral skills.

VisionQuest Carefully regulated, intensive supervision program designed to improve the social and psychological experiences of juveniles; reintegrative program to improve one's educational and social skills; wilderness program.

Waiver *See* **Transfer.**

Waiver hearing Request by prosecutor to transfer juvenile charged with various offenses to a criminal or adult court for prosecution; waiver motions make it possible to sustain adult criminal penalties.

Waiver motion Formal request by prosecutor to send juvenile's case from juvenile court to criminal court.

Walnut Street Jail Reconstructed from earlier Philadelphia Jail in 1790; first real attempt by jail officials to classify and segregate prisoners according to age, gender, and crime seriousness; introduced idea of solitary confinement.

Wilderness experiments Experience programs that include a wide array of outdoor programs designed to improve a juvenile's self-worth, self-concept, pride, and trust in others.

With prejudice To dismiss charges, but those same charges cannot be brought again later against the same defendant.

Without prejudice To dismiss charges, but those same charges can be brought again later against the same defendant.

Workhouses Early penal facilities designed to use prison labor for profit by private interests; operated in shires in the mid-sixteenth century and later.

XYY theory Explanation of criminal behavior suggesting that some criminals are born with extra Y chromosome, characterized as the "aggressive" chromosome compared with the passive X chromosome; extra Y chromosome produces greater agitation, greater aggressiveness, and criminal propensities.

Youth Service Bureaus (YSBs) Various types of diversion programs operated in the United States for delinquency-prone youth.

Youth Services/Diversion (YS/D) Program Established in Orange County, California, with the goals of reducing family dysfunction and teaching youth responsibility; instilling self-esteem and self-confidence through family counseling sessions.

Youth squads Teams of police officers in police departments whose responsibility is to focus on particular delinquency problems and resolve them.

Youth-to-Victim Restitution Project Program operated by the juvenile court in Lincoln, Nebraska, based on the principle that youths must repay whatever damages they inflicted on victims; enforcement of restitution orders decreased recidivism among delinquent offenders.

Zone of transition An area nearest the center of a city undergoing rapid social change; believed to contain high rates of crime and delinquency.

Bibliography

AARONS, N.M., M.B. POWELL, AND J. BROWNE (2004). "Police Perceptions of Interviews Involving Children with Intellectual Disabilities: A Qualitative Inquiry." *Policing and Society: An International Journal of Research and Policy* **14**:269–278.

ABATIELLO, JENNIFER D. (2005). "Juvenile Competency and Culpability: What the Public Deserves." Unpublished paper presented at the annual meeting of the Academy of Criminal Justice Sciences, Chicago (March).

ABRAMSON, ALANA MARIE (2003). "Sustainable Relationships and Competing Values: Restorative Justice Initiatives and the Police: A Case Study." *Police Practice and Research* **4**:391–398.

ADAMS, MIKE S., JAMES D. JOHNSON, AND T. DAVID EVANS (1998). "Racial Differences in Informal Labeling Effects." *Deviant Behavior* **19**:157–171.

ADMINISTRATIVE OFFICE OF THE U.S. COURTS (2001). *The U.S. Probation and Pretrial Services System.* Washington, DC: Administrative Office of the U.S. Courts.

AGNEW, ROBERT (2002). "Experienced, Vicarious, and Anticipated Strain: An Exploratory Study on Physical Victimization and Delinquency." *Justice Quarterly* **19**:603–632.

ALEXANDER, RUDOLPH JR. (2000). *Counseling, Treatment, and Intervention Methods with Juvenile and Adult Offenders.* Belmont, CA: Thomson Learning.

ALFORD, SUSAN (1998). "The Effectiveness of Juvenile Arbitration in South Carolina: Professionals Need Not Apply." *APPA Perspectives* **22**:28–34.

ALOISI, MICHAEL AND JENNIFER LeBAROON (2001). *The Juvenile Justice Commission's Stabilization and Reintegration Program: An Updated Recidivism Analysis.* Trenton: Juvenile Justice Commission Research and Evaluation Unit, New Jersey Department of Law and Public Safety.

ALTSCHULER, DAVID M. AND TROY L. ARMSTRONG (2001). "Reintegrating High-Risk Juvenile Offenders into Communities: Experiences and Prospects." *Corrections Management Quarterly* **5**:72–88.

AMERICAN BAR ASSOCIATION (2001). *Justice by Gender: The Lack of Appropriate Prevention, Diversion, and Treatment Alternatives for Girls in the Justice System.* Washington, DC: American Bar Association/National Bar Association.

AMERICAN CORRECTIONAL ASSOCIATION (2005). *2005 Directory.* College Park, MD: American Correctional Association.

American Jails (1998). "Tennessee: A New Sheriff's Office Program Gives Children a Look Inside Jail." *American Jails* **12**:98.

ANCHORAGE YOUTH COURT (2005). "Youth Courts Strive for Sustainability." *Gavel* **16**:1–4.

APPA Perspectives (2004a). "APPA Resolves Support for Youth Courts." *APPA Perspectives* **28**:8.

APPA Perspectives (2004b). "Project Safe Neighborhoods: Incorporating and Training Probation and Parole Professionals to Reduce Gun Crime." *APPA Perspectives* **28**:9.

ANDERSON, C.A. ET AL. (2003). "The Influence of Media Violence on Youth." *Psychological Science in the Public Interest* **4**:81–110.

ANDERSON, JAMES F. AND LARONISTINE DYSON (2001). *Legal Rights of Prisoners: Cases and Comments.* Lanham, MD: University Press of America.

ARCHWAMETY, TEARA AND ANTONIS KATSIYANNIS (2000). "Academic Remediation, Parole Violations, and Recidivism Rates among Delinquent Youths." *Remedial and Special Education* **21**:161–170.

ARMSTRONG, GAYLENE STYVE (2001). *Private vs. Public Operation of Juvenile Correctional Facilities.* New York: LFB Scholarly Publishing.

ARMSTRONG, TROY L. (1988). "National Survey of Juvenile Intensive Probation Supervision." *Criminal Justice Abstracts* **20**:342–348.

ARMSTRONG, TROY L. (1991). *Intensive Interventions with High-Risk Youths: Promising Approaches in Juvenile Probation and Parole.* Monsey, NY: Criminal Justice Press.

ARTHUR, LINDSAY G. (2000). "Punishment Doesn't Work!" *Juvenile and Family Court Journal* **51**:37–42.

ARTHUR, R. (2004). "Young Offenders: Children in Need of Protection." *Law and Policy* **36**.

ASHFORD, JOSE B. AND CRAIG WINSTON LeCROY (1988). "Decision-Making for Juvenile Offenders in Aftercare." *Juvenile and Family Court Journal* **39**:45–58.

ASHFORD, JOSE B. AND CRAIG WINSTON LeCROY (1993). "Juvenile Parole Policy in the United States: Determinate Versus Indeterminate Models." *Justice Quarterly* **10**:179–195.

ASSOCIATED PRESS (1997). "Girl Found Guilty in Toddler's Death." February 18, 1997.

ASSOCIATED PRESS (2001). "Arkansas Gets Tough on Violent Youths." March 5, 2001.

AUERHAHN, KATHLEEN (2003). *Selective Incapacitation and Public Policy: Evaluating California's Imprisonment Crisis.* Albany: State University of New York Press.

AUERHAHN, KATHLEEN (2004). "California's Incarcerated Drug Offender Population, Yesterday, Today, and Tomorrow: Evaluating the War on Drugs and Proposition 36." *Journal of Drug Issues* **34**:95–120.

AUSTIN, ANDREW (2003). "Does Forced Sexual Contact Have Criminogenic Effects? An Empirical Test of Derailment Theory." *Journal of Aggression, Maltreatment, and Trauma* **8**:41–66.

AUSTIN, JAMES, MICHAEL JONES, AND MELISSA BOLYARD (1993). *The Growing Use of Jail Boot Camps.* Washington, DC: U.S. Department of Justice, Office of Justice Programs.

AYERS, WILLIAM (1997). *A Kind and Just Parent: The Children of Juvenile Court.* Boston: Beacon Press.

AYERS-SCHLOSSER, LEE (2005). "2004 Juvenile Justice Summit: The Oregon Update." Unpublished paper presented at the annual meeting of the Academy of Criminal Justice Sciences, Chicago (March).

BABB, SUSAN AND PETER C. KRATCOSKI (1994). "The Juvenile Justice Assistants Program." *Juvenile and Family Court Journal* **45**:43–499.

BACHMAN, RONET AND ROBERT PERALTA (2001). "The Relationship Between Drinking and Violence in an Adolescent Population: Does Gender Matter?" *Deviant Behavior: An Interdisciplinary Journal* **23**:1–19.

BAIRD, S. CHRISTOPHER (1985). "Classifying Juveniles: Making the Most of an Important Management Tool." *Corrections Today* **47**:32–38.

BAKER, AMY J. L., MEL SCHNEIDERMAN, AND ROB PARKER (2001). "A Survey of Problematic Sexualized Behaviors of Children in the New York City Child Welfare System." *Journal of Child Sexual Abuse* **10**:67–80.

BAKER, MYRIAM L., JANE NADY SIGMON, AND M. ELAINE NUGENT (2001). *Truancy Reduction: Keeping Students in School.* Washington, DC: Office of Juvenile Justice and Delinquency Prevention.

BALLIF-SPANVIL, B. ET AL. (2004). "Individual Differences in the Use of Violent and Peaceful Behavior in Peer Conflicts among Children Who Have and Have Not Witnessed Interparental Violence." *Journal of Emotional Abuse* **4**:101–123.

BANKS, STEVEN ET AL. (2004) "A Multiple-Models Approach to Violence Risk Assessment among People with Mental Disorder."*Criminal Justice and Behavior* **31**:324–340.

BARNES, ALLAN R. (2005). "Weed and Seed Initiative: An Evaluation Using a Pre/Post Community Survey Approach." Unpublished paper presented at the annual meeting of the Academy of Criminal Justice Sciences, Chicago (March).

BATES, ANDREW ET AL. (2004). "A Follow-Up Study of Sex Offenders Treated by Thams Valley Sex Offender Groupwork Program."*Journal of Sexual Aggression* **10**:29–38.

BAZEMORE, GORDON, JEANNE B. STINCHCOMB, AND LESLIE A. LEIP (2004). "Scared Smart or Bored Straight? Testing Deterrence Logic in an Evaluation of Police-Led Truancy Intervention." *Justice Quarterly* **21**:269–299.

BEDAU, HUGO ADAM (1992). *The Case Against the Death Penalty.* Washington, DC: American Civil Liberties Union, Capital Punishment Project.

BELBOT, BARBARA ET AL. (2004). "Legal Issues in Corrections." *Prison Journal* **84**:287–410.

BELL, CARL C. (2002). "Violence Prevention 101: Implications for Policy Development." In *Perspectives on Crime and Justice: 2000–2001 Lecture Series,* Alfred Blumstein, Laurence Steinberg, Carl C. Bell, and Margaret A. Berger (eds.). Washington, DC: National Institute of Justice.

BENDA, BRENT B. (1999). "A Study of Recidivism of Serious and Persistent Offenders Among Adolescents."*Journal of Criminal Justice* **27**:111–126.

BENDA, BRENT B., ROBERT FLYNN CORWYN, AND NANCY J. TOOMBS (2001). "From Adolescent 'Serious Offender' to Adult Felon: A Predictive Study of Offense Progression." *Journal of Offender Rehabilitation* **32**:79–108.

BERENSON, DAVID AND LEE UNDERWOOD (2001). *Juvenile Sex Offender Programming: A Resource Guide.* Washington, DC: U.S. Office of Juvenile Justice and Delinquency Prevention.

BERNAT, FRANCES P. (2005). "Evaluating Schools at Hope: Alternative Paradigm to Kids at Risk." Unpublished paper presented at the annual meeting of the Academy of Criminal Justice Sciences, Chicago (March).

BERRUETA-CLEMENT, JOHN R. ET AL. (1984). "Preschool's Effects on Social Responsibility." In *Changed Lives: The Effects of the Perry Preschool Program on Youths through Age 19,* John R. Berruta-Clement et al. (eds.). Ypsilanti, MI: High/Scope Press.

BEYER, MARTY, THOMAS GRISSO, AND MALCOLM YOUNG (1997). *More Than Meets the Eye: Rethinking Assessment, Competency, and Sentencing for a Harsher Era of Juvenile Justice.* Washington, DC: American Bar Association Juvenile Justice Center.

BILCHIK, SHAY (1996). *State Responses to Serious and Violent Juvenile Crime.* Pittsburgh, PA: National Center for Juvenile Justice.

BILCHIK, SHAY (1998). *Mental Health Disorders and Substance Abuse Problems Among Juveniles.* Washington, DC: U.S. Department of Justice.

BISHOP, DONNA M. AND CHARLES E. FRAZIER (1996). "Race Effects in Juvenile Justice Decision Making: Findings of a Statewide Analysis." *Journal of Criminal Law and Criminology* **86**:392–414.

BITTLE, STEVEN (2001). *Print Media Treatment of Hate Crime as an Aggravating Circumstance for Sentencing: A Case Study.* Unpublished paper.

BLACK, HENRY CAMPBELL (1990). *Black's Law Dictionary.* St. Paul, MN: West Publishing.

BLACK, MEGHAN C. (2001). *Juvenile Delinquency Probation Caseload, 1989–1998.* Washington, DC: U.S. Department of Justice.

BLEVINS, KRISTIE R. (2005). "The Correctional Orientation of 'Child Savers': The Level, Sources, and Impact of Support for Juvenile Correctional Workers." Unpublished paper presented at the annual meeting of the Academy of Criminal Justice Sciences, Chicago (March).

BLOOM, BARBARA ET AL. (2002). "Moving Toward Justice for Female Juvenile Offenders in the New Millennium: Modeling Gender-Specific Policies and Programs." *Journal of Contemporary Criminal Justice* **37**:37–56.

BOHM, ROBERT M. AND BRENDA L. VOGEL (2004). "More Than Ten Years Later: The Long-Term Stability of Informed Death Penalty Opinions." *Journal of Criminal Justice* **32**:307–327.

BONCZAR, THOMAS P. AND TRACY L. SNELL (2004). *Capital Punishment, 2003.* Washington, DC: U.S. Department of Justice, Bureau of Justice Statistics (November).

BOND-MAUPIN, LISA J., JAMES R. MAUPIN, AND AMY LEISENRING (2002). "Girls' Delinquency and the Justice Implications of Intake Workers' Perspectives." *Women and Criminal Justice* **13**:51–77.

BOONE, HARRY N. JR. (1996). "Electronic Home Confinement: Judicial and Legislative Perspectives." *APPA Perspectives* **20**:18–25.

BOOTS, DENISE PAQUETTE, KATHLEEN M. HEIDE, AND JOHN K. COCHRAN (2004). "Death Penalty Support for Special Offender Populations of Legally Convicted Murderers: Juveniles, the Mentally Retarded, and the Mentally Incompetent." *Behavioral Sciences and the Law* **22**:223–238.

BOTTCHER, JEAN AND TERESA ISORENA (1994). *LEAD: A Boot Camp and Intensive Parole Program: An Implementation and Process Evaluation of the First Year.* Sacramento: Research Division, California Youth Authority.

BOURQUE, BLAIR B., MEL HAN AND SARAH M. HILL (1996). *A National Survey of Aftercare Provisions for Boot Camp Graduates.* Washington, DC: U.S. Department of Justice.

BOWEN, ERICA ET AL. (2002). "Evaluating Probation Based Offender Programs for Domestic Violence Perpetrators: A Pro-Feminist Approach." *Howard Journal of Criminal Justice* **41**:221–236.

BOWERS, DAN M. (2000). "Home Detention Systems." *Corrections Today* **62**:102–106.

BOWERS, KATE J., SHANE D. JOHNSON, AND KEN PEASE (2004). "Prospective Hot-Spotting: The Future of Crime Mapping?" *British Journal of Criminology* **44**:641–658.

BOWMAN, CATHY (2005). "Involvement of Probation and Parole in Project Safe Neighborhoods." New York: Unpublished paper presented at the annual meeting of the American Probation and Parole Association (July).

BOYD, REBECCA J. AND DAVID L. MYERS (2005). "Impact of Risk and Protective Factors for Alcohol Use Among a Rural Youth Sample." Unpublished paper presented at the annual meeting of the Academy of Criminal Justice Sciences, Chicago (March).

BRADLEY, TRACEY (2005). "Holistic Representation: Identifying Success." New York: Unpublished paper presented at the annual training institute of the American Probation and Parole Association (July).

BRAITHWAITE, JOHN (2002). *Restorative Justice and Responsive Regulation.* Oxford, UK: Oxford University Press.

BRANDAU, TIMOTHY J. (1992). *An Alternative to Incarceration for Juvenile Delinquents: The Delaware Bay Marine Institute.* Ann Arbor, MI: University Microfilms International.

BRANDL, STEVEN G. AND DAVID S. BARTOW (EDS.) (2004). *The Police in America: Classic and Contemporary Readings.* Belmont, CA: Wadsworth/Thomson Learning.

BRANK, E.M. AND V. WEISZ (2004). "Paying for the Crimes of Their Children: Public Support of Parental Responsibility." *Journal of Criminal Justice* **32**:465–475.

BRANTINGHAM, PATRICIA L. AND PAUL J. BRANTINGHAM (2004). "Computer Simulation as a Tool for Environmental Criminologists." *Security Journal* **17**:21–30.

BROOKBANKS, WARREN (2002). "Public Policy, Moral Panics, and the Lure of Anticipatory Containment." *Psychiatry, Psychology, and the Law* **9**:127–135.

BROOKS, R.R.W. AND S.H. JEON (2001). "Race, Income, and Perceptions of the U.S. Court System." *Behavioral Sciences and the Law* **19**:249–264.

BROWN, JOE M. (2005). "The Future of Juvenile Justice: Does Determinate Sentencing in Juvenile Court Serve the Same Purpose as Certification to Criminal Court?" Unpublished paper presented at the annual meeting of the Academy of Criminal Justice Sciences, Chicago (March).

BROWN, JUSTIN AND REGINA E. YGNACIO (2002). *Evaluation of the Community Youth Development Program.* Austin, TX: Criminal Justice Policy Council.

BROWNING, KATHARINE AND ROLF LOEBER (1999). *Highlights of Findings from the Pittsburgh Youth Study.* Washington, DC: Office of Juvenile Justice and Delinquency Prevention Programs.

BROWNLIE, E.B. ET AL. (2004). "Early Language Impairment and Young Adult Delinquent and Aggressive Behavior." *Journal of Abnormal Child Psychology* **32**:453–467.

BRYL, JASON ET AL. (2002). "The Recycling of Juvenile Offenders in Selected Texas Counties." Unpublished paper.

BUREAU OF JUSTICE STATISTICS (2005). *Annual Reports.* Washington, DC: U.S. Department of Justice, Bureau of Justice Statistics.

BURGESS, ROBERT AND RONALD AKERS (1966). "Differential Association-Reinforcement Theory of Criminal Behavior." *Social Problems* **14**:128–147.

BURNETT, D.M., C.D. NOBLIN, AND V. PROSSER (2004). "Adjudicative Competency in a Juvenile Population." *Criminal Justice and Behavior* **31**:438–462.

BURRELL, WILLIAM D. (2005). "Leaders for the Future: Two Views of Leadership Development." New York: Unpublished paper presented at the annual meeting of the American Probation and Parole Association (July).

BURRUSS, GEORGE W. JR. AND KIMBERLY KEMPF-LEONARD (2002). "The Questionable Advantage of Defense Counsel in Juvenile Court." *Justice Quarterly* **19**:37–68.

BUTTS, JEFFREY A. (1996a). *Offenders in Juvenile Court, 1994.* Washington, DC: Office of Juvenile Justice and Delinquency Prevention.

BUTTS, JEFFREY A. (1996b). "Speedy Trial in Juvenile Court." *American Journal of Criminal Law* **23**:515–561.

BUTTS, JEFFREY A. AND WILLIAM ADAMS (2001). *Anticipating Space Needs in Juvenile Detention and Correctional Facilities.* Washington, DC: U.S. Department of Justice.

BUTTS, JEFFREY A. AND JANEEN BUCK (2002). *The Sudden Popularity of Teen Courts.* Washington, DC: Urban Institute.

BUTTS, JEFFREY A. AND GREGORY J. HALEMBA (1996). *Waiting for Justice: Moving Young Offenders Through the Juvenile Court Process.* Pittsburgh, PA: National Center for Juvenile Justice.

BUTTS, JEFFREY A. AND JOSEPH B. SANBORN JR. (1999). "Is Juvenile Justice Just Too Slow?" *Judicature* **83**:16–24.

BUTTS, JEFFREY A. AND HOWARD N. SNYDER (1997). *The Youngest Delinquents: Offenders Under Age 15.* Washington, DC: Office of Juvenile Justice and Delinquency Prevention.

BYNUM, TIM (2005). "Evaluating Project Safe Neighborhoods in the Eastern District of Michigan." Unpublished paper presented at the annual meeting of the Academy of Criminal Justice Sciences, Chicago (March).

CADIGAN, TIMOTHY P. (2001). "PACTS." *Federal Probation* **65**:25–30.

CAETI, TORY J., CRAIG HEMMENS, AND VELMER S. BURTON JR. (1996). "Juvenile Right to Counsel: A National Comparison of State Legal Codes." *American Journal of Criminal Law* **23**:611–632.

CAIN, TRAVIS ANN (2002). *JUMP.* Washington, DC: Office of Juvenile Justice and Delinquency Prevention.

CALDAS, STEPHEN J. (1990). "Intensive Incarceration Programs Offer Hope of Rehabilitation to a Fortunate Few: Orleans Parish Prison Does an 'About Face.'" *International Journal of Offender Therapy and Comparative Criminology* **34**:67–76.

CALIFORNIA OFFICE OF CRIMINAL JUSTICE PLANNING (1984). *Governor's Youth Crime Prevention Program.* Sacramento: California Office of Criminal Justice Planning.

CAMPBELL, JUSTIN S. AND CHERISE LEREW (2002). "Juvenile Sex Offenders in Diversion." *Sexual Abuse: A Journal of Research and Treatment* **14**:1–17.

CAMPBELL, JUSTIN S. AND PAUL RETZLAFF (2000). "Juvenile Diversion Interventions: Participant Description and Outcomes." *Journal of Offender Rehabilitation* **32**:57–73.

CAMPBELL, MARY ANN AND FRED SCHMIDT (2000). "Comparison of Mental Health and Legal Factors in the Disposition Outcome of Young Offenders." *Criminal Justice and Behavior* **27**:688–715.

CAMPBELL, TERRENCE W. (2003). "Sex Offenders and Actuarial Risk Assessments: Ethical Considerations." *Behavioral Sciences and the Law* **21**:269–279.

CARLSON, R.G. ET AL. (2004). "Perceived Adverse Consequences Associated with MDMA/Ecstasy Use among Young Polydrug Users in Ohio: Implications for Intervention." *International Journal of Drug Policy* **15**:265–274.

CARMONA, RICHARD H. ET AL. (2004). "The Multisite Violence Prevention Project." *American Journal of Preventive Medicine* **26**:1–79.

CARR, PATRICK, KIM A. LOGIO, AND SHANA MAIER (2003). "Keep Me Informed: What Matters for Victims as They Navigate the Juvenile Criminal Justice System in Philadelphia." *International Review of Victimology* **10**:117–136.

CARRINGTON, PETER J. AND JENNIFER L. SCHULENBERG (eds.) (2004). "The Youth Criminal Justice Act." *Canadian Journal of Criminology and Criminal Justice* **46**:219–389.

CARSWELL, K. ET AL. (2004). "The Psychosocial Needs of Young Offenders and Adolescents from an Inner City Area." *Journal of Adolescence* **27**:415–428.

CARY, PAULINE L. (2005). "ADHD and Juvenile Delinquency: A Review of the Literature." Unpublished paper presented at the annual meeting of the Academy of Criminal Justice Sciences, Chicago (March).

CASELLA, RONNIE (2001). *At Zero Tolerance: Punishment, Prevention, and School Violence.* New York: Peter Lang.

CASTELLANO, THOMAS C. AND MICHAEL FERGUSON (1998). *A Time Study of Juvenile Probation Services in Illinois.* Carbondale: Center for the Study of Crime, Delinquency, and Corrections, Southern Illinois University.

CAUFFMAN, ELIZABETH, LAURENCE STEINBERG, AND ALEX R. PIQUERO (2005). "Psychological, Neuropsychological, and Physiological Correlates of Serious Antisocial Behavior in Adolescence: The Role of Self-Control." *Criminology* **43**:133–176.

CAVENDER, GRAY AND PAUL KNEPPER (1992). "Strange Interlude: An Analysis of Juvenile Parole Revocation Decision Making." *Social Problems* **339**:387–399.

CENTER FOR THE STUDY AND PREVENTION OF VIOLENCE (2002). *Perry Preschool Program.* Boulder, CO: University of Colorado, Boulder.

CHAMBLISS, LAUREN, BERARDINE DOHRN, AND STEVEN DRIZIN (2000). *Second Chances: 100 Years of the Children's Court: Giving Kids a Chance to Make a Better Choice.* Washington, DC: Justice Policy Institute.

CHAMPION, DEAN J. (1994). *Measuring Offender Risk: A Criminal Justice Sourcebook.* Westport, CT: Greenwood Press, 1994.

CHAMPION, DEAN J. (1999). "The Use of Attorneys in Juvenile Courts in Five States: A Trend Analysis 1980–1995. Unpublished paper presented at American Society of Criminology meetings, Toronto, Canada (November).

CHAMPION, DEAN J. (2005a). "Private Counsels and Public Defenders in Texas: A Comparison." Academy of Criminal Justice Sciences, Chicago, (March).

CHAMPION, DEAN J. (2005b). *Probation, Parole, and Community Corrections, 5th ed.* Upper Saddle River, NJ: Prentice Hall.

CHAMPION, DEAN J. AND G. LARRY MAYS (1991). *Juvenile Transfer Hearings: Some Trends and Implications for Juvenile Justice.* New York: Praeger.

CHAPIN, JOHN AND DAVID GLEASON (2004). "Student Perceptions of School Violence: Could It Happen Here?" *Journal of Adolescent Research* **19**:360–376.

CHAPPLE, CONSTANCE L. (2005). "Self-Control, Peer Relations, and Delinquency." *Justice Quarterly* **22**:89–106.

CHAPPLE, CONSTANCE L. AND TRINA L. HOPE (2003). "An Analysis of the Self-Control and Criminal Versatility of Gang and Dating Violence Offenders." *Violence and Victims* **18**:671–690.

CHAPPLE, CONSTANCE L., KURT D. JOHNSON, AND LES B. WHITBECK (2004). "Gender and Arrest among Homeless and Runaway Youth: An Analysis of Background, Family, and Situational Factors." *Youth Violence and Juvenile Justice* **2**:129–147.

CHAPPLE, CONSTANCE L. AND ALEX R. PIQUERO (2004). "Applying Social Learning Theory to Police Misconduct." *Deviant Behavior* **25**:89–108.

CHEN, XIAOMING (2000). "Educating and Correcting Juvenile Delinquents: The Chinese Approaches." *Journal of Correctional Education* **51**:334–346.

CHESNEY-LIND, MEDA ET AL. (1998). *Trends in Delinquency and Gang Membership.* Honolulu: Center for Youth Research, University of Hawaii at Manoa.

CHOI, ALFRED AND WING T. LO (2002). *Fighting Youth Crime: Success and Failure of Two Little Dragons.* Singapore: Times Academic Press.

CLEAR, TODD R. AND HARRY R. DAMMER (2003). *The Offender in the Community 2e.* Belmont, CA: Wadsworth/Thomson Learning.

COCHRAN, JOHN K., DENISE PAQUETTE BOOTS, AND KATHLEEN M. HEIDE (2003). "Attribution Styles and Attitudes Toward Capital Punishment for Juveniles, the Mentally Incompetent, and the Juvenile Death Penalty." *Justice Quarterly* **20**:65–93.

COCOZZA, JOSEPH J. AND KATHLEEN SKOWYRA (2000). "Youth with Mental Health Disorders: Issues and Emerging Responses." *Juvenile Justice* **7**:3–13.

COHEN, ALBERT K. (1955). *Delinquent Boys.* New York: Free Press.

COHN, ALVIN W. (2000). "Electronic Monitoring and Graduated Sanctions." *Journal of Offender Monitoring* **13**:19–20, 24.

COHN, ALVIN W. ET AL. (2002). "What Works in Probation?" *Federal Probation* **66**:4–83.

COOK COUNTY COURT (2002). *The Englewood Evening Reporting Center.* Chicago: Cook County Court.

COPES, HEITH (2003). "Societal Attachments, Offending Frequency, and Techniques of Neutralization." *Deviant Behavior* **24**:101–127.

CORBETT, RONALD P. (2000). "Juvenile Probation on the Eve of the Next Millennium." *APPA Perspectives* **24**:22–30.

Corrections Today (1999a). "National Juvenile Detention Association: Leading the Juvenile Detention Field." *Corrections Today* **61**:20.

Corrections Today (1999b). "Rise in Number of Girls in Colorado Jails." *Corrections Today* **61**:12.

CORWIN, JOE-ANNE (2005). "Juvenile Correctional Education Standards Approved." *Corrections Today* **67**:83.

COSTELLO, JAN C. (2003). "Wayward and Non-Compliant People with Mental Disabilities: What Advocates of Involuntary Outpatient Commitment Can Learn from the Juvenile Court Experience with Status Offenders." *Psychology, Public Policy, and Law* **9**:233–257.

COYNE, RANDALL AND LYN ENTZEROTH (2001). *Capital Punishment and the Judicial Process 2e.* Belmont, CA: Wadsworth.

CRADDOCK, AMY AND LAURA A. GRAHAM (2001). "Recidivism as a Function of Day Reporting Center Participation." *Journal of Offender Rehabilitation* **34**:81–97.

CRAIG, LEAM A., KEVIN D. BROWNE, AND IAN STRINGER (2003). "Treatment and Sexual Offense Recidivism." *Trauma, Violence, and Abuse: A Review Journal* **4**:70–89.

CRAISSATI, JACKIE AND ANTHONY BEECH (2004). "The Characteristics of a Geographical Sample of Convicted Rapists." *Journal of Interpersonal Violence* **19**:371–388.

CRAWLEY, WILLIAM R. ET AL. (2005). "Exploring the Experience of Collective Identity and Conflict in Schooling." Unpublished paper presented at the annual meeting of the Academy of Criminal Justice Sciences, Chicago (March).

CREWS, GORDON A. AND REID H. MONTGOMERY (2001). *Chasing Shadows: Confronting Juvenile Violence in America.* Upper Saddle River, NJ: Prentice Hall.

CROWE, ANN H. (2000). *Jurisdictional Technical Assistance Package for Juvenile Corrections.* Washington, DC: U.S. Office of Juvenile Justice and Delinquency Prevention.

CURRAN, DANIEL J. (1984). "The Myth of a 'New' Female Delinquent." *Crime and Delinquency* **30**:386–399.

CURRY, G. DAVID, SCOTT H. DECKER, AND ARLEN EGLEY JR. (2002). "Gang Involvement and Delinquency in a Middle School Population." *Justice Quarterly* **19**:275–292.

DAHLGREN, DANIEL C. (2005). "Emotional Sociology and Juvenile Delinquency: The Value of Interpreting Emotional Subculture of Gangs." Unpublished paper presented at the annual meeting of the Academy of Criminal Justice Sciences, Chicago (March).

D'ANGELO, JILL M. AND MICHAEL P. BROWN (2005). "Missouri Juvenile Justice Reform Act: Comparison of Case Outcomes from 1994 and 2000." Unpublished paper presented at the annual meeting of the Academy of Criminal Justice Sciences, Chicago (March).

DAVIDSON-METHOT, DAVID G. (2004). "Calibrating the Compass: Using Quality Improvement Data for Outcome Evaluation, Cost Control, and Creating Quality Organizational Cultures." *Residential Treatment for Children and Youth* **21**:45–68.

DAVIES, ANDREW AND GEOFFREY PEARSON (EDS.) (1999). "History of Crime and Modernity." *British Journal of Criminology* **39**:1–174.

DEAN, CHARLES W., J. DAVID HIRSCHEL, AND ROBERT BRAME (1996). "Minorities and Juvenile Case Dispositions." *Justice System Journal* **18**:267–285.

DEATH PENALTY INFORMATION CENTER (2005). *Juveniles on Death Row in the United States 2005.* Washington, DC: Death Penalty Information Center.

DECKER, SCOTT H. (2000). *Increasing School Safety Through Juvenile Accountability Programs.* Washington, DC: U.S. Office of Juvenile Justice and Delinquency Prevention.

DECKER, SCOTT H. (2005). "Evaluating Project Safe Neighborhoods in the Eastern District of Missouri." Unpublished paper presented at the annual meeting of the Academy of Criminal Justice Sciences, Chicago (March).

DEJONG, CHRISTINA AND KENNETH C. JACKSON (1998). "Putting Race into Context: Race, Juvenile Justice Processing, and Urbanization." *Justice Quarterly* **15**:487–504.

DEMBO, RICHARD, KIMBERLY PACHECO, AND JAMES SCHMEIDLER (1997). "Drug Use and Delinquent Behavior Among High Risk Youths." *Journal of Child and Adolescent Substance Abuse* **6**:1–25.

DEMBO, RICHARD AND JAMES SCHMEIDLER (2003). "A Classification of High-Risk Youths." *Crime and Delinquency* **49**:201–230.

DEMBO, RICHARD ET AL. (2000b). "Youth Recidivism Twelve Months After a Family Empowerment Intervention." *Journal of Offender Rehabilitation* **31**:29–65.

DEMUTH, STEPHEN (2004). "Understanding the Delinquency and Social Relationships of Loners." *Youth and Society* **35**:366–392.

DEUKMEDJIAN, JOHN EDWARD (2003). "Reshaping Subjectivities in Canada's National Police Force: The Development of RCMP Alternative Dispute Resolution." *Policing and Society* **13**:331–348.

DEZOLT, ERNEST M., LINDA M. SCHMIDT, AND DONNA C. GILCHER (1996). "The 'Tabula Rasa' Intervention Project for Delinquent Gang-Involved Females." *Journal of Gang Research* **3**:37–43.

DIETRICH, KIM N. ET AL. (2001). "Early Exposure to Lead and Juvenile Delinquency." *Neurotoxicology and Teratology* **23**:511–518.

DIMMICK, SUSAN (2005). "Holistic Representation: Identifying Success." New York: Unpublished paper presented at the annual training institute of the American Probation and Parole Association (July).

DOUGHERTY, JOYCE (1988). "Negotiating Justice in the Juvenile Justice System: A Comparison of Adult Plea Bargaining and Juvenile Intake." *Federal Probation* **52**:72–80.

DOUGLAS, KEVIN S. AND RANDALL KROPP (2002). "A Prevention-Based Paradigm for Violence Risk Assessment: Clinical and Research Applications." *Criminal Justice and Behavior* **29**:617–658.

DOWDEN, C. (ED.) (2003). *The Effectiveness of Substance Abuse Treatment with Young Offenders.* Ottawa: Department of Justice Canada, Research and Statistics Division.

DUBOWITZ, H., S.C. PITTS, AND M.M. BLACK (2004). "Measurement of Three Major Subtypes of Child Neglect." *Child Maltreatment* **9**:344–356.

DURAN, ROBERT (2005). "Manufacturing Gang Fears: A Critique of the Police Suppression Industry." Unpublished paper presented at the annual meeting of the Academy of Criminal Justice Sciences, Chicago (March).

DURST-JOHNSON, C. (ED.) (2004). *Youth Gangs in Literature: Recent Contributions in Exploring Social Issues through Literature.* Westport, CT: Greenwood Press.

DWYER, DIANE C. AND ROGER B. McNALLY (1987). "Juvenile Justice: Reform, Retain, and Reaffirm." *Federal Probation* **51**:47–51.

EDWARDS, IAN (2001). "Victim Participation in Sentencing: The Problems of Incoherence." *Howard Journal of Criminal Justice* **40**:39–54.

EISNER, MANUEL (2002). "Crime, Problem Drinking, and Drug Use: Patterns of Problem Behavior in Cross-National Perspective." *Annals of the American Academy of Political and Social Science* **580**:201–225.

EITLE, DAVID AND TAMELA McNULTY EITLE (2003). "Segregation and School Violence." *Social Forces* **82**:598–615.

EITLE, DAVID, LISA STOLZENBERG, AND STEWART D'ALESSIO (2005). "Police Organizational Factors, the Racial Composition of the Police, and the Probability of Arrest." *Justice Quarterly* **22**:30–56.

ELLSWORTH, THOMAS (1988). "Case Supervision Planning: The Forgotten Component of Intensive Probation Supervision." *Federal Probation* **52**:28–33.

ELLSWORTH, THOMAS, MICHELLE T. KINSELLA, AND KIMBERLEE MASSIN (1992). "Prosecuting Juveniles: *Parens Patriae* and Due Process in the 1990's." *Justice Professional* **7**:53–67.

ELTRINGHAM, SIMON AND JAN ALDRIDGE (2000). "The Extent of Children's Knowledge of Court as Estimated by Guardians ad Litem." *Child Abuse Review* **9**:275–286.

EMERSON, ROBERT M. (1969). *Judging Delinquents.* Chicago: Aldine.

EMPEY, LAMAR T. AND JEROME RABOW (1961). "The Provo Experiment in Delinquency Rehabilitation." *American Sociological Review* **26**:679–695.

ENGRAM, PEGGY A. (2005). "What Do We Know about Children of Incarcerated Parents?" Unpublished paper presented at the annual meeting of the Academy of Criminal Justice Sciences, Chicago (March).

EREZ, EDNA AND KATHY LASTER (1999). "Neutralizing Victim Reform: Legal Professionals' Perspectives on Victims and Impact Statements." *Crime and Delinquency* **45**:530–553.

ERICKSON, KRISTAN GLASGOW AND ROBERT CROSNOE (2000). "A Social Process Model of Adolescent Deviance: Combining Social Control and Differential Association Perspectives." *Journal of Youth and Adolescence* **29**:395–425.

ESBENSEN, FINN AAGE ET AL. (2001). "Youth Gangs and Definitional Issues: When Is a Gang a Gang, and Why Does It Matter?" *Crime and Delinquency* **47**:105–130.

ESCARCEGA, ALEX ET AL. (2004). "Juvenile Corrections." *Corrections Today* **66**:20–86.

ESCHHOLZ, SARAH, MATTHEW MALLARD, AND STACEY FLYNN (2004). "Images of Prime Time Justice: A Content Analysis of 'NYPD Blue' and 'Law and Order.'" *Journal of Criminal Justice and Popular Culture* **10**:161–180.

EVERLE, JANE A. AND ROLAND D. MAIURO (2001). "Introduction and Commentary: Developmental Perspectives on Violence and Victimization." *Violence and Victims* **16**:351–354.

FADER, JAMIE J. ET AL. (2001). "Factors Involved in Decisions on Commitment to Delinquency Programs for First-Time Juvenile Offenders." *Justice Quarterly* **18**:323–341.

FAGAN, JEFFREY A. (1990). "Treatment and Reintegration of Violent Juvenile Offenders: Experimental Results." *Justice Quarterly* **7**:233–263.

FAGAN, JEFFREY AND CRAIG REINARMAN (1991). "The Social Context of Intensive Supervision: Organizational and Ecological Influences on Community Treatment." In *Intensive Interventions with High-Risk Youths: Promising Approaches in Juvenile Probation and Parole,* Troy L. Armstrong (ed.). Monsey, NY: Criminal Justice Press.

FARR, KATHRYN ANN (2000). "Defeminizing and Dehumanizing Female Murderers: Depictions of Lesbians on Death Row." *Women and Criminal Justice* **11**:49–66.

FAULKNER, SAMUEL S. AND CYNTHIA A. FAULKNER (2004). "Poverty as a Predictor of Child Maltreatment: A Brief Analysis." *Journal of Poverty* **8**:103–106.

FELD, BARRY C. (1988). "*In re Gault* Revisited: A Cross-State Comparison of the Right to Counsel in Juvenile Court." *Crime and Delinquency* **34**:393–424.

FELD, BARRY C. (1993a). "Criminalizing the American Juvenile Court." In *Crime and Justice: A Review of Research, Vol. 17,* Michael Tonry (ed.). Chicago: University of Chicago Press.

FELD, BARRY C. (1993b). "Juvenile (In)justice and the Criminal Court Alternative." *Crime and Delinquency* **39**:403–424.

FELD, BARRY C. (2000). *Cases and Materials on Juvenile Justice Administration.* St. Paul, MN: West Group.

FELD, BARRY C. (2001). "Race, Youth Violence, and the Changing Jurisprudence of Waiver." *Behavioral Sciences and the Law* **19**:3–22.

FIELDS, SCOTT A. AND JOHN R. McNAMARA (2003). "The Prevention of Child and Adolescent Violence: A Review." *Aggression and Violent Behavior* **8**:61–91.

FINKELHOR, DAVID AND LISA M. JONES (2004). *Explanations for the Decline in Child Sexual Abuse Cases.* Washington, DC: U.S. Office of Juvenile Justice and Delinquency Prevention.

FINN, MARY A. AND SUZANNE MUIRHEAD-STEVES (2002). "The Effectiveness of Electronic Monitoring with Violent Male Parolees." *Justice Quarterly* **19**:293–312.

FLANNERY, DANIEL J. AND C. RONALD HUFF (EDS.) (1999). *Youth Violence: Prevention, Intervention, and Social Policy.* Washington, DC: American Psychiatric Press.

FLEMING, GARY AND GERALD WINKLER (1999). "Sending Them to Prison: Washington State Learns to Accommodate Female Youthful Offenders in Prison." *Corrections Today* **61**:132–136.

FLEXNER, BERNARD AND ROGER N. BALDWIN (1914). *Juvenile Courts and Probation.* New York: Harcourt.

FLORIDA OFFICE OF PROGRAM POLICY ANALYSIS (1995). *Status Report on Boot Camps in Florida Administered by the Department of Corrections and Department of Juvenile Justice.* Tallahassee: Florida Office of Program Policy Analysis and Government Accountability.

FLORY, CHRIS AND LISA HUTCHINSON-WALLACE (2005). "Juvenile Waivers in Kentucky: Legal Implications." Unpublished paper presented at the annual meeting of the Academy of Criminal Justice Sciences, Chicago (March).

FOX, JAMES A. AND M.W. ZAWITZ (1999). *Homicide Trends in the United States.* Washington, DC: Bureau of Justice Statistics, U.S. Department of Justice, Office of Justice Programs.

FRANTZEN, DURANT (2005). "The Juvenile Death Penalty Goes Under Fire: A Test for the High Court." Unpublished paper presented at the annual meeting of the Academy of Criminal Justice Sciences, Chicago (March).

FRIED, CARRIE S. AND N. DICKON REPPUCCI (2001). "Criminal Decision Making: The Development of Adolescent Judgment, Criminal Responsibility, and Culpability." *Law and Human Behavior* **25**:45–61.

GAARDER, EMILY AND JOANNE BELKNAP (2004). "Little Women: Girls in Adult Prison." *Women and Criminal Justice* **15**:51–80.

GAARDER, EMILY, N. RODRIGUEZ, AND ZATZ, MARJORIE S. (2004). "Criers, Liars, and Manipulators: Probation Officers' Views of Girls." *Justice Quarterly* **21**:547–578.

GAINEY, RANDY R. AND BRIAN K. PAYNE (2003). "Changing Attitudes Toward House Arrest with Electronic Monitoring." *International Journal of Offender Therapy and Comparative Criminology* **47**:196–209.

GARBARINO, JAMES ET AL. (2002). "Trauma and Juvenile Delinquency: Theory, Research, and Interventions." *Journal of Aggression, Maltreatment, and Trauma* **6**:1–264.

GARFINKLE, ELIZABETH (2003). "Coming of Age in America: The Misapplication of Sex-Offender Registration and Community-Notification Laws to Juveniles." *California Law Review* **91**:163–208.

GAVAZZI, STEPHEN M. ET AL. (2000). "The Growing Up FAST Diversion Program: An Example of Juvenile Justice System Program Development for Outcome Evaluation." *Aggression and Violent Behavior* **5**:159–175.

GEARY COUNTY COMMUNITY CORRECTIONS (2002). *Pre-Dispositional Supervision Program.* Geary County, KS: Geary County Community Corrections.

GELBER, SEYMOUR (1990). "The Juvenile Justice System: Vision for the Future." *Juvenile and Family Court Journal* **41**:15–18.

GELSTHORPE, LORAINE R. (1987). "The Differential Treatment of Males and Females in the Criminal Justice System." In *Sex, Gender and Care Work,* Gordon Horobin (ed.). Aberdeen, UK: Department of Social Work, University of Aberdeen.

GEBO, ERIKA (2002). "A Contextual Exploration of Siblicide." *Violence and Victims* **17**:157–168.

GERLER, E.R. JR. (2004). *Handbook of School Violence.* New York: Haworth Press.

GIBSON, MARY (2002). *Born to Crime: Cesare Lombroso and the Origins of Biological Criminology.* Westport, CT: Praeger.

GILLIARD, DARRELL K. AND ALLEN J. BECK (1998). *Prisoners in 1997.* Washington, DC: U.S. Department of Justice.

GITTENS, JOAN (1994). *Poor Relations: The Children of the State of Illinois, 1818–1990.* Urbana: University of Illinois Press.

GLASER, BRIAN A., GEORGIA B. CALHOUN, AND JOHN V. PETROCELLI (2002). "Personality Characteristics of Male Juvenile Offenders by Adjudicated Offenses as Indicated By the MMPI-A." *Criminal Justice and Behavior* **29**:183–201.

GLASER, BRIAN A. ET AL. (2001). "Multi-Observer Assessment of Problem Behavior in Adjudicated Youths: Patterns of Discrepancies." *Child and Family Behavior Therapy* **23**:33–45.

GLICK, BARRY (1998). "Kids in Adult Correctional Systems: An Understanding of Adolescent Development Can Aid Staff In Managing Youthful Offender Populations." *Corrections Today* **60**:96–102.

GLOVER, KIT AND KURT BUMBY (2001). "Reentry at the Point of Entry." *Corrections Today* **63**:68–75.

GLUECK, SHELDON AND ELEANOR GLUECK (1950). *Unraveling Juvenile Delinquency.* New York: Commonwealth Fund.

GOMEZ, FERNANDO AND JUAN JOSE GANUZA (2002). "Civil and Criminal Sanctions against Blackmail: An Economic Analysis." *International Review of Law and Economics* **21**:475–498.

GORDON, JILL A. AND PAGE MALMSJO (2005). "The Impact of Offender Characteristics on Recidivism: An Evaluation of Barrett Juvenile Correctional Center."Unpublished paper presented at the annual meeting of the Academy of Criminal Justice Sciences, Chicago (March).

GOTTFREDSON, DENISE C. AND WILLIAM H. BARTON (1997). *Closing Institutions for Juvenile Offenders: The Maryland Experience.* Lewiston, NY: Edwin Mellin Press.

GOTTFREDSON, DENISE C., GARY D. GOTTFREDSON, AND STEPHANIE A. WEISMAN (2001). "The Timing of Delinquent Behavior and Its Implications for After-School Programs." *Criminology and Public Policy* **1**:61–86.

GOVER, ANGELA R. AND DORIS LAYTON MACKENZIE (2000). "Importation and Deprivation Explanations of Juveniles' Adjustment to Correctional Facilities." *International Journal of Offender Therapy and Comparative Criminology* **44**:450–467.

GOVER, ANGELA R. AND DORIS LAYTON MACKENZIE (2003). "Child Maltreatment and Adjustment in Juvenile Correctional Institutions." *Criminal Justice and Behavior* **30**:374–396.

GOWEN, DARREN (2001). "Analysis of Competing Risks in the Federal Home Confinement Program." *Journal of Offender Monitoring* **14**:5–9, 11.

GREENE, JACK R., VINCENT J. WEBB, AND JACK MCDEVITT (2003). *Policing Gangs and Youth Violence.* Belmont, CA: Wadsworth/Thompson Learning.

GREENLEAF, RICHARD G. (2005). "A Survey of Gang and Non-Gang Members Regarding Their Attitudes Toward the Police, Community, and Crime: A Chicago Study." Unpublished paper presented at the annual meeting of the Academy of Criminal Justice Sciences, Chicago (March).

GREGORIE, TRUDY (2005). "Victims' Rights and Issues: Educating Judicial and Court Personnel." New York: Unpublished paper presented at the annual training institute of the American Probation and Parole Association (July).

GRIFFIN, BRENDA S. AND CHARLES T. GRIFFIN (1978). *Juvenile Delinquency in Perspective.* New York: Harper and Row.

GRISSO, THOMAS (1998). *Forensic Evaluation of Juveniles.* Sarasota, FL: Professional Resource Press.

GUARINO-GHEZZI, SUSAN (1989). "Classifying Juveniles: A Formula for Case-By-Case Assessment." *Corrections Today* **51**:112–116.

GUARINO-GHEZZI, SUSAN AND EDWARD J. LOUGHRAN (2004). *Balancing Juvenile Justice.* New Brunswick, NJ: Transaction.

GUERRA, V.S., S.R. ASHER, AND M.E. DEROSIER (2004). "Effect of Children's Perceived Rejection on Physical Aggression." *Journal of Abnormal Child Psychology* **32**:551–563.

HAAPANEN, RUDY AND LEE BRITTON (2002). "Drug Testing for Youthful Offenders on Parole: An Experimental Evaluation." *Criminology and Public Policy* **1**:217–244.

HAGAN, JOHN, KLAUS BOEHNKE, AND HANS MERKENS (2004). "Gender Differences in Capitalization Processes and the Delinquency of Siblings in Toronto and Berlin." *British Journal of Criminology* **44**:659–676.

HANKE, PENELOPE J. (1996). "Putting School Crime into Perspective: Self-Reported School Victimizations of High School Seniors." *Journal of Criminal Justice* **24**:207–226.

HARIG, T.J. (ED.) (2001). *The Juvenile Electronic Monitoring Project: The Use of Electronic Monitoring Technology on Adjudicated Juvenile Delinquents.* Albany: New York State Division of Criminal Justice Services.

HARRIS, PATRICIA M. ET AL. (1993). "A Wilderness Challenge Program as Correctional Treatment." *Journal of Offender Rehabilitation* **19**:149–164.

HARRIS, RICHARD J. (2000). *Operation Safe Streets Governor's Task Force.* Dover: Delaware Statistical Analysis Center.

HARRIS, VICTORIA AND CHRISTOS DAGADAKIS (2004). "Length of Incarceration: Was There Parity for Mentally Ill Offenders?" *International Journal of Law and Psychiatry* **27**:387–393.

HART, LIKISHA (2005). "Learning Disabilities and Juvenile Delinquency: Examining the Correlation Between Labeling and Delinquent Behavior." Unpublished paper presented at the annual meeting of the Academy of Criminal Justice Sciences, Chicago (March).

HARTWELL, STEPHANIE (2004). "Triple Stigma: Persons with Mental Illness and Substance Abuse Problems in the Criminal Justice System." *Criminal Justice Policy Review* **15**:84–99.

HASSETT, CONNIE WALKER (2002). "Juvenile Conference Committees: Issues in Assessing a Diversionary Court Program." *Journal of Criminal Justice* **30**:107–119.

HAVERKAMP, RITA (2002). "House Arrest with Electronic Monitoring." *Kriminologische Forschungsberichte* **107**:621–629.

HAYNIE, DANA L. ET AL. (2005). "Adolescent Romantic Relationships and Delinquency Involvement." *Criminology* **43**:177–210.

HECKERT, ALEX AND DRUANN MARIA HECKERT (2004). "Using an Integrated Typology of Deviance to Expand Merton's Anomie Theory." *Criminal Justice Studies* **17**:75–90.

HEIDE, KATHLEEN M. (1999). *Young Killers: The Challenge of Juvenile Homicide.* Thousand Oaks, CA: Sage.

HEIDE, KATHLEEN M. (2003). "Youth Homicide: A Review of the Literature and a Blueprint for Action." *International Journal of Offender Therapy and Comparative Criminology* **47**:6–36.

HENDERSON, THOMAS A. ET AL. (1984). *The Significance of Judicial Structure: The Effect of Unification on Trial Court Operations.* Washington, DC: U.S. Government Printing Office.

HENHAM, RALPH (2004). "Conceptualizing Access to Justice and Victims' Rights in International Sentencing." *Social and Legal Studies* **13**:27–55.

HENNESSY, KEVIN ET AL. (2001). "Substance Use Survey Data Collection Methodologies and Selected Papers." *Journal of Drug Issues* **31**:595–728.

HENSLEY, CHRISTOPHER ET AL. (2005). "Exploring the Possible Link Between Childhood and Adolescent Bestiality and Interpersonal Violence." Unpublished paper presented at the annual meeting of the Academy of Criminal Justice Sciences, Chicago (March).

HERMAN, SUSAN AND CRESSIDA WASSERMAN (2001). "A Role for Victims in Offender Reentry." *Crime and Delinquency* **47**:428–445.

HERRING, JOHN (2005). "Adult Justice within the Juvenile Justice System: A Review of Significant Constitutional Cases on Juvenile Proceedings." Unpublished paper presented at the annual meeting of the Academy of Criminal Justice Sciences, Chicago (March).

HEYMAN, BOB ET AL. (2002). "Risk Management in the Rehabilitation of Offenders with Learning Disabilities." *Risk Management: An International Journal* **4**:33–45.

HIL, RICHARD AND ANTHONY MCMAHON (2001). *Families, Crime, and Juvenile Justice.* New York: Peter Lang.

HIRSCHI, TRAVIS (1969). *Causes of Delinquency.* Berkeley: University of California Press.

HODGES, KAY AND CHEONG SEOK KIM (2000). "Psychometric Study of the Child and Adolescent Functional Assessment Scale: Prediction of Contact with the Law and Poor School Attendance." *Journal of Abnormal Child Psychology* **28**:287–297.

HOFFMANN, JOHN P. (2002). "A Contextual Analysis of Differential Association, Social Control, and Strain Theories of Delinquency." *Social Forces* **81**:753–785.

HOGE, ROBERT D. (2001). *The Juvenile Offender: Theory, Research, and Applications.* Boston: Kluwer Academic.

HOGG, RUSSELL AND KERRY CARRINGTON (2003). "Violence, Spatiality, and Other Rurals." *Australian and New Zealand Journal of Criminology* **36**:293–319.

HOLSINGER, ALEX M. AND EDWARD J. LATESSA (1999). "An Empirical Evaluation of a Sanction Continuum: Pathways Through the Juvenile Justice System." *Journal of Criminal Justice* **27**:155–172.

HOLTERMAN, THOM (2001). "Neighborhood-Centered Conflict Mediation in the Netherlands: An Instrument for

Social Cohesion." *Contemporary Justice Review* **4**:41–48.

HOLTFRETER, KRISTY, MICHAEL D. REISIG, AND MERRY MORASH (2004). "Poverty, State Capital, and Recidivism among Women Offenders." *Criminology and Public Policy* **3**:181–216.

HOOD, ROGER (2002). *The Death Penalty: A Worldwide Perspective 3e*. Oxford, UK: Oxford University Press.

HOOTON, EARNEST A. (1939). *Crime and the Man*. Cambridge, MA: Harvard University Press.

HOUCHINS, DAVID E. (2001). "Developing the Self-Determination of Incarcerated Students." *Journal of Correctional Education* **52**:141–147.

HOUK, JULIE M. (1984). "Electronic Monitoring of Probationers: A Step Toward Big Brother?" *Golden Gate University Law Review* **14**:431–446.

HOWELL, JAMES C. AND BARRY KRISBERG (EDS.) (1998). "Juveniles in Custody." *Crime and Delinquency* **44**:483–601.

HOWITT, PAMELA S. AND EUGENE A. MOORE (1991). "The Efficacy of Intensive Early Intervention: An Evaluation of the Oakland County Probate Court Early Offender Program." *Juvenile and Family Court Journal* **42**:25–36.

HSIEH, CHING CHI (1993). "Poverty, Income Inequality, and Violent Crime." *Criminal Justice Review* **18**:182–202.

HUGHES, LORINE A. AND JAMES F. SHORT, JR. (2005). "Disputes Involving Youth Street Gang Members: Micro-Social Contexts." *Criminology* **43**:43–76.

HUNTER, JOHN A. JR. AND DENNIS W. GOODWIN (1992). "The Clinical Utility of Satiation Therapy with Juvenile Sexual Offenders: Variations and Efficacy." *Annals of Sex Research* **5**:71–80.

HURST, HUNTER (1990). "Juvenile Probation in Retrospect." *Perspectives* **14**:16–24.

HUSKEY, BOBBIE L. (1984). "Community Corrections Acts." *Corrections Today* **46**:45.

HWANG, S. AND O. BEDFORD (2004). "Juveniles' Motivation for Remaining in Prostitution." *Psychology of Women Quarterly* **28**:136–146.

ILLINOIS DEPARTMENT OF CORRECTIONS (2000). *Two Year Report on Illinois Department of Corrections' Chicago Southside Day Reporting Center*. Springfield: Illinois Department of Corrections.

INCIARDI, JAMES A. (2003). "The Irrational Politics of American Drug Policy: Implications for Criminal Law and the Management of Drug-Involved Offenders." *Ohio State Journal of Criminal Law* **1**:273–288.

INGRAM, JASON R. ET AL. (2005). "Family Environment, Peers, and Delinquency: A Path Analysis." Unpublished paper presented at the annual meeting of the Academy of Criminal Justice Sciences, Chicago (March).

IRELAND, TIMOTHY O., CAROLYN A. SMITH, AND TERENCE P. THORNBERRY (2002). "Developmental Issues in the Impact of Child Maltreatment on Later Delinquency and Drug Use." *Criminology* **40**:359–400.

IRWIN, K. (2004). "The Violence of Adolescent Life: Experiencing and Managing Everyday Threats." *Youth and Society* **35**:452–479.

JACOBSON, WENDY B. (2000). *Safe from the Start: Taking Action on Children Exposed to Violence*. Washington,

DC: Office of Juvenile Justice and Delinquency Prevention.

JANUS, ERIC S. AND ROBERT A. PRENTK (2003). "Forensic Use of Actuarial Risk Assessment with Sex Offenders: Accuracy, Admissibility, and Accountability." *American Criminal Law Review* **40**:1443–1499.

JENNINGS, MARY ANN AND JOHN GUNTHER (2000). "Juvenile Delinquency in Search of a Practice Model: Family Health, Differential Association, and Social Control." *Journal of Family Social Work* **5**:75–89.

JENSEN, ERIC L. AND LINDA K. METSGER (1994). "A Test of the Deterrent Effect of Legislative Waiver on Violent Juvenile Crime." *Crime and Delinquency* **40**:96–104.

JENSON, JEFFREY M. ET AL. (1995). *Racial Disproportionality in the Utah Juvenile Justice System: Final Report*. Salt Lake City: Social Research Institute, University of Utah.

JOHNSON COUNTY DEPARTMENT OF CORRECTIONS (2002). *Juvenile ISP Conditions & Guidelines*. Johnson County, KS: Johnson County Department of Corrections.

JOHNSON, KAY (2005). "Trauma and Substance Abuse Treatment for Women Offenders." Unpublished paper presented at the annual meeting of the American Probation and Parole Association, New York (July).

JOHNSON, MATTHEW B. (2002). "Juvenile Miranda Case Law in New Jersey: The Relevance of Recording All Custodial Questioning." *Journal of Psychiatry and Law* **30**:3–57.

JOHNSTON, WENDY (2000). "An Innovative Solution to the Problem of Juvenile Offenders in Missouri." *The Journal of Offender Monitoring* **13**:18–38.

JONES, BERNADETTE (1990). "Intensive Probation Services in Philadelphia County." Unpublished paper presented at the American Society of Criminology meetings, Baltimore (November).

JONES, PETER R. ET AL. (2001). "Identifying Chronic Juvenile Offenders." *Justice Quarterly* **18**:479–507.

JONES, RALPH K. AND JOHN H. LACEY (1999). *Evaluation of a Day Reporting Center for Repeat DWI Offenders*. Winchester, MA: Mid-America Research Institute.

JORDAN, KAREEM L. AND TINA FREIBURGER (2005). "The Young and the Ruthless: The Effect of Juvenile Decertification on Court Outcomes." Unpublished paper presented at the annual meeting of the Academy of Criminal Justice Sciences, Chicago (March).

JURICH, SONIA, MARTA CASPER, AND KIM A. HULL (2001). "Training Correctional Educators: A Needs Assessment Study." *Journal of Correctional Education* **52**:23–27.

JUSTICE RESEARCH AND STATISTICS ASSOCIATION (2005). *The Weed and Seed Strategy*. Washington, DC: Justice Research and Statistics Association.

JUVENILE JUSTICE CENTER (2001). *Georgia: An Assessment of Access to Counsel and Quality of Representation in Delinquency Proceedings*. Washington, DC: American Bar Association, Juvenile Justice Center.

KADISH, TARA E. ET AL. (2001). "Identifying the Developmental Strengths of Juvenile Offenders: Assessing Four Life-Skills Dimensions." *Journal of Addictions and Offender Counseling* **31**:85–95.

KAKAR, SUMAN, MARIE-LUISE FRIEDEMANN, AND LINDA PECK (2002). "Girls in Detention: The Results of Focus

Group Discussion Interviews and Official Records Review." *Journal of Contemporary Criminal Justice* **18**:57–73.

KAMMER, JAMES J., KEVIN I. MINOR, AND JAMES B. WELLS (1997). "An Outcome Study of the Diversion Plus Program for Juvenile Offenders." *Federal Probation* **61**:51–56.

KARP, DAVID R. (2001). "Harm and Repair: Observing Restorative Justice in Vermont." *Justice Quarterly* **18**:727–757.

KARP, DAVID R. (2004). "Teen Courts." *APPA Perspectives* **28**:18–20.

KATZ, CHARLES M. (2003). "Issues in the Production and Dissemination of Gang Statistics: An Ethnographic Study of a Large Midwestern Police Gang Unit." *Crime and Delinquency* **49**:485–516.

KATZ, CHARLES M., VINCENT J. WEBB, AND SCOTT H. DECKER (2005). "Using the Arrestee Drug Abuse Monitoring (ADAM) Program to Further Understand the Relationship Between Drug Use and Gang Membership." *Justice Quarterly* **22**:58–88.

KEARNEY, EDMUND M. (1994). "A Clinical Corrections Approach: The Failure of a Residential Juvenile Delinquency Treatment Center." *Juvenile and Family Court Journal* **45**:33–41.

KEARON, WILLIAM G. (1990). "Deinstitutionalization, Street Children, and the Coming AIDS Epidemic in the Adolescent Population." *Juvenile and Family Court Journal* **41**:9–18.

KEILITZ, SUSAN L. ET AL. (1997). *Domestic Violence and Child Custody Disputes: A Resource Handbook for Judges and Court Managers.* Williamsburg, VA: National Center for State Courts.

KELLY, KATHARINE (2005). "Auto Theft and Youth Culture: A Nexus of Masculinities, Femininities, and Car Culture." Unpublished paper presented at the annual meeting of the Academy of Criminal Justice Sciences, Chicago (March).

KEMPF-LEONARD, KIMBERLY AND ERICKA S.L. PETERSON (2000). "Expanding Realms of the New Penology: The Advent of Actuarial Justice for Juveniles." *Punishment and Society* **2**:66–97.

KEMPF-LEONARD, KIMBERLY, PAUL E. TRACY, AND JAMES C. HOWELL (2001). "Serious, Violent, and Chronic Juvenile Offenders: The Relationship of Delinquency Career Types to Adult Criminality." *Justice Quarterly* **18**:449–478.

KENNEDY, SHARON (2005). "Increasing the Effectiveness of Probation and Parole Through Research." Unpublished paper presented at the annual training institute of the American Probation and Parole Association, New York (July).

KERLE, KENNETH E. (1998). *American Jails: Looking to the Future.* Boston: Butterworth-Heinemann.

KILCHLING, MICHAEL (1995). *Victim Interests and Law Enforcement.* Freiburg, Germany: Max Planck Institute.

KINARD, E.M. (2004). "Methodological Issues in Assessing the Effects of Maltreatment Characteristics on Behavioral Adjustment in Maltreated Children." *Journal of Family Violence* **19**:303–318.

KING, DENISE AND ANITA GIBBS (2003). "Is Home Detention in New Zealand Disadvantaging Women and Children?" *Probation Journal* **50**:115–126.

KING, TAMMY (2005). "Juvenile Detention: A Descriptive Study of Rule Infractions." Unpublished paper presented at the annual meeting of the Academy of Criminal Justice Sciences, Chicago (March).

KINGREE, J.B., RONALD BRAITHWAITE, AND TAMMY WOODRING (2001). "Psychosocial and Behavioral Problems in Relation to Recent Experience as a Runaway among Adolescent Detainees." *Criminal Justice and Behavior* **28**:190–205.

KITSUSE, JOHN I. (1962). "Societal Reaction to Deviant Behavior: Problems of Theory and Method." *Social Problems* **9**:247–256.

KLEIN, MALCOLM W., L. ROSENZWEIG, AND M. BATES (1975). "The Ambiguous Juvenile Arrest." *Criminology* **24**:185–194.

KLUG, ELIZABETH A. (2001). "Geographical Disparities among Trying and Sentencing Juveniles." *Corrections Today* **63**:100–107.

KNEPPER, PAUL AND GRAY CAVENDER (1990). "Decision-Making and the Typification of Juveniles on Parole." Unpublished paper presented at the Academy of Criminal Justice Science meetings, Denver, CO (April).

KNOX, GEORGE W., BRAD MARTIN, AND EDWARD D. TROMANHAUSER (1995). "Preliminary Results of the 1995 National Prosecutor's Survey." *Journal of Gang Research* **2**:59–71.

KNOX COUNTY JUVENILE SERVICES (2002). *Electronic Monitoring and House Arrest for Juveniles: A Status Report.* Knoxville, TN: Knox County Juvenile Services.

KNUPFER, ANNE MEIS (2001). *Reform and Resistance: Gender, Delinquency, and America's First Juvenile Court.* New York: Routledge.

KOHLBERG, L. (1981). *The Philosophy of Moral Development.* New York: Harper and Row.

KONTOS, LUIS, DAVID BROTHERTON, AND LUIS BARRIOS (EDS.) (2003). *Gangs and Society: Alternative Perspectives.* New York: Columbia University Press.

KONTY, MARK (2005). "Microanomie: The Cognitive Foundations of the Relationship Between Anomie and Deviance." *Criminology* **43**:107–132.

KOWALSKI, MELANIE AND TULLIO CAPUTO (1999). "Recidivism in Youth Court: An Examination of the Impact of Age, Gender, and Prior Record." *Canadian Journal of Criminology* **41**:57–84.

KRAUSE, WESLEY AND MARILYN D. MCSHANE (1994). "A Deinstitutionalization Retrospective: Relabeling the Status Offender." *Journal of Crime and Justice* **17**:45–67.

KREISEL, BETSY WRIGHT ET AL. (2005). "Juvenile Justice Beyond 100 Years: The Past, The Present, and The Future." Unpublished paper presented at the annual meeting of the Academy of Criminal Justice Sciences, Chicago (March).

KRETSCHMER, ERNEST (1936). *Physique and Character.* London: Kegan Paul, Trench, and Trubner.

KUNTSCHE, E.N. AND H.K. KLINGERMANN (2004). "Weapon-Carrying at Swiss Schools? A Gender-Specific Typology in Context of Victim and Offender-Related Violence." *Journal of Adolescence* **27**:381–393.

KURLYCHEK, MEGAN C. AND BRIAN D. JOHNSON (2004). "The Juvenile Penalty: A Comparison of Juvenile and Adult Sentencing Outcomes in Criminal Court." *Criminology* **42**:485–517.

KYLE, JIM (1998). "The Privatization Debate Continues: Tennessee's Experience Highlights Scope of Controversy Over Private Prisons." *Corrections Today* **60**:88–158.

LAB, STEVEN P., GLENN SHIELDS, AND CONNIE SCHONDEL (1993). "Research Note: An Evaluation of Juvenile Sexual Offender Treatment." *Crime and Delinquency* **39**:543–553.

LAHEY, MARY ANNE, BRUCE A. CHRISTENSON, AND ROBERT J. ROSSI (2000). *Analysis of Trial Court Unification in California.* Sacramento: Judicial Council of California.

LAMB, H. RICHARD, LINDA E. WEINBERGER, AND WALTER J. DECUIR (2002). "The Police and Mental Health." *Psychiatric Services* **53**:1266–1271.

LANDREVILLE, P. (1999). "Electronic Surveillance of Delinquents: A Growing Trend." *Deviance et Societe* **23**:105–121.

LANGAN, PATRICK A. AND DAVID J. LEVIN (2002). *Recidivism of Prisoners Released in 1994.* Washington, DC: U.S. Department of Justice, Office of Justice Programs (June).

LATESSA, EDWARD J. (2005). "Increasing the Effectiveness of Probation and Parole Through Research." Unpublished paper presented at the annual training institute of the American Probation and Parole Association, New York (July).

LATESSA, EDWARD J. AND HARRY E. ALLEN (1999). *Corrections in the Community, 2/e.* Cincinnati, OH: Anderson Publishing.

LAUB, JOHN H. (1987). "Reanalyzing the Glueck Data: A New Look at Unraveling Juvenile Delinquency." Unpublished paper presented at the American Society of Criminology meetings, Montreal, Canada (November).

LAWRENCE, RICHARD A. (1984). "The Role of Legal Counsel in Juveniles' Understanding of Their Rights." *Juvenile and Family Court Journal* **34**:49–58.

LEE, G., RONALD L. AKERS, AND M.J. BORG (2004). "Social Learning and Structural Factors in Adolescent Substance Abuse." *Western Criminology Review* **5**:17–34.

LEE, LEONA (1995). "Factors Influencing Intake Disposition in a Juvenile Court." *Juvenile and Family Court Journal* **46**:43–61.

LEE, LEONA (1996). "Predictors of Juvenile Court Dispositions." *Journal of Crime and Justice* **19**:149–166.

LEIBER, MICHAEL J. (1995). "Toward Clarification of the Concept of 'Minority' Status and Decision Making in Juvenile Court Proceedings." *Journal of Crime and Justice* **18**:79–108.

LEIBER, MICHAEL J. (2002). "Disproportionate Minority Confinement (DMC) of Youth: An Analysis of State and Federal Efforts to Address the Issue." *Crime and Delinquency* **48**:3–45.

LEIBER, MICHAEL J. AND JAYNE M. STAIRS (1999). "Race, Contexts, and the Use of Intake Diversion." *Journal of Research in Crime and Delinquency* **36**:56–86.

LEMERT, EDWIN M. (1951). *Social Pathology.* New York: McGraw-Hill.

LEMERT, EDWIN M. (1967a). *Human Deviance, Social Problems, and Social Control.* Englewood Cliffs, NJ: Prentice-Hall.

LEMERT, EDWIN M. (1967b). "The Juvenile Court—Quests and Realities." In *Task Force Report: Juvenile Delinquency and Youth Crime.* Washington, DC: President's Commission on Law Enforcement and the Administration of Justice.

LEMMON, JOHN H., THOMAS L. AUSTIN, AND ALAN FELDBERG (2005). "Developing an Index of Child Maltreatment Severity Based on Survey Data of Child and Youth Services Professionals." Unpublished paper presented at the annual meeting of the Academy of Criminal Justice Sciences, Chicago (March).

LEMON, NANCY K.D. (2001). *Domestic Violence Law.* St. Paul, MN: West Group.

LENNINGS, C.J. (2002). "Children Who Kill Family Members: Three Case Studies from Australia." *Journal of Threat Assessment* **2**:57–72.

LIBERMAN, AKIVA, W. RAUDENBUSH, AND ROBERT J. SAMPSON (2005). "Neighborhood Context, Gang Presence, and Gang Involvement." Unpublished paper presented at the annual meeting of the Academy of Criminal Justice Sciences, Chicago (March).

LIEB, ROXANNE, LEE FISH, AND TODD CROSBY (1994). *A Summary of State Trends in Juvenile Justice.* Olympia, WA: Washington State Institute for Public Policy.

LIGHTFOOT, E. AND MARK UMBREIT (2004). "An Analysis of State Statutory Provisions for Victim-Offender Mediation." *Criminal Justice Policy Review* **15**:5–25.

LINDSTROM, PETER (1996). "Family Interaction, Neighborhood Context and Deviant Behavior: A Research Note." *Studies on Crime and Crime Prevention* **5**:113–119.

LISTUG, DAVID (1996). "Wisconsin Sheriff's Office Saves Money and Resources." *American Jails* **10**:85–86.

LOBLEY, DAVID, DAVID SMITH, AND CHRISTINA STERN (2001). *Freagarrach: An Evaluation of a Project for Persistent Juvenile Offenders.* Edinburgh, Scotland: The Scottish Executive Central Research Unit.

LOCHNER, LANCE AND ENRICO MORETTI (2004). "The Effect of Education on Crime: Evidence from Prison Inmates, Arrests, and Self-Reports." *American Economic Review* **94**:155–189.

LOFQUIST, WILLIAM S. (2002). "Putting Them There, Keeping Them There, and Killing Them: An Analysis of State-Level Variations in Death Penalty Intensity." *Iowa Law Review* **87**:1505–1557.

LOGALBO, ANTHONY P. AND CHARLENE M. CALLAHAN (2001). "An Evaluation of Teen Court as a Juvenile Crime Diversion Program." *Juvenile and Family Court Journal* **52**:1–11.

LOGAN, CHARLES H. AND SHARLA P. RAUSCH (1985). "Why Deinstitutionalizing Status Offenders is Pointless." *Crime and Delinquency* **31**:501–517.

LOMBARDO, RITA AND JANET DiGIORGIO-MILLER (1988). "Concepts and Techniques in Working with Juvenile Sex Offenders." *Journal of Offender Counseling Services and Rehabilitation* **13**:39–53.

LONDON, ROSS D. (2003). "The Restoration of Trust: Bringing Restorative Justice from the Margins to the Mainstream." *Criminal Justice Studies* **16**:175–195.

LORD, GEORGE F., SHANHE JIANG, AND SARAH HURLEY (2005). "Parental Efficacy and Delinquent Behavior: Longitudinal Analysis of At-Risk Adolescents in Treatment." Unpublished paper presented at the annual meeting of the Academy of Criminal Justice Sciences, Chicago (March).

LOUCKS, ALEXANDER AND EDWARD ZAMBLE (1999). "Predictors of Recidivism in Serious Female Offenders: Canada Searches for Predictors Common to Both Men and Women." *Corrections Today* **61**:26–32.

LUNDMAN, RICHARD J. (2004). "Driver Race, Ethnicity, and Gender and Citizen Reports of Vehicle Searches by Police and Vehicle Search Hits: Toward a Triangulated Scholarly Understanding." *Journal of Criminal Law and Criminology* **94**:309–349.

MACDONALD, JOHN M. (2001). "Analytic Methods for Examining Race and Ethnic Disparity in the Juvenile Courts." *Journal of Criminal Justice* **29**:507–519.

MACDONALD, JOHN M. AND MEDA CHESNEY-LIND (2001). "Gender Bias and Juvenile Justice Revisited: A Multiyear Analysis." *Crime and Delinquency* **47**:173–195.

MACK, DENNIS E. (1992). "High Impact Incarceration Program: Rikers Boot Camp." *American Jails* **6**:63–65.

MACKENZIE, DORIS LAYTON AND JAMES W. SHAW (1993). "The Impact of Shock Incarceration on Technical Violations and New Criminal Activities." *Justice Quarterly* **10**:463–487.

MACKENZIE, DORIS LAYTON, JAMES W. SHAW, AND VONCILE B. GOWDY (1993). *An Evaluation of Shock Incarceration in Louisiana.* Washington, DC: U.S. Department of Justice, Office of Justice Programs.

MACKENZIE, DORIS LAYTON AND DAVID B. WILSON (2001). "The Impact of Boot Camps and Traditional Institutions on Juvenile Residents: Perceptions, Adjustments, and Change." *Journal of Research in Crime and Delinquency* **38**:279–313.

MACKENZIE, DORIS LAYTON ET AL. (2001). *A National Study Comparing the Environments of Boot Camps with Traditional Facilities for Juvenile Offenders.* Washington, DC: U.S. Department of Justice.

MALLICOAT, STACEY L. AND MICHAEL L. RADELET (2004). "The Growing Significance of Public Opinion for Death Penalty Jurisprudence." *Journal of Crime and Justice* **27**:119–130.

MALONEY, DENNIS M., DENNIS ROMIG AND TROY ARMSTRONG (1988). "Juvenile Probation: The Balanced Approach." *Juvenile and Family Court Journal* **39**:1–63.

MARDON, STEVEN (1991). "Training America's Youth." *Corrections Today* **53**:32–65.

MARSH, FRANK H. AND JANET KATZ (EDS.) (1985). *Biology, Crime, and Ethics: A Study of Biological Explanations for Criminal Behavior.* Cincinnati, OH: Anderson Publishing.

MARUNA, SHADD, AMANDA MATRAVERS, AND ANNA KING (2004). "Disowning Our Shadow: A Psychoanalytic Approach to Understanding Punitive Public Attitudes." *Deviant Behavior* **25**:277–299.

MASSACHUSETTS STATISTICAL ANALYSIS CENTER (2001). *Implementation of the Juvenile Justice Reform Act: Youthful Offenders in Massachusetts.* Boston: Massachusetts Statistical Analysis Center.

MASTERS, RUTH E. (2004). *Counseling Criminal Justice Offenders.* Thousand Oaks, CA: Sage Publications.

MASTROFSKI, STEPHEN D. (2004). "Controlling Street-Level Police Discretion." *Annals of the American Academy of Political and Social Science* **593**:100–118.

MATZA, DAVID (1964). *Delinquency and Drift.* New York: Wiley.

MAUME, MICHAEL O. AND MATTHEW R. LEE (2003). "Social Institutions and Violence: A Sub-National Test of Institutional Anomie Theory." *Criminology* **41**:1137–1172.

MAURO, DAVID M. (2005). "Total Gang Awareness." Unpublished paper presented at the annual training institute of the American Probation and Parole Association, New York (July).

MAZEROLLE, PAUL ET AL. (2000). "Onset Age, Persistence, and Offending Versatility: Comparisons Across Gender." *Criminology* **38**:1143–1172.

MAYZER, RONI, KEVIN M. GRAY, AND SHEILA ROYO MAXWELL (2004). "Probation Absconders: A Unique Risk Group." *Journal of Crime and Justice* **32**:137–150.

MCCLUSKEY, J.D. ET AL. (2004). "Who Do You Refer? The Effects of a Policy Change on Juvenile Referrals." *Criminal Justice Policy* **15**:437–461.

MCCOLD, PAUL AND BENJAMIN WACHTEL (1998). *Restorative Policing Experiment: The Bethlehem Police Family Group Conferencing Project.* Bethlehem, PA: Real Justice.

MCCORD, DAVID M. (1995). "Toward a Typology of Wilderness-Based Residential Treatment Program Participants." *Residential Treatment for Children and Youth* **12**:51–60.

MCDEVITT, JACK (2005). "Evaluating Project Safe Neighborhoods in the District of Massachusetts." Unpublished paper presented at the annual meeting of the Academy of Criminal Justice Sciences, Chicago (March).

MCDEVITT, JACK, MARLA DOMINO, AND KATRINA BAUM (1997). *Metropolitan Day Reporting Center: An Evaluation.* Boston: Center for Criminal Justice Policy Research, Northeastern University.

MCDOWALL, DAVID, COLIN LOFTIN, AND BRIAN WIERSEMA (2000). "The Impact of Youth Curfew Laws on Juvenile Crime Rates." *Crime and Delinquency* **46**:76–91.

MCGARRELL, EDMUND (2005). "Comprehensive Examination of the Project Safe Neighborhoods Initiative." Unpublished paper presented at the annual meeting of the Academy of Criminal Justice Sciences, Chicago (March).

MCGEE, ZINA T. AND SPENCER R. BAKER (2002). "Impact of Violence on Problem Behavior among Adolescents." *Journal of Contemporary Criminal Justice* **18**:74–93.

MCGLOIN, J. M., T.C. PRATT, AND J. MAAHS (2004). "Rethinking the IQ-Delinquency Relationship: A Longitudinal Analysis of Multiple Theoretical Models." *Justice Quarterly* **21**:603–635.

MCLEAN COUNTY COURT SERVICES (2002). *Day Reporting Center for Juveniles Possessing Firearms.* McLean County, IL: McLean County Court Services.

MCNEILL, F. AND S. BATCHELOR (2004). "Persistent Offending By Young People: Developing Practice." In *Issues in Community and Criminal Justice: Monograph 3.* London: Napo.

MEARS, DANIEL P. (2001). "Getting Tough with Juvenile Offenders: Explaining Support for Sanctioning Youths as Adults." *Criminal Justice and Behavior* **28**:206–226.

MEARS, DANIEL P. (2003). "A Critique of Waiver Research: Critical Next Steps in Assessing the Impacts of Laws for Transferring Juveniles to the Criminal Justice System." *Youth Violence and Juvenile Justice* **1**:156–172.

MEISEL, JOSHUA S. (2001). "Relationships and Juvenile Offenders: The Effects of Intensive Aftercare Supervision." *Prison Journal* **81**:206–245.

MELDE, CHRIS E. (2005). "Assimilation and Perceived Danger at School: An Examination of Immigrant Youth." Unpublished paper presented at the annual meeting of the Academy of Criminal Justice Sciences, Chicago (March).

MENCKEN, F.C., J. NOLAN, AND S. BERHANU (2004). "Juveniles, Illicit Drug Activity, and Homicides Against

Law Enforcement Officers." *Homicide Studies* **8**:327–349.

MENDEL, RICHARD A. (2001). *Less Cost, More Safety: Guiding Lights for Reform in Juvenile Justice.* Washington, DC: American Youth Policy Forum.

MEREDITH, COLIN AND CHANTEL PAQUETTE (2001). *Victims of Crime Research Series: Summary Report on Victim Impact Statement Groups.* Unpublished paper.

MERIANOS, DOROTHY (2005). "Gender Differences in Mental Health Status among Incarcerated Juveniles." Unpublished paper presented at the annual meeting of the Academy of Criminal Justice Sciences, Chicago (March).

MERLO, ALIDA V. AND PETER J. BENEKOS (2003). "Defining Juvenile Justice in the 21st Century." *Youth Violence and Juvenile Justice* **1**:276–288.

MERTON, ROBERT K. (1957). *Social Theory and Social Structure.* New York: Free Press.

METTS, MICHELLE (2005). "Involvement of Probation and Parole in Project Safe Neighborhoods." New York: Unpublished paper presented at the annual meeting of the American Probation and Parole Association (July).

MILLER, WALTER B. (2001). *The Growth of Youth Gang Problems in the United States: 1970–1998.* Washington, DC: U.S. Office of Juvenile Justice and Delinquency Prevention.

MINER, MICHAEL H. (2002). "Factors Associated with Recidivism in Juveniles: An Analysis of Serious Juvenile Sex Offenders." *Journal of Research in Crime and Delinquency* **39**:421–436.

MINNESOTA CRIME CONTROL PLANNING BOARD (1981). *Minnesota Community Corrections Act Evaluation.* St. Paul: Minnesota Crime Control Planning Board.

MINNESOTA OFFICE OF THE LEGISLATIVE AUDITOR (1995). *Guardians Ad Litem.* St. Paul: Minnesota Office of the Legislative Auditor Program Evaluation Division.

MINOR, KEVIN I., JAMES B. WELLS, AND BRANDI JONES (2004). "Staff Perceptions of the Work Environment in Juvenile Group Home Settings: A Study of Social Climate." *Journal of Offender Rehabilitation* **38**:17–30.

MITCHELL, OJMARRH ET AL. (2000). "The Impact of Individual, Organizational, and Environmental Attributes on Voluntary Turnover among Juvenile Correctional Staff Members." *Justice Quarterly* **17**:333–357.

MOAK, STACY C. AND LISA H. WALLACE (2000). "Attitudes of Louisiana Practitioners toward Rehabilitation of Juvenile Offenders." *American Journal of Criminal Justice* **24**:271–285.

MOAK, STACY C. AND LISA H. WALLACE (2003). "Legal Changes in Juvenile Justice: Then and Now." *Youth Violence and Juvenile Justice* **1**:289–299.

MONROE, JACQUELINE (2004). "Getting a Puff: A Social Learning Test of Adolescents Smoking." *Journal of Child and Adolescent Substance Abuse* **13**:71–83.

MOON, MELISSA M. ET AL. (2000). "Putting Kids to Death: Specifying Public Support for Juvenile Capital Punishment." *Justice Quarterly* **17**:663–684.

MOORE, JOAN (1993). "Gangs, Drugs, and Violence." In S. Cummings and D.J. Monti (eds.) *Gangs: The Origins and Impact of Contemporary Youth Gangs in the United States.* Albany: State University of New York Press.

MOORE COUNTY GOVERNMENT (2002). *Moore County Day Reporting Center.* Moore County, NC: Moore County Government.

MORGAN, ROD (2003). "Thinking about the Demand for Probation Services." *Probation Journal* **50**:7–19.

MOSELEY, IVYANN (2005). "Exposure to Violence and Its Relation to Problem-Solving Strategies." Unpublished paper presented at the annual meeting of the Academy of Criminal Justice Sciences, Chicago (March).

MOYER, IMOGENE (2001). *Criminological Theories: Traditional and Nontraditional Voices and Themes.* Thousand Oaks, CA: Sage.

MUELLER, DAVID AND LISA HUTCHISON-WALLACE (2005). "Verbal Abuse, Self-Esteem, and Peer Victimization." Unpublished paper presented at the annual meeting of the Academy of Criminal Justice Sciences, Chicago (March).

MULFORD, CARRIE FRIED ET AL. (2004). "Legal Issues Affecting Mentally Disordered and Developmentally Delayed Youth in the Justice System." *International Journal of Forensic Mental Health* **3**:3–22.

MURRELL, PAMELA R. (2005). "Advocating for Children in the Juvenile Justice System." Unpublished paper presented at the annual meeting of the Academy of Criminal Justice Sciences, Chicago (March).

MUSICK, DAVID (1995). *An Introduction to the Sociology of Juvenile Delinquency.* Albany: State University of New York Press.

MUSSER, DENISE CASAMENTO (2001). "Public Access to Juvenile Records." *Corrections Today* **63**:112–113.

MYERS, MATTHEW L. (1973). "Legal Rights in a Juvenile Correctional Institution." *Journal of Law Reform* **7**:242–266.

MYERS, BRYAN (2004). "Victim Impact Statements and Mock Jury Sentencing: The Impact of Dehumanizing Language on a Death Qualified Sample." *American Journal of Forensic Psychology* **22**:39–55.

NAFEKH, MARK (2002). *The Statistical Information on Recidivism.* Ottawa, Canada: Correctional Service of Canada, Research Branch.

NATIONAL CENTER FOR JUVENILE JUSTICE (2001). *Petitioned Cases to Juvenile Courts 1997.* Pittsburgh, PA: National Center for Juvenile Justice.

NATIONAL GANG CRIME RESEARCH CENTER (2000). "Preliminary Results of Project GANGMILL: A Special Report of the National Gang Crime Research Center." *Journal of Gang Research* **7**:38–76.

NATIONAL GANG INVESTIGATOR'S ASSOCIATION (2002). *Female Gangs in the United States.* Washington, DC: National Gang Investigator's Association.

NELLIS, MIKE (2004). "'I Know Where You Live': Electronic Monitoring and Penal Policy." *British Journal of Community Justice* **2**:33–55.

NEWMAN, KATHERINE S. (2004). *Rampage: The Social Roots of School Shootings.* New York: Basic Books.

NEW MEXICO JUVENILE JUSTICE DIVISION (2002). *Juvenile Justice Probation and Parole Manual.* Albuquerque: New Mexico Juvenile Justice Division.

NEW YORK STATE DEPARTMENT OF CORRECTIONAL SERVICES (1992). *Guidelines for Volunteer Services.* Albany: New York State Department of Correctional Services.

NIETO, MARCUS (1998). *Probation for Adult and Juvenile Offenders: Options for Improved Accountability.* Sacramento: California Research Bureau.

NORMAN, SHERWOOD (1970). *The Youth Service Bureau: A Key to Delinquency Prevention.* Hackensack, NJ: National Council on Crime and Delinquency.

NUFFIELD, J. (2003). *The Challenges of Youth Justice in Rural and Isolated Areas in Canada.* Ottawa: Department of Justice Canada, Research and Statistics Directorate.

OFFICE OF JUVENILE JUSTICE AND DELINQUENCY PREVENTION (2002). *Female Delinquents.* Washington, DC: U.S. Government Printing Office.

OFFICE OF JUVENILE JUSTICE AND DELINQUENCY PREVENTION (2005). *Juvenile Offenders and Victims: National Report.* Washington, DC: Office of Juvenile Justice and Delinquency Prevention.

OFFUTT, WILLIAM M. JR. (1995). *Of "Good Laws" and "Good Men": Law and Society in the Delaware Valley 1680–1710.* Chicago: University of Illinois Press.

OLIVERO, J. MICHAEL (2005). "Youth at Risk and Measures of Psychopathy." Unpublished paper presented at the annual meeting of the Academy of Criminal Justice Sciences, Chicago (March).

O'MAHONY, DAVID (2000). "Young People, Crime, and Criminal Justice: Patterns and Prospects for the Future." *Youth and Society* 33:60–80.

O'SHAUGHNESSY, R.J. (2004). "Violent Adolescents: Psychiatry, Philosophy, and Politics." *Journal of the American Academy of Psychiatry and the Law* 32:12–20.

OSGOOD, D. WAYNE AND A.L. ANDERSON (2004). "Unstructured Socializing and Rates of Delinquency." *Criminology* 42:519–549.

PALMER, TED (1994). *A Profile of Correctional Effectiveness and New Directions for Research.* Albany: State University of New York Press.

PARENT, DALE (2003). *Correctional Boot Camps: Lessons from a Decade of Research.* Washington, DC: U.S. National Institute of Justice.

PARK, SUYEON (2005). "The Effect of Age of Onset on Violent Crime." Unpublished paper presented at the annual meeting of the Academy of Criminal Justice Sciences, Chicago (March).

PARKER, CHAUNCEY G. (2005). "Expanding the Role of Probation and Parole in Public Safety Partnerships." Unpublished paper presented at the annual training institute of the American Probation and Parole Association, New York (July).

PARRY, C.D. ET AL. (2004). "Trends in Adolescent Alcohol and Other Drug Use." *Journal of Adolescence* 27:429–440.

PARTON, FELICITY AND ANDREW DAY (2002). "Empathy, Intimacy, Loneliness and Locus of Control in Child Sex Offenders." *Journal of Child Sexual Abuse* 11:41–57.

PATCHIN, JUSTIN AND SAMEER HINDUJA (2005). "Bullies Move Beyond the Schoolyard: A Preliminary Look at Cyberbullying." Unpublished paper presented at the annual meeting of the Academy of Criminal Justice Sciences, Chicago (March).

PATRICK, STEVEN ET AL. (2004). "Control Group Study of Juvenile Diversion Programs." *Social Science Journal* 41:129–135.

PENNELL, SUSAN, CHRISTINE CURTIS, AND DENNIS C. SCHECK (1990). "Controlling Juvenile Delinquency: An Evaluation of an Interagency Strategy." *Crime and Delinquency* 36:257–275.

PETERSON, SCOTT (2005). *The Growth of Teen Courts in the United States.* Washington, DC: Office of Juvenile Justice and Delinquency Prevention.

PETERSON, B. MICHELLE, MARTIN D. RUCK, AND CHRISTOPHER J. KOEGL (2001). "Youth Court Dispositions: Perceptions of Canadian Juvenile Offenders." *International Journal of Offender Therapy and Comparative Criminology* 45:593–605.

PIERCE, L. AND V. BOZALEK (2004). "Child Abuse in South Africa: An Examination of How Child Abuse and Neglect Are Defined." *Child Abuse and Neglect* 28:817–832.

PIERCE, CHRISTINE SCHNYDER AND STANLEY L. BRODSKY (2002). "Trust and Understanding in the Attorney-Juvenile Relationship." *Behavioral Sciences and the Law* 20:89–107.

PINGREE, DAVID H. (1984). "Florida Youth Services." *Corrections Today* 46:60–62.

PLATT, ANTHONY M. (2001). "Social Insecurity: The Transformation of American Criminal Justice." *Social Justice* 28:138–155.

PODKOPACZ, MARCY RASMUSSEN, AND BARRY C. FELD (1996). "The End of the Line: An Empirical Study of Judicial Waiver." *Journal of Criminal Law and Criminology* 86:449–492.

POLAN, SUSAN LORI (1994). *CSP Revisited: An Evaluation of Juvenile Diversion.* Ann Arbor, MI: University Microfilms International.

POPE, CARL E., RICK LOVELL, AND HEIDI M. HSIA (2002). *Disproportionate Minority Confinement: A Review of the Research Literature from 1989 through 2001.* Washington, DC: U.S. Department of Justice, Office of Justice Programs.

POPE, CARL E. AND HOWARD N. SNYDER (2003). *Race as a Factor in Juvenile Arrests.* Washington, DC: U.S. Department of Justice, Office of Justice Programs.

PORTERFIELD, AUSTIN L. (1943). "Delinquency and Its Outcome in Court and College." *American Journal of Sociology* 49:199–208.

POTTER, ROBERTO HUGH AND SUMAN KAKAR (2002). "The Diversion Decision-Making Process from the Juvenile Court Practitioners' Perspective." *Journal of Contemporary Criminal Justice* 18:20–38.

POYSER, SAM (2004). "The Role of Police 'Discretion' in Britain and an Analysis of Proposals for Reform." *Police Journal* 77:5–17.

PRATT, JOHN AND ROGER GRIMSHAW (1985). "A Juvenile Justice Pre-Court Tribunal at Work." *Howard Journal of Criminal Justice* 24:213–228.

PROJECT SAFE NEIGHBORHOODS (2005). "Project Safe Neighborhood." Unpublished paper presented at the annual meeting of the Academy of Criminal Justice Sciences, Chicago (March).

RACKMILL, STEPHEN J. (1996). "Printzlien's Legacy, the 'Brooklyn Plan,' A.K.A. Deferred Prosecution." *Federal Probation* 60:8–15.

RANS, LAUREL L. (1984). "The Validity of Models to predict Violence in Community and Prison Settings." *Corrections Today* 46:50–63.

RAPPAPORT, AARON J. (2003). "Unprincipled Punishment: The U.S. Sentencing Commission's Troubling Silence about the Purposes of Punishment." *Buffalo Criminal Law Review* 6:1043–1122.

RASMUSSEN, A. (2004). "Teen Court Referral, Sentencing, and Subsequent Recidivism: Two Proportional Hazards Models and a Little Speculation." *Crime and Delinquency* 50:615–635.

RAY, KATHERINE E. BROWN AND LEANNE FIFTAL ALARID (2004). "Examining Racial Disparity of Male Property Offenders in the Missouri Juvenile Justice System." *Youth Violence and Juvenile Justice* **2**:107–128.

REBELLON, CESAR J. (2002). "Reconsidering the Broken Homes/Delinquency Relationship and Exploring Its Mediating Mechanisms." *Criminology* **40**:103–136.

RECKLESS, WALTER (1967). *The Crime Problem.* New York: Appleton-Century-Crofts.

REDDINGTON, FRANCES P. (2005). "The Status of Juvenile Justice in Chicago." Unpublished paper presented at the annual meeting of the Academy of Criminal Justice Sciences, Chicago (March).

REESE, WILLIAM A. III AND RUSSELL L. CURTIS JR. (1991). "Paternalism and the Female Status Offender: Remanding the Juvenile Justice Double Standard." *Social Science Journal* **28**:63–83.

REGINI, LISA A. (1998). "Combating Gangs: The Need for Innovation." *FBI Law Enforcement Bulletin* **67**:25–32.

REHLING, WILLIAM R. (2005). "Adult Consultation for Minors in Custody During Interrogation." Unpublished paper presented at the annual meeting of the Academy of Criminal Justice Sciences, Chicago (March).

REYNOLDS, K. MICHAEL, RUTH SEYDLITZ, AND PAMELA JENKINS (2000). "Do Juvenile Curfew Laws Work? A Time-Series Analysis of the New Orleans Law." *Justice Quarterly* **17**:205–230.

REYNOLDS, K. MICHAEL ET AL. (1999). "Contradictions and Consensus: Youths Speak Out about Juvenile Curfews." *Journal of Crime and Justice* **22**:171–192.

RHOADES, PHILIP W. AND KRISTINA M. ZAMBRANO (2005). "Leading Practice to Theory: Data Driven Strategic Delinquency Prevention Planning Goes Regional." Unpublished paper presented at the annual meeting of the Academy of Criminal Justice Sciences, Chicago (March).

RIBEAUD, DENIS AND PATRIK MANZONI (2004). "The Relationship Between Defendant's Social Attributes, Psychiatric Assessment, and Sentencing." *International Journal of Law and Psychiatry* **27**:375–386.

RISLER, EDWIN A., RICHARD SUTPHEN, AND JOHN SHIELDS (2000). "Preliminary Validation of the Juvenile First Offender Risk Assessment Index." *Research on Social Work and Practice* **10**:111–126.

RIVERS, ANTHONY L. (2005). "Appropriateness of Juvenile Transfer to Adult Court." Unpublished paper presented at the annual meeting of the Academy of Criminal Justice Sciences, Chicago (March).

RIVERS, JAMES E., RICHARD DEMBO, AND ROBERT S. ANWYL (1998). "The Hillsborough County, Florida Juvenile Assessment Center: A Prototype." *Prison Journal* **78**:439–450.

ROBBINS, IRA P. (1986). "Privatization of Corrections: Defining the Issues." *Federal Probation* **50**:24–30.

ROBERTS, JULIAN V. AND THOMAS GABOR (2004). "Living in the Shadow of Prison: Lessons from the Canadian Experience in Decarceration." *British Journal of Criminology* **44**:92–112.

ROBERTS, JULIAN V., JOAN NUFFIELD, AND ROBERT HANN (2000). "Parole and the Public: Attitudinal and Behavioral Responses." *Empirical and Applied Criminal Justice Research Journal* **1**:1–25.

ROBERTSON, ANGELA A., PAUL W. GRIMES, AND KEVIN E. ROGERS (2001). "A Short-Run, Cost-Benefit Analysis of Community-Based Interventions for Juvenile Offenders." *Crime and Delinquency* **47**:265–284.

ROBINSON, JOHN H. (ED.) (1991). "Symposium on Serious Juvenile Crime." *Notre Dame Journal of Law, Ethics, and Public Policy* **5**:257–264.

ROBINSON, PAUL H. AND JOHN M. DARLEY (1995). *Justice, Liability, and Blame: Community Views and the Criminal Law.* Boulder, CO: Westview Press.

RODRIGUEZ, NANCY AND VINCENT J. WEBB (2004). "Multiple Measures of Juvenile Drug Court Effectiveness: Results of a Quasi-Experimental Design." *Crime and Delinquency* **50**:292–314.

ROGERS, JOSEPH W. (1990). "The Predisposition Report: Maintaining the Promise of Individualized Juvenile Justice." *Federal Probation* **54**:43–57.

ROGERS, CHRISTOPHER (1993). "Gang-Related Homicides in Los Angeles County." *Journal of Forensic Sciences* **38**:831–834.

ROGERS, JOSEPH W. AND JAMES D. WILLIAMS (1995). "The Predispositional Report, Decision Making, and Juvenile Court Policy." *Juvenile and Family Court Journal* **45**:47–57.

ROMERO, ESTRELLA ET AL. (2001). "Values and Antisocial Behavior among Spanish Adolescents." *Journal of Genetic Psychology* **1**:20–40.

ROMIG, DENNIS A. (1978). *Justice for Our Children.* Lexington, MA: Lexington Books.

ROSENBAUM, JILL LESLIE (1996). "A Violent Few: Gang Girls in the California Youth Authority." *Journal of Gang Research* **3**:17–33.

ROSSUM, RALPH A., BENEDICT J. KOLLER, AND CHRISTOPHER MANFREDI (1987). *Juvenile Justice Reform: A Model for the States.* Claremont, CA: Rose Institute of State and Local Government and the American Legislative Exchange Council.

ROWE, DAVID C., ALEXANDER T. VAZSONYI, AND DANIEL J. FLANNERY (1995). "Sex Differences in Crime? Do Means and Within-Sex Variation Have Similar Causes?" *Journal of Research in Crime and Delinquency* **32**:84–100.

ROY, SUDIPTO (2004). "Factors Related to Success and Recidivism in a Day Reporting Center." *Criminal Justice Studies* **17**:3–17.

RUBACK, R. BARRY AND PAULA J. VARDAMAN (1997). "Decision Making in Delinquency Cases: The Role of Race and Juveniles' Admission/Denial of the Crime." *Law and Human Behavior* **21**:47–69.

RUSSELL, BETTY G. (2001). "The TAMAR Project: Addressing Trauma Issues of Offenders in Jails." *American Jails* **15**:41–44.

SALEKIN, RANDALL T., MARIA A. LARREA, AND TRACY ZIEGLER (2002). "Relationships Between the MACI and the BASC in the Assessment of Child and Adolescent Offenders." *Journal of Forensic Psychology Practice* **2**:35–50.

SALEKIN, RANDALL T., RICHARD ROGERS, AND KAREN L. USTAD (2001). "Juvenile Waiver to Adult Criminal Courts: Prototypes for Dangerousness, Sophistication-Maturity, and Amenability to Treatment." *Psychology, Public Policy, and Law* **7**:381–408.

SANBORN, JOSEPH B. JR. (1993). "Philosophical, Legal and Systemic Aspects of Juvenile Court Plea Bargaining." *Crime and Delinquency* **39**:509–527.

SANBORN, JOSEPH B. JR. (2001). "A *Parens Patriae* Figure or Impartial Fact Finder? Policy Questions and Conflicts for the Juvenile Court Judge." *Criminal Justice Policy Review* **12:**311–332.

SANBORN, JOSEPH B. JR. (2005). "Juveniles' Competency to Stand Trial: Wading Throughout the Rhetoric and the Evidence." Unpublished paper presented at the annual meeting of the Academy of Criminal Justice Sciences, Chicago (March).

SANGER, D. ET AL. (2004). "Opinions of Female Juvenile Delinquents about Their Interactions in Chat Rooms." *Journal of Correctional Education* **55:**120–131.

SANGSTER, JOAN (2002). *Girl Trouble: Female Delinquency in English Canada.* Toronto, Canada: Between the Lines.

SANTANA, EDWIN L. (2005). "Total Gang Awareness." Unpublished paper presented at the annual training institute of the American Probation and Parole Association, New York (July).

SAWICKI, DONNA RAU, BEATRIX SCHAEFFER, AND JEANIE THIES (1999). "Predicting Successful Outcomes for Serious and Chronic Juveniles in Residential Placement." *Juvenile and Family Court Journal* **50:**21–31.

SCAHILL, MEGHAN C. (2000). *Female Delinquency Cases, 1997.* Washington, DC: U.S. Department of Justice.

SCHAFFNER, LAURIE (2005). "Gender Responsive Programs for Girls: Theory Into Practice." Unpublished paper presented at the annual meeting of the Academy of Criminal Justice Sciences, Chicago (March).

SCHINKE, S.P. ET AL. (2004). "Reducing the Risks of Alcohol Use among Urban Youth: Three-Year Effects of a Computer Based Intervention With and Without Parent Involvement." *Journal of Studies on Alcohol* **65:**443–449.

SCHLOSSMAN, STEVEN AND ALEXANDER PISCIOTTA (1986). "Identifying and Treating Serious Juvenile Offenders: The View from California and New York in the 1920s." In *Intervention Strategies for Chronic Juvenile Offenders: Some New Perspectives,* Peter W. Greenwood (ed.). New York: Greenwood Press.

SCHMID, KARL H. (2002). "Journalist's Privilege in Criminal Proceedings: An Analysis of United States Courts of Appeals Decisions from 1973–1999." *American Criminal Law Review* **39:**1441–1499.

SCHMIDT, ANNESLEY K. (1998). "Electronic Monitoring: What Does the Literature Tell Us?" *Federal Probation* **62:**10–19.

SCHMIDT, RIK ET AL. (1998). "Measuring Success: The Washington State Juvenile Rehabilitation Model." *Corrections Today* **60:**104–106.

SCHNEIDER, ANNE LARSON AND PETER R. SCHNEIDER (1985). "The Impact of Restitution on Recidivism of Juvenile Offenders: An Experiment in Clayton County, Georgia." *Criminal Justice Review* **10:**1–10.

SCHULENBERG, JENNIFER L. (2003). "The Social Context of Police Discretion with Young Offenders." *Canadian Journal of Criminology and Criminal Justice* **45:**127–157.

SEITER, RICHARD P. AND ANGELA D. WEST (2003). "Supervision Styles in Probation and Parole: An Analysis of Activities." *Journal of Offender Rehabilitation* **38:**57–75.

SEYKO, RONALD J. (2001). "Balanced Approach and Restorative Justice Efforts in Allegheny County, Pennsylvania." *Prison Journal* **81:**187–205.

SHAFER, JOSEPH A., DAVID L. CARTER, AND ANDRA KATZ-BANNISTER (2004). "Studying Traffic Stop Encounters." *Journal of Criminal Justice* **32:**159–170.

SHAW, CLIFFORD R. AND HENRY D. McKAY (1972). *Juvenile Delinquency and Urban Areas* (rev. ed.). Chicago: University of Chicago Press.

SHAW, JAMES W. AND DORIS LAYTON MACKENZIE (1992). "The One-Year Community Supervision Performance of Drug Offenders and Louisiana DOC-Identified Substance Abusers." *Journal of Criminal Justice* **20:**501–516.

SHAWNEE COUNTY DEPARTMENT OF COMMUNITY CORRECTIONS (2002). *Shawnee County Community Corrections.* Topeka, KS: Shawnee County Department of Community Corrections.

SHEARER, ROBERT A. (2002). "Probation Strategies of Juvenile and Adult Pre-Service Trainees." *Federal Probation* **66:**33–42.

SHELDEN, RANDALL G. (1998). "Confronting the Ghost of Mary Ann Crouse: Gender Bias in the Juvenile Justice System." *Juvenile and Family Court Journal* **49:**11–26.

SHELDEN, RANDALL G., SHARON K. TRACY, AND WILLIAM B. BROWN (2001). *Youth Gangs in American Society, 2/e.* Belmont, CA: Wadsworth.

SHELDON, WILLIAM H. (1949). *The Varieties of Delinquent Youth.* New York: Harper.

SHEPHERD, JOANNA M. (2002). "Police, Prosecutors, Criminals and Determinate Sentencing: The Truth about Truth in Sentencing Laws." *Journal of Law and Economics* **45:**409–534.

SHINE, JAMES AND DWIGHT PRICE (1992). "Prosecutors and Juvenile Justice: New Roles and Perspectives." In *Juvenile Justice and Public Policy: Toward a National Agenda,* I.M. Schwartz (ed.) New York: Lexington Books.

SHORT, JAMES F. JR. AND F. IVAN NYE (1958). "Extent of Unrecorded Juvenile Delinquency: Tentative Conclusions." Journal of Criminal Law and Police Science **49:**296–302.

SHUTT, J. EAGLE ET AL. (2004). "Reconsidering the Leading Myths of Stranger Child Abductions." *Criminal Justice Studies* **17:**127–134.

SICKMUND, MELISSA (2004). *Juveniles in Corrections.* Washington, DC: Office of Justice Programs.

SIEGEL, JANE A. AND LINDA M. WILLIAMS (2003). "The Relationship Between Child Sexual Abuse and Female Delinquency and Crime." *Journal of Research in Crime and Delinquency* **40:**71–94.

SILVER, ERIC (2002). "A Cautionary Note on the Use of Actuarial Risk Assessment Tools for Social Control." *Crime and Delinquency* **48:**138–161.

SIMS, BARBARA AND WENBO SHI (1999). "An Assessment of Pennsylvania Intermediate Punishment Programs." *Corrections Management Quarterly* **3:**53–62.

SINCLAIR, JIM (2005). "Victim's Rights and Issues: Educating Judicial and Court Personnel." Unpublished paper presented at the annual training institute of the American Probation and Parole Association, New York (July).

SINGER, SIMON I. (2003). "Incarcerating Juveniles Into Adulthood: Organizational Fields of Knowledge and the Back End of Waiver." *Youth Violence and Juvenile Justice* **1:**115–127.

SMALL, MARGARET AND KELLIE DRESSLER TETRICK (2001). "School Violence: An Overview." *Juvenile Justice* **8**:3–12.

SMITH, BEVERLY A. (1989). "Female Admissions and Paroles of the Western House of Refuge in the 1880s: An Historical Example of Community Corrections." *Journal of Research in Crime and Delinquency* **26**:36–66.

SMITH, ROBERT R. AND VICTOR S. LOMBARDO (2002). "Evaluation Report of the Juvenile Mediation Program." *Corrections Compendium* **27**:1–3, 19.

SMITH, WILLIAM R. AND MICHAEL F. ALOISI (1999). "Prediction of Recidivism Among 'Second Timers' in the Juvenile Justice System: Efficiency in Screening Chronic Offenders." *American Journal of Criminal Justice* **23**:201–222.

SMITH-KHURI, E. ET AL. (2004). "A Cross-National Study of Violence-Related Behaviors in Adolescents." *Archives of Pediatrics and Adolescent Medicine* **15**:539–544.

SNYDER, HOWARD N. (1988). *Court Careers of Juvenile Offenders.* Pittsburgh, PA: National Center for Juvenile Justice.

SNYDER, HOWARD N. (2003). *Juvenile Arrests 2001.* Washington, DC: U.S. Department of Justice, Office of Justice Programs.

SNYDER, HOWARD N., MELISSA SICKMUND AND EILEEN POE-YAMAGATA (1996). *Juvenile Offenders and Victims: 1996 Update on Violence: Statistics Summary.* Pittsburgh, PA: National Center for Juvenile Justice.

SNYDER, HOWARD N., MELISSA SICKMUND, AND EILEEN POE-YAMAGATA (2000). *Juvenile Transfers to Criminal Court in the 1990s: Lessons Learned from Four Studies.* Washington, DC: U.S. Office of Juvenile Justice and Delinquency Prevention.

SOUWEINE, JESSE AND AJAY KHASHU (2001). *Changing the PINS System in New York.* New York: Vera Institute of Justice.

SPRUIT, J.E., ET AL. (1998). "Forensic History." *International Journal of Law and Psychiatry* **21**:315–446.

STAHL, ANNE L. (2001). *Drug Offense Cases in Juvenile Courts, 1989–1998.* Washington, DC: U.S. Department of Justice.

STALANS, LORETTA J. ET AL. (2004). "Identifying Three Types of Violent Offenders and Predicting Violent Recidivism While on Probation: A Classification Tree Analysis." *Law and Human Behavior* **28**:253–271.

ST. CYR, JENNA L. (2003). "The Folk Devil Reacts: Gangs and Moral Panic." *Criminal Justice Review* **28**:26–46.

STEEN, SARA (2001). "Contested Portrayals: Medical and Legal Social Control of Juvenile Sex Offenders." *Sociological Quarterly* **42**:325–350.

STEINBERG, ANNIE, JANE BROOKS, AND TARIQ REMTULLA (2003). "Youth Hate Crimes: Identification, Prevention, and Intervention." *American Journal of Psychiatry* **160**:979–989.

STEINBERG, LAURENCE AND ELIZABETH S. SCOTT (2003). "Less Guilty By Reason of Adolescence: Developmental Immaturity, Diminished Responsibility, and the Juvenile Death Penalty." *American Psychologist* **58**:1009–1018.

STEINER, BENJAMIN, ELIZABETH ROBERTS, AND CRAIG HEMMENS (2003). "Where is Juvenile Probation Today? The Legally Prescribed Functions of Juvenile Probation Officers." *Criminal Justice Studies* **16**:267–281.

STODDARD, CINDY, DAVID MUELLER, AND RICHARD LAWRENCE (2005). "The Constitutionalization of School Discipline: Balancing Students' Rights with School Safety." Unpublished paper presented at the annual meeting of the Academy of Criminal Justice Sciences, Chicago (March).

STOLZENBERG, LISA AND STEWART J. D'ALESSIO (2004). "Capital Punishment, Execution Publicity, and Murder in Houston, Texas." *Journal of Criminal Law and Criminology* **94**:361–379.

STREIB, VICTOR L. (1987). *The Death Penalty for Juveniles.* Bloomington: Indiana University Press.

STUART-RYTER, LOREN (2002). *Youth, Gangs, and the State in Indonesia.* Ann Arbor, MI: University Microfilms International.

STUCKY, THOMAS D. (2003). "Local Politics and Violent Crime in U.S. Cities." *Criminology* **41**:1101–1135.

STURGEON, BILL (2005). "Case Management of Youthful Offenders in the Community." Unpublished paper presented at the annual training institute of the American Probation and Parole Association, New York (July).

STYVE, GAYLENE J. ET AL. (2000). "Perceived Conditions of Confinement: A National Evaluation of Juvenile Boot Camps and Traditional Facilities." *Law and Human Behavior* **24**:297–308.

SUN, IVAN AND BRIAN K. PAYNE (2004). "Social Disorganization, Legitimacy of Local Institutions, and Neighborhood Crime." *Journal of Crime and Justice* **27**:33–60.

SUPANCIC, MICHAEL (2005). "A Back Door Approach to Aggression and Gender Violence in Middle Schools." Unpublished paper presented at the annual meeting of the Academy of Criminal Justice Sciences, Chicago (March).

SUTHERLAND, EDWIN H. (1939). *Principles of Criminology.* Philadelphia: Lippincott.

SUTHERLAND, EDWIN H. (1951). "Critique of Sheldon's Varieties of Delinquent Youth." *American Sociological Review* **16**:10–13.

SWAIN, R.C., K.L. HENRY, AND N.E. BAEZ (2004). "Risk-Taking, Attitudes Toward Aggression, and Aggressive Behavior among Rural Middle School Youth." *Violence and Victims* **19**:157–170.

SWANSON, CHERYL G. (2005). "Incorporating Restorative Justice into the School Resource Officer Model." Unpublished paper presented at the annual meeting of the Academy of Criminal Justice Sciences, Chicago (March).

SWEET, JOSEPH (1985). "Probation as Therapy." *Corrections Today* **47**:89–90.

SWENSON, CYNTHIA CUPIT AND WALLACE A. KENNEDY (1995). "Perceived Control and Treatment Outcome with Chronic Adolescent Offenders." *Adolescence* **30**:565–578.

SWISHER, J.D. ET AL. (2004). "A Cost-Effectiveness Comparison of Two Approaches to Life Skills Training." *Journal of Alcohol and Drug Education* **48**:71–87.

TALWAR, VICTORIA ET AL. (2004). "Children's Conceptual Knowledge of Lying and Its Relation to Their Actual Behaviors." *Law and Human Behavior* **26**:395–415.

TAROLLA, SUSAN M. ET AL. (2002). "Understanding and Treating Juvenile Offenders: A Review of Current Knowledge and Future Directions." *Aggression and Violent Behavior* **7**:125–143.

TAXMAN, FAYE (2005). "Tools of the Trade: Incorporating Science into Practice." Unpublished paper presented at the annual meeting of the American Probation and Parole Association, New York (July).

TERRY-MCELRATH, YVONNE M. AND DUANE C. MCBRIDE (2004). "Local Implementation of Drug Policy and Access to Treatment Services for Juveniles." *Crime and Delinquency* **50**:60–87.

TESKE, STEVEN C. (2005). "Juvenile Detention Reform: Using Collaborative Strategies and Evidence-Based Practices." Unpublished paper presented at the annual training institute of the American Probation and Parole Association, New York (July).

TEXAS JUVENILE PROBATION COMMISSION (2002). *Female Juvenile Offenders.* Austin: Texas Juvenile Probation Commission.

TEXAS YOUTH COMMISSION (1990). *Independent Living: An Evaluation.* Austin: Texas Youth Commission Department of Research and Planning.

TEXAS YOUTH COMMISSION (2005). *Certification Rates in Texas, 1990–1999.* Austin: Texas Youth Commission Department of Research and Planning.

THOMAS, CHRISTOPHER, CHARLES E. HOLZER, AND JULIE A. WALL (2004). "Serious Delinquency and Gang Membership." *Adolescent Psychiatry* **27**:61–81.

THORNTON, ROBERT L. (2005). "Involvement of Probation and Parole in Project Safe Neighborhoods." Unpublished paper presented at the annual training institute of the American Probation and Parole Association, New York (July).

THURMAN, QUINT C. AND JIHONG ZHAO (2004). *Contemporary Policing: Controversies, Challenges, and Solutions.* Los Angeles: Roxbury.

TONRY, MICHAEL (1997). *Intermediate Sanctions in Sentencing Guidelines.* Washington, DC: U.S. National Institute of Justice.

TORBET, PATRICIA AND PATRICK GRIFFIN (2002). "Mission-Driven, Performance-Based, and Outcome-Focused Probation." *APPA Perspectives* **26**:22–25.

TORBET, PATRICIA AND LINDA SZYMANSKI (1998). *State Legislative Responses to Violent Juvenile Crime: 1996–1997 Update.* Washington, DC: U.S. Department of Justice.

TORBET, PATRICIA ET AL. (1996). *State Responses to Serious and Violent Juvenile Crime.* Washington, DC: Office of Juvenile Justice and Delinquency Prevention.

TOTH, REID C. (2005). "Limiting Discretion at Intake: An Analysis of Intake Data from North Carolina Juvenile Courts." Unpublished paper presented at the annual meeting of the Academy of Criminal Justice Sciences, Chicago (March).

TRESTER, HAROLD B. (1981). *Supervision of the Offender.* Englewood Cliffs, NJ: Prentice-Hall.

TRIPLETT, RUTH AND LAURA B. MYERS (1995). "Evaluating Contextual Patterns of Delinquency: Gender-Based Differences." *Justice Quarterly* **12**:59–84.

TROJANOWICZ, ROBERT AND BONNIE BUCQUEROUX (1990). *Community Policing: A Contemporary Perspective.* Cincinnati, OH: Anderson.

TRULSON, CHAD R., JAMES W. MARQUART, AND JANET MULLINGS (2005). "Towards an Understanding of Juvenile Persistence in the Transition to Young Adulthood." Unpublished paper presented at the annual meeting of the Academy of Criminal Justice Sciences, Chicago (March).

TRULSON, CHAD, RUTH TRIPLETT, AND CLETE SNELL (2001). "Social Control in a School Setting: Evaluating a School-Based Boot Camp." *Crime and Delinquency* **38**:57–75.

TUBMAN, J.G., A.G. GIL, AND E.F. WAGNER (2004). "Co-Occurring Substance Abuse and Delinquent Behavior During Early Adolescence: Emerging Relations and Implications for Intervention Strategies." *Criminal Justice and Behavior* **3**:463–488.

TURLEY, ALAN C. (2003). "Female Gangs and Patterns of Female Delinquency in Texas." *Journal of Gang Research* **10**:1–12.

TYLER, KIMBERLY A., LES B. WHITBECK, AND ANA MARI CAUCE (2004). "Risk Factors for Sexual Victimization among Male and Female Homeless and Runaway Youth." *Journal of Interpersonal Violence* **19**:503–520.

ULMER, JEFFREY T. AND BRIAN JOHNSON (2004). "Sentencing in Context: A Multilevel Analysis." *Criminology* **42**:137–177.

UNIVERSITY OF NEW MEXICO (1996). *Evaluation of the Juvenile Community Corrections Program.* Albuquerque, NM: Juvenile Justice Division, New Mexico Children, Youth, and Families Department.

U.S. DEPARTMENT OF JUSTICE (2003). *Weed and Seed Best Practices: Evaluation-Based Series.* Washington, DC: U.S. Department of Justice, Office of Justice Programs.

U.S. GENERAL ACCOUNTING OFFICE (1995a). *Juvenile Justice: Minimal Gender Bias Occurred in Processing Noncriminal Juveniles.* Washington, DC: U.S. General Accounting Office.

U.S. GENERAL ACCOUNTING OFFICE (1995b). *Juvenile Justice: Representation Rates Varied as Did Counsel's Impact on Court Outcomes.* Washington, DC: U.S. General Accounting Office.

U.S. GENERAL ACCOUNTING OFFICE (1996a). *At-Risk and Delinquent Youth: Multiple Federal Programs Raise Efficiency Questions.* Washington, DC: U.S. General Accounting Office.

U.S. GENERAL ACCOUNTING OFFICE (1996b). *Juvenile Justice: Status of Delinquency Prevention Program and Description of Local Projects.* Washington, DC: U.S. General Accounting Office.

URBAN, LYNN S. (2005). "The Effect of a Curfew Check Program on Juvenile Opportunities for Delinquent Activity." Unpublished paper presented at the annual meeting of the Academy of Criminal Justice Sciences, Chicago (March).

VALDEZ, AVELARDO AND STEPHEN J. SIFANECK (2004). "Getting High and Getting By: Dimensions of Drug Selling Behavior among American–Mexican Gang Members in Southern Texas." *Journal of Research in Crime and Delinquency* **41**:82–105.

VAN DIETEN, MARILYN (2002). "Implementing Best Practices: A Story from the Field." *APPA Perspectives* **26**:40–45.

VERESS, K. ET AL. (2004). "Drug-Use Patterns and Risk Factors among Young Offenders in Hungary: An Epidemiological Study." *International Journal of Drug Policy* **15**:285–295.

VESTERGAARD, J. (2004). "A Special Youth Sanction." *Journal of Scandinavian Studies in Criminology and Crime Prevention* **5**:62–84.

VICTOR, JEFFREY S. (2004). "Sluts and Wiggers: A Study of the Effects of Derogatory Labeling." *Deviant Behavior* **25**:67–85.

VINCENT, GINA M. ET AL. (2003). "Subtypes of Adolescent Offenders: Affective Traits and Antisocial Behavior Patterns." *Behavioral Sciences and the Law* **21**:695–712.

VIRGINIA COMMISSION ON YOUTH (1998). *Study of Truants and Runaways.* Richmond: Virginia Commission on Youth.

VISHER, CHRISTY A. (1987). "Incapacitation and Crime Control: Does a 'Lock 'Em Up' Strategy Reduce Crime?" *Justice Quarterly* **4**:513–543.

VOGEL, BRENDA L. AND RONALD E. VOGEL (2003). "The Age of Death: Appraising Public Opinion of Juvenile Capital Punishment." *Journal of Criminal Justice* **31**:169–183.

VOLLMAN, BRENDA AND KAREN J. TERRY (2005). "Reporting Trends for Sexual Abuse Victims." Unpublished paper presented at the annual meeting of the Academy of Criminal Justice Sciences, Chicago (March).

VON EYE, ALEXANDER AND CHRISTOF SCHUSTER (2001). "Methodology for Research on Adolescence: The Need for Innovation." *Journal of Adolescent Research* **16**:95–102.

WADSWORTH, TIM (2000). "Labor Markets, Delinquency and Social Control Theory: An Empirical Assessment of the Mediating Process." *Social Forces* **78**:1041–1066.

WALKER, SAMUEL (2001). *Sense and Nonsense About Crime 5/e.* Pacific Grove, CA: Brooks/Cole.

WALLACE, LISA, KEVIN MINOR, AND JAMES WELLS (2005). "Defining the Differential in Differential Oppression Theory: Exploring the Role of Social Learning." Unpublished paper presented at the annual meeting of the Academy of Criminal Justice Sciences, Chicago (March).

WANG, JOHN Z. (2000). "A Corporation-Based Gang Prevention Approach: Possible? Preliminary Report of a Corporate Survey." *Journal of Gang Research* **7**:13–28.

WARCHOL, GREG L. (2000). "Intensive Supervision Probation: An Impact Evaluation." *Justice Professional* **13**:219–232.

WARD, TONY, RICHARD D. LAWS, AND STEPHEN M. HUDSON (EDS.) (2003). *Sexual Deviance: Issues and Controversies.* Thousand Oaks, CA: Sage.

WARR, MARK (2005). "Making Delinquent Friends: Adult Supervision and Children's Affiliations." *Criminology* **43**:77–106.

WATSON, DONNIE W. ET AL. (2003). "Comprehensive Residential Education, Arts, and Substance Abuse Treatment." *Youth Violence and Juvenile Justice* **1**:388–401.

WEATHERBURN, DON AND JOANNE BAKER (2001). "Transient Offenders in the 1996 Secondary School Survey: A Cautionary Note on Juvenile Justice Diversion." *Current Issues in Criminal Justice* **13**:60–73.

WEEDON, JOEY R. (2002). "Budgetary Concerns within States May Not End Reforms." *On the Line* **25**:1–2.

WEST, ANGELA D. (2005). "Smoke and Mirrors: Measuring Gang Activity with School and Police Data." Unpublished paper presented at the annual meeting of the Academy of Criminal Justice Sciences, Chicago (March).

WHITAKER, ASHLEY (2005). "Children Who Witness Abuse: The Role of An Intern in the Research Process." Unpublished paper presented at the annual meeting of the Academy of Criminal Justice Sciences, Chicago (March).

WIEBUSH, RICHARD G. (1990). "The Ohio Experience: Programmatic Variations in Intensive Supervision for Juveniles." *Perspectives* **14**:26–35.

WIESNER, M. AND M. WINDLE (2004). "Assessing Covariates of Adolescent Delinquency Trajectories: A Latent Growth Mixture." *Journal of Youth and Adolescence* **33**:431–442.

WILKERSON, DAWN (2005). "Organizational Structuring within Juvenile Justice: Why Reform Is Needed." Unpublished paper presented at the annual meeting of the Academy of Criminal Justice Sciences, Chicago (March).

WILLIAMS, JACKSON (2003). "Criminal Justice Policy Innovation in the United States." *Criminal Justice Policy Review* **14**:401–422.

WILLIAMS, KATHERINE AND MARCIA I. COHEN (1993). *Determinants of Disproportionate Representation of Minority Juveniles in Secure Settings: Final Report, Preliminary Findings and Recommendations.* Fairfax, VA: Fairfax Juvenile and Domestic Relations District Court.

WILLIAMSON, DEBORAH, MICHELLE CHALK, AND PAUL KNEPPER (1993). "Teen Court: Juvenile Justice for the 21st Century?" *Federal Probation* **57**:54–58.

WILSON, E. O. (1975). *Sociobiology: The New Synthesis.* Cambridge, MA: Harvard University Press.

WILSON, JAMES Q. AND JOAN PETERSILIA (2002). *Crime: Public Policies for Crime Control.* Oakland, CA: Institute for Contemporary Studies Press.

WILSON, JOHN J. (2001). *1998 National Youth Gang Survey.* Washington, DC: Office of Juvenile Justice and Delinquency Prevention.

WITMER, DENISE (2002). *Parenting of Adolescents.* New York: About, Inc.

WOLFGANG, MARVIN AND FRANCO FERRACUTI (1967). *The Subculture of Violence.* London: Tavistock.

WOLFGANG, MARVIN, ROBERT M. FIGLIO, AND THORSTEN SELLIN (1972). *Delinquency in a Birth Cohort.* Chicago: University of Chicago Press.

WOOD, GINA E. (2001). "Increasing Collaboration Between Family Courts and Juvenile Justice." *Corrections Today* **63**:116–122.

WORDES, MADELINE, TIMOTHY S. BYNUM, AND CHARLES J. CORLEY (1994). "Locking Up Youth: The Impact of Race on Detention Decisions." *Journal of Research in Crime and Delinquency* **31**:149–165.

WORLING, JAMES R. (1995). "Adolescent Sex Offenders Against Females: Differences Based on the Age of Their Victims." *International Journal of Offender Therapy and Comparative Criminology* **39**:276–293.

WORRALL, JOHN L. ET AL. (2004). "An Analysis of the Relationship Between Probation Caseloads and Property Crime Rates in California Counties." *Journal of Criminal Justice* **32**:231–241.

WRIGHT, JOHN PAUL AND FRANCIS T. CULLEN (2004). "Parental Efficacy and Delinquent Behavior: Do Control and Support Matter?" *Criminology* **39**:677–705.

WRIGHT, JOHN PAUL ET. AL. (2001). "'The Root of All Evil?' An Exploratory Study of Money and Delinquent Involvement." *Justice Quarterly* **18**:239–268.

XIAOYING, DONG (2005). "A Study of Young Offenders Who Desist from Re-Offending." Unpublished paper presented at the annual meeting of the Academy of Criminal Justice Sciences, Chicago (March).

YALDA, CHRISTINE A. (2005). "From School Halls to School Walls: Student Perceptions of Effective Campus Security at a Public High School." Unpublished paper presented at the annual meeting of the Academy of Criminal Justice Sciences, Chicago (March).

YAR, MAJID AND SUE PENNA (2004). "Between Positivism and Post-Modernity? Critical Reflections on Jock Young's "'The Exclusive Society.'" *British Journal of Criminology* **44**:533–549.

YEAGER, CLAY R., JOHN A. HERB AND JOHN H. LEMMON (1989). *The Impact of Court Unification on Juvenile Probation Systems in Pennsylvania.* Shippensburg, PA: Center for Juvenile Justice Training and Research, Shippensburg University.

YOUNG, ROBERT L. (2004). "Guilty Until Proven Innocent: Conviction Orientation, Racial Attitudes, and Support for Capital Punishment." *Deviant Behavior* **25**:151–167.

YSTGAARD, M. ET AL. (2004). "Is There a Specific Relationship Between Childhood Sexual and Physical Abuse and Repeated Suicidal Behavior?" *Child Abuse and Neglect* **28**:863–875.

ZACHARIAH, JOHN K. (2002). *An Overview of Boot Camp Goals, Components, and Results.* Washington, DC: Koch Crime Institute.

ZASLAW, JAY G. (1989). "Stop Assaultive *Children*—Project SAC Offers Hope for Violent Juveniles." *Corrections Today* **51**:48–50.

ZIGLER, EDWARD AND NANCY W. HALL (1987). "The Implications of Early Intervention Efforts for the Primary Prevention of Juvenile Delinquency." In *From Children to Citizens: Volume III, Families, Schools, and Delinquency,* James Q. Wilson and Glenn C. Loury (eds.). New York: Springer-Verlag.

ZIMMERMANN, CAROL A. AND EDMUND F. MCGARRELL (2005). "The Effects of Family Group Conferencing and Family Bonding on Delinquency Desistance." Unpublished paper presented at the annual meeting of the Academy of Criminal Justice Sciences, Chicago (March).

ZIMRING, FRANKLIN E. (1998). *American Youth Violence.* New York: Oxford University Press.

Case Index

Name Index

A

Aarons, N.M., 231
Abatiello, Jennifer D., 130, 179, 528
Abramson, Alana Marie, 489, 548
Adams, Mike S., 131
Adams, William, 589
Administrative Office of the U.S. Courts, 543
Agnew, Robert, 116, 119–120
Akers, Ronald, 106, 123
Alarid, Leanne Fiftal, 172
Aldridge, Jan, 332
Alexander, Rudolph Jr., 163
Alford, Susan, 490
Allen, Harry E., 544
Aloisi, Michael F., 183, 298
Altschuler, David M., 177, 183, 505, 561
American Bar Association, 450
American Correctional Association, 84, 180, 183, 295, 539, 570, 589, 599, 614
American Jails, 459
Anchorage Youth Court, 463, 465–477
Anderson, A.L., 83, 124
Anderson, C.A., 124
Anderson, James F., 193–194
Anwyl, Robert S., 614
APPA Perspectives, 79, 462
Archwamety, Teara, 600
Armstrong, Gaylene Styve, 614
Armstrong, Troy L., 177, 183, 233, 376, 505, 517, 561
Arthur, Lindsay G., 548
Arthur, R., 20, 343, 569
Asher, S.R., 69
Ashford, Jose, 449, 599–600
Associated Press, 206, 384
Auerhahn, Kathleen, 410–411
Austin, Andrew, 268
Austin, James, 580
Austin, Thomas L., 131
Ayers, William, 13
Ayers-Scholosser, Lee, 529–530

B

Babb, Susan, 596
Bachman, Ronet, 68
Baez, N.E., 107
Baird, S. Christopher, 506–507, 513
Baker, Amy J.L., 45, 570
Baker, Joanne, 448, 451
Baker, Spencer R., 135
Baldwin, Roger N., 507
Ballif-Spanvil, B., 231, 457
Banks, J., 412
Barnes, Allan R., 133–134
Barrios, Luis, 76
Barton, William H., 60, 62
Bartow, David S., 244, 264
Batchelor, S., 302, 304, 358
Bates, Andrew, 506
Bates, M., 264
Baum, Katrina, 481

Bazemore, S. Gordon, 13
Beccaria, Cesare, 96–97
Beck, Allen J., 163
Becker, Howard S., 115
Bedau, Hugo Adam, 223
Bedford, O., 45
Beech, Anthony, 506
Belbot, Barbara, 219–220
Belknap, Joanne, 60
Bell, Carl C., 72
Benda, Brent B., 302, 408–409
Benekos, Peter J., 30
Bentham, Jeremy, 97
Berenson, David, 133
Berbanu, S., 78
Bernat, Frances P., 455
Berrueta-Clement, John R., 107
Beyer, Marty, 376
Bilchik, Shay, 205, 264, 291, 293, 367, 387, 397
Bishop, Donna M., 297
Bittle, Steven, 155
Black, Henry Campbell, 40, 42, 264, 332
Black, M.M., 253–254, 485
Blevins, Kristie R., 11, 20
Bloom, Barbara, 85
Boehnke, Klaus, 106
Bohm, Robert M., 220, 223, 231
Bolyard, Melissa, 580
Bonczar, Thomas P., 214, 219
Bond-Maupin, Lisa J., 501
Boone, Harry N. Jr., 542
Boots, Denise Paquette, 219, 223
Borg, M.J., 106
Bottcher, Jean, 581
Bourque, Blair B., 578
Bowen, Erica, 127
Bowers, Dan M., 543
Bowers, Kate J., 64
Bowman, Cathy, 79, 343
Boyd, Rebecca J., 127–128
Bozalek, V., 120
Bradley, Tracey, 333, 405
Braithwaite, John, 489
Braithwaite, Ronald, 270
Brame, Robert, 297
Brandau, Timothy J., 302, 448
Brandl, Steven G., 244, 264
Brank, E.M., 69, 302
Brantingham, Paul J., 130
Brantingham, Patricia L., 130
Britton, Lee, 183, 597
Brodsky, Stanley L., 120, 287, 333
Brookbanks, Warren, 165
Brooks, Jane, 133
Brooks, R.R.W., 271, 405
Brotherton, David, 76
Brown, Joe M., 349, 352–353
Brown, Justin, 504
Brown, Michael P., 22, 31, 364
Brown, William B., 246, 257
Browne, J., 231
Browne, Kevin D., 506
Browning, Katharine, 72
Brownlie, E.B., 72, 76, 106

Bryl, Jason, 165
Buck, Janeen, 461, 477, 480
Bucqueroux, Bonnie, 271–272
Bumby, Kurt M., 574–575
Bureau of Justice Statistics, 149, 156, 183. 381
Burrell, William D., 531, 561
Burgess, Robert, 108, 123
Burnett, D.M., 311–312, 316
Burruss, George W. Jr., 147, 165, 286, 329–331, 333
Burton, Velmer S. Jr., 207–208, 211
Butts, Jeffrey A., 234, 294, 316, 319, 322–325, 327, 373, 461, 463, 477, 480, 589
Bynum, Timothy S., 79, 136, 290

C

Cadigan, Timothy P., 539, 542
Caeti, Tory J., 207–208, 211
Cain, Travis Ann, 136
Caldas, Stephen J., 580
California Office of Criminal Justice Planning, 106–107
California Youth Authority, 414
Calhoun, Georgia B., 412, 429
Callahan, Charlene M., 451, 455, 457
Campbell, Justin S., 451, 457, 460
Campbell, Mary Ann, 500
Campbell, Terrence W., 411
Caputo, Tullio, 405–406
Carlson, R.G., 273, 510
Carmona, Richard H., 125. 343
Carr, Patrick, 439
Carrington, Kerry, 19
Carrington, Peter J., 480
Carswell, K., 105, 510
Carter, David L., 243–244
Cary, Pauline L., 124
Casella, Ronnie, 343
Casper, Marta, 589
Castellano, Thomas C., 283
Cauce, Ana Mari, 64
Cauffman, Elizabeth, 112
Cavender, Gray, 600, 606
Center for the Study and Prevention of Violence, 134–136
Chalk, Michelle, 463
Chambliss, Lauren, 313
Champion, Dean J., 155, 168, 287–288, 290, 295, 302, 331, 358–359, 400, 411, 595
Chapin, John, 72
Chapman, Yvonne K., 463, 480
Chapple, Constance L., 63, 69, 77–78, 104, 106, 116, 271, 291, 293
Chen, Xiaoming, 60
Chesney-Lind, Meda, 55, 253, 397
Choi, Alfred, 114
Christenson, Bruce A., 232
Clear, Todd R., 531
Cochran, John K., 219, 223
Cocozza, Joseph J., 44
Cohen, Albert K., 112–113,

Subject Index